Biological Determinants
of
Sexual Behaviour

Biological Determinants
of
Sexual Behaviour

Edited by

J. B. HUTCHISON

*Medical Research Council Unit
on the Development and Integration of Behaviour,
University of Cambridge*

A Wiley–Interscience Publication

JOHN WILEY & SONS
Chichester · New York · Brisbane · Toronto

Library of Congress Cataloging in Publication Data:

Main entry under title:

Biological determinants of sexual behaviour.

  'A Wiley–Interscience publication.'
  1. Sex (Psychology) 2. Sex (Biology) I. Hutchison,
John Bower, 1938-
BF692.B45   599′.05′6   76-57753

ISBN 0 471 99490 1

Photosetting by Thomson Press (India) Limited, New Delhi
and printed and bound at The Pitman Press, Bath

Contributing Authors

Adler, N. T. Department of Psychology, University of Pennsylvania, 3813–15 Walnut Street, Philadelphia 19104, USA

Andrew, R. J. Ethology and Neurophysiology Group, School of Biological Sciences, University of Sussex, Brighton, Sussex, England.

Bancroft, J. Department of Psychiatry, University of Oxford, Oxford, England.

Bateson, P. P. G. Sub-Department of Animal Behaviour, University of Cambridge, Madingley, Cambridge, England.

Cowley, J. J. Department of Psychology, The Queen's University, Belfast, Northern Ireland.

Erickson, C. J. Department of Psychology, Duke University, Durham, North Carolina, USA.

Everitt, B. J. Department of Anatomy, University of Cambridge, Cambridge, England.

Feder, H. H. Institute of Animal Behavior, Rutgers University, 101 Warren Street, Newark, New Jersey 07102, USA.

Fentress, J. C. Department of Psychology, Life Sciences Centre, Dalhousie University, Halifax, Nova Scotia, Canada.

Goldman, B. D. Department of Biobehavioral Sciences, University of Connecticut, Storrs, Connecticut 06268, USA.

Hart, B. L. Department of Anatomy, School of Veterinary Medicine, University of California, Davis, California 95616, USA.

Herbert, J. Department of Anatomy, University of Cambridge, Cambridge, England.

Hutchison, J. B. MRC Unit on the Development and Integration of Behaviour, Sub-Department of Animal Behaviour, University of Cambridge, Madingley, Cambridge, England.

Kelley, D. B. The Rockefeller University, New York, NY 10021, USA.

Keverne, E. B.   *Department of Anatomy, University of Cambridge, Cambridge, England.*

Komisaruk, B. R.   *Institute of Animal Behavior, Rutgers University, 101 Warren Street, Newark, New Jersey 07102, USA.*

Larsson, K.   *Department of Psychology, Unit of Psychobiology, University of Göteborg, Fack, S-400 20 Göteborg 14, Sweden.*

Lisk, R. D.   *Department of Biology, Princeton University, Princeton, New Jersey 08540, USA.*

McEwen, B. S.   *The Rockefeller University, New York, NY 10021, USA.*

McFarland, D.   *Animal Behaviour Research Group, Department of Zoology, University of Oxford, South Parks Road, Oxford, England.*

McGill, T. E.   *Department of Psychology, Williams College, Williamstown, Mass. 01267, USA.*

Malmnäs, C-O.   *Department of Medical Pharmacology, University of Uppsala, Uppsala, Sweden*

Meyerson, B. J.   *Department of Medical Pharmacology, University of Uppsala, Uppsala, Sweden.*

Money, J.   *Department of Psychiatry and Behavioral Sciences, and Department of Pediatrics, The Johns Hopkins University, School of Medicine and Hospital, Baltimore, Maryland 21205, USA.*

Nunez, A. T.   *Animal Behaviour Research Group, Department of Zoology, University of Oxford, South Parks Road, Oxford, England.*

Pfaff, D. W.   *The Rockefeller University, New York, NY 10021, USA.*

Plapinger, L.   *The Rockefeller University, New York, NY 10021, USA.*

Schwartz, M.   *Department of Psychiatry and Behavioral Sciences, and Department of Pediatrics, The John Hopkins University, School of Medicine and Hospital, Baltimore, Maryland 21205, USA.*

Simpson, M. J. A.   *MRC Unit on the Development and Integration of Behaviour, Sub-Department of Animal Behaviour, University of Cambridge, Madingley, Cambridge, England.*

Contents

PART IV: SOCIO-SEXUAL FACTORS   653

Introduction   655

Abbreviations

ACTH	Adrenocorticotrophic hormone
AFP	Alphafoetoprotein
cyclic AMP	Cyclicadenosine-3-5-phosphate
CNS	Central nervous system
COMT	Catechol-O-methyl transferase
CRH	Corticotrophic hormone-releasing hormone
CSF	Cerebro-spinal fluid
DNA	Deoxyribonucleic acid
DA	Dopamine
DES	Diethylstilboestrol
DHP	5α-Dihydroprogesterone
DHT	5α-Dihydrotestosterone
DHTP	5α-Dihydrotestosterone propionate
5,7-DHT	5,7-Dihydroxytryptamine
DOPA	Dihydroxyphenylalanine
DOPS	DL-threo-3, 4-dihydroxyphenylserine
EEG	Electroencephalogram
EMG	Electromyograph
FSH	Follicle stimulating hormone
GTH	Gonadotrophic hormones
GTH/AS	Gonadotrophin antiserum
HCG	Human chorionic gonadotrophin
HPPA	*Para*hydroxyphenylpropanoic acid
5-HT	5-Hydroxytryptamine
5-HTP	5-Hydroxytryptophan
I.U	International Unit
Kd	Dissociation Constant

LH	Luteinizing hormone
LRH	Luteinizing hormone-releasing hormone
LSD	Lysergic acid diethyamide
MAO	Monoamine oxidase
α-MT	α-Methyl-*p*-tyrosine
NA	Noradrenaline
OB	Oestradiol benzoate
OD	Oestradiol dipropionate
OAAD	Ovarian Ascorbic Acid Depletion
PCPA	*Para*chlorophenylalanine
PGE_2	Prostaglandin E_2
PPA	Phenylpropanoic acid
RNA	Ribonucleic acid
S	Svedberg Unit
Tfm	Testicular feminization
TP	Testosterone propionate
TRH	Thyrotrophin releasing hormone

Preface

Sexual behaviour is becoming one of the best documented of behavioural phenomena in both animals and humans. Yet the causal factors that influence its performance remain elusive. This is partly due to difficulty in defining precisely the types of behaviour that can be categorized as sexual. At first sight sexual behaviour as a taxonomic unit needs no definition, because there appears to be a common understanding of its content in terms of coital behaviour immediately associated with the production of the zygote. However, as Beach pointed out (1965), definitions of sexual behaviour tend to vary according to the organism which forms the subject of sexual research. Those studying lower vertebrates such as fish find that the intervals between phases of the reproductive cycle, fertilization, egglaying, nesting, and rearing of the young, are so brief that it becomes difficult to dissect out behaviour associated with fertilization from the various other behavioural elements that form the whole complex of reproductive behaviour. Moreover, in some animals, such as birds for example, the time spent in coital behaviour is relatively insignificant compared with that occupied by the ritualized courtship interactions which serve to facilitate mate selection and the coordination of the reproductive cycle. By contrast, studies of sexual behaviour in subprimate mammals, such as rodents, which have usually been carried out in the laboratory tend to focus on coital behaviour itself to the exclusion of other elements of reproductive behaviour, because coital elements are the most obvious to the observer in such conditions. On the other hand, in infrahuman primates definitions restricted to coital activity would represent a meaningless oversimplification of the complexity of sexual behaviour seen as an interaction not only with a particular partner, but also with other members of the social group. In such cases all genitally-orientated behaviour patterns may have to be categorized as sexual despite an apparent lack of a close association with reproduction. In humans, the definition of sexual behaviour may have to be widened still further, as Beach argues, to include non-reproductive activities which are sexually dimorphic.

When we consider the causation of sexual behaviour, similar classificatory problems are encountered; the background and aims of the researcher may determine the type of behaviour categorized as sexual. To the neuro-scientist interested in brain mechanisms underlying hormone-dependent behaviour, sexual behaviour may be equated with the patterned reflexive movements associated with coitus and its component subunits such as intromission and ejaculation in the male, or lordosis in the female. In studying the relationship between hormones and brain mechanisms of sexual behaviour, the physiologist may be compelled to reduce sexual behaviour to its simplest elements in order to obtain a behavioural endpoint which can be defined with sufficient accuracy to allow experimental variables to be specified, and to make the results of physiological manipulations interpretable. On the other hand, the behavioural scientist interested in the way in which discrete items of behaviour are integrated into functional sequences may have to take the more global view of sexual behaviour in which sexual elements are seen as a relatively small facet of the wider complex of social interactions between an individual and members of that individual's social group. The difficulty with the former approach is that fragmentation of behaviour into elements meaningful to the physiologist may result in descriptions of causal mechanisms which bear little relation to the behaviour observed during normal sexual interactions between male and female. With the latter approach, the danger lies in the complexity of the behavioural situation which may preclude physiological analysis.

The study of causation of sexual behaviour must obviously accommodate both the selective approach of the physiologist and the integrated approach of the behaviourist. This book attempts an accommodation. Its primary aim has been to assemble contributions from a number of authors representing both the physiological and behavioural disciplines whose common interest is the study of mechanisms underlying sexual behaviour. The idea was to bring together in one volume various approaches to the problem which are usually scattered diffusely throughout the neuroendocrine and behavioural literature. This seemed an appropriate time to undertake the task, because on the physiological side major discoveries are being made at a biochemical level which are throwing light on the mode of action of sex hormones on brain systems underlying sexual behaviour; the relationship between sex-hormone levels in the brain and peripheral blood and the cellular effects of these hormones are now more clearly understood. At the same time, the methodology of behavioural science, particularly methods of description and analysis of behaviour used in ethology, are beginning to give an insight into the way in which inter-individual relationships can be defined, and are also showing how the dynamics of these relationships change as a function of social structure and reproductive condition.

A major emphasis in this book has been placed on questions concerning the role of hormones in sexual behaviour. How do hormones act to influence the process of differentiation and development of sexual behaviour? What mechanisms are involved in mediating the action of hormones on neural pathways mediating sexual behaviour in adulthood? What parts of the brain are involved? What determines the specificity of hormonal action and the sensitivity to hormones of the substrate associated with sexual behaviour on which hormones act? To broaden the approach to the causal mechanisms underlying sexual behaviour, these questions have to be seen in the light of behavioural studies which emphasize the role of non-hormonal factors such as genetic effects, sexual experience involving special forms of learning, and the acquisition of skills as a consequence of social interaction, of olfactory and other social and environmental stimuli involved in sexual interaction. In organizing this book into parts, I have attempted to balance physiological studies of sexual behaviour with more general articles discussing the contribution of these non-hormonal factors to the integration of sexual behaviour. Where possible, the parts contain contributions which cover both the relevant human and animal research.

J. B. Hutchison,
MRC Unit on the Development and Integration of Behaviour,
University of Cambridge,
Madingley.

Beach, F. A. (1965) Retrospect and prospect. In: *Sex and Behavior*, F. A. Beach (ed.) Wiley, New York, pp. 535–70.

Editor's Acknowledgements

My editing of the book owed a great deal to the help and advice given to me by Rosemary Hutchison and Robert Hinde. I am grateful to a number of other colleagues in the Sub-Department of Animal Behaviour who have made suggestions concerning the editing, particularly Pat Bateson, Brian Bertram, Rosemary Burley, John Cowley, Judy Dunn, Stephen Holman, and Michael Simpson. I am also indebted to Barry Everitt, Joe Herbert, Barry Keverne, and Roger Short for discussion and their suggestions. My thanks are due to Sally Drummond for help with the manuscripts.

Part I

Developmental Processes

Introduction

The now classical theory of the action of gonadal hormones on the differentitation and development of sexual behaviour, which resulted largely from the work of Phoenix *et al.*, (1959) and Harris and Levine (1965) on the copulatory behaviour of rodents, proposes that in mammals androgen 'organizes' the central nervous system during early development to increase the likelihood that the copulatory behaviour of the genetic male will be displayed in response to appropriate environmental and hormonal stimulation. In the absence of androgen, the copulatory behaviour of the female will develop. This hormonal influence is presumed to be mediated during a prenatal or neonatal critical period, depending on the length of the gestation period, when the central nervous mechanisms underlying sexual behaviour are thought to be specifically sensitive to the differentiating action of androgen. The theory dovetails neatly with the current neuroendocrine hypothesis implicating androgen in the differentiation of the acyclic hypothalamo-pituitary system of the male rat, where, as Goldman describes, androgen is available at exactly the right neonatal period for the differentiating effect.

While few doubts have been expressed about the validity of the theory as applied to the neuroendocrine system, there has been controversy over its application to the differentiation of sexual behaviour. With respect to the rodent data, Beach (1971) in particular has argued cogently for a more critical re-thinking of the mechanism of hormonal action in the light of the behavioural evidence at hand; theories postulating a unitary 'organizing' action of androgen on the motor or 'executive' integrating systems of the brain during development appear suspect. It can be suggested equally well in many cases that the developmental influences of androgen on copulatory behaviour are peripheral rather than central, being mediated by an effect on tactile sensory systems of the genitalia for example. Developmentally androgen can also be seen as altering the sensitivity of the central nervous system to hormones secreted in adulthood rather than necessarily organizing the integrational or motor systems underlying male sexual behaviour.

Although the modes of action of androgen in the sexual differentiation of sexual behaviour have yet to be established fully, there are indications of sex differences in brain structure which may underlie behavioural differences between the sexes. For example, Raisman (1974) has established that some axons of the preoptic area of the cycling female rat contain twice as many dendritic spine synapses as those of the male; a sex difference which appears to depend on the action of androgen during the neonatal period. Dyer *et al.* (1976) have demonstrated that more of the cells projecting to the mediobasal hypothalamus in male rats receive synaptic connections from the amygdala than in females. Nottebohm and Arnold (1976) have found that certain motor nuclei in the avian brain controlling vocal behaviour are larger in the male than the female. Biochemical information is also becoming available on the cellular mechanisms that mediate the action of androgen during the critical period for sexual differentiation of behaviour. Plapinger and McEwen take the view that early androgen effects in the brain are mediated by oestrogens produced by aromatization of the circulating androgen. Both the relevant enzymes for conversion and the intracellular receptor proteins to which oestrogens bind are present in the brain at the critical neonatal period for sexual differentiation in the rat.

Individual differences in sexual display are not contingent entirely upon the hormonal conditions prevailing during early development; such differences can also be related to genetic and experiential factors, to special forms of learning during development, and to environmental stimuli. McGill establishes that in addition to species differences in hormone–behaviour interactions, careful selection of genotype can demonstrate the importance of intraspecific genetic variables in determining hormonal effects in early development. The pattern of external stimulation to which the developing animal is subjected also influences the development of sexual behaviour. In taking this view, Cowley argues that the accelerated development of the brain during the first few days of life makes it vulnerable to the effects of malnutrition. Olfactory stimuli, particularly those from the mother in rodents may play a role in determining feeding behaviour which influences infant nutrition, reproductive condition during development, and ultimately sexual behaviour in adulthood. Larsson suggests that tactile contact established with other individuals during infancy is especially important in the development of sexual behaviour. Deprivation of tactile contact with conspecifics has deleterious effects in the male which appear to be irreversible in primates such as rhesus. Simpson (Part IV) enlarges upon this view by suggesting that special social skills including tactile interaction are learned at particular stages during the development of sexual behaviour in different social contexts. One such context is choice of mate. Ethologists have studied the process of acquiring sexual preference or 'sexual imprinting' extensively in submammalian vertebrates. Some authors, notably Lorenz (1935, 1950) and Hess (1959), have argued that experience at a 'sensitive' period of development creates an ineradicable 'imprint' which determines sexual preference in adulthood irrespective of experience. Bateson points to the necessity for plasticity of learning processes in the determination of sexual preference by arguing from an evolutionary viewpoint: in a rapidly evolving species where phenotypic characteristics may be changing rapidly, it would be disadvantageous for mating preference to develop regardless of early experience.

REFERENCES

Beach, F. A. (1971) Hormonal factors controlling the differentiation, development and the display of copulatory behaviour in the Ramstergig and related species. In: *Biopsychology of Development*, L. Aronson and E. Tobach (eds.), Academic Press, New York, pp. 249–96.

Dyer, R. G., Macleod, N. K. and Ellendorff, F. (1976) Electrophysiological evidence for sexual dimorphism and synaptic convergence in the preoptic and anterior hypothalamic areas of the rat, *Proc. Roy. Soc. Lond. B*, **193**, 421–40.

Harris, G. W. and Levine, S. (1965) Sexual differentiation of the brain and its experimental control, *J. Physiol.* London, **181**, 379–400.

Hess, E. H. (1959) Imprinting, *Science*, **130**, 133–41.

Lorenz, K. (1935) Der Kumpan in der Umwelt des Vogels, *J. f. Ornith.*, **83**, 137–213, 289–413.

Lorenz, K. (1950) The comparative method in studying innate behaviour patterns, *Symp. Soc. Exp. Biol.*, **4**, 221–68.

Nottebohm, F. and Arnold, A. P. (1976) Sexual dimorphism in vocal control areas of the songbird brain, *Science*, **194**, 211–3.

Phoenix, C. H., Goy, R. W., Gerall, A. A., and Young, W. C. (1959) Organizing action of prenatally administered testosterone propionate on the tissues mediating mating behaviour in the female guinea pig, *Endocrinology*, **65**, 369–82.

Raisman, G. (1974) Evidence for a sex difference in the neuropil of the rat preoptic area and its importance for the study of sexually dimorphic functions, *Aggression Res. Publ. A.R.N.M.D.*, **52**, 42–51.

CHAPTER 1

Genetic Factors Influencing the Action of Hormones on Sexual Behaviour

THOMAS E. MCGILL

INTRODUCTION: DEFINITIONS, LIMITATIONS, AND GOALS

This chapter is concerned with genetically determined differences in behavioural response to the presence or absence of various hormones. Genetically determined differences are sometimes called 'innate'. Since such terms often carry surplus meaning, it is important to specify the limitations of 'genetically determined' and 'innate' at the outset.

Hinde and Tinbergen have written:

> In the past the term 'innate' has been applied in ethology to both characters and the differences between characters. Various critics ... have pointed out that the application of the term to characters is misleading, since these are the result of continuous interaction between environment and inherent potentialities throughout development. In this paper, therefore, 'innate' is applied only to differences (Hinde and Tinbergen, 1958).

Despite such statements, there has continued to be misunderstanding over the meaning of the terms. In one of his last papers, a chapter entitled 'Semantic and Conceptual Issues in the Nature–Nuture Problem', the late Daniel S. Lehrman attempted further clarification:

> If we rear two animals in the same environment, and they develop different behavior patterns, it is perfectly clear that the difference in the behavior patterns depends upon differences in the genetic constitution of the animals, and not upon differences in the environment. One might refer to these *differences* as 'innate', meaning only that they depended upon differences in the genome. This use of the term 'innate' would be meaningful and useful, provided it was recognized that the observations that justified the conclusion that the difference between the two animals was a genetic difference do not necessarily imply anything, one way *or* the other, about the extent to which the development of the character concerned is, in either animal, influencible by changes in the environment (Lehrman, 1970).

In this chapter we shall refer to certain behavioural differences as 'genetically determined' or as 'innate' with the understanding that both terms are used with the restrictions outlined by Lehrman.

Each species has its own particular pattern or patterns of reproduction ranging from simple cell division to complex repertories of courtship and copulation. This chapter is exclusively concerned with sexual reproduction in mammalian species, particularly domesticated and laboratory animals. Successful reproduction in mammals can depend upon a host of factors such as season, habitat, food and nesting supplies, parental care, antipredator devices, social organization, etc. These important variables are not considered here. Rather, our emphasis will be on differences in the hormonal conditions necessary for sexual arousal and the performance of the copulatory act. 'Hormonal conditions' will include both the effects of hormones during critical stages of development and their role in adult behaviour. We shall be concerned primarily with recent areas of research and with recent studies within these areas.

It should be emphasized that many of the intra-and interspecific comparisons made below depend upon research conducted by different investigators, in different laboratories, using different experimental procedures. For our immediate purposes, these comparisons are accepted as valid. However, the potential effects of experimental technique upon the conclusions reached should be kept in mind.

Within these restrictions, the chapter reviews some of the literature on genetically determined behavioural and physiological differences among various species and within particular species. To anticipate, the major conclusion is that important species differences in hormone–behaviour interactions can also be observed *within* species by the lucky or judicious selection of different genotypes. Recognition of this fact should greatly simplify the search for underlying physiological mechanisms.

NEONATAL ANDROGENIZATION OF FEMALES

Differences Among Species

Much research over the past 20 years has been concerned with the role of hormones in development. The theoretical issues and the experimental literature are reviewed elsewhere in the present volume (Goldman, Chapter 5; Plapinger and McEwen, this volume Chapter 6). Our purpose at this point is to note briefly those instances where species differences appear in response to hormone treatment. Most of the conclusions, however, must be regarded as tentative since sensitive periods and developmental sequences may vary in unknown ways among species.

Luttge and Whalen (1970) found that as much as 800 μg of androstenedione, testosterone, or 5α-dihydrotestosterone (DHT) injected over the first five days after birth did not inhibit lordosis behaviour in female Sprague–Dawley rats when they were tested in adulthood following oestrogen and progesterone treatment. Conversely, Edwards (1971) determined that neonatal androstenedione, testosterone, or testosterone propionate (TP) reduced lordosis frequency in Swiss–Webster mice.

Whether or not neonatal androgen treatment increases the masculine 'response potential' (Beach, 1971) of female mammals has been a matter of disagreement (Whalen and Edwards, 1967). Part of the problem may be the tendency of investigators to institute androgen treatment in adulthood prior to any behavioural tests, or to make only a few brief observations before injections begin. These procedures have served to mask differences between neonatally androgenized females and oil injected controls, since androgen treatment of either group greatly increases masculine behaviour. More recent studies leave little doubt that neonatally administered TP indeed increases masculine response potential. Manning and McGill (1974) have shown that neonatally androgenized female mice are capable of the complete range of masculine behaviour, including the ejaculatory reflex, without androgen injections in adulthood. Södersten (1973a) has reported similar findings for female rats.

We have recently found another possible reason for the failure of previous investigators to observe ejaculatory responses in neonatally androgenized females under androgen treatment in adulthood (McGill et al., 1976). Two groups of neonatally androgenized females were matched on the basis of ejaculation latency, defined as the time from first intromission to the ejaculatory reflex. One group of 18 animals (Group A) was injected daily with 100μg TP in 0.04 ml arachis oil. A second group of animals (Group B) received the oil vehicle only. Injections continued for 10 weeks with weekly behavioural tests occurring during the last 9 weeks, or until the animals had exhibited the ejaculatory reflex on three tests. Following these tests, subjects were 'rested' (no tests; no injections) for six to nine weeks and then the treatments were reversed: Group A animals received the oil vehicle and Group B animals received TP. A further nine-week period of behavioural testing followed treatment reversal. Fig. 1 shows the results for ejaculation latency in the two treatment periods. In both cases females receiving TP therapy took significantly longer to reach the ejaculatory threshold. This inhibition of the ejaculatory reflex by androgen in adulthood may account for the failure of previous investigators to observe the response since most designs used a time-limit observation period.

Until neonatally androgenized females of other species are intensively studied prior to androgen treatment in adulthood the question of species differences in masculine response potential will remain unanswered.

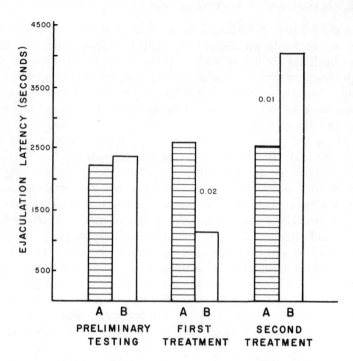

Fig. 1. Response (ejaculation latency) of neonatally androgenized B6D2F$_1$ female mice to testosterone propionate (TP) in adulthood. First treatment: Group A received 100 μg of TP daily. Second treatment: Group B received 100 μg of TP daily

Differences Within Species

We have noted that treatment with androgen during a sensitive period in development can defeminize and/or masculinize females of some mammalian species. Vale *et al.* (1973) suggested that the behavioural changes produced in females by neonatal androgenization may be due to the activation of genes during the sensitive period of development. If this is the case, then changing the genotype might change the response to the hormone treatment. As a test of this hypothesis, Vale, *et al.* injected female mice of the inbred strains A, BALB/c and C57BL/6 with either TP, oestradiol benzoate (OB), or the oil vehicle on the third day of life. In adulthood the animals were tested for response to an oestrous female. About a week later, after receiving injections of estradiol benzoate and progesterone, the experimental females were tested for feminine responses to a sexually vigorous untreated C57BL/6 male. Significant interactions between genotype and neonatal treatment effects were found for 10 of 19 comparisons. For example, the lordosis response of C57BL/6 females was relatively insensitive to neonatal androgen or oestrogen while the other two strains showed significant reductions in the number of lordosis responses as a result of neonatal steroid treatment. The authors conclude that '. . . the effects of neonatal hormone treatment cannot be considered separately from those of genotype.' They suggest that some of the previous discrepancies in the effects of neonatal treatment might be due to genotypic differences in the samples selected for study.

NEONATAL ANDROGENIZATION OF MALES

Differences Among Species

Although not much research has examined the effects of androgen injections in intact, neonatal males, what has been done indicates possible species differences in regard to this variable. For male rats, neonatally administered TP had no effect upon mount or intromission rates or on the proportion of animals mounting, achieving intromission, or ejaculating (Feder, 1967; Whalen, 1964). Vale et al. (1974) found that the proportion of male house mice exhibiting mounts, intromissions, and ejaculatory responses could be increased by neonatal TP treatment. Since they also found strain differences, the results are discussed in the next section.

Differences Within Species

Vale et al. (1974) injected intact male mice of the inbred strains A, BALB/c, and C57BL/6 with 1 mg TP on the third day of life. When tested with receptive females in adulthood, BALB/c and C57BL/6 showed the largest treatment effects; males of the A strain '. . . appeared generally refractory, as did the DBA/2 in the hands of Campbell and McGill' (1970).

HORMONAL INDUCTION OF RECEPTIVITY IN FEMALES

Differences Among Species

There are differences in the hormonal treatment required to induce a state of behavioural receptivity in females of different species. In 1961 Young reviewed the literature in this field and reported that cats, dogs, ferrets, goats, and monkeys can be brought into heat by injections of estrogen alone, whereas the guinea pig requires progesterone a day or so after the oestrogen injection. The ewe also requires both oestrogen and progesterone but the sequence is reversed from that of the guinea pig; normal heat behaviour in the ewe is not displayed unless oestrogen is preceded by progesterone. To further complicate the issue, large amounts of progesterone terminate oestrus in the rabbit, ferret, sheep, and goat. Differences similar to some of these species differences also exist among genotypes within particular species.

Differences Within Species

Gorzalka and Whalen (1974) injected ovariectomized groups of CD-1 and Swiss–Webster mice with oestrogen followed 41 hours later by progesterone once a week for seven weeks. For the next five weeks, 5α-dihydroprogesterone (DHP) was substituted for the progesterone. The animals were then returned to progesterone for four weeks, followed by two weeks when only oestrogen and the oil vehicle were used. Forty-eight hours after oestrogen, the treated females were placed into the home cages of sexually experienced male mice of the same strain. A test continued until the male had mounted the experimental female 10 times. The ratios of female lordotic responses to the male's mounts were calculated. Fig. 2 shows the results. Both strains required five weekly treatments before maximum receptivity with progesterone occurred. Over the seven week period, the CD-1 strain had significantly higher ratios of lordoses to mounts.

During weeks 8–12 when DHP was substituted for progesterone, the receptivity of both strains dropped significantly. However, during the five weekly treatments, the CD-1 females progressively increased in responsiveness to

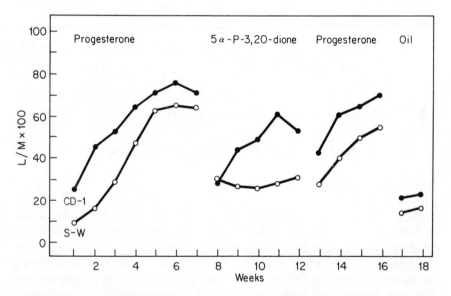

Fig. 2. Mean receptivity quotients (lordosis responses/mounts with pelvic thrusting × 100) for castrated female mice of the CD-1 and Swiss–Webster strains. All females were oestrogen-primed 48 h before testing and received progesterone, 5 —pregnane— 3, 20-dione, or oil vehicle 7 h. before testing (Gorzalka and Whalen, 1974) (Reproduced by permission of Holden-Day Inc.)

dihydroprogesterone until their ratios approached that seen under progesterone treatment. The Swiss–Webster mice failed to respond to dihydroprogesterone; their ratio of lordotic responses to mounts did not change over the five weeks of testing.

During weeks 13–16 when the animals were again administered progesterone, the results were essentially similar to the first series of seven weeks. Thus, the receptivity of CD-1 females is increased by DHP while Swiss–Webster mice fail to respond to this substance. The authors suggest '. . . that progesterone and dihydroprogesterone facilitate receptivity through independent systems.'

In a replication and extension of these findings, Gorzalka and Whalen (1976) repeated the experiment using the original two strains and their reciprocal F_1 hybrids. All four strains showed the progressive increase in lordosis responses as a result of progesterone treatment over six weeks. Under DHP treatment, there was a similar increase in receptivity over the six weeks of testing for the CD-1 animals and for both hybrid groups. Once again, the Swiss–Webster mice failed to respond to this hormone. The levels of response of Swiss–Webster mice receiving DHP were not significantly different from levels of receptivity in female mice receiving only oestrogen and the oil vehicle.

The results suggest that sensitivity to dihydroprogesterone is a dominant trait that is not significantly influenced by sex-linkage or maternal effects. The investigators also noted considerable variability in the groups that did respond to DHP; some members of the 'responding' genotypes were not, in fact, 'responding'. Since the results were found for genetically heterogeneous outbred strains, it might be possible to select within the CD-1 or the F_1 lines for 'responders' and 'non-responders'. Obviously, the animals would have to be bred prior to ovariectomy and the determination of the phenotype. Gorzalka and Whalen's results also suggest that a similar survey of genetically homogeneous inbred lines might prove profitable and might simplify the search for the underlying physiological mechanisms.

Goy and Young (1957) ovariectomized two inbred strains and one heterogeneous strain of guinea pigs. When these females were given different amounts of oestrogen followed by a constant amount of progesterone there were consistent strain differences in such elements as latency and duration of oestrus, male-like mounting behaviour, and maximum lordosis responses. These differences persisted over a range of hormone treatments. 'In general, therefore, the principle established for the male (guinea pig), that supraliminal quantities of gonadal hormone do not alter the characteristic pattern of the behaviour can be extended to the female'. The patterns of inheritance of some of these strain differences in the response of female guinea pigs to ovarian hormone have been partially illuminated (Goy and Jakway, 1959).

In 1971 Thompson and Edwards compared the induction of receptivity in ovariectomized house mice of the inbred C57BL/6 strain to that of the outbred Swiss–Webster strain. They found that the inbred C57BL/6 females exhibited a greater capacity for response and responed significantly faster to weekly treatment with oestrogen and progesterone than did the Swiss–Webster females.

RETENTION OF SEXUAL BEHAVIOUR AFTER CASTRATION IN MALES

Differences Among Species

The relationships between gonadal hormones and behaviour in male mammals have usually been examined by castration followed by observation of postcastration sexual behaviour and the effectiveness of androgens, usually TP, in re-establishing sexual responses. Response to castration has been studied in prepubertal and in postpubertal males with or without sexual experience. Species differences in response to the latter variable have been found. For example, sexually experienced male cats are significantly superior to inexperienced cats in retention of sexual responsiveness following castration (Rosenblatt and Aronson, 1958a). For the rat (Bloch and Davidson, 1968), precastration sexual experience does not significantly facilitate retention of the behaviour after removal of the gonads in adulthood.

In sexually experienced males, there again appear to be large species differences in retention of elements of sexual behaviour following castration. These differences seem to be systematic and led to the hypothesis that dependence on gonadal hormones decreases with increasing development of the forebrain (Beach, 1942, 1947, 1969 but see Hart, 1974). According to this notion, castrated rodents should lose sexual behaviour more rapidly than castrated carnivores, and in most instances this has been the case. The record for the rat is currently held by an animal that exhibited an ejaculatory reflex 147 days after removal of the gonads (Davidson, 1966). Rosenblatt and Aronson (1958b) reported that one of their castrated cats exhibited intromissions on almost every test for $3\frac{1}{2}$ years. Beach (1969) described a beagle who successfully exhibited the ejaculatory reflex and locked with a female 64 months after castration.

In the next section we will describe an exception to this general progression and suggest that genetic differences within a species are as important as genetic differences among species in determining retention of sexual responsiveness following removal of the gonads.

Differences Within Species

To repeat: species differences in retention of sexual behaviour after castration have been found. These differences have led to the hypothesis that dependence on hormones from the gonads decreases with evolutionary development of the forebrain (Beach, 1942, 1947, 1969). A series of experiments using inbred house mice and their progeny has established some important exceptions to the generally observed progression. In the first experiment (McGill and Tucker, 1964), B6D2F$_1$ hybrid male mice resulting from a cross between C57BL/6 females and DBA/2 males retained the ejaculatory reflex significantly longer after castration than did males of either of the inbred parent strains. McGill and Tucker suggested that degree of heterozygosity might be correlated with retention of the reflex after castration. This hypothesis was tested by studying 10 different genotypes that had, theoretically at least, six different degrees of heterozygosity (McGill and Haynes, 1973). A significant correlation between heterozygosity and retention of the ejaculatory reflex after castration was found.

McGill and Manning (in press) further pursued the problem by use of a diallelic design involving the C57BL/6, DBA/2, and BALB/c inbred strains and their six possible F$_1$ groups. They found, as had Champlin *et al.* (1963), that heterosis *per se* does not produce superior retention of the ejaculatory reflex following removal of the gonads; only the B6D2F$_1$ hybrid was significantly superior to the inbred parental strains in retention of the reflex. In some males of this genotype complete sexual behaviour, including the ejaculatory reflex, was observed more than two years after castration and many of these males exhibited ejaculatory patterns regularly up to a few weeks, or days, and in one case hours, of death. The authors concluded that '... genotypic differences *within a species* are among the most important variables determining retention of sexual behaviour after castration.'

RESPONSE OF CASTRATED MALES TO STEROID TREATMENTS

Differences Among Species

Once postcastration sexual behaviour has declined to a low level, injections of TP are usually successful in restoring all elements of copulatory behaviour in all mammalian species (Young, 1961). The next major section considers the response to TP in more detail. More recent studies have involved the effectiveness of other androgens, and of oestrogen, singly and in various combinations.

Some of these studies have established that aromatizable androgens such as testosterone, androstenedione, or androstenediol (or their propionates) are capable of restoring male sexual behaviour in a number of species (Alsum and Goy, 1974; Beyer *et al.*, 1973; Christensen *et al.*, 1973; Luttge and Hall, 1973; Parrott, 1975; Whalen and DeBold, 1974).

Species differences become apparent when the effectiveness of non-aromatizable androgens, such as dihydrotestosterone, are considered (see also Hutchison, this volume Chapter 9.). Non-aromatizable androgens failed to restore intromission or ejaculatory patterns in experienced castrated rats (Feder, 1971; Whalen and Luttge, 1971) and failed to initiate these responses in inexperienced castrates (Beyer, *et al.*, 1973). In hamsters, on the other hand, high doses of DHT induced both intromissions and ejaculatory responses (Whalen and DeBold, 1974). Similar results using moderate doses of dihydrotestosterone propionate (DHTP) have been found for the prepubertally castrated guinea pig (Alsum and Goy, 1974). Rabbits also responded to DHTP following castration (Beyer and Rivaud, 1973).

There also appears to be a species difference in the response of castrated males to OB. Thus oestrogen initiated the full range of behavioural responses in inexperienced castrated rats (Baum and Vreeburg, 1973; Davidson, 1969; Pfaff, 1970; Södersten, 1973b). Prepubertally castrated guinea pigs, however, did not respond to injections of OB (Alsum and Goy, 1974). (Age at castration may account for this 'species difference'.)

Once again, some of these differences can be found in different genotypes within particular species.

Differences Within Species

Luttge and Hall (1973) studied the differential effectiveness of testosterone and its metabolites androstenedione, DHT, and androstanedione in the induction of sexual behaviour in male mice of two outbred strains, CD-1 and Swiss–Webster. Males of both strains were castrated prepubertally (32 days of age) and housed in groups of 10 for five weeks. They were then observed in a 10-minute test with an oestrous female. The males remained in isolation, except for weekly 10-minute tests, for the duration of the experiment. For the first week, the castrates were given daily injections of the vehicle and then another sex test. After the second sex test, the males were assigned to groups which received either vehicle, testosterone, androstenedione, DHT, or androstanedione. Hormone doses increased from 100 μg per day to 500 μg per day over the next five weeks. Behavioural parameters measured included mounts with palpations, mounts with thrusts, mounts with intromissions, and ejaculations. The duration of each of these events was recorded.

Testosterone treatment resulted in sexual behaviour in both strains but it was much more effective in the Swiss–Webster strain where a higher percentage of males displayed intromissions, and where two of the twelve males exhibited a single ejaculatory response near the end of a 10-minute test period. Dihydrotestosterone was almost as potent as testosterone in the Swiss–Webster strain, while it had essentially no behavioural effects in the CD-1 strain. Androstenedione resulted in the display of mating behaviour in some Swiss–Webster males and in a lesser number of CD-1 males. Androstanedione failed to induce mating behaviour in either strain. From measures of sexual accessory structures taken after sacrifice of the experimental animals, the authors concluded '. . . that different androgen metabolites are differentially effective in different target tissues and in the induction of different behaviours.' They further noted '. . . that different androgen metabolites can have different behavioural effects in different species and even in different strains within the same species.'

A more recent study (Luttge, *et al.*, 1974) has essentially replicated the previous finding of behavioural stimulation via DHT in castrated Swiss–Webster mice. However, these investigators reported the puzzling fact that the stimulating effects of DHT only occurred when the substance was dissolved in olive oil and benzyl benzoate (20:80, v:v). When dissolved in propylene glycol, DHT was ineffective in stimulating the complete display of male sexual behaviour.

EJACULATION LATENCY AND TESTOSTERONE PROPIONATE

Differences Among Species

This section is concerned with the relationship between ejaculation latency and dose of TP in castrated males. A striking species difference in response to this treatment has recently been discovered.

In 1952 and 1953 Grunt and Young performed classic experiments involving the response of castrated male guinea pigs to different amounts of TP. They first gave male guinea pigs ten preliminary tests and placed them in high, medium, and low groups on the basis of their 'sex-scores'. The animals were then castrated and, after the sex-scores had reached a uniformly low level, they were injected daily with 25 μg TP per 100 g of body weight. Under this constant hormone dosage, the individual animals returned to the high, medium, or low score that had characterized them prior to gonadectomy. Daily TP injections of 50, 75, and 100 μg per 100 g body weight produced the same results and were no more effective than the smaller dose. In a later experiment, Riss and Young (1954) selected 8 low scoring, intact males and injected them daily for 30 days with 500μg TP per 100 g body weight. Even this large dose was ineffective in raising the level of sexual performance of these animals. Young and his colleagues concluded that they were dealing with a somatic (presumably neural) threshold and that doses of androgen above that threshold were ineffective in changing the animal's behaviour.

Beach and Holz-Tucker (1949) working with male rats took a different approach. Rather than using a composite 'sex-score', they measured several specific behavioural variables such as latency to the first mount and number of intromissions preceding the ejaculatory response. After six weekly mating tests were observed and quantified, the males were castrated and divided into groups that received different daily injections of TP ranging from 1 μg to 500 μg. They found several dose-dependent behavioural differences. For example, the logarithm of the latency to mount the oestrous female was inversely proportional to the amount of androgen injected daily. Of particular interest for present purposes were the results for ejaculation latency, defined as the number of seconds between the first mount (whether or not accompanied by intromission) and the first ejaculation. Beach and Holz-Tucker found:

... that rats receiving plain oil or 1 microgram of androgen invariably took longer to ejaculate than they had in preoperative tests. [Other] males ejaculated in an average of 265 seconds before operation and 281 seconds after castration while they were receiving 25 micrograms of hormone per day. When the dosage was raised to 75 micrograms the average time needed to achieve ejaculation decreased to 257 seconds. Rats receiving 50 or 100 micrograms per day ejaculated more quickly in postoperative tests than they had before castration; and under the influence of 500 micrograms of androgen per 24 hours castrated males displayed the most marked decrease in the number of seconds elapsing before ejaculation (255 seconds as normal and 211 seconds as castrate, significant at the 5 percent level) (Beach and Holz-Tucker, 1949, p. 447).

Whalen and DeBold (1974) examined the effect of increasing doses of testosterone, DHT, and androstenedione on the sexual behaviour of castrated male hamsters. In general, these androgens produced progressively shortened ejaculation latencies with increases in dose.

Using one strain of house mice we have recently obtained results that are

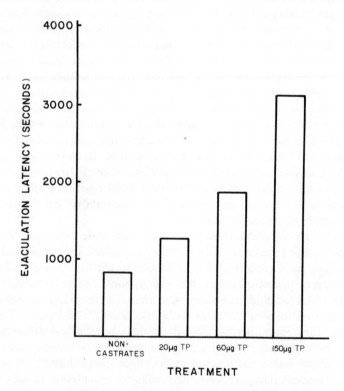

Fig. 3. Response (ejaculation latency) of prepubertally castrated B6D2F$_1$ male mice to different doses of TP injected daily

the direct opposite of those that Beach and Holz-Tucker found for rats and that Whalen and DeBold found for hamsters. McGill *et al.*, (1976) castrated B6D2F$_1$ males at 3–4 weeks of age. (This homogeneous F$_1$ strain results from crossing inbred C57BL/6 females with inbred DBA/2 males; as is noted on p. 21, the genotype of these mice may be an important variable affecting the results of this experiment.) At seven weeks of age daily injections of 20 μg TP were begun for 13 animals. Thirteen other animals received 60 μg and a final 13 animals received 150 μg daily. An intact control group of 30 males received daily oil injections. Sex tests were conducted on a weekly basis during weeks 8–13 while daily injections continued throughout. Several behavioural parameters were scored but the most striking effect was observed for ejaculation latency (defined as the time from the first intromission to the beginning of the ejaculatory reflex). An average latency was determined for each animal and then a mean of these means was calculated for each group. Fig. 3 presents the results and shows that ejaculation latency was proportional to the amount of hormone injected daily. Statistical tests indicated significant differences between the 150 μg group and both the 20 μg group and the non-castrated males. The difference between the 60 μg group and the intact animals was also statistically significant. The number of intromissions preceding ejaculation followed the same rank order and statistically significant differences were found for the same comparisons.

The males in the experiment just described were castrated prior to puberty. Therefore, we repeated the experiment using males who were castrated at 10 weeks of age after experiencing three precastration ejaculations. In addition, we added a group that was injected with 500 μg of TP daily. Injections began on the day of castration and continued for nine weeks. Weekly sex tests occurred during the last eight weeks. Once again, a mean of means was determined for the 12 to 15 males in each group. These averages are indicated on Fig.4.

An analysis of variance showed a significant treatment effect. Mann–Whitney U-tests revealed that the 500 μg group had significantly longer ejaculation latencies than all other groups. The 150 μg animals were significantly different from the 20 μg and intact groups, while the 60 μg males had significantly longer latencies than intact control males. There was no significant difference between the intact males and the 20 μg group.

The number of intromissions preceding ejaculation followed the same rank order with only minor discrepancies in significant differences and p values.

It is clear that the general relationship between ejaculation latency and daily dose of TP that was found for prepubertally castrated males also occurred when animals were castrated after puberty and sexual experience.

The response of castrated B6D2F$_1$ house mice to exogenously administered androgen is clearly different from the response of castrated guinea pigs, hamsters, and rats to similar treatment. The possibility that similar differences

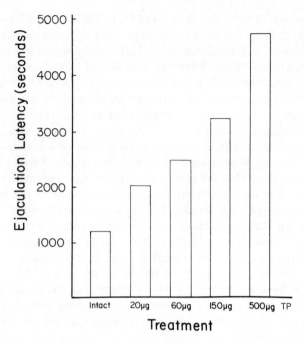

Fig. 4. Response (ejaculation latency) of postpubertally castrated B6D2F$_1$ male mice to different doses of TP injected daily

can be observed in different genotypes within a species is discussed in the next section.

Differences Within Species

Species differences in response of castrated males to injections of TP were described above. Castrated male rats and hamsters tended to ejaculate more rapidly with increasing doses of TP. B6D2F$_1$ male mice, on the other hand, exhibited ejaculation latencies in proportion to the amount of TP injected daily. Do similar differences in response to this androgen exist among different genotypes within particular species?

In 1963 Champlin et al. castrated CD2F$_1$ male mice (resulting from crosses between BALB/c females and DBA/2 males) and found that the animals rapidly lost sexual responsiveness. After sexual behaviour had reached a low level, castrates were injected with either 32 μg or 1024 μg TP daily. These treatments restored sexual behaviour in both groups, but there was no significant difference in ejaculation latency between those animals receiving 32 μg and those receiving 1024 μg. Thus, the results of Champlin et al. are in clear contradiction to those reported for B6D2F$_1$ mice above. (It should be kept in mind that these two strains have different inbred mothers but both have DBA/2 fathers.)

There would appear to be no doubt as to the phenomenon when the subjects are B6D2F$_1$ males, since significant results were found for both prepubertally and postpubertally castrated animals. But the possibility exists that the Champlin *et al.* study was somehow in error, perhaps because relatively few animals were observed. The experiment involving CD2F$_1$ castrates is currently being repeated but interesting experiments are suggested regardless of the outcome of that replication.

Let us suppose that Champlin *et al.* were correct and that CD2F$_1$ males do not exhibit a directly proportional response between ejaculation latency and daily dose of TP. This result would suggest a further hypothesis. Studies reviewed above have demonstrated the remarkable capacity of B6D2F$_1$ males to retain all elements of sexual behaviour for months and even years following castration. Three experiments have shown rapid loss of sexual responsiveness for castrated CD2F$_1$ males (Champlin *et al.*, 1963; McGill and Manning, in press; and an unpublished replication of McGill and Manning). Perhaps genotypes capable of exhibiting sexual responses in the absence of gonadal androgens respond differently to different amounts of exogenous androgens than do genotypes that are dependent upon gonadal androgens for the maintenance of sexual behaviour.

Other interesting questions arise if Champlin *et al.* were incorrect and castrated males, CD2F$_1$, along with all other genotypes of the house mouse species, exhibit ejaculation latencies in proportion to daily TP injections. Radioimmunoassays of plasma testosterone levels have established that BALB/c males have $2\frac{1}{2}$ to 3 times as much endogenous androgen as do B6D2F$_1$ males (Albelda, 1975). This difference is also reflected in the ejaculation latencies of the two genotypes: BALB/c males require approximately 60 min to reach the ejaculatory threshold while B6D2F$_1$ males require about 20 min (McGill, 1962, 1970). Other results from radioimmunoassay plasma testosterone analyses indicate that genotypes not differing greatly from B6D2F$_1$ in ejaculation latency (C57BL/6; DBA/2; D2B6F$_1$) do not differ greatly in plasma testosterone levels. If a cause–effect relationship between blood androgen level and ejaculation latency obtains, it should be possible to take any unstudied strain of house mice, measure one variable and predict the other. Furthermore, some of the other strain differences in sexual behaviour found by previous investigators (Levine *et al.*, 1965; McGill, 1962, 1970b: Vale and Ray, 1972) may be associated with different endogenous androgen levels. It should be noted that this result would not 'explain' all strain differences in house mouse sexual behaviour. For example, BALB/c males with high endogenous plasma testosterone exhibit long latencies from the introduction of an oestrous female until the first mount. Castrated B6D2F$_1$ males on high androgen levels do not exhibit mount latencies similar to those seen in BALB/c males.

To reiterate, the discovery of a linear relationship between daily TP dose and ejaculation latency in B6D2F$_1$ male mice results in interesting research ideas whether the phenomenon is genotype specific or occurs in all house mice. (For example, how do these castrates respond to other steroids?) It also raises the question as to whether other species, or genotypes within species, exhibit a similar response.

'SINGLE-GENE' EFFECTS AND THEIR MECHANISM

A useful method of studying the interactions between genes, hormones, and sexual behaviour is through the use of animals carrying particular point mutations. Alternatively, the effects of short segments of particular chromosomes can be studied by manipulating genotype through special breeding schemes (Bailey, 1971). When working with such subjects, we move a step closer to the reciprocal problems of the biochemical actions of genes directing the production of hormones and of hormones controlling the actions of genes. Such experiments are especially valuable in the study of behavioural differences when such differences are under the control of relatively few genes. Although this area of research is not highly developed, particularly in regard to sexual behaviour, some interesting leads have been published in recent years.

One promising new source of genetic analysis leading towards hormone–behaviour interactions controlled by single genes or short segments of chromosomes involves the use of recombinant inbred strains (Bailey, 1971). Details of the production of recombinant lines are beyond the scope of this chapter but, in brief, two highly inbred strains are crossed, the F_1's are mated, and then several further strains are produced by inbreeding from the F_2 generation.

Using mice bred by this technique, Eleftheriou and Kristal (1974) have studied the genetic control of auditory and visual facilitation of ovulation in females. When immature female mice were injected with pregnant mare's serum and then exposed to either an intermittently ringing bell or a flashing, high intensity light, different genotypes were either 'high responding' (facilitation of ovulation) or 'low responding' (no facilitation of ovulation). By matching the strain distribution patterns of the recombinant inbred lines, Eleftheriou and Kristal were able to characterize a gene exerting a major effect on the character. The gene is located on chromosome four (linkage group VIII). Analysis of behavioural differences in responding and unresponding genotypes has not been performed but may well result in important findings.

Part of this chapter has been concerned with the effects of neonatal androgenization on the masculine and feminine response potential of adult males and females. We have noted species and strain effects. However, it was also pointed out that normal females increase in masculine responsiveness when given TP in adulthood. In other words, they already have the capacity to respond to androgens even though their potential may be increased by neonatal treatment with steroid hormones.

The ability of mammals of either sex to respond in any way to either endogenous or exogenous androgen has been attributed to a single locus of the X chromosome (at least in mice and presumably in all mammals). The importance of this gene in providing the necessary (but not sufficient) conditions for response to androgen has been elucidated by extensive investigations of a mutation, called *Testicular feminization* (Tfm), which has been found in man, rats, mice, cattle, and possibly in dogs. The mutation occurs on the regulatory locus on the X chromosome which mediates response of all target cells to androgenic steroids (Itakura and Ohno, 1973). Externally, mutant-bearing males appear female, although the vagina is blind. Androgen-producing testes are enclosed in the body cavity, but neither a male nor a female duct system is present.

Only recently has attention centred upon the possible behavioural effects of this mutation (Ohno *et al.*, 1974). Ohno *et al.* found that mice carrying the mutant gene exhibited neither masculine nor feminine sexual behaviour when given brief tests after injection with the appropriate hormones. Furthermore, they did not attack other males introduced into their home cages. The lack of masculine behaviour was attributed to the absence of normal neonatal androgenization of particular neurones in the brains of mutant mice; even though the Tfm/y animal produces neonatal androgens no cell in his body is capable of responding to the steroids.

But why was no feminine behaviour observed? The authors hypothesized that '. . . in accordance with the more recent view, oestradiol is the real imprinting agent of masculinization as well as feminization of the brain: a strong imprinting leads to masculinization, while a weak imprinting causes feminization.' If testosterone is present, it is converted within the cells to oestradiol causing a 'strong imprinting'. The normal feminization process is presumed to be due to a low concentration of steroids during the sensitive stage of development. Since the cells of Tfm animals are unaffected by androgen there is no source of oestradiol for either strong or weak imprinting, and thus no masculine or feminine behaviour.

It should be noted that this hypothesis differs from previous notions which attributed masculinization to the presence of steroids during critical stages of development, while feminization was due to the absence of these steroids. Ohno and his colleagues postulate that some sort of neural imprinting is also necessary for feminine response potential to develop. I hope it is also fair to note that the procedures used for inducing and testing oestrous behaviour in these feminized males would be considered inadequate by experienced workers in hormone–behaviour interactions. More extensive observations are required before one can firmly conclude that these animals have no feminine response potential.

Another point mutation that has increased our knowledge of gene–hormone interaction has recently been described in humans (Imperato-McGinley *et al.*, 1974). The mutation is an autosomal recessive that produces male pseudo-hermaphrodites born with ambiguous external genitalia, but generally raised as females. At puberty, however, there is marked virilization: the voice deepens, muscle mass increases, the testes descend, and the individuals prove to be fertile. 'The phallus enlarges to become a functional penis, and the change is so striking that these individuals are referred to by the townspeople as "guevedoces"—penis at 12 (years of age) .... Psychosexual orientation is unequivocally male.' The authors have been able to relate this form of male pseudohermaphroditism to defects in androgen metabolism caused by the recessive genes.

In individuals affected by the mutation, the enzyme involved in the conversion of testosterone to dihydrotestosterone is not present in normal amounts resulting in incomplete prenatal masculinization of those structures, including the external genitalia, that depend upon such conversion for prenatal growth and differentiation. At puberty, muscle mass, growth of the phallus and scrotum, voice change, and the development of male 'sex drive' occur in response to testosterone secretion. However, prostate growth, facial hair, recession of the hairline at the temples, and acne do not occur, and thus are presumed to be mediated by DHT.

Not all genes involved in sexual behaviour induce their effects via hormones. Genes also affect behaviour by means of alterations in protein synthesis, which may or may not depend upon the presence of particular hormones. Certain substances are known to interfere with protein synthesis in one way or another. One example is cycloheximide which inhibits synthesis by a direct action at the ribosomal level. If sexual responses depend upon such activity in particular areas of the brain, then the infusion of cycloheximide into these areas should (reversibly) abolish sexual behaviour. Such effects have indeed been demonstrated for steroid-induced sexual receptivity (lordosis) in the female rat (Quadagno and Ho, 1975) and for mounting behaviour in male mice (Quadagno et al., 1976). In the latter case, reversible cycloheximide-induced interruption of masculine responses in male mice was not the result of interference with androgen production since plasma testosterone levels did not differ significantly between cycloheximide-infused and saline-infused animals.

Other chemicals such as hydroxyurea and alpha-amanitin which interfere with DNA and RNA activity respectively have been found to protect neonatal female rats from the sterilizing effects of exogenous androgen (Salaman, 1974).

These few examples illustrate how the study of 'single-gene effects', and interference with gene functions, can bring us closer to an understanding of the interactions among genes, hormones, and behaviour.

SUMMARY

We have reviewed genetic factors influencing the action of hormones on sexual behaviour by examining differences among speices and differences within species. Differences similar to those seen when species were compared have also been found when various genotypes within a species have been examined. The following examples were given:

(1) Females of different species respond differently in the degree of masculinization and/or deferminization produced by neonatal androgen treatment. So do different genotypes within species.

(2) Males of different species appear to differ in their responses to neonatally administered androgens, as do males of different inbred strains.

(3) Females of different species differ in the hormonal induction of receptivity. Females of different outbred strains and inbred strains exhibit some similar differences.

(4) Males of different species differ in retention of various elements of sexual behaviour after castration. The whole range of sexual responsiveness following removal of the gonads observed in males of different species can also be seen when genotype is varied within house mice.

(5) After castration and the loss of sexual behaviour, males of different species respond in different ways to different steroids. Mice of different outbred strains exhibit some of the same differences.

(6) Castrated males of different species respond differently in terms of ejaculation latency to injections of testosterone propionate. Some evidence exists that different genotypes within a species also exhibit differential responsiveness to this treatment.

This list of examples, combined with the promising results from the study of single gene and chromosome segment effects, points to the importance of manipulating genetic variables within particular species. As such research progresses, *some* (perhaps including those mentioned in this chapter) of the known species differences may disappear. But the use of different genotypes *within a species* is a powerful tool to further elucidate the physiological differences that underlie differences in sexual behaviour.

ACKNOWLEDGEMENTS

I thank Lee C. Drickamer, Gail Hall, Laura Marino, and Christina Williams for critical reading of the manuscript and for their help in the literature search. Research from my laboratory was supported by Research Grant 07495 from the Institute of General Medical Sciences, U.S. Public Health Service. Hormone preparations were generously supplied by the Schering Corporation, Bloomfield, New Jersey.

REFERENCES

Albelda, S. (1975) Examination of plasma testosterone levels in B6D2F$_1$ male mice before and after non-contact sexual exposure and following intracranial cycloheximide infusions. *Unpublished senior honors thesis*, Williams College.

Alsum, P., and Goy, R. W. (1974) Actions of esters of testosterone, dihydrotestosterone, or estradiol on sexual behaviour in castrated male guinea pigs, *Horm. Behav.*, 5, 207–17.

Bailey, D. W. (1971) Recombinant-inbred strains; an aid to finding identity, linkage, and function of histocompatibility and other genes, *Transplantation*, 11, 325–7.

Baum, M. J., and Vreeburg, J. T. M. (1973) Copulation in castrated male rats following combined treatment with estradiol and dihydrotestosterone, *Science*, **182**, 283–5.

Beach, F. A. (1942) Central nervous mechanisms involved in the reproductive behavior of vertebrates, *Psychol. Bull.*, **39**, 200–26.

Beach, F. A. (1947) Evolutionary changes in the physiological control of mating behavior in mammals, *Psychol. Rev.*, **54**, 297–315.

Beach, F. A. (1969) Locks and beagles, *Amer. Psychol.*, **24**, 971–89.

Beach, F. A. (1971) Hormonal factors controlling the differentiation and display of copulatory behavior in the Ramstergig and related species. In: *The Biopsychology of Development*, E. Tobach, L. R. Aronson, and E. Shaw (eds.), Academic Press, New York, pp. 249–96.

Beach, F. A., and Holz-Tucker, A. M. (1949) Effects of different concentrations of androgen upon sexual behavior in castrated male rats, *J. Comp. Physiol. Psychol.*, **42**, 433–5.

Beyer, C., Larsson, K., Pérez-Palacios, G., and Morali, G. (1973) Androgen structure and male sexual behavior in the castrated rat, *Horm. Behav.*, **4**, 99–108.

Beyer, C., and Rivaud, N. (1973) Differential effect of testosterone and dihydrotestosterone on the sexual behavior of pre-puberally castrated male rabbits, *Horm. Behav.*, **4**, 175–80.

Bloch, G. J., and Davidson, J. M. (1968) Effects of adrenalectomy And experience on postcastration sex behavior in the male rat, *Physiol. Behav.*, **3**, 461–5.

Campbell, A. B., and McGill, T. E. (1970) Neonatal hormone treatment and sexual behavior in male mice, *Horm. Behav.*, **1**, 145–50.

Champlin, A. K., Blight, W. C., and McGill, T. E. (1963) The effects of varying levels of testosterone on the sexual behaviour of the male mouse, *Anim. Behav.*, **11**, 244–5.

Christensen, L. W., Coniglio, L. P., Paup, D. C., and Clemens, L. G. (1973) Sexual behavior of male golden hamsters receiving diverse androgen treatment, *Horm. Behav.*, **4**, 223–9.

Davidson, J. M. (1966) Characteristics of sex behavior in male rats following castration, *Anim. Behav.*, **14**, 266–72.

Davidson, J. M. (1969) Effect of estrogen on the sexual behavior of male rats, *Endocrinology*, **84**, 1365–72.

Edwards, D. A. (1971) Neonatal administration of androstenedione, testosterone or testosterone propionate: Effects on ovulation, sexual receptivity and aggressive behavior in female mice, *Physiol. Behav.*, **6**, 223–8.

Eleftheriou, B. E., and Kristal, M. B. (1974) A gene controlling bell- and photically-induced ovultion in mice, *J. Reprod. Fert.*, **38**, 41–7.

Feder, H. H. (1967) Specificity of testosterone and estradiol in the differentiating neonatal rat, *Anat. Rec.*, **157**, 79–86.

Feder, H. H. (1971) The comparative actions of testosterone propionate and 5-androstan, 17–01–3-one propionate on the reproductive behavior, physiology, and morphology of male rats, *J. Endocrinol.*, **51**, 241–52.

Gorzalka, B. B., and Whalen, R. E. (1974) Genetic regulation of hormone action: Selective effects of progesterone and dihydro-progesterone (5α-pregnane-3, 20-dion) on sexual receptivity in mice, *Steroids*, **23**, 499–505.

Gorzalka, B. B., and Whalen, R. E. (1976) Effects of genotype on differential behavioral responsiveness to progesterone and 5-α-dihydroprogesterone in mice, *Behav. Genet.*, **6**, 7–15.

Goy, R. W., and Jakway, S. J. (1959) The inheritance of patterns of sexual behavior in female guinea pigs, *Anim. Behav.*, **7**, 142–9.

Goy, R. W., and Young, W. C. (1957) Strain differences in the behavioral responses of female guinea pigs to alpha-estradiol benzoate and progesterone, *Behaviour*, **10**, 340–54.

Grunt, J. A., and Young, W. C. (1952) Differential reactivity of individuals and the response of the male guinea pig to testosterone propionate, *Endocrinology*, **51**, 237–48.

Grunt, J. A., and Young, W. C. (1953) Consistency of sexual behavior patterns in individual male guinea pigs following castration and androgen therapy, *J. Comp. Physiol. Psychol.*, **46**, 138–44.

Hart, B. L. (1974) Gonadal androgen and sociosexual behavior of male mammals: A comparative analysis, *Psych. Bull.*, **81**, 383–400.

Hinde, R. A., and Tinbergen, N. (1958) The comparative study of species-specific behavior. In: *Behavior and Evolution*, A. Roe and G. G. Simpson (eds.), Yale University Press, New Haven pp. 251–68.

Imperato-McGinley, J., Guerrero, L., Gautier, T., and Peterson, R. E. (1974) Steroid 5α-reductase deficiency in man: An inherited form of male pseudohermaphroditism, *Science*, **186**, 1213–15.

Itakura, H., and Ohno, S. (1973) The effect of the mouse x-linked testicular feminization mutation on the hypothalamuspituitary axis. 1. Paradoxical effect of testosterone upon pituitary gonadotrophs, *Clin. Genet.*, **4**, 91–7.

Lehrman, D. (1970) Semantic and conceptual issues in the nature–nurture problem. In: *Development and Evolution of Behavior*, L. R. Aronson, E. Tobach, D. S. Lehrman, J. S. Rosenblatt (eds.), Freeman, San Francisco, pp. 17–52.

Levine, L., Barsel, G. E., and Diakow, C. A. (1965) Interaction of aggressive and sexual behavior in male mice, *Behaviour*, **25**, 272–80.

Luttge, W. G., and Hall, N. R. (1973) Differential effectiveness of testosterone and its metabolities in the induction of male sexual behavior in two strains of albino mice, *Horm. Behav.*, **4**, 31–43.

Luttge, W. G., Hall, N. R., and Wallis, C. J. (1974) Studies on the neuroendocrine, somatic, and behavioral effectiveness of testosterone and its 5-α-reduced metabolites in Swiss–Webster mice, *Physiol. Behav.*, **13**, 553–61.

Luttge, W. G., and Whalen, R. E. (1970) Dihydrotestosterone, androstenedione, testosterone: Comparative effectiveness in masculinizing and defeminizing reproductive systems in male a .d female rats, *Horm. Behav.*, **1**, 265–81.

Manning, A. and McGill, T. E. (1974) Neonatal androgen and sexual behaviour in female house mice, *Horm. Behav.*, **5**, 19–31.

McGill, T. E. (1962) Sexual behaviour in three inbred strains of mice, *Behaviour*, **19**, 341–50.

McGill, T. E. (1970) Genetic analysis of male sexual behavior. In: *Contributions to Behavior-Genetic Analysis: The Mouse as a Prototype*, G. Lindzey and D. D. Thiessen (eds.), Appleton-Century-Crofts, New York, pp. 57–88.

McGill, T. E., Albelda, S., Bible, H. H., and Williams, C. L. (1976) Inhibition of the ejaculatory reflex in B6D2F$_1$ mice by testosterone propionate, *Behav. Biol.*, **16**, 373–8.

McGill, T. E., and Haynes, C. M. (1973) Heterozygosity and retention of ejaculatory reflex after castration in male mice, *J. Comp. Physiol. Psychol.*, **84**, 423–9.

McGill, T. E., and Manning, A. Genotype and retention of the ejaculatory reflex in castrated male mice, *Anim. Behav.*, in press.

McGill, T. E., and Tucker, G. R. (1964) Genotype and sex drive in intact and in castrated male mice, *Science*, **145**, 514–15.

Ohno, S., Geller, L. N., and Young Lai, E. V. (1974) Tfm mutation and masculinization *versus* feminization of the mouse central nervous system, *Cell*, **3**, 235–42.

Parrott, R. F. (1975) Aromatizable and 5-α-reduced androgens: Differentiation between central and peripheral effects on male rat sexual behavior, *Horm. Behav.*, **6**, 99–108.

Pfaff, D. W. (1970) Nature of sex hormone effects on rat sex behavior: Specificity of effects and individual patterns of response, *J. Comp. Physiol. Psychol.*, **73**, 349–58.

Quadagno, D. M., Albelda, S., McGill, T. E., and Kaplan, L. (1976) Intracranial cyclo-heximide: Effect on male mouse sexual behavior and plasma testosterone, *Pharmacol. Biochem. Behav.*, **4**, 185–9.

Quadagno, D. M., and Ho, G. (1975) The reversible inhibition of steroidinduced sexual behavior in intracerebral cycloheximide, *Horm. Behav*, **6**, 19–26.

Riss, W., and Young, W. C. (1954) The failure of large quantities of testosterone propionate to activate low drive male guinea pigs, *Endocrinology*, **54**, 232–5.

Rosenblatt, J. S., and Aronson, L. R. (1958a) The influence of experience on the behavioral effects of androgen in prepuberally castrated male cats, *Anim. Behav.*, **6**, 171–82.

Rosenblatt, J. S., and Aronson, L. R. (1958b) The decline of sexual behaviour in male cats after castration with special reference to the role of prior sexual experience, *Behaviour*, **12**, 285–338.

Salaman, D. F. (1974) The role of DNA, RNA, and protein synthesis in sexual differentiation of the brain, *Prog. in Brain Res.*, **41**, 349–62.

Södersten, P. (1973a) Increased mounting behavior in the female rat following a single neonatal injection of testosterone propionate, *Horm. Behav.*, **4**, 1–17.

Södersten, P. (1973b) Estrogen-activated sexual behavior in male rats, *Horm. Behav.*, **4**, 247–56.

Thompson, M. L., and Edwards, D. A. (1971) Experiential and strain determinants of the estrogen–progesterone induction of sexual receptivity in spayed female mice, *Horm. Behav.*, **2**, 299–305.

Vale, J. R., and Ray, D. (1972) A diallel analysis of mouse sex behavior, *Behav. Genet.*, **2**, 199–209.

Vale, J. R., Ray, D., and Vale, C. A. (1973) The interaction of genotype and exogenous neonatal androgen and estrogen: Sex behavior in female mice, *Develop. Psychobiol.*, **6**, 319–27.

Vale, J. R., Ray, D., and Vale, C. A. (1974) Neonatal androgen treatment and sexual behavior in males of three inbred strains of mice, *Develop. Psychobiol.*, **7**, 483–8.

Whalen, R. E. (1964) Hormone-induced changes in the organization of sexual behavior in the male rat, *J. Comp. Physiol. Psychol.*, **57**, 175–82.

Whalen, R. E., and DeBold, J. F. (1974) Comparative effectiveness of testosterone, androstenedione, and dihydrotestosterone in maintaining mating behavior in the castrated male hamster, *Endocrinology*, **95**, 1674–9.

Whalen, R. E., and Edwards, D. A. (1967) Hormonal determinants of the development of masculine and feminine behavior in male and female rats, *Anat. Rec.*, **157**, 173–80.

Whalen, R. E., and Luttge, W. G. (1971) Testosterone, androstenedione, and dihydrotestosterone: Effects on mating behavior of male rats, *Horm. Behav.*, **2**, 117–25.

Young, W. C. (1961) The hormones and mating behavior. In: *Sex and Internal Secretions*, W. C. Young (ed.), 3rd edn., Williams and Wilkins, Baltimore, pp. 1173–239.

CHAPTER 2

Early Experience and Sexual Preferences

P. P. G. BATESON

INTRODUCTION

Why choose one sexual partner rather than another? As in any other study of behaviour, such a question can be answered in a variety of ways (Tinbergen, 1963). We can analyse the external and internal events controlling the observed choice at the time of its occurrence. We can examine the consequences of the action and investigate how they might increase the chances of that individual propagating itself or its relations. We can assemble a plausible account of the evolutionary history of the behaviour pattern. Finally, looking less far back in time, we can investigate how the preferences developed in the lifetime of the individual. This last problem concerning the developmental origins of mate selection has excited particular interest. Lorenz (1935) first stimulated the attention of other ethologists by vividly describing bizarre sexual preferences in birds, apparently generated by abnormal rearing conditions. In his famous paper, subsequently translated in full into English (Lorenz, 1970), he closely linked the development of sexual preferences to the way in which many birds will rapidly form an attachment to their mother early in life. At a particular stage in development, he argued, experience leaves an ineradicable imprint on the bird—an imprint which determines the kinds of animals or objects with which the bird will subsequently attempt to mate.

In the intervening years most research has been focused on the short-term effects of 'imprinting' on social preferences shown early in life. Young ducklings, for example, rapidly restrict their filial preferences to their own mother in their natural environment, and to a human keeper when reared by hand. This process is known as 'filial imprinting'. Even though interpretations differ markedly (compare Hess, 1973 with Bateson, 1971), the evidence for the phenomenon now seems quite secure. By degrees a considerable body of evidence has also accumulated in favour of the view that in some species and under certain conditions early (or relatively early) experiences can exert a profound effect on mate selection by one and sometimes both of the sexes. (Note the qualifications which can be of considerable biological significance.) When it is found, a process restricting sexual preferences to an experienced class of objects exhibits many of the same features as filial imprinting. However, the processes are not necessarily identical. What exactly happens, then, when mating preferences are influenced by early experience? What conditions must be satisfied? Are special processes involved? In this chapter I shall attempt to provide some answers to these questions.

The first part of this chapter consists of a brief review. It opens with some general remarks about the evolution of sexual imprinting, the possibility of analogous processes in mammals (including man), and the ways in which species and sex differences are interpreted. I then survey the major factors that are known to influence the development of sexual preferences or are presumed to have such an influence on the basis of studies of filial imprinting. For the most part I have not given details of the studies. A good introductory account to experiments on sexual imprinting can be found in Brown (1975). Klinghammer (1967) and Immelmann (1972) have provided excellent and comprehensive reviews. This chapter updates their reviews and is primarily intended to provide a reasonably complete access to the available evidence.

As will become evident, a variety of factors influence the outcome of sexual imprinting. Therefore, in the second part of the chapter I have offered a working model which brings these different factors together. I appreciate that models are not to everyone's taste and suggest that those with little appetite for theoretical details jump from the end of the review section to p. 48 where the main conclusions and predictions from the model are brought together.

THE EVOLUTION OF SEXUAL IMPRINTING

Why should it be necessary for a bird to *learn* what its future mating partner will look like? On the face of it, a mating preference that developed regardless of the special experience had by a bird in early life might seem the safer evolutionary strategy. However, an unlearned preference could be disadvantageous in a rapidly evolving species in which plumage characteristics were rapidly changing (Bateson, 1966; see also Dilger and Johnsgard, 1959). Unless some way could be found of linking the determinants of the preference to the determinants of the plumage, one might expect mating preferences to be acquired—particularly after a period of rapid evolution. This argument was developed further by Immelmann (1975) only to be criticized by Krebs (1976) who believed that it implies group selection. Even though that heresy no longer seems particularly wicked, I think Krebs is wrong. If selection pressure for a change in plumage characteristics was strong, but the cost of such a change was a loss in mating efficiency in birds with unlearned preferences, the selection pressure on individuals to learn the characteristics of their future mates would inevitably have been high.

A quite different explanation is suggested by an animal's need to strike an optimal balance between inbreeding and outbreeding. When particular combinations of genes are necessary for an adaptive outcome, wholesale genetic recombination arising from sexual reproduction between two unrelated individuals could be disruptive and provide a selection pressure for, among other things, mating with a relation. The outcome of such selection would be to minimise the disrupting effects of recombination. To be set against this, other selection pressures could operate against inbreeding—the most powerful being the need to increase genetic diversity (a conventional explanation for sexual reproduction). One would expect an optimal balance to be struck between inbreeding and outbreeding; in other words a balance between positive and negative assortative mating. But such assortative mating requires recognition of relations. How is the animal to respond selectively to its kin?

Averhoff and Richardson (1976) have proposed a system by which the fruit fly, *Drosophila melanogaster*, can avoid mating with closely related individuals using pheromones that are specific to a particular genotype. They imply that a fly's ability to detect a particular pheromone is also related to its genotype but do not propose a mechanism by which the production of a pheromone and the development of a detection mechanism can be genetically linked. It is possible that even in the fruit fly the detection mechanism develops as a consequence of exposure to it own pheromone and I certainly wish to propose that one of the only ways in which birds can visually recognise a related individual is by learning. The suggestion is that sexual imprinting provides a means by which birds can mate with their kin—the assumption being that kin tend to look alike. On this argument early experience sets a bird's standard and subsequently when selecting a mate the bird opts for some slight discrepancy from that standard, the degree of discrepancy being determined ultimately by the optimal trade-off point between inbreeding and outbreeding.

Whether or not this explanation is correct, the involvement of sexual imprinting in assortative mating is well established. In particular the studies on the polymorphous snow goose (Cooke *et al.*, 1976) suggest that the geese tend to mate with the colour morph to which they were exposed early in life. It should be pointed out that the snow goose studies were triggered by an interest in the role of imprinting in evolution—an area of active theorizing. The question of how imprinting might give rise to new species in evolution is discussed extensively in other reviews (Brown, 1975; Immelmann, 1972, 1975a, 1975b) and I shall not pursue it further here. In conclusion, it is worth emphasizing that whether assortative mating is described as slightly negative (such as avoidance of mating with parents and siblings) or slightly positive (such as avoidance of mating with unrelated individuals) depends very much on definition and the nature of the choice available to the animal.

SEXUAL IMPRINTING IN MAMMALS

If strong evolutionary pressures promoted the involvement of learning in the development of birds' mating preferences, analogous processes would surely be expected in mammals which have, if anything, a much greater capacity to learn than birds. (See also Larsson, this volume Chapter 3 for discussion of the role of experience in the development of mammalian mating behaviour.) Considerable anecdotal evidence suggests that many species of mammals kept as pets will indeed form attachments to their human owners, but systematic studies are not numerous (Beauchamp and Hess, 1973; Deutsch and Larson, 1974). The evidence for some influence of early olfactory experience on mate selection in mice is particularly convincing (Mainardi et al., 1965). Since the dominant sensory modality of many mammals is olfactory rather than visual it is perhaps not surprising that olfactory experience should play an important role in the determination of their social preferences (see Müller-Schwarze, 1974).

What about mate selection in man? Popular accounts of the origins of human behaviour are rather prone to adopt imprinting as the explanation for fetishism, homosexuality, and, indeed, normal sexual proclivities. But the evidence for an imprinting-like process operating early in development is remarkably poor. On the other hand, there are clear signs that humans are generally homogamous—we prefer to form lasting pair bonds with people of the same body type as ourselves (Lewis, 1975). The inference from such data might be that we choose as a sexual partner someone who looks like one of our parents did when we were children. However, as Lewis points out, the evidence could simply arise from a straightforward limitation of choice; if people live in relatively homogeneous communities they may have little opportunity to select a mate with markedly dissimilar appearance from themselves. But even if, as seems likely, an element of active assortative mating is involved, our mating preferences are almost certainly affected by experience occurring late in adolescence and doubtless they are also influenced by a variety of social pressures (Eckland, 1968). While an imprinting-like process is unlikely to play a decisive part in the determination of human pair-bonds, the influences of early social experience, mediated in subtle and indirect ways, may well play a contributory role. That is not saying very much but it is probably all that can be said about the origins of most people's sexual preferences.

SPECIES AND SEX DIFFERENCES

As has already been noted, a statement about sexual imprinting in birds is hedged around with qualifications. Species seem to differ markedly in the extent to which their sexual preferences are determined by early experience. For example, Schutz (1965) found that while the mating preferences of male mallard were easily manipulated by rearing them with another species of duck, those of greylag geese were difficult to shift away from their own species. Such differences can be biologically significant. But it is important to appreciate that they may arise for a wide variety of reasons and the evidence does not necessarily indicate that the preferences of a seemingly 'unimprintable' species are, indeed, uninfluenced by their early experience. For instance, in particular cases the length of exposure may have been too short or, from the outset of the experiment, the birds may have been too strongly biassed against the species to which they were exposed. Without careful parametric studies, species differences in sexual imprinting are not easy to interpret.

That having been said, it would be surprising if the mating preferences of brood parasites like the cuckoo were much affected by experience with their foster parents. Similarly, it would be odd if birds such as female mallard, which are cared for exclusively by their mothers in early life, were greatly influenced by their *early* experience when they come to select a mate. Knowledge of a species' biology can obviously help us to decide in which species and in which sexes early experience is likely to play an important role in the determination of sexual preferences.

Interpretation of sex differences, like species differences, is not as straightforward as might at first seem. The occurrence of mating frequently depends on the preferences of both partners. Consequently, if only one of the birds in a potential cross-species mating has been fostered by the other species, mating between the two species may be prevented by the normally-reared bird. A very interesting field study by Harris (1970) illustrates the point. Harris put fertile eggs of herring gulls in the nests of the closely related lesser black-backed gulls and also made the reciprocal swap. Subsequently the hatched young were ringed and as far as possible their mating behaviour was observed when they returned to the breeding colonies as adults. The cross-fostered birds were much more likely to mate with the other species than the normally-reared birds, but the cross-fostered females showed a significantly stronger tendency to mate with the foster species than the cross-fostered males. Does it follow, that the male gulls are less influenced by their early experience than the females (cf. Brown, 1975)? It does not, since all the cross-fostered males may have attempted to mate with the species that fostered them and those that failed were simply rejected by the normal females. Indeed, Harris attributed the differences between the sexes to the dominant role which the female normally plays in mate selection. It should be noted that the complications imposed on studies of sexual imprinting by the behaviour of a potential mate can sometimes be overcome by offering the birds, in whose preferences the experimenter is interested, a choice between the stuffed and mounted skins of the relevant species (Immelmann, 1969).

In laboratory studies, even those involving tight control over the test stimuli, sex differences may arise because one of the sexes is relatively passive in at least the early stages of pair formation. This appears to be the case in female pigeons and doves (Warriner et al., 1963; Brosset, 1971). A controversy over the interpretation of apparent sex differences in zebra finches can almost certainly be resolved in similar terms. Immelmann (1969) had shown that male zebra finches are dramatically influenced by their early experience. Walter (1973), however, failed to show such an influence in females. Subsequently, Sonnemann and Sjölander (1977) showed that, by using sensitive choice tests, female zebra finches can, indeed, reveal a sexual preference for the species that reared them.

An unequivocal difference between the sexes in sexual imprinting points, of course, to the differences in the ways in which sexual preferences develop. Careful studies may show that one of the sexes does not learn at all or that the sexes learn in different ways. Alternatively, in one sex the effects of early learning may be suppressed in adult life. Evidence for the last possibility was obtained by Schutz (1975). He found that female mallard, which are only slightly influenced by their earlier social experience (see Klint, 1975), can show the effects of this experience much more strikingly when they are injected with the male hormone testosterone. They were exposed as ducklings to muscovy ducks and subsequently mated normally with male mallard. But after injection with testosterone most females showed sexual interest in the muscovy ducks.

FACTORS INFLUENCING SEXUAL IMPRINTING

The classical notion of imprinting is attractively straightforward: a bird is exposed to an object early in life and later it prefers to mate with the object. In many ways, though, this statement is hopelessly vague. Does it matter what kind of object is used? How long does the bird have to be exposed to the object? At what stage in development must the bird be exposed? Does it matter how the bird is kept before and after the period of exposure? Answers to these questions are critical if we are to obtain some understanding of the mechanism. The brilliant intuitive ethology of Konrad Lorenz must give way to more pedestrian precision. Such precision, however, is scarcely available even in the more extensively investigated filial imprinting. Investigation of sexual imprinting is at the relatively primitive stage of laying bare the conditions that are necessary for its occurrence. Nevertheless, explicit acceptance that sexual imprinting is multiply determined has been an important conceptual advance.

In what immediately follows, I have attempted to isolate the major factors affecting sexual imprinting. I have based the analysis initially on what is known about filial imprinting because the evidence from sexual imprinting is still relatively meagre. Rather than cite detailed evidence I have abstracted a picture which can be found in various guises in the reviews of filial imprinting (Bateson, 1966, 1971, 1972; Hess, 1973; Hoffman and Ratner, 1973; Sluckin, 1972). Those who seek experimental support for the statements made here should consult the reviews.

Stage of Development

An overwhelming body of evidence suggests that filial imprinting can be *started* most readily at a certain stage in development (see reviews and Landsberg, 1976). Now, to describe the developmental determinants of that stage as 'maturational' easily traps one into thinking that the stage is reached independently of any experience. If a broad definition of experience is used, this is clearly false (see Bateson, 1976; Gottlieb, 1976). The general rate of development is affected by all sorts of externally derived factors such as temperature, nutrition, and so forth. What is meant then is that the responsiveness of the developing animal alters when it is left in an environment that is changed neither by the experimenter, nor by the animal itself. Anyway, as a consequence of an increase in responsiveness to suitable objects, a bird is increasingly likely to restrict its preferences to the object to which it has been exposed.

In as much as the causes of the increase in responsiveness are understood they seem to be closely associated with rather general improvements in sensory equipment and motor organization in the cases of filial imprinting in precocial birds and sexual imprinting in some altricial species. However, the evidence suggests that several precocial species start to restrict their sexual preferences long after their filial preferences (Gallagher, 1976, 1977; Schutz, 1971; Vidal, 1976a, 1976b). Conceivably the evidence results from the relatively long time that elapses between exposure and testing in sexual imprinting experiments. In effect, the experimenters might have found the trade-off point between maximizing initial storage of information and minimizing subsequent decay of the stored information. If that explanation is not correct, sexual imprinting must depend, in part, on some change in state (such as a change in hormonal level) specific to sexual responsiveness.

It is often assumed that the increase in readiness to learn is brought about by the same conditions that lead to a subsequent decline. The work on filial imprinting strongly suggests that the decline is dependent on the bird developing a preference for something in its immediate environment. In general, the longer a bird is exposed to one object the less likely it is to respond socially to another object and, as its preferences are increasingly restricted, the more likely it is to avoid the novel object. Such a process is likely to operate in the case of sexual imprinting but the picture may be more complicated since an intrinsic decline in responsiveness could also occur at a certain stage in development. For example, having risen, the endogenous level of a hormone could subside once again. Since sexual responsiveness of adult birds fluctuates between breeding seasons sexual responsiveness may also fluctuate during development. That having been said, it should be emphasized that this complication is no more than a plausible possibility at the moment.

As things stand analysis of the developmental conditions under which sexual imprinting can most readily take place suggests that two intrinsic factors are critical. The first determines the levels of responsiveness before any learning has taken place, the second determines how novel objects will be responded to once learning has begun. Taken together these two factors can adequately account for the descriptive evidence for a 'critical' or 'sensitive period' for imprinting. Apart from the possible complication of a subsequent decline in intrinsic responsiveness, the response to novelty is, however, complicated by two additional facets. First, in the early stages of learning, a bird may actually prefer a novel object (Bateson and Jaeckel, 1976; Jackson and Bateson, 1974). The functional explanation for this may be that the visual characteristics of the parent or future class of sexual partners are so dissimilar when seen from different viewpoints that the young bird must actively work to familiarize itself with those different views in order to facilitate ready recognition at a later stage.

Secondly, the negative response to novel objects is not immutable—particularly in the early stages of developing a restricted preference for the familiar. A steady waning in avoidance occurs as the result of repeated presentation of a novel object, especially when the opportunities for fleeing from the object are restricted (Ratner and Hoffman, 1974). When avoidance has ceased the young birds may start to respond socially to the object. Indeed, Salzen and Meyer (1968) showed that in the first week chicks would, after a day's exposure, prefer to approach the most recently seen object when given a choice between it and an object to which they had previously been exposed and which they had previously preferred. By contrast, some truly remarkable cases of stable sexual preferences have been reported in turkeys (Schein, 1963) and zebra finches (Immelmann, 1969). Such differences may represent species differences or differences between filial and sexual imprinting. However, the stable preferences have all been obtained after, at the very least, several days of exposure. This brings into focus another important factor influencing imprinting.

Length of Exposure

The classical concept of imprinting carries with it a strong implication of a single-shot, all-or-nothing, process. The implication was undoubtedly intended by Lorenz (1970) who wrote: 'I regard it as quite possible that a *single* elicitation of the following response can bring about complete imprinting to the mother.' A staunch advocate of this view remarked at a recent conference that for a bird to be half imprinted would be as absurd as a woman being half pregnant. Notwithstanding this attitude, the consensus of opinion has been moving steadily towards the view that the longer a bird has been exposed to an object in broad terms the more restricted will be its preference for that object (Bateson, 1966; Sluckin, 1972). The consensus is largely supported by evidence from studies of filial imprinting (Bateson, 1974; Bateson and Jaeckel, 1976; Zajonc et al., 1973). But in the case of sexual imprinting, no stable long-term preferences have ever been reported as the result of a few seconds or a few minutes of exposure. Increasingly, careful investigators report that sexual preferences are modifiable long after the stage in development that seems optimal for sexual imprinting (Klinghammer, 1967; Gallagher, 1976; Sherrod, 1974; Vidal, 1976a, 1976b). Evidently it would be a mistake to assume that because a stable preference seems to have been formed when the bird is given an easy series of choices, further subtle modifications to its sexual preferences do not occur.

Other Experience

If the effects of exposure to an object on subsequent preferences are cumulative and if the process is at all reversible, it is important to ask what is going on while the animal is *not* being exposed to the object. If the animal is held under some degree of sensory deprivation, it might be supposed that nothing could take place. But this assumption is not really justifiable. Even with sub-optimal stimuli of the most attenuated kind, some modification to plastic parts of the nervous system could take place. Increasing familiarity with the background discharge of its sense organs might ultimately lead the animal to detect and avoid novelty. In any event, sensory deprivation brings with it other consequences which can greatly complicate the design of long-term experiments. Continued sensory deprivation can lead to degenerative changes which drastically alter an animal's capabilities (Riesen, 1966). The implications for developmental studies of sexual imprinting can be quite serious.

In practice, many investigators of sexual imprinting have opted not to rear their birds in social isolation. When the birds were not being exposed to the 'imprinting species' they had social contact with another species. It has some-times been assumed that such additional experience has no long-term effects— maybe because it occurred outside the period on which the experimenter had focused his attention. But given that preferences are restricted relatively gradually, it is clearly unwise to ignore what Klinghammer (1967) termed 'extraneous social experience'. The muddying effects of different kinds of experience in the period between hatching and adult life almost certainly account for some of the variable results obtained in studies of sexual imprint-ing. Well-designed experiments are beginning to show how different kinds of experience can interact, or counteract. For example, Vidal (1976a, 1976b) exposed male domestic chicks to a model between 30 and 45 days after hatching (as well as other ages). Half the chicks were reared in isolation until testing at 150 days and half were reared with a female. At 150 days they were all given a choice between the model and the stuffed skin of a female hen. The isolated birds responded sexually to the model, the socially reared birds responded sexually to the stuffed hen.

Stimulus Value

Although the popular notion of imprinting is that attachments can be formed to almost any object, it has long been apparent that responsiveness is markedly constrained. Some stimulus objects are much more effective than others. This initial bias interacts with the effects of experience. For instance, in the case of filial imprinting Bateson and Jaeckel (1976) found that when inexperienced day-old chicks were given a choice between a red and a yellow flashing light, they showed a preference of x units for the red light. After exposure to the red light for 60 min, chicks showed a preference of $y + x$ units for red and strikingly after exposure to the yellow light for 60 min another group showed a preference for yellow very close to $y - x$ units (see Fig. 1). In other words, in this experiment the preference of experienced birds was determined by the superimposition of the effects of experience on an initial

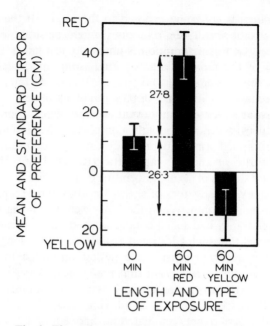

Fig. 1. The preferences of day-old domestic chicks when given a choice between a red rotating flashing light and a yellow one. One group of chicks was untrained, and the other two were previously trained for 60 min either with the red light or the yellow light. (From Bateson and Jaeckel (1976).)

bias. It is unlikely that the simple additive process suggested by these results will usually operate and experience with the initially less effective stimulus would be expected to leave less impact. Nevertheless, the strong hint that preferences are determined by a stable, predetermined bias on the one hand and by a highly plastic process on the other, is important. Certainly, in the work on sexual imprinting investigators have repeatedly reported that notwithstanding considerable experience with another species, birds do, nevertheless, show sexual preferences for their own species (Schutz, 1965).

Immelmann (1972) argued that an initial bias is especially evident when birds such as zebra finches are reared by a mixed pair of foster parents (one of which is a member of their own species and one a member of another species) and subsequently the birds prefer to mate with their own species. This can happen when the zebra finch foster parent is a male as markedly as when it is a female. One possible snag with such experiments is that the foster parent of a different species can detect (from, say, mouth colouration) that the young which it is tending is, from its own species' standpoint, abnormal. As a consequence, it may not direct quite so much parental care towards the young as the zebra finch parent. Klaus Immelmann tells me, though, that adult Bengalese finches, which he and his collaborators generally use as foster parents, take better care of the young zebra finches than do adult zebra finches. So, it seems virtually certain that from an early stage in development some stimuli are much more effective than others and the effects of sexual imprinting are then superimposed on the initial bias. The acquired preference and the initial one, which birds exhibit for their own species and which they presumably do not have to learn, can operate together or in opposition. When they operate in opposition careful experiments may be required to determine how the balance will be struck in particular cases.

INTERACTING FACTORS AND THE NEED FOR A MODEL

The brief foregoing survey suggests that at least four factors influence the development of sexual preferences. Clearly these can interact in numerous ways. Some of the interactions have already been mentioned. Others are hinted at in the literature. For example, Immelmann (1972) wrote that if male zebra finches were to show a sexual preference for a Bengalese finch, they had to be exposed for twice as long to a Bengalese finch when exposure started late than when exposure started early in development. For the most part, however, systematic studies are too scanty for reliable statements to be made about the interactions between the important factors that influence sexual preferences. The paucity of empirical evidence does not reflect any lack of interest but arises from straightforward practical difficulties and from the crude pressures operating on most people actively engaged in research on sexual imprinting. After a bird has been exposed to a particular kind of experience, months or even years may elapse before the effects on sexual behaviour can be assessed. A substantial investment in animals, facilities, and the operations of exposure and testing can be wasted if the experimenter guesses wrongly about the values of independent variables he chooses to manipulate. When commitment to producing positive differences between groups of animals is so great, the absence of a difference can look like a professional disaster. It is no good comforting the experimenter with assurances about the real value of negative evidence if no journal editor will touch the results. Anyway, for better or for worse, real gaps in published knowledge exist.

How should we proceed? A skilled ethologist may make some intelligent guesses about the likely nature of interactions between important factors and he may well be correct. However, it is already evident that the phenomenon is much more complicated than was originally supposed. It is becoming too difficult to juggle mentally with all the known sources of variation and operate by intuition alone. I believe it is now necessary to attempt the formulation of rather more rigorous models than have been used in the past. The major benefit may be merely an improvement in mental hygiene—explicit models tend to expose the assumptions that underpin the arguments of a theorist. Moreover, a working model whose performance can be simulated may suggest lines of enquiry which had not been previously considered.

Clearly a theoretical model is likely to be of most use if its properties are based as closely as possible on the processes that are being simulated. In what follows I have constructed a model of sexual imprinting so that the major parameters correspond as closely as possible to the factors which are known to play a dominant role in determining the long-term effect on sexual preferences. 'Parameter' has become something of a cult word and in the behavioural literature is often used inaccurately as a synonym for 'variable' or 'measure'. I need to use it here in its precise sense of a quantity which is constant in a particular case but which can vary between cases.

PARAMETERS OF THE MODEL

The important external factors in any imprinting experiment are summarized in Fig. 2. They are readily manipulated experimentally and they have all been incorporated as major parameters in the model. In all simulations, when not exposed to condition B (the 'imprinting stimulus'), the model is exposed to condition A. The age of onset of exposure to condition B, the length of exposure to B, and the age of subsequently testing the model's responsiveness to B are all crucial. Equally important are the relative stimulus values of A and B (abbreviated respectively as S_A and S_B). In the simplest case the stimulus values are the same but by varying the value of B in relation to A it is possible, on the one hand, to examine the effects of 'imprinting' with a suboptimal stimulus or, on the other hand, holding a bird in the equivalent of social isolation outside the period of training with B. (The second case is logically equivalent to keeping A normal and making B supernormal since the model deals with the relative stimulus values of A and B.)

Intrinsic processes are inferred. Their modelling requires particular care and involves laying bare a number of assumptions. I have found it conceptually convenient to distinguish *intrinsic responsiveness* and *acquired reduction in responsiveness*. Studies of imprinting suggest that specific experience does not

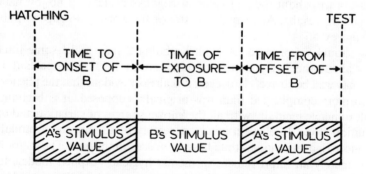

Fig. 2. The major extrinsic factors operating in an imprinting experiment. 'B' is the imprinting object. 'A' refers to the rearing conditions outside the period of imprinting

greatly modify the stage when restriction of preferences can start most readily. Furthermore, a bird with a well-developed mating preference does not neces- sarily manifest that preference at all times of year. These two lines of evidence are, of course, separable, but they both point to the existence of an important internal state factor. I have assumed that acquired restrictions of preference and subsequent manifestations of a mating preference can only occur when the animal is in an appropriate state. In the model the state is specified by a variable termed 'intrinsic responsiveness' (abbreviated as i). In the simplest version of the model, intrinsic responsiveness increases from zero to a prede- termined ceiling value at a specified age and stays at that value. In elaborations of the model which I shall consider later, intrinsic responsiveness fluctuates and the bird can only acquire and show a preference during the periods when intrinsic responsiveness is above zero. In the version used first, intrinsic respon- siveness was increased relatively gradually (see Fig. 3)—although it turned out from computer simulations that a change in the rate of increase did not dramatically alter the model's properties. It should be clear that intrinsic responsiveness is determined by (a) a parameter (or parameters) that specifies the stage (or stages) of development at which i changes, (b) a parameter that determines the way in which i changes and (c) a parameter that determines the upper limit of its fluctuations.

Above all else studies of imprinting show that a specific experience can have a profound influence on the way a bird responds to an object. The principal effect is to restrict preferences to the familiar object. Novel objects, apart

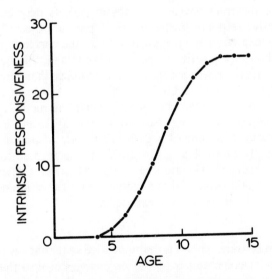

Fig. 3. Changes in intrinsic responsiveness with age. All units are arbitrary. Once intrinsic respon- siveness has risen to its ceiling value it stays there

from being less preferred, may be ignored or even avoided. Therefore, it seemed essential to incorporate into the model an operation that took account of this crucial consequence of imprinting. Therefore, on responding positively to one object the levels of responsiveness to all detectably different objects are reduced from their previous values at a specified rate. The overall amount of the reduction in responsiveness to novel objects is called 'acquired reduction in responsiveness' (abbreviated as n). A potential source of confusion is that this variable increases as a result of a positive response to a dissimilar object. The greater the value of n for a particular object the more likely is the overall responsiveness to that object to be negative since n operates against intrinsic responsiveness (i). The ways in which the value of n is determined by other parameters are described next.

THE MODEL'S OPERATIONS

The prime feature of the model is that its overall responsiveness (abbreviated as r) to an object is determined by the stimulus value of the object (S), the bird's intrinsic responsiveness at the moment (i), and acquired reductions in the bird's responsiveness (n) arising from positive responses to another object. So the overall responsiveness to object B, $r_B = S_B (i - n_B)$. The relationship between S and $(i - n)$ is multiplicative so that it is not possible for the model to give a response to an object if its stimulus value (S) is zero. Furthermore it cannot give a positive social response if intrinsic responsiveness (i) is zero.

At any stage the responsiveness to absent objects may be reduced as a result of a positive response to the currently present object. The amount of the reduction is related to the responsiveness to the currently present object. If the model shows no positive responsiveness to the object in its presence (either because i is zero or because $i - n$ is equal to or less than zero), no increases occur in the values of n for absent objects. Of course, the n value to the currently present object may be greater than zero because the model has already responded positively to something else. An additional feature has been added to simulate the known waning of negative responses such as avoidance when a bird is repeatedly exposed to a novel object: the n value to the currently present object is reduced. The amount of the reduction is determined by the bird's intrinsic responsiveness at the moment and the stimulus value of the object to which it is currently being exposed.

At age t:
$$n_t = n_{t-1} - [(i_{t-1})(S)].$$

The relationship between i and S is multiplicative so that no change in n occurs if i or S is zero. A constraint is placed on changes in n so that it can never become negative, the reason being that it is intended to simulate reductions in responsiveness. What then happens to the responsiveness to object B if n_B is greater than zero? After a period of exposure to B for one unit of age, the value of n at age t is obtained as follows:

$$n_{Bt} = n_{Bt-1} - [(S_B)(i_{t-1})].$$

Consequently the overall responsiveness to B at age t:

$$r_{Bt} = S_B (i_t - n_{Bt}).$$

On exposure to object A, n_B increases at a rate determined by i and S_A. On exposure to B, n_B decreases at a rate determined by i and S_B. If S_A and S_B are the same, recovery of overall responsiveness to B in B's presence will therefore occur at the same rate as did reduction in responsiveness to B when the model was being exposed to A. Such symmetry does not seem altogether plausible since a negative response to B, such as avoidance, might greatly reduce the actual amount of contact with B. Therefore, an additional parameter (abbreviated as Z) has been introduced. The acquired reduction in responsiveness to object B after a positive response to A is: ·

$$n_{Bt} = n_{Bt-1} + (r_{At-1})(Z)$$

when Z is made greater than unity n_B increases more rapidly on exposure to A than it decreases on exposure to B with other things equal.

It is important to draw attention to a number of simplifying assumptions.

(1) A ceiling has been set on the strength of a positive social response. For example, the maximum value for r_A is $S_A i$. However, no ceiling has been set on the strength of a negative response. The purpose of this asymmetry was to simulate the evidence that specific experience *restricts* preferences to the familiar and that the more familiar a bird is with an object, the more extensively it avoids dissimilar objects (except in the early stages of familiarization).

(2) Positive social responses at the time when preferences are first restricted are not treated differently from responsiveness shown towards a preferred mating partner in adult life.

(3) The initial stimulus value of an object is not changed either by experience with that object or by experience with other objects.

(4) The effect of showing positive preference for one object is always to decrease the overall responsiveness to other objects. Heightened responsiveness to slightly novel objects which I have modelled in another paper (Bateson, 1973) has been ignored here.

(5) The complications of generalization gradients have been ignored by simply considering two stimulus conditions, A and B.

(6) The parameters controlling the stage (or stages) at which intrinsic responsiveness changes and the manner in which it changes are unaffected by rearing conditions or short-term factors that influence general arousal.

Probably none of the simplifying assumptions is wholly justified. However, I believe that embellishments which would make the model more realistic would not radically alter its performance.

OUTPUT OF THE MODEL

The performance of the model can be readily simulated on a computer. In presenting the results of such a simulation, a decision must be taken about which dependent variables should be examined. I have opted to present a measure of *preference* because, in a sexual imprinting experiment, the investigator will usually be interested in knowing, whether the species to which the bird was exposed earlier in development, is preferred to another species. In this case the other 'species' is stimulus A, the condition to which the bird was exposed when it was not being trained with stimulus B. It turned out that if the model preferred stimulus B to stimulus A in a choice test, it would also respond sexually to B on its own and not respond sexually to A on its own (and *vice versa*).

In Fig. 4 the results of a simulation are shown in which two parameters, the age of onset of exposure to stimulus B and the stimulus value of B have been varied. The values of other parameters, which are held constant, are given in the figure legend. It should be noted that the stimulus value of A, the condition under which the model is kept when not being exposed to B,

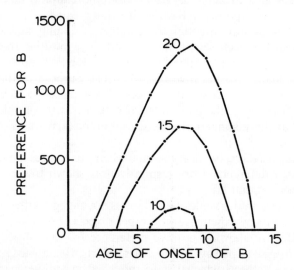

Fig. 4. The results of modelling sexual imprinting with objects (B) of three different stimulus values; the higher B's stimulus value the greater its effect on sexual imprinting. The preference for B when a choice was given at age 50 is shown for different ages of onset. The period of exposure to B was kept constant at 12 units of age. The stimulus value of A was kept at unity. Intrinsic responsiveness increased as shown in Fig. 3. The parameter, Z, that determined the rate at which the acquired reduction of responsiveness, n, was increased was kept constant at 4. All units are arbitrary

is unity. The effect of increasing the stimulus value of B is equivalent either to 'imprinting' the bird with a supernormal stimulus or, at other times, holding the bird in a suboptimal environment (e.g. social isolation). The results of the simulation demonstrate that a striking 'sensitive period' can be obtained— that is there are limited ranges of ages when exposure to B can produce a long-term effect on sexual responsiveness to B. It also shows the relative nature of the 'sensitive period'. The length of the sensitive period, defined in terms of age of onset of exposure, is highly dependent on the relative stimulus values of A and B and, for that matter, on the values of the other parameters. In order to condense the results of varying other parameters, I have presented in Fig. 5 the greatest preference for stimulus B when onset of exposure is varied. This peak value is strongly correlated with the range of ages within which it is possible to start exposure to B and subsequently obtain a positive preference for B. The results merely specify the limits within which it is possible to obtain a positive preference for stimulus B when other parameters are held constant.

A more interesting exercise is to trade-off one parameter value against another—particularly those which correspond to extrinsic factors influencing sexual imprinting. For example, it is obvious from Fig. 5 that the length of

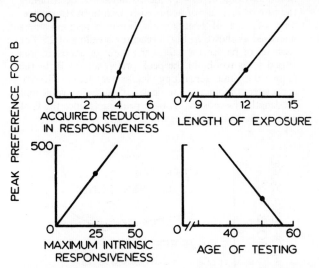

Fig. 5. The results of varying independently four parameters in the model of sexual imprinting while holding the others constant. The value of each parameter when it was not being varied is shown by a dot. 'Acquired reduction in responsiveness' refers to the parameter Z that determines the rate at which n increases (see text). The stimulus values of A and B were kept at unity and the intrinsic responsiveness increased as shown in Fig. 3. For each set of parameter values the age of onset of exposure was varied so as to obtain the peak value for the preference for B. All units are arbitrary

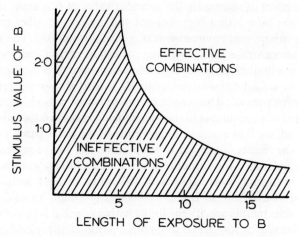

Fig. 6. The results of varying the stimulus value of B and the length of exposure in the sexual imprinting model. The other parameter values were held constant as follows: Stimulus value of A = 1; the parameter Z determining the rate of increase of acquired reduction in responsiveness = 4; age of testing = 50. Intrinsic responsiveness increased as shown in Fig. 3 reaching a ceiling of 25. For each set of parameter values the onset of exposure was varied so as to obtain the peak preference for B. In the figure the line separating ineffective from effective parameter combinations indicates B's stimulus value and the length of exposure giving a peak preference for B of zero at the time of testing.

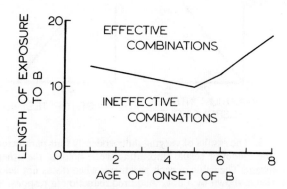

Fig. 7. The results of varying length of exposure and age of onset of exposure in the sexual imprinting model. All other parameter values were the same as for Fig. 6 except B's stimulus value which was kept at unity

exposure can be shortened if the stimulus value of B is increased. If these two parameters are varied systematically it is possible to obtain values for effective combinations of them both. An 'effective combination' means that a positive preference for B is subsequently obtained. These effective combinations are shown in Fig. 6. A striking conclusion is that however optimal a stimulus may be, no preference for it will subsequently be shown if the length of exposure is insufficient. Conversely, if the stimulus is inadequate no amount of exposure to it will be enough to generate a positive preference.

The results of another trade-off are shown in Fig. 7. Here effective combinations of length of exposure and age of onset of exposure are shown. As might have been anticipated there is a stage in development when minimal exposure is needed.

A more subtle point is that if experience intervening between exposure to condition B and testing is important and age of testing is kept constant (as is usually the case in most imprinting experiments) then, in explorations of the sensitive period, the age of onset of exposure is confounded with the amount of experience intervening between the end of exposure and testing. Fig. 8 explores the effects of keeping time from the end of exposure to testing constant while varying the age of onset. It is clear that the results can depend to some degree on which parameters are held constant and which are allowed

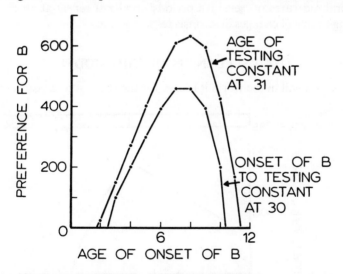

Fig. 8. The preference for B with different ages of onset of exposure when (a) the age of testing was kept constant at 31 and (b) the time from the onset of imprinting to testing was kept constant at 30. Other parameter values were held constant as follows: Stimulus values of A and B = 1; the parameter Z determining the rate of increase of acquired reduction in responsiveness = 4. Intrinsic responsiveness increased as shown in Fig. 3 reaching a ceiling of 25

(often unwittingly) to vary as others, locked in with them, are knowingly altered.

So far, I have considered what may be an extreme case in which all experience after a certain age influences the final preferences to some degree. It is worth considering now a case in which intrinsic responsiveness increases sharply at a certain age and falls back to zero a bit later. Later in life responsiveness rises once again. This variant of the model might be equivalent to state-dependent learning in which a preference is (a) formed at a time when a hormonal level is high, (b) not further modified when that level falls back, and (c) only expressed when the level rises once again in adult life. Such state-dependency would protect a preference formed in early life from the modifying influences of intervening experience. An example is shown in Fig. 9 in which intrinsic responsiveness rises sharply to a ceiling value at age 5, falls back to zero at age 20 and then rises again at 45. The test is at age 50. It should be clear that this modification leads to much more dramatic long-term effects of early experience. The modification embodies a principle closely akin to the classical notion of a critical period—an endogenous increase and subsequent decrease in responsiveness. A particularly interesting feature of this simulation is that no preference for B is shown when exposure starts after the age of 8. However, intrinsic responsiveness does not fall back until the age of 20. In other words, behavioural measures of 'sensitive periods' need not reflect at all closely the underlying timing of changes in intrinsic responsiveness.

THE USEFULNESS OF THE MODEL

With the best will in the world it is easy for the theorist to construct a model

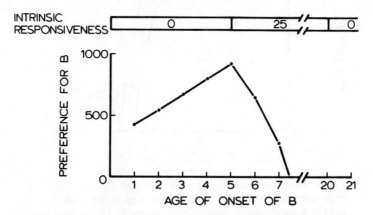

Fig. 9. The preference for B after different ages of onset of exposure when intrinsic responsiveness increased sharply to a value of 25 at age 5 and dropped back to zero at age 20 and increased once again to 25 at age 45. Other parameter values were held constant as follows: Stimulus values of A and B = 1; the parameter Z determining the rate of increase of acquired reduction in responsiveness = 4; age of testing = 50

on the basis of what is known and then come to believe that the moving parts within the model represent reality. So it is obviously important to tread carefully when drawing conclusions about how sexual imprinting does work from purely logical considerations of how it might work. But in as much as the model does draw attention to those logical considerations it has some relevance both to experimental design and to the varieties of inference that can be drawn from actual data. Given that different factors influence the outcome of sexual imprinting, an experimenter ought to be sensitive to the dramatic ways in which those factors may interact and design his experiments accordingly. He should also be alert to the possible intermeshing of those factors so that, for example, manipulation of the age of onset of imprinting may also alter the time from the end of imprinting to testing. At the level of inference, he should be aware that the undoubted phenomenon of a stable sexual preference formed at an early stage in development does not necessarily imply that sexual preferences cannot be modified later in life.

The model is primarily intended to bring together the main factors affecting sexual imprinting. Its performance is, of course, meant to mimic reality. That it does so might seem little cause for congratulation. However, many of the interactions between important determinants of mating preferences are simply not known at the moment. The model enables one to simulate painlessly a very large number of possible experiments which could occupy the lives of many research workers—let alone the lives of their experimental subjects. A great many of those experiments would probably yield negative results in the sense that experience with an object at a certain age would *not* result in the bird showing a mating preference for that object later on. Consequently the model can make certain qualitative predictions about worthwhile lines of enquiry. Particularly useful, I believe, is the suggestion it makes to the experimenter to examine the balance between different factors such as length of exposure and the age at exposure; it predicts in this case that the length of exposure necessary to produce a positive mating preference for the object later in life first decreases with age and then increases. In general, the model suggests that conditions in which sexual imprinting can occur are bordered by innumerable conditions in which it cannot. If precision is eventually to be brought to studies of sexual imprinting it will be necessary to know the factor combinations that are effective in determining a mating preference. One final prediction of the model is worth emphasizing. It suggests that if a classical critical period should indeed exist and endogenous processes do set an upper as well as a lower limit on when experience can restrict sexual preferences, the period of maximum sensitivity as determined by subsequent preferences does not correspond to the timing of the endogenous changes. It starts earlier and is shorter than the internally controlled period. At first this suggestion seems counter-intuitive. However, the lack of correspondence arises because subsequent sexual preferences are not, in the model at any rate, determined simply by the factors that control when modification of sexual preferences is possible.

CONCLUSION

A major aim of this chapter has been to point to some of the possible ways in which early experience can exert a long-term effect on sexual behaviour in the face of potentially disruptive intervening experience. An obvious possibility is that the young animal simply maintains social contact with companions of the same appearance as its parent until such time as pair-formation takes place. However, contact with companions of the same species may be lost and so this procedure is vulnerable—particularly if plasticity of preference is maintained throughout development. A preference formed in early life can have more lasting and stable consequences if the animal avoids contact with objects, both animate and inanimate, that look markedly different from its parent. Alternatively (or in addition) the preference can depend on certain state factors, such as the level of a particular hormone, so that no further modification takes place when those factors are absent. This could be especially valuable as a protective device in, for example, ducks that form mixed feeding flocks with other species outside the breeding season.

Neither maintenance of contact with familiar companions, nor avoidance of novel objects, nor a state-dependent preference requires the postulation of new principles of learning. The long-term effect of early experience on sexual preferences can be generated by the *conditions* under which learning occurs, such as the animal's state, and the *consequences* of learning, such as disregarding an unfamiliar object or avoiding it. The actual mechanisms that produce plastic change in the nervous system and store information can be the same as those used in a wide variety of other contexts in which learning occurs (Hoffman and Ratner, 1973). The processes protecting the specific consequences of early experience from subsequent disruption are sufficient to generate a 'sensitive period' in development. This in itself is interesting but it is important not to be mesmerized by a term which can so easily acquire explanatory overtones but in fact explains little. Both the evidence from studies of imprinting and the computer simulations described here suggest that a sensitive period arises from the interaction of a number of different factors. Furthermore, the length of the period is critically dependent on the values of those parameters—and indeed, on how the period is measured.

Finally it is worth noting that the dependence of sexual imprinting on many different factors makes the phenomenon much more complex and challenging than was at one time believed. The additional involvement of a variety of other processes in the determination of sexual preferences is more than likely in many higher vertebrates—particularly in humans. The most that can probably be said for bold single-process claims for the development of human sexual preferences is that they are easy to grasp. Such explanations have the same status as very long eye lashes—attractive perhaps but almost certainly false.

SUMMARY

This chapter is concerned with the influence of early experience on mating preferences. The first part consists of a discussion of the evolutionary significance of sexual imprinting in birds and a brief review of the factors that influence it. Four factors which can be experimentally manipulated are clearly important: age of the animal, length of exposure to an object, stimulus value of the object and nature of experience with other objects before and after the period of exposure. The ways in which these factors interact are not well understood. In order to predict such interactions two intrinsic processes are postulated: a change in positive social responsiveness occurring independently of the specific effects of experience and a negative response to novel objects arising from experience with a specific object. Next a working model is developed. Among other things, the model indicates that some factors can be balanced against others. For example, factors affecting the responsiveness of a bird to an object may be set against the length for which it is exposed to that object. Up to an important limit, the greater a bird's responsiveness, the shorter the period of exposure required to modify its sexual preferences. In the simplest version of the model, once sexual preferences can be modified, they remain permanently plastic in principle. However, they generally remain stable because behavioural processes such as maintaining contact with the familiar and avoiding the novel protect the preferences against disrupting experience. In an elaboration, plasticity of preferences is only possible during specified periods in development. The model predicts that a behaviourally defined sensitive period would generally be considerably shorter than the actual period in which preferences can be modified. This is because other factors also play important roles in the determination of sexual preferences.

ACKNOWLEDGEMENTS

I am grateful to Jeremy Cherfas, Robert Hinde, Klaus Immelmann, Jean-Marie Vidal, and the Editor of this volume for their comments on earlier drafts of this chapter.

REFERENCES

Averhoff, W. W. and Richardson, R. H. (1976) Multiple pheromone system controlling mating in *Drosophila melanogaster*, *Proc. Nat. Acad. Sci. U.S.A.*, **73**, 591–3.
Bateson, P. P. G. (1966) The characteristics and context of imprinting, *Biol. Rev.*, **41**, 177–220.
Bateson, P. P. G. (1971) Imprinting. In: *Ontogeny of Vertebrate Behavior*, H. Moltz (ed.), Academic Press, New York, pp. 369–78.
Bateson, P. P. G. (1972) The formation of social attachments in young birds. In: *Int. Ornithol. Congress*, K. Voous (ed.), Brill, Leiden, pp. 278–90.
Bateson, P. P. G. (1973) Preference for familiarity and novelty: a model for the simultaneous development of both, *J. Theor. Biol.*, **41**, 249–59.
Bateson, P. P. G. (1974) Length of training, opportunities for comparison and imprinting in chicks, *J. Comp. Physiol. Psychol.*, **86**, 586–9.
Bateson, P. P. G. (1976) Specificity and the origins of behavior. In: *Advances in the Study*

of Behavior Vol. 6, J. Rosenblatt, R. A. Hinde and C. Beer (eds.), Academic Press, New York, pp. 1–20.

Bateson, P. P. G. and Jaeckel, J. B. (1976) Chicks' preferences for familiar and novel conspicuous objects after different periods of exposure, *Anim. Behav.*, **24**, 386–90.

Beauchamp, G. K. and Hess, E. H. (1973) Abnormal early rearing and sexual responsiveness in male guinea pigs, *J. Comp. Physiol. Psychol.*, **85**, 383–96.

Brosset, A. (1971) L'"imprinting", chez les Columbidés—Etude des modifications comportementales au cours du vieillissement, *Z. Tierpsychol.*, **29**, 279–300.

Brown, J. L. (1975) *The Evolution of Behavior*, Norton, New York.

Cooke, F., Finney, G. J. and Rockwell, R. F. (1976) Assortative mating in lesser snow Geese *(Anser caerulescens)*, *Behav. Genet.*, **6**, 127–40.

Deutsch, J. and Larson, K. (1974) Model-oriented sexual behavior in surrogate-reared rhesus monkeys, *Brain, Behav. Evol.*, **9**, 157–64.

Dilger, W. C. and Johnsgard, P. A. (1959) Comments on "species recognition" with special reference to the wood duck and the mandarin duck. *Wilson Bull.*, **71**, 46–53.

Eckland, B. K. (1968) Theories of mate selection, *Eugenics Quarterly*, **15**, 71–84.

Gallagher, J. (1976) Sexual imprinting: effects of various regimens of social experience on mate preference in Japanese quail *(Coturnix coturnix japonica)*, *Behaviour*, **57**, 91–114.

Gallagher, J. E. (1977) Sexual imprinting: a sensitive period in Japanese quail *(Coturnix coturnix japonica)*. *J. Comp. Physiol. Psychol.*, **91**, 72–8.

Gottlieb, G. (1976) The role of experience in the development of behavior and the nervous system. In: *Neural and Behavioral Specificity. Studies on the development of behavior and the nervous system* Vol. 3, G. Gottlieb (Ed.), Academic Press, New York, pp. 25–54.

Harris, M. P. (1970) Abnormal migration and hybridization of *Larus argentatus* and *L. fuscus* after interspecies fostering experiments, *Ibis*, **112**, 488–98.

Hess, E. H. (1973) *Imprinting*, Van Nostrand Reinhold, New York.

Hoffman, H. S. and Ratner, A. M. (1973) A reinforcement model of imprinting: implications for socilization in monkeys and men, *Psychol. Rev.*, **80**, 527–44.

Immelmann, K. (1969) Über den Einfluss frühkindlicher Erfahrungen auf die geschlechtliche Objektfixierung bei Estrildiden, *Z. Tierpsychol.*, **26**, 677–91.

Immelmann, K. (1972) Sexual and other long-term aspects of imprinting in birds and other species. In: *Advances in the Study of Behavior* Vol. 4, D. S. Lehrman, R. A. Hinde and E. Shaw (eds.), Academic Press, New York, pp. 147–74.

Immelmann, K. (1975a) The evolutionary significance of early experience. In: *Function and Evolution in Behaviour*, G. Baerends, C. Beer and A. Manning (eds.), Clarendon Press, Oxford, pp. 243–53.

Immelmann, K. (1975b) Ecological significance of imprinting and early learning. *Ann. Rev. Ecol. Systematics*, **6**, 15–37.

Jackson, P. S. and Bateson, P. P. G. (1974) Imprinting and exploration of slight novelty in chicks, *Nature, Lond.*, **251**, 609–10.

Klinghammer, E. (1967) Factors influencing choice of mate in altricial birds. In: *Early Behavior: Comparative and Developmental Approaches*, H. W. Stevenson, E. H. Hess and H. I. Rheingold (eds.), Wiley, New York, pp. 5–42.

Klint, T. (1975) Sexual imprinting in the context of species recognition in female mallards. *Z. Tierpsychol.*, **38**, 385–92.

Krebs, J. R. (1976) Analysis of function, *Nature, Lond.*, **260**, 196–7.

Landsberg, J.-W. (1976) Posthatch and developmental age as a baseline for determination of the sensitive period for imprinting, *J. Comp. Physiol. Psychol.*, **90**, 47–52.

Lewis, R. A. (1975) Social influences on marital choice. In: *Adolescence in the Life Cycle*, S. E. Dragastin and G. H. Elder (eds.), Wiley, New York, pp. 211–25.

Lorenz, K. (1935) Der Kumpan in der Umvelt des Vögels, *J. Ornithol.*, **83**, 137–213, 289–413.

Lorenz, K. (1970) *Studies in Animal and Human Behaviour* Vol. 1, Methuen, London.

Mainardi, D., Marsan, M., and Pasquali, A (1965) Causation of sexual preference of the house mouse. The behaviour of mice reared by parents whose odour was artificially altered, *Atti della Società Italiana di Scienze Naturali e del Museo Cirico di Storia Naturale di Milano*, **104**, 325–38.

Müller-Schwarze, D. (1974) Olfactory recognition of species, groups, individuals, and physiological states among mammals. In: *Pheromones*, M. C. Birch (ed.), North-Holland Research Monographs Vol. 32, Elsevier, Amsterdam, pp. 316–26.

Ratner, A. M. and Hoffman, H. S. (1974) Evidence for a critical period for imprinting in khaki campbell ducklings *(Anas platyrhynchos domesticus)*, *Anim. Behav.*, **22**, 249–55.

Riesen, A. H. (1966) Sensory deprivation. In: *Progress in Physiological Psychology* Vol. 1, E. Stellar and J. M. Sprague (eds.), Academic Press, New York, pp. 117–47.

Salzen, E. A. and Meyer, C. C. (1968) Reversibility of imprinting, *J. Comp. Physiol. Psychol.*, **66**, 269–75.

Schein, M. W. (1963) On the irreversibility of imprinting, *Z. Tierpsychol.*, **20**, 462–7.

Schutz, F. (1965) Sexuelle Prägung bei Anatiden, *Z. Tierpsychol.*, **22**, 50–103.

Schutz, F. (1971) Prägung des Sexualverhaltens von Enten und Gänsen durch Sozialeindrücke während der Jugendphase, *J. of Neuro-visceral Relations*, Supp. X, 339–57.

Schutz, F. (1975) Der Einfluss von Testosteron auf die Partnerwahl bei geprägt aufgezogenen Stockentenweibchen: Nachweis latenter Sexualprägung, *Verhandlungsbericht der Deutschen Zoologischen Gesellschaft*, **67**, 339–44.

Sherrod, L. (1974) The role of sibling associations in the formation of social and sexual companion preferences in ducks *(Anas platyrhynchos)*: An investigation of the "primacy versus recency" question, *Z. Tierpsychol.*, **34**, 247–64.

Sluckin, W. (1972) *Imprinting and Early Learning* 2nd edn., Methuen, London.

Sonnemann, P. & Sjölander, S. (1977) Effects of cross-fostering on the sexual imprinting of the female zebra finch, *Taeniopygia guttata*, *Z. Tierpsychol.* in press.

Tinbergen, N. (1963) On aims and methods of ethology, *Z. Tierpsychol.*, **20**, 410–33.

Vidal, J.-M. (1976a) *Empreinte filiale et sexuelle—reflexions sur le processus d'attachment d'aprés une etude experimentale sur le coq domestique. Docteur ès Sciences These.* University of Rennes.

Vidal, J.-M. (1976b) L'Empreinte chez les animaux, *La Recherche*, **63**, 24–35.

Walter, M. J. (1973) Effects of parental colouration on the mate preference of offspring in the zebra finch *(Taenioppygia guttata castanotis* Gould), *Behaviour*, **46**, 154–73.

Warriner, C. C., Lemmon, W. B. and Ray, T. S. (1963) Early experience as a variable in mate selection, *Anim. Behav.*, **11**, 221–4.

Zajonc, R. B., Reimer, D. J. and Hausser, D. (1973) Imprinting and the development of object preferences in chicks by mere repeated exposure, *J. Comp. Physiol. Psychol.*, **83**, 434–40.

CHAPTER 3

Experiential Factors in the Development of Sexual Behaviour

KNUT LARSSON

INTRODUCTION

A Survey of Studies on the Role of Experiential Factors in Adult Sexual Behaviour

The first convincing demonstration that an animal's individual experience plays a role in the development of the adult sexual behaviour was reported in the mid-fifties (Valenstein *et al.*, 1955; Valenstein and Goy, 1957; Riss *et al.*, 1955; Valenstein and Young, 1955). They found that social isolation of male guinea pigs from 10 days of age had a deleterious effect on the performance of mating behaviour in adulthood. While sexually aroused by a receptive female, the socially isolated male neither orientated adequately toward the female, nor clasped her hind quarters properly thereby failing to achieve intromission. Interestingly, the impairing effect of social isolation was more marked in strains of genetically homozygotic, low activity males, than in groups of heterozygotic, high activity males. These results were later extended and confirmed by Gerall (1963, 1965).

Similar studies were performed using male rats as experimental subjects. Beach consistently failed to find any impairing effects of social isolation in early infancy on the masculine behaviour of adult rats (Beach, 1942, 1958; Kagan and Beach, 1953). Beach (1958) isolated male rats from their mothers and littermates from 14 days of age. When tested for sexual behaviour in adulthood, isolated rats displayed behaviour which did not differ from that exhibited by their group-reared controls. Results at variance with those of Beach were reported by Zimbardo (1958), who found that isolation impaired the sexual activity of male rats. Folman and Drori (1965) reported two studies, one showing that rats reared in social isolation from 26–30 days of age were unlikely to initiate copulation in adulthood and another showing that social isolation from infancy did not impair sexual behaviour. No explanation was given for the different results obtained. In the light of present day knowledge it could be argued, however, that at 26 days of age the rats may have already acquired experience of importance for adult sexual behaviour. Following these early studies, a number of experiments were reported including those of Gerall *et al.*, (1967), Gruendel and Arnold (1969; 1974), Hard and Larsson (1968), Duffy and Hendricks (1973), the results of which will be discussed below.

Beach (1968) studied the effects of early social isolation in male dogs. One group of five dogs was housed in individual cages and had very limited physical contact with other animals throughout the experiment. Another group was allowed daily physical contact with other male and female dogs for 15 min, while a third group lived with females. The sexual behaviour of the various groups was assessed over an 18-month period in tests with receptive females. The semi-isolates that had only limited physical contact with other dogs showed a deficient sexual behaviour, while the copulatory performances of the controls and the group-reared males were normal. Out of 157 mating tests performed with the isolates, penile insertion was only achieved in 24% of the tests compared to 58% in the controls. Like guinea-pigs and rats, socially deprived dogs in Beach's study did not show any lack of interest in oestrous females. Neither did they show any inability to execute the mounting and thrusting pattern. The poorly coordinated penile insertion exhibited by the deprived dogs was due to the fact that an abnormally high frequency of the mounting responses were inappropriately oriented to the stimulus female. Performances of two of the semi-isolated dogs improved during the course of testing and became equal to that of the control group, but the remaining three dogs in the group showed no tendency to increase the accurancy of their orientation to the female.

Another line of evidence indicating that the individual's social history influences his adult sexual behaviour was reported by Rosenblatt and Aronson (1958a, 1958b). They allowed groups of male cats differing amounts of sexual experience, then castrated them and studied the decline in sexual behaviour. One group of cats was allowed a maximum of heterosexual experience; another group was given no opportunity to copulate. The experienced animals showed only a slow decline of their sexual behaviour, and 15 weeks after castration it was still at a higher level than that shown by the inexperienced cats. In a further experiment the animals were castrated prepuberally and treated with TP in adulthood. Part of the sample of cats were given an opportunity for heterosexual contact; while part of this sample were not permitted access to receptive females during the period of testosterone therapy. Hormone treatment was discontinued thereafter and the animals subjected to weekly tests for sexual behaviour. The group differences were similar to those found in the preceding experiment. Sexual experience acquired either under the influence of injected testosterone or testosterone produced by the male's own gonads delayed the decline of sexual behaviour when hormones were no longer present in the body. The prolonged delay in the decline of sexual behaviour following castration of sexually experienced male cats indicates that a male's sexual experience imparts to its sexual behaviour a degree of independence from hormonal control. The finding that the effects of androgen stimulation were different in sexually inexperienced males as compared with sexually experienced males indicates that testosterone induces added behavioural effects as a result of sexual experience. The results of similar experiments performed on rats will be discussed below.

To obtain primates for experimental purposes, Harlow initiated a breeding programme for rhesus monkeys in the mid-fifties which was to contribute more to our understanding of the influence of early social experience on adult sexual behaviour than any other work. When Harlow started this research, the role of experience in adult sexual behaviour of primates was barely recognized. Bingham (1928) and Yerkes and Elder (1936) reported that sexually inexperienced male primates did not develop complete copulatory patterns in adulthood. Nissen (1954, cited by Riesen, 1971) attempted to raise chimpanzees in the laboratory. Of eight male chimpanzees brought to the nursery within two weeks of birth and raised there without contact with other chimpanzees, only one displayed sexual behaviour in adulthood. This was in contrast to wild chimpanzees which did not show any deficiencies in their reproductive behaviour once they had been adapted to the laboratory.

The first report that the type of breeding situation used by Harlow might result in disturbances in sexual behaviour was published by Mason (1960). He observed three male and three female rhesus monkeys that had been housed in single cages for 28 to 29 months after one month of age. Similar-sized groups of feral born rhesus monkeys were kept as controls. The sexual behaviour of the males was assessed in pair-tests with feral monkeys that had normal social histories and with laboratory born females that had been deprived of social experience. Under both conditions, a striking difference was found between feral and restricted males in the frequency and integration of sexual behaviour. The feral males showed more mounting and thrusting and had sexual episodes of longer duration. Males in the restricted group never clasped the partner's legs with their feet during mounting and frequently assumed inappropriate postures and body orientation. Pelvic thrusting which was not accompanied by mounting was frequent.

Further work on the effects of severe social isolation on masculine sexual behaviour showed that social deprivation for the first six months of life resulted in a nearly complete inability to copulate in adulthood (Harlow and Harlow, 1971; Senko, 1966; Harlow et al., 1966). The deleterious effects of social deprivation appeared to be irreversible. Senko (1966) found that only 2 of 16 males deprived of social contact for the first 19 months of life copulated although they had lived with females for two years before the mating tests were conducted.

It was quickly noted that the sexual deficits produced by social deprivation not only consisted of an inability to orient properly towards the female but involved disturbances in the entire structure of social responsiveness (reviewed by Rosenblatt, 1965). The sexual deficits were only some of the manifestations of a pervasive disorganization of behaviour reflected more subtly by low levels of social grooming (Missakian, 1969; see also Simpson, this volume Chapter 24), high levels of aggression, and a failure to form stable dominance relationships (Mason, 1961), high levels of self-directed behaviour (Mason, 1960), and diminished responsiveness to non-social stimulation (Sackett, 1965). The social aspect of the disturbance in sexual behaviour is demonstrated in the following observations (Deutsch and Larsson, 1974).

As subjects, we used four male rhesus monkeys that had been raised on wire cloth surrogate mothers in Harlow's laboratory. The animals which at the time of the experiment were 10 years of age were exposed to a stationary cloth-covered model (Fig. 1). Three of the four surrogate-raised males explored, groomed, and mounted the model during the 40-min periods of observation while none of the mother-reared monkeys did so. Two of the four males were available for a second test two years later. Both males directed unambiguously social and sexual patterns towards the model in each of the 10 tests performed. One of the males, Bull, exhibited during 7 tests a complete mating sequence including ejaculation. The mounts were properly oriented, interspersed with grooming, and ejaculation was followed sometimes by grooming of the 'genital' region of the model. When presented with female rhesus monkeys none of the

Fig. 1. Bull, one of the surrogate-reared monkeys, mounting the cloth-covered monkey-sized model. Note his clasping of the 'hips' of the model, and his grasping of the 'legs' with one foot. (From Deutsch and Larsson (1974) Brain, Behav., and Evol., **9**, 157–64.)

surrogate-raised males ever showed mounts or sexual approaches. Either the male fled from the female or approached and bit her.

The finding that surrogate-reared males are capable of more or less complete patterns of sexual behaviour with a model, but not with a female monkey, suggests that the sexual failure of these animals resulted not so much from their lack of postural skills as from their inability to adjust to a reciprocally active social object. The surrogate-reared males were clearly disturbed in their encounters with female monkeys. The erratic bouts of aggression of one of the males kept female partners at a distance, while the other male's passivity and withdrawal precluded contact even though females persistently approached and presented to him. The monkeys were thus unable to interpret correctly the signals given to them by their female. Presenting was ignored or elicited withdrawal and fleeing; and fear-grimacing elicited either reciprocal flight or aggression.

The animals used in these studies showed deep disturbances in all aspects of their social behaviour making the sexual deficits perhaps less surprising. Goy and Goldfoot (1974) showed, however, that exposure to less extreme forms of social deprivation than those used in the previous studies resulted in a deficient sexual behaviour in adulthood. The rhesus males were left with their mothers until three months of age and thereafter spent various periods of time with their peers or with adults. While not necessarily deficient in any other aspect of social interactions than sexual behaviour, the males showed delayed development of all parameters of their sexual relationships. Of 23 animals brought up under these conditions and tested for sexual behaviour in adulthood, only 9 displayed intromissions and only 3 ejaculated (Goy and Goldfoot, 1974).

Let me briefly review the results and implications of this examination of the data thus far. In all species studied, including guinea pig, rat, cat, dog, and rhesus monkey, social deprivation in early infancy has deleterious effects on masculine sexual behaviour in adulthood. Social deprivation never suppresses interest in sexual activity. The semi-isolated dogs used by Beach were as interested in female oestrous dogs as were the controls. In so far as masturbatory activity represents a sign of sexual activity, the surrogate-reared rhesus monkeys studied by Harlow were very active sexually. In addition, social deprivation did not impair sexual behaviour by abolishing the capacity of the animal to perform mounting and thrusting. According to Beach, stimulation by the experimenter induced complete erection and ejaculation in the socially deprived dog. The surrogate-reared monkeys studied by Deutsch and Larsson displayed a completely normal mating pattern including ejaculation. A third possible cause of sexual deficit is the complete failure of the socially deprived rhesus monkeys to interact normally with other monkeys. However, Goy and Goldfoot have found sexual deficits similar to those reported by Mason and Harlow in monkeys that have been exposed to less restrictive social environments in infancy and yet appeared to be normal in other aspects of social life. In examining reports of the sexual behaviour of the socially deprived animals, one feature appears to be common to them all: the deprived males lack the perceptual-motor components responsible for appropriate spatial orientation to the receptive female. Describing the behaviour of one of the semi-isolated dogs, Beach (1968) noted that the initial attempts of the dog to mount the female consisted of clasping the female's left haunch or upper leg between his forelegs and then executing pelvic thrusts. This abnormal pattern became established in the animal's behaviour, and during subsequent tests he mounted the female more and more frequently but continued to clasp the bitch's left haunch while thrusting vigorously. Similarly, according to Goy and Goldfoot the socially deprived rhesus monkey, continues for months and years to display an immature type of mounting, in which he stands with his legs on the floor.

The above review was intended to introduce the reader to problems of the role of experiential factors in the development of masculine sexual behaviour. Since our own work has dealt mainly with the rat, the following sections will be devoted to examining in more detail the evidence available concerning the influence of sexual experience on adult sexual behaviour in the rat.

Firstly, experimental evidence will be reviewed indicating that rats subjected to severe restriction of their social contacts in infancy are slow in initiating sexual contacts as adults compared to rats reared under normal social conditions. Secondly, some features of the social interaction in infancy will be discussed in relation to the development of the mating pattern. Thirdly, experimental data will be reviewed suggesting that a male is more dependent on experience for initiating sexual contacts than a female. Finally, experimental results will be reported demonstrating the occurrence of an interaction of hormonal and experiential factors.

Disruption of the Male Rat's Sexual Behaviour Induced by Social Restriction in Infancy

As was indicated in the introduction, the picture of the role of sexual experience in masculine sexual behaviour of the rat was confused when we started our studies in the early 'sixties. In our first investigation (Hård and Larsson, 1968) male rats were reared under three different conditions from birth onwards. Under one condition, peer deprivation, the littermates were removed leaving a single male with his mother until weaning at 25 days of age; thereafter he lived in isolation. The male lived in a separate wooden cage without visual and tactile contact with other animals but allowed auditory and olfactory contact with the rest of the animals in the animal room. Under another condition, isosexual rearing, the male lived with 5 other males. Under a third condition, heterosexual rearing, the male lived with 2 other males and 3 females. Each group consisted of 18 males.

Beginning at 95 days of age, daily mating tests were performed. The male was placed in the mating arena with a sexually receptive female. If no intro-

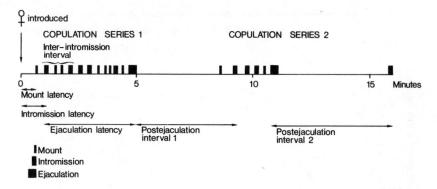

Fig. 2. Showing the course of events during copulation in sexually experienced male rat. After some minutes adaptation to the mating arena, a receptive female is presented to the male. An experienced, intact adult male usually immediately approaches the female and mounts her. Grasping his partner about the flanks, the male straightens his hind legs and raises the penis as high as possible making several rapid piston-like pelvic thrusts (clasping with thrusting). He may dismount after thrusting several times without having penerated the vaginal orifice (mount), or penetration may occur (intromission). After a series of mounts and intromissions, each accompanied by licking of the penis and each separated by a brief inter-intromission interval, ejaculation occurs. The ejaculation response is characterized by a deep, prolonged thrust, easily recognized from the intromission response. The ejaculation is followed by a period of sexual inactivity lasting for about 5 min. He may then again mount the female and after another series of intromissions, now shorter in length and composed of fewer intromissions, ejaculate a second time. This pattern of behaviour may be repeated 8–10 times before the male is sexually exhausted. During the successive series of copulations, progressive changes occur in the behaviour. For more detailed description of the male rat mating pattern see Beach and Jordan (1956), Dewsbury (1966) and Larsson (1956)

Mount and intromission latency is defined as the time from the introduction of the female into the testing arena to the first mount and intromission. Ejaculation latency is the time from the first intromission is a series of intromissions to ejaculation; the postejaculation interval is the period of time from ejaculation to the next following intromission.

The mating arena at present used in our laboratory is a plexiglass cylinder, 60 cm in diameter, the floor covered with shavings. The stimulus females are brought into sexual receptivity by treatment with 20 μg oestradiolbenzoate followed 42 h later by 0.5 mg P. They are dropped into the cage thus starting the test. Various testing routines have been used in our laboratory. The routine now practised is to allow the male a maximum of 15 min in the mating arena unless an intromission has taken place. The test is ended if the mount or intromission latency is > 15 min, if the ejaculation latency is > 30 min, or if the postejaculation interval is > 15 min

mission had occurred after 30 min the test was ended. When, however, intromission took place within 30 min the test continued for an additional 60 min or until ejaculation had been achieved. The daily testing was repeated until the male had ejaculated once. In Fig. 2 the normal copulatory behaviour of the experienced male rat is pictured along a time axis.

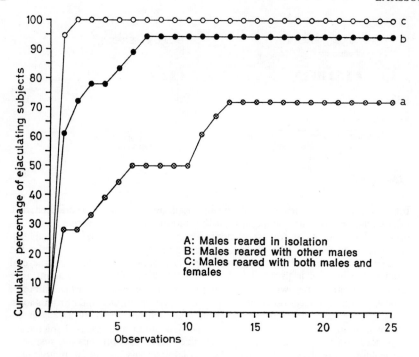

Fig. 3. Cumulative percentage of animals reared under various environmental conditions showing ejaculation in subsequent mating tests. (From Hård and Larsson (1968) Brain, Behav., and Evol., **1**, 405–19.)

At the first test, 4 peer-deprived, 11 isosexually reared, and 17 heterosexually reared males displayed a complete mating pattern. During the course of testing, an increasing number of males started to copulate as indicated in Fig. 3. After 25 days of testing, 5 peer-deprived males still failed to ejaculate while all heterosexually and all but one isosexually reared males ejaculated. In a further attempt to stimulate sexual behaviour in the non-copulating males, the sexually inactive males, that at this time were 125 days old, were placed in cages with an intact female for a period of two weeks. When again tested for sexual activity, 2 peer-deprived and all the isosexually reared males exhibited complete sexual behaviour patterns. Three of the peer-deprived males, however, remained sexually inactive even after this treatment.

These results demonstrate that social restrictions imposed upon the rat during the first three months of life may seriously retard the development of sexual behaviour in adulthood. As described in more detail in the original publication (Hård and Larsson, 1968b), analysis of the mating performance showed that the various components of the mating pattern were differently affected by the rearing conditions. The tendency to approach the female and make tactile contact with her was evident in all of the restricted males from the very first test performed, and in this respect they did not differ from experienced copulators. The character of the interactions differed, however, from those displayed by the experienced male. First, the approaches were poorly oriented, the male climbing upon the head, the sides and the back of the female. Second, no clasping reflex occurred. While the experienced male moved up to the back of the female, clasped her flanks with his forepaws and initiated a series of rapid thrusting movements which might terminate in intromission, the restricted male put his forepaws instead upon the back of the female and only climbed upon her, or he simply turned away without any attempt to mount her. Third, no pelvic thrusting took place. The behavioural deficits very much resembled those previously reported in guinea pigs, reared under socially restricted conditions (Gerall, 1963; 1965).

Even more serious deficits in the behaviour of the socially deprived rat were reported by Gerall et al., (1967) and Gruendel and Arnold (1974). In both of these studies the pups were removed from their mother at 14 days of age and thereafter reared either in isolation or in groups with castrated or intact males and females. During five mating tests in adulthood, Gerall, et al. found that 23 of the 27 group-reared males displayed a complete mating pattern while none of the 30 isolated males ever ejaculted, and only 4 achieved intromission. Similar results were reported by Gruendel and Arnold who found that 16 out of 24 group-reared males achieved intromission compared to 5 out of 22 isolated male rats. The mating tests lasted for only 20 min compared to 60 min in our study (Hård and Larsson, 1968). The time limit of the tests may account for a lower number of ejaculating animals in the study of Arnold and Gruendel compared to ours. The few rats that intromitted without ejaculating may also reflect the time limit of the tests used in this study.

Only one study has been undertaken in which the rats were isolated not only from their peers but also from their mother. Gruendel and Arnold (1969) developed a method of maintaining pups in the absence of their mother from birth onwards: the pups were placed in an incubator containing a warm, moist, pulsating mother surrogate and were fed artificially. One group of pups was placed in incubators with other pups, and another group was reared in incubators in isolation. At 30 days, all rats, including the mother-reared controls, were placed in individual cages with normal rat food provided ad lib. Mating tests performed when the rats were 200 days old revealed grave disturbances in the sexual behaviour of all the group-reared as well as isolated incubator-raised rats. In fact, during four 20-min mating tests, none of them ever displayed any intromission or ejaculation. Mounting was observed in only one single rat. Unfortunately no attempts were made to restore the sexual behaviour by extending the series of tests, or by allowing the males to live together with females for a prolonged period of time, and it is therefore not clear whether the impairment of sexual behaviour was permanent or not. Another critical problem is the possible influence of insufficient nutrition during a critical period of development. Growth-rate was lower for the incubator-raised pups than for mother-reared ones. It is felt, however, that this does not represent a major criticism, because our own research has indicated that postnatal undernutrition up to 20 days after birth does not necessarily suppress or even delay puberty. Although several questions are unanswered, the study reported by Gruendel and Arnold is of great interest and provides us with a most dramatic demonstration of the retarding influence of social deprivation in infancy on sexual behaviour in adulthood.

Masculine sexual behaviour is displayed by the female rat as well as by the male (Södersten, 1972). Interestingly, social restrictions in infancy influence also the development of masculine sexual behaviour in the female. Duffy and Hendricks (1973) isolated females from their littermates when they were 14 days old. When adult the rats were ovariectomized and treated with test-osterone. In comparison with the group-living control females, the isolates exhibited fewer mount and intromission patterns than did the control females. It might be added that the female rat, like the male, shows much climbing and rubbing against the mother rat. Viewing such behaviour patterns as a preliminary to mounting, it may not be surprising to find that isolation delays the occurrence of mounting behaviour in the female as it does in the male. No effects of isolation were observed on lordosis behaviour which was induced subsequently by oestrogen/progesterone treatment. This indicates that female lordosis behaviour, unlike masculine mounting behaviour, is uninfluenced by social isolation in infancy. This is in line with the fact that lordosis in the female as well as in the male is specifically dependent on the hormonal state of the individual.

Several attempts have been made to identify the specific features of the social environment that are critical for the development of sexual behaviour in adulthood. In their study of incubator-raised males, Gruendel and Arnold (1969) found group-reared males as inefficient in performing copulation as animals raised in isolation. The group-reared animals in this study lived, however, with other pups only during the first 30 days of life and were isolated thereafter. This period may have been too short or located too early in the life of the animals to have affected them, particularly as the incubator-raised animals showed a retardation of their weight development. According to Gerall et al. (1967), in terms of preparing the male for adult sexual life, being reared with males is as effective as being reared with females. However, Hård and Larsson (1968b) found that males reared with other males assumed an intermediate position. They were slower in displaying their first mount, intromission, and ejaculation responses than heterosexually-raised males but faster than the isolates. Gerall et al. (1967) removed male rats from their mother and littermates at day 14 and placed the males 'in single cages' so that they could see, hear, and smell one another without having any direct tactile contact. None of these conditions, however, compensated for the lack of direct contact with another animal. Thinking that the sexual deficits of the isolates were secondary perhaps to a general impairment of the brain caused by isolation, Gruendel and Arnold (1974) compared the behaviour of single rats that had lived in cages without access to objects to play with, and rats that had been provided with an abundance of objects. Animals reared in the play-enriched environment showed a markedly increased play activity in adulthood, but their sexual development was impaired.

In conclusion, while the importance of mothering and sibling contacts in infancy for the development of sexual behaviour in adulthood appears to be well established, the question of what factors in early social experience enable the rat to exhibit sexual behaviour in response to a receptive female remains unanswered. This failure may be due to lack of adequate experiments but may also reflect limitations inherent in the experimental approach itself. Firstly, it may be argued that an animal deprived of social contacts from birth, including contact with his own mother, is socially abnormal and an impairment seen in a specific behaviour patterns like those associated with sexual behaviour only reflect an inability to cope with any social situations. This argument may be met by making the social restrictions in infancy less severe, thereby producing animals that are not deficient in all aspects of social behaviour. Secondly, social deprivation in infancy may cause inhibitions that prevent the animal from responsing normally to social stimulation. Rather than being due to lack of specific social skills, it may be argued that the abnormal reactions displayed by the adult reared under socially restricted conditions are due to the presence of aversive reactions that prevent normal sexual interaction. By varying, but not eliminating, the opportunities for social interaction in infancy this problem may be solved.

Developmental Changes in the Social and Sexual Behaviour

Prepubetal Play Behaviour

Like most other mammals, the rat spends his infancy exhibiting an abundance of social activity which we, lacking better terms, may designate play behaviour. Such behaviour is a general phenomenon in infant mammals and its importance for the development of masculine sexual behaviour has been investigated in particular detail by Goy and his collaborators in the rhesus monkey (Goy, 1970). Among the various play patterns displayed by the infant rat, climbing upon littermates and the mother, tumbling beneath her body, and tumbling about may be particularly interesting in the present context. While qualitatively different from mounting in that it is less well oriented towards the partner and not accompanied by pelvic thrusting, climbing on the rear of the female strikingly resembles mounting. Climbing abruptly disappears once the male has exhibited his first mount with thrusting and is rarely seen in the adult experienced male.

A study of the climbing behaviour of the rat as it develops when the male is reared singly or in a group was performed by Hård and Larsson (1971). By climbing we meant any climbing on to another rat whether it occurred from the rear or on to the head, whether the recepient of this behaviour was a male or female, or whether she was made receptive by hormone injections or not. Once a week, from day 17 of age onwards, the males in either group were placed with a receptive female and tested for the following behaviour patterns (a) rear climbing (subject climbs upon the stimulus female from a posterior position and places one or both forepaws on the rear part of her body); (b) head-side climbing (subject climbs upon the anterior part of the female and places one or both forepaws upon her head, or climbs upon the female's side placing one or both forepaws upon her body); (c) mount (subject mounts the female from a posterior position with forelimbs clasped around her flanks and begins pelvic thrusting).

As indicated by Fig. 4, climbing was found to be a rare event between days 17–23, but showed a rapid increase between days 23–31. It is not known when or at what frequency climbing occurs before day 17. The isolated animals tended to display a higher frequency of rear climbing and head-side climbings. After a peak at day 31, the group-reared animals showed a decline in climbing frequency. At day 66, some males performed mounts and intromissions for the first time and further testing was discontinued. In repeating this experiment on females, no difference was found in frequency of climbing exhibited by the two sexes. Gonadectomy was performed when the males and females were 23 days old and the animals were twice tested for climbing behaviour; first at 37 days of age and again at 52 days. No changes in the frequency of climbing were observed following gonadectomy, suggesting that climbing is little, if at all, dependent on gonadal secretions and the sex of the animal, at least during prepuberal age. Climbing behaviour does vary, however, with the rearing conditions; isolated animals were seen to display a much higher rate of climbing activity than group-reared ones. The results obtained raise several unanswered questions. Why did the group-reared rats display fewer climbing bouts than the isolated rats? One possibility is that the isolated males were 'aroused' by meeting another animal while the group-reared males were habituated to social contact. Another possibility is that group rearing produced aversive responses to other animals. Thus, males did not climb the female because they had learned to avoid other rats to protect themselves from attack.

Noting that adult males that had been reared in social isolation displayed an excessive number of climbing responses when presented with receptive females and that this behaviour immediately disappeared once a mount had taken place (mount: clasping the female and thrusting), Gerall, et al., (1967) and Hård and Larsson (1968b) suggested that climbing represents a prelude to mounting and that the sexual deficits seen after social deprivation were due to lack of opportunities to practise climbing. Although this hypothesis still awaits confirmation, a relationship between rearing conditions and occurrence of climbing is suggested by the results obtained above.

The rapidity with which even the sexually inexperienced male assumes a correct mating posture and establishes mating patterns may be partly due to

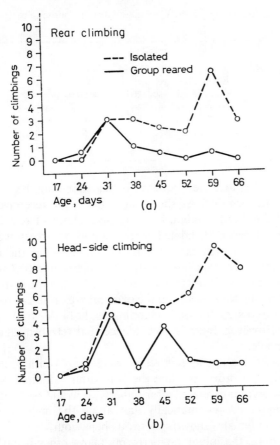

Fig. 4. Median instances of rear-end climbing
and head-side climbing in males reared in isolation
and in groups during 8 successive days of testing.
The isolated males (n = 20) were weaned at day 21
and thereafter reared individually. The group-
reared rats (n = 16) were reared in groups of 8
rats per cage. (From Hård and Larsson (1974)
Brain, Behav., and Evol., 4, 151–61.)

the behaviour of the female. The characteristic ear-wiggling displayed by the
receptive female, her lordosis, her quick spasmodic jumps with stiffly bent
hindlegs, her sniffing and presentation to the male, make it likely that her role
is not at all that of a passive partner. If the male is unwilling to mate, she pushes
him, jumps enticingly away, tugs at his fur and sniffs his genitalia. To evaluate
the importance of the behaviour of the female for the sexual behaviour of the
male, the female of each pair was given a small dosage of tetrabenazine. While
maintaining the females in a state of receptivity, tetrabenazine, in the dosage
injected, more or less immobilizes the female. The sedated female was presented

Table 1. Climbing displayed by 6-week old male rats in response to receptive sedated and non-sedated females

Behaviour component	Female			Group comparison		
	a Receptive non-sedated	b Receptive sedated	c Non-receptive	a–b p	a–c p	b–c p
Rear-end climbing	24	2	16	< 0.01	NS	< 0.01
Head climbing	2	14	6	< 0.01	< 0.02	< 0.01
Side climbing	16	22	33	NS	< 0.02	< 0.02

to 6-week old males, and the frequency of rear climbing, head climbing and side climbing was recorded. As shown in Table 1, the receptive non-sedated female evoked few head climbings but an abundance of rear climbings. By contrast, in the presence of sedated receptive and non-receptive females, the male displayed a very high rate of head climbings. Thus the intact female, receptive or unreceptive, appears to display a behaviour that facilitates rear climbing. Another possible interpretation would be that the sexually attractive female produces olfactory cues from the perineal area whereas sedated females do not. Hence this disorientation in climbing might be due to the absence of an olfactory cue. However, there is no evidence that tetrabenazine changes the odour of the female.

The males participating in this study were reared either individually or with other males. In order to relate the behaviour exhibited before puberty to the sexual behaviour exhibited after puberty, it would be of interest to vary the rearing conditions systematically and allow the male to develop with females, including females showing oestrous behaviour.

Besides climbing, the infant rat performs many other behaviour patterns such as following other males or receptive and unreceptive females, nuzzling other rat's genitals, mutual grooming, and jumping. Bolles and Woods (1964) noted a sudden increases in locomotory activity around the 14th day when the eyes start to open which reached a peak somewhere between 20 and 30 days of age. During this time the rat shows an abundance of activity including fighting, grooming, and sniffing. Interestingly, Gerall et al. (1967) and Gruendel and Arnold (1974) reported more severe deficits in the adult sexual behaviour after having isolated the animals at 14 days of age than did Hård and Larsson (1968a, b), who separated the animals from their mother when they were 25 days old. Since the isolated pups were not provided with mother surrogate in any of these studies but were left alone in their cages, the differences in activity could not be attributed to the surrogate rearing condition.

However fragmentary, the above observations may contribute to an understanding of how the mature mating pattern emerges from the social play pattern displayed by the infant. Rear climbing provides opportunities for the male to bring his penis into contact with the receptive female, and tactile contact results in male pelvic thrusting and finally intromission. When her back is palpated, the receptive female elevates her perineum thus providing the male more easy access to the vaginal opening. Penile contact with the fur of the female, in turn, may reflexively elicit pelvic thrusting. Since lordosis occurs as a response to tactile stimulation of the back, adequate body orientation of the male with respect to the female is a necessary first step in the establishment of the mating pattern. The male may even learn to stimulate the female to evoke lordosis. It should be understood that these sequences of stimuli and response are purely hypothetical until detailed studies have been performed which are based upon filmed behavioural sequences exhibited by males and females reared under various environmental conditions.

Further studies should be undertaken on the development of the various social interaction patterns (grooming, genital sniffing, following) that occur during prepubertal age under different environmental conditions. Given the view that the sexual behaviour emerges from these behaviour patterns, experimentally induced alterations in the development of any of these behaviour patterns will also change the conditions under which sexual behaviour is elicited and hence influence its development.

The Pubertal and Adult Mating Patterns

The sexually experienced rat, in contrast to the sexually inexperienced rat, orientates correctly when presented with a receptive female, and thrusting is elicited at the first encounter with her. It is our impression that once a mount has taken place, a male, whether sexually experienced or not, continues to perform intromissions and eventually ejaculates. Lack of sexual experience seems to hamper the rat mainly in the initial phases of mating. Experience of the complete mating pattern is, however, not entirely without effects on the behaviour. Thus a male allowed repeated experience of mating achieves ejaculation within a shorter period of time and after somewhat fewer mounts and intromissions than a similarly aged inexperienced male (Larsson, 1959; Dewsbury, 1969).

When the complete mating pattern first appears at puberty, the male is only capable or a few ejaculations before he becomes sexually exhausted. The coital pattern at this time has a characteristic appearance consisting of many intromissions preceding ejaculation, a long ejaculation latency, and somewhat longer postejaculatory intervals (the period of time from ejaculation to the next intromission). However the behaviour rapidly changes. The capacity to achieve repeated ejaculations improves, the number of thrusts and mounts before ejaculation decreases, and the response latencies shorten. A month after puberty, the behaviour has largely assumed its adult appearance (Larsson, 1956).

A series of studies was carried out aimed at investigating the basis of these behavioural changes at puberty (Larsson, 1967). According to the results obtained in these studies the age of the animal was an unimportant factor since a rat castrated before puberty responded by displaying a pubertal mating pattern after replacement therapy with testosterone propionate (TP) whether he was 37 or 200 days old. Heterosexual experience was not a critical factor since castrated, hormone-treated rats showed the adult behaviour pattern whether they had had heterosexual experience or not. The determining factor was testosterone. The relationship between hormones and behaviour was not, however, a direct one, as shown by the fact that the effect of a given quantity of hormones varied according to the endocrine history of the animal. A rat castrated before puberty differed, for instance, from an animal operated upon after puberty. Apparently the tissues mediating the mating behaviour become modified under the influence of testicular secretions.

These results raise a number of questions which cannot be answered at present. First, it is not clear whether the changes induced by the hormones are irreversible, or whether, providing that a long enough time has been allowed to pass between the time of castration and the hormone treatment, the effects will disappear. As demonstrated by the experiments described above, after a 4-month period, residual effects of the hormones still remained. Second, it is not clear if the residual effects are due to peripheral or central modifications. After postpuberal castration, penile spines do not completely disappear but a few remain for months and perhaps remain permanently (Södersten and Larsson, 1974).

Infantile Stimulation and Onset of Puberty

A large body of evidence indicates that environmental manipulation in infancy affects the development of neuroendocrine systems and related behaviours in the rat (Levine and Mullins, 1966). Recently some data collected by Stefan Hansen, a student in my laboratory, showed that infantile stimulation may advance the onset of puberty of the male rat.

This study was part of a project on the interaction of nutritional and environmental factors in determining onset of puberty in the male rat. Some of the animals were underfed and some of them were fed normally. Undernourishment was induced by providing the mother with 50% of her normal amount of food, from the day of conception until the pups were 21 days old. The environmental variable was manipulated in the following way. One group (isolates) consisted of male rats that had lived alone with their mothers from the day of birth. In a second group (control) two males and two females lived together with their mother. In a third group (stimulated) two males and two females lived together with their mother and both males were stimulated during the first 21 days of life. Each day the pups were removed from the cage and held, one at a time, for 3 min. After the pups had reached 21 days of age, they were removed from their mothers and placed in single cages until the end of the experiment. All pups were provided with food *ad lib.* after 21 days of

Table 2. Effects of prenatal and early postnatal (until 21st day of age) undernourishment and sensory stimulation during early postnatal age. Indicated are mean number of days before the first occurrence of a mount, an intromission and an ejaculation; mean number of intromissions before ejaculation, when the male for the first time exhibited an ejaculation, and mean body weight at the first mount, intromission, and ejaculation. Each group included 16 rats. The statistical analysis was performed by a 2 × 3 factorial design

	Stimulated	Control	Isolates
Age in days			
Undernutrition	54.1 ± 2.0	61.0 ± 2.9	65.9 ± 2.7
Normal nutrition	57.6 ± 2.3	56.6 ± 2.5	62.3 ± 3.0
Number of intromissions to ejaculation			
Undernutrition	20.1 ± 2.4	16.4 ± 2.0	16.1 ± 2.1
Normal nutrition	21.2 ± 2.5	16.4 ± 2.2	15.0 ± 2.1
Body weight			
Undernutrition	153.5 ± 4.6	181.4 ± 4.7	197.4 ± 4.7
Normal nutrition	202.3 ± 5.4	205.8 ± 5.0	217.6 ± 5.0

Age in days	
Control-Isolates	p. < 0.05
Stimulated-Isolates	p. < 0.01
Intromissions to ejaculation	
Stimulated-Control	p. < 0.05
Stimulated-Isolates	p. < 0.05
Weight:	
Stimulated-Control	p. < 0.05
Stimulated-Isolates	p. < 0.01
Undernutrition-normal	p. < 0.01

age. Daily mating tests were performed when the rats were 45 days of age. The testing was discontinued when the males had ejaculated for the first time. The results obtained are presented in Table 2. The overall variance differed significantly between the groups (p < 0.05). No effects were observed after undernourishment alone. Infantile stimulation, however, had a marked effect in accelerating the onset of puberty. The ejaculatory response was elicited 5–10 days earlier in the stimulated animals. The stimulatory effects occurred independently of whether the rats had been underfed or not. Identical effects were obtained by analysing the mounting and intromission responses.

Hormonal Changes Induced by Social Isolation in Infancy

It is well documented that the reproductive hormones of male rats are altered as a result of sexual activity. Male rats that had lived together with receptive females had heavier seminal vesicles, testes, and penis than males that had lived with other males (Drori and Folman, 1964) or in social isolation (Folman and Drori, 1966). The testes of mated rats contained more testosterone than those of unmated ones (Herz *et al.*, 1969) suggesting that the hypertrophy of the sexual accessory organs might be due to differences in plasma testosterone concentrations. Several recent studies indicate that sexual stimuli are involved in the acute release of testosterone in males of various species including the rat (Purvis and Haynes, 1972). Stimuli related to mating have also been shown to release pituitary hormones in males (Taleisnik *et al.*, 1966) although recent reports suggested that there may not be such an increase (Davidson *et al.*, 1973). In fact, recent evidence indicates that the chronic elevation in plasma hormone levels following sexual experience as reported by earlier workers is difficult to reproduce (Kamel *et al.*, 1975; Södersten *et al.*, unpubl.). Some workers have even found that social isolation results in an increase of androgens (Dessi-Fulgheri *et al.*, 1975). Thus although some doubts exist about the effects of chronic isolation on the reproductive system, the observations reported raise the question of whether the behavioural deficits seen after isolation are the result of endocrine deficits. This question still remains unexplored.

Development of Sexual Behaviour in Sensory Deficient Rats: Effects of Anosmia

To compensate for a deficit in physiological functioning, an intact animal can choose between numerous possibilities. Lacking the sense of smell, the male may use vision or hearing. Deprived of penile sensitivity, he may rely on tactile sensitivity in non-genital regions. The occurrence of compensatory mechanisms makes any attempt to uncover the role of experiential factors more difficult. In this and the next section the importance of experience in sexual behaviour will be discussed using as experimental subjects rats that have been deprived either of smell or of sensitivity in the penis. (See also Cowley, this volume Chapter 4 for the effects of anosmia—induced by bulbectomy—on the development of sexual behaviour.)

Among the various stimuli associated with the oestrous female, odour is of particular importance for sexual arousal. Vision, at least under the conditions of testing used in the laboratory, appears to be of little significance for the sexual behaviour of the rat (Hård and Larsson, 1968a, b) Thus no decrease in sexual activity occurs following enucleation. However, male rats made anosmic by destruction of the olfactory bulbs, continue to copulate, although at a lower rate than normal (Heimer and Larsson, 1967; Larsson, 1971). The initial experiments designed to investigate the role of olfaction in the sexual behaviour of the rat were performed on sexually experienced males. However, the spectrum of stimuli which evoke sexual behaviour presumably increases as the male matures sexually and acquires experience of sexual behaviour. Olfaction may, for example, be important in arousing the male sexually at puberty but once sexual responses have been established to non-olfactory stimuli, olfaction plays a less important role. Therefore, in order to appreciate the role of olfaction in initiating sexual behaviour, experiments should be undertaken in animals which have experienced sexual behaviour prior to being made anosmic. An experiment of this kind was performed by Wilhelmsson and Larsson (1973).

From 10 days postnatally, the rats were reared under four different conditions. In one group, the male rats were reared without littermates and bulbectomized when 30 days of age (peer-deprived, anosmic, n = 19). In a second group, the males lived with two adult female littermates and were operated upon when 30 days old (group-reared, anosmic, n = 18). In addition, two control groups were used, one in which the males lived in isolation (peer-deprived, intact, n = 21) and another in which the males lived in groups (group-reared, intact, n = 20).

Anosmia was induced by olfactory bulbectomy in these experiments. The rostral two-thirds of the olfactory bulbs were removed by suction. Particular care was taken to interrupt the olfactory filaments at their emergence through the cribiform plate. No histology was performed on the particular animals in this study. Histological examination of brains of rats subjected to similar lesions show that the most rostral part of the anterior olfactory nucleus is usually injured. Bleeding occurs easily in the olfactory ventricles causing damage to the deep rostral part of the anterior olfactory nucleus.

During the 26-day period of daily testing of the mating behaviour in adulthood, none of the 19 peer-deprived anosmic rats ever exhibited any intromission or ejaculation and occasional mounts were observed in only one single male (Fig. 5). Since most of the intact peer-deprived controls finally started to copulate, the social deficits could not be attributed to social isolation only. On the other hand, the sexual inactivity could not be due to loss of the sense of olfaction alone, because half of the group-reared anosmic males started to copulate. The total suppression of sexual activity in the anosmic peer-deprived rats was the combined effect of isolation and anosmia. Since the olfactory bulbectomized rats showed a lag in the development of body weight a possible cause of sexual failure was lack of adequate food intake. However, at the time of testing, the operated animals showed a body weight far above that observed in control rats at the age of puberty, making this hypothesis very unlikely.

Another possibility is that the hypophyseal–gonadal system did not develop normally at puberty. In order to test this hypothesis, two further experiments were undertaken. In one experiment the bulbectomy was performed postpubertally when the males were 80 days old. In a second experiment the rats were bulbectomized prepubertally at 30 days of age. Thereafter the males were treated with TP in dosages sufficient to induce and maintain sexual activity in gonadectomized male rats until they were 4 months old. The results obtained

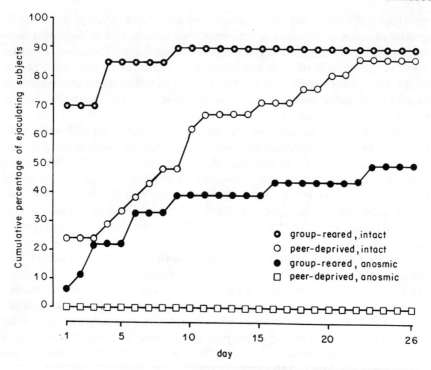

Fig. 5. Cumulative percentage of animals in intact and olfactory bulbectomized rats reared under various environmental conditions. Mating tests were performed each second day during a period of 26 days beginning when the rats were 95 days old (From Wilhelmsson and Larsson (1973) Physiol. Behav., **11**, 227–32.)

failed to support the hypothesis that sexual failure in the bulbectomized rats was due to an endocrine dysfunction. Following postpubertal bulbectomy, 4 of 22 sexually inexperienced males performed intromissions and 1 ejaculated compared to 8 of the 11 bulbectomized, sexually inexperienced rats that achieved intromissions and 7 that achieved ejaculation. Among 33 sexually inexperienced and bulbectomized rats treated with testosterone or oil, only 3 males ejaculated. There were no differences between groups treated with hormone or oil.

In addition to rendering the animal anosmic, removal of the olfactory bulbs may also disrupt brain connections essential for the expression of mating behaviour, and thus anosmia may not be the only cause of the decrement in sexual activity. Several attempts have been made to separate the effects of anosmia from the brain insult caused by olfactory bulbectomy both in rats and other rodents (Alberts and Galef, 1971; Doty and Anisko, 1973; Powers and Winans, 1973) but the results obtained failed to provide a clear answer to the problems posed. Destruction of the olfactory epithelium, removal of the olfactory bulb or interruption of the lateral olfactory tract of sexually experienced male rats produces similar sexual deficits according to our observations (Larsson, 1971). Unfortunately, destruction of the olfactory epithelium may cause non-specific destruction involving many other pathways.

Providing anosmia is the critical factor, one may ask if the sexual deficits are due to inability to respond to the odour of a receptive female or to other qualities of the female. Also, it is not known if the sexual deficits are related to a lowered responsiveness to odoriferous and non-odoriferous features associated with other stimuli from the female. The well-established fact that the male rat needs sexual experience in developing odour preferences for receptive females (Carr et al., 1965; Lydell and Doty, 1972; Stern, 1970) indicates the important role odours play in activating the male rat sexually.

Although the problem still remains unsettled of whether or not the sexual decrement following olfactory bulbectomy is due to anosmia or other factors, the results discussed clearly indicate that sexual experience is involved, and is able to some extent to compensate for the deleterious effects of the operations. Even experience of cohabitation with other males has some facilitatory effects as is evidenced by the fact that in one of the above studies (Larsson, 1975) 4 out of 15 males cohabiting with other males ejaculated compared to 1 of 22 rats that lived without physical contact with other rats. These results also have a methodological implication in that they demonstrate that the effects of a brain operation may be markedly different depending on whether or not the male has had social or sexual experience prior to the operation.

Interaction of Genital Stimulation and Sexual Experience

An important source of sensory stimulation for male sexual behaviour is derived from tactile stimulation of the genital area, particularly the penis. Elimination of the sensory input from the glans penis by local anaesthesia (Carlsson and Larsson, 1964; Adler and Bermant, 1966) or penile deafferentation (Larsson and Södersten, 1973) impairs the sexual performance of the rat. The male continues to mount the female but shows difficulty in achieving intromission and ejaculation.

An attempt to assess the effect of penile deafferentation on sexually inexperienced rats was performed by L. Dahlöf in my laboratory (Dahlöf and Larsson, 1976). Genital deafferentation was accomplished not by interruption of the dorsal penile nerve as in previous experiments but by section of the pudendal nerve, just before it branches into the dorsal penile nerve and enters the penile shaft. This operation deprives the rat of any penile sensitivity. The operation was performed at 14 days of age. Two experimental and two control groups were used. In one of the experimental groups, the male was removed from his littermates at 23 days of age and reared in isolation until the end of the experiment. In the other experimental group, the male lived between 50 and 65 days of age with females that were made receptive by oestrogen treatment. Besides the measures normally used in our laboratory, Dahlöf used two derived measures—total sexual activity per minute composed of the number of mounts and intromissions divided by the ejaculatory latency or, in absence of ejaculation, the length of the test session; and copulatory efficiency percentage: the ratio between mean intromission frequency and mean total activity.

As indicated by Fig. 6 and Table 3 penile deafferentation produced a marked decrease of the sexual activity in both groups. The effect of the operation was, however, more marked among the isolated males than among the group-reared ones. As shown by Table 2, fewer of the isolated operated rats performed intromissions and ejaculations than among the sexually experienced rats. Further, the isolated operated rats showed a significantly lower total sexual activity and a lower copulatory efficiency percentage than the unoperated controls.

No impairment was observed in the operated male's orientation toward the female, and the penis was directed accurately towards the vaginal opening. Since the operation seemed to have deprived the penis of any sensitivity to tactile stimulation we conclude that penile stimulation is not needed for mating. This raises the question of whether the anatomy or behaviour of the female is sufficient to guide the male and then by what means the necessary information is given to the male. No answer to this question is available yet. The results obtained after penile deafferentation in the rat differ from those reported by Aronson and Cooper in cats (1969). The deafferentated cat was unable to orientate adequately towards the female and failed to penetrate the vagina because he could not localize the vaginal orifice. No erectile deficiency was observed in the cat.

The results of penile deafferentation show a striking similarity to those obtained after olfactory bulbectomy. Both operations lowered sexual activity without abolishing it. After both operations the impairment of the sexual behaviour caused by the lesions was markedly aggravated by absence of social and sexual experience. Interestingly, the consequences of the social deprivation were more serious for the olfactorily bulbectomized and the penile deafferentated animals than they were for the intact rats.

Obviously, the effect of a brain lesion or a sensory deficit has to be evaluated with respect to the social history of the individual animal concerned. A sexually experienced male rat is much more resistant to the effects of an operation, than a sexually inexperienced male.

Interaction of Hormones and Experience

A well-known phenomenon in all species, so far studied, is that castration of the male does not immediately abolish sexual behaviour. This is in contrast to the female where ovariectomy immediately abolishes sexual activity in all mammals so far studied except primates. Since androgen produced by the

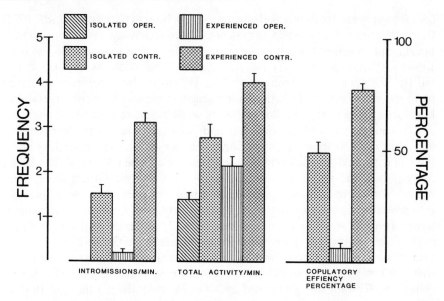

Fig. 6. Effects of pudendal nerve section and social isolation on male rat sexual activity. Comparison between the groups yielded the following results:
Intromissions per minute and total activity per minute $EC > IC > EO > IO$
$$p < 0.002 \quad p < 0.05 \quad p < 0.02$$
Copulatory efficiency percentage
$EC > IC > EO > IO$
$$p < 0.001 \quad p < 0.001 \quad p < 0.001$$
EC, Experienced Controls
IC, Isolated Controls
EO, Experienced Operated
IO, Isolated Operated

Table 3. Number of inexperienced and experienced rats showing various sexual response patterns after pudendal nerve section

	Isolated operated $n = 14$	Isolated controls $n = 12$	Experienced operated $n = 13$	Experienced controls $n = 12$
Mounts	14	12	13	12
Intromissions	6[1]	12	13[1]	12
Ejaculations	1[2]	12	6[2]	12

[1]Experienced operated Isolated operated p. < 0.01
[2]Experienced operated Isolated operated p. < 0.05
Fisher exact probability test (twotailed)

testes disappears from the body within a few hours (Coyotupa *et al.*, 1973) the persistence of masculine sexual behaviour following castration poses a puzzling problem. In the cat, experience of mating prior to castration has been shown to be a major factor in maintaining sexual behaviour as was demonstrated by Rosenblatt and Aronson (1958a, 1958b) in the experiments referred to in the introduction. In order to investigate whether the same observation holds true for the rat the following study was undertaken (Larsson, unpubl.).

The animals were Wistar rats that had been separated from their mothers and were isolated from 21 days of age. (Female rats in our laboratory show their first vaginal and behavioural oestrous cycles when 40 days old.) When 50 days old, the males were divided into three groups. Fifteen males were reared for a month with gonadectomized females that were brought into sexual receptivity once a week by treatment with oestradiol and progesterone (Group A). The Group B rats (n = 12) remained isolated in single cages. In contrast to the males with Group A females the Group C rats (n = 12) lived with gonadectomized females that were not brought into sexual receptivity. When 90 days old, the males were all castrated and tested for sexual behaviour. Testing was performed at 3-day intervals during the first 18 days after the castration and thereafter at 6-day intervals. To avoid disturbing the animals, testing took place in the rat's living cage. Each test lasted for 15 min if no intromission took place and for an additional 30 min if the rat intromitted.

The results obtained in this experiment are presented in Fig. 7. During the first test, three days after the castration, none of the isolated males ejaculated and only half of them intromitted. The majority of the heterosexually-reared males showed a complete mating pattern. Comparing the percentage of animals in the various groups that displayed ejaculations during the first test, the following differences were found: A *vs.* B p < 0.005; A *vs.* C p < 0.05; B *vs.* C p < 0.05. Presumably, due to experience acquired during the first days of testing, an increasing number of the isolates displayed ejaculation during the first two weeks of testing. After this, however, a decline of the sexual activity took place. Extending the comparison to the whole 58-day period of testing, significant differences were found between groups A and B in number of rats showing intromission (p < 0.025) and ejaculation (p. < 0.001), whereas no differences were observed between A and C. A comparison between Groups B and C revealed a significant difference in the proportion of tests in which ejaculation was observed (p < 0.025) but not in the occurence of intromission. The results show that sexual experience acquired prior to castration increases the readiness of the male to initiate sexual activity following castration.

In a further attempt to assess the influence of prior heterosexual experience, at the conclusion of the 58-day period of observation, the rats were injected daily with 100 μg TP. The first testing was performed 3 days after the first injection and was continued at 3-day intervals for 21 days. We predicted that the Group B males, that had a minimum of heterosexual experience, would

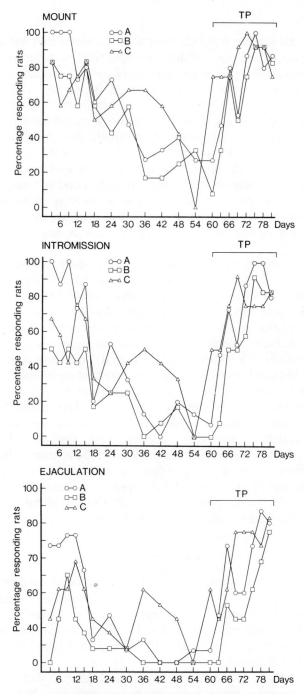

Fig. 7. Percentage of rats showing mount, intromission, and ejaculation on subsequent days after castration (O = day of castration) and after treatment with T propionate. A: rats reared with sexually receptive females; B: rats reared singly; C: rats with social but no hetero-sexual experience

be slower in initiating sexual behaviour than the males that had a maximum of heterosexual experience, or that had cohabited with females. This was found to be true. Comparing the number of daily injections of testosterone that were needed to induce sexual behaviour, the Group A males achieved their first ejaculation (p < 0.01) after a shorter latency than the Group B males. The Group C males, in turn did not deviate from the Group A males, but achieved their first ejaculation more rapidly than the Group B males. The results show that the action of hormones varies with prior experience of mating. The isolates which were sexually inexperienced before the start of testing needed treatment with TP over a longer period of time to attain the same level of performance as the other groups. Rearing males with females, despite the females' sexual inactivity, facilitated male sexual activity in adulthood, suggesting the importance of social experience for the expression of sexual behaviour.

The results obtained on rats are similar to those reported for cats by Rosenblatt and Aronson (1958a, 1958b) and Rosenblatt (1965). They found that half of the sexually experienced animals retained complete patterns of sexual behaviour 5 weeks after castration, while none of the inexperienced cats showed sexual behaviour at this time. When treated with TP after the castration, the experienced animals exhibited mating responses within a shorter period of time and at a higher frequence than did the naive cats. The experimental data obtained on rats and cats indicate that experienced males more readily display sexual behaviour than inexperienced males in the absence of gonadal hormones, or in the presence of low levels of hormones. This suggests that in the intact animal, as in the castrate, an interaction occurs between experiential and hormonal factors in determining the sexual behaviour. It is not clear to what extent experience acquired in the absence of hormones influences hormone-induced sexual behaviour, nor is it known what specific experience is important for sexual behaviour in adulthood. Both hormonal and experiential factors appear to determine this behaviour by influencing the developing organism over long periods of time.

CONCLUSION

At the risk of being repetitive, we will restate some of the conclusions discussed in previous sections and indicate some similarities and dissimilarities in the role that experiential factors play in the development of male sexual behaviour of rats and rhesus monkeys. These are the two species that have been used as experimental subjects in this area of research to the exclusion of almost all other species.

A finding common to the rat and the rhesus monkey is that social deprivation impairs masculine sexual behaviour but seems to have little or no lasting inhibitory influence upon female sexual behaviour (Duffy and Hendricks, 1973; Mason, 1960).

A major difference between the rat and the rhesus monkeys is that in the rat, the deleterious effects of social deprivation in infancy can be easily reversed by sexual experience while in the rhesus monkey the effects of severe social deprivation are irreversible (Harlow, 1966; Senko, 1966; Harlow et al., 1966). Surprisingly enough, in spite of a brain capacity far above that of the rat, a rhesus monkey is unable to readapt.

In the rhesus monkey, social deprivation during the first 6 months of life, resulted in permanent sexual failure in adulthood (Harlow, et al., 1966). No evidence exists for a corresponding period of critical importance for the sexual development of the rat. It appears that any social stimulation after the development of a capacity for locomotion may facilitate sexual behaviour.

The poor sexual performances of socially isolated rhesus monkeys should not be taken as an indication of a lowered sexual interest because the surrogate-reared monkeys masturbated frequently. Neither was absence of intromission due to inability to perform mounting and thrusting as evidenced by the finding that surrogate-reared male rhesus monkeys were perfectly capable of exhibiting a normal copulatory pattern to a model but not to an oestrous female (Deutsch and Larsson, 1974). Rather, the lack of appropriate mounting and insertion appears to be due to a lack of ability to integrate perceptual and motor components in an adequate copulatory pattern. Goy and Goldfoot (1974) have analysed the development of the sexual behaviour in male rhesus monkeys under various rearing conditions. They distinguish between mature mounting involving posterior orientation and clasping of the partner's back with one or both feet, and immature mounting when the male remains standing with both feet on the floor and with hands lightly touching the partner's back. Males reared with their mothers developed a predominance of mature mounts within the first 3 months of life. Males reared with peers, by contrast, developed a predominance of mature mounting only after about 18 months and some continued indefinitely to show immature mountings. A similar inability was observed by Hård and Larsson (1968b) in our study of socially deprived rats. The rats failed to orientate their posture adequately to the female, mounting her from her side or her head rather than from the rear. When mounting from the rear, no thrusting was performed and consequently no intromission took place.

If the hypothesis is correct that a major cause of the sexual deficits of isolated males is impaired perceptual-motor coordination of the behaviour, further studies in species like the rat are of interest because of the ease with which experimental conditions can be arranged in this laboratory species.

Since correctly performed mounting behaviour depends on an adequate mounting partner, preference for the female as a partner might be expected to facilitate adequate mounting. Goy and Goldfoot (1974) studied the choice of mounting partner and found that mother-reared males developed a preference for the mother as a mounting partner within 3 months of age. The peer-reared males never developed such a preference. The mother-reared males chose the more aggressive females to play with, while the less aggressive females were chosen for mounting. Peer-reared males chose males to play with and did not show any preference for the female as a mounting partner. The sexual behaviour thus appears to develop within the framework set by sexually dimorphic behaviour patterns such as play activity. The male shows more rough and tumble play activity, more initiative, and more aggressiveness in his play, and this activity is chiefly directed toward other males. Unfortunately comparable data do not exist for the rat or for any other species.

The socially deprived rhesus monkeys used by Harlow, Mason, and others were unable to interact socially with conspecifics. Hence sexual interaction was prevented. The relationship between sexual behaviour and other social behaviour patterns represents an important aspect of sexual activity of which little is known. In a monkey colony, the social interactions are influenced by dominance relationships and the expression of sexual behaviour is presumably regulated by such relationships. The social integration of the infant monkey in the troop may determine his future sexual behaviour. The same problem applies to other species, including the rat. In view of the immense variation in social organization of different mammalian species, one would expect great variation in the role social interactions play in adult sexual life. It would be interesting to know, for example, how interference with early social interactions among ungulates such as the zebra and the reindeer, which show highly developed social organizations (Espmark, 1971; Klingel, 1967), influence sexual behaviour. Unfortunately no such studies exist.

SUMMARY

In all studies conducted so far which include the rat, guinea pig, cat, dog, and rhesus monkey, deprivation of an individual's tactile contact with conspecifics from early postnatal age until adulthood results in delecterious effects on masculine sexual behaviour. In some species, such as the rhesus monkey, these effects are irreversible. In other species such, as the rat, they are reversible. A lack of ability of the socially deprived male to orientate correctly to the receptive female appears to be common to all species.

Experimental evidence relating to the role of experience in the development of adult masculine sexual behaviour in the rat has been surveyed with particular reference to work performed in our own laboratory. This work indicates that:

(1) The sexual behaviour displayed by the adult rat may be related to various forms of play activity exhibited by the infant. Social isolation may eliminate an important source of stimulation and the male does not gain experience of making the proper contact with the female; this contact facilitates sexual behaviour in adulthood.

(2) Social deprivation has particularly severe consequences for debilitated animals, for example animals that have been castrated and thereby deprived

of hormonal stimulation, olfactorily bulbectomized and thereby made anosmic, or deafferentated so that they have been deprived of tactile stimulation from the penis. Sexually experienced males are less affected by any of these operations than are sexually inexperienced males. A methodological implication of these findings is that the effects of any experimental interference with the normal function of the animal should be evaluated with respect to whether the animal is sexually experienced or not.

ACKNOWLEDGEMENTS

Support for work reported in this chapter has been provided by Swedish Social Research Council and Riksbankens Jubileumsfond. I want to thank Sven Carlsson and Ernest Hård for discussing earlier versions of this manuscript and Claery Persson for typing the manuscript.

REFERENCES

Adler, N. and Bermant, G. (1966) Sexual behavior of male rats: Effects of reduced sensory feedback, *J. Comp. Physiol. Psychol.*, **61**, 240–3.

Alberts, J. R. and Galef, B. G. Jr. (1971) A behavioral test of peripherally-induced olfactory deficit, *Physiol. Behav.*, **6**, 619–21.

Aronson, L. R. and Cooper, M. L. (1969) Mating behaviour in sexuality inexperienced cats after desensitization of the glans penis, *Anim. Behav.*, **17**, 208–12.

Beach, F. A. (1942) Comparison of copulatory behavior of male rats raised in isolation, cohabitation, and segregation, *J. Gen. Psychol.*, **60**, 121–36.

Beach, F. A. (1958) Normal sexual behavior in male rats isolated at fourteen days of age, *J. Comp. Physiol. Psychol.*, **51**, 37–8.

Beach, F. A. (1968) Coital behavior in dogs. III. Effects of early isolation on mating in males, *Behavior*, **30**, 218–38.

Bingham, H. C. (1928) Sex development in apes, *Comp. Psychol. Monogr.*, **5**, 1–165.

Bolles, R. C. and Woods, P. J. (1964) The ontogeny of behaviour in the albino rat, *Anim. Behav.*, **12**, 427–41.

Carlsson, S. G. and Larsson, K. (1964) Mating in male rats after local anesthetization of the glans penis, *Z. Tierpsychol.*, **21**, 854–6.

Carr., W. J., Loeb, L. S., and Dissinger, M. L. (1965) Response of rats to odors, *J. Comp. Physiol. Psychol.*, **59**, 370–7.

Coyotupa, J., Parlow, A. F., and Kovacic, N. (1973) Serum testosterone and dihydrotestosterone levels following orchidectomy in the adult rat, *Endocrinology*, **92**, 1579–81.

Dahlöf, L-G. and Larsson, K. (1976) Interactional effects of pudendal nerve section and social restriction on male rat sexual behavior, *Physiol. Behav.*, **6**, 757–62.

Davidson, J. M., Smith, E. R., and Bowers, C. Y. (1973) Effects of mating on gonadotropin release in the female rat, *Endocrinology*, **93**, 1185–92.

Dessi-Fulgheri, F., Lupo di Prisco, C., and Verdarelli, P. (1975) Influence of long-term isolation on the production and metabolism of gonadal sex steroids in male and female rats, *Physiol. Behav.*, **14**, 495–9.

Deutsch, J. and Larsson, K. (1974) Model-oriented sexual behavior in surrogate-reared rhesus monkeys, *Brain. Behav. Evol.*, **9**, 157–64.

Dewsbury, D. A. (1969) Copulatory behavior of rats (*Rattus Norvegicus*) as a function of prior copulatory experience, *Anim. Behav.*, **17**, 217–23.

Doty, R. L. and Anisko, J. J. (1973) Procaine hydrochloride olfactory block eliminates mounting in the male golden hamster, *Physiol. Behav.*, **10**, 395–7.

Drori, D. and Folman, Y. (1964) Effects of cohabition on the reproductive system, kidneys, and body composition of male rats, *J. Reprod. Fert.*, **8**, 351–9.

Duffy, J. A. and Hendricks, S. E. (1973) Influences of social isolation during development on sexual behavior of the rat, *Anim. Learn. Behav.*, **1**, 223–7.

Espmark, Y. (1971) Mother–young relationship and ontogeny at behaviour in reindeer *(Rangifer tarandus* C.), *Z. Tierpsychol.*, **29**, 42–81.

Folman, Y. and Drori, D. (1965) Normal and aberrant copulatory behavior in male rats *(Rattus Norvegicus)* reared in isolation, *Anim. Behav.*, **13**, 427–9.

Folman, Y. and Drori, D. (1966) Effects of social isolation, and of female odours on the reproductive system, kidneys, and adrenals of unmated male rats, *J. Reprod. Fert.*, **11**, 43–50.

Gerall, A. A. (1963) An exploratory study of the effect of social isolation variables on the sexual behaviour of male guinea pigs, *Anim. Behav.*, **11**, 274–82.

Gerall, H. D. (1965) Effects of social isolation and physical confinement on motor and sexual behavior of guinea pigs, *J. Pers. Soc. Psychol.*, **2**, 460–4.

Gerall, H. D., Ward, I. L., and Gerall, A. A. (1967) Disruption of the male rat's sexual behavior induced by social isolation, *Anim. Behav.*, **15**, 54–8.

Goy, R. W. (1970) Experimental control of psychosexuality, *Phil. Trans. Roy. Soc. Lond.*, **259**, 149–62.

Goy, R. W. and Goldfoot, D. A. (1974) Experiential and hormonal factors influencing development of sexual behavior in the male rhesus monkey. In: *The Neurosciences, Third Study Program*, MIT Press, Cambridge, 571–81.

Gruendel, A. D. and Arnold, W. J. (1969) Effects of early social deprivation on reproductive behavior of male rats, *J. Comp. Physiol. Psychol.*, **67**, 123–8.

Gruendel, A. D. and Arnold, W. J. (1974) Influence of preadolescent experiential factors on the development of sexual behavior in the albino rats, *J. Comp. Physiol. Psychol.*, **86**, 172–8.

Hård, E. and Larsson, K. (1968a) Visual stimulation and mating behavior in male rats, *J. Comp. Physiol. Psychol.*, **66**, 805–7.

Hård, E. and Larsson, K. (1968b) Dependence of adult mating behavior in male rats on the presence of littermates in infancy, *Brain, Behav. Evol.*, **1**, 405–19.

Hård, E. and Larsson, K. (1971) Climbing behavior patterns in prepubertal rats, *Brain, Behav. Evol.*, **4**, 151–61.

Harlow, H. F., Joslyn, W. D., Senko, M. G., and Dopp, A. (1966) Behavioral aspects of reproduction in primates, *J. Anim. Sci.*, **25**, 49–67.

Harlow, H. F. and Harlow, M. K. (1971) Psychopathology in monkeys. In: *Experimental Psychopathology: Recent Research and Theory*, H. D. Kimmel (ed.), Academic Press, New York, pp. 203–29.

Harlow, M. (1966) Learning to love, *Amer. Sci.*, **3**, 244–72.

Heimer, L. and Larsson, K. (1967) Mating behavior of male rats after olfactory bulb lesions, *Physiol. Behav.*, **2**, 207–9.

Herz, Z., Folman, Y., and Drori, D. (1969) The testosterone content of the testes of mated and unmated rats, *J. Endocrinol.*, **44**, 127–8.

Kagen, J. and Beach, F. A. (1953) Effects of early experience on mating behavior in male rats, *J. Comp. Physiol. Psychol.*, **46**, 204–8.

Kamel, F., Mock, E. J., Wright, W. W., and Frankel, A. I. (1975) Alterations in plasma concentrations of testosterone, LH, and prolactin associated with mating in the male rat, *Horm. Behav.*, **6**, 277–88.

Klingel, H. (1967) Soziale Organization und Verhalten freilebender Steppenzebras, *Z. Tierpsychol.*, **24**, 580–624.

Larsson, K. (1956) Conditioning and Sexual Behavior in the Male Albino Rat, Almqvist and Wiksell, Stockholm, pp. 1–269.

Larsson, K. (1959) Experience and maturation in the development of sexual behavior in male puberty rat, *Behaviour*, **14**, 101–7.

Larsson, K. (1967) Testicular hormone and developmental changes in mating behavior of the male rat, *J. Comp. Physiol. Psychol.*, **63**, 223–30.

Larsson, K. (1971) Impaired mating performances in male rats after anosmia induced peripherally or centrally, *Brain, Behav. Evol.*, **4**, 463–71.

Larsson, K. (1975) Sexual impairment of inexperienced male rats following pre- and postpuberal olfactory bulbectomy, *Physiol. Behav.*, **14**, 195–9.

Larsson, K. and Södersten, P. (1973) Mating in male rats after section of the dorsal penile nerve, *Physiol. Behav.*, **10**, 567–71.

Levine, S. and Mullins, R. F. (1966) Hormonal influences on brain organisation in infant rats, *Science*, **152**, 1585–92.

Lydell, K. and Doty, R. L. (1972) Male rat odor preferences for female urine as a function of sexual experience, urine age, and urine source, *Horm. Behav.*, **3**, 205–12.

Mason, W. A. (1960) The effects of social restriction on the behavior of rhesus monkeys. I. Free social behavior, *J. Comp. Physiol. Psychol.*, **53**, 582–9.

Mason, W. A. (1961) The effect of social restriction on the behavior of rhesus monkeys. II. Test of gregariousness, *J. Comp. Physiol. Psychol.*, **54**, 287–90.

Mason, W. A. (1963 Social development of rhesus monkeys with restricted social experience, *Percept. Mot. Skills*, **16**, 263–70.

Missakian, E. A. (1969) Reproductive behavior of socially deprived adult male rhesus monkeys *(Macaca mulatta)*, *J. Comp. Physiol. Psychol.*, **69**, 403–7.

Nissen, H. W. (1954). Development of sexual behavior in chimpanzees. Conference on Genetic, Psychological and Hormonal Factors in the Establishment of Sexual Behavior in Mammals. W. C. Young, Chairman, Lawrence, Kansas: University of Kansas Libraries.

Powers, J. B. and Winans, S. S. (1973) Sexual behavior in peripherally anosmic male hamsters, *Physiol. Behav.*, **10**, 361–8.

Purvis, K. and Haynes, N. B. (1972) The effect of female rat proximity on the reproductive system of male rats, *Physiol. Behav.*, **9**, 401–7.

Resko, J. A. (1967 Plasma androgen levels of the rhesus monkey: Effects of age and season, *Endocrinology*, **81**, 1203–12.

Riesen, A. H. (1971) Nissen's observations on the development of sexual behavior in captive-born, nursery-reared chimpanzees, *The Chimpanzee*, **4**, 1–18.

Riss, W., Valenstein, E. S., Sinks, J., and Young, W. C. (1955) Development of sexual behaviour in male guinea pigs from genetically different stocks under controlled conditions of androgen treatment and caging, *Endocrinology*, **37**, 139–46.

Rosenblatt, J. S. (1965) Effects of experience on sexual behavior in male cats. In: *Sex and Behavior*, F. A. Beach (ed.), John Wiley & Sons, New York, pp. 416–33.

Rosenblatt, J. S. and Aronson, L. R. (1958a) The influence of experience on the behavioural effects of androgen in prepuberally castrated male cats, *Anim. Behav.*, **6**, 171–82.

Rosenblatt, J. S. and Aronson, L. R. (1958b) The decline of sexual behavior in male cats after castration with special reference to the role of prior sexual experience, *Behaviour*, **12**, 285–338.

Sackett, G. P. (1965) Effects of rearing conditions upon the behavior of rhesus monkeys *(Macaca mulatta)*, *Child develop.*, **36**, 855–68.

Sackett, G. P. (1972) Exploratory behavior of rhesus monkeys as a function of rearing experiences and sex, *Develop. Psychol.*, **6**, 260–70.

Senko, M. G. (1966) The effects of early, intermediate, and late experiences upon adult macaque sexual behavior, *Unpubl. Master's Thesis*, Madison, Wisconsin: Univ. of Wisconsin Libraries, pp. 1–102.

Södersten, P. (1972) Mounting behavior in the female rat during the estrous cycle, after ovariectomy, and after estrogen or testosterone administration, *Horm. Behav.*, **3**, 307–20.

Södersten, P., Damassa, D. A., and Smith, E. R. (1977) Sexual behavior in developing male rats, *Horm. Behav.*, **8**, 320–41.

Södersten, P. and Larsson, K. (1974) Lordosis behavior in castrated male rats treated with estradiol benzoate or testosterone propionate in combination with an estrogen antagonist, MER-25, and in intact male rats, *Horm. Behav.*, **5**, 13–8.

Spevak, A. M., Quadagno, D. M., Knoeppel, D., and Poggio, J. P. (1973) The effects of isolation on sexual and social behavior in the rat, *Behav. Biol.*, **8**, 63–73.

Steinach, E. (1936) Zur Geschichte des manlichen Sexual-hormon und seiner Wirkungen am Saugetiere und beim Menschen, *Wein, Klin. Wschr.*, **49**, 164–72.

Stern, J. J. (1970) Responses of male rats to sex odors, *Physiol. Behav.*, **5**, 519–24.

Taleisnik, S., Caligaris, L., and Astrada, J. J. (1966) Effect of copulation on the release of pituitary gonadotropins in male and female rats, *Endocrinology*, **79**, 49–54.

Thomas, T. R. and Neiman, C. N. (1968) Aspects of copulatory behavior preventing atrophy in male rats reproductive system, *Endocrinology*, **83**, 633–5.

Valenstein, E. S. and Goy, R. W. (1957) Further studies of the organization and display of sexual behvior in male guinea pigs, *J. Comp. Physiol. Psychol.*, **50**, 115–9.

Valenstein, E. S., Riss, W. and Young, W. C. (1955) Experiential and genetic factors in the organization of sexual behavior in male guinea pigs, *J. Comp. Physiol. Psychol.*, **48**, 397–403.

Valenstein, E. S. and Young, W. C. (1955) An experiential factor influencing the effectiveness of testosterone propionate in eliciting sexual behavior in male guinea pigs, *Endocrinology*, **56**, 173–7.

Wilhelmsson, M. and Larsson, K. (1973) The development of sexual behavior in anosmic male rats reared under various social conditions, *Physiol. Behav.*, **11**, 227–32.

Yerkes, R. M. and Elder, J. H. (1936) The sexual and reproductive cycles of chimpanzees, *Proc. Nat. Acad. Sci. Washington*, 276–83.

Zimbardo, P. G. (1958) The effect of early avoidance training and rearing conditions upon the sexual behavior of the male rat, *J. Comp. Physiol. Psychol.*, **51**, 764–9.

CHAPTER 4

Olfaction and the Development of Sexual Behaviour

J. J. Cowley

INTRODUCTION

A link between olfaction and the development of sexual behaviour has been present in the minds of investigators for a long time though the systematic and comparative study of the relationship has only recently begun.

A close association between impaired sexual development and defects of the olfactory system was suggested by Ellis (1910) and finds support in a number of clinical studies from the turn of the century and from psychoanalytic writings (for reviews see Brill, 1932; Wiener, 1966, 1967a, 1967b; Comfort, 1971). While acknowledging the part played by olfactory stimuli in eliciting 'sexual excitement' in animals, Krafft-Ebing (1906) considered that only in pathological conditions did odorous substances induce sexual excitement in man. Such views were commonly based not on any analysis of behaviour, which could be attributed to olfaction, but rather on the histological similarity between the erectile tissue of the nose and the genitalia (Krafft-Ebing, 1906; Fabricant, 1960; Ham, 1974). The view that in man odour plays a role in the control of sexual behaviour, in exceptional conditions only, is in keeping with the views of Ellis, who regarded odorants as acting as an allurement for exceptional or abnormal persons only. The dominant sense in sexual behaviour was vision, but with odour there was a built-in latency to respond as a consequence of our having inherited a nervous system which had much in common with that of our animal ancestors.

Experiential factors associated with olfaction and acting early in life were seen as affecting the behaviour of the infant. The child's early interest in the waste products of its body were regarded as being subsequently repressed though the original interest could find expression in other activities and interests (for references see Daly and Senior White, 1930). The modification of the child's behaviour in relation to odorous substances is also seen as critical in the strengthening of the relationship between mother and infant. Fitzherbert (1959) suggests, for example, that the human infant associates the odours of the mother's sweat with the taste of milk, and that the fatty acids, which constitute the breakdown products of both, would facilitate the process. The odours would also provide the toddler with a source to which to orientate itself. Thus the odours of the mother become, through conditioning, synonymous with nourishment.

The odour of the mother is regarded by Kalogerakis (1963) as attractive to the child whereas that of the father is avoided and he regards these features of the family situation as being determinants of the oedipal situation and as having similarities to the phenomena of imprinting. That the odour of children may change with the onset of puberty has been commented on by a number of writers while Ellis quotes Venturi as suggesting that it should be regarded as a secondary sexual characteristic. Sensitivity to odoriferous materials is also said to be heightened at puberty yet without corresponding changes in the threshold of other modalities (for references see Ellis, 1910).

Early studies also drew attention to structural changes in the olfactory organ that occurred at menstruation, thus strengthening the view that there was a link between reproductive hormones and olfaction. As early as 1884 Mackenzie reported that in normal women regular changes in nasal erectile tissue occurred at menstruation and considered that the nasal changes gave rise to an increased sensitivity to odours that preceded menstruation. The term menstruation appears to have been used by some investigators prior to the 1920's, though not by Mackenzie, as synonymous with the period of 'heat' or midcycle receptivity in animals. This was true of Freud (Fitzherbert, 1959), and it may have been used in this way by others. An increase in olfactory sensitivity at midcycle is known from the work of Le Magnen (1952b), (see also Guillot, 1956; Jay, 1965) and may be true of other sensory modalities.

Interest in the odour of the secretions of animals and their use in medicine and in perfumery is evident from the writings of early Greek scholars (Hippocrates, Lucretius). In the 19th century, biologists were well aware of the importance of the sense of smell in reproduction and that in some species the odour of the animal changed with the time of rutting (Althaus, 1882). A description of the occurrence of the 'peculiar glands of mammals' was provided by Owen (1868) who recorded that in the Indian antelope, *Antilope cervicapra*, the doe was attracted to the male by his odour and that castration led to atrophy of the scent glands. The scent of males was considered by Darwin (1871) to be useful in exciting and charming the female rather than as a means of directing the female to the male. The large size of the scent glands with their complex muscular control was regarded as providing through natural selection an advantage when the more odoriferous males were also more successful in mating and having offspring.

A renewed interest has its roots in ethology and more particularly in the emphasis given by ethologists in the 1950's to the part played by releasers (sign stimuli) in evoking behavioural responses (Wilson, 1970). The possibility of odorous substances controlling behaviour in a similar way to visual signals has proved particularly likely in insects where pheromones have been shown to modify sexual development and to exercise a control in such basic activities as food collecting and reproduction. The part played by pheromones in the growth and reproduction of insects is beyond the scope of this article. The extensive use made of chemicals by insects in the control of social behaviour and in the modification of sexual development has its counterpart in mammals, though our knowledge of their role in mammals remains meagre.

Wenzel (1974) has pointed out that with the renewed interest of the role of oldfaction in reproduction, as well as other aspects of behaviour there has been a parallel interest in the mode of functioning of the olfactory system, as such, and particularly in relation to such basic phenomena as attention, learning, and motivation. All three processes are clearly interwoven into that ill-defined and complex series of motor actions which constitute sexual behaviour.

The topic of olfaction has been reviewed by Patton (1950), Wenzel and Sieck (1966), and a recent volume in the *Handbook of Sensory Physiology* series (Beidler, 1971) provides extensive coverage of the structural and functional aspects of the subject as well as reviews of the psychophysics and theories of olfaction. The problem of measurement and the reliability of the techniques for presenting stimuli of standard intensity continues to hinder the systematic study of the subject though the work on pheromones in insects, to which reference has already been made, has directed attention to the advantages to be accrued from organic microanalysis. The presentation of stimuli continues to present formidable problems.

A change in behaviour can be attributed to olfactory stimulation if there is an accompanying change in olfactory reflex (sniffing, orientation to source) and if the source of the stimulation is some distance from the animal. The behavioural criteria must be based, as Pumphrey (1950) has emphasized in discussing 'hearing', on primitive and persistent phylogenetic attributes of the sense that have wide generality across species. Descriptions based on structural and functional features that are limited to particular animals or groups of animals may, because of their specificity, lead to ambiguity or tautological statements.

In assessing the effectiveness of an olfactory source in modifying growth and behaviour it is necessary to show that it is the odorous substance (odorant) that is the necessary and effective stimulus in eliciting the change. The odorant may alter behaviour, it may initiate new patterns, or it may result in the cessation of the behaviour. Thus, the frequency, latency, or intensity of the behaviour may change, though these need not necessarily be correlated with each other. Few, if any, of the studies to be discussed have taken account of these parameters and in most of them growth and behavioural changes are attributed to olfactory stimuli on the basis of circumstantial evidence.

In this chapter, experiments are described in which exogenous hormones administered to infant mice modify sniffing behaviour in a masculine direction.

This is evident in a failure of the mice to discriminate when adult between castrated, vasectomized, and normal males. The change in responsiveness is produced through a close interaction between endogenous and exogenous factors. The action of phermones is implicated in these changes. Lesions of the olfactory tracts in newborn mice block phermone action and so modify growth and sexual development. The severing of the tracts also results in a reduction of food intake which in turn affects the hormonal state. The action of pheromones on sexual development and behaviour needs to be considered in relation to hormonal and nutritional changes which occur during the first few days of life and are responsible for the growth changes in the nervous system that give expression to the behaviour.

THE INTERPRETATION OF SEXUAL BEHAVIOUR

The problem of providing a satisfactory definition of sexual behaviour has been discussed fully by Beach (1965). The whole history of the animal is inextricably involved in the process of sexual development and knowledge of the part played by the exteroceptors in development and in the shaping of sexual behaviour is far from complete. That the social environment contributes to the change is well established (see later) and this in itself suggests that the range of effective stimuli may be wider than hitherto supposed. The gonads of prepubertal animals, while normally functioning at a low level of secretion of gonadal hormone may be activated by endogenous hormones (Donovan and Harris, 1966) and by the action of physical and chemical stimuli. The activation may not lead to the expression of adult patterns of sexual behaviour but it may produce changes that are 'sex related' and which may subsequently become incorporated into the adult behaviour patterns. Thus, the cyclic wheel running of female rats and mice has its counterpart in comparable fluctuations in exploratory behaviour. In the mouse, the peaks of exploratory activity as assessed in an open arena coincide with the pro-oestrous/oestrous period (Foote, 1974) and Burke and Broadhurst (1966) have observed similar changes in the rat. Further, wheel running and exploratory behaviour are 'sex related', female rats being more active than males (Broverman et al., 1968).

In many species of birds the tendency to wander is often the first indication of reproductive behaviour and restless swimming in sticklebacks is a preliminary to nest building (Hinde, 1953). The red deer stag displays a wide range of testosterone-induced behaviour prior to the onset of copulatory behaviour (Short, 1972). Thus, in many species, and in different orders, an increase in activity forms a necessary component of sexual behaviour and this has long been recognized (Hinde, 1953). The age at which the action of young animals can usefully be regarded as components of adult sexuality cannot be readily resolved, as the same movements may be utilized in other activities. Head-lifting as a component of sniffing occurs in day-old female mice and the frequency increases on exposure to a number of artificial and biological odorants.

The same sniffing movements are observed in adult mice when a wire basket enclosing a male is placed in their cage, but the frequency is less if the male is castrated.

Adult sexual behaviour may be observed in infant animals in such activities as chasing and mounting, but the behaviour is poorly organized and the intergation of the movements is dependent on age, experience, and species. Hanby and Brown (1974) have suggested that in Japanese macaques, *Macaca fuscata*, the act of crawling on to the mother's rump (boarding mount) cannot readily be differentiated from a sexual mount by an adult (for further discussion see Simpson, this volume Chapter 24). In this species pelvic thrustings and penis erections are common during the first few weeks of life though the onset of ejaculation does not occur until $4\frac{1}{2}$ years of age. Males and females orientate themselves correctly, however, by two months of age. In rhesus monkeys, Harlow *et al.*, (1972) have described oral, anal, and phallic components, in the development of sexual behaviour which can be regarded as homologous to those described by Freud (1915) in the human child (also Hansen, 1966).

The emergence of sex-related patterns of behaviour has also been described in rhesus monkeys (Harlow and Rosenblum, 1971). Of the three behavioural components involved, 'threat', 'passivity', and 'rigidity', the first two make their appearance at 40 and 30 days respectively, while rigidity, which is an aversive response from an approaching monkey, first appears at about 70 days of age. The postures are seen as predisposing the infants to engage in activities, that are in turn shaped by learning, to produce the adult patterns of reproductive behaviour. A similar emphasis is given to learning in the organizing of copulatory patterns of behaviour in the guinea pig (Valenstein and Goy, 1957). It is probable that features of the environment such as gentling act to modify the components of sexual behaviour and the age at which they find expression. Further, the adult behaviour may itself fail to emerge or appear in a form grossly different from the normal. Environmental stimuli acting on hypothalamic centres regulate endocrine activity and these changes, through modifying the secretions of the animal and therefore behaviour, may in turn affect the growth and behaviour of other members of the species and the environment. Thus, the interactions of members with each other, modify the internal and the external milieu.

Secretions may act olfactorily or be absorbed through the skin or ingested and so bypass the nervous system. In bees, for example, the pheromone involved in inhibiting queen rearing (9-keto-2-decenoic acid) must act on the olfactory receptors whereas the action of the pheromone on ovarian development is more effective if transported by the blood. It is not known, however, whether the pheromones in natural conditions act in this way (Butler and Fairey, 1963 and quoted by Barth, 1970).

In most mammals, social organization may be primarily dependent on olfaction. Individual and sexual recognition may be made on the basis of smell or on a combination of stimuli acting on a number of receptors. Adult male rats readily discriminate between receptive and non-receptive females (Le

Magnen, 1952a) and the same is true of the mouse (Chanel and Vernet-Maury, 1963 and reviewed by Bruce, 1970). Oestrous cats, when introduced into a cage previously occupied by a male, display the same sexual excitement (posturing, rolling, and rubbing) as they would were the male present (Michael and Keverne, 1968). The male ferret shows similar signs of agitation as well as an increase in exploratory behaviour and vocalization when placed in an open field arena in which a female ferret in late oestrus had previously been introduced and then removed (Cowley, unpubl. observ.).

OLFACTION AND NUTRITION IN THE DEVELOPMENT OF SEXUAL BEHAVIOUR

The modification of the social environment early in life can have a marked effect on the growth and sexual development of animals and the presence of other members of the species may be a necessary condition for the integration of the infant behavioural components into adult sexuality. The olfactory system may facilitate these changes through its close association with food-seeking behaviour, but the nutritional state of the animal may also affect olfactory responsiveness.

The presence of littermates may reduce the pace of development because the limited food available has to be shared between more mouths. Thus, female rats reared in large litters grow more slowly and sexual development is delayed as is the onset of wheel running activity (Kennedy and Mitra, 1963). Feeding rat mothers a low protein diet before and during pregnancy and lactation will retard the sensory motor development of their offspring and the frequency with which they sniff and explore an open field when adult will be less than that of comparable control rats; the reduction in sniffing may extend over more than one generation (Cowley and Griesel, 1966). The mechanism through which these and other behavioural changes are mediated is not known though Zamenhoff et al. (1971) have shown decrease in DNA (cell number) in rats of a second generation fed a low protein diet.

In rats whose growth has been reduced through the simple expedient of weaning them early, there is an impairment of spermatogenesis and fertility (Koldovsky et al., 1961; Kubat et al., 1961). Further evidence that adult male rat sexual behaviour may be adversely affected by undernutrition is shown in a recent study in which undernourished rats were shown to be slower in initiating sexual behaviour while some failed to mount at all. There was also an age delay in the occurrence of spermatozoa in the underfed rats at one year of age (Larsson et al., 1974).

Nutrition may not, however, be the only factor involved. Male rats 'weaned' at a late age (42 days) and subsequently tested when adult in an open-field test were *less* active than those weaned at the conventional 21 days of age. In a subsequent experiment male mice were weaned at either 21 or 35 days of age, while a third sample also weaned at the earlier age had a non-lactating adult ('aunt') placed with the litters from 21 to 35 days. The activity of the mice, as in the case of the rats, was less in the late weaned and in the 'aunt' sample than in the early weaned mice. The difference between treatments, in the second study, was only at an acceptable level of significance on the first trial of the test (Cowley *et al.*, 1969). The low activity of the mice with the 'aunt' suggests that it is the presence of the adult female, rather than prolonged lactation, that is responsible for the low activity (see also Fullerton and Cowley, 1971). The sex composition of the litter may also affect the subsequent growth and behaviour of the young. Infant rats raised in single sex litters weigh more than those raised with both male and female littermates and the former were also more active (Brain and Griffin, 1970).

Undernourishing animals in infancy may have widespread effects on their social behaviour when adult. Feeding rats a low protein diet during lactation leads to mothers making fewer contacts and more avoidance responses with their young. The same was true of infant female rats that were fed a low protein diet, early in life, and later tested on their maternal response to malnourished young (Fraňková, 1971). An increase in fighting behaviour, consequent upon early undernutrition, has been reported by Levitsky and Barnes (1972) and and Whatson *et al.*, (1974) while others have reported marked changes in emotionality in an open-field test (Cowley and Griesel, 1964; Fraňková, 1968). The part played by olfaction in these changes cannot be inferred from the studies though the changes in sniffing, in social responsiveness, and sexual development bear certain similarities to those in which olfactory input is modified. It is known, for example, that olfactory stimuli play a critical role in eliciting aggression in mice (Ropartz, 1968; Mackintosh and Grant, 1966) and that removal of the olfactory bulb, in the mouse, leads to a loss of aggressive behaviour (Ropartz, 1968) and an increase in emotionality in the rat (Douglas *et al.*, 1969; Alberts and Friedman, 1972).

The growth of the young may be associated with odour changes that are themselves dependent on nutritional and hormonal conditions. The secretion rate of the sebaceous glands may be influenced by the proportion of carbohydrate to fats in the diet (Rothman, 1929 and cited by Nikkari, 1965). Testosterone enlarges the sebaceous glands and increases the amount of lipid secreted on to the surface of the body while oestrogen has the opposite effect (Nikkari, 1965).

The results of an experiment obtained in collaboration with Ian Hanley (1972) and to be reported in detail elsewhere suggests that the introduction of strongly odorous compounds to the drinking water of mice may affect their aggressive behaviour some time after treatment has been discontinued. In this experiment male mice were given garlic powder (0·825 g/litre) or ground ginger (0·825 g/litre) dissolved in their drinking water from the day they were born and until they were 55 days of age. A third treatment group had the same concentration of garlic but administration was discontinued when the infants were weaned at 21 days. A control sample received normal tap water throughout the experiment. There were initially three litters with four babies in each but, because of the complexity of the testing programme, only three were selected from each litter for testing. All animals were housed in individual cages some three weeks before testing. An aluminium test box (40 × 15 × 10 cm high) with a double hinged perspex lid enabled the behaviour of the animals to be observed and their behaviour was recorded on a check sheet. The contestants were given 5 min to settle after which the sliding door, which divided the box into two equal areas, was lifted to give the mice access to each other. A non-repetitive-lattice design was used to arrange for paired encounters between the mice. The design allowed for the equating of the number of encounters, the spacing of the encounters, and for mice in each treatment to be tested on the same number of occasions (Hanley, 1972). The latency to attack, the number of fighting bouts, the cumulative attacking time (Catlett, 1961), a composite score based on the method of Brain and Nowell (1970) and Banerjee's dominance index (Banerjee, 1971) were the measures recorded during the 5 min test period.

The mice from the control treatment grew at a significantly faster rate ($p < 0.05$) than the other treatments though differences in food consumption, measured between days 20 to 55, were not statistically significant. The sample given ginger drank less liquid than the other samples but there were no other differences in fluid intake between treatments.

On the measures of aggression, analysis of variance showed some evidence of an overall significant difference between treatments on the number of fighting bouts ($p < 0.071$) and on accumulative attacking time ($p < 0.065$) but there were no differences on the latency measure, the composite score, or the dominance index. Further analysis showed that the differences were between the garlic and ginger treatments with the latter sample showing less aggression as measured by number of fighting bouts and the total attacking time. The discontinuation of the garlic at 21 days led to smaller differences between this treatment and the ginger treatment on both measures of aggression ($p < 0.05$ in both instances) than when the garlic was fed until 55 days of age ($p < 0.002$ in both instances). There were no differences between the control and the other treatments though the mean score on latency to attack was longer for the ginger-treated sample than the others and the composite score for this sample also showed them to be less aggressive. The results must clearly be interpreted with caution but considered overall they seem to indicate that the administration of the garlic and the ginger led to a change in the way the mice responded to each other and that this persisted after the treatments had been discontinued. It is not known whether the differences reflect a change in metabolism or a change in the secretion of the animals consequent upon differences in the composition of the substances administered. That they were present some weeks after treatment stopped, though in a less marked form, suggests that whatever factors are operative they lead to a change in the nervous system. Lederer mentions (and is quoted by Wilson and Bossert, 1963) that the caestoreum of the beaver reflects dietary variation, and Ellis (1910) provides other examples. The odour of cow's milk may be tainted with the grasses it eats and particular vegetables give characteristic odours to human urine. The literature on pathological conditions is summarized by Wiener (1967a, 1967b). The harassment of copulating baboon couples was observed in a natural setting by Hall and deVore (1965) and subordinate animals were more often displaced than dominant ones. The harassment may itself reinforce and so maintain the social structure but other features such as size, hormonal state, age, and personal history are no doubt relevant also. In Hanley's study there was no difference in body weight between the ginger and garlic-treated samples so that size does not seem to have been a factor. The difference between the samples in aggression may reflect metabolic and hormonal changes consequent upon the difference in food intake (see p. 000). Alternatively, the volatile substances may have acted to produce selective degeneration of the cells of the olfactory brain. The degeneration of cells in infant mice on exposure to a range of volatile substances has been described by Døving and Pinching (1973) and is discussed later. The cellular changes may form the basis of olfactory imprinting and this, in mice, is associated with mate selection. In invertebrates Kalmus and Ribband (1952) have shown that slight differences in the food supplied to *bee* colonies leads to the production of dissimilar odours by the foragers of the colonies and with the rapid distribution of food between members of the colony there is likely to be established a colony based, at least in part, on the odours of volatile waste products.

RESPONSIVENESS OF INFANT ANIMALS TO ODOROUS SUBSTANCES

The effect of age on human olfactory sensitivity is reviewed by Wenzel and Sieck (1966). Human infants, as judged by the Galvanic Skin Response, respond to odours within 24 h of birth (Crowell *et al.*, 1965) and different substances, and the sequential order in which they are presented, may also affect the response of the neonate (Engen *et al.*, 1963; Engen and Lipsitt, 1965) within a day or two of birth.

The changes in sniffing behaviour of albino rats, early in life, have been documented by Welker (1964) who noted that polypnea frequencies were, on the average, higher than normal resting respiratory rates on the day of birth and that there was a rapid increase in sniffing during the next two days. In our own studies, conducted with Alison Bell, on the albino mouse we have exposed males and female on the day they were born to a number of natural and synthetic compounds. The mice were removed one at a time from their litters and placed in a resting position and at right angles to the observer. A spatula, the tip of which was covered with absorbent cotton wool, was held in a fixed position 1.2 cm in front of the nose of the infant. Sniffing, indicated by the frequency of raising the head in the direction of the spatula, was recorded over a 30-s time interval under standard conditions. Each mouse was exposed to only one test sample so that it was necessary to test a large sample of animals (31 females and 24 males) in each treatment condition.

The frequency of sniffing was recorded when the mice were exposed to smears collected from the vagina of the mother and from her nipple line. Isopropyl alcohol and methanol together with a commercial perfume ('kiku') and a diluted solution of male urine formed the other treatment substances. The urine from two adult males was diluted with 2 ml of normal saline.

The mice responded strongly to many of the substances at this early age and frequency of sniffing varied with the substance to which the mice were exposed. A Friedman two-way analysis of variance showed an overall difference between treatments and further analysis using the Wilcoxon Matched Pairs Test (Siegel, 1956) showed many of the differences to be significant. The results are set out for the male mice in Table 1 and the females in Table 2.

There were also differences between the sexes. The females responded with more sniffing movements in the presence of the perfume than the male mice ($p < 0.01$) and the finding was confirmed when a second sample of mice was tested ($p < 0.02$). In the presence of methanol and isopropyl alcohol the females also made more sniffing movements but only in the case of the former did the differences approach an acceptable level of significance. As the direction of the differences could be predicted a one-tailed test was used ($p < 0.05$). There were no significant differences, at this age, in the response of the male anf female mice to natural substances. The results suggest that at or before birth male and female hormones act differentially on the nervous system and their action finds expression in the differing olfactory responsiveness of the mice to the methanol and to the commercial perfume. The masculinization of female mice which is known to follow the administration of androgens and oestrogens at 4–5 days after birth represents the action of exogenous hormones acting on a system already in the process of differentiation.

The odour of an anaesthetized mother may, however, act to inhibit the activity of rats between 2 and 12 days of age (Schapiro and Salas, 1970) and exposure of infant rats to the presence of nesting material, or the urine from a lactating rat, may have a similar effect. The activity of male rats when exposed to the presence of soiled material was also less than that of females at this age (Cowley and Wise, 1970). In older rats (day 16 onwards) decomposing caeco-trophe from the mother may act to attract the young to the mother (Leon, 1974).

NEONATAL HORMONE ADMINISTRATION AND OLFACTION

The difference between the male and female mice in sniffing behaviour may be of some interest when considered in relation to the sex differences mediated by exposure to testicular androgens and oestrogens on the subsequent sexual behaviour of rats and mice.

The administration of oestrogen to female mice on the day of birth (day 0)

Table 1. Sniffing movements following exposure to test substances—male mice

Treatment	Friedman two-way analysis	Wilcoxon Matched Pairs Signed Rank Test ('T' and 'P' values)				
		Vaginal smear	Nipple smear	Male urine	Saline	Perfume 'Kiku'
Vaginal smear	$\chi r^2 = 11.76$		60.0 < 0.02	73.0 ns	70.0 < 0.02	132.0 ns
Nipple smear				91.0 ns	131.0 ns	61.0 < 0.02
Male urine	$p = < 0.05$				81.5 ns	128.5 ns
Saline						22.0 < 0.01

ns = not significant

Table 2. Sniffing movements following exposure to test substances—female mice

Treatment	Friedman two-way analysis	Wilcoxon Matched Pairs Signed Rank Test ('T' and 'P' values)				
		Vaginal smear	Nipple smear	Male urine	Saline	Perfume 'Kiku'
Vaginal smear	$\chi r^2 = 24.6$		55.5 ns	71.0 ns	12.0 < 0.02	111.0 ns
Nipple smear				120.0 ns	46.0 ns	57.0 < 0.02
Male urine	$p = < 0.001$				43.5 < 0.02	56.5 < 0.02
Saline						28.5 < 0.01

ns = not significant

was found to modify sniffing behaviour in a test situation in which they were exposed, when adult, to a vasectomized and a normal male. The administration of oestrogen also led to an overall decrease in sniffing behaviour in the adult mice (Bell, 1972). Only those aspects of the study which have a bearing on the changes in olfactory behaviour are reported here (see also Bell, 1972). On the day of birth mice of the CSI strain were randomly assigned to one of four treatments. Fifteen mice were injected subcutaneously in the nape of the neck with 0.005 mg of oestradiol benzoate in 0.5 ml arachis oil (Organon Laboratories, Surrey) and a further fifteen mice were injected with the same volume of arachis oil. Two other controls were used. One of ten mice received 0·05 ml of olive oil, while the second sample of ten had a clean hypodermic needle inserted in the same region. Litters of five infants and their mothers were housed in individual cages at a temperature of 21 °C. Lighting was that of normal daylight (November–December) and the animals were fed on Diet 41B (Bruce, 1950).

At 11 weeks of age the mice were placed individually in the centre of an arena made of moulded polythene (60 × 40 × 15 cm high). The floor of the arena was marked into equal areas and the top was covered with a movable wire grid. A vasectomize adult male of the same strain was confined in a wire-mesh basket at one end of the arena and a normal proven male in an identical basket at the opposite end of the arena. The distance between the basket and the floor of the arena was 6 cm. The mice were vasectomized as young adults and at the time of testing they were older than the females. The female mice were tested in the arena for 2 min each day on 3 consecutive days. The number of times the female sniffed at either of the males was recorded together with the number of areas entered in the normal and vasectomized male's halves of the cage.

There were marked differences in the frequency with which the mice sniffed at the vasectomized and at the normal male and these are set out in Table 3. The oestrogen treated mice sniffed at the vasectomized mice more frequently than either the mice that were injected with arachis oil or the control sample. The oestrogen-treated mice also sniffed at the vasectomized male more frequently than the olive oil control, but the differences did not reach an acceptable level of significance.

Table 3. Treatments compared on number of sniffing movements directed at the normal and vasectomized mouse by female mice

Measure	Treatment	'H'	p	Treatments compared	'U'	p
Sniffs at ♂	Oestrogen Arachis Olive Control	18.33	< 0.001	Oestrogen/Arachis Oestrogen/Olive Oestrogen/Control Arachis/Olive Arachis/Control Olive/Control	37.5 3.0 26.5 26.5 42.0 41.0	< 0.01 < 0.001 < 0.01 < 0.01 ns ns
Sniffs at ♂ V.S.	Oestrogen Arachis Olive Control	6.78	< 0.01	Oestrogen/Arachis Oestrogen/Olive Oestrogen/Control Arachis/Olive Arachis/Control Olive/Control	36.5 55.0 41.0 40.5 47.0 40.5	< 0.01 ns < 0.05 ns ns ns

'p' values based on Kruskal–Wallis analysis of variance and Mann-Whitney U tests.
ns = not significant
V.S. = vasectomized male

All three control samples sniffed at the intact male more frequently than the oestrogen-treated mice. There was some indication that amongst the control samples the arachis mice sniffed at the intact male less frequently than the olive oil treated sample. The difference is not great but may reflect on the androgenic activity of arachis oil (Parkes, 1936). The total number of sniffs, irrespective of the male at which they were directed, was also less in the oestrogen-treated and arachis sample than in the other treatments. A Kruskal–Wallis analysis of variance indicated an overall difference between treatments (p < 0.02) and further breakdown using the Mann–Whitney U Test showed that the significant differences were between the oestrogen and the arachis oil and the olive oil control treatments (p < 0.01 in both instances). The oestrogen administration decreased the sniffing behaviour, if we may judge from our study of sniffing in normal day-old mice, in a masculine direction. This is in keeping with what is known of the action of small quantities of exogenous androgens and oestrogens, administered early in life, in subsequently producing a continuous secretion of gonadotrophic hormone from the pituitary. The pattern of gonadal hormone release is correlated with male sexual behaviour and this is reflected in a differential responsiveness to environmental chemicals by normal male and female mice. In the present study, hormone administration to female mice is followed by an increase in frequency of sniffing movements.

Table 4 shows the median number of times the female mice sniffed at the normal and the vasectomized males and a comparison has been drawn for each treatment using the Wilcoxon Matched Pairs Test. In all control treatments the females directed their sniffing significantly more frequently at the normal male than they did at the vasectomized male. Those mice which received oestrogen in infancy did not, however, differentiate between the vasectomized and the normal males.

The injection of testosterone proprionate (TP) and androstenol into female mice at birth leads to a similar failure to differentiate between a normal and, in this instance, a castrated male. The mice were tested in a test situation similar to that already described. The results of the experiment, conducted with M. Ostermeyer are shown in Table 5.

The cues used by female mice to discriminate between normal, vasectomized, and castrated males are unknown. Neaves (1975) has reported that serum testosterone levels were some 20% lower in vasectomized rats as compared with controls though the differences were not statistically significant. Earlier studies (reviewed by Parkes, 1966) have reported changes in seminal fructose in the bull though the results have not been consistent. More recently, Alexander (1972a) has pointed out that the sera of rhesus monkeys, vasectomized some years prior to being examined, had an antibody titre which was several times higher than that of animals recently vasectomized and has suggested that in these monkeys vasectomy results in an autoimmune response to spermatozoa which may aid in the disposal of spermatozoa still being produced (Alexander,

Table 4. Comparison of the median number of sniffing movements directed at the normal and vasectomized male by female mice

Treatment	Median sniffs Male	Vasectomized male	'T'	p
Oestrogen	4.0	4.0	46	ns
Arachis	5.5	3.0	0	< .005
Olive	6.5	3.0	0	< .005
Control	6.0	3.5	1	< .005

'p' values based on the Wilcoxon Matched Pairs Signed Ranks Test.
ns = not significant

Table 5. Comparison of the mean number of sniffing movements directed at the normal and castrated male by female mice

Treatment	N	Mean sniffs Male	Castrated male	'T'	p
Arachis oil	43	7.98	3.79	3.76	< .001
Testosterone Proprionate	46	5.76	5.57	0.67	< .25
Androstenol	40	7.03	6.03	1.54	< .05

'p' values based on the Wilcoxon Matched-Pairs Signed Rank Test.

1972b). A similar autoimmune reaction occurs in man after vasectomy and is discussed by Edwards (1972). An increase in antibodies may suppress male fertility though this is not inevitably so as is evident from studies in which, after vasectomy, the vas deferens is repaired. The secretions present in mice and rats on the penis and surrounding skin may differ in composition and odour as between vasectomized and intact animals though other cues, arising from cellular and tissue changes, associated with the autoimmune response may be used to make the discrimination.

The reduction in the overall sniffing in mice following the administration of oestrogen in infancy suggests that it may not only be a change in the perceptual mechanism (reflected in the failure to discriminate) but also a change in central mechanisms controlling the effectors. The work of Sheridan and Stumpf (1974) has shown that when ^{3}H-testosterone is injected into 2-day old female rats it is concentrated in the preoptic and amygdala region. The projection of fibres from the accessory olfactory bulb (which in turn receives its input from the vomeronasal organ) to the amygdala and preoptic area has been described by Raisman and Field (1971), who have also suggested that the vomeronasal organ and these pathways may be the ones involved in the pheromonal control of gonadotrophin or prolactin secretion. The same authors have provided evidence of an anatomical dimorphism between the female strial part of the preoptic area and that of the male (Field and Raisman, 1974). The incidence of non-amygdaloid dendritic spine synapses is correlated not with the genetic sex but rather with the capacity to provide the appropriate sex related patterns of gonadotrophin secretion. Confirmation of the dimorphic patterns of sniffing behaviour would suggest that at birth, in the mouse, the process of differentiation may already be underway.

PHEROMONES AND SEXUAL DEVELOPMENT

In locusts, phermones can promote somatic development and reproductive growth and the two phases of development are exclusive with the latter not normally beginning until somatic development is complete (Mordue et al., 1970). In Schistocerca, females reared with mature males show accelerated development at both phases and the pheromone has both primer and releaser properties. Its volatile nature enables it to act at a distance although it is more effective in accelerating maturation when the animals are in contact with each other (Loher, 1960, and summarized by Barth, 1970).

Whether phermones act in an analogous way in mice is not known though the persistence of the behavioural changes reported in studies on olfactory imprinting (Mainardi et al., 1965) and Open Field Behaviour (Fullerton and Cowley, 1971) suggest that exposure to odorous substances or adult conspecifics, early in life, may have a more permanent effect on sexual development than exposure at a later age. Further, early exposure may promote somatic growth in mice though others have not invariably found this.

The exposure of neonatal female mice to oestrogens and androgens has a permanent effect on the sexual differentiation of the nervous system and the same is true of pheromones and of undernutrition in the rat. In adult animals the behaviour may be affected by the same conditions but not irreversibly so. On the cellular level it has been suggested that early undernutrition is accompanied by a reduction in cell division and in later life by a reduction in cell size; it is the former which is responsible for the permanent changes (Winnick and Noble, 1965, 1966).

All three treatments, undernutrition, androgenization, and exposure to adult conspecifics lead to changes in Open Field Behaviour and the same is true of animals gentled in infancy (for references see Cowley and Widdowson, 1965). Whether there is a common element in these situations, other than the age factor, that can account for the long-term behavioural effects is not known, but in the case of pheromones the effects are hormone-dependent and their action on the recipient may be a function of its reproductive and nutritional state as well as of age.

In a number of mammalian species, including man, sexual maturation has been shown to be closely dependent on size or weight and factors which facilitate or retard growth will also accelerate or retard the attainment of sexual maturation (see McCance, and Widdowson, 1974).

Kloek (1961), quoting Stieve (1927) reported that the testicles of rabbits showed atrophy, during the winter months, if isolated from females but they remained active in their presence. A male isolated from females requires a time period for the testes to mature and during that time he is unresponsive to the female. The olfactory sense was regarded as exclusively involved in the activation. Atrophy of the testes and of the accessory reproductive organs in rats could be prevented by exposing rats to the odour of females (Steinach, 1936) though Poynter (1939) was unable to confirm his findings. Folman and Drori (1966) report that exposure to female odours had only minor effects on the reproductive system of unmated males living in isolated and in grouped conditions and that though they regarded Steinach's findings valid they considered the reproductive changes to be due to heterosexual mating rather than odour.

The effects of isolation on male sexual behaviour are summarized by Hinde (1966, 1974). Some investigators have reported that isolated rats show an increase in sexual responsiveness (Beach, 1942; Kagan and Beach, 1953) while others have reported that isolates are less successful in their mating behaviour (Zimbardo, 1958) and the same is true of the guinea pig (Valenstein et al., 1955; Gerall, 1963). More recently Goy and Goldfoot (1974) have reported that male peer-raised rhesus monkeys show a delay in the development of adult mating patterns.

The social isolation of animals may itself affect a wide spectrum of behaviour and this has been well illustrated by the extensive and rather ingenious studies of J. P. Henry and his associates at the University of Southern California (Henry et al., 1972). The isolation of mice, at a young age, induced cardiovascular and hormonal changes and the mice fail to develop a stable social order when introduced into an adult community. Whether changes in odour accompany these changes in physiological state is unknown though the fact that even brief periods of isolation may precipitate aggressive behaviour in the mouse suggests that this may be so. The phermones involved are contained in the urine and associated with the coagulating glands of the male genital tract (Mackintosh and Grant, 1966; Ropartz, 1968: Mugford and Nowell, 1971).

A reduction in ovarian activity, consequent upon being housed in all female groups, has been reported by a number of investigators (Andervont, 1944; Van der Lee and Boot, 1955, 1956; Whitten, 1959). The factors involved in the suppression of the oestrous cycle under group living conditions have not been specified though the action of a male in initiating a new cycle (Whitten, 1956a) and in producing a high proportion of matings on the third night after exposure to the male, suggests that a phermone is involved and that it is present in the urine (Marsden and Bronson, 1964, 1965). The removal of the olfactory bulbs may, in some strains but not in others, prevent the suppression of the cycle adding support to the contention that the olfactory pathways are involved (Whitten, 1956b; Whitten and Bronson, 1970).

The reduction of ovarian activity, early in life, may delay the onset of puberty. Andervont (1944) working with the C3H strain found that the oestrous cycles of segregated animals occurred earlier, were more frequent, and lasted longer than those of mice housed in groups of eight per cage and he considered that the crowding, or contact with each other, was responsible for exerting the change in hormonal condition. Housing female mice in groups of four produced a high incidence of true pseudopregnancies and housing the mice individually was a sufficient condition to prevent the pseudopregnancies (Van der Lee and Boot, 1955, 1956). That 'contact' was not a factor in the reduction of the cycles was shown by Whitten (1959). The subdividing of a large cage into smaller units, with perforated or solid partitions, did not prevent the reduction in the cycles though it was less marked than in an undivided cage. A similar reduction in cycles was observed by Whitten when blind mice were grouped together and suggests that visual cues were not the operative ones. Whitten and Bronson (1970) have suggested that the prolonged pseudopregnant cycles reported by van der Lee and Boot (also Dewar, 1959) when mice are housed in small groups and the anoestrus observed in mice in large groups may be due to environmental or strain differences.

Interaction Between Females

A number of studies have reported that pheromones can alter the pace of development. For the main part the studies have concentrated on exposing mice to conspecifics during the preweaning period or for varying lengths of time after they have been separated from the mother. The investigators have restricted themselves almost entirely to the sexual development of the female, though there are exceptions.

The initial studies were set against the background of work on the Bruce and Whitten effect though Castro (1967) also linked his own studies with those on crowding (see Christian, 1959; Christian et al., 1965) and its effects on the suppression of reproduction, while Vandenbergh (1967) associated his studies with those on handling (gentling) and its effects in accelerating sexual maturation. Different centres were clearly following similar lines of thought at much the same time though the investigators were using rather different methods to achieve their effects. (See also Fullerton and Cowley, 1968.)

Castro (1967) housed different numbers of female mice at weaning at 21 days of age in cages of a constant size and was able to demonstrate a linear relationship between the average age of the mice at puberty (assessed by vaginal introitus) and the number of females housed together (density). Other parameters of sexual development were not examined but the magnitude of the relationship was striking.

The urine of adult female mice diluted with water, modifies the rate of sexual maturation when applied daily to the dorsal surface of the nose of infant mice (Cowley and Wise, 1972). The changes in the rate of maturation are dependent on the phase of the reproductive state of the donor female. Urine from adult virgin females delayed sexual development whereas that from pseudopregnant females and females in early pregnancy had an accelerating effect on sexual maturation. Further, the topical application of urine from pseudopregnant donors (and adult male mice) was associated with a higher incidence of pregnancy (Cowley and Wise, 1972). More recently, Colby and Vandenbergh (1974) have shown that urine of adult female donors, housed in groups of 25, and applied to recipients between 24 and 40 days of age resulted in the attaining of first oestrus at an earlier age than mice exposed to urine from castrated males.

The delay in vaginal opening when females are housed in close proximity, but separated by a wire-mesh screen (Fullerton and Cowley, 1971) suggests that the female–female effect in retarding sexual maturation is a real one and that the substances responsible are contained in the urine of virgin female mice (Cowley and Wise, 1972; Colby and Vandenbergh, 1974).

That prolonged exposure is not a necessary condition for producing changes in the reproductive state and behaviour of a female rat exposed to the presence of the urine of another female can be illustrated by an arrangement in which the recipient is housed in a conventional activity wheel and the donor is housed in a cylindrical metal cage some 45 cm above the wheel. The funnel-shaped bottom of the donor's cage allows for urine to be collected and carried down to an area immediately below the activity wheel so that the recipient does not have acess to it.

The recipient is kept in the activity wheel for some weeks prior to being exposed to the urine of the donor and during this time shows the characteristic fluctuations in vaginal oestrus and wheel running. The response of the rat to the urine is dependent on the reproductive state of the donor, and in a proportion of rats this will change as the reproductive state of the donor changes (Cowley and Wise, 1970).

Fig. 1 (rat 22) shows the response of a rat to the presence of the urine from an unmated donor and the changes in activity and in vaginal cornification when the donor is pregnant and lactating. The activity peaks which coincide with vaginal oestrus before exposure are desynchronized while exposure to urine of a pregnant rat produces frequent periods where vaginal oestrus is prolonged and, in this instance, the level of activity is lowered until the litter of the donor rat is born.

The changes in vaginal oestrus and cyclical running can also be demonstrated by placing a paper towel, that has been left for 24 h beneath the living cage of a donor, beneath the wheel. In our experiments, conducted with M. Ostermeyer, we remove the stools and other solid matter, prior to placing the towels beneath the wheel. The towels are changed each day. Fig. 2 shows the changes in vaginal cornification and behaviour of two rats that have been exposed to the urine of a donor that has been mated with a vasectomized male. In both recipients the pattern of running activity is disrupted and in the one there is evidence of persistent vaginal cornification while in the other there are 3 occasions when vaginal cornification persists over two successive days. In this rat, discontinuing exposure to the urine is followed by a return to a normal

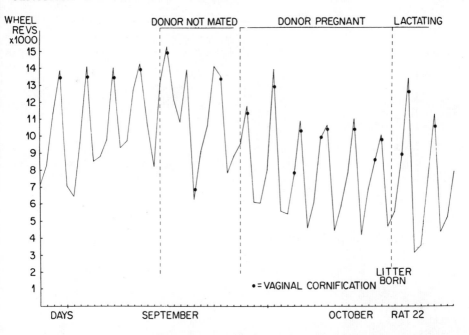

Fig. 1. Record showing spontaneous daily wheel activity changes and vaginal cornification in normal cycling rat before and after exposure to the urine of an adult female donor. The peaks of activity and vaginal oestrus coincide before exposure but are desynchronized by the presence of the urine. When the donor is pregnant vaginal oestrus may be prolonged. There is an increase in the peaks of activity after the donor has littered. The changes in the reproductive state of the donor are shown by the vertical lines

5-day activity cycle, but there is no evidence of a return to normal vaginal cyclicity.

In Fig. 3 the donor has been injected subcutaneously with progesterone (25 mg in 1 ml arachis oil) for 7 consecutive days. One recipient responds with a cessation of cyclic activity and vaginal oestrus. This, 'pseudopregnant' reaction can be contrasted with that of the other recipient which continues to show a normal activity cycle with a single high peak of activity which is not dissimilar to that observed in Fig. 3 (a) or (b). This rat shows evidence of vaginal cornification, on two consecutive days, both after the introduction of normal urine and when the donor has been injected with progesterone.

The response of the rat to the presence of the urine provides a simple method for studying the behavioural changes (activity) that accompany exposure to the changing reproductive state of the donor. In infant mice, the effect of exposure to adult lactating females is to reduce activity and to retard development; the exposure of juvenile mice, for as short a period as three days, delays their sexual maturation (Colby and Vandenbergh, 1974). In the wheel situation the activity and reproductive changes are rapid and the question arises as to

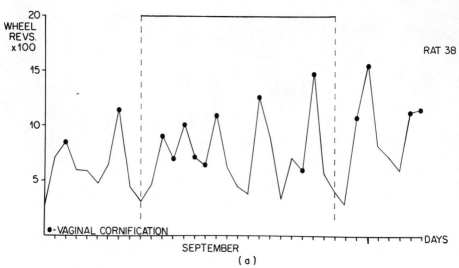

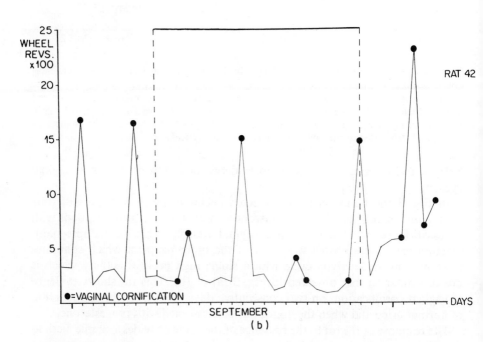

Fig. 2 (a) and (b). The two figures show the daily spontaneous running activity and vaginal cornification before and after exposure to the urine of a donor mated with a vasectomized rat. The discontinuous vertical lines on the left of the figures show the day on which the female donors were mated and the recipient exposed to urine on soiled towels. The discontinuous vertical lines on the right shows the day on which the soiled towels were no longer placed beneath the wheels

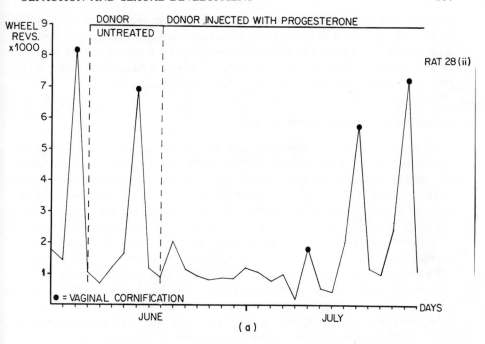

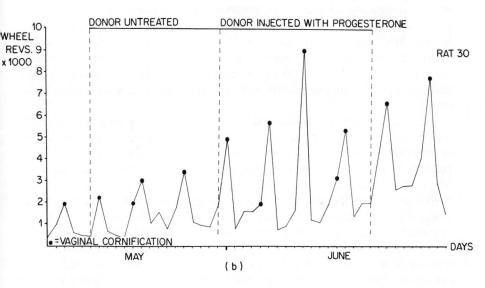

Fig. 3. (a) and (b) show the total daily spontaneous running activity and vaginal oestrus of normal female recipients before and after exposure to the urine of donors injected with progesterone. In Fig. 3 (a) there is a cessation of cyclic activity and of vaginal cornification while the other recipient shows little reaction though there is a peak of activity 10 days after exposure which is similar to that observed in Fig. 2 (b)

whether these primer effects are not the same as those produced by the longer periods of exposure which delay sexual maturation. Confirmation of the similarity would provide us with a simple and useful method of studying the interaction of changes in reproductive state with aspects of behaviour that have long been associated almost exclusively with hormonal fluctuations.

Interaction between Males and Females

The presence of a male mouse in a cage of conspecifics can accelerate female sexual maturation (Castro, 1967; Vandenbergh, 1967) and the same is true if the male is separated from the female by a wire screen (Vandenbergh, 1969; Kennedy and Brown, 1970; Fullerton and Cowley, 1971) or if the soiled bedding material is introduced into the cage of the female (Vandenbergh, 1969; Vandenbergh et al., 1972). The factor(s) responsible for the accelerated sexual development are contained in the urine (Cowley and Wise, 1972; Colby and Vandenbergh, 1974). Adult male rat urine applied to the oral–nasal groove of mice accelerated the onset of first oestrus providing evidence that the active component could act across species (Colby and Vandenbergh, 1974). The seretions from an unfamiliar strain of mice may also affect the growth rate of infant female mice of another strain (Cowley and Wise, 1970). Vandenbergh et al., (1975) have recently attempted to isolate the active component from the urine and they suggest that the pheromone may be a portion of a protein or a substance bound to a protein and that its action is dependent on the female having direct contact with the urine. The question must remain open, but clearly in some studies (e.g. those on infant activity and adult wheel running) the animals do not have access to the secretions; and the behavioural changes may be evoked by different pheromones from those involved in the maturational changes.

The length of time of exposure to the male either before weaning (Kennedy and Brown, 1970) or to urine after weaning has little effect on the age of first oestrus though when urine is applied directly to the nasal region of mice (aged between 21 and 29 days) those which were older showed a more rapid acceleration of first oestrus than those which had the urine applied at the earlier age (Colby and Vandenbergh, 1974). The age range examined is narrow but it may indicate a greater tendency to react to the active substances with the approach of puberty. In an earlier study, adult males were housed prior to weaning in cages with mothers and their litters or with females that had already been weaned. It was found that under the former conditions the mice reached first oestrus at a later age than did those housed with the males after weaning (Vandenbergh, 1967). As adult female mice exercise a retarding action on infant activity and sexual development, as well as restricting their own oestrogenic activity when living in groups, it would seem that in natural conditions there would be an interplay between the activating action of the males and the delaying action of the female secretions. The particular social conditions prevailing could thus either facilitate or retard the development of the 'new' generation. The mothers' history and nutritional state, as well as the number of young to be fed, would further act to promote or retard the development.

Fullerton and Cowley (1971) reported that the presence of adult males during the preweaning period increased, and the presence of adult females decreased the rate of growth of female mice; others have failed to confirm the finding (Vandenbergh, 1967; Kennedy and Brown, 1970). The application of virgin female urine during this period of growth has a retarding effect, though there was no statistically significant difference between females that had had male urine applied to the nasal region and a control group. It was apparent from the growth curves, however, that at the time the experiment was discontinued the males had not yet reached their weight asymptote whereas the control mice had (Cowley and Wise, 1972). A recent study by Colby and Vandenbergh (1974) on the regulatory effects of pheromones on the onset of puberty in the mouse, suggests that under some conditions there is a correlation between body weight, vaginal opening, and first oestrus, but in other experiments the relationship was not present.

The age at which the mice are exposed to the treatments and the method of exposure, may be among other factors that have contributed to the lack of agreement between investigators. Restricting the rate of growth of rats before weaning has a more marked effect in retarding their subsequent growth, than restriction at a later age, and the effects persist well into adult life (reviewed by McCance, 1962; McCance and Widdowson, 1974). The effects of altering the chemical environment may produce similar changes, as suggested by Fullerton's work, by acting on the developing nervous system. Gard et al., (1967) have shown that the gross body movements of infant rats are changed by the chemical environment and the response is dependent on age (Cowley and Wise, 1970). That the exogenous substance may have a permanent effect on the nervous system and the behaviour of the animal is suggested by the studies of olfactory imprinting in mice (Mainardi et al., 1965) and by the changes in Open Field Behaviour (Fullerton and Cowley, 1971).

Interaction between Females and Males

The presence of adult females may accelerate the sexual development of young males. The weight of the testicles of mice exposed to an adult female was greater than that of males exposed to adult males (Vandenbergh, 1971). Fox (1968) has reported similar changes in house mice reared with females from weaning until 37 days of age. The mice reared with females showed higher levels of follicle stimulating hormone (FSH) and there were accompanying growth changes in the epididymis and seminiferous tubules.

That the substances responsible for the changes are airborne is suggested by a study on hamsters. The exposure of hamsters to receptive females or to the odour of vaginal secretions increased plasma testosterone levels (Macrides *et al.*, 1974) while in the pig puberty can be advanced by housing gilts with the boar (Brooks and Cole, 1970).

A division between primer and releaser phermones is often difficult to draw in studies on growth changes, for, as pointed out previously, short periods of exposure (3 days) have been shown to accelerate the onset of puberty in the mouse (Colby and Vandenbergh, 1974) and it is not yet known what the critical time of exposure will be. If the same substances are involved in the maturational process as in the changes of vaginal oestrus and activity in the rat, and they are both susceptible to changes in the reproductive state of the donor, then their action is more that of releaser than of primer effect, and the long-term changes may also be precipitated by the same substances.

In studies where both sexes are present the effects of pheromones may be confounded by the acceleration of copulatory patterns and in those where waste products are directly introduced into the cage, they may, as pointed out elsewhere, provide an additional source of nutrients and steroids (see Cowley and Wise, 1972).

The close interaction between mother and young, prior to weaning, may involves different pheromones from those acting at later ages. Olfactory stimuli from infant rats are known to be involved in the facilitation of the release of prolactin (Grosvenor, 1965) and of corticosteroids (Zarrow *et al.*, 1972), and the failure of bulbectomized rats and mice to care for their offspring (see below) may be associated with a failure to respond appropriately to the infant secretions.

EFFECTS OF LESIONS OF THE OLFACTORY BULBS, EARLY IN LIFE, ON SEXUAL DEVELOPMENT

The review has focused attention on events early in life that modify the subsequent responsiveness of animals to olfactory signals, both during development and when adult, and has been particularly concerned to show that the early modification of the chemical environment may affect the subsequent reproductive and sexual behaviour of the animal. The chemical environment is largely determined by the conspecifics to which the animal is exposed and by the nutrients with which it is supplied. In many laboratory animals, and in man, the olfactory mechanism is geared from a very early age to respond to the chemical changes and these may in turn determine subsequent patterns of responding. The evidence is scattered and incomplete but from both behavioural and electrophysiological studies of a number of species there is evidence of the responsiveness of the system not only to gross changes in the chemical environment but also to more specific olfactory stimuli. (For reviews and references see MacLeod, 1971; Wenzel, 1974.)

Infant rats exposed from 2 weeks of age to different odorous substances, and for varying lengths of time, showed characteristic patterns of cell degeneration in the olfactory bulbs which were dependent on the odorant. The localized nature of the degeneration suggests that the odorants were acting on specific groups of cells in the bulbs (Pinching and Døving, 1974).

On the basis of what has been observed about the responsiveness of infant mice to odorous substances and the neural and behavioural (sniffing) differences between the sexes which are present at birth, one may anticipate that lesions of the olfactory pathways early in life would lead to widespread behavioural changes and that these would be both sex- and age-dependent. That localized morphological changes occur during development after exposure to artificial odorants (see above) suggests that the lesions may have different effects according to their localization within the bulb.

Work in our laboratory by McClelland, Cooper, and Lumsden has concentrated on the effects of lesioning the olfactory bulbs of neonatal mice and attention is largely directed to these studies. The extensive literature on the effects of bulbectomizing *adult* animals is not discussed except where it has particular relevance for the infant studies (see Wenzel, 1974 for examples, and reference to much of this rapidly expanding field).

The problem of accurately placing lesions in the bulbs of neonatal rats and mice are considerable (Orbach and Kling, 1966) and some of the problems are common to those encountered with working on other brain regions in adult animals (Holmes and Ball, 1974). The olfactory bulbs have ready access to limbic structures so that a wide spectrum of autonomic, hormonal, and behavioural changes may ensue from their removal. In young animals these systems are labile and this in itself may make the animal more vulnerable as evidenced by high mortality in the rat during the first week or ten days of life (Tobach *et al.*, 1967) and thereafter a decline in the number of deaths. The high mortality rate in neonatal mice can be reduced by restricting the size and position of the lesions (Fig. 4), and by rearing the young in small litters with control mice as littermates (McClelland and Cowley, 1972; Cooper and Cowley, 1976a, 1976b). The mothers continue to care for their bulbectomized infants though their rate of growth is much reduced and this is no doubt due, at least in part, to a failure to obtain adequate food to sustain normal growth. Locating the mother's nipple and reacting appropriately to it are regarded by Kovach and Kling (1967) as part of the reflex system that is destroyed by bulbectomy and elsewhere we have suggested that bulbectomy may block the action of maternal pheromones (McClelland and Cowley, 1972.). More recently, Lumsden has observed that mice with bilateral anterior lesions of the bulb, placed at 24 h of age, are more active than control mice on days 4, 5, and 6 but thereafter the activity falls rapidly and remains well below that of controls at least up to the time they are 12 days of age. The cross-over between the activity of bulbectomized and control mice is illustrated in Fig. 5. In unilaterally bulbectomized mice there is also an increase in activity at an earlier age than in the controls, though unlike those with bilateral lesions there is a delay of 3 days before the spurt of activity occurs. The activity was measured daily in a constant-temperature oven and with the number of 4 cm squares

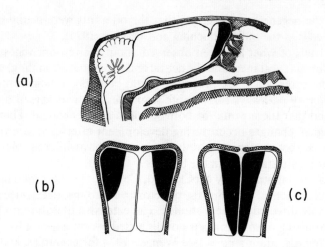

Fig. 4. Drawing of parasagital (above) and transverse
sections (below) of the skull of a mouse. The black area
shows the area of the olfactory bulb removed in anterior
bulbectomy (a), lateral bulbectomy (b), and central
bulbectomy (c). (From McClelland and Cowley, 1972.)

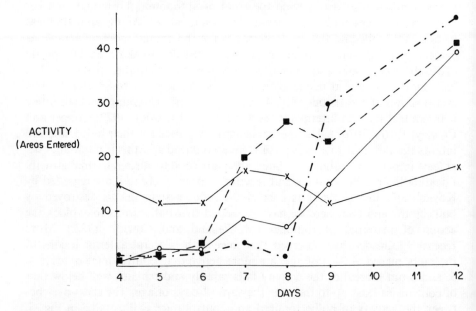

Fig. 5. The total number of areas entered by infant mice with unilateral (———.—)
and bilateral (—×—) lesions of the olfactory bulbs are shown. The lesions were made 24 h
after birth and the mice tested daily between the ages of 4 and 9 days and when 12 days
of age. The activity changes of the control (—.—.—) and control operated mice (o———o)
are also represented

entered in a two-minute period providing the unit. The heightened activity of the mice during the first few days of testing may be due to a failure of the mother's secretions to act on the olfactory centres of the bulbectomized mice. The age period is one in which activity is low when normal mice are exposed to the secretions of the mother (Schapiro and Salas, 1970; Cowley and Wise, 1970). In an earlier study mice bulbectomized at 5 days of age were found to be less active than control mice when tested from the 8th day and the low level of activity persisted until they were mature (McClelland and Cowley, 1972). It would seem that the initial increase in activity is dependent on age.

The age of vaginal opening and of first oestrus were also delayed in mice with lateral and central lesions of the bulb though where only one bulb was removed there was no significant delay in sexual maturation. In the mice with bilateral lesions there was an absence of recurrent cycles and the lesions also affected the fertility of the mice when adult. Mice with lateral and central lesions gave birth to fewer litters than mice with unilateral lesions (McClelland and Cowley, 1972).

In rats 3–19 days of age bilateral section of the olfactory stalk was accompanied by delayed vaginal opening and a slight 'deficiency' in mating (Kling, 1964). The ovaries and uteri of rats bulbectomized at 6 days of age were lighter and vaginal opening was delayed by 10 days. Further, the pattern of change in serum luteinizing hormone (LH) concentration in the bulbectomized rats showed a similar time lag when compared with that of sham-operated animals (Sato et al., 1974). That bulbectomy, early in life, is responsible for poor mothering has been observed in the hamster (Leonard, 1972), the rat (Kling, 1964) and in the mouse in our laboratory (McClelland and Cowley, 1972).

Franck's work on the female rabbit shows a number of similarities to results obtained on the rat and mouse. The rabbits were bulbectomized at 6 weeks of age and of the 21 that survived 19 rejected advances of the male and just under a third of these showed masculine mounting behaviour. The ovaries were atrophic and the genital tract remained immature (Franck, 1966). On the other hand, Leonard has reported normal 4 day oestrous cycles and normal sexual behaviour in hamsters bulbectomized at 10 days of age though there was some evidence, as mentioned previously, of defective mothering. The finding is in keeping with that of Carter (1973) who reported that in the golden hamster removal of the olfactory bulbs failed to alter levels of female receptivity.

Kling (1964) has also reported that male rats bulbectomized between the age of 3–19 days did not show delayed testicular descent and there was active spermatogenesis though all the males failed to mate (see also Orbach and Kling, 1966). In the male mouse Cooper (1973) also observed marked changes in sexual behaviour. The mice were bulbectomized at 24 h of age and subsequently tested when adult. They showed little interest in oestrous females, as judged by frequency of approach, and the little attention they did pay was of a transitory nature. The mice made few attempts to mount the females as compared with control operated and unoperated samples. The mean number of mice achieving intromission was also significantly less than that of a combined control sample (sham operated and undisturbed controls). The testes of the bulbectomized mice though lighter than control-operated mice were not significantly so and the difference was attributable to the lower body weight of the bulbectomized mice.

The studies of bulbectomy in infant animals have been conducted on different species and at different ages and they have been cared for under a variety of social conditions. In the rat and mouse bulbectomy in infancy leads to disturbances of reproductive behaviour in both sexes and these are accompanied in the female rat, mouse, and hamster by retarded growth. Further, in these species, and in the rabbit, ovarian atrophy is associated with the lesions. A disturbance of mothering has been reported in the rat, mouse, and hamster but we do not have information on the rabbit.

The removal of the bulbs in adult female animals has less effect on reproductive behaviour than in the male though there are considerable interspecies differences and the age, and extent of the lesions, may modify the response. In the rabbit, Brooks (1937) reported little change in sexual function while removal of the bulbs in rats is without effect on the oestrous cycle (Rosen et al., 1940) and the same is true of the guinea pig (Donovan and Kopriva, 1965). In the latter, however, the animals took longer to mate and the males were accepted less readily. On the other hand the removal of the bulbs in very young guinea pigs may eliminate adult sexual behaviour (Magnotti, 1936, quoted by Kloek, 1961). In the gilt complete removal induced a permanent condition of anoestrus while partial removal of the bulbs was accompanied by a number of normal cycles (Signoret and Mauleon, 1962). The ovaries of the sample with complete bulbectomy were immature and the uterine weights were reduced, a pattern not dissimilar to that described by Whitten for the adult laboratory mouse.

Adult mice in which the olfactory bulbs are removed do not show the Bruce or Whitten effect and corpora lutea are either absent or atrophic. Further, when paired with normal males for 12 days no copulation plugs were found (Whitten, 1956b). In spayed female rats removal of the bulbs facilitated hormonally induced lordosis (Edwards and Warner, 1972), a finding which contrasts with that reported for the mouse (Thompson and Edwards, 1972). In adult male mice there was no significant difference between the weight of the testes whereas the weight of the accessory glands, and body weight, were less in bulbectomized mice.

In both inexperienced (Beach, 1942) and experienced male rats (Heimer and Larsson, 1967) defects of sexual behaviour have been reported following bilateral bulbectomy though there is some evidence that the copulatory defects are less when the rats are tested with a second female (Bermant and Taylor, 1969). In the hamster (Murphy and Schneider, 1970; Doty et al., 1971; Lisk *et al.*, 1972) and mouse (Rowe and Edwards, 1972) bulbectomy eliminates male sexual behaviour.

SUMMARY AND CONCLUSIONS

The ability of an animal to react to an object while yet some distance from it allows, as Sherrington (1906) has pointed out, for certain preparatory changes to take place in the nervous system that can facilitate approach or withdrawal from the object. The receptors of both taste and smell are sensitive to chemical changes in the environment and the receptors for smell have evolved in relation to such basic aspects of behaviour as finding food and a mate.

In the mouse the olfactory receptors are fully functional at birth and the animal is dependent on the bulbs for its survival. If lesions to the bulbs are restricted, mortality is reduced though the animals continue to grow slowly and are subsequently handicapped in their reproductive behaviour. The nature and extent of the lesions and the age at which they are made are factors of importance and older animals are less affected by the lesions than younger ones.

In a number of laboratory animals the rate of growth has been shown to be retarded following bulbectomy early in life and the question arises as to whether the growth and reproductive changes can be accounted for in terms of reduced food intake. Reducing the rate of growth of mice from 5 days of age, so that they gained weight at the same rate as mice that had the lateral regions of the bulbs removed (lateral bulbectomy) did not produce a marked delay in the onset of first oestrus and the activity of the undernourished mice was greater than that of the lesioned animals (McClelland and Cowley, 1972). Further, undernourishing the animals did not disrupt the cyclical vaginal cornification and fertility was not reduced. It would seem, therefore, that the anorexia cannot entirely account for the reproductive and behavioural changes that accompany the lesions (McClelland and Cowley, 1972, 1973).

Whether the nutritional state of the mother affects the responsiveness of the young is not known but there is some evidence to suggest that the odour of the nest is imprinted on the young and that feeding or exposing mice to odorous substances from an early age may modify their social responsiveness and selection of a mate. Some understanding of the underlying structural changes which may be involved has been provided by the work of Døving and Pinching (1973). Housing rats in an artificial odorous environment causes structural degeneration of cells within the bulbs and the localization of the changes is dependent on the odorous substance (Pinching and Døving, 1974).

Many of the granule cells of the olfactory bulbs of the rat are formed postnatally (Altman, 1969) and as such the bulb may be an area which is particularly susceptible to environmental influences. The bulbs of the rat show consistent electrical activity from the 4th day of age and thereafter the frequency of the rhythm and the amplitude increase until the adult pattern is reached at day

24 (Salas *et al.*, 1969). The odour of the mother produces a significant increase in the electrical activity of the bulbs in rats as young as 6 days of age (Schapiro and Salas, 1970) and the activity of intact rats (and mice) is reduced when they are placed near the mother at about this age and the same is true when young rats are exposed to the urine collected from a lactating mother.

Lesions of the bulb may, however, reduce the action of pheromones, and particularly those of the mother, to which the young would normally respond. They are handicapped by poor sensory coordination and have difficulty in locating the nipple though their strength of grasp remains unimpaired. Further, they are dependent on normal littermates for the maintaining of the sucking stimulus (Cooper and Cowley, 1976a).

Altering the social environment may change the rate of sexual maturation. The features that are responsible for the changes have not been identified, and the number of species is small. That pheromones may be involved is suggested by the change in development that occurs when urine from adult mice is applied to the nasal region of infant mice and by the retarded growth and sexual maturation that accompanies the severing of the olfactory tracts (see above). In so far as the lesions also handicap the infant's ability to obtain food, the nutritional state of the infant may, in turn, modify its responsiveness to the mother's secretions. Undernutrition reduces the frequency of sniffing in mice and it has been shown that the long and irregular cycles that occur in underfed rats can be temporarily shortened by housing them with a male (Cooper and Haynes, 1967). The oestrous cycle in the rat may also be shortened following exposure to the odour of female urine suggesting that under these circumstances the lowering of the plane of nutrition is not a necessary condition for the shortening of the cycle (Chateau *et al.*, 1974). Further, the odour of female urine is more effective in modifying the wheel activity of female rats than male urine though whether this is due to a quantitative or qualitative difference in the active component is not known. The secretions of a pseudopregnant rat or one that has been injected with progesterone have a marked effect on vaginal oestrus and the regular fluctuations in wheel activity of a recipient. The placing of progesterone below the wheel of a recipient did not produce these changes (unpubl. observ.) and it would seem that the recipient may be responding to some factor that is dependent on the pseudopregnant condition or the progesterone for its release.

A number of steroids can alter the cyclic secretion of gonadotrophins, when given early in life, and there is behavioural evidence that androgens which aromatize to oestrogens are more effective in this regard than non-aromatizable forms (Paup *et al.*, 1972).

The pheromone that changes the pace of sexual development in the mouse has not been identified though it has been suggested that it may be a protein fraction or a substance bound to a protein and that rather than acting on the olfactory receptors the pheromone is ingested or absorbed through direct contact (Vandenbergh *et al.*, 1975). A number of criticisms of this interpretation may be made. A number of instances in which there is no direct contact have been described in this chapter. Thus the reduction in activity when infant rats are exposed to the urine of lactating mothers is immediate and occurs when the urine is some distance from the infants. Similarly in the rat, adult wheel activity changes occur in the absence of contact with secretions. It is clear, therefore, that in some instances at least, other factors are operative. There may be different pheromones which effect changes in activity and sexual development, but one pheromone may have primer and releaser effects, as has been described in the desert locust *Schistocerca gregaria* (Loher, 1960). Greater complexity and interdependence of nutritional and pheromonal factors that act during early development is also evidenced by the fact that the stools and urine of rats and mice are a source of nutrients and of steroids (for references see Cowley and Wise, 1972).

A close association between hormonal conditions and olfactory function has long been recognized (see p.000 and also Mortimer *et al.*, 1936) and Barraclough and Cross (1963) have shown that the proportion of hypothalamic neurones excited by odours varies with the oestrous cycle, in prooestrus the proportion of neurones being more than double that at oestrus or dioestrus.

Infant male and female mice respond differently to odorous substances at birth. The injection of oestrogen, at an early age, reduces the frequency of their sniffing when adult and the mice fail to discriminate between normal and vasectomized males. Further, females injected with TP and androstenol, on day 1 of age, also subsequently fail to discriminate between castrated and normal males.

The accelerated development of the brain in the rat and mouse during the first 10 days of life makes it particularly vulnerable to a number of environmental factors at this age and the 'stage of development' may itself be a factor in determining certain common behavioural components irrespective of the pathways which have activated the integration centres. Undernutrition or the administration of steroids early in life may act to depress mitotic activity in the olfactory and associated centres of the brain and natural as well as synthetic substances present in the environment may have a similar action. The effects of neonatal lesions in the olfactory bulbs, with their widespread connections to the hypothalamic and other limbic structures, may also be mimicked by manipulating the nutritional state, the administration of endogenous hormones, or the altering of the pheromonal environment.

ACKNOWLEDGEMENTS

The chapter is dedicated to the memory of Hilda Bruce.

The review was written while at the Sub-Department of Animal Behaviour, Department of Zoology, Madingley, Cambridge. Grateful acknowledgement is made to the students and former students who conducted many of the experiments: Maureen Wood, Alison Bell, Clare Fullerton, Thelma Foote, Tony Cooper, Ian Hanley, Roy McClelland, and David Wise.

REFERENCES

Alberts, J. R. and Friedman, M. I. (1972) Olfactory bulb removal but not anosmia increases emotionality and mouse killing, *Nature*, **238**, 454–5.

Alexander, N. J. (1972a) Long-term effects of vasectomy in the rhesus monkey, *Biol. Reprod.*, **7** (2), Abstr. 89.

Alexander, N. J. (1972b) Vasectomy: long term effect in the rhesus monkey, *J. Reprod. Fert.*, **31**, 399–406.

Althaus, J. von. (1882) Beiträge zue Physiologie und Pathologie des N. Olfactorius, *Archiv fur Psych.*, **12**, 122–40.

Altman, J. (1969) DNA metabolism and cell proliferation. In: *Handbook of Neurochemistry 2, Structural Neurochemistry*, A Lajtha (ed.), Plenum Press, New York, pp. 137–82.

Andervont, H. B. (1944) Influence of environment on mammary cancer, *J. Natl. Cancer Inst.*, **4**, 579–81.

Balázs, R. (1974) Influence of metabolic factors on brain development, *Br. Med. Bull.*, **30**, 126–34.

Banerjee, U. (1971) An inquiry into the genesis of aggression in mice induced by isolation, *Behaviour*, **40**, 86–99.

Barraclough, C. A. and Cross, B. A. (1963) Unit activity in the hypothalamus of the cyclic female rat: effect of genital stimuli and progesterone, *J. Endocrinol.*, **26**, 339–59.

Barth, R. H. (1970) Pheromone–endocrine interactions in insects. In: *Hormones and the Environment. Mem. Soc. Endocrin.*, **18**, G. K. Benson and J. G. Phillips (eds.), University Press, Cambridge.

Beach, F. A. (1942) Analysis of the stimuli adequate to elicit mating behaviour in the sexually inexperienced male rat, *J. Comp. Psychol.*, **33**, 163–207.

Beach, F. A. (1965) Retrospect and Prospect. In: *Sex and Behaviour*, F. A. Beach (ed.), Wiley, New York.

Beidler, L. (1971) *Handbook of Sensory Physiology. IV, Chemical Senses. I Olfaction.* L. Beidler (ed.), Springer Verlag, Berlin.

Bell, A. (1972) The development and behaviour of female albino mice following postnatal administration of sex hormones, *M.Sc. thesis*, The Queen's University, Belfast.

Bermant, G. and Taylor, L. (1969) Interactive effects of experience and olfactory bulb lesions in male rat copulation, *Physiol. Behav.*, **4**, 13–7.

Brain, C. L. and Griffin, G. A. (1970) The influence of the sex of littermates on body weight and behaviour in rat pups, *Anim. Behav.*, **18**, 512–6.

Brain, P. F. and Nowell, N. W. (1970) Some observations on intermale aggression testing in albino mice, *Commun. Behav. Biol.*, **5**, 7–17.

Brill, A. A. (1932) The sense of smell in the neuroses and psychoses, *Psychoanal. Quart.*, **1**, 7–42.

Brooks, C. Mc. C. (1937) The rôle of the cerebral cortex and of various sense organs in the execution of mating activity in the rabbit, *Am. J. Physiol.*, **120**, 544–53.

Brooks, P. H. and Cole, D. J. A. (1970) The effect of the presence of a boar on the attainment of puberty in gilts, *J. Reprod. Fert.*, **23**, 435–40.

Broverman, D. M., Klaiber, E. L., Kobayashi, Y. and Vogel, W. (1968) Roles of activation and inhibition in sex differences in cognitive abilities, *Psychol. Rev.*, **75**, 23–50.

Bruce, H. M. (1950) Feeding and rearing of laboratory animals, *J. Hyg.*, *Camb.*, **48**, 171–83.

Bruce, H. M. (1970) Pheromones, *Br. Med. Bull.*, **26**, 10–13.

Burke, A. W. and Broadhurst, P. L. (1966) Behavioural correlates of the oestrous cycle in the rat, *Nature*, **209**, 223–4.

Butler, C. G. and Fairey, E. M. (1963) The role of the queen in preventing oogenesis in worker honeybees (*A. mellifera* L.), *J. Apicult. Res.*, **2**, 14–8.

Carter, C. S. (1973) Olfaction and sexual receptivity in the female golden hamster, *Physiol. Behav.*, **10**, 47–51.

Castro, B. M. (1967) Age of puberty in female mice: Relationship to population density and the presence of adult males, *Anais. Acad. bras. Cient.*, **39**, 289–91.

Catlett, R. H. (1961) An evaluation of methods for measuring fighting behaviour with special reference to *Mus musculus*, *Anim. Behav.*, **9**, 8–10.

Chanel, J. and Vernet-Maury, E. (1963) Réactions de discrimination olfactive et crise audiogene chez la souris, *C.r. Séanc. Soc. Biol.*, **157**, 1020–4.

Chateau, D., Roos, J., Roos, M., Aron, C. (1974) Mécanismes mis en jeu dans le receourcissement du cycle oestral par les phéromones chez la ratte, *C.r. Séanc. Soc. Biol.*, **168**, 1422–31.

Christian J. J. (1959) In: *Comparative Endocrinology (Proceedings of Columbia University Symposium)*, A. Gorbman (ed.), Wiley, New York.

Christian, J. J., Lloyd, J. A. and Davis, D. E. (1965) The role of endocrines in the self-regulation of mammalian populations, *Rec. Prog. Horm. Res.*, **21**, 501–78.

Colby, D. R. and Vandenbergh, J. G. (1974) Regulatory effects of urinary pheromones on puberty in the mouse, *Biol. Reprod.*, **11**, 268–79.

Comfort, A. (1971) Likelihood of human pheromones, *Nature, Lond.*, **230**, 432–3 and 479.

Cooper, A. J. (1973) Some effects of olfactory bulb lesions on the development and behaviour of male mice, *Ph.D. thesis*, The Queen's University, Belfast.

Cooper, A. J. and Cowley, J. J. (1976a) Neonatal bulbectomy and growth of mice. *Biology of the Neonate*, **29**, 50–65.

Cooper, A. J. and Cowley, J. J. (1976b) Mother-infant interaction in mice bulbectomised early in life, *Physiol. Behav.*, **16**, 453–459.

Cooper, K. J. and Haynes, N. B. (1967) Modification of the oestrous cycle of the underfed rat associated with the presence of the male, *J. Reprod. Fert.*, **14**, 317–20.

Cowley, J. J. and Griesel, R. D. (1964) Low protein diet and emotionality in the albino rat, *J. Genet. Psychol.*, **104**, 89–98.

Cowley, J. J. and Griesel, R. D. (1966) The effect on growth and behaviour of rehabilitating first and second generation low protein rats, *Anim. Behav.*, **14**, 506–17.

Cowley, J. J. and Widdowson, E. M. (1965) The effect of handling rats on their growth and behaviour, *Br. J. Nutr.*, **19**, 397–406.

Cowley, J. J., Williamson, A. J., and Berryman, J. C. (1969) Movement restriction, food intake and behaviour of the mouse. *Proc. VIII Int. Congr. Nutr. Prague.* Excerpta Medica Foundation, Amsterdam.

Cowley, J. J. and Wise, D. R. (1970) Pheromones, growth and behaviour, Ciba Fdn Study Grp. *Chemical Influences on Behaviour*, Churchill, London, pp. 144–70.

Cowley, J. J. and Wise, D. R. (1972) Some effects of mouse urine on neonatal growth and reproduction, *Anim. Behav.*, **20**, 499–506.

Crowell, D. H., Davis, C. M., Chun, B. J., and Spellacy, F. J. (1965) Galvanic skin reflex in newborn humans, *Science*, **148**, 1108–11.

Daly, C. D. and Senior White, R. (1930) Psychic reactions to olfactory stimuli, *Br. J. Med. Psychol.*, **10**, 70–87.

Darwin, C. (1871) The descent of man and selection in relation to sex, John Murray, London.

Dewar, A. D. (1959) Observations on pseudopregnancy in the mouse, *J. Endocrinol.*, **18**, 186–190.

Donovan, B. T. and Harris, G. W. (1966) Neurohumoral mechanisms in reproduction.

In: *Marshall's Physiology of Reproduction*, A. S. Parkes (ed.), **3**, 301–78. Longmans Green, London.

Donovan, B. T. and Kopriva, P. C. (1965) Effect of removal or stimulation of the olfactory bulbs on the estrous cycle of the guinea pig, *Endocrinology*, **77**, 213–7.

Doty, R. L., Carter, C. S., and Clements, L. G. (1971) Olfactory control of sexual behaviour in the male and early-androgenised female hamster. *Horm. Behav.*, **2**, 325–35.

Douglas, R. J., Isaacson, R. L., and Moss, R. L. (1969) Olfactory lesions, emotionality and activity, *Physiol. and Behav.*, **4**, 379–81.

Døving, K. B. and Rinching, A. J. (1973) Selective degeneration of neurones in the olfactory bulb following prolonged odour exposure, *Brain Res.* **52**, 115–29.

Edwards, D. A. and Warner, P. (1972) Olfactory bulb removal facilitates the hormonal induction of sexual receptivity in the female rat, *Horm. Behav.*, **3**, 321–32.

Edwards, R. G. (1972) Immunological influences. In: *Reproduction in Mammals, Book 4 Reproductive Patterns*, C. R. Austin and R. V. Short (eds.), Cambridge University Press, Cambridge.

Ellis, H. (1910) Studies in the psychology of sex, **2**, Part 1. Davis, New York.

Engen, T. Lipsitt, L. P., and Kaye, H. (1963) Olfactory responses and adaptation in the human neonate, *J. Comp. Physiol. Psychol.*, **56**, 73–7.

Engen, T. and Lipsitt, L. P. (1965) Decrement and recovery of responses to olfactory stimuli in the human neonate, *J. Comp. Physiol. Psychol.*, **59**, 312–6.

Fabricant, N. D. (1960) Sexual functions and the nose, *Am. J. Med. Sci.*, **239**, 498–502.

Field, P. M. and Raisman, G. (1974) Structural and functional investigations of sexually dimorphic part of the rat preoptic area. In: *Recent Studies of Hypothalamic Function*. K. L. Lederis and K. E. Cooper (eds.), Karger, Basel.

Fitzherbert, J. (1959) Scent and the sexual object, *Br. J. Med. Psychol.*, **32**, 206–9.

Folman, Y. and Drori, D. (1966) Effects of social isolation and of female odours on the reproductive system, kidneys, and adrenals of unmated male rats, *J. Reprod. Fert.*, **11**, 43–50.

Foote, T. P. (1974) The activity of mice during the oestrous cycle, pregnancy, and lactation, *Ph.D. thesis*, Queen's University, Belfast.

Fox, K. A. (1968) Effects of prepubertal habitation conditions on the reproductive physiology of the small house mouse *J. Reprod. Fert.*, **17**, 75–85.

Franck, H. (1966) Ablation des bulbes olfactifs chez la Lapine impubère. Répercussions sur le tractus génital et le comportement sexuel, *C.r. Séanc. Soc. Biol.*, **160**, 389–91.

Fraňková, S. (1971) Effect of protein-calorie malnutrition on the development of social behaviour in rats, *Dev. Psychobiol.*, **6**, 33–43.

Fraňková, S. (1968) Nutritional and psychological factors in the development of spontaneous behaviour in the rat. In: *Malnutrition, Learning and Behaviour*, N. S. Scrimshaw and J. E. Gordon (eds.), M.I.T. Press, Cambridge, Mass.

Freud, S. (1915) *Drei Abhandlungen zur Sexualtheorie*, Franz Deuticke, Leipzig.

Fullerton, C. and Cowley, J. J. (1968) Mice development following exposure to members of the same strain, *Anim. Behav.*, **16**, 589 (Title only).

Fullerton, C. and Cowley, J. J. (1971) The differential effect of the presence of adult male and female mice on the growth and development of the young, *J. Genet. Psychol.*, **119**, 89–98.

Gard, C., Hård, E., Larsson, K., and Petersson, V. (1967) The relationship between sensory stimulation and gross motor behaviour during the post-natal development in the rat, *Anim. Behav.*, **15**, 563–8.

Gerall, A. A. (1963) An exploratory study of the effect of social isolation variables on the sexual behaviour of male guinea pigs, *Anim. Behav.*, **11**, 274–82.

Goy, R. W. and Goldfoot, D. (1974) Experiential and hormonal factors influencing development of sexual behaviour in the male rhesus monkey. In: *The Neurosciences Third Study Programme*, F. O. Schmitt and F. G. Worden (eds.), M.I.T. Press, Cambridge, Mass.

Grosvenor, C. E. (1965) Evidence that exteroceptive stimuli can release prolactin from the pituitary gland of the lactating rat, *Endocrinology*, **76**, 340–2.

Guillot, M. (1956) Aspect pharmacodynamique de quelques problemes liés à l'olfaction. *Actualités pharmacologiques*, 9-ieme Sêrie, Masson et Cie., Paris.

Hall, K. R. L. and De Vore, I. (1965) Baboon social behaviour. In: *Primate Behaviour*, I. De Vore (ed.), Holt, Rinehart and Winston, New York.

Ham, A. W. (1974) *Histology*, 7th (edn.), Lippincott Co., Philadelphia and Toronto. pp. 720–1.

Hanby, J. P. and Brown, C. E. (1974) The development of sociosexual behaviours in Japanese macaques *(Macaca fuscata)*, *Behaviour*, **49**, 152–96.

Hanley, I. G. (1972) An investigation into the effect of diet changes on aggressive behaviour in albino mice, *B.Sc. dissertation*, Univ. of Belfast.

Hansen, E. W. (1966) The development of maternal and infant behaviour in the rhesus monkey, *Behaviour*, **27**, 107–49.

Harlow, H. F., Harlow, M. K., Hansen, E. W., and Suomi, S. J. (1972) Infantile sexuality in monkeys, *Arch. Sex. Behav.*, **2**, 1–7.

Harlow, H. F. and Rosenblum, L. A. (1971) Maturation variables influencing sexual posturing in infant monkeys, *Arch. Sex. Behav.*, **1**, 175–80.

Henry, J. P., Ely, D. L., and Stephens, P. M. (1972) Changes in catecholamine-controlling enzymes in response to psychosocial activation of the defence and alarm reactions. Ciba Fdn. Symp., **8**, *Physiology, Emotion and Psychosomatic Illness*, Elsevier-Excerpta Medica, Amsterdam.

Heimer, L. and Larsson, K. (1967) Mating behaviour of male rats after olfactory bulb lesions, *Physiol. Behav.*, **2**, 207–9.

Hinde, R. A. (1953) Appetitive behaviour, consummatory act, and the hierarchical organisation of behaviour—with special reference to the great tit *(Parus major)*, *Behaviour*, **5**, 189–224.

Hinde, R. A. (1966) *Animal Behaviour: A Synthesis of Ethology and Comparative Psychology*, McGraw-Hill, New York.

Hinde, R. A. (1974) *Biological Bases of Human Social Behaviour*, McGraw-Hill, New York.

Holmes, R. L. and Ball, J. N. (1974) *The Pituitary Gland*, University Press, Cambridge.

Jay, P. (1965) Field studies. In: *Behaviour of Non-human Primates*, A. M. Schrier, H. F. Harlow, and F. Stollnitz (eds.), Academic Press, New York.

Kagan, J. and Beach, F. A. (1953) Effects of early experience on mating behaviour in male rats, *J. Comp. Physiol. Psychol.*, **46**, 204–8.

Kalogerakis, M. G. (1963) The role of olfaction in sexual development, *Psychosom. Med.*, **25**, 420–31.

Kalmus, H. and Ribband, C. R. (1952) The origin of the odours by which honeybees distinguish their companions, *Proc. Roy. Soc. (B)*, **140**, 50–9.

Kennedy, J. M. and Brown, K. (1970) Effects of male odor during infancy on the maturation, behaviour, and reproduction of female mice, *Dev. Psychobiol.*, **3**, 179–89.

Kennedy, G. C. and Mitra, J. (1963) Body weight and food intake as initiating factors for puberty in the rat, *J. Physiol.*, **166**, 408–18.

Kling, A. (1964) Effects of rhinencephalic lesions on endocrine and somatic development in the rat, *Am. J. Physiol.*, **266**, 1395–400.

Kloek, J. (1961) The smell of some steroid sex-hormones and their metabolites. Reflections and experiments concerning the significance of smell for the mutual relation of the sexes, *Psychiat. Neurol. Neurochir.*, **64**, 309–44.

Koldovský, O., Anděl, J., Dlouhá, H., Faltin, J., Flandera, V., Hahn, P., Kraus, M., Křeček, J., Křečkova, J., Kubát, K., Nouák, M., and Nováková, V. (1961) Late effects of early adaptation: the effect of premature weaning, *Proceedings National Congress, Czechoslovak Physiological Society*, **5**, 133–41.

Kovach, J. K. and Kling, A. (1967) Mechanisms of neonate sucking behaviour in the kitten, *Anim. Behav.*, **15** (1), 91–101.

Krafft-Ebing, R. V. (1906) *Psychopathia Sexualis*, Transl. by F. J. Rebman, Heinemann, London.

Kubat, K., Flandera, V., Hahn, P., and Koldovsky, G. (1971) The effect of early weaning on spermatogenesis in adult rats, *Experientia*, **17**, 463–71.

Larsson, K., Carlsson, S. G., Sourander, P., Forsström, B., Hansen, S., Henriksson, B., and Lingquist, A. (1974) Delayed onset of sexual activity of male rats subjected to pre- and postnatal undernutrition, *Physiol. Behav.*, **13**, 307–11.

Lee, van der S. and Boot, L. M. (1955) Spontaneous pseudopregnancy in mice, *Acta. Physiol. Pharmacol. Neerl.*, **4**, 442–4.

Lee van der S. and Boot, L. M. (1956) II. Spontaneous pseudopregnancy in mice, *Acta Physiol. Pharm. Neerl.*, **5**, 213–5.

Le Magnen, J. (1952a) Les phénoménes olfacto-sexuels chez le rat blanc, *Archs. Sci. physiol.*, **6**, 295–331.

Le Magnen, J. (1952b) Les phénoménes olfacto-sexuels chez l'homme, *Archs. Sci. physiol.*, **6**, 125–60.

Leon, M. (1974) Maternal pheromone, *Physiol. Behav.*, **13**, 441–53.

Leonard, C. M. (1972) Effects of neonatal (day 10) olfactory bulb lesions on social behaviour of female golden hamsters *(Mesocricetus auratus)*, *J. Comp. Physiol. Psychol.*, **80**, 208–15.

Levitsky, D. A. and Barnes, R. H. (1972) Nutritional and environmental interactions in the behavioural development of the rat: Long-term effects, *Science, N. Y.*, **176**, 68–71.

Lisk, R. D., Zeiss, J., and Ciaccio, L. A. (1972) The influence of olfaction on sexual behaviour in the male golden hamster *(Mesocricetus auratus)*, *J. Exp. Zool.*, **181**, 69–78.

Loher, W. (1960) The chemical acceleration of the maturation process and its hormonal control in the male desert locust, *Proc. Roy. Soc. Lond.*, B, **153**, 380–97.

McCance, R. A. (1962) Food, growth, and time, *Lancet* 2, 621–626; 671–6.

McCance, R. A. and Widdowson, E. M. (1974) The determinants of growth and form, *Proc. Roy. Soc. Lond. B*, **185**, 1–17.

McClelland, R. J. and Cowley, J. J. (1972) The effects of lesions of the olfactory bulbs on the growth and behaviour of mice, *Physiol. Behav.*, **9**, 319–24.

McClelland, R. J. and Cowley, J. J. (1973) Olfactory bulb lesions and undernutrition in neonatal mice, *Int. Res. Comm. Syst.*, **73**, 12.

Mackintosh, J. H. and Grant, E. C. (1966) The effect of olfactory stimuli on the agonistic behaviour of laboratory mice, *Z. Tierpsychol.*, **23**, 584–7.

Mackenzie, J. N. (1884) Irritation of the sexual apparatus as an etiological factor in the production of nasal disease, *Am. J. Med. Sci.*, **87**, 360–4.

MacLeod, P. (1971) Structure and function of higher-olfactory centres. In: *Handbook of Sensory Physiology*, **4**, L. M. Beidler (ed.), Springer-Verlag, Berlin, pp. 182–204.

Macrides, F., Bartke, A. Fernandez, F., and d'Angelo, W. (1974) Effect of exposure to vaginal odor and receptive females on plasma testosterone in the male hamster, *Neuroendocrinology*, **15**, 355–64.

Magnotti, T. (1936) L'importanza dell'olfatto sullo sviluppo e funzione degli organi genitali, *Boll. Mal. Orecch.*, **54**, 281.

Mainardi, D., Marsan, M., and Pasquali, A. (1965) Assenza di preferenze sessuali tra ceppi nel maschio di *Mus musculus domesticus*, *Instituto Lombardo—Accademia di Scienze e Lettere*, **99**, 26–34.

Marsden, H. M. and Bronson, F. H. (1964) Estrous synchrony in mice: alteration by exposure to male urine, *Science*, **144**, 1469.

Marsden, H. M. and Bronson, F. H. (1965) The synchrony of oestrus in mice: relative role of the male and female environments. *J. Endocrinol*, **32**, 313–9.

Micheal, R. P. and Keverne, E. B. (1968) Pheromones in the communication of sexual status in primates, *Nature, Lond.*, **218**, 746–9.

Mordue, W., Highnam, K. C., Hill, L., and Luntz, A. J. (1970) Environmental effects upon endocrine-mediated processes in locusts. In: *Hormones and the Environment. Mem. Soc. Endocrin.*, **18**. G. K. Benson and J. G. Phillips (eds.), University Press, Cambridge.

Mortimer, H., Wright, R. P., and Collip, J. B. (1936) The effect of the administration of oestrogenic hormones on the nasal mucosa of the monkey (*Macaca mulatta*), *J. Can. Med. Assoc.*, **35**, 503–10.

Mugford, R. A. and Nowell, N. W. (1971) The preputial glands as a source of aggression-promoting odors in mice, *Physiol. Behav.*, **6**, 247–9.

Murphy, M. R. and Schneider, G. E. (1970) Olfactory bulb removal eliminates mating behaviour in the male golden hamster, *Science*, **167**, 302–4.

Neaves, W. B. (1975) The androgen status of vasectomised rats, *Endocrinology*, **96**, 529–34.

Nikkari, T. (1965) Composition and secretions of the skin surface lipids of the rat: Effects of dietary lipids and hormones, *Scand. J. clin. Lab. Invest. (Suppl.)*, **85**, 1–140.

Orbach, J. and Kling, A. (1966) Effects of sensory deprivation on the onset of puberty, mating, fertility, and gonadal weights in rats, *Brain Res.*, **3**, 141–9.

Owen, R. (1868) *Anatomy of Vertebrates, Vol. III. Mammals*. Longmans Green, London.

Parkes, A. S. (1936) Type and amount of oil influences effects of hormones, *Lancet*, **2**, 674–6.

Parkes, A. S. (1966) The internal secretions of the testis. In: *Marshall's Physiology of Reproduction* 3, A. S. Parkes (ed.), Longmans Green, London, pp. 412–569.

Patton, H. D. (1959) Physiology and smell and taste, *Ann. Rev. Physiol.*, **12**, 469–84.

Paup, D. C., Coniglio, L. P., and Clemens, L. G. (1972) Masculinization of the female golden hamster by neonatal treatment with androgen or estrogen, *Horm. Behav.* 3, 123–31.

Pinching, A. J. and Døving, K. B. (1974) Selective degeneration in the rat olfactory bulb following exposure to different odours, *Brain Res.*, **82**, 195–204.

Poynter, H. (1939) Testis hormone secretion in the rat under conditions of vasectomy or isolation, *Anat. Rec.*, **74**, 355–79.

Pumphrey, R. J. (1950) Hearing, *Symp. Soc. exp. Biol.*, IV, 4–18.

Raisman, G. and Field, P. M. (1971) Sexual dimorphism in the preoptic area of the rat, *Science*, **173**, 731–3.

Ropartz, P. (1968) The relation between olfactory stimulation and aggressive behaviour in mice, *Anim. Behav.*, **16**, 97–100.

Rosen, S., Shelesnyak, M. C., and Zacharias, L. R. (1940) Naso–genital relationship. II. Pseudopregnancy following extirpation of the sphenopalatine ganglion in the rat, *Endocrinology*, **27**, 463–8.

Rowe, F. A. and Edwards, D. A. (1972) Olfactory bulb removal influences on the mating behaviour of male mice, *Physiol. and Behav.*, **8**, 37–41.

Salas, M., Guzman-Flores, C., and Schapiro, S. (1969) An autogenetic study of olfactory bulb electrical activity in the rat, *Physiol. Behav.*, **4**, 699–703.

Salas, M., Schapiro, S., and Guzman-Flores, C. (1970) Development of olfactory bulb discrimination between maternal and food odors, *Physiol. Behav.*, **5**, 1261–4.

Sato, N., Haller, E. W., Powell, R. D., and Henkin, R. I. (1974) Sexual maturation in bulbectomized female rats, *J. Reprod. Fert.*, **36**, 301–9.

Schapiro, S., and Salas, M. (1970) Behavioural response of infant rats to maternal odour, *Physiol. Behav.*, **5**, 815–7.

Sheridan, P. J. and Stumpf, W. E. (1974) Interaction of exogenous steroids in the developing rat brain, *Endocrinology*, **95**, 1749–53.

Sherrington, C. S. (1906) *The Integrative Action of the Nervous System*, Constable, London.

Short, R. V. (1972) Sex determination and differentiation. In: *Reproduction in Mammals, Book 2 Embryonic and Fetal Development*, C. R. Austin and R. V. Short (eds.), Cambridge University Press, Cambridge.

Siegel, S. (1956) Non-parametric statistics for the behavioural sciences, McGraw-Hill, London.

Signoret, J. P. and Mauleon, P. (1962) Action de l'ablation des bulbes olfactifs sur les mecanismes de la reproduction chez la truie, *Ann. Biol. anim. Biochem. Biophys.*, **2**, 167–74.

Steinach, E. (1936) Zur geschichte des männlichen Sexualhormons und geiner Wirkungen om Säugetier und bein Menschen, *Wien. Klin. Waschr.*, **49**, 161.

Stieve, H. (1927) Die Abhängigkeit der Keimdrüssen vom Zustand des Gesamt-korpers und von der Umgebung, *Naturwissenschaften*, **15**, 951.

Thompson, M. L. and Edwards, D. A. (1972) Olfactory bulb ablation and normally induced mating behaviour of male mice, *Physiol. Behav.*, **8**, 37–41.

Tobach, E., Yves, R., and Schneirle, D. C. (1967) Development of olfactory function in the rat pup, *Amer. Zool.*, **7**, 792 (abs.)

Valenstein, E. S. and Goy, R. W. (1957) Further studies on the organisation and display of sexual behaviour in male guinea pigs, *J. Comp. Physiol. Psychol.*, **50**, 115–9.

Valenstein, E. S., Riss, W., and Young, W. C. (1955) Experiential and genetic factors in the organisation of sexual behaviour in male guinea pigs, *J. Comp. Physiol. Psychol.*, **48**, 397–403.

Vandenbergh, J. G. (1967) Effect of the presence of a male on the sexual maturation of female mice, *Endocrinology*, **81**, 345–9.

Vandenbergh, J. G. (1969) Male odour accelerates female maturation in mice, *Endocrinology*, **84**, 658–60.

Vandenbergh, J. G. (1971) The influence of the social environment on sexual maturation in male mice, *J. Reprod. Fert.*, **24**, 383–90.

Vandenbergh, J. G., Drickamer, L. C., and Colby, D. R. (1972) Social and dietary factors in the sexual maturation of female mice, *J. Reprod. Fert.*, **28**, 397–405.

Vendenbergh, J. G., Whitsett, J. M., and Lombardi, J. R. (1975) Partial isolation of a pheromone accelerating puberty in female mice, *J. Reprod. Fert.*, **43**, 515–23.

Welker, W. I. (1964) Analysis of sniffing of the albino rat, *Behaviour*, **22**, 223–44.

Wenzel, B. M. and Sieck, M. H. (1966) Olfaction, *Ann. Rev. Physiol.*, **28**, 381–434.

Wenzel, B. M. (1974) The olfactory system and behaviour. In: *Limbic and Autonomic Nervous System Research*, L. V. Di Cara (ed.), Plenum, New York.

Whatson, T. S., Smart, J. L., and Dobbing, J. (1974) Social interactions among adult male rats after early undernutrition *Br. J. Nutr.*, **32**, 413–9.

Whitten, W. K. (1956a) Modifications of the oestrous cycle of the mouse by external stimuli associated with the male, *J. Endocrinol.*, **13**, 399–404.

Whitten, W. K. (1956b) The effect of removal of the olfactory bulbs on the gonads of mice, *J. Endocrinol.*, **14**, 160–3.

Whitten, W. K. (1959) Occurrences of anoestrus in mice caged in groups *J. Endocrinol.*, **18**, 102–7.

Whitten, W. K. and Bronson, F. H. (1970) The role of pheromones in mammalian reproduction. In: *Advances in Chemoreception, I, Communication by Chemical Signals*, J. W. Johnston, D. G. Moulton, and A. Turk (eds.), Appleton-Century-Crofts, New York.

Wiener, H. (1966) External chemical messengers. 1. Emission and reception in man, *N. Y. State J. Med.*, **66**, 3153–70.

Wiener, H. (1967a) External chemical messengers. II, Natural history of Schizophrenia, *N. Y. State J. Med.*, **67**, 1144–65.

Wiener, H. (1967b) External chemical messengers. III. Mind and body in Schizophrenia, *N. Y. State J. Med.*, **67**, 1287–310.

Wilson, E. O. (1970) *Advances in Chemoreception. Vol. I. Communication by Chemical Signals.* J. W. Johnston, D. G. Moulton, and A. Turk (eds.), Appleton-Century-Crofts, New York.

Wilson, E. O. and Bossert, W. H. (1963) Chemical communication among animals, *Rec. Prog. Horm. Res.*, **19**, 673–710.

Winnick, M. and Noble, A. (1965) Quantitative changes in DNA, RNA, and protein during prenatal and postnatal growth in the rat, *Devl. Biol.*, **12**, 451–66.

Winnick, M. and Noble, A. (1966) Cellular response in rats during malnutrition at various ages, *J. Nutr.*, **89**, 300–6.

Zamenhof, S., van Marthens, E., and Grauel, L. (1971) DNA (cell number) in neonatal brain: Second generation (F_2) alteration by maternal (F_0) protein restriction, *Science*, **172**, 850–1.

Zarrow, M. X., Schlein, P. A. Denenberg, V. H., and Cohen, H. A. (1972) Sustained corticosterone release in lactating rats following olfactory stimulation from the pups, *Endocrinology*, **91**, 191–6.

Zimbardo, P. G. (1958) The effect of early avoidance training and rearing conditions upon the sexual behaviour of the male rat, *J. Comp. Physiol. Psychol.*, **51**, 764–9.

CHAPTER 5

Developmental Influences of Hormones on Neuroendocrine Mechanisms of Sexual Behaviour: Comparisons with other Sexually Dimorphic Behaviours

BRUCE D. GOLDMAN

INTRODUCTION

Among mammals, and probably other vertebrate classes as well, sexually dimorphic aspects of adult sexual behaviour (i.e. qualitative and quantitative differences in masculine or feminine behaviours) are largely determined by the action of gonadal hormones during early development. Our present knowledge in this area owes a great deal to earlier studies of the role of hormones in the development of neural centres which control the pattern of pituitary gonadotrophic hormone release. Such investigations clearly demonstrated that the feminine, or cyclic, pattern of gonadotrophin secretion is absent in males of some species as a result of the action of testicular hormone on the brain during very early life. This is a 'classic' example of a developmental effect of hormones, and similar developmental effects have been shown to be present in cases of sexually dimorphic behaviours. Thus, studies related to the development of sexually dimorphic patterns of hormone secretion will be reviewed here as an introduction to analogous work on behaviour.

SEXUAL DIFFERENTIATION AND REGULATION OF PITUITARY GONADOTROPINS

The studies of Pfieffer (1936) demonstrated that the presence of testicular tissue during the first few days after birth resulted in a failure to develop a capacity for cyclical release of gonadotrophins. Genetic female rats which received testicular grafts during infancy failed to ovulate; genetic males castrated at birth and implanted with ovarian tissue during adulthood showed corpora lutea formation, indicative of cyclic release of gonadotrophins (Pfieffer, 1936; Harris, 1964). A large number of investigations in many laboratories have indicated since that neonatal testicular hormone(s) is responsible for suppressing the development of the capacity for cyclical release of gonadotrophins—i.e. neonatal steroids direct development towards the 'masculine', or tonic, pattern of secretion. Indeed, a single injection of androgen given during the first few days of life will render a genetic female rat permanently incapable of supporting ovulatory cycles.

It was first believed that the effect of neonatal testicular hormone in masculinizing the regulatory mechanisms for gonadotrophin secretion in the rat was exerted at the level of the pituitary gland (Pfieffer, 1936). However, Harris and Jacobson (1952) showed that the rat pituitary does not undergo sexual differentiation. Thus, it appeared most likely that the site of sexual dimorphism was in the central nervous system (CNS) and that the sex differences in patterns of pituitary hormone secretion were imposed upon the pituitary via neural regulation of the gland.

As further evidence for a central site of sexual differentiation, it was shown that ovaries from an 'androgen-sterilized' genetic female rat (i.e. a female made anovulatory by exposure to exogenous androgen neonatally) will develop corpora lutea following transplantation to a normal female. Ovaries from normal females will not show corpora lutea formation when transplanted to males castrated in adulthood (Harris, 1964). These observations appear to prove that the ovary itself is not permanently altered by early exposure to androgen.

It has been established that tonic secretion of gonadotrophins is largely regulated by the arcuate nucleus, while cyclic release of an ovulatory surge of gonadotrophin is 'triggered' by the preoptic (Everett, 1964), or possibly the suprachiasmatic (Clemens and Smalstig, 1975), region. Destruction of the preoptic area renders the female anovulatory (although ovarian follicular maturation still occurs), and electrical stimulation of the preoptic region can induce lutenizing hormone (LH) release and ovulation. Therefore, it has been suggested that neonatal testicular steroid may act to 'masculinize' the preoptic region, but little direct evidence for the specific site of action is available. Nevertheless, anatomical evidence for sexual dimorphism in the (CNS) has recently been presented (Field and Raisman, 1974). Untreated male rats and females treated with testosterone proprionate (TP) on day 4 of life showed reduced numbers of non-strial dendritic spine synapses in the strial part of the preoptic area as compared to untreated females or females receiving TP on day 16 of life. Unfortunately, the specific function of these synapses is unknown, but the effect of neonatal androgen treatment appeared to be limited to the strial part of the preoptic area (Table 1). Recent work suggests that the suprachiasmatic nuclei may be more important than the preoptic region for triggering cyclic LH release in the rat (Clemens and Smalstig, 1975).

Table 1. Sexual dimorphism in the preoptic area

Numbers of non-strial dendritic spine synapses $\pm$ (SEM) per 10 grid squares (1.8×10^4 μm^2) in the strial part of the preoptic area

Genetic sex	Treatment	Synapses	Functional status of adult
Female	None	53 ± 3	Cyclic
	1.25 mg TP on day 4	35 ± 2	Non-cyclic
	1.25 mg TP on day 16	54 ± 5	Cyclic
Male	None	33 ± 2	Non-cyclic
	Castrated on day 0	50 ± 3	Cyclic
	Castrated on day 7	39 ± 4	Non-cyclic

TP = testosterone propionate; day 0 = the day of birth. Data taken from a total count of 50,773 synapses in 64 rats.

(From Field and Raisman, 1974)

The action of testicular hormones on the development of brain centres for control of gonadotrophins has been studied in only a few mammalian species other than the rat (see also Plapinger and McEwen, this volume Chapter 6). The female mouse (Barraclough and Leathem, 1954; Edwards, 1971) and the hamster (Swanson, 1966; Brown and Goldman, unpubl. data) both developed the 'anovulatory syndrome' following neonatal treatment with androgen, and male hamsters castrated at birth and implanted with ovaries in adulthood showed corpora lutea formation (Swanson, 1970). However, working with the rhesus monkey, Karsch et al. (1973) have reported that following castration of an adult male 'ovulatory surges' of LH can be elicited following oestrogen treatment. These LH surges appear to be similar to those observed in female monkeys. Thus, it may be that sexual differentiation of the central mechanisms controlling gonadotrophin release does not occur in this species. This may be related to the observation that surgical disruption of anterior connections to the medial basal hypothalamus did not consistently prevent ovulation in the rhesus monkey (Krey et al., 1975). A similar operation does lead to ovulatory failure in rats.

NEONATAL HORMONES AND SEXUAL BEHAVIOUR

Many studies have been directed toward the developmental effects of testicular hormones on sexually dimorphic behaviours. With few exceptions, these studies have been carried out in mammals and mostly in rodents. The results in the rat and the hamster are described here. The rat has been employed as a 'model' in many studies of this topic but, as indicated here, even such a closely related species as the hamster appears to show some significant divergences from the patterns observed in the rat.

Female rats do not display feminine patterns of sexual behaviour (e.g. 'hopping and darting', lordosis) following ovariectomy. However, these patterns of sexual behaviour are readily restored by treatment with oestrogen and progesterone. Male rats castrated in adulthood usually do not show feminine sexual behaviour even when administered large doses of oestrogen and progesterone. In contrast, adult female rats will display some elements of masculine sex behaviour (e.g. mounting) following androgen treatment (see also Feder, this volume Chapter 12). However, the complete pattern of male behaviour, including movements associated with intromission and ejaculation, is displayed only very infrequently by the androgen-treated female. These observations form the major basis for the study of sexual differentiation of sex behaviour in this species (Edwards and Thompson, 1970; Barraclough and Gorski, 1962).

Male rats which are castrated shortly after birth will readily display feminine sexual behaviours (e.g. hopping, ear-wiggling, lordosis) following treatment with oestrogen and progesterone in adulthood. Treatment with androgen at birth reverses this effect of castration. Similarly, female rats treated with large doses of androgen neonatally usually do not display lordotic behaviour following treatment with ovarian hormones in adulthood. However, it should be noted that females treated with low doses of androgen neonatally are sometimes quite capable of displaying feminine sexual behaviour even though cyclic release of pituitary gonadotrophins is not present in these animals (Barraclough and Gorski, 1962).

A neonatally castrated male rat usually does not show the complete pattern of masculine sexual behaviour in adulthood. The frequency of mounting may be similar to that displayed by intact males, but intromissions are generally displayed only infrequently and ejaculatory behaviour is even less common in such animals. A similar pattern of behaviour has been observed in neonatally androgenized genetic females. The failure of the androgenized female rat to display the complete pattern of masculine sexual behaviour in adulthood has been attributed to a possibly important role of sensory receptors in the male genitalia (Beach, 1968). Although the external genitalia of the androgenized female are somewhat masculinized, complete masculine development is, of course, not achieved.

More recently, the complete masculine pattern of sexual behaviour *has* been observed in female rats treated chronically with high doses of oestrogen in adulthood (Dr. Sachs, pers. commun.). These animals usually develop pituitary tumours, and the behavioural displays may be a result of pressure exerted by the tumours on the neighbouring hypothalamic tissue. Nevertheless, these observations suggest a hitherto unsuspected capacity for the performance of masculine mating behaviour even in females which received no hormonal treatment prior to adulthood.

The data which have been obtained on Syrian hamsters are somewhat confusing, primarily because results from different laboratories do not always agree.

It is, however, generally agreed that male hamsters retain a greater 'bisexual' potential as compared to male rats in that male hamsters consistently display lordotic responses following treatment with oestrogen and progesterone in adulthood (Tiefer and Johnson, 1971). Indeed, intact males of this species occasionally display lordosis even without any hormone treatment (Goldman, unpubl. observ.). The lordotic behaviour of the male hamster is very similar to that of the female except that the lordosis posture is usually not maintained for as long a time in males (Tiefer and Johnson, 1971).

In one study treatment with a large dose of TP shortly after birth almost completely eliminated the capacity to display feminine sexual behaviour in both male and female hamsters (Eaton, 1970). In another study neonatal TP did not disrupt the capacity for ovarian cyclicity or lordotic behaviour in female hamsters, although the treated animals did show enhanced mounting behaviour (Whitsett and Vandenberg, 1975). The reason for the different outcomes of these similar studies is unknown. However, the time of treatment with steroid may be especially critical in the hamster. We observed the 'anovulatory syndrome' in female hamsters treated with TP beginning on the day of birth but failed to find any effect in a second experiment when androgen treatment was initiated on the day after birth (Brown and Goldman, unpubl. data). If one accepts the positive results as being more indicative of *potential* effects of the hormone then the report of Eaton (1970) shows that the feminine pattern of behaviour can be blocked by neonatal exposure to androgen even though such behaviour is still displayed to some extent by male hamsters. These observations suggest that the neonatal male hamster does not secrete sufficient androgen to completely 'masculinize' the CNS.

Treatment of neonatally castrated hamsters and intact females with androstenedione or free testosterone for the first 20 days of life resulted in animals which were capable of displaying moderate levels of lordotic behaviour in adulthood (Tifer and Johnson, 1975), and in another study neonatally administered testosterone failed to reduce oestrogen/progesterone-induced lordosis in male hamsters (Coniglio et al., 1973). These treatments did increase the capacity of the female hamsters to display mounting behaviour. The various effects of neonatal steroid treatments observed in different studies of the hamster probably reflect differences in dosage, time of administration, and type of steroid used. It would be of interest to determine the identity of the predominant testicular steroid(s) in the neonatal hamster and to compare blood levels of steroid in this species to those observed in the rat. Even though (see below) the effect of testicular androgen in these species may be mediated by conversion to oestrogen in the brain, it is not yet clear to what extent such conversion is a prerequisite for 'androgenization'. Furthermore, species differences may exist in testicular products and in the importance of aromatization to oestrogens.

It should be noted here that even in the rat free testosterone was relatively ineffective in reversing the effects of neonatal castration or in 'defeminizing' genetic females (Luttge and Whalen, 1970). This may well be due to the shorter biological half-life of free testosterone as compared to TP. In general, the pattern of development in the hamster appears to be similar to that in the rat except that the neonatal male hamster either secretes less testicular hormone or is less sensitive to such hormone as compared to the rat.

In both the female rat and the mouse treatment with steroids must be administered during the perinatal period to 'masculinize' the pattern of adult sexual behaviour (Harris, 1964). The same is true for male rats castrated at birth (Beach et al., 1969). In the guinea pig and the rhesus monkey the hormone treatment must be given during foetal life (Phoenix et al., 1959; Goy, 1970), and this is probably related to the longer period of gestation in these species.

The results obtained in a variety of mammalian species may be summarized as follows: exposure to gonadal steroid hormones during a 'critical period' in early life (foetal or neonatal) tends to direct the development of various sexually dimorphic physiological and behavioural systems toward the masculine pattern; in the absence of sufficient quantities of such steroids the pattern of development is feminine. It now appears that in order to fully understand the mechanics of this process one must consider the possibility that the circulating hormonal agent (androgen) which is responsible for masculinization may need to be aromatized to form oestrogen before it can affect CNS development.

MECHANISM OF ACTION

The mechanism of action of neonatal steroids in sexual differentiation of neural pathways which regulate sexual behaviour is an area of considerable current interest. This is particularly so in view of accumulating evidence that, at least in the rat, androgen may not be the agent which is directly responsible for 'masculinizing' the brain. Rather, it appears that circulating androgens may enter brain cells and be converted to estrogens which then act within the cell nucleus (see also this volume, Plapinger and McEwen, Chapter 6).

While considerable work has been directed towards determining the significance of the aromatization of androgens in the developing brain, few clues exist as to the way in which steroid hormones affect the cellular machinery to achieve sexual dimorphism in the CNS. The induction of persistent vaginal oestrus by neonatal androgen treatment has been prevented by concurrent administration of inhibitors of DNA and RNA synthesis, but it is not clear whether the synthesis of a new species of DNA and/or RNA is involved (i.e. DNA or RNA coding for new proteins). The effects on sex behaviour were not examined in these studies, but lordotic behaviour can be inhibited in adult female rats by treatment with actinomycin D, a blocker of DNA synthesis. Arai and Gorski (1968a) reported that phenobarbitone administered concurrently with androgen prevented the neural masculinizing effect of neonatal androgen. However, Brown-Grant et al. (1971) were unable to repeat this result. The discrepancies between these two studies cannot be explained at present.

Considerable controversy exists as to the nature of the active testicular hormone during neonatal sexual differentiation. This controversy began with the observation that oestrogen is at least as effective as androgen in 'masculinizing' the brain of the genetic female rat (Edwards and Thompson, 1970). Further studies indicated that androgen can be converted to oestrogen within the human foetal brain (Naftolin et al., 1971) and in the adult rat hypothalamus (Naftolin et al., 1974). Also, oestrogen has been measured in the blood of the newborn female rat (Weisz and Gunsaluz, 1973). The latter observation might actually appear to be in opposition to a physiological role of oestrogen in masculinization of the CNS unless larger quantities of oestrogen are found in the blood of newborn males as compared to neonatal females. Nevertheless, the possibility that conversion of androgen to oestrogen within the brain is important in sexual differentiation is supported by the observation that dihydrotestosterone (DHT), which cannot be converted to oestrogen, is also ineffective in causing masculine differentiation of the CNS. However, this is not conclusive evidence, particularly since the natural hormone, testosterone, is also relatively ineffective as compared to TP (Brown-Grant et al., 1971). This may be due to the slower metabolism of the propionate derivative, although the 17 β-propionate derivatives of dihydrotestosterone and 5α-androstanedione were also comparatively ineffective (Brown-Grant et al., 1971). The hypothesis that the biological half-life of the injected steroid may well be important receives support from the results of Arai and Gorski (1968b, 1968c) indicating that an exposure time of 6–12 h is required for the action of androgen on the neonatal rat brain. With these observations in mind, it would appear advisable in future studies to use dihydrotestosterone propionate (DHTP), or, better, implants of DHT, rather than injections of the free alcohol of dihydrotestosterone.

SENSITIVITY TO HORMONES

It has often been stated that the neonatally androgenized rat is insensitive to oestrogen and/or progesterone in adulthood. With respect to the usual definition of the term 'sensitivity' this would mean that in the androgenized female larger doses of oestrogen and progesterone are required to produce a state in which feminine sexually receptive behaviour (e.g. lordosis) can be elicited. Actually, this hypothesis has not, to the author's knowledge, been critically tested. In most studies in which attempts have been made to induce feminine sexual behaviour in male rats or in androgenized females only one regimen of oestrogen and progesterone has been used. In fact, it seems that the term 'insensitive' has often been used when the data actually suggest virtually total refractoriness to sex hormones. In future studies it would be of interest to attempt several doses of each steroid and to extend the period of treatment. This would help to determine whether neonatal androgens render the animal relatively insensitive to female sex hormones or whether the effect is one of total refractoriness to these hormones.

If insensitivity to hormones is a factor in the development of sexual dimorphism in behaviour, it would seem most likely that the male–female differences in sensitivity might be present in the CNS since the CNS appears to be the most important site for hormone action in regulating behaviours in adulthood. However, it must be remembered that species-specific odours are involved in elicitation of sexual and aggressive behaviours in many mammalian species and also that the sensory nerves innervating the perineal area of the female rat appear to become more sensitive to mechanical stimulation under the influence of oestrogen (Komisaruk et al., 1972). Therefore, it is possible that differences in sensitivity to hormones could be at least partly the result of changes in peripheral receptors.

Some evidence does exist for a specific failure to respond to androgens in adulthood. This is illustrated by a strain of rat which displays the 'androgen-insensitivity' syndrome. Androgen-insensitive males of this strain are pseudohermaphrodites with an XY-karyotype, inguinal testes, well-developed Leydig cells, and a failure of development of the germinal epithelium. These animals are phenotypically female, and the pattern of urinary corticosteroid excretion, hepatic steroid metabolism, and saccharine preference are all feminine. The development of the female phenotype may be due to target organ insensitivity to androgens as suggested by a deficiency of androgen-binding proteins (Bardin et al., 1973).

An apparently similar situation occurs in humans showing the syndrome of testicular feminization. These individuals are genetic males but are phenotypically female and are generally raised with a female gender identity. The testes of these individuals sometimes produce normal amounts of androgens, but the target tissues fail to respond. The suppression of masculine development in both the human testicular feminization syndrome and in the pseudohermaphroditic rat is so complete as to suggest that the syndrome is initiated very early in life, probably prior to birth. It is not certain, however, whether a primary insensitivity to androgen occurs during foetal life even though androgen production may be normal.

Finally, if altered sensitivity to hormones in adulthood is involved in the normal mechanism of sexual differentiation of behaviour, one may ask whether the altered sensitivity is specifically directed toward certain hormones. Male rats castrated in adulthood will display masculine sexual behaviour in response to treatment with either androgen or oestrogen. Females ovariectomized in adulthood will display feminine sexual behaviour following oestrogen and progesterone or following androgen and progesterone treatment. Pfaff and Zigmond (1971) observed that neonatally castrated male rats showed a reduction in male sex behaviour regardless of whether androgen or oestrogen was used to stimulate the behaviour in adulthood. Similarly, neonatally androgenized female rats performed very few lordotic responses in tests for female sex behaviour regardless of whether oestrogen + progesterone or testosterone + progesterone was used as the hormonal stimulus. These results suggest that exposure to androgen neonatally causes a general refractoriness (or insensitivity?) to hormonal stimulation of female sexual behaviour in adulthood and that the absence of neonatal androgen leads to a general refractoriness to hormonal stimulation of male sex behaviour.

ROLE OF THE PITUITARY IN SEXUAL DIFFERENTIATION

The adult pituitary does not show evidence of irreversible sexual dimorphism (Harris and Jacobson, 1952). This does not mean, however, that the pituitary has no role in sexual differentiation. Since the adult testis is largely under pituitary control, it is of importance to inquire whether this is also true for the foetal and/or neonatal testis, especially with respect to the masculinizing effects of the testicular hormones. The studies of Jost (1953) indicated that decapitation (and, consequently, hypophysectomy) of the male rabbit foetus at days 18–22 of gestation resulted in a failure of development of the typical male sex accessories. These findings suggest that the testicular hormones required for masculinization of the reproductive tract are pituitary-dependent. Unfortunately, this animal preparation cannot be studied beyond the time of parturition. Hypophysectomy of the neonate is also not a feasible procedure for long-term studies.

Measurement of the levels of gonadotrophic hormones in the blood can help to answer questions regarding pituitary control of gonadal function. LH and follicle-stimulating hormone (FSH) are essential to the regulation of gonadal growth in both sexes. These hormones are secreted by the anterior pituitary gland and are present in varying concentrations in the blood of adult animals. More recently, LH and FSH have also been detected in the blood of neonatal rats (Goldman et al., 1971; Goldman and Gorski, 1971; Ojeda and Ramirez, 1972) and mice (Selmanoff, Ph.D. Thesis, unpubl.). Both hormones are present only in very low concentrations in neonate males, but the hormone levels increase markedly within one day following castration in the rat. The rapid increase in serum gonadotrophin levels following castration in the neonatal male is similar to that observed in the adult (Goldman et al., 1971), and Goldman and Gorski (1971) were able to reverse the castration response by the administration of androgen (Table 2). These observations indicate that the gonadotrophic hormone (GTH) secretory system is operational at birth, as is the response of this system to the negative feedback effects of androgen. The neonatal female shows higher blood levels of both LH and FSH as compared to littermate males, and a similar sex difference has been observed in human infants (Faiman and Winter, 1971). Although it was first suggested that at least in the rat the high GTH levels might be due to a failure of the neonatal ovary to produce sufficient steroids to inhibit gonadotropin secretion (Goldman et al., 1971), it now appears that the oestrogen concentration in the blood of neonatal female rats is quite high (Weisz and Gunsalus, 1973). However, the circulating oestrogen may be biologically inactive by virtue of being

Table 2. Inhibition of gonadotrophin secretion by testosterone propionate (TP) in castrated neonatal male rats

Treatment	No. rats	LH (ng/ml serum)	FSH (ng/ml serum)
Intact, untreated, day 6	4	< 0.9	− − − **
Castrated day 5:			
Oil day 6	6	3.4	667
3 µg TP day 6	11	<0.9	500
Oil day 6	5; 5*	4.0; 7.5	600; 1000
30 µg TP day 6	6; 6*	<0.9; 0.9	407; 383
Oil days 6 and 7	6	7.8	793
3 µg TP days 6 and 7	9	<0.9	253
Oil days 6 and 7	3	8.8	867
30 µg TP days 6 and 7	6	<0.9	280

*Two groups of controls and corresponding experimental groups are summarized here. The first group of oil-treated animals were littermates of the first group of TP-treated rats, and the second group of controls were litter mates of the second group of experimentals. (< 0.9, undetectable level of hormone.)
**Serum of intact males was not assayed for FSH.
(Data from Goldman and Gorski, 1971)

bound to an α-globulin (see also Plapinger and McEwen, this volume Chapter 6).

In relation to the observations described above, it would be of interest to know at what stage of life the pituitary comes under the control of hypothalamic releasing hormones. Presumably, in order for such control to be exerted, a pathway for the efficient transfer of releasing hormones from the hypothalamus to the pituitary would be required. Early studies suggested that the portal vascular system was not well developed at birth; however, more recent studies indicate that small molecules such as the hypothalamic peptide hormones probably can be transported by the portal vessels as early as the second day of life in the rat (Florsheim and Rudko, 1968). Furthermore, elevated serum LH levels have been observed following the injection of luteinizing hormone-releasing hormone (LRH) in the neonatal rat (Root et al., 1975), indicating that the neonatal pituitary is responsive to hypothalamic releasing hormone.

The question remains whether neonatal pituitary gonadotrophins are functional in the rat. To answer this question rats were treated with an antiserum raised against ovine LH. The antiserum to LH was raised by repeated subcutaneous injection of ovine LH emulsified in Freund's complete adjuvant in rabbits. Several rabbits were used and each produced antisera capable of neutralizing both LH and FSH. Three of the antisera were combined for use in these studies. This antiserum could be shown to neutralize the biological activity of both LH or FSH of rat origin. The administration of gonadotrophin antiserum (GTH/AS) to newborn male rats (days 1–5 of age) of the Sprague–Dawley strain resulted in the development of males which failed to impregnate

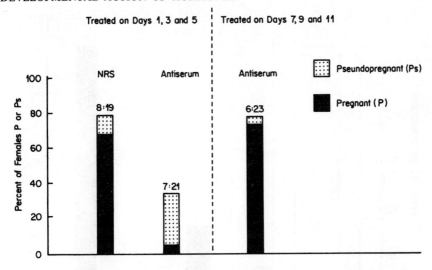

Fig. 1. Percentages of pregnancies and pseudopregnancies resulting from pairings of normal female rats with adult males that had received normal rabbit serum (NRS) or gonadotrophin antiserum (GTH/AS) during neonatal life. (Left) Treated on days 1, 3, and 5; (right) treated on days 7, 9, and 11. The first number above each bar denotes the number of males used; the second number indicates the total number of females used. Each male was used in at least two separate tests. (From Goldman and Mahesh, 1970.)

females in adulthood (i.e. failed to induce pregnancies in females with which they were housed), even though their testes appeared normal at the time of testing (Fig. 1). When the antiserum treatment was delayed until 7–11 days of age, this effect was not observed, suggesting that the necessary quantity of gonadotrophin had already been secreted prior to 7 days of age (Goldman and Mahesh, 1970). This result was also obtained in a second strain (Long–Evans) of rats. Furthermore, it was found that the antiserum-treated males displayed very few intromissions when paired with oestrous females in behavioural tests (Fig. 2). Since male rats require several intromissions before achieving an ejaculation, it seems likely that the decreased ability to achieve intromissions would severely reduce the likelihood of the successful impregnation of females by the antiserum-treated males (Goldman et al., 1972). In further behavioural tests it was found that male rats treated neonatally with GTH/AS displayed high levels of female sexual behaviour following treatment with oestrogen and progesterone in adulthood (Fig. 2); indeed, their level of performance (lordosis quotient) was not statistically different from that of normal female rats (Goldman et al., 1972). The reduction in some aspects of masculine sexual behaviour and the increased potential to display feminine behaviour after neonatal treatment with GTH/AS was again demonstrated in a later study (McCullough et al., 1974).

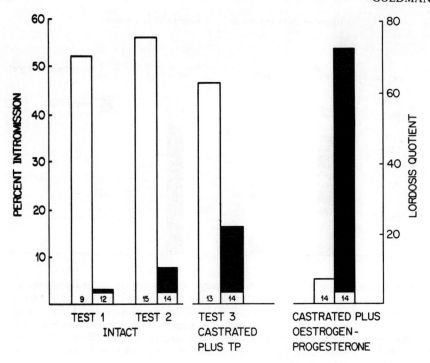

Fig. 2. Influence of neonatal treatment with NRS (open bars) or GTH/AS (closed bars) on masculine and feminine sexual behaviours of male rats following treatment with sex steroids in adulthood. Per cent intromission is equal to (number of intromissions/number of mounts) x 100. In each case the behaviour of antiserum-treated males was significantly different from that of control males (p < 0.001, Mann-Whitney U-test). (From Goldman *et al.*, 1972.)

The author interprets the above-described results as follows: Neonatal gonadotropins (LH and/or FSH) are required to stimulate the rat testis to produce sufficient hormone (probably androgen) for masculinization of the systems which regulate patterns of sexual behaviour in adulthood. Thus, neonatal antiserum treatment is somewhat similar in effect to neonatal castration. In support of this explantion, Arai and Serisawa (1973) observed that neonatal injection of LH or human chorionic gonadotrophin (HCG), but not FSH, was able to advance the process of masculinization of the GTH control centre in the rat. Since this effect was not obtained when the rat pups were castrated prior to administration of HCG, the authors concluded that the exogenous GTH was probably acting via the testes. More recently, Warren *et al.* (1975) reported that treatment with HCG induced a large increase in testicular content of testosterone in rats as early as day 15.5 of foetal life. The effect was observed at all ages studied thereafter up to 20 days after birth. Leydig cells are present at birth in the rat testes and these cells show an abundance of the steroidogenic enzyme, 3β-ol dehydrogenase during the first few days of life. The enzyme content then declines until near the time of puberty (Niemi and Ikonen, 1963). Thus, the time course of development of this enzyme in the Leydig cells parallels the developmental curve for the concentration of testosterone in the blood (Resko *et al.*, 1968).

It should be noted that the hypothesis proposed above does not explain one additional observation which was replicated in three studies in which this author has participated. Namely, it was found that neonatal treatment with GTH/AS failed to 'demasculinize' the systems which regulate cyclic release of GTH—i.e. male rats treated with GTH/AS neonatally failed to show formation of corpora lutea when castrated and implanted with ovarian tissue in adulthood. This was somewhat surprising since rats castrated at birth are able to support a sufficiently cyclic pattern of GTH secretion to allow for corpora lutea formation. It may be that some androgen is produced during neonatal life even when GTH is blocked (by GTH/AS), and this small amount of steroid may be sufficient to masculinize the system which regulates GTH release without affecting systems regulating sexual behaviour. Indeed, there is evidence that the GTH release system may be more sensitive to the masculinizing effect of androgen as compared to the system which controls sexual behaviour (Barraclough and Gorski, 1962).

As mentioned earlier, the direction of sexual differentiation is firmly established during foetal life in those species with long gestation periods. It would be of interest to know whether placental and uterine gonadotropins—i.e. human and monkey chorionic gonadotrophins, pregnant mare serum gonadotrophin—produced by some of these species are effective in stimulating the foetal gonads. If so, the maternal gonadotrophins of pregnancy may have a role in sexual differentiation. For example, it may be that the foetal pituitary gonadotrophic cells are suppressed by maternal steroids, necessitating another source of gonadotrophins to stimulate early testicular function.

PITUITARY AND TESTICULAR HORMONES AND SEXUAL DIFFERENCES IN MATERNAL BEHAVIOUR

The physiological mechanisms underlying maternal behaviour have been studied in only a few mammalian species. Some degree of hormonal regulation is indicated, but it has been difficult to isolate the role of hormones in maternal behaviour because other factors, especially previous experience with young, are also of much significance. Nevertheless, in addition to hormonal effects which may 'activate' maternal behaviour there is also some evidence for developmental effects of hormones on the behaviour.

Virgin female rats begin to display some elements of maternal behaviour (e.g. pup retrieval, licking of pups, crouching, and nest-building) after several consecutive days of exposure to rat pups even when no other treatment is administered. This process of development of maternal behaviour via exposure to pups has been called 'sensitization'. Male rats of the Long–Evans strain usually failed to display all the above-mentioned aspects of maternal behaviour despite 7 consecutive days of exposure to pups, while both intact and ovariec-tomized females usually showed all behaviours after an average latency of 4–5 days (Table 3). These observations suggest a sexual dimorphism in the behaviours, possibly with an endocrine basis. This is further confirmed by the finding that 6 of 8 males castrated at birth displayed all four aspects of maternal behaviour with an average latency of 5 days exposure to pups. Males treated with GTH/AS in infancy also showed considerably more maternal behaviour than untreated or normal rabbit serum-treated males and were not significantly different from virgin females in this respect (Table 3). Thus, in the Long–Even strain, maternal behaviour, like sexual behaviour, appears to be sexually dimorphic and is probably suppressed by testicular hormones secreted during neonatal life under the influence of gonadotrophins.

The findings in the Purdue–Wistar rat were somewhat different in that adult males and females did not differ significantly in the time required for sensitiza-tion to pups. In fact, 24-day-old male rats became sensitized with a latency of only 1.3 ± 0.5 days while older males (30–54 days) required 4.5–7.5 days for sensitization. Females showed a similar 'developmental' pattern. However, when a different behavioural test was used, the Purdue–Wistar rats also de-monstrated some degree of sexual dimorphism with respect to maternal behaviour. Specifically, when adult rats were treated with a 'maternal' hormone regimen (oestradiol benzoate and progesterone for 20 days, followed by prolac-tin on the morning of the 21st day) females showed a greater tendency to retrieve pups from one arm of a T-maze than did males (Table 4). Since similar sex differences were not observed following hormone treatment when pups were placed in the home cage, it may be that dimorphism in maternal be-haviour in this strain appears only when the testing procedure is such as to require strong motivational factors. In the same study, neonatally castrated males responded like control females and neonatally androgenized females behaved like control males. Therefore, the findings suggest that the sexual dimorphism in maternal responsiveness is mediated by the presence or absence of androgen neonatally; neonatal androgen apparently inhibits the full develop-ment of maternal responsiveness in adulthood (Bridges *et al.*, 1973). Evidence also exists for an effect of foetal androgens on the ontogeny of maternal be-haviour in the rabbit (Anderson *et al.*, 1970; Fuller *et al.*, 1970).

HORMONAL CONTROL OF SEX DIFFERENCES IN AGGRESSIVE BEHAVIOUR

The term 'aggressive behaviour' has been used to refer to a broad class of complex behaviour patterns. These patterns include predatory behaviour, territorial defence, defence of the young, and inter-male behaviour related to the establishment and maintenancy of hierarchies (Conner, 1972). It is there-

Table 3. Percentage of adult rats showing four aspects of maternal behaviour (retrieval, licking, crouching and nest building) after neonatal gonadectomy or treatment with gonadotrophin antiserum (GTH/AS) or normal rabbit Serum (NRS)

Group	Percentage to show all behaviour
Intact females (N = 11)	72.72[a]‡ [b]‡
Ovariectomized females (N = 11)	54.54[a] * [b]
Intact males (N = 15)	6.67
GTH/AS males (N = 14)	50.00 [a]*†[b]*
Males castrated at birth (N = 8)	75.00 [a]*,[b] *
NRS males (N = 14)	14.28

[a] Significantly different from intact males.
[b] Significantly different from NRS males.

*p 0.05
†p 0.01 ——— Analysed with X^2
‡p 0.001

(Data from McCullough et al., 1974.)

Table 4. Percentage of adult rats retrieving pups in the T-maze. Numbers in parentheses are N

Genetic sex	Neonatal treatment	Adult treatment	
		Vehicle	Hormone
Male	Sham castrate	0.0 (11)	11.6 (17)
	Castrate	0.0 (11)	42.9 (14)
Female	None	5.9 (17)	48.0 (25)
	Oil	12.5 (16)	42.9 (14)
	TP	25.0 (12)	5.6 (18)

(Data from Bridges et al., 1973.)

fore difficult to define the differentiating effects of hormones on specific types of aggressive behaviour. Moreover these studies have usually been carried out under laboratory conditions, and the relevance of the particular behaviour being examined to particular situations such as those enumerated above has often been unclear.

Male mice show strong aggressive responses towards other males but not towards females. Female mice are not aggressive toward conspecifics of either sex. These sex differences appear to be at least partly due to an action of testicular hormone, and at least part of this action may be exerted upon the developing CNS. Thus, female mice and neonatally castrated male mice often fail to display aggression when treated with androgen in adulthood, but mice treated with androgen neonatally are capable of showing aggression in adulthood irrespective of sex or neonatal castration (Bronson and Desjardins, 1969; Bronson and Desjardins, 1970).

Edwards (1970) reported that massive doses of TP (100 μg/day for 20 days) administered to ovariectomized female mice between 30 and 50 days of life resulted in increased adult aggression. The question arises whether this effect represents a 'developmental' effect of androgen on the adult (or almost adult) brain or whether it is simply a case of supplying pharmacological doses of steroid to 'drive' a system already present in the female. This problem has been further studied by Barkley (1974), who found that adult mice showed different sensitivities to androgen administered in adulthood depending on sex and treatment during infancy. Male mice castrated in adulthood showed complete restoration of fighting behaviour following implantation of a silastic capsule containing 0·3 mg testosterone. Males castrated at 25 days of age (prepuberally) required a 1 mg implant; male mice castrated on the day of birth showed some aggression with a 1 mg implant in adulthood but required a 10 mg implant for a display of aggressive behaviour comparable to that of a male castrated in adulthood. Females ovariectomized in adulthood also required a 10 mg implant to induce aggressive behaviour (Barkley, Ph.D. Thesis, unpubl.). A summary of the data is presented in Table 5. Implants of these same sizes were placed in castrated adult male mice and after 4 weeks the animals were sacrificed. Serum concentrations of testosterone and accessory organ weights are shown and compared to intact male controls in Table 6. Based on accessory organ weights the 1 mg implant would appear to restore 'physiological' androgen levels; however, all implanted groups showed lower serum testosterone than intact males. The reason for this apparent discrepancy is not known.

The data described above suggest that various degrees of sensitivity to androgen may be displayed by adult mice with females and neonatal castrates being least sensitive—i.e. the process of sexual differentiation with respect to aggressive behaviour may involve the development of differential sensitivity to androgen. One may then ask whether sensitivity to androgen can be enhanced by exposure to androgen in adulthood or whether this effect is confined

Table 5. Relationship between size of testosterone implant
and aggressive behaviour in male and female mice

Treatment	0.3 mg	1 mg	10 mg
Male castrated in adulthood	13/18*	8/10	10/10
Male castrated at 25 days of age	4/14	14/15	—
Male castrated at birth	0/9	5/9	9/9
Female ovariectomized in adulthood	0/8	—	6/10

*Number of mice displaying aggressive behaviour total number
tested.

(Data from Barkley, 1974.)

Table 6. Acessory organ weights and serum testosterone in castrated male mice receiving
Testosterone implants*

Treatment	Seminal vesicle wt. (mg/g body wt. ± SE)	Ventral prostate wt. (mg/g body wt. ± SE)	Serum testosterone (ng/ml)
Intact (8)**	7.9 ± 0.9	0.55 ± .05	18.1 ± 5.3
Castrate + oil implant (8)	0.7 ± 0.1	0.23 ± .02	1.1 ± 0.1
Castrate + 0.3 mg implant (11)	2.2 ± 0.5	0.26 ± .03	1.5 ± 0.4
Castrate + 1 mg implant (8)	7.6 ± 0.7	0.49 ± .04	3.4 ± 0.4
Castrate + 5 mg implant (10)	8.5 ± 0.7	0.58 ± .04	4.5 ± 0.4

*Silastic implants were placed subcutaneously at the time of castration. The animals were sacrificed
four weeks later.
**(Number of animals)

(Data from Barkley, 1974.)

to early life. Barkley attempted to answer this question by implanting adult,
ovariectomized female mice with 10 mg testosterone capsules; testing for
aggression after 3 weeks, replacing the 10 mg implants with 0·3 mg implants
and retesting after a further 3-week period. These females displayed about the
same level of aggressive behaviour on both tests (i.e. about 60% of the animals
fought), but females given 0·3 mg implants without prior exposure to androgens
failed to fight at all. The observations suggest that the adult nervous system is
still capable of being sensitized to androgen by exposure to high levels of
steroid. Furthermore, these results also suggest that the pubertal rise in circulating testosterone may be partly responsible for sensitization of the CNS. This
may be of some relevance in determining levels of aggression in adulthood.
Selmanoff (1974) found that the highly aggressive DBA strain of mouse shows
an abrupt pubertal rise in serum testosterone while the less aggressive C57BL

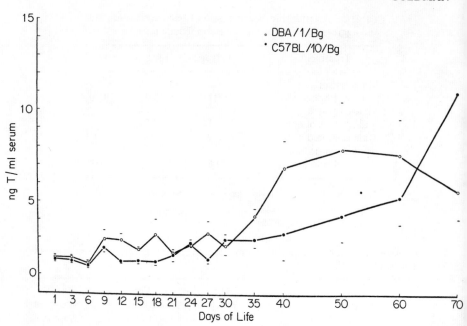

Fig. 3. Concentrations of testosterone in the serum of DBA/1 and C57BL/10 male mice at ages 1 through 70 days of life. Values are plotted as mean ± SEM

strain shows a much more gradual rise in serum testosterone. These two strains have about equal serum testosterone levels in adulthood (Fig. 3). Both strains show precipitous increases in serum levels of FSH and LH prior to the pubertal increases in serum testosterone (Figs. 4 and 5).

The question of when the CNS loses its capacity to be permanently altered by the action of steroid hormones deserves further study. The observations described above suggest that the neural system which mediates aggressive behaviour may retain more plasticity in adulthood compared to the system which mediates sexual behaviour. It should be noted that relevant experiments have not been carried out to determine critically whether patterns of sexual behaviour can be permanently modified during adulthood by exposure to hormones. Nevertheless, it appears to be generally believed that they cannot; and, if true, it would be most interesting to compare the mechanisms by which steroids exert developmental effects on the systems mediating sexual and aggressive behaviours, respectively.

In highly social mammals such as rhesus monkeys and humans it is difficult to evaluate the role of hormones in aggressive behaviour since social structure and 'culture' are obviously important here, and these factors may tend to mask hormonal effects. Rose et al. (1971) reported a correlation between plasma testosterone and dominance rank as well as aggressive behaviour in a

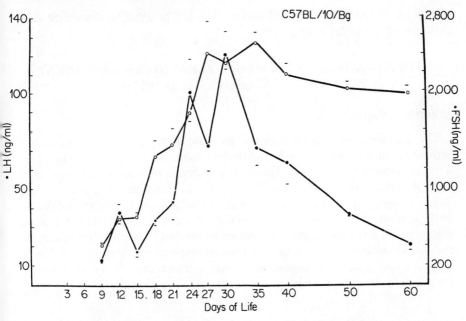

Fig. 4. Concentrations of LH and FSH in sera obtained from male DBA/1 mice at ages 1 through 60 days. Values are plotted as mean ± SEM. The standards were NIAMD-rat LH-RP-1 and NIAMD-rat FSH-RP-1

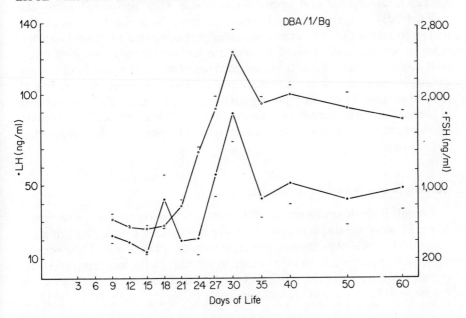

Fig. 5. Concentrations of LH and FSH in sera obtained from male C57BL/10 mice at ages 1 through 60 days. Values are plotted as mean ± SEM

colony of 34 rhesus monkey. However, it is not possible to draw firm conclusions regarding cause and effect.

OTHER SEXUALLY DIMORPHIC BEHAVIOURS DEPENDENT UPON EARLY EXPOSURE TO HORMONES

Micturition Posture in Dogs

The leg elevation posture assumed by male dogs during urination is not present in females and cannot be induced by hormone treatment during adulthood in females (Berg, 1944). However, treatment with androgen soon after birth is capable of inducing the display of this behaviour in genetic female dogs without further hormone treatment in adulthood (Martins and Valle, 1948). Beach (1970) studied this problem more thoroughly and presented evidence that testicular hormone secreted before birth is probably responsible for development of the male-like micturition response in genetic males. These dogs are still somewhat responsive to the masculinizing effects of androgen for a short period after birth.

Emergence and Open-field Behaviour in Rats

Neonatally androgenized female rats performed differently from control females in emergence and open-field tests—i.e. they performed more like males. Males and androgenized females emerge from the home cage less frequently and with a greater average latency as compared to control females. Also, males and androgenized females are less active in the open-field test than control females. Neonatally castrated males behaved similarly to control females in these tests. Since all animals used in these experiments were castrated prior to testing, the results probably cannot be attributed to different patterns of gonadal hormone secretion during adulthood. Thus, it appears that exposure to androgen neonatally has an organizing effect upon the behaviours (Pfaff and Zigmond, 1971).

Juvenile Social Behaviour in Monkeys

Juvenile male rhesus monkeys differ from their female agemates with respect to the frequency of display of the following behaviours: threat, play initiation, rough and tumble play, pursuit play, and mounting behaviour. These sexually dimorphic patterns of social interaction appear to be independent of the presence of the gonads after birth, but they are modified (e.g. 'masculinized') by exposure to TP *in utero* (Goy and Goldfoot, 1973).

EVOLUTIONARY ASPECTS

The developmental effects of sex hormones upon sexually dimorphic behaviours have received very little attention in non-mammalian vertebrates. However, some information is available regarding the mechanisms of morphological sexual differentiation in birds, amphibians, and fishes. Since these mechanisms show differences from the mammalian pattern, they will be reviewed here; perhaps, the findings related to morphological differentiation may provide clues to the ontogeny of sexually dimorphic behaviours in lower vertebrates.

In mammals the male is digametic (XY) and the female is homogametic (XX) with respect to the sex chromosomes. In birds this situation is reversed with the female being digametic (ZW) and the male homogametic (ZZ). In amphibians both patterns exist with males being the digametic sex in frogs and females being digametic in toads and salamanders. In birds, amphibians, and fishes cases of complete sex-reversal have been reported—i.e. cases in which individuals of a given genetic sex are able to function reproductively as the opposite sex. In fact, true hermaphroditism has been reported in many fishes (Atz, 1964) and in some frogs (Kolter, 1963). These are cases in which an individual produces both sperm and ova and can function as both male and female. Complete sex-reversal has never been reported in a mammal although cases of pseudohermaphroditism are fairly common and can be obtained experimentally. The absence of complete sex-reversal in mammals suggests a more rigid mechanism of gonadal sex determination as compared to some of the other vertebrate classes.

An indication of hormonal involvement in sexual differentiation in amphibians has been obtained in two types of experiments. First, when two urodele (*Ambystoma*) embryos of opposite genetic sex are grafted together to form parabiotic 'twins', ovarian development is inhibited in the female, and she becomes partially or totally sterilized. These results suggest that the testis produces a substance which inhibits ovarian development possibly by acting on the pituitary of the female partner to inhibit gonadotrophins which might be needed for ovarian development. However, the nature of the substance is not known nor is its site of action.

A second type of observation which suggests hormonal involvement in sexual differentiation in amphibia is derived from experiments in which larval anurans are treated with gondal sex hormones during a critical stage of development. In *Xenopus*, a species in which the female is the digametic sex, completely sex-reversed animals have been obtained by treatment with oestrogen. Thus genetic males (ZZ) are obtained which have the phenotype and functional characteristics of females (Burns, 1961; Witschi and Dale, 1962). If larva are treated with androgens during development, the result is that genetic females become pseudohermaphrodites which are phenotypically and behaviourally masculine, but are sterile (Witschi, 1965). In *Rana*, where the male is digametic, complete sex-reversal of genetic females has been obtained by treating the tadpoles with androgen (Burns, 1961).

Similar cases of complete sex-reversal have been reported in a few species of fishes following treatment with steroids soon after hatching. The species in which these sex-reversals have been obtained experimentally are not included among the many fishes in which true hermaphroditism is the rule. However, one such species, the rice-field eel (*Monopterus albus*), has been studied. The rice-field eel normally reproduces first as a female, then as a male—the fish is protogynous. A functional reversal of the gonadal type from ovary to testis has been obtained in this fish by treatment with pituitary gonadotrophins, suggesting that high levels of gonadotrophins may be 'male-determining' while low levels may be 'female-determining' (Tang *et al.*, 1974a). When female rice-field eels were treated with androgens no significant ovarian changes were noted (Tang *et al.*, 1974b). These observations suggest that sex-reversal may be triggered by the pituitary in the rice-field eel.

In birds there is some evidence that the ovary produces hormones which are responsible for feminization during early development. Thus, transplantation of ovarian tissue into male chicks led to feminization of the testes of the recipient. Similar results have been obtained when testicular and ovarian tissues are cultured together *in vitro*; the testis fails to affect the ovary, but the ovary feminizes the testis. Further evidence for the 'direction' of sexual differentiation by the ovary has been obtained in studies of the development of sex accessories and secondary sexual characteristics in the duck. Very young duck embryos were castrated by irradiating the germinal ridges. In such birds the syrinx always developed into the enlarged male type regardless of genetic sex. Similarly, the genital tubercle developed into a penis in all birds in which the X-ray-induced castration was complete. Confirmation of the effects of ovarian secretions on directing the development of the genital tubercle and the syrinx was obtained from studies performed *in vitro* where these embryonic tissues were cultured in the absence of gonadal tissue. If the tubercle and syrinx are removed before gonadal differentiation has occurred, they develop into the male type; if removed after gonadal differentiation has been established, these tissues show a developmental pattern appropriate to their genetic sex.

The eggs of Japanese quail have been treated with estradiol benzoate and TP. Both compounds tended to demasculinize males but failed to masculinize females or defeminize either sex. In these birds the male displays more 'bisexual' behaviour than the female; that is, males show both male and female copulatory patterns depending upon the hormonal milieu in adulthood, while females display little sexual behaviour of any sort when treated with androgen in adulthood. This is the reverse of the mammalian pattern where the female is more 'bisexual', and birds possess a ZZ-ZW chromosomal system (Adkins and Adler, 1972). Thus, evidence from amphibians, birds, and mammals suggests a possible correlation between the chromosomal sex-determining mechanism and the developmental effects of sex steroids. Steroids seem to direct differentiation more effectively in the direction of the heterozygous sex. However, the evidence supporting this conclusion is of a very preliminary nature; a concerted effort to investigate this topic might prove very worthwhile.

SUMMARY AND CONCLUSIONS

In mammals sexual differentiation of several physiological and behavioural systems is largely under hormonal control. Testicular hormone(s) secreted during early life imposes a 'masculine' pattern of development, whereas in the absence of steroid hormones or in the presence only of the hormones normally produced by the developing ovary development proceeds in the 'feminine' direction. Recent evidence suggests that the hypothalamic–pituitary–gonadal axis is functional at birth or very shortly thereafter in the rat. In the male rat pituitary gonadotrophins stimulate the production of the testicular androgen which is required for certain aspects of masculine differentiation.

It appears that circulating androgens can be aromatized to form oestrogens in the brain. Several lines of evidence suggest that aromatization is a necessary step in the masculinizing action of androgens. More information is required to determine whether conversion of androgens to oestrogens is a phenomenon which is important in all mammals and whether the conversion is important with respect to masculine development of a wide variety of sexually dimorphic parameters. Considerable further work will be required to determine how steroid hormones exert developmental effects at the cellular level.

REFERENCES

Adkins, E. K. and Adler, N. T. (1972) Hormonal control of behavior in the Japanese quail, *J. Comp. Physiol. Psychol.*, **81**, 27–36.

Anderson, C. O., Zarrow, M. X., and Denenberg, V. H. (1970) Maternal behavior in the rabbit: Effect of androgen treatment during gestation upon the next-building behavior of the mother and her offspring, *Horm. Behav.*, **1**, 337–45.

Arai, Y. and Gorski, R. A. (1968a) Protection against the neutral organizing effect of exogenous androgen in the neonatal female rat, *Endocrinology*, **82**, 1005–9.

Arai, Y. and Gorski, R. A. (1968b) Critical exposure time for androgenization of the developing hypothalamus in the female rat, *Endocrinology*, **82**, 1010–4.

Arai, Y. and Gorski, R. A. (1968c) Critical exposure time for androgenization of the rat hypothalamus determined by antiandrogen injection, *Proc. Soc. Exp. Biol. Med.*, **127**, 590–3.

Arai, Y. and Serisawa, K. (1973) Effect of gonadotropins on neonatal testicular activity and sexual differentiation of the brain in the rat, *Proc. Soc. Exp. Biol. Med.* **143**, 656–60.

Atz, J. W. 1964. Intersexually in fishes. In: *Intersexuality in Vertebrates Including Man*, C. N. Armstrong and A. J. Marshall (eds.), Academic Press, New York, pp. 145–232.

Bardin, C. W., Bullock, L. P., Sherins, R. J., Mowszcowicz, I., and Blackburn, W. R. (1973) Androgen metabolism an mechanism of action in male pseudohermaphroditism: A study of testicular feminization, *Rec. Prog. Horm. Res.*, **29**, 65–109.

Barkley, M. S. (1974) Testosterone and the ontogeny of sexually dimorphic aggression in the mouse, *Ph.D. Thesis*, University of Connecticut.

Barraclough, C. A. and Gorski, R. A. (1962) Studies on mating behaviour in the androgen-sterilized female rat in relation to the hypothalamic regulation of sexual behavior, *J. Endocrinol.*, **25**, 175–82.

Barraclough, C. A. and Leathem, J. H. (1954) Infertility induced in mice by a single injection of testosterone propionate, *Proc. Soc. Exp. Biol. Med.*, **85**, 673–4.

Beach, F. A. (1968) Factors involved in the control of mounting behavior by female mammals. In: *Perspectives in Reproduction and Sexual Behavior*, M. Diamond (ed.), Indiana University Press, Bloomington, pp. 83–131.

Beach, F. A. (1970) Hormonal effects on socio-sexual behavior in dogs. In: *Mammalian Reproduction*, M. Gibran and E. J. Plotz (eds.), Springer-Verlag, New York.

Beach, F. A., Noble, R. G., and Orndoff, R. K. (1969) Effects of perinatal androgen treatment on responses of male rats to gonadal hormones in adulthood, *J. Comp. Physiol. Psychol.*, **68**, 490–7.

Berg, I. A. (1944) Development of behavior: The micturition pattern in the dog, *J. Exp. Psychol.*, **34**, 343–68.

Bridges, R. S., Zarrow, M. X., and Denenberg, V. H. (1973) The role of neonatal androgen in the expression of hormonally induced maternal responsiveness in the adult rat, *Horm. Behav.*, **4**, 315–22.

Bronson, F. H. and Desjardins, C. (1969) Aggressive behavior and seminal vesicle function in mice: Differential sensitivity to androgen given neonatally, *Endocrinology*, **85**, 971–4.

Bronson, F. H. and Desjardins, C. (1970) Neonatal androgen administration and adult aggressiveness in female mice, *Gen. Comp. Endocrinol.*, **15**, 320–5.

Brown-Grant, K., Munck, A., Naftolin, F., and Sherwood, M. R. (1971) The effects of administration of testosterone propionate alone or with a phenobarbitone and of testosterone metabolites to neonatal female rats, *Horm. Behav.*, **2**, 173–82.

Burns, R. K. (1961) Role of hormones in the differentiation of sex. In: *Sex and Internal Secretions*, Vol. I, W. C. Young (ed.), Williams and Wilkins Co., Baltimore, pp. 76–158.

Clemens, J. A. and Smalstig, E. B. (1975) Differential effect of preoptic area lesions and suprachiasmatic nuclei lesions on reproductive function in the rat. Program of the 57th Annual Meeting of the Endocrine Society, New York, NY, June 18–20, p. 178.

Coniglio, L. P., Paup, D. C., and Clemens, L. G. (1973) Hormonal factors controlling the development of sexual behavior in the male golden hamster, *Physiol. Behav.*, **10**, 1087–94.

Conner, R. L. (1972) Hormones, biogenic amines, and aggression. In: *Hormones and Behaviour*, S. Levine (ed.), Academic Press, New York, pp. 209–33.

Eaton, G. (1970) Effect of a single prepubertal injection of testosterone propionate on adult bisexual behavior of male hamsters castrated at birth, *Endocrinology*, **87**, 934–40.

Edwards, D. A. (1970) Post-natal androgenization and adult aggressive behavior in female mice, *Physiol. Behav.*, **5**, 465–7.

Edwards, D. A. (1971) Neonatal administration of androstenedione, testosterone or testosterone propionate: Effects on ovulation, sexual receptivity and aggressive behavior in female mice, *Physiol. Behav.*, **6**, 223–8.

Edwards, D. A. and Thompson, M. L. (1970) Neonatal androgenization and estrogenization and the hormonal induction of sexual receptivity in rats, *Physiol. Behav.*, **5**, 1115–9.

Everett, J. W. (1964) Central neural control of reproductive functions of the adenohypophyses, *Physiol. Rev.*, **44**, 373–431.

Faiman, C. and Winter, J. S. D. (1971) Sex differences in gonadotrophin concentrations in infancy, *Nature*, **232**, 130–1.

Field, P. M. and Raisam, G. (1974) Structural and functional investigations of a sexually dimorphic part of the rat preoptic area. In: *Recent Studies of Hypothalamic Function*, Int. Symp. Calgary, Karger, Basel, pp. 17–25.

Florsheim, W. H. and Rudko, P. (1968) The development of the portal system in the rat, *Neuroendocrinology*, **3**, 89–98.

Fuller, G. B., Zarrow, M. X., Anderson, C. O., and Denenberg, V. H. (1970) Testosterone propionate during gestation in the rabbits: Effect on subsequent maternal behavior, *J. Reprod. Fert.*, **23**, 285–90.

Goldman, B. D. and Mahesh, V. B. (1970) Induction of infertility in male rats by treatment with gonadotropin antiserum during neonatal life, *Biol. Reprod.*, **2**, 444–51.

Goldman, B. D. and Gorski, R. A. (1971) Effects of gonadal steroids on the secretion of LH and FSH in neonatal rats, *Endocrinology*, **89**, 112–5.

Goldman, B. D., Grazia, Y. R., Kamberi, I. A., and Porter, J. C. (1971) Serum gonadotropin concentrations in intact and castrated neonatal rats, *Endocrinology*, **88**, 771–6.

Goldman, B. D., Quadagno, D. M., Shryne, J., and Gorski, R. A. (1972) Modification of phallus development and sexual behavior in rats treated with gonadotropin antiserum neonatally, *Endocrinology*, **90**, 1025–31.

Goy, R. W. (1970) Experimental control of psychosexuality. In: *A Discussion of the Determination of sex*, G. W. Harris and R. G. Edwards (eds.), London, *Phil. Trans. Roy. Soc. B*, **259**, 149–62.

Goy, R. W. and Goldfoot, D. A. (1973). Hormonal influences on sexually dimorphic behavior. In: *Handbook of Physiology*, Section 7, Volume II, Chap. 9, American Physiological Society, Washington, D. C.

Harris, G. W. (1964) Sex hormones, brain development and brain function, *Endocrinology*, **75**, 627–48.

Harris, G. W. and Jacobson, D. (1952) Functional grafts of the anterior pituitary gland, *Proc. Roy. Soc. B*, **139**, 263–76.

Jost, A. (1953) Problems of fetal endocrinology: The gonadal and hypophyseal hormones, *Rec. Prog. Horm. Res.*, **8**, 379–418.

Karsch, F. J., Dierschke, D. J., and Knobil, E. (1973) Sexual differentiation of pituitary function: Apparent difference between primates and rodents, *Science*, **179**, 484–6.

Kolter, P. C. (1963) A hermaphroditic bullfrog, *Turtox News*, **41**, 290–3.

Komisaruk, B. R., Adler, N. T., and Hutchison, J. (1972) Genital sensory field: Enlargement by estrogen treatment in female rats, *Science*, **178**, 1295–8.

Krey, L. C., Butler, W. R., and Knobil, E. (1975) Surgical disconnection of the medial basal hypothalmus and pituitary function in the rhesus monkey. I. Gonadotropin secretion, *Endocrinology*, **96**, 1073–87.

Luttge, W. G. and Whalen, R. E. (1970) Dihydrotestosterone, androstenedione, testosterone: Comparative effectiveness in masculinizing and defeminizing reproductive systems in male and female rats, *Horm. Behav.*, **1**, 265–81.

Martins, T. and Valle, J. R. (1948) Hormonal regulation of the micturition behavior of the dog, *J. Comp. Physiol., Psychol.*, **41**, 301–11.

McCullogh, J., Quadagno, D. M., and Goldman, B. D. (1974) Neonatal gonadal hormones: effect on maternal and sexual behavior in the male rat. *Physiol. Behav.*, **12**, 183–8.

Naftolin, F., Ryan, K. J., and Petro, Z. (1971) Aromatization of androstenedione by the diencephalon, *J. Clin. Endocrinol.*, **33**, 68–70.

Naftolin, F., Ryan, K. J., and Petro, Z. (1974) Aromitization of androstenedione by the anterior hypothalamus of adult male and female rats, *Endocrinology*, **90**, 295–8.

Niemi, M. and Ikonen, M. (1963) Histochemistry of the Leydig cells in the postnatal prepubertal testes of the rat, *Endocrinology*, **72**, 443–8.

Ojeda, S. R. and Ramirez, V. D. (1972) Plasma level of LH and FSH in maturing rats: Response to hemigonadectomy, *Endocrinology*, **90**, 446–72.

Pfaff, D. W. and Zigmond, R. E. (1971) Neontal androgen effects on sexual and non-sexual behavior of adult rats tested under various hormone regimens, *Neuroendocrinology*, **7**, 129–45.

Pfieffer, C. A. (1936) Sexual differences of the hypophyses and their determination by the gonads, *Am. J. Anat.*, **58**, 195–226.

Phoenix, C. H., Goy, R. W., Gerall, A. A., and Young, W. C. (1959) Organizing action of prenatally administered testosterone propionate on the tissues mediating mating behaviour in the female guinea pig, *Endocrinology*, **65**, 369–82.

Resko, J. S., Feder, H. H., and Goy, R. W. (1968) Androgen concentrations in plasma and testis and developing rats, *J. Endocrinol.*, **40**, 485–91.

Root, A. W., Shapiro, B. H., Duckett, G. E., and Goldman, A. S. (1975) Effect of synthetic luteinizing hormone-releasing hormone in newborn rats, *Proc. Soc. Exp. Biol. Med.*, **148**, 631–3.

Rose, R., Holaday, J., and Bernstein, J. (1971) *Nature* (London) **231**, 336.

Selmanoff, M. F. (1974) Genetic variation and the role of testosterone in the development and adult expression of aggression in inbred mice, *Ph.D. Thesis*, University of Connecticut.

Swanson, H. H. (1966) Modification of the reproductive tracts of hamsters of both sexes by neonatal administration of androgen or oestrogen, *J. Endocrinol*, **36**, 327–8.

Swanson, H. H. (1970) Effects of castration at birth in hamsters of both sexes on luteinization of ovarian implants, oestrous cycles, and sexual behaviour, *J. Reprod. Fert.*, **21**, 183–6.

Taber, E. (1964) Intersexuality in birds. In: *Intersexuality in Vertebrates Including Man*, C. N. Armstrong and A. J. Marshall (eds.), Academic Press, N. Y., p. 285.

Tang, F., Chan, S. T. H., and Lofts, B. (1974a) Effect of steroid hormones on the process of sex-reversal in the rice-field eel, *Monopterus albus* (Zuiew), *Gen. Comp. Endocrinol.*, **24**, 227–41.

Tang, F., Chan, S. T. H., and Lofts, B. (1974b) Effect of mammalian luteinizing hormone on the natural sex-reversal of the rice-field eel, *Monopterus albus* (Zuiew) *Gen. Comp. Endocrinol.*, **24**, 242–8.

Tiefer, L. and Johnson, W. A. (1971) Female sexual behavior in male golden hamsters, *J. Endocrinol.*, **51**, 615–20.

Tiefer, L. and Johnson, W. (1975) Neonatal androstenedione and adult sexual behavior in golden hamster, *J. Comp. Physiol. Psychol.*, **88**, 239–47.

Warren, D. W., Haltmeyer, G. C., and Eik-Nes, K. B. (1975) The effect of gonadotrophins on the fetal and neonatal rat testis. *Endocrinology*, **96**, 1226–9.

Weisz, J. and Gunsalus, P. (1973) Estrogen levels in immature female rats: True or spurious—ovarian or adrenal? *Endocrinology*, **93**, 1057–65.

Whitsett, J. M. and J. G. Vandenbergh (1975) Influence of testosterone propionate administered neonatally on puberty and bisexual behavior in female hamsters, *J. Comp. Physiol. Psychol.*, **88**, 248–55.

Witschi, E. (1965) Hormones and embryonic induction, *Arch. Anat. Microscop. Morphol. Exp.*, **54**, 601–11.

Witschi, E. and Dale, E. (1962) Steroid hormones at early developmental stages of vertebrates, *Gen. Comp. Endocrinol.*, (Suppl) **1**, 356–61.

CHAPTER 6

Gonadal Steroid–Brain Interactions in Sexual Differentiation

LINDA PLAPINGER
BRUCE S. MCEWEN

INTRODUCTION

Cellular Mechanisms of Hormone Action

Beginning with observations on the inverterbrate steroid hormone ecdysone (Clever and Karlson, 1960), it has become increasingly evident that steroid hormones exert at least some of their effects at the level of gene expression (O'Malley and Means, 1974). The pioneering studies of Jensen and Jacobson (1962) established the concept for oestrogens that target tissues such as the uterus accumulate and retain a radioactively labelled form of the hormone by a limited-capacity, selective, binding mechanism, and subsequent studies have amply documented this for other steroid hormones and other target tissues (King and Mainwaring, 1974).

The *limited capacity binding* of steroid hormones by a target tissue is due to the presence of receptor sites in the cytoplasm and cell nuclei of the target cells. *Retention* is a term which will be used to refer to binding of a hormone by these receptors. *Uptake* refers only to the entry of a hormone into a tissue, and implies nothing about binding. A pattern common to all target tissues is the entry of the steroid hormone into the cell, attachment to a soluble and presumably cytoplasmic receptor, and translocation to the cell nucleus, where it resides for a period of time (several hours) in association with the chromatin (see Fig. 1). During this time the hormone receptor complex initiates changes in gene transcription which in turn lead to changes in protein formation and thereby alter cell structure and function. It should be noted that thyroid hormone may well have a similar mode of interaction with the cell nucleus, though the role for cytoplasmic receptors in the interaction of this hormone with the nucleus is less certain (Oppenheimer *et al.*, 1974). Other hormones such as epinephrine, adrenocorticotrophic hormone (ACTH), glucagon, and possibly

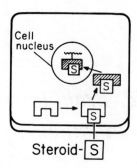

Fig. 1. Diagrammatic representation of a mechanism of
steroid hormone action. The steroid molecule enters the
target cell and binds to a soluble protein receptor. The
steroid-receptor complex is then translocated to the cell
nucleus, and forms an association with chromatin

hypothalamic releasing factors, appear to act on cell surface receptors and
activate formation of cyclic adenosine-3-5-phosphate (cyclic AMP) (Robison
et al., 1971).

With respect to steroid hormones it is clear that some cells of the mature
brain and pituitary contain for oestradiol and for glucocorticoids a receptor
mechanism of the type described above. The situation for androgens and
progestins is confounded by factors which will be discussed below.

Properties and Topography of Steroid Receptors in Mature CNS and Pituitary

Oestrogens

Receptor sites for oestradiol are found in pineal (Marks *et al.*, 1972); in
anterior pituitary (Notides, 1970); and in a number of brain regions of rats:
predominantly in basomedial hypothalamus, medial preoptic area, and corticomedial amygdala; to a lesser extent in midbrain central grey, ventral hippocampus (McEwen *et al.*, 1972a; Pfaff and Keiner, 1973; Ginsburg *et al.*, 1974;
McEwen *et al.*, 1975a); and in spinal cord (Keefer *et al.*, 1973). Autoradiography
reveals neurons to be labelled in these CNS regions (Anderson and Greenwald,
1969; Attramadal, 1970; Stumpf, 1970; Pfaff and Keiner, 1973; Keefer *et al.*,
1973). The same autoradiographic studies also reveal the detailed topography
of these 'oestrophilic neurons'. Within the anterior pituitary, 60–80% of the
cells are labelled after a ^{3}H-oestradiol injection (Stumpf, 1968). The topography of 'oestrophilic neurons' within CNS, described above for the rat, is
similar to that observed in brains from other vertebrates, e.g., amphibia,
birds, and mammals including primates (Morrell *et al.*, 1975).

Soluble oestrogen receptors in brain and pituitary are similar to those found in uterus, having a sedimentation coefficient in sucrose density gradients of $\approx$ 8S at low ionic strength, a high affinity (Kd $\approx 10^{-10}$M) for oestradiol-17β, and a preference for active oestrogens such as oestradiol-17β and diethylstilboestrol (Notides, 1970; Eisenfeld, 1970; Kato et al., 1970; Mowles et al., 1971; Plapinger and McEwen, 1973; Ginsburg et al., 1974). Cell nuclear retention of labelled ^{3}H-oestradiol in vivo is observed in pituitary and in brain regions, paralleling the autoradiographic distribution of 'oestrophilic neurons' (McEwen et al., 1975a). The cell nuclear receptor is reported to have a sedimentation coefficient of 5–7S (Mowles et al., 1971; Vértes and King, 1971) while the uterine nuclear receptor is generally believed to sediment at $\approx$ 5S (Jensen and deSombre, 1973).

Androgens

Uptake of labelled testosterone by pituitary and brain tissue of the rat is less intense than that of labelled oestradiol, but in general the same brain regions are most heavily labelled by the two hormones (Zigmond, 1975). Autoradiographic studies reveal that $\approx$ 15% of rat pituitary cells, mostly basophils, are labelled after a ^{3}H-testosterone injection (Sar and Stumpf, 1973b), while as noted above 60–80% of the cells are labelled after ^{3}H-oestradiol. In the medial preoptic area of the rat a majority of the cells are labelled by both ^{3}H-testosterone and ^{3}H-oestradiol (Stumpf, 1970; Sar and Stumpf, 1973a). This clearly indicates overlap of cells binding the two labels, but may well be explained by the known conversion of ^{3}H-testosterone to ^{3}H-oestradiol, referred to as aromatization (Fig. 2).

Oestrogen formation occurs predominantly in limbic structures (and not in pituitary) of foetal as well as neonatal and adult members of a variety of species (Ryan et al., 1972; Reddy et al., 1973; Weisz and Gibbs, 1974; Lieberburg and McEwen, 1975a, 1975b). In fact, the conversion of testosterone to either oestradiol or 5α reduced metabolites complicates the interpretation of any labelling experiment with ^{3}H-testosterone. With respect to oestradiol as a metabolite, male rat brains are known to contain oestrogen receptors with a topography closely resembling that in female rat brains (Maurer and Wooley, 1974), and ^{3}H-oestradiol has been recovered from brain cell nuclei after in vivo ^{3}H-testosterone administration to adult males (Lieberburg and McEwen, 1975b). With respect to 5α-dihydrotestosterone (DHT) (Fig. 2) as a metabolite, several laboratories have presented evidence for soluble androgen binding macromolecules in brain and pituitary (Ginsburg et al. 1971; Jouan et al., 1973; Kato and Onouchi, 1973; Monbon et al., 1973; Naess et al., 1975). DHT formation occurs predominantly in mes- and diencephalon and in pituitary of the rat (Massa et al., 1972; Denef et al., 1973), and formation in the latter structure is under feedback control by gonadal secretion (Denef et al., 1973; Kniewald and Milkovíc, 1973; Thien et al., 1974).

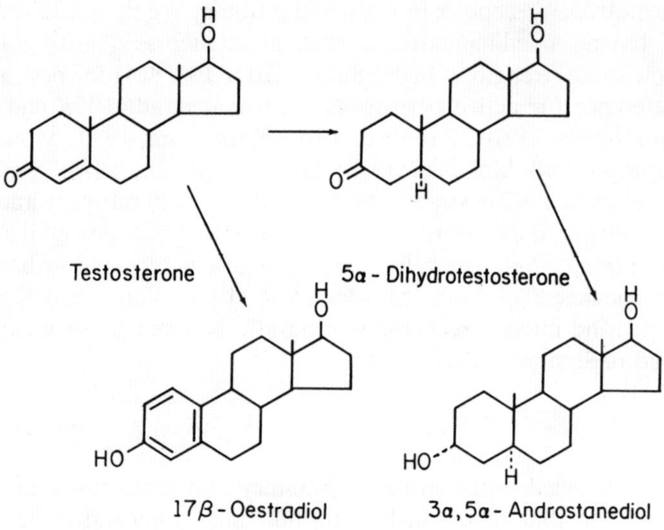

Fig. 2. Some pathways of androgen metabolism. One pathway involves the conversion of testosterone to oestradiol, referred to as aromatization

Glucocorticoids

In sharp contrast to oestrogens, glucocorticoids such as corticosterone and cortisol do not concentrate in pituitary or hypophysiotrophic region but rather in cell nuclei of hippocampus, septum, and amygdala of adrenalectomized animals (McEwen *et al.*, 1972a; Knizley, 1972; Stumpf, 1972; Warembourg, 1974). This pattern has been observed in the Pekin duck (Rhees *et al.*, 1972), the rat (Gerlach and McEwen, 1972), the guinea pig (Warembourg, 1974) and the rhesus monkey (Gerlach *et al.*, 1976). Autoradiography indicates that neurons are the predominant cellular sites of ³H-corticosterone accumulation (Gerlach and McEwen, 1972) but glial cells are also known to respond to glucocorticoids and appear to have some glucocorticoid receptors (deVellis *et al.*, 1971, 1974). The CNS glucocorticoid receptors have been discussed previously with respect to a variety of neural, behavioural, and neuroendocrine effects (McEwen, 1974).

Progestins

Progesterone, like testosterone, is likely to undergo one of a number of metabolic transformations. The conversion to 5α-dihydroprogesterone (DHP) occurs in brain and pituitary tissue and appears to be carried out by the same enzyme responsible for the 5α reduction of testosterone (Massa and Martini, 1971/2; Karavolas and Herf, 1971; Robinson and Karavolas, 1973). Progesterone competition for the 5α-reductase may explain some of the antiand-rogenicity of this steroid (Massa and Martini, 1971/2).

Another progesterone metabolite, 20α-hydroxyprogesterone, is produced by ovarian tissue. The study of progesterone–brain interactions is thus, like that of testosterone, complicated by the question of metabolites which may mediate the hormonal effects and is additionally complicated at the level of the receptor sites by the difficulty in demonstrating which sites are specific for progesterone.

Studies of the fate of systemically injected ^{3}H-progesterone and ^{3}H 20α-hydroxyprogesterone have shown that highest uptake occurs in the midbrain region, somewhat lower uptake in hypothalamus, and still lower uptake in cerebral cortex and hippocampus of rat and guinea-pig brains (Wade and Feder, 1972; Wade et al., 1973). Midbrain and hypothalamus in the guinea pig are both sites where progesterone implants exert inhibitory and excitatory effects, respectively, on mating resembling physiological effects of the hormone given systemically. This pattern of uptake is, however, similar to that observed for ^{3}H-corticosterone and ^{3}H-oestradiol in guinea-pig brains when binding sites for those hormones are saturated either by endogenous or exogenous hormones. These facts have suggested that an interaction of the steroid with lipids in the brain, and not with specific receptors, determines the pattern of uptake. Attempts to saturate and thereby reveal limited-capacity binding sites for ^{3}H-progesterone using unlabelled progesterone have proven uniformly unsuccessful and have tended to suggest that specific progesterone receptor sites either may not exist at all or be so few in number as to escape detection. There is, however, evidence which tends to support the idea of progesterone receptor sites in brain and pituitary. First, Sar and Stumpf have reported autoradiographic localization of binding of radioactivity injected as ^{3}H-progesterone in neurons of the basomedial hypothalamus of the spayed, oestrogen-primed guinea pig (Sar and Stumpf, 1973c). Unlabelled progesterone abolishes this uptake, while unlabelled cortisol is without effect. According to these authors, oestrogen priming is required for ^{3}H-progesterone accumulation. Similar results have been reported for cytosol binding of ^{3}H-progesterone in pituitary and median eminence region of spayed, oestrogen-primed rats: a progesterone-saturable binding component was detected which could not be saturated by unlabelled corticosterone (Seiki and Hattori, 1973). Second, adrenalectomy apparently produces an increase in tissue uptake of ^{3}H-progesterone in brain (Whalen and Gorzalka, 1974). Not only does adrenalectomy remove one source of endogenous progesterone, it also unmasks glucocorticoid-binding sites in the brain to which progesterone is able to bind (Grosser et al., 1973). One peculiarity about the interaction of progesterone with glucocorticoid receptors is that the progesterone is not extensively translocated to the cell nuclei, as is the case for corticosteroids. Progesterone can in fact block nuclear transloca-tion of ^{3}H-corticosterone, presumably by occupying soluble receptor sites (McEwen and Wallach, 1973). Progesterone is therefore an antiglucocorticoid and has been shown to block a number of glucocorticoid effects on thymus, chick neural retina, and hepatoma tissue culture cells (see McEwen, 1974). Thus in principle progesterone might exert some neural effects on reproductive function via an antiglucocorticoid action. A major argument against this hypothesis is that glucocorticoids are normally present in large excess over circulating progesterone, thus reducing the efficacy of progesterone as a competitive inhibitor.

Receptor Function in Activational Effects

The implied action of cell nuclear steroid hormone receptors is the regulation of genomic activity, especially in the production of RNA molecules along a DNA template. Secondary changes in cellular protein synthesis, directed by the altered population of RNA's, would be responsible for hormone effects on cellular structure and function (O'Malley and Means, 1974). While it is outside the scope of this chapter to review such effects of steroid hormones (see Luine and McEwen, 1976 for further review), it is important in relating this mode of hormone action to behaviour and neuroendocrine function to summarize briefly evidence for genomic involvement in steroid hormone action on the brain and pituitary. To do so, we will focus on oestrogen effects on female sexual behaviour and gonadotrophin secretion in the rat.

A fundamental clue is timing. Peak oestradiol levels in early pro-oestrus precede by some hours both the LH surge and the onset of behavioural oestrus. The time lag is also seen in experiments on ovariectomized rats showing lag periods of 20 or 30 h for the induction by oestrogen of lordosis responding (Green et al., 1970) and an LH surge (Jackson, 1972), respectively. The duration of ^{3}H-oestradiol on brain and pituitary cell nuclear receptor sites following a single injection appears to be less than 12 h (McEwen et al., 1975a), and the intervening time up to 20 or 30 h would seem to be due to a sequence of hormone-initiated metabolic events which includes RNA and protein synthesis, as will now be indicated.

Another important piece of evidence for genomic involvement is the effectiveness of an RNA synthesis inhibitor, Actinomycin D, in preventing oestrogen induction of lordosis responding (Terkel et al., 1973; Whalen et al., 1974) or the LH surge (Jackson, 1972). Actinomycin D must be given before oestradiol to block the LH surge (Jackson, 1972) and is effective 6–12 h after oestradiol (but not later) in blocking behavioural oestrus (Terkel et al., 1973; Whalen et al., 1974).

A third piece of evidence relating directly to the cell nuclear oestrogen receptor sites is the effectiveness of antioestrogenic compounds such as clomiphene, MER-25, and CI 628 to prevent both the LH surge (Shirley et al., 1968; Labhsetwar, 1970) and behavioural oestrus (Meyerson and Lindström, 1968, Arai and Gorski, 1968a; Komisaruk and Beyer, 1972; Whalen and Gorzalka, 1973; Södersten, 1974). These antioestrogens are known to accumulate selectively and for long periods of time in target cell nuclei and in so doing make the receptor system unavailable to the natural oestrogen (Clark *et al.*, 1974). As in the case of Actinomycin D, these antioestrogens must be given before or shortly after oestrogen treatment to be effective on behaviour (Meyerson and Lindström, 1968; Arai and Gorski, 1968a; Komisaruk and Beyer, 1972; Whalen and Gorzalka, 1973; Södersten, 1974) or must be given on dioestrus day 2 of the normal cycling female to block the LH surge (Shirley *et al.*, 1968; Labhsetwar, 1970).

Organizational Effects of Gonadal Steroids

In addition to the reversible activational effects of gonadal steroids in adult animals, these same steroids are capable of permanently altering reproductive tract and neural development when exposed to these tissues during a critical period of foetal or early neonatal life (Burns, 1961; Jost, 1970; Goy, 1970a). According to this generally accepted scheme, the male reproductive tract and brain differentiate under the influence of androgen secreted prenatally (e.g., primates, guinea pig) or neonatally (e.g., rat and hamster) while the female pattern appears in the absence of testicular secretion. These long-lasting effects clearly must involve the target cell genome as a direct or indirect mediator, and a fundamental question which must be answered is whether receptor sites for these developmental effects resemble those for the activational effects of the same hormone.

In the urogenital tract, DHT promotes male differentiation of the urogenital simus (anlage of the prostate) and the urogenital tubercle (analage of the external genitalia) and 5α reductase is present prior to the onset of testosterone synthesis by the gonads (see Wilson, 1973; Schultz and Wilson, 1974). In the Wolffian duct (anlage of the epididimis, vas deferens, and seminal vesicle) the appearance of DHT formation follows the irreversible differentiation of this tissue, and thus testosterone itself (which is required for this differentiation to occur) or some other metabolite than DHT is responsible for initiating irreversible differentiation of this embryonic tissue (Wilson, 1973).

Autoradiographic studies have revealed the accumulation of radioactivity injected as ³H-testosterone in neurons of preoptic area, hypothalamus, and amygdala of neonatal male and female rat brains and competition for this uptake by unlabelled oestradiol as well as by testosterone, but not by unlabelled DHT (Sheridan *et al.*, 1974b). A virtually identical pattern of neural uptake has been reported for ³H-oestradiol in neonatal brains and has been shown to be reduced by unlabelled testosterone and oestradiol (Sheridan *et al.*, 1974a). A recent study has shown that as much as 50% of cell nuclear bound radioactivity 2 h after an injection of ³H-testosterone into five-day-old male or female rats is actually ³H-oestradiol (Lieberburg and McEwen, 1975a). It thus appears that conversion of testosterone to oestradiol (aromatization) may play an important role in the fate of testosterone in the neonatal brain and conceivably in the developmental effects of testosterone as well. It is the purpose of the following discussion to review the evidence for the participation of aromatization in the sexual differentiation of the brain. Three experimental approaches will be summarized. First, we will consider the effects of exogenous testosterone, administered to females during the critical period, on some of the adult sexually dimorphic characteristics. Where appropriate information is available, we will compare these effects of testosterone administration with those resulting from early exposure to exogenous oestrogens or other metabolites of testosterone. Of particular importance is the degree to which the effects of these steroids approximate the sexual differentiation of the normal male. Second, we will review the effects of various inhibitors of oestrogen and androgen action, administered during the critical period in conjunction with exogenous testosterone. Third, biochemical and anatomical aspects of sexual differentiation will be described, namely, the studies of aromatization in foetal or neonatal brain tissue and measurements of gonadal steroid (especially oestrogen) receptors. Finally, we will summarize evidence that a protective mechanism exists to prevent endogenous foetal or neonatal oestrogens from having deleterious effects upon the brain and reproductive tract.

SEXUAL DIFFERENTIATION OF GONADOTROPHIN SECRETION

Androgen Effects

Anovulatory Sterility

Long-term treatment of adult female rats with testosterone propionate (TP) interrupted cyclic processes of the normal female reproductive axis, and thereby caused protracted periods of infertility in those animals. After cessation of treatment, however, there was complete restoration of normal reproductive functions (Mazer and Mazer, 1939; Huffman, 1941). These reversible effects of exogenous androgen on the differentiated female reproductive axis are in striking contrast with effects observed in adult female rats which had received prolonged TP treatment starting soon after birth. Such prepuberally androgenized females were sterile as adults, long after the exogenous hormone had been withdrawn (Wilson *et al.*, 1940; Wilson *et al.*, 1941; Bradbury, 1941). Furthermore, when only single systemic injections of TP were administered to female rats (Greene and Burrill, 1941; Barraclough, 1961) or mice (Barraclough and Leatham, 1954; Barraclough, 1955) during the first five postnatal days, the great majority of treated animals were sterile in adulthood. These early studies thus demonstrated the unique effects of testosterone on the undifferentiated mammalian female reproductive axis; effects which cause modifications of subsequent developmental processes, resulting in a permanently sterile animal. Such actions of a hormone are known as 'organizational' actions. The single-injection type of experimental design made it possible to delineate precisely the critical period of sensitivity to androgen imprinting, and provided the model for numerous related subsequent experiments.

Neonatally induced sterility is a result of failure to ovulate. While the ovaries of such neonatally androgenized females are not as sensitive to exogenous luteinizing hormone (LH) as are normal ovaries (Mennin et al., 1974), ovarian insensitivity cannot be considered to represent the major deficit responsible for the anovulatory state, since ovulation did occur in these ovaries when they were transplanted into normal ovariectomized female hosts (Bradbury, 1941; Gorski and Wagner, 1965; Harris and Levine, 1965). Similarly, pituitaries of neonatally androgenized sterile females, transplanted into the emptied sella turcicas of normal female rats, were able to support normal reproductive function in some of the recipients (Segal and Johnson, 1959). More recently, the sexual neutrality, with regard to capacity for LH secretion, of pituitaries from androgenized females has been confirmed in experiments comparing responsiveness to synthetic luteinizing hormone releasing hormone (LRH) in pituitaries from androgenized and normal female rats (Mennin et al., 1974). The primary defect, then, in this type of anovulatory sterility seems to reside in neural mechanisms regulating gonadotrophin secretion.

Results of early studies in which histological characteristics of ovaries, uteri, and vaginas of androgenized females were investigated, and in which the occurrence of ovulation was utilized as the parameter in assessing the effects of various hormonal and neurophysiological manipulations, suggested that in the neonatally androgenized female the pituitary secretes both follide stimulating hormone (FSH) and LH at fairly constant and relatively low rates, but does not have the cyclic neural stimulus required for the normal preovulatory surge of LH secretion. Later work, which directly measured concentrations of gonadotrophins and releasing hormones in the intact and experimentally manipulated androgenized female, tended to confirm the original predictions. Both types of experiments have almost exclusively utilized the rat, although the phenomenon of permanent anovulatory sterility induced by pre- or neonatal exposure to androgens has also been observed in the hamster (Swanson, 1966), the guinea pig (Brown-Grant and Sherwood, 1971), the mouse (Barraclough and Leatham, 1954, Barraclough, 1955), but not in the rhesus monkey (Goy, 1970b, Treloar et al., 1972).

The typical ovary of an adult rat rendered permanently anovulatory by neonatal androgen administration is significantly smaller than ovaries from normal female rats. Histological examination has revealed that it contains follicles in all stages of maturation, including many large vesicular follicles, and hypertrophied interstitial tissue, but no corpora lutea. Uterine weights of these animals are lower than normal uterine weights, with few glandular elements. Vaginal smears persistently contain cornified epithelial cells (Barraclough, 1961; Barraclough and Gorski, 1961; Gorski and Barraclough, 1963; Harris and Levine, 1965; Mullins and Levine, 1968a). The existence of vesicular follicles and interstitial hypertrophy suggested that LH secretion must occur in the androgenized rat. In addition, the cornified vaginal epithelium reflects oestrogenic stimulation and therefore provided further, indirect, evidence for the continual presence of some level of circulating LH, while the relatively unstimulated uterus indicated that oestrogen concentration never reaches peak levels which exist in the normal female during pro-oestrus or that uterine tissue is subnormally sensitive to oestrogen action (Barraclough, 1961; Barraclough and Gorski, 1961; Gorski and Barraclough, 1963; Harris and Levine, 1965; van Rees and Gans, 1966).

Injection of 1.25 mg of TP into either two-day- or five-day-old female rats had identical sterilizing effects. When the androgen treatment was delayed until 20 days, no incidence of anovulatory sterility was observed. TP treatment on day 10 led to intermediate results: only 40% of ten treated animals exhibited the anovulatory syndrome (Barraclough, 1961). A comparison of the effects (observed at 100 days of age) of different doses of TP, each administered at day 5, revealed that 10 μg is the minimum dose which causes anovulatory sterility in the majority (71%) of treated animals. If the 10 μg dose was not administered until day 8, then the incidence of anovulatory sterility observed after 120 days was drastically reduced (one out of 14 animals) (Gorski, 1968). As little as 5 μg of TP was effective when the dose was divided into 5 one μg doses given on postnatal days 1–5 (McDonald and Doughty, 1974). In contrast, when the treatment was not initiated until postnatal day 15, even prolonged treatment with extremely large doses of TP (36mg, 3 times/week for 4 weeks) did not prevent the later occurrence of ovulation (Wilson et al., 1941).

These biological characteristics of the neonatally androgenized sterile female rat suggest a certain parallelism between this experimentally induced defect and the type of gonadotrophin regulating mechanism which differentiates in the normal male. It has of course been known for many years that pituitaries of normal intact or adult-gonadectomized male rats do not periodically release LH in amounts sufficient for induction of ovulation in ovarian grafts (Goodman, 1934; Pfeiffer, 1936; Gorski and Wagner, 1965; Harris and Levine, 1965). The exceptions to these findings was reported by Kempf (1950), who grafted ovaries intrasplenically into adult male rats, castrated the rats three days later, and subsequently observed many corpora lutea in the grafts. Since, under those conditions, the ovarian secretions directly entered the liver and were presumably destroyed before they reached the general circulation, gonadotropin secretion was apparently occurring with little or no negative feedback regulation by gonadal steroids. High levels of LH, typical for a castrated animal, were therefore circulating, and were responsible for the luteinization observed in the grafted tissues (Kempf, 1950). As in the case of the androgenized female, male pituitaries are capable of supporting ovulation in normal females (Harris and Jacobsohn, 1952). The concept of early determination, by products of the neonatal testis, of this masculine mode of gonadotrophin regulation is derived from the widely known early work of

Pfeiffer (1936). He found that neonatal castration altered differentiation of the reproductive axis in male rats to the extent that ovulation occurred in ovarian grafts when these animals were adults (Pfeiffer, 1936). These observations have subsequently been verified (Gorski and Wagner, 1965). The effectiveness of the 10 μg dose of TP in females encourages one to think in terms of the physiological relevance of the neonatally androgenized female. And, at least in terms of the anovulatory state, a single injection of 10 μg of TP seems to mimic the effects of implanting littermate testes into neonatal females (Pfeiffer, 1936; Gorski and Wagner, 1965). In addition, the critical neonatal period in which male differentiation can be modified by castration is roughly the same as the period in which the female brain is sensitive to exogenous testosterone action (Gorski and Wagner, 1965). Finally, the histological appearance of ovarian grafts placed into neonatally androgenized females resembles that of grafts in adult-gonadectomized males (Gorski and Wagner, 1965).

Gonadotrophin and Steroid Levels in the Androgen-sterilized Female

Whether measured by bioassay (Matsuyama *et al.*, 1966) or radioimmunoassay (Brown-Grant *et al.*, 1971, Naftolin *et al.*, 1972; Kawakami and Terasawa, 1972; Mallampati and Johnson, 1973), pituitary concentrations of LH in intact neonatally androgenized female rats were found to be lower than peak concentrations in normal females during pro-oestrus, and similar to those of normal females during oestrus (Matsuyama *et al.*, 1966; Naftolin *et al.*, 1972; Kawakami and Terasawa, 1972), but lower than concentrations in the normal male (Mallampati and Johnson, 1973). Although Barraclough and Haller (1970) observed high concentrations of plasma LH in intact, neonatally androgenized female rats, subsequent investigations indicated that circulating levels of LH in these animals are approximately equal to basal (non-surge) levels in normal intact females (Brown-Grant *et al.*, 1971; Naftolin *et al.*, 1972; Kawakami and Terasawa, 1972), and to plasma LH concentrations in normal intact males (Naftolin *et al.*, 1972; Mallampati and Johnson, 1973). As predicted by earlier investigations, no evidence has been reported for cyclic changes in pituitary or serum levels of LH in the neonatally androgenized female rat, and to that extent, the patterns of LH secretion in the normal male and androgenized female are similar.

Another parameter which shows a difference between the androgenized female and the normal male is the concentrations of FSH, in both pituitary and plasma. This was always found to be markedly higher in intact males than in intact neonatally androgenized or normal females, as determined by bioassay (Johnson, 1972) and radioimmunoassay (Johnson, 1971; Mallampati and Johnson, 1973). However, adult circulating levels of FSH are not lower in neonatally castrated than in adult castrated males. This case of sexual dimorphism is not therefore a function of neonatal testicular secretions, but of other unknown factors (Taleisnik *et al.*, 1970; Johnson, 1972). Considered in that light, it is not surprising that neonatal androgenization does not 'masculinize' the female with respect to FSH secretion.

Discrepant results have been reported concerning circulating concentrations of oestradiol in the neonatally androgenized female rat. Naftolin *et al.* (1972), using a competitive protein binding assay, found adult plasma oestradiol levels in females treated with 1.25 mg of TP on postnatal day 5 to be lower than normal female pro-oestrous values. Cheng and Johnson (1973/4) compared oestradiol levels, measured by radioimmunoassay, in females injected neonatally with 50 μg of TP, with those of neonatally oil-injected controls. They reported high values for the androgenized females, equivalent to control pro-oestrous values.

Plasma testosterone concentrations in androgenized female rats approximated those in the normal female in oestrus, and were lower than normal concentrations during di-oestrus and pro-oestrus. Ovariectomy obliterated this difference, indicating an ovarian source of the cyclicity of circulating testosterone concentrations in normal females (Falvo *et al.*, 1974). The apparent absence of cyclic testosterone secretion in the androgenized rat might significantly modify reproductive function since it has been shown, by administration of antibodies to testosterone, that endogenous testosterone is obligatory for the pro-oestrus surge of FSH in normal females (Gay and Tomacari, 1974).

Positive Feedback

As indicated in the brief summary above, abnormalities of the hormonal milieu in the neonatally androgenized rat are complex. However, one defect which seems indisputable and which is undoubtedly a major cause of the anovulatory state is the apparent absence of a neurally generated cyclic surge of LH secretion. This property of the androgenized female is also characteristic of the normal male rat. It therefore seems worthwhile to consider some of the information available regarding differences in regulatory mechanisms which might underlie this dimorphism in patterns of LH secretion.

One major aspect of gonadotrophin regulation involves the stimulatory action of gonadal and/or adrenal steroids, generally referred to as positive feedback. It has been firmly established, by numerous direct and indirect experimental approaches, that the midcycle peak of oestradiol secretion is a prerequisite for the prevulatory surge of LH in the rat (Hohlweg, 1934; Kempf, 1950; Dörner and Döcke, 1964; Ferin *et al.*, 1969; Caligaris *et al.*, 1971; Neill *et al.*, 1971; Swerdloff *et al.*, 1972; Mann and Barraclough, 1973: Kalra, 1975), the hamster (Labhsetwar, 1972; Norman and Spies, 1974), and the rhesus monkey (Spies and Niswender, 1972; Karsch *et al.*, 1973a, Sundram *et al.*, 1973; Ferin *et al.*, 1974). In the case of the rat, the pro-oestrous surge of prolactin secretion is also apparently contingent upon prior stimulatory action of oestradiol (Neill *et al.*, 1971). In addition, progesterone (possibly of adrenal origin) seems to have some essential, although less clearly defined, role in the positive feedback regulation of LH secretion in the rat (Swerdloff *et al.*, 1972; Mann and Barraclough, 1973).

It has been frequently hypothesized that the acyclicity of LH secretion in neonatally androgenized female rats might reflect diminished sensitivity to the actions of oestradiol and/or progesterone which normally serve to stimulate LH secretion ('positive feedback' actions), and experiments have been designed to investigate the validity of this hypothesis. Dörner and Döcke (1964), investigating corpus luteum formation in transplanted or endogenous ovaries following oestradiol administration, observed that in both normal males and neonatally androgenized females the LH secretory system is insensitive to positive feedback actions of oestrogen. These findings apparently contradicted earlier results of Kempf (1950). He grafted ovaries into the eyes of adult male rats, castrated them three days later and, after five weeks, injected them with oestradiol (500 I.U.). Surprisingly the oestrogen treatment resulted in corpus luteum formation in the ovarian grafts (Kempf, 1950). (The presence of corpora lutea in ovarian tissue is an indication that ovulation has taken place. The occurrence of ovulation, in turn, is considered to reflect the prior occurrence of a surge of LH secretion).

In more recent experiments, the endpoint considered for determining whether positive feedback had taken place was the circulating concentration of LH, rather than the occurrence of ovulation, and the possibly confusing variable of ovarian sensitivity to LH was thereby eliminated (Mennin and Gorski, 1975). As already stated, the pituitary of the androgenized female is competent to respond normally to LRH and to the steroidal hormone environment of a normal female. Therefore, any altered sensitivity to positive feedback observed in this experimental model must be of neural origin.

Neill (1972) measured, by radioimmunoassay, LH concentrations in blood drawn from aortic catheters at two hour intervals, starting 23 h after a second injection of oestradiol benzoate (OB), the first one having been administered 47 h before sampling began. He compared the LH response to OB in normal and neonatally androgenized female rats, all ovariectomized in adulthood. A surge of LH secretion was observed in normal ovariectomized female rats in the afternoon of testing. No such stimulatory effect of oestradiol on LH secretion could be detected in ovariectomized females which had been treated with 50 μg of TP on postnatal day five. Of particular interest, for our purpose of considering the physiological relevance of neonatal androgenization to normal sex differentiation, is the fact that under identical experimental conditions normal male rats gonadectomized in adulthood also did not have elevated plasma concentrations of LH following OB treatment. In six out of 12 male rats castrated within 24 h after birth and tested in the same way in adulthood, however, a surge of LH secretion was observed (Neill, 1972). Similarly, although not precisely comparable to these results with castrated adults, a second injection of OB did not stimulate LH secretion in 28-day-old intact male rats. This result contrasted with the situation observed in intact females of the same age (Caligaris *et al.*, 1972).

More recently, Mennin and Gorski (1975) confirmed Neill's findings, using a slightly different experimental procedure. Normal ovariectomized adult rats were compared with ovariectomized adult rats which had been treated with 10 μg of TP during the critical period for neonatal androgenization (within 72 h after birth). A first, priming, injection of OB significantly reduced plasma LH levels in both groups of animals and—without further treatment—levels remained depressed for four days, indicating that negative feedback was operative. In the group of normal animals which were given a second injection of OB, LH concentrations rose at 6 p.m. on the following day. The next morning (46 h after the second injection), LH levels were depressed, but they rose again at 6 p.m. that evening. This stimulatory effect of oestradiol on LH secretion in normal ovariectomized rats—manifested only at certain times of the day—was comparable to the effects observed by other investigators (Caligaris *et al.*, 1971) and conforms to the idea of a limited diurnal period of neural responsiveness to hormonal triggers. In striking contrast to these results in normal females, however, Mennin and Gorski found that, in the neonatally androgenized, OB-primed ovariectomized rat, LH secretion was not stimulated by OB at any of the postinjection times investigated (Mennin and Gorski, 1975).

Mechanisms involving oestrogenic stimulation of prolactin secretion are also apparently modified in the neonatally androgenized female rat. Circulating levels of prolactin, determined by radioimmunoassay, were consistently low in normal females injected with oil two weeks after ovariectomy. Normal ovariectomized females injected twice with OB had afternoon surges of prolac-in secretion on three consecutive days following the second OB injections, while prolactin levels remained low in gonadectomized neonatally androgenized females and normal males, whether treated with oil or OB. Prolactin secretion was stimulated by OB treatment in 6 of 12 neonatally castrated males.

According to the information available, therefore, diminished neural sensitivity to the positive feedback actions of oestradiol in the neonatally androgenized female rat seems to be a reality, and might be one causal factor in the occurrence of anovulatory sterility. In addition, this relative insensitivity of the androgenized female brain is apparently analogous to the situation in the normal male. That conclusion must be considered tentative, however, in the light of the early results reported by Kempf (1950) which cannot at the present time by satisfactorily explained. It should be pointed out here that a refractoriness to oestrogenic stimulation does not seem to exist in the primate male brain. When castrated male rhesus monkeys were given silastic implants of oestradiol, so that circulating levels always approximated basal levels in the intact female, an acute increment of exogenously administered oestradiol (comparable to the midcycle peak in females) resulted in a measurable surge of LH secretion, indistinguishable from that observed in identically treated females (Karsch *et al.*, 1973b). These findings are concordant with the failure of pre- or neonatal testosterone administration to lead to anovulatory sterility in the female rhesus monkey (Treloar *et al.*, 1972; Goy, 1970b; Karsch *et al.*, 1973b), despite marked masculinizing effects of such treatment on genital morphology and social and sexual behaviour.

It is even less clear whether sexual dimorphism exists in the rat brain with regard to sensitivity to progesterone stimulation of LH release. Neither can it be stated with certainty that the androgenized female and normal female rat brains are differentially sensitive to progesterone.

A number of observations are consistent with the concept of a relative insensitivity of both normal male and neonatally androgenized female rats to the stimulatory action of progesterone on LH secretion. Mennin and Gorski (1975) observed a late afternoon rise in plasma LH levels on three consecutive days after progesterone injections into normal, OB-primed, adult-ovariectomized rats. However, progesterone did not ever stimulate LH secretion in neonatally androgenized, OB-primed, adult-ovariectomized rats (Mennin and Gorski, 1975). These results are consistent with earlier failures to induce ovulation by progesterone administration to adult female rats which had been treated neonatally with 1.25 mg (Barraclough and Gorski, 1961) or 10 μg (Gorski and Barraclough, 1963) of TP. In addition, Brown-Grant and Naftolin (1972) observed no rise in plasma LH concentrations in intact adult male rats or in neonatally androgenized (1.25 mg of TP) intact adult females, 5 h after systemic injections of progesterone. The same dose of progesterone administered to normal females in pro-oestrus caused significant elevations of plasma LH 5 h later, prior to the time when the preovulatory LH surge occurs in normal pro-oestrous females not treated with progesterone (Brown-Grant and Naftolin, 1972). Progesterone also did not stimulate LH secretion in OB-primed intact immature male rats (Caligaris *et al.*, 1972).

The above observations are, however, contradicted by results of a study reported by Taleisnik *et al.* (1969). In this study, using a bioassay for measuring plasma LH levels, no effect of exogenous progesterone was observed on circulating LH concentrations in OB-primed adult male rats, whether they had been castrated as adults or as neonates. But OB-primed ovariectomized females— both normal and neonatally androgenized (1.25 mg of TP)—exhibited progesterone-induced increases in plasma LH concentrations (Taleisnik *et al.*, 1969). These results suggest that a sex difference exists with respect to the LH response to progesterone, but that this sex difference is not a function of the presence or absence of neonatal testicular secretions. In the same study, plasma LH concentrations of neonatally castrated and adult-castrated males, as well as of ovariectomized normal females, *were* elevated by progesterone after TP priming (Taleisnik *et al.*, 1969), suggesting that the sexual dimorphism observed might not directly reflect differences in sensitivity to P itself, but rather reflect a sexually dimorphic response to the initial hormone-priming injection.

Underlining the inconclusiveness of these observations is the fact that ovulation has been observed in ovarian grafts in adult-castrated male rats treated with exogenous progesterone (Kempf, 1950). This finding also emphasizes the point that, while the male rat brain does not cyclically generate secretion of an ovulatory amount of LH under physiological conditions, such activity can be induced by appropriate experimental manipulation. The problem of potential sexual dimorphism of the rat brain to progesterone, with respect to gonadotrophin regulation, must at this point be considered as unresolved.

Negative Feedback

While some aspects of the mechanisms regulating cyclic stimulation of gonadotrophin secretion are clearly aberrant in neonatally androgenized adult female rats, it would seem that the negative feedback mechanisms, by which gonadal steroids maintain relatively low secretory levels of LH and FSH during non-surge stages of the female reproductive cycle, and at all times in the male, are operative in the neonatally androgenized adult female. Reports of the degree to which negative feedback actually works in the intact androgenized female, and to which it *can* work in ovariectomized animals treated with exogenous steroids, have been somewhat inconsistent. Similarly, the existence of differential sensitivities to negative feedback actions of endogenous and exogenous gonadal steroids in normal male and female rats is controversial (for review, see Taleisnik *et al.*, 1971). But most experimental data seem to indicate that development of this regulatory mechanism is only slightly (Morrison and Johnson, 1966; Van Rees and Gans, 1966; Neill, 1972) or not at all (Harris and Levine, 1965; Taleisnik *et al.*, 1969; Taleisnik *et al.*, 1970; McDonald and Doughty, 1972a; Hayashi, 1974, Mennin and Gorski, 1975) modified by neonatal exposure to androgen.

Response to Direct Stimulation of the Brain

Other types of investigations have been made, in addition to those of sensitivity of the brain to steroid hormones, as part of the effort to characterize the functional defects responsible for acyclicity of gonadotrophin secretion. A major field of research has involved studies of the effects of electrochemical or electrical stimulation of brain regions in the neonatally androgenized rat known to have positive (or negative) influence on ovulation in the normal female. This type of manipulation is considered to represent a direct, if artificial, activation of neural components which, when physiologically triggered by hormonal, environmental, or self-generating cues, normally stimulate (or inhibit) gonadotrophin release. Thus, abnormal results obtained by such manipulation in the neonatally androgenized female rat might point to the neural locus of the defect involved in anovulatory sterility.

The major brain regions investigated in these studies have been the medial basal hypothalamus, normally involved in maintaining tonic rates of gonadotrophin secretion and—most relevant for the sterile female—the preoptic area, the integrity of which is essential for the cyclic surge of gonadotrophins (for review, see Flerko, 1968).

Early work, employing the occurrence of ovulation as the endpoint for evaluating responsiveness to electrical stimulation, indicated that both the medial basal hypothalamus (arcuate and ventromedial nuclei) and the preoptic area of neonatally androgenized female rats are subnormally responsive to electrical stimulation, unless the animals are primed with exogenous progesterone (Barraclough and Gorski, 1961; Gorski and Barraclough, 1963), although ovulation did occur in five out of ten 10 μg TP-treated rats, after hypothalamic stimulation, without progesterone priming (Gorski and Barraclough, 1963). Other investigations yielded conflicting results, indicating that the preoptic area of the neonatally androgenized rat is supranormally sensitive to electrochemical stimulation, with respect to the ovulatory response (Terasawa et al., 1969).

Recently the problem has been reinvestigated, and the criterion used for determining a positive response to electrochemical stimulation was circulating levels of LH. Considering the above-mentioned ovarian insensitivity of the androgenized rat to LH, but the normal pituitary sensitivity to LRH (Mennin et al., 1974), LH concentration is a more reasonable endpoint than is the occurrence of ovulation, for evaluating brain responsiveness to extrinsic stimulation (Kubo et al., 1975). Thus, Kawakami and Terasawa (1972) observed elevated serum concentrations of LH following electrical stimulation of the preoptic area of androgenized females. More recently, Kubo et al. (1975) reported the results of a thorough study in which normal and neonatally androgenized females were treated in parallel, and compared in terms of their ovulatory and LH responses to electrochemical stimulation of the medial-basal-septal-preoptic complex. In agreement with some earlier work, only a low percentage of androgenized females ovulated, at any current strength used. However, significant peaks of plasma LH concentrations were observed in a large proportion of these animals, 90 min after stimulation with either 20 or 40 μA of current. The LH response in androgenized females did not differ, in frequency or intensity, from that response in normal females. Kubo et al. thus concluded that, '. . . the pathway from the DBB [diagonal band of Broca] to the pituitary in A [neonatally androgenized] rats appears functionally intact.' Kubo et al., 1975).

These findings are of special interest when considered in the light of an earlier report that ovulation occurred in ovarian grafts in adult-gonadectomized male rats, following electrochemical stimulation of the hypothalamus (Moll and Zeilmaker, 1965) or the medial preoptic area (Quinn, 1966). Furthermore, stimulation of the preoptic area of normal males resulted in elevations of plasma LH levels 3 h later (Velasco and Taleisnik, 1969a). Thus, similarities exist between the neural circuitries of the normal male, the neonatally androgenized female, and the normal female. If sexual dimorphism of gonadotrophin secretion (perhaps partially mediated by a dimorphic sensitivity to positive feedback) is ultimately derived from an intrinsic dimorphism within the preoptic area, then it most likely is one of subtle morphological or biochemical factors not detectable by gross stimulation techniques.

Alternatively, this dimorphism might in part reside in brain regions whose inputs to the preoptic area normally modulate cyclic activity. Pertinent to this last possibility is the fact that electrochemical stimulation of the amygdala of neonatally androgenized female rats did not induce ovulation and had no effect on serum LH concentration (Kawakami and Terasawa, 1972). In contrast, LH secretion was significantly enhanced in normal intact female rats in oestrus or dioestrus, 3 h after stimulation of the medial amygdaloid nucleus (Velasco and Taleisnik, 1969a). Chemical stimulation (by implantation of crystalline carbachol) of the basolateral amygdaloid complex of gonadecto-mized, OB-primed female rats resulted in elevations of plasma LH 5 h later (Velasco and Taleisnik, 1969a). But, comparable to the results obtained with androgenized females, neither of these two modes of amygdaloid stimulation had an effect on LH secretion in intact or castrated males, respectively (Velasco and Taleisnik, 1969a). Finally, electrical stimulation of the dorsal hippocampus of neonatally androgenized female rats led to increased levels of serum LH and FSH (Kawakami and Terasawa, 1972), while that brain region reportedly has an inhibitory influence on gonadotrophin secretion in normal females (Velasco and Taleisnik, 1969b; Kawakami and Terasawa, 1972).

In summary, limited exposure of neonatal female rodents to exogenous testosterone modifies—in still undefined ways—subsequent differentiation of mechanisms which regulate gonadotrophin secretion. Cyclic activity of components of the reproductive axis does not naturally occur in such neonatally treated animals, although it can be induced by various experimental manipulations. In a number of ways, this androgenized female reproductive axis resembles that of the normal male. Considerable evidence exists to support the idea that the effects of exogenous testosterone on the undifferentiated female brain provide a realistic model for normal differentiation of the male brain, in the presence of endogenous testicular secretions. This evidence does not, however, preclude the possibility that the active organizing agent in both cases is an oestrogen derived from testosterone.

Oestrogen Effects

Acute Paranatal Oestrogenization

The possibility that oestrogen may be the active agent, both in the normal male and in the prepuberally androgenized female, was raised indirectly decades ago by Wilson et al: '... in unpublished studies we have observed that early postnatal administration of estrogens produces structural and functional abnormalities that are somewhat similar to and, in some instances, more severe than those obtained with androgens.' (Wilson *et al.*, 1941). More specific examples of the organizational actions of oestrogens on the female reproductive axis had previously been reported by Greene *et al.* in 1940. They treated pregnant rats with multiple injections of oestradiol dipropionate (OD) or unconjugated oestradiol in total doses ranging from 2.0 to 50.0 mg. Eleven of the female offspring were studied as adults. In each case, external genitalia were morphologically abnormal. Ten of these eleven prenatally oestrogenized rats had ovaries which completely lacked corpora lutea (Greene *et al.*, 1940). Similar observations were made of adult female rats which had received single injections of OD (dose not specified) on postnatal day one (Greene and Burrill, 1941), or daily injections of oestrogen (100–200 I.U. oestrogen daily) on postnatal days one through ten (Turner, 1941). In 1944, Hale reported the occurrence of various abnormalities of reproductive function in adult female rats which had been exposed to various amounts of diethylstilboestrol (DES) for limited postnatal periods. Although Hale did not present specific results of each of his various treatment schedules, he did remark that even rats exposed to the smallest doses of DES, for the shortest times (e.g., a 0.0005% solution of DES sprayed one to five times on the nesting material of 2–8-day-old rats) had reproductive abnormalities. Merklin (1953) administered single injections of 10 μg of OD to ten-day-old female mice. As adults 6 of 15 treated mice failed to become pregnant during 70 days of being housed with males. Two others delivered only three offspring each and killed them on the first day of life. Ovaries of the infertile mice contained only 2–4 corpora lutea each.

In 1963, Gorski made a detailed investigation of the long-term effects of single injections of OB to five-day-old female rats and observed anovulatory sterility which differed in two respects from that produced by TP. As in the ovaries of neonatally TP-treated females, ovaries of adults which had been exposed neonatally to 100 μg of OB were significantly smaller than normal ovaries, and contained many large follicles but no corpora lutea. Unlike TP-treated rats, OB-treated rats did show cyclic variations in vaginal smears, but cornified epithelial cells were present during approximately 50% of the time. As was the case with TP-treated females, exogenous progesterone did not induce ovulation in these sterile females. However, unlike the situation in TP treated females, electrical stimulation of the hypothalamus was ineffective in inducing ovulation in OB treated females even after progesterone priming. Compensatory ovarian hypertrophy 20 days after unilateral ovariectomy was normal, suggesting that a normal negative feedback of FSH had existed. The minimum effective dose of OB administered on day five, for induction of this anovulatory syndrome in more than 50% of treated rats, was 5 μg. Thus, with the exceptions of the partial vaginal cyclicity and the ineffectiveness of hypothalamic stimulation, the effects of neonatal oestrogenization resembled those of neonatal androgenization (Gorski, 1963). Furthermore,

5 μg of OB, as well as 10 μg of TP, administered on postnatal day four, was able to prevent 'feminization' of the reproductive axis in male rats that had been castrated on day two (Gorski and Wagner, 1965).

Other investigators also observed the anovulatory state in female rats which had been treated neonatally with 50 (Harris and Levine, 1965), 20–200 (Whalen and Nadler, 1965), 5.0 (Zucker and Feder, 1966), 10–500 (Mullins and Levine, 1968a), or 100 (Feder, 1967; Hendricks and Gerall, 1970) μg of OB or OD. The vaginal smear characteristics of these neonatally-oestrogenized females were less consistent than was the ovarian histology. Whalen and Nadler (1965) and Mullins and Levine (1968a) observed, as did Gorski (1963), some degree of vaginal cyclicity, while Harris and Levine (1965) and Hendricks and Gerall (1970) reported that vaginal smears were more persistently pre-dominated by cornified cells.

Ladosky (1967) administered 100 μg of DES to one-or ten-day old female Wistar rats, and studied vaginal and ovarian histology when the animals reached adulthood. Ovaries of the day one-treated females contained follicles of various maturational stages, but no luteal tissue. In this study, vaginal smears from day 1-treated animals persistently contained cornified cells. DES administration on day 10 did not alter reproductive development, according to the above criteria (Ladosky, 1967). Kincl et al. (1965) compared relative potencies of a number of oestrogenic compounds in the induction of anovula-tory sterility in Wistar rats. The criterion used was the absence of luteal tissue in ovaries removed when the treated animals were 45 days old. The following compounds, administered on postnatal day five, are listed in order of decreasing effectiveness: moestranol (0.1 μg resulted in anovulatory sterility in 8 out of 8 rats treated), ethynyloestradiol, oestriol, and 17β-oestradiol, unconjugated. The minimum effective doses of DES and OB were not determined, since each was effective at the lowest dose tested (50 μg and 30 μg, respectively). The relative potencies of these oestrogens, with respect to this criterion, were unrelated to their relative oestrogenic potencies in older animals (Kincl et al., 1965).

Recently Doughty et al. (1975) reported that 11β-methoxy-17 ethynyl-oestradiol (RU 2858) induced the anovulatory syndrome when as little as 0.5 ng were administered daily to female rats during the first five days after birth. With this same multiple injection regime, OB was effective at a daily dose of 100 ng (Doughty et al., 1975). A very weak oestrogen, o, p-DDT, also has been reported to induce anovulatory sterility. This compound, an isomer of DDT, prises 15–20% of the technical grade of the pesticide. 100 μg of this substance was the lowest dose which, when injected three times into female rats—on postnatal days two, three and four—resulted in anovulatory sterility in the majority of cases. In addition, animals treated in this way had significantly lower than normal serum concentrations of LH and FSH, 21–26 days after ovariectomy, when they were 290 days old (Gellert et al., 1974). Anovulatory sterility was also induced in hamsters treated with 150 μg of OB on day two (Swanson, 1966).

Chronic Prepuberal Oestrogenization

Unfortunately, little work has been done to further characterize the anovulatory state induced by acute neonatal oestrogenization. Another type of prepuberal oestrogenization, involving multiple administrations of fairly large doses of oestrogens to female rats during the first 30 days after birth, has been studied rather extensively. This treatment, however, apparently modifies development of the reproductive axis to a far greater extent than is the case with single injections of either androgens or oestrogens. Results of these investigations are therefore not necessarily applicable to the situation resulting from acute neonatal hormone administration. Vaginal smears taken from such chronically treated females after puberty are generally of the di-oestrous type at all times. Such modified females are therefore referred to as 'persistent di-oestrous' rats (Wilson, 1943; Arai, 1963; Arai, 1965; Arai and Masuda, 1970). Their ovaries are atrophic and contain only small follicles (Wilson, 1943; Arai, 1963; Arai, 1965). Pituitary LH content and hypothalamic LRH content, both determined by the ovarian ascorbic acid depletion (OAAD) method, were lower than normal in 120-day-old persistent di-oestrous rats, some time after ovariectomy (Arai, 1963). Castration cells could not be detected in pituitaries of adult persistent di-oestrous rats, six weeks after gonadectomy (Arai, 1965). Electrochemical stimulation of the preoptic area of adult persistent di-oestrous rats could not induce ovulation. In contrast, other females in this study received daily injections of small doses (10 μg) of oestrone for the first 10 days of life. Vaginal smears of adult animals in this group were generally filled with cornified cells (persistent vaginal oestrus), and electrochemical stimulation of the preoptic area resulted in ovulation in six of eight persistent vaginal oestrous animals (Arai and Masuda, 1970).

Summary

Thus, it would seem at this point that limited neonatal exposure to oestrogens modifies sex differentiation in ways which might be comparable to the effects of neonatal androgenization. More prolonged exposure to oestrogens, however, seems to have deleterious effects not only on development of mechanisms governing pituitary cyclicity, but also on the mechanism for tonic release of gonadotrophins, resulting in chronically subnormal levels of LH and FSH secretions; consequently, ovarian morphology and physiology remain essentially immature.

Effects of Other Metabolites of Testosterone

In addition to the efficacy of various oestrogens as neonatal masculinizing agents, information is available regarding the relative potencies of aromatizable *versus* non-aromatizable androgens for neonatal determination of the anovulatory syndrome. This information is also congruent with the theory that an oestrogen is the obligatory compound for this aspect of sex determination.

DHT is a steroid whose A ring is saturated and therefore cannot be aromatized to form oestradiol (Gual *et al.*, 1962). This androgen is potent in stimulating peripheral reproductive tissues in the adult male rat (for review, see Liao and Fang, 1969), but does not masculinize the female rodent brain. This has been demonstrated for a wide range of doses of both the free alcohol (Luttge and Whalen, 1970; McDonald, 1971; Brown-Grant *et al.*, 1971; Whalen and Luttge, 1971; Arai, 1972, Ulrich *et al.*, 1972), and the propionate ester, DHTP (Brown-Grant *et al.*, 1971; McDonald and Doughty, 1972a; McDonald and Doughty, 1974). Consistently negative results have been obtained whether the endpoints investigated were absence of ovarian luteal tissue (Luttge and Whalen, 1970; McDonald, 1971; Whalen and Luttge, 1971; Arai, 1972; McDonald and Doughty, 1972a; Ulrich *et al.*, 1972; McDonald and Doughty, 1974), decreased ovarian weight (McDonald, 1971; McDonald and Doughty, 1972a; Ulrich *et al.*, 1972; McDonald and Doughty, 1974), or the occurrence of persistent vaginal cornification (McDonald, 1971; Brown-Grant *et al.*, 1971; McDonald and Doughty, 1972a; Ulrich *et al.*, 1972; Mc-Donald and Doughty, 1974). In addition, neither 100 nor 500 μg of DHT administered to 5-day old male rats was able to reverse the effects of castration on day of birth (Arai, 1972).

The ineffectiveness of DHT as a neural organizing agent is in contrast with its capacity to modify differentiation of peripheral reproductive tissues of the neonatal female rat. Thus, as is the case for treatment with TP, neonatal administration of DHTP resulted in premature opening of the vaginal membrane (McDonald and Doughty, 1972a; 1974), and an abnormally increased anogenital distance (McDonald and Doughty, 1974). DHT also induced the neonatal female rat phallus to develop an enhanced sensitivity to exogenous testosterone stimulation when the animals were adults (Luttge and Whalen, 1970; Whalen and Rezek, 1974). The process of masculinization of the brain is therefore apparently distinct from that of peripheral tissues, in the sense that different masculinizing agents are required for each process.

Other examples of non-aromatizable androgens which are also incapable of induction of the anovulatory syndrome in neonatal rats are: androstanediol (Brown-Grant *et al.*, 1971; McDonald and Doughty, 1974); and androsterone (McDonald and Doughty, 1974). On the other hand, androstenedione (Luttge and Whalen, 1970; McDonald and Doughty, 1974) and 19-hydroxytestosterone (McDonald and Doughty, 1974), which are aromatizable, both lead to anovulatory sterility when administered to neonatal rats.

SEXUAL DIFFERENTIATION OF PATTERNS OF BEHAVIOUR

Androgen Effects

As is the case with the differentiation of gonadotrophin regulating mechanisms, the development of sexually dimorphic patterns of mammalian behaviour can be permanently influenced by actions of testosterone during critical foetal or neonatal periods. This phenomenon is more difficult to study than is the influence of early androgen on development of specific physiological endpoints, since even the simplest behavioural patterns represent complex interactions of not easily defined or dissectible neural and non-neural stimuli and responses, and are strongly influenced by many environmental as well as intrinsic factors. Furthermore, it is often found that a particular trait, conveniently designated as 'masculine' or 'feminine', is not exclusively inherent to a particular sexual genotype. The neural substrates for both 'masculine' and 'feminine' patterns of behaviour seem to be present in adult males and females. The dimorphism would seem to reside in the thresholds for activation of these substrates, by hormonal or other factors. The extent of this quantitative dimorphism varies, depending upon the particular trait, species, and individual being studied. In only some cases does the early hormonal milieu normally imposed by the genotype—i.e., the presence or absence of foetal or neonatal testicular secretions—determine the mode of development for each substrate (Beach, 1968; Goy, 1970b; Goy and Phoenix, 1971).

With these limitations in mind, we will consider the early effects of androgens on sexually dimorphic mating behaviour patterns in rodents, concentrating primarily on the 'defeminizing', rather than the masculinizing, aspects of androgenic influences.

The guinea pig was the first laboratory rodent in which the effects of exogenous testosterone on development of mating behaviour patterns was studied. This was a convenient species for investigation in one sense: the stereotypic traits under consideration are more sex-specific in the guinea pig than in some other species of rodents. Thus—while under certain conditions, the normal male guinea pig will display lordosis and the normal female will mount other females—in general, mounting activity is limited to males, and lordosis, to females (particularly when measured in gonadectomized animals treated with gonadal hormones) (Beach, 1968; Goy, 1970b; Goy and Phoenix, 1971).

When pregnant guinea pigs were treated with large doses of TP, their female offspring had strongly masculinized external genitalia. When these pseudohermaphroditic females were gonadectomized as adults and tested for the lordosis response to manual stimulation after oestrogen plus progesterone replacement therapy, they were found to have a significantly suppressed capacity for lordosis, compared to gonadectomized females which had not been exposed to testosterone in utero. In addition, the prenatally treated, adult gonadectomized females responded to testosterone replacement therapy with a markedly higher frequency of mounting behaviour than did normal gonadectomized females. These effects of prenatal testosterone were evident as late as one year after birth and were therefore considered to be irreversible, in contrast to the temporary inhibition of normal lordosis behaviour caused by postnatal administration of testosterone to the female guinea pig (Phoenix et al., 1959). These observations agreed with earlier findings that prenatal testosterone treatment irreversibly masculinizes adult mating behaviour in female guinea pigs (Dantchakoff, 1938).

Since the critical period for the action of androgen in sexual differentiation of the guinea pig is prenatal, the converse of the above experiments—namely, castration of male foetuses—could not readily be done. It was therefore not determined to what degree differentiation of the substrates for sex-specific mating behaviour traits in the normal male is dependent upon products of the foetal testis. Consequently, it could not be directly established that experimental androgenization of female foetuses realistically mimics the effects of foetal testicular secretions. However, results of other studies, in which both lordosis and mounting activities were studied at different times after birth, demonstrated a parallelism between development of the potentials for these activities in normal males and in prenatally androgenized females. This parallelism was independent of the presence of gonads during development and thus suggested that the behavioural endpoints of prenatal androgenization might reflect physiologically relevant actions of testosterone on the foetal brain (Goy et al., 1967).

In the rat, sexual differentiation of neural mechanisms underlying mating behaviour is determined postnatally. As is the case for development of gonadotrophin regulating mechanisms, the ontogeny of mechanisms subserving sexually dimorphic mating behaviour is irreversibly imprinted within a few days after birth. The particular course which will be taken depends upon whether testes are present during this critical period (Grady et al., 1965; Feder and Whalen, 1965; Feder et al., 1966; Whalen and Edwards, 1967; Zucker, 1967; Goldfoot et al., 1969; Stern, 1969; Pfaff and Zigmond, 1971).

In this species, the tendency of gonadectomized adults given testosterone replacement therapy to mount receptive females is not as exclusively a masculine trait as it is in the guinea pig. Gonadectomized, adult-testosterone treated female rats will readily mount other females (Grady et al., 1965; Harris and Levine, 1965; Whalen and Edwards, 1967; Beach, 1968; Mullins and Levine, 1968a; Stern, 1969; Pfaff and Zigmond, 1971; Whalen and Luttge, 1971). Quantitative comparisons of this trait in gonadectomized adult males and females have yielded conflicting results. Some investigators have reported that females exhibit mounting behaviour less often than do males, under identical testosterone replacement regimes (Grady et al., 1965). Others have reported that while the percentage of females which would mount was no different from the percentage of males mounting, the mean frequency of mounts was lower for females than for males (Whalen and Edwards, 1967). Still others observed no quantitative difference between male and female mounting activities (Mullins and Levine, 1968b; Pfaff and Zigmond, 1971). Since the occurrence of mounting behaviour under these conditions (in the gonadectomized, testosterone treated adult) does not appear to be strongly sex-specific, it is not surprising that neonatal castration of males does not result in diminished mounting behaviour in adulthood (Grady *et al.*, 1965; Whalen and Edwards, 1967; Goldfoot *et al.*, 1969; Pfaff and Zigmond, 1971). Thus, the capacity to mount receptive females develops autonomously in both male and female rats, or at least does not seem to be a function of actions of the neonatal testis.

Lordosis, in response to mounting by sexually active males, or to experimental manual stimulation occurs only rarely in adult male rats gonadectomized after the neonatal period and treated with oestrogen and progesterone (Grady *et al.*, 1965; Feder and Whalen, 1965; Feder *et al.*, 1966; Zucker, 1967; Whalen and Edwards, 1967; Goldfoot *et al.*, 1969; Clemens *et al.*, 1970; Edwards and Thompson, 1970; Pfaff and Zigmond, 1971; Whalen *et al.*, 1971), compared with the frequency of lordosis in the gonadectomized, oestrogen—progesterone treated female rat, or in the intact female during oestrus. Davidson (1969) found that, although short-term hormone replacement therapy resulted in negligible lordosis responses, long-term treatment with high doses of oestrogen could induce near-maximal responses in adult-castrated Long-Evans male rats. Whalen *et al* (1971), however, using similar hormone replacement conditions, only observed minimal levels of lordosis in adult-castrated Sprague–Dawley males. These discrepant findings might reflect strain differences, but even in the Davidson study the male sensitivity to oestrogen was strikingly lower than that of females of the same strain (Davidson, 1969). When male rats are castrated within the first few days after birth, their capacities for lordosis as adults are markedly increased, to levels approximating that of the normal female (Grady *et al.*, 1965; Feder and Whalen, 1965; Feder *et al.*, 1966; Whalen and Edwards, 1967; Goldfoot *et al.*, 1969; Stern, 1969; Pfaff and Zigmond, 1971; Whalen *et al.*, 1971).

Sexual dimorphism in the rat, with respect to mating behaviour, is therefore primarily a matter of a reduced lordosis response in the male rat. It should be pointed out that the neural substrate for even this strongly sex-specific behaviour pattern, although normally inactive, seems to be present in normal adult male rats. Thus, for example, serotonergic and adrenergic mechanisms involved in lordosis in female rats are also demonstrable in males (see Meyerson and Malmnas, this volume Chapter 16). When serotonin or β adrenergic receptor blockers were directly applied to the hypothalamus of oestrogen-primed intact males (presumably acting to inhibit inhibitory actions of serotonergic or β adrenergic neurons on lordosis) lordosis was induced to a degree comparable to that induced in identically treated ovariectomized females (Crowley *et al.*, 1975; Ward *et al.*, 1975). But, the presence of the testes in the neonatal male permanently limits the capacity to express this potential.

The male rat brain is sensitive to this determinative effect of testicular secretions only during the first week after birth, since castration on day seven (Zucker, 1967) or day ten (Grady *et al.*, 1965) has no influence on later lordosis activity.

As is the case with the guinea pig, exposure of female rats to exogenous testosterone during the critical period modifies development of neural substrates for mating behaviour in ways which for the most part seem to duplicate the effects of endogenous testicular secretions in the male.

As would be expected from the limited (or non-existent) sexual dimorphism of mounting activity in the adult rat, results of investigations into the effects of administration of testosterone to neonatal females have been equivocal, with respect to this parameter. Although Harris and Levine (1965) and Sheridan et al. (1973) reported a higher incidence of mounting by neonatally androgenized females than by neonatally oil injected control females (all ovariectomized and given testosterone replacement therapy as adults), other investigators observed no such effect of neonatal androgenization (Whalen and Edwards, 1967; Mullins and Levine, 1968a; Whalen et al., 1969; Pfaff and Zigmond, 1971). Södersten (1973), however, did observe a significantly enhanced incidence of mounting in neonatally androgenized females, when they were intact and after ovaiectomy and oestrogen replacement therapy, but not after testosterone replacement therapy.

Development of female rat receptivity, again measured by the frequency of the lordosis response in the adult, is profoundly affected by the actions of exogenous testosterone during the neonatal period. Early investigations involved prolonged administration of large doses of testosterone, beginning either prenatally (Wilson et al., 1940) or postnatally (Wilson et al., 1940, 1941), and continuing in both cases for several weeks after birth. Such extensively androgenized females were not receptive to males as intact adults, or after ovariectomy and oestrogen–progesterone replacement therapy, unless the dose of oestrogen was increased 40-fold above that required to elicit lordosis in the normal female (Wilson et al., 1940, 1941). When the testosterone treatment was limited to the prenatal period (Wilson et al., 1940), the potential for lordosis was not severely affected, and when androgen administration was not initiated until postnatal day 15, later receptivity was normal (Wilson et al., 1941). Ovariectomy at birth did not prevent these effects of prolonged testosterone treatment (Wilson et al., 1941); they did not therefore seem to be mediated by alterations of gonadal steroid patterns during development.

Barraclough and Gorski (1962) administered single injections of 1.25 mg of TP to five-day-old females and found that they were not receptive to mounting attempts by male rats as adults, either intact or ovariectomized and oestrogen–progesterone treated. Administration of only 10 μg of TP on day five led to less drastic and more disparate abnormalities of mating behaviour. Direct observations were not made in this case, but the presence of sperm in vaginal lavages was taken as an index of sexual receptivity. Some of these females were receptive at all times investigated, others were only sporadically receptive, but none showed regular cyclicity of receptiveness typical of the normal female. Mating behaviour after ovariectomy was not studied in these animals (Barraclough and Gorski, 1962).

Numerous studies on the effects of neonatal exposure to testosterone on development of sexual receptivity have subsequently substantiated the earlier findings. Most of these involved administration of single injections of from 100 μg to 2.5 mg of TP to female rats at some time during the first postnatal week, and then direct observations of the lordosis response to mounting in these females as adults, after they had been ovariectomized and given hormone replacement therapy. Almost invariably under these conditions, the neonatally androgenized females were deficient in their potential for displaying lordosis, compared with that potential in normal females or females which had been injected neonatally with the oil vehicle (Harris and Levine, 1965; Gerall, 1967; Whalen and Edwards, 1967; Mullins and Levine, 1968a; Clemens et al., 1970; Edwards and Thompson, 1970; Pfaff and Zigmond, 1971; Whalen et al., 1971; Blizard and Denef, 1973). Negative results were reported by Clemens et al. (1969), who administered ony 10 μg of TP on postnatal day one or two. That same dose given to four- or six-day-old female rats, however, was effective in modifying development of receptivity (Clemens et al., 1969). In apparent contrast with the findings of Clemens et al. (1969), other investigators later reported a reduced lordosis quotient (number of lordoses/number of mounts x 100) in a group of female rats which had been treated with 10 μg of TP on the day of birth (Sheridan et al., 1973). Examination of their data, though, reveals the reported decrement to be extremely small. Clemens et al. (1969) concluded that the neural substrate for this trait is most sensitive to the organizational influence of testosterone a few days after birth. The relative ineffectiveness of prenatal androgenization in the rat (Wilson et al., 1940) is evidence in favour of this hypothesis. In addition, 100 μg of TP administered to female rats on the day of birth had no effect on later sexual receptivity while the same dose administered on day five was effective (McDonald and Doughty, 1972a). Doughty and McDonald (1974), however, observed no abnormalities of lordosis in adult females which had been treated with 30 μg of TP, either on postnatal day one or five.

It would therefore seem that the minimum effective single dose of TP, with respect to 'defeminization' of mating behaviour, is greater than that for 'defeminization' of gonadotrophin regulating mechanisms, and that both the 10 μg and the 30 μg doses were marginal. When such a marginal dose is administered at a time of presumed maximal sensitivity, then perhaps it might or might not be effective, as a function of interlaboratory variations, such as rat strain. The possibly increased sensitivity after birth could involve maturation of a number of (unknown) factors which comprise the process of neonatal sexual determination. The fact that larger doses of TP were sometimes effective if administered on day one (2.5 mg (Whalen and Edwards, 1967), 100 μg (Clemens et al., 1970)) or day two (200 μg (Pfaff and Zigmond, 1971)) suggests that the brain is at least somewhat sensitive to TP at this time, although the possibility that some residual hormone continues to circulate at a later time cannot be excluded. Furthermore, information regarding the most efficient means of neonatal androgenization indicates that, whether or not the brain is most sensitive on day four or five, the process of masculinization can be

initiated on day one as the first step in an ongoing process. Thus, as with determination of gonadotrophin regulating mechanisms, testosterone is most effective for limiting development of female sexual receptivity if it is administered
daily, during the first days after birth. Using this multiple injection procedure,
Sheridan et al., (1973) found that 0.5 μg of TP, injected twice daily on postnatal
days one through ten, resulted in diminished receptivity. McDonald and
Doughty (1974) obtained an effect with only five daily injections (days one
through five) of 1 μg of TP, while, as mentioned above, the same investigators
observed no effect of a single injection of 30 μg of TP administered on day
one or five (Doughty and McDonald, 1974).

It should be noted that even with the more efficient multiple injection procedure, five daily injections of 1 μg of non-propionated testosterone did not
result in behaviourally abnormal females (McDonald and Doughty, 1973/4).
Whalen and Rezek (1974), however, implanted silastic capsules containing
2.0 mg of non-propionated testosterone into one-day-old female rats, and
removed the implants on day ten. These animals had significantly decreased
lordosis responses as adults, compared with responses of control rats which
had been implanted with cholesterol. Since steroids are slowly and continuously
released from silastic capsules (Bullock, 1970), the previously observed difference in potencies of testosterone and TP therefore most likely reflected different lengths of time for which sensitive neonatal tissues were exposed to the
two compounds (Whalen and Rezek, 1974).

The development of female-type receptivity is also inhibited in neonatally
castrated males if they are treated with testosterone during the critical postnatal
period (Whalen and Edwards, 1967; Mullins and Levine, 1968b). Although,
as described above, neonatal castration results in males who display lordosis
as frequently as do normal females, neonatal administration of testosterone
can prevent this effect and the resulting adult males are as unreceptive as are
normal males castrated in adulthood. Mullins and Levine (1968b) reported
that the males were more sensitive to testosterone, with respect to subsequent
defects in the lordosis response, than were females studied in a separate experiment (Mullins and Levine, 1968a). Neonatally castrated, TP-injected males
had significantly lower lordosis quotients than did neonatally castrated, oil-
injected males, whether they had received 10, 100, or 1000 μg of TP (Mullins
and Levine, 1968b), while the lordosis response was signicantly abnormal only
in the groups of females which had been treated with 100 μg or more of TP
after birth (Mullins and Levine, 1968a). Furthermore, even at the higher dose
levels, the absolute values of lordosis quotients were lower for males than for
females (Mullins and Levine, 1968b). However, in the female study, the ovaries
were not removed until the animals were adults, and it had subsequently been
shown that the presence of ovaries until puberty can significantly attenuate,
although not prevent, the organizational effects of TP on substrates for mating
behaviour (Blizard and Denef, 1973; Hendricks and Duffy, 1974). Whalen
and Edwards (1967), who gonadectomized both males and females at the time

of TP injection (2.5 mg, day one), reported no sex difference in the subsequent lordosis responses.

Since the lordosis response in the rat is almost completely dependent upon the activational actions of oestrogen alone or, more optimally, of oestrogen and progesterone or, least effectively, of testosterone (a normal ovariectomized female will scarcely ever show lordosis unless she has received prior hormone replacement therapy), the defect caused by neonatal testosterone possibly involves a diminished sensitivity to one or all of these hormones. Clemens and co-workers reported no significant defects in lordosis behaviour in ovariectomized adult females treated with 10 μg of TP on postnatal day four or six (Clemens et al., 1969) or with 100 μg of TP on postnatal day one, two, four, or six (Clemens et al., 1970), when they were tested after oestrogen administration alone. Ovariectomized adult rats in the same neonatal treatment groups, however, displayed significantly lower lordosis quotients compared with neonatally oil-treated controls, when they were tested after oestrogen plus progesterone treatment (Clemens et al., 1969, 1970). They concluded that testosterone acts neonatally to modify development of neural sensitivity to progesterone only. However, Harris and Levine (1965) had observed diminished sexual receptivity in neonatally TP-treated, compared with neonatally oil-treated, females, after adult ovariectomy and administration of testosterone alone. These results suggested a more generalized defect in neonatally androgenized females than the specific reduced progesterone sensitivity suggested by Clemens et al. Blizard and Denef (1973) administered only oestrogen replacement therapy to ovariectomized adult females which had been treated postnatally with TP or oil, and observed a significantly lower lordosis quotient in the TP-treated group. Similar results were obtained by other investigators, with various doses and times of oestrogen replacement (Edwards and Thompson, 1970; Whalen et al., 1971). Finally, Pfaff and Zigmond (1971) directly compared lordosis behaviour in neonatally androgenized *versus* oil control females, ovariectomized as adults and given either oestradiol, oestradiol plus progesterone or testosterone plus progesterone replacement therapy. In each case, the mean lordosis to mount ratio was significantly reduced in the neonatal TP, compared with the neonatal oil, group. The absolute mean lordosis/mount value for control females was highest after oestrogen plus progesterone treatment and lowest after testosterone plus progesterone, but even the lowest response in control females was significantly greater than that in the corresponding group of neonatally androgenized females. Similarly, males castrated as adults displayed few to no lordoses after each of the hormone replacement therapies, while the responses of neonatally castrated males approximated those of the normal females (Pfaff and Zigmond, 1971). Consideration of these results led Pfaff and Zigmond to describe the organizational actions of endogenous testicular secretions in the normal male, or of exogenous testosterone in the androgenized female, as leading to '... a behaviour-specific change rather than a hormone-specific change ...' (Pfaff and Zigmond,

1971). The earlier failure of Clemens *et al.* to find a difference in receptivities of neonatally androgenized and of normal females after only oestrogen replacement therapy might reflect the low dose and short duration of their oestrogen therapy regime, and the consequently very low levels of lordosis observed in their control females (Clemens *et al.*, 1969, 1970).

The hamster is markedly sexually dimorphic with respect to both mounting and lordosis activities. Thus, lordosis in an adult-castrated, oestrogen–progesterone treated male is relatively rare and an adult-ovariectomized, testosterone treated female will rarely mount another female (Eaton, 1970; Carter *et al.*, 1972; Tiefer and Johnson, 1975). When male hamsters were castrated on the day of birth, their adult potentials for both lordosis and mounting resembled those of normal females (Eaton, 1970; Carter *et al.*, 1972; Tiefer and Johnson, 1975). Castration on postnatal day six had no such determinative effect on mating behaviour (Carter *et al.*, 1972). Administration of a single injection of 500 μg of TP (Eaton, 1970), or of multiple injections of 10 μg of non-propionated testosterone on postnatal days one through 20 (Tiefer and Johnson, 1975), in conjunction with castration on the day of birth, prevented the effects of castration on both parameters. Similarly, adult female hamsters which had been treated with testosterone neonatally displayed abnormal lordosis behaviour after ovariectomy and oestrogen–progesterone therapy, either in terms of decreased durations of lordosis (Carter *et al.*, 1972; Coniglio *et al.*, 1973; Tiefer and Johnson, 1975) or of diminished percentages of animals showing lordosis (Whitsett and Vandenbergh, 1975). In addition, adult-ovariectomized, testosterone treated females which had been androgenized neonatally mounted other females with significantly greater frequency than did control females (Carter *et al.*, 1972; Paup *et al.*, 1972; Tiefer and Johnson, 1975).

The majority of data described in the preceding pages support the hypothesis that exogenous testosterone can, during restricted periods of neural lability, alter the female rodent brain in ways which result in a permanently defeminized potential for mating behaviour. For each species considered, the end results of these alterations resemble the appropriate end results of the actions (during the same time period) of testicular secretions in the normal male. Once again, the question arises concerning the ultimate identity of the masculinizing agent: Do the organizational effects of endogenous hormone in the normal male, and of exogenous testosterone in the female, result from direct actions of testosterone on the brain or are they mediated by an oestrogenic metabolite of testosterone?

Oestrogen Effects

Results of the few studies which investigated mounting behaviour in adult female rats treated neonatally with OB were inconsistent. Both Levine and Mullins (1964) and Hendricks and Gerall (1970) reported an increased frequency of mounting in adult female rats which had received single injections of 100 μg of OB on postnatal day four, compared with mounting frequency in females which had received only oil injections neonatally. (Mounting behaviour was studied in ovariectomized adults after testosterone replacement therapy.) Mullins and Levine (1968a) later extended their investigations, comparing the effects of various neonatal doses of OB (10–500 μg on day four) on later mounting activity. In this experiment, they had a positive effect (increased frequency of mounting) only with the 100 μg dose: neither lower nor higher doses were effective in this regard (Mullins and Levine, 1968a). Other investigators observed no difference between potentials for mounting behaviour in groups of adult rats which had been ovariectomized and injected with 100 μg of OB, ovariectomized and not injected or simply sham ovariectomized, on the day of birth (Whalen and Edwards, 1967). Since the entire problem of the possible influence of early testicular secretions on adult mounting behaviour in the rat is presently unresolved, these inconsistent results with neonatal oestrogenization are not particularly disturbing. The effects of neonatal administration of oestrogens, and of androgens other than testosterone, on the lordosis response are more relevant to the question of normal sex differentiation in the rat. The available information in this area does not seem as conclusive as does information regarding the effects of these various hormones on differentiation of gonadotrophin regulating mechanisms. Table 1 summarizes some of the organizing effects of androgens and oestrogens on development of receptivity in the female rat.

In most instances, administration of oestradiol to neonatal females has been at least as effective as administration of testosterone in altering development of sexual receptivity (Whalen and Nadler, 1963; Levine and Mullins, 1964; Whalen and Nadler, 1965; Zucker and Feder, 1966; Gerall, 1967; Whalen and Edwards, 1967; Mullins and Levine, 1968a; Hendricks and Gerall, 1970; Edwards and Thompson, 1970). In each of these cases, a single injection of from 5 μg to 500 μg of OB was given on postnatal day four or five (with the exception of two experiments, in which the OB was administered on the day of birth (Whalen and Edwards, 1967; Edwards and Thompson, 1970)), and a deficient adult lordosis response to mounting was observed in these neonatally oestrogenized females, after ovariectomy and oestrogen–progesterone replacement treatment, or after just oestrogen replacement therapy (Edwards and Thompson, 1970). It should also be noted that neonatal administration of oestrogen has been shown to prevent the feminizing effects of neonatal castration on development of receptivity in male rats (Feder and Whalen, 1965; Whalen and Edwards, 1967; Mullins and Levine, 1968b). Zucker and Feder (1966) obtained a significant effect on females with only 5 μg of OB, while Mullins and Levine (1968a) reported the minimum effective dose to be 33 μg. In the same experiment, Mullins and Levine (1968a) found the minimum effective dose of TP to be 100 μg.

A most impressive example of oestrogen-induced sexual differentiation is the report of Doughty *et al.* (1975) of diminished receptivity in adult-ovariectomized oestrogen- and progesterone treated female rats which had received as little as 100 ng of OB or 1 ng of RU 2858 per day on postnatal days one to five. This is in contrast to the minimum effective dose (1 μg daily) of multiple neonatal injections of TP (Sheridan *et al.*, 1973; McDonald and Doughty, 1974). Two μg of DES, administered daily to two- through four-day old female hamsters resulted in an enhanced capacity for mounting activity (Paup *et al.*, 1972) and a diminished duration of lordosis (Coniglio *et al.*, 1973). All of the above observations had actually been prognosticated by a study reported in 1943. Female rats received multiple neonatal injections of OD (total doses ranged from 0.037 to 2.4 mg) during the first four weeks after birth. As ovariectomized, oestrogen–progesterone primed adults, these pre-puberally oestrogenized females failed to produce lordosis in response to manual stimulation. Other animals, whose prepuberal oestrogen treatment lasted for the same absolute amount of time but was not initiated until postnatal day 15, exhibited normal lordosis responses as adults (Wilson, 1943). Despite the impressiveness of these various results of neonatal oestrogenization, there have been exceptions. Without presenting specific data, Hale (1944) reported that the majority of a large number of female rats which had been subjected to various regimes of pre- and/or postnatal administration of DES or oestrone, copulated when housed with males, although only one of 36 females tested became pregnant (Hale, 1944). Gorski (1963) checked vaginal lavages of neonatally oestrogenized rats for the presence of sperm, as an index of receptivity. Sperm were present, although in no regular cyclic pattern, in 13 of 18 females which had been treated with 100 μg of OB on postnatal day five. This apparent receptivity existed despite the fact that as low a neonatal dose as 5 μg of OB was sufficient for induction of anovulatory sterility (Gorski, 1963). Whalen and Nadler argued that the occurrence of copulation does not necessarily indicate normal receptivity; that male rats could force intromission in the absence of a normal lordosis response, and that therefore direct observation is required in order to determine whether female mating behaviour is normal (Whalen and Nadler, 1965). However, Harris and Levine (1965) observed mating behaviour directly in adult-ovariectomized, oestrogen–progesterone treated females which had received single injections on postnatal day four of 500 μg of TP, 50 μg of OB, or oil. Although none of the neonatal TP females was receptive, seven of twelve neonatal OB females displayed 'full receptivity', and five, 'partial receptivity'. Partial receptivity was defined as consisting of a lordosis response in the absence of a normal crouching position (Harris and Levine, 1965).

These negative reports are difficult to reconcile with the relative abundance of positive results obtained with oestrogenic compounds. It is of course possible that, as Whalen and Nadler proposed, the copulatory activity reported by both Hale (1944) and Gorski (1963) did not represent normal female receptivity. It is also possible, but less likely, that, for the particular strains of rat employed by Harris and Levine, 50 μg of OB was simply insufficient to modify development of behaviour patterns, despite the fact that it led to anovulatory sterility (Harris and Levine, 1965). But some data obtained with various androgens is not totally consistent with the hypothesis that aromatization of testosterone is an obligatory first step in masculinization of the rat brain, with respect to mating behaviour.

Effects of Other Metabolites of Testosterone

As has been observed for differentiation of gonadotrophin regulating mechanisms, DHT, a non-aromatizable androgen, has not been found to have an organizing influence on substrates for mating behaviour in rats (Brown-Grant et al., 1971; Whalen and Luttge, 1971; McDonald and Doughty, 1972a; McDonald and Doughty, 1974; Whalen and Rezek, 1974). McDonald and Doughty (1974) compared the relative potencies of a number of aromatizable and non-aromatizable androgens, for neonatal sex determination (see Table 1). Female rats were injected once daily, on postnatal days one through five, with oil, 1 μg of TP, or 10 μg of one of the following compounds: androstenedione-enol-propionate, 19-hydroxy testosterone propionate (both aromatizable), 5α-dihydrotestosterone propionate, 5α-androstanedione-enol-propionate, androsterone propionate, 5α, 3α-androstanediol dipropionate, or 5α, 3β-androstanediol dipropionate (all non-aromatizable). In addition, a tenth group received single injections of 100 μg of 5α, 3β-androstanediol dipropionate on postnatal day one. All of the aromatizable androgens were effective in causing anovulatory sterility, and none of the non-aromatizable androgens (with the exception of one, which was later found to be impure) was effective in this regard. However, the results of these neonatal treatments on development of sexual receptivity (measured by the lordosis response in ovariectomized oestrogen–progesterone treated adults) were strikingly different: Only TP and androsterone propionate had significant effects on this parameter (McDonald and Doughty, 1974). Stern (1969) administered 20 daily injections (from day one to day 20) of androstenedione, and did observe an effect on lordosis, in females which had received daily doses of 50 μg or more. Similarly, Whalen and Rezek (1974) reported subnormal receptivity in female rats which had contained silastic implants of 2.0 mg of androstenedione, during postnatal days one through ten. Goldfoot et al. (1969), on the other hand, could not prevent the effects of neonatal castration of male rats, on sexual receptivity, with multiple neonatal injections of 250 μg of that androgen.

McDonald and Doughty suggested that, '... if exposure to estrogen during the neonatal period is responsible for the suppression of female behaviour, our results suggest that testosterone is the most effective means of supplying an estrogenic precursor to the brain.' (McDonald and Doughty, 1974). This interpretation does not, however, account for the effectiveness of the non-aromatizable androsterone as a defeminizing agent for the behavioural endpoint.

Initial results with the hamster were consistent with the theory that aromatization of androgens is a prerequisite for organizing neural substrates of mating behaviour. A 100 μg daily dose of androsterone (non-aromatizable) injected into females on days two through four had no effect on capacity for mounting behaviour (Paup *et al.*, 1972) or lordosis response (Coniglio *et al.*, 1973) in adulthood, while neonatally administered androstenedione (aromatizable) was as potent as testosterone in producing females with enhanced mounting activity and diminished sexual receptivity (Tiefer and Johnson, 1975).

Recent findings of Gerall *et al.* (1975) indicate that in hamsters DHT, given neonatally, does reduce lordosis duration in adulthood, and this, together with the effectiveness of androsterone in rats (McDonald and Doughty, 1974), leaves open the possibility that non-aromatizable androgens may play some role in the sexual differentiation of the brain. Gerall and co-workers implanted silastic pellets containing either testosterone (aromatizable), androsterone, DHT (non-aromatizable) or nothing (controls) into two-day old female, and two-day old male (castrated on day five) hamsters, and studied the lordosis response when these neonatally treated hamsters were adults. All animals were gonadectomized for the lordosis studies (females ovariectomized as adults), and primed with OB and progesterone. The response was measured in terms of duration of lordosis. Testosterone, DHT, and androsterone, implanted into neonatal females, altered development of the capacity for female-type mating behaviour, as reflected in diminished durations of lordosis, compared with durations in control hamsters. Testosterone and DHT, but not androsterone, implanted into neonatal males had similar effects. In each case, however, the effect of DHT or androsterone was considerably smaller than that of testosterone (Gerall *et al.*, 1975).

The discrepancy between these results in the hamster and the previous failures to obtain an effect with neonatally administered DHT in the rat (e.g., Whalen and Rezek, 1974) might of course reflect a species difference in mechanisms underlying the organization of neural substrates of mating behaviour. Alternatively, it might reflect differences in the behavioural measures, since most experiments with rats involved measurements of frequencies, rather than durations, of lordosis, while Gerall *et al.* (1975) reported only lordosis durations. Gerall *et al.* suggested that the discrepancy can be explained by the lower effective circulating dose resulting from a systemic injection of hormone, compared with that resulting from a silastic implant of the same hormone (Gerall *et al.*, 1975). This explanation cannot, however, account for the failure of Whalen and Rezek (1974) to obtain an effect of DHT (also implanted neonatally in silastic pellets) on development of the capacity for lordosis in female rats.

The possibility must be considered that oestrogens and non-aromatizable androgens may both be involved in sexual differentiation, with the additional possibility that substrates for neuroendocrine events, female behaviour patterns, and male behaviour patterns may show differential sensitivities to these two classes of steroids. In this connection, Goldfoot and Van Der Werff ten

Table 1. Effects of neonatal hormone treatment on the lordosis response in ovariectomized adult female rats

A: *Neonatal treatment with aromatizable androgens*

Reference	Neonatal treatment			Behaviour testing in ovariectomized adults	
	Hormone	Dose	Age (days after birth)	Hormone Treatment Prior to Testing **	Subnormal Lordosis Response ***
Barraclough and Gorski, 1962	testosterone propionate	1.25 mg	5	E →P	+
Harris and Levine, 1965		500 µg	4	E→P	+
Harris and Levine, 1965		500 µg	4	T	+
Gerall, 1967		1.25 mg	5	E→P	+
Whalen and Edwards, 1967		2.50 mg	1	E→P	+
Mullins and Levine, 1968a		*100 µg	5	E→P	+
Clemens et al., 1969		10 µg	1 or 2	E or E→P	−
Clemens et al., 1969		10 µg	4, or 6	E→P	+
Clemens et al., 1969		10 µg	4, or 6	E	−
Clemens et al., 1970		100 µg	1,2,4, or 6	E→P	+
Clemens, et al., 1970		100 µg	1,2,4, or 6	E	−
Edwards and Thompson, 1970		100 µg	1	E→P	+
Edwards and Thompson, 1970		100 µg	1	E	+
Whalen et al., 1971		250 µg	1	E→P	+
Whalen et al., 1971		250 µg	1	E	+
Pfaff and Zigmond, 1971		200 µg	2	E→P	+
Pfaff and Zigmond, 1971		200 µg	2	T→P	+
Pfaff and Zigmond, 1971		200 µg	2	E	+
McDonald and Doughty, 1972a		100 µg	1	E→P	−
McDonald and Doughty, 1972a		100 µg	5	E→P	+
Blizard and Denef, 1973		100 µg	4	E	+
Sheridan et al., 1973		*20 × 0.5 µg	1–10	E→P	+
McDonald and Doughty, 1974		5 × 1.0 µg	1–5	E→P	+

Table 1 contd.

Reference	Hormone	Dose	Age (days after birth)	Hormone treatment prior to testing **	Subnormal lordosis response ***
Doughty and McDonald, 1974	non-propionated testosterone	30 μg	1 or 5	E→P	−
Whalen and Rezek, 1970		2.0 mg silastic implant	1–10	E→P	+
McDonald and Doughty, 1974	19-hydroxy testosterone propionate	5 × 10.0 μg	1–5	E→P	−
Stern, 1969	androstenedione	*20 × 50 μg	1–20	E→P	++
Whalen and Rezek, 1974	androstenedione	2.0 mg silastic implant	1–10	E→P	+
McDonald and Doughty, 1974	androstenedione-enol-propionate	. 5 × 10.0 μg	1–5	E→P	−

B: *Neonatal treatment with non-aromatizable androgens*

Reference	Neonatal treatment — Hormone	Dose	Age (days after birth)	Behaviour testing in ovariectomized adults — Hormone treatment prior to testing **	Subnormal lordosis response ***
Whalen and Luttge, 1971	dihydrotestosterone	5 × 800 μg (prenatal) +4 × 200 μg	16–20 (gestation) + 1–4	E→P	−
Whalen and Rezek, 1974	dihydrotestosterone	2.0 mg silastic implant	1–10	E→P	−
McDonald and Doughty, 1972a	dihydrotestosterone propionate	100 μg	1 or 5	E→P	−
McDonald and Doughty, 1974	dihydrotestosterone propionate	5 × 10 μg	1–5	E→P	−
McDonald and Doughty, 1974	androstanedione-enol-propionate	5 × 10 μg	1–5	E→P	−
McDonald and Doughty, 1974	5α, 3α-androstanediol dipropionate	5 × 10 μg	1–5	E→P	−
McDonald and Doughty, 1974	5α, 3β-androstanediol dipropionate	5 × 10 μg	1–5	E→P	−
McDonald and Doughty, 1974	5α, 3β-androstanediol dipropionate	100 μg	1	E→P	−
McDonald and Doughty, 1974	androsterone propionate	5 × 10 μg	1–5	E→P	+

Table 1 Contd.

C: Neonatal treatment with oestrogens

Reference	Neonatal treatment			Behaviour testing in ovariectomized adult	
	Hormone	Dose	Age (days after birth)	Hormone treatment prior to testing **	Subnormal lordosis response ***
Whalen and Nadler, 1963	oestradiol benzoate	200 μg	4	E→P	+
Levine and Mullins, 1964		100 μg	4	E→P	+
Harris and Levine, 1965		50 μg	4	E→P	−
Whalen and Nadler, 1965		* 50 μg	4	E→P	+
Zucker and Feder, 1966		5 μg	4	E→P	+
Gerall, 1967		250 μg	5	E→P	+
Whalen and Edwards, 1967		100 μg	1	E→P	+
Mullins and Levine, 1968a		* 33 μg	4	E→P	+
Edwards and Thompson, 1970		100 μg	1	E→P	+
Edwards and Thompson, 1970		100 μg	1	E	+
Hendricks and Gerall, 1970		100 μg	4	E→P	+
Doughty et al., 1975	11βmethoxy, 17ethynyl-oestradiol (RU 2858)	5 × 100ng	1–5	E→P	+
Doughty, et al., 1975		5 × 1.0ng	1–5	E→P	+

*minimum effective dose tested
**E = oestrogen treatment
T = testosterone treatment
E → P = oestrogen treatment followed by progesterone treatment
T → P = testosterone treatment followed by progesterone treatment
***+ = subnormal lordosis response
− = normal lordosis response

Bosch (1975) did observe, in female guinea pigs, facilitatory, 'masculinizing' effects of prenatal treatment with DHTP on the display of male-type mounting behaviour, while this same prenatal treatment did not have a 'defeminizing' effect on the lordosis response.

EFFECTS OF ANTAGONISTS OF OESTROGEN AND ANDROGEN ACTION ON SEXUAL DIFFERENTIATION OF THE BRAIN

In the preceding pages we have presented some experimental data which demonstrate the efficacy of exogenously administered oestrogenic compounds in modifying certain aspects of sex differentiation of the female rodent brain. In addition, we have described work which suggests that only those androgenic compounds which can be aromatized to oestrogen are effective in this regard, at least with respect to differentiation of gonadotrophin regulating mechanisms. Information presently available, concerning the relative potencies of aromatizable *vs.* non-aromatizable androgens with respect to differentiation of behavioural mechanisms, remains equivocal. While we have indicated so far that oestrogen *can* be effective as an imprinting agent, we have not described work which rigorously substantiates the proposal that conversion of androgen to oestrogen is obligatory for normal sex determination. One approach to this problem is an investigation of the effects of antagonists of oestrogen and testosterone action on sex determination. According to the aromatization hypothesis, oestrogen antagonists should attenuate or prevent the organizing effects of either exogenous or endogenous androgen, while specific testosterone antagonists should have no such effect.

Unfortunately, only a limited number of such investigations have been made, and the information they have generated is not entirely consistent. MER-25, a drug which antagonizes a fairly wide range of oestrogenic but not androgenic actions (Lerner, 1964), is at this point the only antioestrogen which has been employed. In 1972, McDonald and Doughty reported that 500 μg of this oestrogen antagonist was able to protect five-day old female rats against the organizing actions of 30 μg of TP. If the MER-25 was administered six hours prior to injection of TP, ovarian weight and histology were normal when the animals were 110 days old. Vaginal smears taken before ovariectomy showed cyclic variation. In contrast, adults which had been treated with TP alone on day five, or with 100 μg of MER-25 administered concurrently with TP, had reduced ovarian weights, absence of corpora lutea, and constant cornification in vaginal smears. 100 or 500 μg of MER-25 injected alone on day five had no effects on any of these adult parameters (McDonald and Doughty, 1972b). These results were partially confirmed in a similar study made later by the same investigators (Doughty and McDonald, 1974). In this study, as little as 100 μg of MER-25 was able to protect five-day old females against the development of anovulatory sterility, again when it was administered six hours before, but not concurrently with, 30 μg of TP. However, as much as 500 μg

of MER-25 was ineffective in antagonizing the actions of 30 μg of TP administered six hours later, if the two drugs were given on the day of birth. In the
same study, sexual receptivity of the neonatally treated rats was examined after
ovariectomy and hormone replacement therapy in adulthood. Since 30 μg
of TP, administered alone either on day one or day five, had no significant
effect on subsequent numbers of animals showing lordosis, or on mean lordosis
quotient, no conclusions could be made concerning the potential effects of
the oestrogen antagonist on these behavioural parameters (Doughty and
McDonald, 1974).

Daily injections of 1 μg of non-propionated testosterone from postnatal
days one through five also resulted in anovulatory sterility and, under those
conditions of neonatal androgenization, the effects were prevented by administration of 100 μg of MER-25 six hours before each testosterone injection
(McDonald and Doughty, 1973/4). But as indicated above, this dose of the
non-propionated testosterone was ineffective in altering development of
sexual receptivity. However, despite the absence of a behavioural effect of
testosterone alone, or of MER-25 alone, the group of animals which had been
treated neonatally with MER-25 six hours before the daily testosterone injections had a mean lordosis quotient which was significantly lower than that of
the testosterone-only treatment group (McDonald and Doughty, 1973/4).
This curious phenomenon raises the presently inexplicable possibility that
MER-25 might potentiate the organizing actions of testosterone on substrates
for mating behaviour, in striking contrast with the apparent antagonistic
effect of MER-25 on induction of anovulatory sterility.

The issue is further confounded by results reported by Brown-Grant (1974).
He observed no difference between the incidences of anovulation at 160 days
of age in groups of rats which had been treated on postnatal day five with:
50 μg of TP, 50 μg of TP plus 500 μg of MER-25, or 50 μg of TP preceded
by six hours with 500 μg of MER-25. But when 500 μg of MER-25 was administered concurrently with *100* μg of TP on day five, the incidence of anovulation
on day 160 was significantly lower than it was for animals treated with 100 μg
of TP alone, even though MER-25 given six hours prior to 100 μg of TP was
ineffective. In the same study, the incidence of anovulation as a result of neonatal treatment with 10 μg of OB was significantly reduced by administration of
500 μg of MER-25, either concurrently with or six hours prior to injection of
the oestrogen (Brown-Grant, 1974). The criterion that Brown-Grant used to
determine whether ovulation had occurred was simply the mascroscopic
appearance of the ovaries at laparotomy, and his confusing results might
reflect the relative unreliability of that method, compared with histological
examination of ovarian tissue.

Gottlieb *et al.* (1974) implanted silastic pellets containing either free testosterone or TP into two-day old female hamsters and administered daily
injections of either MER-25 or vehicle, from day two through day ten, when
the implants were removed. 100% of animals in each of these four neonatal

treatment groups had no corpora lutea on day 50. In addition, the mean duration of lordosis response (tested after hormone replacement therapy between 80 and 110 days of age) for each of these groups was significantly lower than that of control animals. Gottlieb *et al.* suggested that this apparent failure of MER-25 to modify the effects of androgen on development of either ovarian cyclicity or sexual receptivity in the hamster might be attributable to the fact that the animals had not been exposed to the antioestrogen prior to implantation of the androgen-containing pellets (Gottlieb *et al.*, 1974). Similarly, the majority of female rats, which had received 50 µg injections of TP immediately after intrahypothalamic implants of 10 µg of MER-25 on postnatal day two, exhibited anovulatory sterility in adulthood (Hayashi, 1974).

It might be tentatively concluded from most of the data of McDonald and Doughty that when MER-25 is administered to neonatal female rats some hours before testosterone administration, the oestrogen antagonist can prevent the masculinizing effects of testosterone, with respect to differentiation of gonadotrophin regulating mechanisms. Results which are discordant with this conclusion might reflect species differences, parameters investigated, or the relative doses of MER-25 and testosterone. The last point seems important in light of the fact that at certain relatively low, but not high, doses, MER-25 is itself weakly oestrogenic. Thus, it can mildly stimulate uterine growth and alkaline phosphatase activity in immature ovariectomized mice (Lerner, 1964) and, when MER-25 was administered to lactating rats, the female offspring were sterile as adults (Lerner *et al.*, 1958). Perhaps most pertinent to this problem is the fact that MER-25, compared with other related drugs (such as CI628 or nafoxidine), is not a very efficient antagonist of oestrogen action in the adult rat (McEwen *et al.*, unpubl. data). Again, evidence is missing at the present time which might support—or disprove—the theory that aromatization of testosterone is a prerequisite for its masculinizing effect on differentiation of mating behaviour patterns. Clearly, more experiments must be done, preferably with other oestrogen antagonists, before more definitive conclusions can be made, with respect to both gonadotrophin regulation and mating behaviour. (See Note on p. 218.)

Cyproterone acetate is a specific androgen antagonist which directly inhibits testosterone action at the site of the target tissue (Neumann and von Berswordt-Wallrabe, 1966). It is therefore of interest that when the drug was administered daily to male rats, during the first two weeks after birth, and the animals were later castrated and given ovarian implants, corpora lutea were in some cases observed in the implanted ovarian tissue (Neumann *et al.*, 1967). Furthermore, the incidence of anovulatory sterility in neonatally TP-treated female rats was reduced by neonatal cyproterone acetate treatment concurrent with TP administration (Wollman and Hamilton, 1967; Arai and Gorski, 1968b).

These protective effects of an androgen antagonist against neonatal masculinization do not, however, preclude the possibility of obligatory aromatization of an androgen. The molecular mechanism of cyproterone acetate inhibition is not known. It might interfere with testosterone uptake by neural receptor molecules and this in turn might be a necessary first step in the aromatization process, perhaps in terms of making a sufficient amount of the hormone available to the aromatizing enzyme. Alternatively, the drug might directly compete with the androgen at the level of enzyme interaction. It has in fact been found that cyproterone can partially inhibit *in vitro* biosynthesis of oestrogenic metabolites from androstenedione in a preparation of human placental microsomes (Schwarzel *et al.*, 1973). An interesting parallel exists in this regard between cyproterone and progesterone: the latter can also protect neonatal female rats against masculinization if administered together with TP (Kincl and Maqueo, 1965); and, like cyproterone, progesterone can partially inhibit *in vitro* synthesis of oestrogens from the androstenedione substrate (Schwarzel *et al.*, 1973). Experiments are being planned in this laboratory to investigate the possible inhibition by cyproterone acetate of *in vivo* aromatization of testosterone in the neonatal rat. But, as is the case with the MER-25 experiments, at the present time the cyproterone acetate data have raised important, but still unanswered, questions.

OCCURRENCE OF AROMATIZATION AND THE EXISTENCE OF OESTROGEN RECEPTORS IN THE DEVELOPING BRAIN

In the preceding pages we have presented some evidence supporting the idea that the normal processes of masculinization of the mammalian brain might be mediated by estrogenic metabolite(s) of endogenous aromatizable testicular secretions. At the present time the hypothesis must still be considered viable, but tentative. It remains to be considered whether aromatization of androgens actually can occur in mammalian tissues during critical periods for sex differentiation. As will be discussed below, results of *in vitro* experiments have demonstrated that the necessary enzyme (aromatase) is present in the foetal human and neonatal rat brain. It has also been shown that, at least in the neonatal rat, some proportion of exogenous testosterone is aromatized *in vivo* to form oestrogens recoverable from the brain. Moreover, the neonatal brain appears to contain 'receptor' sites for oestrogens.

When homogenates of human foetal hypothalamic (Naftolin *et al.*, 1971a; Ryan *et al.*, 1972) or hippocampal (Naftolin *et al.*, 1971b; Ryan *et al.*, 1972) tissue were incubated with radioactive androstenedione, oestrone and oestradiol were formed. The absolute levels of each estrogenic product were very low, always representing less than 1% of total radioactivity extracted from the incubates, but they were nevertheless high enough to be identified by crystallization procedures. Homogenates of human foetal cerebral cortex, on the other hand, produced negligible to non-detectable levels of oestrone and oestradiol from the same labelled precursor (Naftolin *et al.*, 1971a, 1971b; Ryan *et al.*, 1972). Similar results were obtained with neural tissues from foetal and neonatal rats (Reddy *et al.*, 1974). These experiments clearly show that a functional aromatizing system exists in the developing mammalian brain, and the regional specificity of its action suggests possible physiological significance.

Weisz and Gibbs (1974) injected five-day-old female rats with tritiated testosterone. Ten, 15 or 30 min later, animals were sacrificed and various radioactive metabolites were extracted, isolated, and identified from whole tissue suspensions of different brain regions. The results were comparable to those of the *in vitro* experiments: small amounts (again, less than 1% of total extractable radioactivity) of tritiated oestradiol were identified in hypothalamus, amygdala, and septal area, but not in cerebral cortex (Weisz and Gibbs, 1974).

More recently, Lieberburg and McEwen (1975a) reasoned that, since exogenously administered oestradiol is concentrated and retained by cell nuclei of limbic structures in the adult rat brain, the search for oestrogenic metabolites of injected testosterone might be more fruitful if investigations were made at the nuclear level. They injected five-day-old male and female rats with tritiated testosterone and two hours later sacrificed the animals and prepared purified nuclear fractions from pooled hypothalamic–preoptic area–amygdaloid tissue, and from cerebral cortex. Oestradiol was extracted and quantified from whole homogenates and from nuclear fractions (Table 2). As was the case in the earlier work, levels of radioactivity identified as tritiated oestradiol were higher in whole tissue homogenates of the pooled limbic regions than in homogenates of cerebral cortex, but all of these levels represented less than 1% of total radioactivity present. However, tritiated oestradiol present in nuclear fractions of the limbic regions comprised 34–54% of total nuclear radioactivity, while in nuclear fractions of cerebral cortex, from zero to 24% of total radioactivity

Table 2. Levels of total radioactivity and oestradiol-17β in whole homogenates and cell nuclei of neonatal rat brains

Brain region	Experiment	Radioactivity (fmoles/mg protein)			
		Homogenate		Nuclei	
		Total	Oestradiol-17β	Total	Oestradiol-17β
Cortex	A	539	3.3	13.8	0.2
	B	401	0.4	8.6	2.1
	C	399	1.0	13.1	0.8
	D	704	U	13.2	U
Limbic	A	469	3.9	38.6	15.6[a]
	B	400	3.6	41.6	20.8[a]
	C	462	3.2	42.7	23.1
	D	744	2.4	39.6	13.4

U = Undetectable levels

[a] Concentrations of oestradiol-17β corrected for recovery, determined from final crystallization, were 16.8 and 20.1 fmoles/mg for A and B respectively. Oestradiol-17β recoveries averaged 52.6 ± 10.2%.

From Lieberburg and McEwen (1975a).

could be identified as oestradiol. In addition, the concentrations of oestradiol (fmoles per mg protein) recovered in limbic cell nuclear fractions always substantially exceeded (by a factor of 4–7) those concentrations in corresponding whole homogenates. This was not the case for the cerebral cortex (Lieberburg and McEwen, 1975a). These results are consistent with autoradiographic studies showing accumulation of radioactivity injected as ^{3}H-testosterone in neurons of preoptic area, hypothalamus, and amygdala and competition for this uptake by unlabelled oestradiol as well as testosterone but not by unlabelled DHT (Sheridan et al., 1974b).

Since the testosterone was systemically injected in these experiments, it could not be definitively established that the oestradiol recovered from the brain had been formed there or had entered the brain after peripheral aromatization. Yet aromatase is present in foetal and neonatal brain tissue (see above), and for reasons which will be described in the last section of this chapter it appears unlikely that small amounts of circulating oestradiol would enter the brain and attach to intracellular receptor sites. The fact that oestradiol formed from testosterone is concentrated and retained within cell nuclei indicates the possible existence of a selective receptor mechanism for the hormone in limbic regions of the developing rat brain, quantitatively comparable to those of the adult female rat brain (Lieberburg and McEwen, 1975a).

Whether or not sexual differentiation involves oestrogen, it is important to consider the evidence for oestrogen 'receptor' sites in neonatal brains, since some experimental data suggest that the neonatal brain–pituitary axis can respond to the hormone. Thus, OB administered on day one leads to altered brain serotonin levels on days 12–14 (Giulian et al., 1973). Moreover, ovarian products exert negative feedback effects on gonadotrophin secretion during the first two weeks of postnatal life (Gerall and Dunlap, 1971; Caligaris et al., 1972, 1973). Initial attempts to demonstrate selective uptake of tracer doses of ^{3}H-oestradiol by hypothalamus of neonatal rats revealed, with the exception of median eminence, generally uniform uptake across all neural structures (Alvarez and Ramirez, 1970; Kato et al., 1971a; Presl et al., 1970) and little, if any, limited capacity cell nuclear accumulation of ^{3}H-oestradiol (Plapinger and McEwen, 1973; Vertes et al., 1973). Most of the above-mentioned reports also agree that the typical adult neural patterns of in vivo ^{3}H-oestradiol uptake following tracer doses of this steroid appear during the fourth postnatal week of life (Presl et al., 1970; Kato et al., 1971a) and are correlated with the emergence in hypothalamus, preoptic area, and amygdala at this time of high levels of limited capacity cell nuclear retention of ^{3}H-oestradiol (Plapinger and McEwen, 1973) and with the predominance at this time of ^{3}H-oestradiol, relative to ^{3}H-oestrone and other metabolites, in median emincence after systemic administration of ^{3}H-oestradiol (Presl et al., 1973).

The exception to the above is the report of Kulin and Reiter (1972) of higher hypothalamic than cerebral cortex tissue levels of radioactivity after incubation of neonatal rat tissue fragments in vitro at 37° C. These different results are due to the use of higher levels of ^{3}H-oestradiol than were achieved in the *in vivo* experiments described above, and are in keeping with results of more recent *in vivo* experiments (McEwen *et al.*, 1975b, and Maclusky *et al.*, 1976) which used higher doses of ^{3}H-oestradiol and revealed cell nuclear receptor sites as early as postnatal day three. Binding of ^{3}H-oestradiol to these cell nuclear receptors can be prevented by prior injection of an antioestrogenic compound, CI 628, as well as by unlabelled oestradiol-17β but not by a variety of other unlabelled steroids such as progesterone, DHT and 3β,5α-androstanediol, indicating that it has the specificity characteristic of oestradiol receptor systems in the adult brain, pituitary, and uterus (McEwen *et al.*, 1975b and unpubl.). These results are consistent with autoradiographic studies showing labelling of neurons in the hypothalamus, preoptic area, and amygdala after injections of 1 μg of ^{3}H-oestradiol into neonatal female rats (Sheridan *et al.*, 1974a).

These observations bear some relationship to the observed developmental time course of hypothalamic (Kato *et al.*, 1971b, 1974) and pooled hypothalamus, preoptic area, and amygdala (Plapinger and McEwen, 1973) cytosol 'receptor' sites of the adult type. These are detectable by sucrose density gradient analysis at day seven and increase steadily during subsequent postnatal development (Kato *et al.*, 1971b, 1974; Plapinger and McEwen, 1973). Detection of cytosol binding sites in rats during the first three postnatal weeks of life is made difficult by the presence of a second class of oestradiol binding proteins (see pp 199–201). However, using procedures which minimize oestrogen binding by this protein, Barley *et al.* (1974) have reported the detection in rats at postnatal day five of an oestradiol binding protein with some of the properties expected of a cytosol receptor.

As to the discrepancy between the low dose and high dose experiments with ^{3}H-oestradiol regarding the age of appearance of cell nuclear retention, the most attractive explanation appears to involve the second class of oestradiol binding proteins which will be described in the next section. Because they are present in large amounts in all parts of the brain (Plapinger *et al.*, 1973), their presence would tend to mask regional differences in ^{3}H-oestradiol retention at the tissue level due to actual receptor sites until they are no longer detectable (around postnatal day 21), and might in addition tend to retard the association of *low doses* of ^{3}H-oestradiol with the receptor sites. In addition there are in the cerebral cortex of neonatal rats cell nuclear and cytosol receptor sites similar in all respects to those found in limbic areas (Barley *et al.*, 1974; McEwen *et al.*, 1975b). Because these sites are present in concentrations comparable to those observed in the amygdala and preoptic area (but lower than those observed in the hypothalamus), their presence would also tend to obscure 'regional' differences in ^{3}H-oestradiol retention of the type seen in the adult brain. These cerebral cortex receptor sites disappear during the third postnatal week of life. Their function remains a total enigma since the cortex apparently lacks the ability to convert testosterone to oestradiol (see above).

Before leaving the subject of the uptake and retention of labelled gonadal steroids from the blood, studies of DHT should also be mentioned. The ability of the brain and pituitary to convert ^{3}H-testosterone to ^{3}H-DHT is well established by postnatal day five (Chamberlain and Rogers, 1972; Denef et al., 1974; Weisz and Gibbs, 1974), and DHTP, given on day one, has been shown, like TP, to delay vaginal opening and to depress brain serotonin levels measured on day 12 (McDonald, 1971; Giulian et al., 1973). (As discussed by Meyerson, this volume Chapter 16, serotonin has been implicated in neural mechanisms underlying sexual behaviour.) The neonatal rat brain takes up radioactivity injected as ^{3}H-testosterone from the blood, and while there is higher accumulation in pituitary than in brain tissue, there appears to be no regional localization of tissue accumulation of total radioactivity (Alvarez and Ramirez, 1970; McEwen et al., 1970; Weisz and Philpott, 1971; Barnea et al., 1972; Lobl and Schapiro; 1972; Tuohimaa and Niemi, 1972), in contrast to the localization of oestradiol as a testosterone metabolite in limbic and hypo-thalamic structures (see Table 2). Cell nuclear retention of ^{3}H-DHT or of unmetabolized ^{3}H-testosterone in neonatal brain tissue has so far not been studied, and thus the existence of neonatal brain cell nuclear receptors for these two gonadal steroids remains to be established.

PROTECTION FROM DELETERIOUS EFFECTS OF ENDOGENOUS FOETAL OR NEONATAL OESTROGENS

Whether or not oestrogenic compounds actually mediate the processes of sexual differentiation in the normal male, one point is apparent: oestrogen can dramatically alter the ontogeny of the reproductive axis, if undifferentiated tissues are exposed to the hormone during a critical period. This point can be illustrated by examples of the effects of exogenous oestrogens on the differen-tiation of peripheral reproductive tissues, as well as by the previously sited examples of effects on the brain.

Direct effects of oestrogen on the development of external genitalia were observed clinically in four human females, whose mothers had been chronically treated with DES during pregnancy (Bongiovanni et al., 1959). These children had markedly enlarged clitorii, requiring surgical alteration, while no further signs of virilization could be detected in either the patients or their mothers.

Perhaps the most extensively studied example of the effects of oestrogen on developing tissues is the case of vaginal pathology resulting from pre-or neonatal administration of the hormone. Abnormalities of vaginal morphoge-nesis have been observed in newborn (Greene et al., 1940) and late foetal (Forsberg, 1960) rats, following in utero exposure to relatively large doses of various exogenous oestrogenic compounds. Similarly, atypical cervico-vaginal cytology and biochemistry have been detectable in neonatal mice, shortly after postnatal administration of oestrogens (Forsberg, 1969, 1970, 1972; Forsberg and Kvinnsland, 1972; Takasugi and Kamishima, 1973). Some aspect(s) of such oestrogen-induced disorganization of cervico-vaginal differentiation have long-term, apparently irreversible, consequences. These include, in mice: constant cornification of superficial epithelium (Dunn and Green, 1963; Takasugi and Bern, 1964; Kimura and Nandi, 1967; Kimura et al., 1967); epidermoid hyperplasia (Takasugi and Bern, 1964; Kimura and Nandi, 1967); transplantable neoplasia (Dunn and Green, 1963; Takasugi, 1972; and retention of patches of columnar epithelial cells interspersed with normal stratified squamous epithelium (Forsberg, 1969). In many cases, these late pathological manifestations of neonatal oestrogenization persist following ovariectomy in adulthood; they therefore seem independent of further oestrogenic stimulation (Kimura and Nandi, 1967; Kimura et al., 1967; Forsberg, 1969; Takasugi, 1972).

The most serious and immediate implication of such experimental findings is their possible relevance to the recently increased incidence of primary adenocarcinoma of the vagina in young women. The great majorityof these cases have been linked to intrauterine exposure to DES and related synthetic oestrogens (Herbst et al., 1972a). Vaginal adenosis (the presence of benign glandular epithelium in the normally aglandular vagina) was frequently observed in these patients, as well as in others who had been exposed to DES in utero but did not have overt carcinomas. These observations led Herbst to postulate that a differentiated vagina containing glandular elements is the crucial aberration resulting from prenatal stilboestrol action; that this aberration provides the cellular substrate for future carcinogenesis (Herbst et al., 1971; Herbst, 1972; Herbst et al., 1972b). Furthermore, it is believed that the adenosis represents retention of Mullerian tissue in regions of the foetal vagina in which Mullerian tissue is normally displaced by proliferating urogenital sinus epithelium (Herbst and Scully, 1970; Herbst, 1972; Herbst et al., 1972a; Herbst et al., 1972b).

One question which persistently emerges from a consideration of these data is: if exogenous oestrogens can so severely and variously modify differentiation of neural and reproductive tissues, then why, under normal circumstances of gestation, does endogenous maternal oestrogen have no deleterious effect on foetal development? While, for the rat brain, it is true that the period of greatest sensitivity to gonadal hormones appears to be some time after birth, that does not seem to be the case for the peripheral tissues in the rat or in the human. And, although systematic studies have not yet been done with oestrogens, it is known that in other species, the critical periods of brain sensitivity to testosterone are during gestation. This is so for development of mating behaviour traits in the guinea pig, as described earlier, as well as for development of certain sexually dimorphic patterns of social behaviour in the rhesus monkey (see Young et al., 1964). Furthermore, findings in a recent study of various behavioural parameters in young men whose (diabetic) mothers had been treated with oestrogens and progestins during pregnancy tentatively suggest that oestrogen might modify psychosexual differentiation in human males (Yalom *et al.*, 1973). Then, again, how are foetal tissues apparently unaffected by endogenous oestrogens, which circulate at relatively high concentrations during primate (Mishell *et al.*, 1973; Challis *et al.*, 1974; Tullner and Hodgen, 1974; de Hertogh *et al.*, 1975) and subprimate (Waynforth and Robertson, 1972; Challis *et al.*, 1973) gestation?

Herbst, considering the latent carcinogenic effects of DES on human foetuses, suggested that the specific structure of the non-steroidal synthetic oestrogen exclusively endows it with the property of disrupting differentiation (Herbst *et al.*, 1972a). However, this cannot account for the data from rodent experiments: no qualitative differences have been reported between the pathological consequences of pre- or neonatal treatment with oestradiol and those of treatment with DES. A more generalizable solution seems feasible. Foetuses might normally be protected against endogenous oestrogen by a mechanism which prevents the hormone from entering foetal tissues. If this were the case, then either natural steroidal oestrogens–introduced in quantities which would exceed the capacity of the protective mechanism–or synthetic (steroidal or non-steroidal) oestrogens—which could not be recognized by such a system— would be free to act on vulnerable foetal tissues.

There exists a likely molecular candidate for serving such a protective function. This is alphafoetoprotein (AFP), the alpha-globulin transiently present in foetoneonatal serum and in amniotic fluid of a wide variety of mammalian species, including the human (Bergstrand and Czar, 1956, 1957; Abelev *et al.*, 1963; Gitlin and Boesman, 1966; Stanislawski-Birencwajg, 1967; Slade and Budd, 1972). Although the existence of AFP has been recognized for a number of years, its physiological function has not been understood. More recently, investigators have studied oestradiol-binding properties of a serum protein in foetal and neonatal rats (Nunez *et al.*, 1971a, 1971b, 1971c; Raynaud *et al.*, 1971). This molecule has a stereospecific affinity for 17β-oestradiol and is present, in progressively diminishing concentrations, in the male and female rat, from late gestation through the fourth week of postnatal life (Raynaud *et al.*, 1971). A number of similarities between properties of the binding protein and of AFP led to further investigation, and it was finally confirmed that, in the rat and mouse, AFP *is*, in fact, the foetoneonatal oestradiol-binding protein (Uriel *et al.*, 1972; Aussel *et al.*, 1973). A similar, immunochemically related, oestradiol-binding macromolecule in the foetal and neonatal rat brain has been studied in this laboratory (Plapinger *et al.*, 1973; Plapinger and McEwen, 1975). The precise physiocochemical and functional relationships of this brain molecule to serum AFP are presently under investigation.

The possibility has been raised that AFP, by binding to oestradiol, prevents the hormone from interacting with foetal tissues (Soloff *et al.*, 1972; Uriel and de Nechaud, 1973; Plapinger *et al.*, 1973). This hypothesis was merely speculative, based primarily on knowledge of the oestradiol-binding property of AFP and of the approximate correlations between the species-specific periods of peak AFP concentrations and of major sensitivities to gonadal hormones. For example, in the human, AFP concentrations decline to barely detectable levels by the time of birth (Gitlin and Boseman, 1966). In the rat, on the other hand, substantial amounts of AFP persist during the neonatal period (Raynaud, 1973), when it might in fact serve to protect still sensitive neural tissues against oestradiol which might be present in maternal milk (Lacassagne and Nyka 1934; Hain, 1935; Green, 1937; Lerner et al., 1958; Darling et al., 1974).

At the present time, however, there is a growing body of information which provides more substantive, although still indirect, support for the hypothesis that AFP has a protective role in normal organogenesis. The information can be classified according to three categories of clinical and experimental data. In all three cases, the same basic reasoning can be applied: the capacities of three oestrogenic compounds to interact with undifferentiated tissues seem to be inversely related to their respective in vitro binding affinities for AFP. Thus, in the rat, 17 β-oestradiol has a high specific affinity for, and DES has a very low specific affinity for, AFP, while RU 2858 (the synthetic steroidal oestrogen) does not specifically bind to AFP at all (Raynaud et al., 1971).

The first category consists of the clinical data on the incidence of vaginal adenocarcinoma in young women. As already stated, the phenomenon has been positively correlated with intrauterine exposure to DES (Herbst et al., 1972a). Although comparative data for offspring of women who might have been treated with oestradiol is not available, it seems possible that the potency of DES might reflect its low binding affinity for AFP. A great proportion of the administered synthetic material, unbound by the serum protein, might therefore have had an enhanced capacity for intracellular localization within foetal tissues.

The second category of evidence for the AFP protection hypothesis concerns the data from experiments which compared the potencies of oestradiol, RU 2858, and DES, for exerting effects on pre- and postnatal rat tissues. The first such experiment compared relative capacities of two of these oestrogens for inducing rat uterine growth, in vivo. In very young animals, when concentrations of AFP are high, oestradiol had no effect on uterine growth at any dose used, while RU 2858 was effective at all doses. This divergence in potencies diminished with increasing age, while plasma concentrations of AFP were declining, until day 28, when AFP was no longer detectable. At this time, the effects of RU 2858 and oestradiol on uterine growth were quantitatively equivalent (Raynaud, 1973). Another experiment compared the potencies of oestradiol and RU 2858 in exerting deleterious effects on urogenital tissues of the male rat foetus (Vannier and Raynaud, 1975). While prenatal administration of either oestrogen resulted in several morphological aberrations, the minimum effective dose of RU 2858 was significantly lower than that of oestradiol for each endpoint studied (Vannier and Raynaud, 1975). A third comparative experiment was recently reported by Doughty et al. (1975), and already described in this paper. It involved determining the minimum effective doses of RU 2858 and OB (administered as daily injections on postnatal days one through five), for modifying sexual differentiation of the reproductive axis. It will be recalled that the minimum effective dose of RU 2858, for inducing anovulatory sterility and diminished sexual receptivity, was 0.5 and 1.0 ng/day, respectively, while that of OB was 100 ng/day for both parameters (Doughty *et al.*, 1975). Analogous results were obtained by Kincl *et al.* (1965) when the effectiveness of DES for inducing anovulatory sterility in neonatal female rats was compared with that of oestradiol.

Finally, experiments performed in this laboratory yielded results which provide further indirect evidence in favour of the protection hypothesis. These entailed determinations of the relative capacities of the three hormones to become intracellularly localized in the neonatal female rat brain. In an initial study, it was found that an approximately physiological dose of systemically injected tritium labelled oestradiol does not become concentrated within cell nuclei of the neonatal brain, in regions where comparable doses are known to be concentrated and retained by cell nuclei in the adult female rat (Plapinger and McEwen, 1973). These results were interpreted as indicating that nuclear binding sites for oestradiol do not yet exist in the neonatal rat brain. More recently, however, McEwen *et al.* (1975b) repeated the experiment with much larger doses of the labelled hormone, and found, as was described earlier, that once a certain circulating concentration was exceeded, considerable amounts of radioactivity were concentrated in brain cell nuclei of neonatal female rats. These findings are in agreement with results of an autoradiography study in which similar high doses of tritiated oestradiol were employed (Sheridan *et al.*, 1974a). Furthermore, McEwen and co-workers compared dose effectiveness of the three labelled oestrogens for *in vivo* nuclear uptake in the neonatal female rat brain, and found them to have the following order of increasing effectiveness: oestradiol, DES, RU 2858 again inversely related to respective binding affinities for AFP (McEwen *et al.*, 1975b).

All of these findings are consistent with predictions which would evolve from the protection hypothesis. If AFP, by sequestering maternal oestradiol, normally provides a molecular barrier between the hormone and sensitive foetal tissues, then oestrogenic compounds which cannot be bound by AFP would be more likely to reach intracellular compartments of the foetus and thereby exert effects on differentiating tissues. In addition, the hypothesis is attractive because it could be included in a model for sexual differentiation of the brain via aromatization of endogenous testosterone. Since testosterone is not significantly bound by rat AFP (Raynaud *et al.*, 1971), it could easily enter foetal or neonatal brain tissue. There it could be acted on by aromatase within brain cells and the oestradiol thus formed could interact with intracellular (distinct from the extracellular AFP) binding sites, with consequent sexual determination. The results of the study by Lieberburg and McEwen (1975a), described in the preceding section, suggest that this hypothetical sequence of events actually occurs in the rat.

Attractive as the AFP protection hypothesis is, problems remain which must be resolved before any definitive conclusions can be made. The first of these problems is the controversy about oestradiol binding to human AFP. Although some investigators have observed binding (Uriel *et al.*, 1972; Arnon *et al.*, 1973), others have reported negative findings, with human material (Nunez *et al.*, 1974 Swartz and Soloff, 1974). One possible explanation for the inconsistent findings might be that, in some human samples, existing binding sites are already saturated with endogenous oestradiol. It is obviously imperative that this controversy be resolved before the AFP protection hypothesis can be considered universally applicable.

Another problem concerns some experimental evidence that endogenous ovarian secretions (presumably oestradiol) exert physiological effects in the neonatal rat. Two examples of such effects are negative feedback on gonadotrophin secretion and stimulation of brain serotonin levels. When rats were ovariectomized on day one, serum concentrations of LH (Caligaris *et al.*, 1972) and of FSH (Caligaris *et al.*, 1973) were increased on day ten, compared with those of intact females. Similarly hemiovariectomy of neonatal rats resulted in compensatory ovarian hypertrophy of the remaining ovary, indirectly suggesting enhanced rates of gonadotrophin secretion after removal of one ovary (Gerall and Dunlap, 1971). Brain concentrations of serotonin are transiently higher in female rats than they are in males during the second week after birth. Ovariectomy on day one resulted in diminished serotonin levels on day twelve, approximating those of intact males of the same age (Giulian *et al.*, 1973).

It would therefore seem that endogenous oestradiol is normally effective, with respect to these two parameters, in the presence of AFP. Rat plasma concentration of AFP, measured by *in vitro* oestradiol-binding activity, is still relatively high during the second postnatal week (Raynaud, 1973). It would be of interest to know if the active ovarian component in these instances is actually oestradiol and, if so, whether it is present in concentrations which exceed the (undetermined) *in vivo* oestradiol-binding capacity of AFP at that time.

A third type of action of prepuberal ovarian secretions is that of attenuation of the masculinizing effects of neonatally administered TP (Blizard and Denef, 1973; Hendricks and Duffy, 1974). Since in these experiments ovaries were not removed until at least day 20, it is not possible to say at what time during the prepuberal period they were effective.

Finally, if AFP has a protective function for the mammalian foetus, then it remains to be demonstrated that an experimentally induced deficit in functional AFP would lead to abnormalities of differentiation caused by endogenous oestrogen alone. Intravenous injection, into pregnant rabbits, of antiserum against rabbit AFP resulted in an increased incidence of foetal mortality, compared with no foetal mortality in control pregnant rabbits injected with normal sheep serum (Slade, 1973). Similar results were obtained when antiserum against rat AFP was administered to pregnant rats (Smith, 1973).

Would surviving offspring of similarly treated pregnant animals have developmental aberrations comparable to those induced by exogenous oestrogens? This question presents a challenge for future experimental work.

SUMMARY AND CONCLUSIONS

Certain sexually dimorphic behavioural and physiological characteristics of several mammalian species reflect sexual dimorphism of components of the mature brain. The presence of testes during a relatively brief critical foetal or neonatal period will irreversibly determine the differentiation of these neural components in a masculine direction. If the testes are absent during the critical period, differentiation will proceed irreversibly in a feminine direction. Such effects of foetal or neonatal testicular products, termed 'organizational' effects, can be mimicked to a large extent, in animals of either genetic sex, by administering various gonadal hormones during the critical period. We have reviewed some aspects of the organizational actions of gonadal hormones, primarily with respect to two sexually dimorphic components of the rodent brain: neural substrates for regulation of pituitary gonadotrophin secretion; and neural substrates for patterns of mating behaviour. Particular emphasis has been placed on an evaluation of the aromatization hypothesis. According to this hypothesis, the organizational effects of androgenic hormones (either endogenous, secreted by the foetal or neonatal testes, or exogenous, administered experimentally during the critical period) are mediated by the conversion of these hormones to oestrogens (aromatization). If this were the case, then the active agent responsible for organizing the brain for masculine type differentiation would be an oestrogenic hormone.

We have reviewed some existing data accumulated from a number of different experimental approaches and considered them in light of the aromatization hypothesis. These approaches include: qualitative and quantitative comparisons of the organizational actions of various exogenously administered oestrogens and androgens; studies of the effects of oestrogen and androgen antagonists on sexual differentiation of the brain; studies of the aromatization process during the critical period for sex differentiation; and studies of oestrogen receptors in the undifferentiated brain.

A majority of the evidence is consistent with the aromatization hypothesis and, at least in terms of differentiation of gonadotrophin regulating mechanisms in the rat brain, is suggestive of the validity of the hypothesis. A few inconsistencies exist however, particularly with respect to differentiation of rodent mating behaviour patterns. These inconsistencies raise some doubts concerning the idea that aromatization of androgens must mediate *all* aspects of neural sex differentiation. At present, the aromatization hypothesis can still be considered a viable, but tentative, working hypothesis. A great deal more work remains to be done, involving a variety of animal species and a variety of experimental endpoints, before it can be accepted as a universally applicable explanation of the mechanism underlying normal sex differentiation of the mammalian brain.

We have concluded this chapter with a discussion of a possible mechanism by which the undifferentiated female brain, and other components of the undifferentiated female reproductive axis, are normally protected against the potentially harmful actions of endogenous oestrogens.

ACKNOWLEDGEMENTS

The work performed in this laboratory was supported by research grant NS 07080 from The National Institutes of Health, and by Rockefeller Foundation grant RF 70095 for research in reproductive biology.

We would like to thank Ms. Freddi Berg and Ms. Deborah Vetter for their editorial assistance in the preparation of this manuscript.

REFERENCES

Abelev, G. J., Perova, D. S., Khramkova, N. I., Postnikova, Z. A., and Irlin, I. S. (1963) Production of embryonal α-globulin by transplantable mouse hepatomas, *Transplantation*, **1**, 174–80.

Alvarez, E., and Ramirez, V. (1970) Distribution curves of ^{3}H-testosterone and ^{3}H-estradiol in neonatal female rats, *Neuroendocrinology*, **6**, 349–60.

Anderson, C. H., and Greenwald, S. S. (1969) Autoradiographic analysis of estradiol uptake in the brain and pituitary of the female rat, *Endocrinology*, **85**, 1160–5.

Arai, Y. (1963) The content of luteinizing hormone of the anterior pituitary and of luteinizing hormone releasing factor of the hypothalamus in estrogen-induced persistent-diestrous rats, *Proc. Japan Acad.*, **39**, 605–9.

Arai, Y. (1965) Failure of ovariectomy to induce pituitary castration reaction in estrogen-induced persistent-diestrous rats, *Proc. Japan Acad.*, **41**, 163–8.

Arai, Y. (1972) Effect of 5α-dihydrotestosterone on differentiation of masculine pattern of the brain in the rat, *Endocrinol. Jap.*, **19**, 389–93.

Arai, Y., and Gorski, R. A. (1968a) Effect of anti-estrogen on steroid induced sexual receptivity in ovariectomized rats, *Physiol. Behav.* **3**, 351–3.

Arai, Y., and Gorski, R. A. (1968b) Critical exposure time for androgenization of the rat hypothalamus determined by anti androgen injection, *Proc. Soc. Exp. Biol. Med.*, **127**, 590–3.

Arai, Y., and Masuda, S. (1970) Effect of electrochemical stimulation of the preoptic area on induction of ovulation in estrogenized rats, *Endocrinol. Jap.*, **17**, 237–9.

Arnon, R., Teicher, E., Bustin, M., and Sela, M. (1973) Preparation of antisera to α-fetoprotein making use of estradiol affinity column, *FEBS Letters*, **32**, 335–8.

Attramadal, A. (1970) Cellular localization of ^{3}H-oestradiol in the hypothalamus: an autoradiographic study in male and female rats, *Zelt. Fur Zallforschung*, **104**, 572–81.

Aussel C., Uriel, J., and Mercier-Bodard, C. (1973) Rat alpha-fetoprotein: isolation, characterization and estrogen-binding properties, *Biochimie*, **55**, 1431–7.

Barley, J., Ginsburg, M., Greenstein, B. D., MacLusky, N. J., and Thomas, P. J. (1974) A receptor mediating sexual differentiation? *Nature*, **252**, 259–60.

Barnea, A., Weinstein, A., and Lindner, H. R. (1972) Uptake of androgens by the brain of the neonatal female rat, *Brain Res.*, **46**, 391–402.

Barraclough, C. A. (1955) Influence of age on the response of preweanling female mice to testosterone propionate, *Am. J. Anat.*, **97**, 493–521.

Barraclough, C. A. (1961) Production of anovulatory sterile rats by single injections of testosterone propionate, *Endocrinology*, **68**, 62–7.

Barraclough, C. A. and Gorski, R. A. (1961) Evidence that the hypothalamus is responsible for androgen-induced sterility in the female rat, *Endocrinology*, **68**, 68–79.

Barraclough, C. A. and Gorski, R. A. (1962) Studies on mating behavior in the androgen-sterilized female rat in relation to the hypothalamic regulation of sexual behavior, *J. Endocrinol.*, **25**, 175–82.

Barraclough A., and Haller, E. W. (1970) Positive and negative feedback effects of estrogen on pituitary LH synthesis and release in normal and androgen sterilized female rats, *Endocrinology*, **86**, 542–51.

Barraclough, C. A. and Leatham, J. H. (1954) Infertility induced in mice by a single injection of testosterone propionate, *Proc. Soc. Exp. Biol. Med.*, **85**, 673–4.

Beach, F. A. (1968) Factors involved in the control of mounting behavior by female mammals. In: *Perspectives in Reproduction and Sexual Behavior*, M. Diamond, (ed.), Indiana University Press, Bloomington, pp. 83–131.

Bergstrand, C. G. and Czar, B. (1956) Demonstration of a new protein fraction in serum from the human fetus, *Scand. J. Clin. Lab. Invest.*, **8**, 174.

Bergstrand, C. G. and Czar, B. (1957) Paper electrophoretic study of human fetal serum proteins with demonstration of a new protein fraction, *Scand. J. Clin. Lab. Invest.*, **9**, 277–86.

Blizard D. and Denef, C. (1973) Neonatal androgen effects on open-field activity and sexual behavior in the female rat: The modifying influence of ovarian secretions during development. *Physiol. Behav.*, **11**, 65–9.

Bongiovanni, A. M., Di George, A. M., and Grumbach, M. M. (1959) Masculinization of the female infant associated with estrogenic therapy alone during gestation: Four cases, *J. Clin. Endocrinol. Metab.*, **19**, 1004–11.

Bradbury, J. T. (1941) Permanent after-effects following masculinization of the infantile female rat, *Endocrinology*, **28**, 101–6.

Brown-Grant K. (1974) Failure of ovulation after administration of steroid hormones and hormone antagonists to female rats during the neonatal period, *J. Endocrinol.*, **62**, 683–4.

Brown-Grant, K., Munck, A., Naftolin, F., and Sherwood, M. R. (1971) The effects of the administration of testosterone propionate alone or with phenobarbitone and of testosterone metabolites to neonatal female rats, *Horm. Behav.*, **2**, 173–82.

Brown-Grant, K. and Naftolin, F. (1972) Facilitation of luteinizing hormone secretion in the female rat by progesterone, *J. Endocrinol.*, **53**, 37–46.

Brown-Grant, K., and Sherwood, M. R. (1971) The 'early androgen sydrome' in the guinea pig, *J. Endocrinol.*, **49**, 277–91.

Bullock, D. W. (1970) Induction of heat in ovariectomized guinea pigs by brief exposure to estrogen and progesterone, *Horm. Behav.*, **1**, 137–43.

Burns, R. K. (1961) Role of Hormones in the Differentiation of Sex. In: *Sex and Internal Secretions*, Vol. I, W. C. Young, (ed.), Williams and Wilkins, Baltimore, pp. 76–158.

Caligaris, L., Astrada, J. J., and Taleisnik, S. (1971) Release of luteinizing hormone induced by estrogen injection into ovariectomized rats, *Endocrinology*, **88**, 810–5.

Caligaris, L., Astrada, J. J., and Taleisnik, S. (1972) Influence of age on the release of luteinizing hormone induced by oestrogen and progesterone in immature rats, *J. Endocrinol.*, **55**, 97–103.

Caligaris, L., Astrada, J. J., and Taleisnik, S. (1973) Development of the mechanisms involved in the facilitatory and inhibitory effects of ovarian steroids on the release of follicle-stimulating hormone in the immature rat, *J. Endocrinol.*, **58**, 547–54.

Carter, C. S., Clemens, L. G., and Hoekema, D. J. (1972) Neonatal androgen and adult sexual behavior in the golden hamster, *Physiol. Behav.*, **9**, 89–95.

Challis, J. R. G., Davies, I. J., Benirschke, K., Hendricks, A. G., and Ryan, K. J. (1974) The concentrations of progesterone, estrone and estradiol-17β in the peripheral plasma of the rhesus monkey during the final third of gestation, and after the induction of abortion with PGF2α. *Endocrinology*, **95**, 547–53.

Challis, J. R. G., Davies, I. J., and Ryan, K. J. (1973) The concentrations of progesterone, estrone, and estradiol-17β in the plasma of pregnant rabbits, *Endocrinology*, **93**, 971–6.

Chamberlain, J. and Rogers, A. W. (1972) The appearance of dihydrotes tosterone-³H in the diencephalon of neonatal rats after subcutaneous injection of testosterone ³H, *J. Steroid Biochem.*, **3**, 945–7.

Cheng, H. C. and Johnson, D. C. (1973/74) Serum estrogens and gonadotropins in developing androgenized and normal female rats, *Neuroendocrinology*, **13**, 357–65.

Clark, J. H., Peck, E. J., and Anderson, J. N. (1974) Oestrogen receptors and antagonism of steroid hormone action, *Nature*, **251**, 446–8.

Clemens, L. G., Hiroi, M., and Gorski, R. A. (1969) Induction and facilitation of female mating behavior in rats treated neonatally with low doses of testosterone propionate, *Endocrinology*, **84**, 1430–8.

Clemens, L. G., Shryne, J., and Gorski, R. A. (1970) Androgen and development of progesterone responsiveness in male and female rats, *Physiol. Behav.*, **5**, 673–8.

Clever, U. and Karlson, P. (1960) Induktion von puff-veranderungen in den Speicheldrusenchromosomen von *Chironomus Tentans* durch Ecdyson, *Exp. Cell Res.*, **20**, 623–6.

Coniglio, L. P., Paup, D. C., and Clemens, L. G. (1973) Hormonal specificity in the suppression of sexual receptivity of the female golden hamster, *J. Endocrinol.*, **57**, 55–61.

Crowley, W. R., Ward, I. L., and Margules, D. L. (1975) Female lordotic behavior mediated by monoamines in male rats, *J. Comp. Physiol. Psych.*, **88**, 62–8.

Dantchakoff, V. (1938) Sur les effets de l'hormone male dans un jeune cobaye femelle traité depuis un stade embryonnaire (inversions sexuelles), *C. R. Soc. Biol.*, **127**, 1255–8.

Darling, J. A. B., Laing, A. H., and Harkness, R. A. (1974) A survey of the steroids in cows' milk. *J. Endocrinol.*, **62**, 291–7.

Davidson, J. M. (1969) Effects of estrogen on the sexual behavior of male rats, *Endocrinology*, **84**, 1365–1372.

De Hertogh, R., Thomas, K., Bietlot, Y., Vanderheyden, I., and Ferin, J. (1975) Plasma levels of unconjugated estrone, estradiol, and estriol and of HCS throughout pregnancy in normal women, *J. Clin. Endocrinol. Metab.*, **40**, 93–101.

de Kloet, R., Wallach, G., and McEwen, B. S. (1975) Differences in corticosterone and dexamethasone binding to rat brain and pituitary, *Endocrinology*, **96**, 598–609.

Denef, C., Magnus, C., and McEwen, B. S. (1973) Sex differences and hormonal control of testosterone metabolism in rat pituitary and brain, *J. Endocrinol.*, **59**, 605–21.

Denef, C., Magnus, C., and McEwen, B. S. (1974) Sex-dependent changes in pituitary 5α-dihydrotestosterone and 3α-androstanediol formation during postnatal development and puberty in the rat, *Endocrinology*, **94**, 1265–74.

de Vellis, J., Inglish, D., Cole, R., and Molson, J. (1971) Effects of hormones on the differentiation of cloned lines of neurons and glial cells. In: *Influence of Hormones on the Nervous System*, D. Ford, (ed.), Karger, Basel, pp. 25–39.

de Vellis, J., McEwen, B. S., Cole, R., and Inglish, D. (1974) Relations between glucocorticoid binding and glycerolphosphate dehydrogenase inductions in a rat glial cell line, *Trans. Am. Soc. Neurochem.*, **5**, 125.

Dörner, G. and Döcke, F. (1964) Sex-specific reaction of the hypothalamo-hypophysial system of rats, *J. Endocrinol.*, **30**, 265–6.

Doughty, C., Booth, J. E., McDonald, P. G., and Parrott, R. F. (1975) Effects of oestradiol-17β, oestradiol benzoate, and the synthetic estrogen, RU 2858 on sexual differentiation in the neonatal female rat, *J. Endocrinol.*, **67**, 419–24.

Doughty, C. and McDonald, P. G. (1974) Hormonal-control of sexual differentiation of the hypothalamus in the neonatal female rat, *Differentiation*, **2**, 275–85.

Dunn, T. B. and Green, A. W. (1963) Cysts of the epididymis, cancer of the cervix, granular cell myoblastoma and other lesions after estrogen injection in newborn mice, *J. Nat. Canc. Inst.*, **31**, 425–55.

Eaton, G. (1970) Effect of a single prepubertal injection of testosterone propionate on adult bisexual behavior of male hamsters castrated at birth, *Endocrinology*, **87**, 934–40.

Edwards, D. A. and Thompson, M. L. (1970) Neonatal androgenization and estrogenization and the hormonal induction of sexual receptivity in rats, *Physiol. Behav.*, **5**, 1115–9.

Eisenfeld, A. J. (1970) ³H-estradiol: *In vitro* binding to macromolecules from the rat hypothalamus, anterior pituitary and uterus, *Endocrinology*, **86**, 1313–8.

Falvo, R. E., Buhl, A., and Nalbandov, A. V. (1974) Testosterone concentrations in the peripheral plasma of androgenized female rats and in the estrous cycle of normal female rats, *Endocrinology*, **95**, 26–9.

Feder, H. H. (1967) Specificity of testosterone and estradiol in the differentiating neonatal rat, *Anat. Rec.*, **157**, 79–86.

Feder, H. H., Phoenix, C. H., and Young, W. C. (1966) Suppression of feminine behaviour by administration of testosterone propionate to neonatal rats, *J. Endocrinol.*, **34**, 131–2.

Feder, H. H. and Whalen, R. E. (1965) Feminine behavior in neonatally castrated and estrogen-treated male rats, *Science*, **147**, 306–7.

Ferin, M., Dyrenfurth, I., Cowchock, S., Warren, M., and Vande Wiele, R. L. (1974) Active immunization to 17β-estradiol and its effects upon the reproductive cycle of the rhesus monkey, *Endocrinology*, **94**, 765–76.

Ferin, M., Tempone, A., Zimmering, P. E., and Vande Wiele R. L. (1969) Effect of antibodies to 17β-estradiol and progesterone on the estrous cycle of the rat, *Endocrinology*, **85**, 1070–8,

Flerko, N. (1968) The experimental polyfollicular ovary. In: *Endocrinology and Human Behaviour*, R. P. Michael, (ed.), Oxford University Press, London, pp. 119–138.

Forsberg, J.-G. (1960) Effect of sex hormones on the development of the rat vagina, *Acta Endocrinol.*, **33**, 520–31.

Forsberg, J.-G. (1969) The development of atypical epithelium in the mouse uterine cervix and vaginal fornix after neonatal oestradiol treatment, *Br. J. Exp. Path.*, **50**, 187–95.

Forsberg, J.-G. (1970) An estradiol mitotic rate-inhibiting effect in the Mullerian epithelium in neonatal mice, *J. Exp. Zool.*, **175**, 369–74.

Forsberg, J.-G. (1972) Estrogen, vaginal cancer, and vaginal development, *Am. J. Obstet. Gynec.*, **113**, 83–7.

Forsberg, J.-G. and Kvinnsland, S. (1972) The appearance and distribution of vaginal antigen during the differentiation of the cervicovaginal epithelium in normal and estradiol-treated mice, *J. Exp. Zool.*, **180**, 403–12.

Gay, V. L. and Tomacari, R. L. (1974) Follicle-stimulating hormone secretion in the female rat: Cyclic release is dependent on circulating androgen, *Science*, **184**, 75–7.

Gellert, R. J., Heinrichs, W. L., and Swerdloff, R. (1974) Effects of neonatally-administered DDT homologs on reproductive function in male and female rats, *Neuroendocrinology*, **16**, 84–94.

Gerall, A. A. (1967) Effects of early postnatal androgen and estrogen injections on the estrous activity cycles and mating behavior of rats, *Anat. Rec.*, **157**, 97–104.

Gerall, A. A. and Dunlap, J. L. (1971) Evidence that the ovaries of the neonatal rat secrete active substances, *J. Endocrinol.*, **50**, 529–30.

Gerall, A. A., McMurray, M. M., and Farrell, A., (1975) Suppression of the development of female hamster behaviour by implants of testosterone and non-aromatizable androgens administered neonatally, *J. Endocrinol.*, **67**, 439–45.

Gerlach, J. L. and McEwen, B. S. (1972) Rat brain binds adrenal steroid hormone: Radioautography of hippocampus with corticosterone, *Science*, **175**, 1133–6.

Gerlach, J. L., McEwen, B. S., Pfaff, D. W., Moskovitz, S., Ferin, M., Carmel, P. W., and Zimmerman, E. A. (1976) Cells in regions of rhesus monkey brain and pituitary retain radioactive estradiol, corticosterone and cortisol differentially, *Brain Res.*, **103**, 603–12.

Ginsburg, M., Greenstein, B.D., MacLusky, N. J., Morris, I.D., Thomas, P. J. (1971) Dihydrotestosterone binding in brain and pituitary cytosol of rats, *J. Endocrinol.*, **61**, XXIV.

Ginsburg, M., Greenstein, B. D., MacLusky, N. J., Morris, I. D., and Thomas, P. J. (1974) An improved method for the study of high-affinity steroid binding: Oestradiol binding in brain and pituitary, *Steroids*, **23**, 773–92.

Gitlin, D. and Boesman, M. (1966) Serum α-fetoprotein, albumin, and γG-globulin in the human conceptus, *J. Clin. Invest.*, **45**, 1826–38.

Giulian, D., Pohorecky, L. A., and McEwen, B. S., (1973) Effects of gonadal steroids upon brain 5-hydroxytryptamine levels in the neonatal rat, *Endocrinology*, **93**, 1329–35.

Goldfoot, D. A., Feder, H. H., and Goy, R. W. (1969) Development of bisexuality in the male rat treated neonatally with androstenedione, *J. Comp. Physiol. Psych.*, **67**, 41–5.

Goldfoot, D. A. and van der Werff ten Bosch, J. J. (1975) Mounting behavior of female guinea pigs after prenatal and adult administration of the propionates of testosterone, dihydrotestosterone, and androstanediol, *Horm. Behav.* **6**, 139–48.

Goodman, L. (1934) Observations on transplanted immature ovaries in the eyes of adult male and female rats, *Anat. Rec.*, **59**, 223–52.

Gorski, R. A. (1963) Modification of ovulatory mechanisms by postnatal administration of estrogen to the rat, *Am. J. Physiol.*, **205**, 842–4.

Gorski, R. A. (1968) Influence of age on the response to paranatal administration of a low dose of androgen, *Endocrinology*, **82**, 1001–4.

Gorski, R. A. and Barraclough, C. A. (1963) Effects of low dosages of androgen on the differentiation of hypothalamic regulatory control of ovulation in the rat, *Endocrinology*, **73**, 210–6.

Gorski, R. A. and Wagner, J. W. (1965) Gonadal activity and sexual differentiation of the hypothalamus, *Endocrinology*, **76**, 226–39.

Gottlieb, H., Gerall, A. A., and Thiel, A. (1974) Receptivity in female hamsters following neonatal testosterone, testosterone propionate, and MER-25. *Physiol. Behav.*, **12**, 61–8.

Goy, R. W. (1970a) Early hormonal influences on the development of sexual and sex-related behavior. In: *The Neurosciences: Second Study Program*, F. O. Schmitt, (ed.), Rockefeller University Press, New York, pp. 196–206.

Goy, R. W. (1970b) Experimental control of psychosexuality. *Phil. Trans. Roy. Soc. London (B)*, **259**, 149–62.

Goy, R. W. and Phoenix, C. H. (1971) The effects of testosterone propionate administered before birth on the development of behavior in genetic female rhesus monkeys. In: *Steroid Hormones and Brain Function*, C. H. Sawyer, and R. A. Gorski, (eds.), University of California Press, Berkeley, pp. 193–201.

Goy, R. W., Phoenix, C. H., and Meidinger, R. (1967) Postnatal development of sensitivity to estrogen and androgen in male, female, and pseudohermaphroditic guinea pigs, *Anat. Rec.*, **157**, 87–96.

Grady, K. L., Phoenix, C. H., and Young, W. C. (1965) Role of the developing rat testis in differentiation of the neural tissues mediating mating behavior, *J. Comp. Physiol. Psychol.*, **59**, 176–82.

Green, R., Luttge, W. G., and Whalen, R. E. (1970) Induction of receptivity in ovariectomized rats by a single intravenous injection of estradio—17 beta. *Physiol. Behav.*, **5**, 137–41.

Greene, R. R. (1937) Production of experimental hypospadias in the female rat, *Proc. Soc. Exp. Biol. Med.*, **36**, 503–10.

Greene, R. R. and Burrill, M. W. (1941) Postnatal treatment of rats with sex hormones: The permanent effects on the ovary, *Am. J. Physiol.*, **133**, 302–3.

Greene, R. R., Burrill, M. W., and Ivy, A. C. (1940) Experimental intersexuality. The effects of estrogens on the antenatal sexual development of the rat, *Am. J. Anat.*, **67**, 305–45.

Grosser, B. I., Stevens, W., and Reed, D. J. (1973) Properties of corticosterone-binding macromolecules from rat brain cytosol, *Brain Res.*, **57**, 387–95.

Gual, C., Morato, T., Hayano, M., Gut, M., and Dorfman, R. I. (1962) Biosynthesis of Estrogens, *Endocrinology*, **71**, 920–5.

Hain, A. M. (1935) The effect (a) of litter-size on growth and (b) of oestrone administered during lactation (rat), *Quart. J. Exp. Physiol.*, **25**, 303–13.

Hale, H. B. (1944) Functional and morphological alterations of the reproductive system of the female rat following prepuberal treatment with estrogens, *Endocrinology*, **35**, 499–506.

Harris, G. W. and Jacobsohn, D. (1952) Functional grafts of the anterior pituitary gland, *Proc. Roy. Soc. (B)*, **139**, 263–76.

Harris, G. W. and Levine, S. (1965) Sexual differentiation of the brain and its experimental control, *J. Physiol.*, **181**, 379–400.

Hayashi, S. (1974) Failure of intrahypothalamic implants of antiestrogen, MER-25, to inhibit androgen sterilization in female rats, *Endocrinol. Jap.*, **21**, 453–7.

Hendricks, S. E. and Duffy, J. A. (1974) Ovarian influences on the development of sexual behavior in neonatally androgenized rats, *Develop. Psychobiol.*, **7**, 297–303.

Hendricks, S. E. and Gerall, A. A. (1970) Effect of neonatally administered estrogen on development of male and female rats, *Endocrionology*, **87**, 435–9.

Herbst, A. L. (1972) Stilbestrol and vaginal cancer in young women. *CA.*, **22**, 292–5.

Herbst, A. L., Kurman, R. J., Scully, R. E., and Poskanzer, D. C. (1972a) Clear-cut adenocarcinoma of the genital tract in young females. Registry Report, *New Eng. J. Med.*, **287**, 1259–64.

Herbst, A. L., Kurman, R. J., Scully, R. E. (1972b) Vaginal and cervical abnormalities after exposure to stilbestrol *in utero.*, *Obstet. Gynecol.*, **40**, 287–98.

Herbst, A. L. and Scully, R. E. (1970) Adenocarcinoma of the vagina in adolescence. A report of 7 cases including 6 clear-cell carcinomas (So-called mesonephromas), *Cancer*, **25**, 745–57.

Herbst, A. L., Ulfelder, H., and Poskanzer, D. C. (1971) Adenocarcinoma of the vagina. Association of maternal stilbestrol therapy with tumor appearance in young women, *New Eng. J. Med.*, **284**, 878–81.

Hohlweg, V. (1934) Veränderungen des Hypophysenvorderlappens und des Ovariums nach Behandlung mit grossen Dosen von Follikel-Horman, *Klin. Wochenschrift*, **13**, 92–5.

Huffman, J. W. (1941) Effect of testosterone propionate upon reproduction in the female, *Endocrinology*, **29**, 77–9.

Jackson, G. L. (1972) Effect of actinomycin D on estrogen-induced release of luteinizing hormone in ovariectomized rats, *Endocrinology*, **91**, 1284–7.

Jensen, E. V. and deSombre, E. R. (1973) Estrogen-receptor interaction, *Science*, **182**, 126–34.

Jensen, E. V. and Jacobson, H. I. (1962) Basic guides to the mechanism of estrogen action, *Rec. Prog. Horm. Res.*, **18**, 387–408.

Johnson, D. C. (1971) Serum follicle-stimulating hormone (FSH) in normal and androgenized male and female rats, *Proc. Soc. Exp. Biol. Med.*, **138**, 140–44.

Johnson, D. C. (1972) Sexual differentiation of gonadotropin patterns, *Am. Zool.*, **12**, 193–205.

Jost, A. (1970) Hormonal factors in the sex differentiation of the mammalian foetus, *Phil Trans. Roy. Soc. London (B)*, **259**, 119–30.

Jouan, P., Samperez, S., and Thieulant, M. L. (1973) Testosterone "receptors" in purified nuclei of rat anterior hypophysis, *J. Steroid Biochem.*, **4**, 65–74.

Kalra, S. P. (1975) Observations on facilitation of the preovulatory rise of LH by estrogen, *Endocrinology*, **96**, 23–8.

Karavolas, H. J. and Herf, S. M. (1971) Conversion of progesterone by rat medial basal hypothalamic tissue to 5α-pregnane-3, 20-dione, *Endocrinology*, **89**, 940–2.

Karsch, F. J., Weick, R. F., Butler, W. R., Dierschke, D. J., Krey, L. C., Weiss, G., Hotchkiss, J., Yamaji, T., and Knobil, E. (1973a) Induced LH surges in the rhesus monkey: strength-duration characteristics of the estrogen stimulus, *Endocrinology*, **92**, 1740–7.

Karsch, F. J., Dierschke, D. J., and Knobil, E. (1973b) Sexual differentiation of pituitary function: apparent difference between primates and rodents, *Science*, **179**, 484–6.

Kato, J. and Onouchi, T. (1973) 5α-dihydrotestosterone "receptor" in the rat hypothalamus, *Endocrinol. Jap.*, **20**, 429–32.

Kato, J., Atsumi, Y., and Inaba, M. (1970) A soluble receptor for estradiol in rat anterior hypophysis, *J. Biochem. (Tokyo)*, **68**, 759–61.

Kato, J., Sugimura, N., and Kobayashi, T. (1971a) Changing patterns of the uptake of estradiol by the anterior hypothalamus, the median eminence and the hypophysis in the developing female rat. In: *Hormones in Development, Proceedings, Conference, Nottingham, September 1968*, M. Hamburgh and E. J. W. Barrington, (eds.), Appleton Century and Crofts, New York, pp. 689–703.

Kato, J., Atsumi Y., and Inaba, M. (1971b) Development of estrogen receptors in the rat hypothalamus, *J. Biochem. (Tokyo)*, **70**, 1051–3.

Kato, J., Atsumi, Y., and Inaba, M. (1974) Estradiol receptors in female rat hypothalamus in the developmental stages and during pubescence, *Endocrinology*, **94**, 309–17.

Kawakami, M. and E. Terasawa, 1972. A possible role of the hippocampus and the amygdala in the androgenized rat: Effect of electrical or electrochemical stimulation of the brain on gonadotropin secretion, *Endocrinol. Jap.*, **19**, 349–58.

Keefer, D. A., Stumpf, W. E., and Sar, M. (1973) Estrogen-topographical localization of estrogen-concentrating cells in the rat spinal cord following ^{3}H-estradiol administration, *Proc. Soc. Exp. Biol. Med.*, **143**, 414–7.

Kempf, R. (1950) Contribution a l'étude du méchanisme de liberation des hormones gonadotropes hypophysaires chez le rat, *Arch. Biol.*, **61**, 501–94.

Kimura, T., Basu, S. L., and Nandi, S. (1967) Nature of induced persistent vaginal cornification in mice. III. Effects of estradiol and testosterone on vaginal epithelium *in vitro*, *J. Exp. Zool.*, **165**, 497–504.

Kimura, T. and Nandi, S. (1967) Nature of induced persistent vaginal cornification in mice. IV. Changes in the vaginal epithelium of old mice treated neonatally with estradiol or testosterone, *J. Nat. Canc. Inst.*, **39**, 75–84.

Kincl, F. A. and Maqueo, M. (1965) Prevention by progesterone of steroid-induced sterility in neonatal male and female rats, *Endocrinology*, **77**, 859–62.

Kincl, F. A., Pi, A. F., Maqueo, M., Lasso, L. H., Oriol, A., Dorfman, R. I. (1965) Inhibition of sexual development in male and female rats treated with various steroids at the age of five days, *Acta Endocrinol.*, **49**, 193–206.

King, R. J. B. and Mainwaring, W. I. P. (1974) *Steroid-Cell Interactions, University Park Press*, Baltimore, 440 pp.

Kniewald, Z. and Milković S. (1973) Testosterone: A regulator of 5-α reductase activity in the pituitary of male and female rats, *Endocrinology*, **92**, 1772–5.

Knizley, H., Jr. (1972) The hippocampus and septal area as primary target sites for corticosterone, *J. Neurochem.*, **19**, 2737–45.

Komisaruk, B. R. and Beyer, C. (1972) Differential antagonism, by MER-25, of behavioral and morphological effects of estradiol benzoate in rats, *Horm. Behav.*, **3**, 63–70.

Kubo, K., Mennin, S. P., and Gorski, R. A. (1975) Similarity of plasma LH release in androgenized and normal rats following electrochemical stimulation of the basal forebrain, *Endocrinology*, **96**, 492–500.

Kulin, H. E. and Reiter, E. O. (1972) Ontogeny of the *in vitro* uptake of tritiated estradiol by the hypothalamus of the female rat, *Endocrinology*, **90**, 1371–4.

Labhsetewar, A. P. (1970) The role of oestrogens in spontaneous ovulation: Evidence for positive oestrogen feedback in the 4 day oestrus cycle, *J. Endocrinol.*, **47**, 481–93.

Labhsetwar, A. (1972) Role of estrogens in spontaneous ovulation: evidence for positive feedback in hamsters, *Endocrinology*, **90**, 941–6.

Lacassagne, A. and Nyka, W. (1934) A propos d'une pathogéne de l'adéno-carcinome mammaire: recherche de la folliculine dans le colostrum, *C. R. Soc. Biol.*, **116**, 844–5.

Ladosky, W. (1967) Anovulatory sterility in rats neonatally injected with stilbestrol, *Endokrinologie*, **52**, 259–61.

Lerner, L. J. (1964) Hormone antagonists: inhibitors of specific activities of estrogen and androgen, *Rec. Prog. Horm. Res.*, **20**, 435–90.

Lerner, L. J., Holthaus, F. J., Jr., and Thompson, C. R. (1958) A non-steroidal estrogen antagonist 1-(p-2-diethylamino-ethoxypheny)-1-phenyl-2-p-methoxyphenyl ethanol, *Endocrinology*, **63**, 295–318.

Levine, S. and Mullins, R. Jr. (1964) Estrogen administered neonatally affects adult sexual behavior in male and female rats, *Science*, **144**, 185–7.

Liao, S. and Fang, S. (1969) Receptor-proteins for androgens and the mode of action of androgens on gene transcription in ventral prostate, *Vitamins and Hormones*, **27**, 17–90.

Lieberburg, I. and McEwen, B., (1975a) Estradiol-17β: A metabolite of testosterone recovered in cell nuclei from limbic areas of neonatal rat brains, *Brain Res.*, **85**, 165–70.

Lieberburg, I. and McEwen, B. S. (1975b) Estradiol-17β: A metabolite of testosterone recovered in cell nuclei from limbic areas of adult male rat brains, *Brain Res.*, **91**, 171–4.

Lierburg, I., Wallach, G., and McEwen, B. S. (1977) The effects of an inhibitor of aromatization (1,4,6 androstatariene-3,17-dione) and an anti-estrogen (CI628) on in vivo formed testosterone metabolites recovered from neonatal rat brain tissues and purified cell nuclei. Implications for sexual differentiation of the rat brain. *Brain Res.*, **128**, 176–81.

Lobl, R. T. and Schapiro, S. (1972) Developmental alterations in uptake and retention of [^{3}H]testosterone in female rats, *J. Endocrinol.*, **54**, 359–60.

Luine, V. N. and McEwen, B. S. (1977) Steroid hormone receptors in brain and pituitary: Topography and possible functions, In: *Sexual Behavior*, R. W. Goy, and D. W. Pfaff, (eds.) Plenum Press, New York. In press.

Luttge, W. G. and Whalen, R. E. (1970) Dihydrotestosterone, androstenedione, testosterone: Comparative effectiveness in masculinizing and defeminizing reproductive systems in male and female rats, *Horm. Behav.*, **1**, 265–81.

Maclusky, N. J., Chaptal, C., Lieberburg, I. and McEwen, B. S. (1976). Properties and subcellular inter-relationships of presumptive estrogen receptor macromolecules in the brains of neonatal and prepubertal female rats. *Brain Res.*, **114**, 158–65.

Mallampati, R. S. and Johnson, D. C. (1973) Serum and pituitary prolactin, LH, and FSH in androgenized female and normal male rats treated with various doses of estradiol benzoate, *Neuroendocrinology*, **11**, 46–56.

Mann, D. R. and Barraclough, C. A. (1973) Role of estrogen and progesterone in facilitating LH release in 4-day cyclic rats, *Endocrinology*, **93**, 694–9.

Marks, B. H., Wu, T. K., Goldman, H. (1972) Soluble estrogen binding protein in the rat pineal gland, *Res Comm. in Chem. Path. and Pharm.*, **3**, 595–600.

Massa, R. and Martini, L. (1971/72) Interference with the 5α reductose system: A new approach for developing antiandrogens, *Gynecol. Invest.*, **2**, 253–70.

Massa, R., Stupnicka, E., Kniewald, Z., and Martini, L. (1972) The transformation of testosterone into dihydrotestosterone by the brain and the anterior pituitary, *J. Steroid Biochem.*, **3**, 385–99.

Matsuyama, E., Weisz, J., and Lloyd, C. W. (1966) Gonadotropin content of pituitary glands of testosterone-sterilized rats, *Endocrinology*, **79**, 261–7.

Maurer, R. A. and Woolley, D. E. (1974) Demonstration of nuclear ³H-estradiol binding in hypothalamus and amygdala of female, androgenized-female, and male rats, *Neuroendocrinology*, **16**, 137–47.

Mazer, M. and Mazer, C. (1939) The effect of prolonged testosterone propionate adminis- tration on the immature and adult female rat, *Endocrinology*, **24**, 175–181.

McDonald, P. G. (1971) Some biological actions of dihydrotestosterone (DHT), *J. Reprod. Fert.*, **25**, 309–10.

McDonald, P. G. and Doughty, C. (1972a) Comparison of the effect of neonatal adminis- tration of testosterone and dihydrotestosterone in the female rat, *J. Reprod. Fert.*, **30**, 55–62.

McDonald, P. G. and Doughty, C. (1972b) Inhibition of androgen-sterilization in the female rat by administration of an antioestrogen, *J. Endocrinol.*, **55**, 455–6.

McDonald, P. G. and Doughty, C. (1973/74) Androgen sterilization in the neonatal female rat and its inhibition by an estrogen antagonist, *Neuroendocrinology*, **13**, 182–8.

McDonald, P. G. and Doughty, C. (1974) Effect of neonatal administration of different androgens in the female rat: Correlation between aromatization and the induction of sterilization, *J. Endocrinol.*, **61**, 95–103.

McEwen, B. S. (1974) Adrenal steroid binding to presumptive receptors in the limbic brain of the rat, In: *Neuroendocrinologie de l'Axe Corticotrope*, P. Dell, (ed.), *Inserm. Colloque*, Vol. 22, 1973, Paris, pp. 79–94.

McEwen, B. S., Lieberburg, I., Chaptal, C., and Krey, L. C. (1977) Aromatization: important for sexual differentiation of the neonatal rat brain, *Hormones and Behavior*. In press.

McEwen, B. S., Magnus, C., and Wallach, G. (1972b) Soluble corticosterone-binding macromolecules extracted from rat brain, *Endocrinology*, **90**, 217–26.

McEwen, B. S., Pfaff, D. W., Chaptal, C., and Luine, V. (1975a) Brain cell nuclear retention of ³H estradiol doses able to promote lordosis: Temporal and regional aspects, *Brain Res.*, **86**, 155–61.

McEwen, B. S., Pfaff, D. W., and Zigmond, R. E. (1970) Factors influencing sex hormone uptake by rat brain regions. III. Effects of competing steroids on testosterone uptake, *Brain Res.*, **21**, 29–38.

McEwen, B. S., Plapinger, L., Chaptal, C., Gerlach, J., and Wallach, G. (1975b) Role of fetoneonatal estrogen binding proteins in the association of estrogen with neonatal brain cell nuclear receptors, *Brain Res.*, **96**, 400–406.

McEwen, B. S. and Wallach, G. (1973) Corticosterone binding to hippocampus: Nuclear and cytosol binding *in vitro*, *Brain Res.*, **57**, 373–86.

McEwen, B. S., Zigmond, R. E., and Gerlach, J. L. (1972a) Sites of steroid binding and action in the brain. In: *Structure and Function of Nervous Tissue*, Vol. 5, G. H. Bourne, (ed.), Academic Press, New York, pp. 205–91.

Mennin, S. P. and Gorski, R. A. (1975) Effects of ovarian steroids on plasma LH in normal and persistent estrous adult female rats. *Endocrinology*, **96**, 486–91.

Mennin, S. P., Kubo, K., and Gorski, R. A. (1974) Pituitary responsiveness to luteinizing hormone-releasing factor in normal and androgenized female rats, *Endocrinology*, **95**, 412–6.

Merklin, R. J. (1953) Reproductive performance of female mice treated prepuberally with a single injection of estradiol dipropionate, *Endocrinology*, **53**, 342–3.

Meyerson, B. J. and Lindström, L., (1968) Effects of an oestrogen antagonist ethamoxytriphentol (MER-25) on oestrous behaviour in rats, *Acta Endocrinol.*, **59**, 41–8.

Mishell, D. R., Thorneycroft, I. H., Nagata, Y., Murata, T., and Nakamura, R. M., (1973) Serum gonadotropin and steroid patterns in early human gestation, *Am. J. Obstet. Gynecol.*, **117**, 631–42.

Moll, J. and Zeilmaker, G. (1965) Induction of ovulation by hypothalamic stimulation in castrated male rats bearing ovarian transplants, *Acta Endocrinol.*, Suppl. 100 (Abstract), 146.

Monbon, M., Loras, B., Reboud, J. P., and Bertrand, J. (1973) Uptake, binding, and metabolism of testosterone in rat brain tissues, *Brain Res.*, **53**, 139–50.

Morell, J. I., Kelley, D. B., and Pfaff, D. W. (1975) Sex steroid binding in the brains of vertebrates: Studies with light microscopic autoradiography. In: *Brain Endocrine Interaction II.* K. M. Knigge, D. E. Scott, H. Kobayshi, Miura-shi, and S. Ishii (eds.), Karger, Basel, pp. 230–56.

Morrison, R. L. and Johnson, D. C. (1966) The effects of androgenization in male rats castrated at birth, *J. Endocrinol.*, **34**, 117–23.

Mowles, T. F., Ashkanazy, B., Mix, Jr., E., and Sheppard, H. (1971) Hypothalamic and hypophyseal estradiol-binding complexes, *Endocrinology*, **89**, 484–91.

Mullins, R. F., Jr., and Levine, S. (1968a) Hormonal determinants during infancy of adult sexual behavior in the female rat, *Physiol. Behav.*, **3**, 333–8.

Mullins, R. F., Jr. and Levine, S. (1968b) Hormonal determinants during infancy of adult sexual behavior in the male rat, *Physiol. Behav.*, **3**, 339–43.

Naess, O., Attramadal, A., and Aakvaag, A., (1975) Androgen binding proteins in the anterior pituitary, hypothalamus, preoptic area, and brain cortex of the rat, *Endocrinology*, **96**, 1–9.

Naftolin, F., Brown-Grant, K., and Corker, C. S. (1972) Plasma and pituitary luteinizing hormone and peripheral plasma oestradiol concentrations in the normal oestrous cycle of the rat and after experimental manipulation of the cycle, *J. Endocrinol.*, **53**, 17–30.

Naftolin, F., Ryan, K. J., and Petro, Z. (1971a) Aromatization of androstenedione by the diencephalon, *J. Clin. Endocrinol. Metab.*, **33**, 368–70.

Naftolin, F., Ryan, K. J., and Petro, Z. (1971b) Aromatization of androstenedione by limbic system tissue from human foetuses, *J. Endocrinol.*, **51**, 795–6.

Neill, J. D. (1972) Sexual differences in the hypothalamic regulation of prolactin secretion, *Endocrinology*, **90**, 1154–9.

Neill, J. D., Freeman, M. E., and Tillson, S. A. (1971) Control of the proestrus surge of prolactin and luteinizing hormone secretion by estrogens in the rat, *Endocrinology*, **89**, 1448–53.

Neumann, F., Hahn, J. D., and Kramer, M. (1967) Hemmung von testosteronabhängigen differenzierungs-vorgangen der männlichen ratte nach der geburt, *Acta Endocrinol.*, **54**, 227–40.

Neumann, F. and von Berswordt-Wallrabe, R. (1966) Effects of the androgen antagonist cyproterone acetate on the testicular structure, spermatogenesis, and accessory sexual glands of testosterone-treated adult hypophysectomized rats, *J. Endocrinol.*, **35**, 363–71.

Norman, R. L. and Spies, H. G. (1974) Neural control of the estrogen-dependent twenty-four-hour periodicity of LH release in the golden hamster, *Endocrinology*, **95**, 1367–72.

Notides, A. C. (1970) Binding affinity and specificity of the estrogen receptor of the rat uterus and anterior pituitary, *Endocrinology*, **87**, 987–92.

Nunez, E., Engelmann, F., Benassayag, C., Savu, L., Crepy, O., and Jayle, M.-F. (1971a) Mise en evidence d'une fraction protéique liant les oestrogènes dans le serum de rats impuberes, *C. R. Acad. Sci. (Paris)*, Serie D, **272**, 2396–9.

Nunez, E. Savu, L., Engelmann, F., Benassayag, C., Crepy, O., and Jayle, M.-F. (1971b) Origine embryonnaire de la protéine serique fixant l'oestrone et l'oestradiol chez la ratte impubere, *C. R. Acad. Sci. (Paris)*, Serie D, **273**, 242–5.

Nunez, E., Engelmann, F., Benassayag, C., and Jayle, M.-F. (1971c) Identification et purification preliminaire de la foeto-proteine liant les estrogènes dans le serum de rats nouveau-nés, *C. R. Acad. Sci. (Paris)*, Serie D, **273**, 831–4.

Nunez, E., Vallette, G., Benassayag, C., and Jayle, M.-F. (1974) Comparative study on the binding of estrogens by human and rat serum proteins in development, *Biochem. Biophys. Res. Comm.*, **57**, 126–33.

O'Malley, B. W. and Means, A. R. (1974) Female steroid hormones and target cell nuclei, *Science*, **183**, 610–20.

Oppenheimer, J. H., Schwartz, H. L., and Surks, M. I. (1974) Tissue differences in the concentration of triiodothyronine nuclear binding sites in the rat: Liver, kidney, pituitary, heart, brain, spleen and testis, *Endocrinology*, **95**, 897–903.

Paup, D. C., Coniglio, L. P., and Clemens, L. G. (1972) Masculinization of the female golden hamster by neonatal treatment with androgen or estrogen, *Horm. Behav.*, **3**, 123–31.

Pfaff, D. W. and Keiner, M. (1973) Atlas of estradiol-concentrating cells in the central nervous system of the female rat, *J. Comp. Neurol.*, **151**, 121–58.

Pfaff, D. W. and Zigmond, R. E. (1971) Neonatal androgen effects on sexual and non-sexual behavior of adult rats tested under various hormone regimes, *Neuroendocrinology*, **7**, 129–45.

Pfeiffer, C. A. (1936) Sexual differences of the hypophysis and their determination by the gonads, *Am. J. Anat.*, **58**, 195–225.

Phoenix, C. H., Goy, R. W., Gerall, A. A., and Young, W. C. (1959) Organizing action of prenatally administered testosterone propionate on the tissues mediating behavior in the female guinea pig, *Endocrinology*, **65**, 369–82.

Plapinger, L. and McEwen, B. S. (1973) Ontogeny of estradiol-binding sites in rat brain. I. Appearance of presumptive adult receptors in cytosol and nuclei, *Endocrinology*, **93**, 1119–28.

Plapinger, L. and McEwen, B. S. (1975) Immunochemical comparison of estradiol-binding molecules in perinatal rat brain cytosol and serum, *Steroids*, **26**, 255–65.

Plapinger, L., McEwen, B. S., and Clemens, L. E. (1973) Ontogeny of estradiol-binding sites in rat brain. II. Characteristics of a neonatal binding macromolecule, *Endocrinology*, **93**, 1129–39.

Presl, J., Herzmann, J., Röhling, S., and V. Figarova, (1973) Developmental changes in regional distribution of estrogenic metabolites in the female rat hypothalamus, *Endocrinologia Experimentalis*, **7**, 189–92.

Presl, J., Rohling, S., Horsky, J., and Herzmann, J. (1970) Changes in uptake of ^{3}H-estradiol by the female rat brain and pituitary from birth to sexual maturity, *Endocrinology*, **86**, 899–900.

Quinn, D. L., (1966) Luteinizing hormone release following preoptic stimulation in the male rat, *Nature*, **209**, 891–2.

Raynaud, J.-P. (1973) Influence of rat estradiol binding plasma protein (EBP) on uterotrophic activity. *Steroids*, **21**, 249–58.

Raynaud, J.-P., Mercier-Bodard, C., and Baulieu, E. E. (1971) Rat estradiol binding plasma protein (EBP). *Steroids*, **18**, 767–88.

Reddy, V., Naftolin, F., and Ryan, K. J. (1973) Aromatization in the central nervous system of rabbits: Effects of castration and hormone treatment, *Endocrinology*, **92**, 589–94.

Reddy, V. V. R., Naftolin, F., and Ryan, K. J. (1974) Conversion of androstenedione to estrone by neural tissues from fetal and neonatal rats, *Endocrinology*, **94**, 117–21.

Rhees, R. W., Abel, J. H., Jr., and Haack, D. W. (1972) Uptake of tritiated steroids in the brain of the duck *(Anas platyrhynchos)*. An autoradiographic study, *Gen. Comp. Endocrinol.*, **18**, 292–300.

Robinson, J. A. and Karavolas, H. J. (1973) Conversion of progesterone by rat anterior pituitary tissue to 5α-pregnane-3,20-dione and 3α-hydroxy-5α-pregnane-20-one, *Endocrinology*, **93**, 430–4.

Robison, G. A., Butcher, R. W., and Sutherland, E. W. (1971) *Cyclic AMP*, Academic Press, New York, 531 pp.

Ryan, K. J., Naftolin, F., Reddy, V., Flores, F., and Petro, Z. (1972) Estrogen formation in the brain, *Am. J. Obstet. Gynecol.*, **114**, 454–60.

Sar, M. and Stumpf, W. E. (1973a) Autoradiographic localization of radioactivity in the rat brain after the injection of 1,2-³H-testosterone. *Endocrinology*, **92**, 251–6.

Sar, M. and Stumpf, W. E. (1973b) Cellular and subcellular localization of radioactivity in the rat pituitary after injection of 1,2-³H-testosterone using dry-autoradiography, *Endocrinology*, **92**, 631–5.

Sar, M. and Stumpf, W. E. (1973c) Neurons of the hypothalamus concentrate ³H progesterone or its metabolites, *Science*, **182**, 1266–8.

Schultz, F. M. and Wilson, J. D. (1974) Virilization of the Wolffian duct in the rat fetus by various androgens, *Endocrinology*, **94**, 979–86.

Schwarzel, W. C., Kruggel, W. G., and Brodie, H. J. (1973) Studies on the mechanism of estrogen biosynthesis. VIII. The development of inhibitors of the enzyme system in human placenta, *Endocrinology*, **92**, 866–80.

Segal, S. J. and Johnson, D. C. (1959) Inductive influence of steroid hormones on the neural system: Ovulation controlling mechanisms, *Archives d'Anat. Microscop. Morph. Exp.*, **48**, 261–74.

Seiki, K. and Hattori, M. (1973) *In vivo* uptake of progesterone by the hypothalamus and pituitary of the female ovariectomized rat and its relationship to cytoplasmic progesterone-binding protein, *Endocrinol. Jap.*, **20**, 111–9.

Sheridan, P. J., Sar, M., and Stumpf, W. E. (1974a) Autoradiographic localization of ³H-estradiol or its metabolites in the central nervous system of the developing rat, *Endocrinology*, **94**, 1386–90.

Sheridan, P. J., Sar, M., and Stumpf, W. E. (1974b) Interaction of exogenous steroids in the developing rat brain, *Endocrinology*, **95**, 1749–53.

Sheridan, P. J., Zarrow, M. X. and Denenberg, V. H. (1973) Androgenization of the neonatal female rat with very low doses of androgen, *J. Endocrinol.*, **57**, 33–45.

Shirley, B., Wolinsky, J., and Schwartz, N. B. (1968) Effects of a single injection of an estrogen antagonist on the estrous cycle of the rat, *Endocrinology*, **82**, 959–68.

Slade, B. (1973) Antibodies to α foetoprotein cause foetal mortality in rabbits, *Nature*, **246**, 493–4.

Slade, B. and Budd, S. (1972) Localization of α-fetoprotein in fetal and newborn rabbits, *Biol. Neonate*, **21**, 309–20.

Smith, J. A. (1973) Effect of antibody to alphafetoprotein on the development of chicken and rat embryos, *Arch. Immunol. Therap. Exp.*, **21**, 163–73.

Södersten, P. (1973) Increased mounting behavior in the female rat following a single neonatal injection of testosterone propionate, *Horm. Behav.*, **4**, 1–17.

Södersten, P. (1974) Effects of an estrogen antagonist, MER-25, on mounting behavior and lordosis behavior in the female rat, *Horm. Behav.*, **5**, 111–22.

Soloff, M. S., Morrison, M. J., and Swartz, T. L. (1972) A comparison of the estrone–estradiol-binding proteins in the plasmas of prepubertal and pregnant rats, *Steroids*, **20**, 597–608.

Spies, H. G. and Niswender, G. D. (1972) Effect of progesterone and estradiol on LH release and ovulation in rhesus monkeys, *Endocrinology*, **90**, 257–61.

Stanislawski-Birencwajg, M. (1967) Specific antigens of rat embryonic serum, *Cancer Res.*, **27**, 1982–9.

Stern, J. J. (1969) Neonatal castration, androstenedione, and the mating behavior of the male rat, *J. Comp. Physiol. Psych.*, **69**, 608–12.

Stumpf, W. E. (1968) Cellular and subcellular ³H-estradiol localization in the pituitary by autoradiographs, *Z. Zellforsch.*, **92**, 23–33.

Stumpf, W. E. (1970) Estrogen-neurons and estrogen-neuron systems in the periventricular brain, *Am. J. Anat.*, **129**, 207–17.

Stumpf, W. E. (1972) Estrogen, androgen, and glucocorticosteroid concentrating neurons in the amygdala, studied by autoradiography. In: *Advances in Behavioral Biology, Vol. 2 The Neurobiology of the Amygdala*, B. E. Eleftheriou, (ed.), Plenum Press, New York, pp. 763–74.

Sundram, K., Tsong, Y. Y., Hood, W., and Brinson, A. (1973) Effect of immunization with estrone-protein conjugate in rhesus monkeys, *Endocrinology*, **93**, 843–7.

Swanson, H. H. (1966) Modification of the reproductive tract of hamsters of both sexes by neonatal administration of androgen or oestrogen, *J. Endocrinol.*, **36**, 327–8.

Swartz, S. K. and Soloff, M. S. (1974) The lack of estrogen binding by human α fetoprotein, *J. Clin. Endocrinol. Metab.*, **39**, 589–91.

Swerdloff, R. S., Jacobs, H. S., and Odell, W. D. (1972). Synergistic role of progestogens in estrogen induction of LH and FSH surge, *Endocrinology*, **90**, 1529–36.

Takasugi, N. (1972) Carcinogenesis by vaginal transplants from ovariectomized, neonatally estrogenized mice into ovariectomized normal hosts, *Gann*, **63**, 73–7.

Takasugi, N. and Bern, H. A. (1964) Tissue changes in mice with persistent vaginal cornification induced by early postnatal treatment with estrogen, *J. Nat. Canc. Inst.*, **33**, 855–65.

Takasugi, N. and Kamishima, Y. (1973) Development of vaginal epithelium showing irreversible proliferation and cornification in neonatally estrogenized mice: An electron microscope study, *Development, Growth, and Differentiation*, **15**, 127–40.

Taleisnik, S., Caligaris, L., Astrada, J. J. (1969) Sex difference in the release of luteinizing hormone evoked by progesterone, *J. Endocrinol.*, **44**, 313–21.

Taleisnik, S., Caligaris, L., and Astrada, J. J. (1970) Positive feedback effect of progesterone on the release of FSH and the influence of sex in rats, *J. Reprod. Fert.*, **22**, 89–97.

Taleisnik, S., Caligaris, L., and Astrada, J. J. (1971) Sex differences in hypothalamo–hypophysial function. In: *Steroid Hormones and Brain Function*, C. H. Sawyer, and R. A. Gorksi, (eds.), University of California Press, Berkeley, pp. 171–84.

Terasawa, E., Kawakami, M., and Sawyer, C. H. (1969) Induction of ovulation by electro-chemical stimulation in androgenized and spontaneously constant-estrous rats. *Proc. Soc. Exp. Biol. Med.*, **132**, 497–501.

Terkel, A. S., Shryne, J., and Gorski, R. A. (1973) Inhibition of estrogen facilitation of sexual behavior by the intracerebral infusion of actinomycin-D, *Horm. Behav.*, **4**, 377–86.

Thien, N. C., Duval, J., Samperiz, S., and Jouan, P. (1974) Testosterone 5α-reductase of microsomes from rat anterior hypophysis: Properties, increase by castration, and hormonal control, *Biochimie*, **56**, 899–906.

Tiefer, L. and Johnson, W. (1975) Neonatal androstenedione and adult sexual behavior in golden hamsters, *J. Comp. Physiol. Psychol.*, **88**, 239–47.

Treloar, O. L., Wolf, R. C., and Meyer, R. K. (1972) Failure of a single neonatal dose of testosterone to alter ovarian function in the rhesus monkey, *Endocrinology*, **90**, 281–4.

Tullner, W. W. and Hodgon, G. D. (1974) Effects of fetectomy on plasma estrogens and progesterone in monkeys (Macaca mulatta), *Steroids*, **24**, 887–97.

Tuohimaa, P. and Niemi, M. (1972) Uptake of sex steroids by the hypothalamus and anterior pituitary of pre- and neonatal rats, *Acta Endocrinol. Copenh.*, **71**, 37–44.

Turner, C. D. (1941) Permanent genital impairments in the adult rat resulting from the administration of estrogen during early life, *Am. J. Physiol.*, **133**, 471–2.

Ulrich, R., Yuwiler, A., and Geller, E. (1972) Failure of 5α-dihydrotestosterone to block androgen sterilization in the female rat, *Proc. Soc. Exp. Biol. Med.*, **139**, 411–3.

Uriel, J. and Nechaud, de (1973) An outline of the physiopathology of rat α fetoprotein. In: *Alpha-Fetoprotein and Hepatoma*, H. Hirai, and T. Miyaji, (eds.), University Park Press, Baltimore, pp. 35–47.

Uriel, J., de Nechaud, B., and Dupiers, M. (1972) Estrogen-binding properties of rat, mouse, and man fetospecific serum proteins. Demonstration by immuno-autoradiographic methods, *Biochem. Biophys. Res. Commun.*, **46**, 1175–80.

Vannier, B. and Raynaud, J. P. (1975) Effect of estrogen plasma binding on sexual differentiation of the rat fetus, *Molec. Cell. Endocrinol.*, **3**, 323–37.

van Rees, G. P. and Gans, E. (1966) Effect of gonadectomy and oestrogen on pituitary LH content and organ weights in androgen-sterilized female rats, *Acta Endocrinol.*, **52**, 471–7.

Velasco, M. E. and Taleisnik, S. (1969a) Release of gonadotropins induced by amygdaloid stimulation in the rat, *Endocrinology*, **84**, 132–9.

Velasco, M. and Taleisnik, S. (1969b) Effect of hippocampal stimulation on the release of gonadotropin, *Endocrinology*, **85**, 1154–9.

Vértes, M., Barnes, A., Lindner, H. R., and King, R. J. B. (1973) Studies on androgen and estrogen uptake by rat hypothalamus. In: *Receptors for Reproductive Hormones. Advances in Experimental Medicine and Biology, Vol. 36*, B. W. O'Malley, and A. R. Means, (eds.), Plenum Press, New York, pp. 137–73.

Vértes, M. and King, R. J. B. (1971) The mechanism of oestradiol binding in rat hypothalamus: Effect of androgenization, *J. Endocrinol.*, **51**, 271–82.

Wade, G. N. and Feder, H. H. (1972) Uptake of [1,2-^{3}H] 20αhydroxypregn-4-en-3-one, [1,2-^{3}H] corticosterone, and [6,7-^{3}H] estradiol 17β by guinea pig brain and uterus: Comparison with uptake of [1,2-^{3}H] progesterone, *Brain Res.*, **45**, 545–54.

Wade, G. N., Harding, C. F., and Feder, H. H. (1973) Neural uptake of [1,2-^{3}H] progesterone in ovariectomized rats, guinea pigs and hamsters: Correlation with species differences in behavioral responsiveness, *Brain Res.*, **61**, 357–67.

Ward, I. L., Crowley, W. R., Zemlan, F. P., and Margules, D. L. (1975) Monominergic mediation of female sexual behavior, *J. Comp. Physiol. Psych.*, **88**, 53–61.

Warembourg, M. (1974) Etude radioautographique des retroactions centrales des corticosteroides ^{3}H chez le rat et le cobaye. In: *Neuroendocrinologie de l'axe Corticotrope. Brain-Adrenal Interactions*, P. Dell, (ed.), INSERM, Paris, pp. 41–66.

Waynforth, H. B. and Robertson, D. M. (1972) Oestradiol content of ovarian venous blood and ovarian tissue in hypophysectomized rats during late pregnancy, *J. Endocrinol.*, **54**, 79–85.

Weisz, J. and Gibbs, C. (1974) Metabolites of testosterone in the brain of the newborn female rat after an injection of tritiated testosterone, *Neuroendocrinology*, **14**, 72–86.

Weisz, J. and Philpott, J. (1971) Uptake and metabolism of testosterone by the brain of the newborn rat. In: *Influence of Hormones on the Nervous System*, D. Ford, (ed), Karger, Basel, pp. 282–95.

Whalen, R. E. and Edwards, D. A. (1967) Hormonal determinants of the development of masculine and feminine behavior in male and female rats, *Anat. Rec.*, **157**, 173–80.

Whalen, R. E., Edwards, D. A., Luttge, W. G., and Robertson, R. T. (1969) Early androgen treatment and male sexual behavior in female rats, *Physiol. Behav.* **4**, 33–9.

Whalen, R. E. and Gorzalka, B. B. (1973) Effects of an estrogen antagonist on behavior and on estrogen retention in neural and peripheral target tissues, *Physiol. Behav.*, **10**, 35–40.

Whalen, R. E. and Gorzalka, B. B. (1974) Estrogen–progesterone interactions in uterus and brain of intact and adrenalectomized immature and adult rats, *Endocrinology*, **94**, 214–23.

Whalen, R. E., Gorzalka, B. B., DeBold, J. F., Quadagno, D. M., Kan-Wha-Ho, G., and Hough, Jr., J. C. (1974) Studies on the effects of intracerebral actinomycin D implants on estrogen-induced receptivity in rats, *Horm. Behav.*, **5**, 337–43.

Whalen, R. E. and Luttge, W. G. (1971) Perinatal administration of didhydrotestosterone to female rats and the development of reproductive function, *Endocrinology*, **89**, 1320–2.

Whalen, R. E., Luttge, W. G., and Gorzalka, B. B. (1971) Neonatal androgenization and the development of estrogen responsivity in male and female rats, *Horm. Behav.*, **2**, 83–90.

Whalen, R. E. and Nadler, R. D. (1963) Suppression of the development of female mating behavior by estrogen administered in infancy, *Science*, **141**, 273–4.

Whalen, R. E. and Nadler, R. D. (1965) Modification of spontaneous and hormone-induced sexual behavior by estrogen administered to neonatal female rats, *J. Comp. Physiol. Psych.*, **60**, 150–2.

Whalen, R. E. and Rezek, D. L. (1974) Inhibition of lordosis in female rats by subcutaneous implants of testosterone, androstenedione or dihydrotesterone in infancy, *Horm. Behav.*, **5**, 125–8.

Whitsett, J. M. and Vandenbergh, J. G. (1975) Influence of testosterone propionate administered neonatally on puberty and bisexual behavior in female hamsters, *J. Comp. Physiol., Psych.*, **88**, 248–55.

Wilson, J. D. (1973) Testosterone uptake by the urogenital tract of the rabbit embryo, *Endocrinology*, **92**, 1192–9.

Wilson, J. G. (1943) Reproductive capacity of adult female rats treated prepuberally with estrogenic hormone, *Anat. Rec.*, **86**, 341–63.

Wilson, J. G., Hamilton, J. B., and Young, W. C. (1941) Influence of age and presence of the ovaries on reproductive function in rats injected with androgens, *Endocrinology*, **29**, 784–9.

Wilson, J. G., Young, W. C. and Hamilton, J. B., (1940) A technic suppressing development of reproductive function and sensitivity to estrogen in the female rat, *Yale J. Biol. Med.*, **13**, 189–203.

Wollman, A. L. and Hamilton, J. B. (1967) Prevention by cyproterone acetate of androgenic, but not of gonadotropic, elicitation of persistent estrus in rats, *Endocrinology*, **81**, 350–6.

Yalom, I. D., Green, R., and Fisk, N. (1973) Prenatal exposure to female hormones. Effect on psychosexual development in boys, *Arch. Gen. Psychiat.*, **28**, 554–61.

Young, W. C., Goy, R. W., and Phoenix, C. H. (1964) Hormones and sexual behavior, *Science*, **143**, 212–8.

Zigmond, R. E. (1975) Binding and metabolism of steroid hormones in the central nervous system. In: *Handbook of Psychopharmacology*, L. L. Iverson, S. D. Iverson, and S. H. Snyder, (eds.), Plenum Press, New York, Volume 5, pp. 239–328.

Zucker, I. (1967) Suppression of oestrous behaviour in the immature male rat, *Nature*, **216**, 88–9.

Zucker, I. and Feder, H. H. (1966) The effect of neonatal reserpine treatment on female sex behavior of rats, *J. Endocrinol.*, **35**, 423–4.

Note added in proof (see p. 192)

Recent experiments from our laboratory and from several other laboratories have established that inhibitors of the conversion of testosterone to estradiol and a potent estrogen antagonist, CI 628, block the action of testosterone on sexual differentiation of the rat brain (see Lieberburg *et al.*, 1977; McEwen *et al.*, 1977, for data and references).

Part II

Integration of Sexual Behaviour:
Physiological Mechanisms

Introduction

Studies of mechanisms underlying sexual behaviour have always been constrained by the technologies of brain research. Conceptually, the neurological techniques employed at the beginning of the century are surprisingly similar to their modern descendants. For example, research into the neural control of sexual clasping behaviour involved in the amplexus of frogs, representing some of the earliest work on brain mechanisms of sexual behaviour, employed a variety of techniques ranging from electrostimulation of the brain and local application of pharmacological agents to transection and more specific ablation of areas of the brain (Tarchanoff, 1887; Goltz, 1869; Steinach, 1910; Baglioni, 1911). While the technological refinements of current methodology have not resulted in any general theory applicable to central nervous mechanisms underlying sexual behaviour, there is increasing evidence that hindbrain and spinal coordination systems are involved in the control of complex polysynaptic reflexive movements involved in copulatory patterns of mammals, as Hart describes, and in lower vertebrates such as frogs (Hutchison, 1967). Studies employing lesioning techniques and electrostimulation also implicate parts of the limbic system, and particularly hypothalamic and preoptic areas in the control of sexual behaviour (Hart, 1974). The specificity of both techniques is often in question however (Harris and Michael, 1964), and it becomes difficult to distinguish between the effects of secondary physiological damage, and effects on mechanisms specific to sexual behaviour.

A major difficulty in studying neural mechanisms of sexual behaviour lies in their hormone dependency. There is a consensus of opinion, however, that in adulthood the steroid sex hormones influence the brain directly to increase or decrease the readiness of central integrative mechanisms to mediate the effects of the patterned sensory stimulation necessary for the elitciation of sexual behaviour. The most rapid advances are being made in determining which parts of the brain are involved in sex-hormone action. Kelley and Pfaff in taking a comparative view suggest that in a variety of vertebrate forms, ranging from fish to primates, sex steroids are concentrated in discrete limbic areas which appear to form a phylogenetically stable system of hormone-sensitive cells. Hart shows that steroid-concentrating cells also occur in the spinal cord. Although neuroanatomical work gives no functional view of the mode of action of sex hormones, there is some agreement between the diencephalic areas, notably in the hypothalamus, delimited by direct implantation of steroids into the brain which appear to be associated with male and female sexual behaviour, and the areas indicated by autoradiographic measurement of the uptake of isotopically labelled androgen and oestrogen.

While the areas in the brain sensitive to steroids and associated with sexual behaviour are beginning to be clarified, the modes of action of sex hormones on the brain remain to be determined. There are some indications now of the complexity of the problem and the difficulty of making any generalizations covering the multiplicity of hormonal effects that have been discovered. Feder argues that there is a difference in specificity of the relationship between hormones and sexual behaviour between male and female rodents. In the adult female, the action of oestrogen is specifically related to female copulatory behaviour. But in the male a distinction can be drawn between 'appetitive' components leading to copulation, which may be influenced by a general alteration of metabolic activity induced by a wide range of steroids, and consummatory behaviour involving copulatory activities which are more specifically affected by androgen and its oestrogenic metabolites. Hutchison takes the view that the action of androgen on male sexual behaviour depends ultimately on the concentration of hormone in the brain, and on the hormonal sensitivity of the brain cells mediating male sexual behaviour. This 'sensitivity' may be determined by the endocrine condition of the animal and environmental variables such as photoperiod and social stimuli. Lisk, in specifying the hormonal determinants of behaviour involved in female sexual receptivity to the male, suggests that progesterone may modulate the action of oestrogen in brain cells. The work of the latter author suggests that further knowledge of hormonal action on mechanisms of behaviour will depend upon biochemical investigation at the cellular level.

Rapid advances are being made in the field of neurotransmitter physiology, particularly in the identification of monoaminergic pathways. Meyerson and Malmnäs point to the evidence from pharmacological studies which implicate serotonergic and dopaminergic activity in the control of sexual behaviour of both male and female mammals. Although it is difficult at present to see precise functional relationships, there seems little doubt that the action of hormones on the central nervous system will eventually be clarified in terms of specific neurotransmitter effects. As Everitt points out, the use of new techniques which allow manipulation of monoamines at the level of the brain will help to clarify the role of monoaminergic neurones in sexual behaviour.

A major difficulty in studying brain mechanisms of sexual behaviour lies with the behavioural terminology; definition of behavioural variables often lags behind the increasing sophistication of neuroendocrine techniques. For example, in rodent studies 'lordosis' is used by some authors to represent the female copulatory response to the male, while others use the term 'sexual receptivity'. This inconsistency can lead to difficulties in the consideration of causal mechanisms. As Komisaruk shows, lordosis, as a reflexive component of female copulatory behaviour in the rat, can be elicited in the total absence of ovarian hormones, whereas female receptivity, defined more comprehensively as a complex of female responses necessary for male intromission and ejaculation, requires oestrogenic stimulation. The emphasis on adequate behavioural definition in physiological studies is carried further by Herbert who finds that the stimulus value of the female, or 'attractivity', in infrahuman primates such as rhesus may have a completely different hormonal basis from that underlying her readiness to mate, or 'receptivity'. In the former case, oestrogens acting peripherally are implicated, in the latter, androgens are thought to act centrally. As regards human sexual behaviour, Bancroft sounds a note of caution by stressing that there is no simple relationship between hormones and sexual behaviour in the male or the female. Here the difficulties of behavioural description are very apparent. With more definitive descriptions of sexual behaviour and avoidance of unitary intervening variables such as 'libido' a distinction between general and more specific actions of hormones on sexual behaviour may be possible.

Sex hormones are traditionally seen as influencing 'sexual' systems to the exclusion of other motivational systems. Andrew argues that this is partly a consequence of the current use of dyadic laboratory tests for sexual behaviour which employ fully sexually active animals in situations where the animals are free from disturbance by conspecifics. Such situations may exclude the performance of behaviour such as courtship which is influenced by a multiplicity of motivational factors. Andrew argues that the action of hormones, and androgens in particular, can be seen in terms of an influence on attentional mechanisms which may determine the balance between competing motivational systems. For example, in situations where distracting or conflicting stimuli interfere with the initiation of copulatory behaviour, shifts of attention could prevent or delay consummatory behaviour by allowing other motivational systems to become dominant. In Andrew's view persistence of attention to stimuli associated with sexual behaviour in the male may be promoted by androgens.

REFERENCES

Baglioni, S. (1911) Zur Kenntis der Zentrentätigkeit bei der sexuallen klammerung der Amphibien, *Zentralbl. f. Physiol.*, **25**, 233–8.

Goltz, F. (1869) *Beitrage zur Lehre von den Funktionen den Nervecentren des Frosches*, August Hirschwald, Berlin.

Harris, G. W. and Michael, R. P. (1964) The activation of sexual behaviour by hypothalamic implants of oestrogen, *J. Physiol. London*, **171**, 275–301.

Hart, B. L. (1974) Gonadal androgen and sociosexual behaviour of male mammals: a comparative analysis, *Psych. Bull.*, **81**, 383–400.

Hutchison, J. B. (1967) A study of the neural control of sexual clasping behaviour in *Rana angolensis* Bocage and *Bufo regularis* Reuss with a consideration of self-regulatory hindbrain systems in the Anura, *Behaviour*, **28**, 1–57.

Steinach, E. (1910) Geschlechstrieb und echt sekundäregeschlechtsmerkmale als Folge der innersekretorischen Funktion der Keimdrüsen, *Zentralbl. f. Physiol.*, **24**, 551–6.

Tarchanoff, J. R. (1887) Zur Physiologie des Geschlechtsapparates des frosches, *Arch. f. d. ges. Physiol. des Menschen v. d. Thiere* (Pflüger) **40**, 330–51.

CHAPTER 7

Generalizations from Comparative Studies on Neuroanatomical and Endocrine Mechanisms of Sexual Behaviour

Darcy B. Kelley and Donald W. Pfaff

INTRODUCTION

The effects of sex hormones on behaviour have been investigated in a number of vertebrate species. Recent studies on neural–endocrine interactions in representatives of different vertebrate classes indicate that certain aspects of sex hormone interactions with the brain have widespread phylogenetic validity (Morrell *et al.*, 1975a). This chapter reviews data on three different classes of interactions: (1) sex hormone effects on behaviour, (2) neural tissue involved in sex behaviour, and (3) binding of steroid sex hormones by cells in brain regions mediating reproductive behaviour. Studies on different vertebrates offer an opportunity to discover general principles as well as phylogenetic trends in hormone–brain–behaviour interactions.

EFFECTS OF GONADAL HORMONES ON SEX BEHAVIOUR

Steroid hormones of gonadal origin are common to all vertebrates. Androgens and oestrogens have been described in mammals, birds, reptiles, amphibians, and fish (Barrington, 1968; Ozon, 1972). Although it is generally true that the role of these hormones is to regulate reproductive functions, the form of regulation varies widely in different species. Investigations of the effects of sex hormones have included behavioural as well as physiological functions. The control of sex behaviour by androgens and oestrogens has been studied most extensively in mammals. Information on other vertebrates has been accumulated more slowly. Recent experiments have broadened the scope of our understanding of non-mammalian forms and a review of these questions now may help to shed some light on the hormonal regulation of sex behaviour in all vertebrates.

Mammals

Hormone effects on sex behaviour in mammals have been reviewed extensively elsewhere (Beach, 1948; Young, 1961; Phoenix et al., 1967; Lisk, 1973; Hart, 1974a). Certain aspects of endocrine control in mammals are reviewed here in order to provide a basis for comparison with other vertebrate classes which have not been as extensively investigated. In general, gonadectomy abolishes many reproductive behaviours. Which sex behaviours are affected and the time courses involved vary depending on the species. Testosterone, a major mammalian androgen, will restore some aspects of male sex behaviour to castrates of many species. Oestradiol with progesterone restores receptivity to ovariectomized females.

In some mammals, testosterone metabolites have also been shown to affect male sex behaviour. Low doses of oestradiol induce castrated male rats to display simple mounting and mounting with thrusts nearly as effectively as higher doses of testosterone (Pfaff, 1970). Another testosterone metabolite, dihydrotestosterone (DHT), is capable of restoring most of the complete male sex pattern to castrated guinea pigs (Alsum and Goy, 1974). The behavioural effectiveness of these metabolites varies from species to species. DHT is effective in restoring male sex behaviour in Swiss–Webster mice (Luttge et al., 1974) and rhesus monkey (Phoenix, 1974) but not in rats. Oestradiol is effective in rats (Pfaff, 1970) but not in guinea pigs (Alsum and Goy, 1974). The behavioural effectiveness of DHT and oestradiol may be linked, in that species behaviourally sensitive to one hormone have to date been found not to be sensitive to the other (Alsum and Goy, 1974). Neither of these metabolites, however, has actions identical to those of testosterone. In both guinea pig and rhesus monkey, for example, DHT is more effective than testosterone in some measures of behaviour and less effective in others (Alsum and Goy, 1974; Phoenix, 1974). The combination of oestradiol and DHT has proven effective in restoring male sex behaviour to castrated rats (Larsson and Sodersten, 1973; Feder et al., 1974a; Baum et al., 1974) and this synergism has been observed for mounting in female hamsters as well (Noble, 1974).

The sexual receptivity of many female mammals can be restored after castration by injections of oestradiol and progesterone. These effects have been especially well documented in rats. Oestrogen and progesterone have been found to act synergistically in the control of the lordosis reflex (Beach, 1948; Davidson, 1972; Pfaff et al., 1973; Kow et al., 1974a). In female rodents (rats and hamsters), testosterone alone is not sufficient to restore sex behaviour to ovariectomized females (Pfaff, 1970; Tiefer, 1970). Injections of testosterone supplemented by progesterone, however, reproduced part of the oestradiol effect on feminine behaviour (Pfaff, 1970; Whalen and Hardy, 1970). In the rhesus monkey, hormonal control of female receptivity presents a somewhat different picture. Oestradiol appears to be important in influencing the female monkey's attractiveness to the male (Michael and Welegalla, 1968). This effect may be mediated by the production of sexually attractive pheromones within the female's vagina (Michael et al., 1971). Recent studies have indicated, however, that the female rhesus's sexual receptivity may depend on the secretion of androgens, especially testosterone (Herbert and Trimble, 1967). The origin of these androgens in the intact female appears to be the adrenal (Everitt and Herbert, 1971).

Birds

Castration has been shown to reduce or eliminate sex behaviour in male and female birds of many different species. In general, androgen acts on castrates to restore male sex behaviour and oestrogen restores sex behaviour to females. Hinde (Hinde and Steel, 1964; Hinde et al., 1963), in the canary and Lehrman (1961, 1965), in the ring dove, have demonstrated that the display of the full repertoire of courtship, copulation, and incubation behaviour results from the interaction of sex hormones with the gradual unfolding of behaviour sequences involving both the male and the female. The transition from sexual to parental behaviour was postulated by Hinde and Lehrman to be involved with alterations in hormone secretion to include higher levels of progesterone and prolactin secretion (Beer, 1973). Erpino (1969) found that progesterone strikingly reduced the male sex behaviour seen in castrated pigeons after testosterone administration. He postulated that the suppression of sex behaviour by progesterone in male and female birds was instrumental in facilitating parental behaviour. In another Columbiform, the ring dove, progesterone has little effect on female sex behaviour restored by oestrogen although it does lead to incubation and nesting responses (Cheng and Silver, 1975). Incubation responses can be elicited in castrated males treated with testosterone alone (Silver and Feder, 1973). Furthermore, although incubation in female doves follows a rise in blood levels of progesterone, no such rise is seen in males (Silver et al., 1974). Thus, while exogenous progesterone promotes a transition from courtship to incubation behaviour in male ring doves (Cheng, 1975), the role of endogenous progesterone is not clear. In females, a sharp rise in progesterone is associated with ovulation and with incubation (Cheng, 1974). These data suggest that hormone facilitation of incubation may be different for males and females in this species.

The effects of testosterone and oestradiol on sexual courtship in the male ring dove have been compared (Hutchison, 1970). There was some variability in the display of one component of courtship, nest soliciting. Castrated males who did not display this behaviour during preoperative tests could not be induced to nest solicit after testosterone treatment although all other aspects of courtship were restored. Treatment with oestradiol, on the other hand, induced nest soliciting in all castrates regardless of preoperative levels of the behaviour. Oestradiol was less effective in restoring other aspects of male sex behaviour. Whereas testosterone induced both chasing and bowing, oestradiol led to less chasing and no bowing. Thus the effects of sex hormones on behaviour in birds have been shown to depend upon the particular response investigated. Although these data might appear to suggest that oestradiol plays some role in the endogenously regulated courtship of male doves, it should be noted that oestradiol has not been detected in dove peripheral plasma at any phase of courtship (Korenbrot et al., 1974). Under experimental conditions where oestradiol levels in females during courtship rose from < 40 pg/ml to a mean of 85 pg/ml, no detectable (< 7 pg/ml) oestradiol was found in males. Conversion of testosterone to oestradiol could, however, occur in the CNS.

Oestradiol has also been shown to affect male sex behaviour in photoperiodically castrated male quail (Adkins and Adler, 1972). In males of this species, testosterone stimulated both courtship and copulation; oestradiol was ineffective in maintaining courtship but did stimulate copulation. Adkins and Adler also investigated the necessary hormonal conditions for initiating male sex behaviour in females and vice versa. After oestradiol administration, males could be induced to display receptive behaviours similar to those shown by sexually active females. Females, however, displayed little sex behaviour of any sort after treatment with testosterone. Differences in the responses of males and females to the same sex hormone have also been noted in ring doves (Hutchison, 1970; Cheng, 1975). These experiments indicate that the genetic sexes may differ in their capacity to display heterotypical sex behaviour in several bird species.

Reptiles

Testosterone has been shown to restore the normal pattern of male courtship behaviour in castrated Anolis carolinesis (Noble and Greenberg, 1940; Crews, 1974). Testosterone will also induce courtship behaviour out of season in another male lizard, Uta stansburiana (Ferguson, 1966). Oestradiol induces oestrous behaviour in ovariectomized female Anolis (Noble and Greenberg, 1941a); changes in female receptivity have been correlated with follicular development (Crews, 1973). In addition to effects on courtship in males, testosterone has been shown to produce male sex behaviour in castrated females. The results of oestradiol treatment on male courtship have not been reported. Testosterone, however, will produce female receptive behaviour in castrated male and female Anolis (Noble and Greenberg, 1940, 1941b) in addition to its effects on male behaviour. One unexplored possibility is that testosterone may be metabolized to an oestrogen in the lizard.

Amphibians

Castration has been shown to abolish male sex behaviour and secondary sex characteristics in a number of anuran amphibians (Steinach, 1894; Dodd,

1960; Palka and Gorbman, 1973). Oestrogens have been measured in the plasma of several anurans (Ozon, 1972). Testosterone levels in frogs using radio-immunoassay have also been described (D'Istria *et al.*, 1974). Whereas testosterone will restore secondary sex characteristics to males, reinstating male sex behaviour has been more difficult. In one report, Greenberg (1942) observed mating calling following testosterone treatment in *Acris gryllus*. Palka and Gorbman (1973) investigated the effects of a variety of steroids including testosterone, oestradiol and DHT on male sex behaviour in *Rana pipiens*. Under the conditions of their experiments, none of the steroids was effective in reinstating male sex behaviour. Kelley and Pfaff (1976) however, have recently reported successful restoration by androgens of male sex behaviour in the South African clawed frog, *Xenopus laevis* (Fig. 1). In these studies, clasping of females by sexually active male frogs was abolished by castration. Testosterone and dihydrotestosterone restored clasping to castrates. Oestradiol administered at a number of different dose levels was ineffective with regard to male sex behaviour. Testosterone was also effective in producing male sex behaviour in castrated female *Xenopus*. In *Xenopus laevis*, it is possible to completely, functionally sex-reverse animals by hormonal manipulations in larval stages (Chang and Witschi, 1955; Mikamo and Witschi, 1963, 1964). From behavioural experiments (Kelley and Pfaff, 1976), it is evident that even adult female frogs retain the capacity for androgen-activated male sex behaviour.

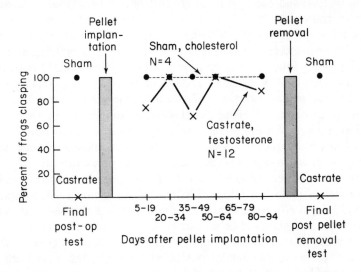

Fig. 1. Percent of adult, male *Xenopus laevis* clasping gonado-trophin-primed females following castration, replacement therapy with 10 mg testosterone pellets into the dorsal lymph sac and then testosterone pellet removal. Sham males received a sham operation instead of castration and were implanted with 10 mg cholesterol pellets into the dorsal lymph sac. (From Kelley and Pfaff, 1976.)

Although the predominant ovarian oestrogen in anurans has proved to be oestradiol (Ozon, 1972), the behaviourally active hormones for female sex behaviour have not yet been identified in this group.

A comparative theory on hormonal control of sex behaviour has been advanced by Adkins (Adkins and Adler, 1972; Adkins, 1973). Briefly, this theory states that the homogametic sex (XX: females, mammals; males, birds) is the neutral sex in terms of development of genitalia and of psychosexuality; this sex is also the most inherently bisexual. Thus Adkins notes that in rats, the female is homogametic (XX), developmentally labile (can be masculinized by neonatal hormones) and bisexual (displays more mounting than the male displays lordosis). In Japanese quail, the male is homogametic, developmentally labile and bisexual. Among mammals, exceptions to this generalization would appear to be the hamster, where the male normally displays more female sex behaviour than the female does male sex behaviour. In other vertebrates, Kelley and Pfaff (1976) have pointed out in *Xenopus laevis* that although the female is heterogametic (WZ), she can readily be induced to clasp with testosterone.

Fish

A number of authors (Aronson, 1959; Hoar, 1965; Liley, 1969; Fiedler, 1974) have reviewed the hormonal control of sex behaviour in teleosts. In general, castration has been found to reduce male and female sex behaviour in many species. As Aronson (1959) has pointed out, the effects of castration vary in different species, particularly with regard to nest building and aggression. Liley (1968) found that receptivity in sexually experienced female guppies persisted as long as 20 weeks after gonadectomy. In a later (1972) study, Liley found that the sexual behaviour of virgin female guppies was considerably reduced by ovariectomy. Thus, in these fish, differences in the effects of castration appear to depend on the sexual experience of the individual. Variable results of castration in other species may also reflect interaction with experiential variables as well as species differences in hormone sensitivity.

Androgens have been shown to restore castration-reduced sexual behaviours in a number of male fish (Hoar, 1962; Wai and Hoar, 1963; Smith, 1969; Johns and Liley, 1970; Reinboth, 1972). Oestradiol has also been shown to play a similar role in female sex behaviour (Liley, 1972; Stacey and Liley, 1974). One interesting aspect of the hormonal control of fish sex behaviour is the apparent direct action of gonadotrophins on mating. In the stickleback (Hoar, 1962; Wai and Hoar, 1963) the effect of testosterone on agonistic behaviour and nest building was shown to interact with the photoperiod, an effect presumably mediated by gonadotrophin. Gonadotrophin administration alone failed to restore female sex behaviour to hypophysectomized, gonadectomized female guppies (Liley and Donaldson, 1969); gonadotrophins appear to act synergistically with ovarian hormones in the regulation of receptivity. In this respect, it is interesting to note that Pfaff (1973) and Moss and McCann (1973) have reported facilitatory effects of a gonadotrophin releasing hormone, luteinizing hormone releasing hormone, LRH, on female sex behaviour in ovariectomized, hypophysectomized, oestrogen-primed female rats.

Fish have also been investigated to determine hormonal conditions necessary for one genetic sex to display sex behaviour more characteristic of the other sex. Male sex behaviour can be produced in female guppies by testosterone treatment (Clemens et al., 1966). The behaviour of a chichlid was also 'completely masculinized' by testosterone treatment (Reinboth, 1972). In guppies, Liley (1972) reports that methyltestosterone, although it did not restore sexual receptivity to male courtship in castrated females, did produce 'male like' behaviours in some females. Wai and Hoar (1963), however, found that methyltestosterone did not produce male sex behaviour in gonadectomized, adult female sticklebacks under conditions identical to those producing male sex behaviour in males. These studies indicate that the ability of testosterone to produce male sex behaviour in females appears to vary somewhat among the fish species studied.

Summary

The generalizations to be drawn from these studies are that in vertebrates, exogenously administered testosterone is an active hormone in restoring male sex behaviour to castrated males and oestradiol is active in restoring sexual receptivity to castrated females.

The possibility that in some cases these sex hormones act through a metabolite has been examined in mammals and, to a lesser extent, in other vertebrates as well. Regarding metabolites of testosterone, in mammals quite marked species differences in the effects of DHT and oestradiol on male sex behaviour have been noted. Although there is less information on this subject in non-mammalian vertebrates, different effects of sex steroid metabolites have been observed across species.

The general action of testosterone in promoting male sex behaviour and of oestradiol in promoting female receptivity may be modified by the action of other sex hormones. A good example is that of progesterone whose behavioural functions exhibit certain species differences: progesterone appears to increase female receptivity in many mammals, while in birds it decreases masculine sex behaviour and promotes parental behaviour. The presence of progesterone of luteal origin is not common to all vertebrates so that we might readily accept the differing roles of this hormone in different species. In speaking of the role of sex steroids in reproductive physiology, Hisaw (1959) has said 'it is not hormones which have evolved but the uses to which they are put.' The applicability of this statement can be extended to include the control of sexual behaviour as well.

PREOPTIC AND HYPOTHALAMIC INVOLVEMENT IN
THE CONTROL OF SEX BEHAVIOUR

In mammals, a number of studies have implicated the preoptic and hypothalamic regions of the brain in the regulation of reproduction, including
sex behaviour and gonadotrophin secretion. Although less extensive, investigations of brain regions involved in sex behaviour in other vertebrates have been
carried out as well. A comparison of the roles of the preoptic and hypothalamic
areas in a number of different vertebrates reveals certain phylogenetic
similarities of function in the control of sex behaviour.

Mammals

Male-typical Behaviour

A number of well-controlled studies in a variety of mammalian species have
strongly implicated the medial preoptic area in the control of male sex behaviour. Large bilateral lesions of this region can abolish male copulatory
behaviour in rats (Larsson and Heimer, 1964; Heimer and Larsson, 1966/67;
Lisk, 1968; Giantonio et al., 1970; Chen and Bliss, 1974). Of the complete
male sexual response, only infrequent mounting of females by lesioned males
is generally described (reviewed by Hart, 1974b). Essentially similar effects
have been reported in male cats (Hart et al., 1973) and dogs (Hart, 1974b).
In contrast to the behaviour of lesioned rats and cats, some dogs did exhibit
light pelvic thrusting when mounting but no intromissions were observed.

Malsbury (1971) and van Dis and Larsson (1971) have reported facilitation
of male sex behaviour by electrical stimulation of the medial preoptic area
in male rats. Roberts et al. (1967) have elicited complete male sex behaviour
pattern in opossums by stimulation of the preoptic region. MacLean and Ploog
(1962) in the squirrel monkey and Robinson and Mishkin (1966) in the rhesus
evoked ejaculation by electrical stimulation of the preoptic region. Perachio
and his colleagues (Perachio et al., 1969; Perachio et al., 1973) have more
recently found that electrical stimulation of the preoptic-anterior hypothalamic
region will result in stimulus-bound sexual behaviour in male rhesus. Support
for the hypothesis that some lesion and stimulation effects in males may be
due to androgen-concentrating cells in the proptic region has come from hormone implant studies. Studies by Davidson (1966), Lisk (1967), and Johnston
and Davidson (1972) have implicated the preoptic area as the most sensitive
region for restoring male sex behaviour to castrate rats by implantation of
small quantities of testosterone directly into the brain.

The preoptic area has also been shown to be involved in the male sex behaviour of female rats (Singer, 1968; Dörner et al., 1968a, 1968b; 1969).
Whereas preoptic lesions abolished male sex behaviour in females, female sex
behaviour was unaffected (Singer, 1968). Conversely, anterior hypothalamic

lesions abolished lordosis while sparing male sex behaviour (Singer, 1968; Dörner et al., 1969). Implants of testosterone into the preoptic-anterior hypothalamic region of females produced male sexual behaviour (Dörner et al., 1968b). Oestradiol will also facilitate mounting in females; brain areas where implants facilitated female sex behaviour were posterior to preoptic areas involved in male sex behaviour (Dörner et al., 1968a). These data indicate the existence of separate neuroanatomical loci for facilitating male and female sex behaviour.

Female-typical Behaviour

Lesions of preoptic tissue have not consistently been found to reduce female sex behaviour (Singer, 1968). Indeed, one study of ovariectomized female rats has indicated (Fig. 2) that preoptic lesions reduce the quantity of oestradiol necessary to restore sexual receptivity (Powers and Valenstein, 1972). From studies of this sort, the suggestion has been made (Law and Meagher, 1958; Powers and Valenstein, 1972) that the preoptic area exerts a tonic inhibitory effect on lordosis behaviour. This suggestion may also receive some support from studies that indicate that electrical stimulation of the medial preoptic area disrupts lordosis in female hamsters (Malsbury and Pfaff, 1973) and rats (Moss et al., 1974).

On the other hand, lesions of hypothalamic structures, posterior to the preoptic area, have been shown to reduce female sex behaviour in a number of mammalian species (rat, Singer, 1968; guinea pig, Goy and Phoenix, 1963; rabbit, Sawyer, 1959; cat, Sawyer and Robison, 1956). In the female hamster,

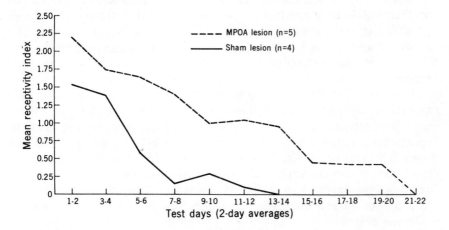

Fig. 2. Sexual receptivity of female rats with bilateral medial preoptic lesions and females with sham lesions following a single injection of oestradiol benzoate (2 μg/kg). Animals were given progesterone (0.5 mg) 6 h before each daily behaviour test. (From Powers and Valenstein, 1972.)

for example, lesions of the ventromedial nucleus reduced lordosis; the degree of reduction was proportional to the extent of damage to the ventromedial region (Kow *et al.*, 1974b). The neuroanatomical locus for lesion effects appears to vary somewhat from species to species: the rat may differ from the hamster in that anterior hypothalamic lesions are more effective than damage to the ventromedial region (Singer, 1968; Kow *et al.*, 1974b).

Implants of oestradiol into the hypothalamus will facilitate female sex behaviour in many species. Neuroanatomical sites where lesions reduce female sexual responses appear to be located posteriorly to regions where implants facilitate lordosis. Thus, for example, medial preoptic area hormone implants increase, and anterior hypothalamic lesions decrease lordotic responses in rats (Lisk, 1962; Singer, 1968). Similar implant and lesion pairs are found in hamsters (anterior hypothalamic implants, Ciaccio and Lisk, 1973/74; ventromedial hypothalamic lesions, Kow *et al.*, 1974b), guinea pigs (anterior hypothalamic and ventromedial hypothalamic implants, Morin and Feder, 1974; medial hypothalamic and lateral arcuate lesions, Goy and Phoenix, 1963), and rabbits (ventromedial hypothalamic and premammillary implants, Palka and Sawyer, 1966a; mammillary lesions, Sawyer, 1959). Although the precise neuroanatomical locus for both lesion and implant effects may be different from species to species, the more posterior location of effective lesion sites compared to effective oestradiol implant sites does appear to be a constant feature.

Lisk and his co-workers (Lisk, 1962; Ciaccio and Lisk, 1973/74) have reported that the neural region where oestradiol implants are most effective in increasing female sexual behaviour is the medial preoptic area for rats and the anterior hypothalamus for hamsters. Using autoradiography, Floody and Pfaff (1974) have reported a lower ratio of medial preoptic to anterior hypothalamic oestrogen-concentrating cells in hamsters than in rats. This species difference in hormone binding may be involved in neuroanatomical differences in the effectiveness of oestradiol implant sites between rats and hamsters.

The effects of heterotypical hormone implants into the brain have been reported in rabbit and rhesus monkey. In rabbits (Palka and Sawyer, 1966b), implants of testosterone into the ventromedial premammillary region of the hypothalamus resulted in a behavioural oestrus indistinguishable from that shown following similar implants of oestradiol. Everitt and Herbert (1975) report that testosterone implanted into the hypothalamus of adrenalectomized female rhesus induces sexual receptivity; the testosterone is presumed to mimic the effects of adrenal androgen which they believe is normally responsible for female libido.

Birds

The neural control of courtship and copulation has been investigated in domestic chicken and in Columbiformes (pigeons and ring doves). In fowl,

Barfield (1965b) and Meyer (Meyer and Salzen, 1970; Meyer, 1974) have studied the effects of hypothalamic lesions on male sexual behaviour. In adult chickens, Barfield (1965b) reported that lesions in the preoptic area interrupted copulatory behaviour. In chicks, Meyer (1974) reports that symmetrical lesions in the medial preoptic area disrupted precocial copulation. Auto-radiographic studies on testosterone uptake in the male chicken brain (Barfield et al., 1977) have revealed binding in the medial preoptic area. A similar uptake picture was found by Meyer (1973) for the male chick. The technique of hor-mone implantation into the brain has also been used in fowl by Barfield (1965a, 1969) and in male chicks (Gardner and Fisher, 1968). Copulatory behaviour, but not aggressive or courtship behaviour, was observed in adult birds with small implants of testosterone in the preoptic area (Fig. 3a, 3b) (Barfield, 1969). It should be noted that many behavioural elements of aggressive behaviour in fowl are common to courtship as well. In chicks (Gardner and Fisher, 1968), androgen stimulation of the preoptic region will activate male sexual behaviour.

Åkerman (1966) has examined the effects of electrical brain stimulation on reproductive behaviour in pigeons. Bowing resulted from stimulation by electrodes placed in the ventromedial forebrain and particularly in the preoptic area. Preening movements and nest demonstration (= nest soliciting, Hutchi-son, 1967) often followed intense bowing elicited by preoptic stimulation. Male sexual behaviour following preoptic area stimulation was observed in both males and females. Hutchison (1967, 1971) and Barfield (1971) have reported that implants of TP in the preoptic and anterior hypothalamic areas of ring doves will restore the full courtship display to castrates. Unlike data from the chicken, no neuroanatomical separation of sites activating courtship, copula-tory and aggressive components of reproductive behaviour was seen (Barfield, 1971). Hutchison (1970, 1971, 1974) however, has postulated that the different components of the reproductive display are differentially sensitive to androgen with aggressive components being less sensitive than nest-orienta-tion behaviour. Finally, it should be noted that the areas thought to control these behaviours in the ring dove, notably the preoptic area, have also been shown autoradiographically to concentrate both oestradiol (Martinez-Vargas et al., 1974a) and testosterone (Martinez-Vargas et al., 1974b). Preoptic implants of oestradiol (Hutchison, 1971) will activate chasing and nest soliciting but not bowing in males.

In reviewing studies on hormonal effects on sex behaviour in birds earlier, it was noted that systemically administered progesterone reduced male sex behaviour and promoted incubation behaviour. Similar results (Komisaruk, 1967; Hutchison, 1974) have followed brain implants of progesterone. Proges-terone, acting at the level of the hypothalamus, reduces aggressive and court-ship behaviours relative to nest-oriented behaviours. Sites for this effect and for the incubation promotion effect appear to differ somewhat (Komisaruk, 1967) but are found generally in the preoptic-anterior hypothalamic area.

We noted in male mammals that in the medial preoptic area, lesions decrease

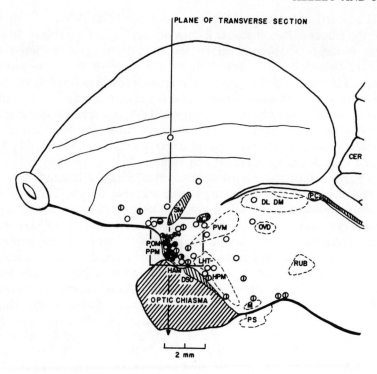

Fig. 3(a). Parasaggital section demonstrating testosterone propionate
implant sites in the brain of male chickens. Implant positions indicated
are 0.5 to 1.5 mm lateral to midline. The box around the anterior hypothalamic-preoptic region indicates the area magnified in (b). Cross-
hatched areas represent fibre tracts. Symbols and abbreviations are
given in Fig. 3(b)

and stimulation increases sex behaviour, and androgen implants promote
copulation. Neurons in the medial preoptic region concentrate testosterone
(Pfaff, 1968; Sar and Stumpf, 1973). Data presented here for chicken and dove
indicate that these generalizations can be extended to include some male birds
as well.

Frogs

Recent autoradiographic results (Kelley et al., 1975; Morrell et al., 1975b;
Kelley and Pfaff, 1975) indicate that testosterone and oestradiol are concentrated
by cells in the anterior preoptic area of male anf female frogs. Since hormone
uptake sites in hypothalamic regions of other vertebrates have been implicated
in the control of sex behaviour, we might expect that these regions would play
similar roles in frogs as well.

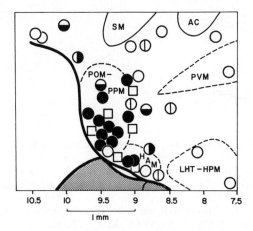

Fig. 3(b). Magnification of the anterior hypothalamic-preoptic region
of the fowl brain shown in Fig. 3(a). The scale gives anterior–
posterior coordinates. Symbols show the position of implant tips.
Areas enclosed by broken lines show sites of major nuclei and fibre
tracts are shown by unbroken lines. Symbols: single implants –●,
copulate; ◕ mount only; o, no sex behaviour; bilateral implants –◑,
copulate; ⊙, no sex behaviour, ◻ ,cholesterol implants. Abbreviations
used in figures: AC, anterior commissure; Cer, cerebellum; DL, M, n.
dorsolateralis, medialis; DSO, supraoptic decussation; HAM, n.
hypothalamicus anterior medialis; HPM, n. hypothalamicus posterior
medialis; LHT, n. hypothalamicus lateralis; M, n. mammilaris; OVD,
n. ovoidalis; PC, posterior commissure; POM-PPM, n. praeopticus
medialis-paraventricularis magno-cellularis (preoptic nuclear complex);
PS, position of pituitary stalk; PVM, n. paraventricularis magnocellu-
laris; SM, tractus septomescencephalicus. (From Barfield, 1969.)

The anuran preoptic area (POA) has been implicated in some aspects of
reproductive behaviour in both males and females. A study of Aronson and
Noble (1945) indicated that the preoptic area was involved in the 'swimming
response' of the male to the oestrous female in *Rana pipiens*. The importance of
the preoptic area in male mate orientation prior to amplexus has been confirmed
by Schmidt (1968) in a number of anuran species. The preoptic area has also
been shown to be involved in the male's release of the female at the termination
of oviposition (Aronson and Noble, 1945). In females, lesions of the POA in
Hyla cinerea and *Bufo fowleri* demonstrate that this region is essential in female
anuran orientation to male mating calling (Schmidt, 1969).

In addition to effects on orientation, lesions of the preoptic area also eliminate
mating calling (Schmidt, 1968). Electrical stimulation of this region (Schmidt,
1966, 1968, 1973, 1974) and of the region of the 'arcuate' nucleus (Schmidt,
1974) elicits normal mating calling in male anurans of a number of different
species. Although stimulation of other brain regions will also elicit vocaliza-

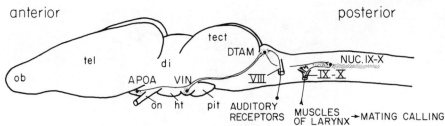

Fig. 4. Proposed neural pathways for mating vocalizations in the frog brain (after Schmidt, 1974). Pathways have been superimposed on a side view of the *Xenopus laevis* brain. Pathways have been schematically diagrammed as single neurons (●────<) whose cell bodies are indicated by black dots (●) and whose terminations are indicated by branchings (────<). Abbreviations: APOA, anterior preoptic area; di, diencephalon; DTAM, dorsal tegmental area of the medulla; ht, hypothalamus; Nuc. IX–X, nucleus of cranial nerves IX–X; ob, olfactory bulb; on, optic nerve; pit, pituitary; tect, tectum; tel, telencephalon; VIN, ventral infundibular nucleus; VIII, eight cranial nerve; IX–X, ninth–tenth cranial nerves

tions, only the preoptic area and arcuate give rise to normal mating calling. Frog calling results from actions of the laryngeal muscles during inspiration and expiration (Schmidt, 1972). These muscles are innervated by the laryngeal branch of the vagus nerve which exits from the medulla with cranial nerves IX–X (Schmidt, 1966, 1969). The cell bodies whose axons leave with nerves IX–X lie in a lateral columnar nucleus in the medulla (Schmidt, 1971, 1973, 1974). Schmidt has recently (1973, 1974) proposed a model for the central control of anuran mating calling. A 'vocal pulse generator' which acts on motor neurons of nucleus IX–X has been found in the sub-cerebellar tegementum. This area (the 'pre-trigeminal nucleus', Schmidt, 1974) is presumed to correlate sensory information from tactile and auditory receptors. This region also appears to be involved in male sexual clasping in *Xenopus laevis* (Hutchison and Poynton, 1963; Hutchison, 1964). Patterned neural input arising from androgen receptors in the preoptic area is presumed to act on the 'pre-trigeminal nucleus' to effect mating calling. In Fig. 4, the neural pathways proposed by Schmidt for mating calling have been superimposed on a lateral view of the *Xenopus laevis* brain. In Fig. 7, testosterone-concentrating regions (see Kelley *et al.*, 1975) have been indicated as stippled areas. All of the areas in the anuran brain from which Schmidt can electrically stimulate vocalizations are areas which contain androgen-concentrating cells. It is of interest that androgensensitive courtship vocalizations in songbirds may also be modulated by brain areas which concentrate testosterone (Zigmond *et al.*, 1972a, 1973; Arnold, 1974; Arnold *et al.*, 1976).

Fish

A number of studies have investigated the effects of forebrain lesions on reproductive behaviour in fish; these studies, however, used very large lesions

(Kamrin and Aronson, 1954; Overmier and Gross, 1974); or very dorsal ablations (Segaar and Niewenhuys, 1963) and so effects, if any, on preoptic tissue are difficult to evaluate. Demski and Knigge (1971) have investigated the effects of electrical stimulation of various brain regions in the bluegill. Stimulation of courtship behaviour in mature males was evoked from electrodes in the preoptic area. Following the termination of preoptic stimulation, nest building and sweeping were frequently observed. These male sex behaviours have been observed after preoptic electrical stimulation in both males and females; nest building has been shown to be androgen-dependent in several species of sunfish (Smith, 1969). Preoptic lesions disrupt the spawning reflex in male killifish (Macey et al., 1974). In the green sunfish, preoptic stimulation will also evoke semen release (Fig. 5 and Fig. 6) (Demski et al., 1973, 1975). Whether brain regions implicated in sex behaviour also concentrate male sex hormone in fish (as has been shown in other vertebrates, see Morrell et al., 1975a for review) being investigated in our laboratory at present.

Summary

Preoptic and hypothalamic neurons are involved in the regulation of sex behaviour in a wide variety of vertebrate species. The medial preoptic area has been strongly implicated in male sex behaviour in mammals, birds, amphibia, and fish. Central nervous system control of female sex behaviour has been investigated primarily in mammals. Lesion-induced decrements in female receptivity appear to be located in the hypothalamus, posterior to the tissue critical for male sex behaviour. Thus it appears that different neural substrates underlie male and female sex behaviour. These findings, in conjunction with autoradiographic localization of hormone-concentrating neurons (see following section), suggest that such neurons mediate hormone effects on sex behaviour.

STEROID SEX HORMONE BINDING IN THE BRAINS OF VERTEBRATES: COMPARATIVE ASPECTS

Features Which Are Common

Sex steroid concentrating cells have been found, using autoradiography, in the brains of mammals (Michael, 1965; Pfaff, 1968; Stumpf, 1968; Pfaff and Keiner, 1973; Pfaff et al., 1974; Floody and Pfaff, 1974; Morrell and Pfaff, 1975; Anderson, 1975), birds (Zigmond et al., 1972a, 1973; Meyer, 1973; Arnold et al., 1976; Barfield et al., 1977), frogs (Kelley et al., 1975; Morrell et al., 1975b; Kelley and Pfaff, 1975) and a fish (Morrell et al., 1975a). Results of these autoradiographic studies are in good agreement with biochemical investigations of steroid hormone binding in rats (Eisenfeld and Axelrod, 1966; Kato and Villee, 1967; McEwen et al., 1970a, 1970b; McEwen and Pfaff,

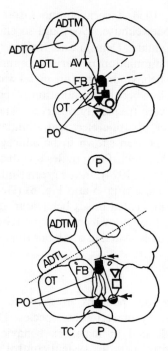

Fig. 5. Representative transverse sections of the brain of the green
sunfish, *Lepomis cyanellus*, depicting Prussian blue marked stimulation sites from which sperm release could be elicited by electrical
stimulation at 100 μA or less. Solid symbols represent marked
positions within 10 μA of the lowest threshold obtained along the
electrode tract. Open symbols represent sites not necessarily within
10 μA of the lowest threshold. Symbols: circles, stimulation sites
with thresholds of 0–25 μA; squares, stimulation sites with thresholds of 26–50 μA; triangles (pointed up), stimulation sites with
thresholds of 51–75 μA; triangles (pointed down), stimulation
sites with thresholds of 76–100 μA; dotted lines, Prussian blue
marked electrode tracks that were negative for sperm release at
100 μA; dashed lines, reconstructed electrode tracks; solid line
between arrows, part of an electrode track showing the locus of
points from which sperm release was evoked at 10 μA. Abbreviations: ADTC, area dorsalis telencephali pars centralis; ADTL,
area dorsalis telencephali pars lateralis; ADTM, area dorsalis
telencephali pars medialis; AVT, area ventralis telencephali; FB,
forebrain bundles; OT, optic tract; P, pituitary; PO, preoptic area;
TC, transverse commissure. (From Demski, Bauer and Gerald,
1975.)

1970, 1973), hamsters and guinea pigs (Feder *et al.*, 1974b; Gorzalka and
Whalen, 1974), rabbits (Chader and Villee, 1970), rhesus monkey (Gerlach
et al., 1974, 1975) and ring dove (Stern, 1972; Zigmond *et al.*, 1972b). The
existence of hormone-concentrating cells in these diverse species suggests that

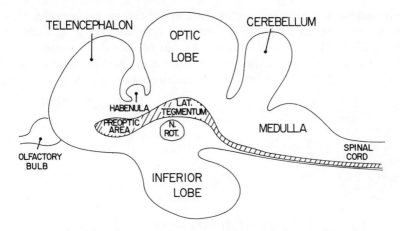

Fig. 6. Schematic diagram of neural regions involved in electrically evoked sperm release in green sunfish. Loci of positive stimulation points (hatched area) are indicated on a composite parasaggital representation. Abbreviation: N. ROT, nucleus rotundus. (From Demski, Bauer and Gerald, 1975.)

sex steroid binding by neurons may be a common, if not universal, vertebrate phenomenon.

A comparison of binding sites in vertebrates (Morrell *et al.*, 1975a) has revealed that sex steroids are accumulated by neurons in discrete brain regions that represent a phylogenetically stable core of hormone-concentrating neural structures. The general features of this neuroanatomical distribution include binding in the preoptic area, the tuberal region of the hypothalamus, various components of the limbic forebrain and mesencephalic regions deep to the tectum. Regions which concentrate sex hormones have been implicated, using other techniques, in the control of gonadotropin secretion and in sex behaviour.

Features Which Are Particular: Possible Correlates

Species Specializations in Locations of Hormone-concentrating Neurons: Functional Correlates

Certain interesting additions to the general vertebrate pattern of hormone binding are found in the zebra finch and in a frog, *Xenopus laevis*. In the zebra finch (Arnold, 1974; Arnold *et al.*, 1976) cells of nucleus MAN of the neostriatum, the caudal nucleus of the hyperstriatum ventrale and the tracheosyringealis part of nucleus hypoglossus of the medulla concentrate androgen. These regions are thought to be involved in the control of song (Arnold, 1974; Nottebohm *et al.*, 1976) which is androgen-dependent in birds. The hypoglossus is particularly interesting because it contains the cells whose axons innervate the syringeal musculature (the syrinx is the organ controlling bird song).

Androgen but not oestrogen uptake in a motor cranial nerve nucleus (IX–X) has also been demonstrated in the frog, *Xenopus laevis* (Fig. 7; Kelley *et al.*, Kelley, 1975; Morrell *et al.*, 1975b). As can be seen from comparison with Fig. 4, nucleus IX–X and many other brain areas postulated to control frog vocalizations (Schmidt, 1974) contain androgen-concentrating cells. Mating

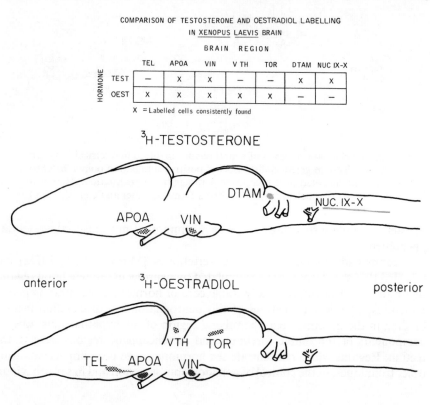

COMPARISON OF TESTOSTERONE AND OESTRADIOL LABELLING
IN <u>XENOPUS</u> <u>LAEVIS</u> BRAIN

BRAIN REGION

		TEL	APOA	VIN	V TH	TOR	DTAM	NUC IX-X
HORMONE	TEST	—	X	X	—	—	X	X
	OEST	X	X	X	X	X	—	—

X = Labelled cells consistently found

^{3}H-TESTOSTERONE

anterior ^{3}H-OESTRADIOL   posterior

Fig. 7. A lateral view of the frog brain: regions containing autoradiographically demonstrated oestradiol and testosterone-concentrating cells in the brain of *Xenopus laevis* (after Kelley *et al.*, 1975; Morrell *et al.*, 1975b) are indicated schematically. Brain regions containing many, very heavily labelled cells (oestradiol: APOA, VIN) are indicated in heavy stipple. Areas with fewer labelled cells (oestradiol: TEL, VTH, TOR; testosterone: APOA, VIN) are indicated in medium stipple. Brain regions containing the smallest number of more lightly labelled cells (testosterone: DTAM, Nuc. IX-X) are indicated in light stipple.

While the pattern of testosterone retention differs from that of oestradiol, male and female brains do not differ in the topography of hormone-concentrating sites. Thus the sex steroid retention pattern in *X. laevis* appears to be determined by the hormone and not by the genetic sex (Kelley *et al.*, 1975; Morrell *et al.*, 1975b.)

Abbreviations: APOA, anterior preoptic area; DTAM, dorsal tegmental area of the medulla; NUC. IX-X, nucleus of the ninth-tenth cranial nerves; TEL, telencephalon (ventral striatum, ventral lateral septum, rostral amygdala); TOR, torus semicircularis; VIN, ventral infundibular nucleus; VTH, ventral thalamus calling in frogs is hormone dependent. The autoradiographically demonstrated binding of testosterone in brain regions involved in androgen-dependent vocalizations may represent functionally important avian and anuran specializations of the general vertebrate pattern.

Quantitative Differences in Binding: Correlations with Circulating Hormone Levels

Biochemical and autoradiographic techniques have been used to investigate binding of sex steroids in brain; there are good correlations between findings with these two methods (McEwen and Pfaff, 1973). Autoradiographic methods allow us to pinpoint the exact neuroanatomical loci of hormone-binding cells. Biochemical techniques are more useful for quantitative determinations of brain receptor affinity for hormones.

Both oestradiol and testosterone are concentrated in limbic and hypothalamic tissues of the rat (Eisenfeld and Axelrod, 1966; Kato and Villee, 1967; McGuire and Lisk, 1968; Pfaff, 1968; Stumpf, 1968; Sar and Stumpf, 1973; Naess *et al.*, 1975). Autoradiographic studies indicate that the topography of uptake in male and female brains is quite similar; also the hormones tend to be concentrated by the same nuclear groups (Pfaff, 1968). However, the number of labelled cells and the intensity of labelling following testosterone administration is generally less than that seen with oestradiol using the autoradiographic technique (Pfaff, 1968). These comparisons agree with biochemical studies (McEwen and Pfaff, 1970; McEwen *et al.*, 1970a, 1970b) in which the pattern of testosterone uptake among 9 brain regions studied was very similar to that observed for oestradiol, but was lower in magnitude. For example, radioactive oestradiol concentration by brain structures is 4–9 times the level seen in the blood whereas, testosterone concentration is only 1–2 times blood level (McEwen *et al.*, 1970a). The lower magnitude of testosterone uptake could be due either to less radioactivity per cell or to fewer radioactive cells, or to both, as seen in some autoradiograms. Studies in whole tissue on steroid hormone competition in the uptake of testosterone (McEwen *et al.*, 1970b) and oestradiol (McEwen and Pfaff, 1970) have revealed that unlabelled oestradiol competes more effectively with radioactive oestradiol for hypothalamic binding sites than 'cold' testosterone does with radioactive testosterone. In the same brain regions, oestradiol is as effective in competing for uptake sites with ^{3}H-testosterone as is testosterone itself. In contrast, testosterone does not compete effectively against ^{3}H-oestradiol. Some of these competition effects may be due to metabolism of testosterone to oestradiol, either peripherally or in the CNS. In competition studies using the nuclear fraction from tissue in the preoptic-hypothalamic region, Zigmond and McEwen (1970) found that while a concurrent injection of non-radioactive oestradiol reduced nuclear uptake of ^{3}H-oestradiol, a similar injection of non-radioactive testosterone had no significant effect. *In vitro* studies using hypothalamic tissue slices in the rabbit (Chader and Villee, 1970) also demonstrated loss of nuclear binding of ^{3}H-oestradiol after 'cold' oestradiol but not 'cold' testosterone competition. These studies indicate that 'binding strength' of oestradiol in rat brain is greater than testosterone and that oestradiol has the more specific uptake system.

Oestradiol circulates in much lower amounts than testosterone. Using competitive protein binding and radioimmunoassay, peak oestradiol levels in peripheral blood of cycling females are generally in the range of 20 to 50 pg/ml (Brown-Grant et al., 1970; Butcher et al., 1974; Kalra and Kalra, 1974) whereas testosterone generally circulates at maxima of 2,000 to 10,000 pg/ml (Gomes et al., 1973; Harris and Barthe, 1974). An interesting parallel may be drawn with behavioural data in the rat. At a much smaller dose, oestradiol is as effective as testosterone in facilitating male sex behaviour (Pfaff, 1970). Testosterone alone is not effective in restoring female sex behaviour to castrates. Thus oestradiol (a) circulates at low levels in the blood; (b) is more effective per μg than testosterone in facilitating behaviour; and, (c) is associated with high-affinity, highly specific binding in rat brain. Testosterone circulates at higher levels, is less effective per μg in sex behaviour facilitation, and is less strongly and specifically bound in brain tissue.

These quantitative comparisons can be extended by considering progesterone in the female rat. Progesterone circulates in concentrations much higher than those of oestradiol (Butcher et al., 1974; Shaikh and Shaikh, 1975). Over 100 μg of progesterone is required for full effectiveness in tests of female sex behaviour in female rats (Powers, 1970; Davidson and Levine, 1969). Progesterone binding in rat brain tissue is quantitatively so weak that the existence of classical, specific cytosol or nuclear receptors is still in doubt (Whalen and Luttge, 1971; Wade and Feder, 1972). If such progesterone binding occurs, it must be less strong and specific than that of oestradiol in female rat brain. In a separate comparison across species, Wade et al. (1973) report that the binding affinity for progesterone in brain was greatest for guinea pig, followed by hamster, and then rat. The sensitivity of female sex behaviour to progesterone in these species also follows the pattern, guinea pig > hamster > rat.

Feder et al. (1974b) have recently compared the behavioural effectiveness and uptake of oestradiol in three different rodent species: rat, guinea pig, and hamster. The behavioural effectiveness of oestradiol in promoting lordosis in ovariectomized rats and guinea pigs are quite similar. Hamsters, however, require 20–50 times as much oestradiol before 100% of the animals display lordosis (all females were, in addition, progesterone primed). In biochemical studies, rats and guinea pigs had much greater tissue/plasma concentration ratios for oestradiol in hypothalamus than did hamsters (see also Gorzalka and Whalen, 1974). In addition, the degree of elevation of hypothalamic affinity for hormone relative to other brain regions was less for hamsters than for the other two species. Perhaps reflecting the lower affinity of the hamster brain for oestradiol, Floody and Pfaff (1974) in an autoradiographic study have reported that fewer oestrogen-concentrating neurons are present in the female hamster brain than in the female rat. Baranczuk and Greenwald (1973) have measured the maximum amount of oestradiol in the peripheral plasma of the cycling hamster: in their radioimmunoassay system, hamster blood levels of oestradiol on day 4 of the cycle were, on average, 186 pg/ml whereas, maximum blood levels reported for 2 rats in the same radiommunoassay system were, on average, 87 pg/ml. If valid, these data would suggest that oestradiol circulates at levels 2–3 times higher in the hamster than in the rat. In this comparison across species, there is the suggestion that the species with higher blood levels of oestradiol (hamster) is the species in which oestradiol is less effective behaviourally (per microgram) and whose brains demonstrate lower target tissue affinity for the hormone.

Thus, among sex steroids in rodents, certain comparisons can be made between circulating levels and brain binding. Under conditions where circulating levels are very low, the affinity of receptor systems in the brain for the hormone seems to be high. This is precisely what is required to ensure that adequate quantities of each steroid reach appropriate target neurons. Moreover, in competition studies (especially between oestrogens and androgens, to date) it seems that the hormone circulating in lower concentrations will have the more specific receptor system in brain tissue. This is exactly what is needed to protect that steroid's receptor system from interference by other steroid hormones circulating in larger quantities.

Summary and Conclusions

Sex steroid hormone-concentrating cells are found in discrete regions of the brain in several diverse vertebrate species. Preoptic, tuberal-hypothalamic and limbic forebrain structures apparently constitute a phylogenetically stable core of hormone-concentrating regions, and have been implicated in the control of gonadotropin secretion and sex behaviour. Androgen-concentrating CNS regions thought to be involved in courtship vocalizations in an avian and an anuran species may represent specializations of the general vertebrate pattern.

Regarding affinity and specificity of hormone binding by neurons, differences between oestradiol, testosterone and progesterone exist in the rat. In comparisons across species, the binding strength of oestradiol in rat brain was greater than that found in hamster brain. Both within and between species, binding strength in brain is inversely correlated with circulating blood levels and directly correlated with the behavioural effectiveness of the sex hormone. The greater the binding affinity and specificity of the sex steroid, the greater its behavioural effectiveness per microgram and the lower the circulating hormone level in the blood. High affinity binding for hormones circulating at low levels may ensure adequate hormone concentrations in the brain. High specificity for hormone circulating at low levels may protect receptor systems from interference by competing steroids circulating at higher levels.

REFERENCES

Adkins, E. (1973) Hormones and behavior: An evolutionary and genetic perspective. Presented in symposium *Genes, Hormones, and Reproductive Behavior* at 13th Int. Congr. Ethology.

Adkins, E. K. and Adler, N. T. (1972) Hormonal control of behavior in the Japanese quail, *J. Comp. Physiol. Psychol.*, **81**, 27–36.

Åkerman, B. (1966) Behavioural effects of electrical stimulation in forebrain of the pigeon. I. Reproductive behaviour, *Behaviour*, **26**, 323–38.

Anderson, C. (1975) Localization of cells retaining ^{3}H-estradiol in the forebrain of rabbits, *Anat. Rec.*, **181**, 287–92.

Arnold, A. (1974) Behavioral effects of androgen in zebra finches *(Poephila guttata)* and a search for its sites of action. *Thesis*, Rockefeller University, New York.

Arnold, A., Nottebohm, F. and Pfaff, D. W. (1976) Hormone concentrating cells in vocal control and other areas of the brain of the zebra finch *(Poephila guttata) J. Comp. Neur.*, **165**, 487–512.

Aronson, L. R. (1959) Hormones and reproductive behavior: Some phylogenetic considerations. In: *Comparative Endocrinology*, A Gorbman (ed.), John Wiley and Sons, Inc, New York, pp. 98–120.

Aronson, L. R. and Noble, G. K. (1945) The sexual behavior of anura. 2. Neural mechanisms in *Rana pipiens*, *Bull. Am. Mus. Nat. Hist.*, **86**, 83–140.

Alsum, P. and Goy, R. (1974) Actions of esters of testosterone, dihydrotestosterone or estradiol on sexual behavior in castrated male guinea pigs, *Horm. Behav.*, **5**, 207–17.

Baranczuk, R. and Greenwald, G. (1973) Peripheral levels of estrogen in the cyclic hamster, *Endocrinology*, **92**, 805–11.

Barfield, R. J. (1965a) Induction of aggressive and courtship behavior by intracerebral implants of androgen in capons, *Am. Zool.*, **5**, 203 (abstract).

Barfield, R. J. (1965b) Effects of preoptic lesions on the sexual behavior of male domestic fowl, *Am. Zool.*, **5**, 686–7 (abstract).

Barfield, R. J. (1969) Activation of copulatory behavior by androgen implanted into the preoptic area of the male fowl, *Horm. Behav.*, **1**, 37–52.

Barfield, R. J. (1971) Activation of sexual and aggressive behavior by androgen implanted into the male ring dove brain, *Endocrinology*, **89**, 1470–6.

Barfield, R., Ronay, G., and Pfaff, D. W. (1977) Autoradiographic localization of androgen-concentrating cells in the brain of the chicken, in prep.

Barrington, E. (1968) Phylogenetic perspectives in vertebrate endocrinology. In: *Perspectives in Endocrinology*, E. Barrington and C. Jorgensen (eds.), Academic Press, New York, pp. 1–46.

Baum, M., Sodersten, P., and Vreeburg, J. (1974) Mounting and receptive behavior in the ovariectomized female rat: Influence of estradiol, dihydrotestosterone and genital anesthetization, *Horm. Behav.*, **5**, 175–90.

Beach, F. A. (1948) *Hormones and Behavior*, Harper and Brothers, New York.

Beer, C. (1973) Behavioral components in the reproductive biology of birds. In: *Breeding Biology of Birds*, D. Farner (ed.), National Academy of Sciences, Washington, pp. 323–45.

Brown-Grant, K., Exley, D., and Naftolin, F. (1970) Peripheral plasma oestradiol and luteinizing hormone concentrations during the oestrous cycle of the rat, *J. Endocrinol.*, **48**, 295–6.

Butcher, R., Collins, W., and Fugo, W. (1974) Plasma concentration of LH, FSH, prolactin, progesterone, and estradiol-17β throughout the 4-day estrous cycle of the rat, *Endocrinology*, **94**, 1704–8.

Chader, G. and Villee, C. (1970) Uptake of oestradiol by the rabbit hypothalamus, *Biochem. J.*, **118**, 93–7.

Chang, C. Y. and Witschi, E. (1955) Breeding of sex-reversed males of *Xenopus laevis* Daudin, *Proc. Exp. Biol. Med.*, **89**, 150–2.

Chen, J. and Bliss, D. (1974) Effects of sequential preoptic and mammillary lesions on male rat sexual behavior, *J. Comp. Physiol. Psychol.*, **87**, 841–7.

Cheng, M.-F. (1974) Ovarian development in the female ring dove in response to stimulation by intact and castrated male ring doves, *J. Endocrinol.*, **63**, 43–53.

Cheng, M.-F. (1975) Induction of incubation behavior in male ring doves *(Streptopelia risoria)*: A behavioural analysis. *J. Reprod. Fert.*, **42**, 267–76.

Cheng, M.-F. and Silver, R. (1975) Estrogen–progesterone regulation of nest building and incubation behavior in ovariectomized ring doves *(Streptopelia risoria)*, *J. Comp. Physiol. Psychol.*, **88**, 256–63.

Ciaccio, L. and Lisk, R. (1973/74) Central control of estrous behavior in the female golden hamster, *Neuroendocrinology*, **13**, 21–8.

Clemens, H., McDermitt, C., and Inshee, T. (1966) The effects of feeding methyl testosterone to guppies for 60 days after birth, *Copeia*, (1966) 280–4.

Crews, D. (1973) Behavioral correlats to gonadal state in the lizard *(Anolis carolinensis)*, *Horm. Behav.*, **4**, 307–13.

Crews, D. (1974) Castration and androgen replacement on male facilitation of ovarian activity in the lizard *(Anolis carolinensis)*, *J. Comp. Physiol. Psychol.*, **87**, 963–9.

Davidson, J. M. (1966) Activation of the male rat's sexual behavior by intracerebral implantation of androgen, *Endocrinology*, **79**, 783–94.

Davidson, J. (1972) Hormones and reproductive behavior. In: *Reproductive Biology*, H. Balin and S. Glasser (eds.), Excerpta Medica, Amsterdam, pp. 877–918

Davidson, J. and Levine, S. (1969) Progesterone and heterotypical behavior in male rats, *J. Endocrinol.*, **44**, 129–30.

Demski, L., Bauer, D., and Gerald, J. (1975) Sperm release evoked by electrical stimulation of the fish brain: a functional-anatomical study, *J. Exp. Zool.*, **191**, 215–32.

Demski, L., Gerlad, J., and Bauer, D. (1973) Semen release evoked by electrical stimulation of the fish brain, *Anat. Rec.*, **175**, 305.

Demski, L. and Knigge, K. (1971) The telencephalon and hypothalamus of the bluegill *(Lepomis macrochirus)*: Evoked feeding, aggressive and reproductive behavior with representative frontal sections, *J. Comp. Neural.*, **143**, 1–16.

D'Istria, M., Delrio, A., Botte, V., and Chieffi, A. (1974) Radioimmunoassay of testosterone, 17β-oestradiol and oestrone in the male and female plasma of *Rana esculenta* during sexual cycle, *Steroids Lipids Res.*, **5**, 42–8.

Dodd, J. M. (1960) Gonadal and gonadotropic hormones in lower vertebrates. In: *Marshall's Physiology of Reproduction Vol. I*, part 2, A. S. Parkes (ed.), Longmans Green, *London*, pp. 417–582.

Dörner, G., Döcke, F., and Hinz, G. (1969) Homo- and hypersexuality in rats with hypothalmic lesions, *Neuroendocrinology*, **4**, 20–4.

Dörner, G., Döcke, F., and Moustafa, S. (1968a) Homosexuality in female rats following testosterone implantation in the anterior hypothalamus, *J. Reprod. Fert.*, **17**, 173–5.

Dörner, G., Döcke, F., and Moustafa, S. (1968b) Differential localization of a male and a female hypothalamic mating centre, *J. Reprod. Fert.*, **17**, 583–6.

Eisenfield, A. and Axelrod, J. (1966) Effect of steroid hormones, ovariectomy, estrogen pretreatment, sex and immaturity on the distribution of ^{3}H-estradiol, *Endocrinology*, **79**, 38–42.

Erpino, M. (1969) Hormonal control of courtship behaviour in the pigeon *(Columbia livia)*, *Anim. Behav.*, **17**, 401–5.

Everitt, B. and Herbert, J. (1971) The effects of dexamethasone and androgens on sexual receptivity of female rhesus monkeys, *J. Endocrinol.*, **51**, 575–88.

Everitt, B. and Herbert, J. (1975) The effects of implanting testosterone propionate into the central nervous system on the sexual behavior of adrenalectomized female rhesus monkeys *Brain Res.*, **86**, 109–20.

Feder, H., Naftolin, E., and Ryan, K. (1974a) Male and female sexual responses in male rats given estradiol benzoate and 5α-Androstan-17β-el-3-one Propionate, *Endocrinology*, **94**, 136–41.

Feder, H., Siegel, H., and Wade, G. (1974b) Uptake of [6,7-³H]Estradiol-17β in ovariectomized rats, guinea pigs, and hamsters: Correlation with species differences in behavioral responsiveness to estradiol, *Brain Res.*, **71**, 93–103.

Ferguson, G. W. (1966) Effect of follicle-stimulating hormone and testosterone propionate on the reproduction of the side blotched lizard *(Uta stansburiana)*, *Copeia*, **1966**, 495–8.

Fieldler, K. (1974) Hormonale kontrolle des verhaltens bei fischen, *Fortschritte der Zoologie*, **22**, 268–309.

Floody, O. and Pfaff, D. (1974) Steroid hormone and aggressive behavior: Approaches to the study of hormone-sensitive brain mechanisms for behavior. In: *Aggression* (Res. Pub. Assn. Res. Nerv. Ment. Dis., Vol. 52) S. Frazier (ed.), Waverly Press, Boston, Massachusetts, pp. 149–85.

Gardner, J. E. and Fisher, A. E. (1968) Induction of mating in male chicks following preoptic implantation of androgen. *Physiol Behav.*, **3**, 709–12.

Gerlach, J., McEwen, B., Pfaff, D., Moskovitz, S., Ferin, M., Carmel, P., and Zimmerman, E. (1974) Corticosterone, cortisol, and estradiol bind differentially to specific cell groups in Rhesus monkey brain and pituitary, *Abstracts, Soc. for Neurosci.* (4th Annual Meeting), 224.

Gerlach, J., McEwen, B., Pfaff, D., Moskovitz, S., Carmel, P., Ferin, M., Zimmerman, G., and Zimmerman, E. (1976) Cells in regions of rhesus monkey brain and pituitary retain radioactive estradiol, corticosterone and cortisol differentially. *Brain Res.*, **103**, 603–12.

Giantonio, G. W., Lund, N. L., and Gerall, A. A. (1970) Effect of diencephalic and rhinencephalic lesions on the male rat's sexual behavior, *J. Comp. Physiol. Psychol.*, **73**, 38–46.

Gomes, W., Hall, R., Jain, S., and Boots, L. (1973) Serum gonadotropin and testosterone levels during loss and recovery of spermatogenesis in rats, *Endocrinology*, **93**, 800–9.

Gorzalka, B. and Whalen, R. (1974) Accumulation of estradiol in brain, uterus, and pituitary: Strain, species, suborder and order comparisons, *Brain, Behav. Evol.*, **9**, 376–92.

Goy, R. and Phoenix, C. (1963) Hypothalamic regulation of female sexual behaviour; establishment of behavioural oestrus in spayed guinea-pigs following hypothalamic lesions, *J. Reprod. Fert.*, **5**, 23–40.

Greenberg, B. (1942) Some effects of testosterone on the sexual pigmentation and other sex characters of the cricket frog *(Acris gryllus)*, *J. Exp. Zool.*, **91**, 435–51.

Harris, M. and Barthe, A. (1974) Concentration of testosterone in testis fluid of the rat, *Endocrinology*, **95**, 701–6.

Hart, B. L. (1974a) Gonadal androgen and sociosexual behavior of male mammals: A comparative analysis, *Psychol. Bull.*, **81**, 383–400.

Hart, B. L. (1974b) Medial preoptic-anterior hypothalamic area and sociosexual behavior of male dogs. *J. Comp. Physiol. Psychol.*, **86**, 328–49.

Hart, B. L., Haugen, C. M., and Peterson, D. M. (1973) Effects of medial preoptic-anterior hypothalamic lesions on mating behavior of male cats, *Brain Res.*, **54**, 177–91.

Heimer, L. and Larsson, K. (1966/67) Impairment of mating behavior in male rats following lesions in the preoptic-anterior hypothalamic continuum, *Brain Res.*, **3**, 248–63.

Herbert, J. and Trimble, M. (1967) Effect of oestradiol and testosterone on the sexual receptivity and attractiveness of female rhesus monkey, *Nature*, **216**, 165–6.

Hinde, R., Bell, R., and Steel. E. (1963) Changes in sensitivity of the canary brood patch during the natural breeding season, *Anim. Behav.*, **11**, 553–60.

Hinde, R. and Steel, E. (1964) Effect of exogenous hormones on the tactile sensitivity of the canary brood patch, *J. Endocrinol.*, **30**, 355–9.

Hisaw, F. L. (1959) Endocrine adaptations of the mammalian estrous cycle and gestation, *Comp. Endocrinol., Proc. Columbia Univ. Symp.*, Cold Spring Harbor, New York, 1958, 533–52.

Hoar, W. S. (1962) Hormones and the reproductive behavior of the male three-spined stickleback *(Gasterosteus aculeatus)*, *Anim. Behav.*, **10**, 247–66.

Hoar, W. S. (1965) Comparative physiology: Hormones and reproduction in fishes, *Ann. Rev. Physiol.*, **27**, 51–70.

Hutchison, J. B. (1964) Investigations on the neural control of clasping and feeding in *Xenopus laevis* (Daudin), *Behaviour*, **24**, 47–65.

Hutchison, J. B. (1967) Initiation of courtship by hypothalamic implants of testosterone propionate in castrated doves *(Streptopelia risoria)*, *Nature*, **216**, 591–2.

Hutchison, J. B. (1970) Differential effects of testosterone and oestradiol on male courtship in barbary doves *(Streptopelia risoria)*, *Anim. Behav.*, **18**, 41–51.

Hutchison, J. B. (1971) Effects of hypothalamic implants of gonadal steroids on courtship behavior in Barbary doves *(Streptopelia risoria)*, *J. Endocrinol.*, **50**, 97–113.

Hutchison, J. B. (1974) Differential hypothalamic sensitivity to androgen in the activation of reproductive behavior. In: *The Neurosciences, The Third Study Program*, F. Schmitt and F. Worden (eds.), MIT Press, Boston, Massachusetts, pp. 593–8.

Hutchison, J. B. and Poynton, J. C. (1963) A neurological study of the clasp reflex in *Xenopus laevis* (Daudin), *Behaviour*, **22**, 41–63.

Johns, L. and Liley, N. (1970) The effects of gonadectomy and testosterone treatment on the reproductive behavior of the male blue gourami *(Trichogaster trichopterus)*, *Can. J. Zool.*, **48**, 977–87.

Johnston, P. and Davidson, J. (1972) Intracerebral androgens and sexual behavior in the male rat, *Horm. Behav.*, **3**, 345–57.

Kalra, S. and Kalra, P. (1974) Temporal interrelationships among circulatory levels of estradiol. progesterone, and LH during the rat estrous cycle: Effects of exogenous progesterone, *Endocrinology*, **95**, 1711–8.

Kamrin, R. P. and Aronson, L. R. (1954) The effects of forebrain lesions on mating behavior in the male platyfish *(Xiphophorus maculatus)*, *Zoologica*, **39**, 133–40.

Kato, J. and Villee, C. (1967) Factors affecting uptake of estradiol, 6-7-³H by the hypophysis and hypothalamus, *Endocrinology*, **80**, 1133–42.

Kelley, D. B. (1975) Central nervous system localization of sex hormones and their effects on reproductive behavior in the South African clawed frog *(Xenopus laevis)*, *Thesis*, The Rockefeller University, New York.

Kelley, D. B., Morrell, J. I., and Pfaff, D. W. (1975) Autoradiographic localization of hormone-concentrating cells in the brain of an amphibian *(Xenopus laevis)*, I. Testosterone, *J. Comp. Neurol.*, **164**, 47–61

Kelley, D. B. and Pfaff, D. W. (1975) Locations of steroid hormone-concentrating cells in the central nervous system of *Rana pipiens, Abstracts, Soc. for Neurosci.* (5th Annual Meeting), 438.

Kelley, D. B. and Pfaff, D. W. (1976) Hormone effects on male sex behavior in adult South African clawed frogs *(Xenopus laevis)*, *Horm. Behav.*, **7**, 159–82.

Komisaruk, B. R. (1967) Effects of local brain implants of progesterone on reproductive behavior in ring doves, *J. Comp. Physiol. Psychol.*, **64**, 219–24.

Korenbrot, C., Schomberg, D., and Erickson, C. (1974) Radioimmunoassay of plasma estradiol during the breeding cycle of ring doves *(Streptopelia risoria)*, *Endocrinology*, **94**, 1126–32.

Kow, L.-M., Malsbury, C., and Pfaff, D. (1974a) Effects of progesterone on female reproductive behavior in rats: Possible modes of action and role in behavioral sex differences. In: *Reproductive Behavior*, W. Montagna and W. Sadler (eds.), Plenum Press, New York, pp. 179–210.

Kow, L.-M., Malsbury, C., and Pfaff, D. (1974b) Effects of medial hypothalamic lesions on the lordosis response in female hamsters, *Abstracts, Soc. for Neurosci.*, (4th Annual Meeting), 291.

Larsson, K. and Heimer, L., (1964) Mating behavior of male rats after lesions in the preoptic area, *Nature*, **202**, 413–4.

Larsson, K. and Sodersten., P. (1973) Sexual behavior in male rats treated with estrogen in combination with dihydrotestosterone, *Horm. Behav.*, **4**, 289–99.

Law, T. and Meagher, W. (1958) Hypothalamic lesions and sexual behavior in the female rat, *Science*, **128**, 1626–7.

Lehrman, D. (1961) Hormonal regulation of parental behavior in birds and infrahuman mammals. In: *Sex and Internal Secretions*, W. Young (ed.), Williams and Wilkins, Baltimore, Maryland, pp. 1268–1382.

Lehrman, D. (1965) Interactions between internal and external environments in the regulation of the reproductive cycle of the ring dove. In: *Sex and Behavior*, F. Beach (ed.), Wiley New York, pp. 355–80.

Liley, N. R. (1968) The endocrine control of reproductive behaviour in the female guppy *(Poecilia reticulata* Peters*)*, *Anim. Behav.*, **16**, 318–31.

Liley, N. R. (1969) Hormones and reproductive behavior in fishes. In: *Fish Physiology, III*, W. S. Hoar and D. J. Randall (eds.), Academic Press, New York-London, pp. 73–116.

Liley, N. R. (1972) The effects of estrogens and other steroids on the sexual behavior of the female guppy *(Poecilia reticulata)*, *Gen. Comp. Endocrinol. Suppl.*, **3**, 542–52.

Liley, N. and Donaldson, E. (1969) The effects of salmon pituitary gonadotropin on the ovary and the sexual behavior of the female guppy *(Peocilia reticulata)*, *Can. J. Zool.*, **47**, 569–73.

Lisk, R. (1962) Diencephalic placement of estradiol and sexual receptivity in the female rat, *Am. J. Physiol.*, **203**, 493–6.

Lisk, R. D. (1967) Neural localization for androgen activation of copulatory behavior in the male rat, *Endocrinology*, **80**, 754–61.

Lisk, R. D. (1968) Copulatory activity of the male rat following placement of preoptic-anterior hypothalamic lesions, *Exp. Brain Res.*, **5**, 306–13.

Lisk, R. (1973) Hormonal regulation of sexual behavior in polyestrous mammals common to the laboratory. In: *Handbook of Physiology. Section 7: Endocrinology, Vol. II, part I*, R Greep (ed.), American Physiological Society, Washington, pp. 223–60.

Luttge, W., Hall, N., and Wallis, C. (1974) Studies on the neuroendocrine, somatic, and behavioral effectiveness of testosterone and its 5α reduced metabolites in Swiss–Webster mice, *Physiol. Behav.*, **13**, 553–61.

Macey, M., Pickford, G., and Peter, R. (1974) Forebrain localization of the spawning reflex response to exogenous neurohypophysial hormones in the killifish *(Fundulus heteroclitus)*, *J. Exp. Zool.*, **190**, 269–80.

MacLean, P. and Ploog, D. (1962) Cerebral representation of penile erection, *J. Neurophysiol.*, **25**, 29–55.

Malsbury, C. (1971) Facilitation of male rat copulatory behavior by electrical stimulation of the medial preoptic area, *Physiol. Behav.*, **7**, 797–805.

Malsbury, C. and Pfaff, D. (1973) Suppression of sexual receptivity in the hormone-primed female hamster by electrical stimulation of the medial preoptic area, *Abstracts, Soc. for Neurosci.* (3rd Annual Meeting), 122.

Martinez-Vargas, C., Sar, M., and Stumpf, W. (1974a) Localization of estrogen in the avian brain, Eastern Regional Conference on Reproductive Behavior, Atlanta, Georgia.

Martinas-Vargez, M., Sar, M., and Stumpf, W. (1974b) Brain targets for androgens in the dove *(Streptopelia risoria)*, *Am. Zool.*, **14**, 1285.

McEwen, B., and Pfaff, D. (1970) Factors influencing sex hormone uptake by rat brain regions. I. Effects of neonatal treatment, hypophysectomy, and competing steroid on estradiol uptake, *Brain Res.*, **21**, 1–16.

McEwen, B., and Pfaff, D. W. (1973) Chemical and physiological approaches to neuro-endocrine mechanisms: Attempts at integration. In: *Frontiers in Neuroendocrinology*, L. Martini and W. F. Ganong (eds.), Oxford University Press, New York, pp. 267–335.

McEwen, B., Pfaff, D., and Zigmond, R. (1970a) Factors influencing sex hormone uptake by rat brain regions. II. Effects of neonatal treatment and hypophysectomy on testosterone uptake, *Brain Res.*, **21**, 17–28.

McEwen, B., Pfaff, D., and Zigmond, R. (1970b) Factors influencing sex hormone uptake by rat brain regions. III. Effects of competing steroids on testosterone uptake, *Brain Res.*, **21**, 29–38.

McGuire, J. and Lisk, R. (1968) Estrogen receptors in the intact rat, *Proc. Nat. Acad. Sci.*, **61**, 497–503.

Meyer, C. C. (1973) Testosterone concentrations in the male chick brain: An autoradiographic study, *Science*, **180**, 1381–3.

Meyer, C. (1974) Effects of lesions in the medial preoptic region on precocial copulation in the male chick, *Horm. Behav.*, **5**, 377–81.

Meyer, C. C. and Salzen, E. A. (1970) Hypothalamic lesions and sexual behavior in the domestic chick, *J. Comp. Physiol. Psychol.*, **73**, 365–76.

Michael, R. P. (1965) Oestrogens in the central nervous system, *Br. Med. Bul.*, **21**, 87–90.

Michael, R., Keverne, E., and Bonsall, R. (1971) Pheromones: Isolation of male sex attractants from a female primate, *Science*, **172**, 964–6.

Michael, R. and Welegalla, J. (1968) Ovarian hormones and sexual behaviour of the female rhesus monkey *(Macaca mulatta)* under laboratory conditions, *J. Endocrinol.*, **41**, 407–50.

Mikamo, K. and Witschi, E. (1963) Functional sex-reversal in genetic females of *Xenopus laevis*, induced by implanted testes, *Genetics*, **48**, 1411–21.

Mikamo, K. and Witschi, E. (1964) Masculinization and breeding of the WW *Xenopus*, *Experientia*, **20**, 622–3.

Morin, L. and Feder, H. (1974) Intracranial estradiol benzoate implants and lordosis behavior of ovariectomized guinea pigs, *Brain Res.*, **70**, 95–102.

Morrell, J. I., Kelley, D. B. and Pfaff, D. W. (1975a) Sex steroid binding in the brains of vertebrates: Studies with light microscopic autoradiography. In: *The Ventricular System in Neuroendocrine Mechanisms, Proceedings of the Second Brain-Endocrine Interaction Symposium*, K. Knigge, D. Scott, and M. Kobayashi (eds.), Karger, Basel, pp. 230–56.

Morrell, J. I., Kelley, D. B., and Pfaff, D. W. (1975b) Autoradiographic localization of hormone-concentrating cells in the brain of an amphibian *(Xenopus laevis)* II. Estradiol. *J. Comp. Neurol.*, 164, 63–78.

Morrell, J. and Pfaff. D. (1975) Autoradiographic localization of ^{3}H-estradiol in the brain of the female mink *(Mustela vison)*, *Anat. Rec.*, **181**, 430–1.

Moss, R. and McCann, S. (1973) Induction of mating behavior in rats by luteinizing hormone-releasing factor, *Science*, **181**, 177–9.

Moss, R. L., Paloutzian, R. F., and Law, O. (1974) Electrical stimulation of forebrain structures and its effect on copulatory as well as stimulus-bound behavior in ovariectomized hormone-primed rats, *Physiol. Behav.*, **12**, 997–1004.

Naess, O., Attramadal, A., and A. Aakvaag. (1975) Androgen binding proteins in the anterior pituitary, hypothalamus, preoptic area, and brain cortex of the rat, *Endocrinology*, **96**, 1–9.

Noble, G. K. and Greenberg, B. (1940) Testosterone propionate, a bisexual hormone in the American chameleon, *Proc. Soc. Exp. Biol. Med.*, **44**, 460–2.

Noble, G. K. and Greenberg, B. (1941a) Effects of seasons, castration, and crystalline sex hormones upon the urogenital system and sexual behavior of the lizard *(Anolis carolinensis)*, I. The adult female, *J. Exp. Zool.*, **88**, 451–79.

Noble, G. K. and Greenberg, B. (1941b) Induction of female behavior in male *Anolis carolinensis* with testosterone propionate, *Proc. Soc. Exp. Biol. Med.*, **47**, 32–7.

Noble, R. (1974) Estrogen plus androgen induced mounting in adult female hamsters, *Horm. Behav.*, **5**, 227–34.

Nottebohm, F., Stokes, T., and Leonard, C. (1976) Central control of song in the canary *(Serinus canaria)*, *J. Comp. Neurol.*, **165**, 457–86.

Overmier, J. and Gross, D. (1974) Effects of telencephalic ablation upon nest-building and avoidance behaviors in East African mouthbreeding fish *(Tilapia mossambica)*, *Behav. Biol.*, **12**, 211–22.

Ozon, R. (1972) Estrogens in fishes, amphibians, reptiles, and birds. In: *Steroids in Nonmammalian Vertebrates*, D. R. Idler (ed.), Academic Press, New York, pp. 390–413.

Palka, Y. and Gorbman, A. (1973) Pituitary and testicular influenced sexual behavior in male frogs *(Rana pipiens)*, *Gen. Comp. Endocrinol.*, **21**, 148–51.

Palka, Y. and Sawyer, C. (1966a) The effects of hypothalamic implants of ovarian steroids on oestrous behaviour in rabbits, *J. Physiol.*, **185**, 251–69.

Palka, Y. S. and Sawyer, C. H. (1966b) Induction of estrous behaviour in rabbits by hypothalamic implants of testosterone, *Am. J. Physiol.*, **211**, 225–8.

Perachio, A. A., Alexander, M., and Marr, L. D. (1973) Hormonal and social factors affecting evoked sexual behavior in rhesus monkeys, *Am. J. Phys. Anthropol.*, **38**, 227–32.

Perachio, A., Alexander, M., and Robinson, B. (1969) Sexual behavior evoked by telestimulation. In: *Proceedings of the Second International Congress of Primatology, Vol. 3*, H. O. Hofer (ed.), S. Karger, Basel, Switzerland, pp. 68–74.

Pfaff, D. W. (1968) Autoradiographic localization of radioactivity in rat brain after injection of tritiated sex hormones, *Science*, **161**, 1355–6.

Pfaff, D. (1970) Nature of sex hormone effects on rat sex behavior: Specificity of effects and individual patterns of response, *J. Comp. Physiol. Psychol.*, **73**, 349–58.

Pfaff, D. (1973) Luteinizing hormone-releasing factor potentiates lordosis behavior in hypophysectomized ovariectomized female rats, *Science*, **182**, 1148–9.

Pfaff, D. W., Diakow, C., Zigmond, R., and Kow, L.-M. (1973) Neural and hormonal determinants of female mating behavior in rats. In: *The Neurosciences, Vol. III*, F. O. Schmitt *et al.* (eds.), MIT Press, Boston, Massachusetts, pp. 621–46.

Pfaff, D. W. and Keiner, M. (1973) Atlas of estradiol-concentrating cells in the central nervous system of the female rat, *J. Comp. Neurol.*, **151**, 121–58.

Pfaff, D., Moskovitz, S., Gerlach, J., McEwen, B., Carmel, P., Ferin, M., and Zimmerman, E. (1974) Autoradiographic localization of cells which bind estradiol or corticosterone in the brain and pituitary of the female rhesus monkey, *Proc. Int. Congr. Physiol. Sci.*, New Delhi.

Phoenix, C. (1974) Effects of dihydrotestosterone on sexual behavior of castrated male rehesus monkeys, *Physiol. Behav.*, **12**, 1045–55.

Phoenix, C., Goy, R., and Young, W. (1967) Sexual behavior: General aspects. In: *Neuroendocrinology, Vol. II*, L. Martini and W. Ganong (eds.), Academic Press, New York, pp. 163–239.

Powers, J. B. (1970) Hormonal control of lordosis in ovariectomized rats by intracerebral progesterone implants, *Brain Res.*, **48**, 311–25.

Powers, B. and Valenstein, E. (1972) Sexual receptivity: Facilitation by medial preoptic lesions in female rats, *Science*, **175**, 1003–5.

Reinboth, R. (1972) Some remarks on secondary sex characters, sex, and sexual behavior in teleosts, *Gen. Comp. Endocrinol. Suppl.*, **3**, 565–70.

Roberts, W., Steinberg, M., and Means, L. (1967) Hypothalamic mechanisms for sexual, aggressive and other motivational behaviors in the opossum, *Didelphis virginiana*, *J. Comp. Physiol.*, **64**, 1–15.

Robinston, B. W. and Mishkin, M. (1966) Ejaculation evoked by stimulation of the preoptic area in monkey, *Physiol Behav.*, **1**, 269–72.

Sar, M. and Stumpf, W. (1973) Autoradiographic localization of radioactivity in the rat brain after the injection of 1,2-^{3}H-testosterone, *Endocrinology*, **92**, 251–6.

Sawyer, C. H. (1959) Effects of brain lesions on estrous behavior and reflexogenous ovulation in the rabbit, *J. Exp. Zool.*, **142**, 227–46.

Sawyer, C. H. and Robison, B. (1956) Separate hypothalamic areas controlling pituitary gonadotrophic function and mating behavior in female cats and rabbits, *J. Clin. Endocrinol.*, **16**, 914–5.

Schmidt, R. S. (1966) Central mechanisms of frog calling, *Behaviour*, **26**, 251–85.

Schmidt, R. S. (1968) Preoptic activation of frog mating behavior, *Behaviour*, **30**, 239–57.

Schmidt, R. S. (1969) Preoptic activation of mating call orientation in female anurans, *Behaviour*, **35**, 114–27.

Schmidt, R. S. (1971) A model of the central mechanisms of male anuran acoustic behavior, *Behaviour*, **39**, 288–317.

Schmidt, R. S. (1972) Action of intrinsic largyngeal muscles during release calling in leopard frog, *J. Exp. Zool.*, **181**, 233–44.

Schmidt, R. (1973) Central mechanisms of frog calling, *Amer. Zool.*, **13**, 1169–77.

Schmidt, R. S. (1974) Neural correlates of frog calling. Trigeminal tegmentum, *J. Comp. Physiol.*, **92**, 229–54.

Segaar, J. and Nieuwenhuys, R. (1963) New etho-physiological experiments with male *Gasterosteus aculeatus* with anatomical comment, *Anim. Behav.*, **63**, 331–44.

Shaikh, A. and Shaikh, S. (1975) Adrenal and ovarian steroid secretion in the rat estrous cycle temporally related to gonadotropins and steroid levels found in peripheral plasma, *Endocrinology*, **96**, 37–44.

Silver, R. and Feder, H. (1973) Role of gonadal hormones in incubation behavior of male ring doves *(Streptopelia risoria)*, *J. Comp. Physiol. Psychol.*, **84**, 464–71.

Silver, R., Reboulleau, C., Lehrman, D., and Feder, H. (1974) Radioimmunoassay of plasma progesterone during the reproductive cycle of male and female ring doves *(Streptopelia risoria)*, *Endocrinology*, **94**, 1547–54.

Singer, J. J. (1968) Hypothalamic control of male and female sexual behavior in female rats, *J. Comp. Physiol. Psychol.*, **66**, 738–42.

Smith, R. (1969) Control of prespawning behaviour of sunfish *(Lepomis gibbosus* and *L. megalotis)*. I. Gonadal androgen, *Anim. Behav.*, **17**, 279–85.

Stacey, N. and Liley, N. (1974) Regulation of spawning behaviour in the female goldfish, *Nature*, **247**, 71–2.

Steinach, E. (1894) Untersuchen zur vergleichenden physiologie der männlichen geschlectsorgane insbesondere der accesorischen geschlectsdrusen, *Plügers Arch.*, **56**, 304–38.

Stern, J. M. (1972) Androgen accumulation in hypothalamus and anterior pituitary of male ring doves—influence of steroid hormones, *Gen. Comp. Endocrinol.*, **18**, 439–49.

Stumpf, W. E. (1968) Estradiol-concentrating neurons: Topography in the hypothalamus by dry-mount autoradiography, *Science*, **162**, 1001–3.

Tiefer, L., (1970) Gonadal hormones and mating behavior in the adult golden hamster, *Horm. Behav.*, **1**, 189–202.

van Dis, H. and Larsson, K. (1971) Induction of sexual arousal in the castrated male rat by intracranial stimulation, *Physiol. Behav.*, **6**, 85–6.

Wade, G. and Feder, H. (1972) [1,2-^{3}H] Progesterone uptake by guinea pig brain and uterus: Differential localization, time-course of uptake and metabolism, and effects of age, sex, estrogen-priming, and competing steroids, *Brain Res.*, **45**, 525–43.

Wade, G., Harding, C., and Feder, H. (1973) Neural uptake of [1,2-^{3}H] progesterone in ovariectomized rats, guinea pigs and hamsters: Correlation with species differences in behavioral responsiveness, *Brain Res.*, **61**, 357–67.

Wai, E. and Hoar, W. (1963) The secondary sex characters and reproductive behavior of gonadectomized sticklebacks treated with methyl testosterone, *Can. J. Zool.*, **41**, 611–28.

Whalen, R. and Hardy, D. (1970) Induction of receptivity in female rats and cats with estrogen and testosterone, *Physiol. Behav.*, **5**, 529–33.

Whalen, R. and Luttge, W. (1971) Differential localization of progesterone uptake in brain. Role of sex, estrogen pretreatment, and adrenalectomy. *Brain Res.*, **33**, 147–55.

Young, W. (1961) The hormones and mating behavior. In: *Sex and Internal Secretions*, W. Young (ed.), The Williams and Wilkins Co., Baltimore, Maryland, pp. 1173–239.

Zigmond, R. and McEwen, B. (1970) Selective retention of oestradiol by cell nuclei in specific brain regions of the ovariectomized rat, *J. Neurochem.*, **17**, 889–99.

Zigmond, R., Nottebohm, F., and Pfaff, D. (1972a) Distribution of androgen-concentrating cells in the brain of chaffinch. *IV Int. Congr. Endocrinol.*, abstract # 340.

Zigmond, R., Stern, M., and McEwen, B. (1972b) Retention of radioactivity in cell nuclei in the hypothalamus of the ring dove after injection of ^{3}H-testosterone, *Gen. Comp. Endocrinol.*, **18**, 450–453.

Zigmond, R., Nottebohm, F., and Pfaff, D. (1973) Androgen-concentrating cells in the midbrain of a songbird, *Science*, **179**, 1005–1007.

CHAPTER 8

Increased Persistence of Attention Produced by Testosterone, and its Implications for the Study of Sexual Behaviour

R. J. ANDREW

INTRODUCTION

The facilitation by androgens of specific patterns of behaviour such as male copulation is well established in vertebrates. This is true of male chicks (review, Andrew, 1975a–1975c), just as of many other species of birds and mammals. Less attention has been paid to the possibility of more general effects of hormones which may have consequence for a very wide range of behaviour. Recently (Andrew and Rogers, 1972; other references below), evidence has been obtained from studies with male chicks that testosterone affects attentional mechanisms.

Most of the present paper is devoted to a review of the evidence for the existence of such an effect of testosterone on the persistence of attention, and to a discussion of its character in the light of selective attention theory. The effect is of interest in its own right in that it provides a way of directly manipulating important mechanisms which seemed previously inaccessible, and of studying them in animals rather than man. However, it is clearly also important for studies of hormonal effects on behaviour to establish whether the effect is one which is produced in normal males by physiological levels of testosterone. Evidence that this is probably so in adult fowl and in some mammals (mice and men) is given in a penultimate section. Finally, the ways in which changes in attentional mechanisms due to androgens might affect male sexual behaviour, are briefly considered.

It may be helpful at this point to summarize the main features of the hypothesis which seems to best explain the effects of testosterone on attention. This rests upon a number of the concepts of human selective attention theory

(Broadbent, 1971); a fuller treatment of the application of such theory to animal data, and its possible extension to cover a wider range of situations, is given elsewhere (Andrew, 1976). Human beings (and chicks) can and do select for examination those stimuli with particular characteristics, even when there are a large number of available stimuli, and choice must be rapid; the criteria used in such selection and the way in which they are applied will be here termed 'rules of selection'. At the same time, other stimuli are partially or completely excluded from attention. Broadbent (1971) stresses the importance of the distinction between two categories of rules of selection: filtering and response set. The term 'response set' is used in human studies because selection in such cases involves complete recognition which is potentially able to be manifested at once in a specific response. Thus in the case of verbal material, the identification of a particular word is usually treated as a 'response', since the word is often spoke, and even if it is not, it could be spoken if the subject were to be so instructed. In filtering, a simple physical characteristic such as colour can be used to select stimuli for examination, whilst in response set a variety of parameters have to be considered, no one of which is adequate to identify the type of stimulus which is being selected. Filtering may be exemplified in the case of visual search by selection of all stimuli which are coloured red, whilst response set would be necessary to select digits from an array in which digits and letters were mixed together. The distinction between filtering and response set is not absolute even in man (Broadbent, 1971; pp. 182–6), since it is difficult to define precisely what constitutes a simple single characteristic such as might be used in filtering. However, the distinction between these two strategies of selection proves to be important in animal, as well as in human studies. Search tests in which one or other strategy is imposed by the conditions of the test are discussed here for the chick.

After a stimulus has been selected for attention, further analysis is necessary before recognition is complete, and appropriate response can occur (if it is called for). Attention theorists treat this further analysis in terms of the 'activation' of a particular set of central specifications out of a population of such specifications, which have been elaborated as a result of previous experience. Different authors use different terms for these in human studies (e.g. 'category state', Broadbent, 1971; 'dictionary unit', Treisman, 1960); 'recognition unit' (Kahneman, 1973) seems the most suitable for animal work. If a particular recognition unit is activated by the input from the stimulus, then recognition has occurred, and if a response is called for (such as speaking a word, or pecking a grain) it can occur. Activation depends both on the characteristics of the perceptual input provided by the stimulus and on the threshold of activation (Treisman, 1960), at that moment, of recognition units which receive the input. The effectiveness of perceptual input in activating a particular unit depends on the preciseness of the correspondence between the various parameters specified in the input and by the unit; the process is effectively one of retrieval. The threshold is affected by past experience (being low if the corresponding stimulus is a common one), and can be temporarily lowered by immediately prior experience of the stimulus or by cues which are usually associated with the stimulus.

The application of such a model of attentional processes to data from chick search tests is discussed in detail below. In brief, the most important type of event in such data is a shift from one type of freely available target to another. Such a shift is to be explained on the present model as a shift to a new rule of selection (p. 256). Chicks tend to continue a particular rule once it has come into use. A change to a new rule appears often to be associated with examination of a type of target which is not currently being taken: such examination would be expected to tend to result in the activation of the recognition unit corresponding to it. Human studies (Broadbent, 1971, p. 164 *et seq.*) show that a new rule of selection may come into use in consequence; in the chick data this would be reflected in a period of choice of the new target. The reasons for the failure of the previous rules of selection to exclude the new target, and so to prevent its examination, appear to be various. In the chick the best established is the strictness with which the crucial criterion is applied during filtering (see p. 261).

Much of the data which I will discuss are from tests in which the effects of changes in a familiar stimulus are important. Little systematic attempt has been made to use the theory of selective attention to explain such effects. Kahneman (1973, p. 81) briefly discusses a 'recursive path of attention control' which increases the amount of information obtained about a stimulus when there is a mismatch between recognition unit and stimulus. Such an increase depends in part on the receptor reflexes of the orientation response, which are evoked when there is mismatch between 'neuronal model' and stimulus input (Sokolov, 1960); Kahneman explicitly accepts an equivalence between neuronal model and recognition unit in this context.

I shall assume that sustained comparison between input and an activated recognition unit may occur when a changed stimulus is examined, and that it is the mismatch resulting from such comparison which sustains attention on the changed stimulus (see Andrew, 1975, for a fuller discussion). I shall distinguish two types of situation which involve stimulus change. In the first, the change occurs in a stimulus which is irrelevant to the response in hand. The effectiveness of the changed stimulus in catching and holding attention is measured by the duration of the interruption of the ongoing response (e.g. approach to a goal). In the second type, the change is in the stimulus which is being attended; again interruption or postponement of response is measured. In the first case, the changed stimulus tends to be excluded, whilst in the second it is selected. In either case, once comparison resulting in mismatch begins, attention will be concentrated on the changed stimulus.

We can now consider the effect of testosterone on attentional processes in male chicks. In all of the experimental tests so far applied this appears to involve an increased persistence in use of whatever rule of selection is currently in operation. In search situations, this in general terms results in a decreased likelihood of shift to choice of a second alternative target; note that once such shift has occurred, choice of the second target is more persistent in its turn. In tests using stimulus change, greater persistence of rules of selection means that irrelevant stimuli (i.e. ones not associated with the goal) are more effectively excluded: birds which have received testosterone are in fact less distracted by such change. On the other hand, they are equally or more affected by change in goal stimuli (i.e. ones which are not attenuated).

Other tests will be considered in the sections which follow, and in each case an attempt will be made to explain the results in terms of the effect just described. Male chicks which received testosterone (a single dose of testosterone oenanthate; in most cases 12.5 mg, a dose which is also maximally effective in facilitating responses like attack, Andrew, 1975a–1975c) will be referred to as Ts, and controls as Cs. Chicks were not gonadectomized in studies discussed in this section.

EVIDENCE THAT TESTOSTERONE AFFECTS ATTENTION IN CHICKS

The Lack of Direct Effects on Hunger

Many of the tests which will be discussed use food reinforcement. It is important therefore to establish whether testosterone changes the effectiveness of such reinforcement. It is improbable that this is the case on the following grounds:

(1) The distribution and duration of feeding bouts over several days under *ad lib.* conditions do not differ between Ts and Cs (P. Clifton, pers. commun.).

(2) The rate of key operation (and so the frequency of feeding) is very similar in Ts and Cs working for food on a continuous reinforcement schedule, when both have similar previous deprivation (Messent, 1973).

(3) The changes in pattern of food search produced by testosterone were present to the same extent over a wide range of deprivation levels (Andrew and Rogers, 1972). These were 5 h, 3 h, 1 h and 0 h, the latter being achieved by giving 1 ml 0.5 M glucose into the crop, just before testing. After 5 h all chicks feed very rapidly and persistently, whilst in contrast only pecking with no ingestion occurs after 0 h: nevertheless the same differences between Ts and Cs in patterns of selection of grains for pecking were present in both cases. Thus, even if food deprivation were more or less effective in Ts than in Cs (which does not appear to be the case), this could not explain the differences between Ts and Cs which are found in food search tests.

Food Search Tests

Each chick is trained to eat both red or yellow foodgrains by exposure to these separately in the home cage on different days (Rogers, 1971; Andrew and Rogers, 1972; Rogers, 1974). These exposures are so arranged that one colour is usually preferred, given a free choice such as is afforded by a local clump of grains in which both colours are present. It is essential that non-preferred as well as preferred food should have been eaten in the past, or the bird may not peck at all in the test. Tests are conducted in the home cage, which has a transparent front through which the chick can see the open laboratory, so that it is completely accustomed to the sight of human beings. As a result, pecking over test floors, which can be introduced under the cage by raising it slightly from the bench, can be scored with the observer's face at a few centimetres from the chick. Chicks will often pursue a particular grain with repeated pecks, if it is sent bouncing by the first peck, and it is important that only each fresh choice of a new grain should be scored.

The type of food sought can be altered in chicks, which do not have too strong a preference, by priming: this involves allowing the chick to feed on one colour of food and then moving the cage with a minimum of disturbance to a test floor. The food used in priming usually continues to be chosen for some time on the test floor (Andrew and Rogers, 1972; Dawkins, 1971).

Two main conditions of search have been studied (Rogers, 1971; Andrew and Rogers, 1972; Andrew, 1972a). In the first (pebble floor) the chick has to find its preferred food on a floor covered with pebbles which closely resemble preferred food in size, shape, and colour, and which are firmly stuck down; non-preferred food is also present at the same frequency as preferred food and pebbles. Under these conditions, several parameters have to be used with care whilst searching for preferred food, if pecks at pebbles are to be avoided, (as they are, by both Ts and Cs). Search of this sort (which approximates to response set) is likely to completely exclude non-preferred food from examination since this differs from preferred food far more than do pebbles): search should be largely taken up with the rejection of pebbles and identification and pecking of preferred food.

As might be expected from the 'persistence of attention' hypothesis, Ts show very long runs on preferred food. Cs, on the other hand, often interpolate runs of pecks at non-preferred food, as would be predicted if they were more likely to change the rules of selection with which they started search (Table 1).

In the second condition of search, only preferred and non-preferred food grains are present (plain floor). In order to understand the patterns of choice obtained (Table 1), it is necessary to consider also the readiness with which search is moved from one place to another. This can be done by distributing the food in small clumps. Ts then prove to make more pecks before moving to a new clump than do Cs. This is not due to a primary effect of testosterone on locomotion, since on a pebble floor the reverse is true. It almost certainly reflects instead a more persistent specification of area of search in Ts, since this has been independently demonstrated (e.g. by more frequent returns to a particular point at which food has been found, Andrew, unpubl.).

Table 1. Patterns of choice on plain and pebble floors

		Clumps					
		1	2	3	4	5	6
Pebble floor:							
targets P, N, pebble	T	PPPP	PPP	PPPP	PPPP	PPPP	PP
	C	PPPP	PPPN	NNN	NNNN	PPP	PPP
Plain floor:							
targets P, N	T	PPPN	PPPP	PPPN	PPPPN	PPP	PPPP
	C	PPPP	PPP	PPPN	NNN	PPPP	PPP

P = preferred food,   N = non-preferred food.

Typical patterns of choice by Ts and Cs are illustrated above for floors on which food grains (and pebbles, if present) are distributed in small clumps.

Commonly both Ts and Cs take only preferred food over long periods of search, as might be expected in a test in which preferred food can so easily be located. Higher readiness to shift to non-preferred food is shown to be present in Cs, under these circumstances also, by the fact that they are more likely to begin to take non-preferred food when preferred food has become very scarce.

However, if pecks at non-preferred food are made more likely (e.g. by priming with non-preferred food just before the test) a new pattern of choice tends to appear. Ts then often peck one or more non-preferred grains immediately before moving to another clump. This does not involve a full change to a new target of search since preferred food is at once taken again at the next clump. Cs once again show themselves to be more ready to show such a full change; although such interpolated pecks at non-preferred food are rarer in Cs, when they do occur they are usually followed by choice of non-preferred food at the next clump, resulting in a relatively long peck at non-preferred food.

Single intrusive responses to a normally excluded stimulus, rather like interpolated pecks at non-preferred food, occur in human studies when filtering (p. 256) is in use, but not when response set (p. 256) is in use (Broadbent, 1971, p. 178). Search on a plain floor is in fact likely to involve filtering, since selection on a single obvious parameter such as hue or saturation (see Rogers, 1971, for evidence that either may be used) would be enough to allow efficient choice of preferred food. The interpolated non-preferred pecks thus probably represent failures of exclusion, which do not occur (or are very rare) when the much more extensive and careful procedures of response set are in operation. The basic difference in search situations between Ts and Cs would then be that failure of exclusion tends to lead to a change of rule of selection in Cs, but is unlikely to do so in Ts.

An explanation in terms of brief failure of exclusion depends on the theoretical assumption that the recognition unit for non-preferred food has a relatively low threshold in birds in which intrusive pecks at non-preferred food occur, so that activation may occur despite relative exclusion; this would agree with the fact that such pecks are made more likely by prior priming with non-preferred food (above). A frequently used human example is that a subject often notices the presentation of his own name, even when this occurs in a message which he is otherwise excluding, since his attention is fully occupied in repeating a message presented by another voice. (Note that attention to a particular voice makes use of filtering with formant pitch as cue; Broadbent, 1971).

Further evidence for this explanation of intrusive pecks at non-preferred food is provided by manipulation of the main parameter likely to be used in filtering selection (Rogers and Andrew, in prep.). The accuracy of this parameter for red food can be varied by the dyeing procedure: if the food is dyed superficially, as was done in all the experiments so far discussed, small patches will often flake off, leaving some grains with yellow portions. If, on the other hand, the food is dyed as a powder and then made up into grains, the chick never sees anything other than uniform red grains. Chicks with either type of experience can be trained also to accept yellow food by the usual procedure of providing yellow food by itself on separate days. However, when both are compared in search for uniformly red food on a plain floor, under conditions when Ts with training on variable red food are showing single pecks at non-preferred food before moving to a new clump, Ts with training on food which is uniformly red are found (in the same experiment) not to give any such pecks. This is not because they are unprepared to take yellow food at all, since they occasionally do show a full shift to yellow, which is then continued as a definite run. It is rather that single pecks in error no longer occur when specifications which describe hue and saturation in narrow precise terms are in use. (It should be noted that Ts with experience of variable red food also show occasional full shifts, so that it is only in the presence or absence of error pecks that the two groups differ.)

A final feature of the search experiments which must be mentioned is that testosterone produces increased persistence of attention even when no visual exposure to food is allowed between injection and test; (the chicks being maintained by croploading). This confirms that it is the use rather than the elaboration of recognition units and rules of selection that the hormone affects (Rogers, 1971; Andrew and Rogers, 1972).

Distractibility Tests

Two different tests will be discussed. In the first, novel and conspicuous changes, and in the second novel changes were presented, whilst the chick was engaged in a well practised task.

In the first test (Archer, 1974a), chicks were trained to run along a runway to a food dish. When they would do this reliably and rapidly, two types of stimuli were presented: (a) two black and white cards half way down the blue-painted runway and on each side of it, or (b) a black and white food dish (containing food) in place of the usual transparent food dish. The latency to feed was measured for 3 consecutive tests in which one or other change was present, and was compared in each individual with control tests carried out before and after. The two changes were presented in the order runway–food dish in half the chicks, and food dish–runway in the other half. Cs were much more delayed by the runway changes than were Ts, whereas the reverse was true of the food dish change. Change in itself thus could not be said to be more effective in either Ts or Cs. Instead Ts were affected less by change in stimuli irrelevant to the task, but more by change in relevant stimuli.

Selective attention theory provides a straightforward explanation for this otherwise somewhat paradoxical finding. It seems reasonable to assume that attention is concentrated on the food dish whilst the runway is being traversed; certainly, if a similar food dish is presented in an alcove part way down the runway, the chick is likely to notice it and feed (Archer, 1974a). The activation of the food dish recognition unit and the introduction of appropriate rules of selection is likely to occur at entry to the runway. Thus Rogers (unpubl.) has shown that chicks can be trained to use the appearance of the walls of the test chamber (e.g. black v. white) as a cue to determine the type of food for which they will search.

Any effect of a change in the appearance of the runway wall thus represents a failure of exclusion, followed by a period of response to the change, once it is noticed. This period is here assumed to involve comparison between the change, and a recognition unit corresponding to the normal appearance of the runway wall. It has further been assumed (above) that the mismatch which will result is the cause of the concentration of attention on the changed stimulus which is obvious in the chicks. It will be seen that exclusion of a changed stimulus is potentially unstable; once the stimulus is noticed, mismatch causes a shift of attention which amounts at least temporarily, to a breakdown of exclusion.

Greater persistence in use of rules of selection corresponding to the food dish, due to testosterone, should increase exclusion of stimuli associated with the runway wall. The behaviour of the chicks as well as the lesser delay in Ts agree with this proposition: Ts often check only briefly at the change or pass it slowly and cautiously, looking forward at the goal, in a way which suggests some continuing exclusion of input from the changed stimulus. Cs on the other hand, commonly fail to show any further interest in the food dish.

Increased persistence due to testosterone would be expected to have quite different consequences when the food dish itself is changed. Both Ts and Cs should have activated the recognition unit for the food dish, and so should both respond to mismatch. This state is likely usually to be terminated by a shift to a rule of selection for food grains, since food grains are readily visible when standing near the dish. Such a shift of attention to food would be likely to be delayed by increased persistence (since this would tend to sustain activation of the recognition unit for the dish, and the associated rules of selection). The fact that Ts take longer to feed than Cs after a change in the food dish can thus be explained.

In the second test, Messent (1973) used a Skinner box with two keys, which were illuminated from behind. The positive key, whose operation delivered food, could be distinguished by colour from the negative, whose operation produced a five second period in which neither key worked and the key lights were out. The two colours alternated every 20 s between the two keys, which were adjacent (being actually the two halves of a split key), so that it was possible for a chick which was examining one key to be able to see clearly any change in the other. Changes in the colour of the positive stimulus affected Ts and Cs equally, as measured by the slowing or withholding of any key pecks. On the other hand, such a change in the negative stimulus affected Ts significantly and markedly less than Cs. The same was true when the cage illumination was changed from white to a pink tinge. Here none of the stimulus changes were such as to make the stimulus more intrinsically conspicuous. They must have affected the chicks by their novelty. Once again, irrelevant changes affected Ts much less than Cs. On the other hand, this time Ts were apparently not more disturbed by a change in the stimulus which was attended. The crucial difference between the two tests probably lies in the fact that in the case of the Skinner box, response can be resumed only when the changed positive stimulus can be treated as an acceptable match for the appropriate recognition unit (The processes involved are certainly complex. They may include both learning the characteristics of the new stimulus, and the effects of an increasing delay without reinforcement; the important point here is that there is no reason to suppose them to be sensitive to testosterone.) Shift to a rule selecting another stimulus is here of no help.

Inhibition of Response and Extinction

It is important to distinguish short term effects of persistence, in particular of persistence of attention to a particular stimulus or to a series of stimuli concentrated within a particular area, from the ability to withhold or inhibit response to a particular stimulus, after a series of experiences in which the response was unrewarded. The first type of effect sometimes results in Ts emitting 'inappropriate' responses—such as pecks at non-preferred food just before leaving an area in which preferred food has been exhausted—which are absent or less frequent in Cs. This is not because Cs are better able to inhibit such responses, but because of the greater likelihood in Cs of shifting attention to a new area. Messent (1973) has provided another example of this sort. Chicks were trained to turn small caps to obtain food. The caps were distributed in groups of five, each placed on an elevated block. In an experiment in which food was present on only one block, Ts turned significantly more caps on both this block and on the blocks without food. Since the effect was present whether or not food was found as a result of the immediately preceding responses, it seems probable that once again an effect of persisting in attention to a particular area was involved: note that response to a series of different though adjacent stimuli was involved.

On the other hand, a variety of studies has shown there to be no differences between Ts and Cs in the rate of extinction or its final completeness. Messent (1973), using relatively large numbers of chicks (28 Cs, 20 Ts) found no such differences in extinction of key pecking in a Skinner box discrimination in which food reward was withheld, after training on continuous reinforcement. (In addition, even when extinction was almost complete, both groups retained the original discrimination, almost as well as at the end of training.) Archer (1974b) found that the time taken to reach a food dish increased in a very similar way in Ts and Cs over eight massed extinction trials, which followed training to run from a start box down a runway to feed from the dish. Ts were marginally faster than Cs on later trials but never significantly so.

Andrew (1972a, and unpubl.) found no consistent (and certainly no significant) differences between Ts and Cs in the distribution or total duration of time spent looking in an empty food dish within a single extinction session. However, there was a very marked and significant difference in the amount of time spent in searching over the floor, proceeding progressively away from the food dish; although food had never been available away from the food dish, the behaviour was so like that of a chick looking for food that this seems its most probable explanation, particularly as it was markedly increased by increases in deprivation. In Ts such behaviour disappeared progressively, whilst in Cs it continued, extending over the whole test area. Andrew (1972a) interpreted this finding as showing that Ts remained dominated by the original stimulus (i.e. the food dish) even after response to it had been inhibited. This is supported by the fact that Ts remain more continuously and for longer on the dais in which the food dish was sunk. Indications of such an effect were present in the study of Archer (1974b) in the middle trials of the extinction series, and it may be that the shorter trials gave insufficient time for its development.

A classic test for reduced ability to inhibit inappropriate responses is that of key operation on a DRL schedule (i.e. a reinforcement schedule on which response must be withheld for a specified time following each key operation, if reinforcement is to be received). Rats with medial septal lesions typically give bouts of rapid responding immediately after reinforcement, even when they have learned to withhold response for the specified interval at other times (Ellen et al., 1964). Messent (1973) confirmed the existence of such an effect in chicks with medial septal lesions on a DRL-10 schedule: the test is thus applicable to chicks. When Ts and Cs were compared on such a schedule no marked differences emerged. Both, unlike the septal animals, progressively reduced the number of very short intertrial intervals, but neither showed spacing at the full 10 s interval which was demanded of them. However, Ts did come to show a significant increase in intervals somewhat shorter than 10 s, which was quite absent in Cs. Thus, if anything, Ts were better able to withhold responses than were Cs.

In summary, all studies indicate that, although the increased persistence of attention upon stimuli within a particular area, which is shown by Ts, may lead to the emission of additional responses, this is accompanied by an ability to inhibit inappropriate response which is equal (or perhaps superior) to that of Cs.

Conflict and Frustration

If Ts inhibit responses to a particular stimulus or type of stimulus when they cease to be reinforced, but do not shift attention as readily to other stimuli as as do Cs, it would be expected that they would be exposed to the frustrating consequences of non-reinforcement for longer, in any particular extinction test. It is interesting therefore, that a number of responses, which are thought to be associated with conflict, are more frequent in Ts during such tests.

The response whose association with non-reinforcement is best attested from other studies, is that of adjunctive drinking. Falk (1972) has shown that, when water is available during periods when food reinforcement is withheld, drinking in excess of physiological need occurs in both rats and pigeons. In general, the longer the exposure to non-reinforcement the greater the amount of water which is drunk. In a recent experiment (Andrew, unpubl.), Ts were shown to drink markedly and significantly more frequently than Cs, when no food could be found under caps of the type already described.

Bill shaking is much more frequent in Ts in frustration situations than in Cs (empty food dish in runway: Archer, 1974b, Andrew, 1972a). The causation of the movement is complex: it is associated (when not evoked by dirt or damp on the bill) with periods of sustained attention to conspicuous visual stimuli (Andrew and de Lanerolle, 1975). It is possible therefore that bill shakes are causally associated with the brief periods of immobility which also became commoner in Ts than in Cs in frustration situations (Andrew, 1972a, and unpub.): Archer (1974b) has suggested that such behaviour may represent periods of locked visual attention.

However this may be, the most important point for the present argument is that bill shaking is characteristic of periods of frustration, and is commoner in Ts than in Cs.

Escape and Freezing

It is important to establish whether testosterone has any direct effect on escape or freezing before proceeding to a discussion of tests in which novel stimuli are presented. Most of the relevant evidence has been provided by Archer in a series of open field studies. The commonest response in such tests which is unambiguously identifiable as an escape response, is jumping at the chamber wall. In three very different novel environments (Archer, 1973a), there were no consistent (and certainly no significant) differences between Ts and Cs in frequency of jumping. It is unlikely that amount of ambulation in the open field is related in any simple way to running in escape or to freezing, but it is still worth noting that this too did not differ between Ts and Cs. Finally, Andrew (1975c) found no difference between Ts and Cs, when placed in a strange small chamber, either in frequency of jumps or of intention jumps, or in movements of burrowing against the wall.

Differences were obtained between Ts and Cs in various measures which might be affected by differences in the likelihood of freezing. However they were not consistent with a primary effect of testosterone on freezing. Ts began locomotion (as measured by moving off the area of floor on which they had been standing) sooner after introduction into an open field (Archer, 1973a, b, and unpubl.). They also passed more quickly than Cs into full locomotion after the first food movement had occurred. When a loud bell was rung outside the open field some time after the beginning of the test (Archer, 1973b, and unpubl.) Ts again began locomotion sooner after the immobility induced by the bell; they also moved their heads sooner, so that it is reasonable to speak of a reduction in freezing time. However, the opposite result was obtained (Archer, unpubl.) when the bell was placed in the centre of the field where it was clearly visible; Ts now remained immobile for longer than Cs.

Exact comparison with the previous experiment is impossible, since the bell was rung this time at the beginning of the test, but it is clear that either Ts or Cs can remain immobile for longer according to the conditions of testing.

Overall, testosterone does not appear directly to facilitate or depress either fleeing or freezing.

Scanning Attention and Peeps

When placed in a strange chamber at 5°C, Ts peep far less than do Cs (Andrew, 1963, 1972a); the same is true in open fields and other novel environments at room temperature (Archer, 1973a, 1973c). The effect is probably only to a slight extent a consequence of the replacement of peeps by other calls, since this occurs in both sexes, and is probably reflected in the cold chamber by an increase in short calls and warbles, which are shown by both males and females (Andrew, 1975c). The main reduction in peeps due to testosterone is shown by males alone, and results from the interpolation of periods of silence, rather than periods of short calls.

There is evidence suggesting that the main reduction in peeping, which (like changes in persistence of attention, Andrew, 1972b) is confined to males, may be an indirect consequence of attentional changes. Whenever a peeping chick can be persuaded to fixate a specific stimulus, peeps at once decrease in intensity or disappear; Andrew (1972a) suggested, on the basis of this observation, that the main decrease in peeping shown by Ts might be due to a greater likelihood of sustaining attention on particular stimuli in an environment full of strange and disturbing stimuli. Archer (1973c), using a small novel chamber, found that testosterone reduced not only peeps but also the scanning head movements which typically accompany them: Ts showed both fewer total head movements and also fewer head movements in one direction before reversing. There was also a marked and significant correlation in Ts between the number of such head movements and the number of peeps, which further supports a shared causation for the two behaviours.

Finally, inhibition of locomotion (and other responses such as pecking) is usually marked during peeping. Such inhibition, peeping, and scanning may be in fact different aspects of a syndrome of behaviour which is more fully developed in Cs than in Ts during periods in a novel environment. Both Andrew (1972a) and Archer (1973c) have suggested the following hypothesis to explain this basic difference. A strange environment presents a variety of stimuli which call for examination. As a result, Cs pass into a state in which continuous scanning comes to dominate behaviour; peeps and inhibition of response are directly associated with such scanning. The full development of this state is opposed in Ts by the fact that they repeatedly sustain attention on particular localized strange stimuli. This in its turn is a consequence of the increased persistence of attention which is shown by Ts in the various quite different tests which have been discussed in earlier sections.

This hypothesis still awaits proper testing: it would predict, for example, that the presence of a few conspicuous local features should increase the difference between Ts and Cs by reducing scanning and peeping in Ts more than in Cs.

Novel Objects Presented in the Home Cage

Four phases of behaviour can be distinguished in chicks following the induction of a localized change in the home cage (Andrew and Clayton, unpubl.). In the first phase, 'calling and response', the bird accompanies or alternates investigation of the object with a variety of responses, such as calling (short calls of a number of types), locomotion, and head and body shakes. In the second phase, 'silent investigation', the bird remains almost or quite silent, and more or less immobile, except for investigatory head movements. Short calls are typically given by chicks whenever they are induced to respond by a conspicuous or significant stimulus (Andrew and de Lanerolle, 1975). When calls are given without overt locomotion, pecking or similar response, there are often signs of incipient response such as slight movement of head or body. The absence of calling during silent investigation thus suggests that even incipient response to the changed stimulus is absent. 'Escape' (jump, look up, burrow against the wall) forms the third phase, whilst resumption of maintenance activities is the last. The first three phases can alternate and do not occur in any fixed order.

The results which are about to be discussed were obtained using chicks held in almost complete auditory and visual isolation in sound attenuating cages, whose interior could be video-recorded through a small darkened aperture; since the camera was housed in a darkened room and moved on a silent wormdrive, the arrival and departure of the camera lens at the aperture only very rarely affected the chicks' behaviour even slightly. The novel stimulus might be either a pattern projected on a screen at the end of the cage, or a small three dimensional object slid silently up into sight between the transparent inner shell of the cage and the outer soundproofing shell. Similar results were obtained with both methods, but only those from the second will be discussed here.

Again, as in open field and similar tests, the proportion of chicks showing escape jumps did not differ between Ts and Cs. In addition, there was no difference between Ts and Cs in the average total amount of time spent in looking up, a characteristic low intensity form of escape jumping which was shown by nearly all birds.

The basic difference between Ts and Cs in this test was that the changes induced by the novel stimulus lasted for longer in Ts. Thus Cs returned to normal maintenance activities sooner than Ts. This was particularly clear in the case of feeding; the first bout of feeding after the introduction of the novel stimulus was of usual length in Cs but was commonly interrupted in Ts by one or more brief periods of locomotion (commonly to return to investigation of the stimulus). Even when a sustained bout of feeding was finally given by Ts, there were signs that the animal was not fully relaxed. During normal behaviour Ts and Cs both commonly stretch during brief breaks in feeding or at its end. After the introduction of a novel stimulus, this remained true of Cs but not of Ts, which now rarely stretched at all. Cs also showed a normal period of sleep earlier than did Ts. It should be emphasized that Ts and Cs do not differ, when undisturbed, in the duration or distribution of sleep or of feeding periods (P. Clifton, pers. commun.).

Ts showed significantly more responses which are characteristic of the calling and response phase: these include head and body shaking (replicated in a different and larger home cage, Archer, unpubl.), and wing flapping in sudden locomotion. The total duration of the phase was higher in Ts but not significantly so, certainly in part because of frequent interruptions due to locomotion. Cs on the other hand, showed significantly more silent investigation, which was much less interrupted.

It will be seen that Ts show signs of being affected by a localized stimulus change for considerably longer than Cs. Ts and Cs were equally likely to show escape behaviour, even when the lowest intensity behaviour was considered, and it will be remembered that a direct effect of testosterone on fear responses is improbable on evidence from other tests (see p. 262). The differences obtained are readily explicable, on the other hand, by increased persistence of attention in Ts: more specifically, they would be expected to result from an increased persistence in use of a rule of selection specifying the position at which the stimulus change has occurred, together with continued activation of the recognition unit for the former state of that part of the environment. It is interesting that signs of being affected by the stimulus change may persist in Ts (but not Cs) through relatively long periods of response to other stimuli, such as periods of feeding. The mechanism responsible for increased persistence of attention is thus apparently capable of sustaining or reasserting attention to a particular stimulus, despite intervening periods in which attention is apparently directed to other stimuli. A similar conclusion (but for behaviour during a much shorter period of time) is suggested by the behaviour shown by Ts whilst passing the change in the runway wall (see p. 262).

Changes in Likelihood of Targetting to Peripheral Stimuli

The much greater scanning shown by Cs in open field and similar tests might be explicable by a direct depression by testosterone of targetting to stimuli in the peripheral visual field. However, it is improbable that such an effect could explain most of the results which have been described. In the case of food search over a pebble floor, the greater readiness of Ts to move to a new area of search is not to be so explained: in fact, it is more compatible with an opposite type of effect. In addition, Rogers (1971) showed that, despite hoods which confined vision approximately to the binocular field (c. 45° on either side of the median plane), there were marked and significant differences between Ts and Cs, in search over a plain floor: these differences could not have involved the peripheral visual field. The hoods were effective, in that they caused Cs to show the same pattern of search on a continuous plain floor that they showed without hoods on a floor with clumps of food separated by 9 cm spaces of bare floor (i.e. they effectively broke the continuous floor up into more discrete areas of search.)

Similar arguments may be advanced for the other tests. Thus, in the runway, it was common for Ts to stop at least momentarily when they reached the novel panels (which would usually lie in peripheral vision); they differed from Cs in that they then tended to pass the panels sooner and proceed on their way. In the case of changes in discriminating stimuli presented on a split key, nearly all chicks faced the key, so that both stimuli were seen binocularly. Here, differences in effectiveness of peripheral stimuli could not have been involved.

Conclusion

All of the results which have been discussed in the preceding sections are explicable by a single type of behavioural change. This is in the most general terms as follows: when alternative acceptable targets and/or distracting but irrelevant stimuli are present, Ts respond for longer to the stimulus or type of stimulus to which they have begun to respond. In the absence of such alternative targets or distractions, on the other hand, Ts do not show longer bouts of each type of behaviour (e.g. feeding). Increased persistence of response in Ts, when it occurs, is not due to inability to inhibit non-reinforced or punished responses. Further, in some situations, it can be shown that there is persistence of attention in Ts even after inhibition of response; such persistence of attention would explain all of the types of persistence of response to a particular type of stimulus which have been observed in Ts.

The increased persistence of attention shown by Ts amounts to a more effective exclusion of stimuli to which the animal is not directly attending. Such more effective exclusion appears not to be based on a simple perceptual change such as reduced effectiveness of stimuli in the peripheral visual field but to involve more central mechanisms.

There are hints that, as in humans, exclusion does not preclude analysis of excluded stimuli, at least in a preliminary or abbreviated form. Thus, if an excluded stimulus is conspicuous or significant, Ts show signs of noticing it (even though they are less affected by it), just as humans show signs of noticing their own name even when it is presented on an excluded channel. However, work is only now beginning on this aspect of persistence of attention in chicks.

EVIDENCE THAT THE EFFECT OF TESTOSTERONE ON ATTENTION IS PHYSIOLOGICAL

Relatively high doses of testosterone (a single dose of 5–12.5 mg of a long-acting ester, testosterone oenanthate, in a 40–100 gm chick) are required to produce increased persistence of attention in the young male chick. However, this is also true of the other effects of testosterone in the chick: thus comb growth and copulation have a dosage threshold (1–5 mg oenanthate), which is a little lower than that for attack and attentional changes (Andrew, 1972b; 1975a–1975c). Schleidt (1970) has noted that turkey poults also require much larger doses of androgen than do adults in order to produce the same facilitation of sexual behaviour. It is possible that plasma proteins which bind androgens in the adult are absent or at very low levels in the chick and that renal elimination is therefore very rapid; alternatively, membrane transport systems or specific binding proteins may be lacking in the target cells.

Rogers (1974) has provided direct evidence that the normal secretion of androgens by the testis increases persistence of attention in domestic cocks. In the same food search tests that have been used in chicks, cocks differed from castrates (and hens) in the same way as Ts differ from Cs. Testosterone injections caused castrates to show the same patterns of search as intact cocks. Human studies also suggest an effect of physiological levels of androgen on attention. Much of the evidence has been reviewed elsewhere (Andrew, 1972a). In brief, men who are known to have chronically high androgen (as judged by physique and hairiness: Broverman *et al.*, 1964) or who have received additional testosterone, score differently from other men in a number of cognitive tests. Two main types of result may be distinguished.

Firstly, men with high endogenous levels of androgen perform unusually well on tests which require very rapid recognition of a small number of standard stimuli ('speed of naming repeated objects': Broverman *et al.*, 1964).

Marcel (unpubl.) has provided a technique by which effects of this kind can be analysed in a more fundamental way than has previously been possible. He used a test in which the time to recognize (speak) a digit briefly flashed up on a screen was carefully measured. The latency to speak proved to be very much shorter when the same digit was presented as had immediately been shown. However, there was also significant shortening when a digit was presented which was close to the previously presented digit in the usual sequence of digits. The effect was asymmetric in that it was more marked for digits following the previously presented digit than for ones preceding it, again showing a relation to the usual order in which digits are rehearsed. In such tests, men with high androgen levels showed a more marked facilitation of response by the preceding presentation of a digit close in the usual digit order to the one currently presented.

Androgens thus sustain the ability to respond rapidly to exactly the stimulus to which response has just occurred or to stimuli which are closely associated with it by the rules of association used for digits. It is important that this occurs under conditions which allow effects of direction of gaze and peripheral perceptual effects to be largely excluded. An approach of this sort offers a direct way of investigating the mechanisms affected by testosterone: it could readily be adapted, for example, to measure differences in the ability to select amongst a number of stimuli.

A typical example of the second class of human tests affected by testosterone is as follows: high androgen men are slow to find a pattern embedded in more complex figures (Broverman *et al.*, 1968). It seems unlikely, in view of the evidence just considered, that they are more likely to forget what they are looking for than other subjects. The explanation which was advanced earlier (Andrew, 1972a) remains the most likely: high androgen men are more persistent in each attempt to compare the sought-for pattern with any one particular part of the main pattern in a particular orientation. As a result they are likely to be delayed in finding the correct part.

Finally, effects of testosterone on persistence of attention are now under way in rodents. Archer (unpubl.) has found such an effect in a comparison of intact and castrate male mice, and castrate mice with testosterone therapy, using a variant of the chick runway test. The results which were obtained were broadly similar to those of the chick runway study. Changes in the runway wall were relatively less effective than changes in the food dish in mice with either exogenous or testicular androgens, whilst the reverse was true of castrates which did not receive testosterone.

CONCLUSION: POSSIBLE EFFECTS OF INCREASED PERSISTENCE OF ATTENTION ON BEHAVIOUR SUCH AS COPULATION

Differences in persistence of attention are likely to have their greatest effect in situations in which distracting stimuli or some obstacle or dispute make it difficult to carry out a particular response. Shifts of attention will at the very least delay access to the goal, and may very well prevent it altogether. If attempts to copulate with a not fully cooperative female are taken as an example, at least three types of factors which might lead to a complete shift of attention may be distinguished. Firstly, the female herself is likely to present stimuli other than those tending to evoke copulation: if attention shifts more than briefly to her threat or attacks, then the male is likely to emit new responses such as attack or fleeing in place of copulation attempts. Secondly, attention to the stimuli which evoke copulation is itself likely to sustain motivation to copulate. Each distraction (such as a fall during attempts to mount), which causes a temporary shift of attention, is an opportunity for other motivational systems to become dominant. Finally, even if copulatory behaviour continues to dominate, there may come a point at which attention will shift from the first female, and the male will begin to respond to or search for others; this would be possible in species in which the male has access to more than one female within the social group, or in which the male moves through the territories of different females in turn.

I would not wish to argue that differences in persistence of attention are likely markedly to affect most of the usual measures of intensity of copulation. Tests which use fully receptive females, with no competition from other males, are likely to measure changes specific to copulation (as was intended by their designers).

Other measures taken in studies of sexual behaviour do seem likely to be affected by changes in persistence of attention, even if in complex, and as yet not entirely predictable ways. Periods of courtship displays or other preliminaries to copulation, during which the female is unresponsive or repeatedly drives the male off, are likely to be prolonged in males with high persistence of attention. In general, we know too little about the exact stimuli to which the animal is attending in such situations to make detailed and unambiguous predictions. Thus, during courtship many male birds display at a nest site and may gather nest material (review, Andrew, 1961). Since, at the same time, they usually show signs of observing the female, and may follow if she moves away, it is impossible to say whether such particular phases of courtship would tend to be prolonged or not by high persistence of attention. Other difficulties are raised by lack of information about the stimuli and situations which are effective in terminating precopulatory behaviour when the female is unresponsive. In particular, it is not clear to what extent certain stimuli associated with the female are reinforcing to precopulatory behaviour, even when copulation is not possible. The chick findings would suggest that, if and when precopulatory behaviour can be treated as essentially unreinforced in the absence of copulation, it should cease as quickly in persistent as in non-persistent animals. However, persistence of attention would still have some effect in that it would make it likely that the male would continue to pay attention for longer to the female; he should be quicker therefore to respond to any change in her behaviour.

There are similar problems in making predictions about possible effects of persistence of attention on the organization of successive copulations in species with repeated mounts. If the motivational changes after copulation lead to a shift of attention away from the female (e.g. towards cleaning the penis, or grooming behaviour) it is possible that increased persistence of attention might even extend intercopulatory intervals.

The obvious next step is thus to compare males which differ in persistence but are equally ready to copulate, and to endeavour to settle some of these problems experimentally. In order to be able to do this it is necessary to find some means of reliably blocking the effect on persistence, whilst leaving direct effects of testosterone on copulation untouched, before any firm conclusions can be drawn.

The sensible species to pick for such an investigation seemed to be the domestic fowl, in which the effects on persistence is firmly established. The approach taken so far has been to cut specific lateral hypothalamic tracts in chicks which have received testosterone. A tract between midbrain and paraventricular nucleus has been shown to be necessary for the performance of anything but the lowest levels of copulation by interruption at a number of points (Mitchell and Andrew, 1976). Another tract, originally identified as having a relatively specific involvement in attack (Andrew and Mitchell, in prep.), has now proved in a first series of experiments also to be necessary for the effect of testosterone on persistence of attention. There is other evidence which suggests that the facilitation of attack and increased persistence of attention are bound up together in male chicks. Both occur in response to testosterone in male chicks but not in females, and both require a dosage higher than that which is necessary specifically to facilitate copulation (Andrew, 1975a, 1975b). It is thus possible that this sort of approach will eventually permit the study of behaviour in animals in which copulation has been facilitated by testosterone without the changes in persistence, which in species like the domestic fowl, are normally produced at the same time.

It may be worth bearing in mind the possibility of such separation of normally associated effects when using androgen implants in the CNS. Thus Barfield (1964) has shown that facilitation of copulation can be obtained by preoptic implants of testosterone propionate (TP) in capons, without any accompanying facilitation of attack or courtship. In view of the resemblances between attack and persistence noted above, such animals deserve examination for evidence of increased persistence. They may offer an alternative means of studying the interactions between copulation and increased persistence.

ACKNOWLEDGEMENTS

I am extremely grateful to the Science Research Council and Medical Research Council of the U.K. for their support of the work which has been discussed here.

REFERENCES

Andrew, R. J. (1961) The displays given by passerines in courtship and reproductive fighting, *Ibis*, **103a**, 315–48, 549–79.

Andrew, R. J. (1963) Effects of testosterone on the behaviour of the domestic chick, *J. Comp. Physiol. Psychol.*, **56**, 933–40.

Andrew, R. J. (1972a) Recognition processes and behaviour, with special reference to effects of testosterone in persistence, *Adv. Study Behav.*, **4**, 175–208.

Andrew, R. J. (1972b) Changes in search behaviour in male and female chicks, following different doses of testosterone, *Anim. Behav.*, **20**, 741–50.

Andrew, R. J. (1975a) Effects of testosterone on the behaviour of the domestic chick. I. Effects present in males but not in females, *Anim. Behav.*, **23**, 139–55.

Andrew, R. J. (1975b) Effects of testosterone on the behavior of the domestic chick. II. Effects present in both sexes, *Anim. Behav.*, **23**, 156–68.

Andrew, R. J. (1975c) Effects of testosterone on the calling of the domestic chick in a strange environment, *Anim. Behav.*, **23**, 169–78.

Andrew, R. J. (1976) Attentional mechanisms and animal behaviour. In: *Growing Points in Ethology*, R. A. Hinde and P. P. G. Bateson (eds.), Cambridge, 1976.

Andrew, R. J. and de Lanerolle, N. (1975) The effects of muting lesions on emotional behaviour and behaviour normally associated with calling, *Brain, Behav. Evol.* **10**, 377–99.

Andrew, R. J. and Mitchell, J. (in prep.) A hypothalamic tract of importance in attack.

Andrew, R. J. and Rogers, L. (1972) Testosterone, search behaviour and persistence. *Nature*, **237**, 343–46.

Archer, J. (1973a) The influence of testosterone on chick behavior in novel environments, *Behav. Biol.* **8**, 93–108.

Archer, J. (1973b) Effects of testosterone on immobility responses in the young male chick, *Behav. Biol.*, **8**, 551–56.

Archer, J. (1973c) A further analysis of responses to a novel environment by testosterone-treated chicks, *Behav. Biol.*, **9**, 389–96.

Archer, J. (1974a) The effects of testosterone on the distractibility of chicks by irrelevant and relevant novel stimuli, *Anim. Behav.*, **22**, 397–404.

Archer, J. (1974b) Testosterone and behaviour during extinction in chicks, *Anim. Behav.*, **22**, 650–55.

Barfield, R. J. (1964) Induction of copulatory behaviour by intracranial placement of androgen in capons, *Am. Zool.*, **4**, 301.

Broadbent, D. (1971) Decision and stress, Academic Press, London.

Broverman, D. M., Broverman, I. K., Vogel, W., Palmer, R. D., and Klaiber, E. L. (1964)

The automatization cognitive style and physical development, *Child Develop.*, **35**, 1343–59.

Broverman, D. M., Klaiber, E. L., Kobayashi, Y., and Vogel, W. (1968) Roles of activation and inhibition in sex differences in cognitive abilities, *Psychol. Rev.*, **75**, 23–50.

Dawkins, M. (1971) Perceptual changes in chicks: another look at the 'search image' concept, *Anim. Behav.*, **19**, 566–74.

Ellen, P., Wilson, A. S. and Powell, E. W. (1964) Septal inhibition and timing behaviour in the rat, *Exp. Neurol.*, **10**, 120–32.

Falk, J. L. (1972) The nature and determinants of adjunctive behaviour. In: *Schedule Effects: Drug, Drinking, Aggression*, R. M. Gilbert and J. D. Keehn (eds.), Univ. Toronto Press, pp. 148–73.

Green, D. M. and Swets, J. A. (1966) *Signal Detection Theory and Psychophysics*, John Wiley, New York.

Kahneman, D. (1973) *Attention and Effort*, Prentice Hall, Englewood Cliffs, New Jersey.

Messent, P. R. (1973) Distractibility and persistence in chicks, *D. Phil. Thesis*, University of Sussex, U.K.

Mitchell, J. and Andrew, R. J. (1976) A copulatory system in the hypothalamus and tegmentum of the domestic chick. *J. Comp. Physiol. Psychol.*, **90**, 643–52.

Moray, N. (1969) *Attention: Selective Processes in Vision and Hearing*, Hutchison, London.

Rogers, L. (1971) Testosterone, isthmo–optic lesions and visual search in chickens, *D. Phil. Thesis*, University of Sussex, U.K.

Rogers, L. (1974) Persistence and search influenced by natural levels of androgens in young and adult chickens, *Physiol. Behav.*, **12**, 197–204.

Schleidt, W. M. (1970) Precocial sexual behavior in turkeys (*Meleagris gallopavo* L.), *Anim. Behav.*, **18**, 760–61.

Sokolov, E. N. (1960) Neuronal models and the orienting reflex. In: *The Central Nervous System and Behaviour*, M. A. B. Brazier (ed.), Josiah Macy, New York, pp. 187–276.

Treisman, A. M. (1960) Contextual cues in selective listening, *Q. J. Exp. Psychol.*, **12**, 242–48.

CHAPTER 9

Hypothalamic Regulation of Male Sexual Responsiveness to Androgen

J. B. HUTCHISON

INTRODUCTION

In the early fifties, Young and his colleagues demonstrated that male guinea pigs differed individually in the level of sexual behaviour displayed or, as they termed it, in the 'strength of the sex drive' (Grunt and Young 1952, 1953). The importance of their finding lay not in their observation of individual differences in sexual behaviour, but rather in the fact that these individual differences were reflected in the degree of behavioural response to androgen therapy following castration. Despite differing dosages of androgen, the level of male sexual response was found to be highly correlated with the level shown prior to castration. This was surprising in view of the well-established view of endocrinologists that the effectiveness of a given hormonal sex steroid in inducing regeneration of a target tissue in gonadectomized animals could be directly related to the amount of steroid injected. However, on the basis of their work, Young and his co-workers put forward the hypothesis that in-individual variability in male sexual responsiveness to androgens was due to differences between individuals in the 'reactivity of their tissues' to androgens. Whether this hypothesis referred to the action of androgen on responsive areas of the brain or peripheral tissues was not determined nor could reactivity be defined in physiological terms. But their hypothesis has a remarkable predictive value in the light of present knowledge of the physiology of brain–hormone interactions. A development of their hypothesis, and one which will be carried further in this chapter, is that the brain contains steroid-sensitive cells which may influence or perhaps determine the level of male sexual behaviour in specified conditions of external stimulation.

The chances of associating male sexual behaviour with cellular events in the brain have improved considerably as a consequence of the increase in knowledge of the way in which steroid hormones influence regulatory mechanisms in target cells. Studies of the fate of radioactively labelled sex hormones in known peripheral target tissues of the male such as the rat seminal vesicle and prostate (Stern and Eisenfeld, 1971) have indicated that the hormonal steroid enters the target cell, binds to specific receptor proteins in the cytoplasm, and then moves to the cell nucleus in conjunction with receptor proteins. The hormone–receptor complex initiates changes in genomic function and RNA synthesis which in turn modify the physiological characteristics of the target cell. It has become clear that the brain can be regarded as a target organ for hormonal steroids, because cells of certain areas, notably of the preoptic and anterior hypothalamic areas, contain high affinity steroid-binding proteins (reviewed by Zigmond, 1975; Plapinger and McEwen, this volume Chapter 6). A number of studies involving an assessment of the effects of chronic intracerebral implants of androgen have also indicated that these same brain areas are closely associated with the mechanisms underlying male sexual behaviour (reviewed by Hutchison, 1976).

The purpose of this chapter is to discuss whether differences in the effectiveness of androgen on male sexual behaviour can be related to the functional properties of steroid-sensitive cell systems in the brain. Beach has pointed out that the effect of hormones is to 'increase or decrease the probability that a given response will occur under carefully specified conditions of current external stimulation and previous history of the individual' (Beach, 1974). The question to be considered here is what factors operate to determine the effectiveness of hormones not only in relation to the probability of occurrence of a particular behavioural response, but also their operational effectiveness in terms of the degree to which the response is displayed. The question implies that the steroid-sensitive mechanisms in the brain underlying components of sexual behaviour are variable in their response to hormones. I shall employ the term "responsiveness" to denote the variable capacity or potential of the androgen-sensitive mechanisms in the brain to mediate certain levels of particular types of sexual behaviour in response to androgen, given predictable patterns of sensory stimulation to elicit the behaviour. The term is intentionally restricted here to the interaction between brain mechanisms underlying patterns of sexual behaviour and androgen, and is not intended to have a unitary meaning (see Hinde, 1960 for further discussion of unitary drives) because, as will be seen later in this chapter, brain mechanisms underlying different sexual behaviour patterns may differ in their 'responsiveness' to androgen.

Factors which may influence the brain to change male sexual responsiveness can usefully be considered to act at two levels; the first relates to the action of androgen directly on the central nervous system (CNS) and the second to the action of androgen on peripheral sensory mechanisms which may influence afferent input to brain mechanisms of behaviour. The former topic will be discussed in this chapter, the latter has not been studied extensively (reviewed by Cooper and Aronson, 1974) and will not be dealt with in detail here. The main thesis that I shall put forward is that differences in the effectiveness of steroid hormones with regard to male sexual behaviour are determined not by short-term fluctuations in hormone level, but by changes in the 'sensitivity' of steroid-sensitive cells in the brain which are a consequence of long-term fluctuations in hormone level. There is, however, ample evidence reviewed elsewhere in this volume that differences in behavioural response to hormones can be related to genetic differences within species (reviewed by McGill, this volume Chapter 1); to experiential factors (Larsson, this volume Chapter 3), special forms of learning such as sexual imprinting (Bateson, this volume Chapter 2). It must also be emphasized that male sexual behaviour seldom occurs in the absence of interaction with a female. Variability in male sexual behaviour is necessarily also a function of individual differences in the behaviour of the female and dynamic changes in her stimulus value during sexual interactions which may influence the 'nexus' (Hinde, 1970) of inter-individual stimuli and which determine the course of behaviour during the reproductive cycle. This chapter will concentrate on variability in male sexual behaviour which can be considered to be minimally influenced by the stimulus value of the female, and therefore to be intrinsic to the male.

SHORT-TERM CHANGES IN ANDROGEN LEVEL

Peripheral Levels and Behaviour

With the development of biochemical methods for the identification of sex hormones in peripheral blood plasma, accurate information is becoming available on rapid fluctuations in the level of trophic and steroid sex hormones in male animals undergoing normal reproductive cycles. The majority of male mammals studied so far show evidence of a regular rhythmicity in these hormones which in some cases is clearly circadian in nature (Moor and Younglai, 1975) and has a duration of several hours. However, it has also been possible to correlate external events, such as the incidence of stimuli associated with the initiation of sexual behaviour, with sudden elevations in plasma levels of male sex hormones occurring over time periods measured in minutes rather than hours. Whether such elevations are a consequence or a cause of changes in male sexual behaviour is a topic currently receiving much attention, and at first sight, the evidence is suggestive of a causal relationship in some cases. Several examples have been noted where acute release of testosterone and luteinizing hormone (LH) accompanies male sexual behaviour. Thus the sight or smell of the female is claimed to be sufficient stimulus to elevate plasma testosterone levels before mating has occurred in the male rabbit (Saginor and Horton, 1968), the bull (Katongole et al., 1971) and in the male rat (Purvis and Haynes, 1974). In the male hamster, a rapid increase in plasma testosterone after exposure to vaginal odour is comparable to increases that occur after pairing with a female (Macrides et al., 1974). Similarly, male house mice which have been paired with a female for one week show an elevation in plasma testosterone concentration 30 to 60 min after the resident female is replaced by another female (Macrides et al., 1975). This elevation appears to be a specific response to a strange female as it does not occur if the resident female is replaced by a male. Elevation in plasma testosterone level is also correlated with copulatory behaviour in male rhesus monkeys (Rose *et al.*, 1972). Copulatory behaviour also results in an elevation of plasma testosterone within approximately 45 min in the male rabbit (Haltmeyer and Eik-Nes, 1969; Saginor and Horton, 1968), 60 min in the bull (Katongole *et al.*, 1971; Smith *et al.*, 1973), and 5 min of the first intromission in the male rat (Purvis and Haynes, 1974).

Few experiments of this type have been carried out in sub-mammalian vertebrates. But in birds such as the barbary dove *(Streptopelia risoria)*, which has an elaborate visually mediated courtship display (Hutchison, 1970a; Lovari and Hutchison, 1975), a more specific effect of sexual interaction on peripheral testosterone levels has been demonstrated recently. Feder *et al.* (1977) have shown that male plasma testosterone levels are almost doubled within 4 hours of pairing with the female; the consequent elevation in plasma testosterone appears to accompany the initial phase of the courtship interaction. In contrast, pairing with a male or occupation of the breeding cage has no such effect. Interestingly, levels of 5α-dihydrotestosterone (DHT) of male doves are elevated to approximately ten times their basal levels within the same period (Feder *et al.*, 1977). This hormone, although an important androgen (Wilson, 1975) as an activator of peripheral tissues, such as the prostate and seminal vesicle in mammals, is not normally found in large quantities in the peripheral circulation.

Whether or not an increase in LH concentration accompanies the early stages of male sexual behaviour, and whether increases in LH precede an elevation in plasma testosterone concentration is a subject of controversy, particularly in the mammalian literature. Katongole *et al.* (1971) recorded a significant increase in plasma LH of the bull which was 'possibly associated with the teaser cow being led past the bull on her way to the covering yard'. By contrast, mating itself had no appreciable effect on LH level, presumably because it was already elevated. The elevation in plasma testosterone not large in this example. In subsequent studies of sexual stimulation of the bull (Convey *et al.*, 1971; Gombe *et al.*, 1973) plasma LH increases were found to be slight and insignificant, casting some doubt on the phenomenon. Moreover, increases in plasma LH could not be correlated with copulatory behaviour in male rats (Spies and Niswender, 1971; Davidson *et al.*, 1973) and adult human males (Stearns *et al.*, 1973; Lincoln, 1974). Lincoln (1974) has suggested from studies of the human male that elevation in plasma LH may, in any event, be irrelevant to rapid increases in plasma testosterone, because transitory increases in androgens of testicular origin are likely to be accounted for by increased blood flow through the testis. The human testis is relatively slow to respond to endogenous LH and, as Lincoln points out, a sexual stimulus which increases plasma LH concentration could not be expected to produce an elevation in plasma testosterone for 30–90 min thereafter (i.e. the time period quoted for plasma testosterone increases in the bull and rabbit). If the slow response to elevated plasma LH levels is common to other mammalian species, temporal correlations between changes in LH induced by sexual stimuli, 'sexual excitement' or the act of coitus and elevations in plasma testosterone, which are thought to be causally related to male sexual behaviour, become all the more difficult to establish.

Even if more adequate correlations between rapid changes in LH or testosterone level and behaviour can be established in the future, it is unlikely that such changes have any immediate influence on male sexual responsiveness, in terms of the response of brain mechanisms underlying male sexual behaviour to androgen. The rapid elevations in testosterone described above might be seen rather as having a general influence on the functional capacity of such mechanisms during performance of the behaviour, or peripheral effects which increase male attractiveness (Keverne et al., 1977) to the female.

More recently, this problem has been complicated by the discovery that elevation in both plasma testosterone and LH may be a consequence of increased familiarity with the mating situation. Thus Kamel et al. (1975) found that although acute elevations in plasma concentration of testosterone and LH could be correlated with mating behaviour in the male, plasma testosterone and LH of male rats also rose significantly when they were alone in the arena used for testing sexual behaviour or were with anoestrous females. They interpreted these data as suggesting 'anticipation of a mating encounter', and speculate that the 'anticipatory rise may function to initiate or facilitate male mating behaviour'. They cite an apparently similar anticipatory effect in the human male, reported anonymously (1970), where increase in beard growth, which was presumably testosterone mediated, preceded sexual activity. However, it is equally plausible, as these authors point out, that elevation in plasma hormones is a result of non-sexual social stimuli that occur when a different social environment is encountered.

In long-term studies of Talapoin monkeys, Keverne et al. (1977) have demonstrated the importance of social environment in determining increases in plasma testosterone levels which are a consequence of interaction with the females. Thus males which are dominant in the social hierarchy show marked elevations in plasma testosterone level after mating interactions, whereas subordinate males show no such increases. Interestingly, visual and olfactory contact are insufficient to elevate plasma testosterone. Despite increased interest in looking at the female and masturbatory activity, dominant males separated from females by wire partitions showed no significant elevation in plasma testosterone.

Brain Hormone Levels and Behaviour

Little is known at present about the way in which rapid fluctuations in androgen levels measured at the periphery relate to the functioning of brain mechanisms of male sexual behaviour. In fact, it is only very recently (Challis *et al.*, 1976) that attempts have been made, using radioimmunoassay techniques, to compare plasma androgen level with the endogenous steroid pool in the adenohypophysis and brain. In the male rat, testosterone levels in the hypothalamus and cortex exceed those of the plasma (4.1, 4.0 ng/g, hypothalamus, cortex; ≥ 1.8 ng/ml, plasma). Following castration and a period of 3 weeks before the tissues were sampled, testosterone concentrations were reduced to negligible amounts (< 0.13, ≤ 0.08 ng/g; ≤ 0.004 ng/ml) indicating that brain levels of testosterone reflect levels in the periphery, at least after gross manipulation of the endocrine system. The clearance rates of androgens in the brain clearly differ; substantial levels of androstenedione remain in the hypothalamus for at least 21 days after castration (1.4 ng/g). Nothing appears to be known, however, of the relationship between smaller fluctuations of testosterone level, such as those induced by sexual stimuli or the experience of sexual behaviour, and the endogenous androgen pool in the brain. Attempts to study this relationship are complicated by the variety of possible routes by which testosterone reaches the relevant hormone-sensitive areas of the brain. For example, there is little doubt that androgen reaches the preoptic and anterior hypothalamic cells via the capillary network within the hypothalamus. However, testosterone is known to pass into the cerebrospinal fluid (CSF) after intravenous injection into castrated or intact rhesus monkeys (David and Anand-Kumar, 1974). The CSF represents a potential source of androgen that may be important in regulation of gonadotrophin release. This could also be the case with regard to activation of sexual behaviour.

Experimentally, an obvious method to study the relationship between brain androgen level and behavioural mechanisms would be to alter brain androgen level directly and observe the behavioural consequences given the standardized conditions of external stimulation necessary to evoke the male behaviour. In practice, this has proved difficult for two technical reasons. First, there are at present no effective methods for accurately controlling the amount of steroid applied to local areas of the brain in quantities sufficient for the activation of behaviour. Second, male copulatory behaviour is highly dependent on peripheral sensory input which may itself be directly linked to hormonal action (Hart, this volume Chapter 10). Male precopulatory behaviour in mammals has not been studied to any extent, but what data there are suggest that it is brief, highly variable (Burley, 1976) and in many cases, particularly in rodents, initiated by female pheromones. The nature of avian precopulatory courtship behaviour, consisting of elaborate, visually mediated displays which are sterotyped in form and within limits predictable in sequence, has made the study of the effects of varying brain androgen levels on behaviour a possibility. One attempt has been made using solid testosterone propionate (TP) implants of differing surface areas which were designed to release hormone into the brain in minute quantities, but at different rates (Hutchison, 1970b). Using three differently sized implants positioned unilaterally into the anterior hypothalamus and preoptic area of castrated male doves, it was found that there was a direct relationship between the size of the implant (and therefore presumed diffusion rate into the brain tissue) and the structure of the behavioural interaction induced with standardized test females. Thus castrates that had received 'high diffusion' implants showed full courtship behaviour consisting of aggressive and nest-orientated components. But castrates receiving 'low diffusion' implants displayed only the nest-orientated components. This finding leads to the hypothesis that different types of sexual behaviour may depend on different concentrations of androgen in the hypothalamus and that the effects of androgen on mechanisms underlying male sexual behaviour may depend both on effective hormone concentration in the anterior hypothalamus, and on the threshold of 'sensitivity' of the brain mechanisms underlying the particular behaviour pattern to androgen (Fig. 1). The physiological mechanisms underlying sensitivity are still a matter for speculation, but a differential affinity for steroids of cell populations associated with mechanisms underlying

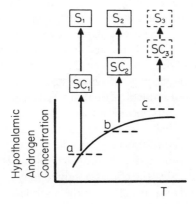

Fig. 1. Components of a possible threshold mechanism underlying units of sexual behaviour with differing levels of responsiveness to androgen. Hypothalamic androgen, which is assumed to show an hypothetical increase over time (T), activates specified androgen-sensitive cell populations (SC_1, SC_2, SC_3 .....^{n}) with differing thresholds of sensitivity to hypothalamic androgen concentrations (a, b, c) specifically associated with brain systems S_1, S_2, S_3 .....^{n}) integrating the units of sexual behaviour. In the example, hypothalamic androgen is assumed to rise to concentrations below threshold for SC_3

particular behaviour patterns, possibly involving receptor proteins, has been suggested (see Hutchison, 1976 for further discussion).

In view of the findings of Moss *et al.* (1975), discussion of the direct effects on the brain of short-term changes in androgen level must take into account the possibility that androgen may operate in synergy with or as a background to the action of a second class of hormones; the polypeptide hypothalamic releasing hormones, which are known to be involved in the control of the gonadotrophic hormonal system of the pituitary. In rats, luteinizing hormone-releasing hormone (LRH) has been detected in a band of tissue extending from the medial preoptic area through the ventral hypothalamus to the median eminence-arcuate nucleus region, from which LRH is presumably released into the portal capillaries to influence synthesis and release of the gonado-trophic hormones. Moss has found that a single 500 ng dose of synthetic LRH injected systemically into ovariectomized rats primed with doses (0.25 mg) of oestrone that are subthreshold for lordosis evoke this behaviour within 2 h of injection, suggesting a very rapid action of the releasing hormone on mechanisms of female copulatory behaviour given an oestrogen background. The effects obtained with male copulatory behaviour were not as striking. Though a similar dose of LRH injected into castrate male rats primed with TP given in subthreshold doses decreased the latency to ejaculation, suggesting that LRH facilitates the display of copulatory behaviour. The significance of LRH in the hormonal control of male sexual behaviour is not altogether clear from these experiments, because there are no cases in which LRH acts alone to activate sexual behaviour; the behavioural effects of the releasing hormone, when given in conditions of steroidal priming, never exceed those of the steroid hormone given alone. In addition, as these hormonal treatments have been given systemically, the effects obtained may be mediated not directly by the brain but indirectly via an action on the peripheral sensory system associated with sexual behaviour. Studies of the role of releasing hormones on male behaviour have not so far involved analyses of behaviour at a sufficient level of complexity to answer any of these questions, but more convincing evidence may come to light in the future. One point that does seem to be clear is that the behavioural actions of the releasing hormones are not a consequence of induced elevations in gonadotrophin hormone (GTH) level. For exogenous GTH does not appear to influence male sexual behaviour in the conditions used in the experiments described above (Moss *et al.*, 1975).

To conclude, attempts are being made to correlate rapid elevations in both gonadotrophin and androgen level with changes in the male sexual behaviour of mammals and also birds. However, even in carefully controlled behavioural test situations, such correlations do not establish the premise that rapidly rising androgen levels cause changes in the functioning of brain mechanisms of male sexual behaviour. These short-term elevations in androgen level are probably in many cases a consequence of sexual interaction rather than a cause of behavioural change. Perhaps a more important criticism of the view that rapidly changing hormone levels can influence male sexual behaviour can be put forward on behavioural grounds. As ethologists have pointed out, apparently simple male sexual activities can be shown to be part of a complex causal nexus of events which have to be seen in the context of the dynamics of the changing relationship between male and female during the reproductive cycle. To give one example, Hinde (1970) has shown that the copulatory attempts of the male chaffinch *(Fringilla coelebs)* result in conflicting tendencies in the female to flee from the male, attack the male, or solicit copulation—each may involve 'differing motivational states'. In this sort of situation, it is impossible to attribute the continuation of the sexual interaction to a unitary effect of a male hormone on brain mechanisms of male behaviour (see Fentress, this volume Chapter 18 for further discussion).

There is experimental evidence, however, that the predominant type of male behaviour displayed in an interaction, such as the aggressive courtship of the male dove described above, may require a certain minimum level or concentration of androgen in the hypothalamus. Speculation on the mode of action of a hormone-sensitive brain system capable of responding differentially to androgen level leads to the conclusion that for such a system to operate, steroid-sensitive cells comprising the androgen-sensitive threshold mechanism, described above, would have to be 'programmed' to 'ignore' rapid fluctuations in hormone level and to 'respond' to the modal level of hormone over a given time period. This is because it is difficult to envisage a system which would respond preferentially to rapid elevations in hormone level caused by sexual stimuli and not to respond to normally occurring rhythmic fluctuations or changes in level relating to other conditions such as emotional stress for example. The rapid release of testicular androgen in response to sexual stimuli, possibly occurring independently of the gonadotrophic system, may be required, however, for sperm maturation and preparation of the male reproductive tract for transport of sperm (Macmillan and Hafs, 1967). Conceivably, the androgen-sensitive behavioural mechanism is structured to prevent behavioural response to the rapid elevations in androgen level necessary for spermatogenesis and sperm transport.

LONG-TERM CHANGES IN ANDROGEN LEVEL

The short-term changes in androgen level described in the previous section can be contrasted with the prolonged seasonal changes in androgen level seen in many temperate species of mammals, such as the ferret *(Putorius vulgaris)* (Herbert, 1971) whose pattern of pituitary LH and testicular secretion of androgen is regulated by seasonal changes in daylength. Photoperiodic regulation of testicular activity is also characteristic of many species of birds (Rowan, 1926; Menaker and Keatts, 1968; Lofts *et al.*, 1970). For example long (18L/6D) photoperiods imposed on male quail *(Coturnix coturnix)* that have been subjected to a series of short photoperiods stimulate a rapid elevation in LH and testicular growth within 1 day of exposure to a long photoperiod (Follett and Farner, 1966).

In this section I shall be concerned with whether androgenic target cells in the preoptic and anterior hypothalamic areas associated with male sexual behaviour remain stable in their sensitivity to androgen during long-term changes in the secretory pattern of the testis. More specifically, is behavioural responsiveness to androgen as high during periods of very low endogenous androgen level as it is during periods of high androgen level? This question can be answered experimentally by studying the effects of exogenous androgen on behaviour in conditions where a prolonged androgen deficit is imposed either by gonadectomy or manipulation of environmental stimuli, such as photoperiod, which are known to influence the pituitary–gonad axis.

Indirect Evidence for Variable Brain Sensitivity to Androgen

Although it has been known for some time that the type of sexual behaviour induced by androgen therapy in castrated males may be qualitatively similar to that shown before castration, Riss and Young (1954) were able to demonstrate quantitatively that the sexual behaviour of castrated male guinea pigs was restored to precastration levels irrespective of the dosage used. 'Low drive' males, which normally displayed little sexual behaviour when given dosages of androgen 20 times higher than those necessary to restore behaviour showed no increase in the incidence or level of display. They interpreted this as indicating that it was 'unlikely that low drive was a consequence of androgenic insufficiency' and that the 'character of the behaviour was determined by the nature of the soma and substrate on which the hormones act rather than the amount of hormone, providing of course the threshold for the somatically determined level had been exceeded'. The results on which this conclusion was based were derived from a composite score of sexual behaviour and can perhaps be criticized on the grounds that if the component patterns of sexual behaviour had been measured in detail, dose-response effects might have been shown similar to those obtained by parametric studies where a dose-dependent decrease in ejaculation latency was demonstrated in castrated male rats (Beach and Holz-Tucker, 1949) and castrated male hamsters (Whalen and de Bold, 1974). In castrated male doves, a dose-dependent increase in chasing behaviour can also be demonstrated (Hutchison, in prep.). However, as Fig. 2 indicates, interpretation of such an increase becomes difficult if more than one behaviour pattern has been measured. Thus with a larger hormone dose an increase in one type of behaviour, chasing, can be related to changes in display of another, nest soliciting. The degree of change differs according to the steroid or combination of steroids used in therapy. In this example, the relative changes are unlikely to depend on the time limit of the test, because the actual display of courtship occupies only a relatively small proportion of the test period.

Recent work with the male dove *(Streptopelia risoria)* (Hutchison, 1971)

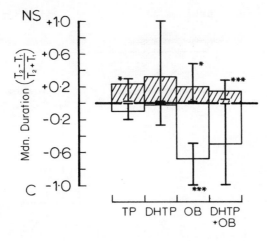

Fig. 2. The effects on the courtship of castrated male doves of increasing the intramuscular dosage of various androgens and oestrogen (TP, testosterone propionate; DHTP, 5α-dihydrotestosterone propionate; OB, oestradiol monobenzoate; DHTP + OB, hormones injected together). Initial therapy (T_1) consisted of 10 daily 300 μg doses in saline; in the subsequent therapy (T_2) 5 daily 600 μg doses were given. Differences in the effects of dosage on chasing (C) and nest soliciting (NS) courtship patterns are expressed as a ratio $(T_2 - T_1)/(T_2 + T_1)$ where T_1 and T_2 are the medians of the daily durations of display; the daily duration is the sum of the duration of bouts of display of the pattern within a 3-min test period with a female (see also Hutchison, 1971). T_1 and T_2 are compared statistically; *$p < 0.05$, ***$p < 0.01$ (Wilcoxon Matched Pairs Test, two-tailed)

indicates that individual differences in male courtship are maintained following castration and androgen therapy. Thus males (P males), that displayed the aggressive components of courtship in the absence of the nest-oriented courtship displays before castration, behave similarly if treated systemically or implanted intrahypothalamically with TP. There also proved to be quantitative differences in behavioural responsiveness to both exogenous androgen and oestrogen between the two groups (Fig. 3) (Hutchison, in prep.). The P castrates showed significantly lower levels of courtship and vocal behaviour, indicating that the mechanisms underlying courtship in this group were less sensitive not only to androgen, but also to oestrogens. Therefore, consistent qualitative

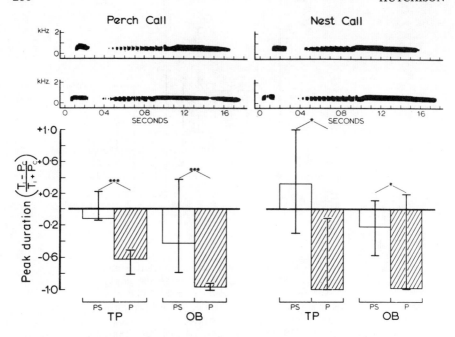

Fig. 3. Differential responsiveness of hormone-dependent vocal behaviour (perch call and nest call illustrated by sound spectrographs; 2 examples of each call type) of castrated male doves whose precastration behaviour consisted of either aggressive and nest-orientated courtship (PS males) or aggressive courtship only (P males) (see also Hutchison and Lovari, 1976). Groups of P and PS males received either testosterone propionate (TP) or oestradiol monobenzoate (OB) as 10 daily injections of 300 μg/day. Differences in effectiveness of hormone treatment (T_1) relative to precastration vocal behaviour (P_c) are expressed as $(T_1 - P_c)/(T_1 + P_c)$ where P_c and T_1 represent peak durations of display. The peak duration is the longest of the daily durations of display during a 10-min observation period. (Daily duration is described in Fig. 1.) The doves were caged individually in that they were in auditory contact, but in visual isolation. P and PS groups are compared statistically; *p < 0.05, ***p < 0.01

differences in precastration sexual behaviour can be correlated with both the structure of the behaviour induced by therapy and responsiveness to exogenous hormones, irrespective of the precise structure of the steroid in this case.

Individual differences in the retention of male sexual behaviour following castration are undoubtedly due partly to experiential factors. The experience of performing behaviour appears to make the mechanisms underlying male sexual behaviour less sensitive to the effects of castration. Thus Rosenblatt and Aronson (1958) found that few male cats with no prior sexual experience intromitted in mating tests following castration. By contrast, sexually experienced males continued to intromit for weeks after castration. As McGill (this volume Chapter 1) points out, genotypic differences within a species also serve to influence both the retention of male sexual behaviour after castration and the behaviour restored by androgen therapy. However, there is also evidence to suggest that mechanisms underlying sexual behaviour change in their sensitivity to exogenous androgen as a direct consequence of the androgen deficit imposed by castration. Thus Hutchison (1969, 1974a) has reported three observations which provide circumstantial evidence for a postcastration decline in behavioural sensitivity to androgen. First, significantly more TP injections were required to initiate courtship behaviour in long-term castrates than in short-term castrates. Second, the component patterns of courtship were not usually restored to precastration levels even with large dosages of TP. Third, in a sample of castrated male doves of similar age and sexual experience, a proportion showed no courtship response to daily TP injections, although the remainder all responded to therapy within 1 to 3 days. Doubling the dosage of TP induced courtship in all the castrates that had previously failed to respond to treatment (Hutchison, 1976). The latter result indicates that a decline in sexual responsiveness to androgen occurs more rapidly in some males than others. Similarly, Davidson and Bloch (1969) found that the dosage of TP required to restore ejaculatory behaviour to precastration levels in castrated male rats, given immediately after daily tests had indicated the disappearance of the behaviour, was significantly higher than the minimum dose required to initiate and maintain the display of this behaviour after castration. Two studies of female rats also indicate a postgonadectomy decline in behavioural responsiveness to exogenous hormone therapy. Thus ovariectomized rats show higher levels of lordosis behaviour when treatment is initiated on the day after ovariectomy than when treatment is delayed for 6 weeks (Damassa and Davidson, 1973). Beach and Orndoff (1974) have also reported that oestrogen and progesterone treatment declines in effectiveness when the period of hormonal deprivation exceeds 30 days. These latter workers concluded that 'the response of CNS mechanisms to exogenous estrogen decreases after oestrogen deprivation'. The decline in the 'crawling response' of the female rat, which does not depend on tactile stimulation from male mounting, would appear to support their conclusions. A decline in female copulatory behaviour could be due, however, to deficits in sensory input from the perineal area, which is influenced by oestrogen (Komisaruk et al., 1972; Kow and Pfaff, 1974).

None of the studies reviewed above answers the question posed at the beginning of this section. Although suggestive of a decreasing sensitivity to exogenous hormone following gonadectomy, the results of these studies, which all involve systemic treatments of hormone, do not establish whether the decline in sensitivity to hormone specifically involves the brain. The changes in effectiveness of exogenous hormone could equally well be due to changes in peripheral metabolism and transport of hormone or to changes in afferent input from sensory structures. In male rats and cats for example, penile epidermal papillae decline uniformly after castration (Aronson and Cooper, 1968; Phoenix et al., 1976). Because these papillae are associated with encapsulated nerve endings, reduction in copulatory behaviour following castration may be due to diminished sensory input from the penis. In fact, the problem is difficult to study using male rat copulatory behaviour, because abnormalities in behaviour may be due to deficiencies in both sensory feedback from the penis and in the functioning of spinal reflex mechanisms coordinating copulatory behaviour which are thought to depend on the influence of androgen (Beach and Levinson, 1950; Hart, 1967 and this volume Chapter 10) which in long-term castrates may not adequately reverse the effects of a prolonged androgen deficit. A second difficulty in using rodents and other mammals is that the display of male sexual behaviour depends on olfactory cues and may continue for many months after castration (see McGill, this volume Chapter 1 and Hart, this volume Chapter 10). In contrast to mammalian copulatory behaviour, avian precopulatory courtship behaviour consists of stereotyped, visually mediated courtship displays which do not, as far as is known, depend on olfactory stimuli, but which are highly androgen-dependent. Moreover there appears to be no direct relationship between androgen-dependent sensory structures and male courtship behaviour.

Direct Evidence for Variable Brain Sensitivity to Androgen

In view of the possibility that peripheral metabolic changes might influence the transport of hormone in the brain, the hypothesis that prolonged androgen deficit causes a decline in the sensitivity of the brain to androgen can only be tested by measuring the behavioural effectiveness of hormone applied directly to local areas of the brain. There are four prerequisites for this study. First, that the course of the behavioural interaction with the female is determined mainly by the male, and is consistent in the testing situation used; the latter requires the use of females which respond in a predictable way to the male. Second, that the males are homogeneous in the type of courtship displayed before castration. Third, that the level of behavioural analysis is sufficiently accurate to expose individual differences in response to hormonal treatment. Fourth, that the hormonal stimulus is applied as a brief pulse of hormone directly to the androgen-sensitive area of the brain. The latter point is important because assessment of the hormonal 'sensitivity' of the behavioural system at a given time after castration requires that the androgen applied locally to the brain does not create prolonged high concentrations of hormone that might compensate for any decline in the functional capacity of the hormone-sensitive mechanisms. These prerequisites have been fulfilled to some extent by using the male dove. The courtship interaction, homogeneity of the male courtship response to standardized test females, and the androgen-dependence of the male courtship displays are described in detail elsewhere (Hutchison, 1970a). There is also circumstantial evidence that the solid, crystalline implants that have been used for studies of the central action of androgen in the male dove do have a relatively brief effect on behaviour. Thus the majority of castrates with unilateral intrahypothalamic implants consistently begin to display courtship 2–3 days after implantation, a peak in response occurs after 3–4 days and the response rapidly disappears within 6–8 days (Hutchison, 1976). In contrast, systemically treated castrates show a progressive rise in levels of behaviour presumably due to the cumulative effects of androgen. The transient nature of the response to intrahypothalamic implants is probably due to the effects of gliosis in masking diffusion from the implant (Hutchison, 1971). That there is no long-term 'storage' of the effects of the implant on either the hypothalamic cells responsive to testosterone or the extra-hypothalamic mechanisms underlying courtship is indicated by the lack of response of castrates tested for courtship on day 10 instead of day 1 after implantation (Hutchison, 1976 and in prep.).

The experiment carried out to answer the question of whether central changes in sensitivity to androgen are responsible for the postcastration decline in effectiveness of androgen therapy has been described previously (Hutchison, 1974b, 1976). I shall refer only to the major findings which serve as a background to a discussion of interpretation of the results. In this experiment, castrated male doves, selected as being behaviourally homogeneous prior to castration, received intrahypothalamic TP implants 15, 30, and 90 days after castration. The implants were effective in restoring courtship in 15-day castrates, somewhat less effective in the 30-day castrates and markedly less effective in the long-term (90-day) castrate (Fig. 4). That this is not an irreversible insensitivity to androgen in the long-term castrates was indicated by treating 90-day castrates intramuscularly with large doses of TP. The display of courtship was re-established after a few days delay (Fig. 5). This delay proved to be significantly longer than the response latency of the short-term castrates, suggesting that a period of hormonal priming (termed precursory sensitization, Hutchison, 1976) is required in long-term castrates before the androgen-sensitive brain mechanism mediates courtship behaviour.

Levels of Interpretation

The immediate question raised by these results is whether the focus for changes in brain functioning responsible for the ineffectiveness of hypothalamic implants lies within the hypothalamus itself, or whether it involves extra-hypothalamic brain mechanisms underlying courtship. It could be argued that a prolonged androgen deficit may cause a functional change in extra-hypothalamic systems or that they either fail to respond to testosterone-induced activity in hypothalamic cells or actively inhibit the response of these cells to androgen. There is some justification for implicating the anterior hypothalamus and preoptic areas alone, because implants of TP in this region are maximally effective in inducing courtship display. If the effects of testosterone are mediated by cells in this area, changes in the celluar action of testosterone may be responsible for the ineffectiveness of TP in long-term cas-

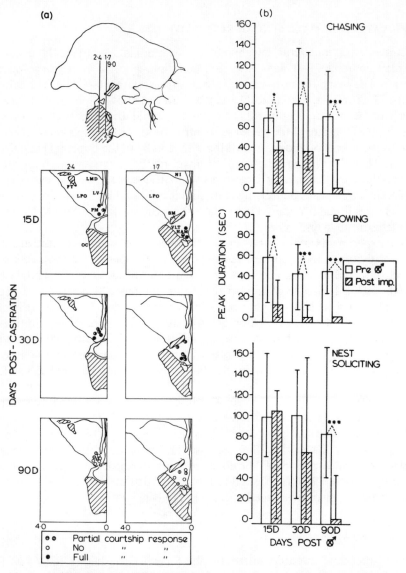

Fig. 4. Comparison between courtship shown before castration and following implantation of testosterone propionate in the preoptic-anterior hypothalamic area 15, 30, and 90 days after castration (a). Each symbol (circle) denotes the tip of a unilateral implant; shading within the symbol indicates the behavioural response. Peak durations of courtship shown before castration are indicated by open bars; postimplantation peak durations by crosshatched bars. The data are expressed as medians and ranges, and are derived from Hutchison (1974b). Precastration and postimplantation peak durations are compared statistically *p < 0.05, ***p < 0.001 (Wilcoxon Matched Pairs Test, one-tailed). FT, tractus frontothalamicus; HAM, nucleus hypothalamicus anterior medialis; LMD, lamina medullaris; LPO, lobus parolfactorius; LV, lateral ventricle; NI neostriatum intermediale; OC, optic chiasma; PM, nucleus preopticus medialis; SM, tractus septomesencephalius; VLT, nucleus ventrolaterialis. (Modified from Hutchison, 1974b)

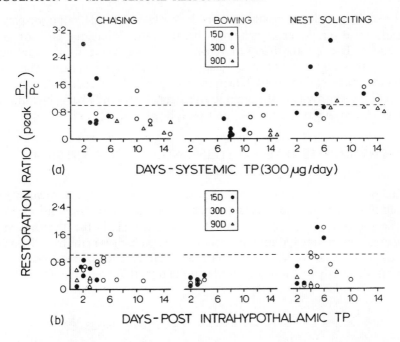

Fig. 5. Restoration of aggressive and nest-orientated courtship behaviour in castrated male doves by (a) TP treatment initiated 15 days, 30 days, and 90 days after castration, and (b) intrahypothalamic TP implants positioned 15 days, 30 days, and 90 days after castration. In (a) and (b) the relationship between precastration (P_c) and posttreatment (P_t) peak duration are expressed as a restoration ratio (P_t/P_c). The dotted lines indicate where precastration peak durations are equal to postimplantation peak durations (ratio value 1.0). (Modified from Hutchison, 1974b.)

trates. This interpretation, leading to a research strategy which involves analysis of the metabolism of testosterone in hypothalamic cells, will be considered in the final section of this paper.

The results can also be interpreted in terms of non-hormonal factors which might indirectly influence brain cell systems sensitive to androgen. For it will be argued that, first, the long period of visual isolation from other birds in which the castrates were maintained, second, the lack of experience of performing courtship during the period of visual isolation or third, the lack of androgen-dependent social stimuli such as the vocal behaviour during the post-castration period, might influence responsiveness to intrahypothalamic androgen. The period of visual isolation would not appear to be of significance in itself, because the males were kept in a similar condition for a comparable period (90 days) before castration without any discernible effects on their behaviour (Hutchison, 1974b). The second argument, suggesting that the changes in mechanisms underlying courtship behaviour are an indirect consequence of the androgen deficit resulting from lack of 'use' in mediating display is difficult to disprove experimentally, because the behaviour is androgen-dependent. Use of androgen to reinstate the behaviour would confound attempts to study non-hormonal changes in the control system. The third argument, that environmental factors and particularly social stimuli may influence the sensitivity of the brain to androgen, is currently being investigated and will be considered in the section that follows.

ENVIRONMENTAL FACTORS AND CENTRAL CHANGES IN ANDROGEN SENSITIVITY

The principal question to be discussed here is whether environmental stimuli influence brain mechanisms underlying male sexual responsiveness to androgen directly by action on the CNS and particularly the hypothalamus, or whether environmental stimuli act indirectly via changes in the hypothalamo-pituitary-gonad axis which influences the gonadal secretion of androgen, and in turn the sensitivity to androgen of cells in the hypothalamus (Fig. 6).

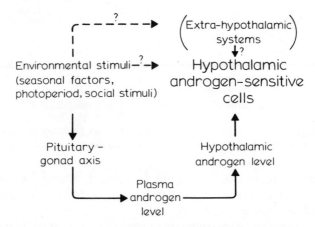

Fig. 6. Two suggested routes by which environmental factors could influence the sensitivity of brain mechanisms of sexual behaviour to androgen. The first, represented by dotted arrows, indicates an action of environmental stimuli on the brain, either directly on hypothalamic cells sensitive to androgen or on extrahypothalamic systems which influence the androgen-sensitive cells. The second, represented by solid arrows, indicates an effect of environmental factors which act via the neuro-endocrine system to induce a long-term change in hypothalamic androgen level which subsequently changes the sensitivity of the brain to androgen either by a direct action on hypothalamic androgen-sensitive cells, or indirectly via extrahypothalamic systems associated with these cells

Photoperiod

Circumstantial evidence suggesting that photoperiod directly influences the brain to induce behavioural refractoriness to systemically injected oestrogen has been advanced by several recent studies. In the most extensive of these studies, Steel and Hinde (1972) have presented evidence that photoperiod is critical for the initiation of nest-building in female canaries by systemic oestrogen treatment, an effect thought to be independent of gonadotrophin level (see also Hinde and Steel, 1977). The effectiveness of oestrogen on the oestrous behaviour of the ewe has also been found to vary with season (Fletcher and Lindsay, 1971; Raeside and Mcdonald, 1959).

An example more relevant to the issue of male sexual responsiveness to androgen has been described by Morin et al. (1976) for a highly photoperiodic species, the male hamster. These workers tested the hypothesis that the substrate underlying reproductive behaviour is less responsive in castrated hamsters maintained under short photoperiods than in those maintained under long photoperiods to the activational effects of systemic androgen. Long-term androgen deprivation had little effect on behavioural responsiveness to subcutaneous TP implants in males maintained on a long daylength (14L/10D). But a similar group maintained on a short daylength (2L/22D) showed little response to TP implants despite an obvious peripheral action of the androgen in stimulating active flank glands to levels exceeding those obtained in castrates kept on long daylengths. Their work suggests an effect of photoperiod on male sexual responsiveness to androgen. However, the development of 'behavioural refractoriness' appears to be contingent also upon the prolonged absence of circulating androgen, because long-term castrates maintained on the short daylength, and given TP implant therapy at the time of castration, showed a response to TP implants similar to that of the group maintained on the long photoperiod. Presumably, the initial therapy may have induced behavioural effects, such as sex-related changes in activity, which may have indirectly facilitated the behavioural response to the second TP implant. However, the results are consistent with an influence of photoperiod on mechanisms underlying male sexual responsiveness to androgen. A seasonal decline in responsiveness of the rutting behaviour of the red deer stag (*Cervus elaphus*) to systemic androgen (Lincoln et al., 1972) suggests a similar phenomenon. As in the case of the testosterone insensitivity of the male hamster, there was visible evidence that the testosterone implants were functionally active (velvet and hard horn on the antlers in this case). Whether the results obtained with systemic treatments in male hamsters and red deer represent an effect of photoperiod on the androgen-sensitivity of the brain remains to be established by experiments involving application of hormone directly to the brain.

An analogous effect suggesting a change in hypothalamic sensitivity to androgen has been demonstrated in studies of the hypothalamo–pituitary axis of male hamsters (Turek *et al.*, 1975). Thus the castration-induced elevation in LH and follicle stimulating hormone (FSH) usually occurring in males maintained on a long daylength regime (14L/10D) is not seen in castrates maintained under a short daylength regime (6L/18D), suggesting that the 'non-inductive' photoperiod may reduce the sensitivity of the neuroendocrine system to androgenic feedback, possibly via a direct retino-hypothalamic tract, pineal gland effect or as a result of a gradual decline in steroid levels themselves. A comparable decline in sensitivity to androgenic feedback occurs as a consequence of the seasonal decline in androgen level in the snow-shoe hare *(Lepus americanus)* (Davis and Meyer, 1973).

Demonstration of a direct effect of photoperiod on responsiveness to androgen in male doves has proved difficult. Intrahypothalamic implants of TP were found to be more effective in initiating aggressive courtship behaviour in long-term (90-day) castrates maintained on a 13L/11D photoperiod than in long-term castrates maintained on a short photoperiod (Table 1). However, the effect was not very marked (Hutchison, 1974c) and both short and long daylength groups of 90-day castrates showed an overall decline in responsiveness to intrahypothalamic TP relative to short-term (15-day) castrates. The difference in effectiveness of TP implants between long and short photoperiod 90-day castrates could be due to an indirect effect mediated by higher gonadotrophin level in the long photoperiod group in view of the possibility that gonadotrophin levels are probably lower in castrates maintained on a short photoperiod (see Hinde *et al.*, 1974 for a similar effect in the female canary).

Table 1. Effects of photoperiod and duration of the period between castration and implantation on the courtship response to intrahypothalamic testosterone propionate in male doves

Condition prior to castration*		Photoperiod		Pre-implantation period	Courtship peak durations**(s) median (range)		
testes	courtship	pre♂	post♂	(days)	chasing	bowing	nest sol.
1	D	C	14	14	30	76 (15–77)	4 (0–2)	25 (3–92)
2	D	C	14	14	90	0[b] (0–23)	—	0[b] (0–63)
3	D	C	14	6	90	—	—	0[c] (0–18)
4	R	NC	6	6	30	14.5[a] (0–23)	0 (0–10)	—

*D, testes fully developed; R, testes regressed; C, full courtship; NC, no courtship displayed.
**Groups 2, 3, 4 are compared statistically with group 1 (Mann–Whitney U-test) two-tailed
   [a]$p < 0.05$; [b]$p < 0.02$; [c]$p < 0.002$,
—Behaviour not displayed.

To assess the influence of gonadotrophin level on the response to intrahypo-thalamic implants of TP, male doves were established on short daylengths (6 L/18 D) for a month before castration and compared with a group maintained in similar conditions on a long photoperiod (14 L/10 D) (Hutchison, 1976). The short day (SD) group showed a pronounced decline in testicular weight and courtship behaviour prior to castration. After intrahypothalamic implanta-tion of TP, there were no significant differences between the groups in duration of courtship response (Table 1), but the SD group displayed aggressive court-ship during significantly fewer daily tests. If it can be assumed that this level of gonadotrophin differed immediately prior to castration and subsequently between these groups, the overall similarity in behavioural effects of implants suggests that gonadotrophin level, photoperiod, and sexual experience im-mediately prior to castration have little influence on the effectiveness of in-trahypothalamic TP. However, males brought into the laboratory with sea-sonally regressed testes in early winter appear to be markedly less sensitive to intrahypothalamic TP than birds implanted at other times of the year (Hutchison, 1976). The difference in effects of photoperiod on male sexual responsiveness to androgen may reflect not only the obvious phylogenetic differences between mammalian and avian forms, but also differences between a highly photoperiodic species, the hamster, and one that is less photoperiodic, the dove.

Social Stimuli

There appear to be no reports in the literature of the influence of social stimuli on the effectiveness of androgen in inducing male sexual behaviour. In doves, this effect has been studied by utilizing the social environment of males in visual isolation, but auditory contact as an experimental variable. In such conditions, the male utters a series of vocalizations (Fig. 3) which are thought to serve as 'contact calls', and which, since they disappear after castration at a similar rate to courtship behaviour, are clearly hormone-dependent. Therefore males subjected to long-term androgen deprivation following castration fail to vocalize and consequently do not hear their own vocalizations or those of other males. It can be argued that this social depriva-tion could contribute to the decline in behavioural effectiveness of intra-hypothalamic implants in conditions of long-term androgen deficit. In order to study this possibility (Hutchison, in prep.), two groups of long-term cas-trates (90-days) were maintained in visual isolation in conditions that allowed one group to hear the vocalizations of sexually active males, and auditorily isolated the other group. A third group of 90-day castrates which could hear vocalizations received a priming dose of TP ($3 \times 300\mu g$) after 70 days which brought them into a condition where they would vocalize. All three groups received intrahypothalamic implants 90 days after castration and were tested for courtship behaviour. Castrates which received neither vocalizations nor the hormonal priming doses showed the least response to the intrahypothalamic implants (Fig. 7). The group that were subjected to vocalizations without the hormonal priming doses were intermediate in their response to implants between the other groups. These results suggest that social stimulation in the form of vocalizations from sexually active males can compensate partly for the decline in responsiveness to intrahypothalamic androgen. However, the decline in sensitivity of the brain to testosterone would appear to be contingent upon the absence of endogenous androgen, because the priming dosages combined with vocal stimulation had the greatest compensatory effect.

The results of the studies reviewed above indicate a direct effect of both environmental factors and long-term androgen deprivation on the behavioural responsiveness to androgen. Whether these variables have different foci of action on the brain has yet to be resolved. But it is conceivable that the influence of environmental factors such as short photoperiod or deprivation of social stimuli are mediated by an effect of low circulating hormone levels on the sensitivity of hypothalamic cells to androgenic steroids. The final section of this chapter is concerned with the possible cellular mechanisms that may be involved.

BIOCHEMICAL FACTORS AND CENTRAL CHANGES IN ANDROGEN SENSITIVITY

Androgen Uptake and Behaviour

Before discussing biochemical changes induced in the brain by prolonged androgen deficit, it is necessary to establish whether hormone-induced cellular events can be related to sexual behaviour. Some evidence is coming to light to suggest that there may be a basis for this relationship. Using the lordosis behaviour of the female rat, McEwen et al. (1975) have demonstrated that the duration of retention of ^{3}H-oestradiol on nuclear receptors in the basomedial hypothalamus lasts for less than 12 h. By contrast, lordosis does not appear until at least 20–24 h after intravenous injection or intrahypothalamic implantation of oestradiol. The behavioural effects of the hormone appear to be expressed in the absence of occupied nuclear receptor sites in areas of the brain known to be sensitive to oestrogen, suggesting that the intervening time to appearance of the behavioural effect of oestradiol is due to metabolic events in the cell initiated by the hormone. Intracranial application of actinomycin D, an RNA synthesis inhibitor, blocks the induction of lordosis by oestrogen, suggesting that the cellular events initiated after nuclear binding of oestrogen involve the genome. A further relationship between oestrogen and lordosis behaviour has been established by a comparison of hypothalamic oestrogen affinities and threshold differences in the induction of lordosis behaviour by oestradiol between rats, guinea pigs and hamsters (Feder et al., 1974). Thus ovariectomized rats and guinea pigs have a higher hypothalamic affinity for

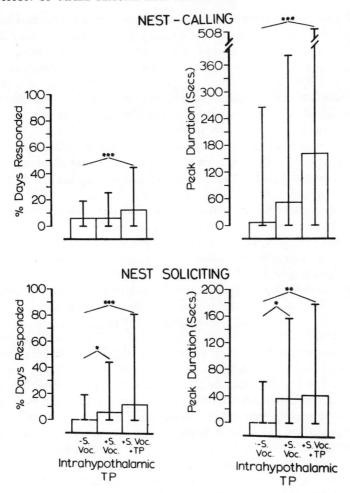

Fig. 7. The vocal (nest calling) and courtship (nest soliciting) behaviour of long-term castrated male doves that received implants of TP in the preoptic-anterior hypothalamic region. Three groups are compared (see text) (a) castrates in auditory and visual isolation (-S. Voc.), (b) castrates in visual isolation which were able to hear the vocalizations (perch calls and nest calls) of sexually active males (+ S. Voc.), (c) castrates in visual isolation which were able to hear vocalizations of sexually active males and which received 3 priming dosages of intramuscular TP 70 days after castration (+ S. Voc. + TP). Percentage days responded, the number of days when a particular behaviour was displayed expressed as a percentage; peak total duration, the longest of the daily durations of display during either a 3-min courtship test or 10-min observation of vocal behaviour

^{3}H-oestradiol (as indicated by tissue/plasma ratios) than hamsters. The former species are also more responsive behaviourally to exogenous oestrogen than are hamsters. These workers suggest that species differences in behavioural response to steroid hormones may be partly a function of differential target tissue affinity for the hormone and speculate that individual differences in male behavioural responsiveness to androgen may be due to similar factors. There do appear to be differences in plasma testosterone levels between 'high activity' adult male guinea pigs (showing ejaculation during 2 behavioural tests) and 'low activity' males (showing no ejaculations) (Harding and Feder, 1976a). However, no differences in brain uptake or metabolism of ^{3}H-testosterone could be detected between high and low activity males (Harding and Feder, 1976b).

The relationship between retention of androgen in target cells within the hypothalamus and the induction of male behaviour has not been investigated. Unfortunately many of the data from studies with intrahypothalamic implants in birds and mammals involve spaced behavioural observations which preclude analysis of latency of effect. But they do indicate a substantial delay in behavioural activation, ranging from one to several days after implantation of TP (Table 2). In castrated male doves, significant nuclear binding to hypothalamic cells occurs within 1 h of intravenous injection of ^{3}H-testosterone (Zigmond and Hutchison, in prep.). The duration of retention is unknown at present. However, the expression of male courtship behaviour clearly requires the sustained action of androgen on the hypothalamus (Hutchison, 1976). As described above, this could be demonstrated by testing for the behavioural effects of intrahypothalamic TP implants in the period after the peak response to implants normally occurs. Little behavioural response was obtained from implanted castrates unless behavioural testing was initiated soon (within 12 h) after implantation. It would appear probable that in the male dove, whose sexual behaviour is highly androgen-dependent, the functioning of the mechanisms underlying courtship requires the continuous action of androgen; an action which is likely to involve secondary metabolic effects of the hormone on brain cells occurring after nuclear binding of testosterone has taken place.

Variability in Androgen-binding

On the basis of studies in rats of the inverse relationship between peak uptake of ^{3}H-oestradiol and the period between ovariectomy and intravenous injection of hormone (McGuire and Lisk, 1969), Lisk, (1971) has suggested that oestradiol receptor molecules become inactivated during the prolonged absence of circulating oestrogen. This hypothesis could not be established conclusively because the labelled oestradiol was injected intravenously, and delays in uptake of oestradiol may have been due to peripheral factors rather than the steroid-binding properties of hypothalamic cells. However, following this argument, the tentative suggestion could be made (Hutchison, 1969)

Table 2. Studies of the action of testosterone on male sexual behaviour using intrahypothalamic implants

Author	Species	Type of behaviour	Latency (days)	Duration (days)	Post-operative period (days)	Type	Implant
Barfield (1969)	Capon	Copulation Courtship waltzing	4–17	34	?	Bilateral	Fused in 27 gauge tubing
Barfield (1971)	Dove	Copulation Aggression	?	?	21	Bilateral	0.5 mg fused, spherical, or powder in 22 gauge tube
Cristensen and Clemens (1974)	Rat	Copulation	?	?	Variable (21 days no ejaculation)	Bilateral	Replaceableconnulae containing powder, 15 μg/3 days × 5
Davidson (1966	Rat	Copulation	5–6	?	Variable (21 days no ejaculation)	Unilateral	Fused inside 22 gauge tube or pellet ejected
Hutchison (1967, 1971)	Dove	Courtship	1–4	5–8	30	Unilateral	33 μg fused, spherical
Johnson and Davidson (1972	Rat	Copulation	6–8	7	Variable (21 days no ejaculation)	Unilateral	180–220 μg powder in tube
Kierniesky and Gerall (1973)	Rat	Copulation	6	9	Variable (28–37 days no ejaculation)	Bilateral	Fused in 20 gauge tube
Lisk (1967)	Rat	Copulation	10–21	?	Variable (14 days no mounting)	Bilateral	179 μg fused, spherical or fused inside 200 μm diameter tube

? Information not available.

that one factor responsible for the ineffectiveness of TP implants in long-term castrated male doves is an increased degradation or inactivation of hypothalamic 'receptor' macromolecules that bind testosterone. A similar suggestion has been made on the basis of behavioural studies of the female rat to account for the apparent decline in effectiveness of oestrogen in inducing lordosis behaviour. As Damassa and Davidson (1973) put it: 'receptor mechanisms in relevant target tissues decline in sensitivity as time elapses after removal of trophic hormone, possibly due to atrophy of certain structures and/or breakdown of biosynthetic mechanisms.' Beach and Orndoff (1974) have also concluded from similar experimental evidence that 'the response of CNS mechanisms to exogenous estrogen decreases after estrogen deprivation.' There appears to be a consensus of opinion therefore that a decline in sensitivity of receptor systems in the brain for steroid hormones may account for the postgonadectomy decline in sexual responsiveness to these steroids.

This hypothesis is difficult to test with regard to androgen action on the brain in mammals, because the testosterone-binding system in the hypothalamus appears to have a lower affinity for androgen than does the analogous system in the female for oestrogen (see Kelley and Pfaff, this volume Chapter 7 for further discussion). Limited-capacity binding of testosterone occurs to a small degree in nuclear fractions of cells obtained from the hypothalamo–preoptic area and the amygdala of castrated rats (McEwen and Pfaff, 1970). The binding of testosterone to soluble cytoplasmic macromolecules from hypothalamic tissue obtained from adult castrated rats has been described in a number of studies (reviewed by Naess et al., 1975; Zigmond, 1975, Farquar et al., 1976, McEwen, 1976). Thus the hypothalamus of the male rat appears to have androgen-reactive cells. But the concentration and kinetics of uptake do not differ from the cortex (Naess and Attramadal, 1974). This is possibly because cells taking up androgen constitute only a small proportion of the total cell population in the hypothalamo–preoptic area, and a selective concentration of radioactivity in this brain area may be masked when total uptake is measured. As regards the macromolecule constituting the receptor, the soluble form in the cytoplasm is thought to have a sedimentation rate constant of 8.65S (Kato and Onouchi, 1973) or 6–7S (Naess et al., 1975). However, as Zigmond (1975) has pointed out, the data available suggest that either there are fewer androgen than oestrogen binding sites in the mammalian brain, or the binding of androgen is weaker than that of oestrogen.

There have been few studies of androgen uptake and retention in birds. But the results available suggest that the avian hypothalamus may contain testosterone-specific macromolecules in hypothalamic cell nuclei. Subcellular fractionation studies have shown that, after intravenous injection of ^{3}H-testosterone in castrated male barbary dove, the concentration of radioactivity is fourteen times higher in purified nuclei isolated from the whole hypothalamus than in nuclei isolated from the cerebrum (Zigmond et al., 1972). Preliminary results (Hutchison and Zigmond, 1976 and unpubl. data) indicate that the binding of testosterone in nuclear cell fractions from the anterior hypothalami of the castrated male barbary doves is of the limited-capacity type. Thus the nuclear binding of ^{3}H-testosterone was reduced by 97% when the labelled hormone was preceded by unlabelled testosterone, a competitive reduction in binding that compares well with that obtained from a known peripheral target tissue, the vas deferens (99% reduction in binding). No competition effect could be detected in whole tissue homogenates. The regional uptake of ^{3}H-testosterone has also been studied in the brain of the castrated male dove using autoradiography (Martinez-Vargas, pers. commun.). Concentrations of labelled cells were found following ^{3}H-testosterone injection in the preoptico–strial region; the basal hypothalamic region, the amygdaloid area and the midbrain nucleus intercollicularis. The distribution is very similar to that observed after injection of ^{3}H-oestradiol (Martinez-Vargas et al., 1976), though labelling of cells in all regions was less intense after ^{3}H-testosterone injection.

Given that the dove hypothalamus of the male dove contains a saturable receptor system for testosterone, it was possible to test the hypothesis that a prolonged androgen deficit influences the binding of testosterone to nuclear receptors by comparing binding in long- and short-term castrates, matched according to their display of courtship before castration, and in a similar endocrine condition prior to castration as judged by testicular weight (Hutchison and Zigmond, 1976; Zigmond and Hutchison, in prep.). ^{3}H-testosterone was injected intramuscularly 7 or approximately 90 days after castration. The results indicate that nuclear radioactivity was higher in the 90-day group than in the 7-day group, suggesting that more ^{3}H-testosterone is bound in the long-term castrates (Fig. 8). Contrary to our predictions it would appear that the hypothalamus of the long-term castrate has a greater capacity for testosterone-binding than the short-term castrate. It could be argued that because the labelled hormone was injected intramuscularly, the differences in nuclear radioactivity were due to differences between 7- and 90-day castrates in plasma-binding proteins, metabolism or clearance of the hormone. However, as there was no significant difference between whole tissue homogenates prepared from the hypothalami of the two groups, the same concentrations of hormone appear to have reached the brain.

It could also be argued that the difference in uptake of testosterone between long- and short-term castrates is due to residual binding of enodogenous androgen which gradually dissociates from the plasma-binding proteins. However, this process is likely to be completed 2–3 days after castration, and is therefore unlikely to contribute to the difference in binding between 7- and 90-day castrates. Increases in testosterone-binding in the long-term castrates would appear to indicate, therefore, an increase in available hypothalamic binding sites for testosterone.

There are few reports of differences in nuclear binding in the mammalian hypothalamus that might be a function of long-term androgen deficit. This is presumably due to difficulties in identifying saturable nuclear binding in hypo-

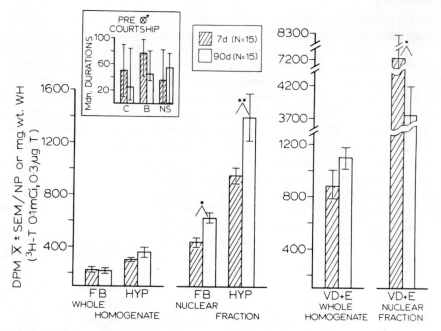

Fig. 8. Uptake of ³H-testosterone in male doves which had been castrated 90 or 7 days before intramuscular injection of isotope. Bound radioactivity is expressed as mean DPM/mg wet weight for whole tissue homogenates (WH) or as DPM/nuclear pellet for the nuclear fractions (NP) of forebrain (FB), hypothalamus (HYP) and vas deferens (VD + E) samples. Levels of precastration behaviour (C, chasing, B, bowing, NS, nest soliciting), which were not significantly different between 7- and 90-day castrates are shown in the insert. 7- and 90-day groups are compared statistically, **p < 0.01 *p < 0.05, Student T-test. (After Zigmond and Hutchison, in prep.)

thalamic cells. However, in their studies of testosterone-binding in the cytosol fraction, Naess and Attramadal (1974) found that, although the pattern of testosterone uptake was basically similar in male rats castrated 2 or 30 days before injection of the isotope, cytosol macromolecules isolated from the anterior hypothalamus, cortex, adenohypophysis, and prostate of 2-day castrates contained higher levels of radioactivity than the 30-day group. These authors do not point to the significance of their result, but it would appear that endogenous testosterone dissociating from plasma-binding proteins after castration does not compete for binding sites with tracer dosages given 2 days after castration. Studies of testosterone uptake in male rats castrated 24 h prior to the injection of ³H-testosterone showed markedly less (by a factor of 20) testosterone-binding in pooled nuclear fractions of hypothalamic tissue (Monbon et al., 1974) than rats castrated 48 h prior to isotope injection; a result which is in the direction of the difference in nuclear binding described above for long and short-term castrated male doves.

A major study (McEwen et al., 1974) of the binding of corticosterone to hippocampal cells of male rats is of relevance to the interpretation of increased binding of testosterone in castrated doves. These workers found a biphasic increase in cell nuclear binding sites of the hippocampus following bilateral adrenalectomy. The first phase occurred after 2 h and could probably be accounted for in terms of a disappearance of endogenous corticosterone from binding sites; the second phase was detectable 18 h after adrenalectomy and reached a plateau 2–7 days later, indicating an elevation in amount of binding protein in the hippocampus. As these authors point out, the elevation could be due to the manufacture of new binding proteins or the 'unmasking' of pre-existing binding sites. This suggests an apparent negative feedback control of a brain corticosteroid-binding protein by the adrenal gland which may be of physiological significance, because 'changes in level of brain corticosteroid-binding protein may occur in rats subjected to prolonged periods of either excessive or reduced levels of corticosteroid secretion and not only under the abnormal conditions of adrenalectomy'. This is an important point in view of the suggestion that fluctuations in the hormone-specific receptors may be influenced by endogenous hormonal conditions. If such an interpretation of the testosterone-binding data obtained from long-term castrates can be made, it can be suggested that the level of endogenous testosterone-binding in the brain may be related to the level of testosterone-binding in peripheral plasma. Whether or not such an interpretation is valid will depend on further work.

The purpose of studying changes in hypothalamic testosterone uptake as a function of time after castration was undertaken initially to test the hypothesis that the binding mechanism is inactivated in the prolonged absence of endogenous androgen. This clearly was not demonstrated in our experiments and theoretically an increase in binding sites for testosterone might be expected to produce an increase in effect of the hormone on the target cell associated with behaviour. The question of whether the pronounced increase in hypothalamic binding of testosterone in long-term castrates can be related to the decline in behavioural sensitivity to intrahypothalamic TP remains unanswered. It is only possible to speculate on the basis of the evidence available at present, but it can be suggested that although a prolonged androgen deficit results in an overall increase in testosterone-binding sites, there is a proportional decrease in binding sites occupied by testosterone 'relevant' for components of sexual behaviour due to an increase in other testosterone-binding sites which are 'irrelevant' for sexual behaviour. This theory is obviously highly speculative and there is no evidence as yet as to whether particular cells or binding sites for testosterone are differentiated to bear any special relationship to sexual behaviour or any other neuroendocrine function of the hypothalamus.

Androgen Metabolism

In addition to the possible effects on testosterone-binding in the hypothalamus, long-term fluctuations in androgen level may influence the metabolism of testosterone in the brain. Testosterone is converted within the mammalian brain to a number of Δ^4 reduced metabolites by reduction of the Δ^4-3-ketone group notably by the 5α-steroid reductase enzyme which is probably associated with the cell endoplasmic reticulum. (See also Feder, this volume Chapter 12). *In vitro* studies of testosterone metabolism in incubated slices of selected brain regions of male and female rats indicate that the principal metabolite in all regions of the brain is 5α-dihydrotestosterone (DHT) (5α-androstan-17β-ol-3-one). Androstenedione (4-androstene-3, 17- dione) and 3α-androstanediol (3α, 17β-dihydroxy-5α-androstone) are also consistently formed (Denef and McEwen, 1972). The pattern of conversion to DHT differs according to the brain area. Thus in males, the highest conversion rate to DHT is in the midbrain, exceeding the cortex by 2–3 orders of magnitude. The midbrain is closely followed by the hypothalamus and thalamus. Metabolism to DHT in the preoptic region, hippocampus, and cerebellum exceeds the cortex only slightly. There appear to be no regional differences in the formation of androstanediol and androstenedione (Denef *et al.*, 1973). In terms of both somatic and neuroendocrine effects DHT has an androgenic potency equivalent to testosterone in stimulating growth of peripheral target organs such as the rat seminal vesicles and prostate (Wilson and Gloyna, 1970; Feder, 1971) and in a negative feedback effect on the release of pituitary LH. Significant conversion of labelled testosterone to DHT accompanies these stimulatory effects (Bruchovsky and Wilson, 1968; Robel *et al.*, 1971; Bruchovsky, 1971) and DHT is accumulated in both cell nuclei and cytoplasm. This metabolite has also been detected in the hypothalamus and pituitary of rats (Jaffe, 1969; Stern and Eisenfeld, 1971) and doves after systemic injection of ^{3}H-testosterone (Stern, 1972), but it is not clear from this work whether testosterone is converted peripherally and transported to the brain or converted within the brain. Incubated slices of rat pituitary, amygdala, and cortex all convert testosterone to DHT (Kniewald *et al.*, 1970) confirming that the 5α-reductase enzymes, essential for the conversion, are present in brain tissue. Other studies (Zigmond and Hutchison, in prep.) using thin-layer chromatography to estimate proportion of radioactivity associated with metabolites in nuclear fractions following injection of ^{3}H-testosterone into long-term castrated male doves (Fig. 9) indicate that there is substantial conversion of testosterone to DHT. Because ^{3}H-testosterone was injected systemically, *in vitro* studies are required to establish whether the conversion occurred centrally or peripherally. However, if the assumption is made that conversion takes place in the hypothalamus, the hypothesis can be put forward that the ineffectiveness of TP implants in long-term castrates is due to increased conversion of testosterone to behaviourally inactive metabolites. Whether or not testosterone is increasingly converted to DHT after castration in the male dove remains to be established. But increased 5α-reductase activity occurs in the hypothalamus (Denef *et al.*, 1973) and hypophysis (Thien *et al.*, 1974) after castration in male rats. Behavioural

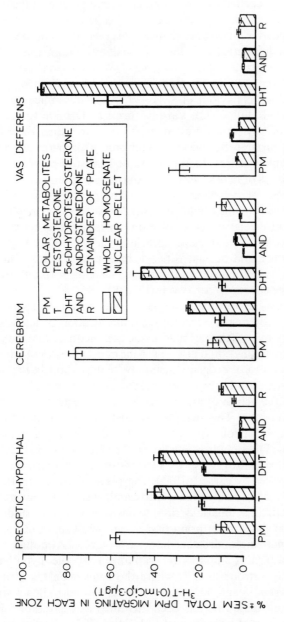

Fig. 9. Radioactivity associated with various androgens after intramuscular injection of ³H-testosterone in long-term (90-day) castrates determined by thin-layer chromatography. (After Zigmond and Hutchison, in prep.)

evidence that DHT is ineffective as regards male courtship behaviour would help to substantiate this hypothesis.

There is some dispute regarding the behavioural potency of DHT. Much of the work has been carried out in mammals where potency appears to depend on the species examined. For example, DHT is less effective in inducing male couplatory behaviour in castrated male rats, whether injected systemically (Feder, 1971) or implanted into the hypothalamus (Johnston and Davidson, (1972) than in castrated male hamsters (Whalen and De Bold, 1974), guinea pigs (Alsum and Goy, 1974) or rhesus monkeys (Phoenix, 1974). DHT restores male sexual behaviour in Swiss–Webster house mice but not in other strains (Luttge and Hall, 1973). Various forms of DHT have been implanted intrahypothalamically into castrated male doves to assess the effects of this metabolite on courtship behaviour (Hutchison in preparation) and dihydro-testosterone propionate (DHT) appears to be almost as potent as testosterone in terms of numbers of males showing a courtship response after implantation. But the low levels of behaviour were far lower than those induced by TP (Fig. 10). As a potential metabolite of testosterone, DHT is therefore probably of little significance relative to testosterone in the central activation of male courtship behaviour. This does not preclude the possibility that DHT is as-sociated with other androgen-sensitive behavioural systems. Thus the vocal behaviour of castrated male doves is far more responsive to intrahypothalamic DHTP than is the courtship behaviour (Fig. 10).

Although increased conversion of testosterone to DHT, as an inactive me-tabolite, could theoretically decrease the concentration of testosterone avail-able to bind to hypothalamic cells associated with sexual behaviour, 5α-reduction of testosterone could also lower the concentration of androgen avail-able for conversion to oestrogen which may be important in the activation of male sexual behaviour. There is now evidence that aromatization may be an essential step in the action of androgens on brain mechanisms of mammalian male sexual behaviour. This evidence consists mainly of the demonstration that male sexual behaviour cannot be restored in castrated male rats using non-aromatizable DHT, androstanediol, and androsterone, but can be restored using aromatizable androgens such as the testosterone, androstenedione, and-rostenediol (reviewed by Parrott, 1975). There is also little doubt that the mam-malian brain has the capacity to aromatize androgens (i.e. convert to C_{18} phe-nolic steroids with an aromatic A ring) to oestrogen. In vitro studies (Naftolin et al., 1972) have shown that brain tissue from adult male and female rats is capable of aromatizing androstenedione to oestrone. Although only a small percentage ($\leq 1.0\%$) is apparently aromatized by the hypothalamus, the concentration of oestrone in cells where the conversion takes place may be high. Thus between 35 and 50% of cell nuclear bound radioactivity in limbic structures of adult male rats has been identified as oestradiol following ^{3}H-testosterone injection (Lieberburg and McEwen, 1975). So far the aromatiza-tion of testosterone to oestradiol has not been demonstrated in the endogenous steroid pool of the brain.

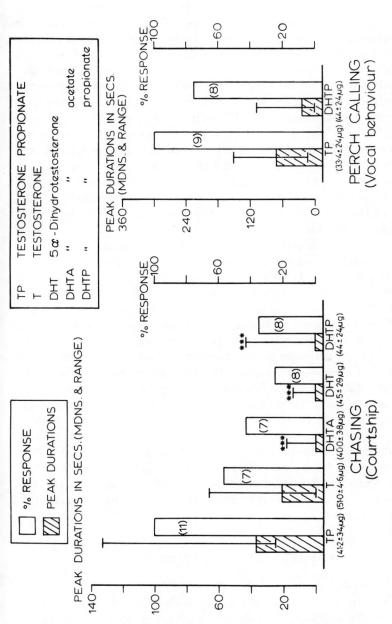

Fig. 10. Comparison between the effects of intrahypothalamic testosterone and its presumed metabolite 5α-dihydro-testosterone on patterns of courtship (chasing) and vocal behaviour (perch calling) in groups of castrated male doves. The bracketed figures within the histograms indicate sample numbers, bracketed figures below the ordinate indicate mean implant weights ± standard error of the mean. Groups implanted with testosterone propionate are compared statistically with all the other implanted groups. (***p < 0.002; Mann–Whitney U test, two-tailed.)

Whether aromatization of testosterone in the hypothalamus is of any significance in mediating the action of androgens in brain mechanisms of dove courtship behaviour has yet to be resolved. If this is the case, there is some significance in the discovery that hypothalamic implants of oestradiol monobenzoate (OB) not only induce longer durations of nest-orientated behaviour in male castrates (nest soliciting, Hutchison, 1971), but are also more effective in restoring these behaviour patterns to precastration levels than TP (reviewed by Hutchison, 1976). In contrast, OB implants induce virtually no aggressive courtship (chasing and bowing). Changes in metabolism of testosterone in the hypothalamus of long-term castrates that involve a decline in effective level of testosterone and an increase in DHT are more likely to influence the androgen-sensitive aggressive courtship patterns than nest-orientated courtship which appears to be less specific in its steroid sensitivity. The apparent differential hormonal sensitivity of these two components of male courtship be-behaviour serves to illustrate the difficulties of establishing the manner in which changes in androgen metabolism, consequent upon a long-term androgen deficit, may influence the hypothalamic or other hormone-sensitive brain cells underlying male courtship.

Discussion of possible cellular factors involved in changes in hormonal sensitivity of brain mechanisms underlying male sexual behaviour must take into account the very recent findings on the influence of hormones on neurotransmitters. This work is still in its early stages. However, there seems little doubt that the binding of androgen to cellular receptors and genomic effects of the hormone represent an initial stage in an array of hormonal actions on the brain. Subsequent effects of prolonged hormonal deficit could well involve the influence of androgen on catecholamines, which have been implicated in the control of male sexual behaviour (Everitt, this volume Chapter 17 and Meyerson and Malmnas Chapter 16). For example, gonadectomy influences the hypothalamic activity of tyrosine hydroxylase, the rate-limiting enzyme for catecholamine synthesis (Kizer et al., 1974). Lack of a behavioural effect of androgen in long-term castrates might be due to changes in the synthesis or axonal and dendritic transport of newly synthesized enzyme. Such effects are purely speculative at present, and as McEwen (1976) points out that there seems little doubt that the action of hormonal steroids on the brain are multiple, involving not only the biosynthesis of neurotransmitters but also their postsynaptic receptors.

SUMMARY AND CONCLUSIONS

There is increasing evidence that androgen influences male reproductive behaviour by direct action on a discrete area of the brain, the anterior hypothalamic–preoptic complex. This chapter explores factors underlying the action of androgen on the brain which contribute to variability in behavioural responsiveness of the male.

A distinction can be drawn between short-term, rapid fluctuations in plasma androgen level, which appear to be immediate consequences of sexual stimuli, and the long-term changes in androgen level which accompany seasonal fluctuations in testicular secretion. Little is known at present about the way in which fluctuations in androgen level measured at the periphery relate to concentration of androgen in the brain or to the functioning of brain mechanisms of male sexual behaviour. Analysis of the temporal relationship between rapid elevation of androgen level and male behaviour provides little evidence for a facilitatory effect of change in androgen level on the display of male sexual behaviour. In contrast, long-term deficits in endogenous androgen level have profound effects on male sexual responsiveness to exogenous androgen. Thus an inverse relationship can be demonstrated between the behavioural effects of intrahypothalamic implants of testosterone propionate and the period between castration and implantation in the male dove, indicating that hypothalamic or other brain mechanisms associated with the hormonal activation of male precopulatory courtship behaviour become less sensitive to androgen with time after castration. The diminishing effectiveness of intrahypothalamic implants on male courtship behaviour may be a function of the changing steroid-binding properties of intracellular androgen receptors within the hypothalamus. However, social (vocalizations) or photoperiodic stimuli act to compensate partially for the effects of the prolonged androgen deficit. These environmental stimuli may act directly on androgen receptors of hypothalamic cells or indirectly via extrahypothalamic systems mediating the responsiveness of these cells to androgen.

This chapter emphasizes the point that relationships between androgen and brain mechanisms of sexual behaviour are likely to be understood not in terms of the short-term availability of hormone, but in terms of when and to what degree cells in the brain associated with sexual behaviour are 'sensitive' to circulating androgen. The hormonal sensitivity of such cells may be a function of the availability or affinity of specific cytoplasmic and nuclear macromolecules for androgen. But changes in metabolism of the hormone and chemistry of the androgen-sensitive cell are undoubtedly also involved.

We are a long way from understanding the dynamics of the relationship between steroid hormones and the cellular mechanisms associated with hormone-dependent behaviour. Until more direct evidence is forthcoming attempts to link cellular and behavioural events must at best remain highly speculative. There is no doubt that the dynamics of male sexual display are also influenced by other factors such as the behaviour of the female partner, prior sexual experience, and reproductive condition.

ACKNOWLEDGEMENTS

I am grateful to Robert Hinde, Rosemary Hutchison and Barry Keverne for their comments on the manuscript. The work reported in this Chapter received generous support from the Medical Research Council.

REFERENCES

Alsum, P. and Goy, R. W. (1974) Actions of esters of testosterone, dihydro-testosterone or estradiol on sexual behaviour in castrated male guinea pigs, *Horm. Behav.*, **5**, 207–17.

Anon. (1970) Effects of sexual activity on beard growth in man *Nature*, **226**, 869–70.

Aronson, L. A. and Cooper, M. L. (1968) Desensitization of the glans penis and sexual behavior in cats. In: *Perspectives in Reproduction and Sexual Behavior*. M. Diamond (ed), Indiana University Press, Bloomington, pp. 51–82.

Barfield, R. J. (1969) Activation of copulatory behavior by androgen implanted into the preoptic area of the male fowl. *Horm. Behav.*, **1**, 37–52.

Barfield, R. J. (1971) Activation of sexual and aggressive behaviour by androgen implanted into the male ring dove brain, *Endocrinology*, **89**, 1470–76.

Beach, F. A. (1974) Behavioral endocrinology and the study of reproduction. *Biology of Reproduction*, **10**, 2–18.

Beach, F. A. and Holtz. Tucker, A. M. (1949) Effects of different concentrations of androgen upon sexual behavior in castrated male rats. *J. Comp. Physiol. Psychol.*, **42**, 433–453.

Beach, F. A. and Levinson, G. (1950) Effects of androgen on the glans penis and mating behavior of castrated male rats, *J. Exp. Zool.*, **144**, 159–71.

Beach, F. A. and Orndoff, R. K. (1974) Variation in responsiveness of female rats to ovarian hormones as a function of preceding hormonal deprivation, *Horm. Behav.*, **5**, 201–5.

Bruchovsky, N. (1971) Comparison of the metabolites formed in rat prostate following the *in vivo* administration of seven natural androgens, *Endocrinology*, **89**, 1212–22.

Bruchovsky, N. and Wilson, J. D. (1968) The conversion of testosterone to 5α-androstan-17β-ol-3-one by rat prostate *in vivo* and *in vitro*, *J. Biol. Chem.* **343**, 2012–21.

Burley, R. A. (1976) The integration of oestrous behaviour in the female Mongolian gerbil, *Ph.D. Thesis*, Cambridge Univ.

Challis, J. R. G., Naftolin, F., Davies, J., Ryan, K. J., and Lanman, T. (1976) Endogenous Steroids in neuroendocrine tissues, In: *Subcellular Mechanisms in Reproductive Neuroendocrinology*. F. Naftolin, K. J. Ryan and I. J. Davies (eds), Elsevier, Amsterdam, pp. 247–263.

Christensen, L. W. and Clemens, L. G. (1974) Intra-hypothalamic implants of testosterone or estradiol and resumption of masculine sexual behaviour in long-term castrated male rats, *Endocrinology*, **95**, 984–90.

Convey, E. M., Bretschneider, E., Hafs, H. D. and Oxender, W. D. (1971) Serum levels of LH, prolactin and growth hormone after ejaculation in bulls, *Biol. Reprod.*, **5**, 20–4.

Cooper, K. K. and Aronson, L. R. (1974) Effects of castration on neural afferent responses from the penis of the domestic cat, *Physiol. Behav.*, **12**, 93–107.

Damassa, D. and Davidson, J. M. (1973) Effect of ovariectomy and constant light on responsiveness to estrogen in the rat, *Horm. Behav.*, **4**, 269–79.

David G. F. X. and Anand-Kumar, T. C. (1974) Transfer of steroid hormones from blood to cerebrospinal fluid in the rhesus monkey *Neuroendocrinology*, **14**, 114–20.

Davidson, J. M. (1966) Activation of the male rat's sexual behavior by intra-cerebral implantation of androgen, *Endocrinology*, **79**, 783–94.

Davidson, J. M. and Bloch, G. J. (1969) Neuroendocrine aspects of male reproduction, *Biol. Reprod.*, **1**, 67–92.

Davidson, J. M., Smith, E. R., and Bowers, C. Y. (1973) Effects of mating on gonadotrophin release in the female rat, *Endocrinology*, **93**, 1185–92.

Davis, G. J. and Meyer, R. K. (1973) Seasonal variation in LH and FSH of bilaterally castrated snow-shoe hares, *Gen. Comp. Endocrinol.*, **20**, 61–8.

Denef, C. and McEwen, B. S. (1972) Regional and sex differences in the metabolism of testosterone in the rat brain. Proceedings of the IVth International Congress of Endocrinology, *Excerpta Medica, International Congress Series* No. 256 (abstract 302).

Denef, C., Magnus, C., and McEwen, B. S. (1973) Sex differences of testosterone metabolism in rat pituitary and brain, *J. Endocrinol.*, **59**, 605–21.

Farquhar, M. N., Namiki, H., and Gorbman, A. (1976) Cytoplasmic and nuclear metabolism of testosterone in brains of neonatal and prepubertal rats, *Neuroendocrinology*, **20**, 358–72.

Feder, H. H. (1971) The comparative actions of testosterone propionate and 5α-androstan-17β ol-3-one propionate on the reproductive behaviour, physiology, and morphology of male rats, *J. Endocrinol.*, **51**, 241–52.

Feder, H. H., Siegel, H. and Wade, G. N. (1974) Uptake of [6,7-³H] estradiol-17β in ovariectomized rats, guinea pigs, and hamsters: Correlation with species differences in behavioural responsiveness to estradiol, *Brain Res.*, **71**, 93–103.

Feder, H. H., Story, A., Goodwin, D., and Reboulleau, C. (1977) Testosterone and "5α-dihydrotestosterone" levels in peripheral plasma of male and female ring doves *(Streptopelia risoria)* during the reproductive cycle, *Biol. Reprod.*, **16**, 666–77.

Fletcher, I. C. and Lindsay, D. R. (1971) Effect of oestrogen on oestrous behaviour and its variation with season in the ewe, *J. Endocrinol.*, **50**, 685–96.

Follett, B. K. and Farner, D. S. (1966) The effect of the daily photoperiod on gonadal growth, neuro-hypophysical hormone content and neuro-secretion in the hypothalamo-hypophysial system of the Japanese quail *(Coturnix coturnix japonica)*, *Gen. Comp. Endocrinol.*, **7**, 111–24.

Gombe, S., Hall, W. C., McEntree, K., Hansel, W., and Pickett, B. W. (1973) Regulation of blood levels of LH in bulls: influence of age, breed, sexual stimulation and temporal fluctuations, *J. Reprod. Fert.*, **35**, 493–503.

Grunt, J. A. and Young, W. C. (1952) Differential reactivity of individuals and the response of the male guinea pig to testosterone propionate, *Endocrinology*, **51**, 237–48.

Grunt, J. A. and Young, W. C. (1953) Consistency of sexual behavior patterns in individual male guinea pigs following castration and androgen therapy, *J. Comp. Physiol. Psychol.*, **46**, 138–44.

Haltmeyer, C. L. and Eik-Nes, K. B. (1969) Plasma levels of testosterone in male rabbits following copulation, *J. Reprod. Fert.*, **19**, 273–7.

Harding, C. F. and Feder, H. H. (1976a) Relation between individual differences in sexual behaviour and plasma testosterone levels in the guinea pig, *Endocrinology*, **98**, 1198–205.

Harding, C. F. and Feder, H. H. (1976b) Relation of uptake and metabolism of [1,2,6,7-³H] testosterone to individual differences in sexual behaviour in male guinea pigs, *Brain Res.*, **105**, 137–49.

Hart, B. L. (1967) Testosterone regulation of sexual reflexes in spinal male rats, *Science N.Y.*, **155**, 1283–84.

Herbert, J. (1971) The role of the pineal gland in the control by light of the reproductive cycle of the ferret. In: *Ciba Foundation Symposium on the Pineal Gland*, G. E. W. Wolstenholme and J. A. Knights (eds.), Churchill, London, pp. 303–27.

Hinde, R. A. (1953) The Conflict between drives in the courtship and copulation of the chaffinch, *Behaviour*, **5**, 1–31.

Hinde, R. A. (1960) Energy models of motivation. *Sym. Soc. exp. Biol.*, **14**, 199–213.

Hinde, R. A. (1970) *Animal Behaviour: A Synthesis of Ethology and Comparative Psychology*, 2nd edn., McGraw-Hill, New York.

Hinde, R. A. and Steel, E. (1977) The influence of daylength and male vocalizations on the estrogen-dependent behavior of female canaries and budgerigars with discussion of data from other species. In: *Advances in the Study of Behavior*, 7 J.S. Rosenblatt, R. A. Hinde, E. Shaw, and C. Beer (eds.), Academic Press, N. Y., in press.

Hinde, R. A., Steel, E. and Follett, B. K. (1974) Effect of photoperiod on oestrogen-induced nest-building in ovariectomized or refractory female canaries *(Serinus canarius)*, *J. Reprod. Fert*, **40**, 383–99.

Hutchison, J. B. (1967) Initiation of courtship by hypothalamic implants of testosterone propionate in castrated doves *(Streptopelia risoria)*, *Nature, London*, **216**, 591–2.

Hutchison, J. B. (1969) Changes in hypothalamic responsiveness to testosterone in male Barbary doves *(Streptopelia risoria)*, *Nature, London*, **222**, 176–7.

Hutchison, J. B. (1970a) Differential effects of testosterone and oestradiol on male courtship in Barbary doves *(Streptopelia risoria)*, *Anim. Behav.*, **18**, 41–52.

Hutchison, J. B. (1970b) Influence of gonadal hormones on the hypothalamic integration of courtship behaviour in the Barbary dove, *J. Reprod. Fert. (Suppl.)*, **11**, 15–41.

Hutchison, J. B. (1971) Effects of hypothalamic implants of gonadal steroids on courtship behaviour in Barbary doves *(Streptopelia risoria)*, *J. Endocrinol.*, **50**, 97–113.

Hutchison, J. B. (1974a) Differential hypothalamic sensitivity to androgen in the activation of reproductive behaviour. In: *The Neurosciences, Third Study Volume*, O. Schmidt and F. G. Worden (eds.), M.I.T. Press, Cambridge, Mass., pp. 593–9.

Hutchison, J. B. (1974b) Post-castration decline in behavioural responsiveness to intrahypothalamic androgen in doves, *Brain Res.*, **80**, pp. 1–10.

Hutchison, J. B. (1974c) Effect of photoperiod on the decline in behavioural responsiveness to intrahypothalamic androgen in doves *(Streptopelia risoria)*, *J. Endocrinol.*, **63**, pp. 783–4.

Hutchison, J. B. (1976) Hypothalamic mechanisms of sexual behaviour, with special reference to birds. In: *Advances in the Study of Behaviour, Vol. 6*, J. S. Rosenblatt, R. A. Hinde, E. Shaw, and C. Beer (eds), Academic Press, New York, pp. 159–200.

Hutchison, J. B. and Lovari, S. (1976) Effects of male aggressiveness on behavioural transitions in the reproductive cycle of the Barbary dove. *Behaviour*, **59**, 296–318.

Hutchison, J. B. and Zigmond, R. E. (1976) Post-castration decline in male sexual responsiveness to androgen: hypothalamic factors. International Society of Psychoneuroendocrinology. VIIth International Congress (abstract).

Jaffe, R. B. (1969) Testosterone metabolism in target tissues: hypothalamic and pituitary tissues of the adult rat and human foetus, and immature rat epiphysis, *Steroids*, **14**, 483–98.

Johnston, P. and Davidson, J. M. (1972) Intracerebral androgens and sexual behavior in the male rat, *Horm. Behav.*, **3**, 345–57.

Kamel, F., Mock, E. J., Wright, W. W., and Frankel, A. I. (1975) Alterations in plasma concentrations of testosterone, LH, and prolactin associated with mating in the male rat, *Horm. Behav.* **6**, 277–88.

Kato, J. and Onouchi, T. (1973) 5 Alpha-Dihydrotestosterone 'receptor' in the rat hypothalamus, *Endocrinology, Japon.*, **20**, 641- 44.

Katongole, C. B., Naftolin, F. and Short, R. V. (1971) Relationship between blood levels of luteinizing hormone and testosterone in bulls, and the effects of sexual stimulation, *J. Endocrinol.*, **50**, 457–66.

Keverne, E. B., Meller, R. E. and Martinez-Arias, A. M. (1977) Dominance, aggression and sexual behaviour in social groups of talapoin. monkeys. In: *Proceedings of the Sixth Congress of the International Primatological Society*, (Eds D. J. Chivers, J. Herbert) Academic Press, London (In Press).

Kierniesky, N. C. and Gerall, A. A. (1973) Effects of testosterone propionate implants in the brain on the sexual behavior and peripheral tissue of the male rat, *Physiol. Behav.*, **11**, 633–40.

Kizer, J. S., Palkovits, M., Zivin, J., Brownstein, M., Saavendra, J. M., and Kopin, I. J. (1974) The effect of endocrinological manipulations on tyrosine hydroxylase and dopamine hydroxylase activities in individual hypothalamic nuclei of the adult male rat. *Endocrinology*, **95**, 799–812.

Kniewald, Z., Massa, R. and Martini, L. (1970) The transformation of testosterone into dihydrotestosterone by the anterior pituitary and the hypothalamus. In: *Third International Congress on Hormonal Steroids. Excerpta med. Int. Congr. Ser.*, **210**, 59.

Komisaruk, B. R. Adler, N. T. and Hutchison, J. B. (1972) Genital sensory field: enlargement by estrogen treatment in female rats, *Science*, **178**, 1295–8.

Kow, L-M, and Pfaff, D. W. (1973/4) Effects of estrogen treatment on the size of the receptive field and response threshold of pudendal nerve in the female rat, *Neuroendocrinology*, **13**, 299–313.

Lieberburg, I. and McEwen, B. S. (1975) Estradiol-17β: a metabolite of testosterone recovered in cell nuclei from limbic areas of neonatal rat brains, *Brain Res.*, **85**, 165–70.

Lincoln, G. A. (1974) Luteinising hormone and testosterone in man, *Nature*, **252**, 232–3.

Lincoln, G. A., Guinness, F. and Short, R. V. (1972) The way in which testosterone controls the social and sexual behavior of the red deer stag *(Cervus elaphus)*, *Horm. Behav.*, **3**, 375–96.

Lisk, R. D. (1967) Neural localization for androgen activation of copulatory behavior in the male rat, *Endocrinology*, **80**, 754–61.

Lisk, R. D. (1971) The physiology of hormone receptors, *Am. Zoologist*, **11**, 755–67.

Lofts, B., Follett, B. K., and Murton, R. K. (1970) Temporal changes in the pituitary-gonadal axis, *Mem. Soc. Endocrinol.*, **18**, 545–75.

Lovari, S. and Hutchison, J. B. (1975) Behavioural transitions in the reproductive cycle of Barbary doves *(Streptopelia risoria* L.) *Behaviour* 53, 126–150.

Luttge, W. G. and Hall, N. R. (1973) Differential effectiveness of testosterone and its metabolites in the induction of male sexual behavior in two strains of albino mice, *Horm. Behav.*, **4**, 31–43.

Luttge, W. G., Hall, N. R., Wallis, C. J., and Campbell, J. C. (1975) Stimulation of male and female sexual behavior in gonadectomized rats with estrogen and androgen therapy and its inhibition with concurrent anti-hormone therapy, *Physiol. Behav.*, **14**, 65–73.

MacMillan, K. L. and Hafs, H. D. (1967) Semen output of rabbits ejaculated after varying sexual preparation, *Proc. Soc. Exp. Biol. Med.*, **125**, 1278.

Macrides, F., Bartke, A., Fernandez, F. and D'Angelo, W. (1974) Effect of exposure to vaginal odour and receptive females on plasma testosterone in the male hamster, *Neuroendocrinology*, **15**, 355–64.

Macrides, F., Bartke, A. and Delterio, S. (1975) Strange females increase plasma testosterone levels in male mice, *Science*, **189**, 1104–6.

Martinez-Vargas, M. C., Stumpf, W. E. and Sar, M. (1976) Antomical distribution of estrogen target cells in the avian CNS: A comparison with the mammalian CNS, *J. Comp. Neurol.*, **167**, 83–104.

McEwen, B. (1976) Steroid receptors in neuroendocrine tissues: topography, subcellular distribution and functional implications. In: *Subcellular Mechanisms in Reproductive Neuroendocrinology*. F. Naftolin, K. J. Ryan, I. J. Davies (eds). Elsevier, Amsterdam, pp. 277–305.

McEwen, B. S. and Pfaff, D. W. (1970) Factors influencing sex hormone uptake by rat brain regions. 1. Effects of neonatal treatment, hypophysectomy, and competing steroid on estradiol uptake, *Brain Res.*, **21**, 1–16.

McEwen, B. S., Wallach, G. and Magnus, C. (1974) Corticosterone binding to hippocampus: Immediate and delayed influences of the absence of adrenal secretion, *Brain Res.*, **70**, 321–34.

McEwen, B., Pfaff, D. W., Chaptal, C. and Luine, V. N. (1975) Brain cell nuclear retention of [^{3}H] estradiol doses able to promote lordosis: temporal and regional aspects, *Brain Res.*, **86**, 155–61.

McGuire, J. L. and Lisk, R. D. (1969) Localization of estrogen receptors in the rat hypothalamus, *Neuroendocrinology*, **4**, 289–95.

Menaker, M. and Keatts, H. (1968) Extraretinal light perception in the sparrow. II. Photoperiodic stimulation of testis growth, *Proc. Nat. Acad. Sci.*, **60**, 146–51.

Monbon, M., Loras, B., Rebaud, J. P., and Bertrand, J. (1974) Binding and metabolism of testosterone in the rat brain during sexual maturation—1. Macromolecular binding of androgens, *J. Steroid Biochem.*, **5**, 417–23.

Moor, B. C. and Younglai, E. V. (1975) Variations in peripheral levels of LH and testosterone in adult male rabbits, *J. Reprod. Fert.*, **42**, 259–66.

Morin, L. P., Fitzgerald, K. M., Rusak, B., and Zucker, I. (1977) Circadian organization and neural mediation of hamster reproductive rhythms, *Psychoneuroendocrinology*, **2**, 73–98.

Moss, R. L., McCann, S. M. and Dudley, C. A. (1975) Releasing hormones and sexual behaviour. In: *Hormones, Homeostasis and the Brain. Progress in Brain Res.*, **42**, W. H. Gispen, Tj. B. van Wimersma Greidanus, B. Bohus, and D. de Wied (eds.), Elsevier, Amsterdam, pp. 37–46.

Naess, O. and Attramadal, A. (1974) Uptake and binding of androgens by the anterior pituitary gland, hypothalamus, preoptic area, and brain cortex of rats, *Acta Endocrinol.*, **76**, 417–30.

Naess, O., Attramadal, A., Aakvaag, A. (1975) Androgen-binding proteins in the anterior pituitary, hypothalamus, preoptic area, and brain cortex of the rat. *Endocrinology*, **96**, 1–9.

Naftolin, F., Ryan, K. J., and Petro, Z. (1972) Aromatization of androstenedione by the anterior hypothalamus of adult male and female rats, *Endocrinology*, **90**, 295–8.

Parrott, R. F. (1975) Aromatizable and 5α-reduced androgens: Differentiation between central and peripheral effects on male rat sexual behaviour. *Horm. Behav.*, **6**, 99–108.

Phoenix, C. H. (1974) Effects of dihydrotestosterone on sexual behavior of castrated male rhesus monkeys, *Physiol. Behav.*, **12**, 1045–55.

Phoenix, C. H., Copenhaver, K. H. and Brenner, R. M. (1976) Scanning electron microscopy of penile papillae in intact and castrated rats, *Horm. Behav.*, **7**, 212–27.

Purvis, K. and Haynes, N. B. (1974) Short-term effects of copulation, human chorionic gonadotrophin injection and non-tactile association with a female on testosterone levels in the male rat, *J. Endocrinol.*, **60**, 429–39.

Raeside, J. I. and McDonald, M. F. (1959) Seasonal changes in oestrous response by the ovariectomized ewe to progesterone and oestrogen, *Nature*, **184**, 458–9.

Riss, W. and Young, W. C. (1954) The failure of large quantities of testosterone propionate to activate low drive male guinea pigs, *Endocrinology*, **54**, 232–5.

Robel, P. Lasnitzki, I., and Baulieu, E. E. (1971) Hormone metabolism and action: testosterone and metabolites in prostate organ culture, *Biochemie*, **53**, 81–97.

Rose, R. M., Gordon, T. P. and Bernstein, I. S. (1972) Plasma testosterone levels in the male rhesus: influences of sexual and social stimuli, *Science*, **178**, 643–5.

Rosenblatt, J. S. and Aronson, L. R. (1958) The decline of sexual behavior in male cats after castration with special reference to the role of prior sexual experience, *Behaviour*, **12**, 285–338.

Rowan, W. (1926). On photoperiodism, reproductive periodicity, and the annual migration of birds and certain fishes. *Proc. Boston. Soc. nat. Hist.*, **38**, 147–189.

Saginor, M. and Horton, R. (1968) Reflex release of gonadotropin and increased plasma testosterone concentration in male rabbits during copulation, *Endocrinology*, **82**, 627–30.

Smith, O. W., Mongkonpunya, K., Hafs, H. D., Convey, E. M. and Oxender, W. D. (1973) Blood serum testosterone after sexual preparation or ejaculation, or after injections of LH or prolactin in bulls, *J. Anim. Sci.*, **37**, 979–84.

Spies, H. G. and Niswender, G. D. (1971) Levels of prolactin, LH, and FSH in the serum of intact and pelvic neurectomized rats, *Endocrinology*, **88**, 937–43.

Stearns, E. L., Winter, J. S. D., and Faiman, C. (1973) Effects of coitus on gonadotropin, prolactin, and sex steroid levels in man, *J. Clin. Endocr. Metab.*, **37**, 687–91.

Steel, E. and Hinde, R. A. (1972) The influence of photoperiod on oestrogenic induction of nest building in canaries, *J. Endocrinol.*, **55**, 265–78.

Stern, J. M. (1972) Androgen accumulation in hypothalamus and anterior pituitary of male ring doves; influence of steroid hormones, *Gen. Comp. Endocrinol.*, **18**, 439–49.

Stern, J. M. and Eisenfeld, A. J. (1969) Androgen accumulation and binding to macromolecules in seminal vesicles: Inhibition by cyproterone, *Science*, **166**, 233–5.

Stern, J. M. and Eisenfeld, A. J. (1971) Distribution and metabolism of ³H-testosterone in castrated male rats; effects of cyproterone, progesterone and unlabelled testosterone, *Endocrinology*, **88**, 1117–25.

Thien, N. C., Duval, J., Samperez, S. and Jouan, P. (1974) Testosterone 5α-reductase of microsomes from rat anterior hypophysis: properties, increase by castration, and hormonal control, *Biochimie*, **56**, 899–906.

Turkel, F. W., Elliot, J. A., Alvis, J. D. and Menaker, M. (1975) The interaction of castration and photoperiod in the regulation of hypophyseal and serum gonadotropin levels in male golden hamsters, *Endocrinology*, **96**, 854–60.

Whalen, R. E. and De Bold, J. F. (1974) Comparative effectiveness of testosterone, androstenedione and dihydrotestosterone in maintaining mating behavior in the castrated male hamster, *Endocrinology*, **95**, 1674–9.

Wilson, J. D. (1975) Metabolism of testicular androgens. In: *Handbook of Physiology Vol. 5*, D. W. Hamilton and R. O. Greep (eds.), American Physiological Society, Washington D. C., pp. 491–508.

Wilson, J. S. and Gloyna, R. E. (1970) The intranuclear metabolism of testosterone in the accessory organs of reproduction, *Rec. Prog. Horm. Res.*, **26**, 309–30.

Zigmond, R. D. (1975) Binding, metabolism and action of steroid hormones in the contral nervous system. In: *Handbook of Psychopharmacology 5*, L. L. Iverson, S. D. Iversen, and S. H. Snyder (eds.), Plenum Press, New York, pp. 239–326.

Zigmond, R. E. Stern, J. M., and McEwen, B. S. (1972) Retention of radio-activity in cell nuclei in the hypothalamus of the ring dove after injection of ³H-testosterone, *Gen. Comp. Endocrinol.*, **18**, 450–3.

CHAPTER 10

Hormones, Spinal Reflexes, and Sexual Behaviour

BENJAMIN L. HART

INTRODUCTION

No analysis of the biological determinants of sexual behaviour is complete without a consideration of spinal reflexes. Behavioural signs of receptivity in several female animals are usually assumed to include reflexive responses. The important responses of erection and ejaculation in males are known to be mediated at the spinal level—even in human males. Neurologists working with human paraplegics sustaining relatively complete transection of the spinal cord have been aware of the embarrassment suffered by patients from accidental triggering of penile erection. Ejaculation can also be evoked from many human patients suffering from traumatic transection of the spinal cord (Munro et al., 1948; Riddoch, 1917; Talbot, 1955; Zeitlan et al., 1957). In fact in some instances paraplegics have been able to impregnate their wives. The degree to which endogenous and exogenous gonadal steroids influence the sexual reflexes of males and females is obviously important in understanding the total picture of hormonal control of sexual behaviour.

Sexual reflexes are among the most complex of all reflexive activity. In the male, for example, one stimulus can evoke seminal expulsion resulting from contraction of smooth muscle, glandular secretions, and rhythmic contractions of striated muscle. This type of visceral–somatic integration is not commonly seen in other reflexes.

A historical survey of experimental studies of reflexive mechanisms involved in sexual behaviour of male and female vertebrates has been presented in an excellent review by Beach (1967). The review documents that species-specific copulatory patterns consist, in part, of reflexes mediated by the spinal and myelencephalic areas which are capable of functioning after separation from more rostral parts of the central nervous system (CNS). It was noted by Beach that the spinal and myelencephalic mechanisms are capable of functioning at some level in the absence of testicular and ovarian hormones. At the time there was insufficient experimental evidence to indicate the degree to which gonadal hormones may modulate the sexual reflexes.

The purpose of the present chapter is to review the research on sexual reflexes of mammals that has occurred since the earlier review by Beach, and particularly to emphasize the influence that gonadal hormones apparently have on these reflexes.

It is appropriate to mention two historical lines of research. First the relatively simple copulatory pattern of male frogs and toads in which the male clasps the female (amplexus) throughout the period of oviposition and fertilizers the eggs as they emerge from the cloaca, has provided many investigators with a convenient animal model of sexual reflexes. The early work of Steinach (1910) and Aronson and Nobel (1945), and the more recent studies by Hutchison (1964, 1967), and Hutchison and Poynton (1963) in locating a myelencephalic region that mediates amplexus have provided an excellent model of the role of cephalic disinhibition in the display of sexual reflexes.

The second historical line relates to a paragraph by Sherrington (1906) in a textbook regarding reflexes he observed in spinal male dogs. He states:

In the dog, after transection above the lumbar region, movements due to the skeletal musculature are easily excited from certain genital regions. Touching the preputial skin evokes bilateral extension at the knees and ankles, and to a less extent at the hip joints; accompanying this there is depression of the tail. If, though, the skin more posteriorly to the glans penis be pressed, the posterior end of the body is curved downwards, pushing the penile bone forward. These reflex movements suggest themselves as belonging to the act of copulation, and the suggestion is strengthened by the failure to obtain similar movement on touching analogous parts of the spinal bitch.

This paragraph provided the initial basis for much of the research discussed in this review.

SPINAL REFLEXES IN GENERAL

Before going on to a specific discussion of sexual reflexes we might briefly consider experimental work on reflexes in general. One of the experimental preparations used by Sherrington (1910; 1947) was a dog or cat in which the cerebral hemispheres were surgically separated from the rest of the brain. Such an animal is capable of reflexive behaviour and exhibits responses which are more than just meaningless immutable movements in response to specific stimuli. For him, each movement seemed to have an obvious functional meaning. His decerebrate dogs would walk or run, scratch parts of their bodies that had been tickled, and if a thorn or needle was stuck into the foot, the foot was withdrawn while the other legs pushed the animal away from the stimulus through extensor movements. If milk was placed in the mouth it was swallowed and unpalatable solutions such as acid were rejected. He even mentions that when water was placed on the leg there was a shaking movement as if to remove the water. Sherrington stressed that the reflexes were not identical each time they occurred. A reflex response to a weak stimulus would often be weak and to a strong stimulus more intense or longer lasting.

Since the work of Sherrington there has been a great deal of disagreement and confusion about the nature of the reflex and the role of reflexes in behaviour. Sherrington apparently concluded that since the study of reflexes became so complex the 'simple reflex' was an improbable but useful fiction.

There seems to be no readily acceptable anatomical or physiological definition of a reflex. For the purposes of this paper reflexes will be considered repeatable, stereotyped responses which are evoked by relatively specific stimuli and which do not require conscious mediation or even awareness. They are mediated in localized areas of the brain stem and spinal cord. Except for the monosynaptic stretch (knee jerk) reflex, all reflexes are polysynaptic. Through the interneurons involved in polysynaptic reflexes there is a great deal of opportunity for complex neural processing and integration to occur within the reflex system.

Sherrington's decerebrate preparation turned out to be almost too complex for studying reflexive behaviour so it has been useful to turn to responses mediated in more restricted parts of the nervous system. This involves isolating and studying a portion of the nervous system that mediates the reflex and comparing the response of the isolated part with some complete behavioural sequence. The lower part of the spinal cord has been particularly easy to isolate surgically, and chronic spinal animals are easily and humanely cared for.

In isolating a section of the nervous system, such as the spinal cord, there is a sudden deprivation of tonic facilitatory and inhibitory descending influences (Chambers et al., 1973). For a period of time afterwards, reflexes are depressed or not even evocable, presumably because the isolated neurons are suffering from transient or even permanent transneuronal degeneration. This depression of reflex activity in the isolated cord is referred to as spinal shock. Many or most spinal neurons seem to recover from the effects of transection and continue to function in a relatively normal or even hyperreflexive manner. The development of denervation hypersensitivity, and even the sprouting of new collateral fibres from parent axons have been suggested as mechanisms by which neurons compensate for the loss of supraspinal influences (Stavraky, 1961).

Simple reflexes usually gain normal strength within a few hours or days after spinal transection, but complex reflexes such as those involved in sexual responses do not appear normal for weeks. The degree of encephalization of a species (the localization of behavioural functions in higher brain areas) is apparently related to the duration of spinal shock. In rats spinal reflexes seem to recover to full strength more rapidly than in dogs and cats. In primates reflexes take even longer to recover.

A number of spinal reflexes of the dog, cat, and monkey are known (Hart, 1973a; Kellogg et al., 1946; Sherrington, 1906, 1947). The most intensively studied is the limb withdrawal reflex which is activated by nociceptive stimulation of the limbs. Others are crossed extension, knee jerk, scratching, and defecation.

Some of the more complicated spinal reflexes involving striated muscle are standing and walking. These reflexes involve complex interactions of opposing sets of flexor and extensor muscles. Sherrington observed that a dog in which the cerebral hemispheres had been removed was capable of walking or standing when placed on a treadmill; the speed of walking was related to the speed of the treadmill. In a study involving kittens and puppies, Shurrager and Dykman (1951) transected the spinal cords of very young animals and found that they later showed a surprising degree of walking ability including jumping and running for short distances. Some dogs with a chronic midthoracic transection in adulthood will display walking; this reflex is facilitated by administration of strychnine, a drug which blocks postsynaptic inhibition. This indicates, interestingly, that there is a degree of intrinsic spinal inhibition normally associated with the walking reflex (Hart, 1971a).

SPINAL REFLEXES AND SEXUAL BEHAVIOUR OF MALES

General Reflexive Mechanisms

The sexual reflexes of males are complex reactions involving dilation of arterioles supplying erectile tissue, emptying of secretory products from the accessory sexual glands, contraction of the striated extrinsic penile muscles and movements of the limbs, pelvis, and back. (These are responses seen in animals with a midthoracic transection. Movements of the front legs and neck might be expected in animals with a high cervical transection but such animals would be extremely difficult to maintain for observations after recovery from spinal shock because of respiratory paralysis since the nerve supplying the diaphragm originates in the midcervical region.) The afferent arm involves, of course, receptors in ths penis. Sectioning the dorsal nerve of the penis prevents copulatory responses. Monkeys with such an operation show a marked decline in mounting (Herbert, 1973), whereas cats (Aronson and Cooper, 1968) and rats (Larsson and Södersten, 1973) persist in mounting.

There are receptors located over the surface of the penis that certainly influence sexual responses but are probably not involved in evoking ejaculatory reflexes. The encapsulated nerve endings beneath the cornified papillae found on the surface of the glans penis of the rat (Beach and Levinson, 1950) are probably the best example of such receptors. These receptors are undoubtedly affected by topical anaesthetization; copulation is blocked by surface anaesthetization of the glans penis of the rat as it is by sectioning of the dorsal nerve (Adler and Bermant, 1966; Carlsson and Larsson, 1964). However, receptors involved in triggering penile movement, erection, and ejaculation are probably deep pressure receptors located in the body of the penis, proximal to the glans. Such receptors have not been described histologically for any animal species. However, in rats (Hart, 1968a) and dogs (Hart, 1967a) only pressure stimulation of the body of the penis—not stimulation of the glans—will evoke erection and/or ejaculation. Typical anaesthetization of the glans penis of spinal male rats does not block the elicitation of sexual reflexes because presumably deep pressure receptors are still able to function (Hart, 1972a). The more superficial receptors over the glans would appear to function in the male's ability to detect the vaginal orifice.

An analysis of the role that spinal mechanisms play in postural adjustments, copulatory movements, penile erection, and ejaculation involves several conceptual questions. An important consideration is the issue of whether certain responses in the intact male are a direct manifestation of some spinal reflexes. Conceivably the brain could, in intact animals, qualitatively alter spinal activity. Thus reflexes observed in the spinal preparation might only be fragments of copulatory responses rather than complete behavioural units. Also involved is the question of supraspinal facilitation and inhibition of sexual reflexes. Manual stimulation of the penis of normal, intact male rats and dogs rarely evokes the same intensity of penile erection and limb movements as that seen in intact animals during copulation (Hart, 1967a; 1968a). Conceivably this difference could be due to lack of necessary supraspinal facilitation or pronounced supraspinal inhibition of reflex activity. If sexual reflexes of spinal animals match the intensity of comparable responses in intact animals during copulation then it could be assumed that sexual reflexes in the intact animal during copulation are displayed under conditions of reduction of inhibition rather than facilitation. Another consideration is whether the postejaculatory refractory period is at least partially a reflection of spinal cord refractoriness. A third point relates to the possible action of gonadal androgen on sexual reflexes, especially the erectile and ejaculatory responses mediated at the spinal level. In mammals castration often leads to an apparent inability of animals to achieve intromission and the ejaculatory pattern although mounting and thrusting continue at a high rate (Hart, 1974; Young, 1961). This suggests that spinal reflexes involved in erection and ejaculation may be altered more readily than neural mechanisms mediating other sexual responses such as pursuit of the female and mounting.

The animal in which complete spinal transection has been made in the midthoracic region is probably the best experimental subject in which to attempt to answer these questions. The midthoracic level is well above those segments most involved in the mediation of sexual reflexes, but is low enough to allow the animal complete use of the front legs so that it is able to move about and easily obtain food and water. The chronic spinal animal can be tested repeatedly and used as its own control in certain experiments.

There is some difficulty in interpreting data from chronic spinal animals because of postsurgical changes in excitability in the isolated spinal cord. There is also a possibility of altered reflex function if neurons, especially the small interneurons, die because of a transient interference with the blood supply following surgery. Allowing experimental subjects to fully recover from spinal shock reduces the importance of these factors. In some of the studies reviewed here which focus on hormonal alteration of sexual reflexes, extra precautions were taken by testing subjects after the same duration of time following transection but maintaining some animals on a certain hormonal treatment while withdrawing the hormone from others; later hormone treatment for the two groups of subjects was reversed.

Sexual Reflexes in Male Dogs

When placed with a receptive female, a male dog will usually first investigate the genital region and possibly make a few attempts at playing with the female. He then usually mounts without thrusting once or twice before exhibiting a mount which includes pelvic thrusting. Intromission is achieved as a result of 'trial and error' thrusting, usually after three or four mounts. Complete intromission generally occurs within 3–4 min and is followed by a highly stereotyped response. The front legs are pulled posteriorly, the tail deflected downwards and there is an initiation of stepping activity of the rear legs along with intense pelvic movement or oscillaton. Ejaculation commences during this response which I will refer to as the intense ejaculatory reaction. This reaction which lasts for usually 15–30 s, is followed by a genital lock of 10–30 min duration. Except for twisting and turning at the beginning of the lock, the dogs remain quite passive throughout the lock although the female may drag the male around. In the male, intermittent rhythmic contractions of the external anal sphincter, which contracts simultaneously with the bulbocavernosus (bulbospongiosus) muscle, may occasionally be seen or palpated during the lock. These contractions tend to subside when the dogs are standing quietly and to recur when the female or male moves. After separation from the lock the male licks the genital area and exposed penis. If the female licks the penis the male often exhibits a lordosis or arching of the back. Lordosis is also seen as the penis is withdrawn into the sheath.

Because of the paralysed condition of the spinal subject it is difficult to make a direct comparison between the copulatory responses of spinal and intact subjects. One procedure which allows some degree of quantitative comparison is electromyographically (EMG) monitoring the contractions of the striated penile muscles along with visual observation of limb movements, penile erection, and seminal expulsion. In experiments on dogs we decided to use EMG monitoring of three penile muscles, and to the extent possible, make comparisons between spinal and intact dogs (Hart, 1967a; 1972b; Hart and Kitchell, 1966). In Fig. 1 contractions of the ischiourethral, ischiocavernosus and bulbocavernosus muscles are shown during manual elicitation of an ejaculatory

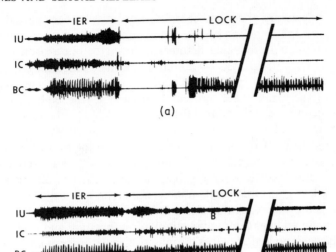

Fig. 1. (a) Representative electromyographic recordings from the ischiourethral (IU), ischiocavernosus (IC) and bulbocavernosus [bulbospongiosus] (BC) muscles during an intense ejaculatory reaction (IER) and simulated lock of a spinal male dog (break in record indicates a long section has been removed). (From Hart, 1967a. Copyright 1967 by the American Psychological Association. Reprinted by permission.) (b). Electromyographic recordings from the same muscles as in (a) during copulation in an intact male dog illustrating contractions during IER and initial part of the copulatory lock. (From Hart, 1972b. Copyright 1972 by the American Psychological Association. Reprinted by permission.)

response in a spinal dog. In the same figure comparable recordings from the same muscles are shown for an intact male dog during copulation. The patterns of contraction are similar enough to indicate that ejaculatory responses are a direct manifestation of spinal reflex activity and do not require supraspinal integration or even facilitation.

Based on contraction patterns of the striated penile muscles, erection, seminal expulsion, and movements of the posterior trunk and hind legs, one can discern four different sexual reflexes in spinal male dogs (Hart, 1967a). One of the reflexes was evidently seen by Sherrington (1906) in his earlier work. This was a response involving shallow thrusting along with partial erection and is elicited by rubbing the preputial sheath over the collum of the penis. The second reflex is characterized by lordosis of the back, a strong extension of the rear legs and rapid detumescence if the penis is erect. This reflex is elicited by touching or rubbing the coronal area of the penis. These two reflexes, which do not involve seminal expulsion, appear to play different roles in copulation. The reflex characterized by shallow pelvic thrusting probably contributes to the male dog's ability to achieve complete intromission once partial intromission is obtained. The reflex characterized by lordosis and rapid detumescence may be important in inducing detumescence if, for one reason or another, penile erection has progressed too far during the male's mounting and thrusting for him to achieve complete intromission since complete engorgement of the bulb of the glans would prevent intromission (the bulb engorges after intromission and keeps the animal locked).

The other two reflexes involves erection and ejaculation. By applying pressure and rubbing the body of the penis just proximal to the glans, the intense ejaculatory reaction is evoked. As in the non-spinal subject, this reaction is 15–30s in duration and involves intense pelvic movement, strong alternate stepping of the back legs plus rapid penile tumescence along with expulsion of seminal fluid. This is the only reflex that seems to have a rather short, definite duration with an abrupt ending. Continuing stimulation (pressure and rubbing) on the body of the penis no longer evokes the intense ejaculatory response, presumably because of a refractory period. However, if the body of the penis is still held and then pressure applied to the penile tip (urethral process) a fourth reflex is elicited. No leg movements occur during this latter reflex, but erection of the penis is maintained for 10–30 min along with continuation of seminal expulsion. This reflex seems to 'run down' after 10–30 min as rhythmic contractions of the bulbocavernosus muscle subside and detumescence of the penis occurs. This reflex appears to be represented in the intact male dog by responses which occur when the sexual partners are locked following the intense ejaculatory reaction; it is referred to as the simulated lock.

Effects of Testosterone on Sexual Reflexes of Male Dogs

The sexual reflexes described above were examined and evaluated on chronic spinal male dogs which were castrated prior to spinal transection but maintained on daily injections of replacement testosterone. The most logical question to ask regarding these reflexes, after first determining what aspects of sexual behaviour they relate to, is the effects of testosterone withdrawal on both their intensity and duration.

Behavioural studies of the effects of castration on copulatory behaviour in non-spinal male dogs have shown that while some males may retain their motivation to copulate, as evidenced by continued mounting and pelvic thrusting, there is an impairment of responses involved in intromission. Specifically, when dogs continue to copulate following castration, there is a rather pronounced decline in the duration of the copulatory lock. Some dogs also show a reduction of the intense ejaculatory reaction (Beach, 1970; Hart, 1968b). Since the intense ejaculatory reaction and the genital lock appear to be manifestations of spinal reflexes, spinal male dogs were studied to determine if the sexual reflexes were altered by testosterone.

In a study of the effects of testosterone alteration in spinal animals, half of the subjects were maintained on testosterone replacement while the other half were given no androgen. After a series of tests for sexual reflexes, including the intense ejaculatory reaction and a simulated lock, the hormone injection schedules were reversed for the two groups (Hart, 1968c).

The most obvious effect of withdrawal of testosterone was a marked reduction in duration of the simulated lock. Dogs that were first tested with testosterone injections and then taken off the hormone had a simulated lock duration reduced from 11.6 to 4.2 min after 60 days. Dogs that initially received no testosterone had a lock duration of 2 min which was extended to 10.5 min after 60 days of testosterone treatment. The mean duration of the intense ejaculatory reaction as measured by the duration of rhythmic contraction in the bulbocavernosus muscle was also affected by testosterone. These changes are illustrated in typical subjects in Fig. 2. Another effect of testosterone withdrawal was an apparent elevated threshold or sensitivity to elicitation of the intense ejaculatory reaction inasmuch as this reflex could not be evoked from some subjects in which testosterone injections were no longer given. Interestingly, there was no evident change in the postejaculatory refractory period as a function of testosterone withdrawal or administration. There was also no change in the response pattern or intensity of skeletal movements in the reflexes involving pelvic thrusting and lordosis.

The experiments on the effects of testosterone on sexual reflexes of dogs did not involve a direct examination of the question of whether the effect of the hormone was primarily on peripheral sensory receptors, effector mechanisms or on spinal neurons. This question will be dealt with in the following section on spinal sexual reflexes of the male rat and in the general discussion of androgen influence on spinal neurons.

Sexual Reflexes in Male Rats

Our initial work on sexual reflexes involved dogs because Sherrington's observations had indicated that a strong correlation could probably be made between spinal responses and copulatory behaviour. When it became apparent that an analysis of the effects of androgen on sexual reflexes was the next logical step we turned our attention primarily to the male rat because copulatory behaviour had been studied more thoroughly in this species than any other, and behavioural studies on the effects of castration revealed that we could expect more rapid changes in sexual reflexes as a function of alteration of androgen level than in the dog (Davidson, 1966a). Since a male rat displays a series of brief copulatory intromissions (approximately 0.33s in duration) before an ejaculation and has no lock, we were also interested in learning the degree to which differences in copulatory behaviour between dogs and rats was represented by species-specific differences in sexual reflexes.

The most surprising finding on spinal male rats was that, unlike the dog, erection and ejaculation could not be evoked by simply touching or rubbing

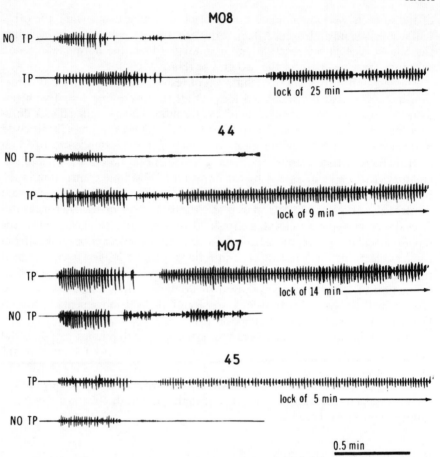

Fig. 2. Examples of electromyographic recordings from the bulbocavernosus muscle of 4 spinal male dogs during the elicitation of an intense ejaculatory reaction (initial series of contractions on each tracing) and simulated lock (onset of rhythmic contractions after a brief pause). Recordings were taken after 60 days of testosterone propionate administration (TP) and 60 days after withdrawal of testosterone propionate (no TP). (From Hart, 1968c.)

part of the penis. The only body movement that could be evoked by touching the tip of the penis was kicking. Through trial and error it was learned that holding the preputial sheath behind the glans would result in the occurrence of a series or cluster of genital responses every 2–3 min (Hart, 1968a). A standard test for evoking these reflexes consisted of restraining the head, front legs, and thorax of subjects in a glass cylinder, retracting the penile sheath and holding it in this manner for a specified period (Fig. 3).

Most standard tests were 30 min in duration and the sheath was held back constantly for the duration of the test. Generally, each cluster of responses began

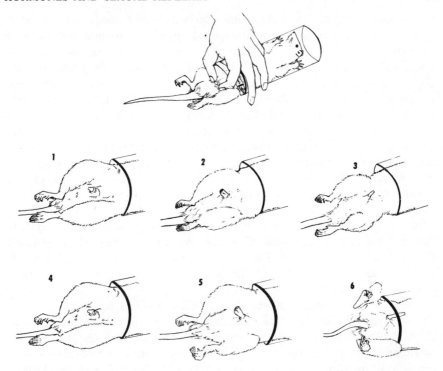

Fig. 3. Responses in a typical response cluster of a test for sexual reflexes in a spinal male rat showing: (1) quiescent stage before onset of response cluster, (2) response cluster beginning with a brief penile erection, (3) a quick flip which generally followed several erections, (4) brief quiescence stage within a response cluster, (5) another erection within the response cluster, and (6) a long flip which generally occurred near the end of a response cluster. (From Hart, 1968a.)

with three or four partial or complete erections. The penis during some erections became so engorged it resembled a flared cup. The tumescence and detumescence of each erection took about 1 s and some erections were followed immediately by a quick dorsal flip of the glans. These flips had a duration of less than 1 s and are referred to as quick flips. The quick flip was accompanied by no body or pelvic movement. After one to three quick flips there usually occurred a third response consisting of an erection of the glans followed immediately by a long extended flip of the glans. This response had a duration of 1–2 and is referred to as a long flip. A long flip was accompanied by a strong ventral flexion of the pelvis. When additional pressure was applied to the sides of the penis during a long flip the duration and intensity of the long flip often increased and the glans remained briefly engorged in the flip position.

Although the genital responses in spinal male rats obviously have something to do with sexual behaviour the reflexes do not relate as logically to sexual behaviour as in the dog. The mating pattern of the male rat is characterized by a series of usually 5–15 brief intromissions which culiminate in an ejaculatory response. Intromissions are usually spaced 30–60 s apart and may occur as frequently as every 5 or 10 s. The type of genital stimulation used to evoke sexual reflexes in spinal rats is probably not comparable to the genital stimulation received by the male rat during copulation. In addition, the occurrence of genital responses as clusters appears to have little resemblance to the copulatory responses displayed during mating. Furthermore, in our tests of spinal animals we have rarely observed seminal expulsion (as we did in dogs) which makes it particularly difficult to interpret exactly which of the responses are related to ejaculation. The long flip reaction appears to resemble both intromission and ejaculatory responses. How the response cluster interval might relate to the events in the mating sequences is also unclear. The response cluster interval, usually 2–3 min, is considerably longer than the interval between intromissions and shorter than the period of time between an ejaculation and the first intromission of another copulatory series. If the response cluster interval is a reflection of sexual refractoriness, then it is probably related to what is called the absolute phase (or physiological minimum) of the post-ejaculatory interval.

The genital responses observed during reflex tests of spinal male rats have also been seen in the intact male rats fitted with a plastic collar which prevents the oral genital grooming that normally occurs after intromissions and ejaculations (Hart and Haugen, 1971). With genital grooming prevented, brief erections of the glans penis were usually observed after intromissions. Follow-int withdrawal of the male from the female after ejaculations there occurred erections, quick flips, and long flips identical to those seen in our spinal subjects. One possibility that arises from the observations on male rats prevented from genital grooming is that following ejaculations part of a cluster of responses occurs and if oral genital grooming is prevented the responses are overt and quite obvious. Otherwise the male rat normally licks the penis and suppresses or inhibits the remainder of a response cluster.

Effects of Testosterone on Sexual Reflexes of Male Rats

Initial attempts to examine the effects of testosterone on sexual reflexes of male rats involved an experiment where male rats were castrated and subsequently given injections of testosterone (Hart, 1967b). Following transection and recovery from spinal shock they were tested for sexual reflexes while still receiving testosterone injections. The subjects were then separated into two groups so that one group could be taken off testosterone while the other was maintained on the androgen; later, when the initial group was again given testosterone, the second group was taken off. In this manner the possible influence of further recovery of spinal shock on the intensity or frequency of sexual reflexes was controlled for in the experimental design.

Fig. 4 illustrates the effects of the testosterone withdrawal and administra-

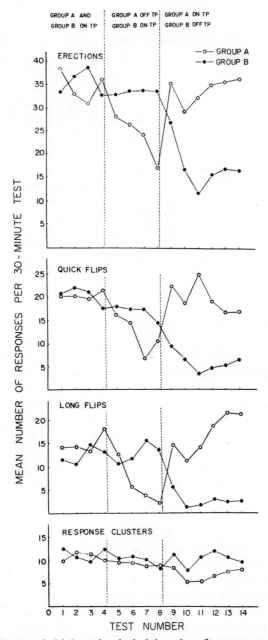

Fig. 4. Influence of withdrawal and administration of testosterone on number of erections, quick flips, long flips, and response clusters per test for spinal male rats. Tests were conducted at 2-day intervals. When hormone withdrawal is indicated there was no injection given on the day of the last test which was conducted while the animals were on testosterone proprionate (TP). When readministration of hormone is indicated, the first injection was given 48 h before the first test which was conducted while the animals were on testosterone. (From Hart, 1967b.)

tion. All of the genital responses, erections, quick flips, and long flips, were promptly altered by testosterone withdrawal and administration. Interestingly, the timing mechanism related to the control of the clusters of responses was not effected. The most striking aspect of this experiment was the very rapid response to testosterone alteration. Within four days after withdrawal of testosterone and within two days after testosterone replacement, there were significant changes in the frequency of genital responses.

The above experiment suggested that the decline in ejaculatory and intromission responses of non-spinal male rats following castration is at least partially due to the influence of withdrawal of gonadal androgen at the spinal level. However, since the testosterone was administered subcutaneously, it could not be determined whether the effect was a reflection of peripheral action of testosterone on receptors (and possibly effectors) or a central action on neural tissue in the cord. Our initial approach to this next question was rather direct. The experiment was conceptualized from the study by Davidson (1966b) on castrated (non-spinal) animals in which the activation of male rat sexual behaviour had been evoked by the implantation of testosterone into preoptic and anterior hypothalamic areas. In this study the localized effect on some parts of the brain was evident because of precautions taken to demonstrate that increases in sexual activity could not be attributed to elevated systemic levels of the hormone as a result of vascular absorption from the implantation site.

We attempted to implant crystalline testosterone propionate (TP) into segments of the spinal cord which mediate the sexual reflexes and to monitor absorption of the implanted androgen into systemic circulation by gross and microscopic examination of the accessory sex organs (at the present time it would be more reasonable to conduct this experiment by monitoring serum levels of androgen by radioimmunoassay).

Castrated male rats were transected and maintained without testosterone replacement until recovery from spinal shock (Hart and Haugen, 1968). The subjects were then screened for those showing a particularly low level of sexual reflex activity; these animals received spinal implants of either TP or cholesterol. Results, shown in Fig. 5, revealed that the testosterone-implanted subjects exhibited a pronounced increase in long flips whereas cholesterol-implanted subjects actually showed a decline.

Although the results indicated that testosterone has a facilitatory influence on sexual reflexes by means of direct action on spinal neural tissue, there is a problem in interpretation. It is known now that papillae on the surface of the penis are more sensitive to testosterone than accessory sexual organs (Davidson et al., 1970). It could be that sensory receptors of the penis which evoke sexual reflexes (as yet still not indentified) may be also stimulated by low levels of testosterone which are not sufficient to stimulate accessory sexual organs.

A different way to approach this question is by the use of special steroids such as dihydrotestosterone (DHT). This agent has been found to maintain normal size and morphology of the penis in castrated rats much more effectively

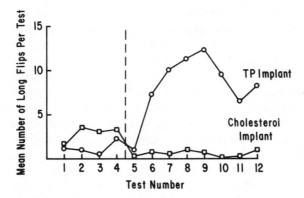

Fig. 5. Effects of spinal implantation of testosterone in spinal male rats. The graph shows the number of long flips per 30-min test for sexual reflexes conducted every 2 days before and after spinal implantation (indicated by vertical dashed line) of either testosterone propionate or cholesterol. (From Hart and Haugen, 1968.)

than sexual behaviour (Feder, 1971; Johnston and Davidson, 1973; Whalen and Luttge, 1971) although in large enough amounts (1 mg) this steroid will also activate behaviour in many castrated male rats (Paup *et al.*, 1975).

Castrated spinal male rats, maintained initially on daily injections of TP, were given a series of baseline tests for sexual reflexes. Some subjects were then given no steroid, others switched to daily injections of a low level (25 μg) of DHT and still others were left on testosterone (Hart, 1973b). Those switched to the low level of DHT, showed a significant decline in sexual reflexes, paralleling the decline of subjects receiving no steroid after the initial testosterone treatment. (As will be mentioned later, a higher dose (200 μg) of DHT daily will maintain or activate sexual reflexes in spinal male rats.) Those continuing to receive testosterone showed no decline in reflexes. The penile papillae and length and weight of the penile shaft in the DHT-treated subjects were markedly greater than in subjects taken off testosterone. Results from this experiment clearly indicated that changes in sexual reflexes induced by testosterone could not be accounted for by only androgenic influences on peripheral tissues, and the results were consistent with the hypothesis that androgen may directly activate spinal neural elements.

Effects of Testosterone on Spinal Neurons: Conceptual Issues

With this background on male rats it is probably appropriate to address the issue of androgen influences on spinal neurons in a more general way. It should be emphasized first that there are androgen-sensitive areas of the penis that may indirectly influence sexual reflexes and sexual behaviour either through modulating the sensory input to the CNS or affecting responses such as erection or penile movement. The most frequently cited examples are the penile papillae found over the surface of the glans penis of the rat (Beach and Levinson, 1950) and cat (Aronson and Cooper, 1967) and which atrophy or regenerate as the animals are castrated or given androgen replacement respectively. It is, in fact, hard to imagine that changes in the size or structure of papillae would not have some influence on sexual responses. It is interesting to note, however, that in an analysis of cutaneous sensitivity threshold and pattern of neuron discharge in nerves from the penis of the cat, Cooper and Aronson (1974) found that the penis of castrates was no less sensitive than that of intact animals. The size of striated penile muscles that play a role in erection and ejaculation in the dog (Hart, 1970a), and presumably in other species, is also influenced by androgen (Hayes, 1965). One would expect this to alter the strength of muscle contractions and thus the degree of erection (but not necessarily the pattern or frequency of muscle contractions or erections which have been recorded in the studies mentioned above).

It is also obvious that gonadal androgen influences sexual behaviour of males by acting on certain, specific neural elements in the brain. Testosterone is concentrated by neurons in several areas including parts of the hypothalamus, preoptic nuclei, and limbic structures (Sar and Stumpf, 1973). Testosterone implant studies have led some investigators (Davidson, 1966b; Johnston and Davidson, 1973; Lisk, 1967) to postulate that the medial preoptic-anterior hypothalamic area is the one major androgen responsive area for the activation of male sexual behaviour and others (Kierniesky and Gerall, 1973) to speculate that there may be several such androgen responsive areas.

There is no logical reason for not postulating that spinal neurons involved in sexual reflexes are also modulated by testosterone levels. However, because of the conventional manner of looking at the spinal cord as mainly a relay station between the limbs and trunk on one hand and the brain on the other, there is a tendency to overlook the complexity of behavioural mediation that can occur in the spinal cord. I have mentioned above phenomena such as the postejaculatory refractory period in spinal male dogs and the timing of genital response clusters in spinal male rats which undoubtedly require complex spinal neural processing. Another example of neural complexity at the spinal level is the recent work on habituation of responses and classical conditioning in spinal animals. Quantitative relationships between various stimulus parameters and the degree of habituation of spinal reflexes have been studied in spinal cats (Thompson and Spencer, 1966). Habituation of reflexes in spinal animals shares all the characteristics of habituation that have thus far been evident in intact animals (Groves et al., 1969). Even a type of classical conditioning can occur at the spinal level (Patterson et al., 1973; Durkovic, 1975). In terms of capability for complex neural processing, spinal neurons seem to be qualitatively no different than those located in the brain. Finally, there is now evidence of selective uptake of androgen by spinal cord neurons, which lends additional support to the notion that neurons involved in spinal sexual reflexes are indeed modulated by androgen.

Very recently Sar and Stumpf (1977) have observed the accumulation of ³H-DHT in nuclei of motor neurons of the ventral horn of the cervical, thoracic, and lumbar regions of the spinal cord of the male rat (Fig. 6). (Sexual reflexes that have been studied have usually involved analyses of animals with midthoracic transections. This precludes observation of the action of hormones on neck and front leg movements that would involve upper thoracic and cervical neurons.) It is probably safe to conclude that testosterone would also be concentrated by such neurons. However, since Sar and Stumpf found that DHT was concentrated by spinal neurons, it is appropriate to mention that when 200 μg DHTP is given to spinal male rats daily, sexual reflexes are facilitated to the same degree as with the injection of a comparable amount of TP (Hart, unpubl. observ.).

If there is reason to believe that testosterone may have a modulating, con-current effect on some spinal elements related to sexual reflexes of adult animals, then the question arises as to the possible involvement of testosterone in the developmental aspects of sexual reflexes. There is evidence that the presence of androgen in infancy is necessary for the complete differentiation of the neural substrate for male behaviour in rats, guinea pigs, monkeys, and presumably

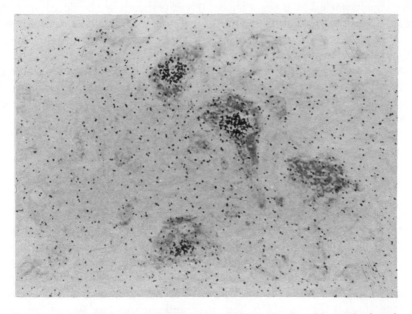

Fig. 6. Autoradiogram of the thoracic spinal cord of orchiectomized and adrenalectomized rat after injection of ³H-dihydrotestosterone, showing nuclear concentration of radioactivity in motor neurons of ventral horn, x 540. (Sar, M. and Stumpf, W. E., 1977. Copyright 1977 by the American Association for the Advancement of Science.)

other mammals (Phoenix *et al.*, 1968). Most male rats, for example, castrated on or before the fourth or fifth day after birth and given exogenous testosterone in adulthood show a high degree of sexual motivation when tested with receptive females but apparently cannot complete the mating sequence with an ejaculatory pattern; male rats castrated after 10 days of age generally exhibit the complete mating pattern (Gerall *et al.*, 1967; Grady *et al.*, 1966; Hart, 1968d; Larsson, 1966). Since we are assuming that the ejaculatory reflex is mediated at the spinal level, it is possible that there is some neonatal influence of testosterone on the development of spinal elements mediating this reflex.

In one experiment we found that male rats castrated four days after birth and later transected and given injections of testosterone in adulthood displayed severe impairment in genital responses corresponding to an inability of the subjects to ejaculate prior to transection (Hart, 1968d).

One difficulty in interpreting the above experiment is that in addition to resulting in impairment of sexual reflexes, neonatal castration also results in incomplete phallic development even when the adult male rat is given testosterone. Thus the inability to ejaculate might be considered secondary to a lack of phallic development and restriction of the penile sensory field.

In a further experiment male rats were castrated at 7 days of age and then given testosterone in adulthood (Hart, 1972c). About half of these 7-day castrates were capable of ejaculation. Thus in this experiment we could compare the sexual reflexes of ejaculators and non-ejaculators for which penile development might be the same. The non-ejaculators, when transected, showed a pronounced impairment in sexual reflexes when compared with the ejaculators. The ejaculators had only slightly longer and heavier penes than the non-ejaculators and the number of papillae on a cross-sectional area did not differ. Thus, the difference between the 7-day ejaculators and non-ejaculators could probably not be attributed to differences in penile development. These results are suggestive of a developmental as well as an activational role of androgen on spinal neural elements involved in sexual reflexes; however, this question obviously needs further work and analysis.

SPINAL REFLEXES AND SEXUAL BEHAVIOUR OF FEMALES

In males the work on sexual reflexes can more or less be limited to stimulation of the penis and observation of specific copulatory responses such as erection, ejaculation, penile movements, and limb movements. In females a consideration of the various sensory regions and peripheral responses makes spinal sexual reflexes more difficult to interpret. For example, three different sensory regions are: (1) the surface of the vulva and surrounding perineum, (2) the clitoris, and (3) walls of the vagina and posterior cervix. Conceivably, stimulation of each of the different areas could evoke different reflexes.

The complexity in approaching an analysis of the sensory areas is illustrated by the limited work which has been done. In spinal cats, stimulation of the clitoris and vaginal wall produces no visible reaction (Hart, 1971b). Yet in the intact cat, probing of the vagina with a glass rod evokes the copulatory cry and the typical postcoital rubbing and rolling. The latter responses are not eliminated by denervation of the clitoris and surrounding area; denervation of the vagina does, however, eliminate these responses (Diakow, 1971). In spinal female dogs stimulation of the clitoris evokes rhythmic contraction of the posterior walls of the vagina (Hart, 1970b).

Smooth muscle in the ovarian soma, walls of the oviduct, uterus, and vagina may be controlled by spinal or supraspinal reflexes as may be vasocongestion of the vagina and clitoris. These are responses which have not been studied in spinal animals and hardly at all in intact subjects. The reason is obvious; whereas contraction of genital tract smooth muscle in males leads to visible seminal expulsion, and genital vasocongestion is evident by penile erection, comparable responses would be difficult to observe in the female. Movement of limbs and postural adjustments such as lordosis or lateral curvature of the spine that reflexively follow stimulation of the external genitalia are readily apparent and these are the responses that have received attention in spinal female mammals. The peripheral sensory field activating these responses is known. The lordosis response of female rats (non-spinal), for example, is markedly impaired by cutaneous denervation of the perineum, tail base, and flanks (Kow and Pfaff, 1976).

The three species that will be considered in regard to spinal sexual reflexes are the cat, dog, and rat. Each of these species illustrates a different perspective or issue involved in understanding the role of spinal mechanisms in female receptive behaviour. The question of oestrogenic facilitation of these reflexes will be discussed when the reflexes are described for each species. However, as Fig. 7 illustrates, oestrogen-concentrating neurons have been observed in the spinal cord of rats using autoradiography (Keefer et al., 1973; Stumpf and Sar, 1976) so the topic of oestrogen activation of spinal neural elements will receive a separate consideration.

Sexual Reflexes in Female Cats

Attempts to understand spinal mechanisms in sexual behaviour of cats goes back to a publication by Maes (1939) in which he mentions that in spinal female cats stimulation of the perineal region evoked dorsal flexion of the pelvis, treading or stepping of the back legs, and lateral deviation of the tail. These are all responses which are prominent in the receptive behaviour of oestrous female cats. Maes reported that these reflexes could only be evoked in his spinal cats if the female was in natural or induced oestrus when the transection was performed.

In a publication appearing very shortly afterwards, Bard (1940) stated that in an experiment he conducted with Bromley, the responses of pelvic elevation, treading and tail deviation could be evoked from spinal female cats regardless

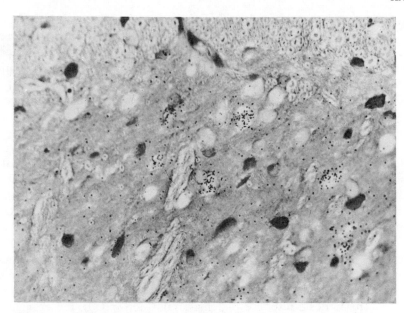

Fig. 7. Autoradiogram of the substantia gelationosa of spinal cord of ovariectomized rat after injection of ³H-oestradiol showing nuclear concentration of
radioactivity in neurons, x 540. (Reproduced from Stumpf and Sar, 1976,
p. 60 by courtesy of Marcel Dekkes, Inc.)

of their hormonal state. Both Maes and Bard leave out essential methodological
details regarding their experiments and neither Maes nor Bard and Bromley
maintained their spinal subjects until reflex function had stabilized after
recovery from spinal shock. Therefore, they were unable to compare the same
subjects before and after administration of an oestrogen.

In an attempt to re-evaluate this problem, female cats were first spayed and
injected with oestrogen to determine how readily treading and tail deviation
were evoked by male cats and by manual stimulation. The animals were subjected to a midthoracic transection and maintained with no hormonal stimulation
until recovery from spinal shock. These reflexes were then evaluated in a series
of tests before and after oestrogen administration (Hart, 1971b).

We found that treading and lateral tail deviation in response to tactile
stimulation of the perineal region were evoked in most spinal subjects after,
but not before, administration of oestrogen. Pelvic elevation, which was
reported by both Maes and Bard, was not seen. This is probably because transection in our cats was midthoracic whereas in those studied by Maes and
Bard it was apparently in the cervical region and therefore the entire set of
back muscles was able to respond together in a reflex manner.

In this experiment on cats we found that not all spinal animals may respond
in the same manner to hormonal treatment. In tests before oestrogen administration one animal did display moderate treading (with no tail deviation)

and another tail deviation (with no leg treading) while 7 subjects exhibited no responses. Following oestrogen administration treading and deviation of the tail were seen in 7 of 9 subjects. In the two subjects which showed partial responses before oestrogen administration there was an intensification of these reflexes. In two subjects no reflexes were seen even after prolonged oestrogen administration. Interestingly, prior to transection, these two animals exhibited strong receptive behaviour to male cats and one displayed receptive responses to manual stimulation. Thus it is also clear that facilitation from more cranial areas of the spinal cord or brain may be important for the full display of receptive responses in the rear quarters.

The intact female cat usually displays a copulatory after-reaction consisting of a brief period of arousal and excitement followed by rolling and rubbing on the floor. This response can also be induced in intact female cats by inserting a glass rod into the vagina. This type of stimulation evoked no sexual response from spinal females.

Sexual Reflexes in Female Dogs

An examination of sexual responses of spinal female dogs offered an opportunity to not only study spinal mechanisms involved in the receptive posture but also contractions of muscles surrounding the vagina during stimulation of the clitoris (Hart, 1970b). Under the conditions of both natural and induced oestrus, signs of receptivity in the female dog include lateral curvature of the rear quarters (towards the male), looping or arching the tail to the side and vertical movement of the genital orifice when the male begins pelvic thrusting. Following complete intromission by the male, and engorgement of the glans penis resulting in a genital lock, most females exhibit a vigorous twisting and turning reaction lasting 5–30 s.

In our studies of spinal dogs we were able to observe lateral curvature of the rear quarters evoked by stimulation of the vulva or perineum (looping of the tail to the side was not possible to evaluate because in spinal subjects we found it necessary to dock the tail for sanitary reasons). It was also possible to monitor, electromyographically, the contraction of the constrictor muscle (constrictor vestibuli) of the posterior vagina and vulva (Hart, 1970b).

As in the study of spinal female cats, spayed females were tested, after recovery from spinal shock, for sexual reflexes before and after oestrogen administration. Two of the 7 animals showed a lateral curvature of the rear quarters towards the side of perineal stimulation before oestrogen administration. Five subjects showed this response following oestrogen administration; subjects showing this response prior to oestrogen administration exhibited an increase in intensity of the response after oestrogen. Lateral curvature was accompanied by tonic unilateral contraction of the constrictor muscle as illustrated in Fig. 8(a); this response was also facilitated by oestrogen. Both the lateral curvature and unilateral contraction of the constrictor muscle are

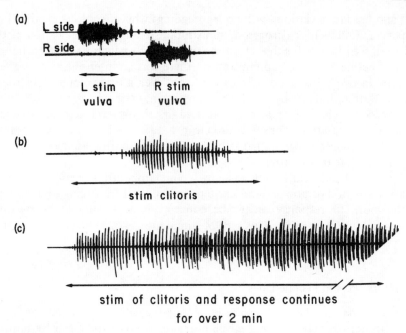

Fig. 8. Electromyographic activity in the constrictor vestibuli muscle of spinal females in response to two types genital stimulation (arrows indicate duration of stimulation). (a) Tonic contraction to stimulation of vulva on ipsilateral side. There was a recording needle in both the left and right sides of the muscle. (b) and (c) Rhythmic contractions of two different durations evoked by clitoral stimulation of the same spinal female on different days. (From Hart, 1970b.)

probably activated in the intact dog when the male licks, or rubs his penis against, the perineal region. The genital region of the female is then oriented towards the male and unilateral contraction of the constrictor muscle functions to move the genital orifice in line with the penis.

When the clitoris of spinal dogs was stimulated by digital palpation, bilateral rhythmic contractions occurring at about 1 per second were evoked from the constrictor muscle. This is illustrated in Fig. 8 (b) and (c). The duration of these contractions varied from 0.10 min to over 2 min. There was also some ventral flexion of the pelvis and leg stepping during these reactions. Neither the latency to the onset of the rhythmic contractions, duration of the contractions, nor limb or trunk movements were influenced by oestrogen administration.

The constrictor muscle of female dogs is homologous to the bulbocavernosus (bulbospongiosus) muscle of males. In spinal male dogs, rhythmic contraction of the bulbocavernosus muscle, at the rate of about 1 per second is characteristic of the intense ejaculatory reaction which is evoked by penile stimulation. Thus, there appears to be a spinal reflex in females that is in some respects homologous to the ejaculatory reflex of males. The same response is possibly similar to the rhythmic contractions of the wall of the vagina in human females that accompany the experience of orgasm (Masters and Johnson, 1966).

The primary evidence that this reflex occurs in intact female dogs during actual copulation is that in the first minute or so of the genital lock, rhythmic contractions of the anal sphincter muscle are visually apparent. Since the anal sphincter and the constrictor muscles tend to contract as a unit, the constrictor muscle is undoubtedly contracting as well.

In a separate aspect of the study of female sexual reflexes in dogs, 6 adult spinal males receiving TP were examined for the 'female' lateral curvature response by stroking the skin over the perineal and scrotal regions (Hart, 1970b). A series of tests were conducted before and after injections of oestradiol. One dog showed lateral curvature during one test prior to oestrogen treatment, whereas 5 of the 6 dogs showed this response after oestrogen treatment. Our analysis of sexual reflexes in both male (Hart, 1967a, 1968c) and female dogs (Hart, 1970b) illustrate, therefore, that both males and females have at least some of the spinal mechanisms for display of responses typically associated with the opposite sex.

Sexual Reflexes in Female Rats

Because of the stereotyped nature, reference is often made to the lordosic posture of sexually receptive female rodents as the manifestation of a spinal reflex. However, the experimental basis for this assumption is quite limited. Dempsey and Rioch (1939) were unable to evoke a lordotic posture from spinal female guinea pigs. However, this may have been due to the presence of spinal shock since the animals were apparently tested shortly after transection.

The female rat was a logical species to evaluate this response. The rat is the most common laboratory animal for the study of sexual behaviour and the receptive posture of females has been examined extensively from the standpoint of the effects of hormones and drugs. The lordosic quotient (ratio of lordoses to male mounts) is a standard laboratory measure of this response.

When we initially started this project we felt it would be fairly easy to demonstrate a lordosis in spinal females and, since genital responses of spinal male rats were affected by androgen, we expected to find the lordosic reflex of female rats facilitated by oestrogen. Two procedures were used in an attempt to evoke lordosis from spinal subjects. One was manual stimulation consisting of digital palpation in the perineal and flank regions. The other was to allow sexually active male rats to mount the spinal females. Spayed females were studied prior to hormone administration and after the administration of a regimen of oestrogen and progesterone injections that readily induce receptivity in intact female rats (Hart, 1969).

Lordosis could not be reliably or consistently evoked from any subject regardless of hormonal treatment. Seven out of 9 subjects in one experiment and 6 out of 8 in another showed a moderate arching of the back on at least one test before or after hormone treatment. However, with a paralysis of the back legs it was hard to evaluate whether the occasional arching represented true lordosis. Under conditions of no hormone, oestrogen alone, and oestrogen plus progesterone, the frequency of the response did not vary. Essentially the same results were found by Pfaff *et al.* (1972).

The absence of a clear lordosic response in spinal female rats has been taken by Pfaff *et al.* (1972) to indicate that in the rat supraspinal mechanisms are necessary for the display of the lordosic reflex. It is difficult to imagine that receptive postures and movements are spinally mediated in the cat and dog but not in the rat which is a less encephalized species according to our conventional manner of viewing CNS evolution. It is conceivable that with the appropriate methodological techniques (as yet unknown) a sexually receptive response such as lordosis will be found in rats.

Effects of Oestrogen on Spinal Neurons: Conceptual Issues

We have basically the same problem in determining the locus action of oestrogen on sexual reflexes of females as we did with testosterone in males. Particular areas of the hypothalamus, preoptic region, amygdala, and other limbic areas concentrate oestradiol (Pfaff and Keimer, 1973; Stumpf, 1968; 1970; 1971; Stumpf and Sar, 1971, 1976). From studies involving the activation of sexual behaviour by oestrogen implants (Harris and Michael, 1964; Palka and Sawyer, 1966; Lisk, 1962) it is clear that oestrogen can affect brain structures resulting in supraspinal facilitation of spinal reflexes involved in receptive behaviour.

As discussed here, there is, for some cats and dogs, evidence for facilitation of sexual reflexes at the spinal level as well. Some of this could be attributed to an oestrogen-induced enlargement of the peripheral genital sensory field as demonstrated in rats (Komisaruk *et al.*, 1972; Kow and Pfaff, 1973). It is very significant that there are oestrogen-concentrating cells in the female rat spinal cord (Keefer *et al.*, 1973; Stumpff and Sar, 1976). This lends strong support to the possibility of activation of spinal neurons by oestrogen and raises the possibility that similar neurons exist in the spinal cords of cats and dogs. Perhaps it is best, at this point, to postulate that in the female, as in the male, there are three general sites of action of oestrogen in influencing receptive behaviour: the brain, spinal cord, and peripheral genital sensory field.

CONCLUSION

As mentioned at the beginning of this chapter, no analysis of the biological determinants of sexual behaviour is complete without a consideration of spinal sexual reflexes. Reflexes that play an obvious role in sexual behaviour have been described for both male and female animals. In males the most important reflexes are erection and ejaculation; in females reflexive aspects of the receptive posture are the most interesting.

At first approach it would seem as though experimental work on spinal sexual reflexes should be straightforward and relatively uncomplicated. As is evident to the reader, an understanding of the role of sexual reflexes in mating behaviour is not simple. Take, for example, the work that has been discussed in regard to the rat. According to conventional neuroanatomy and neurophysiology this species is less encephalized in CNS function than the dog or cat and one would expect, correspondingly, that spinal sexual reflexes in the rat would more closely resemble sexual behaviour than in the dog and cat. However, just the opposite has been found. Sexual reflexes in the male rat are very difficult to correlate with mating behaviour. In the female rat no type of sexual reflex has been evoked, regardless of hormonal treatment, and yet in spinal female dogs and cats elements of the receptive posture are easily elicited.

Several experiments have shown that spinal sexual reflexes are not static immutable responses but are responses that may be modulated at the spinal level. Gonadal hormones of both sexes may have quantitative influences on sexual reflexes at the spinal level in at least some species. Might we expect these sexual reflexes to be modulated in other ways? The recent observations of habituation of spinal neurons and the occurrence of classical conditioning in spinal elements should make us aware of the possibility that these processes may also occur in the spinal elements mediating sexual reflexes as well.

For experimental work it is necessary to isolate neural elements mediating reflexes in the spinal cord in order to study them. In this isolated or spinal preparation we can still identify parts of the typical reflex system including the afferent arm extending from sensory receptors in the genitalia, the central mediating elements within the spinal cord, and the effector arm innervating the smooth muscle of genital organs and genital vasculature, as well as some of the striated muscle of the trunk and limbs. However, by isolating a reflex system we are creating an artifactual situation. In the intact animal responses that we normally think of as being activated by the afferent arm of a reflex are also activated or facilitated by supraspinal structures. Thus female cats and dogs may show the full receptive posture just in the presence of the male with no tactile stimulation to the genitalia. In male animals, including human males, erection and ejaculation occur under some circumstances without penile stimulation. The isolated reflex system, therefore, lends itself to only a partial understanding of the role of reflexive responses in the behaviour of the intact animal. In the future we will probably continue to isolate parts of the CNS in order to study sexual reflexes more completely and to understand how the neural elements of some reflex systems may be influenced by hormones and possibly other factors. However, from the behavioural standpoint the most important work will be related to understanding how reflexes are integrated into the total behavioural system of normal functioning animals.

ACKNOWLEDGEMENT

Research supported by grant MH 12003 from the National Institute of Mental Health, U.S. Public Health Service.

REFERENCES

Adler, N. and Bermant, G. (1966) Sexual behavior of male rats: Effects of reduced sensory feedback, *J. Comp. Physiol. Psychol.*, **61**, 240–3.

Aronson, L. R. and Cooper, M. L. (1967) Penile spines of the domestic cat: Their endocrine-behavior relations, *Anat. Rec.*, **157**, 71–8.

Aronson, L. R. and Cooper, M. L. (1968) Desensitization of the glans penis and sexual behavior in cats. In: *Perspectives in Reproduction and Sexual Behavior*, M. Diamond (ed.), University of Indiana Press, Bloomington.

Aronson, L. R. and Nobel, G. K. (1945) The sexual behavior of Anura. 2. Neural mechanisms controlling mating in the male leopard frog *(Rana pipens)*, *Bull. Am. Mus, Nat. Hist.*, **86**, 87–135.

Bard, P. (1940) The hypothalamus and sexual behavior. *Res. Publications Assoc. Nervous and Mental Disorders*, **20**, 551–79.

Beach, F. A. (1967) Cerebral and hormonal control of reflexive mechanisms involved in copulatory behavior, *Physiol. Rev.*, **47**, 289–316.

Beach, F. A. (1970) Coital behavior in dogs: VI. Long-term effects of castration upon mating in the male, *J. Comp. Physiol. Psychol.*, **70**, (3, Pt. 2).

Beach, F. A. and Levinson, G. (1950) Effects of androgen on the glans penis and mating behavior of castrated male rats, *J. Exp. Zool.*, **144**, 159–71.

Carlson, S. G. and Larsson, K. (1964) Mating in male rats after local anesthetization of the glans penis, *Zeitshrief Tierpsychology*, **21**, 854–6.

Chambers, W. W., Lui, C. N., and McCouch, G. P. (1973) Anatomical and physiological correlates of plasticity in the central nervous system, *Brain, Behav. and Evol.*, **8**, 5–27.

Cooper, K. K. and Aronson, L. R. (1974) Effects of castration on neural afferent responses from the penis of the domestic cat, *Physiol. Behav.*, **12**, 93–107.

Davidson, J. M. (1966a) Characteristics of sex behaviour in male rats following castration, *Anim. Behav.*, **14**, 266–72.

Davidson, J. M. (1966b) Activation of the male rat's sexual behavior by intracerebral implantation of androgen, *Endocrinology*, **79**, 783–94.

Davidson, J. M., Johnston, P., Bloch, G. J., Smith, E. R., and Weick, R. F. (1970) Comparative responses to androgen of anatomic, behavioral, and other parameters. Third International Congress on Hormonal Steroids. Hamburg. *Excerpta Medica International Congressional Series*, **219**, 727–30.

Dempsey, E. W. and Rioch, D. M. (1939) The localization in the brain stem of the oestrus responses of the female guinea pig, *J. Neurophysiol.*, **2**, 9–18.

Diakow, C. (1971) Effects of genital desensitization on mating behavior and ovulation in the female cat, *Physiol. Behav.*, **7**, 47–54.

Durkovic, R. G. (1975) Classical conditioning, sensitization and habituation in the spinal cat, *Physiol. Behav.*, **14**, 297–304.

Feder, H. H. (1971) The comparative actions of testosterone propionate and 5α-andros-tran-17βol-3-one propionate on the reproductive behaviour, physiology, and morphology of male rats, *J. Endocrinol.*, **51**, 241–52.

Gerall, A. A., Hendrick, S. E., Johnson, L. L., and Bounds, T. W. (1967) Effects of early castration in male rats on adult sexual behavior, *J. Comp. Physiol. Psychol.*, **64**, 206–212.

Grady, K. L., Phoenix, C. H., and Young, W. C. (1965) Role of the developing rat testis in differentiation of the neural tissues mediating behavior, *J. Comp. Physiol. Psychol.*, **56**, 176–82.

Groves, P. M., Lee, D., and Thompson, R. F. (1969) Effects of stimulus frequency and intensity on habituation and sensitization in acute spinal cats, *Physiol. Behav.*, **4**, 383–8.

Harris, G. W. and Michael, R. P. (1964) The activation of sexual behaviour by hypothalamic implants of oestrogen, *J. Physiol.*, **171**, 275–301.

Hart, B. L. (1967a) Sexual reflexes and mating behavior in the male dog, *J. Comp. Physiol. Psychol.*, **64**, 388–99.

Hart, B. L. (1967b) Testosterone regulation of sexual reflexes in spinal male rats, *Science*, **155**, 1282–4.

Hart, B. L. (1968a) Sexual reflexes and mating behavior in the male rat, *J. Comp. Physiol. Psychol.*, **65**, 453–60.

Hart, B. L. (1968b) Role of prior experience in the effects of castration on sexual behavior of male dogs, *J. Comp. Physiol. Psychology.*, **66**, 719–25.

Hart, B. L. (1968c) Alteration of quantitative aspects of sexual reflexes in spinal male dogs by testosterone, *J. Comp. Physiol. Psychology.*, **66**, 726–30.

Hart, B. L. (1968d) Neonatal castration: Influence on neural organization of sexual reflexes in male rats, *Science*, **160**, 1135–6.

Hart, B. L. (1969) Gonadal hormones and sexual reflexes in the female rat, *Horm. Behav.*, **1**, 65–71.

Hart, B. L. (1970a) Reproductive system—Male. In: *The Beagle as an Experimental Dog*, A. C. Andersen (ed.), Ames, Iowa State University Press, pp. 296–312.

Hart, B. L. (1970b) Mating behavior in the female dog and the effects of estrogen on sexual reflexes, *Horm. Behav.*, **2**, 93–104.

Hart, B. L. (1971a) Facilitation by strychnine of reflex walking in spinal dogs, *Physiol. Behav.*, **6**, 627–8.

Hart, B. L. (1971b) Facilitation by estrogen of sexual reflexes in female cats, *Physiol. Behav.*, **7**, 675–8.

Hart, B. L. (1972a) Sexual reflexes in the male rat after anesthetization of the glans penis, *Behav. Biol.*, **7**, 127–30.

Hart, B. L. (1972b) The action of extrinsic penile muscles during copulation in the male dog, *Anat. Rec.*, **173**, 1–6.

Hart, B. L. (1972c) Manipulation of neonatal androgen: Effects on sexual responses and penile development in male rats, *Physiol. Behav.*, **8**, 841–5.

Hart, B. L. (1973a) Reflexive behavior. In: *Perspectives on Animal Behavior*, G. Bermant (ed.), Scott, Foresman, Glenview, Ill. pp. 171–193.

Hart, B. L. (1973b) Effects of testosterone propionate and dihydrotestosterone on penile morphology and sexual reflexes of spinal male rats, *Horm. Behav.*, **4**, 239–46.

Hart, B. L. (1974) Gonadal androgen and sociosexual behavior of male mammals: A comparative analysis, *Psychol. Bull.*, **81**, 383–400.

Hart, B. L. and Haugen, C. M. (1968) Activation of sexual reflexes in male rats by spinal implantation of testosterone, *Physiol. Behav.*, **3**, 735–8.

Hart, B. L. and Haugen, C. M. (1971) Prevention of genital grooming in mating behavior of male rats *(rattus norvegicus)*, *Anim. Behav.*, **19**, 230–2.

Hart, B. L. and Kitchell, R. L. (1966) Penile erection and contraction of penile muscles in the spinal and intact dog, *Am. J. Physiol.*, **210**, 257–61.

Hayes, K. J. (1965) The so-called 'levator ani' of the rat, *Acta Endocrinologica*, **48**, 337–47.

Herbert, J. (1973) The role of the dorsal nerves of the penis in the sexual behavior of the male rhesus monkey, *Physiol. Behav.*, **10**, 293–300.

Hutchison, J. B. (1964) Investigations on the neural control of clasping and feeding in *Xenopus laenis* (Daudin), *Behaviour*, **24**, 47–66.

Hutchison, J. B. (1967) A study of the neural control of sexual clasping behaviour in *Rana angolensis* bocage and *Bufo regularis* reuss with a consideration of self-regulatory hindbrain systems in the anura, *Behaviour*, **28**, 1–57.

Hutchison, J. B. and Poynton, J. C. (1963) A neurological study of the clasp reflex in *Xenopus laevis* (Daudin), *Behaviour*, **22**, 41–63.

Johnston, P. (1973) Davidson, J. M. Intracerebral androgens and sexual behavior in the male rat, *Horm. Behav.*, **3**, 345–57.

Keefer, D. A., Stumpf, W. E., and Sar, M. (1973) Topographical localization of estrogen-concentrating cells in the rat spinal cord following ³H-estradiol administration, *Proc. Soc. Exp. Biol. Med.*, **143**, 414–7.

Kellogg, W. N., Deese, J., and Pronko, W. N. (1946) On the behavior of the lumbo-spinal dog, *J. Exp. Psychol.*, **36**, 503–11.

Kierniesky, N., and Gerall, A. A. (1973) Effects of testosterone propionate implanted in the brain on the sexual behavior and peripheral tissue of the male rat, *Physiol. Behav.*, 633–40.

Komisaruk, B. R., Adler, N. T., and Hutchison, J. (1972) Genital sensory field: Enlargement by estrogen treatment of female rats, *Science*, **178**, 1295–8.

Kow, L. M. and Pfaff, D. W. (1973) Effects of estrogen treatment on the size of receptive field and response threshold of pudendal nerve in the female rat, *Neuroendocrinology*, **13**, 299–313.

Kow, L. M. and Pfaff, D. W. (1976) Sensory requirements for the lordosis reflex in female rats, *Brain Res.*, **101**, 47–66.

Larsson, K. (1966) Effect of neonatal castration upon the development of mating behavior of the male rat, *Zeitshrief Tierpsychology*, **13**, 867–73.

Larsson, K. and Södersten, P. (1973) Mating in male rats after section of the dorsal penile nerve, *Physiol. Behav.*, **10**, 567–71.

Lisk, R. D. (1962) Diencephalic placement of estradiol and sexual receptivity in the female rat, *Am. J. Physiol.*, **203**, 493–6.

Lisk, R. D. (1967) Neural localization for androgen activation of copulatory behavior in the male rat, *Endocrinology*, **80**, 754–61.

Liu, C. N., Chambers, W. W., and McCouch, G. P. (1966) Reflexes in the spinal monkey *(Macaca mulatta)*, *Brain*, **89**, 349–58.

Maes, J. P. (1939) Neural mechanisms of sexual behaviour in the female cat, *Nature*, **144**, 598–599.

Masters, W. H. and Johnson, V. E. (1966) *Human sexual response*, Little, Brown and Co., Boston.

Munro, D. H., Horne, H. W., and Paull, D. P. (1948) The effect of injury to the spinal cord and cauda equina on the sexual potency of men, *New Eng. J. Med.*, **239**, 903–11.

Palka, Y. S. and Sawyer, C. H. (1966) The effects of hypothalamic implants of ovarian steroids on oestrus behavior in rabbits, *J. Physiol.*, **185**, 251–67.

Patterson, M. M., Cegawski, C. F., and Thompson, R. F. (1973) Effects of a classical conditioning paradigm on hind-limb flexor nerve response in immobilized spinal cats, *J. Comp. Physiol. Psychol.*, **84**, 88–97.

Paup, D. C., Mennin, S. P., and Gorski, R. A. (1975) Androgen- and estrogen-induced copulatory behaviour and inhibition of luteinizing hormone (LH) secretion in the male rat, *Horm. Behav.*, **6**, 35–46.

Pfaff, D. W. and Keimer, M. (1973) Atlas of estradiol-concentrating cells in the central nervous system of the female rat, *J. Comp. Neurol*, **151**, 121–58.

Pfaff, D., Lewis, C., Diakow, C., and Keimer, M. (1972) Neurophysiological analysis of mating behavior responses as hormone-sensitive reflexes. In: *Progress in Physiological Psychology*, Vol. 5. E. Stellar and J. Sprague (eds.), Academic Press, New York, pp. 253–97.

Phoenix, C. H., Goy, R. W., and Resko, J. A. (1968) Psychosexual differentiation as a function of androgenic stimulation. In: *Perspectives in Reproduction and Sexual Behavior*, M. Diamond (ed.), Indiana University Press, Bloomington.

Riddoch, G. (1971) The reflex functions of the completely divided spinal cord in man, compared with those associated with less severe lesions, *Brain*, **40**, 264–402.

Sar, M. and Stumpf, W. E. (1973) Autoradiographic localization of radioactivity in the rat brain after the injection of 1,2-³H-testosterone, *Endocrinology*, **92**, 251–6.

Sar, M., and Stumpf, W. E. (1977) Androgen concentration in motor neurons of cranial nerves and spinal cord, *Science*, **197**, 77–9.

Sherrington, C. S. (1906) The spinal cord, In: *Textbook of Physiology*. E. A. Sharpey-Schafer (ed.), Edinburgh, Scotland.

Sherrington, C. S. (1910) Flexion-reflex of the limb, crossed estension-reflex, and reflex stepping and standing, *J. Physiol.*, **40**, 28–121.

Sherrington, C. S. (1947) *The Integrative Action of the Nervous System*. Yale University Press, New Haven.

Shurrager, P. S. and Dykman, R. A. (1951) Walking spinal carnivores. *J. Comp. Physiol. Psychol.*, **44**, 252–62.

Stavraky, G. W. (1961) *Supersensitivity Following Lesions of the Nervous System*. University of Toronto Press, Toronto.

Steinach, E. (1910) Geschlechtstrieb und echt sekundare Geschlechtsmerkale als Falge der imersekretorischen Funktion der Keimdrüsen, *Zent. Physiol.*, **24**, 551–66.

Stumpf, W. E. (1968) Estradiol-concentrating neurons: Topography in the hypothalamus by dry-mount autoradiography, *Science*, **162**, 1001–3.

Stumpf, W. E. (1970) Estrogen-neurons and estrogen-neuron systems in the periventricular brain, *Am. J. Anat.*, **129**, 207–18.

Stumpf, W. E. (1971) Probable sites of estrogen receptors in brain and pituitary, *J. Neuro-Visceral Relations*, Suppl. X, 51–64.

Stumpf, W. E. and Sar, M. (1971) Estradiol concentrating neurons in the amygdala, *Proc. Soc. Exp. Biol. Med.*, **136**, 102–6.

Stumpf, W. E. and Sar, M. (1976) Autoradiographic localization of estrogen, androgen, progestin, and glucocorticosteroid in 'target tissues' and 'non-target tissues'. In: *Receptors and Mechanism of Action of Steroid Hormones*, J. Pasqualini (ed.), Marcel Dekker, New York.

Talbot, H. S. (1955) The sexual function in paraplegia, *J. Urology*, **73**, 91–100.

Thompson, R. F. and Spencer, W. A. (1966) Habituation: A model phenomenon for the study of neuronal substrates of behaviour, *Psychol. Rev.*, **73**, 16–43.

Whalen, R. E. and Luttge, W. G. (1971) Testosterone, androstenedione and dihydrotestosterone: Effects on mating behavior of male rats, *Horm. Behav.*, **2**, 117–25.

Young, W. C. (1961) The hormones and mating behavior. In: *Sex and Internal Secretions*, W. C. Young (ed.), Williams & Wilkins, Baltimore.

Zeitlin, A. B., Cottrell, T. L., and Lloyd, F. A. (1957) Sexology of the paraplegic male, *Fertil. Steril.*, **8**, 337–44.

CHAPTER 11

The Nature of the Neural Substrate of Female Sexual Behaviour in Mammals and its Hormonal Sensitivity: Review and Speculations

BARRY R. KOMISARUK

INTRODUCTION

In rats, oestrogen concentration in ovarian venous plasma starts to rise in late dioestrus and reaches peak levels at about noon on the day of prooestrus (Yoshinaga *et al.*, 1969). The progesterone level in ovarian venous plasma reaches a peak 7 h later (Hashimoto *et al.*, 1968). This pattern of steroid secretion induces sexual receptivity during the evening of prooestrus (see reviews by Everett, 1961; Schwartz, 1970; Sawyer, 1975; Feder, 1977). Although oestrogen alone can induce sexual receptivity in rats (Davidson *et al.*, 1968), oestrogen and progesterone act synergistically in facilitating various components of female receptivity, including lordosis, hopping, and rapid head movements which produce vibration of the ears (Beach, 1942). Oestrogen and progesterone also act synergistically to increase both the effectiveness of weak genital stimuli in eliciting lordosis and increase the intensity of the lordosis response (degree of arching the back: Diakow *et al.*, 1973). (For a recent review of oestrogen–progesterone synergy, see Kow *et al.*, 1974.)

In the absence of these hormones, what is the condition of the neural substrate on which the hormones act? Beach (1948) has stated that 'Behaviour which is unquestionably under hormonal influence may be ... so strongly affected by stimuli from the environment that external events ... elicit the reaction in the absence of the hormones.' This statement is supported by recent findings in which lordosis in rats can be elicited by sensory stimuli similar to those provided by the male, under hormonal conditions that are considerably different from those of prooestrus. That is, sexually unreceptive rats can be made receptive to males by manual stimulation of the vagina with a glass rod (Rodriguez-

Sierra *et al.*, 1975a) and rats that are dioestrous or ovariectomized (Komisaruk and Diakow, 1973), ovariectomized–adrenalectomized (Larsson *et al.*, 1974), or hypophysectomized–ovariectomized (Crowley *et al.*, 1976c, Rodriguez-Sierra *et al.*, 1975b), all of which received no hormonal treatment, showed lordosis when vaginal stimulation was applied in conjunction with manual stimulation of the flanks and the perineum. Similarly, Beyer *et al.* (1969) observed sexual receptivity in 14 of 63 rabbits after ovariectomy in the absence of exogenous hormone treatment, and 7 of 11 of those that mated also showed sexual receptivity after subsequent adrenalectomy (see also Beyer, 1967). Thus, the neural substrate of the female mating posture, lordosis, can be activated by appropriate sensory stimuli even in the apparent absence of the hormones which normally facilitate it. In the present paper, I shall emphasize some possible implications of viewing lordosis in terms of its sensorimotor aspects independently of its hormonal control. As an introduction, however, it may be helpful to review studies of the hormone-sensitive system underlying the lordosis response. These can be grouped into several main types of studies, which have sought to eliminate lordosis through lesions of the brain, spinal cord, or peripheral nervous system; facilitate or inhibit it with electrical stimulation or local application of sex steroids; identify the neural regions which accumulate sex steroids; and record the neural responses to sex steroid administration and/or to sensory stimuli that are relevant to sexual behaviour.

EFFECTS OF NEURAL LESIONS ON FEMALE MATING RESPONSES

Peripheral Nervous System

While 'highly receptive rats may display hopping, ear vibration, and lordosis even though the male does not approach them' (Beach, 1947) normally, lordosis is elicited by direct contact with the male. When the male rat mounts the female in copulation, he straddles the female's dorsal surface with his forelegs, grasping her flanks with his forepaws near her hind legs and contacting her thighs with his hind legs, and her back with his nose and chin (Pfaff *et al.*, 1974). As the female starts to show lordosis, the male makes rapid repetitive pelvic movements, and thrusts his penis adjacent to the base of her tail aimed diagonally toward the female's vaginal orifice (Adler *et al.*, in prep.). In response to this stimulation, the female stands immobile with her legs extended, elevates her rump in the lordosis posture, in which there is a marked dorsiflexion of her spine; her head as well as her rump become elevated while her thoracic region becomes depressed (Komisaruk, 1971a, Komisaruk and Diakow, 1973; Pfaff *et al.*, 1974). The male performs several rapid shallow thrusts and then may show a deep intromittive thrust which lasts approximately 300 ms, after which he dismounts rapidly (Bermant, 1965). The female starts to move into the lordosis posture before intromission occurs, and if intromission or ejaculation occurs, she maintains her head elevation and immobility longer than if intromission does not occur (Diakow, 1975). If the skin of the flank, rump, and perineal areas is denervated locally, the female does not show lordosis to mounting by males (Kow and Pfaff, 1976; Rodriguez-Sierra and Komisaruk, in prep.). If the genital tract (uterus and vagina) is removed, the female still shows lordosis in response to the male's mounts (Ball, 1934). However, if the pelvic nerve, which innervates the genital tract (Clegg and Doyle, 1967; Abrahams and Teare, 1969; Komisaruk et al., 1972a) is cut, thus blocking, at least in part, the sensory effect of the intromittive and ejaculatory stimuli, then lordosis and immobility are shortened to durations closer to those of mounts without intromissions (Diakow, 1970).

Oestrogen administration increases the size (Komisaruk et al., 1972a) and sensitivity (Kow and Pfaff, 1973) of the sensory field of the pudendal nerve, which innervates the perigenital area. Mechanical stimulation of this area is adequate to elicit lordosis in highly receptive females (Kow and Pfaff, 1976; pers observ.). In addition, the size and sensitivity of this field is greater in sexually receptive, naturally oestrous rats than in unreceptive, dioestrous females (Adler, Komisaruk, and Davis, 1974). This facilitation of sensory input may be one of the ways in which oestrogen increases the female rat's responsiveness to stimulation that is adequate for elicitation of lordosis. Oestrogen has a comparable effect on the trigeminal nerve field of the face, the functional significance of which is not known (Bereiter and Barker, 1975).

After removal of the uterus and proximal vagina (and/or abdominal sympathectomy) female cats still show lordosis and allow intromission (Bard, 1935). However, the 'afterreaction' to intromission ('vigorous rolling, rubbing, squirming, and licking') was abolished by these extirpations. Removal of the sacral portion of the spinal cord also abolished the afterreaction. Diakow (1967, 1968), and Aronson and Diakow (1971a) confirmed these findings by showing that in cats, after removal of the pelvic plexus which innervates the vagina and uterus, mating still occurred. But the afterreaction was less vigorous, the copulatory cry occurred less frequently, and the male was not dislodged after copulation. In rabbits, local anaesthetization of the vagina and vulva did not affect the 'copulatory reflex' (Fee and Parkes, 1930). In guinea pigs there was an indication that mating did not occur after pelvic nerve transection (Donovan and Traczyk, 1965).

These studies indicate that there are at least two separate afferent neural pathways involved in female mating responses: one from the body surface and a second from the internal genital tract. First, in rats, stimulation of the body surface surrounding the genital area is adequate to elicit lordosis under appropriate hormonal conditions. Second, vagino-cervical stimulation, while not in itself adequate to elicit lordosis can nevertheless facilitate the lordosis elicited by skin stimulation (Komisaruk, 1971a; Komisaruk and Diakow, 1973). In those studies, even under hormonal conditions in which skin stimulation is not adequate to elicit lordosis, vagino-cervical stimulation, if added to the skin stimulation elicits lordosis. Vagino-cervical stimulation applied without concurrent skin stimulation will almost always fail to elicit lordosis even under hormonal conditions which are optimal for eliciting the lordosis response to skin stimulation. In earlier reports of vagino-cervical stimulation inducing lordosis in rats, concurrent skin stimulation was always applied, and the effects of vagino-cervical stimulation without concurrent skin stimulation were not reported (Long and Evans, 1922; Beach, 1944; Carlson and DeFeo, 1965). Carlson and DeFeo (1965) reported that pelvic neurectomy abolished this lordosis-inducing effect of vagino-cervical stimulation. We have confirmed and extended this finding in that ovariectomized, oestrogen-treated rats showing a moderate lordosis response to skin (flank-perineal area) stimulation displayed a markedly increased lordosis response when vagino-cervical stimulation was added (Komisaruk and Diakow, 1973), whereas ovariectomized, oestrogen-treated pelvic-neurectomized rats which showed a comparable moderate lordosis response to skin stimulation showed no increase in lordosis intensity when vagino-cervical stimulation was added (Diakow and Komisaruk, unpubl. observ.). Furthermore, after denervation of the skin of the entire posterior half of the body, except for several millimetres in the perigenital area, oestrogen-treated rats failed to show lordosis in response to manual stimulation. However, with the addition of vagino-cervical probing, lordosis was elicited, although it was ineffective when applied alone. Thus, vagino-cervical sensory activity acts synergistically with the perigenital skin sensory activity in the elicitation of lordosis (Rodriguez-Sierra and Komisaruk, in prep.).

Spinal Cord

In spinal animals, components of the female mating responses have been elicited by genital stimulation, but the extent to which ovarian hormones influence the responses is variable. Thus, in oestrous cats, treading and deviation of the tail was elicited by perineal tapping after spinal transection (Maes, 1939; Bard, 1940; Hart, 1971), and Maes (1939) and Bard (1940), but not Hart (1971) also elicited lordosis or pelvic elevation in response to perineal tapping in these preparations. Although Maes and Hart found that oestrogen administration facilitated the response, suggesting that the spinal system underlying the response is oestrogen-sensitive, all were able to elicit at least some of the responses, and Bard emphasized that both spinal anoestrous females and spinal males could show the responses. In spinal dogs, oestrogen facilitates the lateral curvature of the rear quarters and tail deviation in response to stroking the skin on the side of the vulva (Hart, 1970). In spinal ovariectomized rats, arching of the back (lordosis), hind leg extension, and tail deviation could be elicited occasionally by manual palpation in the flank region provided by a male rat mounting the female, but the frequency of occurrence and intensity of the response was not affected by treatment with oestrogen and progesterone. In guinea pigs treated with oestrogen and progesterone, spinal transection at L2-T5 eliminated all oestrous-type responses (Dempsey and Rioch, 1939). It is noteworthy that at least in some species, the neural system underlying lordosis and other components of the mating posture is to some extent functional in the apparent absence of ovarian hormones.

In rats, transection of the lateral, but not the dorsolateral spinothalamic tract or dorsal columns, disrupted locomotion and blocked or reduced the lordosis intensity (Kow and Pfaff, 1973). However, in guinea pigs, unilateral transections which interrupted the dorsal column, Lissaur's tract and 'other regions' in the dorsal quadrant, blocked oestrous responses to ipsilateral but not contralateral stimulation (Dempsey and Rioch, 1939).

Brain

Midbrain

In a recent study, Herndon (1976) found that midbrain lesions in the catecholamine (norepinephrine and dopamine) and serotonin pathways produced severe deficits in sexual receptivity in rats. Administration of d-amphetamine, which releases catecholamines, partially reversed the effects of lesions in the catecholamine pathways. The lordosis response to manual stimulation using cervical probing was, however, not blocked except in the rat with the largest lesion. In earlier studies, hormone-primed cats and guinea pigs with transections through the midbrain at the intercollicular level showed decerebrate rigidity and 'in no case was any response obtained which even remotely resembled oestrous behaviour' Dempsey and Rioch, 1939). Transections rostral to the midbrain permitted oestrous responses (e.g. treading, pelvic elevation, hind leg extension) to be elicited by genital stimulation. However, in similar decerebrate cats, Bard (1940) elicited 'a sort of wobbling movement of the body and pelvis which is a little suggestive of oestrual treading' by rubbing the vulval and perineal areas. Oestrous and anoestrous female and male cats showed these movements as a response to genital stimulation. Thus, The extent to which the components of oestrous behaviour persist in the absence of the forebrain and in the various hormonal states of the animals is contradictory, and part of the problem lies in the implicit disagreement on the definition of an 'oestrous response'. That is, does the movement itself, or the hormonal sensitivity of the movement, constitute the diagnostic characteristic of 'oestrous response'? For further discussion, see Beach (1967).

Forebrain

The studies of forebrain (di-and telencephalic) lesions or ablations on female sexual behaviour present a particular difficulty for comparison with the effects of lower brain stem or spinal transections. In the lower brain stem or spinal transection studies, the implicit assumption is that sexual behaviour will be essentially abolished, and the question is which, if any, components persist. In contrast, in the forebrain lesion or ablation studies, the implicit assumption is that sexual behaviour will be essentially normal, and the question is which, if any, components are abolished. This leads to an apparent discrepancy; components of female sexual behaviour persist after brain stem or spinal transections but female mating behaviour is abolished by certain diencephalic lesions. This apparent discrepancy can be resolved partially if one keeps in mind that in the forebrain lesion studies, which abolished female mating behaviour, the investigators did not report whether 'local components' of the mating response persisted. This can be contrasted with the lower brain stem and spinal transection studies, in which the persistence of 'local components' was the principal topic. It is possible, although not demonstrated, that after forebrain lesions that abolish mating behaviour, the same individuals would still show the types of response shown by spinal females.

Hypothalamus. In rats, the lordosis response to mounting by males was abolished by (a) central hypothalamic lesions in the region of the posterior border of the optic chiasm even though the rats continued to show vaginal oestrous cycles or were tested with oestrogen and progesterone (Law and Meagher, 1958); (b) anterior hypothalamic but not preoptic lesions after exogenous oestrogen and progesterone administration (Singer, 1968). Mating behaviour, as indicated by the presence of a vaginal plug and sperm in the vaginal smear, was also abolished by ventromedial hypothalamic lesions which did not disturb the oestrous cycle (Kennedy and Mitra, 1963). Lesions of the medial forebrain bundle (lateral hypothalamus) had no effect upon lordosis and soliciting behaviour in spayed rats treated with oestrogen and progesterone (Rodgers and Law, 1967; Hitt *et al.*, 1970). Knife cuts caudal to the suprachiasmatic nucleus reduced the incidence of mating in rats as determined by the presence of sperm in the vaginal smear; knife cuts rostral to the suprachiasmatic nucleus or through the mamillary nuclei were relatively ineffective in this regard (Kalra and Sawyer, 1970). However, in a different study, similar knife cuts at the posterior border of the optic chiasm did not prevent mating (Rodgers and Schwartz, 1972). The discrepancy might be due to the manner of testing employed. Kalra and Sawyer made the cut before 11.00h on the day of prooestrus, using a short-acting anaesthetic (Brevital), placed the females with males at 18.00 that evening, and determined whether sperm were present in the vaginal smears the next morning. In contrast, the lesioned rats in the study by Rodgers and Schwartz showed constant vaginal oestrus, high uterine weights, and constant behavioural receptivity over a period of several weeks after the surgery, suggesting a 'steady state of high oestrogen ... secretion rates.' The latter study therefore provided an extended period during which oestrogen and/or recovery of function could operate.

Lesions of the anterior hypothalamus abolished mating behaviour in ovariectomized rats treated with oestrogen and progesterone; systemic administration of d-amphetamine restored their receptivity, suggesting that facilitation of catecholaminergic neurotransmission is involved in lordosis responsiveness (Herndon and Neill, 1973). In other species, hypothalamic lesions 'between the optic chiasma and the attachment of the infundibular stalk' abolished oestrous behaviour without disrupting ovarian cycles (Dey et al., 1940) in guinea pigs, and in the same species, oestrous behaviour was inhibited by lesions at the 'level of the posterior border of the optic chiasma' (Brookhart et al., 1940) or in the 'midventral hypothalamus' (the smallest effective lesions being 'at the level of the anterior infundibular protuberance in the lateral extensions of the arcuate nucleus and adjacent ventral regions') (Goy and Phoenix, 1963). In ewes, mating behaviour was inhibited by destruction of 'an area immediately above the anterior median eminence' without affecting ovarian cycles (Clegg and Ganong, 1960). In cats, anterior hypothalamic lesions blocked mating behaviour even after exogenous oestrogen and pregnant mare serum administration, and mamillary lesions blocked mating behaviour in rabbits (Sawyer and Robison, 1956). Lesions of the 'sensory thalamus' were reported to reduce the lordosis response in ovariectomized oestrogen–progesterone-treated rats (Diakow, 1971b). Certain hypothalamic lesions facilitate the lordosis response in rats. Thus, Law and Meagher (1958) found that rats with 'anterior hypothalamic lesions in the preoptic area and posterior hypothalamic damage in the premamillary region' mated in dioestrus.

Extra-hypothalamic Forebrain Areas. Powers and Valenstein (1972) and Numan and Komisaruk (in prep.) found that lesions in the medial preoptic area of ovariectomized rats reduced the quantity of oestrogen needed to induce sexual receptivity. Similarly, Taleisnik et al. (1970) observed ear quivering elicited by finger pressure applied to the flanks and noted that 'this reaction, often seen during normal mating, could also be evoked in some spayed oestrogen-progesterone-treated rats, but in the brain-operated animals the threshold of the response seemed to be considerably reduced.' Komisaruk et al. (1972b) observed that after ablation of the septum by aspiration, ovariectomized rats mated significantly earlier and had higher lordosis quotients than control rats in which either the brain was intact or the cortex overlying the septum was removed. Furthermore, even without exogenous hormone administration, these ovariectomized, septal-ablated rats showed an intense and significantly more pronounced lordosis dorsiflexion posture (quantified photographically) than the control rats in response to vagino-cervical probing applied in conjunction with flank-perineum palpation Fig. 1). This is reminiscent of the report by Goy and Phoenix (1963) that two female guinea pigs displayed behavioural oestrus in the absence of exogenous hormone after lesions which were 'anterior, and possibly medial' to the midventral hypothalamic lesions that inhibited receptivity after exogenous hormone in the same study.

Nance et al. (1975a) found that septal lesions facilitated the lordosis response in female rats treated with oestrogen or testosterone, and in prepubertally castrated males treated with oestrogen (Nance et al., 1975b). In other studies, septal lesions did not block sexual receptivity (Dempsey and Rioch,

1939; Sawyer, 1959). It is interesting in this respect that electrical stimulation of the septum in cats generated 'pelvic movements, small jolting of the back pelt, raising of the tail and peculiar mewing . . . and vulvo-vaginal contraction' (Galeano et al., 1964).

These studies taken together suggest that a forebrain system may tonically inhibit a lordosis-activating system which can be activated in the absence of ovarian hormones, and that ovarian hormones may inhibit the inhibitory mechanisms. An additional possibility is that ovarian hormones may activate a lordosis-activating system, because oestrogen enhances the lordosis response which has already been potentiated by the septal ablation (Komisaruk et al., 1972b). An alternative possibility is that the septal or preoptic lesions increase the sensitivity of a lordosis-activating system to oestrogen, neurotransmitter, and/or sensory stimulation. For further discussion of disinhibition of the lordosis response, see Beach (1967) and Kow, et al. (1974).

Neocortical ablation did not abolish mating behaviour in rats (Davis, 1939). Indeed, this operation facilitated mating responses in ovariectomized, oestrogen–progesterone-treated rats (Beach, 1944). In that study, although the ablation increased the variability of the responses, other notable effects were that some females displayed (a) lordosis in response to stimuli which had not elicited this reaction prior to operation (pipette in the vagina, grasp of experimeter's hand, male's preliminary investigation), (b) maintenance of the lordosis posture 'long after the male had dismounted', and (c) increases in the frequency of ear-wiggling and hopping. Consistent with this, the lordosis quotient was increased by application of potassium chloride to the neocortex of ovariectomized, oestrogen-treated rats (Clemens et al., 1967) or electrical stimulation of the neocortex (Ross et al., 1973), both of which can induce spreading cortical depression.

Mating behaviour has been reported to be facilitated by lesions in other non-hypothalamic brain regions. After lesions that included the amygdaloid nuclei, there was an increased tendency for cats to show lordosis in response to genital stimulation while they were in vaginal anoestrus (Gastaut, 1952; Schreiner and Kling, 1953; Green et al., 1957). Zouhar and De Groot (1963) reported frequent mating during dioestrus and anoestrus of gestation, after lesions in the medial habenular nuclei, amygdaloid complex or stria terminalis, but not lateral habenula, septum, fornix, olfactory bulbs, or mamillary complex. However, habenular lesions were reported to decrease receptivity and increase avoidance of the males by the females in vaginally oestrous rats (Rodgers and Law, 1967), and also increased rejection behaviour and reduced soliciting behaviour in rats (Modianos et al., 1974). Moss (1971) reported that olfactory bulb lesions increased the lordosis quotient in sexually naive and experienced ovariectomized oestrogen–progesterone-treated, and normally cycling, rats. We have confirmed this finding in ovariectomized oestrogen-treated rats (Rodriguez-Sierra and Komisaruk, in prep.), and Edwards and Warner (1972) showed that this was not due to peripheral anosmia. Sawyer (1959) found that after combined olfactory bulb ablation and fornix transection, three of five female rabbits were 'hypersexual' in that they 'repeatedly mounted and accepted the male at a time when their vaginal orifices appeared pale and anoestrous.' However, olfactory bulb lesions in hamsters did not affect female sexual receptivity (Carter, 1973), and attenuated receptivity in mice (Thompson and Edwards, 1972).

Mating behaviour persisted after ablation of neocortex and olfactory bulbs (rabbits: Brooks, 1937); olfactory bulbs, amygdaloid nuclei, septum, and fornix (rabbits: Sawyer, 1959); neocortex, hippocampus, and most of the caudate and putamen (guinea pigs: Dempsey and Rioch, 1939); and neocortex and parts of rhinencephalic cortex (cats: Bard and Rioch, 1937; Bard, 1940). Behavioural afterreactions to mating or vaginal stimulation were observed in the cats (Bard, 1936, 1940). For further discussion, see the reviews by Sawyer (1960, 1962b); Beach (1967), Lisk (1967), Diakow (1974), Pfaff, et al. (1974); Kow, et al. (1974).

UPTAKE OF STEROID HORMONES IN THE BRAIN IN RELATION TO BEHAVIOURAL RESPONSIVENESS

Recent studies indicate that radioactively labelled steroid hormones injected systemically are accumulated in some of the same brain regions that had previously been implicated in the control of sexual behaviour on the basis of lesion studies. In the rat, radioactively labelled oestradiol was found to accumulate in the following hypothalamic nuclei: ventromedial, arcuate, anterior, lateral, posterior, premamillary; and in the medial preoptic, lateral and triangular septal, lateral habenular nuclei; also in the bed nucleus of the stria terminalis, lateral central gray of the mesencephalon, and in the substantia gelatinosa of the spinal cord (Stumpf, 1968, 1970; Stumpf and Sar, 1971; Pfaff and Keiner, 1973; Keefer et al., 1973). The relationship between the neural sites of oestrogen accumulation and the effects of lesions on female sexual behaviour is variable. Thus, although the following relationships appear contradictory, they raise interesting questions as to the various processes underlying neural and hormonal interactions in the control of female sexual behaviour. Ventromedial hypothalamic nucleus: high oestrogen uptake, lesions block female mating behaviour; medial preoptic nucleus: high oestrogen uptake, lesions facilitate female mating behaviour; neocortex: low oestrogen uptake, lesions facilitate female mating behaviour.

An interesting hypothesis regarding the functional significance of steroid hormone uptake in the brain is that the higher the affinity of the brain for oestrogen or progesterone, the lower the minimally effective dose of the hormones for inducing female sexual receptivity, i.e. the more sensitive the behaviour is to the hormone. Thus, 'activation of female copulatory behaviour requires a far lower dose of esterified estradiol in rats and guinea pigs than in hamsters ... and ... rats and guinea pigs had a much higher affinity for

... the estradiol (as indicated by tissue/plasma concentration ratios) ... than hamsters in uterus, anterior pituitary, and hypothalamus' (Feder et al., 1974). Furthermore, in the case of injected progesterone, neural affinity was directly related to behavioural sensitivity; affinity and sensitivity in the guinea pig being greater than in hamster, where in turn they were greater than in the rat (Wade et al., 1973). Similarly, the female rat's greater behavioural responsiveness to oestrogen than the male may be due at least in part to a higher affinity for oestrogen by the brain in females (see Kow et al., 1974 for review and see Hutchison, and Kelley and Pfaff, this volume Chapters 9 and 7 respectively for further discussion).

INDUCTION OF SEXUAL RECEPTIVITY BY DIRECT APPLICATION OF STEROID HORMONES TO THE BRAIN

Oestrogen

It is intriguing that direct application of sex steroids to certain regions of the brain induce animals to display complex behavioural patterns in response to previously ineffective stimuli. This is perhaps even more surprising than the demonstration that lesions can abolish the behaviour and that the sex steroids accumulate in particular neural regions. The mechanisms by which direct implantation of hormones influence behaviour are not known. These could include modulation of the effectiveness of sensory activity, modulation of neural activity more closely related to the motor output, and/or to some sort of integrative modulatory activity. In some, but not all cases, the effective implantation sites correspond to those at which lesions disrupt the behaviour and/or where there is uptake of the radioactively labelled hormones. There is, of course, no reason to expect a priori that hormonal implantation will activate sexual behaviour by an effect on the same region affected by lesions which abolish the behaviour, because components of the behaviour could be activated by the hormone acting in multiple brain regions which function in parallel. Furthermore, the behaviour could be blocked at a hormonally-insensitive modulating and/or efferent pathway in a region that is remote from the hormone-sensitive area(s). Thus, in ovariectomized (Lisk, 1962; Chambers and Howe, 1968) or ovariectomized, oestrogen treated (Ross et al., 1971) rats, female mating behaviour was activated by oestradiol implants in the medial-basal preoptic-suprachiasmatic area. Since in rats, oestrogen uptake occurs in the medial preoptic area (Stumpf, 1968; Pfaff and Keiner, 1973) and lesions in the medial preoptic area increase the behavioural responsiveness to systemically injected oestrogen (Powers and Valenstein, 1972) it is possible that oestrogen acts there by inhibiting neural activity (see Kow, et al., 1974 for further discussion).

A different process may occur in the ventromedial hypothalamus in female rats, where oestrogen implants induce sexual receptivity (Dorner et al., 1968),

and enable systemically administered progesterone to facilitate sexual receptivity (Lisk and Barfield, 1975) and where lesions suppress sexual receptivity (Law
and Meagher, 1968; Kennedy and Mitra, 1963). In other species, the effective
sites for facilitating oestrous behaviour with direct oestrogen implantation
differ somewhat from those in rats, and are not always congruent with areas
where lesions block oestrous behaviour. Thus, in rabbits, oestrogen implants
in the premamillary-ventromedial hypothalamic area facilitated female mating
behaviour (Palka and Sawyer, 1966), whereas mating behaviour was abolished
not by lesions in this region but in the mamillary bodies (Sawyer and Robison,
1956; Sawyer, 1959). In cats, oestrogen implants in the posterior hypothalamus
were effective in inducing sexual receptivity (Harris and Michael, 1964) but
in a simultaneous comparison between anterior lateral hypothalamic and
posterior medial hypothalamic sites, implants in anterior lateral hypothalamic
sites induced sexual receptivity in a higher proportion of the cats (Sawyer,
1962a). Furthermore, lesions in the anterior hypothalamus in cats abolished
mating behaviour (Sawyer and Robison, 1956). In guinea pigs, the most effective
sites for facilitation of the lordosis response by oestrogen implants after systemic
progesterone treatment were in the arcuate-ventromedial area and basal anterior
hypothalamic-preoptic area (Morin and Feder, 1974c). Similarly, lesions in
the arcuate nucleus and adjacent ventral regions abolished sexual receptivity
in guinea pigs despite exogenous oestrogen–progesterone administration
(Goy and Phoenix, 1963), whereas two ovariectomized, hormonally untreated
females with lesions which seem to corespond to the more rostral effective
site of Morin and Feder (1974c) showed behavioural oestrus without exogenous
hormones, a relationship similar to that in rats. In hamsters, oestrogen implants
in the anterior dorsal hypothalamus, but not in other sites which were found to
be effective in rats, facilitated oestrous behaviour when tested after systemic
progesterone treatment (Ciaccio and Lisk, 1973/74; Lisk et al., 1972; and
see Lisk, this volume Chapter 13).

Progesterone

Progesterone implants in the brain have also been shown to facilitate or
inhibit oestrous behaviour. In ovariectomized oestrogen-treated rats, progesterone inserted through cannulae chronically implanted into the midbrain
reticular formation, but not the preoptic, ventromedial or anterior hypothalamic areas, facilitated lordosis behaviour within 15 min (Ross et al., 1971).
In contrast, Powers (1972) found that progesterone implanted into the medial
basal hypothalamus but not the midbrain reticular formation did facilitate
sexual receptivity. Progesterone implanted into the caudate nucleus also
facilitated the lordosis response in rats (M. Yanase, pers. commun.). In guinea
pigs, the lordosis response was facilitated by progesterone implants in the
basal hypothalamus (Morin and Feder, 1974b). Inhibition of oestrous behaviour in animals primed with sex steroids has been observed after nore-

thindrone (a synthetic progestagen) into the mamillary bodies (Kanematsu and Sawyer, 1965) and by progesterone implanted near the midbrain substantia nigra (Morin and Feder, 1974a). In view of the possibility that the dopaminergic neurons whose cell bodies are located in the substantia nigra might be activated by the progesterone and thereby inhibit the lordosis response, Crowley, Feder, and Morin (1976a) systemically administered the dopaminergic agonist, apomorphine, and found that lordosis was indeed suppressed.

SENSORY AND HORMONAL INFLUENCES ON NEURAL ACTIVITY

Recording of neural activity has provided another approach to the question of how hormones affect the nervous system and facilitate the elicitation of female sexual behaviour by adequate sensory stimulation. These studies have taken several forms, such as (a) do hormones alter spontaneous neural activity and if so, are the effects specific to particular regions of the nervous system and/or to specific hormones? (b) do hormones alter neural responses to sensory stimuli which are relevant to sexual behaviour? (c) does sensory stimulation that is relevant to sexual behaviour induce specific patterns of neural activity in discrete regions of the nervous system? The main shortcoming of any study of this type is that the findings are at best only a correlate of the behaviour; the studies do not in themselves demonstrate whether any alteration in neural activity is directly or indirectly involved in any behavioural change. With this reservation, let us review such studies and some conclusions that can be drawn from them.

Neural Activity During Naturally Changing Hormonal Conditions

Spontaneous and evoked neural activity has been shown to vary in relation to naturally occurring changes in hormonal condition and in response to systemically injected steroid hormones. The firing activity of neuronal populations in the arcuate nucleus was found to increase during late dioestrus and through the afternoon of prooestrus (Kawakami et al., 1970), the time when oestrogen secretion is increasing (Yoshinaga et al., 1969). Similarly, single neurons in the preoptic area and anterior hypothalamus were found to fire faster in prooestrus than in the other stages of the oestrous cycle (Moss and Law, 1971; Dyer et al., 1972), an effect not seen in the cingulate cortex or lateral septum (Moss and Law, 1971). Consistent with these findings, although measured differently, the proportion of slowly firing neurons in the preoptic- suprachiasmatic and arcuate areas was found to be lowest in prooestrus and late dioestrus, an effect that was abolished by ovariectomy (Yagi and Sawaki, 1973). Other indices of brain excitability also showed changes in relation to changes in hormonal states. The current threshold for inducing local seizure activity by stimulating the dorsal hippocampus was lowest during prooestrus–oestrus (Terasawa and Timiras, 1968b), and a decrease in brain impedance was observed 2–6 days prior to oestrus in guinea pigs (Malven *et al.*, 1967). Hippocampal and amygdaloid seizure thresholds also showed a decrease as puberty approached, but a comparable change did not occur in neonatally ovariectomized rats (Terasawa and Timiras, 1968a). In 7–11 day pseudopregnant rats, the percentage of hypothalamic neurons excited by mechanical probing of the cervix was lower than that in cyclic rats, and this was reversed by removing the pseudopregnant ovaries before commencing the unit recording (Cross and Silver, 1965). The EEG pattern in the hypothalamus has been reported to be different in oestrous rabbits from the pattern obtained with pregnant rabbits (Ishziuka *et al.*, 1954). The genital sensory field, recorded from the pudendal nerve in rats, was found to be significantly larger and more sensitive in oestrous, sexually receptive females than in dioestrous, unreceptive females (Adler *et al.*, 1974).

Neural Activity in Response to Exogenously Administered Ovarian Hormones

Administration of oestrogen or progesterone has been shown to alter both spontaneous and evoked neuronal activity. Injection of oestrogen intravenously altered spontaneous firing rats in hypothalamic neurons with a mean latency of about 15 min (Yagi and Sawaki, 1973); intraperitoneal injection of oestrogen or progesterone altered the pattern of the EEG in dorsal hippocampus and septum within 30 min, and within 5 min of direct crystalline application of either steroid into the lateral septum, an increase was observed in the amplitude of the EEG recorded there (Innes and Michal, 1970). Within 3 min of direct application of crystalline progesterone into the preoptic area of awake cats, characteristic sleep waves in the cortical EEG as well as behavioural sleep were observed (Heuser *et al.*, 1967). Similarly, sleeplike activity in the EEG was induced within minutes after intravenous administration of progesterone Kobayashi *et al.*, 1962; Arai *et al.*, 1967; Ramirez *et al.*, 1967; Komisaruk *et al.*, 1967; Lincoln, 1969b; Terasawa and Sawyer, 1970). Spontaneous firing rate activity of neurons in hypothalamus as well as cortex and thalamus changed in relation to the EEG (e.g. increased during EEG arousal and decreased during EEG sleeplike activity) after progesterone administration (Komisaruk, *et al.*, 1967; Lincoln, 1969b), although in arcuate-median eminence neurons (Terasawa and Sawyer, 1970), effects of progesterone on neuronal activity were often independent of the EEG pattern, suggesting a more specific effect on these neurons.

Hormonal Modulation of Evoked Neural Responses

Electrically-evoked Activity

Neural activity which is evoked by sensory or intracranial electrical stimulation has also been shown to vary in relation to changes in hormonal state. Kawakami and Sawyer (1959) showed that administration of progesterone alters the voltage threshold for electrical stimulation of the midbrain reticular formation to induce EEG arousal (the arousal threshold) from sleep in oestrogen-primed ovariectomized rabbits. These findings were confirmed by Endroczi (1967, 1971). The threshold decreased over several hours after progesterone administration, during which time the rabbits became sexually receptive. After 24 h, the threshold was markedly elevated and the rabbits were unreceptive. A second type of threshold (the EEG afterreaction threshold) was determined in rabbits showing slow wave sleep. It was the voltage threshold for electrical stimulation of the ventromedial hypothalamus to induce paradoxical sleep. Differential effects on the two thresholds were observed after administration of estradiol benzoate (OB), testosterone propionate (TP), or certain progestational contraceptive drugs, such as norethynodrel (Sawyer and Kawakami, 1961; Kawakami and Sawyer, 1967), which blocked ovulation but not mating behaviour. Since the EEG afterreaction threshold was elevated but the arousal threshold was not, they hypothesized that the former was more closely related to the ovulatory mechanism and the latter was more closely related to sexual receptivity. In further support of this hypothesis, Delalutin, a long-acting progestational agent, prolonged sexual receptivity and the ability to ovulate and concomitantly delayed the elevation of the two thresholds. The relationship of these thresholds to receptivity and ovulation is not clear, since the events occur naturally in the awake animal. It is possible that equivalent changes in brain excitability occur even during waking, although starting at a different baseline.

Alterations in the amplitude of mono- and polysynaptic responses in the spinal cord were reported following administration of oestrogen and progesterone (Kawakami, 1960). The amplitude of the late but not early components of the evoked potentials generated by stimulation of the sciatic nerve or sacral roots and recorded from the midbrain reticular formation or arcuate nucleus was altered by exogenous oestrogen (Kawakami and Terasawa, 1967). Similarly, Endroczi (1969) reported alterations of evoked potentials recorded in the lower brain stem and hypothalamus within 5–10 min of an intravenous injection of progesterone.

Responses of hypothalamic neurons to sensory stimulation have been reported to be modulated by sex hormones, as discussed below. (For further discussion, see reviews by Sawyer, 1966, 1967; Beyer and Sawyer, 1969; Komisaruk, 1971.)

Responses to Vaginal Stimulation

Behavioural and Hormonal. Changes in neural activity resulting from vaginal stimulation are of considerable interest because of the variety of neuroendocrine and behavioural processes which are activated by vaginal stimulation occurring during mating behaviour, and because of the modulating effect of the sex steroids on the effectiveness of vaginal stimulation on these processes. Ovulation normally occurs in certain species including cats and rabbits in response to vaginal stimulation, and in cats denervation of the genital tract interferes with ovulation and the behavioural afterreaction (Diakow, 1971a). This effect is modulated by sex steroids, for oestrous (Sawyer and Markee, 1959), but not anoestrous rabbits (Sawyer and Everett, 1959) ovulate in response to vaginal stimulation. The proportion of rabbits that ovulate in response to vaginal stimulation is increased by administration of oestrogen (Sawyer and Markee, 1959) or progesterone (Sawyer and Everett, 1959).

Vaginal stimulation resulting from mating also induces ovulation in other species under conditions in which their normally spontaneous ovulation does not occur, e.g. after administration of barbiturate (Everett, 1967), chlorpromazine (Harrington et al., 1966), during light-induced persistent oestrus (Dempsey and Searles, 1943; Brown-Grant et al., 1973; Smith and Davidson, 1974); earlier than normal during the oestrous cycle (Aron et al., 1966), or in immaturity (Zarrow and Clark, 1968). In rats, the release of luteinizing hormone (LH) which results from mating (Moss and Cooper, 1973; Smith and Davidson, 1974) can increase the number of ova released (Rodgers, 1971). This may have behavioural significance in the activation of lordosis responsiveness which persists for several hours after a brief application of cervical probing, even in ovariectomized, hormonally-untreated rats (Rodriguez-Sierra et al., 1975a). That is, luteinizing hormone-releasing hormone (LRH) induced sexual receptivity in oestrogen-treated rats when injected systemically (Moss and McCann, 1973; Pfaff, 1973) or into the hypothalamus (Moss and Foreman, 1976; Rodriguez- Sierra and Komisaruk, in prep.), suggesting that it may be released in the brain and act locally to facilitate mating behaviour. Prostaglandin E_2 (PGE_2) has been shown to release LH in rats (Chobsieng et al., 1975) and induces sexual receptivity when implanted into the hypothalamus (Hall et al., 1975). When we injected PGE_2 intraperitoneally, in ovariectomized-hysterectomized, hormonally-untreated rats, using a blind test procedure, manual stimulation of the flanks and perineum (without cervical probing) induced lordosis in six of nine rats within 20 min, whereas only one of eight controls responded (Rodriguez-Sierra and Komisaruk, in prep.). Vaginal stimulation resulting from mating behaviour also induces prolactin release, and denervation of the genital tract by pelvic neurectomy interferes with this effect (Spies and Niswender, 1971) and the pregnancy and pseudopregnancy associated with it (Kollar, 1953; Carlson and DeFeo, 1965). Vaginal stimulation in hamsters at the time of artificial insemination also increases the proportion of pups born alive 17 days later (Diamond, 1972).

Vaginal stimulation resulting from mating behaviour or applied artifically can (a) facilitate female sexual behaviour (Koster, 1943; Green et al., 1970; Larsson et al., 1974; Rodriguez-Sierra et al., 1975a) in rats; (b) exert inhibitory (pacing) control over the female's timing of successive copulations (Bermant,

1961; Peirce and Nuttall, 1961; Bermant and Westbrook, 1966); and (c) attenuate the duration of the sexually receptive period in rats (Blandau *et al.*, 1941; Hardy and DeBold, 1972), rabbits (Beyer and Rivaud, 1969), guinea pigs (Goldfoot and Goy, 1970), hamsters (Carter and Schein, 1971; Carter, 1972) and lizards (Crews, 1973). In rats, rapidly repeated manual elicitation of lordosis by cervical probing plus flank-perineum palpation habituates the response; oestrogen-pretreated ovariectomized females showed significantly more successive lordoses until habituation (mean: 7.2 ± 0.2) than the oil-treated controls (4.2 ± 0.2) and a more rapid recovery of the lordosis response to original levels (mean: 6 h) than the oil-treated controls (mean: 60 h) (Rodriguez-Sierra, Velez, and Komisaruk, in prep.).

Neural. In several species, vaginal stimulation in oestrous but not anoestrous cats has been shown to induce an afterreaction recorded electrophysiologically, a response which may have an onset latency of several minutes and persist for minutes, or in certain cases, hours. One form that the afterreaction takes is a high amplitude, slow-wave, sleeplike activity (Porter *et al.*, 1957) which Lissak (1962) claims to have confirmed. It may continue into paradoxical sleep (e.g. Sawyer, Kawakami and Kanematsu, 1966: awake rabbits). Similar induction of a slow-wave sleeplike EEG pattern (not paradoxical sleep) resulted from vaginal stimulation predominantly in prooestrous rats (Ramirez *et al.*, 1967). A possible indication of a 'dearousal' effect of vaginal stimulation is that Kurtz (1975) found that in awake rats, the frequency of the theta rhythm slowed more during intromission or ejaculation than during mounts without intromission. An indication of hormonal modulation of the neuronal effect of vaginal stimulation is that Blake and Sawyer (1972) found that neurons in the medial preoptic area and arcuate nucleus showed an increase in firing activity which persisted for about 2.5 h after vaginal stimulation was applied during the evening of prooestrus but not dioestrus. Similarly, electromechanical stimulation of the cervix in rabbits induced an increase in neuronal activity in the premamillary area, that started almost immediately and persisted for about 30 min (Faure *et al.*, 1967). A relationship between the sleeplike afterreaction to vaginal stimulation and the stage of the oestrous cycle was reported by Zolovick and Eleftheriou (1971) in deermice. They found that ovariectomized, pregnant, or dioestrous females all showed an arousal-like response, in contrast to oestrous females, which showed a sleeplike afterreaction. Oestrogen reinstated the sleeplike afterreaction in some females. The behavioural afterreaction to cervical probing (which is characterized by vigorous movements, rolling, rubbing, sliding, twisting, and licking the vagina: Bard, 1940; Zitrin and Beach, 1945, in oestrous but not anoestrous cats) was accompanied by increased activity of hypothalamic and mesencephalic reticular formation neurons (Beyer *et al.*, 1971b). This activity was reduced by restraining the cats during the afterreaction, suggesting that it was more closely related to the motor activity than the sensory stimulation. This is reminiscent of the findings by Komisaruk and Olds (1968) that the activity of hypothalamic and mesencephalic reticular formation neurons in awake rats was more closely related to the behaviour being shown by the individual than to the stimuli that were applied. It is noteworthy that the response, to vaginal stimulation, of brain stem neurons in freely moving cats was very different from the response to vaginal stimulation in Flaxedil-immobilized cats (Alcaraz et al., 1969).

Hormonal modulation of the responses of hypothalamic neurons to vaginal stimulation and other modalities of sensory stimulation (e.g. olfactory, pain, cold) have been demonstrated in rats. The nature of the responses (e.g. proportion of neurons excited or inhibited) varies over the oestrous cycle (Barraclough and Cross, 1963) and in relation to pseudopregnancy (Cross and Silver, 1965) and persistent oestrus or estrogen administration (Lincoln and Cross, 1967; Cross, 1964), Vaginal stimulation-sensitive neurons in cats in the medullary reticular formation (Rose and Sutin, 1973), pons (Rose, 1973), and midbrain (Rose, 1975), but not thalamus (Rose and Sutin, 1971) showed an increase in probability of responding to other types of tactile and mechanical stimulation after oestrogen administration. In rats, neurons in the region of the dorsal midbrain which accumulates oestrogen (Pfaff et al., 1974), and which when stimulated electrically generates tail and rump movements (Pfaff et al., 1974), respond to tactile stimulation in skin areas contacted by the male during mating, but the responses were not affected by hormonal treatment (Malsbury et al., 1972). Anterior hypothalamic neurons were reported to respond selectively to cervical probing, but the effects of hormones on these neurons was not reported (Lincoln, 1969a). These findings must be viewed with caution for there are many possibilities for artifacts. For example, although Porter et al. (1957) claimed that the afterreaction to vaginal stimulation which they observed occurred only in oestrous, and not anoestrous cats, Sutin and Michael (1970) found no such difference. Holmes and Egan (1973) described characteristic 30–40 Hz EEG waves in the amygdala in female cats during mating and the behavioural afterreaction. However, Gault and Leaton (1963) described similar activity in the olfactory bulbs and amygdala in cats, which could be eliminated by occluding the nostrils. Thus the activity occurring during and after mating could be generated by a change in respiratory pattern and only indirectly by vaginal stimulation. Similarly, a synchronization of the cortical EEG and decrease in brainstem multiunit activity was observed during perineal tapping or perineal self-licking in cats (Beyer et al., 1971a). However, because the change in brain activity also occurred during eating and 'adoption of a relaxed posture' the authors concluded that it was related to 'relaxation behaviour' rather than specifically to genital stimulation. In a related context, the ability of progesterone to selectively block the effect of vaginal stimulation, but not other stimulus modalities, such as cold and pinch, on hypothalamic neurons (Barraclough and Cross, 1963) could be explained on a different basis from that of hormonal specificity. That is, all the stimuli elicit non-specific arousal, progesterone suppresses non-specific arousal, vaginal stimulation is the weakest of these arousing stimuli, and therefore the effect of vaginal stimulation is most strongly suppressed by progesterone, leading to an apparently specific effect. When attention was paid to this reservation, no effects of progesterone on responses to cervical stimulation were found which were independent of the non-specific EEG arousal–sleep balance (Komisaruk et al., 1967; Lincoln, 1969b).

One of the main difficulties in interpreting many of these neurophysiological studies is that the effects of genital stimulation have not been distinguished consistently from the effects of other types of sensory stimulation. Thus, when neuronal activity or the EEG changes in response to genital stimulation, it is not clear whether or not the effect is due to an induced change in the non-specific arousal level is response to the genital stimulus. That is, a variety of sensory stimuli or changes in the experimental conditions can generate effects indistinguishable from those observed in response to genital stimulation (see Margherita et al., 1965). The problem is that the neurophysiological correlates of genital stimulation can be less specifically related to the genital stimulation than are the natural consequences of genital stimulation, e.g. induction or inhibition of sexual behaviour and elicitation of ovulation. It seems valid to conclude, however, that gonadal hormones as well as genital stimuli do elicit observable changes in at least hypothalamic and lower brain stem neural activity, and the hormones alter the responses to genital stimuli. The relationship of the observed effects to the naturally occurring physiological event, however, requires considerable clarification.

THE NATURE OF THE NEURAL SUBSTRATE OF LORDOSIS IN THE ABSENCE OF OVARIAN HORMONES

Lordosis as an Extension-dominated, Flexion-suppressed Motor Pattern

Having reviewed evidence that hormones can act locally in the nervous system and can alter the excitability of neurons, it might be instructive to consider the properties of the neural system on which the hormones act when they are present in amounts that are insufficient to facilitate sexual behaviour, or are absent. The motor pattern of lordosis is not restricted to female mating behaviour, for it occurs in several other contexts. This suggests that it might be a component of a more general neural system, which also happens to be hormone-sensitive.

From a purely descriptive standpoint, all of the major components of the lordosis posture, the elevation of the head and rump with dorsiflexion of the spine, and extension of the fore- and hind legs share a particular postural characteristic. In each of these components, extensor muscle activation predominates over flexors. This contention is based in part on the distinct similarity between the lordosis posture in rats and the component of the 'air-righting' reflex in immature rabbits and cats that Warkentin and Carmichael (1939) describe as 'general body extension' which includes 'extensor-arching of the

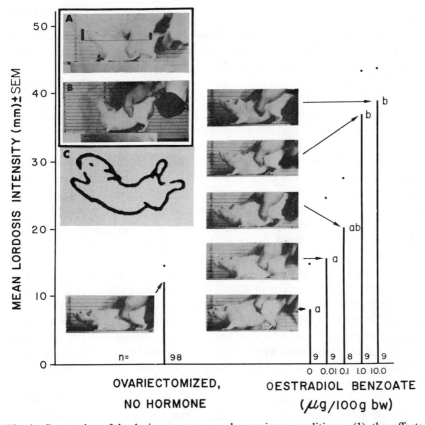

Fig. 1. Composite of lordosis responses under various conditions: (1) the effects of oestradiol benzoate on the lordosis response to flank-perineal palpation in conjunction with cervical probing. The bars (and dots above them) represent the group mean ($\pm$ S.E.M.) lordosis 'intensity' measured photographically in the various groups (number of rats in each group is shown along the abscissa). The photographs pointing to each bar are of the individual in each group that is closest to the mean for its group. Groups with different letters differ significantly from each other (Duncan test, $p < 0.05$). Thus, groups 0 and 0.01 differ from groups 1 and 10, but none differ from 0.1. (From Komisaruk and Diakow, 1973.) (2) Inset A shows the method of measuring lordosis 'intensity'. Each rat is photographed against a millimetre grid and the sum, in millimetres, of the elevations of the tip of the nose and top of the rump (marked here as vertical bars) above the lowest part of the back (horizontal line) form the lordosis intensity for that individual. A is an ovariectomized, hormonally-untreated rat showing lordosis. (3) Inset B is a representative example of a *septal ablated* ovariectomized, hormonally-untreated rat showing intense lordosis to the combined cervical and flank-perineal stimulation (see Komisaruk *et al.*, 1972). Inset C is photocopied from the study by Warkentin and Carmichael (1939). It is shown upside down in order to emphasize the postural similarities to lordosis. This is a drawing made from a motion picture film of the 'air-righting' reflex in a 13-day-old rabbit. The rabbit was suspended upside down by its legs and then dropped. At this age, rabbits fail to 'right' themselves and hit a ground cushion with their nose and rump first, in an extension-dominated posture. Note that extension involves the limbs and the characteristic curvature of the nose–back–rump continuum

back'. (I am indebted to J. S. Rosenblatt for pointing out this similarity.) Fig. 1 (c) shows the similarity between these two postures. The immature rabbit (up to 13 days of age) and cat fall to the ground in this posture when dropped upside down, for the flexor component of the 'air-righting' reflex has not yet matured fully. Thus it is a relatively 'pure' form of extensor activation. An extension posture in humans is the Moro reflex. The back is arched in the same way, the head is thrown back, and the arms, fingers, and sometimes the legs, extend. This extensor reflex can be elicited by suddenly dropping out support from a supine infant (Peiper, 1963; Prechtl, 1965). Marked extension of the hind legs accompanies arching of the back in neonatal rats when the mother licks the anogenital region, thereby inducing urination and defecation, according to studies by Capek and Jelinek (1956) and M. Friedman pers. commun.). Extension of the hind leg, specifically an increase of the angle formed at the knee by the femur and shank bones, characterizes the lordosis posture in rats on the basis of cinegraphic analyses (Pfaff et al., 1974). In our own studies, probing against the vaginal cervix induces hind leg extension, (a) in rats in which the spinal cord was transected at the midthoracic level (Komisaruk and Larsson, 1971); (b) in intact rats standing on a table; (c) in intact rats whose hind legs were lifted off the table by the experimenter lifting the tail; and (d) in rats suspended by the nape of the neck. Fig. 2 illustrates (d). The initial flexed position is maintained while the rat is suspended by the nape of the neck. When the probe is then pushed against the vaginal cervix, the limbs and digits extend tonically.

In support of the extensor-activating effect of vaginal stimulation, marked hind leg extension occurs just before the foetus emerges from the birth canal in the pronghorn antelope (Müller-Schwartze, 1975 (film)). However, there are species differences in mating posture in relation to the effect of vaginal stimulation. Thus, during copulation female cats normally show alternate treading (extension) movements of the hind legs from a crouched position, in which all four legs are flexed, while female dogs stand up with their legs extended rigidly, which functions to support the weight of the male (Beach, 1967). Vaginal stimulation in decerebrate cats showing extensor rigidity induces a 'most striking collapse of the extensor rigidity of the forelegs' and a 'moderate flexion of the hind legs', but the hind legs 'retain fair extensor tone' (Bard, 1940). Furthermore, 'when the cat is held in the standing position this response results in a crouching posture'. In contrast, vaginal stimulation in ten decerebrate dogs gave 'not the slightest trace of such a reaction' which is 'perhaps significant in view of the fact that a crouch is not a part of the oestrous behaviour of the female dog' (Bard, 1940).

The extension resulting from stimulation of the anogenital area in neonatal rats, and from vaginal stimulation in adult rats, suggests that lordosis during mating behaviour may be induced and/or facilitated by the same genital sensory–extensor motor link. A possible relationship between falling induced extension and mating behaviour is not as evident. However, the following speculation is tempting. The Moro reflex and the righting reflex are activated

Fig. 2. Extension of limbs induced by cervical probing. Left: holding an awake rat by the nape of the neck induces prolonged tonic flexion of the limbs and digits. Probing the vaginal cervix (right) induces prolonged tonic extension in the limbs and digits. (Szechtman and Komisaruk, unpubl. observ.)

by dropping the head, thereby generating activity in the vestibular system. This extension is not necessarily due to stimulation of neck stretch receptors in the case of the human Moro reflex, for it occurs even in infants whose head remains fixed in relation to its shoulders and trunk by a plaster cast (Prechtl, 1965). This has adaptive significance for protecting the head, as seen in the mature air-righting reflex (Warkentin and Carmichael, 1939) or in the case of a child who trips and falls while running; in both cases, the arms go out and the head goes back. Vestibular stimulation-induced extension is probably involved in the lordosis response in mating behaviour in rats. Highly receptive rats show ear wiggling, (rapid head movements which produce vibration of the ears: Beach, 1942). The head vibrates along the longitudinal axis so that each ear is alternately higher, then lower, than the other, about 25 times per second, based upon cinegraphic analysis (Komisaruk and Larsson, unpubl. observ.). This most likely generates potent vestibular input. This head vibration in the rat may be a kind of behavioural self-stimulation in which the female potentiates her own subsequent lordosis response intensity. The possibility that the head vibration is a ritualized display does not deny the possibility that it also is a form of behavioural self-stimulation. The two are not mutually exclusive. The afferent stimulation generated by an individual's own movements may well be a motivating factor for the further performance of the movement.

The rigid extensor pattern of lordosis in rats might provide additional physical support for the weight of the male while the mounts the female, and may have a similar function in other species, such as in sow, which stand rigidly immobile during coitus (Signoret, 1970) and dogs (Beach, 1967). Lesions of the lateral vestibular nucleus depress (Modianos and Pfaff, 1975a) and electrical stimulation facilitates (Modianos and Pfaff, 1975b) lordosis responding. Perhaps this involves the extensor-facilitating role of the vestibular system.

The Role of Vaginal Stimulation in Facilitating Extension and Lordosis, while Suppressing Flexion and Pain

The extension induced by vaginal stimulation simultaneously blocks flexion responses (e.g. leg withdrawal in response to foot pinch: Komisaruk and Larsson, 1971). This might occur if cervical probing activated both extensors and flexors but the extensors were stronger, thereby preventing limb flexion. However, when, in lightly anaesthetized rats, we cut flexor muscles free in the leg so that they contracted in response to foot pinch unopposed by extensors, cervical probing still blocked the muscle contraction (Naggar and Komisaruk, unpubl. observ.). The blockage apparently occurs before the final motor pathway, because when we generated hind limb movement by electrical stimulation of the pyramidal tract, the movement was *not* blocked by cervical probing (Komisaruk, 1974). We then determined whether cervical probing blocks other responses to noxious stimulation.

There seems to be a gradient of effectiveness of inducing immobilization and suppressing responses to noxious stimulation, the greatest effect being exerted in the tail and hind limbs and a much weaker effect being exerted on the face (Komisaruk and Larsson, 1971). Nevertheless cervical probing markedly and significantly elevated the current threshold needed to elicit vocalization in response to tail shock in awake rats (Crowley *et al.*, 1976d). In that test situation, the rats often vocalized spontaneously between successive shocks, in the non-shock interval, while they were receiving cervical probing, indicating that the cervical probing did not block their *ability* to vocalize. Furthermore, vocalization can be elicited by placing one's hand under the rat's ventral surface and lifting the rat suddenly. This is probably a startle response. When we applied vagino-cervical stimulation by means of a balloon inflated in the vagina and attached it to a flexible tube in order to avoid possibly painful stimulation as we lifted the rats, they vocalized during the lifting, although the vocalization in response to foot pinch was suppressed by the same balloon stimulus (Komisaruk and Wallman, 1977). Thus, they were capable of vocalizing during the vagino-cervical stimulation, but only the response to the noxious pinch stimulus was suppressed.

Using an additional approach to circumvent the problem that cervical probing may simply be preventing the rat from making a behavioural response, rather than having an analgesic effect, we performed the following experiment (Ross and Komisaruk, in prep.). Rats were first trained to press a lever in order to terminate skin shock. They were then divided into two groups: The experimental group was confronted with unavoidable skin shock and allowed to press a lever, thereby obtaining cervical probing while the shock remained on. If these rats did not press the lever, they did not get the cervical probing, but they still received the skin shock. Thus, they were given the option of obtaining cervical probing. The control group also received the unavoidable shock, but when they pressed the lever, they did not get the cervical probing. The lever-pressing response in the control rats soon extinguished and the rats passively took the shock. In contrast, the experimental rats continued pressing the lever for cervical probing during the unavoidable shock for significantly more trials. This procedure circumvents the problem of immobilization induced by cervical probing, and these findings suggest that cervical probing ameliorates the aversive properties of skin shock. The females that pressed the lever for cervical probing did so almost exclusively after the shock came on; they virtually never pressed for cervical probing during the intertrial inervals of approximately one minute. If the probing by itself were rewarding we would expect the rats to show a high spontaneous rate of lever pressing. Since this did not occur, we conclude tentatively that the cervical probing, while not rewarding in and of itself, may nevertheless ameliorate the effects of the shock.

In order to obtain neurophysiological evidence as to whether cervical probing may actually block pain, we recorded the responses to noxious and non-noxious stimulation of neurons in the ventrobasal complex of the thalamus, before and during cervical probing. Responses to pinch were markedly attenuated by cervical probing (Fig. 3). In neurons that responded to both pinch and touch, the cervical probing attenuated the response to pinch but not the response to touch (Fig. 4). On a group basis, the pinch-sensitive neurons (n = 24) increased their mean (± SEM.) firing rate (spikes per second) from 3.9 ± 1.2 (their spontaneous level) to 22.5 ± 6.7 during pinch, and during pinch applied concurrently with cervical probing, their firing rate was only 9.1 ± 2.7, a significant attenuation of the response to pinch. In contrast, the touch-sensitive neurons (n = 11) increased their firing rate from 4.2 ± 2.1 (their spontaneous level) to 14.6 ± 4.9 during touch, and during touch applied concurrently with cervical probing, their firing rate was 18.3 ± 5.6, which was not a suppression. This effect was not due to a differential action of cervical probing on the firing rates *per se* because in both pinch- and touch-sensitive neurons, cervical probing had an equivalent effect on increasing firing rates over the spontaneous levels (10.2 ± 3.4: pinch-sensitive neurons, 8.7 ± 4.5: touch-sensitive neurons). The selective suppression of responses to pinch is also not necessarily due to some units responding to pinch and different units responding to touch, because the differential effect was seen in single neurons (Fig. 5) (Komisaruk, and Wallman, 1973; Komisaruk, 1974; Komisaruk and Wallman, 1977). Furthermore, we found that the blockage of responses to pinch by cervical probing occurred despite maintenance of an aroused condition (by occluding the nares), and that the effect is probably not due to

SUPPRESSION OF RESPONSE TO PINCH BY CERVICAL PROBING

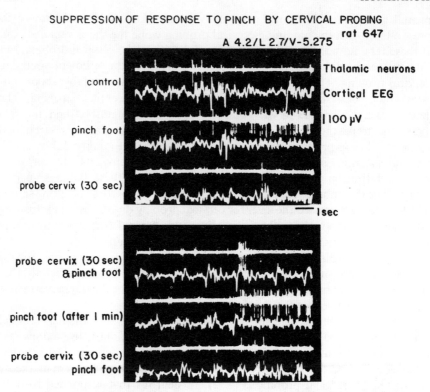

Fig. 3. After a control period showing low spontaneous activity (top unit trace), foot pinch was applied and maintained throughout the second half of the sweep (next unit trace down), resulting in a marked activation of the unit. After the foot pinch was released, and the unit activity returned to 'baseline', probing the cervix continuously for 30 s did not noticeably alter the unit activity from the control condition (third unit trace down). However, when the cervix was probed for 30 s and then the foot pinch was applied and maintained throughout the second half of the sweep, while the cervix was still being probed, only a short burst of activity occurred (fourth unit trace down), indicating a marked attenuation of the response compared to pinch without cervical probing (second unit trace down). Note that this is a multi-unit recording and that the response of the population as whole was suppressed. One minute after cervical probing was released, foot pinch was again applied and maintained throughout the second half of the sweep (fifth unit trace down), and the full response was seen again. When the cervical probing plus foot pinch procedure was repeated, attenuation of the response to pinch was seen again (bottom unit trace). The corresponding EEG records suggest a stronger arousal during pinch alone than during pinch combined with cervical probing or probing alone

distraction. In the latter case, we substituted for the cervical probing a variety of intense stimuli which had little or no effect on the neurons being studied (i.e. their relative lack of effect was similar to the relative lack of effect of the cervical probing applied alone). In those cases, the substituted stimuli had no

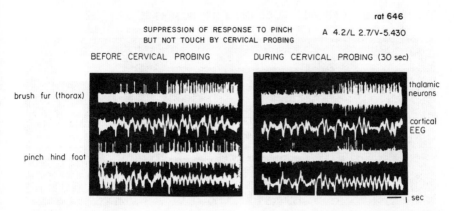

Fig. 4. The units at this recording site (nucleus ventralis thalami) were activated when either repetitive brushing of the fur or pinching the foot were applied throughout the second half of each sweep. During cervical probing, there was no apparent change in the response to tactile stimulation, whereas the unit (but not EEG) response to foot pinch was attenuated

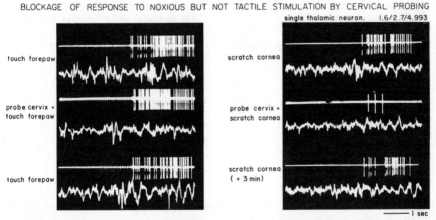

Fig. 5. Light touch applied to the forepaw and scratching the cornea (throughout the second half of each sweep) both activated this single neuron. Cervical probing attenuated the response to the noxious stimulus, but not to the light touch stimulus.

suppressive effect on the neuronal response to pinch, although the cervical probing did have a suppressive effect (Fig. 6).

Another argument against the possibility that the antinociceptive effect of cervical probing is due to selective attention to the probing is that even in spinal-transected rats cervical probing blocked the leg withdrawal response to foot pinch, suggesting that cervical probing may block nociceptive input at the spinal level. Further study is needed to resolve this problem. Our findings of a suppressive effect of cervical probing on responses of ventrobasal thalamic

"DISTRACTION" CAN NOT ACCOUNT FOR BLOCKAGE
OF RESPONSE BY CERVICAL PROBING.   single thalamic neuron

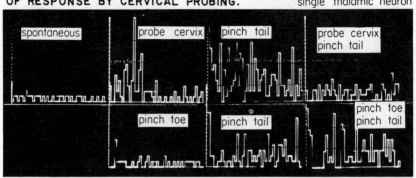

30 sec.

Fig. 6. The effect of a noxious stimulus (pinching the tail) was suppressed by cervical probing but this effect was not mimicked by a different type of intense stimulation (pinching a toe). This suggests that cervical probing suppressed the response to pinch by some means other than distraction. Each segment depicts the firing pattern of the single thalamic neuron for a 30 s period (recorded in 60 one-half-second bins) during the application of the stimuli as labelled. The smallest-sized 'blip' is one action potential. Vertical height represents the number of spikes per 'bin'. In this example, compared with spontaneous activity (top, 1st left segment) probing the cervix induces an initial activation of the unit (top, 2nd segment), and the strong long-lasting activation of the unit, induced by applying an alligator clip to the tail (top, 3rd segment), is markedly suppressed by applying cervical probing concurrently with the tail pinch (top, 4th segment). In contrast, a strong distracting stimulus, applying an alligator clip to the toe, (bottom, 2nd segment) did not activate this particular neuron, although pinching the tail (bottom, 3rd segment) did activate it again. When pinching the toe was substituted for probing cervix (bottom, 4th segment) no suppressive effect was observed. Thus, although the toe pinch was presumably at least as intense a distracting stimulus as the cervical probe, it did not have the suppressive effect on the neuron that the cervical probing had

neurons to noxious stimulation are supported by recent studies. Petty (1975) found that cervical probing suppressed responses to noxious stimulation in neurons of the mesencephalic central grey in awake rats (an area in which electrical stimulation induces analgesia: Reynolds, 1969; Mayer *et al.*, 1971) and cervical probing blocked responses to pinch in neurons of the nucleus reticularis gigantocellularis of the medulla (Hornby and Rose, 1976).

The findings reviewed in this section can be summarized concisely as follows: at least in rats, vaginal stimulation *induces extension* of the limbs and facilitates the elicitation of lordosis, which is an extension-dominated pattern. Simultaneously, vaginal stimulation *suppresses flexion* (withdrawal) responses, as well as vocalization, conditioned behavioural, and thalamic neuronal, responses to noxious stimulation. These findings suggest that vagino-cervical stimulation may suppress the perception of pain.

How the Female Rat may Modulate her Sensory Perception by Using her Muscles

Does Vaginal Stimulation both Intensify Non-noxious Input and Attenuate Noxious Input?

Several authors have suggested that intromissions and ejaculations may be aversive in female rats. Peirce and Nutall (1961) found that when female rats were provided with an elevated escape compartment attached to an arena containing sexually active males, '. . . following copulation, feats of "broken-field running" occurred in which the female might jump completely over one male, side-step another, and, from the center of the arena, make a wild leap to the lip of the escape compartment.' They suggested that 'the fact that work is done to avoid the male indicates that the motivational change involves more than a possible reduction in sexual drive: an aversive drive is also present.' The findings by Bermant and Westbrook (1966) could be interpreted similarly. That is, if intromission or ejaculation is more aversive than mounts without intromission, then the female would wait longer to reinitiate sexual contact after the intromittive stimuli. The possibility that numerous intromissions are aversive is also supported by the finding of Hardy and DeBold (1972) that the waning of receptivity and increase of rejection behaviour resulting from numerous (more than 40) intromissions is counteracted by using a vaginal mask to prevent intromissions. However, the mating behaviour studies cited above could also be interpreted to mean that the intromittive stimuli are more 'satisfying' and thus the female waits longer before obtaining the stimulation and seeks less of it.

If the intromittive stimuli are to some extent aversive, then the apparently antinociceptive component of the vaginal sensory input may attenuate the aversive component and facilitate the female's willingness to obtain intromittive stimuli, several of which at least in the rat, are necessary prior to ejaculation in order for pregnancy to occur (Adler, 1969). Furthermore, analgesia induced by genital tract distention may also have significance in parturition as the foetuses pass through the cervix and vagina, perhaps generating their own suppression of pain in doing so. This could attenuate stress responses in the parturient female.

Thus, vaginal stimulation may have a dual effect, (a) increasing the perceived intensity of relatively low intensity tactile stimulation of the genital skin (this may be the means by which vaginal stimulation potentiates the lordosis-inducing effect of flank-perineum palpation (Komisaruk and Diakow, 1973), and (b) attenuating the noxious properties of the intromittive stimulation. The processes are not necessarily mutually exclusive. Such a combination of intensified non-noxious, plus partially attenuated aversive, genital stimulation resulting from intromissions could well be highly arousing. The relative intensity of these components, depending on their decay rates after stimulation, could influence the temporal pattern of the female's approach to, and withdrawal from, the male.

Vaginal stimulation may attenuate the *perception* of intense stimulation, thus allowing the female to accept intense levels of sensory stimulation which are normally aversive. Simultaneously, however, excitation along other afferent pathways projecting from this intense input might remain unattenuated. This would generate high levels of excitation of various (e.g. neuroendocrine, autonomic) efferent systems which may function optimally at high excitation levels or which may have high thresholds for activation.

A comparable process might underly the copulatory behaviour–ejaculatory systems in males. That is, perhaps intense afferent stimulation is necessary to generate the explosive autonomic discharge at ejaculation and the genital sensory input simultaneously attenuates the perception of the aversive properties of the intense stimulation. According to Kinsey *et al.* (1948), in humans 'the genitalia of many adult males become hypersensitive immediately at and after orgasm, and some males suffer excruciating pain and may scream if movement is continued or the penis even touched. The males in the present group become similarly hypersensitive before the arrival of actual orgasm, will fight away from the partner, and may make violent attempts to avoid climax, although they derive definite pleasure from the situation. Such individuals quickly return to complete the experience, or to have a second experience if the first was complete'.

A Possible Relationship Between Lordosis and Acupuncture Analgesia

By what processes could genital stimulation attenuate aversive properties of sensory stimulation? There is some evidence that acupuncture needling analgesia may be mediated by mechanical stimulation of deep muscle and/or tendon receptors, because the acupuncture effect was abolished by local anaesthetization of the deep tissue, but not the skin, surrounding the acupuncture needle (Chang, 1973; Chiang *et al.*, 1973). Furthermore, stretching the Achilles tendon induces immobilization and is widely used in veterinary practice in order to produce immobility for administering injections (Kaada, 1974). In the female, cervical probing and intromissions may have a comparable effect by exerting stretch on deep muscle receptors. In addition, it is tempting to speculate that when the female rat shows the intense tonic muscular contraction which characterizes lordosis, or when the male shows vigorous copulatory movements, they are, through their own behavioural movements, generating afferent activity in their own deep muscle and tendon receptors, by which they may be activating intrinsically an analgesic process. In this regard, the expressions 'gritting one's teeth' or 'biting the bullet' as a means of overcoming physical or ideational pain, may not be just fanciful metaphors.

A Possible Reafferent Process in the Lordosis Response

The above considerations imply that the female rat may alter her perception of stimulation applied by the male by tensing the muscles which she uses in lordosis. In addition, she might intensify the sensory input which she receives from the genital skin by elevating her rump and exposing it to the male's thrusting. The latter possibility is made more plausible by a consideration of the striking copulatory behaviour of female porcupines. Just prior to copulation, the female raises her tail, backs up and pushes against the male's nose and head with her genitals. During copulation, the female pushes actively against the thrusts of the male. If copulatory contact is broken, the female re-establishes contact by backing up to the male (Shadle, 1946). It seems likely that the female porcupine organizes her own bodily movements to increase the intensity of genital stimulation, rather than simply reacting to stimulation provided by the male.

The studies by Peirce and Nuttall (1961), Bermant and Westbrook (1966) and McClintock and Adler (Adler, 1974) indicate that a significant role is played by the female rat in initiating and timing her contact with the male. Similarly, Meyerson and Lindstrom (1973) showed that oestrogen induces female rats to actively seek out certain environmental stimuli, rather than only facilitating the response of the females to the male (see Meyerson and Malmnas, this volume Chapter 16 for experimental details). In this case, the possibility that oestrogen changes the female rat's perception of, or criteria for, appropriate sensory input is more plausible than the possibility that the oestrogen changes the excitability of specific motor patterns for approaching the male.

Since sensory thresholds fluctuate in relation to the oestrous cycle in rats (tactile: Adler *et al.*, 1974) and the menstrual cycle in women (thermal: Kenshalo, 1966; visual: Diamond *et al.*, 1972), it is possible that ovarian hormones might alter the perception of the 'resting' pattern of sensory input. In response to this, the individual might then organize her own behaviour towards achieving optimal sensory input, using her body to obtain appropriate stimulation, rather than passively responding to specific sensory stimulation.

Some Possible Parallels in Humans

The process of an individual using its own motor movements to generate and modulate sensory input could make use of the processes described above. This may be similar to our own perception of, and response to, an itch, which we satisfy by increasing our intensity of scratching. The scratching is perceived as increasing the sensory input and simultaneously as satisfying or inhibiting the itch. Similarly, when we stretch in order to squeeze away aches in muscles, we show arm extension and opisthotonus. In the case of sexual behaviour, the hormones might induce aching or related sensory activity in the genital area and its dermatomally related muscles. Then tactile and muscle afferent activity, generated actively and passively, might suppress the aching. The suppression might be perceived, as in the case of itch, as satisfying, surmounting, overcoming squeezing away, dissipating, etc. the irritating stimulus.

In this regard, it is interesting to note that orgasmic capability is reported to be abolished by anterolateral spinal transection performed clinically in order to block pain (Elliott, 1969) and that as pain sensation recovers after a prolonged interval, so does orgasmic capability (D. Price, pers. commun.). Conversely, the application of painful stimulation to heighten the perceived intensity of orgasm (J. Money, personal communication) might be due in part to the ability of genital stimulation to surmount (i.e. suppress) intense sensory input, thereby altering its perceived nature. By a crude analogy, this may be likened to a pressure cooker. Normally, boiling (= orgasm) limits the amount of heat (= excitatory, including aversively intense, effect of genital stimulation) that can be absorbed. Applying the lid of the pressure cooker (= inhibitory effect of genital stimulation) allows the contents to absorb more heat before reaching the boiling point. The more pressure (= genitally stimulated inhibition) is applied, the more heat (= perceived intensity of genital and other excitatory input) can be absorbed (= tolerated) before boiling (= orgasm) occurs at the elevated temperature (= higher orgasmic intensity). At least part of the perception of a more intense orgasm may be due to the increased proprioceptive afferent activity generated from the somatic and visceral muscles, whose contractions had been more strongly activated by the increased sensory stimulation.

Indeed, the process in which proprioceptive input, which is generated by muscular contraction, inhibits unpleasant, irritating, or painful (nociceptive) sensory input, and all its physical and metaphorical ramifications, may be a general principle underlying the motivation of species-characteristic behaviour patterns, and genital orgasm may be just an extreme case of this general principle. Non-genital 'orgasms' may normally be represented by behaviour patterns such as stretching and yawning, sneezing, coughing, urinating, defecating, vomiting, and perhaps even chewing, swallowing, breathing, blinking, sobbing, crying, grasping, etc., and their myriad metaphorical equivalents. In an anthropomorphic sense, organisms may find pleasurable, and therefore seek out, situations or activities in which they can both generate and also surmount, squeeze away, dissipate, or in any sense attenuate, unpleasant sensory input by self-generated muscular activity.

Visceral–Somatic Interactions in Lordosis

The effect of vagino-cervical stimulation on the response to skin stimulation involves a convergence between sensory input of visceral and somatic origin. The genital tract is considered visceral for the following reasons. Embryonically, the distal vagina, rectum, and urinary bladder are derivatives of the cloaca, hind-gut and allantois, which in turn are derivatives of the splanchnic mesoderm (hypomere mesenchyme) (Arey, 1954, p. 324). The cervix and proximal vagina are derivatives of the Müllerian ducts which in turn are derivatives of the mesodermal mesomere (Arey, 1954, p. 325; Walter and Sayles, 1949, pp. 164–167). The genital tract is comprised of smooth muscle which is innervated by the pelvic (parasympathetic) and hypogastric (sympathetic) nerves.

Under oestrogenic stimulation, the somatic stimulation alone (flank-perineum palpation) can elicit lordosis only occasionally (Komisaruk, 1971a). When the two stimuli are applied jointly, with oestrogenic pretreatment, lordosis occurs in almost every case, and is almost invariably of greater intensity than when either stimulus is applied alone (Komisaruk and Diakow, 1973). When the two stimuli are applied jointly, with oestrogenic pretreatment, lordosis occurs in almost every case, and is almost invariably of greater intensity than when either stimulus is applied alone (Komisaruk and Diakow, 1973). In ovariectomized rats with very low doses of oestrogen, or in the absence of exogenous oestrogen, the somatic and visceral stimuli are each essentially unable to elicit lordosis when applied alone, but when they are applied simultaneously, lordosis is induced in at least half the rats which we have tested (Komisaruk and Diakow, 1973). Thus, there appear to be powerful additive effects of visceral and somatic stimuli in this system.

The ability of visceral (cervical) stimulation to induce tonic somatic muscular contraction (e.g. leg extension) and block the polysynaptic reflexes (e.g. leg flexion to foot pinch) is consistent with other findings. Eble (1960) showed that compression of a fallopian tube in rabbits induces local contraction of the paravertebral muscles. In cats, distention of the uterine horn, bladder, or rectum can inhibit hind limb polysynaptic reflexes (Evans and McPherson, 1958) and polysynaptic reflex responses of the hind leg are suppressed during spontaneous contractions of the urinary bladder (McPherson, 1966). Inhibition of polysynaptic reflexes of the leg can be obtained by stimulation of the pelvic nerve (a branch of which innervates the vagina: Komisaruk, et al., 1972), splanchnic nerve, or sympathetic chain (Evans and McPherson, 1960). Other studies, e.g. Fields et al. (1970), Selzer and Spencer (1969a, 1969b), and Pomeranz et al. (1968) have shown that a single spinal cord neuron can respond to both somatic and visceral stimulation. For example, the same spinal cord neuron responded to stimulation of the sensory nerve which innervates the skin of the back and to compression of the urinary bladder (Fields, et al., 1970). This represents convergence between a cutaneous (somatic) nerve and the sensory component of the pelvic (visceral) nerve. Convergence of vaginal and genital skin afferents onto single neurons has been reported by Rose (1973, 1975) and Rose and Sutin (1971, 1973). The findings of convergence of somatic and visceral input onto the same spinal neuron have been utilized to account for the phenomenon of referred pain. That is, when visceral irritation activates a spinal sensory neuron, one cannot tell whether the true origin of the input to that neuron is from the viscera or from the body surface, so the origin of the pain is often misinterpreted as coming from the body surface at the same dermatomal level. This is the so-called 'dermatomal rule' of Ruch

(1961). Examples of referred pain are arm and chest pains occurring when an embolism occludes the coronary artery, or in the case of abdominal soreness accompanying inflammation of the appendix. Selzer and Spencer (1969a, 1969b) reported that single neurons in the spinal cord in cats which respond to stimulation of the skin of the thigh, also respond to stimulation of the splanchnic (visceral) nerve. Furthermore, this visceral nerve stimulation increased the responsiveness to the skin stimulation. This is direct evidence of visceral stimulation converging and summating with skin stimulation onto the same neuron. Selzer and Spencer (1969a, 1969b) proposed that this could be the basis of cutaneous hyperalgesia which occurs as a result of visceral pain. Similarly, Miller and Waud (1925) showed that in decerebrate cats, stroking the abdominal wall elicits a moderate contraction of the abdominal muscles. When they applied traction to the intestines, they obtained a marked increase in the surface area on the abdomen from which they could elicit the abdominal contraction, and also an increase in the intensity of the contraction. These findings also support the concept of hyperalgesia of the skin resulting from stimulation of the viscera and functional convergence between the somatic and visceral systems. According to Ruch (1961), hyperalgesia and referred pain are thought to be based on the same mechanism of convergence of visceral and somatic input onto the same spinal neurons. Perhaps most relevant to the present discussion is the referral of pain to the perigenital and perianal region, thighs, lower abdomen, and back when the foetus passes through the birth canal (Bonica, 1972). This indicates the likelihood of a dermatomally restricted convergence of pain input between the (visceral) genital tract and (somatic) thighs, flanks, and perineum in women. It is likely that this functional convergence is related to the synergistic effects of flank-perineal and vagino-cervical stimulation in the lordosis response in rats.

An implicit assumption that I am making is that visceral and somatic convergence for tactile and/or pressure input follows the same principles as visceral and somatic convergence for nociceptive input, but this requires specific testing. Furthermore, the mechanism by which visceral (pressure?) stimulation (cervical probing) attenuates the effects of somatic noxious (pinch) stimulation is not known.

The above discussion has applied to visceral and somatic interactions in pain sensation, but it is likely that a parallel interaction exists for non-nociceptive systems as well. Indeed, this seems to be the case in Fields, et al. (1970) study showing convergence onto the same spinal neuron between cutaneous input from the surface of the lower back and moderate distention input from the bladder.

Convergence of visceral and tactile stimuli onto the same spinal neurons could also play a vital role in the survival of neonatal rodents. Neonatal guinea pigs do not urinate or defecate and die, unless they receive anogenital tactile stimulation, which is provided by the mother as she licks them (Beach, 1966; Harper, 1972). In adults, distention of the bladder or rectum is an adequate stimulus to elicit bladder or rectum contraction, which results in voiding, an example of a viscero-visceral reflex. Perhaps this reflex is not fully mature in the neonatal rodents and thus bladder or rectal distention does not activate the visceromotor reflex. When the mother licks the pups' anogenital region, perhaps she provides somatic tactile input from the anogenital region and this input summates with the bladder or rectal input and thereby activates the visceromotor efferents for voiding. Beach (1966) and Boling *et al.* (1939) observed that this perineal stimulation induced the lordosis posture as well as urination and defecation in neonatal guinea pigs. It is of particular interest, as Beach noted, that on some occasions, tactile stimulation of rump alone, *not* the anogenital region, could induce urination and defecation. This is further evidence that lumbosacral and perineal somatic afferents may converge on pelvic visceral afferents to activate lordosis and/or voiding. Kuru (1965) has demonstrated that electrical stimulation of the pelvic nerve elicits a so-called pelvico-perineo-abdominal reflex, which is mediated by the medulla. In this response, electrical stimulation of the pelvic nerve, which receives sensory input from the rectum and bladder, as well as from the vagina and cervix, induces a marked *relaxation* of the muscles of the perineum and also *contraction* of the muscles of the abdomen and diaphragm. Thus, the same reflex may be utilized in urination, defecation, and parturition. In this regard, it is also of interest that lordosis in guinea pigs is accompanied by dilatation of the vaginal orifice (Boling, *et al.*, 1939). Thus, this pelvico-perineo-abdominal reflex may also be utilized in mating behaviour and activated by somatic perineal stimulation which converges with visceral pelvic nerve input.

Beach (1966) has shown that lordosis accompanies urination and defecation induced by tactile stimulation of the perigenital area in neonatal male as well as female guinea pigs, and Capek and Jelinek (1956) and Friedman (pers. commun.) have shown that extension of the hind limbs accompanies this response in rats. Flexion in this situation would physically interfere with the reception of tactile stimuli from the mother by the pups, and would be maladaptive.

Thus it seems possible that lordosis in response to tactile stimulation of the flanks and perineal area may be a special case in which the general principle is activation of the extensor system by convergence of visceral and somatic afferents. Visceral and somatic input apparently converge and summate to facilitate extension, pain blockage, and perineal relaxation. Thus a common mechanism may exist for urination, defecation, mating behaviour, and parturition. That is, extension and lordosis, defecation, urination, parturition, and female mating readiness, may all share common properties of immobility, extension, and pain blockage, which involve somatic and visceral sensory convergence and summation. It may be helpful, therefore, to view the lordosis response, which is characteristic of mating behaviour in rodents as a special, hormone-sensitive, case of a more general organizational pattern of the nervous system.

SUMMARY AND CONCLUSIONS

Neural aspects of female sexual behaviour in mammals are reviewed, based primarily on analysis of the effects of lesioning and hormonal implantation, and on recording of neural activity.

Findings are reviewed which show that with appropriate sensory stimulation, the lordosis response (at least in rats and rabbits) can be elicited in the absence of ovarian, adrenal, and/or pituitary hormones. Oestrogen and progesterone synergize in facilitating the lordosis response. A conclusion based on these findings is that hormones play a facilitatory but not obligatory role in the elicitation of lordosis in certain species.

This conclusion is less surprising when lordosis is viewed as a motor pattern which appears in behavioural contexts that are not uniquely sexual, such as in the case of neonatal rats and guinea pigs showing components of lordosis when urinating or defecating in response to licking of the ano-genital area by the mother.

Evidence is reviewed of visceral mechanisms being closely related to components of somatic muscular activity associated with lordosis. For example, probing against the vaginal cervix facilitates lordosis in rats, dilation of the vaginal orifice or relaxation of the perineal musculature may accompany lordosis in both sexual and excretory contexts, hind-leg extension occurs during passage of the foetus through the birth canal, and direct stimulation of the visceral genito-urinary system modulates somatic reflexes. The possible relationship between these viscero-somatic processes and referred sensation is discussed with reference to mating behaviour.

Evidence is presented which indicates that the suppression of flexor reflexes by visceral genital tract stimulation is associated with a pain-blocking effect, and the possible adaptive significance of this effect in mating behaviour and parturition is discussed.

Speculations are presented on the possible relationships between pain blockage and afferent stimulation generated by passive or active stimulation of muscle stretch receptors, such as that which occurs during intromission, acupuncture analgesia, orgasm, and other intense muscular activity such as sneezing or stretching.

The common properties of female mating behaviour, parturition, urination, and defecation suggest that the lordosis response may be a special, hormone-sensitive, case of a more general organizational pattern of the nervous system.

ACKNOWLEDGEMENTS

Contribution No. 251 from the Institute of Animal Behaviour. I thank Mr. K. Kearney, Ms. N. Jachim, and Ms. W. Cunningham for their excellent technical assistance. The research and writing was supported by U.S.P.H.S. grant MH 13279 and Research Career Development Award 5KO2-MH 14711.

U.S.P.H.S. center grant MH 08604 (J. S. Rosenblatt), and by funds provided by the Alfred P. Sloan Foundation.

REFERENCES

Abrahams, V. C. and Teare, J. L. (1969) Peripheral pathways and properties of uterine afferents in the cat, *Can. J. Physiol.*, **47**, 576–7.

Adler, N. T. (1969) Effects of the male's copulatory behavior in successful pregnancy of the female rat, *J. Comp. Physiol. Psychol.*, **69**, 613–22.

Adler, N. T. (1974) The behavioral control of reproductive physiology. In: *Reproductive Behavior*, W. Montagna and W. A. Sadler, (eds.), pp. 259–86. Plenum Press, New York.

Adler, N. T., Komisaruk, B. R., and Davis, P. (1974) Sensory field of the pudendal nerve in female rats: changes over the estrous cycle, *Society for Neuroscience Abstracts*, 4th Annual Mtg., 1974, p. 113.

Alcaraz, M., Guzman-Flores, C., Salas, M., and Beyer, C. (1969) Effect of estrogen on the responsivity of hypothalamic and mesencephalic neurons in the female cat, *Brain Res.*, **15**, 439–46.

Arai, Y., Hiroi, M., Mitra, J., and Gorski, R. A. (1967) Influence of intravenous progesterone administration on the cortical electroencephalogram of the female rat, *Neuroendocrinology*, **2**, 275–82.

Arey, L. B. (1954) *Developmental Anatomy* (6th edn.), W. B. Saunders, Phil.

Aron, C., Asch, G., and Roos, J. (1966) Triggering of ovulation by coitus in the rat, *Int. Rev. Cytol.*, **20**, 139–72.

Ball, J. (1934) Sex behavior of the rat after removal of the uterus and vagina, *J. Comp. Psychol.*, **18**, 419–22.

Bard, P. (1935) The effects of denervation of the genitalia on the oestrual behavior of cats, *Am. J. Physiol.*, **113**, 5.

Bard, P. (1936) Oestrual behavior in surviving decorticate cats, *Am. J. Physiol.*, **116**, 4–5.

Bard, P. (1940) The hypothalamus and sexual behavior, *Res. Publ. Assoc. Res. Nervous Ment. Dis.*, **20**, 551–79.

Bard, P. and Rioch, D. McK. (1937) A study of four cats deprived of neocortex and additional portions of the forebrain, *Bull. Johns Hopkins Hospital*, **60**, 73–146.

Barraclough, C. A. and Cross, B. A. (1963) Unit activity in the hypothalamus of the cyclic female rat: effect of genital stimuli and progesterone, *J. Endocrinol.*, **26**, 339–59.

Beach, F. A. (1942) Importance of progesterone to induction of sexual receptivity in spayed female rats, *Proc. Soc. Exp. Biol. Med.*, **51**, 369–71.

Beach, F. A. (1944) Effects of injury to the cerebral cortex upon sexually-receptive behavior in the female rat, *Psychosomatic Med.*, **6**, 40–55.

Beach, F. A. (1947) A review of physiological and psychological studies of sexual behavior in mammals, *Physiol. Rev.*, **27**, 240–307.

Beach, F. A. (1948) *Hormones and Behavior* (2nd edn.), Cooper Square Publishers Inc., p. 249.

Beach, F. A. (1966) Ontogeny of 'coitus-related' reflexes in the female guinea pig, *Proc. Nat. Acad. Sci.*, **56**, 526–33.

Beach, F. A. (1967) Cerebral and hormonal control of reflexive mechanisms involved in copulatory behavior, *Physiol. Rev.*, **47**, 289–316.

Bereiter, D. A. and Barker, D. J. (1975) Facial receptive fields of trigeminal neurons: increased size following estrogen treatment in female rats, *Neuroendocrinology*, **18**, 115–24.

Bermant, G. (1961) Response latencies of female rats during sexual intercourse, *Science*, **133**, 1771–3.

Bermant, G. (1965) Rat sexual behavior: photographic analysis of the intromission response, *Psychon. Sci.*, **2**, 65–6.

Bermant, G. and Westbrook, W. H. (1966) Peripheral factors in the regulation of sexual contact by female rats, *J. Comp. Physiol. Psychol.*, **61**, 244–50.

Beyer, C. (1967) Variaciones periodicas en la actividad del mecanismo cerebral relacionado con la conducta sexual en la ausencia de hormones gonadales. IV Simposio Panamericano de Farmacologia y Terapeutica, Academia Nacional de Medicine, Mexico, D. F., 24–26 Agosto 1967, pp. 61–6.

Beyer, C. (1971) Effect of estrogen on brain stem neuronal responsivity in the cat. In *Steroid Hormones and Brain Function*, C. H. Sawyer and R. A. Gorski, (eds.), UCLA Press, Berkeley, pp. 121–6.

Beyer, C., Almanza, J., Torre, L. de la, and Guzman-Flores, C. (1971a) Brain stem multi-unit activity during 'relaxation' behavior in the female cat, *Brain Res.*, **29**, 213–22.

Beyer, C., Almanza, J., Torre, L. de la, and Guzman-Flores, C. (1971b) Effect of genital stimulation on the brain stem multi-unit activity of anestrous and estrous cats, *Brain Res.*, **32**, 143–50.

Beyer, C., Cruz, M. L., and Rivaud, N. (1969) Persistence of sexual behavior in ovariecto-mized-adrenalectomized rabbits treated with cortisol, *Endocrinology*, **85**, 790–3.

Beyer, C. and Rivaud, N. (1969) Sexual behavior in pregnant and lactating domestic rabbits, *Physiol. Behav.*, **4**, 753–7.

Beyer, C., and Sawyer, C. H. (1969) Hypothalamic unit activity related to control of the pituitary gland. In: *Frontiers in Neuroendocrinology*, W. F. Ganong and L. Martini, (eds.), Oxford University Press, New York, pp. 255–87.

Blake, C. A. and Sawyer, C. H. (1972) Effects of vaginal stimulation on hypothalamic multiple-unit activity and pituitary LH release in the rat, *Neuroendocrinology*, **10**, 358–70.

Blandau, R. J., Boling, J. L., and Young, W. C. (1941) The length of heat in the albino rat as determined by the copulatory response, *Anat. Rec.*, **79**, 453–63.

Boling, J. L., Blandau, R. J., Wilson, J. G., and Young, W. C. (1939) Postparturitional heat responses of newborn and adult guinea pigs, data on parturition, *Proc. Soc. Exp. Biol. Med.*, **42**, 128–32.

Bonica, J. J. (1972) *Principles and Practice of Obstetric Analgesia and Anesthesia*, F. A. Davis Co., Phil.

Brookhart, J. M., Dey, F. L., and Ranson, S. W. (1940) Failure of ovarian hormones to cause mating reactions in spayed guinea pigs with hypothalamic lesions, *Proc. Soc. Exp. Biol.*, **44**, 61–4.

Brooks, C.McC. (1937) The role of the cerebral cortex and of various sense organs in the excitation and execution of mating activity in the rabbit, *Am. J. Physiol.*, **120**, 544–53.

Brown-Grant, K., Davidson, J. M., and Greig, F. (1973) Induced ovulation in albino rats exposed to constant light, *J. Endocrinol.*, **57**, 7–22.

Capek, K., and Jelinek, J. (1956) The development of the control of water metabolism. I. The excretion of urine in young rats. *Physiol. Bohemoslov.*, **5**, 91–6.

Carlson, R. R. and DeFeo, V. J. (1965) Role of the pelvic nerve *vs.* the abdominal sympa-thetic nerves in the reproductive function of the female rat, *Endocrinology*, **77**, 1014–22.

Carter, C. S. (1972) Postcopulatory sexual receptivity in the female hamster: The role of the ovary and adrenal, *Horm. Behav.*, **3**, 261–5.

Carter, C. S. (1973) Olfaction and sexual receptivity in the female golden hamster, *Physiol. Behav.*, **10**, 47–51.

Carter, C. S. and Schein, M. W. (1971) Sexual receptivity and exhaustion in the female golden hamster, *Horm. Behav.*, **2**, 191–200.

Chambers, W. F. and Howe, G. (1968) A study of estrogen-sensitive hypothalamic centers using a technique for rapid application and removal of estradiol, *Proc. Soc. Exp. Biol. Med.*, **128**, 292–4.

Chang, H.-T. (1973) Integrative action of thalamus in the process of acupuncture for analgesia, *Scientia Sinica*, **16**, 25–60.

Chiang, C.-Y., Chang, C.-T., Chu, H.-L. and Yang, L.-F. (1973) Peripheral afferent pathway for acupuncture analgesia, *Scientia Sinica*, **16**, 210–7.

Chobsieng, P., Naor, Z., Koch, Y., Zor, U., and Lindner, H. R. (1975) Stimulation effect of prostaglandin E_2 on LH release in the rat: evidence for hypothalamic site of ACTH, *Neuroendocrinology*, **17**, 12–7.

Ciaccio, L. A. and Lisk, R. D. (1973/74) Central control of estrous behavior in the female golden hamster, *Neuroendocrinology*, **13**, 21–8.

Clegg, M. T. and Doyle, L. L. (1967) Role in reproductive physiology of afferent impulses from the genitalia and other regions, In: *Neuroendocrinology*, L. Martini and W. F. Ganong, (eds.), Academic Press, New York, pp. 1–17.

Clegg, M. T. and Ganong, W. F. (1960) The effect of hypothalamic lesions on ovarian function in the ewe, *Endocrinology*, **67**, 179–86.

Clemens, L. G., Wallen, K., and Gorski, R. A. (1967) Mating behavior: facilitation in the female rat after cortical application of potassium chloride, *Science*, **157**, 1208–9.

Crews, D. (1973) Coition-induced inhibition of sexual receptivity in female lizards *(Anolis carolinensis)*, *Physiol. Behav.*, **11**, 463–8.

Cross, B. A. (1964) Electrical recording techniques in the study of hypothalamic control of gonadotrophin secretion. In *Proc. 2nd Int. Congr. Endocrinol.*, London, August 1964. Excerpta Med. Int. Congr. Ser. No. 83. pp. 513–6.

Cross, B. A. and Silver, I. A. (1965) Effect of luteal hormone on the behaviour of hypothalamic neurones in pseudopregnant rats, *J. Endocrinol.*, **31**, 251–63.

Crowley, W. R., Feder, H. H., and Morin, L. R. (1976a) Role of monoamines in sexual behavior of the female guinea pig, *Pharmac. Biochem. Behav.*, **4**, 67–71.

Crowley, W. R., Rodriguez-Sierra, J. F., and Komisaruk, B. R. (1976b) Effect of vaginal stimulation in rats: modulation by catecholamines and steroids, *Fed. Proc.*, **35**, 668.

Crowley, W. R., Rodriguez-Sierra, J. F., and Komisaruk, B. R. (1976c) Hypophysectomy facilitates sexual behavior in female rats. *Neuroendocrinology*, **20**, 328–38.

Crowley, W. R., Jacobs, R., Volpe, J., Rodriguez-Sierra, J. F., and Komisaruk, B. R. (1976d) Analgesic effect of vaginal stimulation in rats: modulation by graded stimulus intensity and hormones. *Physiol. Behav.*, **16**, 483–8.

Davidson, J. M., Smith, E. R., Rodgers, C. H., and Bloch, G. J. (1968) Relative thresholds of behavioral and somatic responses to estrogen, *Physiol. Behav.*, **3**, 227–9.

Davis, C. D. (1939) The effect of ablations of neocortex on mating, maternal behavior, and the production of pseudopregnancy in the female rat and on copulatory activity in the male, *Am. J. Physiol.*, **127**, 374–80.

Dempsey, E. W. and Rioch, D. McK. (1939) The localization in the brain stem of the oestrous responses of the female guinea pig, *J. Neurophysiol.*, **2**, 9–18.

Dempsey, E. W. and Searles, H. F. (1943) Environmental modification of certain endocrine phenomena, *Endocrinology*, **32**, 119–28.

Dey, F. L., Fisher, C., Berry, C. M., and Ranson, S. W. (1940) Disturbances in reproductive functions caused by hypothalamic lesions in female guinea pigs, *Am. J. Physiol.*, **129**, 39–46.

Diakow, C. (1970) Effects of genital desensitization on the mating pattern of female rats as determined by motion picture analysis, *Am. Zool.*, **10**, 486.

Diakow, C. (1971a) Effects of genital desensitization on mating behavior and ovulation in the female cat, *Physiol. Behav.*, **7**, 47–54.

Diakow, C. (1971b). Effects of brain lesions on the mating behavior of rats, *Am. Zool.*, **11**, 617.

Diakow, C. (1974) Male–female interactions and the organization of mammalian mating patterns, In: *Advances in the Study of Behavior* Vol. 5, J. S. Rosenblatt, R. A. Hinde, C. G. Beer and E. Shaw (eds.), Academic Press, New York, pp. 227–68.

Diakow, C. (1975) Motion picture analysis of rat mating behavior, *J. Comp. Physiol. Psychol.*, **89**, 704–12.

Diakow, C. A. and Aronson, L. R. (1967) The role of genital sensation in the maintenance of sexual behavior in the female cat, *Am. Zool.*, **7**, 799–800.

Diakow, C. A. and Aronson, L. R. (1968) Effects of genital desensitization on mating behavior and ovulation in the female cat, *Am. Zool.*, **8**, 748.

Diakow, C., Komisaruk, B., and Pfaff, D. (1973) Sensory and hormonal interactions in eliciting lordosis. *Fed. Proc.*, **32**, 241.

Diamond, M. (1972) Vaginal stimulation and progesterone in relation to pregnancy and parturition, *Biol. Reprod.*, **6**, 281–7.

Diamond, M., Diamond, A. L., and Mast, M. (1972) Visual sensitivity and sexual arousal levels during the menstrual cycle, *J. Nerv. Ment. Dis.*, **155**, 170–5.

Donovan, B. T., and Traczyk, W. (1965) Interruption of the hypogastric and pelvic nerve supply to the uterus and the occurrence of pregnancy in the guinea-pig. *J. Endocrin.*, **33**, 335–6.

Dörner, G., Döcke, F., and Moustafa, S. (1968) Differential localization of a male and a female hypothalamic mating centre, *J. Reprod. Fert.* **17**, 583–6.

Dyer, R. G., Pritchett, C. J., and Cross, B. A. (1972) Unit activity in the diencephalon of female rats during the oestrous cycle, *J. Endocrinol.*, **53**, 151–60.

Eble, J. N. (1960) Patterns of response of the paravertebral musculature to visceral stimuli, *Am. J. Physiol.*, **198**, 429–33.

Edwards, D. A. and Warner, P. (1972) Olfactory bulb removal facilitates the hormonal induction of sexual receptivity in the female rat, *Horm. Behav.*, **3**, 321–32.

Elliott, H. C. (1969) *Textbook of Neuroanatomy*, J. B. Lippincott Co., Phil.

Endröczi, E. (1967) Neural and hormonal regulations of the patterns of sexual behavior. Symposium on Reproduction. *Cong. Hungr. Soc. for Endocr. and Metabol.*, K. Lissak, (ed.), Akademiai Kiado, Budapest, pp. 39–63.

Endröczi, E. (1969) Effect of sex hormones on the electrical activity of brain stem and diencephalon in castrated female rats, *Acta Physiol. Acad. Sci. Hung.*, **35**, 31–9.

Endröczi, E. (1971) The role of brainstem and limbic structures in regulation of sexual behavioural patterns, *J. Neuro-visceral Rel.*, Suppl., **10**, 263–76.

Evans, M. H. and McPherson, A. (1958) The effects of stimulation of visceral afferent nerve fibers on somatic reflexes, *J. Physiol. Lond.*, **140**, 201–12.

Evans, M. H. and McPherson, A. (1960) The effects of electrical stimulation of visceral afferent nerve fibres on monosynaptic and polysynaptic reflex responses, *J. Physiol.*, **150**, 105–13.

Everett, J. W. (1961) The mammalian female reproductive cycle and its controlling mechanisms. In: *Sex and Internal Secretions*, Vol. 1, W. C. Young, (ed.), Williams and Wilkins Co., Baltimore, pp. 497–555.

Everett, J. W. (1967) Provoked ovulation or long-delayed pseudopregnancy from control stimuli in barbiturate-blocked rats, *Endocrinology*, **80**, 145–54.

Faure, J.-M., Vincent, J.-D., Bensch, Cl., Favarel-Garrigues, F., and Dufy, B. (1967) Activities elementaires dans l'hypothalamus au cours de l'ovulation chez la lapine chronique. *J. Physiol. Paris*, **59**, 405.

Feder, H. H. (1977) Regulation of sexual behavior by hormones in female non-primates. In: *Handbook of Sexology*, H. Musaph and J. Money (eds.), ASP Biological and Medical Press (Elsevier), Amsterdam, pp. 393–411.

Feder, H. H., Siegel, H., and Wade, G. N. (1974) Uptake of (6,7-³H) estradiol-17β in ovariectomized rats, guinea pigs, and hamsters: correlation with species differences in behavioral responsiveness to estradiol, *Brain Res.*, **71**, 93–103.

Fee, A. R. and Parkes, A. S. (1930) Studies on ovulation. III. Effect of vaginal anesthesia on ovulation in the rabbit, *J. Physiol. Lond.*, **70**, 385–88.

Fields, H. L., Partridge, Jr., L. D., and Winter, D. L. (1970) Somatic and visceral receptive field properties of fibers in ventral quadrant white matter of the cat spinal cord, *J. Neurophysiol.*, **33**, 827–37.

Galeano, C., Roig, J. A., and Sommer-Smith, J. A. (1964) Conditioning of subcortical telencephalic stimulation effects. *Electroenceph. Clin. Neurophysiol.*, **17**, 281–93.

Gastaut, H. (1952) Correlations entre le systeme nerveux vegetatif et le systëme de la vie de relation dans le rhinencephale, *J. Physiol. Paris*, **44**, 431–70.

Gault, F. P. and Leaton, R. N. (1963) Electrical activity of the olfactory system, *Electroenceph. Clin. Neurophysiol.*, **15**, 299–304.

Goldfoot, D. A. and Goy, R. W. (1970) Abbreviation of behavioral estrus in guinea pigs by coital and vagino-cervical stimulation. *J. Comp. Physiol. Psychol.*, **72**, 426–34.

Goy, R. W. and Phoenix, C. H. (1963) Hypothalamic regulation of female sexual behaviour; establishment of behavioural oestrus in spayed guinea-pigs following hypothalamic lesions, *J. Reprod. Fert.*, **5**, 23–40.

Green, J. D., Clemente, C. D., and DeGroot, J. (1957) Rhinencephalic lesions and behavior in cats. *J. Comp. Neurol.*, **108**, 505–45.

Green, R., Luttge, W. G., and Whalen, R. E. (1970) Induction of receptivity in ovariectomized female rats by a single intravenous injection of estradiol-17β, *Physiol. Behav.*, **5**, 137–141.

Hall, N. R., Luttge, W. G., and Berry, R. B. (1975) Intracerebral prostaglandin E_2: effect upon sexual behavior, open field activity and body temperature in ovariectomized female rats, *Prostaglandins*, **10**, 877–88.

Hardy, D. F. and DeBold, J. F. (1972) Effects of coital stimulation upon behavior of the female rat, *J. Comp. Physiol. Psychol.*, **78**, 400–8.

Harper, L. V. (1972) The transition from filial to reproductive function of 'coitus-related' responses in young guinea pigs, *Dev. Psychobiol.*, **5**, 21–34.

Harrington, F. E., Eggert, R. G., Wilbur, R. D., and Linkenheimer, W. H. (1966) Effect of coitus on chlorpromazine inhibition of ovulation in the rat, *Endocrinology*, **79**, 1130–4.

Harris, G. W. and Michael, R. P. (1964) The activation of sexual behavior by hypothalamic implants of oestrogen, *J. Physiol.*, **171**, 275–301.

Hart, B. L. (1969) Gonadal hormones and sexual reflexes in the female rat, *Horm. Behav.*, **1**, 65–71.

Hart, B. L. (1970). Mating behavior in the female dog and the effects of estrogen on sexual reflexes. *Horm. Behav.*, **2**, 93–104.

Hart, B. L. (1971) Facilitation by estrogen of sexual reflexes in female cats, *Physiol. Behav.*, **7**, 675–8.

Hashimoto, I., Henricks, D. M., Anderson, L. L., and Melampy, R. M. (1968) Progesterone and pregn-4-en-20α-ol-3-one in ovarian venous blood during various reproductive states in the rat, *Endocrinology*, **82**, 333–41.

Herndon, Jr., J. G. (1976) Effects of midbrain lesions on female sexual behavior in the rat, *Physiol. Behav.*, **17**, 143–8.

Herndon, J. G. and Neill, D. B. (1973) Amphetamine reversal of sexual impairment following anterior hypothalamic lesions in female rats, *Pharmac. Biochem. Behav.*, **1**, 285–8.

Heuser, C., Ling, G. M., and Kluver, M. (1967) Sleep induction by progesterone in the pre-optic area in cats, *Electroenceph. Clin. Neurophysiol.*, **22**, 122–7.

Hitt, J. C., Hendricks, S. E., Ginsberg, S. I., and Lewis, J. H. (1970) Disruption of male, but not female, sexual behavior in rats by medial forebrain bundle lesions, *J. Comp. Physiol. Psychol.*, **73**, 377–84.

Holmes, J. E. and Egan, K. (1973) Electrical activity of the cat amygdala during sexual behavior, *Physiol. Behav.*, **10**, 863–7.

Hornby, J. B. and Rose, J. D. (1976) Responses of caudal brain stem neurons to vaginal and somatosensory stimulation in the rat and evidence of genital–nociceptive interactions, *Exp. Neurol.*, **51**, 363–76.

Innes, D. L. and Michal, E. K. (1970) Effects of progesterone and estrogen on the electrical activity of the limbic system, *J. Exp. Zool.*, **175**, 487–92.

Ishizuka, N., Kurachi, K., Sugita, N., and Yoshii, N. (1954) Studies on the relationship between EEG of the hypothalamus and sexual function, *Med. J. Osaka Univ.*, **5**, 729–40.

Kaada, B. (1974) Mechanisms of acupuncture analgesia, *T. norske Loegeforen*, **94**, 422–31.

Kalra, S. P. and Sawyer, C. H. (1970) Blockade of copulation-induced ovulation in the rat by anterior hypothalamic deafferentation, *Endocrinology*, **87**, 1124–8.

Kanematsu, S. and Sawyer, C. H. (1965) Blockage of ovulation in rabbits by hypothalamic implants of norethindrone, *Endocrinology*, **76**, 691–9.

Kawakami, M. (1960) Effect of sex hormones upon the spinal segmental discharges. In: *Sex Hormones and Brain* Kyodoisho, Tokyo (in Japanese), pp. 106–8.

Kawakami, M., and Sawyer, C. H. (1959) Neuroendocrine correlates of changes in brain activity thresholds by sex steroids and pituitary hormones. *Endocrinology*, **65**, 652–68.

Kawakami, M. and Sawyer, C. H. (1967) Effects of sex hormones and antifertility steroids on brain thresholds in the rabbit, *Endocrinology*, **80**, 857–71.

Kawakami, M. and Terasawa, E. (1967) Differential control of sex hormones and oxytocin upon evoked potentials in the hypothalamus and midbrain reticular formation, *Jap. J. Physiol.*, **17**, 65–93.

Kawakami, M., Terasawa, E., and Ibuki, T. (1970) Changes in multiple unit activity of the brain during the estrous cycle, *Neuroendocrinology*, **6**, 30–48.

Keefer, D. A., Stumpf, W. E., and Sar, M. (1973) Estrogen-topographical localization of estrogen-concentrating cells in the rat spinal cord following ^{3}H-estradiol administration, *Proc. Soc. Exp. Biol. Med.*, **143**, 414–7.

Kennedy, C. C. and Mitra, J. (1963) Hypothalamic control of energy balance and the reproductive cycle in the rat, *J. Physiol. Lond.*, **166**, 395–407.

Kenshalo, D. R. (1966) Changes in the cool threshold associated with phases of the menstrual cycle, *J. Appl. Physiol.*, **21**, 1031–9.

Kinsey, A. C., Pomeroy, W. B., and Martin, C. E. (1948) *Sexual Behaviour in the Human Male*. W. B. Saunders Co., Philadelphia.

Kobayashi, T., Kobayashi, T., Takezawa, S., Oshima, K., and Kawamura, H. (1962). Electrophysiological studies on the feedback mechanisms of progesterone. *Endocrinol. Japon.*, **9**, 302–20.

Kollar, E. J. (1953) Reproduction in the female rat after pelvic nerve neurectomy, *Anat. Rec.*, **115**, 641–58.

Komisaruk, B. R. (1971a) Induction of lordosis in ovariectomized rats by stimulation of the vaginal cervix: hormonal and neural interrelationships. In: *Steroid Hormones and Brain Function*, C. H. Sawyer and R. A. Gorski (eds.), UCLA Press, Berkeley, pp. 127–41.

Komisaruk, B. R. (1971b) Strategies in neuroendocrine neurophysiology, *Am. Zool.*, **11**, 741–54.

Komisaruk, B. R. (1974) Neural and hormonal interactions in the reproductive behavior of female rats. In: *Reproductive Behavior*, E. Montagna and W. A. Sadler (eds.), Plenum Press, New York, pp. 97–129.

Komisaruk, B. R., Adler, N. T., and Hutchison, J. (1972a) Genital sensory field: enlargement by estrogen treatment in female rats, *Science*, **178**, 1295–8.

Komisaruk, B. R., Ciofalo, V., and Latranyi, M. B. (1976) Stimulation of the vaginal cervix is more effective than morphine in suppressing a nociceptive response in rats. In: *Advances in Pain Research and Therapy* Vol. 1, J. J. Bonica and D. Albe-Fessard (eds.), Raven Press, New York, pp. 439–43.

Komisaruk, B. R. and Diakow, C. (1973) Lordosis reflex intensity in rats in relation to the estrous cycle, ovariectomy, estrogen administration and mating behavior, *Endocrinology*, **93**, 548–57.

Komisaruk, B. R. and Larsson, K. (1971) Suppression of a spinal and a cranial nerve reflex by vaginal or rectal probing in rats, *Brain Res.*, **35**, 231–5.

Komisaruk, B. R., McDonald, P. G., Whitmoyer, D. I., and Sawyer, C. H. (1967) Effects of progesterone and sensory stimulation on EEG and neuronal activity in the rat. *Exp. Neurol.*, **19**, 494–507.

Komisaruk, B. R. and Olds, J. (1968) Neuronal correlates of behavior in freely moving rats, *Science*, **161**, 810–3.

Komisaruk, B. R. and Wallman, J. (1973) Blockage of pain responses in thalamic neurons by mechanical stimulation of the vagina in rats, *Soc. Neurosci.*, 3rd Ann. Mtg., p. 315.

Komisaruk, B. R., and Wallman, J. (1977) Antinociceptive effects of vaginal stimulation in rats: neurophysiological and behavioral studies, *Brain Res.*, in press.

Komisaruk, B. R., Larsson, K., and Cooper, R. (1972b) Intense lordosis in the absence of ovarian hormones after septal ablation in rats. *Soc. Neurosci.*, 2nd. Ann. Mtg., p. 230.

Koster, R. (1943) Hormone factors in male behavior of the female rat, *Endocrinology*, **33**, 337–48.

Kow, L. M. and Malsbury, C. W., and Pfaff, D. W. (1974) Effects of progesterone on female reproductive behavior in rats: possible modes of action and role in behavioral sex differences. In: *Reproductive Behavior*, W. Montagna and W. A. Sadler (eds.), Plenum, Press, New York, pp. 179–210.

Kow, L. M. and Pfaff, D. W. (1973) Spinal tract transections and the lordosis reflex in female rats, *Physiologist*, **16**, 367 (abstract).

Kow, L. M. and Pfaff, D. W. (1976) Sensory requirements for the lordosis reflex in female rats, *Brain Res.*, **101**, 47–66.

Kuehn, R. E. and Beach, F. A. (1963) Quantitative measurement of sexual receptivity in female rats, *Behaviour*, **21**, 282–99.

Kurtz, R. G. (1975) Hippocampal and cortical activity during sexual behavior in the female rat, *J. Comp. Physiol. Psychol.*, **89**, 158–69.

Kuru, M. (1965) Nervous control of micturition, *Physiol. Rev.*, **45**, 425–94.

Larsson, K., Feder, H. H., and Komisaruk, B. R. (1974) Role of the adrenal glands, repeated matings and monoamines in lordosis behavior of rats, *Pharmac. Biochem. Behav.*, **2**, 685–92.

Law, R. and Meagher, W. (1958) Hypothalamic lesions and sexual behavior in the female rat, *Science*, **128**, 1626–7.

Lincoln, D. W. (1969a) Response of hypothalamic units to stimulation of the vaginal cervix: specific *versus* non-specific effects, *J. Endocrinol.*, **43**, 683–4.

Lincoln, D. W. (1969b) Effects of progesterone on the electrical activity of the forebrain, *J. Endocrinol.*, **45**, 585–96.

Lincoln, D. W. and Cross, B. A. (1967 Effect of oestrogen on the responsiveness of neurones in the hypothalamus, septum, and preoptic area of rats with light-induced persistent oestrus, *J. Endocrinol.*, **37**, 191–203.

Lisk, R. D. (1962) Diencephalic placement of estradiol and sexual receptivity in the female rat, *Am. J. Physiol.*, **203**, 493–6.

Lisk, R. D. (1967) Sexual behavior: hormonal control. In: *Neuroendocrinology* Vol. 2, L. Martini and W. F. Ganong (eds.), Academic Press, New York, pp. 197–239.

Lisk, R. D. and Barfield, M. A. (1975) Progesterone facilitation of sexual receptivity in rats with neural implantation of estrogen, *Neuroendocrinology*, **19**, 28–35.

Lisk, R. D., Ciaccio, L. A., and Reuter, L. A. (1972) Neural centers of estrogen and progesterone action in the regulation of reproduction. In: *Biology of Reproduction—Basic and Clinical Studies*, J. T. Velardo and B. A. Kasprow (eds.), p. 71–87.

Lissak, K. (1962) Olfactory-induced sexual behaviour in female cats. In: *Excerpta med. Found. Congr. Ser.*, pp. 652–6. Brain-Gonad Symposium, Proc. Int. Cong. Physiol., Leiden, 1962.

Long, J. A. and Evans, H. M. (1922) The oestrous cycle in the rat and its associated phenomena, *Mem. Univ. Calif.*, **6**, 1–148.

Maes, J. P. (1939) Neural mechanism of sexual behaviour in the female cat, *Nature*, **144**, 598–9

Malsbury, C. W., Kelley, D. B., and Pfaff, D. W. (1972) Responses of single units in the dorsal midbrain to somatosensory stimulation in female rats. In: *Progress in Endocrinology*, C. Gual (ed.), Excerpta Medica, pp. 229–33.

Malven, P. V., Whitmoyer, D. I., and Sawyer, C. H. (1967) Arousal thresholds and tissue-electrode impedance in guinea pigs, *Am. J. Physiol.*, **212**, 1209–14.

Margherita, G., Albritton, D., MacInnes, R., Hayward, R., and Gorski, R. A. (1965) Electroencephalographic changes in ventromedial hypothalamus and amygdala induced by vaginal and other peripheral stimuli. *Exp. Neurol.*, **13**, 96–108.

Mayer, D. J., Wolfle, T. L., Akil, H., Carder, B., and Liebeskind, J. C. (1971) Analgesia from electrical stimulation in the brainstem of the rat, *Science*, **174**, 1351–4.

McPherson, A. (1966) Vesico-somatic reflexes in the chronic spinal cat, *J. Physiol. Lond.*, **185**, 197–204.

Meyerson, B. J. and Lindstrom, L. H. (1973) Sexual motivation in the female rat. A methodological study applied to the investigation of the effect of estradiol benzoate, *Acta Physiol.*, *Scand.* suppl. **389**, 1–80.

Miller, F. R. and R. A. Waud (1925) Viscero-motor reflexes. IV. *Am. J. Physiol.*, **73**, 329–40.

Modianos, D. T., Hitt, J. C., and Flexman, J. (1974) Habenular lesions produce decrements in feminine but not masculine sexual behavior in rats, *Behav. Biol.*, **10**, 75–87.

Modianos, D. T. and Pfaff, D. W. (1975a) Brainstem lesions and lordosis in female rats, *Fedn. Proc.*, **34**, 396.

Modianos, D. T. and Pfaff, D. W. (1975b) Facilitation of the lordosis reflex by electrical stimulation of the lateral vestibular nuclei, *Neurosci. Abstr.*, **1**, 457.

Morin, L. P. and Feder, H. H. (1974a) Inhibition of lordosis behavior in ovariectomized guinea pigs by mesencephalic implants of progesterone, *Brain Res.*, **70**, 71–80.

Morin, L. P. and Feder, H. H. (1974b) Hypothalamic progesterone implants and facilitation of lordosis behavior in estrogen-primed ovariectomized guinea pigs, *Brain Res.*, **70**, 81–93.

Morin, L. P. and Feder, H. H. (1974c) Intracranial estradiol benzoate implants and lordosis behavior of ovariectomized guinea pigs, *Brain Res.*, **70**, 95–102.

Moss, R. L. (1971) Modification of copulatory behavior in the female rat following olfactory bulb removal, *J. Comp. Physiol. Psychol.*, **74**, 374–82.

Moss, R. L. and Cooper, K. J. (1973) Temporal relationship of spontaneous and coitus-induced release of luteinizing hormone in the normal cyclic rat, *Endocrinology*, **92**, 1748–53.

Moss, R. L. and Foreman, M. M. (1976) Potentiation of lordosis behavior by intra-hypothalamic infusion of synthetic luteinizing hormone-releasing hormone, *Neuroendocrinology*, **20**, 176–81.

Moss, R. L. and Law, O. T. (1971) The estrous cycle: its influence on single unit activity in the forebrain, *Brain Res.*, **30**, 435–8.

Moss, R. L. and McCann, S. M. (1973) Induction of mating behavior in rats by luteinizing hormone-releasing factor, *Science*, **181**, 177–9.

Müller-Schwarze, D. (1974) *Antilocapra americana* (Antilocapridae) birth and behavior of the newborn. In: *Encyclopedia Cinematographica*, G. Wolf, (ed.), Film E 2057. Institut fur den Wissenschaftlichen Film.

Nance, D. M., Shryne, J., and Gorski, R. A. (1975a) Effects of septal lesions on behavioral sensitivity of female rats to gonadal hormones, *Horm. Behav.*, **6**, 59–64.

Nance, D. M., Shryne, J., and Gorski, R. A. (1975b) Facilitation of female sexual behavior in male rats by septal lesions: an interaction with estrogen, *Horm. Behav.*, **6**, 289–99.

Palka, Y. S., and Sawyer, C. H. (1966) The effects of hypothalamic implants of ovarian steroids on oestrous behaviour in rabbits. *J. Physiol.*, **185**, 251–69.

Peiper, A. (1963) *Cerebral Function in Infancy and Childhood*, 3rd rev. edn., B. Nagler and H. Nagler (trans.), International Behavioral Sciences Series, Consultants Bureau, New York.

Peirce, J. T., and Nuttall, R. L. (1961) Duration of sexual contacts in the rat. *J. Comp. Physiol. Psych.*, **54**, 585–7.

Petty, L. C. (1975) Alteration of activity of single units in the mesencephalic central grey produced by cervical probing, noxious stimuli and their combination in the awake freely moving female rat, Unpubl. doctoral dissertation. Virginia Commonwealth University, Richmond.

Pfaff, D. W. (1968) Uptake of ^{3}H-estradiol by the female rat brain. An autoradiographic study. *Endocrinology*, **82**, 1149–55.

Pfaff, D. W. (1973) Luteinizing hormone-releasing factor potentiates lordosis behavior in hypophysectomized ovariectomized female rats, *Science*, **182**, 1148–9.

Pfaff, D. W., Diakow, C., Zigmond, R. S., and Kow, L. M. (1974) Neural and hormonal determinants of female mating behavior in rats. *The Neurosciences 3rd Study Program*, F. O. Schmitt and F. G. Worden (eds.), MIT Press, Cambridge, Mass., pp. 621–46.

Pfaff, D. W. and Keiner, M. (1973) Atlas of estradiol-concentrating cells in the central nervous system of the female rat, *J. Comp. Neurol.*, **151**, 121–58.

Pomeranz, B., Wall, P. D., and Weber, W. V. (1968) Cord cells responding to fine myelinated afferents from viscera, muscle, and skin. *J. Physiol.*, **199**, 511–32.

Porter, R. W., Cavanaugh, E. B., Critchlow, B. V., and Sawyer, C. H. (1957) Localized changes in electrical activity of the hypothalamus in estrous cats following vaginal stimulation, *Am. J. Physiol.*, **189**, 145–51.

Powers, J. B. (1972) Facilitation of lordosis in ovariectomized rats by intracerebral progesterone implants, *Brain Res.*, **48**, 311–25.

Powers, B. and Valenstein, E. S. (1972) Sexual receptivity: facilitation by medial preoptic lesions in female rats, *Science*, **175**, 1003–5.

Prechtl, H. F. R. (1965) Problems of behavioral studies in the newborn infant. In: *Advances in the Study of Behavior* Vol. 1, D. S. Lehrman, R. A. Hinde, E. Shaw (eds.), Academic Press, New York, pp. 75–98.

Ramirez, V. D., Komisaruk, B. R., Whitmoyer, D. I., and Sawyer, C. H. (1967) Effects of hormones and vaginal stimulation on the EEG and hypothalamic units in rats, *Am. J. Physiol.*, **212**, 1376–84.

Reynolds, D. V. (1969) Surgery in the rat during electrical analgesia induced by focal brain stimulation, *Science*, **164**, 444–5.

Rodgers, C. H. (1971) Influence of copulation on ovulation in the cycling rat, *Endocrinology*, **88**, 433–6.

Rodgers, C. H., and Law, O. T. (1967) The effects of habenular and medial forebrain lesions on sexual behavior in female rats. *Psychonom. Sci.*, **8**, 1–2.

Rodgers, C. H., and Schwartz, N. B. (1972) Diencephalic regulation of plasma LH, ovulation, and sexual behavior in the rat. *Endocrinology*, **90**, 461–5.

Rodriguez-Sierra, J. F., Crowley, W. R., and Komisaruk, B. R. (1975a) Vaginal stimulation in rats induces prolonged lordosis responsiveness and sexual receptivity, *J. Comp. Physiol. Psychol.*, **89**, 79–85.

Rodriguez-Sierra, J. F., Crowley, W. R., and Komisaruk, B. R. (1975b) Hypophysectomy facilitates lordosis responding in female rats, *Neuroscience Abstr.*, **1**, 435. 5th Annual Mtg.

Rose, J. D. (1973) Pontine unit responses to genital stimulation in estrous and anestrous cats, *Brain Res.*, **62**, 291–6.

Rose, J. D. (1975) Responses of midbrain neurons to genital and somatosensory stimulation in estrous and anestrous cats, *Exp. Neurol.*, **49**, 639–52.

Rose, J. D. and Sutin, J. (1971) Responses of single thalamic neurons to genital stimulation in female cats, *Brain Res.*, **33**, 533–9.

Rose, J. D. and Sutin, J. (1973) Responses of single units in the medulla to genital stimulation in estrous and anestrous cats, *Brain Res.*, **50**, 87–99.

Ross, J., Claybaugh, C., Clemens, L. G., and Gorski, R. A. (1971) Short latency induction of estrous behavior with intracerebral gonadal hormones in ovariectomized rats, *Endocrinology*, **89**, 32–8.

Ross, J. W., Gorski, R. A., and Sawyer, C. H. (1973) Effect of cortical stimulation on estrous behavior in estrogen-primed ovariectomized rats, *Endocrinology*, **93**, 20–5.

Ruch, T. C. (1961) Pathophysiology of pain. In: *Neurophysiology*, T. C. Ruch, H. D. Patton, J. W. Woodbury and A. L. Towe (eds.), W. B. Saunders Co., Phil., pp. 350–68.

Sawyer, C. H. (1959) Effects of brain lesions on estrous behavior and reflexogenous ovulation in the rabbit, *J. Exp. Zool.*, **142**, 227–46.

Sawyer, C. H. (1960) Reproductive behavior. In: *Handbook of Physiology. Neurophysiology* Vol. 2, J. Field, H. W. Magoun, and V. E. Hall (eds.), Amer. Physiol. Soc., Washington, D.C., pp. 1225–40.

Sawyer, C. H. (1962a) Induction of estrus in the ovariectomized cat by local hypothalamic treatment with estrogen, *Anat. Rec.*, **144**, 280.

Sawyer, C. H. (1962b) Gonadal hormone feed-back and sexual behavior. *Proc. I.U.P.S. XXII Int. Cong, Leiden. Excerpta Med. Int. Cong. Series* no. 47, 642–9.

Sawyer, C. H. (1966) Effects of hormonal steroids on certain mechanisms in the adult brain, *Excerpta Med. Int. Congr. Series* no. 132, 123–35.

Sawyer, C. H. (1967) Some endocrine aspects of forebrain inhibition, *Brain Res.*, **6**, 48–59.

Sawyer, C. H. (1975) Neuroendocrine control of ovulation. In: *The Nervous System* Vol. 1, D. B. Tower (ed.), Raven Press, N. Y.

Sawyer, C. H. and Everett, J. W. (1959) Stimulatory and inhibitory effect of progesterone on the release of pituitary ovulating hormone in the rabbit, *Endocrinology*, **65**, 644–51.

Sawyer, C. H. and Kawakami, M. (1961) Interactions between the central nervous system and hormones influencing ovulation. In: *Control of Ovulation*, C. A. Villee (ed.), Pergamon Press, pp. 79–100.

Sawyer, C. H., Kawakami, M., and Kanematsu, S. (1966) Neuroscience aspects of reproduction. In: *Endocrines and the Central Nervous System, Res. Publ. Assoc. Res. Nerv. Ment. Dis.*, **43**, 59–85.

Sawyer, C. H. and Markee, J. E. (1959) Estrogen facilitation of release of pituitary ovulating hormone in the rabbit in response to vaginal stimulation, *Endocrinology*, **65**, 614–21.

Sawyer, C. H. and Robison, B. (1956) Separate hypothalamic areas controlling pituitary gonadotropic function and mating behavior in female cats and rabbits, *J. Clin. Endocrinol. Metab.*, **16**, 914–5.

Schreiner, L., and Kling, A. (1953) Behavioral changes following rhinencephalic injury in the cat. *J. Neurophysiol.*, **16**, 643–59.

Schwartz, N. B. (1970) Control of rhythmic secretion of gonadotropins. In: *The Hypothalamus*, L. Martini, M. Totter, and F. Fraschini (eds.), Academic Press, New York, pp. 515–28.

Selzer, M. and Spencer, W. A. (1969a) Convergence of visceral cutaneous afferent pathways in the lumbar spinal cord, *Brain Res.*, **14**, 331–48.

Selzer, M. and Spencer, W. A. (1969b) Interaction between visceral and cutaneous afferents in the spinal cord: reciprocal primary afferent fiber depolarization, *Brain Res.*, **14**, 349–66.

Shadle, A. R. (1946) Copulation in the porcupine, *J. Wildlife Manag.*, **10**, 159–62.

Signoret, J. P. (1970) Reproductive behaviour of pigs, *J. Reprod. Fert.*, **11**, 105–17.

Singer, J. J. (1968) Hypothalamic control of male and female sexual behavior in female rats, *J. Comp. Physiol. Psychol.*, **66**, 738–42.

Smith, E. R. and Davidson, J. M. (1974) Luteinizing hormone releasing factor in rats exposed to constant light: effects of mating, *Neuroendocrinology*, **14**, 129–38.

Spies, H. G. and Niswender, G. D. (1971) Levels of prolactin, LH, and FSH in the serum of intact and pelvic-neurectomized rats, *Endocrinology*, **88**, 937–43.

Stumpf, W. E. (1968) Estradiol-concentrating neurons: topography in the hypothalamus by dry-mount autoradiography, *Science*, **162**, 1001–3.

Stumpf, W. E. (1970) Estrogen-neurons and estrogen-neuron systems in the periventricular brain, *Am. J. Anat.*, **129**, 207–18.

Stumpf, W. E. and Sar, M. (1971) Estradiol-concentrating neurons in the amygdala, *Proc. Soc. Exp. Biol. Med.*, **136**, 102–6.

Sutin, J. and Michael, R. P. (1970) Changes in brain activity following vaginal stimulation in estrous and anestrous cats, *Physiol. Behav.*, **5**, 1043–51.

Taleisnik, S., Velasco, M. E., and Astrada, J. J. (1970) Effect of hypothalamic deafferentation on the control of luteinizing hormone secretion, *J. Endocrinol.*, **46**, 1–7.

Terasawa, E. and Sawyer, C. H. (1970) Diurnal variation in the effects of progesterone on multiple unit activity in the rat hypothalamus, *Exp. Neurol.*, **27**, 359–74.

Terasawa, E. and Timiras, P. S. (1968a) Electrophysiological study of the limbic system in the rat at onset of puberty, *Am. J. Physiol.*, **215**, 1462–7.

Terasawa, E. and Timiras, P. S. (1968b) Electrical activity during the estrous cycle of the rat: cyclic changes in limbic structures, *Endocrinology*, **83**, 207–16.

Thompson, M. L. and Edwards, D. A. (1972) Olfactory bulb ablation and hormonally induced mating in spayed female mice, *Physiol. Behav.*, **8**, 1141–6.

Wade, G. N., Harding, C. F., and Feder, H. H. (1973) Neural uptake of (1,2-^{3}H) progesterone in ovariectomized rats, guinea pigs and hamsters: correlation with species differences in behavioral responsiveness, *Brain Res.*, **61**, 357–67.

Walter, H. E. and Sayles, L. P. (1949) *Biology of the Vertebrates* 3rd edn., Macmillan Co., N. Y.

Warkentin, J. and Carmichael, L. (1939) A study of the development of the air-righting reflex in cats and rabbits, *J. Genet. Psychol.*, **55**, 67–80.

Yagi, K. and Sawaki, Y. (1973) Feedback of estrogen in the hypothalamic control of gonadotropin secretion. In: *Neuroendocrine Control*, K. Yagi and S. Yoshida (eds.), Univ. Tokyo Press, pp. 297–325.

Yoshinaga, K., Hawkins, R. A., and Stocker, J. F. (1969) Estrogen secretion by the rat ovary *in vivo* during the estrous cycle and pregnancy, *Endocrinology*, **85**, 103–12.

Zarrow, M. X. and Clark, J. H. (1968) Ovulation following vaginal stimulation in a spontaneous ovulator and its implications, *J. Endocrinol.*, **40**, 343–52.

Zitrin, A. and Beach, F. A. (1945) Discussion of paper by C. G. Hartman: The mating of mammals, *N. Y. Acad. Sci.*, **46**, 23–40.

Zolovick, A. J. and Eleftheriou, B. E. (1971) Hormonal modulation of hypothalamic unit activity and EEG response to vaginal stimulation in the deermouse, *J. Endocrinol.*, **49**, 59–69.

Zouhar, R. L. and de Groot, J. (1963) Effects of limbic brain lesions on aspects of reproduction in female rats, *Anat. Rec.*, **145**, 358.

CHAPTER 12

Specificity of Steroid Hormone Activation of Sexual Behaviour in Rodents

H. H. FEDER

INTRODUCTION

The question of the specificity of hormones in relation to the expression of sexual activity exists within a variety of contexts. One might wish to frame the question in terms of tissue specificity. For example, hormones may act on tissues outside the nervous or reproductive system (Kappas and Palmer, 1963; Kincl, 1965; Landau, 1973) and thereby influence sexual responses in an indirect fashion. Alternatively, hormones may act preferentially on only some portions of the central nervous system (CNS) (anatomical specificity: Davidson and Bloch, 1969; Pfaff and Keiner, 1973; Lisk, 1973) and they may influence various tissues with heightened or subdued intensity according to factors such as time of day (Everett, 1961; Meier, 1969; Everitt et al., 1975), season of year (Amoroso and Marshall, 1960), stage of development (all manifestations of temporal specificity: Price and Ortiz, 1944; Diamond and Cerney, 1966; Goy et al., 1967; Lisk, 1973), evolutionary history of the animal (species specificity: Barrington, 1968; Wade et al., 1973; Feder et al., 1974; Gorzalka and Whalen, 1974), or genetic sex of the animal (sex specificity: Goodale, 1918; Price and Pannabecker, 1959). Furthermore, hormonal specificity may be studied in terms of the types of behavioural responses activated (response specificity: Beach, 1961; Young, 1961) or the particular molecular form of the hormone activating the response (chemical specificity: Beach, 1961; Young, 1961). This review will focus primarily on sex specificity, response specificity, and chemical specificity by examining the relation of genetic sex to certain sexual responses in adult rodents and lagomorphs subjected to treatments with a variety of chemical forms of androgen, oestrogen, and progestin.

Controversy over the extent of chemical specificity of hormonal influences over sexual behaviours can be caricatured as consisting of two extreme viewpoints. On the one hand, authors such as Eayrs (1952) and Kinsey et al. (1953) concluded that there is virtually no specific relation between a hormone and the behaviour it activates or suppresses. For example, Young (1961) cites the conclusion of Kinsey *et al.* that the so-called sex hormones are merely 'among the physiologic agents which step up the general level of metabolic activity in an animal's body, including the level of its nervous function and therefore of its sexual activity.' On the other hand, authors such as Steinach (1940) and Sand (1919) argued for a very specific relationship between hormones and sex behaviour. They believed that ovarian hormones activated feminine behaviour equally well in gonadectomized genetic females and males, and that testicular hormones activated masculine behaviour equally well in gonadectomized genetic males and females. In fact, the reasoning of these early authors led them to expect that a gonadectomized animal would show alternating periods of male and female behaviour if given simultaneous transplants of an ovary and a testis. A short excerpt from Steinach (1940) nicely illustrates his perspective on the problem:

> The simultaneous implantation of both an ovary and a testicle into an animal, previously rendered neuter by castration, resulted in the manifestation of both male and female attributes. The sexual duality was not only physical (technically known as androgyny), but it also manifested itself in the simultaneous occurrence of inclinations typical of both sexes, so that the experimental animal exhibited both homosexuality (inclination toward the like sex) and heterosexuality (inclination toward the opposite sex). When I came to sum up the result of masculinization and feminization, it was legitimate to draw the conclusion that the sexual life of every creature—whether in the male, female, hermaphrodite, or some other transitional, that is intersexual, form—is determined by the hormone-producing sex glands, and by the quality, and quantity, of the hormone they furnish.

Contained in this excerpt are several assumptions that have since been shown to be unwarranted, but that nevertheless retain some influence to this day. For this reason it seems useful to make these assumptions explicit and examine them before proceeding to a detailed discussion of hormonal specificity.

The first of these assumptions is that adult mammals are rendered sexually neutral by gonadectomy. That this is not the case is demonstrated by experiments illustrating the influences of genotype (McGill and Haynes, 1973), exposure to hormones during perinatal differentiation (Phoenix *et al.*, 1959; Grady *et al.*, 1965) and prior sexual experiences (Rosenblatt and Aronson, 1958) on the sexual bias or the sexual capability of gonadectomized animals. Thus, it is not only the nature of the hormone administered, but also the character of the substrate or soma on which the hormone acts, that determines the nature of a behavioural response to a hormone (Young, 1969). A second implicit assumption is that females produce only 'female hormone' (oestrogen and progestin) and males produce only 'male hormone' (androgen). However, female mammals secrete androgens (Savard, 1968; Gay and Tomacari, 1974) and the mammalian testis secretes oestrogens (Engel, 1973). Some of the and-

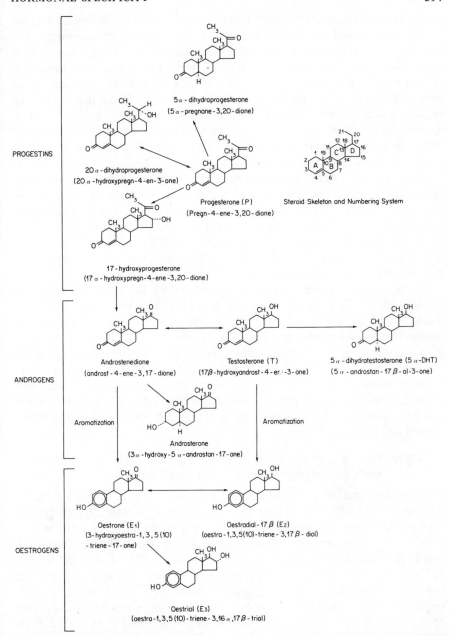

Fig. 1. Basic pathways from progesterone to other progestins, to androgens, and to oestrogens. Arrows pointing in one direction indicate irreversible reactions, arrows pointing in both directions indicate reversible reactions. The steroids depicted are those most extensively discussed in the text, and the figure is not meant as a complete map of steroid pathways. A single arrow does not necessarily imply that only a single metabolic step is involved.

rogens secreted by the gonads can be converted to oestrogens by a process called 'aromatization' (Klyne, 1960). (See Fig. 1 for biochemical pathways.) The significance of this process for behavioural studies will be apparent in later sections of this review. A third assumption is that sexual duality of behaviour is clear-cut. However, female mammals of many species display elements of behaviour that are ordinarily associated with masculinity (e.g. mounting behaviour) even when no surgical or hormonal manipulation has been performed (Beach, 1968). In the absence of experimental interventions male mammals also display behaviours ordinarily designated as feminine (e.g. presenting posture in rhesus macaques) (Goy, 1970). In view of these data it is preferable to speak of particular behavioural responses after hormone treatment (e.g. lordosis, mounting, intromission, etc.) rather than of 'masculine' or 'feminine' responses (Beach, 1971). It would be even more preferable to analyse hormone–behaviour interactions by referring to particular aspects of a response (e.g. latency to lordosis, intensity of individual lordosis response, duration of lordosis) rather than to the entire response (lordosis), but this approach would be too unwieldy for the present review.

Neither of the extreme viewpoints represented by Kinsey et al. (1953) and by Steinach (1940) is widely accepted today. There is ample evidence both for a measure of specificity and a measure of non-specificity in the relationships between hormones and sexual responses. In order to review some of the recent data, eight possible interactions among sexual specificity, response specificity, and chemical specificity in rodents will be considered. Previously, this type of review has been presented by Beach (1961) and by Young (1961), and systematic experiments designed to test these eight relationships within the context of a single study have been carried out in rats (Pfaff, 1970) and in ring doves (Cheng and Lehrman, 1975).

GENETIC FEMALES AND THE EFFECTS OF OESTROGENS AND PROGESTINS ON LORDOSIS RESPONSES

When in oestrus, female rodents readily assume a lordotic posture (concave arching of the back) after being mounted by a male (Komisaruk, 1974). Biochemical measurements of steroids in the systemic circulation or in the ovarian vein of rats, hamsters, and guinea-pigs (Naftolin et al., 1972a; Baranczuk and Greenwald, 1973; Joshi et al., 1973; Schwartz, 1974; Shaikh and Shaikh, 1975) indicate that oestradiol-17β levels begin to increase about 24 h prior to onset of lordosis behaviour, and that a substantial increase in progesterone secretion occurs almost simultaneously with the onset of this behaviour (Feder et al., 1968a, b; Lukaszewska and Greenwald, 1970; Feder et al., 1971). These studies also show that secretion of other oestrogens (e.g. oestrone) and other progestins (e.g. 20α-dihydroprogesterone) are, in general, not as consistently associated with lordosis, and it is reasonable to suppose that oestradiol and progesterone are the hormones most intimately associated with facilitation of lordosis in these species.

Table 1. Eight relationships among behavioural responses, classes of steroid hormones and genetic sex. The particular steroids listed are those that are most extensively examined in the text

Behavioural responses	Hormones	Genetic Sex	Relationship page number in text
LORDOSES	Oestrogens (± Progestins), Oestradiol-17β, Oestrone, Oestriol	FEMALE	398
	Progesterone, 5α-Dihydroprogesterone, 20α-Dihydroprogesterone	MALE	403
	Androgens, Testosterone, 5α-Dihydrotestosterone	FEMALE	404
		MALE	405
MOUNTS, INTROMISSIONS, EJACULATIONS	Androgens, Testosterone, 5α-Dihydrotestosterone	MALE	406
		FEMALE	409
	Oestrogens, Oestradiol-17β, Oestrone	MALE	408
		FEMALE	410

Oestrogens

Experimental studies bolster this supposition. In ovariectomized rats, oestradiol was more potent in facilitating lordosis than oestrone, oestrone-3-sulphate or oestriol (Beyer et al., 1971). Similarly, in ovariectomized guinea pigs the 3-benzoate oester of oestradiol was more effective in promoting lordosis than the corresponding ester of oestrone. Oestriol also facilitated lordosis in ovariectomized guinea pigs (Feder and Silver, 1975). Although metabolic interconversions occur between oestradiol and oestrone (Villee, 1961), administration of radioactive oestriol does not result in the appearance of radioactive oestradiol or oestrone in brain tissue homogenates of guinea pigs (I.T. Landau and H. H. Feder, unpubl. observ.). These data indicate that a range of naturally occurring oestrogenic substances is capable of facilitating lordosis, and that an absolutely specific relation between oestradiol and lordosis does not obtain. However, this degree of non-specificity does not mean that the relationship between oestrogens and behaviour is not amenable to further biochemical study. The uterus, like the neural tissues mediating lordosis, is capable of exhibiting responses to a variety of oestrogens, including oestriol (Anderson et al., 1975), but this has not prevented major advances in the understanding of mechanisms of oestrogen action in the uterus.

The mechanisms whereby oestradiol promotes lordosis are not known, but it is apparent that protein receptors for oestradiol exist in higher concentrations in neurones of the preoptic area and hypothalamus than in neurones of other brain areas (McEwen and Pfaff, 1973; McEwen et al., 1974). A current working hypothesis is that translocation of the oestradiol receptor complex from the cytoplasm to the cell nucleus of hypothalamic neurones mediates the production of increased RNA and protein synthesis, and that this synthetic activity somehow facilitates lordosis (Whalen et al., 1974). Oestriol (and possibly other oestrogens) may be sufficiently similar in chemical structure to oestradiol to be able to attach to these same receptor molecules and thereby initiate biochemical events leading to the display of lordosis. Recently, it was demonstrated that oestriol could attach to uterine receptors normally responsive to oestradiol, but that the oestriol receptor complex was not retained in uterine nuclei for as long an interval as the oestradiol receptor complex (Anderson et al., 1975). Perhaps a similar situation accounts for the suboptimal effects of oestriol on lordosis. In support of this notion, I. T. Landau has found, with in vivo preparations, that radioactive oestriol is not retained in whole homogenates of guinea-pig hypothalamus for as long as radioactive oestradiol (unpubl. observ.).

Progestins

Injections of progesterone into ovariectomized, oestrogen-primed rats and guinea pigs facilitate lordosis far more effectively than injections of other progestins (Meyerson, 1972; Whalen and Gorzalka, 1972; Wade and Feder, 1972a;

Czaja *et al.*, 1974). The compound 20α-dihydroprogesterone, which is secreted copiously by non-pregnant rats (Hashimoto *et al.*, 1968; Uchida *et al.*, 1969) is quite ineffective in facilitating lordosis in this species (Langford and Hilliard, 1967; Meyerson, 1972). Similarly, only very high doses of 20α-dihydroprogesterone facilitate lordosis in oestrogen-primed guinea pigs (Zucker and Goy, 1967). However, even this slight effect may be attributable to metabolic conversion of injected 20α-hydroprogesterone to progesterone. For example, Wade and Feder (1972b) showed that about 5 to 11% of radioactivity recovered from guinea-pig brain homogenates after systemic injection of 20α-dihydroprogesterone had chromatographic properties of progesterone. Similar considerations may account for lordosis-promoting properties of pregnenolone (Zucker and Goy, 1967), a steroid that is known to be a metabolic precursor of progesterone (Fieser and Fieser, 1959). The steroid 17α-hydroxyprogesterone lacks lordosis-facilitating properties in guinea-pigs (Byrnes and Shipley, 1955; Zucker and Goy, 1967; Wade and Feder, 1972a), but corticosterone is capable of promoting this response when given in large doses, even though corticosterone is not converted to progesterone in guinea pigs (Wade and Feder, 1972a, 1972b).

A somewhat special case may be presented by the progestin 5α-dihydroprogesterone (5α-pregnan-3, 20-dione, DHP). This steroid and its metabolite 3α-hydroxy-5α-pregnan-20-one, are capable of facilitating lordosis in guinea pigs (Wade and Feder, 1972a; Czaja *et al.*, 1974) and rats (Whalen and Gorzalka, 1972; Meyerson, 1972) but less effectively than progesterone. The argument has been made that the lower potency of DHP is an artefact caused by reduced bioavailability of this substance when it is systemically injected (Czaja *et al.*, 1974). According to this view, progesterone may serve as a circulating 'pre-hormone' (Baird *et al.*, 1968) but upon reaching critical central neural structures it is metabolized to DHP and sequestered from influences that would otherwise reduce the bioavailability of this metabolite. The sequestered DHP may then be responsible for influencing lordosis. A parallel situation has been shown to exist for testosterone and its 5α-reduced metabolite, 5α-dihydrotestosterone (DHT) in male genital tract tissues (Wilson, 1975), but judgement on the behavioural role of DHP must be reserved until further data are collected. For example, one would like to know whether intracranial implants of DHP are more effective than corresponding implants of progesterone in facilitating lordosis. Another experiment that might be useful would consist of administering progesterone along with an agent that prevents 5α-reduction to determine whether lordosis would still be facilitated by progesterone in the absence of its reduction to DHP.

The problem of specificity of progestins in promotion of lordosis is cloudier than for oestrogens. While there is no conclusive evidence that oestrogen interaction with protein receptors in diencephalic neurones is a *sine qua non* for oestrogenic facilitation of lordosis, such an hypothesis seems reasonable, and is strongly supported by data from techniques as disparate as lesioning

(Brookhart *et al.*, 1940; Sawyer, 1960; Lisk, 1973), implantation of oestrogens intracranially (Lisk, 1962; Ciaccio and Lisk, 1973; Morin and Feder, 1974a), autoradiography (Stumpf, 1968; Pfaff and Keiner, 1973), scintillation counting of brain homogenates (Eisenfeld and Axelrod, 1965; Kato and Villee, 1967; Wade and Feder, 1972b; McEwen and Pfaff, 1973), and brain cell nuclei (Zigmond and McEwen, 1970; Feder and Wade, 1974), administration of anti-oestrogens (Arai and Gorski, 1968; Komisaruk and Beyer, 1972; Ross *et al.*, 1973; Whalen and Gorzalka, 1973; Luttge *et al.*, 1975), and administration of protein synthesis inhibitors (Whalen *et al.*, 1974). The situation for the progestins offers a marked contrast. Lesion techniques have not established crucial sites for the action of progesterone on lordosis. Intracranial implantation studies suggest that a rather circumscribed area in the medial basal hypothalamus regulates lordosis-facilitating effects of progesterone in ovariectomized, oestrogen-primed guinea pigs (Morin and Feder, 1974b), but this behavioural effect of progesterone in rats is found when intracranial implants of the steroid are placed in medial basal hypothalamus (Powers, 1972), midbrain reticular formation (Ross *et al.*, 1971), and caudate-putamen (Yanase and Gorski, 1975). No specific antiprogestins appear to be available for studying brain effects of progestins. Autoradiographic studies suggest the presence of nuclear receptors for progestins in guinea-pig hypothalamus (Sar and Stumpf, 1973), but there is disagreement concerning this finding (Warembourg cited in Atger *et al.*, 1974). Scientillation counting techniques suggest higher brain uptake of radioactive progesterone in midbrain than in hypothalamus, and higher uptake in hypothalamus than in cerebral cortex of guinea pigs, rats, and hamsters (Wade *et al.*, 1973). While some evidence for a limited-capacity cytoplasmic receptor for progesterone exists in rat and guinea-pig hypothalamus (Seiki and Hattori, 1973; C. Iramain, pers. commun.) there is, as yet, no conclusive evidence that the midbrain progesterone uptake mechanism is of the high-affinity, limited-capacity category (Whalen and Luttge, 1971a; Wade and Feder, 1972c; Luttge and Wallis, 1973). No data indicate that blockade of protein synthesis inhibits lordosis-promoting effects of progesterone in guinea pigs (Wallen *et al.*, 1972), but progesterone seems to increase amino-acid incorporation into brain protein in this species (Wade and Feder, 1974). Thus, it appears that although progesterone is the most effective progestin for facilitating lordosis, the mechanism by which this chemical specificity is achieved is not certain. Even if receptor proteins for progesterone do exist in brain, we do not have adequate support, at this time, for the conclusion that such receptor molecules play a crucial role in mediating behavioural responses to progesterone administration.

Aside from its facilitatory actions on lordosis, progesterone also is capable of suppressing lordosis in guinea pigs, hamsters, and rats (Whalen and Nakayama, 1965; Goy *et al.*, 1966; Lisk, 1969; Feder, 1976). Czaja *et al.* (1974) demonstrated that systemically injected progesterone was more effective in suppressing lordosis than other progestins but the cellular basis of this selectivity is unknown. This review will not deal with inhibitory effects of progesterone, and the above-mentioned papers should be consulted for further information.

GENETIC MALES AND THE EFFECTS OF OESTROGENS AND PROGESTINS ON LORDOSIS RESPONSES

Adult, castrated male rats can be induced to display lordosis when given oestrone, oestradiol or oestriol preparations (reviewed in Young, 1961 and Beach, 1961; Pfaff, 1970; Södersten and Larsson, 1974; Larsson et al., 1976) with oestradiol being the most potent of these oestrogens as is the case for genetic females. Young (1961) and Beach (1961) point out that while the promotion of lordosis in males by oestrogens occurs, the responses are usually of short duration, incomplete and more difficult to elicit (that is, higher doses of oestrogen are required) than in females. Presumably, this sex difference in behavioural responsiveness to oestrogen administered alone or in combination with progesterone (Davidson, 1969; Arén-Engelbrektsson et al., 1970) is attributable to an action of endogenous aromatizable testicular steroids on the differentiating nervous system of perinatal animals. Thus, genetic females given injections of aromatizable androgens (Edwards and Thompson, 1970; Gerall and Kenny, 1970; Whalen et al., 1971; Carter and Landauer, 1975) during perinatal differentiation possess a reduced responsiveness to lordosis-promoting actions of oestrogen in adulthood, and genetic males given anti-androgen (Ward, 1972) or castrated during an appropriate perinatal period possess an enhanced ability to display lordosis after oestrogen treatment in adulthood (Grady et al., 1965; Gerall et al., 1967). It may be that genetic factors in addition to perinatal hormonal factors, contribute to the sex difference in lordosis-facilitating effects of oestrogen, but this possibility has not been examined.

An interesting finding is that progesterone does not readily synergize with oestrogen in male rats to facilitate lordosis as it does in females (Davidson, 1969; Davidson and Levine, 1969; Clemens et al., 1969; Clemens et al., 1970; Franck et al., 1973). The origin of this lack of responsiveness to progesterone in males may be related to the secretion of testicular hormones during perinatal life and/or to genetic factors. The ways in which either or both of these factors bring about a sex difference in responsiveness to lordosis-facilitating actions of progesterone are a matter for speculation. One might venture that males take up less progesterone in neural tissues than females. However, this was not been shown to be the case when brain homogenates of ^{3}H-progesterone injected rats and guinea pigs were examined (Whalen and Luttge, 1971a; Wade and Feder, 1972c). Possibly, there are sex differences in the quantity of cytoplasmic or nuclear receptors for progesterone that are obscured by using whole homogenates for analysis. An alternative possibility is that males are less capable of metabolizing progesterone to DHP, or some other progestin, in brain areas crucial to the display of lordosis. The peripheral metabolism or binding of progesterone to plasma proteins may also differ between sexes in such a way as to permit more progesterone reach the brain of a female than a male.

GENETIC FEMALES AND THE EFFECTS OF ANDROGEN ON LORDOSIS RESPONSES

It has been known for many years that androgen administration to ovariectomized rats (Beach, 1942) or rabbits (Klein, 1952) leads to an increased likelihood that lordosis will be displayed. More recent research indicates that a proportion of the administered androgen is aromatized to oestrogen (Naftolin *et al.*, 1972b), and the oestrogenic compound so formed is thought to be the significant hormonal factor in the facilitation of lordosis. Experiments supporting this contention include the administration of aromatizable or non-aromatizable androgens to gonadectomized rabbits (Beyer *et al.*, 1970). Only the aromatizable androgens seemed to be effective in facilitating lordosis in rabbits and in rodents (Beyer and Komisaruk, 1971) with the unexplained exception that very prolonged treatment of rats with the non-aromatizable androgen DHT also promoted lordosis (Beyer *et al.*, 1971a). Furthermore, when administration of antioestrogenic compounds was combined with injection of the aromatizable androgens, lordosis responses decreased (Whalen *et al.*, 1972; Beyer and Vidal, 1971; Luttge *et al.*, 1975).

Biochemical experiments have shown that hypothalamic whole homogenates from rats contained a small, but measurable, percentage of oestrogen after androgens such as testosterone or androstenedione were administered (Naftolin *et al.*, 1972b; Weisz and Gibbs, 1974). However, the extremely small magnitude of this conversion ($< 1\%$) left its significance for behaviour in some doubt. Other experiments with hypothalamic cell nuclear fractions, rather than with whole homogenates, seem more convincing in this respect. The percentage of oestrogen in rat cell nuclei from the hypothalamus was as high as 45% after administration of androgen to females or males (Lieberburg and McEwen, 1975a, 1975b).

When Young, in 1961, surveyed the relationship between feminine behaviour and androgens in females he viewed as remote the possibility that metabolic conversion of the androgens to oestrogens could be a significant factor. Today, in considering lordosis behaviour of non-primate female mammals this possibility no longer seems remote. Indeed, a great deal of evidence cited in this chapter points to the importance of oestrogen (directly or via aromatization of androgens) in the activation of lordosis responses. It would be of considerable interest to determine whether any aspects of feminine behaviour in female primates are as closely tied to aromatization of androgens as lordosis is in non-primates. Some workers have found increases in the frequency of display of the 'present' posture in ovariectomized rhesus macaques when these animals were given (aromatizable) testosterone preparations but not when they were given (non-aromatizable) DHT preparations (D. Goldfoot, pers. commun.). However, there may be an important role for androgens of adrenal origin in primate feminine behaviour (particularly 'receptivity') that is not entirely referable to aromatization of these secretions (Everitt et al., 1972). The possibility that adrenal androgens or other adrenal secretions potentiate the action of exogenous aromatizable androgens in activating lordosis in rodents might also be examined.

GENETIC MALES AND THE EFFECTS OF ANDROGENS ON LORDOSIS RESPONSES

Typically, lordosis responses are difficult to elicit in males treated with either oestrogen or androgen (Young, 1961). However, lordotic responses have been observed in male hamsters (Tiefer, 1970), rats (Beach, 1941) and mice (Engel, 1942) given aromatizable androgens alone or in combination with progesterone. It seems highly probable that the lordosis-activating properties of androgen in males are attributable to aromatization as is the case for genetic females. Brain tissues of both sexes possess the ability to convert androgen to oestrogen (Lieberburg and McEwen, 1975a, 1975b).

Apparently, genetic male rats are less sensitive than females to the lordosis-facilitating effects of androgen injection in combination with progesterone (Pfaff, 1970). One group of workers (Dörner and Hinz, 1967) has suggested that deprivation of testicular secretions during perinatal differentiation of genetic male rats results in an enhancement, in adulthood, of the lordosis-potentiating effects of androgen. This is an intriguing possibility, but the effect requires confirmation by more rigid behavioural observations than those reported.

SUMMARY

In summary, the relationships between steroid hormones and lordosis behaviour of rodents and lagomorphs seem even more specific than was supposed 15 years ago. The effects of androgens on lordosis now seem predominantly, if not entirely, attributable to their conversion to oestrogens. However, the ability to activate lordosis is not limited to a solitary oestrogen (oestradiol-17β). Oestrone, oestriol (Beyer et al., 1971b; Feder and Silver, 1974), stilboestrol (Michael, 1973), and even the antioestrogens enclomiphene and zuclomiphene (Ross et al., 1973; W. A. Walker and H. H. Feder, unpubl. data) are all capable of facilitating lordosis to varying degrees in a variety of non-primate females. A widely held notion is that all of these substances become bound to a common steroid receptor protein in diencephalic neurones and initiate a common biochemical process that ultimately facilitates the expression of lordosis. A correlate is that once this biochemical process has been set in motion by oestrogen, the oestrogen plays no further significant role in promotion of lordosis, and it disappears fairly rapidly from binding sites within the nervous system (Michael, 1962). The fact that oestrogens and aromatizable androgens facilitate lordosis more readily in genotypic females than males suggests that the oestrophilic binding proteins are present in higher concentration in females than males. This suggestion has been a point of much contention, but some recent data favour its adoption (Vertes and King, 1971; Whalen and Massicci, 1975). Furthermore, species that are highly sensitive to lordosis-promoting effects of oestrogen (rat, guinea pig) take up and retain more ^{3}H-oestradiol in hypothalamus than species that are relatively insensitive to oestrogen (hamster) (Feder et al., 1974b; Kelley and Pfaff, this volume Chapter 7).

Although this conception of mediation of the lordosis response through oestrophilic receptor molecules is reasonable, there are some data that do not, as yet, appear to fit it comfortably. For example, Baum and Vreeburg (1975) report that the affinity of some antioestrogens (MER-25, 5α-DHT, 3α-androstenediol) for oestrogen receptors is not correlated with their ability to inhibit the stimulatory effects of ovarian hormones on lordosis. Another set of data collected from guinea pigs deals with a different aspect of the problem. These data suggest that, in addition to whatever effects oestrogens (and related substances) have on initiating biochemical processes (Bullock, 1970) leading to lordosis, they also have effects on lordosis that are related to their prolonged residence in diencephalic tissues. Thus, a second dose of oestrogen administered about 36–40 h after the first dose, causes an increase in the duration of lordosis behaviour (Collins et al., 1938; Joslyn and Feder, 1971), while an injection of the antioestrogen MER-25 about 40 h after oestrogen treatments causes decrements in lordosis behaviour (Feder and Morin, 1974). Moreover, direct measurements of radioactivity in hypothalamus indicate that substantial quantities of oestradiol remain 36 h after subcutaneous injection of ^{3}H-oestradiol benzoate (OB) dissolved in oil vehicle (Eaton et al., 1975). This route of injection of the benzoate ester of oestradiol is the same as that generally used to induce behavioural responses in female guinea pigs and is therefore more relevant than data on retention of radioactivity collected by intravenous or intraperitoneal administration of small quantities of free oestradiol dissolved in alcohol or benzene solutions. It is conceivable that in some species, such as the rat, oestrogen acts on lordosis predominantly or exclusively by initiating RNA or protein synthesis (Quadagno and Ho, 1975). In other species, such as the guinea pig, this early initiation phase may be followed by a 'maintenance' phase during which the continued presence of oestrogen in the nervous system is influential in regulating some aspects of the lordosis response.

GENETIC MALES AND THE EFFECTS OF ANDROGENS ON MOUNTING, INTROMISSION, AND EJACULATION

The term 'mounting' will refer to behaviour in which one animal approaches another from behind and grasps the flanks of the mounted animal with the forepaws. This behaviour may or may not be accompanied by rapid pelvic thrusting by the mounting animal. 'Intromission' will refer to a behaviour pattern in which a mount with thrusting ends in an unusually deep thrust is followed by a backward lunge at dismount. 'Ejaculation' will refer to a behaviour pattern in which a series of deep thrusts is followed by a release of the mounting clasp, a slow raising of the forelegs, and a refractory period during which no sexual activity occurs (Beach, 1961; Young, 1961; Malsbury and Pfaff, 1974).

As a rule, testosterone (in free or esterified form) has been used experimentally to reinduce mounting, intromission and ejaculation responses in castrated male subjects (reviewed in Beach, 1961; Young, 1961). In the last several years interest in the activity of androgens other than testosterone has been expressed by several authors. The compound DHT received much attention because it is convertible neither to testosterone nor to oestrogens (Dorfman and Ungar, 1965). At first, experiments with this compound in castrated rats and hamsters indicated that moderate doses administered systemically over a period of several weeks were ineffective in restoring or maintaining mounting, intromission or ejaculation (McDonald et al., 1970a; Feder, 1971; Whalen and Luttge, 1971b; Beyer et al., 1973; Christensen et al., 1973). However, the generalizability of these data to other species seems questionable, and even the position that DHT is completely ineffectual in potentiating mounting, intromission, and ejaculation in rats has been eroded. First, in species such as guinea pigs (Alsum and Goy, 1974), and rabbits (Beyer and Rivaud, 1973), hamsters (Whalen and DeBold, 1974) and in some strains of mice (Luttge and Hall, 1973), preparations of DHT restore, in varying degrees, mounting, intromission, and ejaculation behaviours. Second, in rats, large doses of DHT preparations result in restoration of ejaculation in 55% of castrated animals (Paup et al., 1975), and intracerebral implants of DHT propionate, though less effective than corresponding implants of TP, were slightly more effective than implants of cholesterol in this respect (Johnston and Davidson, 1972). Several explanations for the differential behavioural potency of DHT among species or strains are plausible. For example, one might suppose that species or strains that are highly sensitive to the restorative actions of DHT on mounting, intromission, and ejaculation behaviours contain a higher brain concentration of DHT receptors than the relatively insensitive species or strains. Another possibility is that there is a reduced bioavailability of exogenous DHT in responsive as compared with unresponsive species or strains (e.g. faster metabolic clearance rate in the unresponsives). Still another possibility is that DHT must act in combination with adrenal oestrogens to restore various aspects of male behaviours, and the appropriate balance between DHT and adrenal oestrogen is struck more readily in responsive species

Whatever explanation eventually emerges, it seems clear that the non-aromatizable androgen DHT is capable of restoring male copulatory responses in castrated animals of a number of species. The non-aromatizable androgen androsterone (3α-hydroxy-5α-androstan-17-one) was also found to potentiate mounting behaviour, but not intromission, in male hamsters (Christensen *et al.*, 1973). Another compound that is presumably not aromatized but yet potentiates the retention of ejaculatory responses in castrated rats is cyproterone or its acetate (Bloch and Davidson, 1971). All of these data suggest that the expression of male mating responses is not rigidly dependent on the presence of steroids that are transformable either to testosterone or to oestradiol.

Several other androgenic substances have also been tested for behavioural effects. Androstenedione (androst-4-ene-3, 17-dione) and androstenediol (androst-5-ene-3β, 17β-diol) were found to stimulate mounting, intromission, and ejaculation in castrated rats (Luttge and Whalen, 1970; Moralí, *et al.*, 1974). The impact of these data is reduced by the fact that both of these steroids can be biotransformed to testosterone, and then presumably, to oestradiol (Dorfman and Ungar, 1965). Compounds that were ineffective in restoring complete copulatory behaviour to castrated rats include: dehydroepiandrosterone (3β-hydroxyandrost-5-en-17-one), androstanedione (5α-androstane-3, 17-dione), androstanediol (5α-androstane-3α, 17β-diol), 5β-androstanediol (5β-androstane-3α, 17β-diol) and 11β-hydroxyandrostenedione (11β-hydroxyandrost-4-ene-3, 17-dione) as well as the synthetic compound fluoxymesterone (Beach and Westbrook, 1968; Beyer *et al.*, 1973).

It may be mentioned in passing that several androgens possessing the capability to induce penile growth do not restore masculine sexual responses in castrated animals (Parrott, 1975). Other papers should be consulted for a consideration of the relative contribution of peripheral and central factors to the expression of masculine behaviours (Beach, 1971; Goy and Goldfoot, 1973; Hart, 1974).

GENETIC MALES AND THE EFFECTS OF OESTROGENS ON MOUNTING, INTROMISSION, AND EJACULATION

The frequency of mounting, intromission, and ejaculation responses increases in castrated male rats when they are given oestradiol preparations (Ball, 1939; Beach, 1942a; Davidson, 1969; Pfaff and Zigmond, 1971; Södersten, 1973). Oestradiol seems more effective in this respect than oestrone or oestriol in rats (Larsson *et al.*, 1976), but in castrated guinea pigs oestrone reinstated mounting and intromission patterns more effectively than OB (Antiliff and Young, 1956). This latter result is puzzling and is deserving of replication because it is unusual for oestrone (and in a non-esterified form, at that) to produce stronger behavioural effects than esterified oestradiol. The basis of this effectiveness of oestrone in male guinea pigs is unknown, and is even more surprising because significant proportions of the radioactivity recovered from hypothalamus after subcutaneous injection of ^{3}H-oestradiol or ^{3}H-oestrone are in the form of ^{3}H-oestradiol (Wade and Feder, 1972b; Eaton *et al.*, 1975; I. T. Landau and H. H. Feder, unpubl. data). Perhaps the heightened effectiveness of oestrone in guinea pigs is related to the fact that oestrone rather than oestradiol is the predominant oestrogen found in extra-hypothalamic neural tissues, such as cerebral cortex, after administration of ^{3}H-oestradiol or ^{3}H-oestrone (Wade and Feder, 1972b; Eaton et al., 1975; I. T. Landau and H. H. Feder, unpubl. data).

Some authors have suggested that aromatization is an obligatory biochemical step in the activation of various male behaviours (McDonald et al., 1970a). One line of evidence for this idea, as mentioned on p. 407, is that in certain rodent species aromatizable androgens readily activate mounting, intromission, and ejaculation, while non-aromatizable androgens do not. Another line of evidence is that oestrogen administration increases mounting and intromission pattern frequency in castrated rats (Pfaff, 1970), hamsters (Clemens cited in Christensen and Clemens, 1974), and guinea pigs (Antliff and Young, 1956) and increases ejaculation pattern frequency in rats (Södersten, 1973). Furthermore, some experiments demonstrate that antioestrogens inhibit steroid-induced activation of male copulatory responses (Luttge, 1974). However, just as there are incongruities in the evidence related to the use of aromatizable and non-aromatizable androgens (see p. 407), there are weakness associated with the evidence collected by the use of oestrogens and antioestrogens. First, high dosages of systemically administered oestrogen are required to fully activate complete male copulatory behaviour in male rats unless the oestrogen is administered in combination with DHT (Larsson et al., 1973; Baum and Vreeburg, 1973; Feder et al., 1974a; Södersten, 1973). It was believed that the DHT exerted this synergistic effect on behaviour primarily because of its actions on penile morphology and growth, but more recent evidence indicates that DHT may also act on the CNS to produce facilitatory influences upon behaviour (Baum et al., 1974; Paup et al., 1975; Södersten, 1975). Thus, although oestrogens are undoubtedly capable of activating masculine sexual responses their action may be potentiated enormously by DHT, or possibly by other androgens, some of which could be of adrenal origin (Gorzalka et al., 1975). Second, even though some antioestrogenic compounds have been shown to inhibit steroid-induced mounting, intromission, and ejaculation, there are other reports that antioestrogens failed to inhibit TP-induced masculine behaviours (Whalen et al., 1972; Baum and Vreeburg, 1975). If these negative findings are not due merely to inappropriate dosages of antioestrogens, they suggest further caution in attributing hormonal activation of masculine sexual responses exclusively to aromatization of androgens.

GENETIC FEMALES AND THE EFFECTS OF ANDROGENS ON MOUNTING, INTROMISSION, AND EJACULATION

Activation of mounting behaviour by testosterone preparations has been reported in female rats, guinea pigs and rabbits (Hu and Frazier, 1939; Ball, 1940; Beach, 1942; Koster, 1943; Klein, 1952; Goy and Young, 1958; McDonald et al., 1970b, but is not seen often in female hamsters (Beach, 1968;

Tiefer, 1970). In some instances, high doses of androgen also stimulate intromission patterns of behaviour in genetic female rats (Beach, 1942; Södersten, 1972). The conceptual issues surrounding the role of aromatization of androgens in activating mounting behaviour in genetic males have already been discussed (pp. 406–408), and since these issues probably also apply to genetic females, they will not be repeated in this section.

Rather, another perspective on the problem of hormonal specificity, recently emphasized by Goldfoot and Van Der Werff Ten Bosch (1975) will be discussed. These authors found that injection of DHT propionate to adult female guinea pigs did not stimulate mounting behaviour, even when genetic females were given TP treatment prenatally. Because adult, genetic male guinea pigs do exhibit increased mounting behaviour in response to DHT propionate treatment in adulthood (Alsum and Goy, 1974), the authors suggested 'the possibility that mechanisms determining sensitivity to specific steroids may not be mediated exclusively by steroids during critical periods of embryological differentiation.' Evidence that genetic factors can determine sexual specificity for steroids is also suggested by the earlier work of Price and Pannabecker (1959) with foetal genital tract tissues and possibly by the fact that adult females of some strains of guinea pigs mount after receiving TP treatment whereas females of other strains do not (Goy and Young, 1958). It might be interesting to know whether strains of guinea pigs in which the females do not display mounting after receiving TP in adulthood do not do so because of properties of the same genetic loci implicated by Goldfoot and Van Werff Ten Bosch as accounting for sex differences in responsiveness to steroid hormones.

GENETIC FEMALES AND THE EFFECTS OF OESTROGENS ON MOUNTING, INTROMISSION, AND EJACULATION

Young (1961) described the relationship between oestrogen and masculine responses in females as a commonly occurring one. Indeed, oestrogen can potentiate not only mounting, but intromission and ejaculatory patterns as well in adult female rats (Pfaff, 1970; Södersten, 1973; Emery and Sachs, 1975). However, Beach and Rasquin (1942) showed that mounting can be displayed by female rats in the absence of hormones of ovarian origin and Södersten (1974) has shown that antioestrogens that suppress lordosis responses in oestrogen-treated rats fail to suppress mounting behaviour. Although alternative explanations are possible, these data suggest that hormonal regulation of mounting behaviour in females, as in males, may be complicated by non-specific actions of hormones and by non-hormonal environmental influences.

An interesting situation is presented in guinea pigs with regard to mounting behaviour. Oestrogen and a subsequent injection of progesterone facilitate the display of mounting in genetic females of the Topeka strain, but this combination of hormones is ineffective in stimulating mounting in males of the same strain. When genetic females of this strain are subjected to androgenization during foetal life they are 'masculinized' (i.e., their responsiveness to mounting behaviour promoting actions of androgens is enhanced in adulthood) and 'defeminized' (i.e. their responsiveness to lordosis facilitating actions of oestrogen and progesterone is reduced in adulthood). One might expect that such prenatally androgenized females would fail to exhibit mounting in response to oestrogen and progesterone just as their genetic male counterparts fail to mount in response to oestrogen and progesterone (Young, 1969). However, this is not the case. The prenatally androgenized females mounted as frequently as adult normal females after receiving oestrogen and progesterone (Goy *et al.*, 1964). Like the data for androgens cited on p. 410 these data suggest that sex differences in genotype account for some sex differences in responsivity to steroid hormones.

SUMMARY

The data on the specificity of the relationship between mounting, intromission, and ejaculation and steroid hormones seem to me to be far more difficult to interpret than the corresponding data on lordosis behaviour and steroids. The following paragraphs are intended as a speculation on this problem.

Many authors have remarked that male sexual behaviour appears to consist of two 'functions' or 'mechanisms' that have been dichotomized variously as contrection *vs.* detumescence, arousal *vs.* executive or consummatory, excitability *vs.* capacity for response, appetitive *vs.* consummatory, and precopulatory *vs.* copulatory (see reviews by Young, 1961; Hart, 1974). In male rodents, aspects of behaviour such as ano-genital sniffing and (sometimes) mounting are classified as appetitive or precopulatory and are usually thought to be dependent on neural activity of forebrain structures such as the medial forebrain bundle. On the other hand, intromission and ejaculatory responses are categorized as consummatory or copulatory acts that are mediated by the medial preoptic area and spinal cord (Hart, 1974; Malsbury and Pfaff, 1974). Mounting behaviour is sometimes also considered as belonging to the category of consummatory behaviours (Malsbury and Pfaff, 1974), and perhaps it is reasonable to describe mounting behaviour as having bases in both appetitive and consummatory groundwork and acting as a kind of behavioural bridge between these separable functions. If there is a dichotomy between appetitive and consummatory mechanisms, the question of whether there are different rules of hormonal specificity for these two mechanisms must be raised. (This dichotomy is accepted for purposes of discussion. Probably, multiple mechanisms are involved in masculine behaviour, each with its own rules of hormonal specificity.) It is conceivable, for example, that the appetitive function could be relatively non-specifically activated through a general alteration of metabolic activity inducible by a relatively wide range of androgens or oestrogens. Other non-specific arousing factors such as electric shock to the tail or to the skin of the back might also affect the appetitive function (Barfield and Sachs, 1968; Caggiula and Eibergen, 1969; Goldfoot and Baum, 1972; Crowley and Ward, 1974) providing that there is a backdrop of hormonal stimulation (Barfield and Sachs, 1970). The hormonal stimuli and the electrical shock stimuli are presumably similar in that they render the animal ready to attend to external cues, but they could be dissimilar in that the hormonal stimulation might more tightly focus the animal's attention to external cues leading to copulatory opportunities, while stimulation of the tail or the skin of the back might increase an animal's attentiveness to all external cues, including those that lead to aggression and eating as well as those that could lead to copulation (Caggiula, 1972; Antelman et al., 1975). One would think that hormonal stimulation of mounting, which has both appetitive and consummatory aspects, would involve neural and other tissues not having specific steroid receptor molecules as well as neural tissues bearing such receptors.

If there is adequate hormonal and non-hormonal stimulation, and an oestrous female is present, the full copulatory pattern can be displayed. Like the lordosis pattern of the female (also a consummatory behaviour), the ejaculatory response of the male should be capable of being displayed in the absence of hormonal stimulation of specific sites in the medial preoptic area and/or spinal cord, but the threshold for response should be expected to be high. One might predict that the consummatory portions of male sexual behaviour are subserved by a more specific range of hormones acting at more specific sites than the hormones affecting the appetitive system. The categories of hormones subserving the appetitive function may overlap among species because this function need not require great specificity, but the types of hormones mediating the consummatory system may not overlap as much, because this system requires more specificity. Thus, in male rats, aromatization of testosterone to oestradiol (plus a synergistic action of DHT) is especially effective in facilitating ejaculation (Larsson et al., 1973; Baum and Vreeburg, 1973), while in male guinea pigs reduction of testosterone to DHT is especially effective in facilitating ejaculation (Alsum and Goy, 1974). From this hypothetical scheme some further thoughts emerge:

(1) Without metabolism to other steroids, testosterone may be involved in the activation of the appetitive mechanism, particularly through general metabolic effects on extra-hypothalamic tissues.

(2) Metabolism of testosterone to oestradiol (e.g. in rats) or to DHT (e.g. in guinea pigs) in the diencephalon (and/or spinal cord) might act to selectively lower the threshold of the consummatory function.

(3) The fact that both appetitive and consummatory sexual responses decline after castration indicates that both functions are hormonally mediated. However, ejaculation responses usually diminish at a faster rate than appetitive behaviours such as ano-genital sniffing and bridge behaviours such as mounting (Young, 1961).

This suggests that appetitive behaviours might be retained because of genetic factors (e.g. heterosis) (McGill and Haynes, 1973) that tend to keep strains of animals in a higher stage of general vigour or arousal, or because of environmental factors (e.g. previous sexual experience) (Rosenblatt and Aronson, 1958) that tend to permit an animal to focus on cues for copulation. (An alternative explanation for the difference in rate of decline of appetitive and consummatory behaviours after castration is that sensory input from the penis (important for intromission and ejaculation behaviours) decreases as a result of lack of androgen. The magnitude or significance of this androgen-dependent sensory input for consummatory behaviours may exceed the significance of androgen-dependent sensory input for appetitive behaviours.) This formulation helps to account for strains of animals or individual animals that continue to copulate for prolonged periods after removal of testicular and adrenal steroids. Such animals, by virtue of favourable genetic or experiential factors, would be more likely to perform appetitive sexual behaviours that, once started, can lead to consummatory behaviours. This notion also accounts for the finding that there is no difference in resting level of plasma testosterone among guinea pigs that ejaculate during each of three sex tests, guinea pigs that mount and intromit but do not ejaculate, and guinea pigs that show no response to the female at all (Harding and Feder, 1976). Despite their normal levels of plasma testosterone, the completely non-responsive animals presumably fail to attend to or to appropriately interpret cues from their partners.

(4) A behaviour such as mounting may be displayed fairly readily by genetic females as well as by genetic males (Beach, 1968). This degree of overlapping of behaviour patterns between the sexes may be attributable to the involvement of the relatively non-specific appetitive mechanism in the activation of mounting. However, even though both males and females exhibit mounting behaviour, the normal functional significance of this behaviour may differ between the sexes. In the male, mounting serves as the predecessor to intromission and ejaculation. In the female, mounting behaviour shown near the time of spontaneous oestrus (Young, 1961; Beach, 1968) may serve as a soliciting behaviour whose purpose is to contribute to arousing the male by somatosensory stimulation so that he will attempt to copulate, and thereby induce the expression of the consummatory lordosis response.

(5) Finally, it may be that under normal conditions appetitive and consummatory sexual behaviours are regulated by the same hormones. This would be economical in terms of function. Perhaps this account for the sex differences in guinea pigs with regard to hormonal mediation of mounting. Oestradiol and progesterone effectively mediate not only lordosis in female guinea pigs, but also the mounting behaviour that often precedes lordosis (Young and Rundlett, 1939; Diamond, 1965). Testosterone and DHT mediate not only intromission and ejaculation in males, but also the mounting behaviour that precedes ejaculation. It would be uneconomical (but not theoretically impossible) if, for example, DHT were solely responsible for stimulating mounting

in a female guinea pig, and oestradiol and progesterone were solely responsible for activating lordosis in the same animal.

CONCLUSIONS

In writing this essay, I have come to the conviction that if we ask the question 'How specific is the relation between steroid hormones and the expression of sexual behaviour?' we can only receive answers that boil down to 'very specific' or 'not specific at all'. In fact, as I suggested at the beginning, these answers are the essence of the two extreme positions adopted by Steinach and by Kinsey, respectively. The review of recent literature presented here, appears to lead to a third conclusion. Namely, neither of these extreme viewpoints is valid, and 'the truth' lies somewhere between them. Yet, there seems little satisfaction to be gained by favouring any of these three answers. I suspect the question itself is sterile, and would recommend that we substitute for it questions such as: 'How do particular genetic, developmental, hormonal, neural, and environmental factors modulate the sensitivity of portions of the nervous system to the biochemical effects of certain steroid hormones which interest us because of their consequences for behaviour?' Questions such as these will not close us off to possible hormone–behaviour relationships that are independent of limited capacity receptor mechanisms and will not be so vague as to discourage research.

A current trend of thought in psycho–endocrine research is that steroid-specific, limited-capacity receptors mediate the effects of steroids on behaviour. Although a research strategy based on this idea will almost undoubtedly result in at least a partial affirmation of it, proponents should bear in mind that the idea has simplistic assumptions in it that are a throwback to early arguments about specificity. For example, the assumption is implicit that 'activation' of a behaviour is a unitary process. However, as we have seen, activation of a behaviour such as mounting might have quite different bases than activation of a behaviour such as lordosis.

In contrast to those engaged in psycho–endocrine research are many bio-chemists and other 'hard scientists' whose unpublished prejudice is that the relationships between hormones and behaviour are unpredictable and capricious. That sexual behaviour is influenced by non-hormonal factors, by non-specific hormonal factors, and by specific hormonal factors does not, however, render the interactions among these factors unpredictable, but instead complicates and enriches them.

ACKNOWLEDGEMENTS

I thank William Crowley, Margaret Johns, Babetta Marrone, and Jay Rosenblatt for reading the manuscript. Thanks are also due to D.A. Goldfoot and R. W. Goy for helpful discussions and for access to unpublished data from their laboratory. Invaluable assistance with preparation of the manuscript was given by Winona Cunningham and Cynthia Banas.

The writing of this essay and the research from my laboratory were supported by USPHS Grant NIH-HD 04467 and NIMH Research Scientist Development Award K2-MH-29006. Contribution Number 233 of the Institute of Animal Behaviour.

REFERENCES

Alsum, P. and Goy, R. W. (1974) Actions of esters of testosterone, dihydro-testosterone, or estradiol on sexual behavior in castrated male guinea pigs, *Horm. Behav.*, 5, 207–17.

Amoroso, E. C. and Marshall, F. H. A. (1960) External factors in sexual periodicity. In: *Marshall's Physiology of Reproduction* Vol I Part 2, 3rd edn., A. S. Parkes (ed.), Longmans Green & Co., London, pp. 707–831.

Anderson, J. N., Peck, E. J., Jr., and Clark, J. H. (1975) Estrogen-induced uterine responses and growth: relationship to receptor estrogen binding by uterine nuclei, *Endocrinology*, 96, 160–7.

Antelman, S. M., Szechtman, H., Chin, P., and Fisher, A. E. (1975) Tail pinch induced eating, gnawing and licking behavior in rats: dependence on the nigro-striatal dopamine system, *Brain Res.*, in press.

Antliff, H. R. and Young, W. C. 1956. Behavioral and tissue responses of male guinea pigs to estrogens and the problem of hormone specificity. *Endocrinology* 59, 74–82.

Arai, Y. and Gorski, R. A. (1968) Effects of anti-estrogen on steroid induced sexual receptivity in ovariectomized rats, *Physiol. Behav.*, 3, 351–3.

Arén-Engelbrektsson, B., Larsson, K., Södersten, P., and Wilhelmson, M. (1970) The female lordosis pattern induced in male rats by estrogen, *Horm. Behav.*, 1, 181–8.

Atger, M., Baulieu, E.-E., and Milgrom, E. (1974) An investigation of progesterone receptors in guinea pig vagina, uterine cervix, mammary glands, pituitary and hypothalamus, *Endocrinology*, 94, 161–7.

Baird, D., Horton, R., Longcope, C., and Tait, J. F. (1968) Steroid prehormones, *Persp. Biol. Med.*, 11, 384–421.

Ball, J. (1939) Male and female mating behavior in prepubertally castrated male rats receiving estrogens, *J. Comp. Psychol.*, 28, 273–83.

Ball, J. (1940) The effect of testosterone on the sex behavior of female rats, *J. Comp. Psychol.*, 29, 151–65.

Baranczuk, R. and Greenwald, G. S. (1973) Peripheral levels of estrogen in the cyclic hamster, *Endocrinology*, 92, 805–12.

Barfield, R. J. and Sachs, B. D. (1968) Sexual behavior: Stimulation by painful electric shock to the skin in male rats, *Science*, 161, 392–4.

Barfield, R. J. and Sachs, B. D. (1970) Effect of shock on copulatory behavior in castrate male rats, *Horm. Behav.*, 1, 247–53.

Barrington, E. J. W. (1968) Phylogenetic perspectives in vertebrate endocrinology. In: *Persp. Endocrinol.*, E. J. W. Barrington and C. Barker Jørgensen (eds.), Academic Press, N. Y., pp. 1–46.

Baum, M. J., Sodersten, P., and Vreeburg, J. T. M. (1974) Mounting and receptive behavior in the ovariectomized female rat: Influence of estradiol, dihydro-testosterone, and genital anesthetization, *Horm. Behav.*, 5, 175–90.

Baum, M. J. and Vreeburg, J. T. M. (1973) Copulation in castrated male rats following combined treatment with estradiol and dihydrotestosterone, *Science*, 182, 283–5.

Baum, M. J. and Vreeburg, J. T. M. (1975) Failure of MER-25 to disrupt TP-induced copulation in castrated male rats: An argument against the aromatization hypothesis?

Paper presented at Eastern Conf. on Reproductive Behavior, Nags Head, North Carolina.

Beach, F. A. (1941) Female mating behavior shown by male rats after administration of testosterone propionate, *Endocrinology*, **29**, 409–12.

Beach, F. A. (1942) Male and female mating behavior in prepubertally castrated female rats treated with androgens, *Endocrinology*, **31**, 673–8.

Beach, F. A. (1942a) Copulatory behavior in prepubertally castrated male rats and its modification by estrogen administration, *Endocrinology*, **31**, 679–83.

Beach, F. A. (1961) *Hormones and Behavior*, Cooper Square Publishers, N. Y.

Beach, F. A. (1968) Factors involved in the control of mounting behavior by female mammals. In: *Perspectives in Reproduction and Sexual Behavior*, M. Diamond (ed.), Indiana University Press, Bloomington, pp. 83–132.

Beach, F. A. (1971) Hormonal factors controlling the differentiation, development, and display of copulatory behavior in the ramstergig and related species. In: *The Biopsychology of Development*, E. Tobach, L. R. Aronson, and E. Shaw (eds.), Academic Press, N. Y., pp. 249–96.

Beach, F. A. and Rasquin, P. (1942) Masculine copulatory behavior in intact and castrated female rats, *Endocrinology*, **31**, 393–409.

Beach, F. A. and Westbrook, W. H. (1968) Dissociation of androgenic effects on sexual morphology and behavior in male rats, *Endocrinology*, **83**, 395–8.

Beyer, C. and Komisaruk, B. (1971) Effects of diverse androgens on estrous behavior, lordosis reflex, and genital tract morphology in the rat, *Horm. Behav.*, **2**, 217–25.

Beyer, C., Larsson, K., Pérez-Palacios, G., and Morali, G. (1973) Androgen structure and male sexual behavior in the castrated rat, *Horm. Behav.*, **4**, 99–108.

Beyer, C., Morali, G., and Cruz, M. (1971a) Effect of 5α-dihydrotestosterone on gonadotropin secretion and estrous behavior in the female Wistar rat, *Endocrinology*, **89**, 1158–61.

Beyer, C., Morali, G., and Vargas, R. (1971b) Effect of diverse estrogens on estrous behavior and genital tract development in ovariectomized rats, *Horm. Behav.*, **2**, 275–7.

Beyer, C. and Rivaud, N. (1973) Differential effect of testosterone and dihydrotestosterone on the sexual behavior of prepubertally castrated male rabbits, *Horm. Behav.*, **4**, 175–80.

Beyer, C. and Vidal, N. (1971) Inhibitory action of MER-25 on androgen-induced oestrous behaviour in the ovariectomized rabbit, *J. Endocrinol.*, **51**, 401–2.

Beyer, C., Vidal, N., and Mijares, A. (1970) Probable role of aromatization in the induction of estrous behavior by androgens in the ovariectomized rabbit, *Endocrinology*, **87**, 1386–9.

Bloch, G. J. and Davidson, J. M. (1971) Behavioral and somatic responses to the antiandrogen cyproterone, *Horm. Behav.*, **2**, 11–25.

Brookhart, J. M., Dey, F. L., and Ranson, S. W. (1940) Failure of ovarian hormones to cause mating reactions in spayed guinea pigs with hypothalamic lesions, *Proc. Soc. Exp. Biol.*, **44**, 61–4.

Bullock, D. W. (1970) Induction of heat in ovariectomized guinea pigs by brief exposure to estrogen and progesterone, *Horm. Behav.*, **1**, 137–44.

Byrnes, W. W. and Shipley, E. G. (1955) Guinea pig copulatory reflex in response to adrenal steroids and similar compounds, *Endocrinology*, **57**, 5–9.

Caggiula, A. R. (1972) Shock-elicited copulation and aggression in male rats, *J. Comp. Physiol. Psychol.*, **80**, 393–397.

Caggiula, A. R. and Eibergen, R. (1969) Copulation evoked by painful peripheral stimulation, *J. Comp. Physiol. Psychol.*, **69**, 414–9.

Carter, C. S. and Landauer, M. R. (1975) Neonatal hormone experience and adult lordosis and fighting in the golden hamster, *Physiol. Behav.*, **14**, 1–6.

Cheng, M.-F. and Lehrman, D. (1975) Gonadal hormone specificity in the sexual behavior of ring doves, *Psychoneuroendocrinology*, **1**, 95–102.

Christensen, L. W. and Clemens, L. G. (1974) Intrahypothalamic implants of testosterone or estradiol and resumption of masculine sexual behavior in long-term castrated male rats, *Endocrinology*, **95**, 984–90.

Christensen, L. W., Coniglio, L. P., Paup, D. C., and Clemens, L. G. (1973) Sexual behavior of male golden hamsters receiving diverse androgen treatments, *Horm. Behav.*, **4**, 223–9.

Ciaccio, L. A. and Lisk, R. D. (1973) Central control of estrous behavior in the female golden hamster, *Neuroendocrinology*, **13**, 21–8.

Clemens, L. G., Hiroi, M., and Gorski, R. A. (1969) Induction and facilitation of female mating behavior in rats treated neonatally with low doses of testosterone propionate, *Endocrinology*, **84**, 1430–8.

Clemens, L. G., Shryne, J., and Gorski, R. A. (1970) Androgen and development of progesterone responsiveness in male and female rats, *Physiol. Behav.*, **5**, 673–8.

Collins, V. J., Boling, J. L., Dempsey, E. W., and Young, W. C. (1938) Some quantiative studies of experimentally-induced sexual receptivity in spayed guinea pigs, *Endocrinology*, **23**, 188–96.

Crowley, W. R. and Ward, O. B., Jr. (1974) Male copulatory behavior induced in female rats by peripheral electric shock, *Physiol. Behav.*, **13**, 129–31.

Czaja, J. A., Goldfoot, D. A., and Karavolas, H. J. (1974) Comparative facilitation and inhibition of lordosis in the guinea pig with progesterone, 5α-pregnane-3, 20-dione, or 3α-hydroxy-5α-pregnan-20-one. *Horm. Behav.*, **5**, 261–74.

Davidson, J. M. (1969) Effects of estrogen on the sexual behavior of male rats, *Endocrinology*, **84**, 1365–72.

Davidson, J. M. and Bloch, G. J. (1969) Neuroendocrine aspects of male reproduction, *Biol. Reprod.*, **1**, 67–92.

Davidson, J. M. and Levine, S. (1969) Progesterone and heterotypical sexual behavior in male rats, *J. Endocrinol.*, **44**, 129–30.

Diamond, M. (1965) The antagonistic actions of testosterone propionate and estrogen and progesterone on copulatory patterns of the female guinea pig, *Anat. Rec.*, **151**, 449 (Abstr.).

Diamond, M. and Cerny, V. A. (1966) The effect of age on female sex behavior in the guinea pig, *Am. Zool*, **6**, 301 (Abstr.).

Dorfman, R. I. and Ungar, F. (1965) *Metabolism of Steroid Hormones*, Academic Press, N. Y.

Dörner, G. and Hinz, G. (1967) Homosexuality of neonatally castrated male rats following androgen substitution in adulthood, *German Med. Month*, **12**, 1–7.

Eaton, G., Goy, R. W., and Resko, J. A. (1975) Brain uptake and metabolism of estradiol benzoate and estrous behavior in ovariectomized guinea pigs, *Horm. Behav.*, **6**, 81–97.

Eayrs, J. T. (1952) Sex differences in the maturation and function of the nervous system in the rat, *Ciba Fdn. Colloq. Endocrinol.*, **3**, 18–33.

Edwards, D. A. and Thompson, M. L. (1970) Neonatal androgenation and estrogenization and the hormonal induction of sexual receptivity in rats, *Physiol. Behav.*, **5**, 1115–9.

Eisenfeld, A. J. and Axelrod, J. (1965) Selectivity of estrogen distribution in tissues, *J. Pharmacol. Exp. Ther.*, **150**, 469–75.

Emery, D. E. and Sachs, B. D. (1975) Ejaculatory pattern in female rats without androgen treatment, *Science* **190**, 484–6.

Engel, L. L. (1973) The biosynthesis of estrogens. In: *Handbook of Physiology* Sect. 7, Vol. 2, Part 1, R. O. Greep (ed.), American Physiological Society, Washington, D. C., pp. 467–84.

Engel, P. (1942) Female mating behavior shown by male mice after treatment with different substances, *Endocrinology*, **30**, 623.

Everett, J. W. (1961) The mammalian reproductive cycle and its controlling mechanisms. In: *Sex and Internal Secretions* 3rd edn., W. C. Young (ed.), Williams & Wilkins, Baltimore, pp. 497–555.

Everitt, B. J., Fuxe, K., Hökfelt, T., and Jonsson, G. (1975) Studies on the role of monoamines in the hormonal regulation of sexual receptivity in the female rat. In: *Sexual Behavior: Pharmacology and Biochemistry*, M. Sandler and G. L. Gessa (eds.), Raven Press, N. Y., pp. 152–3.

Everitt, B. J., Herbert, J., and Hamer, J. D. (1972) Sexual receptivity of bilaterally adrenalectomized female rhesus monkeys, *Physiol. Behav.*, **8**, 409–15.

Feder, H. H. (1971) The comparative actions of testosterone propionate and 5α-androstan-17β-ol-3-one propionate on the reproductive behaviour, physiology and morphology of male rats, *J. Endocrinol.*, **51**, 241–52.

Feder, H. H. (1976) Regulation of sexual behaviour by hormones in female non-primates. In: *Textbook of Sexology* H. Musaph and J. Money (eds.), Elsevier, Amsterdam.

Feder, H. H., Brown-Grant, K., and Corker, C. S. (1971) Pre-ovulatory progesterone, the adrenal cortex and the 'critical period' for luteinizing hormone release in rats, *J. Endocrinol.*, **50**, 29–39.

Feder, H. H. and Morin, L. P. (1974) Suppression of lordosis in guin– pigs by ethamoxytriphetol (MER-25) given at long intervals (34–46 h) after estradiol benzoate treatment, *Horm. Behav.*, **5**, 63–72.

Feder, H. H., Naftolin, F., and Ryan, K. J. (1974a) Male and female sexual responses in male rats given estradiol benzoate and 5-α-androstan-17β-ol-3-one propionate, *Endocrinology*, **94**, 136–41.

Feder, H. H., Resko, J. A., and Goy, R. W. (1968a) Progesterone levels in the arterial plasma of pre-ovulatory and ovariectomized rats, *J. Endocrinol.*, **41**, 563–9.

Feder, H. H., Resko, J. A. and Goy, R. W. (1968b) Progesterone concentrations in the arterial plasma of guinea pigs during the oestrous cycle, *J. Endocrinol.*, **40**, 505–13.

Feder, H. H., Siegel, H. and Wade, G. N. (1974b) Uptake of (6, 7-³H) estradiol-17β in ovariectomized rats, guinea pigs, and hamsters: Correlation with species differences in behavioral responsiveness to estradiol, *Brain Res.*, **71**, 93–103.

Feder, H. H. and Silver, R. (1974) Activation of lordosis in ovariectomized guinea pigs by free and esterified forms of estrone, estradiol-17β, and estriol, *Physiol. Behav.*, **13**, 251–5.

Feder, H. H. and Wade, G. N. (1974) Integrative actions of perinatal hormones on neural tissues mediating adult sexual behavior, In: *The Neurosciences* Vol 3 F. O. Schmitt and F. G. Worden (eds.), MIT Press, Cambridge, Mass., pp. 583–6.

Fieser, L. F. and Fieser, M. (1959) *Steroids*, Van Nostrand Reinhold, N. Y.

Franck, J. A., Ward, I. L., and Crowley, W. R. (1973) Lordotic responding in male rats treated with central progesterone. Paper presented at Eastern Psychological Association, Washington, D. C.

Gay, V. L. and Tomacari, R. L. (1974) Follicle-stimulating hormone secretion in the female rat: cyclic release is dependent on circulating androgen, *Science*, **184**, 75–7.

Gerall, A. A., Hendricks, S. E., Johnson, L. L., and Bounds, T. W. (1967) Effects of early castration in male rats on adult sexual behavior, *J. Comp. Physiol. Psychol.*, **64**, 206–212.

Gerall, A. A. and Kenny, A. M. (1970) Neonatally androgenized female's responsiveness to estrogen and progesterone, *Endocrinology*, **87**, 560–6.

Goldfoot, D. A. and Baum, M. J. (1972) Initiation of mating behavior in developing male rats following peripheral electric shock, *Physiol. Behav.*, **8**, 857–63.

Goldfoot, D. A. and Van Der Werff Ten Bosch (1975) Mounting behavior of female guinea pigs after prenatal and adult administration of the propionates of testosterone, dihydrotestosterone, and androstenediol, *Horm. Behav.*, **6**, 139–48.

Goodale, H. D. (1918) Feminized male birds, *Genetics*, **3**, 276–99.

Gorzalka, B. B., Rezek, D. L., and Whalen, R. E. (1975) Adrenal mediation of estrogen-induced ejaculatory behavior in the male rat, *Physiol. Behav.*, **14**, 373–6.

Gorzalka, B. B. and Whalen, R. E. (1974) Accumulation of estradiol in brain, uterus and pituitary: strain, species, suborder and order comparisons, *Brain, Behav. Evol.*, **9**, 376–92.

Goy, R. W. (1970) Experimental control of psychosexuality, *Phil. Trans. Roy. Soc. Lond. B*, **259**, 149–62.

Goy, R. W., Bridson, W. E., and Young, W. C. (1964) Period of maximal susceptibility of the prenatal female guinea pig to masculinizing actions of testosterone propionate, *J. Comp. Physiol. Psychol.*, **57**, 166–74.

Goy, R. W. and Goldfoot, D. A. (1973) Hormonal influences on sexually dimorphic behavior. In: *Handbook of Physiology* Sect. 7, Vol. 2, Part 1 R. O. Greep (ed.), American Physiological Society, Washington, D. C., pp. 169–86.

Goy, R. W., Phoenix, C. H., and Meidinger, R. (1967) Postnatal development of sensitivity to estrogen and androgen in male, female, and pseudohermaphroditic guinea pigs, *Anat. Rec.*, **157**, 87–96.

Goy, R. W., Phoenix, C. H., and Young, W. C. (1966) Inhibitory action of the corpus luteum on the hormonal induction of estrous behavior in the guinea pig, *Gen. Comp. Endocrinol.*, **6**, 267–75.

Goy, R. W. and Young, W. C. (1958) Responses of androgen-treated spayed female guinea pigs to estrogen and progesterone, *Proc. Am. Soc. Zool., Anat. Rec.*, **131**, 560.

Grady, K. L., Phoenix, C. H., and Young, W. C. (1965) Role of the developing rat testis in differentiation of the neural tissues mediating mating behavior, *J. Comp. Physiol. Psychol.*, **59**, 176–82.

Harding, C. F. and Feder, H. H. (1976) Relation between individual differences in sexual behavior and plasma testosterone levels in the guinea pig, submitted for publication.

Hart, B. L. (1974) Gonadal androgen and sociosexual behavior of male mammals: A comparative analysis, *Psychol. Bull.*, **81**, 383–400.

Hashimoto, I., Henricks, D. M., Anderson, L. L., and Melampy, R. M. (1968) Progesterone and pregn-4-en-20α-ol-3-one in ovarian venous blood during various reproductive states in the rat, *Endocrinology*, **82**, 333–41.

Hu, C. K. and Frazier, C. N. (1939) Masculinization of adult female rabbit following injection of testosterone propionate, *Proc. Soc. Exp. Biol. Med.*, **42**, 820–3.

Johnston, P. and Davidson, J. M. (1972) Intracerebral androgens and sexual behavior in the male rat, *Horm. Behv.*, **3**, 345–57.

Joshi, H. S., Watson, D. J. and Labhsetwar, A. P. (1973) Secretion of oestradiol, oestrone, 20-dihydroprogesterone and progesterone during the oestrous cycle of the guinea-pig, *J. Reprod. Fert.*, **35**, 177–81.

Joslyn, and Feder, H. H. (1971) Facilitatory and inhibitory effects of supplementary estradiol benzoate given to ovariectomized, estrogen-primed guinea pigs, *Horm. Behav.*, **2**, 307–14.

Kappas, A. and Palmer, R. H. (1962) Selected aspects of steroid pharmacology, *Pharmacol. Rev.*, **15**, 123–67.

Kato, J. and Villee, C. A. (1967) Preferential uptake of estradiol by the anterior hypothalamus of the rat, *Endocrinology*, **80**, 567–75.

Kincl, F. A. (1965) Anabolic steroids, In: *Methods in Hormone Research* Vol 4, Part B R. I. Dorfman (ed.), Academic Press, N. Y., pp. 21–76.

Kinsey, A. C., Pomeroy, W. B., Martin, C. E., and Gebhard, P. H. (1953) *Sexual Behavior in the Human Female*, W. B. Saunders, Philadelphia, pp. 729–48.

Klein, M. (1952) Administration of sex hormones and sexual behavior, *Ciba Fdn. Colloq. Endocrinol.*, **3**, 323–37.

Klyne, W. (1960) *The Chemistry of the Steroids*, Methuen, London.

Komisaruk, B. R. (1974) Neural and hormonal interactions in the reproductive behavior of female rats. In: *Reproductive Behavior* W. Montagna and W. A. Sadler (eds.), Plenum Press, N. Y., pp. 97–130.

Komisaruk, B. R. and Beyer, C. (1972) Differential antagonism, by MER-25, of behavioral and morphological effects of estradiol benzoate in rats, *Horm. Behav.*, **3**, 63–70.

Koster, R. (1943) Hormone factors in the male behavior of the female rat, *Endocrinology*, **33**, 337–48.

Landau, R. L. (1973) The metabolic influence of progesterone. In: *Handbook of Physiology* Sect. 7, Vol. 2, Part 1 R. O. Greep (ed.), American Physiological Society, Washington, D. C., pp. 573–89.

Langford, J. and Hilliard, J. (1967) Effect of 20α-hydroxypregn-4-en-3-one on mating behavior in spayed female rats, *Endocrinology*, **80**, 381–3.

Larsson, K., Beyer, C., Moralí, G., Pérez-Palacios, G., and Södersten, P. (1976) Effects of estrone, estradiol, and estriol combined with dihydrotestosterone on mounting and lordosis behavior in castrated male rats, *Horm. Behav.*, in press.

Larsson, K., Södersten, P. and Beyer, C. 1973. Sexual behavior in male rats treated with estrogen in combination with dihydrotestosterone, *Horm. Behav.*, **4**, 289–99.

Lieberburg, I. and McEwen, B. S. (1975a) Estradiol-17β: A metabolite of testosterone recovered in cell nuclei from limbic areas of neonatal rat brains, *Brain Res.*, **85**, 165–70.

Lieberburg, I. and McEwen, B. S. (1975b) Estradiol-17β: A metabolite of testosterone recovered in cell nuclei from limbic areas of adult male rat brains, *Brain Res.*, **91**, 171–4.

Lisk, R. D. (1962) Diencephalic placement of estradiol and sexual receptivity in the female rat, *Am. J. Physiol.*, **203**, 493–6.

Lisk, R. D. (1969) Mechanisms regulating sexual activity in mammals, *J. Sex Res.*, **6**, 220–8.

Lisk, R. D. (1973) Hormonal regulation of sexual behavior in polyestrous mammals common to the laboratory. In: *Handbook of Physiology* Sect. 7, Vol. 2, Part 1 R. O. Greep (ed.), American Physiological Society, Washington, D. C., pp. 223–60.

Lukaszewska, J. H. and Greenwald, G. S. (1970) Progesterone levels in the cyclic and pregnant hamster, *Endocrinology*, **86**, 1–9.

Luttge, W. G. (1975) Effects of anti-estrogens on testosterone-stimulated male sexual behavior and peripheral target tissues in the castrate male rat, *Physiol. Behav.*, **14**, 839–46.

Luttge, W. G. and Hall, N. R. (1973) Differential effectiveness of testosterone and its metabolites in the induction of male sexual behavior in two strains of albino mice, *Horm. Behav.*, **4**, 31–43.

Luttge, W. G., Hall, N. R., Wallis, C. J., and Campbell, J. C. (1975) Stimulation of male and female sexual behavior in gonadectomized rats with estrogen and androgen therapy and its inhibition with concurrent anti-hormone therapy, *Physiol. Behav.*, **14**, 65–73.

Luttge, W. G. and Wallis, C. J. (1973) *In vitro* accumulation and saturation of ^{3}H-progestins in selected brain regions and in the adenohypophysis, uterus, and pineal of the female rat, *Steroids*, **22**, 493–502.

Luttge, W. G. and Whalen, R. E. (1970) Dihydrotestosterone, androstenedione, testosterone: Comparative effectiveness in masculinizing and defeminizing reproductive systems in male and female rats, *Horm. Behav.*, **1**, 265–81.

Malsbury, C. W. and Pfaff, D. W. (1974) Neural and hormonal determinants of mating behavior in adult male rats. In: *Limbic and Autonomic Nervous Systems Research*, L. V. DiCara (ed.), Plenum, N. Y., pp. 85–136.

Meier, A. H. (1969) Diurnal variations of metabolic responses to prolactin in lower vertebrates, *Gen. Comp. Endocrinol. Suppl.*, **2**, 55–62.

Meyerson, B. (1972) Latency between intravenous injection of progestins and the appearance of estrous behavior in estrogen-treated rats, *Horm. Behav.*, **3**, 1–9.

Michael, R. P. (1962) Oestrogen-sensitive systems in mammalian brains, *Exc. Med. Int. Congr. Ser.*, **47**, 650–2.

Michael, R. P. (1973) The effects of hormones on sexual behavior female cat and rhesus monkey. In: *Handbook of Physiology* Sect. 7, Vol. 2, Part 1, R. O. Greep (ed.), The American Physiological Society, Washington, D. C., pp. 187–221.

Morali, G., Larsson, K., Pérez-Palacios, G., and Beyer, C. (1974) Testosterone androstenedione, and androstenediol: Effects on the initiation of mating behavior of inexperienced castrated male rats, *Horm. Behav.*, **5**, 103–10.

Morin, L. P. and Feder, H. H. (1974a) Intracranial estradiol implants and lordosis behavior of ovariectomized guinea pigs, *Brain Res.*, **70**, 95–102.

Morin, L. P. and Feder, H. H. (1974b) Hypothalamic, progesterone implants and facilitation of lordosis behavior in estrogen-primed ovariectomized guinea pigs, *Brain Res.*, **70**, 81–93.

McDonald, P., Beyer, C., Newton, F., Brien, B., Baker, R., Tan, H. S., Sampson, C., Kitching, P., Greenhill, R., and Pritchard, D. (1970a) Failure of 5αdihydrotestosterone to initiate sexual behavior in the castrated male rat, *Nature*, **227**, 964–5.

McDonald, P. G., Vidal, N., and Beyer, C. (1970b) Sexual behavior in the ovariectomized rabbit after treatment with different amounts of gonadal hormones, *Horm. Behav.*, **1**, 161–72.

McEwen, B. S., Denef, C. J., Gerlach, J. L., and Plapinger, L. (1974) Chemical studies of the brain as a steroid hormone target tissue. In: *The Neurosciences* Vol 3, F. O. Schmitt and F. G. Worden (eds.), MIT Press, Cambridge, Mass., pp. 599–620.

McEwen, B. S. and Pfaff, D. W. (1973) Chemical and physiological approaches to neuro-endocrine mechanisms: Attempts at integration. In: *Frontiers in Neuroendocrinology* W. F. Ganong and L. Martini (eds.), Oxford University Press, N. Y., pp. 267–335.

McGill, T. E. and Haynes, C. M. (1973) Heterozygosity and retention of ejaculatory reflex after castration in male mice, *J. Comp. Physiol. Psychol.*, **84**, 423–9.

Naftolin, F., Brown-Grant, K., and Corker, C. S. (1972a) Plasma and pituitary luteinizing hormone and peripheral plasma oestradiol concentrations in the normal oestrous cycle of the rat and after experimental manipulation of the cycle, *J. Endocrinol.*, **53**, 17–30.

Naftolin, F., Ryan, K. J., and Petro, Z. (1972b) Aromatization of androstenedione by the anterior hypothalamus of adult male and female rats, *Endocrinology*, **90**, 295–8.

Parrott, R. F. (1975) Aromatizable and 5α-reduced androgens: differentiation between central and peripheral effects on male rat sexual behavior, *Horm. Behav.*, **6**, 99–108.

Paup, D. C., Mennin, S. P., and Gorski, R. A. (1975) Androgen- and estrogen-induced copulatory behavior and inhibition of luteinizing hormone (LH) secretion in the male rat, *Horm. Behav.*, **6**, 35–46.

Pfaff, D. (1970) Nature of sex hormone effects on rat sex behavior: Specificity of effects and individual patterns of response, *J. Comp. Physiol. Psychol.*, **73**, 349–58.

Pfaff, D. and Keiner, M. (1973) Atlas of estradiol-concentrating cells in the central nervous system of the female rat, *J. Comp. Neurol.*, **151**, 121–58.

Pfaff, D. W. and Zigmond, R. E. (1971) Neonatal androgen effects on sexual and non-sexual behavior of adult rats tested under various hormone regimes, *Neuroendocrinology*, **7**, 129–45.

Phoenix, C. H., Goy, R. W., Gerall, A. A., and Young, W. C. (1959) Organizing action of prenatally administered testosterone propionate on the tissues mediating mating behavior in the female guinea pig, *Endocrinology*, **65**, 369–82.

Powers, J. B. (1972) Facilitation of lordosis in ovariectomized rats by intracerebral implants, *Brain Res.*, **48**, 311–25.

Price, D. and Ortiz, E. (1944) The relationship of age to reactivity in the reproductive system of the rat, *Endocrinology*, **34**, 215–39.

Price, D. and Pannabecker, R. (1959) Comparative responsiveness of homologous sex ducts and accessory glands of fetal rats in culture, *Arch. Anat. Microscop. Morphol. Exp.*, **48**, 233–44.

Quadagno, D. M. and Ho, G. K. W. (1975) The reversible inhibition of steroid-induced sexual behavior by intracranial cycloheximide, *Horm. Behav.*, **6**, 19–26.

Rosenblatt, J. S. and Aronson, L. R. (1958) The decline of sexual behavior in male cats after castration with special reference to the role of prior sexual experience, *Behaviour*, **12**, 285–338.

Ross, J., Claybaugh, C., Clemens, L. G., and Gorski, R. A. (1971) Short latency induction of estrous behavior with intracerebral gonadal hormones in ovariectomized rats, *Endocrinology*, **89**, 32–8.

Ross, J. W., Paup, D. C., Brant-Zawadzki, M., Marshall, J. R., and Gorski, R. A. (1973) Effects of *cis-* and *trans*-clomiphene in the induction of sexual behavior, *Endocrinology*, **93**, 681–5.

Sand, K. (1919) Experiments on the internal secretion of the sexual glands, especially on experimental hermaphroditism. *J. Physiol.*, **53**, 257–63.

Sar, M. and Stumpf, W. E. (1973) Neurons of the hypothalamus concentrate (^{3}H) progesterone or its metabolites, *Science*, **182**, 1266–8.

Savard, K. (1968) The biogenesis of steroids in the human ovary. In: *The Ovary*, H. C. Mack, (ed.), Charles C. Thomas Co., Springfield, pp. 10–26.

Sawyer, C. H. (1960) Reproductive behavior. In: *Handbook of Physiology* Vol. 2, J. Field (ed.), American Physiological Society, Washington, D. C., pp. 1225–40.

Schwartz, N. B. (1974) The role of FSH and LH and of their antibodies on follicle growth and on ovulation, *Biol. Reprod.*, **10**, 236–72.

Seiki, K. and Hattori, M. (1973) *In vivo* uptake of progesterone by the hypothalamus and pituitary of the female ovariectomized rat and its relationship to cytoplasmic progesterone-binding protein, *Endocrinol. Japon.*, **20**, 111–9.

Shaikh, A. A. and Shaikh, S. A. (1975) Adrenal and ovarian steroid secretion in the rat estrous cycle temporally related to gonadotropins and steroid levels found in peripheral plasma, *Endocrinology*, **96**, 37–44.

Södersten, P. (1972) Mounting behavior in the female rat during the estrous cycle, after ovariectomy, and after estrogen or testosterone administration, *Horm. Behav.*, **3**, 307–20.

Södersten, P. (1973) Estrogen-activated sexual behavior in male rats, *Horm. Behav.*, **4**, 247–56.

Södersten, P. (1974) Effects of an estrogen antagonist, MER-25, on mounting behavior and lordosis behavior in the female rat, *Horm. Behav.*, **5**, 111–21.

Södersten, P. (1975) Mounting behavior and lordosis behavior in castrated male rats treated with testosterone propionate, or with estradiol benzoate or dihydrotestosterone in combination with testosterone propionate, *Horm. Behav.*, **6**, 109–26.

Södersten, P. and Larsson, K. (1974) Lordosis behavior in castrated male rats treated with estradiol benzoate or testosterone propionate in combination with an estrogen antagonist, MER-25, and in intact male rats, *Horm. Behav.*, **5**, 13–8.

Steinach, E. (1940) *Sex and Life*, Viking Press, N. Y.

Stumpf, W. E. (1968) Estradiol-concentrating neurons: Topography in the hypothalamus by dry-mount autoradiography, *Science*, **162**, 1001–3.

Tiefer, L. (1970) Gonadal hormones and mating behavior in the adult golden hamster, *Horm. Behav.*, **1**, 189–202.

Uchida, K., Kadowaki, M., and Migake, T. (1969) Ovarian secretion of progesterone and 20α-hydroxy-pregn-4-en-3-one during rat estrous cycle in chronological relation to pituitary release of luteinizing hormone, *Endocrinol. Japon.*, **16**, 227–37.

Vertes, M. and King, R. J. B. (1971) The mechanism of oestradiol binding in rat hypothalamus: Effect of androgenization, *J. Endocrinol.*, **51**, 271–82.

Villee, C. A. (1961) Some problems of the metabolism and mechanism of action of steroid sex hormones. In: *Sex and Internal Secretions* 3rd edn., W. C. Young (ed.), Williams & Wilkins, Baltimore, pp. 643–65.

Wade, G. N. and Feder, H. H. (1972a) Effects of several pregnane and pregnene steroids on estrous behavior in ovariectomized estrogen-primed guinea pigs, *Physiol. Behav.*, **9**, 773–5.

Wade, G. N. and Feder, H. H. (1972b) Uptake of (1, 2-³H) 20α-hydroxypregn-4-en-one, (1, 2-³H) corticosterone, and (6, 7-³H) estradiol-17β by guinea pig brain and uterus: Comparison with uptake of (1, 2-³H) progesterone, *Brain Res.*, **45**, 545–54.

Wade, G. N. and Feder, H. H. (1972c) 1, 2-³H Progesterone uptake by guinea pig brain and uterus: Differential localization, time-course of uptake and metabolism, and effects of age, sex, estrogen-priming, and competing steroids. *Brain Res.*, **45**, 525–43.

Wade, G. N. and Feder, H. H. (1974) Stimulation of (³H) leucine incorporation into protein by estradiol-17β or progesterone in brain tissues of ovarietomized guinea pigs, *Brain Res.*, **73**, 545–9.

Wade, G. N., Harding, C. F., and Feder, H. H. (1973) Neural uptake of (1, 2-³H) progesterone in ovariectomized rats, guinea pigs, and hamsters: Correlation with species differences in behavioral responsiveness, *Brain Res.*, **61**, 357–67.

Wallen, K., Goldfoot, D. A., Joslyn, W. D., and Paris, C. A. (1972) Modification of behavioral estrus in the guinea pig following intracranial cycloheximide, *Physiol. Behav.*, **8**, 221–3.

Ward, I. L. (1972) Female sexual behavior in male rats treated prenatally with an anti-androgen, *Physiol. Behav.*, **8**, 53–6.

Weisz, J. and Gibbs, C. (1974) Metabolites of testosterone in the brain of the newborn female rat after an injection of tritiated testosterone, *Neuro-endocrinology*, **14**, 72–86.

Whalen, R. E., Battie, C., and Luttge, W. G. (1972) Anti-estrogen inhibition of androgen induced sexual receptivity in rats, *Behav. Biol.*, **7**, 311–20.

Whalen, R. E. and DeBold, J. F. (1974) Comparative effectiveness of testosterone, andros-. tenedione and dihydrotestosterone in maintaining mating behavior in the castrated male hamster, *Endocrinology*, **95**, 1674–9.

Whalen, R. E. and Gorzalka, B. B. (1972) The effects of progesterone and its metabolites on the induction of sexual receptivity in rats, *Horm. Behav.*, **3**, 221–6.

Whalen, R. E. and Gorzalka, B. B. (1973) Effects of an estrogen antagonist on behavior and on estrogen retention in neural and peripheral target tissues, *Physiol. Behav.*, **10**, 35–40.

Whalen, R. E., Gorzalka, B. B., DeBold, J. F., Quadagno, D. M., Ho, G. K., and Hough, J. C., Jr. (1974) Studies on the effects of intracerebral actinomycin D implants on estrogen-induced receptivity in rats, *Horm. Behav.*, **5**, 337–43.

Whalen, R. E. and Luttge, W. G. (1971a) Differential localization of progester-one uptake in brain, role of sex, estrogen pretreatment and adrenalectomy, *Brain Res.*, **33**, 147–55.

Whalen, R. E. and Luttge, W. G. (1971b) Testosterone, androstenedione, and dihydrotestosterone. Effects on mating behavior of male rats, *Horm. Behav.*, **2**, 117–25.

Whalen, R. E., Luttge, W. G. and Gorzalka, B. B. (1971) Neonatal androgenization and the development of estrogen responsivity in male and female rats, *Horm. Behav.*, **2**, 83–90.

Whalen, R. E. and Massicci, J. (1975) Subcellular analysis of the accumulation of estrogen by the brain of male and female rats, *Brain Res.*, **89**, 255–64.

Whalen, R. E. and Nakayama, K. (1965) Induction of oestrous behavior: facilitation by repeated hormone treatments, *J. Endocrinol.*, **33**, 525–6.

Wilson, J. D. (1975) Metabolism of testicular androgens. In: *Handbook of Physiology* Sect. 7, Vol. 5, D. W. Hamilton and R. O. Greep (eds.), American Physiological Society, Washington, D. C., pp. 491–508.

Yanase, M. and Gorki, R. A. (1975) Sites of estrogen and progesterone facilitation of lordosis behavior in the spayed rat, *Fed. Proc.*, **34**, 340 (Abstr).

Young, W. C. (1961) The hormones and mating behavior. In *Sex and Internal Secretions* 3rd edn., W. C. Young (ed.), Williams & Wilkins, Baltimore, pp. 1173–239.

Young, W. C. (1969) Psychobiology of sexual behavior in the guinea pig. In: *Advances in the Study of Behavior* Vol. 2, D. S. Lehrman, R. A. Hinde, and E. Shaw (eds.), Academic Press, N. Y., pp. 1–110.

Young, W. C. and Rundlett, B. (1939) The hormonal induction of homosexual behavior in the spayed female guinea pig, *Psychosomat. Med.*, **1**, 449–60.

Zigmond, R. E. and McEwen, B. S. (1970) Selective retention of estradiol by cell nuclei in specific regions of the ovariectomized rat, *J. Neurochem.*, **17**, 889–99.

Zucker, I. and Goy, R. W. (1967) Sexual receptivity in the guinea pig: Inhibitory and facilitatory actions of progesterone and related compounds, *J. Comp. Physiol. Phychol.*, **64**, 378–83.

CHAPTER 13

The Regulation of Sexual 'Heat'

ROBERT D. LISK

INTRODUCTION: THE OESTROUS CYCLE AND SEXUAL HEAT PERIOD

The literature on sexual behaviour in female mammals tends to use the terms oestrus and sexual heat synonymously. However, the term oestrus is used with reference to at least three separate events: (a) as a term designating the ovulatory cycle (oestrous cycle); (b) in short cycle animals like rat, mouse, and hamster to refer to a specific stage of the cycle (oestrus); (c) to designate the time during the cycle at which the female will accept the male and allow mating. Furthermore, the oestrous stage of the cycle is not the period throughout which the female allows the male to mate. To avoid the confusion inherent in the multiple usages for the term oestrus, this chapter will use the term sexual heat or simply heat as the preferred designation for that stage of the ovulatory cycle during which mating takes place. All non-primate mammals investigated, except the rabbit (Beyer et al., 1969), allow the male to copulate only when the ovaries are present and undergoing cycles of follicle maturation. Hormonal integration of primate sexual behaviour is discussed in Chapter 14 of this volume.

For a complete copulation to occur, the female must be willing to remain stationary. There is usually a flattening of the back and elevation of the perianal region may occur along with lateral deflection of the tail. This posture is known as lordosis, and serves as the basis for detecting sexual heat. Quantitative assessments of the degree of sexual responsiveness of the female to the male can be made and these have been referred to as copulatory quotients or receptivity scores. Beach (1944) designated the copulatory quotient as the number of lordotic responses divided by the number of times the female is mounted by the male multiplied by 100. Although most workers use this as their standard scoring system, more elaborate systems have been devised for measuring sexual receptivity. The female rat in heat shows darting and crouching movements plus quivering of the ears produced by rapid sideways shaking of the head; Ball (1937) has incorporated these behaviours as part of her scoring system.

In the rat arching of the perianal region occurs at lordosis and numerical values have been assigned based on the degree of arching. A composite score based on degree of arching, whether darting occurs, plus the duration of the sutained lordosis posture after the male dismounts (Gerall and Dunlap, 1973) has been employed and is termed the receptivity score. The degree of arching of the head and tail region of the rat during lordosis has also been quantified by photographing the animal against a millimetre grid (Komisaruk and Diakow, 1973).

As seen above, sexual receptivity provides a qualitative score which measures degree of sexual responsiveness. Receptivity scores are derived from a composite of factors which include both a variety of behavioural elements shown by the female during sexual heat and may include qualitative aspects of the lordosis posture itself. Sexual receptivity scores are difficult to translate into a uniform scale to allow direct comparison among various experiments since even within a single species some of the elements which are utilized in the composite score, e.g., hopping, darting, ear wiggling, in the rat may be absent in certain strains of animals. Also, all workers do not utilize the same elements of behaviour in calculating their sexual receptivity scores. For most studies of sexual behaviour the percentage or fraction of animals responding to the treatment is given. By designating this responding group as the fraction showing sexual heat, a comparison can be made of the effectiveness of hormone treatments in relation to percentage of responders. Furthermore, this simple dichotomy of responder *versus* non-responder is applicable across different experimental designs within, as well as across, species.

Assumption of the lordotic posture in response to artificial stimulation, usually pressure on the back plus 'fingering' of the perianal region, has been described for several species of rodents. When cervical probing is employed in addition to 'fingering' lordosis can be elicited in rats throughout most of the oestrous cycle while lordosis in response to mating attempts by the male occurs only on the night during which ovulation takes place. In ovariectomized rats treated with exogenous hormone cervical probing plus 'fingering' results in a high percentage of the animals displaying lordosis while significantly fewer or no animals may respond when mounted by the male (Komisaruk and Diakow, 1973; Lisk, 1973). Thus, in studies of sexual heat, the appropriate test stimulus is the response of the female to the male.

While oestrous cycle length may be four to six days for the small polyoestrus mammals like rat, hamster, and mouse or two to three weeks for the ungulates and 60 to 90 days for the canidae, the period of sexual heat has a maximum duration of about 15% of the oestrous cycle length for all species examined. To maximize fertility this limited period of sexual heat must be tied to the time of ovulation. Thus, an interaction might be expected between the mechanism for triggering ovulation and the mechanism for determining onset of heat.

In this chapter the following questions will be addressed. What is the mechanism for ensuring the concurrence of sexual heat and ovulation? Since sexual heat occurs only when the sex steroids oestrogen and progesterone are present, what is the role of these hormones both individually and combined in relation to onset of heat and duration of heat? What factors are involved in termination of heat? Following mating the hormones necessary for heat must continue to be produced to support pregnancy yet the pregnant animal only rarely if ever shows sexual heat. Does age at first exposure to sex hormone affect sexual heat? The hormones must act on the neural substrate to modify the sexual responses of the animal. Are there specific sites in the brain at which the hormones act to facilitate heat? Finally, what is the cellular mechanism by which hormones act to regulate sexual heat?

Mating cannot occur until the female and male make contact. In some species at least, it is the female who becomes more active during the heat period and actively seeks out and makes contact with other animals. The literature on the rat has been reviewed and re-examined by Meyerson and Lindström (1973) who used three methods: open field to study orientation of the female to a male; increasing barrier technique in which an electric grid had to be crossed to gain access to the male; a runway choice to investigate preference for a certain animal. The data from the three methods indicated that in ovariectomized animals oestradiol benzoate (OB) was effective in increasing activity and male-seeking behaviour after two to four days of treatment at $1\mu g/100$ g body weight. This dosage and duration of oestrogen treatment is similar to that required for heat.

Ram-seeking activity could be induced in all ewes but only when injected with a dosage of oestrogen greatly in excess of that required to induce heat (Lindsay and Fletcher, 1972). Female dogs, when in heat, if free to wander will spend more time visiting tethered males than tethered females, although, when not in heat, no preference is shown (LeBoeuf, 1967). The tendency to wander more widely and the period of immobility during copulation both tend to expose the female to more danger from predators. Thus, the development of mechanisms for the limitation of sexual heat compatible with fertility might be expected. Although changes in activity patterns can be used to detect the approach of the period during which the female will permit copulation, throughout this chapter onset of sexual heat will be used in the strict sense as the beginning of the period during which the female stands and allows copulation to occur. The duration of heat is a measure of the total interval of time over which copulations occur and thus termination of heat is defined as the female being unwilling to continue to stand still and permit the male to copulate.

For most of the history of reproductive biology it has been technically possible to measure with precision only two events in the oestrous cycle, the period of sexual heat and the time of ovulation. Now it is possible to measure the blood levels of the various hormones and so graph the hormonal events which occur throughout the oestrous cycle. A picture of the relationship between blood levels of hormones, onset of sexual heat, and time of ovulation can be obtained. Oestrous cycles show several basic patterns. These will be outlined before discussing the blood levels of hormone which are characteristic of the phases of the ovulatory cycle.

Oestrous cycles can be divided into two phases: a follicular phase followed by a luteal phase. In the follicular phase the follicle with enclosed ovum increases in diameter and becomes a hormone-secreting structure (mostly oestrogen). At maturity either the whole structure breaks down (atresia) or the follicle ruptures, releasing the ovum. Ovulation occurs either as a spontaneous event or is triggered as a result of the act of mating (reflex ovulation). Following rupture of the follicle the remaining follicle cells undergo a further differentiation to form a new structure, the corpus luteum. The phase of the cycle following ovulation is referred to as the luteal phase. This generalized description of the oestrous cycle has been modified several times with similar modifications appearing in unrelated orders of mammals (Everett, 1961).

Most species have a two-phase oestrous cycle with ovulation occurring as a spontaneous event. Thus, the follicular phase ends with ovulation occurring spontaneously followed by a luteal phase. Cycle lengths depending on species are typically 18 to 28 days in duration with the follicular phase occupying half or less of the total cycle length. Cycle length can be shortened to a minimum by eliminating the luteal phase altogether. This is seen in rats, mice, and hamsters where the cycle length is four days. This appears to be the minimum time required for maturation of the follicle so that ovulation is possible. The corpus luteum is actually formed in mice, rats, and hamsters but it does not become an active hormone-secreting structure and therefore has no effect on the next group of follicles to develop. Only as a result of mating does the corpus luteum become an active hormone secreting gland (progesterone is the main secretory product) and the cycle is extended by 8 days in hamster and 12 days in rat and mouse. Thus, the luteal phase is added only when the hormonal products (progesterone) would be necessary for pregnancy maintenance. Another group of animals including the cat and rabbit have a pure follicular cycle (during the breeding season mature follicles capable of ovulation are continuously available) with the mature follicles being maintained for two to three days after which atresia occurs and a new set of follicles matures. Rupture of the follics (ovulation) occurs only following the act of mating (reflex ovulation) resulting in formation of corpora lutea which are active progesterone-secreting organs. Thus, in reflex ovulators mating is required both for ovulation to occur and to achieve the luteal phase of the oestrous cycle.

Role of the Ovaries and the Ovarian–Hypothalamic–Pituitary Feedback System

Most determinations of blood levels of hormone have been made for the 4-day follicular cycle. If the ovulatory cycle is defined as terminating with ovulation this will be day 4 of the 4-day cyclic animal like rat and hamster. Blood levels of oestrogen begin to rise on day 2 and peak by day 3 [prooestrus, rat (Yoshinaga et al., 1969; Naftolin et al., 1972); hamster (Shaikh, 1972; Baranczuk and Greenwald, 1973; Labhsetwar et al., 1973)]. Shortly after oestrogen level peaks a surge of gonadotropin (luteinizing hormone, LH) can be detected in the blood (Naftolin et al., 1972; Labhsetwar et al., 1973). Within several hours of the LH surge blood levels of progesterone have markedly increased (Schneider et al., 1970; Labhsetwar et al., 1973). Onset of heat occurs on the evening of prooestrus several hours after the increased blood levels of progesterone are detected [rat (Feder et al., 1968a; Mann and Barraclough, 1973); hamster (Leavitt and Blaha, 1970; Lukaszewska and Greenwald, 1970); guinea pig (Feder et al., 1968b)]. Ovulation occurs some 10 to 14 h after the LH surge in rat and hamster (Schwartz, 1972). These relationships have been diagrammed for the hamster (Fig. 1). The above observations imply that the maturing follicles secrete the oestrogen necessary to induce the luteinizing hormone (LH) surge which acting on the ovary results in increased progesterone output and follicular rupture, thus sexual heat and ovulation are tied together.

In the 4-day cycle it can further be shown that progesterone release is the factor controlling heat onset. Heat can be advanced by 24 h in the 5-day cyclic rat (Zucker, 1967) and 4-day cyclic hamster (Reuter et al., 1970) and up to 18 h in the 4-day cyclic rat (Barfield and Lisk, 1970) by injection of exogenous progesterone. As shown in Fig. 2 for the hamster, progesterone injection early in the cycle can delay both sexual heat and ovulation or result in early heat unaccompanied by ovulation. If the LH surge is blocked (see Fig. 1), both sexual heat and ovulation are inhibited (hamster, Bosley and Leavitt, 1972), however, sexual heat can be induced by injection of progesterone.

The guinea pig is the only species to date with both a follicular and luteal phase to its oestrous cycle in which increased progesterone output in the preovulatory animal (during follicular phase of the cycle) is essential for onset of heat (Feder et al., 1968b). Injection of progesterone is effective in some guinea pigs in inducing heat up to 4 days early in the 17-day cycle (Joslyn et al., 1971). In other species, e.g., cow, sow, sheep, onset of heat (Stabenfeldt et al., 1969a, 1969b, 1969c) does not occur until 24 to 72 h after progesterone has reached its low point in the cycle (less than 1 ng/ml plasma). Although oestrogen levels are rising at this time, careful examination in cows starting 60 h prior to sexual heat showed that no clear-cut oestradiol peak occurred (Lemon et al., 1975). In the ewe a peak of oestradiol (200 pg/ml) occurred 24 h prior to heat (Cox et al., 1971). However, no change in progesterone levels occurred. Thus, in the long cycle animal, with the exception of the guinea pig, the most uniform hormonal event signalling onset of heat was the decline of progesterone levels to less than 1 ng/ml plasma.

Ovariectomized animals do not show sexual heat. Oestrogen treatment for 24 h or longer will induce heat in some species, e.g., rat, cat, rabbit, while in others progesterone must be added after 24 h of oestrogen treatment before the animals show sexual heat, e.g., hamster. In the ewe, although oestrogen is

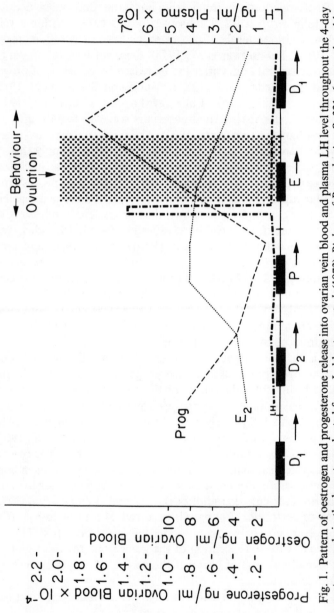

Fig. 1. Pattern of oestrogen and progesterone release into ovarian vein blood and plasma LH level throughout the 4-day oestrous cycle in the hamster, adapted from Labhsetwar *et al.* (1973) *Biology of Reproduction*, **8**, 321–6, reproduced by permission of Academic Press. The period of sexual heat (behaviour) and the time of ovulation are indicated based on data in Reuter *et al.* (1970) *Endocrinology*, **86**, 1287–97. Black bar = 10 h dark period; line = 14 h light period with short vertical line indicating 'noon'; midnight by definition = midpoint of dark period. Days of cycle are dioestrus day 1 (D1), dioestrus day 2 (D2), prooestrus (P), oestrus (E)

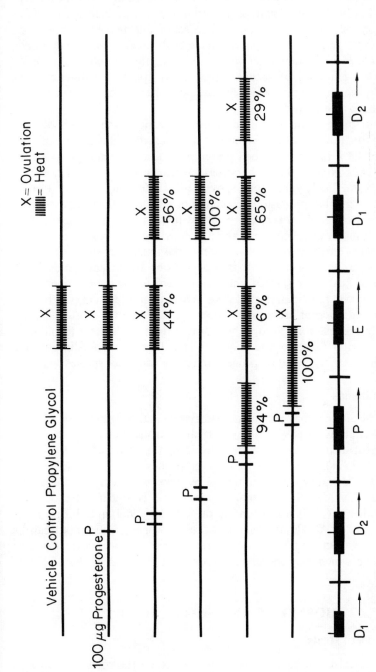

Fig. 2. Effect of progesterone on the timing of sexual heat and ovulation in the 4-day cyclic hamster. Progesterone (100 μg) was given as a single injection at the intervals indicated. The duration of sexual heat and occurrence of ovulation are indicated with the percentage of the population showing heat noted. Sexual heat was determined by placing females with sexually active males for 10 min out of each hour. Adapted from data in Reuter et al. (1970) *Endocrinology*, 86, 1287–97. P = time of progesterone injection. See Fig. 1 for key to other symbols

required for sexual heat, it is possible to induce sexual heat only if the animals have received prior treatment with progesterone (Moore and Robinson, 1957). The pattern of oestrogen and progesterone secretion during the ovulatory cycle does not differ in the ewe, cow or pig (compare Stabenfeldt *et al.*, 1969a, 1969b, 1969c; Cox *et al.*, 1971; Lemon *et al.*, 1975). Thus, the stimulus value of the hormones for facilitation of sexual behaviour is apparently different. The mechanism by which progesterone facilitates oestrogen action to induce sexual heat in the sheep awaits study.

In addition to the facilitatory role of progesterone for the onset of heat, an inhibiting function can also be demonstrated. Sexual heat is not maintained beyond about 24 h in the continued presence of oestrogen and progesterone (rat, Lisk, 1969; Nadler, 1970; hamster, Ciaccio and Lisk, 1971a; rabbit, Makepeace *et al.*, 1937; guinea pig, Goy *et al.*, 1966). During times of continuous oestrogen plus progesterone secretion, e.g., pregnancy and pseudopregnancy (Powers and Zucker, 1969) or the luteal phase of the cycle (Goy *et al.*, 1966) animals rarely show heat and if injected with oestrogen and progesterone in dosages effective in the ovariectomized animal they show little or no responsiveness to the hormones. It is progesterone which apparently limits the duration of heat since species which show heat following treatment with oestrogen alone will remain in heat as long as oestrogen is present (rat, rabbit). Only after the addition of progesterone does the heat become of limited duration and only progesterone need be withdrawn from the system to induce a second heat period (Ciaccio and Lisk, 1971b). Thus, both facilitation and duration of heat are regulated by progesterone in a variety of species.

Role of the Adrenals

In the rat the adrenal may play an accessory role in timing the onset of heat. Although adrenalectomized rats show normal oestrous cycles with ovulation and sexual heat, acute adrenalectomy can delay the onset of heat (Nequin and Schwartz, 1971). Acute ovariectomy in prooestrus can advance onset of heat and this advance can be inhibited by prior dexamethasone injection (Barfield and Lisk, 1974). Adrenal progesterone is under adrenocortico trophic hormone (ACTH) control in the rat, (Resko, 1969) and during stress when high levels of ACTH are released adrenal progesterone output can be equivalent to ovarian output. Thus, the rat adrenal is an important source of progesterone which may modify the onset and duration of the period of sexual heat.

HORMONES AND SEXUAL HEAT

Oestrogen-induced Heats

The ovariectomized animal has been used to study the roles of oestrogen and progesterone for heat onset and duration. In most experiments the hormones are suspended in an oil vehicle and given as a series of subcutaneous injections. In general, those species examined have a minimal latency of 24 to 72 h between injection of oestrogen and onset of heat. Using a dosage more than 10 times as large as that required to induce heat (100 μg oestradiol) and intravenous injection, some rats were reported to show heat as early as 16 h with the maximal number of animals responding by 24 h (Green et al., 1970). Increased dosage of oestrogen does not shorten the latency to onset of heat, however increased dosage of oestrogen does increase the duration of the heat period (cat, Peretz, 1968; ewe, Fletcher and Lindsay, 1971; sow, Signoret, 1967; rat, Quadagno et al., 1972). Also in the rat the duration of lordosis was found to be proportional to the oestrogen dosage (Hardy and DeBold, 1971a). Injection of a variety of oestrogens (oestradiol, estrone, estriol) at 1 or 4μg/day for 10 days into adult ovariectomized female rats showed that oestradiol was the most potent for induction of lordosis. No clear relationship could be demonstrated between the lordosis-inducing potency and genital tract effects such as uterine weight gain and vaginal cornification (Beyer et al., 1971). Thus, different mechanisms of hormone action may be involved in promoting the behavioural effects and physiological changes in the genital tract.

Oestrogen Plus Progesterone-induced Heats

Progesterone can have a facilitatory or inhibitory effect on heat induction and intensity depending upon the sequencing of the hormone injections and the species being studied. Simultaneous injection of oestrogen and progesterone does not result in induction of heat in any species studied. Oestrogen must be present for a least 24 h before the addition of progesterone facilitates sexual heat (hamster, Ciaccio, 1970; guinea pig, Dempsey et al., 1936; rat, Arai and Gorski, 1968; sow, Signoret, 1971). The ewe is the only exception among species studied to date (see p. 429). The amount of oestrogen required to prime the system so that progesterone can synergize appears to vary with species, some being highly sensitive to oestrogen (rat 1–2 μg/kg body weight, Powers and Valenstein, 1972; guinea pig 2–5 μg/kg body weight, Goy and Young, 1957) and others less sensitive (hamster 90 μg/kg body weight, Feder et al., 1974). Similarly, the amount of progesterone given as a single injection to synergize with oestrogen suggest differing sensitivities exist for various species (guinea pig 10 μg/100g body weight, Wade and Feder, 1972b; hamster 50 μg/100g body weight, Reuter et al., 1970; rat 100 μg/100g body weight, Powers and Valenstein, 1972). Synergistic effects of progesterone for induction of heat are not necessary in all species, e.g., pig, cat, cow. In the guinea pig, the length of the heat period was found to show a positive correlation with the amount of oestrogen present at the time of progesterone injection (Joslyn and Feder, 1971). Oestrogen action for maintenance of heat is not terminated at the time of progesterone synergism since oestrogen removal by ovariectomy (Ciaccio and Lisk, 1971a) or inactivation by injection of an antioestrogen about the time of progesterone injection (Feder and Morin, 1974) results in a significant decrease of the duration of heat.

In contrast to the species just examined, the ewe requires a reverse sequence of hormone priming, first progesterone then oestrogen, to induce heat (Robinson, 1955). Following progesterone priming the behavioural responsiveness to oestrogen decreases with time or repeated injections of oestrogen (Scaramuzzi et al., 1971). Thus, repeated conditioning of the system by progesterone appears necessary to maintain the oestrogen sensitivity of the ewe so that it is within the range of oestrogen levels found in the blood as a result of ovarian secretion (Moore et al., 1969). This hypothesis is consistent with the observation that the first ovulation of each season is unaccompanied by heat (Thorburn et al., 1969). Thus, only after the first set of corpora lutea have secreted progesterone is the system able to respond to oestrogen during the second ovulatory cycle to bring the animal into heat. Is this a mechanism peculiar to the sheep or only an extreme example of a general function of progesterone?

An answer to this question has been provided by a study of heifers tested with bulls for presence of sexual heat, Carrick and Shelton (1969) found that repeated induction of heat using high dosage of oestrogen (10 mg OB) induced a refractoriness to heat induction by lower dosage of oestrogen (400 μg). However, if these animals are given 10 mg progesterone for five days they again show a normal response to 400 μg OB on day 3 following the last progesterone injection. Repeated pretreatment with progesterone is necessary for normal responsiveness to be maintained to subsequent low dosage of oestrogen. Thus, in the heifer progesterone appears to be exerting a preconditioning effect similar to that observed in the ewe.

The first ovulations of animals reaching puberty are often not accompanied by heat—so called 'silent' ovulations have been noted in 100% of sheep and about 75% of heifers. By the third ovulation sexual heat is apparent in 80% of heifers (Morrow, 1969). Similar observations have been found for pubertal rats (Blandau and Money, 1943) and hamsters Diamond and Yanagimachi, 1970). During the first few oestrous cycles 'silent' ovulations occur and sexual receptivity is reduced. Only after one to three cycles have occurred do the multiple events which make up the ovulatory cycle appear to be properly coordinated so that a high percentage of the matings are fertile. Hormone injections given to very young animals fail to induce sexual heat. Sequential oestrogen and progesterone treatment do not induce heat before about day 20 in the rat and day 21 in the guinea pig (Wilson and Young, 1941). The silent ovulations and reduced sensitivity to hormones reported in the young animals may be another example of reduced oestrogen sensitivity in the absence of a progesterone preconditioning period.

Progesterone Regulation of Length of Heat

In those species in which progesterone synergizes in the oestrogen-primed animal to facilitate heat the facilitatory phase is of finite duration and is followed

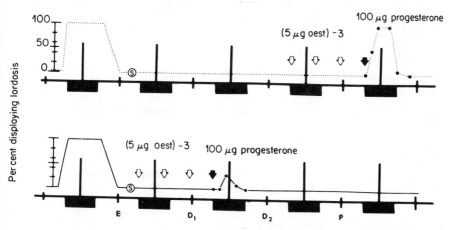

Fig. 3. Effectiveness of sequential oestrogen–progesterone treatment for induction of sexual heat in the hamster in relation to the length of time from the preceding period of sexual heat. The animals were ovariectomized on oestrus (E) after termination of sexual heat and exogenous hormone treatment was started immediately or 48 h later; from Ciaccio and Lisk (1971) *Am. J. Physiol.*, **221**, 936–42. Reproduced with permission of the American Physiological Society. S = time of spaying; open arrows indicate time of oestradiol-17β injection (5 μg); black arrow indicates time of progesterone injection. Y axis indicates per cent of test population responding to mating attempts of male by showing lordosis. Other symbols similar to Fig.1.

by a phase in which the animals are refractory to further oestrogen and progesterone treatment for induction of heat. Thus, the addition of progesterone appears to programme the length of the heat period (rabbit, Marshall and Hammond Jr., 1945; rat, Lisk, 1969; Nadler, 1970; hamster, Ciaccio and Lisk, 1971b; guinea pig, Morin and Feder, 1973). An experiment illustrating this for the intact hamster is shown in Fig. 3.

Ovariectomy of hamsters at the end of the heat period followed by immediate replacement therapy with oestrogen and progesterone resulted in a failure to induce a new heat period (Fig. 3). However, when the same hormonal regimen was started 48 h after ovariectomy all the animals came into heat. Thus, the physiological levels of progesterone produced during the cycle are clearly capable of making the animal insensitive to the action of the sex steroids for induction of heat.

Ovariectomized, oestrogen primed hamsters were used to determine which parameters of progesterone are important for (a) heat duration, (b) induction of a refractory state to further progesterone induced heat (Ciaccio and Lisk, 1971b). The total progesterone injection was always 200 μg. When this was given as a single injection in sesame oil, 100% of hamsters tested remained in heat for 20 h while if the vehicle for the progesterone was propylene glycol, heat was only 14 h in duration (Fig. 4). Fig. 4 also shows that progesterone is released very rapidly from the propylene glycol with blood levels during the

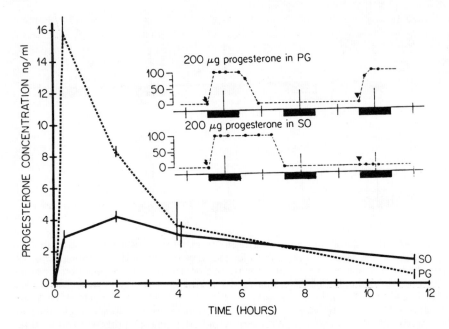

Fig. 4. Blood levels of progesterone (ng/ml) and (inset) length of sexual heat in ovariec-tomized hamsters when a standard dose of progesterone (200 μg) is given in different injection vehicles. Propylene glycol (PG) as injection vehicle results in a 14 h heat period while sesame oil (SO) results in a 20 h heat period. Ordinate main graph shows blood concentration of progesterone (ng/ml). Ordinate, inset, shows per cent of animals in sexual heat when tested with males at the times indicated by black circles. First progesterone injection was given at time indicated by black arrow; second progesterone injection at time indicated by black triangle. Animals had been oestrogen-primed for 5 days. Behavioural data from Ciaccio and Lisk (1971) *J. Endocrinol.*, **50**, 201–7. Reproduced by permission of Journal of Endocrionology Ltd. Blood levels of proges-terone from Reuter and Lisk, unpublished. The longest heat resulted from hormone injection in SO which produced a slow steady release of progesterone (plasma level ∼ 4 ng/ml. This group also showed no sexual heat following a second progesterone injection

first hour, reaching 4 times those found for the animals receiving progesterone in sesame oil. However, by 12 h the animals receiving progesterone in the propylene glycol vehicle had blood progesterone levels significantly lower than the animals receiving progesterone in the sesame oil vehicle. To determine whether this low blood level of progesterone was the reason for the shorter heat period in the propylene glycol groups, attempts were made to duplicate the 20 h heat period produced by the 200 μg progesterone in sesame oil by administering the total dosage of 200 μg of progesterone in propylene glycol as a series of injections (4 × 50 μg) spread over various intervals of time (Fig. 5). As the time between progesterone injections was increased, heat duration was lengthened but 100% of the animals did not remain in heat.

Since a rapid release of progesterone occurs from the propylene glycol vehicle (Fig. 4), repeated injections of progesterone in this vehicle will result in a series of progesterone peaks in the systemic circulation. Under this type of condition, some of the animals fail to respond to the later injections of progesterone (bottom half of Fig. 5) and, in addition, most animals remain refractory to 200 μg of progesterone given 48 h later. Thus, it appears that the peak blood levels of progesterone produced as a result of hormone released from the propylene glycol vehicle make the hamsters insensitive to further injections of progesterone which produce similar peak levels of progesterone

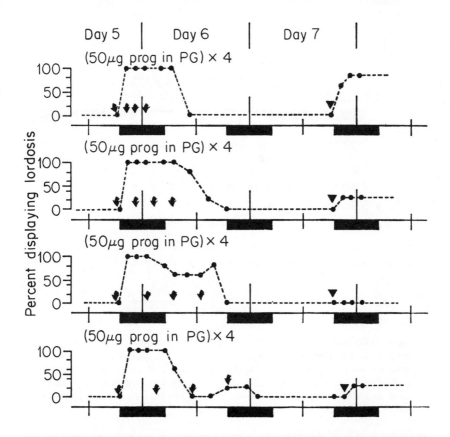

Fig. 5. Failure to maintain or reinitiate heat in ovariectomized, oestrogen-primed hamsters by repeated treatment with progesterone. All animals received a 150 μg pellet of oestradiol-17β subcutaneously on day 0 (not shown). Initial progesterone treatments (200 μg total) were in propylene glycol (PG) and injected at various time intervals beginning at lights off (horizontal black bar) on day 5 after start of oestrogen treatment. At lights off on day 7 the animals' responsiveness to progesterone-induced heat was retested following subcutaneous implantation of a 200 μg pellet of crystalline progesterone. (From Ciaccio and Lisk (1971) *J. Endocrinol.*, **50**, 201–7. Reproduced by permission of Journal of Endocrinology Ltd.)

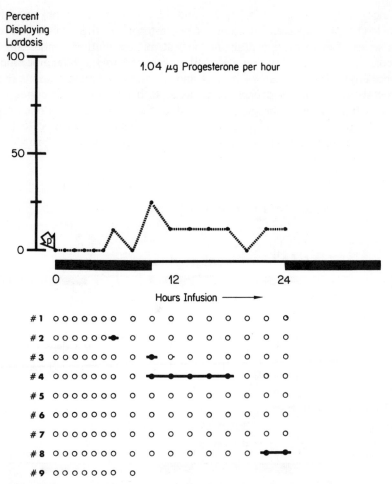

Fig. 6. Effect of infusion rate of progesterone on percentage of animals showing sexual heat and duration of sexual heat. Spayed oestrogen-primed hamsters were infused via the jugular vein with 1.04 μg progesterone per hour. Open circles in lower half indicate 10 min tests with males. A solid circle indicates female which displayed lordosis. (From Lisk, Reuter, Davison and Schwarz, unpubl.)

in the blood. Thus, the refractory state in which no response occurred on further injection of progesterone appeared to result from high blood levels of hormone maintained over some minimal interval of time.

Since the low and slowly declining blood level of progesterone produced by injection in sesame oil vehicle resulted in 100% of the animals tested showing the longest duration of heat, we next decided to examine the possibility that a low but constant blood level of progesterone would result in a lengthened heat period. Our experiments to date suggest that the higher the blood level of progesterone used to initiate heat, the shorter the duration of the heat period. Ovariectomized hamsters were given a constant oestrogen source. Progesterone dissolved in propylene glycol was infused into the jugular vein at rates from 1 to 4 μg per hour. Infusion of progesterone at 1.0 μg/h was almost totally ineffective (Fig. 6). At 2.08 μg/h all the animals tested showed heat and 24 h later all were still in heat; some animals were still receptive to the male at 72 h (Fig. 7). When the amount of progesterone infused per hour was again doubled (4.16 μg/h) the heat duration was greatly shortened and resembled the 16–18 h duration seen in the intact animal (Fig. 8).

This series of experiments suggests that a greatly extended heat is possible

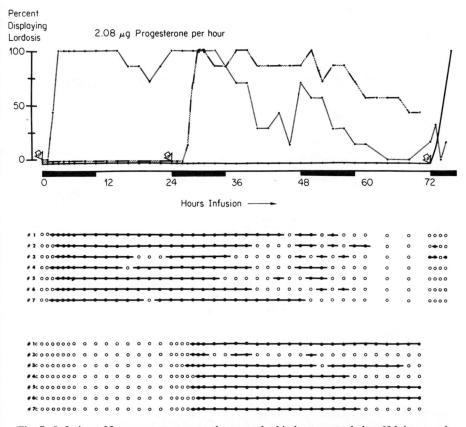

Fig. 7. Infusion of 2 μg progesterone per hour resulted in heats extended to 60 h in spayed oestrogen-primed hamsters. Progesterone infusion was started at arrows marked P, i.e., 0, 24, or 72 h, the latter two groups of animals were infused with vehicle only up to the time that the progesterone infusion was started. The results are independent of the length of vehicle infusion. The lower half of the figure shows lordosis responses (solid circles) when females were tested with males.

Females 1 to 7 received progesterone starting at time 0. Females 1c to 7c received progesterone starting at 24 h. (From Lisk, Reuter, Davison and Schwarz, unpubl.)

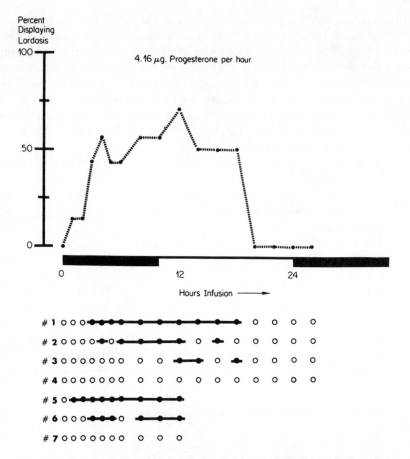

Fig. 8. Infusion of progesterone at 4 µg per hour resulted in a heat period similar to that found in intact cyclic animals. For further details, see legend to Fig. 6. (From Lisk, Reuter, Davison and Schwarz, unpubl.)

in the hamster and that blood level of progesterone is the critical factor for 'programming' of the duration of heat, or, put in other terms, the concentration of progesterone which initiates and maintains heat also predetermines the termination of heat. A further experiment was carried out to determine whether the gradual decline in response in the 2.08 µg/h group seen after 24 h was due to progesterone or some toxic effect of the vehicle. When propylene glycol was injected for 24 h followed by progesterone at 2.08 µg/h, the response was similar to the first 24 h of progesterone infusion (Fig. 7) which suggests that the gradual decline in the response is due to a developing refractoriness to the progesterone.

These studies suggest that the blood levels of progesterone which occur during the oestrous cycle are necessary not just to synergize with oestrogen for induction of heat but the concentration of progesterone in the circulation may be important for programming the length of the heat period. Since progesterone levels are highest during the luteal stage of the cycle if progesterone remained facilitatory for sexual heat the animal would continue to mate throughout half or more of the total period of each ovulatory cycle. The energy utilized in seeking out a mate and the exposure to predation resulting both from the increased wandering behaviour and during the mating act would not have an adaptive advantage. Since no mature ova are present during the luteal phase, the mating would be without consequence for fertility. Thus, a selective advantage probably exists for maintenance of a short period of sexual heat tightly correlated with the period of ovulation. Mechanisms have therefore evolved which result in the same hormone, progesterone, being facilitatory for the first few hours but on continued presence of progesterone the animal becomes insensitive to the action of the hormone. Although the mechanism by which progesterone can exert this dual function remains unknown, one possibility will be discussed later in this chapter under cellular mechanisms p. 454.

Although the biphasic response to progesterone in regulation of heat can be demonstrated in rat, hamster, mouse, and rabbit, in the rat the biphasic effect is seen only at physiological levels of oestrogen (Lisk, 1969; Nadler, 1970). If high levels of oestrogen are maintained, the inhibitory effect of progesterone is not observed.

NON-HORMONAL STIMULI AND THE SEXUAL HEAT PERIOD

Exposure of female rats to the mating situation in the absence of hormone priming (i.e., no oestrogen and progesterone) had no effect on response to males (lordosis/mount ratio) in a subsequent test; however, if the female rats were both hormone primed and exposed to males in the mating situation a significantly greater response to the males was observed in subsequent tests (Gerall and Dunlap, 1973). In the hamster, Noble (1973) reported that copulatory stimulation increased the mean total time spent in lordosis during a subsequent series of mounts. The amount of copulatory stimulation appears to be an important factor in this regard since exposure to the male for 4 h reduced the amount of time the female hamster spent in lordosis during an immediately subsequent 600 s test (Carter, 1972). The amount of time lordosis is displayed during a standard 10 min mating test declines with repeated testing in the hamster (Carter and Schein, 1971) and in the rat exposure to 50 mounts reduces the frequency and degree of arching of head and perianal region during subsequent lordosis (Hardy and DeBold, 1971b). Coitus and vaginal stimulation are reported to abbreviate the heat period in the guinea pig (Goldfoot and Goy, 1970) and rat (Blandau et al., 1941).

Maintaining female mice in groups can suppress oestrous cyclicity by induction of a state of pseudopregnancy or anoestrus (Whitten, 1966). Introduction of males tends to immediately initiate a new cycle of follicle development with the result that most animals come into heat in synchrony on the third night after introduction of the males.

Female hamsters maintained in groups fail to mate when placed with males although the ovulatory cycle is not blocked (Lisk et al., 1974). Introduction of a ram can synchronize onset of sexual heat in a flock of ewes and also initiate the breeding season earlier than when ewes are maintained without a ram (Fraser, 1968). In many species of wild and domestic ungulates the males show nuzzling, nudging, and licking about the genital region of the female. It appears that this behaviour may be important for induction of full heat behaviour in the female. Thus, a variety of adaptations has evolved to synchronize heat to the presence of the male. The appropriate tests have not been undertaken so the mechanisms by which external stimuli affect heat remain unknown. One likely possibility is that exposure to males and the behaviour of the males towards the female could result in earlier release of hormones during the cycle or increase the circulating level of hormone in the female.

NEONATAL HORMONE MANIPULATION AND RESPONSIVENESS OF THE ADULT ANIMAL TO HORMONE FOR INDUCTION OF SEXUAL HEAT

Long Term Castration

Rats ovariectomized as adults require a lower total dosage of oestrogen and a shorter exposure period to oestrogen for induction of sexual heat when oestrogen treatment is begun immediately versus 30 days or more after ovariectomy (Damassa and Davidson, 1973; Beach and Orndoff, 1974). Thus, the rat's sensitivity to hormone appears to decrease with time following castration. (See Hutchison, this volume Chapter 9, for further discussion.) Also in rats ovariectomized prepubertally and not injected with hormones for six or more months oestrogen alone had little effect for induction of heat (progesterone had to be given to the oestrogen-primed animals), whereas animals ovariectomized as adults responded to oestrogen alone (Lisk and Suydam, 1967).

Perinatal Exposure to Sex Steroid Hormones

Hormone injections into very young mammals fail to facilitate sexual heat. In the rat heat cannot be induced by hormone injections before about 20 days of age (Wilson and Young, 1941). While guinea pigs did not respond to hormone injections at seven days of age, heat was induced by oestrogen plus progesterone treatment at 21 days of age (Wilson and Young, 1941). Oestrogen injections given within a few days of birth to the female have not been found to facilitate responsiveness to subsequent treatment with oestrogen plus progesterone. However, there are several reports that low dosage (5 to 50 μg) TP treatment facilitated the copulatory quotient to oestrogen in the adult rat (Mullins and Levine, 1968; Clemens *et al.*, 1969). These studies are in contrast to a large body of literature which indicates that perinatal injection of female young either with the female sex steroid, oestrogen, or the male sex steroid, androgen, results in adults which are anovulatory and show reduced sensitivity or complete absence of response for induction of sexual heat on treatment with oestrogen plus progesterone.

Male mammals castrated as adults show a greatly reduced sensitivity to oestrogen plus progesterone induced sexual heat. Following long term oestrogen treatment, Davidson (1969) reported that male rats show a copulatory quotient approaching that of the female. However, in the male progesterone fails to synergize with oestrogen to increase the copulatory quotient. This difference in responsiveness between genetic males and females for oestrogen plus progesterone induction of lordosis has been examined by a variety of techniques.

Male rats castrated within three days of birth are similar to females in responsiveness when injected in adulthood with oestrogen plus progesterone (Feder and Whalen, 1965; Lisk and Suydam, 1967). If castrated within 24 h of birth and given ovarian grafts, males when mature show 5-day cycles and sexual heat occurs on the night of prooestrus (Van der Schoot and Zeilmaker, 1972). When androgens are blocked from reacting with their target tissues by daily injection of a potent antiandrogen, cyproterone acetate, male rats in which treatment was started prenatally show lordotic responses identical to those shown by genetic females (Ward, 1971). These experiments, which are more recent representatives of the many studies on this subject, support the contention that the presence of the testis as a source of androgenic hormone during the perinatal period makes the male less responsive to the effects of oestrogen plus progesterone for induction of the lordosis response.

The female rat ovariectomized at birth (Lisk and Suydam, 1967; Gerall *et al.*, 1972a) is capable of showing sexual heat when injected with exogenous oestrogen plus progesterone in adulthood. However, injection of androgens prenatally or up to day five postnatally results in a reduced percentage of female rats which display heat following oestrogen injection (Barraclough and Gorski, 1962; Gerall, 1967; Ward and Renz, 1972) and there is no facilitation of the percentage of animals responding, or increase in the copulatory quotient, on addition of progesterone (Edwards and Thompson, 1970). The decrease in percentage of the population showing sexual heat appears to be proportional to the amount of androgen injected during the neonatal period (Napoli and Gerall, 1970). Similar findings have been reported for the hamster (Eaton, 1970; Ciaccio and Lisk, 1971c; Paup *et al.*, 1974). Again the larger the dosage of androgen given during the neonatal period the smaller the fraction of animals showing sexual heat following injection of exogenous oestrogen followed by progesterone (Gottlieb *et al.*, 1974). Although the preceding reports are in agreement with the fact that the presence of the testis as an androgen source during the neonatal period results in reduced sexual heat, there are also a large number of studies which show that oestrogen injection into the perinatal rat or hamster can result in absence of sexual heat in the adult animal. OB (200–250 µg) given as a single injection by day 5 post birth in the rat severely suppresses the copulatory quotient (Whalen and Nadler, 1963; Gerall, 1967) or completely eliminates sexual heat (Levine and Mullins, 1964) and injection of exogenous oestrogen plus progesterone is without effect. A similar observation was noted for the hamster (Paup *et al.*, 1974). The male rat orchidectomized within 6 h of birth shows sexual heat when exogenous oestrogen plus progesterone is injected in adulthood. However, if following orchidectomy at 6 h a single injection of OB (10 µg or larger) is given on day 3 or 5 post birth (Gerall *et al.*, 1972b) the males when adult show little or no sexual heat when exogenous oestrogen plus progesterone is injected.

Thus, in the absence of hormonal stimulation during the perinatal period sexual heat can be induced by injection of exogenous oestrogen plus progesterone in the adult animal regardless of genetic sex. Injection of male hormone (androgen) or female hormone (oestrogen) results in a reduced percentage of the population responding as adults and a reduced copulatory quotient in those animals which do show sexual heat following injection of oestrogen.

A separate, easily quantified behaviour pattern which correlates with the period of sexual heat in the rat is the pattern of locomotor activity. This is usually quantified by counting revolutions of a wheel in which the animal is free to run. During the night of sexual heat a doubling of the amount of wheel running occurs. Neonatal treatment with oestrogen which renders animals anovulatory as adults also results in a significantly decreased amount of wheel running (Kawashima and Shinoda, 1968). When ovariectomized and given daily oestrogen injections, those animals which received neonatal oestrogen injections responded with a lesser increase or no change in wheel running while the control animals showed the largest increase in running. A similar effect was found by Gerall (1967) as a result of neonatal oestrogen or androgen treatment and further studies showed that the depression in oestrogen-induced wheel running was proportional to the dosage of androgen given the neonatal rat. When 1250 µg TP was given as a single injection on day 5 there was a complete suppression of oestrogen-induced wheel running (Gerall *et al.*, 1972b). Therefore the increased activity shown by rats during the period of sexual heat is correlated with the animals' sensitivity to oestrogen. When oestrogen sensitivity is decreased by manipulation of the animal's hormone environment during the neonatal period, all oestrogen-sensitive response systems, i.e., control of ovulation, increased locomotor activity, and sexual heat are severely disrupted or completely suppressed. Thus, both physiological and behavioural responses to oestrogen may be regulated through pathways which have in common an oestrogen-sensitive substrate.

SITES OF HORMONE ACTION FOR REGULATION OF SEXUAL HEAT

Oestrogen-sensitive Sites

Studies on the localization of the oestrogen-sensitive neural substrate necessary for the expression of lordosis have been undertaken for several mammalian species. The total area found to be oestrogen-sensitive and its anatomical localization differs among the species examined. The rat shows heat following implantation of a single oestrogen-bearing probe of surface area 17 to 32 $\mu m^2 \times 10^3$ with the preoptic area and anterior hypothalamus the most sensitive locus of action (Lisk, 1962). Other species which have been examined require a larger surface area of the neural substrate exposed to oestrogen for sexual heat to be facilitated. When large surface areas of oestrogen are used (blobs of hormone on the end of stainless steel rods) sexual heat is found in cats bearing oestrogen implants throughout the entire basal hypothalamus from preoptic area to mamillary bodies (Harris and Michael, 1964; Michael, 1965). When an oestrogen probe of more restricted surface areas was employed (67 $\mu m^2 \times 10^3$), following bilateral implants, heat was induced only if the implants ended in the anterior hypothalamus (Sawyer, 1963). In the ewe oestrogen implants in the anterior hypothalamus but not the posterior hypothalamus resulted in sexual heat (Signoret, 1970; Domanski et al., 1972a). In contrast, the most oestrogen-sensitive site in the rabbit is located in the posterior hypothalamus in the ventromedial premamillary region (Palka and Sawyer, 1966). In none of the studies was latency from hormone implantation to onset of sexual heat less than 24 h. Thus, direct application of hormones to the oestrogen-sensitive neural structures does not decrease the latency to response established by systemic injection of hormone.

In many species induction of heat is greatly facilitated by the addition of progesterone to the oestrogen-primed animal. Thus, exploration of the oestrogen-sensitive substrate can also be carried out by employing localized application of oestrogen to neural structures followed at various intervals by systemic injection of progesterone. In the adult rat bearing neural implants of oestrogen for 72 h the addition of systemic progesterone results in sexual heat in animals with oestrogen implants throughout the basal medial hypothalamus from preoptic to mamillary bodies when the surface area of oestrogen implant is 31 $\mu m^2 \times 10^3$ (Lisk and Barfield, 1975). However, if the oestrogen surface area is 17 $\mu m^2 \times 10^3$ the synergistic effects were not found. In the hamster, neither subcutaneous (Ciaccio and Lisk, 1973/74) nor brain implantation of oestrogen results in sexual heat. However, when hamsters bearing oestrogen implants of surface area 71 $\mu m^2 \times 10^3$ within the dorsal anterior hypothalamic area are given a subcutaneous injection of progesterone (200 μg) sexual heat occurs within 2–3 h of the progesterone injection. When bilateral implantation of oestrogen probes were made (31 $\mu m^2 \times 10^3$) laterally on both sides of the

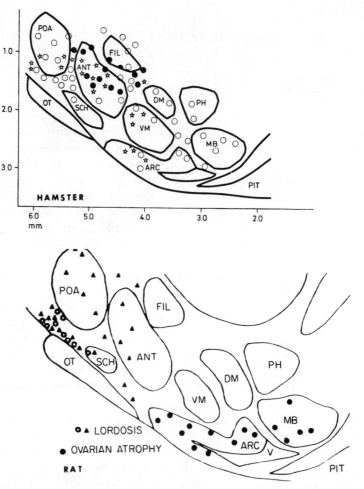

Fig. 9. Oestrogen-sensitive sites for sexual heat in rat and hamster. Left-hand side shows distribution of oestrogen-sensitive sites for hamster. ● 23G (450 μm diameter) sexual heat; ○23G no sexual heat; ✶ 27G (250 μm diameter) no sexual heat. Heat was shown only following systemic injection of progesterone. Rat, ▲ 27G (250 μm diameter) and ○ 30G (150 μm diameter) oestradiol implants which resulted in sexual heat without addition of progesterone; ● 27G implants which blocked the ovarian cycle. Right-hand side shows distribution of oestrogen-sensitive sites in three classes of rats, females ovariectomized as adults (top), females ovariectomized on the day of birth (middle), and males orchidectomized on the day of birth (bottom). Animals were tested for sexual heat at 72 h (E72) or 264 h (E264) after brain implantation of oestrogen. The animals were also tested at 5.5 h after addition of progesterone (E72 P5.5; E264 P5.5). The symbols on each panel indicate the location of the oestrogen implant and the type of hormone treatment for which a response occurred. For details concerning fraction responding, see Table 1. In all cases sexual heat was tested by mating the test animals with males. The hamster data are adapted from Ciaccio and Lisk (1974) *Neuroendocrinology*, **13**, 21. The rat data are adapted from Lisk (1962) *Am. J. Physiol.*, **203**, 493; Lisk and Barfield (1975) *Neuroendocrinology*, **19**, 28. AHA,

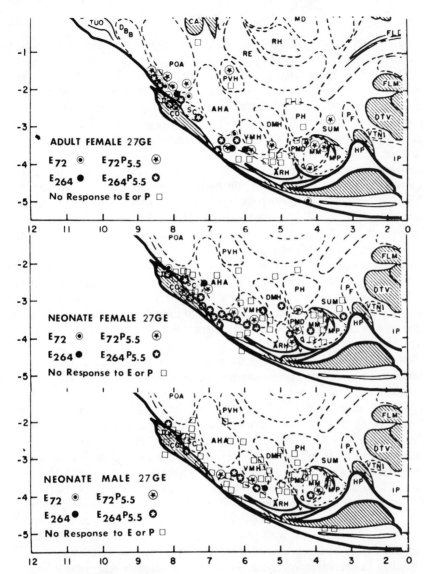

ANT anterior hypothalamic nucleus; ARC, ARH arcuate nucleus; CA anterior commissure; CO,OT optic chiasm; DBB diagonal band of Brocca; DM, DMH dorsomedial nucleus; DTV decussation of ventral tegmentum; FIL, PVH paraventricular (filiform) nucleus; FLD fasciculus of longitudinal dorsalis; FLM fasciculus of longitudinal medialis; HP habenular-inter penducular tract; IP interpenduncular nucleus; MB mamillary bodies; MD mediodorsal thalamic nucleus; MM medial mamillary nucleus; MP posterior mamillary nucleus; PF parafasicular thalamic nucleus; PH posterior hypothalamic nucleus; PIT pituitary; PMD dorsal premamillary nucleus; POA preoptic area; RE reunions thalamic nucleus; RH rhomboideus thalamic nucleus; SCH suprachiasmatic nucleus; SUM supramamillary area; TUO olfactory tubericle; VM, VMH ventromedial hypothalamic nucleus; VTN ventral tegmental nucleus neural region in which the hormone resulted in onset of sexual heat, all the animals failed to show sexual heat.

The oestrogen-sensitive neural sites for rat and hamster are shown in Fig. 9. For both species the responses of the animals are measured in relation to oestrogen alone and measured again following systemic treatment with progesterone. The sexual heat response to oestrogen alone occurs only in the rat. The oestrogen-sensitive substrate occupies a more compact area in the hamster brain than in the rat brain, however, in the hamster brain a larger surface area must be exposed to oestrogen than is necessary in the rat brain before progesterone synergism is effective for facilitation of heat. This apparent difference in the direct sensitivity of the neural substrate to oestrogen in the hamster correlates with the observation that induction of sexual heat via systemic injection of hormones requires a larger dosage of oestrogen in the hamster as compared to the rat (Feder et al., 1974; Powers and Valenstein, 1972).

The guinea pig has an oestrogen-sensitive neural substrate of similar anatomical localization to that seen in the rat. Bilateral oestrogen-bearing tubes of 31 $\mu m^2 \times 10^3$ surface area facilitated heat following systemic injection of progesterone when the oestrogen tubes were located in the basal medial hypothalamus between preoptic area and mamillary bodies (Morin and Feder, 1974a).

Sheep show a reversal of the usual oestrogen-progesterone synergism for induction of heat. Prior progesterone injection in the sheep is required before oestrogen can induce sexual heat or following progesterone treatment a lower dosage of oestrogen is effective (Robinson, 1955). When progesterone (5 mg/day for 5 days) was given to sheep with neural implants of oestrogen (Signoret, 1970) within 48 h of the termination of progesterone treatment all sheep came into heat regardless of the location of oestrogen implant in the brain. Sheep bearing oestrogen implants in the anterior hypothalamus showed no heat as long as progesterone injections were given (Domanski et al., 1972b). However, heat occurred within 48 h of the end of progesterone injections and while the animals which did not receive progesterone showed heat only for 24–30 h, in those treated with progesterone the sexual response was easier to elicit and sexual heat was extended to three to six days in duration.

Studies in the rat employing ³H-labelled oestrogen and autoradiography to detect hormone retention by neurons has demonstrated a system of oestrogen-retaining neurons extending from the septum throughout the hypothalamus with some labelling in the amygdala and brainstem (Pfaff, 1968; Stumpf, 1970; Pfaff and Keiner, 1972). In the rat oestrogen has been implanted into the hypothalamic, amygdala, and brainstem portion of this system. Lordosis responses were observed after oestrogen implants only when localized to the preoptic and anterior hypothalamus. Following systemic injection of progesterone heat was also seen in animals with oestrogen implants throughout the medial basal hypothalamus to the mamillary region and, in addition, the amygdala (Lisk and Barfield, 1975). Few responses were found following oestrogen implantation in the reticular formation in rat (Lisk and Barfield, 1975). Thus, not all oestrogen-retaining neurons are related to systems mediating sexual heat. Implantation of oestrogen into the arcuate nucleus blocks the ovulatory cycle in the intact rat (Lisk, 1960). Implantation of oestrogen into arcuate neurons is without effect on sexual heat in the ovariectomized rat while implantations both anterior to and posterior to this nucleus are effective for induction of heat. Thus, separate oestrogen-sensitive systems can be described both anatomically and functionally by use of implantation techniques which allow one to follow the responses of the animal and determine the functional significance of the hormone-retaining neurons.

The oestrogen-sensitivity of the neural system which regulates heat has been examined for the rat (Table 1) by studying the response of three classes of animals to oestrogen induced heat and oestrogen plus progesterone induced heat (Lisk and Barfield, 1975). These are adult females ovariectomized for 11 days, adult females ovariectomized on the day of birth, and adult males orchidectomized on the day of birth. The fraction of animals responding to males by showing lordosis when mounted was examined following short term (72 h) and long term (264 h) oestrogen implantation of either 17 or 31 $\mu m^2 \times 10^3$ surface area into various brain structures. Analysis according to implant location (Table 1) showed a significantly larger fraction responded to oestrogen along only when the oestrogen implant had a surface area of 31 $\mu m^2 \times 10^3$ and was localized in the preoptic-anterior hypothalamic region of animals ovariectomized as adults. When responses were measured 5.5 h after a systemic injection of progesterone a significant increase in the fraction responding occurred for 72 h of oestrogen priming for implantations in the posterior hypothalamus of animals ovariectomized as adults. Following 264 h of oestrogen priming with a surface area of 31 $\mu m^2 \times 10^3$ plus addition of progesterone, a significant increase in the fraction of animals responding was observed for the amygdala group of animals ovariectomized as adults and for preoptic-anterior hypothalamus and medial hypothalamus of neonatally ovariectomized females. When total oestrogen–progesterone responses were measured the neonatally ovariectomized females also showed a significant effect for the 17 $\mu m^2 \times 10^3$ surface area implants in the medial hypothalamus. Neonatally gonadectomized males showed no oestrogen–progesterone synergistic effects for any brain regions examined. Thus, females ovariectomized as adults showed a differential oestrogen sensitivity in the neural substrate while those ovariectomized as neonates required the addition of progesterone before a significant fraction of animals responded for any implant location. However, when oestrogen–progesterone responses are studied the only difference between animals ovariectomized as adults and those ovariectomized as neonates was the failure of the latter group to respond to implantation of oestrogen in the amygdala. The males showed no oestrogen–progesterone synergistic effects indicating that by birth in the rat the neuronal substrate in the male for steroid-induced sexual heat is already significantly less sensitive than

Table 1. Fraction of test population showing sexual heat (lordosis quotient > 30%) for rats ovariectomized as adults plus females and males gonadectomized on the day of birth. Oestrogen sensitivity within the brain (17 μm^2 or 31 $\mu m^2 \times 10^3$ surface area) and synergistic oestrogen–progesterone effects are examined. Data analysis by Fisher exact probability test or McNemar test for related samples. Adopted from Lisk and Barfield (1975) Neuroendocrinology, **19**, 28

Animal type	Oestrogen 72 h	Oestrogen 264 h	OE72 + P5.5 h	OE264 + P5.5 H	Totals Oestrogen	Totals Progesterone
Adult ♀ E₂ (31 μm^2)						
Poa-Ant. hyp.	6/15	1/15 (.031)	6/15	5/15	7/15	11/15 (.05)
Med. hyp.	2/20	2/20	4/20	4/20	4/20	8/20
Post hyp.	0/7	0/7	5/7 (.031)	0/7	0/7	5/7 (.031)
Reticular	1/20	0/20	0/20	2/20	1/20	2/20
Amygdala	0/19	0/19	1/19 (.008)	7/19	0/19	8/19 (.004)
Adult ♀ E₂ (17 μm^2)						
Poa-Ant. hyp.	0/50	0/50	1/50	3/50	0/50	4/50
Med. hyp.	0/17	0/17	2/17	0/17	0/17	2/17
Post hyp.	0/7	0/7	0/17	0/7	0/7	0/7
Amygdala	0/17	0/17	0/17	0/17	0/17	0/17
Neonate ♀ E₂ (31 μ^2)						
Poa-Ant. hyp.	1/21	2/21	1/21 (.031)	7/21	3/21	8/21 (.031)
Med. hyp.	0/28	0/28	3/28 (.001)	11/28	0/28	14/28 (.001)
Post. hyp.	0/15	0/15	2/15	2/15	0/15	4/15
Reticular	0/20	0/20	0/20	3/20	0/20	3/20
Neonate ♀ E₂ (17 μm^2)						
Poa-Ant. hyp.	0/18	2/18	2/18	1/18	2/18	3/18
Med. hyp.	0/25	0/25	3/25	4/25	0/25	7/25 (.008)
Reticular	0/12	0/12	0/12	0/12	0/12	0/12
Neonate ♂ E₂ (31 μm^2)						
Poa-Ant. hyp.	0/21	1/21	2/21	3/21	1/21	5/21
Med. hyp.	0/31	1/31	2/31	3/31	1/31	5/31
Post. hyp.	0/10	0/10	1/10	1/10	0/10	2/10
Reticular	0/15	0/15	0/15	3/15	0/15	3/15
Neonate ♂ E₂ (17 μ^2)						
Poa-Ant. hyp.	0/11	0/11	1/11	1/11	0/11	2/11

the neuronal substrate in the female. This complements the studies (pp. 442–444) which indicate that perinatal androgen treatment can reduce the sensitivity of the female to the sexual heat inducing effects of oestrogen. Also the finding that oestrogen alone was ineffective for inducing heat in females ovariectomized on the day of birth agrees with the study by Lisk and Suydam (1967) suggesting that progesterone is required to achieve full oestrogen sensitivity (see p. 442) in such animals.

Since in all the preceding experiments a localized source of oestrogen was employed, it is possible that the oestrogen–progesterone synergism is occurring at the same set of neurons. Localization of the progesterone-sensitive system for regulation of sexual heat has been explored by using systemic injection of oestrogen followed by localized placement of crystalline progesterone.

Progesterone-sensitive Sites

In the rat Ross et al. (1971) reported that progesterone implanted in to the medial reticular formation of animals primed with 2 μg of OB for three days facilitated lordosis in 15 min while similar implants were not effective in the preoptic area. Progesterone facilitation in the oestrogen-primed guinea pig has been reported for the ventromedial-arcuatepremaillary region (Morin and Feder, 1974b). Progesterone is observed to have a biphasic effect on sexual receptivity in the oestrogen-primed animal (p. 433), for the first 24 h following progesterone injection sexual heat is facilitated but then in the continued presence of progesterone, further expression of sexual heat is inhibited. In the rat this biphasic effect of progesterone on sexual heat was expressed regardless of the locus of oestrogen implant in the brain (Lisk, 1970; Lisk and Barfield, 1975). In their studies on the rabbit, progesterone inhibition of sexual heat could not be demonstrated when oestrogen was implanted at the most sensitive part of the neural substrate (Palka and Sawyer, 1966). These workers also determined the threshold dose of oestrogen necessary to bring individual rabbits into heat. Following bilateral implantation of progesterone into the neural oestrogen-sensitive sites, only 20 to 30% of the females showed a partial elevation of the threshold dose of oestrogen required to induce sexual heat. In the guinea pig an inhibitory site for progesterone was found in an area extending from the midreticular formation to the midsubstantia nigra. When oestrogen-primed animals had bilateral implants of progesterone in this region a systemic injection of progesterone 48 h later resulted in only 41% showing sexual heat and this was abbreviated in duration in comparison to the controls (Morin and Feder, 1974c).

The neuronal substrate for progesterone regulation of sexual heat has not been as well explored as that for oestrogen. With one exception (Sar and Stumpf, 1973), the autoradiographic technique has failed to demonstrate selective retention of progesterone by neurons. However, in the guinea pig, Sar and Stumpf (1973) reported that ovariectomized oestrogen-primed animals show concentration of radioactivity in neurons in the preoptic-anterior hypothalamus and the arcuate nucleus.

The amount of radioactivity retained by a tissue can also be quantified by grinding up the tissue and extracting the labelled material with suitable solvents. The extract can then be counted using liquid scintillation spectrometry. When this method is employed and regional areas of the brain examined the highest concentration of radioactivity was found for midbrain in rat, hamster, guinea pig, and mouse (Wade and Feder, 1972b; Wade et al., 1973; Luttge et al., 1974). If the animals are pretreated with unlabelled hormone prior to the injection of ^{3}H-progesterone no difference in binding was noted for guinea pig (Wade and Feder, 1972b) or mouse (Luttge et al., 1974). This is in marked contrast with the oestrogen-retaining system where pretreatment with unlabelled hormone always results in a significant decrease in binding of the labelled steroid. Thus, the progesterone system has the characteristics of a non-specific system, i.e., no saturation by prior treatment with unlabelled hormone. Also, the level of differential in binding among various areas of the brain varies only by about 2 times and concentration is only two fold above blood, thus the amount bound is also very low in relation to the oestrogen system.

Cellular Mechanisms of Hormone Action

Neural binding of oestrogen or progesterone as an initial step in the mechanism of action for the hormonal regulation of sexual heat has been reviewed by Lisk et al. (1972a, 1972b). Recent reviews on the biochemistry of receptor systems and actions of sex hormones provide detailed information on nuclear uptake of oestrogens and progesterone in a variety of target tissues and the regulation of cytosol to nuclear uptake and binding (Williams-Ashman and Reddi, 1971; Jensen and DeSombre, 1973; O'Malley and Means, 1974). It is not possible to discuss this vast literature here. It is clear that for the anatomical loci at which implantation of oestrogen facilitates lordosis one can show by autoradiographic techniques the existence of populations of oestrogen-binding neurons. Furthermore, the system is specific for oestrogen since pretreatment with testosterone, progesterone or adrenal corticoid hormones does not block the binding of oestradiol. Only prior treatment with oestradiol will inhibit binding of a subsequent injection of radiolabelled oestradiol. Thus, the system is specific and of limited capacity. Similar statements cannot be made about the progesterone system as noted previously.

Is there a relationship between the target tissue's ability to bind hormone and the ability of sex steroids to facilitate sexual heat? A model is available to examine this hypothesis since animals exposed to hormones perinatally (pp. 442–444) give reduced responses or fail to show heat when injected as adults with oestrogen and progesterone. Although there are reports suggesting no change in amount of oestrogen found in neural tissue from animals treated perinatally with androgen, most recent reports indicate a decrease in amount of oestrogen bound by neonatally hormone-treated animals for the anterior hypothalamus, a region essential to oestrogen facilitated sexual heat. This finding occurs whether total tissue binding of oestrogen is measured (Maurer and Woolley, 1971, 1975) or cytosol and nuclear oestrogen binding are measured separately (Vertes et al., 1974; Maurer and Woolley, 1974). In studies from my laboratory, reduced oestrogen binding was found following either perinatal oestrogen or androgen treatment (McGuire and Lisk, 1969).

When oestrogen binding to target tissues in the rat was sampled at multiple points following injection of a tracer dose of ^{3}H-oestrogen the latency to maximum binding increased with time after ovariectomy (McGuire and Lisk, 1968). This relationship between binding and time after ovariectomy suggested that oestrogen might act at the target cell level to regulate its own binding. This concept was examined further in the hamster by ovariectomizing a group of animals on the morning of oestrus and determining tissue binding of a tracer dose of ^{3}H-oestradiol at 6 h, 1, 3, and 14 days following ovariectomy (Fig. 10, top panels). For the oestrogen target-tissues (arcuate, anterior hypothalamus, pituitary, and uterus) significantly increased oestrogen binding was noted on days 1 and 3 compared to 6 h and 14 day ovariectomized animals, while no change in binding occurred for the non-target tissues. Another group of hamsters ovariectomized on the morning of oestrus was rested 14 days then given a physiological dose of unlabelled oestrogen (200 μm diameter tubing filled with oestradiol-17β and implanted subcutaneously) and at 3, 6, 48, or 72 h after adding the unlabelled oestrogen a similar tracer dose of ^{3}H-oestrogen to that given the previous group of hamsters was injected (2μCi, 2, 4, 6, 7- ^{3}H-oestradiol-17β per 100 g body weight). For the arcuate, anterior-hypothalamus a significant increase in ^{3}H-oestrogen binding was found for all test times (Fig. 10, bottompanels). Significant increases in ^{3}H-oestrogen binding also occurred for the other target tissues while little or no changes occurred in the non-target tissues. Thus, in both rat and hamster we found that hormone binding in the target tissues shows a dynamic pattern with the amount of binding being related to the immediately preceding hormonal exposure of the tissue.

When this relationship was examined in female rats treated perinatally with androgen or oestrogen, a priming dose of unlabelled oestrogen 6 to 72 h in duration always resulted in less ^{3}H-oestrogen binding than that seen for rats not given perinatal hormone treatment (Fig. 11). Thus, the dynamic response of the normal animal, i.e., increased hormone binding as a result of oestrogen priming is absent in the perinatally oestrogen- or androgen-treated animals. When target tissues from these animals is incubated in vitro with ^{3}H-oestradiol significantly less radioactivity is retained in the nuclear fraction as measured per μg DNA (Fig. 12). From our studies and those by Vertes et al. (1974), it is reasonable to conclude that one reason for the reduced sensitivity or complete lack of response to hormone by perinatally hormone-treated animals is a reduction in hormone binding by target tissues from these animals. Thus,

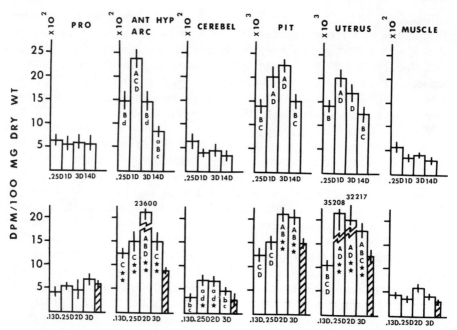

Fig. 10. Oestrogen retention by various tissues of the hamster (top panels) as a function of the time interval since ovariectomy; (botton panels) as a function of the interval of oestrogen priming. All animals were ovariectomized on the morning of day-4 of the cycle (oestrus) and at the interval in days indicated on the bar graphs were examined for ^{3}H-oestrogen retention. In the bottom panels 14 day ovariectomized animals (diagonal stripped bars) were given a physiological dose of oestrogen defined operationally as that treatment which would prime the system so that after 72 h exposure to oestrogen, addition of a pellet of progesterone would result in most animals becoming behaviourally receptive within 2 to 4 h. This was achieved by use of a piece of 22 gauge hypodermic tubing (450 μm lumen diameter) filled with crystalline oestradiol-17β. One end of the tubing was plugged with paraffin wax and the tube placed subcutaneously. Animals were injected intravenously with 2 μCi/100 g body weight (5.44 ng), 2, 4, 6, 7 ^{3}H-oestradiol, 100 Ci/mmol and autopsied 1 h later. For statistical evaluation of differences the four open bargraphs for each tissue are considered as ABCD or abcd. The significance of differences was determined by student's t-test with ABCD = 0.005 and abcd = 0.05. All bargraphs for a tissue containing A, a differ significantly from the first (A, a bargraph) for that issue etc. Comparisons with the 14-day ovariectomized controls (diagonally striped bars) ** = 0.005. Thin lines at top of bargraph indicate SEM. (Ciaccio and Lisk unpubl.)

hormone retention is probably an important initial step in the mechanism of events by which sexual heat is activated.

Animals brought into heat by oestrogen alone remain in heat indefinitely (pp. 432–433) as long as oestrogen continues to be present. However, when heat is induced as a result of sequential treatment with oestrogen followed by progesterone the heat is of finite duration regardless of the continued availability of oestrogen and progesterone to the animal (pp. 434–441). One possible reason for the programming of the length of heat by progesterone

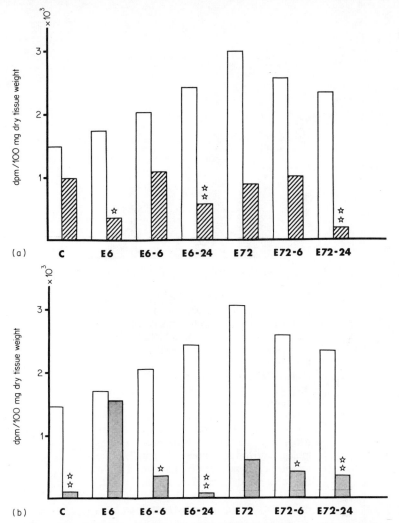

Fig. 11. Total tissue retention of ^{3}H-labelled hormone in the preoptic-anterior hypothalamic area of the rat. (Fig. 11a) normal females (open bars) *versus* females given an injection of 200 μg oestradiol benzoate (cross-hatched bars) on the day of birth and (Fig. 11b) females given an injection of 500 μg testosterone propionate (stipped bars) on the day of birth. Animals about 100 days old were examined 7 days after ovariectomy and in response to oestrogen priming with a subcutaneous oestrogen source of 31 μm^2 × 10^3 surface area which was present for the time in hours indicated (e.g., E6 = 6 h of oestrogen priming). A minus sign preceding a number indicates the oestrogen source was removed that number of hours prior to pulsing the animals with ^{3}H-labelled steroid. For all groups ^{3}H-oestradiol was injected intra-peritoneally at the end of the oestrogen priming period (2 μCi 2, 4, 6, 7-^{3}H-oestradiol 17-β, 100 Ci/m mol, per 100 g body weight) and ^{3}H activity was measured 2 h later. Activity is expressed as dpm/100 mg dry weight of tissue ×10^3 and indicates group means (N = 10). The neonatally steroid-treated animals show less retention; a single asterisk indicates a significant difference at 0.05, a double asterisk at 0.01 by Student's t-test. (From Lisk and Reuter, unpubl.)

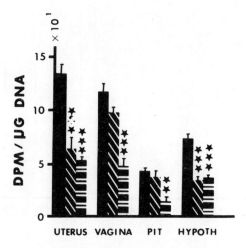

Fig. 12. Steroid retention in purified nuclei from the target tissues of normal *versus* neonatally steroid-injected rats (as in Fig. 11). Adult animals were ovariectomized for one week and the tissue removed, homogenized and incubated for 1 h at 37 °C in 1×10^{-8} molar ^{3}H-oestradiol. A purified nuclear preparation was obtained and radioactivity measured. Activity is expressed as dpm/µg DNA; from Lisk and Reuter, unpublished. Black bar—control females; diagonal stripes—neonatally oestradiol benzoate-treated females; horizontal stripes—neonatally testosterone propionate-treated females. Thin bar indicates standard error of mean. Two stars = 0.01; three stars = 0.001 significant difference in comparison to controls by Mann-Whitney U

is the observation by Ciaccio and Lisk (1972) which shows that the oestrogen-sensitive target tissues on being primed with oestrogen and exposed to progesterone for as little as 4 h show a decreased ability to retain oestrogen (Fig. 13). When adult female rats ovariectomized for 14 days (Fig. 13) are given a priming dose of oestrogen (B) a significant increase in oestrogen binding is found. However, if progesterone is present for the last 4 h of the oestrogen-priming period (C) significantly less of a tracer dose of ^{3}H-oestradiol is bound by the tissue. Systemic injection of 15 µg of oestradiol-17β was given to saturate the specific oestrogen retention system. The low level of ^{3}H-oestrogen binding which still occurs (D) results from the non-specific binding component which is unsaturable. Thus, the binding in excess of the level shown in D probably represents the amount of specific receptor for oestrogen in the system. All neural tissue does not respond similarly. Only a low level of binding occurs in the amy-

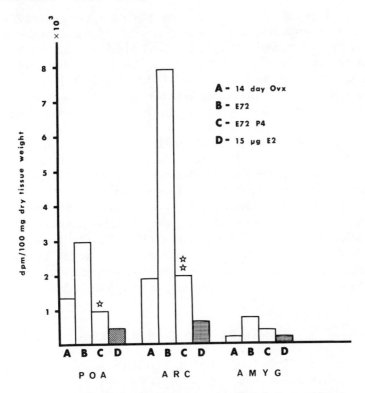

Fig. 13. Effect of pretreatment with oestradiol alone or with oestradiol plus progesterone on total tissue retention of a tracer dose of
^{3}H-oestradiol. Tissues examined were preoptic-anterior hypothalamus (POA), medial hypothalamus (ARC), and amygdala
(AMYG). Oestrogen treatment was achieved by a s.c. placement of a
piece of 22G hypodermic tubing lumen diameter 450 μm. The tubing
was filled with crystalline hormone with one end exposed to the
tissues, the opposite end plugged with paraffin wax. Progesterone
treatment was achieved by placing a 50 mg pellet of crystalline
hormone s.c. A tracer dose of ^{3}H-oestrogen was injected intravenously
(2 μCi/100 g body weight 5.44 ng) 2, 4, 6, 7 ^{3}H-oestradiol, 100 Ci/
mmole and animals were autopsied 2 h later. After 72 h (E72) of
oestrogen priming the addition of progesterone for as little as 4 h
(P4) resulted in a significant reduction in ^{3}H-oestrogen retention
with the level of retention after progesterone treatment being similar
to that found in the 14 day ovariectomized animals. (From Lisk and
Reuter, unpubl.)

gdala and the oestrogen or progesterone treatments have very little effect on
the amount of binding. This series of observations suggests that in oestrogen-
sensitive cells the addition of progesterone inhibits oestrogen binding. If oestrogen binding is required for synthesis of some product which is required for
expression of sexual heat, as soon as the oestrogen-dependent product has been

utilized, heat should terminate. If no new product can be synthesized in the presence of progesterone, heat should be blocked as long as progesterone remains in the system. Only after progesterone withdrawal can a new cycle of oestrogen-mediated product synthesis occur. Progesterone has a dual role in many species. It is required for initiation of heat which occurs only following oestrogen priming; if progesterone action requires utilization of a product synthesized during the oestrogen-priming period the rate of utilization of this product could determine the length of heat. Thus, progesterone interacting with the oestrogen binding system could, through effects on oestrogen-dependent product synthesis, provide a direct means for programming the length of sexual heat. What this hypothetical product is remains unknown. A minimum of 24 h of oestrogen priming is required before progesterone can facilitate sexual heat. On addition of progesterone another 2 to 4 h elapses before sexual heat is expressed. Thus, long intervals of time are available for product synthesis and many interactions at the molecular level could occur. One probable class of products which are affected by oestrogen and progesterone are the neurotransmitters and it may be that oestrogen and progesterone regulate heat through changes in availability of a variety of transmitter substances.

SUMMARY AND CONCLUSIONS

Sexual heat in mammals is restricted, with the possible exception of some primates, to a period of no more than 15% of the total cycle length and occurs about the time of ovulation. Two steroids made in the ovaries, oestrogen and progesterone, are necessary to sexual heat. The role of these steroids in regulation of the heat period differs among the species. Oestrogen, if given in high enough dosage, can result in the occurrence of heat in some species, however, few measurements of oestrogen levels in the systemic circulation have been made during various stages of the oestrous cycle. Therefore, we do not know whether sexual heat can result only from pharmacological levels of circulating oestrogen resulting from exogenous hormone injection. It is necessary to determine whether sexual heat is facilitated with blood levels of oestrogen in the physiological range resulting from the animal's endogenous secretion or whether at physiological levels of oestrogen one must add progesterone to facilitate sexual heat.

When heat can be initiated by oestrogen alone, the duration of heat appears to be indefinite, continuing for as long as oestrogen is present. However, when progesterone is used to initiate heat, although progesterone acts only in the oestrogen-primed animal, the heat is always of limited duration, often less than 24 h. If oestrogen and progesterone injections are continued, no further display of heat occurs until progesterone is removed. Then, following a period in which oestrogen alone is present the addition of progesterone will again initiate a heat period of limited duration. For one species, the ewe, this relationship between oestrogen and progesterone is reversed. The ewe requires prior treatment with progesterone before an injection of oestrogen is effective for initiation of heat. Studies with heifers, pigs, and goats show that heat occurs within 24 to 48 h after progesterone has reached its low point for the cycle. Thus, following progesterone treatment there may be an increased sensitivity to oestrogen in some species. Progesterone, therefore, appears to occupy a key regulatory role in which at least three separate actions have been identified: (1) sensitization of the system to oestrogen so that treatment with lower doses of oestrogen will be effective for initiation of heat, (2) initiation of heat in the oestrogen-primed animal, (3) termination of heat.

Anatomical localization of the neural substrate on which oestrogen acts to facilitate sexual heat has been well mapped for several species. The oestrogen-sensitive cells are localized mostly within the preoptic-hypothalamic continuum with the exact localization varying from species to species. Subcellular studies on the oestrogen-sensitive cells have been possible using ^{3}H-oestrogen, and it is clear that when oestrogen binding to the nuclear fraction of the cell is decreased oestrogen-induced effects are not expressed. Similar studies for elucidation of the progesterone-sensitive substrate have not had as great a success. ^{3}H-progesterone does not reveal specific localizations in the brain. If local implantation of oestrogen is used and heat is facilitated by systemic injection of progesterone, it might be concluded that since the oestrogen effect is local progesterone must be acting in the same area.

The mechanism of hormone action for the regulation of sexual heat remains largely unknown. There is compelling evidence that oestrogen acts at the nuclear level on cells scattered throughout the hypothalamus. Since oestrogen binding and sequestration in the nucleus reaches peak levels within an hour and heat is not expressed until 24 h after the start of oestrogen treatment, many biochemical events could occur prior to the overt behaviour being expressed. As shown in this chapter, progesterone regulates heat by affecting at least three separate events. No specific receptor for progesterone has been detected in the nervous system. Local implantations of hormone have not proven a highly successful technique for mapping the anatomical localization of the neural substrate on which progesterone acts. There is a suggestion that progesterone may exert some of its effects through modulation of the amount of oestrogen binding. Thus, one key to the multiple actions of progesterone in regulation of sexual heat may be in determining the relationships between progesterone treatments and the amount of oestrogen binding which occurs in the oestrogen-sensitive neural substrate.

ACKNOWLEDGEMENT

Unpublished results from the author's laboratory were supported by grants from the National Science Foundation.

REFERENCES

Arai, Y. and Gorski, R. A. (1968) Effect of anti-estrogen on steroid induced sexual receptivity in ovariectomized rats, *Physiol. Behav.*, **3**, 351–3.

Aron, C. and Asch, G. (1963) Action exercée par la testostérone ou cours même du cycle oestral sur le comportement sexuel et sur l'activité ovarienne de la ratte, *Comp. Rend. Soc. Biol.*, **157**, 645–48.

Ball, J. (1937) A test for measuring sexual excitability in the female rat, *Comp. Psychol. Monograph*, **14**, 1–37.

Baranczuk, R. and Greenwald, G. S. (1973) Peripheral levels of estrogen in the cyclic hamster, *Endocrinology*, **92**, 805–12.

Barfield, M. A. and Lisk, R. D. (1970) Advancement of behavioral estrus by subcutaneous injection of progesterone in the 4-day cyclic rat, *Endocrinology*, **87**, 1096–8.

Barfield, M. A. and Lisk, R. D. (1974) Relative contributions of ovarian and adrenal progesterone to the timing of heat in the 4-day cyclic rat, *Endocrinology*, **92**, 571–5.

Barraclough, C. A. and Gorki, R. A. (1962) Studies on mating behavior in the androgen-sterilized female rat in relation to the hypothalamic regulation of sexual behaviour, *J. Endocrinol.*, **25**, 175–82.

Beach, F. A. (1942) Male and female mating behavior in prepuberally castrated female rats treated with androgens, *Endocrinology*, **31**, 673–8.

Beach, F. A. (1944) Effects of injury to the cerebral cortex upon sexually-receptive behavior in the female rat. *Psychosomat. Med.*, **6**, 40–55.

Beach, F. A. and Orndoff, R. K. (1974) Variation in the responsiveness of female rats to ovarian hormones as a function of preceding hormonal deprivation, *Horm. Behav.*, **5**, 201–5.

Beyer, C., Cruz, M. L., and Rivaud, N. (1969) Persistence of sexual behavior in ovariectomized-adrenalectomized rabbits treated with cortisol, *Endocrinology*, **85**, 790–3.

Beyer, C., McDonald, P., and Vidal, N. (1970) Failure of 5a-dihydrotestosterone to elicit estrous behavior in the ovariectomized rabbit, *Endocrinology*, **86**, 939–41.

Beyer, C., Morali, G., and Vargas, R. (1971) Effect of diverse estrogens on estrous behavior and genital tract development in ovariectomized rats, *Horm. Behav.*, **2**: 273–7.

Blandau, R. J., Boling, J. L., and Young, W. C. (1941) The length of heat in the albino rat as determined by the copulatory response, *Anat. Rec.*, **79**, 453–63.

Blandau, R. J., and Money, W. L. (1943) The attainment of sexual maturity in the female albino rat as determined by the copulatory response, *Anat. Rec.*, **86**, 197–215.

Bosley, C. G. and Leavitt, W. W. (1972) Dependence of preovulatory progesterone on critical period in the cyclic hamster, *Am. J. Physiol.*, **222**, 129–33.

Carrick, M. J. and Shelton, J. N. (1969) Oestrogen-progesterone relationship in the induction of estrus in spayed heifers, *J. Endocrinol.*, **45**, 99–109.

Carter, C. S. (1972) Postcopulatory sexual receptivity in the female hamster: the role of the ovary and adrenal, *Horm. Behav.*, **3**, 261–5.

Carter, C. S. and Schein, M. W. (1971) Sexual receptivity and exhaustion in the female golden hamster, *Horm. Behav.*, **2**, 191–200.

Ciaccio, L. A. (1970) Estrogen and progesterone: factors involved in the regulation of estrous behavior in the female hamster *(Mesocricetus auratus)*, *Ph.D. Thesis*, Princeton University.

Ciaccio, L. A. and Lisk, R. D. (1971a) The hormonal control of cyclic estrus in the female hamster, *Am. J. Physiol.*, **221**, 936–42.

Ciaccio, L. A. and Lisk, R. D. (1971b) Progesterone: role in regulating the period of sexual receptivity in the female hamster, *J. Endocrinol.*, **50**, 201–7.

Ciaccio, L. A. and Lisk, R. D. (1971c) Estrogens: effects on development and activation of neural systems mediating receptivity. In: *Influence of Hormones on the Nervous System*,

Proc. Int. Soc. Psychoneuroendocrinology, Brooklyn, Basel Karger Press, pp. 441–50.

Ciaccio, L. A. and Lisk, R. D. (1972) Effect of hormone priming on retention of ³H-oestradiol by males and females, *Nature New Biol.*, **236**, 82–3.

Ciaccio, L. A. and Lisk, R. D. (1973/74) Central control of estrous behavior in the female golden hamster, *Neuroendocrinology*, **13**, 21–8.

Clemens, L. G., Hiroi, M., and Gorski, R. A. (1969) Induction and facilitation of female mating behavior in rats treated neonatally with low doses of testosterone propionate, *Endocrinology*, **84**, 1430–8.

Cox, R. I., Mattner, P. E., and Thorburn, G. D. (1971) Changes in ovarian secretion of oestradiol-17β around oestrus in the sheep. *J. Endocrinol.*, **49**, 345–6.

Damassa, D. and Davidson, J. M. (1973) Effects of ovariectomy and constant light on responsiveness to estrogen in the rat, *Horm. Behav.*, **4**, 269–79.

Davidson, J. M. (1969) Effects of estrogen on sexual behavior of male rats, *Endocrinology*, **84**, 1365–72.

Dempsey, E. W., Hertz, R., and Young, W. C. (1936) The experimental induction of oestrus (sexual receptivity) in the normal and ovariectomized guinea pig, *Am. J. Physiol.*, **116**, 201–9.

Diamond, M. and Yanagimachi, R. (1970) Reproductive development in the female golden hamster in relation to spontaneous estrus, *Biol. Reprod.*, **2**, 223–9.

Domanski, E., Prezekop, F., and Skubiszewski. B. (1972a) The role of the medial basal hypothalamus in the control of ovulation and sexual behavior in sheep, *Acta Neurobiol Exp.*, **32**, 753–62.

Domanski, E., Prezekop, F., and Skubiszewski, B. (1972b) Interaction of progesterone and estrogens on the hypothalamic center controlling estrous behavior in sheep, *Acta Neurobiol. Exp.*, **32**, 763–6.

Eaton, G. (1970) Effect of a single prepubertal injection of testosterone propionate on adult bisexual behavior of male hamsters castrated at birth, *Endocrinology*, **87**, 934–40.

Eayers, J. T. and Glass, A. (1962) The ovary and behavior. In: *The Ovary* Vol II, S. Zuckerman (ed.), Academic Press, New York, pp. 381–433.

Edwards, D. A. and Thompson, M. L. (1970) Neonatal androgenization and estrogenization and the hormonal induction of sexual receptivity in rats, *Physiol. Behav.*, **5**, 1115–9.

Everitt, B. J. and Herbert, J. (1971) The effects of dexamethasone and androgens on sexual receptivity of female rhesus monkeys, *J. Endocrinol.*, **51**, 575–88.

Everitt, J. W. (1961) The mammalian female reproductive cycle and its controlling mechanisms. In: *Sex and Internal Secretions* Vol I, W. C. Young (ed.), The Williams and Wilkins Co., Baltimore, pp. 495–555.

Feder, H. H. and Morin, L. P. (1974) Suppression of lordosis in guinea pigs by ethamoxytriphetol (MER-25) given at long intervals (34–46 h) after estradiol benzoate treatment, *Horm. Behav.*, **5**, 63–71.

Feder, H. H., Resko, J. A., and Goy, R. W. (1968a) Progesterone levels in the arterial plasma of pre-ovulatory and ovariectomized rats, *J. Endocrinol.*, **41**, 563–9.

Feder, H. H., Resko, J. A., and Goy, R. W. (1968b) Progesterone concentrations in the arterial plasma of guinea pigs during the oestrous cycle, *J. Endocrinol.*, **40**, 505–13.

Feder, H. H., Siegel, H., and Wade, G. N. (1974) Uptake of 6, 7-³H-estradiol-17β in ovariectomized rats, guinea pigs, and hamsters: correlation with species differences in behavioral responsiveness to estradiol, *Brain Res.*, **71**, 93–103.

Feder, H. H. and Whalen, R. E. (1965) Feminine behavior in neonatally castrated and estrogen-treated male rats, *Science*, **147**, 306–7.

Fletcher, I. C. and Lindsay, D. R. (1971) Effect of oestrogen on oestrous behaviour and its variation with season in the ewe, *J. Endocrinol.*, **50**, 685–96.

Fraser, F. A. (1968) *Reproductive Behaviour in Ungulates*, Academic Press, London.

Gerall, A. A. (1967) Effects of early postnatal androgen and estrogen injections on the estrous activity cycles and mating behavior in rats, *Anat. Rec.*, **157**, 97–104.

Gerall, A. A. and Dunlap, J. L. (1973) The Effect of experience and hormones on the initial receptivity in female and rats, Physiol. Behav., **10**, 851–4.

Gerall, A. A., Dunlap, J. L., and Hendricks, S. E. (1972a) Effect of ovarian secretions on female behavioral potentiality in the rat, *J. Comp. Physiol. Psychol.*, **82**, 449–65.

Gerall, A. A., Stone, L. S., and Hitt, J. C. (1972b) Neonatal androgen depresses female responsiveness to estrogen, *Physiol. Behav.*, **8**, 17–20.

Goldfoot, D. A. and Goy, R. W. (1970) Abbreviation of behavioral estrus by coital and vagino-cervical stimulation. *J. Comp. Physiol. Psychol.*, **72**, 426–34.

Gottlieb, H., Gerall, A. A., and Thiel, A. (1974) Receptivity in female hamsters following neonatal testosterone, testosterone propionate, and MER-25. *Physiol. Behav.*, **12**, 61–8.

Goy, R. W., Phoenix, C. H., and Young, W. C. (1966) Inhibitory action of the corpus luteum on the hormonal induction of estrous behavior in the guinea pig, *Gen. Comp. Endocrinol.*, **6**, 267–75.

Goy, R. W. and Young, W. C. (1957) Strain differences in the behavioral responses of female guinea pigs to α-estradiol benzoate and progesterone, *Behavior* **10**, 340–54.

Green, R., Luttge, W. G., and Whalen, R. E. (1970) Induction of receptivity in ovariectomized female rats by a single intravenous injection of estradiol-17β, *Physiol. Behav.*, **5**, 137–41.

Hardy, D. F. and DeBold, J. F. (1971a) The relationship between levels of exogenous hormones and the display of lordosis by the female rat, *Horm. Behav.*, **2**, 287–97.

Hardy, D. F. and DeBold, J. R. (1971b) Effects of mounts without intromission upon the behavior of female rats during the onset of estrogen induced heat, *Physiol. Behav.*, **7**, 643–5.

Harris, G. W. and Michael R. P. (1964) The activation of behavior by hypothalamic implants of oestrogen, *J. Physiol. London.*, **171**, 275–301.

Jensen, E. V. and DeSombre, E. R. (1973) Estrogen-receptor interaction, *Science*, **182**, 126–34.

Joslyn, W. D. and Feder, H. H. (1971) Facilitatory and inhibitory effects of supplementary estradiol benzoate given to ovariectomized, estrogen-primed guinea pigs, *Horm. Behav.*, **2**, 307–14.

Joslyn, W. D., Wallen, K., and Goy, R. W. (1971) Cyclic changes in sexual response to exogenous progesterone in female guinea pig, *Physiol. Behav.*, **7**, 915–7.

Kawashima, S. and Shinoda, A. (1968) Spontaneous activity of neonatally estrogenized female rats, *Endocrinol. Japon.*, **15**, 305–12.

Komisaruk, B. R. and Diakow, C. (1973) Lordosis reflex intensity in rats in relation to the estrous cycle, ovariectomy, estrogen administration and mating behavior, *Endocrinology*, **93**, 548–57.

Labhsetwar, A. P., Joshi, H. S., and Watson, D. (1973) Temporal relationships between estradiol, estrone, and progesterone secretion in the ovarian venous blood and LH in the peripheral plasma of cyclic hamster, *Biol. Reprod.*, **8**, 321–6.

Leavitt, W. W. and Blaha, G. C. (1970) Circulating progesterone levels in the golden hamster during the estrous cycle, pregnancy, and lactation, *Biol. Reprod.*, **3**, 353–61.

LeBoeuf, B. J. (1967) Interindividual associations in dogs, *Behaviour*, **29**, 268–95.

Lemon, M., Pelletier, J., Saumande, J., and Signoret, J. P. (1975) Peripheral plasma concentrations of progesterone, oestradiol-17β, and luteinizing hormone around oestrus in the cow, *J. Reprod. Fert.*, **42**, 137–40.

Levine, S. and Mullins Jr. R. F. (1964) Estrogen administered neonatally affects adult sexual behavior in male and female rats, *Science*, **144**, 185–7.

Lindsay, D. R. and Fletcher, I. C. (1972) Ram-seeking activity associated with oestrous behavior in ewes, *Anim. Behav.*, **20**, 452–6.

Lisk, R. D. (1960) Estrogen-sensitive centers in the hypothalamus of the rat, *J. Exp. Zool.*, **145**, 197–208.

Lisk, R. D. (1962) Diencephalic placement of estradiol and sexual receptivity in the female rat, *Am. J. Physiol.*, **203**, 493–6.

Lisk, R. D. (1969) Progesterone: biphasic effects on the lordosis response in adult or neonatally gonadectomized rats, *Neuroendocrinology*, **5**, 145–60.

Lisk, R. D. (1970) Mechanisms regulating sexual activity in mammals, *J. Sex Res.*, **6**, 220–8.

Lisk, R. D. (1973) Hormonal regulation of sexual behavior in polyestrus mammals common to the laboratory, *Handbook of Physiology-Endocrinology* II, Part I, American Physiological Society, Washington D. C., pp. 223–60.

Lisk, R. D. and Barfield, M. A. (1975) Progesterone facilitation of sexual receptivity in rats with neural implantation of estrogen, *Neuroendocrinology*, **19**, 28–35.

Lisk, R. D., Ciaccio, L. A., and Reuter, L. A. (1972a) Neural centers of estrogen and progesterone action in the regulation of reproduction. In: *Biology of Reproduction— Basic and Clinical Studies*, J. T. Velardo and B. A. Kasprow (eds.), III Pan American Congress of Anatomy New Orleans, pp. 71–87.

Lisk, R. D., Ciaccio, L. A., and Reuter, L. A. (1972b) Neural receptor mechanisms for estrogens and progesterone and the regulation of ovulation and sex-related behavior in mammals, *Gen. Comp. Endocrinol. Suppl.*, 3, 553–64.

Lisk, R. D., Reuter, L. A., and Raub, J. A. (1974) Effects of grouping on sexual receptivity in female hamsters, *J. Exp. Zool.*, **189**, 1–6.

Lisk, R. D. and Suydam, A. (1967) Sexual behavior patterns in the prepubertally castrated rat, *Anat. Rec.*, **157**, 181–90.

Lukaszewska, J. H. and Greenwald, G. S. (1970) Progesterone levels in the cyclic and pregnant hamster, *Endocrinology*, **86**, 1–9.

Luttge, W. G., Wallis, C. J., and Hall, N. R. (1974) Effects of pre- and post-treatment with unlabeled steroids on the *in vivo* uptake of [^{3}H] progestins in selected brain regions, uterus, and plasma of the female mouse, *Brain Res.*, **71**, 105–15.

Makepeace, A. W., Weinstein, G. L., and Friedman, J. M. (1937) The effect of progestin and progesterone on ovulation in the rabbit, *Am. J. Physiol.*, **119**, 512–6.

Mann, D. R. and Barraclough, C. A. (1973) Changes in peripheral plasma progesterone during the rat 4-day estrous cycle; an adrenal diurnal rhythm, *Proc. Soc. Exp. Biol. Med.*, **142**, 1226–9.

Marshall, F. H. A. and Hammond, J., Jr. (1945) Experimental control by hormone action of the estrous cycle in the ferret, *J. Endocrinol.*, **4**, 159–68.

Maurer, R. and Woolley, D. (1971) Distribution of ^{3}H-estradiol in clomiphene-treated and neonatally androgenized rats, *Endocrinology*, **88**, 1281–7.

Maurer, R. A. and Woolley, D. E. (1974) Demonstration of nuclear ^{3}H-estradiol binding in hypothalamus and amygdala of female, androgenized female, and male rats, *Neuroendocrinology*, **16**, 137–47.

Maurer, R. A. and Woolley, D. E. (1975) ^{3}H-estradiol distribution in female, androgenized female, and male rats at 100 and 200 days of age, *Endocrinology*, **96**, 755–65.

McGuire, J. L. and Lisk, R. D. (1968) Estrogen receptors in the intact rat, *Proc. Nat. Acad. Sci.*, **61**, 497–503.

McGuire, J. L. and Lisk, R. D. (1969) Oestrogen receptors in androgen or oestrogen sterilized female rats, *Nature*, **221**, 1068–9.

Meyerson, B. J. and Lindström L. H. (1973) Sexual motivation in the female rat, *Acta Physiol. Suppl.*, 389, 1–80.

Michael, R. P. (1965) Oestrogens in the central nervous system, *Brit. Med. Bull.*, **21**, 87–90.

Moore, N. W., Barrett, S., Brown, J. B., Schindler, I., Smith, M. A., and Smyth, B. (1969) Oestrogen and progesterone content of ovarian vein blood of the ewe during the oestrus

464   LISK

cycle, *J. Endocrinol.*, **44**, 55–62.

Moore, N. W. and Robinson, R. J. (1957) The behavioral and vaginal responses of the spayed ewe to oestrogen injected at various times relative to the injection of progesterone, *J. Endocrinol.*, **15**, 360–5.

Morin, L. P. and Feder, H. H. (1973) Multiple progesterone injections and the duration of estrus in ovariectomized guinea pigs, *Physiol. Behav.*, **11**, 861–5.

Morin, L. P. and Feder, H. H. (1974a) Intracranial estradiol implants and lordosis behavior of ovariectomized guinea pigs, *Brain Res.*, **70**, 95–102.

Morin, L. P. and Feder, H. H. (1974b) Hypothalamic progesterone implants and facilitation of lordosis behavior in estrogen-primed ovariectomized guinea pigs, *Brain Res.* **70**, 81–93.

Morin, L. P. and Feder, H. H. (1974c) Inhibition of lordosis behavior in ovariectomized guinea pigs by mesencephalic implants of progesterone, *Brain Res.*, **70**, 71–80.

Morrow, D. A. (1969) Estrous behavior and ovarian activity in prepuberal and post-puberal dairy heifers, *J. Dairy Sci.*, **52**, 224–7.

Mullins, R. F. Jr. and Levine, S. (1968) Hormonal determinants during infancy of adult sexual behavior in the female rat, *Physiol. Behav.*, **3**, 333–8.

Nadler, R. D. (1970) A biphasic influence of progesterone on sexual receptivity of spayed-female rats, *Physiol. Behav.*, **5**, 95–7.

Naftolin, F., Brown-Grant, K., and Corker, C. S. (1972) Plasma and pituitary luteinizing hormone and peripheral plasma oestradiol concentrations in the normal oestrous cycle of the rat and after experimental manipulation of the cycle, *J. Endocrinol.*, **53**, 17–30.

Napoli, A. M. and Gerall, A. A. (1970) Effect of estrogen and anti-estrogen on reproductive function in neonatally androgenized female rats, *Endocrinology*, **87**, 1330–7.

Nequin, L. G. and Schwartz, N. B. (1971) Adrenal participation in the timing of mating and LH release in the cyclic rat, *Endocrinology*, **88**, 325–31.

Noble, R. G. (1973) Facilitation of the lordosis response of the female hamster *(Mesocricetus auratus)*, *Physiol. Behav.*, **10**, 663–6.

O'Malley, B. W. and Means, R. (1974) Female steroid hormones and target cell nuclei, *Science*, **183**, 610–20.

Palka, Y. S. and Sawyer, C. H. (1966) The effects of hypothalamic implants of ovarian steroids on oestrous behavior in rabbits, *J. Physiol. London*, **185**, 251–69.

Paup, D. C., Coniglio, L. P., and Clemens, L. G. (1974) Hormonal determinants in the development of masculine and feminine behavior in the female hamster, *Behav. Biol.*, **10**, 353–63.

Peretz, E. (1968) Estrogen dose and the duration of the mating period in cats, *Physiol. Behav.*, **3**, 41–3.

Pfaff, D. W. (1968) Uptake of ^{3}H-estradiol by female rat brain. An autoradiographic study, *Endocrinology*, **82**, 1149–55.

Pfaff, D. (1970) Nature of sex hormone effects on rat sex behavior: specificity of effects and individual patterns of response, *J. Comp. Physiol. Psychol.*, **73**, 349–58.

Pfaff, D. W. and Keiner, M. (1972) Estradiol-concentrating cells in the rat amygdala as part of a limbic-hypothalamic hormone-sensitive system. In: *The Neurobiology of the Amygdala*, B. E. Eleftheriow (ed.), Plenum, New York, pp. 775–85.

Powers, J. B. and Valenstein, E. S. (1972) Individual differences in sexual responsiveness to estrogen and progesterone in ovariectomized rats, *Physiol. Behav.*, **8**, 673–6.

Powers, J. B. and Zucker, I. (1969) Sexual receptivity in pregnant and pseudopregnant rats, *Endocrinology*, **84**, 820–7.

Quadagno, D. M., McCullough, J., and Langan, R. (1972) The effect of varying amounts of exogenous estradiol benzoate on estrous behavior in the rat, *Horm. Behv.*, **3**, 175–9.

Resko, J. A. (1969) Endocrine control of adrenal progesterone secretion in the ovariecto-mized rat, *Science*, **164**, 70–1.

Ross, J., Claybough, C., Clemens, L. G. and Gorski, R. A. (1971) Short latency induction of estrous behavior with intracerebral gonadal hormones in ovariectomized rats, *Endocrinology*, **89**, 32–8.

Robinson, T. J. (1955) Quantitative studies on the hormonal induction of oestrous in spayed ewes, *J. Endocrinol.*, **12**, 163–73.

Reuter, L. A., Ciaccio, L. A. and Lisk, R. D. (1970) Progesterone: regulation of estrous cycle, ovulation and estrous behavior in the golden hamster, *Endocrinology*, **86**, 1287–97.

Sar, M. and Stumpf, W. E. (1973) Neurons of the hypothalamus concentrate ^{3}H progesterone or its metabolites, *Science*, **182**, 1266–8.

Sawyer, C. H. (1963) Induction of estrus in the ovariectomized cat by local hypothalamic treatment with estrogen, *Anat. Rec.*, **145**, 280.

Scaramuzzi, R. J., Tillson, S. A., Thorneycroft, I. H., and Coldwell, B. V. (1971) Action of exogenous progesterone and estrogen on behavioral estrus and luteinizing hormone levels in the ovariectomized ewe, *Endocrinology*, **88**, 1184–9.

Schneider, T., Piacsek, B., and Gay, V. (1970) Simultaneous measurements of progesterone and 20α-OH-pregn-4-ene-3-one in ovarian venous blood and of luteinizing hormone in systemic blood on the afternoon of proestrus in the rat, *Fed. Proc.*, **29**, 381 Abs.

Schwartz, N. B. (1972) Mechanisms controlling ovulation in small animals. *Handbook of Physiology-Endocrinology* II, Part I, American Physiological Society, Washington D. C., p. 125.

Shaikh, A. A. (1972) Estrone, estradiol, progesterone and 17α-hydroxy-progesterone in the ovarian venous plasma during the estrous cycle of the hamster, *Endocrinology*, **91**, 1136–40.

Signoret, J. P. (1967) Durée du cycle oestrien et de l'oestrus chez la truie. Action due benzoate d'oestradiol chez la femalle ovariectomisée, *Ann. Biol. Anim. Biochem. Biophys.*, **7**, 407–21.

Signoret, J. P. (1970) Action d'implants de benzoate d'oestradiol dans l'hypothalamus sur le comportement d'oestrus de la brebis ovariectomisée, *Anim. Biochem. Biophys.*, **10**, 549–66.

Signoret, J. P. (1971) Etude de l'action inhibitrice de la progesterone sur l'apparition due compartment sexuel induit par injection d'oestrogens chez la true et la brebis ovariectomisées, *Ann. Biol. Anim. Biochem. Biophys.*, **11**, 489–94.

Stabenfeldt, G. H., Akins, E. L., Ewing, L. L., and Morrissette, M. C. (1969a) Peripheral plasma progesterone levels in pigs during the estrous cycle. *J. Reprod. Fert.*, **20**, 443–9.

Stabenfeldt, G. H., Ewing, L. L., and McDonald, L. E. (1969b) Peripheral plasma progesterone levels during the bovine oestrous cycle, *Fertility*, **19**, 433–42.

Stabenfeldt, G. H., Holt, J. A., and Ewing, L. L. (1969c) Peripheral plasma progesterone levels during the ovine estrous cycle, *Endocrinology*, **85**, 11–5.

Stumpf, W. E. (1970) Estrogen-neurons and estrogen-neuron systems in the diencephalon and amygdala, *Am. J. Anat.*, **129**, 207–18.

Thorburn, G. D., Bassett, J. M. and Smith, I. D. (1969) Progesterone concentration in the peripheral plasma of sheep during the oestrous cycle, *J. Endocrinol.*, **45**, 459–69.

Van der Schoot, P. and Zeilmaker, G. H. (1972) Aspects of the function of ovarian grafts in neonatally castrated male rats, *Endocrinology*, **91**, 389–95.

Vertes, M., Barnea, A., Lindner, H. R. and King, R. J. B. (1974) Studies on androgen and estrogen uptake by rat hypothalamus. In *Receptors for Reproductive Hormones*, B. W. O'Malley and A. R. Means (eds.), Plenum, New York, pp. 137–73.

Wade, G. N. and Feder, H. H. (1972a) Effects of several pregnane and pregene steroids on estrous behavior in ovariectomized estrogen-primed guinea pigs, *Physiol. Behav.*, **9**, 773–5.

Wade, G. N. and Feder, H. H. (1972b) [1,2-^{3}H] Progesterone uptake by guinea pig brain and uterus: differential localization, time-course of uptake and metabolism, and the effects of age, estrogen-priming, and competing steroids, *Brain Res.*, **45**, 525–43.

Wade, G. N., Harding, C. F. and Feder, H. H. (1973) Neural uptake of [1,2-³H] progesterone in ovariectomized rats, guinea pigs, and hamsters: correlation with species differences in behavioral responsiveness, *Brain Res.*, **61**, 357–67.

Ward, I. L. (1972) Female sexual behavior in male rats treated prenatally with an antiandrogen, *Physiol. Behav.*, **8**, 53–6.

Ward, I. L. and Renz, F. J. (1972) Consequences of perinatal hormone manipulation on the adult sexual behavior of female rats, *J. Comp. Physiol. Psychol.*, **78**, 349–55.

Whalen, R. E., Battie, C., Luttge, W. G. (1972) Anti-estrogen inhibition of androgen induced sexual receptivity in rats, *Behav. Biol.*, **7**, 311–20.

Whalen, R. E. and Hardy, D. R. (1970) Induction of receptivity in female rats and cats with estrogen and testosterone, *Physiol. Behav.*, **5**, 529–33.

Whalen, R. E. and Nadler, R. D. (1963) Suppression of the development of female mating behavior by estrogen administered in infancy, *Science*, **141**, 273–4.

Whitten, W. K. (1966) Pheromones and mammalian reproduction. In: *Advances in Reproductive Physiology*, Vol I, A. McLaren (ed.), Logos Press, London, pp. 155–77.

Williams-Ashman, H. G. and Reddi, A. H. (1971) Actions of vertebrate sex hormones, *Ann. Rev. Physiol.*, **33**, 31–83.

Wilson, J. F. and Young, W. C. (1941) Sensitivity to estrogen studied by means of experimentally induced mating responses in the female guinea pig and rat, *Endocrinology*, **29**, 779–83.

Yoshinaga, K., Hawkins, R. A. and Stocker, J. F. (1969) Estrogen secretion by the rat ovary *in vivo* during the estrous cycle and pregnancy, *Endocrinology*, **85**, 103–12.

Zucker, I. (1967) Progesterone in the experimental control of the behavioral sex cycle in the female rat, *J. Endocrinol.* **38**, 269–77.

CHAPTER 14

Neuro–Hormonal Integration of Sexual Behaviour in Female Primates

J. HERBERT

INTRODUCTION

The neural and humoral systems of primates seem to have evolved at different rates. Though details may differ, the general pattern of the secretion of hormones from the gonads of both male and female primates resembles that observed in non-primates. Thus, the principal androgen of primates is testosterone, whose secretion is modulated by (among other factors) the time of day, season of the year (in some species), and by the receipt of behavioural signals from other animals, including both sexual and aggressive stimuli. Similarly, the females' ovaries secrete, in cyclic fashion, oestradiol and progesterone, the former determining the midcycle surge of LH, the latter the duration of the luteal phase of the cycle, as in many non-primates. There seems nothing distinctive about the endocrine function of the primate gonads, though much more needs to be known about the way hormones are secreted, and metabolized, throughout the various primate species. At first sight, quite different conclusions are reached when one considers the primate brain. The enormous development of the neocortex, together with its associated subcortical structures, differentiates primates from non-primates. The olfactory system regresses, whilst the visual system shows increasing elaboration. And yet, the structure and hormone-binding characters of those parts of the brain which are the primary targets of hormone action (e.g. the hypothalamus, amygdala and septum) are not so very different from corresponding structures in rats, cats, or sheep. The little we know about 'primary' neuroendocrine interactions in primates (i.e. the way hormones act upon the primate's brain) suggests that this comparison may be extended: for example, the anterior hypothalamus, the septum, and the amygdala of the female monkey's brain specifically bind oestrogen as do the same regions of the rat brain (Pfaff, 1976); high oestrogen levels induce luteinizing hormone (LH) release in rats and monkeys (though the extent to which this is truly a neuroendocrine interaction is now debated)

(Knobil, 1974). So the study of the neuroendocrinology of behaviour in primates can be resolved into considering what features distinguish primates from non-primate mammals and their smaller brains, and what may be considered to be the basically similar mechanisms in the two groups. It would be an over-implication to think of a monkey as possessing something akin to a rodent hypothalamus surrounded by a primate neocortex. Nevertheless, we might expect primates to show a greater variability and flexibility in their sexual activity—as in many other aspects of their behaviour—primarily because their neocortex is so large.

Whilst the ability of primates to adapt their behaviour is a principal interest of students of primates, this property constitutes a hinderance to unravelling basic neuroendocrine mechanisms, since the latter may be overshadowed, or compensated for, by other neural functions. This is quite different from saving that hormone-sensitive mechanisms are less important (Ford and Beach, 1952). One approach to primate behaviour is deliberately to minimize these other variables (eg. partner preferences; interfering effects of aggression; etc) so that basic mechanisms can be revealed (Herbert, 1974). Thereafter, one must proceed to ask different, progressively more elaborate questions about primate sexual activity, particularly about the way other factors modify simple neuroendocrine interactions.

The study of primate sexual behaviour tends to suffer from the assumption that such basic mechanisms must resemble those in the rat and other rodents, the subjects of so many years' investigations. Even this, as we shall see, is questionable (Herbert, 1976).

HORMONAL POINTS OF ACTION

It is very well recognized that steroid hormones operate on particular target tissues, which are then specifically activated and which constitute the physio-logical response to secretion of such steroids (Zigmond, 1975). It is also possible to apply the same kind of reasoning to behaviour, so that a behaviour pattern can be dissected, cut into its parts, to determine which component is specifically altered by a given hormone. Thus, it is no longer sufficient to say that a particular category of behaviour (e.g. sexual or aggressive) is altered by hormones; it is more informative to attempt to determine which component of what be-haviour (e.g. sexual receptivity; liability to attack by other males, etc.) has changed. In such behavioural contexts, we may speak of a hormone having a *somatic* point of action; that is, the tissue upon which the hormone acts to produce its effects on behaviour, and a *behavioural* point of action; the com-ponent of behaviour changed as a result of alteration in the function of the hormone-sensitive tissue (Herbert, 1974). Ultimately, each hormonally-induced change should be specified in a precise way; thus, eventually we might be able to say that the given hormone alters sexual receptivity by depressing a particular component of behaviour as a result of altering the function of a given part of the brain in a clearly defined way.

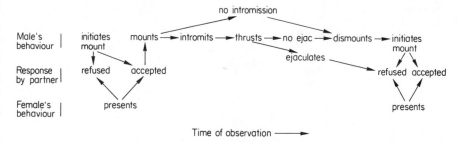

Fig. 1. Diagrammatic representation of part of the mounting sequence of the male rhesus monkey. The behaviours and responses resulting in a mount are shown;several such mounts normally occur before the male ejaculates. A mount can be initiated either by the male (above) or the female (below). Several points during the ensuing interaction are critical in determining the behavioural pattern (e.g. accepted/refused; intromits/no intromission; ejaculates/no ejaculation). The female's role is normally limited to determining whether a mount shall, or shall not, be initiated. Her attractiveness is measured by her ability to cause the male to respond sexually to her invitations; her proceptivity by the incidence of such invitations ('presents') and her receptivity by her response to sexual initiatives from the male. (From Herbert, 1974. Reproduced by permission of Elsevier/ North-Holland Biomedical Press.)

In order to dissect out behaviour it is obviously important to measure and distinguish its different components during sexual interaction. In general one does this by separating actions from reactions. Thus, measuring the level of a particular component of the male's (or female's) behaviour gives essential information. Equally important, but quite different, is the way each animal responds to a given behavioural component displayed by the other. A hormone may alter the latter without necessarily changing the former, or may alter the former as a result of an effect upon the latter.

As an example of behavioural analysis, Fig. 1 shows in diagrammatical form the components of sexual interaction which occur between a male and female rhesus monkey. In this species a series of mounts, each with intromission and a number of thrusts, occurs before the male finally ejaculates. Fig.1 shows that a mount may be initiated by the male or by the female; the male by clasping the female, the female by offering a sexual invitation (Fig. 2) to the male. Each animal may either accept or refuse the others invitation; if this is refused then the sequence comes temporarily to an end, to be repeated a little while later. If the invitation is accepted, the male mounts. From then on, most of the sequence depends upon him. It will be seen from Fig. 1 that the outcome of most components is binary; that is, a given response either does or does not occur. If the male, after mounting, does not intromit then the sequence comes to an end; if he intromits he will then thrust, if he thrusts he may not ejaculate (in which case he will dismount and the sequence will be repeated some time later), if he ejaculates he then enters a refractory phase when sexual interaction comes to an end until sexual responsiveness is restored. By measuring each behavioural component separately, and determining the effects of a given

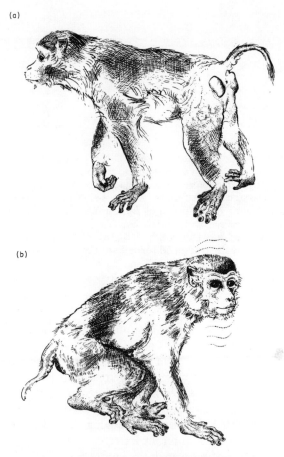

Fig. 2. Sexual invitations offered by female rhesus
monkeys. (a) The full 'presentation' posture, with
the female's tail deviated to expose the genitalia.
(b) The 'head duck' in which the female bobs her
head up and down, at the same time half raising
her perineum from the ground

hormonal or neural factor upon them, one can locate precisely the behavioural
point of action of the hormone (Herbert, 1974).

BEHAVIOURAL COMPONENTS OF THE FEMALE'S
SEXUAL INTERACTION

It is possible to separate the female primates sexual behaviour into three
components: attractiveness, proceptivity, and receptivity.

Attractiveness

Attractiveness is defined as the value the female has as a sexual stimulus for the male (Baum *et al.*, 1977). It can be further subdivided into two components, behavioural and non-behavioural. The female's behaviour itself affects the male's response to her. For example, an aggressive female or one who grooms a given male a great deal may, in this way, modify her attractiveness. More particularly, altering her sexual invitations (presentations) may accentuate a female's attractiveness. As we shall see, invitational behaviour is better defined as *proceptivity* (Beach, 1976), so that we are in danger of confusing attractiveness with proceptivity. In discussions of endocrine function in the female it is more convenient to limit attractiveness to non-behavioural qualities. These form the second component of attractiveness, and comprise somatic features of the female which determine her value as a sexual stimulus for a given male, though it is likely that the frequency of a female's interactions may itself alter the males response to them (Beach, 1976).

Attractiveness is measured, in rhesus monkeys, in two ways. If a male responds consistently to an invitation by attempting to mount, the female is highly attractive. However, a highly attractive female may be emitting non-behavioural signals at such an intensity that the male mounts without the necessity of her offering an invitation. Thus, a high proportion of male-initiated mounts is also an index of maximal attractiveness. It is important to recognize that both parameters can be influenced by individual qualities (for example, dominance), so that in studies of hormonal action it is the change induced by hormonal alterations rather than absolute values which is important. Another way of studying attractiveness is to make the male perform an operant task (e.g. bar pressing) for access to the female (Keverne, 1976). Changes in his performance may then be related to the female's attractiveness, though the assumption that he is pressing for sexual contact with her rather, say, than social activity (e.g. the opportunity to groom) has to be accounted for by using appropriate controls.

Hormones and Attractiveness

Withdrawing treatment from ovariectomized oestrogen-treated female monkeys reduces their sexual interaction with a male. A most consistent finding accompanying this change is a decrease in both the behavioural parameters defined above which together define attractiveness (Fig. 3). Giving progesterone to the oestrogen-treated female has a similar effect (Fig. 4) (Dixson *et al.*, 1973). Further analysis of these findings has shown that the vagina is the point of action of these hormones in rhesus monkeys which determines attractiveness. Oestrogen introduced directly into a female rhesus monkey's vagina accentuates her attractiveness (Herbert, 1966; Michael and Saayman, 1968) apparently because it promotes the formation of a mixture of aliphatic acids that functions as a stimulating 'pheromone' (Michael *et al.*, 1972; Keverne, 1976). These are discussed more fully by Keverne (this volume, Chapter 22). Several other species of primates, including female chimpanzees, baboons,

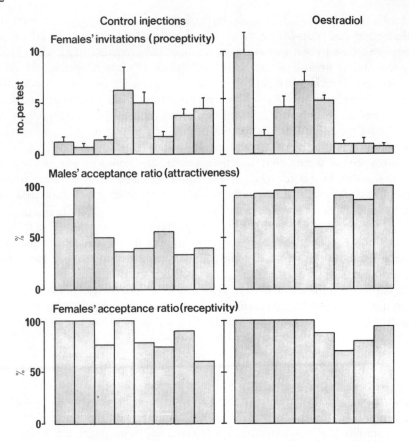

Fig. 3. The effect of treating ovariectomized females with oestradiol (15–25 μg/day) on their proceptivity (sexual invitations offered to the male), attractiveness (proportion of invitations accepted by the male), and receptivity (proportion of the male's attempts to mount accepted by the female). Data from 8 females. (From Baum *et al.*, 1977. Reproduced by permission of Plenum Publishing Corporation.)

mangabeys, and talapoins respond to oestrogen by developing large oedematous swellings of the 'sexual skin', the oestrogen-sensitive area covering the perineum. Whether this acts as a sexual attractant, in addition to the olfactory signals originating from the vagina, is not yet definitely established, though talapoin males pay much more attention to the sexual skin of females if it is swollen (Dixson *et al.*, 1973).

A female's attractiveness depends upon several qualities in her, including those determining the preference of a male for a particular kind of female. The hormone-dependent part, we have seen, is regulated by oestrogen acting upon the females genitalia and this causes behaviourally significant stimuli to be transmitted to the male, thus altering his behaviour, as in the case of the behaviour of non-primates. This demonstrates that the relatively underdeveloped

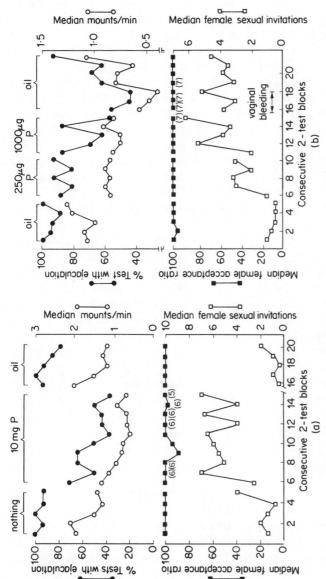

Fig. 4. The effect of giving progesterone (P) to oestrogen-treated ovariectomized female rhesus monkeys on (above) two parameters of the male's sexual activity (mounts and ejaculations) and(below) two of the females—receptivity (per cent male's attempts accepted) and proceptivity (sexual invitations). In (4a) 10 mg/day progesterone were given subcutaneously. In (4b) 250 μg/day or 1000 μg/day progesterone were given intravaginally. The latter treatment replicated the behavioural effects of the former. (From Baum et al., 1977. Reproduced by permission of Plenum Publishing Corporation.)

olfactory system of primates still has an important role in their sexual behaviour.

The antagonistic effect of progesterone on attractiveness when given systemically can also be replicated if the hormone is introduced directly into the vagina (Fig. 4b). Very small amounts, insufficient to raise plasma levels significantly, cause the same changes in the males' behaviour as much larger amounts given to females by intramuscular injection (Baum et al., 1976). It seems likely that, just as progesterone antagonizes the effects of oestrogen on the cellular proliferation of the vaginal wall, so it opposes the formation of the olfactory substance which is promoted by high plasma levels of oestrogen.

Though they are most firmly established in rhesus monkeys, observations on a number of other species of primates suggest that signals from the female vagina, either olfactory or visual, play an important part in regulating sexual interaction between female and the male (e.g. Dixson et al., 1973). Whilst the importance of olfactory components came as somewhat of a surprise to those used to thinking of the primate olfactory system as having regressed, the role of visual components is more immediately acceptable, since this part of the primate brain is well developed and there are striking changes in appearance and colouration of many primate females during their sexual cycle.

As well as studying the direct effects hormones have upon attractiveness, it is also most important to consider the interaction between attractiveness and other components of behaviour, and this becomes critical in analysing a hormone's somatic point of action. If a treatment changes a female's sexual attractiveness as a result of an effect upon non-behavioural cues, this will be reflected in corresponding alterations in the male's behaviour. The female, in turn, may respond to the male's changed response to her by altering her own behaviour towards him (eg. her proceptivity) (Baum et al., 1977). If this fact is not appreciated, alterations in the female's behaviour induced in this way may quite erroneously be attributed to the hormone acting directly on neural mechanisms within the female regulating her behaviour (eg. proceptivity). The critical relationship between the female's attractiveness and her proceptivity will be discussed further below.

Proceptivity

Proceptivity refers to behavioural gestures used by females which serve to induce the male to attempt to mount (Beach, 1976) (Fig. 2). The rhesus monkey, for example, may offer sexual invitations (eg. presentations, Zuckerman, 1932) which must be separated clearly from the response of a female to a mounting attempt initiated by the male (an index of the females receptivity—see below). A female monkey offering such a sexual invitation is doing so either because of non-behavioural sexual stimuli emanating from the male, or as a result of some behaviour (eg. an approach movement or an attempt to mount) displayed by him. But an important point is that a female's invitations qualify as 'proceptive' only if they are not an immediate response contingent on the behaviour of the male; though the definition of what constitutes 'contingent' must seem arbitrary, in practice this is usually self-evident. If a female is made to perform some operant task to gain access to a male, then this is also a measure of her proceptive behaviour, given that it can be safely assumed (from control procedures) that she is performing this task to copulate with him. Proceptivity is not to be equated with sexual 'drive' or 'arousal' and is not a measure of it. This follows from the finding that altering a female's sexual attractiveness may simultaneously alter her proceptive behaviour. Thus, the sexual invitations she offers are a product of at least three factors: her hormonal condition, the stimuli emanating from the male, and his response to her behavioural or non-behavioural signals. These points are further amplified below, but it can be noted now that a highly attractive female may offer very few sexual invitations because the male is mounting her at maximal rate without the requirement that she do so. It would be quite incorrect to conclude that her sexual 'drive' or 'arousal' was at a low level in this situation.

Hormones and Proceptivity

Two hormones can alter proceptivity. The first, androgen, seems to act directly on the female CNS to modulate proceptive behaviour. The second, progesterone, seems to act indirectly as described above and stimulates the female's proceptivity secondarily to the effect it has on the male's behaviour towards the female. Whether oestrogen has any role in the control of proceptivity is still uncertain.

Injecting ovariectomized females with testosterone stimulates their proceptivity (Trimble and Herbert, 1968): they offer more sexual invitations to the male, even though (unless they are given oestrogen) they remain unattractive. Tested in an operant situation, they bar-press with greater eagerness for access to the male after they are given androgen. These experimental findings recall earlier clinical ones; women treated with androgen reported increased 'libido' (eg. Salmon and Geist, 1943). Because such procedures necessarily increased testosterone levels above those normally found in the female, it is more informative to consider what happens when androgens are removed. This can be accomplished by bilateral adrenalectomy combined with ovariectomy, subsequently giving females corticoid replacement therapy to keep them healthy. Proceptivity declines sharply after this operation, even though the females—being given oestrogen—remain attractive (Everitt et al., 1972) (Fig. 5). Though only a limited number of steroids has been tried so far, testosterone or androstenedione (two of the principal adrenal androgens) are the only ones that have been found capable of restoring proceptive behaviour to normal. This behavioural analysis, together with failure to find significant changes in the vaginal epithelium after testosterone therapy, suggests that androgens act directly upon neural mechanisms in the female to stimulate proceptivity and not indirectly (eg. via the male) as is the case, for example,

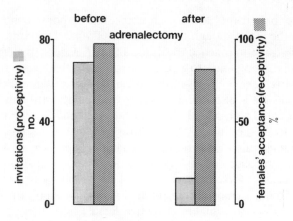

Fig. 5. The effects of bilateral adrenalectomy (with cortisol replacement) on the female's sexual invitations (proceptivity) and acceptance ratio (receptivity) in 15 oestrogen-treated females

for progesterone (see below). Subsequent studies on adrenalectomized female monkeys in which testosterone has been implanted directly into the brain supports this interpretation (see below). It is noteworthy that bilateral adrenalectomy (but not ovariectomy) has been reported to reduce 'libido' in women (Waxenburg et al., 1959).

If an ovariectomized female monkey is given oestrogen, sexual behaviour between her and the male is stimulated provided they are compatible, as we have seen. But this is not accompanied by equally reliable changes in the female's proceptivity (eg. sexual invitations). This does not necessarily indicate that the hormone has no direct action on proceptivity, for such an action may be overlain by dramatic changes in the female's attractiveness which occur when she is given oestrogen. The interdependence between the female's attractiveness and proceptive behaviour is revealed by giving progesterone to an oestrogen-treated rhesus monkey. Her sexual invitations (eg. proceptivity) increase (Baum et al., 1976). This is not, however, the result of a directly stimulating effect of progesterone upon the female's CNS, similar to that seen in rodents and ungulates (Zucker and Goy, 1967), since a much smaller amount of progesterone (about 1/40th) given intravaginally has a similar effect upon the female's behaviour, yet causes no appreciable elevation in blood levels of progesterone (Baum et al., 1976). Behavioural analysis shows that progesterone decreases attractiveness (see above). Thus, it may be that the female offers more sexual invitations to the male because he is now responding sluggishly to her as a result of decrements in non-behavioural signals (eg. pheromones).

Two conclusions follow this argument. The first (a general one) is that changes in proceptive behaviour after hormone treatment do not necessarily indicate, by themselves, the hormone's site of action, and the second (more particularly) is that progesterone acts on the female's genitalia to change both her attractiveness (directly) and her proceptivity (indirectly via the male).

Is there a role for oestrogen in the neural control of the female's proceptivity? Since androgen deficiency causes such a profound decline of proceptivity even in oestrogen-treated females (Everitt and Herbert, 1971; Everitt et al., 1972), the latter cannot substitute for the former. This implies that aromatization of androgen to oestrogen (Ryan et al., 1972) cannot be the mechanism whereby androgens restore receptivity to adrenalectomized females. However, dihydrotestosterone (DHT) apparently fails to stimulate proceptivity in ovariectomized females, in contrast to testosterone (D. A. Goldfoot, pers. commun.), which argues against the 5α-reductase pathway being responsible for the effect of a supposed testosterone 'pre-hormone'. Oestrogen can still elicit LH release in adrenalectomized monkeys (Knobil, 1974), suggesting that the central effect of oestrogen is not dependent upon adrenal androgens—i.e. the latter are not playing a permissive role—though it should be noted that in this context it is not yet certain to what degree oestrogen acts directly on pituitary (rather than upon the brain) and changes its sensitivity to luteinizing hormone-releasing hormone (LRH). However, although oestrogen withdrawal from ovariectomized monkeys causes them to become unattractive, their proceptivity is not stimulated (Baum et al., 1977). This suggests that oestrogen may, in circumstances such as these, play a part in regulating proceptivity (since the 'expected' stimulation does nor appear), but this is not conclusive evidence and further experimentation is required.

Stilboestrol implanted into the female monkey's brain is said to stimulate proceptivity (Michael, 1969, 1971). However, in these experiments, implants in both the 'effective' and 'control' areas altered the male's sexual activity, presumably because enough hormone leaked from the implants to act upon the female's vagina and hence stimulate her attractiveness. Furthermore, effective sites were apparently found in both hypothalamus and midbrain (Michael 1969, 1971). The problems which attend analysis of changes in proceptivity on the face of coincident alterations in attractiveness have already been emphasized.

Johnson and Phoenix (1976) report findings which they consider evidence against such a function for androgen in female rhesus. Unfortunately, the method they use (testing each female once only under each treatment) is unsuitable for detecting endocrine-dependent changes, since aggression was high and sexual behaviour very variable. Nevertheless, they demonstrated marked decrements in 'presentations' (i.e. sexual invitations) in females treated with dexamethasone (which would be expected to decrease adrenal output, though no measurements are reported) which is consistent with earlier findings. Replacement therapy with an androgen, necessary to substantiate or refute such findings, was evidently not carried out. They concluded that testosterone is effective only to the extent that it is aromatized to oestrogen, but (as they point out) dexamethasone effects are not counteracted by giving oestradiol which argues against this interpretation. They also suggest that some hypothetical balance is necessary between the two hormones, a different conclusion and one which is more in agreement with previous work.

Receptivity

Receptivity is the willingness of the female to accept the male's attempts to mount her (Beach, 1976). It is measured therefore as a response to the male and thus critically differs from proceptivity in this regard (as Beach, 1976, points out). Many factors (such as the male's persistence or dominance, or sexual attractiveness) may influence this component of the female's behaviour. Thus, highly attractive females may possibly show changes as a result of the way the male behaves towards her—for example, a highly persistent male may, because of this behaviour, alter apparent levels of receptivity in the female. In other words, there may be interdependence between attractiveness and receptivity as been attractiveness and proceptivity. On the other hand, it is difficult to determine whether there is any relationship between receptivity and proceptivity because oestrogen-treated females are usually highly receptive and therefore hormone-induced increases in this behaviour are unlikely; those females that are not highly receptive are usually eliminated experimentally by selection procedures.

Hormones and Receptivity

Although androgen withdrawal (as by adrenalectomy) seems to reduce receptivity as predictably as it does proceptivity (Everitt et al., 1972), the changes in receptivity are usually rather less. For example, before adrenalectomy only 4 out of 15 animals in a particular experiment ever refused to allow the male to mount during the ten observations made on each, but after operation there were 14 refusals. This seems a striking reduction in receptivity, and so it may be; but examining the data in another way, it is also true that the females accepted between 75–80% of the male's mounting attempts even after adrenalectomy (compared with about 100% before operation), whereas proceptive behaviour was less than 25% of what it had been before the adrenals had been removed (Fig. 5). Thus, whilst androgen withdrawal decreases receptivity, the extremely unreceptive state characterizing, say, an untreated ovariectomized cat or rat is not observed in female monkeys. Does this mean that the female primates' sexual receptivity is, at least partly, hormone independent? Or that oestrogen, which was given to females, was responsible for their residual receptivity? The critical experiments necessary to answer these questions have not been reported.

The widespread supposition that progesterone decreases receptivity in female monkeys is also suspect. Some ovariectomized females given 5 μg/day oestradiol and 25 mg/day progesterone were certainly unreceptive (though others were not) (Michael *et al.*, 1968). But this dose is likely to produce plasma levels at least three times the physiological range (which is about 10 ng/ml). Recently similar females given 10 mg/day progesterone (plasma levels 5.2–14.5 ng/ml) showed no unreceptivity, but only decreased attractiveness (Baum *et al.*, 1976). In fact, the entire behavioural pattern induced by systemic progesterone could be reproduced by very much smaller amounts given intravaginally raising, the question of whether progesterone, *per se*, has any direct effect upon the female monkeys CNS in regulating her sexual behaviour.

THE HORMONAL BASIS OF BEHAVIOURAL CHANGES DURING THE MENSTRUAL CYCLE

Changes in sexual interaction which correlate with the phase of the cycle have been described in several species of apes and monkeys (Nadler, 1975; Eaton, 1973). Many exceptions seem to occur though it is not always clear how far these represent different species, individuals, conditions of study, or methods of measurement (Rowell, 1972). In general, the more the primary interaction between male and female is separated from variables such as aggression, or interference with other animals, and the more detailed the measurements, the greater the likelihood for detecting rhythmic changes in behaviour occurring during the female's menstrual cycle. Maximal interaction usually occurs at midcycle, and minimal levels during the luteal phase. Follicular-phase levels may be intermediate, or even approach those at midcycle, and before menstruation there may be a resurgence of sexual activity. Some non-endocrine factors, particularly the composition of groups and the phase relationship between the cycle of different females, may markedly modify this pattern (Rowell, 1972). Nevertheless, it is possible, on the basis of the experimental evidence presented above, to account for behavioural rhythms in terms of underlying fluctuations in oestrogen, progesterone, and androgens during the cycle.

It is becoming apparent that most of the behavioural fluctuations induced by hormones during the menstrual cycle may be ascribed to changes in the female's attractiveness (Eaton, 1973). Thus, at midcycle, oestrogen levels are at their highest, and this induces vaginal changes which ensure maximal attractiveness. Conversely, the rising levels of progesterone during the luteal phase result in decreasing attractiveness, which remits as the corpus luteum wanes just before menstruation (Everitt and Herbert, 1972).

Changes in the female's proceptive behaviour during the cycle also occur, though less prominently. Maximal levels at midcycle have been reported in rhesus monkeys by some (Carpenter, 1942; Loy, 1970; Czaja and Bielert, 1975) but not others (Michael and Wellagala, 1968), and in talapoin monkeys (Scruton and Herbert, 1970) (Fig. 6) pig-tail macaques (Goldfoot, 1971) baboons (Saayman, 1968) and some others (see Rowell, 1972). It is likely that

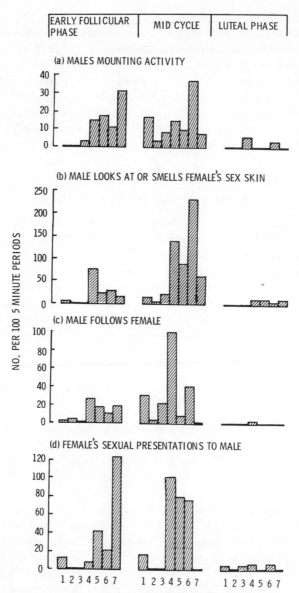

Fig. 6. Changes in sexual interaction during the menstrual cycle of the female talapoin monkey. (From Scruton and Herbert, 1970. Reproduced by permission of the Zoological Society of London.)

such findings are related to the increasing androgen secretion from the ovaries (eg. androstenedione) which occurs near ovulation (Hess and Resko, 1973). Receptivity usually remains high throughout the cycle, though occasional exceptions have been described (Michael and Wellagala, 1968). As we have seen, there is debate over whether progesterone in physiological amounts can reduce receptivity in rhesus females, though the increased reduction in her attractiveness taking place during the luteal phase might make unreceptivity difficult to determine, since the males attempt to mount unattractive females less vigorously. It is important to recognize that the unvarying level of receptivity in monkeys is the parameter giving rise to the suggestion that behaviour in these animals is relatively less hormone-sensitive than in other species; but if other components are considered carefully, this supposed distinction becomes much less certain. The behavioural bases on which such comparisons are made need to be clearly stated if they are to be convincing.

It ought also to be recognized that day-to-day fluctuations in hormone levels during the menstrual cycle are not reproduced by the relatively steady conditions resulting from treating ovariectomized or adrenalectomized animals with steroids. We do not know whether the way a hormone acts upon behaviour is influenced by rising or falling levels, or the way its secretion follows that of other steroids in a particular sequence (as, for example, the well recognized sequence for progesterone and oestrogen in sheep and rats). Furthermore there are some hormones (eg. 17α-hydroxyprogesterone) known to be released during the primates' cycle whose behavioural role has not yet been assessed.

CEREBRAL MECHANISMS REGULATING THE FEMALES BEHAVIOUR

The neural mechanisms responsible for the way hormones modify sexual behaviour in female primates are still relatively unexplored. However, it appears that a small implant of solid testosterone propriate (TP) into the anterior hypothalamus can restore both preceptive and receptive behaviour to adrenalectomized females, whereas implants in other areas examined (including part of the posterior hypothalamus, thalamus, and midbrain) were ineffective (Everitt and Herbert, 1975) (Fig. 7). This site corresponds with that demonstrated to be oestrogen-sensitive in the rat, since it is here that oestrogen implants can facilitate, or lesions prevent, oestrous (i.e. receptive) behaviour (Davidson, 1972). In so far as the behaviours studied and the brain areas implanted in monkeys and rats seem similar, a tentative conclusion is that the hormonal-sensitive systems of the two may be very similar in their anatomical organization, but differ in the endocrine stimulus required to activate them. As we have seen, androgens are necessary to activate the system in female rhesus monkeys, whereas oestrogen is required in rats, though the role of oestrogen in monkeys is still uncertain.

Further similarities between rats and monkeys appear from the preliminary information available on the neurochemical basis of sexual behaviour in the two species. Reducing cerebral 5-hydroxytryptamine (5-HT) levels, or administering drugs which act as 5-HT antagonists, facilitate oestrous behaviour in rats by increasing oestrogen sensitivity, so that doses of oestrogen not other-

LOCATION OF IMPLANTS IN ANT. HYPOTHALAMUS/PREOPTIC AREA
IN EIGHT ADRENALECTOMISED MONKEYS.

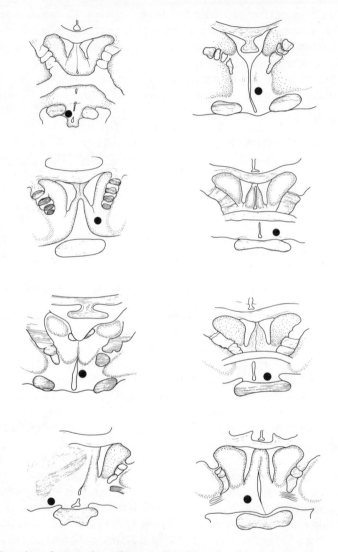

Drawing of coronal section passing through midpoint of implant.

Site of implant not to scale.

Fig. 7. Location of testosterone propionate implants (black circles) restoring sexual activity in adrenalectomized-ovariectomized oestrogen-treated female rhesus monkeys. Each drawing shows the site of an implant in the brain of a different female. (From Everitt and Herbert, 1975. Reproduced by permission of Elsevier/North-Holland Biomedical Press.)

wise able to induce receptive behaviour now become capable of so doing (Meyerson, 1964; Meyerson and Lewander, 1970). Increasing 5-HT activity has the opposite effect (Meyerson, 1970). In the same way, reducing 5-HT synthesis by giving the drug *p*-chlorophenylalanine (an inhibitor of tryptophan hydroxylase) restores proceptivity in adrenalectomized monkeys (Gradwell *et al.*, 1975). However, it should be noted that depleting 5-HT (or any other amine) cannot substitute for the action of oestrogen in the female rat, whereas the action of androgens can, it seems, be replicated in this way in the monkey. We could speculate that there are minute amounts of androgens present even in adrenalectomized and ovariectomized monkeys, or that oestrogen can produce a metabolic substance mimicking, to some degree, the effects of androgenic hormones. Thus, we are not necessarily driven to the conclusion that there is a fundamental distinction between the relationship between 5-HT systems and oestrogen in the rat, and androgens in the monkeys. Such arguments, however, beg another question: whether altering 5-HT activity in this way is, in reality, demonstrating a specific role for the transmitter in sexual behaviour. 5-HT-containing systems have been implicated in sleep/ waking cycles, eating and drinking behaviour (Weissman and Harbert, 1972), and in the hormonal control of the pituitary (see below) amongst others, and thus changing their activity by systemic pharmacological means may have generalized effects on neural function. For example, they might change the sensitivity of the animal to various stimuli, both behavioural and chemical, which influence its own behaviour. The effect this would have upon the animals behaviour will depend upon the circumstances in which it is studied. This is particularly important in the case of 5-HT, since it has been suggested that this amine may, in some way, be related to the neural basis of mood (Korf and Van Praag, 1970), and changes in this parameter could easily alter many characteristics of behaviour in monkeys (as in humans). There is, however, no evidence at present which suggests that 5-HT alters mood in experimental primates, and its role even in humans is still debated.

The second neurochemical system which has still to be implicated in the female primate's behaviour is that containing peptides. There is increasing suspicion—and some evidence—that peptides which are known to be concerned in pituitary function (eg. LRH) are also concerned in other aspects of reproduction, including sexual behaviour. It is not surprising if this should be the case: peptides (eg. angiotensin) are known to control drinking behaviour (Fitzimons, 1972) and may be implicated in sleep. Both behaviours are also modulated by monoamines. LRH can substitute for the action of progesterone in oestrogen-treated rats (Moss and McCann, 1973), and is said to augment sexual performance in some impotent men not responsive to testosterone (Mortimer *et al.*, 1974), though these findings need corroboration and amplification. If one takes as a model the way that LRH is known to alter pituitary function, it then becomes possible that steroids may modify the response of cells to the peptides, and this may apply as much to neurons as to cells in the pituitary itself. If this were the case, then the role of monoamines in behaviour would be (again by analogy with what is known about the control of the pituitary) one of modulating peptide release, rather than directly interacting with steroids or steroid-containing neurons, and whether an animal responds to these peptides depends upon the amount of steroid reaching parts of the brain sensitive to both. Alternatively, it is also possible that steroids may regulate neural sensitivity to amines by changing the synthesis of proteins thought to be part of the neuronal amine-receptor mechanism. We should recall that all oestrogen and androgen-binding neural areas also seem to receive a large aminergic input.

CORRELATIONS BETWEEN THE NEUROENDOCRINE CONTROL OF BEHAVIOUR AND OF THE MENSTRUAL CYCLE IN PRIMATES

Primates (as well as rodents) have a mechanism for ensuring that copulation

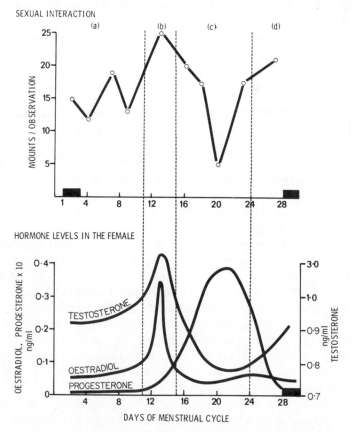

Fig. 8. Possible correlation between rhythmic changes in (above) sexual interaction between pairs of intact rhesus monkeys and (below) fluctuations in hormone levels in the female

is most frequent at midcycle, when ovulation also occurs (Herbert, 1976b) (Fig. 8). In rodents this is accomplished by the midcycle surge of oestrogen, which induces both LH release and sets in action the neural mechanisms. for sexual behaviour (particularly receptivity). In primates, too, a midcycle oestrogen surge causes LH release (Knobil, 1974) and, as we have seen, induces maximal sexual attractiveness. Though oestrogen stimulates both sexual behaviour and LH release in primates as it does in rodents, there is a significant difference between the action of the hormone in the two groups. In primates, oestrogen acts principally on peripheral mechanisms (in the vagina) to increase attractiveness whereas in the rat the effect is a direct one upon the CNS, thus activating the female's behaviour.

Progesterone in rats may act in low dosage synergistically with oestrogen to provoke the release of LH from the pituitary. In the same way, it also combines with oestrogen to induce maximal sexual receptivity. In female primates, on the other hand, progesterone can prevent the induction of the LH surge by oestrogen (Knobil, 1974), though there is some recent evidence suggesting (not entirely convincingly) that, under certain circumstances, progesterone may act synergistically in primates as in rats (Clifton et al., 1976). In rats, as in other rodents, progesterone has a biphasic effect upon receptivity. Initially this is stimulating, but then the hormone causes behavioural refractivity to oestrogen so that the animal becomes unreceptive despite the continuing presence of high oestrogen levels (Zucker and Goy, 1967). On the other hand, in primates the argument that progesterone acts directly upon the CNS in regulating sexual behaviour is, at the moment, insecure. Progesterone thus diminishes sexual interaction in rodents and primates by different mechanisms. Although the hormone has a potent effect upon the central nervous mechanism regulating gonadotrophin secretion in primates, its effect upon behaviour is minimal and this means that a female's receptivity or proceptivity is not reduced during the luteal phase in the presence of progesterone levels as it is in the rat. These findings suggest that the nature of the neural receptors regulating sexual behaviour in the female primate differ from those controlling the pituitary. Those regulating behaviour are sensitive to androgen and relatively insensitive to progesterone, whereas those regulating the pituitary are sensitive to oestrogen and also to progesterone. This separation between the neural systems subserving sexual behaviour in the female and the control of the pituitary on the basis of their endocrine affinities distinguishes the situation in the primate from that in the rat. In particular the special role of androgen in the control of sexual activity in the female primates is not found in subprimates; but there is no corresponding difference in the control of the pituitary.

CONSIDERATIONS ON THE ROLE OF ANDROGENS IN THE DIFFERENTIATION OF NEUROENDOCRINE MECHANISMS IN FEMALE PRIMATES

It is possible that the distinctive role played by androgens in adult female primates is reflected in an equally marked separation of their function in sexual differentiation of primates compared to non-primates. In female rats, it is well known, a critical event during early life is whether the neonatal brain experiences gonadal steroids (Harris and Levine, 1962). If it does, as a result of these hormones being secreted from the infantile gonad, or if such hormones are given experimentally, then two main consequences follow: the ability of the animal to display a lordotic (i.e. feminine) response to treatment with appropriate hormones is diminished, and the neuroendocrine system also becomes insensitive to the positive feedback of oestrogen so that the animal fails to experience regular oestrous cycles and becomes continually vaginally oestrus, a condition characterized by absence of ovulation and by the normal rhythmic secretion of hormones (Harris, 1964). There is also a second behavioural consequence: the animal becomes more responsive to androgens, and is thus more likely to show male type responses after androgen treatment (i.e. male mounting behaviour) in the presence of an oestrous female, than is a normal female treated in the same way (Davidson, 1972). We are still not entirely sure how widely these conclusions can be generalized to species other than rodents.

The evidence in the female primate is rather different, and may be correlated with the individual role androgens play in adult sexual life. If female rhesus monkeys are treated during intrauterine life with androgen, they are born with heavily masculinized genitalia, as would be expected from similar experiments carried out in rodents. However, as they grow up, it becomes clear that the modifying effect of androgens upon the neuroendocrine system is significantly different in primates and rodents. In the first place, when such females reach puberty they show regular menstrual cycles and ovulate in a manner entirely comparable to normal females (Goy, 1968). Providing we can rule out some experimental parameter (i.e. dose of hormone or time of treatment) this suggests a distinct difference between the sensitivity to androgen of the prenatal primate's neuroendocrine system and that of the rodent both neonatally, as in the rat, and prenatally, as in the guinea pig. Information about the behaviour of such monkeys is much less complete. During infantile life it is certainly true that androgen-treated female monkeys show greater amounts of male type play behaviour and more infantile mounting of other monkeys than normal females (Goy, 1968). But whether they will display in their adult life the inability to exhibit feminine responses to the attempts of a normal male to mount them is not yet established. Clinical evidence suggests otherwise. Adrenogenital girls, who have been exposed to relatively high levels of androgen during prenatal life, are not, it appears, in general prevented from showing normal feminine responses to the male (Money, 1972).

The distinction between the response to androgens of primate and non-primate neuroendocrine systems is further emphasized in a second context by recent work on normal males. If a normal male monkey is castrated, and then given an oestrogen surge experimentally, LH is released from the pituitary in a way which seems analogous to that of the female (Knobil, 1974). This is not obtained in the rat, since one consequence of the presence of neonatal androgen is prevention of the positive feedback effect of oestrogen upon LH discharge from the pituitary. Thus, in both behavioural and hypophysial function, the effect of androgen on the development of primates is different from rodents.

Although the connection is by no means clear, it may be that this early insensitivity to the potential 'defeminising' action of androgen in female primates relates in some way to the role the hormone has in adult life. If, as seems possible, androgen is the main hormone in both males and females which regulates levels of the animals' sexual 'motivation' it follows that the mechanisms responsible for differentiation of the nervous system into the 'masculine' or 'feminine' type may also react differently to the hormone in early life. It must be recognized that the effect of prenatal androgen on adult 'female' behaviour is quite a different question from that concerning the role of androgens in the development of the capacity of primates to display masculine behaviour. Such a masculinizing effect is well documented in rodents, though whether the primary site of such an action is within the brain or upon the genitalia is still undecided. As far as the limited information on primates goes, prenatal androgens given to females certainly seem to facilitate the ability of the animals to mount during postnatal life, and increase the behavioural sensitivity of the animal to testosterone so far as this is demonstrated by mounting activity. We may therefore tentatively conclude that androgens in primates may act to facilitate the development of masculine responses, but not to suppress the ability to show feminine ones. This, as appears clear from the previous argument, indicates a distinct difference between the effect the hormones have on infantile primates and rodents. It also has obvious bearing on theories which attempt to explain the genesis of homosexual behaviour on the basis of prenatal hormonal experience in man. Thus, whilst it would not be surprising to find that the development of pronounced 'feminine' type behaviour in human males might be the result of androgen deficit or androgen insensitivity during early life, the evidence is at present against the theory that male-type behaviour (lesbianism) in women results from the induction of masculine type neural systems in the primate brain by abnormal exposure to androgens. Furthermore, attempts to demonstrate 'feminine' or 'masculine' types of pituitary responsiveness to exogenous oestrogen in normal and homosexual men (Dorner et al., 1975) must be interpreted with knowledge that substantial differences between primates and rodents may reside in these mechanisms.

SUMMARY AND CONCLUSIONS

A hormone's action on behaviour can be defined in two ways: behaviourally (indicating the behavioural component altered), or somatically (the tissue on which it operates to alter behaviour). The female rhesus monkey's sexual behaviour can be divided operationally into three components: attractiveness, proceptivity, and receptivity. Each has a hormonally-sensitive controlling element, as well as other factors (often ill-defined) which are not endocrine-dependent. Attractiveness is stimulated by oestrogen acting on the vagina, an action antagonized by progesterone. Proceptivity is androgen-sensitive, and so is much reduced by ovariectomy combined with adrenalectomy. Receptivity is possibly less altered by this operation, though whether the hormonal control of this parameter and proceptivity are truly distinct remains enigmatic. So, too, does the possibility of a central (neural) role for oestrogen in regulating sexual behaviour in female rhesus. Together, changes in progesterone, oestrogen, and androgen can account for rhythmic fluctuation in sexual interaction during the female's menstrual cycle, attractiveness being, perhaps, the principal modulator of behaviour in these circumstances.

Androgen receptors modifying behaviour exist in the female monkey's anterior hypothalamus. Oestrogen, however, is the effective stimulus for evoking the LH surge at midcycle. Thus the two sets of receptors in the monkey (unlike the rat) are differentially sensitive to steroids. Pharmacologically altering amines (5-HT) can replicate the behavioural effects of androgens, though the way the two systems interact within the brain is still poorly understood. Similar findings linking steroids with amines have been made in rodents.

Pre- or neonatal androgenic suppression of 'feminine' behaviour and hypophysial characteristics, so prominent in rodents does not seem to occur in primates. How, or if, this relates to the adult primate's responsiveness to androgen is not yet determined. These differences between rodents and primates need to be taken into account when extrapolations to humans are made as, for example, in attempts to explain the genesis of homosexuality.

ACKNOWLEDGEMENTS

Supported by grants from the Medical Research Council. I thank Debby Hickman for her help in preparing this manuscript.

REFERENCES

Baum, M. J., Everitt, B. J., Herbert, J., and Keverne, E. B. (1977) Hormonal basis of proceptivity and receptivity in female primates, *Arch. Sex. Behav.*, **6**, 173–191.

Baum, M. J., Keverne, E. B., Everitt, B. J., Herbert, J., and de Vrees, P. (1976) Reduction of sexual interaction in rhesus monkeys by a vaginal action of progesterone, *Nature*, **263**, 606–8.

Beach, F. A. (1976) Sexual attractivity, proceptivity, and receptivity in female mammals, *Horm. Behav.*, **7**, 105–38.

Carpenter, C. R. (1942) Sexual behavior of free-ranging rhesus monkeys (*Macaca mulatta*), *J. Comp. Psychol.*, **33**, 113–42.

Clifton, D. K., Steiner, R. A., Resko, J. A. and Spies, H. G. (1976) Estrogen-induced gonadotrophin release in ovariectomized rhesus monkeys and its advancement by progesterone, *Biol. Reprod.*, **13**, 190–4.

Czaja, J. A. and Bielert, C. (1975) Female rhesus sexual behaviour and distance to a male partner: relation to stage of menstrual cycle, *Arch. Sex. Behav.*, **4**, 583–97.

Davidson, J. M. (1972) Hormones and reproductive behaviour. *In: Hormones and Behaviour*, S. Levine (ed.), Academic Press, N.Y.

Dixson, A. F., Everitt, B. J., Herbert, J., Rugman, S., and Scruton, D. M. (1973) Hormonal and other determinants of sexual attractiveness and receptivity in rhesus and talapoin monkeys. *In: Primate Reproductive Behaviour*, C. H. Phoenix (ed.), Karger, Basel.

Dorner, G., Rohde, W., Stahl, F., Krell, L., and Masius, W. G. (1975) A neuroendocrine predisposition for homosexuality in men, *Arch. Sex. Behav.*, **4**, 1–8.

Eaton, G. C. (1973) Social and endocrine determinants of simians and prosimians female sexual behavior. *In: Primate Reproductive Behaviour*. W. Montagna (ed.), Karger, Basel.

Everitt, B. J. and Herbert, J. (1971) The effects of dexamethazone and androgens on sexual receptivity of female rhesus monkeys, *J. Endocrinol.*, **51**, 575–88.

Everitt, B. J. and Herbert, J. (1972) Hormonal corelates of sexual behaviour in sub-human primates, *Danish Med. Bull.*, **19**, 246–58.

Everitt, B. J. and Herbert, J. (1975) The effects of implanting testosterone proprionate into the central nervous system on the sexual behaviour of adrenalectomized female rhesus monkeys, *Brain Res.*, **86**, 109–20.

Everitt, B. J., Herbert, J., and Hamer, J. D. (1972) Sexual receptivity of bilaterally adrenalectomized female rhesus monkeys, *Physiol. Behav.*, **8**, 409–15.

Fitzimons, J. T. (1972) Thirst, *Physiol. Rev.*, **52**, 468–561.

Ford, C. S. and Beach, F. A. (1952) *Patterns of Sexual Behaviour*. Methuen, London.

Goldfoot, D. A. (1971) Hormonal and social determinants of sexual behavior on the pigtail monkey *(Macaca nemestrina)*. *In: Normal and Abnormal Developments of Brain and Behaviour*, G. B. A. Stoelinger and J. J. Van der Werfften Bosch (eds.), University of Leiden Press, pp. 325–42.

Goy, R. W. (1968) Orginizing effect of androgen on the behaviour of rhesus monkeys. *In: Endocrinology of Human Behaviour*. R. P. Michael (ed.), Oxford University Press.

Gradwell, P., Everitt, B. J. and Herbert, J. (1975 5-hydroxytryptamine in the central nervous system and sexual receptivity of female rhesus monkeys, *Brain Res.*, **88**, 281–93.

Harris, G. W. (1964) Sex hormones, brain development, and brain function, *Endocrinology*, **75**, 627–48.

Harris, G. W. and Levine, S. (1962) Sexual differentiation of the brain and its experimental control, *J. Physiol.*, **163**, 42.

Herbert, J. (1966) The effect of oestrogen applied directly to the genitalia upon the sexual attractiveness of the female rehesus monkey, *Excerpta Med. Int. Cong. Sex.*, **3**, 212.

Herbert, J. (1974) Some functions of hormones and the hypothalamus on the sexual activity of primates, *Prog. Brain Res.*, **41**, 331–47.

Herbert, J. (1976a) Hormonal basis of sex differences in rats, monkeys, and humans, *New Scientist* **70**, 284–6.

Herbert, J. (1976b) Relationship between neuroendocrine mechanisms controlling sexual behaviour and ovulation in primates. In *Neuroendocrine Regulation of Fertility*, T. C. Anand Kumar (ed.), Karger, Basel, pp. 286–93.

Hess, D. L. and Resko, J. A. (1973) The effects of progesterone on the patterns of testosterone and estradiol concentrations in the systemic plasma of the female rhesus monkey during the intermenstrual period, *Endocrinology*, **92**, 446–53.

Johnson, D. F. and Phoenix, C. H. (1976) Hormonal control of female sexual attractiveness, proceptivity and receptivity in rhesus monkeys, *J. Comp. Physiol. Psychol.*, **90**, 473–83.

Keverne, E. B. (1976) Sexual receptivity and attractiveness in the female rhesus monkey. *In: Advances in the Study of Behaviour Vol. 7*. J. S. Rosenblatt and R. A. Hinde (eds.), Academic Press, N. Y.

Knobil, E. (1974) On the control of gonadotrophin secretion in the rhesus monkey, *Rec. Prog. Horm. Res.*, **30**, 1–46.

Korf, J. and Van Praag, H. M. (1970) The intravenous probenicid test: a possible aid in evaluation of the serotonin hypothesis on the pathogenesis of depression, *Psychopharm.*, **18**, 129–32.

Loy, J. (1970) Perimenstrual sexual behaviour among rhesus monkeys, *Folia Primatologica*, **13**, 286–97.

Meyerson, B. J. (1964) Central nervous monoamines and hormone-induced estrus behavior in the spayed rat, *Acta Physiol. Seand. Physiol.*, **63**, 1–32.

Meyerson, B. J. (1970) Monoamines and hormone-activated oestrous behaviour in the ovariectomized hamster, *Psycho. pharm.*, **18**, 50–7.

Meyerson, B. J. and Lewander, T. (1970) Serotonin synthesis inhibition and oestrous behaviour in female rats, *Life Sci.*, **9**, 661–71.

Michael, R. P. (1969) Neural and non-neural mechanisms in the reproductive behaviour of primates. *In: Progress in Endocrinology*, C. Gjal (ed.), *Excerpta Medica*, Amsterdam, pp. 302–9.

Michael, R. P. (1971) Neuroendocrine factors regulating primate behaviour. *In: Frontiers in Neuroendocrinology*, L. Martin and W. F. Ganong (eds.), Oxford University Press, pp. 359–98.

Michael, R. P., Keverne, E. B., Zumpe, D., and Bonsall, R. W. (1972) Neuroendocrine factors in the control of primate behaviour, *Rec. Prog. Horm. Res.*, **28**, 665–706.

Michael, R. P. and Saayman, G. S. (1968) Differential effects on behaviour of subcutaneous and intravaginal administration of oestrogen in the rhesus monkey *(Macaca mulatta)*, *J. Endocrinol.*, **41**, 231–46.

Michael, R. P., Saayman, G. S., and Zumpe, D. (1968) The suppression of mounting behaviour and ejaculation in male rhesus monkeys by administration of progesterone to their female partners, *J. Endocrinol.*, **41**, 421–31.

Michael, R. P. and Welegalla, J. (1968) Ovarian hormones and the sexual behaviour of the female rhesus monkey *(Macaca mulatta)* under laboratory conditions, *J. Endocrinol.*, **41**, 407–20.

Money, J. (1972) Clinical aspects of prenatal steroidal action on sexually dimorphic behaviour. *In: Steroid Hormones and Brain Function*, C. Sawyer and R. A. Gorski (eds.), University California Press, pp. 325–28.

Mortimer, C. H., McNeilly, A. S., Fisher, R. A., Murray, M. A. F., and Besser, G. M. (1974) Gonadotrophic-releasing hormone therapy in hypogonadal males with hypothalamic and pituitary dysfunction, *Brit. Med. J.*, **4**, 617–21.

Moss, R. L. and McCann, S. M. (1973) Induction of mating behaviour in rats by luteinizing hormone-releasing factor, *Science N. Y.*, **181**, 177–9.

Nadler, R. D. (1975) Sexual cyclicity in captive lowland gorillas, *Science*, **189**, 813–4.

Pfaff, D. W. (1976) The neuroanatomy of sex hormone receptors in the vertebrate brain. *In: Neuroendocrine Regulation of Fertility*, T. C. Anand Kumar (ed.), Karger, Basel, pp. 30–45.

Rowell, T. E. (1972) Female reproductive cycles and social behaviour in primates, *Adv. Study Behav.*, **4**, 69–105.

Ryan, K. J., Naftolin, F., Reddy, V., Flores, F., and Petro, Z. (1972) Estrogen function in the brain, *Am. J. Obstet. Gynec.*, **114**, 404–60.

Saayman, G. S. (1968) Oestrogen, behaviour and the permeability of a troop of chacma baboons, *Nature*, **220**, 1339–400.

Salmon, V. J. and Geist, G. H. (1943) The effect of androgens upon libido in women, *J. Clin. Endocr. Metab.*, **3**, 235–8.

Scruton, D. M. and Herbert, J. (1970) The menstrual cycle and its effects upon behaviour in the talapoin monkey *(Miopithecus talapoin)*, *J. Zool. Lond.*, **142**, 419–36.

Trimble, M. R. and Herbert, J. (1968) The effects of testosterone or oestradiol upon the sexual and associated behaviour of the adult female rhesus monkey, *J. Endocrinol.*, **42**, 171–85.

Waxenburg, S. F., Drellich, M. G., and Sutherland, A. M. (1959) The role of hormones in human behaviour I Changes in female sexuality after adrenalectomy, *J. Clin. Endocrinol.*, **19**, 193–202.

Weissman, A. and Harbert, C. A. (1972) Recent developments relating serotonin and behaviour, *Am. Rep. Med. Chem.*, **7**, 48–58.

Zigmond, R. E. (1975) Binding metabolism and action of steroid hormones in the central nervous system. *In: Handbook of Psychopharmacology Vol. 5*, L. L. Iversen, S. D. Iversen, and S. H. Snyder (eds.), Plenum, N. Y., pp. 239–328.

Zucker, I and Goy, R. W. (1967) Sexual receptivity in the guinea pig: inhibitory and facilitatory actions of progesterone and related compounds, *J. Comp. Physiol. Psychol.*, **64**, 378–83.

Zuckerman, S. (1932) *Social life of monkeys and apes*, Kegan Paul, London.

CHAPTER 15

The Relationship Between Hormones and Sexual Behaviour in Humans

JOHN BANCROFT

INTRODUCTION

At the present time evidence of the relationship between hormones and behaviour in human sexuality is limited and often conflicting. Until recently much of the data have relied on dubious hormone assay methods. Even with modern assay techniques, there remain major methodological uncertainties. There has been a tendency to extrapolate to humans from animal data in spite of increasing evidence of important species differences. A further major shortcoming has been the superficial and dubiously valid data on human sexual behaviour in endocrine studies. The complexities of evaluating changes in such behaviour have been given scant attention.

This chapter, rather than providing an exhaustive review will briefly consider the principal evidence that we have, and will indicate that as yet most important questions relating to the issue of the relationship between hormones and human sexual behaviour remain to be answered. The evidence is almost exclusively clinical and is of three main types:

(1) Observations of sexual behaviour in patients with endocrine disorders either of prenatal or later onset.

(2) Endocrine assays in people with abnormalities of sexual behaviour.

(3) The observed effects on sexual behaviour or exogenous hormones and antihormones.

Most attention has been paid to the sex steroids and gonadotrophins. Thyroxine, posterior pituitary hormones, and gonadotrophin releasing factors have been considered to a very limited extent.

Human sexuality is undoubtedly complex and is a function not only of the individual but also of the interaction between that individual and others. In order to render this complexity more manageable for our purpose the following components, based on a scheme by Whalen (1966), will be considered.

(i) *Gender identity;* i.e. that part of the individual's identity or self-image that relates to masculinity or femininity. Gender role is the behavioural manifestation of gender identity.

(ii) *Sexual preferences;* i.e. the characteristics of a desirable sexual partner or erotic stimulus.

(iii) *Sexual arousal and arousability;* arousal is the state of sexual excitement or desire at a point in time; arousability is the facility to respond to sexual stimuli with an increase in arousal.

(iv) *Sexual behaviour;* i.e. the occurrence of purposive behaviour of sexual type.

The sexuality of an individual represents a complex interaction between these various components, and they cannot be considered as independent of one another. Gender identity, which is probably the first to be established developmentally, will influence to some extent the establishment of sexual preferences and *vice versa.* Sexual arousability and activity are clearly interrelated (for further consideration of these interrelationships, see Bancroft, 1972).

The three clinical sources of evidence already mentioned will be considered in relation to each of these four components of sexual behaviour.

GENDER IDENTITY

The extent to which gender identity is determined prenatally and early in the postnatal period by hormonal factors has for some time remained a battleground between those favouring the predominance of either prenatal or environmental factors. This controversy has mainly centred on the establishment of the 'core' gender identity, that aspect which involves the belief—'I am a male', or 'I am a female', and which normally becomes established somewhere between the ages of two and four years. Zuger (1970) is a proponent of prenatal determination; Lev-Ran (1974a, b) is of the environmental determination school. Money (Money and Ehrhardt, 1972) and Diamond (1965) both emphasize the interaction between prenatal and environmental factors. Their tendency to disagree with one another, however, leads them to stress the importance of environmental and prenatal factors respectively. Much of this polemic has been sterile and indeed any model which does not take both types of factor into consideration would seem futile. There remain, nevertheless, interesting questions about potency and timing of effect of these hormonal and social-learning factors.

The two main sources of human data are first, the variety of prenatal endocrine abnormalities associated with pseudohermaphroditism; and second, those abnormalities of gender identity not associated with any apparent anatomical or genetic anomaly (i.e. transexualism).

The evidence relating to pseudohermaphoroditism has been extensively reported and discussed in the literature and there will be no purpose in representing it fully here. Only the most crucial points will be considered. The best available source for further information is Money and Ehrhardt (1972), (see also Diamond, 1965 and Money and Schwartz this volume Chapter 23).

The adreno-genital syndrome is the result of an autosomal recessive gene defect in cortisol biosynthesis which in the majority of cases involves a deficiency of the 21-hydroxylase enzyme. The resulting increase in adrenocorticotrophic hormone (ACTH) production, whilst ensuring a virtually normal plasma cortisol level, also leads to overstimulation of androgens. If sufficiently severe, the genetically female child with this defect will be born with a degree of masculinization of the external genitalia. A proportion of such cases in the past have been reared as boys and have usually developed male gender identity. In such cases both the abnormal endocrine state and the sex of assignment and consequent social-learning factors may contribute to the masculine gender identity development. The study of such children tells us relatively little about the role of hormonal factors. Of more interest are those individuals whose condition is diagnosed at birth and who are reared as girls in spite of being virilized. Up to 1950 there was no treatment for this condition; since then continuous treatment with corticosteroids has effectively controlled the androgenization. Ehrhardt and Money have studied two groups of such women, those who were effectively treated from birth, and thus only suffered androgenization *in utero* (Ehrhardt *et al.*, 1968a), and those who were already adolescent or adult when treatment started and who therefore continued to be androgenized throughout childhood (Ehrhardt *et al.*, 1968b). These studies show that in both groups there is definite evidence of 'tomboy' behaviour during childhood, significantly more than in a matched control group. They also showed other features more consistent with the male than the female stereotype, e.g. preference for male clothes and avoidance of self-adornment and subordination of marriage to a career. Although the early and late onset groups did not differ in these respects, they did show other differences which were more noticeable in relation to sexual preferences and behaviour than to gender identity *per se* and will be considered further below.

A further group of interest are the female children of women who were given relatively high doses of progestogens during pregnancy as a means of preventing spontaneous abortion (Ehrhardt and Money, 1967).Certain progestogens appear to have an androgenizing effect on the foetus in these cases, similar to, though less marked than that found in the adreno-genital syndrome. The small number of such cases followed into adolescence once again shows that the majority are 'tomboyish' in behaviour.

In the genetic male, the endocrine anomaly of most relevance is the testicular feminization or androgen insensitivity syndrome. In this, due to a lack of androgen-binding protein in the target cells, the brain and other target organ cells are sensitive to oestrogens but insensitive to testosterone, both hormones being produced in amounts normal for the male. The child is born with feminized external genitalia and in most cases develops a normal external body appearance of a female, except for a lack of sexual hairgrowth, and an unequivocally female gender identity, even to the extent of showing a typically female pattern of verbal-performance discrepancy in IQ testing (Masica and Lewis, 1969). This syndrome may also exist in an incomplete form when some pubic and axillary hair may be present and partial androgenization occurs. The metabolic defect may be qualitatively different in these cases (Rosenfield *et al.*,1971). In a series of such incomplete cases (Money and Ogunro, 1974) gender identity was consistent with the sex of assignment which varied, most being reared as boys.

In cases of Turner's syndrome, in which the chromosomal configuration is XO, the lack of ovarian development and hence absence of oestrogens is associated with a gender identity pattern which is closer to the female stereotype (i.e. the model of essential femininity) than that typically found amongst normal females (Money and Ehrhardt, 1972).

The equivalent in the male to the progestogen-induced hermaphroditism in the female has been observed amongst children of diabetic mothers who received high doses of oestrogens combined with low doses of progestogens in an attempt to reduce the high foetal mortality associated with diabetes (Yalom *et al.*, 1973). A group of 16-year-old male children resulting from these pregnancies were found to be less aggressive and less athletic than untreated controls. A group of such 6-year-old male children differed from controls in teacher's ratings of assertiveness and atheletic ability, although they did not differ in other measures. For some reason the experimental subjects differed more in these respects from control subjects who were born of diabetic mothers but not given hormones, than the 'non-diabetic' controls. These results whilst not conclusive are certainly compatible with a weak intrauterine antiandrogen effect impairing later masculine development.

These various examples of naturally occurring and iatrogenic endocrine abnormalities suggest that the presence of androgens during prenatal development will increase the likelihood of masculine gender identity development whatever the genetic sex. One must be cautious in interpreting such evidence, however, as in most of these cases there may have been sufficient cues of 'masculinization' at birth to influence in some way the parental child-rearing practices and thus enhance masculinity through social learning.

It is also important to realize that there are various androgens which may have different effects in this respect. Androstenedione, a weak androgen, is the precursor of testosterone. Both of these androgens have direct effects on the brain as well as on general metabolism and secondary sexual characteristics. Dihydrotestosterone (DHT), a metabolite of testosterone, is a more potent androgen but in several animal species its effects are largely confined to the development of secondary sexual characteristics, having relatively little effect on the brain (e.g. Johnston and Davidson, 1972). As yet we lack data on this difference in the human, but the following report is noteworthy.

Imperato-McGinley *et al.* (1974) studied a small rural community in the Dominican Republic in which there were 24 genetic males with a 5-α reductase enzyme deficiency, leading to a failure of conversion of testosterone to DHT. These males were born with ambiguous genitalia. The vas deferens, epididymis, and seminal vesicles developed normally, presumably dependent on testosterone. The urogenital sinus was incompletely developed, however, remaining as a blind vaginal pouch with a clitoral-like phallus, labia-like scrotum and inguinal or labial testes. The development of the external genitalia is therefore presumably dependent on DHT. Eighteen of these males were reared as girls; in spite of this, at the onset of puberty not only was there growth of the penile stump and scrotum but also a change to a masculine gender identity with sexual interest directed at the opposite sex. These rather surprising findings were reported very summarily and obviously one needs to know more about the childhood gender identity of these individuals before drawing any firm conclusions. Nevertheless, it looks as though in these cases the presence of testosterone during foetal development and at puberty countered the feminizing effects of their upbringing. The relative importance of hormonal determinants of gender identity therefore remains uncertain.

The most likely explanation for the different effects of testosterone and DHT lies in the fact that the former can be aromatized to oestrogens, whilst the latter cannot. This aromatization process has been shown to occur in the hypothalamus and limbic system of humans as well as rats and rabbits (Ryan et al., 1972; Naftolin et al., 1975). It has been suggested that testosterone has its effects on the brain by being converted to oestrogens. Male sexual behaviour can be restored in castrated male rats (Ryan et al., 1972) and other animals (Fletcher and Short, 1974) by oestrogens, using much smaller doses than are necessary with androgen replacement. As yet this remains to be demonstrated in man, but it is a puzzling possibility that would need to be reconciled with the apparent antiandrogenic effects of oestrogens in the intact human that has already been mentioned in relation to the children of diabetic mothers and will also be discussed further below.

Transexualism is a condition in which the individual either believes himself to be or has a very strong desire to be the gender opposite to that of his genetic and anatomical sex. In addition, such individuals usually have a strong desire to receive sex-reassignment surgery to correct what they see as anatomical aberration, and hormone therapy consistent with their gender identity rather than their gonadal status. Thus the male-to-female transexual seeks oestrogens, and the female-to-male, androgens.

Most transexuals present themselves to clinicians in adult life and it is often difficult to be certain how long the condition has existed. In many cases, possibly the majority, this transexual identity has only been clearly manifested since puberty, evolving from an earlier pattern of fetishistic transvestism (Bancroft, 1972). Some, however, will have experienced their gender identity since early childhood and there are now many documented cases of childhood transexualism, particularly in the male (Green, 1974). It is tempting to suppose that this anomaly of early gender identity development is a manifestation of prenatal or early postnatal endocrine determinants. However, there is as yet no evidence in support of this and endocrine studies of adult male transexuals have failed to show any consistently abnormal pattern (Migeon *et al.*, 1969). The evidence in the female-to-male transexual is limited but more conflicting.

Jones and Samimy (1973) reported a normal endocrine status in three female transexuals. Fulmer (1973), on the other hand, found three out of nine female transexuals to have raised testosterone levels. A recurring problem in investigating the endocrine status of adult transexuals is their tendency to surreptitiously take exogenous hormones, and one cannot exclude this explanation of Fulmer's findings. Furthermore, female-to-male transexualism was not a feature of the females with early- or late-treated adreno-genital syndrome, reported by Ehrhardt *et al.* (1968a, b).

It is possible that in the future either prenatal or early postnatal androgen levels may be shown to be correlated with degrees of later masculinization and that lack of androgens in genetic males at these times may facilitate the development of transexualism. For the moment such relationships are exceedingly speculative.

SEXUAL PREFERENCES

The determination of sexual preference is even more obscure than that of gender identity. It is not clear why most individuals develop heterosexual preferences whilst some become predominantly homosexual. Early attempts to explain the causation of homosexuality were heavily influenced by the desire to demonstrate that it was an innate condition for which the individual could not be held morally responsible. Workers such as Hirschfeld (1944) postulated that homosexuals were examples of a hormonal intersex.

Two sources of evidence can be considered. First, how do sexual preferences develop in those individuals with endocrine abnormalities? and second, are there any endocrine correlates of established sexual preference?

If the presence of androgens prenatally and during childhood increases the likelihood of female object choice, then one might expect homosexual preferences amongst females with the adreno-genital syndrome. In the group of those women treated from birth, reported by Ehrhardt *et al.* (1968a) there was no evidence of homosexuality. Of the 23 females who were not treated until adulthood, 10 reported bisexual fantasies and 4 had bisexual experiences. None was exclusively or predominantly homosexual. However, in contrast Lev-Ran (1974b) reported 18 Soviet females with late treated adreno-genital syndrome; none of these had any homosexual interest. His explanation for this difference was that the sexual mores of Soviet women would make homosexual orientation unlikely. By implication this suggests that the virilization occurring in these women might lead, by means of a phase of sexual uncertainty, to homosexual interest if the social climate permitted. In other words the endocrine factor might facilitate, but not be sufficient for the development of homosexual preferences.

Males with Klinefelter's syndrome (XYY) are known to have a higher than expected incidence of anomalous sexual preferences though not particularly homosexual (Nielsen, 1969). This again could be explained in the same way; genetic and endocrine abnormalities increase the likelihood of abnormal or varied sexual development but are not sufficient for its development.

When we turn to studies of the endocrine status of homosexuals and heterosexuals the reader is entitled to feel confused. Although earlier studies failed to show any association (Perloff, 1965) interest has been reawakened with the introduction of new and better assay methods. Loraine et al. (1970) studied urinary androgen excretion in three male and four female homosexuals. Of the males, two who were exclusively homosexual showed lower urinary testosterone levels than heterosexual controls. The females all showed higher levels of urinary testosterone than controls. In addition the pattern of testosterone excretion during the menstrual cycle was somewhat unusual, though this pattern does vary considerably among normal women (see below). Oestrogen excretion was also lower than in the controls. These findings, whilst of interest, are of uncertain significance. Urinary output of testosterone is a poor indication of endogenous production; the number of homosexual subjects was very small and the method of selection uncertain. Also, rather dubious statistical procedures were used for comparing the homosexuals with the controls.

Kolodny et al. (1971) reported results of plasma testosterone estimations in 30 male homosexuals and 50 male controls, all university student volunteers. Those homosexuals who also had some heterosexual interest or past experience (i.e. rated Kinsey 2, 3, or 4), did not differ from the controls. The group of 15 exclusive or predominantly homosexual subjects (Kinsey 5 and 6) had significantly lower plasma testosterone levels. (Kinsey ratings indicate the relative proportions of homosexual and heterosexual behaviour and interest. Kinsey 5 is 'largely homosexual but with incidental heterosexual history'. Kinsey 6 is 'entirely homosexual'. These ratings are usually applied to a defined time period—e.g. 3 years.) Only one blood sample was assayed in each case. Plasma gonadotrophin levels (Kolodny et al., 1972) were outside the normal range in the 13 homosexuals who had low testosterone levels. Four of these had raised luteinizing hormone (LH) and follicle stimulating hormone (FSH) and on semen analysis were found to be azoospermic. They therefore showed a picture of primary testicular dysfunction. The nine other subjects had low LH levels. It is therefore noteworth that the low testosterone picture was not associated with a consistent pattern of endocrine abnormality. Of importance is the fact that 43% of the homosexual subjects were regular marijuana users. In a more recent study Kolodny has shown that regular marijuana use leads to suppression of testicular function (Kolodny, 1975). Unfortunately the incidence of marijuana use amongst the heterosexual controls is not given, and reanalysis of the data concerning use of marijuana is necessary.

A number of further and usually conflicting reports have followed. Birk *et al.* (1973) estimated plasma testosterone in 19 male homosexuals undergoing psychotherapy. They not only failed to find any correlation with the degree of homosexuality, but the mean level of testosterone for the group was high in the normal range, two of the highest levels being found in Kinsey 5 and 6 males. Doerr *et al.* (1973) studied 32 male homosexuals and failed to find any difference in testosterone levels between Kinsey 5 and 6 homosexuals and the controls. They did, however, find higher oestradiol levels in the homosexual group. Brodie *et al.* (1974) found the plasma testosterone levels in 19 homosexuals (Kinsey 6) to be significantly *higher* than those in their heterosexual controls. Pillard *et al.* (1974) on the other hand found that plasma testosterone levels in 28 homosexual males were somewhat lower than in their heterosexual controls, though showing considerable overlap. In their case the homosexuals in Kinsey 5 and 6 categories had lower testosterone levels than those in categories 3 and 4. In that study they also failed to find any correlation between testosterone levels and a variety of psychological variables including ratings of masculinity and femininity. It is difficult to account for these varied and conflicting results except by assuming that crucial variables had not been controlled. It seems naive, however, to assume that there would be any simple relationship between isolated levels of plasma testosterone and sexual orientation or preference.

A somewhat different approach investigated the pattern of androgen metabolism in homosexuals, in particular the ratio of androsterone to ethiocholanolone in the urine, both of which are the result of reduction of testosterone in the liver and elsewhere (Margolese, 1970; Margolese and Janiger, 1973). These workers found that by using linear discriminant analysis, the androsterone–etiocholanolone ratio discriminated between homosexuals of Kinsey categories 5 and 6 and healthy heterosexual controls. The homosexuals were not significantly different to a small number of physically unhealthy controls, however. There was no difference between groups in the amount of total 17-ketosteroids excreted in the urine. These findings were replicated in a study by Evans (1972) involving 44 homosexual and 111 heterosexual men. If this rather obscure findings is to be further established the nature of the association between the endocrine pattern and homosexual preference will require explanation.

The most likely mechanism mediating between endocrine factors and sexual preferences is the masculinization of the brain, or the lack of it, prenatally and possibly immediately postnatally. Males who for some reason are insufficiently androgenized during early development (as might be the case with the oestrogen-treated sons of diabetic mothers, as discussed earlier) may be left with a hypothalamus that responds to an increase in androgen level at puberty more in the manner of a female than a male. Attempts have therefore been made to identify female-type hypothalamic responses in male homosexuals. The positive oestrogen feedback effect has been considered the most likely indicator of this type of hypothalamic development. In anovulatory females a single dose of oestrogen produces an initial fall in plasma LH followed by a rise above initial values (Van de Wiele et al., 1970). Dörner et al. (1975) sought this response in 21 homosexuals, 5 bisexual and 20 heterosexual men, all attending hospital for treatment of skin or veneral diseases (A bisexual is someone who is attracted to both homosexual and heterosexual partners.) Following two initial blood samples, 20 mg of conjugated oestrogens were given intravenously and further blood samples were taken 24, 48, 72, and 96 h later. Thirteen of the 21 homosexuals showed positive feedback effect compared with 2 of the 20 heterosexuals, and none of the bisexuals. This difference was statistically significant. This positive feedback was considerably less marked and much slower to happen than that observed in women. These authors explained this difference on the grounds that androgens, which are at a higher level in male homosexuals than in heterosexual women, decrease the LH responsiveness of the anterior pituitary to hypothalamic LRH. Plasma testosterone levels were not different in the three groups. The premise on which this investigation was based has recently been questioned. Whereas the prenatally or perinatally determined sexual dimorphism of the hypothalamus is well established in rodents, its existence in primates is less certain. Karsch et al. (1973) found a positive feedback effect of oestrogens in both male and female rhesus monkeys if they were castrated. Stearns et al. (1973) found a comparable positive feedback effect in a small number of castrated human males, primed with oestrogens, when given progestogens. McKinnon (Pers. Commun., 1976) has found a similar effect in occasional otherwise normal males. This positive feedback therefore remains a potentially important form of individual difference especially in the male, whilst its relationship to sexual dimorphism is less certain. The findings of Dörner et al. (1975) whilst of interest, certainly require replication. As yet they are the findings most suggestive of an endocrine difference between homosexual and heterosexual males. In general it seems sensible to consider homosexuals as a heterogenous population so far as sexual development is concerned and their Kinsey ratings may be less relevant in discriminating between aetiological categories than other possible variables. As yet very little attention has been paid to endocrine factors in female homosexuality. Nevertheless the recurring pursuit of an organic basis for homosexuality is likely to continue and whilst it seems improbable that any simple answer will emerge, our understanding of general sexual development may be furthered in the process.

SEXUAL AROUSABILITY AND BEHAVIOUR

The relationship between hormones and sexual arousability and behaviour will be examined in the following ways. What patterns of sexual behaviour occur in cases of hyper and hypo-gonadism? What is the endocrine status of people with reduced sexual arousability or performance? How does sexual behaviour vary with variations in endogenous hormone levels? What are the sexual effects of giving hormones to sexually normal or sexually dysfunctional individuals? What is the effect of sex hormone antagonists on sexual arousability?

Sexual Behaviour in Hyper- and Hypo-gonadal States

Money and Walker (1971) reported 15 cases of females with precocious puberty. They found that the frequency of childhood sex play and subsequent sexual development was not abnormal although the age of onset of masturbation was slightly younger than expected. In males with precocious puberty, most of whom are suffering from adreno-genital syndrome, the situation is a little different. Money and Alexander (1969) reported 18 cases, 4 of them of unknown cause. They found a relatively early onset of sexual responsiveness but the content of sexual imagery tended to be consistent with their social and emotional age, though it was fairly readily susceptible to appropriate sex education. Sexual misconduct was not a problem in either the males or the females.

In the females with untreated or late-treated adreno-genital syndrome, where the picture is virilization rather than precocious puberty, there is some evidence of enhanced sexual arousability though the evidence does not indicate whether this is of early onset (Lev-Ran, 1974a). It is of interest that in Lev-Ran's series several of the women reported virtual cessation of their sexual dreams when treatment of the adreno-genital syndrome, and hence reduction of their endogenous testosterone levels, was instituted.

When considering hypogonadism we are once again largely dependent on Money and his colleagues for details of sexual behaviour and development. Money and Alexander (1967) reported eight cases of anorchia and hyporchia believed to be secondary to deficient blood supply in, or an autoimmune destruction of the gonads. The amount of sexual responsiveness and behaviour in these males in late adolescence and adulthood was variable but in most cases involved some response and in one man this was sufficient to allow regular intercourse, even though orgasm was unassociated with ejaculation. It is perhaps significant in this last case that androgens were prescribed though not certainly taken at the appropriate time for the onset of puberty. If androgens had been taken for even a short time this may have accounted for his greater responsiveness in spite of the continuing hypogonadal state. All eight cases showed increase in sexual responsiveness in addition to other signs of virilization once androgen replacement was started. This increase was also very varied in extent.

Bobrow et al. (1971) reported sexual development and the response to treatment in 13 males with hypogonadotrophic hypogonadism. At least five of these had anosmia and were regarded as cases of Kallman's syndrome (hypogonadotrophic hypogonadism associated with anosmia). The level of pretreatment sexuality was certainly lower in this group than in the anorchic group. When compared with primary testicular failure they showed less sexuality after androgen replacement therapy though most of them increased to some extent. These authors concluded that where prepubertal hypogonadism is concerned, sexuality and the sexual response to androgens is more impaired in hypogonadotrophic types than in primary testicular failure. However, this evidence does not support the earlier notion that androgens during adult life are ineffective if hypogonadism is prepubertal in origin; clearly it is a matter of degree. There is minimal data on the effects of prepubertal castration in males, though there is a substantial amount concerning postpubertal castration (see review by Kinsey *et al.*, 1953). Bremer (1959) in following up a large series in Scandinavia, where castration was used for treatment of sexual offenders, found that the loss of sexual responsiveness, though usual, was by no means inevitable and the timing of its onset was very variable and almost certainly poorly correlated with the reduction in circulating androgens. There is general agreement, however, that with adult castration or postpubertal primary testicular failure (e.g. following mumps orchitis) replacement androgens will more or less restore responsiveness to its previous usual level.

One of the most interesting and relevant pieces of evidence concerning the effects of gonadotrophin-releasing hormones, has been reported by Mortimer *et al.* (1974). Of seven males, with onset of hypothalamic hypogonadism in adulthood, six showed an early improvement in sexual potency, more or less to premorbid levels, which was maintained in spite of levels of circulating androgens that were well below normal and in the range that one would expect to be accompanied by impotence. They also demonstrated that the low total androgen level was not concealing a high free androgen level. Only one of these men showed a gradual rise of free androgens to normal levels. These findings suggest that the increase in potency was a direct result of the effect of gonadotrophin-releasing hormone on the brain and not secondary to gonadotrophin or androgen production. Clearly this exciting finding deserves closer attention. Benkert (1975) has briefly reported two small studies of the effects of releasing hormones on sexual dysfunction. Thyrotropin releasing hormone (TRH) was compared with placebo in a double-blind cross over study of 12 impotent males. No effect of the TRH was observed. Luteinizing hormone releasing hormone (LRH), given by means of nasal spray, was compared with placebo in a further double-blind study of six impotent males. Only three of them received the LRH, but in each case there was a noticeable effect on sexual response, particularly after the LRH was discontinued. Clearly, further work is indicated on the effects of LRH on human sexual response.

The best example of prepubertal primary hypogonadism in the female is Turner's syndrome. Although girls with this syndrome are late-developing, ending up small statured, they are eventually capable of relatively normal sexual relationships except that their vaginal mucosa requires oestrogen replacement to respond normally. Thus the absence of oestrogens prepubertally does not apparently interfere with sexual development other than via the effects on stature and any consequent psycho-social effects. Ovariectomy in the post-pubertal female does not usually produce effects on sexual response, though as with the postmenopausal women, oestrogens may be necessary for a normal vaginal lubrication (Bremer, 1959; Kinsey *et al.*, 1953; Waxenberg, 1963). Adrenalectomy in the female, however, removing as it does the main source of androgen, has a predictable effect in reducing female sexual responsiveness (Waxenberg *et al.*, 1959). This is similar to the effect of 'chemical adrenalectomy' by dexamethasone suppression in some female non-human primates (Everitt and Herbert, 1972), and certainly supports the idea that apart from the oes-trogen-dependent response of vaginal lubrication, sexual arousability in the female is largely dependent on androgens.

What is surprising, therefore, is the relatively normal sexual responsiveness of people with the testicular feminization syndrome. Not only do they develop normally feminine gender identities and patterns of maternal behaviour, but most establish satisfactory heterosexual relationships, and usually are orgasmic though rather passive during coitus (Money and Ehrhardt, 1972). It must be assumed that their sexual arousability has developed in spite of androgen insensitivity, but it may be that conversion of testosterone to oestrogen, mentioned earlier as being possibly important for androgen effects on the brain, will hold the explanation for this otherwise paradoxical finding.

Relationship Between Endogenous Hormone Levels and Sexual Behaviour

In studying the relationship between levels of circulating hormones and sexual activity, various methodological problems arise which have not yet been satisfactorily resolved. It is still unclear what effect sexual activity itself has on androgen production. Raboch and Starka (1972) failed to find any correla-tion between frequency of coital activity and plasma testosterone levels. Fox *et al.* (1972), on the other hand, found plasma testosterone levels in one married man to be higher both shortly before and after coital orgasm than under resting conditions. There was no significant difference between the pre- and postorgasm levels, however, as recorded in this one individual on repeated occasions. Nor was there any postorgasm rise in seven other males in whom orgasm was induced by masturbation. It is of course possible that coitus was more likely to happen at periods of high testosterone levels either because the high level would increase sexual arousability or alternatively, and possibly more likely, because the erotic stimulation involved in the anticipation of coitus may have increased circulating androgen. Contrary to earlier expectations (Ismail and Harkness, 1967) this limited data do not suggest that male orgasm *per se* increases tes-tosterone levels. LH levels were not raised in this study, leaving Lincoln (1974) to suggest that the raised testosterone levels associated with sexual activity may be a function of increased testicular blood flow rather than a response to gonadotrophic stimulation.

An anonymous researcher (Anon, 1970) reported increased beard growth during periods preceding the return to his sexual partner after separation. Change in rate of beard growth is considered to be a valid indicator of the change in testosterone secretion. Lincoln (1974) measured testosterone levels in men during and following the watching of erotic films. This study failed to find any effect of the erotic stimulus on testosterone or LH levels in spite of sexual arousal being reported by most subjects. The time span was short, however. Pirke *et al.* (1974) in a similar study involving direct measurement of penile volume change as well as hormone assays, and carrying on the hormone measurements for longer periods of time after the stimulus, showed a noticeable but quite delayed increase in testosterone levels following erotic films. The association between REM phases of sleep and penile erection is now well established (Fisher *et al.*, 1965). Evans *et al.* (1971) reported increases in testosterone level during sleep associated with REM phases and erections.

The issue therefore remains obscure; until such direct effects of sexual behaviour on hormone levels are clarified, it will remain difficult to interpret those studies where random sampling of blood levels is related to relatively long-term patterns of sexual behaviour. With this qualification, therefore, let us consider the further human data that are available to us.

Heller and Myers (1944) identified a proportion of males with sexual dysfunction as having late onset primary testicular failure. This was typically associated with high gonadotrophin and low testosterone levels. They called the syndrome the 'male climacteric' thus implying that it was some form of ageing process affecting the testes. Unlike most cases of sexual dysfunction in the male, these men predictably responded to exogenous androgen administration. After a flurry of interest in the 'male climacteric' at that time, the notion largely disappeared until recently. A number of studies have now shown that there is a decline in testosterone production with advancing age, though levels of total testosterone are not noticeably affected until the sixth decade or later, and there is much individual variation (Vermeulen *et al.*, 1972; Stearns *et al.*, 1974). The fall in free unbound testosterone, however, is greater and of earlier onset than measurement of total values would suggest, because of an increase in sex hormone binding globulin and subsequent increase in testosterone binding, that accompanies ageing (Vermeulen *et al.*, 1972; Stearns *et al.*, 1974). Rubens *et al.* (1974) studied this change further by means of gonadotrophin releasing hormone and gonadotrophin stimulation studies. They concluded that the lowered testosterone is a result of testicular failure. This is consistent with previously observed increase in LH and FSH levels in males with advancing age, noticeable from the fifth decade onwards. Rubens *et al.* (1974) also reported a significant correlation between free testosterone and LH and FSH levels, indicating that feedback control of gonadotrophin production is dependent on free rather than total testosterone levels.

Thus it seems that ageing quite commonly leads to primary testicular failure, and it is therefore possible that a proportion of late onset sexual dysfunction in the male could be secondary to this process. Careful endocrine assessment of such cases will be necessary, and as yet the predictability of their response to exogenous androgen is somewhat uncertain.

Ismail *et al.* (1970) reported the urinary testosterone levels in 28 impotent males, finding them to be significantly lower than in a group of 14 normal males. Cooper *et al.* (1970) went on to divide the impotent men into those who remained sexually responsive (i.e. with continuing desire and masturbatory activity in spite of their erectile impotence) and those who were not. As the problems in the latter group were typically of longer onset, they labelled the two groups 'psychogenic' and 'constitutional', though the etiological implications of these labels were not adequately substantiated by their data. However, they reported that the 'psychogenic' group with continuing sexual responsiveness had significantly higher testosterone levels than the 'constitutional' group. Once again it remains uncertain whether or not the differing testosterone levels were the *consequence* of differing amounts of sexual activity or interest.

Lawrence and Swyer (1974) found no difference in plasma testosterone levels or testosterone-binding affinities between 27 normal and 27 impotent males. Unfortunately they did not give sufficient details of sexual activity and histories of the impotent men to know whether they were predominantly in Cooper's 'constitutional' or 'psychogenic' categories. Raboch *et al.* (1975) on the other hand, reported significantly lower plasma testosterone levels in males with sexual dysfunction than in normal controls. The levels in the dysfunctional group were similar to those found in a previous group studied, where there were pathological somato-sexual changes (e.g. varicocele or Klinefelter's syndrome). In this pathological group the lower testosterone levels were not associated with a lower level of coital activity (Raboch and Starka, 1973). In contrast, a study by Comhaire and Vermeulen (1975) found that 10 men with varicocele and sexual dysfunction had lower plasma testosterone levels than a group of 23 men with varicocele and no sexual dysfunction, and a third group of 31 men with 'psychogenic' impotence. It is probably significant that the first group was older than the other two, but what is of particular interest is that after surgical treatment of the varicocele, the first group showed a return to normal testosterone levels *and* recovery of potency. The evidence for a relationship between plasma testosterone levels and sexual dysfunction is therefore largely negative, but it remains likely that in some cases this relationship is important and it is possible that in several studies it has been obscured by the failure to control for the appropriate variables.

When we turn to the female we have the advantage and the disadvantage of the menstrual cycle; an advantage because of the built-in and to a large extent predictable variability of hormone levels, a disadvantage because any sampling of hormone levels and behaviour must take the phase of the menstrual cycle into account.

The pattern of oestrogen and progesterone levels during the menstrual cycle has long been established; oestrogen level climbs in the follicular phase and reaches a peak just prior to ovulation and declines in the luteal phase as the progestogen level rises, the latter showing a sharp drop just prior to menstruation and the oestrogen having a second peak during the luteal phase (Short, 1972). The pattern of androgen secretion during the menstrual cycle is much less clear and no doubt complicated by the fact that both the adrenal cortex and ovary contribute to the androgen supply. As yet the data are limited but suggest considerable variability from woman to woman. Levels are likely to be low during the follicular phase, however, showing peaks most commonly at around ovulation or during the luteal phase (Lobotsky et al., 1964; Ismail et al., 1968); in several studies these differences are minimal and not significant (Osborn and Yannone, 1971). Baird et al. (1974) reported androstenedione levels to rise to a peak during the seven days around midcycle and to decline gradually during the luteal phase. There was much variation from day to day but overall the androstenedione levels followed those of oestradiol, though not showing the characteristic midcycle dip of the latter.

The data on coital activity during the human menstrual cycle are both more numerous and more contradictory. Studies by Davis (1929) McCance et al. (1937) and Hart (1960) had shown evidence of peaks of coital activity both before and after menstruation and at midcycle. The midcycle peak occurred in only 6% of Hart's series, 34% of his women showing no predictable peaks anywhere in the cycle.

Udry and Morris (1968) examining data collected by Kinsey and his colleagues earlier and collecting some of their own, reported a high coital rate during the follicular phase tending to reach a maximum around ovulation and then declining in the luteal phase. This pattern was considered to be consistent with a hormonal determination and comparable with data from non-human primates. Activity during the follicular phase of the female rhesus monkey was consistent with oestrogen-determined attractiveness of the female, increasing the likelihood of the male approach (Everitt and Herbert, 1972). The reduction in activity during the luteal phase could be accounted for in two ways; either the rising progestogen level has an antiandrogenic effect, thereby reducing the 'receptivity' or sexual approach behaviour of the female, or it has an antioestrogenic effect reducing the 'attractiveness' of the female to the male, an explanation held by Udry et al. (1973) to be consistent with their observed effects of the contraceptive pill (see below). (As is discussed in Chapter 14 and 22 of this volume, rhesus monkey 'attractiveness' is in part determined by oestrogen-dependent cues such as olfactory phermones or colour changes of the vulva. It remains a possibility that pheromonal cues play a part in human female attractiveness, at least in some cases.) The importance of androgens for the 'receptivity' or responsiveness of the female both primate and human, has already been mentioned. One might therefore suppose that sexual activity would be correlated with peaks of testosterone or androstenedione production in the female. As yet we have no data which enable us to make this correlation but we know that the pattern most commonly observed is for androgen levels to be high either at ovulation or during the luteal phase. The first peak could be consistent with the occasional tendency to midcycle peaking of coital activity; the latter peak, however, is inconsistent with the reported decline of activity during the luteal phase.

James (1971) reanalysed the data of McCance et al. (1937) and Udry and Morris (1968) and added some of his own. By pooling data only from cycles of similar length, he found that the only predictable peak was immediately following menstruation, evidence for a midcycle peak being very slight. Spitz et al. (1975) reported similar findings and concluded that such a pattern must be predominantly determined by psychological rather than hormonal factors. The issue, therefore, remains confused.

As yet we lack any evidence of the endocrine status of sexually dysfunctional women though with current assay techniques such evidence should provide relevant information.

The Effects of Exogenous Hormones on Sexual Behaviour

The study of the effects of the oral contraceptive provides a substantial source of information about the effects of exogenous hormones on the normal female. Regrettably we once again find ourselves with conflicting evidence. This rich source is riddled with methodological pitfalls and few studies have effectively avoided them. Only some of the reports will be mentioned here (for a fuller review see Bancroft, 1974).

Several reports, some involving large numbers of subjects have indicated an increase in coital frequency in women on the pill (e.g. Westoff et al., 1969). Others have reported a noticeable proportion of women with decreased sexual interest or arousability. One of the most substantial reports, prepared by the Royal College of General Practitioners (1974) compared 20,000 pill users with a similar numbers of controls, using self-report measures. Complaints of decreased sexual interest were more than four times as common in the pill-users than in the controls.

It is quite possible that some of the varied results reflect the fact that women experiencing side effects, including loss of sexual response, are likely to stop using the pill and thus may be underrepresented in some studies. Herzberg et al. (1971) compared three groups of women in an uncontrolled study. One group used intrauterine devices, the second used one form of oral contraceptive throughout the study, and the third group changed from one oral preparation to another. Whereas the IUD group showed a steady improvement sexually over the period of the study, the 'no-change' pill group showed an initial improvement which then flattened out, whereas the 'change-pill' group showed a slight but steady deterioration. Those women who changed the pill because of loss of sexual response were significantly more depressed than those who did not. These workers concluded that the increasing improvement with the IUD's was due to an increasing confidence in their efficacy. They also concluded that the benefit of contraceptive security, producing an initial improvement in the second group, was eventually outweighed by some psychopharmacological or endocrine effects of the pill. Against this, however, are the findings by Cullberg et al. (1969) and Grounds et al. (1970) that reduction of sexual arousability as an effect of oral contraceptives was maximal in the first one or two months, thereafter declining.

Grant and Pryse-Davies (1968) reported an association between both depression and reduced sexual interest as side effects and the level of progestogen in the oral contraceptive. Several other workers have suggested that sexual effects may be related to mood changes. Cullberg (1973) examined this possibility in one of the more methodologically satisfactory studies. Using four groups each of 80 women volunteers all using other forms of contraception, he compared the effects of four different preparations, one a placebo, the other three progestogen–oestrogen combinations with varying levels of progestogen. Mild depressive symptoms were significantly more common in the groups receiving active preparations than in the placebo group though there was no significant difference in this respect between the different progestogen levels. Lowered sexual interest, when it occurred, seemed to be associated with mood disturbance and hence Cullberg concluded that these preparations affected sexual function only indirectly by means of mood change.

Morris and Udry (1971) in a double-blind controlled study gave three groups of women, each using other means of contraception, either placebo, a progestogen–oestrogen combination, or an oestrogen–progestogen sequential pill. They found that taking the menstrual cycle as a whole, there was no significant difference in the frequency of sexual intercourse between the three groups. When they examined the data in more detail (Udry and Morris, 1970) they found that the decrease in frequency that they had previously observed during the luteal phase did not occur in the second half of the cycle with women on the pill. By getting the women to record whether their husbands wanted intercourse or not they concluded that the absence of a luteal suppression of coitus was probably due to greater attractiveness of the female to the male during that period of the cycle whilst the women were on the pill. Their explanation was that the endogenous progesterone levels which normally would reduce the female's attractiveness, would themselves be inhibited by the exogenous hormones during a pill cycle, (Udry et al., 1973). Whatever the explanation, it seems probable that oral contraceptives flatten out some of the peaks of high and low coital frequency during the cycle. This is further supported by the findings of Diamond et al. (1972) that the normal peaks of visual sensitivity around the time of ovulation, possibly making coitus more likely, are eliminated by oral contraceptives.

At this stage we can justifiably conclude that for the substantial majority of women oral contraceptives do not directly lower the overall frequency of coitus. We do not yet know whether the quality of the coital experience is affected and it remains probable that there is a small proportion of women who are unduly susceptible to oral contraceptives either by direct effect on sexual responsiveness or via induced mood change.

Exogenous androgens, in particular testosterone, have been used for some time in an attempt to increase sexual responsiveness in men and women. Several of the earlier reports of this effect in women followed the use of androgens for reasons unconnected with sexual response. Shorr *et al.* (1938) gave one group of women oestrogens and a second group oestrogens combined with 25–50 mg of testosterone propionate (TP) daily. They found a significantly greater effect on sexual responsiveness in the latter group. Greenblatt *et al.* (1942) reported the effects of testosterone in 55 women treated for a variety of gynaecological disorders. TP was used in doses ranging from 25–400 mg implanted subfascially. Twenty-two women who had secondary loss of sexual responsiveness all reported an increase following the hormone. In fourteen women with 'mild to moderate' sexual interest and response, eight reported an increase and six no change. In ten with 'good to excessive' sexual interest and response, eight reported no change, one a temporary increase and one, described previously as 'nymphomaniacal', a decrease. Nine women had always been minimally responsive sexually; six of these reported increased responsiveness, three no change. Salmon and Geist (1943) reported a series of 101 women; some were given testosterone parenterally, others orally. Twenty nine of the women were described as having 'primary frigidity' (i.e. general sexual unresponsiveness since puberty); 20 of these were considered to have developed normal sexual responsiveness as a result of treatment; a further four improved but remained anorgasmic. Thirty women had frigidity considered to be secondary to some endocrine state, e.g. surgical menopause, amenorrhoea. Ten out of eleven given androgens alone responded with an increase in sexual responsiveness. Of ten women initially given oestrogens alone, six responded when androgens were subsequently added. Seven out of nine women receiving the combination from the start reported improvement.

The effects reported in these earlier studies were striking and it is remarkable how little attention has been paid in recent years to this use of androgen, particularly in view of the obvious increase in demand for treatment of sexual unresponsiveness in the female. These earlier studies are deficient in various ways, however. They lack appropriate controls and methods of evaluating behavioural change. It is possible that much of the apparent effects were of placebo type and that clinicians have become disillusioned with this application of androgens. Virilizing side effects, which most women would strongly wish to avoid, may have proved a problem, although from most reports they are unlikely to occur with the lower doses of testosterone. Interest in specific treatment tends to wax and wane according to current fashion and it is now time for this aspect to be reinvestigated with modern methods.

The effects of exogenous testosterone on male sexuality are, paradoxically, even less certain. There is no satisfactory study of these effects on the sexually normal male and, such as they are, the data are conflicting (see Kinsey *et al.*, 1953). Testosterone has been used extensively for the treatment of erectile impotence in the male, though the weight of opinion in the literature is that it is ineffective except in those cases where there is primary testicular failure (Cooper, 1972). There have been two controlled studies. In the first a small dose of testosterone combined with a variety of other compounds thought to have some aphrodisiac properties (e.g. yohimbine) was compared with placebo in a double-blind controlled study (Bruhl and Leslie, 1963). A significant drug effect was claimed. The details given were minimal, however, and the methods of assessing change were crude. The second by Jakobovitz (1970) used a combination of methyltestosterone (75 mg daily) with thyroid extract (30 mg daily). Once again details given were extremely limited, and although the study was described as double-blind, description of the design was minimal. A hundred patients were involved, mainly aged 50 to 70. Approximately half received a placebo. A 'favourable response' was noted in 78% of those receiving the active drug, and 45% of those receiving the placebo. Even allowing for the substantial placebo effect, this appears to be a convincing drug effect in an age group where hormonal effects are probably more likely—but the report does not permit confident conclusions and it is possible that the sexual improvement was part of a non-specific improvement in well-being. As with the female, we await satisfactory research. Even in those cases where testosterone is clearly effective, (e.g. primary hypogonadism) we know little of the timing and mechanisms of its action. One single case report (Beumont *et al.*, 1972) in which careful assessment was involved, showed in a hypogonadal male that erections to psychic stimuli (i.e. visual stimuli and imagery) increased after one week on methyltestosterone. In this case the mechanisms of action were not confined to an increase in genital sensitivity as suggested by Perloff (1949), as this would have shown itself in reflexive but not psychic erections.

Recently, as a result of observed effects in a variety of animals (Lidberg, 1972a), interest has been shown in the possibility that oxytocin may enhance human sexual responsiveness. In impotent men, Lidberg (1972b) has found that levels of oxytocinase, the enzyme responsible for the breakdown of oxytocin were higher the longer the duration of the impotence. In three double-blind controlled studies of males with erectile impotence (Lidberg, 1972a; Lidberg and Sternthal, in prep.) a weak effect of oxytocin or oxytocin analogues was demonstrated in comparison with placebo, though in two studies the effect was greater with the lower of the drug dosages used. This suggested a possible curvilinear dose–effect relationship. These rather surprising findings await replication and as yet we lack relevant data on oxytocin levels during normal human sexual response.

The Use of Hormones to Reduce Sexual Responsiveness

The final source of clinical evidence is the pharmacological control of sexual behaviour, particularly in male sexual offenders. Oestrogens have been used for this purpose for many years, either given orally (Golla and Hodge, 1949; Whittaker, 1959; Scott, 1964); or by implants (Field and Williams, 1970). Whilst they have been found effective in many cases, their usefulness has been limited by side effects (e.g. nausea, headaches, and the more irreversible or serious effects such as breast enlargement (gynaecomastia), subsequent mammary carcinoma or thrombotic disease). More recently in the United States, progestogens have been used for this purpose. The possible effects of progesterone in reducing sexual interest and responsiveness in the female have already been mentioned in discussing oral contraceptives. They have been used clinically to control excessive sexual interest in the female (e.g. Kupperman and Studdiford, 1953). Money (1970) reported the effects of medroxy-progesterone acetate in a group of eight male sex offenders. Whilst the behavioural effects were only noticeable in three of the eight cases, these effects were apparently associated with a marked reduction in circulating androgens, presumably due to an antigonadotrophic effect of the progesterone. These effects were reversible.

In Europe attention has focused on a synthetic progestogen which combines progestogen-like antigonadotrophic properties with a direct antiandrogenic effect due to competitive binding at target organ sites. This is cyproterone acetate, an antiandrogen, which has been used extensively in animal research as well as clinically for the control of unwanted sexuality (Briggs and Briggs, 1971; Davies, 1974). A further drug that has been used for this purpose is Benperidol, a butyrephenone, thought to have relatively specific effects on sexual responsiveness (Sterkmans and Geerts, 1966).

Assessing such drug or hormone effects in sexual offenders presents even greater methodological problems than those that have hitherto been described. The reports so far mentioned have been based on clinical impressions. Two studies have employed double-blind cross-over design together with a variety of measures of change, including the physiological measurement of erectile response to erotic stimuli. The first (Tennent et al., 1974) compared Benperidol with Chlorpromazine, a tranquillizer with comparable side effects, and a placebo in twelve male sexual offenders. Each subject received each of the three preparations for six-week periods, the order being varied according to a balanced design. Measurement was carried out at the end of each drug period. Benperidol was more effective than Chlorpromazine or placebo on only one measure, a self-rating of frequency of sexual thoughts. There was no significant effect on frequency of masturbation, sexual attitudes, or erectile response to erotic stimuli (including erotic film). The second study involving another group of twelve sexual offenders (Bancroft et al., 1974) used the same design and measures as the first, but compared the effects of cyproterone acetate, ethinyl oestradiol, and a period of 'no treatment'. The pattern of change in the various measures was similar to that in the first study. The two drugs did not differ significantly from one another in any of the variables. They both differed significantly from 'no treatment' in their effects on frequency of sexual thoughts and masturbation, whereas cyproterone acetate alone produced a weakly significant effect on the erectile response to erotic stimuli. It was thus noticeable that the most marked effects were on the more cognitive measures (i.e. self-rating of sexual thoughts) whilst physiological responses were relatively unaffected, with responses to erotic films continuing strongly throughout the study. This was a somewhat surprising finding as it had often been assumed on the basis of clinical reports that oestrogens impaired the erectile response more than the sexual interest.

In such controlled conditions, therefore, these drugs were shown to have a significant but not particularly marked effect. How did this relate to hormonal changes? Murray *et al.* (1975) reported the endocrine changes in these two studies. In the first, no changes of either testosterone or gonadotrophin levels were found with Benperidol. In the second, both drugs produced marked endocrine changes which were substantially different. Cyproterone acetate produced a significant reduction in plasma testosterone and follicle stimulating hormone (FSH) levels and a slight but non-significant reduction in plasma lutenizing hormone (LH). Ethinyl oestradiol, on the other hand, produced a highly significant increase in plasma testosterone and LH but very little effect on plasma FSH. These unexpected changes with oestrogen were attributed to a substantial increase in the sex hormone binding globulin provoked by the ethinyl oestradiol and leading to an increase in bound inactive testosterone, and masking a fall in free active testosterone. This once again reminds us of the importance of distinguishing between free and bound steroids when looking for relationships between plasma hormones and behaviour. The subjects in these studies were not necessarily normal in their response to oestrogens, and the oestrogen-induced changes were similar to those observed in men with thyrotoxicosis or chronic liver disease (Anderson, 1974); we await results of studies of the hormonal effects of low-dose oestrogens in normal men. Steroid binding in the plasma provides a subtle mechanism by which exogenous hormones can influence levels of circulating free steroids (Burke and Anderson, 1972) and this may be the basis for the behavioural effects of both cyproterone acetate and ethinyl oestradiol. However, there were no apparent hormonal changes with Benperidol and the similarity of the pattern and extent of the behavioural changes with the three compounds suggests that some common mechanism, not reflected in the plasma steroid levels, was operating. If the oestrogen mediation of central androgen effects has to be incorporated into our explanation we are left with a hormonal conundrum.

SUMMARY AND CONCLUSIONS

The evidence of the relationship between hormones and sexual behaviour in humans is considered under the following headings: gender identity, sexual preferences, and sexual arousability and behaviour. The evidence is mainly clinical and is derived from observations of sexual behaviour in patients with endocrine disorders of either prenatal or later onset, endocrine assays in people with abnormalities of sexual behaviour, and the observed effects on sexual behaviour of exogenous hormones such as oral contraceptives, as well as of antihormones.

This review has served to emphasize that our understanding of the relationship between hormones and human sexual behaviour is at a primitive stage. We can conclude with some confidence that hormones, in particular androgens, play a vital role in prenatal development of sexual anatomy. The evidence that prenatal or childhood levels of androgens may influence gender identity development is suggestive, though by no means conclusive. The presence of androgens at puberty appears to be necessary for the development of normal sexual responsiveness, at least in the male, whilst removal of endogenous androgen supply from both male and female adults is highly likely in time to have a negative effect on sexual responsiveness. However, the relationship between circulating levels of steroid hormones or gonadotrophins and sexual interest, responsiveness or behaviour remains almost totally obscure.

It is true that much of the investigation of this relationship to date has been methodologically suspect and there is great scope for better research methods in the future. It is also probably true that much of the research has tackled questions which are too naive or simplistic. There has been a widespread need to find a simple hormonal key to the understanding of human sexual behaviour. There is no reason why we should expect to find simple relationships. Future research must be prepared for greater complexity. We have to allow for considerable individual variation, for curvilinear dose–effect relationships, for the possibly greater importance of the rate of change than of absolute levels of hormones, and for the importance of levels and ratios of the free active moieties rather than of total amounts of circulating steroids. Alongside this greater laboratory sophistication we must establish behavioural measures of more certain validity and relevance. Whether such progress will allow us to consider hormones as important determinants of sexual behaviour in the human remains to be seen.

REFERENCES

Anderson, D. C. (1974) Sex hormone binding globulin, *Clin. Endocrinol.*, **3**, 69–96.

Anon. (1970) Effects of sexual activity on beard growth in man, *Nature*, **226**, 869–70.

Baird, D. T., Burger, P. E., Hearon-Jones, G. D., and Scaramuzzi, R. J. (1974) The site of secretion of androstenedione in non-pregnant women, *J. Endocrinol.*, **63**, 201–12.

Bancroft, J. H. J. (1972) The relationship between gender identity and sexual behaviour: some clinical aspects. In: *Gender Differences: Their Ontogeny and Significance*, C. Ounsted and D. C. Taylor (eds.), Churchill Livingstone, Edinburgh.

Bancroft, J. H. J. (1974) The effects of fertility control on human sexual behaviour. In: *Population and its Problems: a Plain Man's Guide*, H. B. Parry (ed.), Clarendon, Oxford.

Bancroft, J. H. J., Tennent, T. G., Loucas, K., and Cass, J. (1974) Control of deviant sexual behaviour by drugs: behavioural effects of oestrogen and anti androgens. *Br. J. Psychiat.*, **125**, 310–5.

Benkert, O. (1975) Studies on pituitary hormones and releasing hormones in depression and sexual impotence, *Prog. Brain Res.*, **42**, 25–36.

Beumont, P. J. V., Bancroft, J. H. J., Beardwood, C. J., and Russell, G. F. M. (1972) Behavioural changes following treatment with testosterone: a case report. *Psychol. Med.*, **2**, 70–2.

Birk, L., Williams, G. H., Chasin, M., and Rose, L. I. (1973) Serum testosterone levels in homosexual men, *New Engl. J. Med.*, **289**, 1236.

Bobrow, N. A., Money, J., and Lewis, V. G. (1971) Dalayed puberty, eroticism, and sense of smell: A psychological study of hypo-gonadotrophism, osmatic and anosmatic (Kallmann's Syndrome), *Arch. Sex. Behav.*, **1**, 329–44.

Bremer, J. (1959) *Asexualisation: A Follow-up Study of 244 Cases*, Macmillan, New York.

Briggs, M. and Briggs, M. H. (1971) Treatment of male hypersexual conditions by a non-oestrogenic anti-androgen, *Med. J. Zambia*, **5**, 125–9.

Brodie, H. K. H., Gartrell, N., Doering, C., and Rhue, T. (1974) Plasma testosterone levels in heterosexual and homosexual men, *Am. J. Psychiat.*, **131**, 82–3.

Bruhl, E. E. and Leslie, C. H. (1963) Afrodex, double blind test in impotence, *Med. Rec. Ann.*, **56**, 22.

Burke, C. W. and Anderson, D. C. (1972) Sex hormone-binding globulin is an oestrogen amplifier, *Nature*, **240**, 38–40.

Comhaire, F. and Vermeulen, A. (1975) Plasma testosterone in patients with varicocele and sexual inadequacy, *J. Clin. Endocrinol. and Metabol.*, **40**, 824–9.

Cooper, A. J. (1972) Diagnosis and management of 'Endocrine Impotence'. *Br. Med. J.*, **2**, 34–6.

Cooper, A. J., Ismail, A. A. A., Smith, C. G., and Loraine, J. A. (1970) Androgen function in 'Psychogenic' and 'Constitutional' types of impotence. *Br. Med. J.*, **3**, 17–20.

Cullberg, J. (1973) Mood changes and menstrual symptoms with different gestagen/estrogen combinations, *Act. Psychiat. Scand.*, Suppl., 236.

Cullberg, J., Gelli, M., and Jonsson, C. O. (1969) Mental and sexual adjustment before and after six months use of oral contraceptives, *Acta Psychiat. Scand.*, **45**, 259–76.

Davies, T. S. (1974) Cyproterone acetate for male hypersexuality, *J. Internat. Med. Res.*, **2**, 159–63.

Davis, K. B. (1929) *Factors in the Sex Life of 2,200 Women*, Harper and Row, New York.

Diamond, M. (1965) A critical evaluation of the ontogeny of human sexual behavior, *Quart. Rev. Biol.*, **40**, 147–75.

Diamond, M., Diamond, A. L., and Mast, M. (1972) Visual sensitivity and sexual arousal levels during the menstrual cycle, *J. Nerv. Ment. Dis.*, **155**, 170–6.

Doerr, P., Kockott, G., Vogt, H. J., Pirke, K. M., and Dittmar, F. (1973) Plasma testosterone, estradiol and semen analysis in male homosexuals, *Arch. Gen. Psychiat.*, **29**, 829–33.

Dörner, G., Rohde, W., Stahl, F., Krell, L., and Masius, W. G. (1975) A neuroendocrine predisposition for homosexuality in men, *Archiv. Sex. Behav.*, **4**, 1–8.

Ehrhardt, A. A., Epstein, R., Money, J. (1968a) Fetal androgens and female gender identity in the early treated adrenogenital syndrome, *Johns Hopkins Med. J.*, **122**, 160–67.

Ehrhardt, A. A., Evers, K., and Money, J. (1968b) Influence of androgen and some aspects of sexually dimorphic behaviour in women with late-treated adreno-genital syndrome, *Johns Hopkins Med. J.*, **123**, 115–22.

Ehrhardt, A. A. and Money, J. (1967) Progestin-induced hermaphroditism: IQ and psychosexual identity in a study of ten girls, *J. Sex. Res.*, **3**, 83–100.

Evans, J. I., Maclean, A. W., Ismail, A. A. A., and Love, D. W. (1971) Concentrations of plasma testosterone in normal men during sleep, *Nature*, **229**, 261–62.

Evans, R. B. (1972) Physical and biochemical characteristics of homosexual men, *J. Consult. Clin. Psychol.*, **39**, 140–47.

Everitt, B. J. and Herbert, J. (1971) The effects of dexamethasone and androgens on sexual receptivity of female rhesus monkeys. *J. Endocrinol.*, **51**, 575–88.

Everitt, B. J. and Herbert, J. (1972) Hormonal correlates of sexual behaviour in subhuman primates, *Danish Med. Bull.*, **19**, 246–58.

Field, L. H. and Williams, M. (1970) The hormonal treatment of sex offenders, *Medicine, Science and the Law.*, **10**, 27.

Fisher, C., Gross, J., and Zuch, J. (1965) Cycle of penile erections synchronous with dreaming (REM) sleep, *Arch. Gen. Psychiat.*, **12**, 29–45.

Fletcher, T. J. and Short, R. V. (1974) Restoration of libido in castrated red deer stag *(Cervus elaphus)* with oestradiol 17β, *Nature*, **248**, 616–8.

Fox, C. A., Ismail, A. A. A., Love, D. N., Kirkham, K. E., and Loraine, J. A. (1972) Studies on the reltionship between plasma testosterone levels and human sexual activity, *J. Endocrinol.*, **52**, 51–8.

Fulmer, G. P. (1973) Testosterone levels and female-to-male transexualism, *Arch. Sex. Behav.*, **2**, 399–400.

Gabele, A. (1971) Results of treatment of libido disorders in women, *Z-Allgemeinmed.*, **47**, 666–8.

Golla, F. L. and Hodge, S. R. (1949) Hormone treatment of sex offenders, *Lancet*, **1**, 1006.

Grant, E. C. G. and Pryse-Davies, J. (1968) Effect of oral contraception on depressive mood changes and on endometrial monoamine oxidase and phosphatases, *Br. Med. J.*, **3**, 777–80.

Green, R. (1974) *Sexual Identity Conflict in Children and Adults*, Duckworth, London.

Greenblatt, R. B., Mortara, F., and Torpin, R. (1942) Sexual libido in the female, *Am. J. Obstet. Gynec.*, **44**, 658–63.

Grounds, D., Davies, B., and Mowbray, R. (1970) The contraceptive pill, side effects and personality: a report of a controlled double-blind trial. *Br. J. Psychiat.*, **116**, 169–72.

Hart, R. D. A. (1960) Monthly rhythm of libido in married women, *Br. Med. J.*, **1**, 1023–4.

Heller, C. G. and Myers, G. B. (1944) The male climacteric: its symptomatology, diagnosis and treatment, *J. Am. Med. Assoc.*, **126**, 472–7.

Herzberg, B. N., Draper, K. C., Johnson, A. L., and Nicol, G. C. (1971) Oral contraceptives, depression and libido, *Br. Med. J.*, **3**, 495–500.

Hirschfeld, M. (1944) *Sexual Anomalies and Perversions*, Francis Aldor, London.

Imperato-McGinley, J., Guerrero, L., Gautier, T., and Peterson, R. E. (1974) Steroid 5-reductase deficiency in man: an inherited form of male pseudohermaphroditism, *Science*, **186**, 1213–5.

Ismail, A. A. A., Davidson, D. W., Loraine, J. A., Cullen, D. R., Irvine, W. J., Cooper, A. J., and Smith, C. G. (1970) Assessment of gonadal function in impotent men. In: *Reproductive Endocrinology*, W. J. Irvine, (ed.), Livingstone, Edinburgh.

Ismail, A. A. A. and Harkness, R. A. (1967) Urinary testosterone excretion in men in normal and pathological conditions, *Acta Endocrinol.*, **56**, 469–80.

Ismail, A. A. A., Harkness, R. A. H., and Loraine, J. A. (1968) Some observations on the urinary excretion of testosterone during the normal menstrual cycle, *Acta Endocrinol.*, **58**, 685–95.

Jakobovitz, T. (1970) The treatment of impotence with methyl testosterone thyroid, *Fertil. Steril.*, **21**, 32–5.

James, W. H. (1971) The distribution of coitus within the human intermenstruum, *J. Biosoc. Sci.*, **3**, 159–71.

Johnston, P. and Davidson, J. M. (1972) Intracerebral androgens and sexual behaviour in the male rat, *Horm. Behav.*, **3**, 345.

Jones, J. R. and Samimy, J. (1973) Plasma testosterone levels and female transexualism, *Arch. Sex. Behav.*, **2**, 251–6.

Karsch, F. J., Dierschke, D. J., and Knobil, E. (1973) *Science*, **179**, 484.

Kinsey, A. C., Pomeroy, W. B., Martin, C. E., and Gebhard, P. H. (1953) *Sexual Behavior in the Human Female*, Saunders, Philadelphia.

Kolodny, R. C. (1975) Paper presented at 1st Annual meeting of International Academy of Sex Research, Stony Brook, New York. September 1975.

Kolodny, R. C., Jacobs, L. S., Masters, W. H., Toro, G., and Daughaday, W. H. (1972) Plasma gonadotrophins and prolactin in male homosexuals, *Lancet*, **2**, 18–20.

Kolodny, R. C., Masters, W. H., Hendryx, B. S., Toro, G. (1971) Plasma testosterone and semen analysis in male homosexuals, *New Engl. J. Med.*, **285**, 1170–74.

Kupperman, H. S. and Studdiford, W. E. (1953) Endocrine therapy in gynecologic disorders, *Postgrad. Med.*, **14**, 410–25.

Lawrence, D. H. and Swyer, G. I. M. (1974) Plasma testosterone and testosterone binding affinities in men with impotence, oligospermia, azoospermia and hypogonadism, *Br. Med. J.*, **1**, 349–51.

Lev-Ran, A. (1974a) Sexuality and educational level of women with thë late-treated adreno-genital syndrome, *Arch. Sex. Behav.*, **3**, 27–32.

Lev-Ran, A. (1974b) Gender role differentiation in hermaphrodites, *Arch. Sex. Behav.*, **3**, 391–424.

Lidberg, L. (1972a) The effect of Syntocin on patients suffering from impotence, *Pharmakopsychiat.*, **5**, 187.

Lidberg, L. (1972b) Oxytocinase levels in patients suffering from impotence, *Hormones*, **5**, 273.

Lincoln, G. A. (1974) Luteinising hormone and testosterone in man, *Nature*, **252**, 232–3.

Lobotsky, J. H. L., Wyss, E. J., Segre, J., and Lloyd, C. W. (1964) Plasma testosterone in the normal woman, *J. Clin. Endocrinol. Metabol.*, **24**, 1261–5.

Loraine, J. A. Ismail, A. A. A., Adamopolos, D. A., and Dove, G. A. (1970) Endocrine function in male and female homosexuals, *Br. Med. J.*, **4**, 406–8.

McCance, R. A., Luff, M. C., and Widdowson, E. E. (1937) Physical and emotional periodicity in women, *J. Hygiene*, **37**, 571–611.

Margolese, M. S. (1970) Homosexuality: a new endocrine correlate, *Horm. Behav.*, **1**, 151–5.

Margolese, M. S. and Janiger, O. (1973) Androsterone/Etiocholanolone ratios in male homosexuals, *Br. Med. J.*, **3**, 207–10.

Masica, D. N. and Lewis, V. G. (1969) IQ, fetal sex hormones and cognitive patterns: studies in the testicular feminising syndrome of androgen insensitivity, *Johns Hopkins Med. J.*, **123**, 105–14.

Migeon, G. J., Rivarola, M. A., and Forest, M. G. (1969) Studies of androgens in male transsexual subjects; effects of oestrogen therapy. In: *Transexualism and Sex Re-assignment*, R. Green and J. Money (eds.), Johns Hopkins Press, Baltimore.

Money, J. (1970) Use of an androgen-depleting hormone in the treatment of male sex offenders, *J. Sex Res.*, **6**, 165–72.

Money, J. and Alexander, D. (1967) Eroticism and sexual function in developmental anorchism and hyporchia with pubertal failure, *J. Sex. Res.*, **3**, 31–47.

Money, J. and Alexander, D. (1969) Psychosexual development and absence of homosexuality in males with precocious puberty: review of 18 cases, *J. Nerv. Ment. Dis.*, **148**, 111–23.

Money, J. and Ehrhardt, A. A. (1972) *Man and Woman; Boy and Girl.* The differentiation and dimorphism of gender identity from conception to maturity, Johns Hopkins Univ. Press, Baltimore.

Money, J. and Ogunro, C. (1974) Behavioral sexology: ten cases of genetic male intersexuality with impaired prenatal and pubertal androgenisation, *Arch. Sex. Behav.*, **3**, 181–205.

Money, J. and Walker, P. A. (1971) Psychosexual development, maternalism, nonpromiscuity and body image in 15 females with precocious puberty, *Arch. Sex. Behav.*, **1**, 45–60.

Morris, N. M. and Udry, J. R. (1971) Sexual frequency and contraceptive pills, *Soc. Biol*, **18**, 40–5.

Mortimer, C. H., McNeilly, A. S., Fisher, R. A., Murray, M. A. F., and Besser, G. M.

(1974) Gonadotrophin releasing hormone therapy in hypogonadal males with hypothalamic or pituitary dysfunction, *Br. Med. J.*, **4**, 617–21.

Murray, M. A. F., Bancroft, J. H. J., Anderson, D. C., Tennent, T. G., and Carr, P. J. (1975) Endocrine changes in male sexual deviants after treatment with anti-androgens, oestrogens or tranquillizers, *J. Endocrinol.*, **67**, 179–88.

Naftolin, F., Ryan, K. J., Davies, I. J., Reddy, V. V., Flores, F., Petro, Z., Kuhn, M., White, B. J., Takaoka, Y., and Wollin, L. (1975) The formation of estrogens by central neuroendocrine tissues, *Rec. Prog. in Horm. Res.*, Vol. 31.

Nielsen, J. (1969) Klinefelter's syndrome and the XYY syndrome *Acta Psychiatrica Scandinavica*, Suppl. 209.

Osborn, R. H. and Yannone, M. E. (1971) Plasma androgens in the normal and androgenic female: a review, *Obstet. Gynaecol. Survey*, **26**, 195–228.

Perloff, W. H. (1949) Role of hormones in human sexuality, *Psychosom. Med.*, **11**, 133–9.

Perloff, W. H. (1965) Hormones and homosexuality. In: *Sexual Inversion*, J. Marmor (ed.), Basic Books, New York.

Pillard, R. C., Rose, R. M., and Sherwood, M. (1974) Plasma testosterone levels in homosexual men, *Arch. Sex. Behav.*, **3**, 453–9.

Pirke, K. H., Kockott, G., and Dittmar, F. (1974) Psychosexual stimulation and plasma testosterone in man, *Arch. Sex. Behav.*, **3**, 577–84.

Raboch, J., Mellan, J., and Starka, L. (1975) Plasma testosterone in male patients with sexual dysfunction, *Arch. Sex. Behav.*, **4**, 541–5.

Raboch, J. and Starka, L. (1972) Coital activity of men and the levels of plasmatic testosterone, *J. Sex Research*, **8**, 219–24.

Raboch, J. and Starka, L. (1973) Reported coital activity of men and levels of plasma testosterone, *Arch. Sex. Behav.*, **2**, 309–16.

Rosenfield, R. L., Lawrence, A. M., Liao, S., and Landau, R. L. (1971) Androgen and androgen responsiveness in the feminising testis syndrome. Comparison of complete and incomplete forms, *J. Clin. Endocrinol. and Metabol.*, **32**, 625–32.

Royal College of General Practitioners (1974) *Oral Contraceptives and Health*, London, Pitman.

Rubens, R., Dhont, M., and Vermeulen, A. (1974) Further studies on Leydig cell function in old age. *J. Clin. Endocrin. and Metabol.*, **39**, 40–45.

Ryan, K. J., Naftolin, F., Reddy, V., Flores, F., and Petro, Z. (1972) Estrogen formation in the brain, *Am. J. Obstet. Gynec.*, **114**, 454–60.

Salmon, U. J. and Geist, S. H. (1943) The effects of androgens upon libido in women, *J. Clin. Endocrinol.*, **3**, 235–8.

Scott, P. D. (1964) Definition, classification, prognosis, and treatment. In: *Pathology and Treatment of Sexual Deviation*, I. Rosen (ed.), Oxford University Press.

Shorr, E., Papanicolaou, G. N., and Stimmel, B. J. (1938) Neutralisation of ovarian follicular hormone in women by simultaneous administration of male sex hormone, *Proc. Soc. Exp. Biol. Med.*, **38**, 759–62.

Short, R. V. (1972) Role of hormones in sex cycles. In: *Hormones in Reproduction. No. 3. Reproduction in Mammals* series, C. R. Austin and R. V. Short (eds.), Cambridge Univ. Press.

Spitz, C. J., Gold, A. R., and Adams, D. B. (1975) Cognitive and hormonal factors affecting coital frequency, *Arch. Sex. Behav.*, **4**, 249–64.

Stearns, E. L., MacDonnel, J. A., Kaufman, B. J., Padna, R., Lucman, T. S. Winter, J. S. D., and Fairman, C. (1974) Declining testicular function with age. Hormonal and clinical correlates, *Am. J. Med.*, **57**, 761–6.

Stearns, E. L., Winter, J. S. D., and Faiman, C. (1973) Positive feedback effect of progestin upon serum gonadotropins in estrogen-primed castrate men, *J. Clin. Endocrinol. and Metabol.*, **37**, 635–8.

Sterkmans, P. and Geerts, F. (1966) Is benperidol (R4504) the specific drug for the treatment of excessive and disinhibited sexual behaviour? *Acta Neurolog. Psychiat. Belgica*, **66**, 1030–40.

Tennent, T. G., Bancroft, J. H. J., and Cass, J. (1974) The control of deviant sexual behaviour by drugs: a double-blind controlled study of benperidol, chlorpromazin and placebo. *Arch. Sex. Behav.*, **3**, 266–71.

Udry, J. R. and Morris, N. M. (1968) Distribution of coitus in the menstrual cycle, *Nature*, **220**, 593–6.

Udry, J. R. and Morris, N. M. (1970) The effect of contraceptive pills on the distribution of sexual activity in the menstrual cycle, *Nature*, **227**, 502–3.

Udry, J. R., Morris, N. M., and Waller, L. (1973) Effect of contraceptive pills on sexual activity in the luteal phase of the human menstrual cycle, *Arch. Sex. Behav.*, **2**, 205–14.

Van de Wiele, R. L., Bognmil, F., Dyrenfurth, I., Ferin, M., Jewelewicz, R., Warren, M., Rizkallah, J., and Mikhail, G. (1970) Mechanisms regulating the menstrual cycle in women, *Rec. Prog. Horm. Res.*, **26**, 63–95.

Vermeulen, A., Rubens, R., and Verdonck, L. (1972) Testosterone secretion and metabolism in male senescence, *J. Clin. Endocrinol. and Metabol.*, **34**, 730–5.

Waxenburg, S. E. (1963) Some biologic correlates of sexual behavior. In: *Determinants of Sexual Behaviour*, G. Winokur (ed.), Charles C. Thomas, Springfield, Illinois.

Waxenburg, S. E., Drellich, M. G., and Sutherland, A. M. (1959) The role of hormones in human behaviour. I. Changes in female sexuality after adrenalectomy, *J. Clin. Endocrinol. Metabol.*, **19**, 193–202.

Westoff, C. F., Bumpass, L., and Ryder, N. B. (1969) Oral contraception, coital frequency, and the time required to conceive, *Soc. Biol.*, **16**, 1–10.

Whalen, R. E. (1966) Sexual motivation, *Psychol. Rev.*, **73**, 151–63.

Whittaker, L. H. (1959) Oestrogens and psychosexual disorders, *Med. J. of Australia*, **2**, 547.

Yalom, I., Green, R., and Fisk, N. (1973) Prenatal exposure to female hormones—effect on psychosexual development in boys, *Arch. Gen Psychiat.*, **28**, 554–61.

Zuger, B. (1970) Gender role determination: a critical review of the evidence from hermaphroditism, *Psychosom. Med*, **32**, 449–67.

CHAPTER 16

Brain Monoamines and Sexual Behaviour

BENGT J. MEYERSON AND CARL-OLOF MALMNÄS

INTRODUCTION

The use of chemical substances in the investigation of behaviour is justified mainly by the fact that certain chemicals are known to influence neurotransmission in the central nervous system (CNS). The existence of substances which selectively increase or decrease the activity in certain types of neurons make it possible to determine whether specific types of neurons are important for the behaviour studied. Sexual behaviour is activated by the combined action of sensory and hormonal stimuli. Neurotransmission must be involved in the sensory as well as endocrine activation of the behaviour, and in the central nervous processes which maintain the behaviour. When it has become clear that under certain hormonal and sensory stimulus conditions a certain neurotransmitter is implicated in the activation of sexual behaviour, we might extend our investigation and ask whether it is the hormonal, the sensory process or a process initiated but maintained independently of these stimuli which is related in some way to the activity of the neurotransmitter. The hormonal condition, the sensory stimuli, the specific element of the sexual behaviour or instrumental response represent variables that we manipulate in our experimental design. The response is measured under the influence of a drug treatment which has to meet certain requirements if it is to be used as an investigational tool. This chapter will deal with the pharmacological basis for using drugs as investigational tools and describe the available data that suggest a possible role for monoamine neurotransmitters—catecholamines, dopamine and noradrenaline, and the indole amine, serotonin—in the production and maintenance of certain hormone-induced elements of sexual behaviour. Our knowledge in this field is mainly based upon studies in which substances have been used that selectively influence central nervous monoaminergic transmission.

THE CONCEPT OF PSYCHOPHARMACOLOGY

Neuropharmacology can be defined as the study of chemical substances (drugs) that interact with the nervous system. The scope of neuropharmacology includes certain groups of substances. The characteristics of these groups are a common biological response such as anaesthesia (anaesthetics), sleep (hypnotics), prevention of seizures (anticonvulsants), pain relief (analgesics and local anaesthetics) etc. This classification is not always maintained. When the principal action of a substance is known, a neuropharmacological substance might be classified under a specific category such as 'ganglion-blocking drug'. Sometimes a more specific classification is used, such as muscarinic drugs, which refers to the kind of cholinergic receptor to which these substances bind and interact to produce subsequent responses. Such receptor-stimulating substances are called agonists in pharmacology. The effect of an agonist can be blocked by an antagonist, which means an agent which binds to the receptor without producing the subsequent response.

Psychopharmacology is a subunit of neuropharmacology, and broadly defined, it is the study of chemical substances (psychotropic drugs) that affect mood and behaviour. More and more evidence is appearing which indicates that psychotropic drugs influence events intimately involved in the chemical transmission of information between the nerve cells in the central nervous system (CNS). The different psychotropic drugs which are available permit a specific manipulation of different events within the monoaminergic process of neurotransmission. A schematic representation of the process in the monoaminergic synapse is given in Fig. 1. For basic concepts in the field see Cooper *et al.* (1975), Iversen and Iversen (1975) and for more specialized surveys the reader is referred to recent reviews edited by Costa *et al.* (1974), Gispen (1976). Usdin and Bunney (1975) and for specific reviews of the pharmacology of sexual behaviour the reader is referred to Gessa and Sandler (1975).

THE PSYCHOPHARMACOLOGY OF MONOAMINES

In retrospect, the earliest psychopharmacological exploration of monoaminergic mechanisms and behavioural effects were based upon a correlation between the change in cerebral monoamine levels caused by a drug and the effect of the drug on behaviour. Drugs like reserpine were formed to bring about a general depletion of the monoamine stores and monoamine oxidase inhibitors increased the brain amine levels by preventing their metabolic degradation (Fig. 1, Table 1). The gross quantitative changes in amine levels seen after these treatments were thought to correlate with the behaviour syndromes induced by the treatment. Compounds then became available which altered nerve ending transmitter release or reuptake of released transmitters from the synaptic cleft, or interfered directly with the postsynaptic receptors thereby altering the access of the monoamine neurotransmitter to postsynaptic receptors rather than the total intra-axonal content of biogenic amines. The psychotropic effect of tricyclic antidepressants like imipramine is associated with the inhibitory effect these drugs exert on the reuptake of released amines (Fig. 1, Table 1). This causes an increase of the concentration of transmitter

THE SYNAPTIC TRANSMISSION PROCESS·

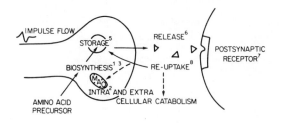

BIOSYNTHETIC PATHWAYS

tyrosine hydroxylase³   decarboxylase⁴   β-hydroxylase
TYROSINE ——→ DOPA ——→ DOPAMINE ——→ NORADRENALINE
                        ↑
                RATE LIMITING STEP
              WHERE PHARMACOLOGICAL
          INTERVENTION IS POSSIBLE FOR
          REDUCING THE BIOSYNTHESIS³
                        ↓
TRYPTOPHAN ——→ 5-HTP ——→ SEROTONIN (5HT)
              tryptophan   decarboxylase⁴
              hydroxylase⁵

FEEDBACK MECHANISMS

A FEEDBACK MEDIATED BY POSTSYNAPTIC RECEPTORS   B FEEDBACK MEDIATED BY PRESYNAPTIC RECEPTORS

NEURONAL LOOPS FEED BACK THE INFORMATION FROM POSTSYNAPTIC   A FEEDBACK MEDIATED BY A DIRECT ACTION OF THE RELEASED
RECEPTORS TO THE CELL BODY OF THE PRESYNAPTIC NEURON.   TRANSMITTER ON PRESYNAPTIC RECEPTORS.

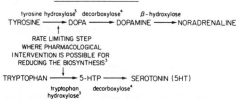

(a)

Fig. 1. (a) *The synaptic transmission process and psychotropic drugs (see also Table 1).* Information is transferred between neurons by means of transmitter substances which exert their action via specific receptors. Receptors are either presynaptic or post-synaptic depending on their location in relation to the synapse. The action of the transmitter is dependent on its biosynthesis, storage, release, effect at receptor site, re-uptake into the nerve terminal, and catabolism. Psychotropic drugs are thought to influence one or several of these events. The figures in the illustration refer to Table 1

In addition to the events mentioned above, the transmission process is influenced by certain feedback mechanisms. The model for these mechanisms is at present partly hypothetical. One of these mechanisms is thought to be mediated by postsynaptic receptors (A) and another one mediated by presynaptic receptors (B). The feedback process means that stimulation of either pre- or postsynaptic receptors inhibits the firing rate of presynaptic neuron. A decrease in the firing rate will subsequently decrease the transmitter turnover (biosynthesis and release) in the presynaptic neuron. Evidence for a direct feedback action on transmitter turnover has also been provided. MAO, monoamineoxidase; 5-HT, 5-hydroxytryptamine; 5-HTP, 5-hydroxytryptophan

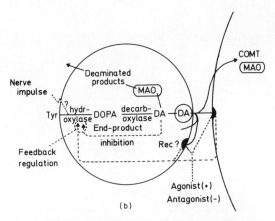

Fig. 1. (b) Schematic illustration of the hypothetical
mechanisms controlling the activity of tyrosine
hydroxylase with a nerve terminal (left) and a
postsynaptic neuron (right)

The release of transmitter (here dopamine, DA)
causes a decrease in transmitter concentration in-
traneuronally, thereby reducing the hypothetical
end-product inhibition of tyrosine hydroxylase. It is
doubtful it the normal concentration of transmitter
in free form is sufficient to cause appreciable end-
product inhibition. Inhibitory transmitter levels
may, however, be reached, for example, after inhibition of monoamine oxidase or interruption of nerve
impulses by axotomy of the nigrostriatal dopamine
tract

The nerve impulses might influence tyrosine
hydroxylase activity, for instance by influencing
the availability of cofactor or hypothetical allosteric
modulator.

Tyrosine hydroxylase activity might also be controlled via postsynaptic or hypothetic presynaptic
monoaminergic receptors, independently of nerve
impulses. Thus, tyrosine hydroxylase activity of the
rat forebrain *in vivo* can be manipulated by a
dopaminergic agonist and antagonist, even after
axotomy. (DOPA, dihydroxyphenylalanine; MAO,
monoamininioxidase; COMT, catecholamine-o-
methyltransferase.)

(From A. Carlsson, 1974. In: *Aromatic Amino
Acids in the Brain*, Ciba Found. Symp. 22. Elsevier,
Amsterdam.)

at the receptor site. Amphetamine is thought to release newly synthetized
catecholamines from storage pools. LSD and apomorphine to act at serotonergic and dopaminergic receptor sites respectively (see Table 1). Thus,
behaviour was found to be influenced by drugs not only by an effect on the gross

content of cerebral monoamines but also by effects associated with synaptic transmitter mechanisms such as neurotransmitter synthesis, release, reuptake, storage and postsynaptic receptor stimulation (see Fig. 1). More recently, studies of drug effects on nerve impulse flow and transmitter synthesis have provided evidence for the view that the CNS monoaminergic activity is modulated by certain feedback mechanisms. Stimulation of postsynaptic receptors might feedback information by neuronal loops to the cell bodies of the presynaptic neuron and in this way influence its firing rate (Fig. 1 (a) A). In addition, an intrasynaptic feedback mechanism has been proposed which involves presynaptic receptors sensitive to the transmitter produced by the neuron (Fig. 1 (b) B). These receptors are thought to regulate transmitter release, modulate the transmitter turnover (synthesis and release) and also control the firing rate of the neuron. The mechanism involved in this modulation of the monoaminergic activity is not known in detail. An account of the different theories would be beyond the scope of this chapter (see Usdin and Bunney, 1975). The exact location of the presynaptic receptors has not been demonstrated; they might not be restricted to a presynaptic distribution. It is feasible that a drug which stimulates a monoaminergic receptor is active at presynaptic as well as postsynaptic receptor sites. Recent data indicate that at least some presynaptic receptors are more sensitive than postsynaptic ones (see Aghajanian and Bunney, 1974). As stimulation of presynaptic receptors has been shown to inhibit the firing rate of the neuron, this means that one and the same receptor-stimulating drug could have opposite functional effects depending on the dosage; low doses preferentially stimulating presynaptic receptors with subsequent inhibition of presynaptic firing rate, and higher doses activating postsynaptic neuronal activity by stimulating postsynaptic receptor sites as well.

Thus, psychotropic drugs could influence behaviour by a primary action on neuronal transmitter mechanisms such as (a) the biosynthesis of the neurotransmitter, (b) the intra-axonal storage of the transmitter, (c) release, uptake, and reuptake mechanisms, (d) stimulation or blockage of postsynaptic receptor sites (e), secondarily, as a consequence of an effect on postulated neuronal feedback mechanisms, neuronal loop feedback or feedback mediated by presynaptic receptors. The drugs which will be considered below have as their proposed action one or several of these mechanisms of action.

GENERAL ASPECTS OF BEHAVIOUR PHARMACOLOGY

One of the main purposes of using psychotropic drugs in the investigation of behaviour is, as mentioned above, to relate evidence of the drug action to the pathways which might be involved in the production of the behaviour. If the behaviour is for example facilitated by a drug which causes increased dopaminergic activity, we can assume that dopaminergic pathways are implicated in the central nervous mediation of that behaviour; the action of the drug

Table 1. Survey of the predominant mechanism of action of some psychotropic drugs used in the investigation of monoamines and sexual behaviour

Compound	Amine	Mechanisms of action
Biosynthesis		*Increased substrate for synthesis* Amino acid precursors
1. DOPA (dihydroxyphenylalanine)	DA (dopamine) and	to the monoamines. In contrast to the amines themselves,
	NA (noradrenaline)	these precursors pass the blood-brain barrier readily.
DOPS (DL-threo-3, 4-dihydroxy-phenylserine)	NA	
5-HTP (5-hydroxytryptophane)	5-HT (serotonin)	
2. Pargyline	NA, DA, 5-HT	*Decreased intra-axonal catabolism* MAO (monoamine oxidase) inhibitor. A general increase of monoamine level is achieved by decreased catabolism. A selective increase of NA, DA or 5-HT achieved by MAOinh. combined with a precursor
		Inhibition of synthesis
3. α-MT (α-methyl-p-tyrosine)	NA, DA	tyrosine hydroxylase inhibitor
PCPA (p-chlorophenylalanine)	NA, DA	tryptophanehydroxylase inhibitor
	5-HT	
4. MK 486 (Lα- (3, 4-dihydroxybenzyl)-α-hydrazine prop. acid.	NA, DA, 5-HTP	*Inhibition of synthesis outside the blood-brain barrier*
R04-4602 (N- (DL-seryl)-N- (2,3,4-trihydroxybenzylhydrazine)	NA, DA, 5-HTP	Decarboxylase inhibitors which do not readily pass into the brain
Storage		*Amine depletion*
5. reserpine	NA, DA, 5-HT	Prevent storage into storage granules
tetrabenazine	NA, DA, 5-HT	
Release		*Displacement of amines from storage pools*
6. D-amphetamine	DA	Increased activity due to release from newly synthesized storage pools. Other actions as well
fenfluramine	5-HT	
Receptor affinity		*Receptor stimulation and blockade resp.*

7. Agonists		
apomorphine	DA	DA-agonist (receptor stimulation)
ET495 (piribedil)	DA	DA-agonist (receptor stimultion)
LSD (lysergic acid diethylamide)	5-HT	5-HT agonist (receptor stimulation)
Antagonists		
Pimozide	DA	DA-antagonist (receptor-blockade)
Phenoxybenzamine	NA	NA-antagonist (receptor-blockade)
Propranolol	β	β-antagonist (receptor-blockade)
Reuptake mechanism		*Increased activity of postsynaptic receptors*
8. Imipramine and other so-called tricyclic antidepressants		Inhibit reuptake of the amines. Different compounds in this group inhibit the reuptake of the different monoamines more or less selectively

The numbers refer to Fig. 1.

being either facilitatory or disinhibitory. In order to draw any conclusions, certain methodological requirements must be fulfilled as to the selectiveness of the drug action, definitions of the hormonal condition, and the stimulus–response situation. These methodological considerations will be discussed below (see also Whalen, 1975; Meyerson and Eliasson, 1976).

Selectiveness in Drug Action

Relationship Between Dose, Time, and Effect

The functional effect of most compounds depends on the dose and the time elapsed after administration. As a rule the spectrum of actions of a compound increases with increasing dose level. The different actions of a compound sometimes have different latences and durations. This means that the achievement of a desired type of drug action is a matter of finding the right dose and right time interval between administration and behavioural observation.

The Use of Drugs with a Common or Different Point of Action but Equivalent Functional Effects

Almost all psychotropic drugs have several actions on the neuronal processes. It is therefore an advantage if several compounds with a common action can be tested on the same behaviour parameter. Another strategy in the study of drugs and behaviour is the comparison of effects on behaviour of compounds with different points of action but a similar or equivalent functional effect.

The Hormonal Condition

The Hormone-induced Response Level

The fact that a certain behaviour pattern, whether sexual or not depends on hormones requires that the effect of the test compound must be studied when the hormone-activated behavioural response is maintained at level which permits stimulatory and inhibitory effects to be seen. For example, if the hormonal condition either induced by exogenous treatment or by endogenous secretion has induced the behavioural response at a maximal response level, we cannot expect to see a stimulatory effect of a psychotropic drug. Further when two hormones, like oestrogen and progesterone, are given to activate the response, the dose–response relationship for both hormones has to be considered. A psychoactive compound might interact with the action of oestrogen, progesterone, or both hormones.

The Time of Treatment

In subjects deprived of a certain endogenous hormone secretion and given hormonal replacement treatment, there is a specific latency to the appearance of the hormone-dependent behaviour. Drugs can be given at a time when the hormone-induced response has developed or can be given at a time when the hormone-induced response is not yet fully developed. This means that depending on when the drug treatment is given, the drug can influence either the neuronal mechanism involved in maintenance of the behaviour when the behaviour is fully induced by the hormonal action, or the mechanism by which the hormone induces the behaviour.

Endogenous Hormone Production

From the above, it is clear that drugs could interfere with the production and maintenance of sexual behaviour by an action on central nervous transmitter mechanisms, such as synthesis, storage, release and elimination (by enzymatic degradation or reuptake) of transmitter substances. However, drugs could also interfere with hormone-induced behaviour indirectly by an effect on the CNS-pituitary hormone secretory systems, and thereby increase or decrease secretion of endogenous hormones significant for the behaviour.

The Stimulus—Response Situation

Sexual Behaviour Parameters, Measures and Stimulus Situation

Neuropharmacological agents might influence different components of sexual behaviour in different ways. The activation and maintenance of a certain element might be facilitated by a certain neurotransmitter, and another component of the sexual behaviour might be inhibited by the same neurotransmitter. Our analysis is thus dependent on how well we can measure the different components of the behaviour separately. It is also essential that the behavioural element under study is clearly defined with respect to its dependence on and relation to other behavioural components. Often one component of behaviour is dependent on the previous one; for instance ejaculation is dependent on intromission and mounting performance. Drugs could act primarily on the behaviour recorded and/or secondarily affect this element by changing a related component. The response in different hormonal and environmental stimulus situations might be influenced differently by one and the same drug treatment, e.g., male–male mounting might be influenced in a different way to heterosexual mounting. Testosterone-activated lordosis behaviour might involve different pathways to oestrogen-induced lordosis behaviour.

Besides a direct or indirect effect on the CNS, drugs could change a relevant sensory input by acting on peripheral sensory receptors, thereby changing the threshold for environmental stimuli. We have also to consider that a drug-treated experimental subject influences the stimulus situation. A drug-treated female might not be a good sexual stimulus for a male and thus the lordosis response might decrease after a certain treatment due rather to inefficient mounting by the male than to the drug treatment *per se*.

Capacity to Display Sexual Behaviour

Coital activity and all instrumental measures of sexual activity require a certain capacity of motor function. The behaviour in different test situations may be influenced differently by drugs. Thus the lordosis response can be elicited in an obviously sedated female, while male mounting will decline substantially even when locomotor activity is slightly decreased. It is an advantage if the effect of the pharmacological treatment on the locomotor ability is evaluated independently. In order to ensure that the effect obtained is specific with regard to the sexual behaviour, it is also an advantage if another behaviour parameter is recorded in parallel with sexual behaviour.

FEMALE SEXUAL BEHAVIOUR

Studies on the pharmacology of female sexual behaviour have mostly been limited to observations of the copulatory response, i.e. the posture taken up by the female on being mounted by the male. Other components of the sexual behaviour such as soliciting behaviour or the effect of drugs on instrumental responses in the analysis of sexually motivated approach behaviour have been studied only to a very small extent. The ovariectomized female laboratory rat, given exogenous hormone treatment (oestradiol benzoate alone or followed by progesterone), has been the most commonly used subject. The quantification of the female copulatory response is expressed either as the proportion of mounts by the male which are followed by female acceptance and lordosis (lordosis quotient, see Kuehn and Beach, 1963; acceptance ratio, see Everitt *et al.*, 1974) or in terms of the percentage of females which display a positive lordosis response after a certain defined number of mounts with a certain time limit (Meyerson 1964a). The lordos/mount-ratio (L/M) measures not only probability of lordosis response but also how often it is possible to elicit the response by repeated stimuli. The central and peripheral nervous mechanisms involved in the initial elicitation of the lordosis response need not necessarily be the same as those mechanisms which make the female respond to repeated stimuli. Thus, psychotropic drugs hypothetically could influence mechanisms involved in the initial elicitation of the lordosis response and/or act on those mechanisms which make the female respond to repeated stimuli.

Monoamines and Female Copulatory Behaviour

Monoamine Oxidase Inhibitors, Monoamine Precursors, Decarboxylase Inhibitors

Monoamines like serotonin, dopamine, and noradrenaline are metabolized by the enzyme monoamine oxidase (MAO, see Fig. 1). Inhibition of this enzyme

Table 2. The effect on oestradiol + progesterone activated lordosis response in ovariecto-mized rats of L-5HTP or L-DOPA in combination with the monoamine oxidase inhibitor pargyline and peripheral decarboxylase inhibitor R04-4602

Treatment mg/kg	LORDOSIS RESPONSE[a] %								Number of animals	runs pooled
	min before (−) and after (+) treatment									
	−90		+30		+90		+180			
	ER[a]	TR	ER	TR	ER	TR	ER	TR		
Saline 0.2 ml	54	71	71	82	73	88	71	79	48	4
L-5HTP, 2.5	52	70	73	79	61	73	45*	55*	33	3
5.0	40	63	60	73	10***	23***	8***	21***	30	3
L-DOPA 2.5	66	79	83	88	67	83	75	83	24	2
5.0	67	75	23***	35***	4***	8***	27***	58*	48	4

Lordosis response was produced by oestradiol benzoate (10 μg/kg s.c.) followed 48 h later by progesterone (0.4 mg/rat s.c.). The −90 min test was conducted 4 h after progesterone inj. Pargyline 25 mg/kg s.c. was given at − 60 min and Ro4-4602 25 mg/kg s.c. at − 30 min. The difference between saline and L-5HTP of L-DOPA treatment tested by the χ^2 test *p < 0.05 ***p < 0.001

[a] Behaviour techniques used:
Female copulatory behaviour: Details of the testing procedures and environmental conditions are described elsewhere (Meyerson, 1964a). Ovariectomized rats (Sprague–Dawley strain, 250–300 g) were kept under reversed day–night rhythm (12 h of light, 12 h of darkness) and tested during the dark period of the cycle. The female was transferred to an observation cage which held a sexually active male to test for the lordosis response. Five to six months were allowed. The estimate of the percentage of lordosis response is based on the number of animals showing a clearcut lordosis response during two of the first three mounts (ER = early responders) or after at least two of the total number of mounts (TR = total responders).

increases the intra-axonal monoamine content and causes a subsequent leakage of monoamines onto postsynaptic receptor sites. As this treatment will lead to an increase of catecholamines as well as serotonin a more selective rise of the CNS level of specific monoamines could be achieved by adding the precursor amino acid of serotonin, 5-hydroxytryptophan (5-HTP), or of catecholamines, dihydroxyphenylalanine (DOPA). These precursors have to be decarboxylated to yield the amines. A selective central nervous increase relative to the periphery is obtained when the monoamine oxidase inhibitor and precursor treatment is combined with a decarboxylase inhibitor which poorly penetrates the blood brain barrier, i.e. the precursor amino acid is decarboxylated to yield the amine only within the CNS.

Different MAO-inhibitors have been shown to inhibit the lordosis response induced by oestradiol benzoate followed 48 h later by a dose of progesterone in the rat, mouse, hamster, and rabbit (induced by oestrogen alone) (Meyerson, 1964a, Meyerson et al., 1973). A subthreshold dose of a MAO-inhibitor in combination with 5-HTP brought about a clearcut inhibition in the rat, whereas an analogous treatment with DOPA had no or a very transient effect (Meyerson, 1964a, 1964c). However, DOPA treatment effectively inhibited the lordosis response when a selective peripheral decarboxylase-inhibitor, RO4-4602 (Bartholinin and Pletscher 1968) was given as well (Tables 1 and 2). The inhibitory effect appeared faster after DOPA (30 min) than after 5-HTP treatment (90 min). The two criteria of response (early response, ER and total response TR) were influenced in the same way after different treatments.

Receptor Stimulating and Receptor Blocking Agents

It has been suggested that LSD has a direct 5-HT receptor-stimulating action and that the compound apomorphine has a direct dopamine receptor-stimulating action. The experimental evidence for this view is mainly bio-chemical but certain functional effects of LSD and apomorphine on serotonin and dopamine-dependent responses have been demonstrated (see Agahjanian et al., 1973, Andén et al., 1967, 1968, Ernst, 1967). LSD as well as apomorphine inhibits the lordotic behaviour in a dose-dependent way (Eliasson et al., 1972; Eliasson and Meyerson, 1973, 1976; Meyerson et al., 1974; Everitt et al., 1975b). Everitt et al. (1974) found that a reduced L/M ratio resulted after treatment with the dopamine receptor-stimulating agent ET495 (Corrodi et al., 1972). Doses (5, 10 μg/kg i.p) of LSD cause a clear increase in L/M ratio in ovariectomized females treated with oestradiol alone (Everitt et al., 1975b). Higher doses were inhibitory (40 μg/kg). How do these qualitatively different effects of LSD fit together? The most likely explanation is that small doses of LSD decrease the activity of the 5-HT neurons; hypothetically, by stimulating mainly presynaptic receptors (see above). Whereas higher doses are required to stimulate postsynaptic 5-HT receptors. A similar bimodal effect by small doses of apomorphine of ET495 has so far not been reported.

Pimozide, an effective dopamine antagonist (Table 1, Andén et al., 1970a) counteracts the effect of apomorphine (Meyerson et al., 1974, Eliasson and Meyerson, 1976) and increases the L/M ratio in female rats treated with oes-trogen alone (Everitt et al., 1975).

Thus, the lordosis response in the female rat is inhibited both by drugs acting on serotonergic receptors and by drugs acting on dopaminergic post-synaptic receptors. The dopamine stimulation is inhibited by the dopamine receptor-blocking agent pimozide. Unfortunately, a drug which blocks central nervous serotonin receptors in an analogous way has not been discovered. Methysergid and cinnanserin have been reported as serotonon antagonists (Dombro and Wooley 1964; Baldratti et al., 1965). The evidence for this antagonism is, however, rather weak. When delivered to specific central nervous sites, Ward et al. (1975) demonstrated that these compounds facilitate the lordotic behaviour in oestrogen-primed female rats. However, when given by the subcutaneous route, methysergide, 5 mg/kg, decreased the number of oestrogen + progesterone treated females that displayed lordosis response (Fechter and Meyerson, in prep.).

Intracerebral application of a β-blocking compound LB-46, facilitated the oestrogen-induced lordosis response (Ward et al., 1975). Whereas an α-adrenergic blocking compound was ineffective in analogous experiments.

The evidence that the lordosis response is inhibited by increased activity in serotonergic and dopaminergic neurons is quite strong. But at present, facilitatory or disinhibitory actions of β-adrenergic receptor blockers are difficult to interpret as too few data are avilable.

Release and Blockage of Axonal Reuptake

Amphetamine, which is thought to displace catecholamines from newly synthesized stores (Glowinsky and Axelrod 1966; Besson et al., 1969), and fenfluramine, a 5-HT releasing agent (Duhault and Verdavainne 1967; Costa et al., 1971), inhibit the oestrogen + progesterone activated lordosis response (Meyerson 1968a, Everitt et al., 1974; Michanek and Meyerson 1975). The amphetamine-induced inhibition of the lordosis response is antagonized by pimozide treatment (dopamine receptor blockage), which does not influence the inhibitory effect of the amphetamine derivative fenfluramine (Michanek and Meyerson 1977). The results indicate that amphetamine and fenfluramine inhibit the lordosis response by different mechanisms of action. Amphetamine might act relatively more on the catecholaminergic neurons (dopamine) with fenfluramine preferentially stimulating the serotonergic activity (see Table 1).

Reuptake into the nerve terminal appears to be the major mechanisms of elimination of monoaminergic transmitters released at the synapse. Inhibition of this reuptake is considered to increase the availability of the monoamine at the receptor site. Imipramine and related tricyclic antidepressive drugs prevent the reuptake of synaptically released monoamines. The reuptake process seems to be specific enough to permit a selective inhibition of the catecholamine reuptake in preference to the serotonin uptake. Tertiary side chain amine compounds like imipramine and amitriptyline are considered to preferentially inhibit serotonin reuptake whereas desimipramine more actively inhibits catecholamine reuptake (Rose and Renyi 1969, Carlsson 1970). The tricyclic compounds have been found to inhibit the lordosis response (Meyerson 1966), and this inhibition is potentiated by monoamine oxidase inhibitors. Antidepressants with a low capacity for influenceing catecholaminergic functions (imipramine and amitriptyline) effectively inhibit the lordosis response, providing further evidence for the hypothesis that serotonergic as well as dopaminergic pathways are involved in the suppression of hormone-activated oestrous behaviour.

Amine Depletors and Synthesis Inhibitors

When the data given above are taken together they suggest that the oestrogen + progesterone activated lordosis response is inhibited by drugs and drug combinations which stimulate serotonergic and dopaminergic synapses by different mechanisms. It can now be asked whether compounds with an opposite effect, that is drugs which deplete or antagonize monoamines, can facilitate the hormone-induced copulatory response. Progesterone treatment is necessary to obtain a lordosis response in the ovariectomized rat, mouse, and hamster when single low doses of oestrogen are used. However, at a certain dose regimen of oestrogen, a low lordosis response can be achieved (Davidson et al., 1968). Both studies on the facilitatory effect of lordosis response by an impairment of monoaminergic transmission have used subjects treated with oestrogen alone. In ovariectomized female rats it has been found that the lordotic response is facilitated by several neuropharmacological compounds such as the amine depletors reserpine and tetrabenazine (Meyerson 1964b; Paris et al., 1971; Ahlenius et al., 1972a), the 5-HT and catecholamine synthesis inhibitors p-chlorophenylalanine (PCPA) and α-methyl-p-tyrosine (α-MT) (Meyerson and Lewander 1970; Ahlenius et al., 1972b; Zemlan et al., 1973; Everitt et al., 1975b), serotonin and β-receptor antagonists (Zemlan et al., 1973; Ward et al., 1975), the muscarinic receptor stimulant pilocarpine (Lindström 1973), the CNS-depressants diethyl ether, hexobarbital, diphenyl-hydantoin and the CNS stimulants strychnine and picrotoxin (Carrer and Meyerson 1976), and by potassium chloride application onto the cerebral cortex (Clemens et al., 1967). As so many different drugs with such a variety of neurotransmitter effects could induce lordosis behaviour in subjects treated with oestrogen alone, it is likely that more than one mechanism is involved in the facilitatory effect on the lordosis response. It is possible that some of these drugs produce their effect on lordosis by inducing progestin release from the adrenals. Thus, the facilitation of the lordosis response might be achieved by an effect of the drug either on the central nervous mechanisms directly involved in the production of the behaviour or by an effect mediated by progestin secretion from the adrenals. Some drugs might have both effects. Evidence for this view has been provided from experiments in which the adrenals have been stimulated or removed.

Adrencorticotrophin hormone (ACTH) induced lordosis and increased plasma concentration of progesterone in oestrogen-treated rats (Feder and Ruff, 1969). Also, reserpine treatment was found to increase the concentration of plasma progesterone in ovariectomized rats (Paris et al., 1971). Adrenalectomy has been shown to prevent the drug-induced copulatory response in the oestrogen-treated female mouse and rat (Uphouse 1970; Eriksson and Södersten 1973; Larsson et al., 1974; Carrer and Meyerson 1976) but there are also reports which show that the lordosis response is facilitated in adrenalectomized oestrogen-treated females by compounds like reserpine, tetrabenazine, PCPA, α-MT, pimozide and methysergid (Meyerson 1964b; Everitt et al., 1975b; Zemlan et al., 1973). In one treatment schedule, PCPA was recently shown to inhibit the lordosis response induced by oestrogen + progesterone in adrenalectomized female rats (Gorzalka and Whalen, 1975). Some of these contradictory results in the rat could be due to the differences in measures of the lordosis behaviour. It is clear that in reports on the drug-induced lordosis response in adrenalectomized animals the full repertoire of oestrous behaviour is not obtained. However, differences in variables like hormonal treatment, time elapsed from adrenalectomy, time elapsed after the drug was given and behaviour tested could also explain differences between experimental results. It is, however, conceivable that an adrenal progesterone release is involved in the drug-induced response seen in the non-adrenalectomized female rat. This effect could very well mask a direct drug effect on functions involved in the production of the copulatory response. The use of adrenalectomized subjects should provide a means to avoid this effect. However, we have also to consider that adrenalectomy might influence drug effects by altering central neuronal function secondary to electrolytic and metabolic changes. Also hypothalamic and pituitary hormonal changes in the adrenalectomized subject might make the adrenalectomized animal inadequate for these studies, unless adequate substitution therapy is given. The difference between adrenalectomized and adrenal intact subjects is definitely not solely a matter of endogenous progestin secretion. In addition to using adrenalectomized subjects other methods of investigating the facilitatory effect on copulatory behaviour of drugs which impair monoaminergic transmission are required.

Investigations in mammals other than the rodentia are sparse. Ovariectomized and adrenalectomized female rhesus monkeys which received PCPA have been observed to present to the male more frequently, an effect which is reversed by 5-HTP treatment (Everitt et al., 1975a). In the female cat, the copulatory behaviour of which is not facilitated by progesterone, PCPA and reserpine have been found to induce certain behaviour patterns normally associated with the oestrous behaviour (Hoyland et al., 1970; Cerny 1975) indicating that a general or more selective serotonin depletion can facilitate certain components of the copulatory behaviour in these mammals.

There is a methodological problem in designing experiments to determine whether a drug facilitates or disinhibits the lordosis response by a direct action on the central nervous mechanisms involved in the production of the behaviour, or by activating endogenous hormone secretion. To study whether certain drugs can facilitate the lordosis response by direct action, experiments have been carried out on ovariectomized female rats treated with a low dose of oestradiol and a maximal dose of progesterone; i.e. a dose which if increased cannot be expected to increase the response. In this case, an increased secretion of progestins should not lead to an increase of the response-level. An increased behavioural response should indicate an effect of the drug that is not related to progestin secretion.

The effect on copulatory behaviour of α-MT and PCPA in ovariectomized females rats which had been treated with a low dose of oestradiol benzoate (OB) and a maximal dose of progesterone is shown in Table 3. It was found that neither PCPA nor α-MT treatment increased the response relative to the group treated with hormone alone. The data in Table 3 show that the lordosis response could not be increased above the level induced by a maximal dose of progesterone by the selective monoamine biosynthesis inhibitors. This experiment does not exclude the possibility that a treatment which decreases serotonergic as well as dopaminergic activity would be more effective in producing

Table 3. The effect on oestradiol + progesterone activated lordosis response in ovariecto-mized rats of dl-p-chlorophenylalanine (PCPA), dl-α-methyl-p-tyrosine (αMT).

TREATMENT		LORDOSIS RESPONSE[a] % h after last inj.				
At h 0 mg/kg	½ mg/rat	5 ER[a]	TR[a]	7 ER[a]	TR	Number of animals runs pooled
A.						
Saline 0.2 ml	prog. 2.0	30	63	41	74	27	3
Saline 0.2 ml	prog. 5.0	48	61	52	74	23	2
PCPA 200	prog. 2.0	17	46	29	50	24	2
PCPA 3 × 100[b]	prog. 2.0	0*	9***	0**	27**	22	2
αMT 200	prog. 2.0	20	40	40	60	10	1

Oestradiol benzoate was given 48 1/2 h before progesterone (prog.). PCPA and αMT was injected intraperitioneally (i.p.) Other treatments were given subcutaneously (s.c.)
[a]See footnote to Table 2.
[b]PCPA 100 mg/kg was given at times 48 h, 24 h before and at time zero.
The difference between saline + prog 2.0 and other treatments was tested by the χ^2 test * p < 0.05 **p < 0.01 ***p < 0.001.

a response than was achieved by the selective monoamine synthesis inhibitors, a possibility which is at present investigated in our laboratory. When PCPA was given 24 and 48 h before progesterone treatment, the response was significantly reduced relative to the oestrogen + progesterone treated group. After eliciting lordosis behaviour in oestrogen-treated females by progesterone, repeated progesterone treatment had little effect. This has been shown mainly in guinea pigs (Zucker and Goy, 1967, but there is also some evidence that this effect exists in rats (Whalen and Nakayama 1965). It is possible that the PCPA injected at 24 and 48 h before the progesterone injection in the present experiment (Table 3) released adrenal progesterone which, by its dual action, inhibited the response expected after exogenous progesterone treatment.

Relationship Between Monoaminergic and Cholinergic Mechanisms

Pilocarpine, arecoline and oxotremorine are compounds which stimulate cholinergic, muscarinic receptors. These muscarinic compounds have been shown to decrease the oestrogen + progesterone activated female copulatory behaviour in the rat and hamster (Lindström and Meyerson 1967; Lindström 1970, 1971, 1972). The combination of compounds acting on monoaminergic synapses and muscarinic agents reveals that the inhibitory effect of the muscarinc compounds is mediated by 5-HT mechanisms. The 5-HT biosynthesis inhibitor PCPA prevents the inhibitory effect of pilocarpine whereas an analogous effect is not seen after the catecholamine inhibitor α-MT.

As increased cholinergic activity (muscarinic receptors) decreases the lordosis response, the possibility that decreased cholinergic activity (muscarinic receptors) has the opposite effect, has been investigated. However, the anticholinergic compounds atropine or scopolamine were not effective in facilitating the lordosis response in ovariectomized rats treated with oestrogen alone.

Instrumental Measures of Heterosexual Approach in the Female Rat

In the observation and test situations used by us (described in detail elsewhere, Meyerson, 1964a) we have observed that during mounting attempts by the male, the female kicks the male with her hindlegs, runs away, and turns around to face the male, sometimes rising on his hindlegs to take up a 'boxing' position. In spite of this if the male achieves a mount a full lordosis response is still seen in the female. Thus, the question can be raised whether lordosis behaviour is a good measure of 'sexual receptivity'. The female's acceptance ratio (a measure of the female's willingness to accept the male, see Everitt *et al.*, 1974) should add further information.

We have recently attempted to investigate the approach of the female towards a sexually active partner. To study the effect of hormones on heterosexual approach behaviour, different techniques were used to measure how the female rat would seek contact with a sexually active male (for details see Meyerson and Lindström, 1973). The methods differ with respect to the behaviour that the subject has to perform to make contact with the stimulus object. In ovariectomized subjects oestrogen induces an obvious increase in the amount of aversive stimuli that the subject is willing to withstand in order to make contact with a sexually active male. The female also spends more time sitting close to the male in an open field arena, and, in a runway-choice situation, there is an increase in the number of trials in which the male was chosen in preference to an oestrous female. In intact females with a five-day oestrous cycle, there is a cyclic variation in these measures with a clear peak in response when the females are in a prooestrous condition (Eliasson and Meyerson, 1975; Meyerson and Lindström, 1973). Although experiments on the psychopharmacology of these instrumental measures of heterosexual approach behaviour are at an early state, decreased biosynthesis of serotonin induced by PCPA treatment appears to increase the amount of aversive stimuli that the female is willing to withstand in order to reach a sexually active male. This effect is only seen if oestrogen is given in combination with the drug. A decreased response following PCPA treatment is obtained when the stimulus male is replaced by water and the subjects are water-deprived (Meyerson *et al.*, 1974). The water-deprivation experiment shows that the increased response achieved after PCPA treatment when the male rat is used as a stimulus is not due to a decreased sensitivity to the aversive foot shock. The same PCPA treatment decreases the time that the female spends in the vicinity of the male in an open field and the preference of a male for an oestrous female measured in the runway-choice situation (Meyerson 1975). The role of serotonin in the regulation of heterosexual approach behaviour in the female rat has to be elucidated by further experiments. By running different methods in parallel and using a diversity of incentives (see Meyerson *et al.*, 1974; Meyerson, 1975), it may be possible to find a psychopharmacological profile which can provide evidence as to which neural pathways are implicated in the behavioural condition which brings the animal to seek heterosexual contact.

MALE SEXUAL BEHAVIOUR

Most studies on the effect of drugs on male sexual behaviour have been carried out on the laboratory rat. These studies have mainly been concerned with the mounting phase of copulatory behaviour, either mounting behaviour as such or its secondary consequences on, for example, ejaculation latency. The aim of these studies has been to elucidate neurotransmitter mechanisms primarily involved in the control of sexual behaviour. From this point of view, it is surprising that most investigators in this field have used intact animals, where behavioural effects secondary to induced alterations in the testicular hormone production cannot be excluded. Methodologically, further problems may arise in intact subjects because most investigators use vigorously copulating intact subjects thus leaving little scope for the facilitatory effects of drugs, at least with regard to the rather crude behavioural measures employed. A simple way of solving both these problems is to use castrated males and administer testosterone in a dosage which, for example, is insufficient to activate mounting in more than a fraction of the total number of subjects (Malmnäs 1973). A great variety of methods has been used, the methods mainly differing with respect to testing procedures (adaptation to the test cage, test duration etc.), hormonal state, and stimulus object. When comparing results from different laboratories, the use of different stimulus situations should be considered. Most studies are performed using a receptive female, mainly an ovariectomized female brought into heat by exogenous oestrogen or oestrogen + progesterone treatment. In a different type of study, drug-effects on male–male 'homosexual' mounting behaviour have been investigated in groups of males which have all received the same treatment (Hoyland *et al.*, 1970; Shillito, 1970; Tagliamonte *et al.*, 1971; Gawienowski and Hodgen, 1971). If homosexual mounting is facilitated by a certain treatment, this could be due either to an increased willingness to display mounting, or equally that the males become attractive as mounting objects with a subsequent increase of male–male mounting. Thus, this is a rather gross technique and extrapolations of data from these experiments to experiments using a standard treated female as a stimulus partner should be made with caution. Another important methodological point is the interdependence of coital elements mentioned above. The evaluation of the influence of drugs on different elements of male copulatory behaviour must be based upon a comparison of experimental and control subjects with equivalent responses in the elements of the coital behaviour preceding the coital element which is studied (i.e. drug effects on ejaculation must be compared in experimental and control subjects with equivalent mounting and intromission patterns. Finally, with regard to how sensitive the male copulatory response is to changes in environmental conditions (odours, noise, temperature, humidity, air pressure, etc.), variables that are not always possible to control, it should be an elementary requirement that controls are run during the same test periods as experimental animals.

Monamines and Male Copulatory Behaviour

Monoamine Oxidase Inhibitors, Monoamine Precursors and Decarboxylase Inhibitors

The effect on copulatory responses of monoamine oxidase inhibitors has consistently been an inhibition of the different elements studied (Soulairac, 1963; Malmnäs and Meyerson, 1970; Tagliamonte et al., 1971, Dewsbury et al., 1972, Malmnäs, 1973). The involvement of monoaminergic mechanisms in the mounting behaviour of male rats is most convincingly demonstrated when monoamine precursors are given after pretreatment with a monoamine oxidase inhibitor and extracerebral decarboxylase inhibitor. The rationale for pretreating the animals with these enzyme inhibitors is to restrict the formation of monoamines in the CNS and to prevent the newly formed monoamines from being subject to oxidative deamination. (Table 1) Low doses of 5-HTP reduce the number of males displaying mounting (Malmnäs and Meyerson, 1970, 1972; Tagliamonte et al., 1972, Malmnäs, 1973). In analogous experiments, DOPA significantly increases the percentage of mounts (Malmnäs and Meyerson, 1972; Malmnäs, 1973). With increasing doses of DOPA, the stimulatory effect reaches a maximum after which an inhibitory effect can be noted (see Fig. 2). There is some variability in the stimulatory effect reported from different laboratories, depending on whether DOPA has been combined with a monoamine oxidase inhibitor and depending on the testing and stimulus situation (Da Prade et al., 1973a, 1973b; Tagliamonte et al., 1973; Hyyppä et al., 1971; Gray et al., 1974). It must be emphasized, however, that some studies in which an excitatory effect has not been obtained have been carried out on animals which may have reached a maximal response level (Hyppä et al., 1971; Gray et al., 1974). By decarboxylation DL-threo-3, 4-hydroxy-phenylserine (DOPS) yields noradrenaline (Table 1). Analogous experiments where monoamine oxidase inhibitors and extracerebral decarboxylase inhibitors precede treatment with DOPS fail to change mount percentage (Malmnäs and Meyerson, 1972; Malmnäs, 1973). Since noradrenalin can be formed from both DOPA and DOPS, whereas DOPA is the only precursor that yields dopamine, the difference in effect between DOPA and DOPS suggests a role for dopamine in the copulatory behaviour of the castrated male rat. Taken together, the experiments using monoamine precursors suggest that serotonin inhibits while dopamine, but not noradrenalin, facilitates copulatory behaviour in the male rat.

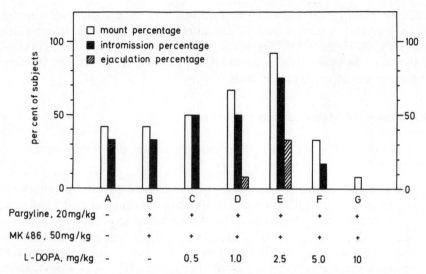

Fig. 2. Dose–response relationship for the effect of L-DOPA on copulatory behaviour in the castrated male rat.

The subjects were castrated as adults and treated with testosterone propionate (0.10 mg/kg/week). Each treatment group was made up of 12 subjects, selected on the basis of copulatory scores in the last test preceding the experimental test (one week prior to the exp. test) in order to make the groups uniform. Drug and saline injections were given at 1.5 h (pargyline), 1.0 h (MK486), and 0.5 h (L-DOPA) prior to the exp. test. A minus sign in the treatment schedule indicates saline treatment. The significance of differences between groups was tested by means of the Fisher exact probability test. Group comparisons

Mount percentage
A *vs.* B; B *vs.* C, D, F, G: p > 0.05
B *vs.* E: p < 0.02
E *vs.* F: p < 0.01
E *vs.* G: p < 0.001

Intromission percentage
A *vs.* B; B *vs.* C, D. F. G: p > 0.05
B *vs.* E: p < 0.05
E *vs.* F, G: p < 0.01

Ejaculation percentage
A *vs.* B; B *vs.* C, D, F, G: p > 0.15
B *vs.* E; E *vs.* F, G: p < 0.05

Receptor Stimulating Agents

Bignami (1966) demonstrated that small doses of LSD increased intromission frequency and decreased both intromission and postejaculatory intervals. The opposite effect was obtained by higher doses. An evident reduction in mount and intromission percentage has been seen after LSD treatment given at doses which do not affect overt copulatory behaviour (Malmnäs, 1973), an effect which is most likely due to stimulation of postsynaptic serotonin receptors. Apomorphine, a dopamine receptor stimulating agent, reduces the number of intromissions occurring before ejaculation (Butcher *et al.*, 1969) increases mount percentage and intromission percentage, and shortens mount latency

(Malmnäs and Meyerson, 1972; Malmnäs, 1973; Tagliamonte *et al.*, 1973). Clonidine is considered to be a central noradrenalin receptor stimulating agent (Andén, *et al.*, 1970b). This compound has little effect on the copulatory behaviour when doses are given which do not affect motor capability (Malmnäs, 1973).

Synthesis Inhibitors and Receptor Blocking Agents

There has been a rapid growth in the literature on the effect of PCPA on different aspects of sexual behaviour which has recently been reviewed by Gessa and Taliamonte (1974). PCPA produces male–male mounting behaviour in male rats under conditions where similar behaviour is either not seen in the control animals or is seen at a significantly lower level. (Tagliamonte *et al.*, 1969). Where a female is used as sexual partner there is a clearcut increase in the number of animals mounting (Malmnäs and Meyerson 1971), and a reduction of latencies to ejaculation (Salis and Dewsbury, 1971, Ahlenius *et al.*, 1971, Malmnäs, 1973).

The facilitatory effect of PCPA is also obtained in adrenalectomized animals (Malmnäs and Meyerson 1971; Malmnäs 1973). However, Gawionowski and Hodgen (1971) reported that it was not possible to induce male–male mounting after hypophysectomy by PCPA treatment in combination with the monoamine oxidase inhibitor pargyline. Whalen and Luttge (1970) found no significant effect of PCPA on the number of mounts and intromissions per ejaculation nor or coital activity preceding satiation. These parameters apparently differ from those for which a stimulatory effect of PCPA has been reported. Increased mounting behaviour after PCPA treatment has also been reported in the rabbit (Perez-Cruet *et al.*, 1971) and cat (Hoyland *et al.*, 1970; Ferguson *et al.*, 1970). Failure to show a stimulatory effect on male–male mounting has also been reported in the cat by Zitrin *et al.* (1970) and in a group of *Macaca speciosa* containing both sexes (Redmond *et al.*, 1971).

In contrast to PCPA treatment, the catecholamine synthesis inhibitor α-MT decreases the mount percentage in castrated male rats (Malmnäs 1973). A general monoamine depletion by reserpine and tetrabenazine also decreases the percentage of males mounting a receptive female (Malmnäs 1973). Some reports are available in which reserpine and tetrabenazine have been found to facilitate some components of copulatory behaviour in intact male rats such as the number of intromissions required to attain ejaculation (Soulairac, 1963; Dewsbury and Davis, 1970; Dewsbury, 1972).

The dopamine receptor blocking agent pimozide decreases the mount percentage and also effectively inhibits the stimulatory effect of apomorphine (Malmnäs 1973) and of DOPA (Malmnäs 1976). No effect has been demonstrated with the α-receptor blocking agent phenoxybenzamine. The β-andrenergic receptor blocking agent propranolol inhibits certain elements of the male copulatory behaviour. Malmnäs recently (1975) demonstrated that while the L-isomer was effective the D-isomer was ineffective, suggesting a role for adrenergic β-receptors in the control of male sexual behaviour in rats because the β-blocking capacity is only achieved by the L-isomer of this agent.

HETEROTYPIC SEXUAL BEHAVIOUR

The effect of psychotropic drugs on heterotypic sexual behaviour has not been investigated very fully. There are two main questions to be anounced. Are the same types of pathways involved in female and male copulatory behaviour in both sexes? Is a sexual response influenced by psychotropic drugs in the same way irrespective of whether the behaviour is induced by oestrogen or testosterone?

Female Copulatory Behaviour in the Male

Lordotic behaviour can be induced in the male rat by oestrogen treatment (Beach, 1942a; Feder and Whalen, 1965; Table 4). In contrast to the female, progesterone does not induce a facilitatory effect when injected after oestradiol (Meyerson, 1968b; Davidson and Levine, 1969).

Dopamine Receptor Stimulation

The oestrogen-induced lordotic behaviour in the adult castrated male rat is inhibited by the dopamine agonist apomorphine (Table 4). The effective dose was similar to the dose required to depress the lordosis response in the female.

Amine Depletors and Biosynthesis Inhibitors

Reserpine, tetrabenazine, PCPA, and α-MT facilitates the occurrence of the lordosis response in male rats castrated as adults and given OB (Meyerson, 1968b; Larsson and Södersten, 1971; Table 4) or testosterone (Luttge, 1975). Also other drugs with a proposed inhibitory effect on serotonergic activity have been used. Thus, direct placement of methysergide and cinnanserin into the hypothalamus of oestrogen-treated male rats elicits the lordotic response significantly more than oestrogen alone (Crowley et al., 1975). The lordosis response was only obtained in the presence of oestrogen pretreatment.

These data indicate that in the male rat decreased monoaminergic activity facilitates oestrogen-activated lordotic behaviour, and increased dopaminergic activity decreases female copulatory behaviour. The relative importance of the different monoamines (dopamine and 5-HT) has still to be elucidated.

The Androgenized Female

It is well established that female rats treated neonatally with androgen show

Table 4. The effect of apomorphine, reserpine, p-chlorophenylalanine (PCPA), and α-methyl-p-tyrosine (α-MT) on oestrogen-activated lordotic behaviour in the adult castrated male rat, and of apomorphine on testosterone activated mounting and lordotic behaviour in the ovariectomized female rat

	Sex	Treatment mg/kg, i.p.		Mount[b] % test: 1	2	N	Lordosis response[a] % test: 1	2	N
A.	Female	apomorphine, 0.10		27	83*	18			
		saline		33	33	18			
B.	Female	apomorphine, 0.10					77	46	13
		0.30					62	15*	13
		Saline, 0.2 ml					67	75	12
C.	Male	apomorphine, 0.15					42	29	24
		0.30					58	17**	24
		Saline, 0.2 ml					38	47	24
D.	Male	reserpine, 1.0					—	83***	36
		p-chlorophenylalanine 4 × 100					—	72***	36
		α-methyl-p-tyrosine 150					—	64**	36
		saline, 0.2 ml					—	25	36

Hormone treatment: A. TP 0.5 mg/kg s.c. 56 h before test. B. TP 1.0 mg/kg s.c. 76 h and progesterone 1.0 mg/rat 4 h before test. C. and D. OB, 25 μg/kg s.c. 54–55 h before test.

Drug treatment: Apomorphine was given 15 min before test 2, reserpine 24 h, p-chlorophenylalanine 78, 54, 30 and 6 h and α-methyl-p-tyrosine 6 h before test 2.

In exp. A and B one week between test and 2, in exp. C one hour between test 1 and 2, in exp. D only one test.

Comparison between test 1 and 2 (A, B, C) or saline vs. drug treatment (D).

*p < 0.05, **p < 0.01, ***p < 0.001. (The Sign test and Fisher exact probability test) The animals were gonadectomized as adults.

[a] The lordotic behaviour in male rats was tested using a similar procedure to that used for females. The males were kept on a weekly dose of oestradiol benzoate (OB) 25 μg/kg s.c.

[b] Male mounting behaviour: Details of the testing procedure and environmental conditions are described elsewhere (Malmnäs, 1973). Castrated male rats (Wistar strain 350–450 g) were tested for copulatory activity with spayed females in oestrogen + progestërone induced behavioural oestrus. The subjects were kept on a weekly dose of terrosterone propionate (TP) (0.10 mg/kg) which maintained the mount percentage at a stable submaximal level.

a lower level of behavioural responsiveness to oestrogen and progesterone treatment than untreated females. This difference was not diminished by amine depletors such as reserpine (Meyerson 1968b). However, the possibility that early androgen treatment will activate inhibitory mechanisms related to the monoaminergic system should be further investigated.

Male Copulatory Behaviour in the Female

In the female rat male like mounting behaviour is activated by testosterone treatment (Beach, 1942b; Södersten, 1972; Table 4). We have just started to investigate how mounting behaviour in the female is influenced by psychotropic drugs. In our experiments mounting behaviour (mounting with pelvic thrusting) was recorded after testosterone treatment and the experimental subjects placed with other females which were brought into heat by oestradiol benzoate + progesterone. The lordosis response to mounting by a vigorous male was tested in the same experimental subjects.

Dopamine Receptor Stimulation

The effect of apomorphine on the male and female copulatory behaviour induced by testosterone propionate in females is shown in Table 4. Apomorphine, 100 μg/kg i.p. increased the mount percentage. In contrast, the lordosis response was not changed by apomorphine at a 100 μg/kg dosage. But the response decreased after apomorphine 300 μg/kg. These data are in agreement with those obtained with TP-induced mounting behaviour in the male, oestrogen-induced lordosis behaviour in the female and oestrogen + progesterone-induced lordosis behaviour in the female.

As to the first question raised above, the data described so far appear to be consistent with the hypothesis that the heterotypic behaviour in one sex has analogous monoaminergic pathways as the homotypic behaviour in the opposite sex.

SUMMARY AND CONCLUSIONS

There is a growing knowledge as to how psychotropic drugs influence different mechanisms involved in the central nervous neurotransmitter process. This knowledge can be used in the investigation of neurotransmitters implicated in the activation and maintenance of different elements of sexual behaviour. This chapter has dealt with the pharmacological basis for using drugs as investigational tools and has introduced data that suggest a possible relationship between monoamines and sexual behaviour.

When the available data are considered, the evidence for an inhibitory effect on the lordotic response in the female rat by increased central nervous serotonergic and dopaminergic activity is well supported. The role of noradrenaline is less clear. Evidence that noradrenaline has an excitatory effect has been discussed by Everitt *et al.* (1974) but the data available are not conclusive. Inhibitory cholinergic mechanisms related to the monoaminergic system seem also to be implicated.

Can suppression of monoaminergic activity substitute for progesterone treatment by a central effect directly involved in the production of female copulatory behaviour? There seems to be some controversy as to whether substitution for progesterone is only possible by the mediation of adrenal secretion. The adrenalectomized subject might, however, not be a good model for answering this question. Drugs which suppress serotonergic and/or dopaminergic

Table 5. Serotonergic and dopaminergic influence on hormone-induced copulatory behaviour in gonadectomized female and male rats

Amine	Tone at receptor sites	LORDOSIS RESPONSE				Mounting (Mount %) TP induced ♂
		OB + Prog induced ♀	OB induced ♀	♂	TP + Prog induced ♀	
Serotonin	increased	decreased				decreased
	decreased	unaffected?	(increased[a])	increased		increased
Dopamine	increased	decreased		decreased	decreased	increased
	decreased	unaffected?	(increased[a])	increased		decreased

[a] Data from OB-induced lordosis response in the female is still controversial

transmission on one hand and progesterone on the other might act on lordotic behaviour in a different manner. For example, progesterone might surmount a tonic inhibitory influence whereas the monoamine-suppressive compounds act to remove it. The present data show that lordotic behaviour is not induced by decreased monoaminergic activity caused by selective synthesis inhibition at a level above that resulting from a maximal dose of progesterone. These data indicate that the facilitatory effect of the synthesis inhibition is achieved solely by endogenous progestin release. The data could also be interpreted as indicating that progesterone activity is equivalent to the suppression of monoaminergic activity in pathways mediating inhibition of the lordotic behaviour; after a maximal progesterone effect no further response could be expected by decreased monoaminergic tone. One could ask why it is so easy to obtain an inhibition of the behaviour when clearcut facilitation seems much more difficult to achieve. If we assume that a tonic inhibition of the lordotic behaviour exists and this involves many different transmitter systems (serotonergic, dopaminergic, cholinergic) linked consecutively, inhibition would be easy to achieve by stimulating only one of the systems. The removal of the inhibition might require impairment of many transmitter functions. It is therefore possible that facilitation of lordotic behaviour on a pharmacological basis requires suppression of several kinds of transmitter systems possibly in combination with stimulation of pathways mediating an excitatory effect on the behaviour.

A further dissociation of the different components of the copulatory behaviour might reveal a differential action of the various monoamines on elements of the behaviour such as acceptance of the male and lordotic behaviour. Instrumental studies of approach towards a partner of the opposite sex are at a very early stage. But it is of particular interest that although oestrogen increases responses in all of the three test situations used, drugs like PCPA increase the response of crossing an aversive barrier to make contact with a male, but decreases heterosexual preference (Meyerson et al., 1974; Meyerson, 1975). The strength of sexual motivation and the sexual preference might be influenced in different ways by psychotropic compounds.

In the male, increased serotonergic tone induces decreased mounting behaviour, while decreased activity leads to increased sexual response. In contrast, manipulating the dopaminergic activity had the opposite effect.

Malmnäs (1973, 1974) found that among males that show no mounting behaviour, female-orientated activity was increased by dopamine stimulating agents, an effect prevented by a dopamine antagonist (Malmnäs 1973, 1976). The same behaviour was decreased by 5-HT stimulation, indicating that monoaminergic control of the male's interaction with the female is not restricted to the copulatory act, but includes elements preceding copulation as well.

The oestrogen-and testosterone-induced lordotic behaviour in the male is not facilitated by progesterone. However, amine depletors and the dopamine agonist apomorphine have facilitatory and inhibitory effects respectively. The testosterone-induced mounting behaviour in the female rat is increased

by apomorphine, a drug which also inhibits the oestrogen- or testosterone +
progesterone-activated lordosis behaviour in the female. These data leave
several questions to be answered as to the role of brain monoamines in the
activation of the oestrogen- and testosterone-induced heterotypic sexual
behaviour. One question, for instance, is whether pathways exist which mediate
inhibition of the heterotypic behaviour while the homotypic behaviour is
activated. It appears that dopaminergic pathways might play such a role:
in both the male and the female, the male type of behaviour is facilitated by
dopaminergic agonists while the female type of behaviour is suppressed by
such agents.

FUTURE RESEARCH DIRECTIONS IN THE FIELD

So far, we can only say that monoaminergic mechanisms seem to be implicated in the copulatory behaviour of the rat. The direct relationship between the
hormonal and sensory processes and the activity in monoaminergic pathways
remains to be investigated. Some attempts have been made to determine
the action of gonadal hormones on the cerebral monoamine content, turnover,
uptake, etc. (Donoso et al., 1969; Meyerson, 1964c; Fuxe and Hökfelt, 1969;
Lichtensteiger, 1969; Meyerson and Lewander, 1970; Bapna et al., 1971;
Tonge and Greengrass, 1971; Kordon and Glowinski, 1972; Everitt et al.,
1975b). The changes in monoamines which have been demonstrated could be
specifically related to the hormonal activation of sexual behaviour. However,
data from different studies are sometimes contradictory and there are many
other neuroendocrine functions in which monoamines are implicated. Therefore, it is at present not feasible to relate the hormone-induced changes in
cerebral monoamines directly to the production of copulatory behaviour.
However, when monoaminergic pathways involved in the copulatory behaviour
have been mapped out, it might be possible to obtain further information
regarding biochemical changes in monoaminergic activity related to the action
of steroid hormonal action on sexual behaviour. Neurotoxic compounds such
as 6-hydroxydopamine (6-OHDA) and 5, 6 and 5, 7-dihydroxytryptamine
(see review edited by Malmfors and Thoenen, 1971; Baumgarten et al., 1974;
Jonsson et al., 1975), which, if applied locally in the brain make selective
lesions in the different monoaminergic neurons, should in combination with
more conventional lesion techniques prove a useful tool in the mapping of
relevant pathways (see Everitt, Chapter 17 this volume for further discussion.)

The scope of this chapter is limited to monoamines and sexual behaviour.
However, we should remember that only a very small proportion of the neurons
in the brain (1–2%) contain either noradrenaline, dopamine, or serotonin;
more neurons contain acetylcholine (about 10%). For the majority of central
neurons, the transmitter is unknown. Certain amino acids have, however,
been proposed as transmitters such as γ-aminobutyric acid (GABA) and
glycine. So far, nothing is known about the possible relationship between
different amino acids and sexual behaviour. This would be of particular interest

in view of the evidence that exists for pathways mediating the inhibition of the copulatory behaviour. Some of these amino acids have been proposed as inhibitory transmitters. A research in the future will probably be based upon the increasing evidence showing that certain peptide hormones may influence central nervous functioning. Psychotropic effects, including effects on sexual behaviour, have been shown after treatment with some of the peptides such as luteinizing hormone releasing hormone (LRH) and adrenocorticotrophic hormone (ACTH) derivatives (for review see Schotman et al., 1976).

Studies on drugs and sexual behaviour have mainly been carried out using the laboratory rat. However, studies on other species are necessary before general conclusions can be drawn.

Research on this topic has been limited to copulatory behaviour. Comparatively little work has been carried out in the field of 'sexual motivation'. We assume in adopting this rather controversial intervening variable that copulatory behaviour is preceded by a condition (hormonally and/or sensorily activated) which results in the animal seeking, orientating towards, and making contact with a sexual partner. The instrumental techniques used to measure the appetitive component of the sexual behaviour should use a variety of incentives to make sure that the motivation can be labelled sexual. There is a strong opposition in certain circles to the use of the term sexual motivation unless the appetitive behaviour has been shown to be directly reinforced by a consummatory act, in this case copulation (see Fentress, this volume, Chapter 18 for further discussion of this problem). There is an equally strong opposition from us to measuring sexual motivation solely in terms of the lordosis response or components of male copulatory behaviour. For the same reasons given to justify the study of drugs on copulatory behaviour, pharmacological studies on sexual motivation must take into account the possibility that appetitive behaviour is dissociated from the consummatory response. The neuronal mechanisms implicated in the activation and maintenance of the appetitive phase might not be identical to those involved in consummatory behaviour. We might even find that certain elements in the appetitive behaviour are facilitated by psychotropic drugs which have an inhibitory action on the display of the copulatory behaviour. To measure sexual motivation in terms of copulatory behaviour alone or even involve copulatory behaviour in the measure of the sexual motivation seems, therefore, hazardous.

In recent years, psychopharmacology has developed rapidly which means that even researchers working within the field have difficulty in keeping abreast of new concepts. The analysis of behaviour also requires long experience and wide knowledge. It seems evident that the most profitable future direction of research in this field must involve more collaborature work both in the field of behavioural pharmacology where drugs are used to investigate behaviour, and in the other field of behavioural pharmacology which has not been dealt with here, namely the use of behaviour to investigate the action of psychotropic drugs.

REFERENCES

Aghajanian, G. K. and Bunney, B. S. (1974) In: *Frontiers in Neurology and Neuroscience Research*, P. Seeman and G. M. Brown (eds.), Ch. 2, The Univ. Toronto Press, Toronto.

Aghajanian, G. K., Bunney, B. S., and Kuhar, M. J. (1973) Use of single unit recording in correlating transmitter turnover with impulse flow in mono-amine neurons. In: *New Concepts in Neurotransmitter Regulation* A. J. Mandell (ed.), Plenum Press, New York, pp. 115–34.

Ahlenius, S., Eriksson, H., Larsson, K., Modigh, K., and Södersten, P. (1971) Mating behavior in the male rat treated with *p*-chlorophenylalanine methyl ester alone and in combination with pargyline, *Psychopharmacologia* Berl., **20**, 383–8.

Ahlenius, S., Engel, J., Eriksson, H., and Södersten, P. (1972a) Effects of a tetrabenzine on lordosis behaviour and on brain monomines in the female rat, *J. Neural. Transm.*, **33**, 155–62.

Ahlenius, S., Engel, J., Eriksson, H., Modigh, K., and Södersten, P. (1972b) Importance of central catecholamines in the mediation of lordosis behaviour in ovariectomized rats treated with estrogen and inhibitors of monoamine synthesis, *J. Neural. Transm.*, **33**, 247–56.

Andén, N. E., Butcher, S. G., Corrodi, H., Fuxe, K., and Ungerstedt, U. (1970a) Receptor activity and turnover of dopamine and noradrenaline after neuroleptics, *Eur. J. Pharmacol.*, **11**, 303–14.

Andén, N. E., Corrodi, H., Fuxe, K., and Hökfält, T. (1968) Evidence for a central 5-hydroxytryptamine receptor stimulation by lysergic acid diethyl-amide, *Br. J. Pharma-Col. Chemother.*, **34**, 1–7.

Andén, N. E., Corrodi, H., Fuxe, K., Hökfelt, T., Hökfelt, C., Rydin, C., and Svensson, T. (1970b) Evidence for a central noradrenaline receptor stimulation by clonidine, *Life Sci.*, **9**, 513–23.

Andén, N. E., Rubenson, A., Fuxe, K., and Hökfelt, T. (1967) Evidence for dopamine receptor stimulation by apomorphine, *J. Pharm. Pharmacol.*, **19**, 627–9.

Baldratti, G., Arcari, G., and Suchowsky, G. K. (1965) Studies on a compound antagonistic to 5-hydroxytryptamine, *Experientia*, **21**, 396–7.

Bapna, J., Neff, N. H., and Costa, E., 1971, A method for studying norepine-phrine and serotonin metabolism in small regions of rat brain: Effect of ovariectomy of amine metabolism in anterior and posterior hypothalamus, *Endocrinology*, **89**, 1345–9.

Bartholini, G. and Pletscher, A. (1968) Cerebral accmumulation and metabolism of C^{14}-DOPA after selective inhibition of peripheral decarboxylase, *J. Pharmacol. Exp. Ther.*, **161**, 14–20.

Baumgarten, H. G., Björklund, A., Lachenmayer, L., Rensch, A., and Rosengren, E. (1974) De- and regeneration of the bulbospinal serotonin neurons in the rat following 5,6- or 5,7-dihydroxytryptamine treatment, *Cell Tissue Res.*, **152**, 271–81.

Beach, F. A. (1942a) Male and female mating behavior in prepuberally castrated female rats treated with androgens, *Endocrinology*, **31**, 373–8.

Beach, F. A. (1942b) Copulatory behavior in prepuberally castrated male rats and its modification by estrogen administration, *Endocrinology*, **31**, 679–83.

Besson, M. J., Cheramy, A., Felty, P., and Glowinski, J. (1969) Release of newly synthesized dopamine from dopamine-containing terminals in the striatum of the rat, *Proc. Nat. Acad. Sci.*, **62**, 741–8.

Bignami, G. (1966) Pharmacological influences on mating behavior in the male rat, *Psychopharmacologia* Berl., **10**, 44–58.

Butcher, L. L., Butcher, S. G., and Larsson, K. (1969) Effects of apomorphine, (+)-amphetamine and nialamide on tetrabenazine-induced suppression of sexual behavior in the male rat, *Eur. J. Pharmacol.*, **7**, 283–8.

Carlsson, A. (1970) Structural specificity for inhibition of (^{14}C)-5-hydroxy-tryptamine uptake by cerebral slices, *J. Pharm. Pharmac.*, **22**, 729–32.

Carlsson, A. (1974) The *in vivo* estimation of rates of trypotophane andtyrosine hydroxylation: effects of alterations in enzyme environment and neuronal activity. In: *Aromatic Amino Acids in the Brain*, CIBA Foundation, Symp., 22 Elsivier, Excerpta Medica, North Holland, Amsterdam, pp. 117–34.

Carrer, H. and Meyerson, B. J. (1976) Effects of CNS-depressants and stimulants on lordosis response in the female rat, *Pharmacol. Biochem. Behav.*, in press.

Cerny, V. A. (1976) The influence of hypothalamically administered reserpine on the sexual behavior of the female cat, *Psychopharmacology*, **50**, 269–74.

Clemens, L. G., Wallen, K., and Gorski (R. A., 1967) Mating behavior: Facilitation in the female rat after cortical application of potassium chloride, *Science*, **157**, 1208–9.

Cooper, J. R., Bloom, F. E., and Roth, R. H. (1975) *The Biochemical Basis of Neuropharmacology*, Oxford Press, New York.

Corrodi, H., Farnebo, L. O., Fuxe, K., Hamberger, B., and Ungerstedt, U. (1972) ET495 and brain catechlamine mechanisms: Evidence for stimulation of dopamine receptors, *Eur. J. Pharmacol.*, **20**, 195–204.

Costa, E., Gessa, G. L., and Sandler, M., eds. (1974) *Advances in Biochemical Psychopharmacology*, Vols. 10 and 11, Raven Press, New York.

Costa, E., Gropetti, A., and Revuelta, A. (1971) Action of fenfluramine on monoamine stores, *Br. J. Pharm.*, **41**, 57–64.

Crowley, W. R., Ward, I. L., and Margules, D. L. (1975) Female lordotic behavior mediated by monoamines in male rats, *J. Comp. Physiol. Psychol.*, **88**, 62–8.

Da Prada, M., Carruba, M., Saner, A., O'Brien, R. A., and Pletscher, A. (1973a) The action of 5,6-dihydroxytryptamine and L-DOPA on sexual behaviour of male rats. In: *Psychopharmacology, Sexual Disorders, and Drug* Abuse, T. A. Ban (ed.), N. Holland Publ. Co., Amsterdam, pp. 517–22.

Da Prada, M., Carruba, M., Saner, A. O'Brien, R. A., and Pletscher, A. (1973b) Action of L-DOPA on sexual behaviour of male rats, *Brain Res.*, **55**, 383–9.

Davidson, J. M. and Levine, S. (1969) Progesterone and heterotypical sexual behavior in the male rat, *J. Endocrinol.*, **44**, 129–30.

Davidson, J. M., Smith, E. R., Rodgers, C. H., and Bloch, G. J. (1968) Relative thresholds of behavioral and somatic responses to estrogen, *Physiol and Behav.*, **3**, 227–9.

Dewsbury, D. A. (1972) Effects of tetrabenazine on the copulatory behavior of male rats, *Eur. J. Pharmacol.*, **17**, 221–6.

Dewsbury, D. A., and Davis, H. N. (1970) Effects of reserpine on the copulatory behavior of male rats, *Physiol. Behav.*, **5**, 1331–3.

Dewsbury, D. A., Davis, H. N., and Janssen, P. E. (1972) Effects of monoamine oxidase inhibitors on the copulatory behavior of male rats, *Psychopharmacologia*, **24**, 209–17.

Dombro, R. S. and Wooley, D. W. (1964) Cinnamides as structural analogs and antagonists of serotonin, *Biochem. Pharmacol.*, **13**, 569–76.

Donoso, A. O., de Gutierrez Moyano, M. B., and Santolaya, R. L. (1969) Metabolism of noradrenal in the hypothalamus of castrated rats, *Neuroendocrinology*, **4**, 12–9.

Duhault, J. and Verdavainne, C. (1967) Modification du taux de sérotonine sérébrale chez le rat par les trifluorométhyl-phényl-2-éthyl aminopropane (fenfluramines 768 S), *Arch. Int. Pharmacodyn. Ther.*, **170**, 276–86.

Eliasson, M. and Meyerson, B. J. (1973) Influence of LSD and apomorphine on hormone-activated copulatory behaviour in the female rat, *Acta Physiol. Scand.*, Suppl. 396, abstr. 129.

Eliasson, M. and Meyerson, B. J. (1975) Sexual preference in female rats during estrous cycle, pregnancy, and lactation, *Physiol. and Behav.*, **14**, 705–10.

Eliasson, M. and Meyerson, B. J. (1976) Comparison of the action of lysergic acid diethylamide and apomorphine on the copulatory response in the female rat, *Psychopharmacologia*, submitted manuscript.

Eliasson, M., Michanek, A., and Meyerson, B. J. (1972) A differential inhibitory action of LSD and amphetamine on copulatory behavior in the female rat, *Acta Pharmacol. Toxicol.*, **31**, Suppl. 1, abstr.

Eriksson, H. and Södersten, P. (1973) Failure to facilitate lordosis behavior in adrenalectomized and gonadectomized estrogen-primed rats with monoamine-synthesis inhibitors, *Horm. Behav.*, **4**, 89–98.

Ernst, A. M. (1967) Mode of action of apomorphine and dexamphetamine on gnawing compulsion in rats, *Psychopharmacologia Berl.*, **10**, 316–23.

Everitt, B. J., Fuxe, K., and Hökfelt, T. (1974) Inhibitory role of dopamine and 5-hydroxytryptamine in the sexual behaviour of female rats, *Eur. J. Pharmacol.*, **29**, 187–91.

Everitt, B. J., Fuxe, K., Hökfelt, T., and Jonsson, G. (1975b) Studies on the role of monoamines in the hormonal regulation of sexual receptivity in th female rat. In: *Sexual Behavior Pharmacology and Biochemistry*, M. Sandler and M. Gessa (eds.), Raven Press, New York.

Everitt ,B. J., Gradwell, P. B., and Herbert, J. (1975a) Humoral and aminergic mechanisms regulating sexual receptivity in female thesus monkeys. In: *Sexual Behavior Pharmacology and Biochemistry*, M. Sandler and G. L. Gessa (eds.), Raven Press, New York.

Feder, H. H. and Ruf, K. B. (1969) Stimulation of progesterone release and estrous behaviour by ACTH in ovariectomized rodents, *Endocrinology*, **69**, 171–4.

Feder, H. H. and Whalen (1965) Feminine behavior in neonatally castrated and estrogen-treated male rats, *Science*, **147**, 306–7.

Ferguson, J., Henriksen, S., Cohen, H., and Mitchell, G. (1970) Hypersexuality and behavioral changes in *cats* caused by administration of *p*-chlorophenylalanine, *Science*, **168**, 499–501.

Fuxe, K., and Hökfelt, T. (1969) Catecholamines in the hypothalamus and the pituitary gland. In: *Frontiers in Neuroendocrinology*, W. F. Ganong and L. Martini (eds.), Oxford Press, Oxford, pp. 61–83.

Gawienowski, A. M. and Hodgen, G. D. (1971) Homosexual activity in male rats after *p*-chlorophenylalanine effects of hypophysectomy and testosterone, *Physiol. Behav.*, **7**, 551–5.

Gessa, G. L. and Sandler, M., eds. (1975) *Sexual Behavior Pharmacology and Biochemistry*, Raven Press, New York.

Gessa, G. L. and Tagliamonte, A. (1974) Role of brain monoamines in male sexual behavior, *Life Sci.*, **14**, 425–36.

Gispen, W. H., ed. (1976) *Molecular and Functional Neurobiology*, Elsevier, Amsterdam.

Glowinski, J., and Axelrod, J. (1966) Effects of drugs on the disposition of H^3-norepinephorine in the rat brain, *Pharmacol. Rev.*, **18**, 775–85.

Gorzalka, B. B. and Whalen, R. E. (1975) Inhibition not facilitation of sexual behavior by PCPA, *Pharmacol. Biochem. Behav.*, **3**, 511–3.

Gray, G. D., Davis, H. N., and Dewsbury, D. A. (1974) Effects of L-dopa on the heterosexual copulatory behavior of male rats, *Eur. J. Pharmacol.*, **27**, 367–70.

Hoyland, V. J., Shillito, E. E., and Vogt, M. (1970) The effect of parachlorophenylalanine on the behavior of cats, *Br. J. Pharmac.*, **40**, 659–67.

Hyyppä, M. Lehtinen, P., and Rinne, U. K. (1971) Effect of L-DOPA on hypothalamic, pineal and striatal monomines on the sexual behaviour of the rat, *Brain Res.*, **30**, 265–72.

Iversen, S. D. and Iversen, L. L. (1975) *Behavioral Pharmacology*, Oxford Univ. Press.

Jonsson, G., Malmfors, T., and Sachs, C., eds. (1975) *Chemical Tools in Catecholamine Research I. 6-Hydroxydopamine as a Denervation Tool in Catecholamine Research*, Elsevier, Amsterdam.

Kordon, L. and Glowinski, J. (1972) Role of hypothalamic monoaminergic neurons in the gonadotrophin release-regulating mechanism, *Neuropharmacology*, **11**, 153–62.

Kuehn, R. E. and Beach, F. A. (1963) Quantitative measurements of sexual receptivity in female rats, *Behaviour*, **21**, 282–99.

Larsson, K., Feder, H. H., and Komisaruk, B. R. (1974) Role of the adrenal glands, repeated matings, and monoamines in lordosis behavior of rats, *Pharmacol., Biochem. Behav.*, **2**, 685–92.

Lichtensteiger, W. (1969) Cyclic variations of catecholamine content in hypothalamic nerve cells during the estrous cycle of the rat, with a concomitant study of the substantia nigra, *J. Pharmacol. Exp. Ther.*, **165**, 204–15.

Lindström, L. H. (1970) The effect of pilocarpine in combination with monoamine oxidase inhibitors, imipramine or desmethylimipramine on oestrous behaviour in female rats, *Psychopharmacologia Berl.*, **17**, 160–8.

Lindström, L. H. (1971) The effect of pilocarpine and oxotremorine on oestrous behaviour in female rats after treatment with monoamine depletors or monoamine synthesis inhibitors, *Eur. J. Pharmacol.*, **15**, 60–5.

Lindström, L. H. (1972) The effect of pilocarpine and oxotremorine on hormone-activated copulatory behavior in the ovariectomized hamster, *Naunyn-Schmiedeberg's Arch. Pharmacol.*, **275**, 233–41.

Lindström, L. H. (1973) Further studies on cholinergic mechanisms and hormone-activated copulatory behaviour in the female rat, *J. Endocrinol.*, **56**, 275–83.

Lindström, L. H. and Meyerson, B. J. (1967) The effect of pilocarpine, oxotremorine and arecoline in combination with methyl-atropine or atropine on hormone activated ostrous behaviour in ovariectomized rats, *Psychopharmacologia*, **11**, 405–13.

Luttge, W. G. (1975) Stimulation of estrogen induced copulatory behavior in castrate male rats with the serotonin biosynthesis inhibitor *p*-chlorophenylalanine, *Behav. Biol.*, **14**, 373–8.

Malmfors, T. and Thoenen, H., eds. (1971) *6-Hydroxydopamine and Catecholamine Neurons*, North-Holland Publ., Amsterdam.

Malmnäs, C. O. (1973) Monoaminergic influence on testosterone-activated copulatory behavior in the castrated male rat, *Acta Physiol Scand.*, Suppl. 395, 1–128.

Malmnäs, C. O. (1975) Effects of D- and L-propranolol on sexual behavior in male rats, *European Neurosciences Meeting*, Munich.

Malmnäs, C. O. (1976) The significance of dopamine, *versus* other catecholamines, for L-DOPA induced facilitation of sexual behavior in the castrated male rat, *Pharmacol. Biochem. Behav.*, **4**, 521–6.

Malmnäs, C. O. and Meyerson, B. J. (1970) Monoamines and testosterone activated copulatory behaviour in the castrated male rat, *Acta Pharmacol. Toxicol.*, **28**, Suppl.

Malmnäs, C. O. and Meyerson, B. J. (1971) *p*-Chlorophenylalanine and copulatory behaviour in the male rat, *Nature*, **232**, 398–400.

Malmnäs, C. O. and Meyerson, B. J. (1972) Monoamines and copulatory activation in the castrated male rat, *Acta Pharmacol Toxicol.*, **31**, Suppl. 1.

Mandell, A. J., ed. (1973) *New Concepts in Neurotransmitter Regulation*, Plenum Press, New York.

Meyerson, B. J. (1964a) The effect of neuropharmacological agents on hormone-activated estrus behaviour in ovariectomized rats, *Arch. Int. Pharmacodyn.*, **150**, 4–33.

Meyerson, B. J. (1964b) Estrus behaviour in spayed rats after estrogen or progesterone treatment in combination with reserpine or tetrabenazine, *Psychopharmacologia*, **6**, 210–8.

Meyerson, B. J. (1964c) Central nervous monoamines and hormone induced estrus behaviour in the spayed rat, *Acta Physiol. Scand.*, **63**, 3–32, Suppl. 241.

Meyerson, B. J. (1966) The effect of imipramine and related antidepressive drugs on estrus behaviour in ovariectomized rats activated by progesterone, reserpine or tetrabenazine in combination with estrogen, *Acta Physiol. Scand.*, **67**, 411–22.

Meyerson, B. J. (1968a) Amphetamine and 5-hydroxytryptamine inhibition of copulatory behaviour in the female rat, *Ann. Med. Exp. Fenn.*, **46**, 394–8.

Meyerson, B. J. (1968b) Female copulatory behaviour in male and androgenized female rats after oestrogen/amine depletor treatment, *Nature*, **217**, 683–4.

Meyerson, B. J. (1975) Drugs and sexual motivation in the female rat. In: Sexual Behavior Pharmacology and Biochemistry, M. Sandler and G. L. Gessa (eds.), Raven Press, New York.

Meyerson, B. J., Carrer, H., and Eliasson, M. (1974) 5-Hydroxytryptamine and sexual behavior in the female rat. In: *Adv. in Biochem. Psychopharm.* Vol II, E. Costa, M. Gessa, and M. Sander (eds.), Raven Press, New York, pp. 229–42.

Meyerson, B. J. and Eliasson, M. (1976) Pharmacological and hormonal control of reproductive behavior. In: *Handbook of Psychopharmacology*, L. L. Iversen, S. D. Iversen, and S. H. Snyder (eds.), Plenum Publ. Corp., New York.

Meyerson, B. J., Eliasson, M., Lindström, L., Michanek, A., and Söderlund, A. C. (1973) Monoamines and female sexual behaviour. In: *Psychopharmacology, Sexual Disorders and Drug Abuse*, T. A. Ban, J. R. Boissier, G. J. Gessa, H. Heimann, L. Hollister, H. E. Lehmann, I. Munkvad, H. Steinberg, F. Sulser, A. Sundwall, and O. Vinar (eds.), N. Holland Publ., pp. 463–572.

Meyerson, B. J. and Lewander, T. (1970) Serotonin synthesis inhibition and estrous behaviour in female rats, *Life Sci.*, **9**, 661–71.

Meyerson, B. J. and Lindström, L. H. (1973) Sexual motivation in the female rat. A methodological study applied to the investigation of the effect of estradiol benzoate, *Acta Physiol. Scand.*, Suppl. 389, pp. 1–80.

Michanek, A., and Meyerson, B. J. (1975) Copulatory behavior in the female rat after amphetamine and amphetamine derivatives. In: *Sexual Behavior, Pharmacology and Biochemistry*, M. Sandler and G. L. Gessa (eds.), Raven Press, New York.

Michanek, A. and Meyerson, B. J. (1977) A comparative study of different amphetamines on copulatory behavior and stereotype activity in the female rat, *Psychopharmacologia*, **53**, 175–83.

Paris, C. A., Resko, J. A., and Goy, R. W. (1971) A possible mechanism for the induction of lordosis by reserpine in spayed rats, *Biol. Reprod.*, **4**, 23–30.

Perez-Cruet, J., Tagliamonte, A., and Gessa, G. L. (1971) Differential effects of *p*-chlorophenylalanine (PCPA) on sexual behavior and on sleep patterns of male rabbits, *Riv. Farmacol. Ter.*, **11**, 27–34.

Redmond, D. E., Maas, J. E., Kling, A., and Graham, C. W. (1971) Social behavior of monkeys selectively depleted of monoamines, *Science*, **174**, 428–30.

Ross., S. B. and Renyi, A. L. (1969) Inhibition of the uptake of triatiated 5-hydroxytryptamine in brain tissue, *Eur. J. Pharmacol.*, **7**, 270–2.

Salis, P. J. and Dewsbury, D. A. (1971) *p*-Chlorophenylalanine facilitates copulatory behaviour in male rats, *Nature*, **232**, 400–1.

Schotman, P., Reith, M. E. A., Van Wimersma Greidanus, Tj. B., Gispen, W. H., and DeWied, D. (1976) Hypothalamic and pituitary peptide hormones and the central nervous system. With special references to the neurochemical effects of ACTH. In: *Molecular and Functional Neurobiology*, W. H. Gispen (ed.), Elsevier Sci. Publ. Co., Amsterdam.

Shillito, E. E. (1970) The effect of parachlorophenylalanine on social interactions of male rats, *Br. J. Pharmacol.*, **38**, 305–15.

Soulairac, M. L. (1963) Étude expérimentale des régulations hormono-nerveuses du comportement sexuel du rat mâle, *Ann. d'Endocr.*, **24**, 1–98, Suppl. to N. 3.

Södersten, P. (1972) Mounting behavior in the female rat during the estrous cycle, after ovariectomy and after estrogen or testosterone administration, *Hormon. Behav.*, **3**, 307–20.

Tagliamonte, A., Fratta, W., Del Fiacco, M., and Gessa, G. L. (1973) Evidence that brain dopamine stimulates copulatory behavior in male rats, *Riv. Farmaco. Ter.*, **4**, 177–81.

Tagliamonte, A., Fratta, W., Mercuro, G., Biggio, G. Camba, R. C., and Gessa, G. L. (1972) 5-Hydroxytryptophan, but not tryptophan, inhibits copulatory behavior in amale rats, *Riv. Farmacol. Ter.*, **3**, 405–9.

Tagliamonte, A., Tagliamonte, P., and Gessa, G. L. (1971) Reversal of pargyline-induced inhibition of sexual behaviour in male rats by *p*-chlorophenylalanine, *Nature Lond.*, **230**, 244–5.

Tagliamonte, A., Tagliamonte, P., Gessa, G. L., and Brodie, B. B. (1969) Compulsive sexual activity induced by *p*-chlorophenylalanine in normal and pinealectomized male rats, *Science*, **166**, 1433–5.

Tonge, S. R., and Greengrass, P. M. (1971) The acute effects of oestrogen and progesterone on the monoamine levels of the brain of ovariectomized rats, *Psychopharmacologia Berl.*, **21**, 374–81.

Uphouse, L. L. (1970) Induction of estrus in mice: possible role of adrenal progesterone, *Horm. Behav.*, **1**, 255–64.

Usdin, E., and Bunney Jr., W. E., eds. (1975) Pre- and postsynaptic receptors, Marcel Dekker Inc., New York.

Ward, I. J., Crowley, W. R., and Zemlan, F. P. (1975) Monoaminergic mediation of female sexual behavior, *J. Comp. Physiol. Psychol.*, **88**, 53–61.

Whalen, R. E. (1975) Methodological considerations in the study of animal sexual behaviour, In: *Sexual Behavior, Pharmacology, and Biochemistry*, M. Sandler and G. L. Gessa (eds.), Raven Press, New York.

Whalen, R. E. and Luttge, W. G. (1970) *p*-Chlorophenylalanine methyl ester: an aphrodisiac? *Science*, **169**, 1000–1.

Whalen, R. E. and Nakayama, K. (1965) Induction of oestrous behaviour: Facilitation by repeated hormone treatments, *J. Endocrinol.*, **33**, 525.

Zemlan, F. P., Ward, I. J., Crowley, W. R., and Margules, D. L. (1973) Activation of lordotic responding in female rats by suppression of serotonergic activity, *Science*, **179**, 1010–1.

Zitrin, A., Beach, F. A., Barchas, J. D., and Dement, W. C. (1970) Sexual behavior of male cats after administration of *para*chlorophenylalanine, *Science*, **170**, 868–9.

Zucker, I. and Goy, R. W. (1967) Sexual receptivity in the guinea pig: Inhibitory and facilitatory actions of progesterone and related compounds, *J. Comp. Physiol. Psychol.*, **64**, 378–83.

CHAPTER 17

A Neuroanatomical Approach to the Study of Monoamines and Sexual behaviour

Barry J. Everitt

INTRODUCTION

There is a considerable body of evidence (see Meyerson and Malmnäs, this volume Chapter 16) which suggests that the biogenic monoamines may play a fundamentally important role in the control by hormones of sexual activity in mammals. Thus, 5-hydroxytryptamine (5-HT) is seen to have an inhibitory role in males and females while dopamine (DA) appears to be inhibitory in females but excitatory in males. Noradrenaline (NA) has proved elusive to define in this context because it is difficult to alter it specifically using drugs, but there is a tendency for it to appear excitatory in both sexes (Malmnäs, 1973; Everitt *et al.*, 1975b). This large quantity of psychopharmacological data persuasively argues for, and is often taken to be evidence which supports the concept that hormones normally act on the CNS to alter behaviour by modulating monoamine neurotransmitter activity. This is not the case—in fact there is little or no direct evidence that the mechanism of action of hormones which induce sexual activity is the same as the mechanism of action of drugs which induce a similar change in sexual activity. Circumstantial evidence that the two are interrelated comes from a number of neurochemical studies in which it is seen that hormones do have marked effects on levels, turnover, and uptake of monoamines and on the activity of their biosynthetic and degrading enzymes (see Everitt, 1976).

Another important approach to this problem is an anatomical one. If hormones are indeed acting on aminergic neurons (or on neurons innervated by them) then selective destruction or stimulation of these neurons either at cell body sites, along their axon projections or at terminal areas should produce predictable changes in sexual behaviour. Stated thus, this approach would seem a simple one. The distribution of amines in the central nervous system (CNS) is well known, at least for the rat. The sites of action of sex steroids on reproductive behaviour (from implantation and lesion experiments) are also quite well known. But to draw these two facets of the problem together has proved difficult and the methodologies underlying experiments in this area of research are fraught with problems of interpretation and control.

This chapter is concerned, then, with a neuroanatomical approach to the study of amines and sexual behaviour. First the organization of aminergic neurons in the brain will be described and will be followed by a brief review of some anatomical experiments which have contributed to our understanding of the complicated interaction between hormones, amines, and sexual activity.

THE DISTRIBUTION OF AMINERGIC NEURONS IN THE CENTRAL NERVOUS SYSTEM

The detailed knowledge that now exists concerning the distribution of aminergic neurons in the brain is due to the development of the highly specific and sensitive Falck–Hillarp histochemical fluorescence technique (See Fuxe and Jonsson, 1973). It is based on the observation that when freeze-dried tissues are reacted with formaldehyde vapour at $+80\,°C$, neuronal monoamines are converted into high intensity fluorophors (without appreciable diffusion if the reaction conditions are optimal). The formaldehyde fluorescence reaction with catecholamines and 5-HT is a two-step reaction involving ring closure followed by dehydrogenation to yield fluorescent 3, 4-dihydroisoquinolines from catecholamines or 3, 4-dihydro-β-carbolines from 5-HT. Specificity of the technique is due to the fact that only 3-hydroxylated β-phenylethlamines and β-(3-indolyl)-ethylamines and their corresponding amino acids give rise to a formaldehyde-induced fluorescence. Thus, in mammalian tissues, the technique mainly demonstrates NA, DA, 5-HT, and their immediate precursors, but if an animal is treated with synthetic amine derivatives of these compounds, then they will also yield fluorescent products (a finding which has been made use of in the case of some neurotoxins—see below). The fact that diffusion of the fluorophors is minimal under correct reaction conditions means that the technique is a very powerful one, since it enables specific neuron systems to be studied at the microscopic level with respect to their transmitter content. Variations on this theme involving, for example, immunofluorescence studies of intraneuronal enzyme specific to DA, NA or 5-HT synthesis and, more recently, studies using labelled amino acid (e.g. proline) intracerebral injections, have allowed these systems of aminergic neurons in the CNS to be very precisely mapped.

A common feature of these neurons is that their cell bodies (with only one or two exceptions) are located exclusively in the medulla, pons, and midbrain, but from these sites they project widely over the CNS, both down the spinal cord and rostrally to the diencephalon and telencephalon, including the neocortex. For fuller details of the distribution of amines in the CNS see Dahlstrom and Fuxe (1965); Fuxe (1965); Ungerstedt (1971); Fuxe and Jonsson (1974); Fuxe et al. (1975).

Noradrenaline Neurons (Fig. 1)

The NA cell groups are designated A1 to A7 (by Dahlstrom and Fuxe, 1965) and are located exclusively in the reticular formation of the medulla and pons. The locus coeruleus NA neurons (A6) innervate the hippocampal formation, cingulate, prepyriform, entorhinal, and periamygdaloid cortex as well as parts of the neocortex. Their axons run together initially as the 'dorsal NA bundle' through the pons and midbrain but, at the rostral level of the mamillary nuclei they turn ventrolaterally to join the medial forebrain bundle (mfb—see below), in which they ascend to the septum and there turn dorsally and caudally in the cingulum. The locus coeruleus also projects to the cerebellum and lower brain stem nuclei. The somewhat larger NA terminals (compared to those in the cortex) found in the subcortical limbic brain (the areas surrounding the DA-rich nucleus accumbens and olfactory tubercle, the nucleus interstitialis stria terminalis, septal nuclei, and large areas of the hypothalamus) originate from other NA cell groups (A1, A2, A5, and A7). Their axons run in the 'ventral NA bundle' in which they ascend in the midreticular formation, turn ventromedially along the medial lemniscus and run rostrally within the mfb. Both the ventral and dorsal bundle components of the ascending NA pathways overlap somewhat in their terminal distribution.

It should be remembered that the most caudal NA cell group A1 (and perhaps A2) also gives rise to NA axons which run down the cord in the anterior and ventral lateral funiculi to terminate in the anterior horn and another system which runs in the dorsal lateral funiculus to terminate in the intermediolateral (sympathetic) column.

Dopamine Neurons (Fig. 1)

The DA cell groups are numbered A8, A9 (the substantia nigra, zona compacta) and A10, all of which are in the midbrain. Of those in the diencephalon, cell group A12 (within the arcuate nucleus of the hypothalamus) is of particular interest because of its relationship via the capillary plexus in the median eminence to the anterior pituitary. The A9 DA cell group in the substantia nigra gives rise to the nigro-striatal DA pathway which runs in the dorsolateral part of the lateral hypothalamus, axons leaving it to fan out in the globus pallidus and enter the caudate-putamen where they terminate. The meso-limbic DA pathway originates primarily in cell group A10 which surrounds the interpeduncular nucleus and perhaps from the medial part of A9. Axons from here ascend medial to the nigro-striatal pathway within the mfb to innervate the nucleus accumbens, olfactory tubercle, central amygdaloid nucleus, lateral septal nucleus, dorsolateral part of the nucleus intersti-

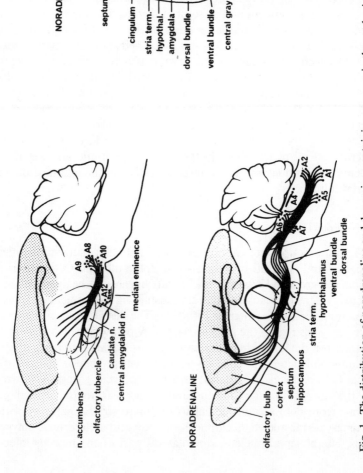

Fig. 1. The distribution of noradrenaline and dopamine-containing neurons in the rat brain. Redrawn from Ungerstedt, 1971. Nomenclature of cell groups, Dahlstrom and Fuxe, 1965

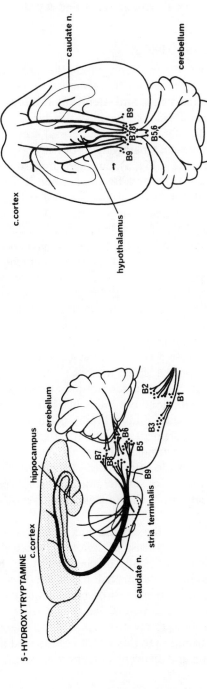

Fig. 2. The distribution of 5-hydroxytryptamine-containing neurons in the rat brain. Redrawn from Fuxe and Jonsson, 1974. Nomenclature of cell groups, Dahlstrom and Fuxe, 1965

tialis stria terminalis, and areas in the nucleus of the diagonal band of Broca. More recently a DA innervation of the limbic cortex (frontal, anterior cingulate, and entorhinal) has been demonstrated and which similarly originates in cell group A10.

5-Hydroxytryptamine Neurons (Fig. 2)

The 5-HT cell groups B1–B9 lie mainly within the raphe nuclei of the brain stem. The most caudal of these (B1–B3) give rise to axons which descend through the spinal cord in the medial and lateral anterior funiculus to terminate in the anterior horn. Other 5-HT axons run in the dorsal lateral funiculus to terminate in the intermediolateral column and dorsal horn.

Ascending 5-HT axons orginate mainly in the dorsal and medial raphe nuclei (B7 and B8) in the midbrain (see Fig. 3), but there are also contributions from groups B9 (in the midbrain), B5 and B6 (in the pons). The axons run first ventrally and then rostrally in two partially separated bundles—the medial and lateral 5-HT bundles—which then join the mfb to course through the lateral hypothalamus, preoptic area and septum where axons join the stria terminals, fornix and cingulum. 5-HT terminals have been demonstrated throughout the hypothalamus (particularly in the suprachiasmatic nucleus), the lateral and medial septal nuclei, corticomedial and basolateral amygdala, hippocampus, caudate nucleus, lateral geniculate nucleus and wide areas of the cerebral cortex. It has recently been shown (Azmitia, pers. commun.) that the dorsal and medial raphe nuclei have separable, regional innervation patterns. This sort of information will prove extremely useful when analysing the functions of such a diverse 5-HT system since it will enable selective and well localized lesions to be placed within it.

From the above, rather abbreviated description it can be seen that aminergic neurons have a wide distribution, but particularly richly innervated areas include the hypothalamus and 'limbic brain' (such as septal nuclei and amygdala). It is, therefore, pertinent to note that these are also areas which take up and bind labelled sex steroids, although the overlap is less than perfect (Pfaff and Keiner, 1973; Wade and Feder, 1972a, 1972b; Zigmond and McEwen, 1970), where implants of sex steroids can induce sexual activity and where lesions may prevent their behaviour-inducing actions (see Davidson, 1972 for review).

The strategies which underly the experiments described below are, at first glance, straightforward. They consist of lesioning (electrolytically or with neurotoxins) or stimulating (electrically or chemically) cell body sites in the brain stem, terminal areas in the diencephalon or axons at various sites along the mfb. It is important, here, to say a little more about the latter structure. From the description above it is apparent that the mfb carries virtually all the *ascending* aminergic projections to the diencephalon and telencephalon. But an equal, perhaps larger contribution to this structure is derived from a number of sites in the rostral forebrain and diencephalon and which *descend* in the mfb to

Fig. 3. Fluorescence photo-micrograph of the 5-hydroxy-tryptamine-containing neurons of the mesencephalic dorsal (B7) and medial (B8) raphe. AS = cerebral aqueduct MB = medial, ascending 5-HT bundle

the midbrain tegmentum (Millhouse, 1969). Along their course, these axons give off many collaterals to neurons along their path as well as long collaterals which, for example, enter the stria medullaris thalami. Neurons in the lateral preoptic-hypothalamic area ('path neurons'—Millhouse, 1969) have dendritic trees which both spread perpendicularly across the mfb and overlap with the more medially placed preoptic and hypothalamic nuclear groups. Axons from these path neurons bifurcate to give rostrally and caudally running branches also within the mfb.

Thus, to speak of a 'lesion in the mfb' brings with it a serious problem of interpretation since, as will be seen, it would appear almost impossible to relate the behavioural sequelae of such a lesion to destruction of any one of its many ascending and descending components.

MONOAMINERGIC PATHWAYS AND THE SEXUAL BEHAVIOUR OF FEMALES

It is important to remember, at this point, two features of the psychopharmacological data reviewed by Meyerson and Malmnäs. One is that drugs which induce or inhibit sexual activity in females do so by replacing (Everitt *et al.*, 1975b), combining with (see Meyerson and Malmnäs, this volume Chapter 16), or interfering with (Everitt *et al.*, 1975b) the action of progesterone. The second is, therefore, the apparent critical presence of oestrogen in these experiments (Everitt, 1976) and those which will be described below. The most commonly used model is that of an ovariectomized, oestrogen-treated female who (if the dose of oestrogen is carefully controlled) is not displaying sexual receptivity and in whom, therefore, facilitatory actions of lesions or implants can be assessed.

It has been reported that progesterone exerts its facilitatory effect on sexual receptivity in the guinea pig when implanted in the midbrain, a site rich in 5-HT cell bodies (Morin and Feder, 1974a, 1974b), although rather different results were obtained by Powers (1972) in the rat. A number of additional studies have shown that progesterone may have this effect when implanted over a wide area of the diencephalon (Ross *et al.*, 1971; Powers, 1972; Ward *et al.*, 1975) and, indeed, injections of the labelled steroid seem to suggest potentially diverse sites of action (Wade and Feder, 1972a, 1972b; Wade *et al.*, 1973). Clemens (1971) has reported that NA facilitated lordosis when placed in midbrain sites sensitive to progesterone, but it is difficult to assess this finding in the absence of histological data which show exact sites of implantation.

A rather surprising finding in view of the well established inhibitory role of 5-HT in oestrous behaviour is that lesions of the dorsal and median raphe nuclei, singly or combined, have no effect on the sexual activity of oestrogen-treated female rats (Sterling and Everitt, to be publ.). Similarly, partial lesions of the DA cell group A10 are without effect (Sterling and Everitt, to be publ.). These three cell groups provide the diencephalon and limbic forebrain with the majority of their 5-HT and DA input and it would be expected, therefore, that their destruction would have effects similar to 5-HT and DA depletion (see also Sheard, 1973 and below).

Kow *et al.* (1974) have suggested that the increase in lordotic behaviour shown by rats with septal lesions (Nance *et al.*, 1974, 1975a) is due to a disruption of 5-HT inputs from the midbrain raphe. Clearly this is not supported by the above experiments, nor by the finding that injections of the neurotoxin

5, 7-dihydroxytryptamine (5, 7-DHT) into the lateral septal nucleus (which caused a 40% decrease in 5-HT uptake there) had no effect on lordotic behaviour in oestrogen-treated female rats (Sterling and Everitt, to be publ.). Electrolytic lesions of the mfb are also without effect on the sexual activity of female rats (Hitt *et al.*, 1970; Modianos *et al.*, 1973) contrary to the effects on males (see below) although, for reasons stated earlier, lesions which cause a total destruction of the mfb are difficult to assess.

A way of avoiding the dilemma of trying to attribute the effects of mfb lesions to destruction of one or other component within it is to make use of both the detailed information concerning 5-HT projections and the neurochemically specific neurotoxin 5, 7-DHT to lesion the ascending 5-HT components of the mfb selectively. If this is done (by injection into the rostral midbrain, see Fig. 4) a large (70%) and selective (telencephalic 5-HT, NA, and diencephalic NA are unaffected) 5-HT denervation of the hypothalamus is achieved. Oestrogen-treated rats lesioned in this way show a significant and permanent (up to 9 months) increase in sexual receptivity (Everitt *et al.*, 1975a). Thus, destruction of these 5-HT neurons has obviated the necessity of using progesterone in inducing receptivity in animals who would not normally display it. A more careful analysis of the extent of 5-HT denervation achieved in other areas (notably the septum) is required before definitive statements about the effects of the lesion can be made, but it is apparent that this approach is potentially a powerful one and could yield much information if applied to DA and NA neurons as well, using the neurotoxin 6-hydroxydopamine.

Similar use of the information concerning the course and distribution of aminergic neurons has been made in a series of experiments involving the implantation of receptor antagonists in diencephalic terminal areas and within the mfb (Ward *et al.*, 1975). Their results showed that 5-HT receptor blockers and β-adrenergic blockers elicited lordosis in oestrogen-treated rats when placed at sites which were also responsive to progesterone. These sites were within the medial anterior hypothalamic and preoptic areas and also at various sites within the mfb. This is at once interesting and puzzling since both postsynaptic receptors (in the hypothalamus) and presynaptic receptors (in the mfb) are undergoing blockade. The former (i.e. blockade of postsynaptic receptors) in this case, should lead to an increase in sexual activity as was observed. The latter, however, should have an opposite effect—a blockade of presynaptic receptors being associated with an increase in activity (i.e. impulse flow) in the neuron (Fuxe *et al.*, 1976). Thus it remains to be seen whether these drugs are indeed acting on the mfb or on path neurons receiving an aminergic input. If the latter is true, then the lateral hypothalamus should be investigated more thoroughly as a potential site of action of progesterone.

Implantation of 5-HT and β-adrenergic antagonists within the anterior or posterior hypothalamus of male rats also caused an increase in lordotic (i.e. 'heterotypical') behaviour whereas systemic progesterone is without effect in males (Crowley *et al.*, 1975). Large septal lesions similarly cause an increase

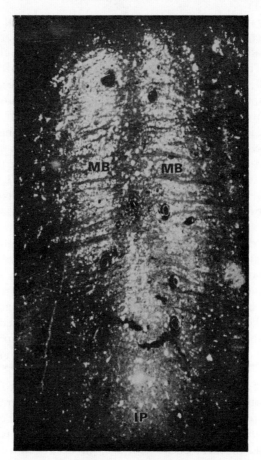

Fig. 4. Fluorescence photomicrograph of medial, ascending 5-HT bundle lesioned by injection of 4 μg 5, 7-dihydroxytryptamine in 2 μl solvent. IP = region of interpeduncular nucleus

in lordosis in male rats—an effect which is greatest if the males are prepubertally castrated (Nance *et al.*, 1975b). In a recent study it was further shown that such males also display a responsiveness to progesterone i.e. progesterone facilitates the display of lordosis in the oestrogen-treated, prepubertally castrate male rat after lesion of the lateral septum (Chambers and Everitt, to be publ.). Furthermore, electrolytic destruction of the septohypothalamic trace, which carries the 5-HT input from the mfb to the lateral septal nucleus, causes a similar alteration in behaviour (Chambers and Everitt, to be publ.).

These findings which relate the septal nuclei, progesterone, and 5-HT in the control of lordotic behaviour in both females and males are far from conclusive but warrant a much closer look. Kow *et al.* (1974) suggest that the projections back from the septum to the midbrain via the stria medullaris, habenula, and fasciculus retroflexus may also be an important component of the raphe–septum system. In this context the results of Rodgers and Law (1967) which show that destruction of the habenula *prevents* the response of oestrogen-primed female rats to progesterone become particularly relevant. Thus, this complicated system of connections between midbrain, septum, and back to the midbrain, part of which seems to involve 5-HT neurons running in the mfb, warrants careful and detailed analysis to dissect out its role in the neuroendo-crine basis of sexual behaviour.

In summary, the anatomical data reviewed above give some basis to the psychopharmacological data relating 5-HT (at least) and sexual behaviour. But the picture is far from clear and will remain so unless use is made of the sophisticated tools available (eg. neurotoxins) to dissect out the system. The data also reflect a bias, not illogically, towards the ascending components of aminergic neurons, but it should be borne in mind that there are substantial 5-HT and NA projections down the spinal cord to anterior horn cells. They are known to play a major part in extensor and flexor reflex activity (Andén, 1968) and, if the nature of the postural response of a female rat to a male's mount is remembered (see Pfaff *et al.*, 1973), these neurons could well represent a (direct or indirect) site of action of steroids which would, therefore, affect the threshold of activation of these reflexes. However, preliminary experiments (Fuxe and Everitt, unpubl.) on the interaction of oestrogen, progesterone, and a number of 5-HT receptor agonists and antagonists in the control of extensor reflex activity in rats yielded little evidence that the spinal cord is a major site where oestrogens may influence the activity of, or response to aminergic neurons. Hart (1969) also using spinally transected animals, has come to a similar conclusion.

MONOAMINERGIC PATHWAYS AND THE SEXUAL BEHAVIOUR OF MALES

As with the psychopharmacological studies of sexual behaviour in females, it must be emphasized here that in similar experiments on males it is critical that testosterone is present for aminergic drugs to affect their sexual activity. Thus, intact animals are often used, both vigorous copulators (in whom so-called 'aphrodisiac' effects are sought out) and 'sexually sluggish' animals (in whom a restoration of activity to the 'norm'—or at least an increase—is expected). But more recently the concept of a low dose of testosterone given to castrates which induces a submaximal response rate has been introduced by Malmnäs (1973) as a model in which both increases and decreases of sexual activity following drug treatment may be measured. As with oestrogen in females, therefore, we are forced to assume that testosterone in males is a critical prerequisite for any modulation of aminergic transmitter activity to result in an alteration in sexual activity. The nature of the relationship between hormone and drug (or, indeed, amine) remains a perpetual problem. Of the studies described below, almost all have used intact males.

Very large lesions of the mesencephalic–diencephalic junction cause an increase in the sexual activity of male rats (Heimer and Larsson, 1964). Although it is difficult to relate the changes in behaviour to destruction of any one structure, it is clear that aminergic pathways were among the ablated structures. The results are particularly interesting since not only did the animals ejaculate in a shorter time and after fewer intromissions, but the postejaculatory refractory period was markedly shortened. It is rare for both preejaculation copulatory performance and postejaculation refractoriness to be affected together in this way (see below).

Sheard (1973) compared the behavioural effects of PCPA (see Meyerson and Malmnäs, this volume Chapter 16) with lesions of the dorsal and medial raphe which caused a comparable lowering of cerebral 5-HT. The lesions, which were quite extensive, caused no increase in sexual activity—in contrast to PCPA. The reasons for the different results may reside in the wider effects of PCPA which also inhibits tyrosine hydroxylase and hence lowers the levels of NA and DA as well as 5-HT in the brain (Ahlenius et al., 1972), or in the unavoidable destruction of adjacent structures by the lesions, or in the nature of the behavioural observations which were not optimal for the measurement of changes in sexual activity. The problems associated with interpreting data derived from experiments using very different behavioural methodologies have been discussed in detail elsewhere (Everitt, 1976. See also Meyerson and Malmnäs, this volume Chapter 16).

There have been numerous investigations of the mfb in males which have involved both electrolytic lesions and electrical stimulation. The immense difficulties in interpreting the results of these experiments in the context of which component(s) of the mfb have been destroyed will become readily apparent.

Maclean and Ploog (1962) reported that penile erection follows electrical stimulation of the mfb in squirrel monkeys. Even though this display need not necessarily be sexual, their results provoked considerable research into the suggestion that the mfb might be an important structure in the neural basis of sexual activity.

Subsequently it has been shown, notably by Caggiula and his colleagues, that electrical stimulation of the mfb in the posterior lateral hypothalamus (from the level of the ventromedial nucleus to the mamillary bodies) results in a stimulation-bound increase in the copulatory performance of male rats (Caggiula and Hoebel, 1966; Caggiula, 1970). An extension of this work (Eibergen and Caggiula, 1973) demonstrated that the facilitatory effects (both a decrease in the latency to ejaculate and in postejaculation refractoriness) could be obtained by stimulating the mfb more posteriorly—down to the caudal extension of this structure in the ventral tegmentum. Stimulation-bound mounting behaviour has also been obtained by electrical stimulation of the mfb in the lateral preoptic area (Madlafousek *et al.*, 1970). Thus, alterations interpreted as increases in sexual activity have been reported to follow electrical stimulation of the anterior–posterior extent of the mfb. These changes may be either in pre- or postejaculatory performance—or both, indeed Caggiula and Szechtman (1972) report that the former (facilitation of ejaculation) was always accompanied by the latter (decreased refractory period). One recent study (Merari and Ginton, 1975) provided contradictory data, since here it was seen that electrical stimulation of the lateral preoptic area caused a decrease in male sexual activity—and it is clear from electrode placements that a number of them were in the mfb.

It has been remarked upon before (Malsbury and Pfaff, 1975) that all the facilitatory effects which follow lateral hypothalamic–preoptic area mfb stimulation also follow stimulation of the medial preoptic area (see Malsbury 1971; van Dis and Larsson, 1971; Merari and Ginton, 1975). The latter is also the most consistently effective site for testosterone implants to activate sexual activity in castrate males (see Davidson, 1972). Neurons in the medial preoptic area project caudally via the mfb to the hypothalamus and brain stem, while brain stem 5-HT, NA, and DA neurons project *inter alia* to the medial preoptic area also via the mfb. Thus a body of circumstantial evidence suggests that testosterone-sensitive neurons in the preoptic area and their aminergic input may interact in some way and, hence, underlly changes in sexual behaviour. This has been reinforced by studies involving destruction of the mfb.

Lesions of the parafornical mfb abolished sexual activity in male rats (and 'masculine' behaviour in androgen-treated females) in a study by Hitt *et al.* (1970). Hendricks continued this work (Hendricks and Scheetz, 1973) and demonstrated that sexual activity in males decreased not only after parafornical mfb lesions, but also after medial preoptic area lesions. In addition, a combination of a unilateral mfb lesion together with a medial preoptic lesion on the contralateral side had the same effect as bilateral lesions in either structure. In discussing their data, they attributed the behavioural deficit to a disruption of the *caudal* projections of the medial preoptic area but then took the puzzling step of treating animals with 5-hydroxytryptophan (the 5-HT precursor) to *reverse* the deficit. It had long been known (see Meyerson and Malmnäs, this volume Chapter 16) that 5-HTP alone can depress sexual activity and, further, if destruction of 5-HT neurons was responsible for the behavioural changes they would be ascending to the preoptic area, not descending from it.

Lesions of the mfb in the lateral hypothalamic–preoptic area junction also produced a clear decrease in the sexual activity (measured as mounts) of castrate male rats treated with testosterone (Modianos *et al.*, 1973). A subsequent study (Hitt *et al.*, 1973) demonstrated two important facts. First, the change in behaviour was not accompanied by any endocrine change. Second the decrement in sexual activity was the consequence of a defect in *initiation* of sexual activity but not in any other measure. Once these lesioned animals began to mount, they continued to ejaculate in an apparently normal way. Caggiula *et al.* (1973) in a similar study, but with lesions of the mfb in the middle and posterior lateral hypothalamus, produced very comparable results i.e. a deficit in initiation of sexual activity but, once begun, the mounting sequence continuing normally. These lesions were also later shown to have no significant effects on testosterone and luteinizing hormone (LH) levels, seminal vesicles, and testes (Cagguila *et al.*, 1975).

The most effective lesions in the early study (Cagguila *et al.*, 1973) both included and extended above the mfb in the posterior hypothalamus. Furthermore, measures of telencephalic NA and 5-HT levels suggested a correlation existed between the copulatory deficit and telencephalic NA, but not 5-HT. Thus, the implication is that lesions which included the dorsal NA bundle (which joins the mfb at this level) were the most effective and that this structure may, therefore, be particularly important in the context of male sexual activity. This is an interesting suggestion and represents one of the first attempts to relate amines and mfb lesions, but there are problems in accepting it—the most important being that total lesions of the mfb rostral to this point would also destroy its dorsal NA bundle component. Why, therefore, should the caudal ones be any more effective? Furthermore, the anterior hypothalamus and preoptic areas have been strongly implicated in the control of sexual behaviour and have a rich aminergic input—a correlation between amine levels and copulatory deficit might best have been sought here. However, Caggiula *et al.* (1973) do point out that differential destruction of 5-HT and DA neurons could be a factor and, more important, emphasize that descending components of the mfb would also have been destroyed.

Two recent studies have utilized the fact that the aminergic components of the mfb are accessible more caudally, in the midbrain, *before* they enter this structure. Lesions in the ventral midbrain, medial to the substantia nigra, produce a large decrease in the postejaculatory refractory period in male rats (Barfield *et al.*, 1975). Ironically, these lesions were in sites similar to those where electrical stimulation was seen to cause the same effect (Eibergen and Caggiula, 1973). The decrease in refractoriness was, apparently, unrelated to alterations in the levels of either 5-HT or NA (the *ventral* NA bundle would have been destroyed in this case). Conversely, a selective lesion of the *dorsal* NA bundle caused a very similar decrease in refractory period which was well correlated with NA depletion in the telencephalon. (Clark *et al.*, 1975). This, unfortunately, runs contrary to Caggiula's earlier suggestion (see above) that the *deficit* in initiating mounting after mfb lesions was due to destruction of the dorsal NA bundle also (see above) although, clearly, the latter lesions would have destroyed everything else in the mfb as well.

Clearly, in summary, there is nothing definitive to say about aminergic neurons and male sexual activity. Two features of the experiments reported do emerge: lesions of the lateral hypothalamic–preoptic mfb cause decreases while lesions of the aminergic components of the mfb more caudally produce increases in sexual activity. Perhaps this can be related to some earlier findings that medial preoptic area lesions abolish intromissions and ejaculations, but some measure of 'sexual arousal' may still be evident (sniffing, pursuit, palpation— but not thrusting; Giantonio et al., 1970).

It may be tentatively suggested, on the basis of some of this information, that the *ascending* monoaminergic neurons (at least 5-HT and NA) participate in the 'arousal' component of male sexual activity. This is evidenced by the fact that their destruction is followed by a decrease in postejaculatory refractoriness. Conversely, the *descending* axons in the mfb (originating *inter alia* in the olfactory bulbs, preoptic area) may be more important in the copulatory (mounting, thrusting, intromitting, and ejaculatory) components of male sexual activity. Clearly, the behavioural sequelae of any lesion of the mfb will depend on the degree to which ascending (aminergic) or descending projections are destroyed. (Whether or not a similar analysis may be applied to the female will depend on the availability of substantially more information than at present.)

However, it must be apparent from the foregoing account that any hypothesis which attempts to separate the ascending and descending components of the mfb in functional terms is extremely speculative, since the data on which it is based lack consistency and control. But a number of refined neuropharmacological techniques are available which, if combined with what is known of the neural basis of sexual behaviour and of the detailed morphology and distribution of aminergic neurons in the brain, may lead to answers now which were not possible a few years ago.

The *nature* of the interaction between hormones and amines remains a major problem. Progesterone may act in the midbrain where there are 5-HT cell bodies and is, therefore, in a position to alter neuronal activity or transmitter synthesis. But oestrogen and testosterone are taken up in areas where there are only amine terminals. Thus, if they interact with this aminergic input, they may do so by altering the postsynaptic response to these transmitters, perhaps by regulating the synthesis of proteins thought to be part of the amine receptor (Greengard, 1976). Alternatively, amines may modulate the sensitivity of the neurons they innervate to steroid hormones. How this might occur remains a key problem for future research, but in another neuroendocrine system where amines and hormones interact (in the control of the anterior pituitary), peptides such as luteinizing hormone releasing hormone (LRH) are also involved. It is also becoming apparent that peptides are putative transmitter substances distributed widely over the brain, found in synaptosomes and are often in close association with monoaminergic neurons (eg. substance P in the substantia nigra). LRH and corticotrophic hormone-releasing hormone (CRH) have also been seen to have effects on the sexual activity of rats, rabbits and, indeed, man (Moss and McCann, 1973; Mortimer et al., 1974; Bertolini et al., 1971; Schotman et al., 1976). Thus, perhaps a more complete way to view the neuroendocrine basis of sexual behaviour is in terms of a a more complicated interaction between hormones, amines, and peptides. This interaction may well not be a direct one between hormones and amines, therefore, and we can look to the pituitary again for some clue. Here we see that steroids are able to alter the response of cells to peptides (Yen *et al.*, 1973), while the amines themselves (particularly DA) alter release of the latter. It is, therefore, of fundamental importance to discover whether or not this form of interaction occurs within, say, the anterior hypothalamus and preoptic area.

SUMMARY AND CONCLUSIONS

The purpose of this chapter has been to provide some neuroanatomical basis for the many pharmacological experiments which have assigned to monoamine neurotransmitters a fundamental role in the regulation by hormones of sexual behaviour. It will have become apparent that such a view of amines and behaviour is a relatively new one and the methodologies underlying an anatomical approach are embryonic, but potentially powerful. It is also clear that a number of studies involving lesions and stimulations within the brain reflect an unawareness of the course of aminergic neurons and, consequently, they have been destroyed or stimulated inadvertently. This is, of course, often unavoidable since detailed knowledge of the distribution of amines in the brain has been available only recently.

The behavioural data are more consistent (and more numerous) for male than for female mammals. In the former, lesions of the mfb are seen to depress sexual activity while electrical stimulation has the opposite effect. However, in the two studies so far conducted, specific destruction of ascending aminergic components of the mfb cause an increase in sexual behaviour—measured as a decrease in the postejaculatory refractory period. Lesions of the mfb have more diverse effects, many of which are similar to lesions of the androgen-sensitive medial preoptic area, taking the form of copulatory deficits (mounting, thrusting, intromitting). On this basis, it has been tentatively suggested that the ascending aminergic elements in the mfb may subserve an initiation or 'arousal' mechanism, while those neurons descending from tel- and diencephalon in the mfb may be more concerned with copulatory performance. This distinction may prove to be artificial but may also form a basis for more experimentation.

A similar analysis, even at such a crude level, is not yet possible for the female. Destruction of the mfb seems not to have any great effect on the female's sexual behaviour, although selective lesions of its ascending 5-HT components or implantation of 5-HT receptor antagonists along its course do cause an increase in oestrous behaviour.

A more careful and selective approach to the study of monoamine neurons and sexual behaviour is badly needed if the data already available are to be understood and if their role (and the role of descending components of the mfb) are to be dissected out. Neurotoxic agents and specific receptor agonists and antagonists are likely to be important tools in this context.

ACKNOWLEDGEMENTS

Part of the work reported here was supported by grants from the British and Swedish Medical Research Councils. I should like to thank Debby Hickman for her help in preparing the manuscript and Raith Overhill for preparing the figures.

REFERENCES

Ahlenius, S., Engel, J., Eriksson, H., Modigh, K., and Södersten, P. (1972) Importance of central catecholamines in the mediation of lordosis behaviour in ovariectomized rats treated with estrogen and inhibitors of monoamine synthesis, *J. Neural Transm.*, **33**, 247–55.

Andén, N.-E. (1968) Discussion of serotonin and dopamine in the extrapyramidal system, *Adv. Pharmacol.*, **6A**, 347.

Barfield, R. J., Wilson, C., and McDonald, P. G. (1975) Sexual behaviour: extreme reduction of postejaculatory refractory period by midbrain lesions in male rats, *Science*, **189**, 147–9.

Bertolini, A., Gentile, G., Greggia, A., Sternieri, E., and Ferrari, W. (1971) Possible role of hypothalamic corticotrophin-releasing factor in the induction of sexual excitation in adult male rats, *Rivista di Farmacologia e Terapia*, **11**, 243–9.

Caggiula, A. R. (1970) Analysis of the copulation-reward properties of posterior hypothalamic stimulation in male rats, *J. Comp. Physiol. Psychol.*, **70**, 399–412.

Caggiula, A. R., Antelman, S. M., and Zigmond, M. J. (1973) Disruption of copulation in male rats after hypothalamic lesions: A behavioural, anatomical, and neurochemical analysis, *Brain Res.*, **59**, 273–87.

Caggiula, A. R., Gay, V. L., Antelman, S. M., and Leggens, J. (1975) Disruption of copulation in male rats after hypothalamic lesions: A neuroendocrine analysis, *Neuroendocrinology*, **17**, 193–202.

Caggiula, A. R. and Hoebel, B. G. (1966) 'Copulation-Reward Site' in the posterior hypothalamus, *Science*, **153**, 1284–5.

Caggiula, A. R. and Szechtman, H. (1972) Hypothalamic stimulation: A biphasic influence on copulation of the male rat, *Behav. Biol.*, **7**, 591–8.

Clark, T. K., Cagguila, A. R., McConnell, R. A., and Antelman, S. M. (1975) Sexual inhibition is reduced by rostral midbrain lesions in the male rat, *Science*, **190**, 169–71.

Clemens, L. (1971) Regulation of sexual behavior in the rat with intracerebral hormone application. Proc. 79th Annual Convention of American Psychological Association.

Crowley, W. R., Ward, I. L., and Margules, D. L. (1975) Female lordotic behaviour mediated by monoamines in male rats, *J. Comp. Physiol. Psychol.*, **88**, 62–8.

Dahlström, A. and Fuxe, K. (1965) Evidence for the existence of monoamine neurons in the central nervous system. I. Demonstration of monoamines in the cell bodies of brain stem neurons. *Acta Physiol. Scand.*, **62**, Suppl. 232, 1–55.

Davidson, J. M. (1972) Hormones and reproductive behaviour. *In: Reproductive Biology*, H. Balin and S. Glasser (eds.), Excerpta Medica, Amsterdam.

Eibergen, R. D. and Caggiula, A. R. (1973) Ventral midbrain involvement in copulatory behaviour of the male rat, *Physiol. Behav.*, **10**, 435–42.

Everitt, B. J. (1976) Cerebral monoamines and sexual behaviour. In: *Handbook of Sexology*, J. Money and H. Musaph (eds.), Elsevier/North-Holland.

Everitt, B. J., Fuxe, K., and Jonsson, G. (1975a) The effects of 5,7-dihydroxytryptamine lesions of ascending 5-hydroxytryptamine pathways on the sexual and aggressive behaviour of female rats, *J. Pharmacol. Paris*, **6**, 25–32.

Everitt, B. J., Fuxe, K., Hökfelt, T., and Johnson, G. (1975b) Pharmacological and biochemical studies on the role of monoamines in the control by hormones of sexual receptivity in the female rat, *J. Comp. Physiol. Psychol.*, **89**, 556–72.

Fuxe, K. (1965) Evidence for the existence of monoamine neurons in the central nervous system. IV. Distribution of monoamine nerve terminals in the central nervous system, *Acta Physiol. Scand.*, **64**, Suppl., 247, 37–85.

Fuxe, K., Everitt, B. J., Agnati, L. F., Freedholm, B., and Jonsson, G. (1976) On the biochemistry and pharmacology of hallucinogens, In: Schizophrenia Today. *Proc. Multidisciplinary Workshop on Schizophrenia Capri*, Pergamon, pp. 135–157.

Fuxe, K., Hökfelt, T., Everitt, B. J., Johansson, O., Jonsson, G., Lidbrink, P., Ljungdahl, Å., and Ogren, S.-O. (1975) Anatomical and functional studies of monoamines in the limbic system, *Proc. VIIth Int. Congr. Neuropathol. Hungary, Excerpta Medica*, pp. 185–90.

Fuxe, K. and Jonsson, G. (1973) The histochemical fluorescence methods for the demonstration of catecholamines. Theory, practice and application, *J. Histochem. Cytochem.*, **21**, 293–311.

Fuxe, K. and Jonsson, G. (1974) Further mapping of central 5-hydroxytryptamine neurons: Studies with the neurotoxic dihydroxytryptamines, *Adv. Biochem. Psychopharmacol.*, **10**, 1–12.

Giantonio, G. W., Lund, N. L., and Gerall, A. A. (1970 Effect of diencephalic and rhinencephalic lesions on the male rat's sexual behaviour, *J. Comp. Physiol. Psychol.*, **73**, 38–46.

Greengard, P. (1976) Possible role for cyclic nucleotides and phosphorylated membrane proteins in postsynaptic actions of neurotransmitters, *Nature*, **260**, 101–8.

Hart, B. L. (1969) Gonadal hormones and sexual reflexes in the female rat, *Horm. Behav.*, **1**, 65–71.

Heimer, L. and Larsson, K. (1964) Drastic changes in the mating behaviour of male rats following lesions in the junction of diencephalon and mesencephalon, *Experientia*, **20**, 460–1.

Hendricks, S. E. and Scheetz, H. A. (1973) Interaction of hypothalamic structures in the mediation of male sexual behaviour, *Physiol. Behav.*, **10**, 711–6.

Hitt, J. C., Byron, D. M., and Modianos, D. T. (1973) Effects of rostral medial forebrain bundle and olfactory tubercle lesions upon the sexual behaviour of male rats, *J. Comp. Physiol. Psychol.*, **82**, 30–6.

Hitt, J. C., Hendricks, S. E., Ginsberg, S. I., and Lewis, J. H. (1970) Disruption of male, but not female, sexual behaviour in rats by medial forebrain bundle lesions, *J. Comp. Physiol. Psychol.*, **73**, 377–84.

Kow, L.-M., Malsbury, C. W., and Pfaff, D. W. (1974) Effects of progesterone on female reproductive behaviour in rats: Possible modes of action and role in behavioural sex differences. *In: Reproductive Behaviour*, W. Montagna and W. A. Sadler (eds.), Plenum, N. Y., pp. 179–210.

MacLean, P. D. and Ploog, D. W. (1962) Cerebral representation of penile erection, *Neurophysiology*, **25**, 29–55.

Madlafousek, J., Freund, K., and Grofova, I. (1970) Variables determining the effect of electrostimulation in the lateral preoptic area on the sexual behaviour of male rats, *J. Comp. Physiol. Psychol.*, **72**, 28–44.

Malmnäs, C.-O. (1973) Monoaminergic influence on testosterone activated copulatory behaviour in the castrated male rat, *Acta Physiol Scand.*, Suppl. 395, 1–128.

Malsbury, C. W. (1971) Facilitation of male rat copulatory behaviour by electrical stimulation of the medial preoptic area, *Physiol. Behav.*, **7**, 797–805.

Malsbury, C. W. and Pfaff, D. W. (1975) Neural and hormonal determinants of mating behaviour in adult male rats. A review. *In: Limbic and Autonomic Nervous Systems Research*, L. V. DiCara (ed.), Plenum, N. Y., pp. 85–136.

Merari, A. and Ginton, A. (1975) Characteristics of exaggerated sexual behaviour induced by electrical stimulation of the medial preoptic area in male rats, *Brain Res.*, **86**, 97–108.

Millhouse, O. E. (1969) A Golgi study of descending medial forebrain bundle, *Brain Res.*, **15**, 341–63.

Modianos, D. T., Flexman, J. E., and Hitt, J. C. (1973) Rostral medial forebrain bundle lesions produce decrements in masculine, but not feminine, sexual behaviour in spayed female rats, *Behav. Biol.*, **8**, 629–36.

Morin, L. P. and Feder, H. H. (1974a) Inhibition of lordosis behaviour in ovariectomized guinea pigs by mesencephalic implants of progesterone, *Brain Res.*, **70**, 71–80.

Morin, L. P. and Feder, H. H. (1974b) Hypothalamic pogesterone implants and facilitation of lordosis behaviour in estrogen-primed ovariectomized guinea pigs, *Brain Res.*, **70**, 81–93.

Mortimer, C. H., McNeilly, A. S., Fisher, R. A., Murray, M. A. F., and Besser, G. M. (1974) Gonadotrophic releasing hormone therapy in hypogonadal males with hypothalamic and pituitary dysfunction, *Br. Med. J.*, **4**, 617–21.

Moss, R. L. and McCann, S. M. (1973) Induction of mating behaviour in rats by luteinizing hormone releasing factor, *Science*, **181**, 177–9.

Nance, D. W., Shryne, J., and Gorski, R. A. (1974) Septal lesions: effects on lordosis behaviour and pattern of gonadotropin release, *Horm. Behav.*, **5**, 73–81.

Nance, D. W., Shryne, J., and Gorski, R. A. (1975a) Effects of septal lesions on behavioural sensitivity of female rats to gonadal hormones, *Horm. Behav.*, **6**, 59–64.

Nance, D. A., Shryne, J., and Gorski, R. A. (1975b) Facilitation of female sexual behaviour in male rats by septal lesions: An interaction with estrogen, *Horm. Behav.*, **6**, 289–99.

Pfaff, D. W., Diakow, C., Zigmond, R. E., and Kow, L.-M. (1973) Neural and hormonal determinants of female mating behaviour in rats. *In: The Neurosciences Vol. III*, F. O. Schmitt *et al.* (eds.), Massachusetts Institute of Technology Press, Boston, pp. 621–46.

Pfaff, D. and Keiner, M. (1973) Atlas of estradiol-concentrating cells in the central nervous system of the female rat, *J. Comp. Neurol.*, **151**, 121–58.

Powers, J. B. (1972) Facilitation of lordosis in ovariectomized rats by intracerebral progesterone implants, *Brain Res.*, **48**, 311–25.

Rodgers, C. H. and Law, O. T. (1967) The effects of habenular and medial forebrain bundle lesions on sexual behaviour in female rats, *Psychonom. Sci.*, **8**, 1–2.

Ross, J. W., Claybaugh, C., Clemens, L. G., and Gorski, R. A. (1971) Short latency induction of oestrous behaviour with intracerebral gonadal hormones in ovariectomized rats, *Endocrinology*, **89**, 32–8.

Schotman, P., Reith, M. E. A., van Wimersma Greidanus, Tj. B., Gispen, W. H., and DeWeid, D. (1976) Hypothalamic and pituitary peptide hormones and the central nervous system with special reference to the neurochemical effects of ACTH. *In: Molecular and Functional Neurobiology*, W. H. Gispen (ed.), Elsevier/North-Holland.

Sheard, M. (1973) Brain serotonin depletion by *p*-chlorophenylalanine or lesions of raphe neurons in rats, *Physiol. Behav.*, **10**, 809–11.

Ungerstedt, Y. (1971) Stereotaxic mapping of the monoamine pathways in the rat brain. *Acta Physiol Scand.*, *Suppl.* 367, 1–48.

van Dis, H. and Larsson, K. (1971) Induction of sexual arousal in the castrated male rat by intracranial stimulation, *Physiol. Behav.*, **6**, 85–6.

Wade, G. N. and Feder, H. H. (1972a) [1,2-^{3}H] progesterone uptake by guinea pig brain and uterus: differential localization, time-course of uptake and metabolism, and effects of age, sex, estrogen-priming, and competing steroids, *Brain Res.*, **45**, 525–43.

Wade, G. N. and Feder, H. H. (1972b) Uptake of [1,2-^{3}H] 20α-hydroxypregn-4-en-3-one, ([1,2-^{3}H] corticosterone, and [6,7-^{3}H] estradiol-7 by guinea pig brain and uterus: comparison with uptake of [1,2-^{3}H] progesterone, *Brain Res.*, **45**, 545–54.

Wade, G. M., Harding, C. G., and Feder, H. H. (1973) Neural uptake of [1,2-^{3}H] progesterone in ovariectomized rats, guinea pigs, and hamsters: correlation with species differences in behavioural responsiveness, *Brain Res.*, **61**, 357–67.

Ward, I. L., Crowley, W. R., Zemlan, F. P., and Margules, D. L. (1975) Monoaminergic mediation of female sexual behaviour, *J. Comp. Physiol. Psychol.*, **88**, 53–61.

Yen, S. S. C., Rebar, R., Vandenberg, G., Ehara, Y., and Siler, T. (1973) Pituitary gonado -
trophin responsiveness to synthetic LRF in subjects with normal and abnormal
hypothalamic-pituitary-gonadal axis, *J. Reprod. Fert.* Suppl. 20, 137–61.

Zigmond, R. E. and McEwen, B. S. (1970) Selective retention of estradiol by cell nuclei
in specific brain regions of the ovariectomized rat, *J. Neurochem.*, **17**, 889–99.

Part III

Patterning of Sexual Behaviour: Theoretical Constructs

Introduction

No explanation of causal mechanisms underlying sexual behaviour would be complete without recourse to physiological information. However, physiological analysis, which may require limitation of behavioural endpoints to purely 'sexual' elements, such as those involved in copulatory behaviour, can lead to conceptual difficulties. Fentress draws attention to the dangers inherent in viewing sexual behaviour in isolation from other behavioural systems; a construct which implies unitary organization of sexual mechanisms and a functional independence of these mechanisms. There are many cases, particularly in the ethological literature, where sexual behaviour can be seen in contexts which suggest conflict between two or more underlying predispositions. For example, courtship behaviour in birds can be blocked by conflicting tendencies to fight with or flee from the potential mate (Hinde, 1970; Tinbergen, 1964). Sexual behaviour may also be influenced by variables which are apparently unassociated, such as handling by the experimenter or position in a social dominance hierarchy. Terms such as 'sexual motivation' or 'drive' used as intervening variables can be taken to imply unitary processes which might preclude analysis of component control systems underlying an array of behavioural subunits.

The contributions in this part are complementary to one another. Fentress emphasizes the necessity for studying the causation of sexual behaviour in terms of 'moment-to-moment' or short-term transitions at the behavioural level to counteract the traditional view that sexual behaviour is static in organization, and argues that the 'dynamic content' in which a given behavioural pattern occurs should be analysed to determine the relationship between separate behaviour patterns and their underlying mechanisms. This is a view shared by Simpson (Part IV). McFarland describes new methods of behavioural analysis, based on systems analysis, which would be required for studying the dynamics of rapid transitions in elements of sexual behaviour.

REFERENCES

Hinde, R. A. (1970) *Animal Behaviour. A Synthesis of Ethology and Comparative Psychology* (2nd edn), McGraw-Hill, New York.
Tinbergen, N. (1964) Aggression and fear in the normal sexual behaviour of some animals. In: *The Pathology and Treatment of Sexual Deviation*, I. Rosen (ed.), Oxford University Press, pp. 1–23.

CHAPTER 18

Conflict and Context in Sexual Behaviour

JOHN C. FENTRESS

INTRODUCTION

When we speak of sexual behaviour we form a distinction between this one class of activities and all others. There are complementary dangers of this approach, however necessary it may be.

On the one hand when a 'system' is defined it often carries the unnecessary and non-logical inference of unitary organization, as pointed out in detail by Hinde (1970). This can obscure the fact that different behavioural components attributed to the same system may be diverse in their control. It is clear, however, that different behavioural components such as soliciting, copulation, and nesting are relatively separable. Different measures of even a single behavioural act such as mounting can reveal important differences in the subcomponents of control. For example, Beach (1955) has shown the separability of factors which influence mount latency and duration in rats as a function of previous experience.

The construct of a behavioural system also often implies that factors 'within the system' are not influenced in their operation and/or expression by factors 'outside the system'. However, there is ample evidence not only that sexual behaviour can be blocked through the concurrent excitation of fleeing, fighting, etc. (below) but also that enhancement of one or more components of the 'sexual system' can occur upon the application of such unobviously associated variables as handling (Larsson, 1956), shock (Barfield and Sachs, 1968; Caggiula and Eibergen, 1969), and general disturbance (Hanby, 1974). The relationship between these positive and negative effects of extrinsic variables upon one or more components of sexual behaviour is not altogether clear. Analysis based within more abstract frameworks such as hierarchical relationships (Dawkins, 1976) and motivational state-spaces (McFarland, 1976) may in the future offer fresh insights (*cf.* boundary-state approach suggested by Fentress, 1973, 1976a, and below).

In this chapter problems of integration are examined primarily at the behavioural level. The major problems can be stated simply:

(1) how does one fractionate the factors which underlie a given class of behaviour?

(2) how does one examine the relationships between factors which underlie different classes of behaviour?

As the chapter progresses an attempt will be made to construct a dynamic framework within which these complementary questions can be examined. The approach provides an alternative to more traditional analyses which stress factors that are (i) unitary, (ii) independent, and (iii) static in their basic organization.

SEXUAL BEHAVIOUR: APPROACHES AND PROBLEMS

Motivational Constructs

Terms such as 'sexual motivation' are frequently applied to the description, classification, and analysis of integrated behaviour patterns which appear to subserve a common goal (eg. copulation). There is often the further implication that a common (unitary) process can be determined which accounts in full for the entire spectrum of behaviour patterns observed. This is rarely, if ever, the case. Motivational constructs are abstractions and approximations which most accurately apply to initial analyses at the behavioural level. In particular, the theme of motivation signals the investigator of the need for examining the interplay between processes intrinsic and extrinsic to the organism, as well as the integration of factors which may contribute to a variety of activity patterns (e.g. Hinde, 1970; Fentress, 1973, 1976a; McFarland and Nunez, this volume Chapter 19). Even for single and relatively simple activity patterns networks of sensory, muscular, and hormonal mechanisms can be determined as analysis proceeds (cf. Fentress, 1976b). Unless carefully applied, therefore, motivational constructs that imply unitary (indivisible) control can be misleading, and actually preclude rather than facilitate refined analysis.

A disturbingly common situation is when an initially descriptive motivational label comes to imply understanding of antecedent causation. For example, statements which attribute increases in copulation to increases in 'sexual drive' are clearly tautological and thus no explanation at all. It is equally erroneous, but by no means uncommon, to treat subcomponents of a complex system (e.g. individual neurons in behaving vertebrates) as if these components are a miniature representation of the operational principles defined at the more complex level. Action potentials and slower postsynaptic potentials are the properties of neurons; drives, as defined for the behaving organism, are not. Our metaphors necessarily change with our levels of analysis.

Most analyses of 'motivation' today are operationally constructed to permit inferences about changes in internal state given constant environmental conditions. This is typically done by examining the type and degree of response to standardized stimulus events (e.g. Hinde, 1970). As analysis proceeds the *range of response* to a given stimulus event as well as the *range of stimuli* that contribute to a given response can be determined. From here more complete evaluation of integrative networks can be made by examining the combined effects of different 'inputs' upon specified combinations of 'output' (Fentress, 1973, 1976a).

As in neurophysiological research it is often possible to infer changes in internal state which are either of intrinsic origin or the consequence of extrinsic events. This can be done even when these changes of intrinsic or extrinsic origin do not in themselves give rise to alterations in behavioural expression. The most common procedure is to test for changes in response to other standardized stimuli. Terms such as 'tendency' or 'predisposition' refer to these operationally derived changes of behavioural state. With further analysis it is possible to determine relationships and priorities among individually defined tendencies in much the same way that Sherrington spoke of relations and priorities among reflexes. The main difference between motivational and reflex analysis is the greater concern with changes of internal state in the former. One can speak of a 'major tendency' when it is expressed in priority to others which may be concurrently activated.

Criteria of System Definition

For any given analysis level there are three major methods used to classify behaviour. Confusion between them is common, and introduces serious consequences for subsequent analysis.

Classification by Functional Endpoint

The most common form of behavioural classification is in terms of the functional endpoints or 'goals'. Thus the category 'sexual behaviour' is used to encompass those activities which appear to lead towards reproduction (e.g., copulation). This is clearly distinct from a classification based upon precise description of movement details or causal antecedents. As the breeding season progresses, for example, a male timber wolf may engage in a wide diversity of individual movements such as pawing, sniffing, rubbing, posturing, and mounting. Each of these activities appears, through analysis of temporal relationships, to lead towards the endpoint of reproduction (Fentress, unpubl.). Terms such as 'aggression,' 'fear,' etc., are similarly embedded in the *consequences* observed or presumed for the constituent activities rather than being based primarily upon detailed description of the motor patterns themselves or prior knowledge of their causal antecedents.

Classification by Movement/Posture

Similar movements may appear in quite different contexts, serve apparently diverse functions from one instant to the next, and differ from one occasion to another in the details of their causal structure. It can be seen, for example, that the upright posture in herring gulls contains motor elements commonly observed in attack or flight behaviour, but which in the context of display may serve an important reproductive function (e.g. Tinbergen, 1952, 1959). Is such a display really aggression or sexual behaviour? From the functional perspective it is related to reproduction; from the descriptive and causal perspectives there is reason to include it under the label of aggression. *(Such rhetorical statements are of course gross simplifications since they assume unitary behavioural systems from each of the perspectives outlined above. A major conclusion of this chapter is that such assumptions are invalid.)*

Classification by Causal Antecedent

By manipulation of several antecedent conditions (e.g. hormonal state, previous experience) separately and in various combinations the investigator is in a position to evaluate the *spectrum* of activities affected *and* their consequences. Such an integrated approach, however, is strikingly rare in the literature on sexual as well as other classes of behaviour. One reason surely is the failure either to recognize the distinction between functional, descriptive, and causal modes of classification, or to assume that any of one of these modes can be directly translated into the other two. Thus while we may clearly recognize the functional distinction between copulation and fighting, this does not imply either the motor patterns involved or the causal antecedents of each are unrelated. Many carnivores such as domestic cats and lions, for example, employ neck bites during copulation. These are similar to the biting movements employed in the capture of prey. To my knowledge the influence of predatory predispositions upon the probability and/or form of copulation in these animals has not been subjected to critical test, but it is certainly an unsafe proposition to assume what the outcome would be! The literature abounds with suggestions of a close affinity between sexual and aggressive behaviour in man (e.g., Freud, 1922), but the animal literature provides caution in making statements of a general nature. Sevenster (1961), for example, has given evidence that strong predispositions towards fighting in sticklebacks interfere with mating in the short term, although the longer-term association between these two functional classes of behaviour (such as measured between breeding and non-breeding seasons) is facilitatory (cf. Fentress, 1973 for further discussion).

Motor patterns of similar appearance may also differ in their control from one context to another. For example, denervation of the sensory branches of the trigeminal nerve produces little difference in the form and probability of face grooming in mice tested in a novel environment. However, grooming in the home cage is strikingly altered (Fentress, 1972). This case is particularly instructive since although the same functional term (grooming) is applied to the different test situations, the details of control differ systematically.

On Levels of Analysis

Terms such as 'sexual behaviour' refer ultimately to integrated activity of the intact organism. It is perhaps obvious, but if not should be made explicit, that our methods of classifying, and hence analysing, behaviour depend upon the level of examination employed (e.g., ecological, organismic, physiological, cellular). Eventually we wish to relate our analyses of isolated mechanisms to their operation in the intact organism. This involves an examination of the interplay between different defined classes of behaviour. In this light, conflict will be examined in terms of its assumptions, implications, and problems. (A more detailed evaluation of analysis levels from the perspective of 'simpler network' approaches can be seen in Fentress, 1976b.)

Ethological Approaches

A major thrust of ethological research has been to examine the dynamic context in which a given act or class of species behaviour occurs. This permits determination of the relationships among separately defined behavioural systems as they operate together in the intact organism.

Many animal species, for example, exhibit systematic seasonal transitions in the probability and relationships among different classes of behaviour. Nowhere is this more clearly evidenced than in the emergence of integrated clusters of activity which together appear to subserve the role of reproduction. In the spring various species of passerine birds set up territories, display reduced tolerance for conspecifics, exhibit intricate patterns of courtship and threat, and eventually mate and rear their young. The search for the physiological (e.g., endocrinological) substrates of these seasonal behavioural activities has been rewarding, and is summarized in detail in other sections of the present volume.

The focus of this chapter is upon the control of short-term, moment-to-moment, transitions at the behavioural level. At one instant a gull may attack its mate, then pull grass from its nest site, followed by a variety of vocalizations and postures, and then prolonged vacillation towards and away from its partner, etc. The birds do not appear as 'single minded' as traditional models, based upon the analysis of experimentally isolated behavioural acts frequently suggest. It seems reasonable, therefore, to assume that the control of a given act of behaviour cannot be divorced entirely from the relationship of this act, and its underlying processes, to others. The general strategy of this type of analysis has been emphasized by the phrase *context of control* (Fentress, 1972). It is fundamental to the construction in ethology of motivational models (e.g., Hinde, 1970, 1972; Fentress, 1973, 1976a).

A moment's reflection makes it abundantly clear that each component of behavioural activity that we can define occurs not only in the general context of factors endogenous and exogenous to the organism defined *in toto*, but more specifically in the context of preceding, subsequent, simultaneous, and/or alternate modes of behavioural expression. It is unlikely in the extreme that these diverse modes of behavioural expression are causally detached from one another in their final expression. If this proposition is accepted, then detailed analysis of both the context and components of a presumed behavioural system is a necessary prerequisite for precise interpretation of the control of that system (cf. Fentress, 1973, 1976a).

THE CONSTRUCT OF CONFLICT

Many classes of behaviour seen during reproduction are incompatible and mutually exclusive. An animal obviously cannot attack its mate, flee, and copulate at the same time. Such activities, however, frequently appear in rapid succession. During these transitions one also frequently observes a variety of 'displays' (i.e., relatively stereotyped postures and sequences, most commonly investigated in birds, which are directed with reference to another member of the species). Occasionally behaviour sequences appear truncated and incomplete (intention movements), directed toward inanimate objects or animals not clearly involved in the interaction (redirected behaviour), or irrelevant to the functional context presumed by the observer to be fundamental (displacement). These various categories are based primarily upon descriptive shorthands. They thus should not be presumed to be either causally unitary or mutually exclusive even at this level. However, they help to convey the richness of behavioural expression that accompanies reproduction in many species.

It is from such descriptive data that ethologists have emphasized the role of conflict in the integration of reproductive sequences. Many lines of evidence have been reviewed previously (cf. Hinde, 1970; Tinbergen, 1952, 1959). Several major lines will be cited here.

Alternation Between Incompatible Tendencies

Animals of many species establish territories during the breeding season. This process is accompanied by rapid alternations between attacking and fleeing from rivals, e.g., at the boundaries of two territories. The situation is superficially similar to the vacillations in behaviour observed in experimentally established approach–avoidance conflicts (e.g., Miller, 1959). Ethologists have extended their analysis of the nexus of behaviour patterns observed during the course of reproduction by specifying alternations between a variety of activities such as attack, flight, remaining in a particular location, and copulation.

Male chaffinches (Fringilla coelebs), for example, not only attack other males of the same species who intrude upon their territory in the early breeding season, but females (potential mates) as well. Only later, and often after a period during which the male alternates between attacking and fleeing from the female, does successful courtship and copulation take place (Hinde, 1953). Similarly a male stickleback (Gasterosteus aculeatus) displays rapid alternations between attacking a female who enters his territory and courtship movements of leading the female towards the nest. The zigzag courtship movements involve an alternation between approaching the female and moving away from her,

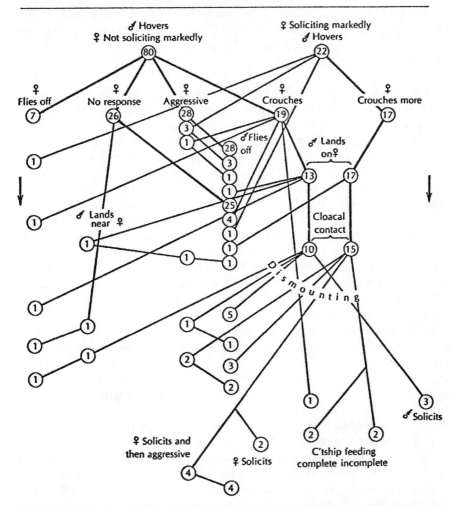

Fig. 1. Diagram of behaviour sequences observed in copulation attempts by male green-finches. Numbers within circles indicate the number of times each situation was observed. Read from top to bottom, starting with hovering by the male over the female, when the female was not soliciting (left) and when the female was soliciting (right). (From Hinde, 1954. Reproduced by permission of E. J. Brill.)

and have themselves been interpreted as a manifestation of conflict (Tinbergen, 1959). Some appreciation for the complexity of behavioural transitions involved in breeding can be seen in the sequences of behaviour involved in copulation attempts by male greenfinches *(Chloris chloris)* as recorded by Hinde (Fig. 1). The alternation and overlap of movement patterns during pair formation and copulation of mammalian species such as wolves *(Canis lupus)* contains a similar if not more subtle richness and diversity (Fentress, unpubl. observ.).

Note that the interpretation of conflict derived from alternating behaviour patterns that appear to subserve different functions is based upon the assumption that two or more underlying behavioural predispositions are simultaneously active even though frequently only one defined class of behaviour (e.g., attack or avoidance or copulation) is observed at any given instant. This assumption is not without its dangers. For example, one might alternatively argue that transitions between attacking and fleeing are due to the *sequential* activation of incompatible predispositions, such as might be triggered by the relative proximity of another animal, its posture at the moment, etc.

There is, however, evidence that factors which predispose an animal to one class of behaviour may be operating during the overt expression of a different class of behaviour. This can perhaps be seen most readily in the context of *behavioural inertia*. Fentress (1968a, 1968b), for example, found that the probability of fleeing as opposed to freezing in response to an overhead moving stimulus was markedly and similarly increased for two species of vole *(Microtus agrestis* and *Clethrionomys britannicus)* when the animals either were locomoting at the time of the stimulus presentation or *had been locomoting* within the preceding ten seconds. This latter observation indicates an inertia of internal state which accompanies locomotion that persists for a period after overt locomotion is replaced by other activities.

Special experimental procedures are necessary to reveal such persistence of internal state. An example directly related to the theme of reproductive behaviour can be seen in the study by Sevenster (1961). He tested the aggressive and sexual responses of male sticklebacks which were presented with other male and female fish in bottles. When the tests were arranged in different combinations Sevenster found that previous aggression affected subsequent sexual responses, and *vice versa*. Thus one can conclude that the processes generated by the first stimulus object 'carry over' into subsequent tests.

This approach involving the analysis of the relationships among sequential behaviour patterns was pioneered by Moynihan (1955) in his analysis of threat postures that accompany reproduction in blackheaded gulls *(Larus ridibundus)*. It has been successfully employed by a number of workers (e.g., Stokes, 1962; Kruijt, 1964; Blurton-Jones, 1968). However, caution must obviously be used in the interpretation of sequential correlations not accompanied by direct experimental procedures (e.g., Hinde, 1970; Fentress, 1972).

Since many courtship and threat displays occur in the transition between incompatible forms of behaviour such as attack, flight, and copulation they are often presumed to have dual (etc.) motivation as their causal base (e.g., Tinbergen, 1959; Hinde, 1970). These analyses will be elaborated more fully below.

Simultaneous Presence and Blending of Behavioural Components

In contexts similar to those which produce alternation between incompatible classes of behaviour, animals may simultaneously display behavioural compo-

Fig. 2. Two Forms of the upright threat posture of the herring gull: (a) posture which accompanies hypothesized tendency to attack; (b) posture more characteristic of potential flight (escape). (From Tinbergen, 1959, as redrawn in Hinde, 1970. Reproduced by permission of E. J. Brill.)

nents that are normally associated with different tendencies (see above). During early stages of a breeding season, for example, female wolves may simultaneously snarl, fold their ears back, and adopt a soliciting posture (pers. observ.). The upright posture in herring gulls *(Larus argentatus)* involves a variable mixture of motor profiles that are seen in attack (e.g., downward-pointed bill and raised carpal joints) and escape (e.g., sleeked feathers) (Fig. 2). The relative predominance of these motor components, combined with an assessment of the broader context in which they occur, makes it possible for the investigator to approximate the relative probabilities of attack and escape (Tinbergen, 1959).

For mammals the blending of motor components often results in a wide spectrum of behavioural profiles (Fig. 3). By comparing these profiles with each other, and relating each to the behavioural and environmental contexts in which it occurs, one can argue that they represent intraction between a definable set of major tendencies (e.g., Schenkel, 1947; Leyhaussen, 1956). While certainly suggestive, the ultimate utility and precision of this approach for clarifying mechanism deserves further analyses. Andrew (1972), for example, has argued that it may often be more fruitful to examine the data in terms of conflict between responses demonstrably incompatible at the effector level rather than on the basis of presumed interactions between more global inter-vening tendencies (see also Hinde, 1972, pp. 177–8, 204–6).

It should be noted that there are at least two distinct forms in which behaviour patterns can be expressed simultaneously. In one case each is seen in apparently full amplitude. In the other case the expression of one reduces the expressed amplitude of another. Either one or both components, to take the simplest case, may thereby be diminished. This distinction can be illustrated by the multiple site brain stimulation studies with domestic chickens by von Holst and von St. Paul (1963). Picking and head turning could be elicited simultaneously without any apparent diminution of the amplitude of either, whereas 'looking around' and 'watching out' reduced the expressed amplitude of each other during simultaneous intracranial electrical stimulation of both. Von Holst and von St. Paul label these interactions *superposition* and *averaging* respectively. Mechanisms responsible for the different profiles are not clear, and brain stimulation studies must obviously be interpreted with considerable caution. Yet the basic approach of electrically produced interacting activity in specified neural loci may still reveal insights in the hands of sensitive investigators. Its full utilization in the study of sexual behaviour and conflict is yet to be implemented.

The Blocking of One Form of Behavioural Expression by Another

If one assumes that different functional classes of behaviour (e.g. sex, feeding, etc.) are incompatible in their expression, then it follows that the expression of one activity may preclude the expression of another. If the activation of the expressed behaviour outlasts activation of another behaviour which is also activated but subsequently blocked, the latter may never reach overt expression. With fluctuations in the relative strengths of presumed tendencies alternation should occur (discussed above). The trick of course, is to demonstrate activation of a given behavioural predisposition if the behavioural output of this predisposition fails to reach overt expression. Again experimental intervention is called for (*cf.* von Holst and von St. Paul, 1963; Hinde, 1970). Often direct manipulations of internal state, such as through electrical stimulation at different sites and strengths, can provide insights.

The next question is whether one should speak of 'conflict' if one or another form of behaviour is not expressed. In cases where the apparent intensity of the expressed behaviour is altered circumstantial evidence can be obtained. (But see Fentress, 1973, for discussion of problems of measuring intensity.) The distinction made by von Holst and von St. Paul (1963) between 'masking' and 'preventing' is instructive here. In the former case one behaviour (e.g., clucking) is blocked by simultaneous stimulation of another site (e.g. brooding). The former occurs momentarily, however, when stimulation of the two sites is stopped simultaneously. In their words, '... when one behaviour pattern makes a second one invisible it is nevertheless possible to show that the latent drive has not been eliminated.' In the case of preventing, such as in the suppression of eating, preening, or crowing by simultaneously stimulated immobility responses, the former set of activities may never achieve overt expression. Detailed analyses of variations in threshold, form of expressed behaviour, etc., are necessary for a clarification of mechanism. Systematic investigations at both the behavioural and neurobiological levels are needed to establish at what stage of processing there is blockage between incompatible activities (e.g., sensory, motor, higher levels of integration). Often it is difficult to separate results which are primarily a function of the type of electrostimula-

Fig. 3A. Body and facial postures in cats as a function of hypothesized tendencies for aggression (increase left to right) and fear (increase from top to bottom). (From Leyhausen, 1956. Reproduced by permission of Paul Parey.)

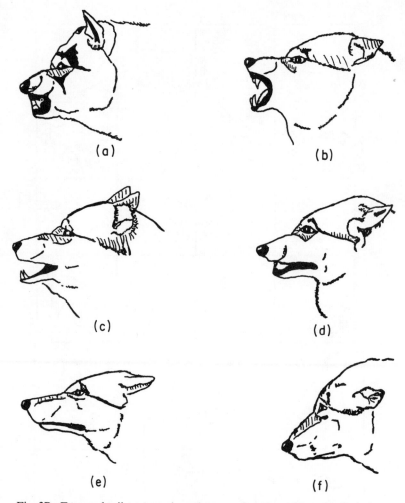

Fig. 3B. Face and tail postures in wolves as a function of presumed motivational state. (From Schenkel, 1948, with legends translated in Thorpe, 1963.
Reproduced by permission of E. J. Brill.)

Studies on the expression of emotion in the wolf.
(a) Fully confident threat.
(b) High intensity threat with slight uncertainty.
(c) Low intensity threat with uncertainty.
(d) Weak threat with much uncertainty.
(e) Anxiety.
(f) Uncertainty with suspicion in the face of the enemy.

tion from those which indicate inherent mechanisms. For example, a few
microseconds difference in duration of stimulation of different neural sites can
greatly affect one's conclusions about preventing as distinct from masking
(J. B. Hutchison, pers. commun.). It is safe to conclude that anything approach-

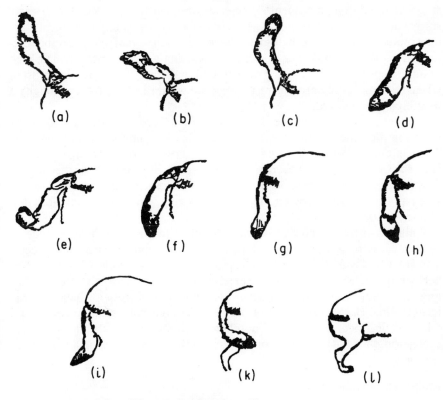

Use of the tail for expression in the wolf.
(a) Self-confidence in social group.
(b) Confident threat.
(c) With wagging; imposing carriage.
(d) Normal carriage (in a situation without social tension).
(e) Somewhat uncertain threat.
(f) Similar to (d) but specially common in feeding and guarding.
(g) Depressed mood.
(h) Intermediate between threat and defence.
(i) Active submission (with wagging).
(k) and (l) Complete submission.

ing a full account of interlocking mechanisms that underlie ethological findings of the relationship between sexual and other behaviour patterns must rely upon painstaking future research efforts that do justice to the full spectrum of behavioural phenomena observed in both field and laboratory investigations.

Truncated and Exaggerated Forms of Behavioural Expression

When a given form of behaviour is initiated by the animal and then blocked, it often occurs in incomplete form. Such incomplete, or preliminary, forms of behavioural expression have been used as evidence for conflict. A common label for incomplete expressions of behaviour that cease after their initial stages is 'intention movement'. These are frequently observed during early stages of mating, for example when copulatory thrusting movements are interrupted by fleeing or fighting. I have observed a male wolf exhibit preliminary thrusting movements when approaching an unreceptive female who in turn snaps at her 'intruder'. These 'intention thrusts' subsequently occurred when the female, still unreceptive, approached within a few feet, even though no overt fighting followed.

Similarly, birds during the early stages of a breeding season may show intention movements of flight upon the approach of another species member. These intention movements are frequently observed during both agonistic and courtship encounters. They can be recognized by alternations between a crouching prelude to flight and an upright posture. Such data have been used to suggest a conflict between fleeing, attacking, and/or copulation (*cf.* Hinde, 1970).

While it is perhaps most common for conflict to diminish the amplitude or completeness of a given class of behaviour, the opposite may also occur. Von Holst and von St. Paul (1963) cite evidence that once an electrically blocked behaviour reaches threshold for expression it may be extremely intense. This type of observation provides further evidence that processes which underlie incompatible classes of behaviour may be activated both simultaneously and relatively independently of one another. If conflict raises the threshold for expression, then the behaviour, once reaching threshold, occurs in an exaggerated form.

Altered Orientation of Behaviour

Male wolves who are blocked from copulation by the snarling and snapping of a female may in turn snap at a third animal or even inanimate objects (pers. observ.). While it is difficult to assess without ambiguity the processes which underlie such observations in the absence of experimental manipulation, a plausible hypothesis is that the male has redirected his biting behaviour away from its source (the female) toward other animals or objects. This in turn would imply that a direct attack on the female is blocked, e.g., by copulatory or avoidance predispositions.

Many analogous observations have been reported in the ethological literature. For example, Moynihan (1955) provided evidence that male black-headed gulls who are inhibited from attacking their mates may attack other birds. Tinbergen (1959) has shown that the pecking of herring gulls in agonistic encounters is frequently oriented towards inanimate objects in the environment. Similar data have been reported for fish (e.g., Rasa, 1969) and a variety of other animal classes.

Generation of Novel Behaviour Patterns

Not infrequently animals which appear to exhibit conflict between two or more major tendencies, such as copulation and flight, break into behaviour patterns that do not have any obvious functional connection with these major tendencies. Such apparently irrelevant behaviour patterns have been given the label 'displacement activities,' a term which is broadly descriptive although underlying mechanisms are probably diverse (e.g., Hinde, 1970; Fentress, 1972; Andrew, 1974).

In a major study van Iersel and Bol (1958) provided evidence that preening in terns (*Sterna* spp.) often occurs during transitions between incubation, attack, and escape. From their experimental data they concluded that preening occurred when major conflicting predispositions were effectively equal; i.e. when they were each strong, intermediate, or weak. Sevenster (1961) analysed the occurrence of displacement fanning (a behaviour which normally functions to aerate eggs in the nest) during the courtship behaviour of sticklebacks. His experiments provided evidence for the role of conflict between such major predispositions as sexual and aggressive behaviour. For example, by independently manipulating factors which underlie sexual and aggressive behaviour (e.g. through the use of fish models) Sevenster was able to demonstrate that fanning most frequently occurs when sexual and aggressive behaviour cancel each other out in a state of effective equality. In Sevenster's view, conflict between sexual and aggressive predispositions releases their inhibition upon parental fanning, which thus can occur in contexts in which it would not otherwise be expected. Factors relevant to fanning, such as carbon dioxide concentration in the water, remain effective under these circumstances.

Displacement activities provide further evidence for the role of conflict in integration of reproductive behaviour. The causal bases of these diverse forms of behavioural expression are still not altogether clear, however. For example, Sevenster's hypothesis of disinhibition of an apparently irrelevant behaviour through mutual antagonism between two or more major behavioural predispositions does not adequately account for possible facilitatory processes of central origin that are partially shared between activities (e.g., Fentress, 1968a, 1968b, 1972, 1973, 1976a). Certainly a careful distinction must be made between irrelevance defined in terms of functional end points and causal antecedents (*cf.* Wilz, 1972). Even the term functional irrelevance must be treated cautiously, for it reveals an assumption on the part of the observer of what an animal 'should be' doing, or 'intends' to do. Such comments aside, the *fact* of initially surprising transitions between activities in reproductive and other contexts points to the potential importance of taking into account multiply associated behavioural activities for a full appreciation of the operation of mechanisms underlying any given subset of these activities.

Displays

The analysis of sexual and related displays in the ethological literature is closely related to the construct of conflict between behavioural propensities. The term display implies communicatory function, and is generally applied to species characteristic movement patterns and/or postures to which other members of the species respond. As noted above displays frequently occur at times where independent evidence suggests that the displaying animal is torn between two or more incompatible forms of behaviour, e. g., attack, avoidance, and/or copulation. The nature of the display can often be related to the particular balance presumed between these different classes of behaviour. In a detailed analysis, for example, Stokes (1962) found that different *combinations* of nine behavioural components in blue tits *(Parus caerulens)* were quite (but not perfectly) reliable predictors of subsequent probabilities of attack, escape, and immobility. Individual components were less reliable predictors of subsequent behaviour than were components in combination. A given component was associated with either increases or decreases in the probability of subsequent behaviour patterns as a function of the broader context within which it occurred.

Tinbergen (1959) has reviewed three major lines of evidence for the hypothesis that displays which accompany reproductive and related activities have their causal origins in the conflict between major behavioural predispositions. *First*, the display itself may contain components that are recognizable as elements in one or more of the major conflicting tendencies. For example, the upright threat posture of the herring gull may resemble the stance normally used to attack another bird, even though in this case no overt attack is forthcoming. In another form of the posture the beak may be pointed slightly upward with the neck drawn in. This posture under other circumstances leads to actual escape (see Fig. 1 and previous discussion). *Secondly*, overt sexual behaviour, attack, or escape may accompany a given display closely in time. As we have seen above this provides useful, if circumstantial, evidence that predispositions towards these activities are present during the performance of the display. Factor analysis and related techniques for quantifying the associations of different classes of behaviour in time have added useful supporting data for this hypothesis (e.g., Wiepkema, 1961; Blurton-Jones, 1972). *Thirdly*, the environmental and behavioural context in which displays occur frequently reveal stimuli which at other times are known to elicit one or more of the major hypothesized behavioural predispositions (e.g., attack, flight, mating, immobility).

A variety of complementary considerations and techniques can obviously be employed in analysing the relationship between conflict and display behaviour. These include detailed observation of patterns which actually accompany the display (such as moving towards or away from the other animal), independent manipulation of variables known to affect one or more behavioural components, systematic cateloguing of the relationships between temporal, quantitative, and qualitative dimensions of behavioural clusters, examining the form of the expressed behaviour in detail with reference to such dimensions as amplitude, speed, duration, completeness, stereotypy, etc. (*cf.* Hinde, 1970; Fentress, 1973). However, for the present purposes, it is more important to examine critically the construct of conflict in sexual behaviour from a conceptual standpoint, and to determine possible implications for the analysis of mechanism.

Summary of Conflict Criteria

Conflict is Based Upon Presumed Goals

When we speak of an animal being in conflict between e.g., sexual behaviour and aggression we most commonly refer to the fact that the animal appears to vacillate between activities which subserve the functions of reproduction and fighting. This leads to two potential problems: (1) such a method of classification based upon presumed goals does not carry the necessary implications about either the details of motor patterns involved, or causal substrates (previous sections); (2) the goals, or functional endpoints, are usually presumed rather than tested directly.

(It can be argued that the three criteria employed by Tinbergen (1959) and others to define conflict in the study of displays include descriptions of movement and causation in addition to function. However, the consistency between these measures is rarely examined, and the concern with function appears paramount. It is well established that quite similar movement patterns can appear in different functional contexts. Wolves, for example, neck-rub not only on odoriforous objects but in play and courtship (pers. observ.). Similar motor patterns that occur in different contexts may also differ in their causation (e.g., Fentress, 1972, for self-grooming in mice). Finally, there is evidence that motivational systems defined as distinct on the basis of functional criteria may have partially overlapping causal roots some of which appear mutually facilitatory (Fentress, 1973, 1976a).

A bird which repeatedly moves towards and away from its mate could, on the basis of presumed function, be defined as being in an approach–avoidance conflict. If, however, it is subsequently determined that this vacillation increases the performer's sexual attractiveness then the vacillatory display might be defined as a function in its own right. At the physiological level *all* acts of behaviour involve some degree of antagonistic interplay between underlying processes (e.g., co-activation of extensor and flexor musculature). We do not speak of a bird in flight as in conflict even though this behaviour involves alternating upward and downward patterns of wing movements, and few would argue that the pelvic thrusting behaviour of animals during copulation involves a conflict even though by certain measures the participating animals vacillate in their proximity to one another! In these cases we presume a common function. Similarly, Andrew (1972) points out that one's interpretation of 'to and fro' behaviour of song birds in the presence of a predator can take on quite different implications if one assumes a conflict between approach (e.g. attack) and avoidance functions as opposed to the unitary goal-state where the prey animal gets a better visual scan of the predator.

Courtship behaviour patterns may combine to serve a common function *even if* based upon conflicting predispositions at the causal level. For example, prolonged courtship may not only serve the immediate goal of promoting mating, but also pair-bonding. Important physiological feedback processes may also depend upon prolonged courtship, such as the stimulation of ovarian development in females to coincide with subsequent copulation (e.g., Lehrman and Friedman, 1969; Adler, this volume Chapter 20). Our conclusions of functional unity *versus* conflict depend in part upon the level of analysis employed and the time scale examined.

Andrew (1972) is particularly critical of the heuristic value in treating display defined on the basis of presumed function in terms of conflict between specific major behavioural predispositions. His arguments basically are that one can often obtain the display when independent evidence suggests that diverse and rather general behavioural predispositions are activated; and the level of analysis involved in the literature on conflicting predispositions is frequently too crude, and unnecessary to the examination of immediate antecedent conditions. (See Blurton-Jones, 1968 and Hinde, 1972 for recent articulate statements of the alternative viewpoint.)

Conflict is Defined at the Level of the Organism

As noted above conflict is defined primarily in terms of the presumed goal states of the intact organism (e.g. obtaining a mate *vs.* flight). We do not therefore speak of conflict during locomotion or respiration *unless* different patterns are involved which appear to underlie incompatible consequences at the organism level (e.g., moving towards or away from a predator, holding one's breath to avoid smoke inhalation in spite of rising levels of blood carbon dioxide). There is a sense of arbitrariness here, at least for one concerned with mechanism.

An important point that is too frequently missed in causal analysis, particularly at physiological levels, is that natural selection operates primarily upon *functions* defined in terms of the organism (e.g., Mayr, 1970). This fact is particularly apparent in the literature on reproduction as a primary constituent of evolutionary success. It is thus to be expected that individual components defined at the descriptive or causal level will form meaningful clusters in terms of organism function. Although I have emphasized previously that it is often advantageous to separate causal, descriptive, and functional categories of behaviour, this obviously does not imply they are unrelated. The issue here is that fundamental constraints may be most apparent at the level of functional endpoints since it is these endpoints which are most directly guided by selection. Such constraints are discussed more fully by McFarland and Nunez, this volume Chapter 19.

A most interesting if somewhat speculative discussion of function generating cause in an evolutionary sense has been provided by Tinbergen (1952). He points out, for example, that although reproductive displays may originate in conflict between major predispositions (e.g., flight, aggression, copulation), they may serve important signal functions which in turn are selected for their predictability and clarity. In such cases, Tinbergen argues, the displays may become *ritualized* and *emancipated* from their original dependence upon conflict (see also Lorenz, 1961, 1965). The fact that descriptively similar movement patterns associated with sexual behaviour may have different causal bases at different stages of ontogeny is also clear (e.g., Kruijt, 1964). Again such differences can often be comprehended best when combined with functional analyses at the organism level.

Conflict is Defined on the basis of Discrete, Coherent, and Antagonistic Control Systems

Terms, such as 'tendency', used to explain conflict behaviour (e.g., Hinde, 1970) assume a cohesion among control elements which is distinct from, and antagonistic to, other complexes of control elements in their operation. Potential difficulties with such conceptualizations, if carried to extremes, can be seen even in relatively simple neurobiological systems. For example, successive locomotor movements in locusts may appear indistinguishable from one another, yet be produced by quite different combinations of activity in flexor and extensor motoneurons (Hoyle, 1964). Also in invertebrates the same muscle groups may be employed, but with altered rules of coupling, in quite different activities such as flight and walking behaviour (Kennedy, 1976). In vertebrates, particularly mammals, similar principles certainly apply but at a much greater level of complexity (Paillard, 1960; Doty, 1976; Evarts, 1976).

Again we are returned to the problem of defining a behavioural system, for without such a definition we cannot in turn either define conflict or examine in a meaningful way the operation of underlying (e.g., physiological) mechanisms. It is probably not surprising that attempts to examine critically ethological models of dual motivation in reproductive and other displays have met with limited success (*cf.* Hinde, 1970).

One of the most thorough behavioural attempts to manipulate presumed conflict in the causation of display is Blurton-Jones' (1968) study of great tits. He first determined stimuli that would reliably elicit three different functional classes of behaviour: attack (a pencil), escape (a small light bulb), and feeding (food held in forceps). Subsequently he presented these stimuli in different combinations to produce conflict. For example, when the escape stimulus was presented in conjunction with the attack stimulus, overt attacks decreased and displays increased. By careful manipulation and observation, he also provided suggestive evidence that different threat displays could be elicited by altering the ratio between the predispositions to flee and attack. Blurton-Jones' approach emphasizes the potential in systematic application of behaviourally defined intervening variables, and should be followed up. More direct attempts to look at mechanisms have had less success.

A pioneering attempt to examine neural mechanisms in conjunction with the dual motivation hypothesis of displays was made by Brown and Hunsperger (1963). These investigators succeeded in eliciting 'pure' escape, 'mixed' attack, threat in cats by stimulating selected regions of the brain stem and forebrain. Combined stimulation of escape and attack regions, however, failed to produce threat behaviour as might be expected on the basis of ethological theory. Secondly, since stimulation of a single site produced threat the authors conclude that the construct of conflict in threat displays is unnecessary. Thirdly, they found that stimulation of escape areas could facilitate rather than suppress threat-attacks; this appears contrary to predictions based upon the hypothesis of inhibitory relationships between attack and escape systems. The authors' conclusions can be and have been criticized on various logical grounds (e.g., Rowell, 1964; Hinde, 1970). For example stimulation of a single neural site may simultaneously activate elements that normally participate in antagonistic behaviour patterns. Their very failure to elicit 'pure' attack also reduces the conclusions that can be drawn from experiments involving the simultaneous activation of different loci. Brain stimulation studies at best must be interpreted cautiously since localized populations of neural elements are activated synchronously although this may never occur in the normal life of the animal. However, at the present time there is no clear confirmatory evidence for the obligatory role of conflict at the level of neural *systems* in the production of reproductive and other display patterns (see also Roberts *et al.*, 1967).

One lesson of recent experiments on neural systems underlying motivated behaviour is that they may intergrade and show dimensions of plasticity to a much greater extent than was previously expected by most investigators (e.g., Valenstein, 1970a). To a large extent this can be attributed to the traditional methodological pitfalls of not allowing the animal sufficient opportunity to engage in diverse behaviour patterns, or not examining with sufficient precision the interplay among a meaningful sample of causal antecedents. The latter necessitates a systematic manipulation of individual and combined variables along qualitative, quantitative, and temporal dimensions (Fentress, 1973).

When such procedures are undertaken and combined with precise description at the level of movement as well as consequence, one achieves a picture of more or less continual intergradations among motor elements in varying combinations (e.g., Golani, 1976). It may well be that a greater appreciation for the *dynamic relationships* at all levels of behavioural organization will lead to a depth of understanding which will obviate the necessity of static constructs defined both within and between behavioural systems (e.g., Fentress, 1973, 1967a). It is apparent that analyses of sexual behaviour and its relationship to conflict has not yet reached this stage.

BOUNDARY-STATE APPROACH TO SEXUAL BEHAVIOUR AND CONFLICT

Our explanations of sexual behaviour and conflict depend upon the assumptions and taxonomic methods we employ. Analytical techniques, no matter how sophisticated, cannot be divorced from these considerations.

Some Problems in Review

At this stage it is useful to summarize major problems.

Classificatory Criteria

Behaviour systems can be defined on the basis of function, movement, or antecedent cause. While these three methods are each important and complementary, they are distinct in detail. Terms such as sexual behaviour, for example, imply functional consequences. Details of motor performance and causation are separable issues.

Analysis levels

Terms such as sexual behaviour and conflict are defined at the organism level. We do not, for example, speak of conflict for the alternating motor patterns of copulation, even though antagonistic relationships between physiological control systems (e.g., at the motor level) can be demonstrated. Antagonistic reltionships occur between mechanisms or systems defined at the motor, sensory, or motivational levels of integration. Only the latter, however, are usually included in behavioural analyses of conflict (cf. Andrew, 1972, this volume). Further, the relationship between mechanism and broader system function cannot be assumed, but must be tested directly. At the level of the organism this involves analysis of the interplay between different classes of behaviour that we have defined.

Presumed Function

Review of the literature reveals that terms such as sexual behaviour and conflict are often based upon presumed *unitary functional endpoints or goals. If we either switch our assumptions of function, or allow the possibility of multiple functions, the very definition of behavioural categories may alter. Thus, interpretations of to and fro behaviour exhibited during courtship might be interpreted (and subsequently analysed) differently if one considers conflict between approach and avoidance tendencies, the role of vacillation in attracting a mate, or longer-term consequences such as altered physiological state of the sexual partner.*

Assumptions of Unitary, Mutually Exclusive, and antagonistic predispositions

Terms such as tendency, drive, or sexual motivation imply a unity of operation of causal elements within the system, and a clear separation of causal elements between systems. This is usually combined with the assumption of antagonistic relationships between systems, a paradoxical indication that the systems are not *separate at the level of the organism. Possible facilitatory relationships between subelements classified into different systems needs further investigation, as does the whole question of partially overlapping systems (Fentress, 1973, 1976).*

Static Representations of Dynamic Processes

Behaviour is defined in terms of dynamic process. *Our categories of behaviour, however, are basically static abstractions. The possibility of dynamic shifts in the boundaries of a given defined system, and thus in the relationship among two or more defined systems, has been inadequately explored. Thus, for example, certain factors may contribute both to aggressive and sexual behaviour, but both the extent and direction of contribution may depend upon the internal dynamics of the organisms.*

The necessity for multiple Measures

Since sexual behaviour and conflict are not entities but abstractions it is critical to employ multiple behavioural and/or physiological measures. This must include not only the measurement of subcomponents defined within the context of the system (e.g., approaching, mounting, thrusting, ejaculation), but also subcomponents normally defined in the context of other systems (e.g., aggressive bites, playful pawing, fearful withdrawal). Each of these measures must also be applied with multiple and explicitly defined criteria. For example, the construct of behavioural intensity can be measured by movement amplitude, duration, stereotypy, completeness, vigour, ease of interruption, etc., and the measures do not necessarily obtain a correlation of 1.0 (Fentress, 1973). Similarly, different time-scales may reveal both positive and negative interactions between variables measured. For example, there may be seasonally determined positive correlations between fighting and sexual behaviour, whereas on shorter time-scales these two classes of behaviour may be negatively correlated (e.g., Sevenster, 1961).

The Necessity for Multiple Manipulations

Rarely do investigators employ a sufficiently broad spectrum of separate manipulations in the study of sexual behaviour or other motivational categories. More rarely still does one find a systematic combination *of independent variables. For this to be done properly the investigator must consider the separate and combined operation of variables defined along three dimensions:* qualitative *(which variable),* quantitative *(how much of the variable), and* temporal *(when the variable is applied and the precise time that various positive, negative, and null effects are observed). Finally, a full appreciation of the causal nexus underlying behaviour can only be achieved if factors initially defined (assumed) as outside of (or antagonistic to) the behavioural system in question are employed.*

The Employment of Both Context and Component Analysis

The construct of a control system depends both upon the context within which that system operates and its subcomponents. At the behavioural level this emphasizes that sexual or other behavioural systems must be examined in conjunction with other defined dimensions of behaviour while at the same time subdivided into constituent parts. Perhaps there is no area where modern behavioural analysis has failed more dramatically than in the combined determination of constituent dimensions within a system and relationships among systems (defined as above). Focus upon both component and context can provide an important corrective to this situation.

Criteria of Excitation and Inhibition in System Definition

Systems in behaviour are usually defined in terms of positive correlations among component elements. When these correlations are separated in time causal connections are frequently inferred. This is a narrow definition of system, however. For example, Sherrington (1906) defined spinal control systems in terms of both synergistic and antagonistic relationships among neuromuscular groups. If increased levels of hormone block the expression of early phases of courtship it does not seem reasonable to exclude these activities from the reproductive system. Yet if the same treatment reduces the occurrence of fighting or fleeing this is often taken as an indication of the separability of these systems from reproduction. This is a further illustration of the potential dangers of confusing descriptive, functional, and causal criteria in system definition. From a causal perspective, if two or more populations of events are systematically related, either positively or negatively, then we have grounds to link them together in our thinking. Whether two or more variables are positively or negatively related may also depend in part upon the intensity or level of these variables, the broader context within which they operate, and the time-span incorporated in a given analysis.

Towards the Study of Dynamic Relationships

Factor, Cluster, and Related Analysis

Wiepkema (1961) applied the techniques of factor analysis in an important study of reproductive behaviour and conflict in bitterlings. From his data he concluded that inferences of conflict behaviour based upon the assumption of unitary and incompatible response tendencies may be misleading. He demonstrated that individual variables could be separated for a given tendency, and that several of these variables could influence more than one tendency. He notes that this problem is precipitated when only a single dependent variable is evaluated; e.g. zigzag frequency as a unitary indicator of sex drive in

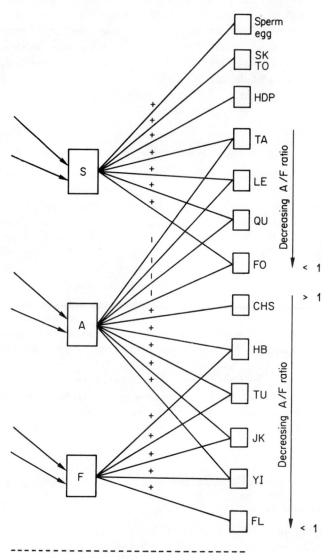

Fig. 4. Causal relations among reproductive activities in the bitterling as measured on the basis of three hypo-thetical motivational factors: sex (S), attack (A), and flight (F). Decreasing attack/flight ratio indicated by the arrows. Abbreviations from top downward: skimming (SK), touching (TO), headdown posture (HDP), tail bending (TA), leading (LE), quivering (QU), following (FO), chasing (CHS), head butting (HB), turning beak (TU), jerking (JK), yielding (YI), fleeing (FL). (From Wiepkema, 1961, as redrawn in Hinde, 1970. Reproduced by permission of the Netherlands Zoological Society.)

sticklebacks. When he applied factor analytic techniques to his data, significant correlations were obtained on the basis of three major sets of causal predispositions: sex (S), attack (A), and fleeing (F). However, the mathematical loading on these hypothetical factors was such to indicate the heterogeneity of causation of behavioural subcomponents within a factor and both positive and negative relationships among subcomponents of different factors (see Fig. 4).

A clear implication of Wiepkema's study is that major behavioural predispositions (such as commonly assumed under such headings as drive and tendency) provide useful approximations for initial research but are limited in the precision to which they can be applied in detailed analysis of integrated behaviour (cf. Hinde, 1970; Andrew, 1972). Three points are relevant: (a) the systems defined in terms of major factors are heterogeneous in their relationship to specific behavioural measures; (b) different factors partially overlap in their control of particular outputs; (c) the overlap between factors thus measured may be both positive (excitatory) and negative (inhibitory). Missing from Wiepkema's data are detailed statements of the precise temporal relationships among variables investigated *in conjunction with* detailed titration of quantitative dimensions.

The careful use of factor analysis can provide a powerful tool in behavioural research as long as one does not treat the factors thus revealed as entities rather than convenient abstractions (cf. Overall, 1964). Dawkins (1976) has recently demonstrated the use of cluster analysis to clarify further the problem of overlapping hierarchies in behaviour, and in a related vein McFarland (1976) has demonstrated that complex motivational relationships can often become more comprehensive through the use of highly abstract 'space-state' approaches (See McFarland and this volume Chapter 19 for further discussion). Sequential analysis also holds considerable promise (e.g., Nelson, 1973; Slater, 1973), although all such methods are in preliminary stages of development (cf. Fentress, 1972, 1973, 1976a).

Relationships at the Level of Social Context

In social species reproductive activities are complexly related to other dimensions of group behaviour. The relationships of individual animals shift in a variety of ways, but generally settle upon stable points between successive transitions (Golani, 1976; Hinde and Stevenson-Hinde, 1976). Formally similar processes can often be determined for relationships defined within the organism (Fentress, 1973, 1976a, b).

Observations that I have made in conjunction with R. Field, H. Parr, and J. Ryon (unpubl.) on the dynamics of reproductive behaviour in captive timber wolves can be used as illustration.

Fighting behaviour among adult females and signs of agonistic reactions of the single adult male toward the females increased markedly with the approach of the breeding season. Antagonistic encounters between the females also significantly increased the probability that the male would show courtship (pawing, rubbing, etc.) and preliminary mounting attempts within the next several minutes. Thus in this context aggression between members of the opposite sex could be said to facilitate sexual behaviour. Upon the approach of a female the male would frequently growl and bristle prior to mount attempts, but our data are insufficient to provide clear evidence of a positive association between sexual behaviour and aggression in this instance. Either intention or full mounting bouts were also often observed after other forms of disturbance or play, as if linked to at present unspecified states of tension or excitement (*cf.* Hanby, 1974).

(Note that terms such as sexual behaviour, aggressive behaviour, excitement, and tension are being used as convenient short-hands from descriptive and functional perspectives only; cf. previous discussion).

The relationship between the two females was stable for more than a year, with the older animal clearly dominant by various criteria of measurement. One consequence was that any intention mounts directed by the male towards the young female were quickly interrupted by direct interference by the older animal. Removal of the older female from the social group for one week resulted in a permanent shift in the social nexus since courtship by the younger female was no longer prevented. Upon reintroduction of the older animal a prolonged fight occurred between the females, lasting for more than an hour, and finally ending with the older animal prostrate on the ground from apparent exhaustion. Upon his own reintroduction to the main pen the male almost immediately approached the prostrate female and performed a protracted series of copulatory thrusts. Group aggression and mating appear interconnected in these animals, since on several other occasions mounting has been observed to closely follow agonistic behaviour. Once the social structure shifted to a new configuration it stabilized. Even today, nearly a year and a half after the older female was again removed to protect her from possible injury, the new stability is clear from observations of the females interacting across a fence. Breeding of the younger female was successful.

Documentation of feeding patterns prior to and after the birth of the pups illustrates dynamic stabilities in social structure relevant to reproductive behaviour at a different level (Table 1). Several months prior to the birth of the pups the male and female both fed yearlings in the pen at frequent intervals, usually by carrying and dropping pieces of food. Just prior to and shortly following the pups' birth the male switched his feeding efforts primarily toward the adult female who in turn ceased feeding the yearlings. No signs of sexual activity were observed during this period. When the newborn animals emerged from the den they were fed by the male, adult female, *and* yearlings. The male was only observed on one occasion to feed the adult female, but continued to feed the yearlings who in turn often carried the food to the pups. The pattern

Table 1. Social feeding and food solicitation behaviour in timber wolves: Observed before breeding season, shortly before and after birth of cubs, and after the cubs were seen outside of the den.

FEEDING BEHAVIOUR

Feeding by:	To:	Before litter Aug. 29/73-Dec. 1/73 N=46		Litter (born Apr. 19/74) Apr. 1/74-May 13/74 N=21		Litter above ground May 14/74-Sept. 14/74 N=35	
		Regurg.	Carry	Regurg.	Carry	Regurg.	Carry
Adult male	Adult female	0	0	16	0	1	0
	Yearlings	36	75	8	26	11	10
	Pups	–	–	–	–	25	8
Adult female	Adult male	0	0	0	0	0	0
	Yearlings	11	29	0	0	0	5
	Pups	–	–	–	–	15	11
Yearlings	Adult male	0	0	0	0	0	0
	Adult female	0	0	0	0	0	0
	Pups	–	–	–	–	19	7

SOLICITATION

Soliciting by:	From:	Before litter Aug. 29/73-Dec. 1/73 N=46	Litter (born Apr. 19/74) Apr. 1/74-May 13/74 N=21	Litter above ground May 14/74-Sept. 14/74 N=35
Adult male	Adult female	5	22	7
	Yearlings	61	16	3
	Pups	–	–	12
Adult female	Adult male	0	0	0
	Yearlings	34	2	0
	Pups	–	–	10
Yearlings	Adult male	0	0	0
	Adult female	0	0	0
	Pups	–	–	22

N = the number of observation nights for each condition.
– = no observations
Numbers within table refer to the number of times each pattern was observed.

of feeding changed as well. For example, the male usually fed the newborn by regurgitation rather than the food carrying he previously showed with the other animals (i.e. yearlings, adult female). This in turn coincided with increase in the proportion of regurgitation to carrying for all social feeding shown by the male within the group.

The purpose of these observations is to emphasize the dynamic (i.e. systematically shifting) relationships between behavioural dimensions associated with reproduction. Decline in sexual behaviour in wolves here is closely followed by increase in care (feeding) of the female, and subsequently the newborn pups, by the male. A major question which is not yet answered is the pattern of causal relations among these diverse reproductive activities. Clearly our models of control must eventually do justice to such behavioural transitions and stabilities if they are to be applied successfully at either the level of organism or social group.

Relationships at the Level of Organism

Observations such as noted in the previous section make it clear that behavioural relationships must be viewed in a dynamic context of positive and negative interactions, both between organisms and in terms of motivational processes within the organism. It is often particularly useful to examine situations in which relationships between presumably distinct or antagonistic behavioural predispositions are positively associated, such as between aggression and sexual behaviour. Observations and analyses of this type are necessary to avoid overgeneralization about the ubiquity of antagonistic associations (conflict). A more ambitious goal not at present realizable is to relate positive and negative relationships to one another within a common dynamic framework that does justice to the distinct features of each.

The affinity between sexual and aggressive patterns of behaviour has long been postulated for man (e.g., Freud, 1922; Gorney, 1972). Certainly there is much evidence that normal seasonal changes and experimentally raised androgen levels can increase fighting as well as courtship and copulation in a variety of vertebrates (e.g., reviews by Hinde, 1970; Archer, 1976). Long-term positive associations between these classes of behaviour are often accompanied by shorter-term negative relationships (e.g., Sevenster, 1961; previous sections). This emphasizes the importance of explicit definition of measurement criteria in drawing conclusions about motivational relationships.

Certain forms of behaviour, such as male–male mounting in primates, are difficult to assign unambiguously to a given motivational system. Hanby (1974) has provided a useful review of the confusion that can occur in discussions of dominance *versus* sexual mounts in primates due to imprecise mixture of causal, contextual, descriptive, and functional criteria. To emphasize the close relationship between these dimensions she utilized the terminology of socio-sexual mounts. In addition to a general literature review, she cites her own evidence that a variety of disturbances can increase mounting (particularly male–male) in Japanese macaques *(Macaca fuscata)*. Increases in male–male mounts occur most commonly *after* periods of disturbance (*cf.* Fentress, 1973; Archer, 1976), and in situations where predispositions for both aggression and copulation appear closely associated.

Other workers have found that male-female copulation can be facilitated by such diverse factors as handling (e.g., Larsson, 1956, for older male rats) shock (e.g., Beach, 1955—but note different measures; Barfield and Sachs, 1968 for sexually experienced male rats; and Caggiula and Eibergen, 1969, for virgin male rats), amphetamine (Bignami, 1966, male rats), food deprivation (e.g., Jarman and Gerall, 1961, guinea pigs; but see also Sachs, 1965, for rats), and novelty (e.g., Andrew, 1956). Fighting, escape, and even exploratory behaviour are often facilitated by similar situations (e.g., Hinde, 1970) although for fighting and escape the findings are often more robust (e.g., Archer, 1976). It is important that in many of these cases maximal enhancement of sexual behaviour occurs either *after* the termination of factors which appear strongly to facilitate other classes of behaviour, such as escape or avoidance responses (e.g., Barfield and Sachs, 1968; Hanby, 1974; Archer, 1976) or *during* less intense and more diffuse changes in arousal, activation, etc. (e.g., Bignami, 1966; Fentress, 1973, 1976a for more general reviews).

Clearly the causal relationships between different classes of behaviour defined primarily from descriptive and/or functional criteria exhibit subtleties that are easily missed if one conceptualizes underlying control systems in unitary, totally independent or mutually antagonistic, and static terms.

The Boundary-state Approach to Dynamic Relationships

It is a truism, but a critical one, that behavioural investigations at all levels are essential to, and an eloquent assay of, the dynamic relationships between animal species and their environments. This implies that in addition to consideration of relatively permanent phenotypic substrates in behaviour, investigations *must* deal explicitly with the dynamic relationships of underlying behavioural systems, not only with respect to time but also with respect to one another. The dynamic context within which a given dimension of behaviour, such as sexual behaviour, occurs is central to the question of mechanism of control.

But what of the very boundaries of a behavioural control system, i.e., the rules of taxonomy in behaviour? Is mounting between male primates really sexual behaviour or some form of dominance or aggression? Do aggressive, or escape control systems conflict in their expression with sexual behaviour, or are the relationships synergestic? Or are the systems independent? A similar list of questions could be extended indefinitely. But what is the importance to the investigator focused upon sexual behaviour? The answer to this depends upon the level and precision of explanation that we are willing to accept.

In my view there are four major sets of problems that present themselves at the behavioural level. The first is that our very taxonomic criteria used to define sexual behaviour too frequently confuse the distinctions that appear if we carefully separate taxonomic factors into explicit languages of description, causation, function, context, analysis level, etc. The second problem occurs if we assume that our categories of behaviour, such as sexual behaviour, are entities in themselves rather than convenient abstractions for analysis. Thirdly, if our categories, which obviously are essential, are assumed to be unitary and mutually exclusive we may miss the opportunity to explore both divisible and overlapping dimensions of expression and control at the organism level. And lastly, there is no *a priori* reason, other than perhaps misguided cultural tradition or intellectual laziness, to presume that the systems we have defined to work with operate within statically confined boundaries which in turn impress the relationships between systems into a single fixed mode.

In writing this chapter it soon became apparent that the distinction between conflict and synergism among systems as defined in behavioural research is often arbitrary and unclear. It also became clear that the study of 'sexual' behaviour has an enormous appeal, not only because of the intellectual challenges and importance to the species' populations in their own right, but also because of the more general questions posed about the components and context of any behavioural dimension we may choose for study.

I offer as a suggestion that we reconsider the boundaries of our taxonomies and analyses of sexual behaviour, with a view to more complete integration into the broader relational dynamics defined at the level of the intact, behaving organism. Certainly sexual behaviour, however, we define it, is influenced by other acts the organism is or could be performing. Sometimes the relationships seem to be antagonistic, and at other times supportive, but we do not yet have a fully clear picture of which occurs at any particular instant.

Here are some thoughts for consideration and further test.

(1) Antagonistic relationships between sexual and other forms of behaviour (such as in conflict situations) are most likely to occur when any one set of predispositions can be independently manipulated to, or otherwise measured at, a high activation level.

(2) When one or more of these behavioural systems is less strongly activated some degree of mutual facilitation, or at least positive correlational relationship, is more likely to be observed.

(3) When the time domain is incorporated in our analyses along with consideration of quantitative and qualitative relationships, diverse behavioural systems are most likely to facilitate rather than block the expression of sexual behaviour during *either* early stages of their activation *or* upon the termination of factors which led to this activation.

This general scheme can be simply illustrated and leads to some simple predictions. For example:

(1) strongly activated attack or escape predispositions will block sexual behaviour;

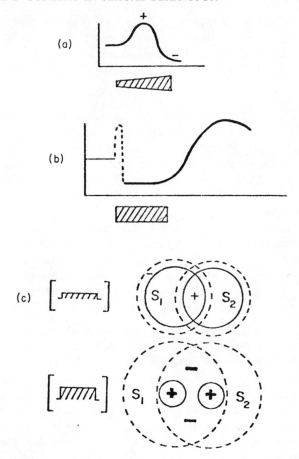

Fig. 5. Model for dynamic relationships between and within two behavioural systems as a function of quantitative and temporal variables. (a) With increasing activation (stippled bar, left to right) of factors not normally included in, for example, sexual behaviour, there may initially be an increase in one or more measures of sexual behaviour, followed by a decrease. (b) When factors not normally included in, for example, sexual behaviour are presented at high levels, there may be a very brief increase in one or more measures of sexual behaviour, followed by a reduction in these measures, and subsequent rebound when the 'extrinsic' factors are removed. (c) Model to suggest that when behavioural systems are weakly activated, excitation (defined behaviourally) is relatively diffuse, with resulting cross-system facilitation likely (top line); whereas when these same behavioural systems are more strongly activated there is a focusing of net excitation and spread of inhibition, with the result that the systems now antagonize the expression of one another (bottom line). For example, S_1 and S_2 could represent information spaces for 'agonistic' and 'sexual' control systems and their relationships. (From Fentress, 1973. Reproduced by permission of Plenum Publishing Corporation.)

(2) attack or escape predispositions at a level below that which produces overt expression of these behaviour patterns *may* facilitate sexual behaviour;

(3) during early stages of activation of attack or escape, and perhaps most clearly during the aftermath of these dimensions of behaviour, sexual activity may be facilitated.

The basic idea being applied here is that the control boundaries within qualitatively defined behavioural systems, and thus the dynamic relationships between systems, may shift in a systematic manner as a function of both quantitative and temporal variables. Thus, for example, positive causal overlap between systems is viewed as most likely during relatively low degrees of 'within system' activation, whereas during higher levels of activation the systems become more tightly focused with respect to the *functionally defined* classes of behaviour they will facilitate rather than block (Fig. 5, Fentress, 1973). This general scheme does not in any way negate the importance of qualitative differences between behavioural systems, species, contexts, etc. Nor can it be equated with traditional models of general activation, since specificities which differentiate one system from another as well as the particular relationships between systems are recognized explicitly (*cf.* Andrew, 1974).

(A further consideration is differential thresholds and 'bandwidths' determined for behavioural outputs that might be defined within a system. Archer (1976), for example, has argued that independent variables such as stress, novelty, etc., may facilitate sexual behaviour only when applied within a very restricted range, while responses such as attack and escape can be elicited over broader ranges. The affinities between attack and escape, and the possible utility of threshold models appears through the observation that escape often replaces attack at very high levels of activation. Many of the relationships between systems may also be conceptualized in terms of differential thresholds of excitation or inhibition, an abstraction that appears compatible with data at the neurobiological level (Fentress, 1973, 1976a). Valenstein (1970b) reviews data from the Soviet literature that appears to agree with this perspective at least in formal terms, but the precision of generalizations between types and levels of analysis must be viewed critically in conjunction with further detailed investigations specifically oriented to their comparison.)

Rather, it is one approach towards seeking unifying rules of dynamic organization that may apply to differing degrees to qualitatively distinguishable behavioural systems, species, etc. While the model has been applied successfully to a variety of behavioural situations (e.g., Fentress, 1972, 1973, 1976a), its detailed applicability to the study of sexual behaviour at the level of the intact organism remains a question for future investigation.

SUMMARY

Sexual behaviour is examined in terms of dynamic relationships among defined dimensions of behavioural organization. The argument emphasizes the need to examine each given dimension of behaviour both in terms of its component elements and in relationship to the broader spatio-temporal context of expression. In short, the relationships *between* behavioural dimensions can clarify mechanisms *within* a given system. It is particularly critical to specify possible distinctions between descriptive, causal, and functional explanations at any given level of analysis.

Sexual behaviour frequently occurs in contexts which suggest conflict between two or more underlying predispositions. Under specified conditions dimensions of sexual behaviour can also be facilitated by factors normally associated with other classes of behviour. Possible relationships between these negative and positive associations are explored within a framework that includes qualitative, quantitative, and temporal parameters.

ACKNOWLEDGEMENTS

This review, and research report herein, were supported in part by U.S. Public Health Service Grant MH 16955, National Research Council of Canada Grant A 9787, and funds from Graduate Studies and Arts and Science, Dalhousie University. I thank my colleagues at Dalhousie for many useful discussions. In particular, I thank H. Parr and J. B. Hutchison for critical reading of the manuscript, and J. Ryon for allowing me to use some of the data she gathered on wolf social behaviour.

REFERENCES

Andrew, R. J. (1956) Fear responses in *Emberiza* spp., *Br. J. Anim. Behav.*, **4**, 125–32.
Andrew, R. J. (1972) The information potentially available in mammal displays. In: *Non-Verbal Communication*, Robert A. Hinde (ed.), Cambridge University Press, pp. 197–204.
Andrew, R. J. (1974) Arousal and the causation of behaviour, *Behaviour*, **51**, 135–65.
Archer, J. (1976) The organization of aggression and fear in vertebrates. In: *Perspectives in Ethology*, Vol. 2, P.P.G. Bateson and P. H. Klopfer (eds.), Plenum Press, New York, pp. 231–98.
Barfield, R. J. and Sachs, B. D. (1968) Sexual behaviour: stimulation by painful electrical shock to skin in male rats, *Science*, **161**, 392–5.
Beach, F. A., Goldstein, A. C., and Jacoby, G. A. (1955) Effects of electroconvulsive shock on sexual behaviour in male rats, *J. Comp. Physiol. Psychol.*, **48**, 173–9.
Bignami, G. (1966) Pharmacologic influences on mating behaviour in the male rat, *Psychopharm. Berlin*, **10**, 44–58.
Blurton-Jones, N. G. (1968) Observations and experiments on causation of threat displays of the great tit *(Parus major)*, *Anim. Behav. Monogr.*, **1**, 2.
Brown, J. L. and Hunsperger, R. W. (1963) Neuroethology and the motivation of agonistic behaviour, *Anim. Behav.*, **11**, 439–48.
Caggiula, A. R. and Eibergen, R. (1969) Copulation of virgin male rats evoked by painful peripheral stimulation, *J. Comp. Physiol. Psychol.*, **69**, 414–9.
Dawkins, R. (1976) Hierarchical organization: a candidate principle for ethology. In: *Growing Points in Ethology*, P. P. G. Bateson and R. A. Hinde (eds.), Cambridge University Press, Cambridge, pp. 7–54.
Doty, R. W. (1976) The concept of neural 'centers' as an explanatory principle, and as a problem. In: *Simpler Networks and Behavior*, J. C. Fentress (ed.), Sinauer Assoc., Sunderland, Mass, pp. 251–65.

Evarts, E. V. (1976) Neuronal representation of acquired movement patterns in primates. In: *Simpler Networks and Behavior*, J. C. Fentress (ed.), Sinauer Assoc., Sunderland, Mass, pp.266–73.

Fentress, J. C. (1968a) Interrupted ongoing behaviour in two species of vole *(Microtus agrestis* and *Clethrionomys britannicus)*. I. Response as a function of preceding activity and the context of an apparently 'irrelevant' motor pattern. *Anim. Behav.*, **16**, 135–53.

Fentress, J. C. (1968b) Interrupted ongoing behaviour in two species of vole *(Microtus agrestis* and *Clethrionomys britannicus)*. II. Extended analysis of motivational variables underlying fleeing and grooming behaviour, *Anim. Behav.*, **16**, 154–67.

Fentress, J. C. (1972) Development and patterning of movement sequences in inbred mice. In: *The Biology of Behavior*, J. Kiger (ed.), Oregon State University Press, Corvallis, pp. 82–132.

Fentress, J. C. (1973) Specific and nonspecific factors in the causation of behaviour. In: *Perspectives in Ethology* Vol. 1, P. P. G. Bateson and P. H. Klopfer (eds.), Plenum Press, New York, pp. 155–224.

Fentress, J. C. (1976a) Dynamic boundaries of patterned behaviour: interaction and self-organisation. In: *Growing Points in Ethology*. P. P. G. Bateson and R. A. Hinde (eds.), Cambridge University Press, Cambridge, pp. 135–69.

Fentress, J. C., ed. (1976b) *Simpler Networks and Behavior*. Sinauer Assoc., Sunderland, Mass.

Freud, S. (1922) *Psycho-analysis*, Hogarth, London.

Golani, I. (1976) Motor interaction sequences as simultaneous and successive routes of convergence. In: *Perspectives in Ethology*, Vol. 2, P. P. G. Bateson and P. H. Klopfer (eds.), Plenum Press, New York, pp. 69–134.

Gorney, R. (1973) *The Human Agenda*, Simon and Schuster, New York.

Hanby, J. P. (1974) Male–male mounting in Japanese monkeys *(Macaca fuscata)*, *Anim. Behav.*, **22**, 836–49.

Hinde, R. A. (1953) The conflict between drives in the courtship and copulation of the chaffinch, *Behaviour*, **5**, 1–31.

Hinde, R. A. (1954) The courtship and copulation of the greenfinch *(Chloris chloris)*, *Behaviour*, **7**, 207–32.

Hinde, R. A. (1959) Unitary drives, *Anim. Behav.*, **7**, 130–41.

Hinde, R. A. (1970) *Animal Behaviour: A Synthesis of Ethology and Comparative Psychology*, 2nd edn., McGraw-Hill Book Company, New York.

Hinde, R. A. ed. (1972) *Non-Verbal Communication*, Cambridge University Press, Cambridge.

Hinde, R. A. and Stevenson, J. (1976) Towards understanding relationships: dynamic stability. In: *Growing Points in Ethology*, P. P. G. Bateson and R. A. Hinde (eds.), Cambridge University Press, Cambridge, pp. 451–79.

Holst, E. von and Saint Paul, U. von (1963) On the functional organisation of drives, *Naturwiss.*, **18**, 409–22.

Hoyle, G. (1964) Exploration of neuronal mechanisms underlying behaviour in insects. In: *Neural Theory and Modeling*, R. F. Reiss (ed.), Stanford University Press, Stanford, pp. 346–467.

Iersel, J. J. A. van and Bol, A. C. A. (1958) Preening of two tern species. A study on displacement activities, *Behaviour*, **13**, 1–88.

Jarmon, H. and Gerall, A. A. (1961) The effect of food deprivation upon the sexual performance of male guinea pigs, *J. Comp. Physiol. Psychol.*, **54**, 306–9.

Kennedy (1976) Properties of neural elements in relation to network function. In: *Simpler Networks and Behavior*. J. C. Fentress (ed.), Sinauer Assoc., Sunderland, Mass., pp. 65–81.

Kruijt, J. P. (1964) Ontogeny of social behaviour in Burmese red junglefowl *(Gallus gallus spadiceus* Bonnaterre), *Behaviour*, Suppl., 12.

Larsson, K. (1963) Non-specific stimulation and sexual behaviour in the male rat, *Behaviour*, **20**, 110–4.

Lehrman, D. and Friedman, M. (1969) Auditory stimulation of ovarian activity in the ring dove *(Streptopelia risoria)*, *Anim. Behav.*, **17**, 494–7.

Leyhausen, P. (1956) Verhaltensstudien bei Katzen, *Z. Tierpsychol.*, *Beiheft*, **2**.

Lorenz, K. (1961) Phylogenetische Anpassung and adaptive Modifikation des Verhaltens, *Z. Tierpsychol.*, **18**, 139–87.

Lorenz, D. (1965) *Evolution and Modification of Behavior*, Univ. of Chicago.

Mayr, E. (1970) *Populations, Species and Evolution*, Belknap Press, Harvard University, Cambridge, Mass., pp. 55–93.

McFarland, D. J. (1976) Form and function in the temporal organization of behaviour. In: *Growing Points in Ethology*, P. P. G. Bateson and R. A. Hinde (eds.), Cambridge University Press, Cambridge.

Miller, N. E. (1959) Liberalization of basic S-R concepts: Extensions to conflict behaviour, motivation, and social learning. In: *Psychology: A Study of Science*, Vol. 2, S. Koch (ed.), McGraw-Hill, New York, pp. 196–292.

Moynihan, M. (1955) Some aspects of reproductive behaviour in the black-headed gull *(Larus ridibundus ridibundus* L.) and related species, *Behaviour*, Suppl., 4, 1–201.

Nelson, K. (1973) Does the holistic study of behaviour have a future? In: *Perspectives in Ethology*, Vol. 1, P. P. G. Bateson and P. H. Klopfer (eds.), Plenum Press, New York, pp. 281–328.

Overall, J. E. (1964) Note on the scientific status of factors, *Psychol. Bull.*, **61**, 270–6.

Paillard, J. (1960) The patterning of skilled moments. In: *Handbook of Physiology: Neurophysiology* Vol. III, J. Field, H. W. Magoun, and V. E. Hall (eds.), American Physiological Society, Washington, D. C., pp. 1679–708.

Rasa, O. A. E. (1971) Appetence for aggression in juvenile damsel fish, *Z. Tierpsychol.*, *Beiheft* 7, 1–70.

Roberts, W. W., Steinberg, M. L., and Means, L. W. (1967) Hypothalamic mechanisms for sexual, aggressive, and other motivational behaviours in the opossum *Didelphis virginiana*, *J. Comp. Physiol. Psychol.*, **64**, 1–15.

Rowell, C. H. F. (1964) Comments on a recent discussion of some ethological terms, *Anim. Behav.*, **12**, 535–7.

Sachs, B. C. (1965) Sexual behaviour of male rats after one to nine days without food, *J. Comp. Physiol. Psychol.*, **60**, 144–6.

Schenkel, R. (1948) Ausdrucks-Studien an Wolfen, *Behaviour*, **1**, 81–130.

Sevenster, P. (1961) A causal analysis of a displacement activity (Fanning in *Gasterosteus aculeatus* L.), *Behaviour*, Suppl., 9, 1–170.

Sherrington, C. S. (1906) *The Integrative Action of the Nervous System*, Yale University Press, New Haven.

Slater, P. J. B. (1973) Describing sequences of behaviour. In: *Perspectives in Ethology*. P. P. G. Bateson and P. H. Klopfer (eds.), Plenum Press, New York, pp. 131–54.

Stokes, A. W. (1962) Agonistic behaviour among the blue tits at a winter feeding station, *Behaviour*, **19**, 118–38.

Thorpe, W. H. (1963) *Learning and Instinct in Animals* 2nd edn., Methuen and Co. Ltd., London.

Tinbergen, N. (1952) Derived activities: their causation, biological significance, origin and emancipation during evolution, *Quart. Rev. Biol.*, **27**, 1–32.

Tinbergen, N. (1959) Comparative studies of the behaviour of gulls *(Laridae)*: a progress report, *Behaviour*, **15**, 1–70.

Valenstein, E. S. (1970a) Stability and plasticity of motivation systems. In: *The Neurosciences. Second Study Program.* Francis O. Schmitt (ed.), The Rockefeller University Press, New York, pp. 207–17.

Valenstein, E. S. (1970b) Pavlovian typology: Comparative comments on the development of a scientific theme. In: *Development and Evolution of Behaviour. Essays in memory of T. C. Schnierla.* L. R. Aronson, E. Tobach, D. S. Lerhman, and J. S. Rosenblatt (eds.), W. H. Feeman and Co., San Francisco, pp. 254–80.

Wiepkema, P. R. (1961) An ethological analysis of the reproductive behaviour of the bitterling, *Archs. Neerl. Zool.*, **14**, 103–99.

Wilz, K. J. (1972) Causal relationships between aggression and the sexual and nest behaviours in the three-spined stickleback *(Gasterosteus aculeatus)*, *Anim. Behav.*, **20**, 335–40.

CHAPTER 19

Systems Analysis and Sexual Behaviour

DAVID MCFARLAND AND ADELINE TAYLOR NUNEZ

INTRODUCTION

It has become commonplace to regard the control of sexual behaviour as non-regulatory (Milner, 1970) or non-homeostatic (Hokanson, 1969). It may seem strange, therefore, to propose that sexual behaviour is an appropriate medium for control systems analysis. The application of systems analysis to the study of feeding (Geertsema and Reddingius, 1974), drinking (Oatley, 1967; McFarland and McFarland, 1968; Toates and Oatley, 1970), and thermoregulatory behaviour (McFarland and Budgell, 1970; Budgell, 1971) has met with some success in recent years, but these topics are physiologically circumscribed and seem far removed from the relatively loosely defined world of sexual behaviour. This view is well expressed by Grossman (1967):

> Although the central regulation of motivational processes appears to be very similar, there are many physiological and psychological differences between homeostatic drives (such as hunger, thirst, sleep, and elimination) which are elicited and reduced directly by changes in the *internal* environment and non-homoestatic drives (such as sexual or emotional arousal and, perhaps, activity itself) which appear to be elicited and reduced by changes in the *external* environment of the organism. The earlier theories of Morgan and Stellar are based primarily on evidence relevant to homeostatic drive mechanisms (i.e. hunger and thirst) and have encountered serious difficulties when applied to such problems as sexual or emotional arousal.

It may appear that what was true for Morgan and Stellar is also going to be true for the application of systems analysis to sexual behaviour. However, one advantage of systems analysis is that it teaches one to be ultra-critical in the assessment of theories, and we may do well to consider the non-homeostatic view of sexual behaviour more carefully.

In general, systems analysis has developed into three main approaches. The classical approach, developed from the study of simple servo-mechanisms, is based on the use of differential equations and their operational equivalents. This approach has been applied to various aspects of biology, including behaviour (e.g. Milsum, 1966; McFarland, 1971), and has been found to be particularly useful in analysing the relationships between particular chosen variables (i.e. input–output relationships). The state-space approach is much more general in its applicability, being well suited to the study of complex multivariable systems with many inputs and outputs. Its application in biology has so far been relatively restricted, but the state-space approach promises to be more powerful in the analysis of complex biological systems. The stochastic approach has been developed to meet the need to handle the variability inherent in biological systems. Such systems are variable in their behaviour by virtue both of their complexity and of their design. In this chapter we discuss the implications of these three aspects of systems analysis for sexual behaviour. It should be realized that very little work has been done on the application of systems analysis to sexual behaviour, so that concrete examples are few. We believe that this is partly the result of a prevalent view, that sexual behaviour is somehow 'different' from other aspects of behaviour, and therefore not amenable to systems analysis. One of our aims is to dispel this attitude. In addition, we attempt a rough sketch of the possible ways in which systems analysis might profitably be applied to the study of sexual behaviour. We hope that readers will take this to be an ideas 'jumble-sale', and not as an attempt to argue a case.

THE CLASSICAL APPROACH

The early studies, which applied classical systems analysis to behavioural problems, used simple feedback theory, and concentrated primarily on problems of orientation (e.g. Mittelstaedt, 1957) and of homeostasis (e.g. McFarland, 1965; Oatley, 1967). The lessons learned from these studies have led to the development of more sophisticated methods of analysis, and have shown that homeostatic mechanisms are much more complex than had previously been realized.

Control Mechanisms and Homeostasis

At the Eighteenth Symposium of the Society for Experimental Biology, held at Cambridge in 1963, topics concerned with the homeostatic mechanisms of animals were discussed. Before the meeting, all contributors agreed to the following definition:

> *Homeostasis* in its widest context includes the coordinated physiological processes which maintain most of the steady states of organisms. Similar general principles may apply to the establishment, regulation, and control

of steady states for other levels or organization. It must be emphasised that homeostasis does not necessarily imply a lack of change, because the 'steady states' to which the regulatory mechanisms are directed may shift with time. But throughout the change they remain under more or less close control.

Such a concept can therefore be applied to organisms at cellular, organ system, individual, and social levels. It may be considered in relation to time intervals ranging from milli-seconds to millions of years. Its essential feature is the interplay of factors which tend to maintain a given state at a given time. (Hughes, 1964).

In the traditional view, 'Homeostatic drives are believed to arise as a direct consequence of internal stimulation that results when an essential physiological process deviates from some optimal level of functioning.' (Grossman, 1967). It is a *sine qua non* of this view of homeostasis that the central nervous system (CNS) be able to monitor the state of the blood, though this was not appreciated by early investigators. Hypothalamic sensitivity to changes in temperature, osmosity, and blood glucose, has been demonstrated, and the roles of these variables in the regulation of feeding and drinking implicated (Grossman, 1967; Hokanson, 1969). The means by which the brain obtains information concerning water and energy balance are not fully understood, and it appears that a number of different cellular mechanisms act in parallel. In addition to regulation of the internal environment, the CNS acts as a controller of negative feedback loops which encompass the external environment. In particular, hunger and thirst differ from some other aspects of homeostasis in that appropriate behaviour is essential for maintenance of the *status quo*. The deprived animal cannot compensate for loss of water or energy, it can only reduce the rate of loss. Thus feeding and drinking behaviour can be regarded as an essential part of homeostasis.

The classical view of feeding and drinking as regulatory processes implies that feeding and drinking are initiated by monitored systemic changes, which can be regarded as inputs to the mechanisms controlling the behaviour. In other words, the output of the control mechanism is changed in response to a change in input. Certain consequences of the output, for example, the oral, alimentary, and systemic consequences of drinking, serve to alter the input, so that a number of feedback loops are formed. Thus feeding and drinking may be said to be under *feedback* control. However, recent work suggests that, in addition to feeding and drinking in response to systemic changes, these activities may occur in anticipation of such changes. In such cases *feedforward* control can be said to exist (McFarland, 1970).

Feedforward can be seen as a phenomenon which enables the animal to anticipate the long-term consequences of behaviour, and to take appropriate action to forestall deviations of the internal steady state. Thus the long-term digestive consequences of food intake generally increase thirst, but instead of drinking as a result of such a thirst increase, many animals drink in advance and thus anticipate the effects of food ingestion (Fitzsimons and Le Magnen, 1969). Similarly, thermoregulation involves water loss, but instead of allowing thirst to build up as a result of this loss, many animals drink in anticipation and thus have water available for thermoregulation (McFarland, 1970; Budgell, 1970, 1971). It appears that the simple picture of homeostasis as a negative feedback mechanism does not adequately account for the results of these studies. We must ask ourselves, therefore, what alternative theoretical framework might serve, and whether the control of sexual behaviour could also be considered in terms of such a framework.

If we ask what principles are involved in the execution, by the animal, of the behaviour patterns that are required to achieve certain physiological consequences, the answer that has traditionally been given is fairly clear. The behaviour is governed by a conventional type of negative feedback mechanism, by which the physiological consequences of behaviour, or their short-term neurological representatives, progressively reduce the level of motivation as the animal becomes more satiated. This is the type of thinking that underlies Cannon's (1932) concept of homeostasis and governs much current research into physiological and behavioural aspects of regulation. However, the simple negative feedback model is not adequate to account for the complexity of the situation that arises in nature. Even the introduction of refinements to the classical regulatory model, such as positive feedback and feedforward (McFarland, 1970), does little to account for the problem of ambivalence in the consequences of behaviour.

The ambivalence problem arises because there may not always be a one-to-one relationship between a particular activity and its physiological consequences. Thus in behavioural thermoregulation the animal may associate a particular activity with a one-dimensional (univalent) consequence, namely a change in body temperature. Feeding behaviour, however, has multidimensional consequences relating to the many nutrients involved. These consequences will be ambivalent when a particular food has a number of components. When the consequences of behaviour are ambivalent, constraints may be set up such that the animal cannot achieve its 'goal' even though the necessary 'commodities' are available in the environment (McFarland and Sibly, 1972). There must be some sort of *adaptive control* (McFarland, 1971) by which the animal is able to change the properties of its regulatory mechanisms to suit environmental circumstances. The adaptive control can occur, either through the medium of physiological acclimatization, or by means of changes in behavioural strategy. Both these processes are likely to be important in the control of sexual behaviour, as will be explained later in this chapter.

An animal that relies on short-term satiation mechanisms to tell it how much to eat or drink at a particular time, must be able to recalibrate those mechanisms in relation to the ultimate physiological consequences of ingestion. Although animals may sometimes be able to detect changes in the constitution of food by taste, this could account for only a few of the many changes that are possible.

It seems more probable that animals learn how much to eat as a result of experiencing the physiological consequences of eating particular foods. In addition to learning how much to eat, animals also have to learn what to eat. As Rozin and Kalat (1971) point out, 'it is hard to believe that the rat comes equipped with prewired recognition systems for each of the many substances for which it can show a specific hunger'. Indeed, it is now known that many animals can learn to avoid or select particular foods, as a result of physiological consequences occurring hours after ingestion (Revusky and Garcia, 1970; Rozin and Kalat, 1971; McFarland, 1973). As another example of learned modification of homeostatic mechanisms, Richter and his associates showed that when physiological regulators were surgically eliminated '...the animals themselves made an effort to maintain a constant environment or homeostasis.' (Richter, 1943). The evidence shows that rats given a suitable environment could compensate behaviourally following parathyroidectomy, adrenalectomy, pancreatectomy, and thyroidectomy. In essence, Richter's thesis is that animals deprived of physiological regulation resort to behavioural measures in maintaining the stability of the internal environment.

Suppose we invert Richter's argument: animals deprived of behavioural opportunity, by suitable alterations to the environment, resort to physiological regulation and acclimatization in achieving internal stability. Moreover, if an animal can survive under such conditions, by virtue of physiological adaptation, it will no longer be motivated to do all its former behaviour. For example, an animal acclimatized to the heat is no longer motivated to sit in the shade. An animal which is short of food may cease to indulge in the expensive luxury of sexual behaviour, and will eventually cease to be sexually motivated. This thesis is discussed at length by Sibly and McFarland (1974), on the grounds that it is necessary to account for physiological stability. It also has important implications for sexual behaviour, which are discussed later in this chapter.

So far we have argued that, to account for the control of such classical 'homeostatic' aspects of behaviour as feeding, drinking, and thermoregulation, it is necessary to take account not only of the negative feedback mechanisms involved, but also of feedforward anticipatory mechanisms, of adaptive control mechanisms permitting changes in behavioural strategy, and of acclimatory mechanisms providing long-term physiological adjustment. We now take a closer look at traditional arguments relating to sexual behaviour, and ask whether the control of sexual behaviour is really different in principle from that of feeding and drinking.

The Control of Sexual Behaviour

Negative Feedback

An enduring myth in discussions on the control of sexual behaviour is that, whereas feeding, drinking, and thermoregulatory behaviour arise from specific internal stimulation and serve to bring the animal back to some optimal state, this does not seem to be the case with sexual behaviour. 'Here we encounter little evidence to suggest that there is physiological deficit which accumulates or a build up of tissue needs which is then returned to some equilibrium as a result of sexual behaviour.' (Hokanson, 1969).

One problem here is that the terms 'deficit' and 'tissue needs' refer to questions about need in relation to survival, and being a question of function, should have no place in a discussion of causal mechanisms. It would be more correct to refer to a 'physiological displacement' being cancelled as a result of behaviour. The question of the extent to which such displacements from normal physiological levels are deleterious to the individual is another matter entirely.

Hokanson's argument now seems to say that feeding, drinking, and thermo-regulatory behaviour form part of negative feedback mechanisms designed to cancel physiological displacements, whereas sexual behaviour does not. However, although such negative feedback mechanisms certainly play a part in controlling these behaviours, feeding and drinking do not, under ad libitum conditions, occur as part of a corrective action of this kind. Evidence from the study of feeding and drinking patterns, in a variety of species and situations (Fitzsimons and Le Magnen, 1969; Kissileff, 1969; Steffens, 1969; McFarland, 1969), shows that such behaviour generally occurs as part of a complex (feed forward) routine designed to obviate physiological displacements, rather than to correct them. Lloyd (1974) has found that meal patterns in doves are organized on a complex 'pre-programmed' basis, quite different from that which would be expected on the basis of homeostasis.

The idea that the control of sexual behaviour does not involve regulatory processes is, of course absurd. Endocrinologists have long been aware of the hormonal regulatory mechanisms involved in the control of the female mammalian reproductive cycle (e.g. Everett, 1964). To propose that sexual behaviour per se plays to feedback role is to assert that sexual behaviour has no consequences that effect future sexual behaviour. As will become clear later in this chapter (pp. 623), there are very many ways in which sexual behaviour feeds back to affect the sexual state of the animal. It is true that sexual behaviour may not be essential for the maintenance of certain internal states, physio-logical regulation being adequate, but the same is also true of thermoregulation and some other typically homeostatic systems.

Satiation

According to Grossman (1967):

Homeostatic drive reduction can occur only when the behaviour of the organism has resulted in a physiological or biochemical process which re-establishes the homeostatic balance. Some learned or unlearned signals may temporarily terminate the drive-instigated behaviour. Such intermediary satiety mechanisms may be essential to bridge the time lag between remedial action and its final physiological effect . . .'

Although the same requirements (i.e. cessation of drive stimulation) apply to the nonhomeostatic drives, the basic processes are quite different. Since nonhomeostatic drives are elicited by specific external stimuli, drive reduction becomes a relatively simple and direct problem of removing the source of stimulation. No complex intermediary mechanisms are required, for the cessation of external stimulation produces immediate and direct effects on the central drive state (Grossman, 1967).

Obviously, when a male loses contact with the female, sexual behaviour may have to stop. However, an animal also has to stop eating if it exhausts the food available at a particular time. There are some species, such as the three-spined stickleback, in which the male chases away the female after fertilization of the eggs, but satiation of sexual behaviour by removal of external stimuli is certainly not the rule. The mechanisms that produce sexual satiation in rats have been investigated for many years, and will be discussed later in this chapter. From the feedback theory point of view, there is no essential differences between the mechanisms involved in the termination of sexual behaviour and those involved in the satiation of feeding or drinking.

Interaction of Internal and External Factors

Whereas homeostatic behaviour appears 'to be elicited by internal stimuli associated with states of disequilibrium, the role of physiological processes in sexual responses has a different emphasis. Here hormonal and neural events seem to prime the organism to produce a readiness to respond, but, to a large extent, it is external stimuli which elicit the reproductive behaviours' (Hokanson, 1969). A similar view is expressed by Grossman (1967).

Their claim is that the interaction of internal and external factors governing sexual behaviour is fundamentally different from that governing homeostatic behaviour, such as feeding and drinking. Although modulation of afferent stimuli by changes in hormonal balance has been demonstrated in some cases (e.g. Barraclough and Cross, 1963; Komisaruk et al., 1972), the evidence is quite insufficient to support the assertion that this type of mechanism is characteristic of sexual behaviour as opposed to homeostatic behaviour. Moreover, much depends upon the use of the term 'elicit'. To maintain that feeding is elicited by internal stimuli implies that appropriate external stimuli are always available. In fact, in those cases where the contribution of external stimuli to feeding or drinking tendency has been carefully measured (see McFarland and Sibly, 1975), it has been found that the roles of internal and external stimuli are comparable.

Attempts to find a global recipe for the interaction of internal and external factors controlling behaviour have been singularly unsuccessful (for a review see McFarland, 1971). From the point of view of systems analysis, however, it is necessary to have some way of representing the interaction in any particular case. This can be done and is discussed in some detail later in this chapter (pp. 632–635). At this stage we should distinguish between doctrinaire assumptions concerning the interaction between internal and external factors, and the empirical determination of the nature of such interactions in particular cases. Since the significance of these interactions in terms of the organization of behaviour is far reaching, no assumptions should be made about them without very careful consideration of the evidence.

Sexual Behaviour of the Rat

We leave, for the moment, the global questions of the animal's behaviour and apply the principles discussed above to one well-defined area of behaviour, the copulatory sequence of the male rat. The rat's sexual behaviour has been extensively studied and manipulated (for example, Larsson, 1956) and, as Brown (1974) points out, these studies accept the same descriptive standards and their results agree very well on a pattern of repeated mounts and intromissions leading to an ejaculation, which is followed by a long refractory period terminated by another series of mounts, intromissions, and ejaculations. This pattern may be repeated seven or eight times, before ejaculations, intromissions, and finally, mounting attempts cease. Quite apart from the importance of reproduction to species' survival and consequent questions about the design of this pattern, the structure of the copulatory sequence has attracted a great deal of investigation.

In the first place, the reliability of its description makes it a good benchmark, allowing comparison between studies and the pooling of information. Also, it is generally assumed that such observable variables as intromission frequency and mount latency reflect some motivational level or apportioning of motivational energy, so that they may be used to assess manipulations of the motivational condition of the animal. One part of the sequence, the refractory period, is unique in the rat's behavioural repertoire. Its anomalous feature is that, although a strong stimulus, such as tail-shock, can reduce the length of the refractory period, there remains an absolute, minimum period when sexual behaviour is completely 'switched off' after an ejaculation (Barfield and Sachs, 1968).

The time course of an ejaculatory series, the number of intromissions, average postejaculatory interval, etc., is fairly predictable (see esp. Brown, 1974). Thus, the components of the expected sequence can be varied and the resulting differences measured; for example, Larsson (1956) finds that increasing the interintromission intervals increases ejaculatory latency. In order to organize the various experimental and descriptive results and to make conclusions and predictions easier, Beach and others have produced verbal models, postulating an interaction between motivational and physiological mechanisms. A more formal model, designed to be mathematically stringent, (Freeman and McFarland, 1974) demonstrates the advantages and constraints of model building because, unlike the more vague verbal codifications, it uses the tested methods of control systems analysis.

The construction of a model begins by arranging the known variables according to some logical scheme of cause and effect, based on classical control theory, and then proceeds by identifying the operations which most economically produce the observed results. Thus, in this case, ejaculations must be preceded by intromissions, and after the ejaculation, there is always a delay before the next mount. Clearly, the hypothetical arrangement must allow not only for logical prerequisites (no intromissions without mounts, or no ejaculation without intromission) but for feedback, cumulative effects, and thresholds.

Beach's model (Beach, 1956) hypothesizes two systems, one controlling the level of the male's arousal (a motivational variable) and the other regulating the progress of the ejaculatory series itself. Freeman and McFarland discuss an arousal mechanism, an inhibitory mechanism, and an ejaculatory mechanism, which are related by explicit constants, operators, or proportional ratios of the experimental variables. The significant differences between the models is that the latter model is quantified: its relationships are expressed mathematically, so that the model can assign discrete values to its hypothetical connectors and generate specific, numerical predictions. In particular, this model takes advantage of the convention that block diagrams and equations, such as the normal series of differential equations, are equivalent descriptions of a system. As a result, the model is not limited to the distinction between numerical experimental data and qualitative controlling mechanisms. Instead, state variables such as inhibition and arousal become directly observable and manipulable.

Fig. 1 illustrates a simplified version of the RATSEX model of Freeman and McFarland (1974). It is worth noting, in view of our discussion above, that this model incorporates both negative and positive feedback loops, and looks

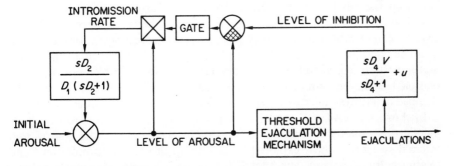

Fig. 1. Simplified version of the model of Freeman and McFarland (1974) for the copulatory behaviour of the male rat. Essentially, level of arousal is increased as a function (indicated by the formula) of intromission rate, provided the level of arousal is greater than the level of inhibition. Ejaculation occurs at a particular level of arousal (threshold), and the level of inhibition is a function (indicated by the formula) of the ejaculations

little different from models which have been proposed for the control of feeding (e.g. Toates, 1974) and drinking (e.g. McFarland and McFarland, 1968).

Once the model is adjusted to fit the experimental results fairly well, it can suggest which variables are most useful as diagnostic or predictive measures. For instance, given the assumed relationships between the three mechanisms of the model, the place of the individual ejaculatory series within the total number of series in the sequence is found to be an accurate predictor of observed variations in intromission frequency, ejaculation latency etc., of that series. Fig. 2 shows results from Larrson's (1956) analysis of rat sexual behaviour, compared with results predicted by the RATSEX model.

Albeit entirely theoretical, such models provide a clear demarcation of systems and assumptions and are more precise than models which remain verbal or pictorial. However, despite the convenience of visualizing the problem using block diagrams, and then solving the consequent state equations, and the mathematical accountability which this method provides, its very stringency limits its applications. In the first place, the model is not a unique description of the behaviour. Freeman and McFarland point this out when they modify sections of their basic model to better fit particular observations. In theory, there can never exist a perfect description, but in practice, flexibility becomes a liability when the quality of the data combined with intuition lead the designer into increasingly unrealistic variations. Compounding this problem is the unambiguous definition of the variables used which is an inherent property of a formal model. Intromissions and ejaculations are real events; the hypothetical mechanisms incorporating them may be labelled whatever the designer finds useful, but no conclusions about, say 'exhaustion' defined in such a model and any other formulation of the same concept in different terms can be made. The model exists only on the level of its information and can specifically predict changes only in its expressed variables. A less constrained type of model can accept combinations of physiological behavioural explanation; however, as we have seen, the conclusions one can draw from such formulations are necessarily less productive than they appear superficially. Furthermore, once an effect of any sort can be tabulated in terms consistent with the rest of the formal model, it can be adopted and used. For example, evidence that an aspect of the sexual motor pattern is controlled by the differential absorption by brain tissue of plasma testosterone could be incorporated into the model, but it would be stripped of its physiological content and take the form of, say, a time constant.

In short, the RATSEX model allows us to summarize a myriad of experimental descriptions in such a way that the exact nature of the control and internal structure can be explored by setting up theoretical formulations and relations. By organizing our knowledge within a logical framework, we can choose experiments that are precisely directed at the hypotheses.

Conclusion

In conclusion, we can see no justifiable basis for distinguishing between

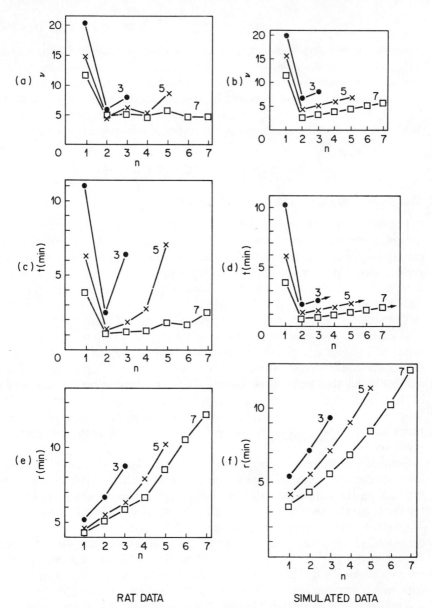

RAT DATA

SIMULATED DATA

Fig. 2. Aspects of the copulatory behaviour of the male rat: observed results compared with simulated behaviour. (a) Intromission frequency *versus* ejaculation number. Each curve is labelled by m, the number of ejaculations occurring in 1 h of observation. n is the ejaculation number. (Data from Larsson, 1956.) (b) Simulated version of (a). (From Freeman and McFarland, 1974.) (c) Ejaculatory latency *versus* ejaculation number. Curves labelled by m, the number of ejaculations occurring in the particular series. (Data from Larsson, 1956.) (d) Simulated version of (c). (From Freeman and McFarland, 1974.) (e) Durations of successive refractory periods. Curves labelled by m. (Data from Larsson, 1956.) (f) Simulated version of (e). (From Freeman and McFarland, 1974.)

homeostatic and non-homeostatic forms of behaviour control. The maintenance of the internal environment is not simply a matter of simple negative feedback processes, but of complex instructions between feedback, anticipatory, adaptive and optimizing control. In these respects the control of sexual behaviour is not fundamentally different from the control of feeding or drinking, as we propose to demonstrate in the remainder of this chapter.

THE STATE-SPACE APPROACH

Models and Principles in the Study of Behaviour

In recent years ethologists have become familiar with the use of models as aids in the explanation of behaviour. By their very nature models require a certain degree of abstraction, which needs to be justified in terms of empirical verification of predictions derived from the model. Thus behavioural models tend to be tied closely to a restricted set of phenomena and are not easily generalized to other aspects of behaviour.

The achievement of precision at the expense of generality, which is characteristic of model making, raises a number of questions concerning the direction in which quantitative behavioural work should develop. A danger of model making is that it is likely to lead to increasing fragmentation into a number of highly technical specialities. The alternative to increased precision is often thought to be increased generally with corresponding loss of rigour. This need not necessarily be so. It is possible to investigate general principles of behaviour without sacrificing theoretical rigour or quantitative empirical precision.

Generalizations from empirical observations can lead to the establishment of laws or rules. For example, if as a rule we find that the strength of a response depends on the summated value of all the stimuli present which are effective for the response, then we are justified in formulating a *Rule of Heterogeneous Summation*. Since this rule was formulated by Seitz (1940), it has received considerable empirical support from a variety of sources and situations (e.g. Heiligenberg *et al.*, 1972; Baerends and Kruijt, 1973). As has been pointed out by Dawkins and Dawkins (1974), rules permit reduction in the quantity of data without undue loss of information. Redundant data are those which do not contribute information because they are predictable from other data. For example, if an observer can state as a rule that activity A will invariably be followed by activity B, he can cut down the quantity of description by first stating the rule, and then discarding all records of B after occurrences of A. Such records of B would be redundant. Thus to look for redundancy is the same as to look for rules. Dawkins and Dawkins (1974) look for redundancy directly by calculating the uncertainty involved in a particular stream of behaviour.

One of the problems involved in model making in the behavioural sciences is that however much we learn about the causation of behaviour in one species, we seem to have to start at square one when we come to investigate another species. Apart from what we learn about methods of investigation, there seems to be little to carry over from one situation to another. Even in the case of the Rule of Heterogeneous Summation, which does seem to be widely applicable, we can never be sure, when we come to a new situation, that the rule will still apply. We have no reason to suppose that stimuli should summate, apart from the fact that they often do.

A set of empirically determined patterns or rules can be represented as a model. The reduction of descriptions to manageable proportions by the elimination of redundancy can be regarded as equivalent to the replacement of raw data by models which more briefly embody the informative parts of the data. However, a model should be more than an elegant redescription of the data. It should also embody an element of hypothesis, which introduces parsimony into the explanation, and from which testable predictions can be derived.

Models are essentially formalizations of empirical observations, and are relatively restricted in their applicability. Principles, on the other hand, are almost tautological in nature, and are general in their applicability. It is often asserted that we should not expect to find general principles in the study of behaviour, because behaviour is anarchic in nature. This pessimistic view hinders that search for general principles, which should underlie any thorough-going analysis of behaviour. Too often the fundamental principles are neglected, perhaps because their relevance to everyday laboratory problems is difficult to perceive, or because the scientist becomes carried away in his enthusiasm for new methods of data analysis. Before discussing, later in this chapter some of the ways in which modern techniques of systems analysis can be applied to the study of sexual behaviour, it may be instructive to consider some general principles.

The Stability of the Internal Environment

A general principle that is familiar to most biologists is expressed in Claude Bernard's dictum 'The stability of the internal environment is the condition for free and independent life.' This principle is very general in its applicability, applying to all species. It is essentially tautological, because what counts as a free and independent life is having a stable environment. Although many species do not have a stable internal environment, according to this principle, neither do they have a free and independent life.

The principle of stability of the internal environment has not been exploited to the full by students of behaviour, largely because they have failed to see its relevance. However, it should be appreciated that every activity must affect the stability of the internal environment, because every activity uses energy and necessitates various physiological regulatory mechanisms. Moreover, the performance of one activity postpones the performance of others, and therefore accentuates those aspects of instability that some of these other activities are designed to minimize. Therefore, the stability of the internal environment must act as a constraint on the way in which motivational systems are designed by natural selection. Consideration of stability is particularly important in the study of interactions between motivational systems, and in the relation between physiological regulation, acclimatization, and behaviour, which are three ways by which internal stability is maintained. These considerations are likely to be of considerable importance in the study of the interaction between the fast and slow processes involved in the control of sexual behaviour.

The internal environment of an animal can be viewed as a system of inter-acting variables, which is subject to influences resulting from changes in the animal's behaviour. The state of any biological system can in principle be characterized in terms of the state variables of the system, the minimal number of state variables necessary for a complete description of the system being the same as the number of degrees of freedom of the system (McFarland, 1971; Milsum, 1966; Rosen, 1970). The state of the internal environment can thus be described in terms of a finite number of physiological state variables, each of which can be represented as an axis of an n-dimensional hyperspace. We represent the state of the physiological environment as a point in an n-dimensional Euclidean space, the axes of which are independent.

In this space there are boundaries determined by the physical possibilities (e.g. negative hormonal levels are impossible), and by values of state variables beyond which the animal cannot live (e.g. certain temperature extremes are lethal). For convenience we might choose as the origin of this physiological space the ideal optimal point on each axis. That is the value of each state variable which is optimal in the biochemical or physiological sense. It may be that this is the state that would be attained were external conditions such as to allow the attainment of any of the states within the boundary. This physiological space is illustrated in Fig. 3.

The adaptive processes, which oppose displacement of physiological state, range between rapid physiological reflexes and slow-acting acclimatization mechanisms. There will generally be a spectrum of such processes, as illustrated in Fig. 4. A physiological displacement results from the sudden transportation to high altitude, and this is initially counteracted by increased rate of breathing. This type of physiological reflex involves high energy expenditure, and such high cost can be alleviated by means of relatively slow-acting acclimatization mechanisms. An increase in the number of circulating red blood corpuscles is the ultimate response involved in acclimatization to high altitude. Such acclimatization does involve some increased cost, but it alleviates the necessity for extreme behavioural or regulatory measures.

We can distinguish three types of process serving to maintain the physiological state of an animal within lethal boundaries: acclimatization, regulation, and behaviour. How do these three processes interact? Sibly and McFarland (1974) show that these processes will generally be vectorially additive, and are therefore alternatives. In the process of adaptation, various combinations of

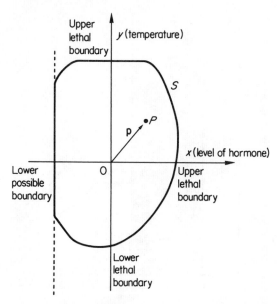

Fig. 3. Physiological space. An hypothetical two-dimensional space, with the origin 0 corresponding to optimal body temperature y and hormone level x. The physiological state is indicated by the position of the point, P, specified by its coordinates, or by the vector **p.** The boundary to the states in which the animal can survive, S, delineates the possible and lethal limits to the values of x and y. (From Sibly and McFarland, 1974.)

régulation, behaviour, and acclimatization may occur. Thus in adapting to high altitudes, the processes regulating respiration initially function with respect to their normal optima. Stability may be maintained through behavioural measures, such as avoiding heavy work, but gradually the individual will become acclimatized, so that the behavioural measures may be relaxed. At the same time regulation may occur directed towards new optima. As another example, consider a man moving from a cold to a hot climate. He may be able to expose himself to the sun, acclimatize quickly, and thus obviate any special behavioural measures. On the other hand, he may seek the shade, and thus postpone his acclimatization. These examples emphasize the point that the degree of regulation, acclimatization, or behavioural response, depends upon the degree of displacement or drift from the adapted or optimal state. The different processes act in parallel, their effects are additive, but at the same time the success of one mechanism obviates the necessity for another.

Our views on the stability of physiological state are not substantially different from the those of other biologists (e.g. Prosser, 1958) and we have outlined the situation as we see it in order to set the stage for a consideration of an important

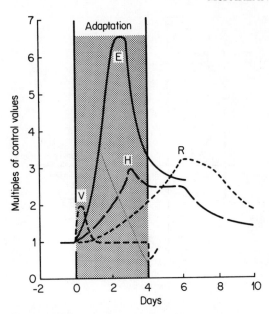

Fig. 4. Adaptive modifications in a man breathing rarefied air (p_{O_2} 85 mm Hg) during 4 days, followed by 6 additional days of deadaptation. V = lung ventilation, E = serum erythropoietin, H = rate of haemoglobin synthesis, R = fraction of reticulocytes in circulating blood. (From Adolph, 1972.)

concern; the stability of motivational systems and their relation to physiological state. A consequence of our representation of motivational space is that shifts in the origin of the space due to acclimatization will be reflected in behavioural changes. For example, an animal deprived of water may attempt to adapt by eating less food, seeking a cooler environment, and reducing its activity. It may sacrifice large portions of its behavioural repertoire, such as reproductive behaviour. The possibility that acclimatization may induce marked changes in motivational systems has received very little attention from research workers, though there is some support for this hypothesis in the field of acclimatization to temperature in fish. Many fish show temperature preferences related to acclimatization temperature (Fry and Hochachka, 1970).

We can deduce, from considerations of physiological regulation and acclimatization, that motivational systems are stable under certain conditions. Moreover, under such conditions motivational state can be deduced from the animal's behaviour, provided that the structure of the environment is known. In order for motivational state to be specified, two questions have to be answered: How many state variables are necessary to describe the state? What are the values of such variables at any particular point in time? The first question is discussed by McFarland and Sibly (1972) and Sibly and

McFarland (1974). They consider that the number of state variables required to specify the motivational state under any particular set of conditions can be determined from knowledge of the structure of the environment, provided that certain conditions hold.

In setting up this type of description, it is assumed (1) that the processes involved in physiological regulation, acclimatization and behaviour can be adequately represented in a Euclidean space; (2) that there are boundaries to this space which delineate all possible stable states; (3) that acclimatization involves a change in physiological state, and that the consequences of behaviour, physiological regulation, and acclimatization add vectorially to counteract imposed physiological displacement.

The relevance of these considerations to the study of sexual behaviour may not be immediately apparent. However, it should be recognized that, under certain conditions, sexual behaviour may be an expensive luxury in that it consumes energy and takes up valuable time that might be more profitably devoted to other behaviour. Let us represent (Fig. 5) the direct consequences of performing sexual behaviour by a vector s_p representing the rate of displacement induced by energy expenditure, etc.; and a vector s_b represents the displacement rate due to postponement of all other behaviour. The resultant s_r is the sum of these effects. Opposing this resultant is a vector s_o representing the combined effect of all the other behavioural and physiological processes, such as feeding, thermoregulation, etc. Any drift resulting from sexual behaviour can be corrected by a component of s_c. However, we can imagine conditions where the 'sphere of influence' of these other processes is insufficient to counteract the effects of sexual behaviour. The theory of Sibly and MacFarland (1974) is

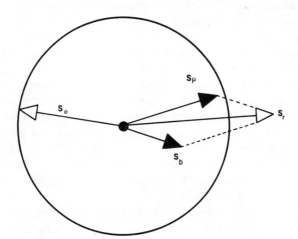

Fig. 5. Vectors in physiological space representing possible effects of sexual behaviour. s_p = sexual performance vectors, s_b = postponement vector, s_r = resultant vector, s_o = other vectors (resultant)

quite explicit as to what will happen in this type of situation. There will be a slow shift of the sphere of influence (more correctly called the regulatory subspace) to another part of the state space, where the consequences of sexual behaviour are not so deleterious, or where the other aspects of behaviour are better able to contain the consequences of sexual behaviour. In other words, acclimatization will take place, so as to minimize the disruptive consequences of sexual behaviour. The term acclimatization is merely a convenience under which to group all slow-acting adjustment, including such annual events as hibernation, migration, and the reproductive cycle. In terms of our example (Fig. 5), there is a region of the state space where sexual behaviour is 'discouraged' (by attenuation of motivational command vectors, see Sibly and McFarland, 1974) and another region where it is facilitated. An annual cycle between these two regions will develop in conjunction with, and sometimes as a consequence of, seasonal climatic changes, etc. This type of formulation, therefore, reaches similar conclusions to those traditionally found in the study of sexual behaviour, but at the same time it provides a means by which sexual behaviour can be integrated with other aspects of the animal's behaviour and physiology. In particular, it permits us to envisage the possibility of accounting for the complete time-budget of the animal in terms of a cost–benefit analysis (McFarland, 1970).

The Principle of Incompatibility

A well-known behavioural tautology is that 'drive can, in its widest sense, be defined as the complex of internal and external states and stimuli leading to a given behaviour' (Thorpe, 1951, 1956). Although behaviour is (tautologically) caused by its causal factors, only one type of behaviour can occur at a time, provided we categorize the behaviour we observe into mutually exclusive classes. McFarland and Sibly (1975) argue that any model of the motivational (i.e. reversible) processes governing the behaviour of an animal can be represented by means of isoclines in a multidimensional causal factor space. The argument is axiomatic, based upon the two prime assumptions: (1) that it is always possible to classify the behavioural repertoire of a species in such a way that the classes are mutually exclusive in the sense that the members of different classes cannot occur simultaneously, and (2) these incompatible actions are uniquely determined by a particular set of causal factors. The isoclines join all points in the space which represent a given 'degree of competitiveness' of a particular 'candidate' for overt behavioural expression. The competition between candidates is an inevitable consequence of the fact that animals cannot 'do more than one thing at a time'.

When we come to the problem of how the various incompatible activities are related to the motivational state of the animal, we can see that each is controlled by a set of causal factors. The causal factors will include variables describing the animal's 'estimate' of the stimuli present in the external environment (e.g. cues to the availability of food), and variables relevant to the animal's internal state. McFarland and Sibly (1975) represent the total motivational

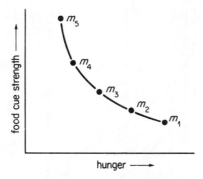

Fig. 6. Feeding tendency as a function of cue strength and hunger. The feeding tendency is the same for points $m_1, \ldots m_5$, and the line joining these points is a motivational isocline. (From McFarland and Sibly, 1975.)

state in a *causal factor space*, in which there is an axis corresponding to each class of causal factor, with the classes defined in terms of some suitable arbitrary criterion. For example, an (hypothetical) animal might have a motivational state that can be represented in a two-dimensional space (Fig. 6), with one axis corresponding to the degree of hunger, and the other to the strength of food cues (i.e. the animal's estimate of the availability of food). Thus the causal factor space has axes corresponding to each class of causal factor. It is clear that there are likely to be a number of motivational states that will map to the same feeding tendency. For example, an animal may have a high hunger but low cue strength (m_1), giving the same feeding strength as if it had a low hunger and high cue strength (m_5). The line joining all those motivational states ($m_1 \ldots m_5$) which give the same behavioural tendency, is an example of a *motivational isocline*.

A simple example is provided by the work of Baerends et al., (1955) on the courtship of the male guppy *Lebistes reticulatus*. The tendency of the male to attack, flee from, and behave sexually towards the female can be gauged from the colour patterns characteristic of each motivational state. In Fig. 7 increasing sexual motivation is plotted as an index of colour change along the abscissa. The effectiveness of the female in eliciting courtship increases with her size and is plotted on the ordinate. The points plotted on the graph represent the relationship between the measures of internal state and external stimulation at which particular patterns of behaviour are observed. If the patterns, p, si, and s are taken to represent increasing values of response strength, and the scaling of the ordinate is taken at face value, then the isoclines obtained represent closely those that would result from multiplication of internal and external factors. In this case the method of quantification is somewhat arbitrary, the scaling on the abscissa depending on the association of the different colour patterns

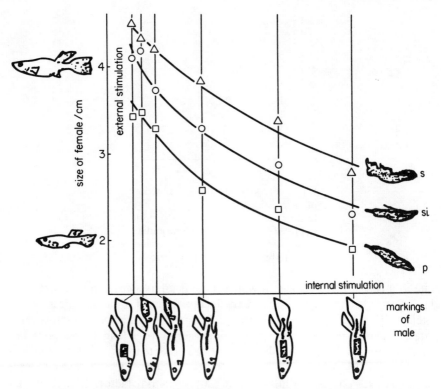

Fig. 7. The influence of the strength of external stimulation (measured by the size of the female) and the internal state (measured by the colour pattern of the male) in determining the courtship behaviour of male guppies. Each curve represents the combination of external stimulus and internal state producing posturing (p), sigmoid intention movements (si), and fully developed sigmoid (s) respectively. (From Baerends *et al.*, 1955.)

with the relative frequency of activities characteristic of sexual tendency and that on the ordinate being arbitrarily linear. Nevertheless, Fig. 7 is a good example of the type of representation that we have in mind. McFarland and Sibly (1975) discuss various ways in which arbitrary scaling can be overcome, but for our present purposes it is sufficient to note only the principle involved.

The importance of motivational isoclines is that their shape is a design feature, which is intimately related to the animal's ecological circumstances. Any decision-making process, in which there is 'totally decidable logical preference', can be expressed as a set of isoclines, or 'indifference curves' (Kaufmann, 1968). The essence of the argument is that, because animal behaviour can always be classified into mutually exclusive and exhaustive categories (i.e. the animal is always doing something), a totally decidable logical preference always exists, albeit inherent in the design of the decision-making machinery (McFarland and Sibly, 1975).

Corresponding to every trajectory in causal factor space is an overt behaviour sequence. Each trajectory crosses a series of regions bounded by the isoclines, so that a corresponding series of changes in behaviour results from any particular trajectory. However, the characteristics of a trajectory are determined largely by the consequences of the behaviour, but the characteristics of the corresponding behaviour sequence are determined jointly by the path of the trajectory and the shape of the isoclines which the trajectory crosses. The trajectories vary from occasion to occasion, but the isocline shape is a design feature, moulded by natural selection, and presumably adapted to the animal's natural way of life. Knowledge of the shape of the isoclines, therefore, is the key to understanding the way in which a particular behavioural system works. Moreover, the hypothesis that the decision-rules, which we represent by isoclines, are designed by natural selection to produce optimal behaviour sequences, is a true hypothesis in that it is testable. Sibly and McFarland (1976) have shown how optimality theory can be used to predict the families of behaviour sequences that should correspond to any hypothesis about the design of decision-rules. Such predictions can be tested by direct observation of behaviour.

THE STOCHASTIC APPROACH

Variability in the behaviour of animals necessitates the use of methods capable of detecting regularities in data, estimating the state of mechanisms in the face of uncertainty, and controlling processes which are subject to random disturbance. Many techniques have been developed in attempting to handle such problems in the physical sciences (see Bendat and Piersol, 1966). Some of these have also been applied in the biological sciences (Milsum, 1966). In behavioural studies there are examples of a wide variety of approaches (Dawkins and Dawkins, 1974; Heiligenberg, 1974; Metz, 1974; Slater, 1973). We are here concerned solely with time-series analysis as applied to behaviour (McFarland, 1971; Lloyd, 1974).

Variability in behavioural data is a phenomenon frequently encountered by research workers. Most commonly it is due to failure to control for random fluctuations in external variables. In some cases variability persists even when careful controls are incorporated into the experimental design. This has led some workers to assume that behavioural systems are by their very nature stochastic processes. An alternative view is that behavioural systems are basically deterministic, and that the problem of variability should be met by attempts to identify the source of the variation and then to specify its cause. This is the aim of time-series analysis. An elementary introduction to this topic can be found in McFarland (1971).

Time-Series Analysis of the Sexual Behaviour of the Hamster

From the sample record of the sexual behaviour of the male hamster illustrated in Fig. 8, one can abstract, for instance, the mean number of mounts or any

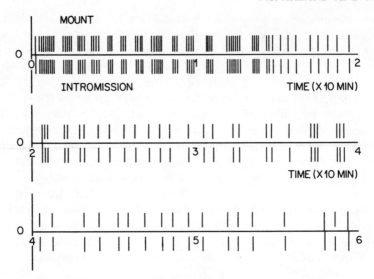

Fig. 8. The pattern of mounts and intromissions of a male hamster in a 1 h session. This particular record is unusual because of the perfect correspondence between mounts and intromissions. In other words, the animal succeeded in intromitting each time he mounted

of the simple measures used to describe rat sexual behaviour, as discussed on pp. 622–624. However, none of these measures adequately describes what we inituitively recognize as the periodicity of the record, nor do they provide a concise, inclusive description that covers the entire sequence. That sort of characterization requires the construction and testing of a formal model, in which must be incorporated a great deal of basic information. The alternative methods of systems description discussed below, namely the techniques of time-series analysis, are designed to isolate the variability of different elements of the sequence in time and frequency, and in relation to one another. This produces a probabilistic rather than a deterministic explanation; we now treat each sexual event not as an element of a block diagram but as a separate, continuous function in time.

The male hamster's sexual behaviour is very like the rat's except that the time constants differ and the refractory period is much shorter (a matter of seconds rather than minutes), and not distinguished by any unusual behaviour. Also, ejaculations are difficult to distinguish from intromissions, and in the experiments reported here they are not recorded, since there does not seem to be any consistent index of their occurrence.

The data were collected as part of a study of male and female preferences for mates. The hamsters were kept in individual cages and maintained under a 10 h dark/14 h light night–day cycle. All the animals were descended from Mesocricetus auratus *stock brought from Syria in 1965, and were approximately five months old. The male subjects were tested for an hour once a week, for up to six weeks, with an ovariectomized female primed with oestradiol benzoate and progesterone. The tests were made just after the room lights went out, under dim red light in an 18" × 24" × 18" Perspex box. The males were never tested twice with the same female. During the test period, the animal's behaviour, divided into 20 possible categories, was continuously recorded by the observer, using an electronic event-recorder on-line to a laboratory computer which transcribed the recording onto paper tape as code words with matching times. The paper tape was edited and analysed at the Oxford University 1906a computer. The analysis programs are modifications of Lloyd's (1974), written in ALGOL 60 and using graphical packages and NAG library routines.*

In Appendix 1 we report on the analysis of observations on the sexual behaviour of hamsters, by means of time-series correlation techniques. Correlation methods have long been used in behavioural analysis, particularly various types of sequential and temporal correlations. These methods have been criticized (McFarland, 1971) on the grounds that no account is taken of the fact that behaviour can vary in intensity as well as in duration or frequency. In the analysis of meal patterns, for example, correlations between meal sizes and meal intervals often give Poisson distributions, implying that successive meals are independent. As energy regulation is known to be accurate in the species studied, and must ultimately be geared to the nutrient properties of the diet, it is obvious that both meal size and intervals between meals must jointly determine the meal pattern. The correlational techniques of time-series analysis take into account joint functions of temporal and intensity factors, and their application to meal-pattern analysis shows this (McFarland, 1971; Lloyd, 1974; Slater, 1973).

The results of the analysis of hamster sexual behaviour are less easy to interpret than those of meal patterns, because we do not have an intuitive understanding of the sexual equivalent of 'nutrient'. However, the analysis does go some way to indicate the rhythmic and arhythmic aspects of copulatory behaviour.

Fig. 9 shows autocorrelations and crosscorrelations for the data shown in Fig. 8. The sample functions or types of behaviour are isolated and paired: mounts and intromission, head grooming and grooming the ano-genital area, and sniffing the bottom of the box and sniffing the female's ano-genital area. The last pairing is done as a check of the correlation technique, and it will not be referred to here.

The results for all seventy data records are highly variable. Furthermore, no single animal is highly consistent. Nevertheless, some conclusions can be made.

(1) Although no one animal can be characterized by all his records, males can be classified by such criteria as degree of periodicity, presence of trend, or number of significant peaks. In other words, an individual may show trend in all the correlations of all his records, but the appearance of the curves may be markedly different in other respects.

(2) The appearance of the curves could not be predicted by knowing the total number of events used to form the correlation function.

(3) In general, the crosscorrelation functions appeared random; thus, they

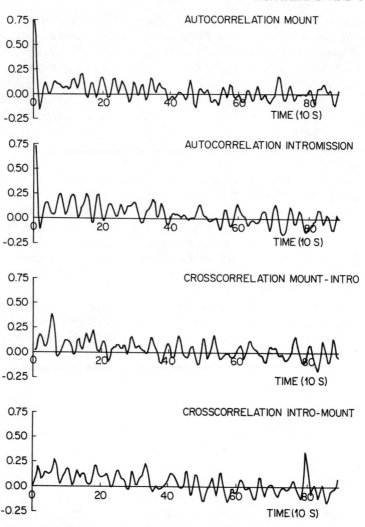

Fig. 9. Autocorrelation and crosscorrelation functions for mounts and intromissions for the animal whose record is shown in Fig. 8

cannot be used to draw positive conclusions about interactions between the different behavioural processes. However, in some cases there are significant crosscorrelations, especially at particular displacements.

(4) Apart from short displacements, neither sexual behaviour nor grooming behaviour values show much periodicity or significant variation from the random pattern. Nevertheless, a substantial minority of individual records (generally belonging to a smaller group of animals as mentioned in (3) above) show significant peaks (coefficient > 0.25), which appear either as isolated peaks or as part of a series of such peaks appearing regularly over the possible

displacements. The first implies the presence of an autoregressive effect near that particular displacement, the second the existence of some periodic process.

(5) The overall shape of the curves may be classified into three types, as shown in Fig. 10.

(6) The overall shape of the grooming autocorrelation functions tends to

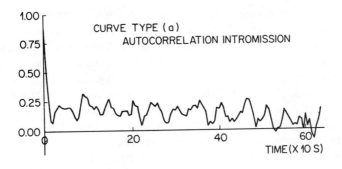

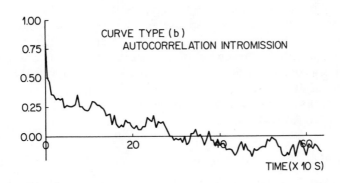

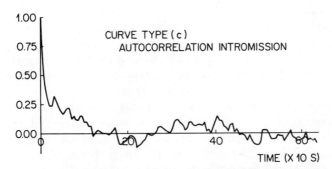

Fig. 10. Three general curve types emerge from the correlation analysis, within reliable displacement increments: (a) a steady average amplitude; (b) a declining level overall; and (c) fluctuating levels. All these types may include periodic elements

resemble that of the intromission curve rather than that of the mount curve. Since grooming the anogenital region is coupled with mounting, this is an unexpected result.

(7) The appearance of the mount curve tends to be more random than that of the intromission curve for those records that were not random-looking overall.

In Appendix 2 we give an outline of the application of power spectral analysis to the sexual behaviour of hamsters. The power (mean square value) of a time-fluctuating variable may be expressed in terms of an amplitude probability distribution. There may be various underlying frequencies represented in the data, and the variation of power with frequency is a measure of the 'power spectrum' of the signal (McFarland, 1971). In the behavioural context, the identification of causal relationship may be to some extent arbitrary, and correlations between different behaviour patterns can be used to determine the nature of their mutual interaction. From the application of power spectral analysis in Appendix 2, it appears that intromissions are controlling mounts in the copulatory behaviour of the male hamster. In Appendix 3 this conclusion is checked by means of impulse–response analysis.

The application of impulse–response identification to biological data was pioneered by McFarland and Lloyd (1972) and an introductory account is given in Lloyd (1974). The aim of this approach is to identify causal relationships within a complex system, by calculating the result that would be expected if one part of the system were to give a 'kick' or 'impulse' to the other. Preliminary results of applying; this approach to the analysis of sexual behaviour are reported in Appendix 3.

Applications of Time-Series Analysis

In conclusion, the methods of time-series analysis and model building expose relationships implicit in the raw data. The former method does so by isolating real effects from random variations and the latter by defining an optimal theoretical mechanism to explain the data. Although neither technique allows us to extend our arguments to include physiological factors such as sperm generation or hormonal release, time-series analysis provides a set of reliable measures to use as behavioural assays for physiological manipulation. Similarly, we are left without a justification for the pattern's existence in the first place. However, it is possible not only to speculate but also to test hypothetical explanations, again using the results of time-series analysis. Current research in this laboratory is directed at this functional question, using the analysis of behaviour to draw inferences about the adaptive nature of the copulatory sequence. Other work has shown directly that behaviour can control reproductive success.

First, experiments by Adler (see this volume Chapter 20) and others have established that at least two patterned features of the rat's first ejaculatory series affect the female's hormonal response. If the female has received an ejaculation and then receives an intromission before the expected refractory period has elapsed, the number of sperm found in her reproductive tract is far less than that found when normal stimulation is received (Adler and Zoloth, 1970).

Intromissions before the ejaculation are necessary to trigger the female's hormonal system to prepare for pregnancy (Adler, 1969); and, finally, if female rats receive an experimentally limited number of intromissions, these intromissions are more effective in inducing pseudopregnancy if they come at long, rather than short, intervals (Edmonds et al., 1972).

In addition, female sexual 'satiety' may influence the design of the male sequence. In both rats (Hardy and DeBold, 1973) and hamsters (Carter, 1973), an hour of vaginal stimulation by the male or some experimental means dramatically reduces the female's receptivity to a subsequent male. Without such stimulation, the female would remain oestrus for up to 12h. The presence of the male or mounting behaviour alone does not produce this exhaustion effect.

Considering these disparate results, we may arrive at two possible and not exclusive explanations for the temporal patterning of sexual behaviour. The stochastic analysis shows some male hamsters to be highly random, although they are capable of a high number of mounts and intromissions. The female's requirement for minimal stimulation, which is optimal if spread out in time, may not be satisfied by a non-periodic sequence, particularly if the male finds the mating situation so fearful that he may show shortened or abnormal refractory periods. In other words, providing the necessary minimum may be a test, requiring the male to be unflustered and coordinated. This test discriminates against young, unproven animals and favours experienced males who have survived long enough to have mated before.

Another hypothesis is that the pattern is the most efficient way for the male to ensure that his sperm, rather than rivals', contribute to the offspring. In theory, the female can accumulate sperm for hours, and pregnant wild Peromyscus carry litters with many fathers. It may be of advantage to the male hamster to fertilize all the eggs, and, in any case, he must prevent another male from mounting the female during his own refractory period, because the sperm from his ejaculation would be eliminated. In addition, if the male can keep the female to himself by repeatedly undertaking ejaculatory series, he can exhaust her so that she will not tolerate the advances of yet another male.

Unfortunately, no studies have been made of social interaction or competition between hamsters of the same sex in a mating situation; results of that type might point to completely different hypothetical justifications. However, the preliminary results of preference tests in this laboratory show that females who have mated with the experimental males show preferences which are uncorrelated with the preferences of females who have never seen the males. These behavioural responses may reflect the physiological options open to the female, and analysis seeking a connection between aspects of the males' performance during the mating segment of the experiment and the female's choice is underway.

Summary and Conclusion

In conclusion, we reiterate our intention that this chapter should be seen as an exploratory forage into the possible applications of systems analysis to sexual behaviour. We reiterate our view that there is no justifiable basis for distinguishing between homeostatic and non-homeostatic forms of behaviour control. The control of any behaviour is extremely complex, involving feedback, anticipatory, adaptive, and optimizing control. In these respects the control of sexual behaviour is not fundamentally different from the control of feeding, drinking or any other aspect of behaviour.

We have outlined three aspects of systems analysis, each of which has its advantages and disadvantages. It should not be thought that these exhaust the relevance of systems analysis to the study of sexual behaviour. Indeed, the major question that emerges from our studies of the copulatory behaviour of the rat and hamster, is why these control systems have been designed in such a particular, and peculiar, fashion. Recent developments in the application of systems analysis to evolutionary theory, especially the application of optimality theory to questions of design of life-histories and of motivational systems (Sibly and McFarland, 1976; McFarland, 1976; Leon, 1976), suggest that it may soon be possible to tackle this type of question.

Appendix 1

Correlation Functions

As the RATSEX model demonstrates, the rats sexual behaviour varies in a predictable fashion according to the total number of ejaculations and the current ejaculation number. Without being able to use the ejaculation as a marker, can we produce a statistical expression of the time-dependence of sexual events?

If we take a sample function of a process and denote it $x(t)$, we may describe the autocorrelation function as the expected value of the product of two variables of this function (Cooper and McGillem, 1967):

$$R_x(t_1, t_2) = E[x(t_1)x(t_2)]$$

It is convenient to regard this sample function as stationary and thus independent of t_0, the time origin. In the case of analysis of sexual behaviour, this assumption is unreasonable, but useful since one objective is to assess the amount of trend. For a stationary function,

$$R_x(t_1 + T, t_2 + T) = E[x(t_1 + T))x(t_2 + T)]$$

which, by setting $T = -t$, becomes

$$R_x(0, t_2 - t_1) = E[x(o)x(t_2 - t_1)]$$

If $\tau = t_2 - t_1$, then we arrive at the usual formulation

$$R_x(\tau) = E[x(t_1)x(t_1 + \tau)]$$

In practice, we must deal with finite records of some unknown process, so that instead of the formal definition

$$R_x(\tau) = \lim_{T \to \infty} \frac{1}{T} \int_{-T}^{T} x(t)x(t + \tau)dt$$

we must use the estimated correlation function

$$\hat{R}_x(\tau) = \frac{1}{T - \tau} \int_{0}^{T-\tau} x(t)x(t + \tau)dt$$

where the maximum time displacement τ is much less than T.

Furthermore, if the data are in digital form, we must calculate the discrete estimate

$$\hat{R}_x(n\Delta t) = \frac{1}{N - n} \sum_{k=0}^{N-n} x_k x_{k+n} \qquad\qquad n = 0,1,2,\ldots,m$$

where m is much less than N. The summation can be divided by $1/N$, which is easier to compute but does introduce a bias (Bendat and Piersol, 1966).

Some important properties of the autocorrelation function which help in its interpretation are:

(1) that if the sample function has a constant component, $\hat{R}_x(t)$ also has a constant component;

(2) that if the sample function has a periodic component, then $\hat{R}_x(t)$ has a periodic component of the same frequency;

(3) that the mean square value of the sample function is given by $\hat{\psi}_x^2 = \hat{R}_x(0)$, since $\psi_x^2 = \lim_{T \to \infty} \int_{-T}^{T} x^2(t)dt$.

Thus a normalized estimate for the correlation function may be obtained by dividing

$$\hat{R}_x(n\Delta t) \text{ by } \hat{R}_x(0);$$

(4) that when the mean of the sample function is equal to zero, the correlation function for non-periodic data will tend to zero over long displacements.

The crosscorrelation function of sample functions $x(t)$ and $y(t)$ may be defined as

$$R_{xy}(\tau) = E[x_1 y_2]$$

or

$$R_{xy}(\tau) = \lim_{T \to \infty} \frac{1}{T} \int_{-T}^{T} x(t)y(t + \tau)dt$$

As with the autocorrelation function, we must deal with single discrete records, so the estimated crosscorrelation function is defined, at time displacements of $n = 0, 1, 2, \ldots, m$ and $N \gg m$,

$$\hat{R}_{xy}(n\Delta t) = \frac{1}{N - n} \sum_{k=0}^{N-n} x_k y_{k+n}$$

Also as above, it is more convenient, although inaccurate, to divide by $1/N$. The function

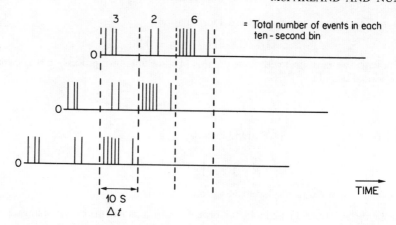

Fig. A 1. Successive displacements of the same record of an event type form the autocorrelation function. The segment here shows the formation of values for the first increment (0–10 s), taken against subsequent increments by shifting the record against itself

may be normalized by division by

$$\sqrt{\hat{R}_x(0)}\,\sqrt{\hat{R}_y(0)}$$

Some properties of the crosscorrelation function are:

(1) That $\hat{R}_{xy}(0)$ does not represent the mean square value of the sample function;

(2) that the maximum of the function does not necessarily occur at $\tau = 0$, although the maximum, wherever it appears, cannot be greater than $|\hat{R}_{xy}(\tau)| = [\hat{R}_x(0)\hat{R}_y(0)]^{1/2}$

Fig. A1 illustrates the general method of finding correlation functions in this type of analysis. Each record is divided into $n\,\Delta t$ units. Here $\Delta t = 10$ s, and the value of, say, $x(t)$ at $k\Delta t$ contains the number of events that occurred at that interval. In the case of autocorrelations, the value of $x(t)$ at all discrete increments from $x(0\Delta t)$ is multiplied by the values at all time differences varying from 0 to m. For crosscorrelation, the values of $x(t)$ are multiplied by the corresponding values of $y(t)$ at all time displacements. The two records may be pictured as shifting against each other: for $\hat{R}_{xy}(\tau)$ correlations, $y(t)$ is shifted along the values of $x(t)$, and for $\hat{R}_x(\tau)$, $x(t)$ is moved with reference to itself.

To prevent falling off the end of the record, the greatest time difference τ (or $n\Delta t$) cannot exceed $N/2$, nor can the increment of t be greater than $N/2\Delta t$. In fact, to prevent biasing by averaging unequal numbers of points, it is advisable to take $m < < N$, as defined above. However, to see the effects of trend it is useful to take the calculations as far as possible into the data. Therefore, the details of correlation functions derived in this study should be evaluated with caution at long time displacements, although their general appearance is of interest.

Appendix 2

Power Spectral Density Functions

As can be seen from Fig. 9, there tends to be no consistent synchronization between the different correlation functions formed from the same record split into its behavioural 'processes'. In order to highlight any frequency dependencies, such as periodicities which may not be obvious, we may take advantage of an important property of correlation functions: they can be transformed from the time domain to the frequency domain by using a Fourier transform. This relationship is defined by

$$G_x(\omega) = 2 \int_{-\infty}^{\infty} R_x(\tau) e^{-j2\pi\omega\tau} d\tau$$

which for real-time functions

$$= 4 \int_0^{\infty} R_x(\tau) \cos 2\pi\omega\tau \, d\tau$$

because $R_x(\tau)$ is an even function of τ (Bendat and Piersol, 1966). $G_x(\omega)$ is the spectral density of the function $x(t)$.

The Fourier transform of $x(t)$ itself is

$$X(j\omega) = \int x(t) e^{-j\omega t} dt$$

which separates $x(t)$ into a series of sinusoids with amplitudes $(\frac{1}{2}\pi) X(j\omega) d\omega$. $(\frac{1}{2})\pi) |X(j\omega)| d\omega$ is the amplitude of the function lying in the frequency range ω to $\omega + \Delta\omega$. Because the mean square value of $x(t)$ represents in energy in the time domain, we may say

$$\int x^2(t) dt = \frac{1}{2}\pi \int |X(j\omega)|^2 d\omega$$

since the right-hand side expressed the energy in the frequency domain. Thus the spectral density of $x(t)$ can be defined as the rate of change of the mean square value with frequency (Bendat and Piersol, 1966).

This analysis used the power spectral density or intensity function to show the frequency properties of the data. This function is defined as

$$I_x(\omega) = \frac{\sigma^2}{\pi} G_x(\omega)$$

The Fourier series expresses the sample function as a series of harmonic terms. Thus, the Fourier transform cannot contain any components of a lower frequency than the function length, but it may contain frequencies higher than the resolution period chosen for the calculations. The Nyquist frequency

$$f_c = 1/2\Delta t$$

is the point where these higher frequencies will start folding back into the lower frequencies, distorting the results. For this reason, the estimate of the power spectral density must be filtered (Bendat and Piersol, 1966).

Two interesting properties of the power spectral density are:

(1) that a sine wave has a power spectral density of infinite amplitude at its frequency but of zero amplitude over the rest of the spectrum. The estimate of the power spectral density used in these analyses truncated this true amplitude;

(2) that the significance or confidence limits of spectral peaks can be calculated. If the sample function $x(t)$ is taken to have zero mean and variation σ^2, then the spectral density $(G_x(\omega))$ is distributed as the sum of squares of the Fourier coefficients a and b, since the Fourier series of $x(t)$ is

$$\sum_{j=1}^{\infty} a_j \sin jx + \frac{1}{2} b_0 + \sum b_j \cos jx$$

and a and b are normally distributed, independent, and have variance $\sigma^2/2\pi$. Thus,

$$2 G_x(\omega) = \frac{2\pi(a^2 + b^2)}{\sigma^2} = \frac{2\pi I_x(\omega)}{\sigma^2}$$

is distributed as χ^2 with two degrees of freedom, and

$$E[G_x(\omega)] = 1$$

$$\text{var } G_x(\omega) = E^2[G_x(\omega)] = 1$$

The same relationship holds for $I_x(\omega)$; accordingly, we may calculate to the 95% confidence limit by multiplying the mean of the spectrum by 4.34 (Lloyd, 1974).

The power crosspectral density function is the Fourier transform of the crosscorrelation function, multiplied by σ^2/π. It may be described as the average product of $x(t)$ and $y(t)$ within a narrow frequency band between ω and $\omega + \Delta\omega$, divided by the frequency interval (Bendat and Piersol, 1966) and multiplied by the variance over π.

Because of the limitations of the estimate of the power spectrum, low frequencies, such as trend, can corrupt their neighbouring harmonics if they have a large amplitude. However, as in the case of the correlation analysis, it does not seem useful to undertake removal of these components, especially since in this initial identification we are seeking to describe the long-term as well as short-term parts of the sexual sequence. For this reason, two types of power spectra are calculated separately on each data record: one, the transform of the correlations reported above, goes halfway through the data, and the second through only one quarter of the data. Comparison of the results shows the effect of trend on its neighbouring frequencies, which are often present in the second power spectrum. An illustration of this comparison is shown in Fig. A2.

For all the data records, the results expressed in the frequency domain are much less variable than shown by the correlation analysis, and although only a minority of spectra show highly significant peaks, most records contain frequency relationships significant at the $\alpha = 0.05$ level.

(1) Results for all behaviour types tend to show a highly significant trend. Intromission shows much more energy at low frequencies, however.

(2) The next harmonic which appears in nearly all the records corresponds to an interval of 8–10; this is especially true for mounts, intromissions, and grooming of the ano-genital area. Crosspectra show the same periodicity.

(3) For a substantial minority of the records, a significant peak in the frequency of both mounts and intromission appears at a period of 30 s.

(4) The shape of the spectra is approximately the same for each individual record, regardless of the behaviour or combinations of behaviour in question.

Appendix 3

Impulse–Response Determination

Another method of system indentification, which is less direct and more artificial because of the assumptions it makes about the data, is impulse–response analysis. The advantage of impulse analysis is that the results clearly differentiate between a dependent and an independent variable. The crosscorrelation and crosspower spectral density functions implicitly contain this sort of information, but their interpretation is not straightforward, although inferences may be drawn. In fact from the ones obtained above, we can conclude that intromissions are the controlling variable and mounts the dependent variable. Impulse–response analysis can be used to check this conclusion.

Impulse–response analysis attempts to describe the effect that the system has on input signals by comparing the input to the system and the output from the system in time. If we make the input x_{k-t} constant from i to $i + 1$, where i is an increment in time, and consider the expected output y' at the kth interval of time, then

$$y'_k = x_{k-i}w_i$$
$$i = -\infty$$

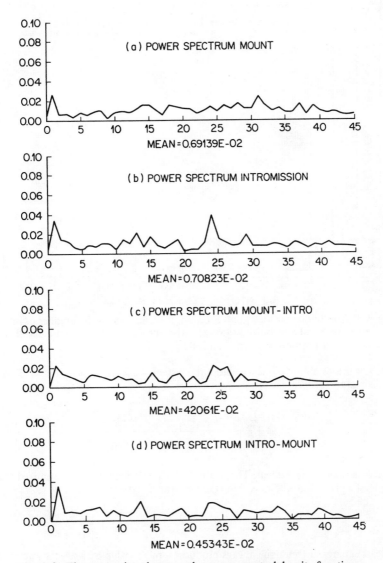

Fig. A 2. The comparison between the power spectral density function for half the length of the record and for one quarter the length (here for mounts) demonstrates that the overall trend of the record, which is significant, does not appear in the shorter function (a). Thus, it is unnecessary to remove the trend so long as it can be observed. Other examples of power spectral are also shown (b), (c), (d)

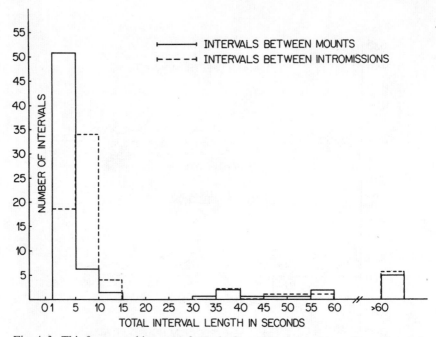

Fig. A 3. This frequency histogram for a single session shows the number of intervals between mounts and intromissions falling within the lengths shown. Note that there are no intervals of a duration between 15 and 30 s

where w is the weighting sequence within the system, which we hope to define. This value w_s is defined by the formula

$$w_s = \frac{\sum\limits_{k=s}^{n} y_k x_{k-s} - \sum\limits_{k=s}^{n} \sum\limits_{i=1+s}^{k} w_i x_{k-i} x_{k-s} T}{\sum\limits_{k=s}^{n} x_{k-s} x_{k-s} T}$$

where T is the time increment. The method of analysis is to find an optimized value of w, by least squares fit technique, using the performance index

$$PI = \sum_{k=-\infty}^{\infty} (y_k - y'_k)^2 = \sum_{k=-\infty}^{\infty} \left(y_k - \sum_{i=-\infty}^{\infty} x_{k-i} w_i\right)^2$$

The least squares fit technique always produces a relationship between the two variables x and y, even though they may be from two entirely independent processes. The performance index which gives the total sums of squares of the difference between the predicted and actual output of the system, which represents the residual error not covered by the estimate, allows us to assess the success of the fit. Furthermore, as Lloyd (1974) has proved, the estimate reaches its optimum when the rate of change of the slope of these confidence values becomes approximately equal to zero. Thus, the interpretation of the numerical results of this method is quite easy.

Using this technique it was found that mounting has a significant ($= 0.05$) effect on intromissions, no doubt because the animal must mount in order to intromit. However,

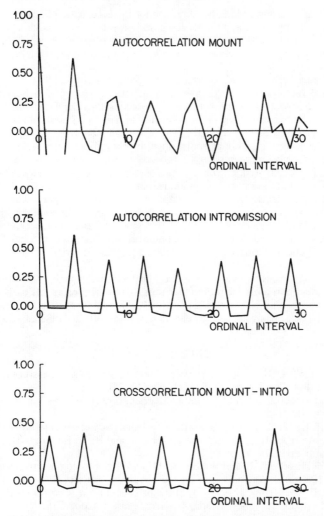

Fig. A 4. This figure shows the correlation functions for the session discussed in Fig. A 3. The abscissa, which in Fig. 9 represented time, here shows the successive numbers of the intervals counted from the first interval between events. The values of these intervals, instead of being the number of events within a time bin, are the total duration of each interval

contrary to expectations from the correlation results, an intromission seems to have no effect on the subsequent mounts.

Correlations of Interval Length

So far we have not uncovered any effects which are nearly as deterministic as intuition and the analysis of the rat data would predict. Since the impulse response analysis shows little controlling relationship in either direction for the occurrence of mounts or of intromissions, we will turn to an analysis of the gaps between events to seek a deterministic element which might impose periodicity on the events themselves. An indication that this is a promising approach is shown in Fig. A3, where a histrogram of interval frequencies is plotted.

Using the same techniques of correlation and power spectral density but not using a strict time base, this analysis finds the average product of the *length* of each interval multiplied by the lengths of all other intervals at every possible *ordinal* displacement. As described above, this result is then expressed in the frequency domain by a Fourier transformation.

The results (e.g., Fig. A4) are dramatic. The relationship between gap-length and order in the sexual sequence is highly periodic, often appearing as a 'pure sinusiod'. There is little evidence of solely autoregressive effects, since the periodicity is obvious in the power spectral density plots as well. Once an event has occurred, the consequence for the next event, i.e., the time until it occurs, is highly constrained.

Even though the hamster data are not comparable to the rat data, particularly because of the lack of an ejaculation criterion, we can, by using time-series analysis, characterize a record as periodic or random, identify the periods, and isolate autoregressive effects. Not only can we show that an animal's total number of mounts and intromissions have a variety of distributions in time, we can also separate these events from the intervals between them.

A great number of possible analyses remain to be done, including the interaction between interval and event and cross-record comparisons. However, even at this early stage, it is clear that time series analysis provides a powerful tool for data reduction and classification, especially in the case of hamster sexual behaviour, where individual differences are marked.

REFERENCES

Adler, N. T. (1969) Effect of the male's copulatory behavior on successful pregnancy of the female rat, *J. Comp. Physiol. Psychol.*, **69**, 613–22.

Adler, N. T. and Zoloth, S. R. (1970) Copulatory behavior can inhibit pregnancy in female rats, *Science*, **168**, 1480–2.

Adolph, E. F. (1972) Some general concepts of physiological adaptations. In: *Physiological Adaptations*, M. K. Yousef, S. M. Horvath, and R. W. Bullard (eds.), Academic Press, London and New York.

Baerends, G. P., Brouwer, R., and Waterbolk, H. Tj. (1955) Ethological studies on *Lebistes reticulatus* (Peters): I. An analysis of the male courtship pattern, *Behaviour*, **8**, 249–334.

Baerends, G. P. and Kruijt, J. P. (1973) Stimulus selection. In: *Constraints on Learning*, R. A. Hinde, and J. Stevenson-Hinde, Academic Press, London.

Barfield, R. J. and Sachs, B. D. (1968) Sexual behaviour: stimulation by painful electric shock to skin in male rats, *Science*, **161**, 392–5.

Barraclough, C. A. and Cross, B. A. (1963) Unit activity in the hypothalamus of the cyclic female rat: effect of genital stimuli and progesterone, *J. Endocrinol.* **26**, 339–59.

Beach, F. A. (1956) Characteristics of masculine 'sex drive'. In: *Nebraska Symposium of Motivation*, M. R. Jones, (ed.), University of Nebraska Press, Lincoln.

Bendat, J. S. and Piersol, A. G. (1966) *Measurement and Analysis of Random Data*, Wiley and Sons, Inc., London and New York.

Brown, R. (1974) Rat copulatory behaviour. In: *Motivational Control Systems Analysis*, D. J. McFarland, (ed.), Academic Press, London.

Budgell, P. (1970) The effect of changes in ambient temperature on water intake and evaporative water loss, *Psychon. Sci.*, **20**, 275–6.

Budgell, P. (1971) Behavioural thermoregulation in the Barbary dove *(Streptopelia risoria)*, *Anim. Behav.*, **19**, 524–31.

Cannon, W. B. (1932) *The Wisdom of the Body*, Keegan Paul, London.

Carter, C. S. (1973) Stimuli contributing to the decrement in sexual receptivity of female golden hamsters *(Mesocricetus auratus)*, *Anim. Behav.*, **21**, 827–34.

Cooper, G. R. and McGillem, C. D. (1967) *Methods of Signal and System Analysis*, New York.

Dawkins, M. and Dawkins, R. (1974) Some descriptive and explanatory stochastic models of decision-making. In: *Motivational Control Systems Analysis*, D. J. McFarland (ed.), Academic Press, London.

Edmonds, S., Zoloth, S. R., and Adler, N. T. (1972) Storage of copulatory stimulation in the female rat, *Physiol. Behav.*, **8**, 161–4.

Everett, J. W. (1964) Central neural control of periodic functions of the adenohypophysis, *Physiol. Rev.*, **44**, 373–431.

Fitzsimons, J. T. and Le Magnen, J. (1969) Eating as a regulatory control of drinking in the rat, *J. Comp. Physiol. Psychol.*, **67**, 273–83.

Freeman, S. and McFarland, D. (1974) RATSEX. An exercise in simulation. In: *Motivational Control Systems Analysis*, D. J. McFarland (ed.), Academic Press, London.

Fry, F. E. J. and Hochachka, P. (1970) Fish. In: *Comparative Physiology of Thermoregulation* Vol. 1, G. C. Whitlow (ed.), Academic Press, New York and London.

Geertsema, S. and Reddinguis, J. (1974) Preliminary considerations in the simulation of behaviour. In: *Motivational Control Systems Analysis*, D. J. McFarland (ed.), Academic Press, London.

Grossman, S. P. (1967) *A Textbook of Physiological Psychology*, John Wiley and Son, New York.

Hardy, D. F. and DeBold, J. F. (1973) Effect of repeated testing on sexual behavior of the rat, *J. Comp. Physiol. Psychol.*, **85**, 195–202.

Heiligenberg, W. (1974) A stochastic analysis of fish behaviour. In: *Motivational Control Systems Analysis*, D. J. McFarland (ed.), Academic Press, London.

Heiligenberg, W., Kramer, U., and Schulz, V. (1972) The angular orientation of the black eye-bar in *Haplochromis burtoni* (Cichlidae, Pisces) and its relevance to aggressivity, *Z. Vergl. Physiol.*, **76**, 168–76.

Hokanson, J. E. (1969) *The Physiological Bases of Motivation*, John Wiley and Sons, New York.

Hughes, G. M. (1964) Homeostasis and feedback mechanisms, *Symposium of the Society for Experimental Biology*. Vol. XVIII. Preface.

Kaufmann, A. (1968) *The Science of Decision-making*, World University Library, Weidenfeld and Nicolson.

Kissileff, H. R. (1969) Food-associated drinking in the rat, *J. Comp. Physiol. Psychol.*, **67**, 284–300.

Komisaruk, B. R., Adler, N. T. and Hutchison, J. B. (1972) Genital sensory field: enlargement by estrogen treatment in the female rat, *Science*, **178**, 1295–8.

Larsson, K. (1956) *Conditioning and Sexual Behaviour in the Male Albino Rat*, Almkvist and Wiksell, Stockholm.

Leon, J. A. (1976) Life histories as adaptive strategies, *J. Theor. Biol.*, in press.

Lloyd, I. H. (1974) Stochastic identification methods. In: *Motivational Control Systems Analysis*, D. J. McFarland (ed.), Academic Press, London.

McFarland, D. J. (1965) Control theory applied to the control of drinking in the Barbary dove, *Anim. Behav.*, **13**, 478–92.

McFarland, D. J. (1969) Mechanisms of behavioural disinhibition, *Anim. Behav.*, **17**, 238–42.

McFarland, D. J. (1970) Recent developments in the study of feeding and drinking in animals, *J. Psychosom. Res.*, **14**, 229–37.

McFarland, D. J. (1971) *Feedback Mechanisms in Animal Behaviour*, Academic Press, London.

McFarland, D. J. (1973) Stimulus relevance and homeostasis. In: *Constraints on Learning*,

J. Stevenson-Hinde (eds.), R. A. Hinde and Academic Press.

McFarland, D. J. (1976) Form and function in the temporal organisation of behaviour. In: *Growing Points in Ethology*, R. A. Hinde, and P. P. G. Bateson, (eds.), Cambridge University Press.

McFarland, D. J. and Budgell, P. (1970) The thermoregulatory role of feather movements in the Barbary dove *(Streptopelia risoria)*, *Physiol. Behav.*, **5**, 763–71.

McFarland, D. J. and Lloyd, I. H. (1972) Determination of a behavioural impulse response by a stochastic identification technique, *Nature*, **236**, 170–2.

McFarland, D. J. and McFarland, F. J. (1968) Dynamic analysis of an avian drinking response, *Med. Biol. Engng.*, **6**, 659–68.

McFarland, D. J. and Sibly, R. (1972) 'Unitary drives' revisited, *Anim. Behav.*, **20**, 548–63.

McFarland, D. J. and Sibly, R. M. (1975) The behavioural final common path, *Phil. Trans. Roy. Soc. B.*, **270**, 265–93.

Metz, J. (1974) Stochastic models for the temporal fine structure of behaviour sequences. In: *Motivational Control Systems Analysis*, D. J. McFarland (ed.), Academic Press, London.

Milner, P. M. (1970) *Physiological Psychology*, Holt, Rinehart and Winston, London.

Milsum, J. H. (1966) *Biological Control Systems Analysis*, McGraw-Hill, New York, London.

Mittelstaedt, H. (1957) Prey capture in mantids. In: *Recent Advances in Invertebrate Physiology: A Symposium*. B. T. Scheer (ed.), University of Oregon Publications, Eugene.

Oatley, K. (1967) A control model for the physiological basis of thirst, *Med. Biol. Engng.*, **5**, 225–37.

Prosser, C. L. (1958) Perspectives of adaptation: theoretical aspects. In: *Handbook of Physiology*. D. B. Dill (ed.), Am. Physiol. Soc., Washington, D. C.

Revusky, S. and Garcia, J. (1970) Learned associations over long delays, *Psychology of Learning and Motivation* Vol. 4.

Richter, C. P. (1943) Total self-regulatory functions in animals and human beings, *Harvey Lectures*, **38**, 63–103.

Rosen, R. (1970) *Dynamical System Theory in Biology*, Wiley, New York.

Rozin, P. and Kalat, J. W. (1971) Specific hungers and poison avoidance as adaptive specialisations of learning, *Psychol. Rev.*, **78**, 459–86.

Seitz, A. (1940) Die Paarbildung bei einigen Cichliden, *Z. Tierpsychol.*, **4**, 40–84.

Sibly, R. and McFarland, D. (1974) A state-space approach to motivation. In: *Motivational Control Systems Analysis*, D. J. McFarland (ed.), Academic Press, London.

Sibly, R. M. and McFarland, D. J. (1976) On the fitness of behaviour sequences, *Am. Natur.*, **110**, 601–17.

Slater, P. (1973) Describing sequences of behaviour. In: *Perspectives in Ethology*, P. P. G. Bateson, and P. H. Klopfer, (eds.), Plenum Press, New York, London.

Steffens, A. B. (1969) Rapid absorption of glucose in the intestinal tract of the rat after ingestion of a meal, *Physiol. Behav.*, **4**, 829–32.

Thorpe, W. H. (1951) The learning abilities of birds, *Ibis* **93**, 1–52; 252–96.

Thorpe, W. H. (1956) *Learning and Instinct in Animals*, Methuen, London.

Toates, F. (1974) Computer simulation and the homeostatic control of behaviour. In: *Motivational Control Systems Analysis*, D. J. McFarland (ed.), Academic Press, London.

Toates, F. M. and Oatley, K. (1970) Computer simulation of thirst and water balance, *Med. Biol. Engng.*, **8**, 71–87.

Part IV

Socio-sexual Factors

Introduction

To what extent do social factors influence the integration of sexual behaviour? An answer to this question depends on the degree to which causal factors underlying sexual behaviour can be distinguished from the complex of factors which determine the more general integration of an individual's social interactions with conspecifics. This in turn requires a distinction between sexual and social behaviour which is not easy to make, particularly in higher mammals. Definitions of sexual behaviour that are limited to the movement patterns involved in coitus could be misleading, because sexual patterns seen in a reproductive context can also have a communicatory function in a social context. For example, in some primate species the 'presentation posture' of the female required for successful insemination can occur as a component of greeting ceremonies, as an appeasement gesture, or to solicit grooming (reviewed by Hinde 1975). Copulatory behaviour itself can have different functional meanings depending on the situation; thus in the establishment of social dominance, male mounting behaviour in primate species may have a signal value indicating rank. The position in the dominance hierarchy may determine when and to whom such behaviour is displayed.

To a biologist, questions concerning the relationship between sexual and social elements of behaviour can best be seen perhaps in a functional perspective. What does the behaviour in question contribute to the reproductive success of the individual and ultimately continuation of the species? Adler sees sexual behaviour as having at least two important functions. The first is to establish the reproductive relationship between individuals of the same species, a process involving behavioural isolating mechanisms. The second is to synchronize the development of male and female reproductive cycles so that the correct temporal relationship is established between seasonal changes and reproduction. This synchronization depends in part upon the functioning of the endocrine system with reference to biological clocks or oscillators which are entrained to environmental stimuli such as photoperiod. Synchronization also depends on the establishment of sexual affiliation early in the reproductive cycle. Erickson points out that adjustment of the sexual cycles of the male and female depend on behavioural signals that ensure compatibility. Reproductive success also depends upon synchrony of the male and female cycles due not only to the effects of environmental stimuli on the reproductive endocrines, but also to social adaptation which depends on mutual recognition of changing behavioural stimuli during the cycle. These social signals have the property in some cases of communicating reproductive condition or possibly influencing the reproductive condition of the sexual partner. As Keverne establishes, female attractiveness to the male in mammals is a function of olfactory cues which both depend on hormones for their secretion and release, and require sensitive olfactory receptor systems. Olfactory cues could well influence specific pathways in the brain associated with the neuroendocrine mechanisms underlying sexual behaviour.

The influences of social factors on sexual behaviour are particularly apparent during development. Simpson suggests that behaviour patterns resulting in tactile experience are directly involved in the development of sexual behaviour in primates. This may be only one facet of the problem, as Simpson points out, because learning may be associated with the development of many special skills concerned, for example, with attention to particular stimuli which enable an individual to learn from events initiated by that individual. Male and female primates may differ in the acquisition of such skills. Because prenatal hormonal condition is known to affect the development of social behaviour in early infancy (Goy, 1970), it is conceivable that sex hormones may influence the capacity of the individual to acquire these skills. In humans, the relationship between hormonal and social influences in the development of sexual behaviour is complicated by cultural factors. Money and Schwartz take the view that both hormonal and cultural determinants contribute to the development of individual gender identity or self-image relating to concepts of masculinity and femininity.

REFERENCES

Goy, R. W. (1970) Experimental control of psychosexuality, *Phil. Trans. Roy. Soc. London B.*, **259**, 149–62.
Hinde, R. A. (1975) *Biological Bases of Human Social Behaviour*, McGraw-Hill, New York.

CHAPTER 20

On the Mechanisms of Sexual Behaviour and Their Evolutionary Constraints

N. T. ADLER

INTRODUCTION

Sexual reproduction involves the coordination of two separate organisms interacting in such a way that progeny are produced. The main foci of this chapter are the mechanisms which produce sexual behaviour in animals and the evolutionary constraints which shape these mechanisms. In this review, behaviour is treated as both a dependent variable produced by the organisms' living machinery and also as an independent variable—a biological adaptation which itself has consequences for the individual, the population, and the species.

Let us start with some definitions. Sexual behaviour is that series of responses of the organism that results in sexual reproduction, while sexual reproduction refers to the production of progeny by sexual means. Reproduction refers simply to the production of progeny and can be achieved by a variety of non-sexual means, such as fission, budding, and parthenogenesis, as well as by sexual means (Dobzhansky, 1955). Reproduction itself is one of the definitive characteristics of all living things. If in the early history of life on this planet there were macromolecular aggregates that did not replicate themselves, they would surely have been supplanted by physiochemical systems that did.

Reproduction, in the sense of simple replication of individuals, however, is not sufficient to ensure survival. It is because of the vagaries of survival that sexuality developed evolutionarily. The 'organic condition' is that procreation does not go unchecked. There is always predation and limitation of resources (food and shelter) that lead to a situation of competition in which organisms, better adapted to a particular set of circumstances, are more likely to survive. Organisms which are sexually reproductive are more likely to survive than organisms which reproduce asexually.

The reason for the advantage of sexuality over asexuality is the richness of genetic permutations it promotes. Because of genetic segregation and recombination, the progeny from a sexual union display a great deal more genetic variability than do the progeny from asexually reproducing organisms (Crow and Kimura, 1970). Offspring from a sexual union can thus survive in a larger range of microenvironments (Brown, 1975), and the genes of the sexually reproducing organisms which generate these offspring consequently enjoy a higher probability of being represented in the next generation. Sex, then, is an adaptation for survival; it is probably the master adaptation.

Once sexuality has been adopted as an evolutionary strategy, however, there are immediately a set of problems which must be solved. Sexuality requires differentiation of two sexual types, male and female, or their prototypes. There is a basic difference between male and female on the cellular level in that the female's egg is specialized to contain the basic nutritive elements for the embryo while the male's sperm are specialized for motility (Trivers, 1972). The basic gametic difference between male and female becomes magnified as more and more of the organism's behaviour and auxiliary reproductive physiology become specialized as secondary sexual adaptations. With even a moderate amount of genital specialization and differentiation, there is a problem of synchronizing the two animals' behaviour so that gametes meet under appropriate conditions and lead to the production of viable young.

In this chapter, I will discuss four general classes of synchronization involving the coordination of male and female reproductive behaviour.

(1) The first class deals with the establishment of a relationship between two appropriate organisms. Generally, the sexual partners are from the same species. They must be reproductively mature and competent to produce, and sometimes care for, offspring. Sexual solicitation and responsiveness are often involved in an organism's selection of the biologically appropriate mate and, in the case of interspecific isolating mechanisms, in the rejection of unsuitable mates.

(2) In addition to arranging for the right mate, sexual behaviour helps ensure that reproduction occurs at the right place and the right time. Mating seasons and territories are biological phenomena that facilitate adequate climatic and geographical conditions for reproduction. The choice of a biotically adequate territory requires a way for the organism to evaluate the resources in an area and to gain social control of the chosen area. The occurrence of a breeding season often requires sexual behaviour to be tied to a seasonally accurate 'biological clock'.

(3) Once the place and partner are chosen, the more reflexological aspects of copulatory behaviour lead to the union of sperm and egg. Concentrating on mammals, and the commitment of that class to internal fertilization and pregnancy, reproduction requires the mechanical positioning of the male's penis in the female's vagina. This positioning is accomplished by the genital reflexes of copulation. Copulatory stimulation also induces the male to ejaculate a sufficient number of sperm to ensure fertilization (*cf*. Hart, This Volume Chapter 10) and can facilitate the movement of sperm through the female's reproductive tract (p. 685).

(4) Once the female has received (or is about to receive) the male's sperm, her physiological and behavioural status is often altered by copulatory stimulation. If she is in the early stages of the ovarian cycle, copulation may induce ovulation (p. 680). In some species, like the rat, copulatory stimulation can trigger the secretion of progestational hormones necessary for uterine implantation of the ovum. Finally, the female's behaviour may be altered by copulatory stimulation. Just as in the initial stages of courtship, when it was important that sexual contact between inappropriate organisms be prevented (e.g., prevention of interspecific mating), sexual responsiveness is sometimes turned off *after* copulation in order to protect the products of an appropriately completed mating. This 'turning off' prevents disruption of pregnancy by subsequent copulatory stimulation (p. 685).

THE CHOICE OF MATE

The Correct Species—General Considerations

Perhaps the most important characteristic of a mate is that it be a member of the same species as the sexual partner. The species is a basic unit of biological organization and classification; it is a 'supra-individual biological system' (Dobzhansky, 1970, p. 353). The essential difference between groups of individuals that comprise *populations* within a species and individuals that comprise different *species* is the degree of genetic flow between groups: species are groups of interbreeding natural populations that are reproductively isolated from other such groups (Mayr, 1969).

Since distinct species are adapted to different ecological niches, interspecific mating is likely to produce organisms that are ill-adapted to either of the niches of the parent species. There are consequently biological adaptations which prevent interspecific mating and thus promote species integrity.

The beginnings of reproductive isolation between groups will come about merely as a by-product of general genetic divergence as two populations begin the process of speciation (Muller, 1942). This incipient divergency may be illustrated by the reproductive behaviour patterns of the semi-species, *Drosophila paulistorum;* semi-species are populations which have partly completed the process of speciation. Gene exchange is still possible among semi-species, but not as freely as among conspecific populations (Mayr, 1963).

Crosses between two semi-species of *Drosophila paulistorum* (Braillian and Amazonian) produced females that were anatomically and physiologically apparently normal (Ehrman, 1960). These hybrid females, however, would not accept a complete copulatory sequence from any male. They rejected not only the males of both parent strains but also rejected hybrid males. The genetic contributions by the parents of the female hybrids were apparently so discordant that the hybrid females could not perform the complete mating sequence and constantly adopted the rejection posture of this species (lowering the head and raising the abdomen so the vaginal orifice is inaccessible to the male).

The generalized copulatory pattern of male Drosophilids consists of the following four elements: (1) orientation to the female; (2) wing vibration; (3) licking the female's genitalia; and (4) attempts at copulation. It is now known that the wing vibration of the male produces acoustic signals that stimulate the female and that there is species-specificity in these signals (Bennet-Clark and Ewing, 1968). However, when Ewing (1970) examined the courtship songs of six semi-species in the *paulistorum* group, he found considerable similarity between them. Single sinusoidal pulses of sound of approximately 3 ms duration were produced by all the semi-species examined, and in five of the six groups, the interpulse intervals of the song were not significantly different from one another. Thus, at this *early* stage of reproductive isolation, differences in song do not contribute to whatever isolation there is, although for fully formed species songs do serve as species-specific mating signals (see below).

The Correct Species—Reproductive Isolating Mechanisms

Although there is already some general divergence in the behavior of semi-species, as the degree of isolation between emerging species continues, there evolve isolating mechanisms which function to prevent mating between members of these separate species.

If species occupy different geographical zones (i.e., they are allopatric), the members of their groups will not meet; so reproduction is prevented by means extrinsic to the organisms themselves. If species, however, live in the same region (i.e., they are sympatric), then other mechanisms, intrinsic to the organisms themselves, are needed to prevent the production of interspecific hybrids.

Dobzhansky (1970) lists several of these phenomena that act as *reproductive isolating mechanisms*. This list includes: the reduction in the viability or fertility of the hybrid zygotes; anatomical differences in the organisms' genital structures; and ecological or habitat isolation in which populations concerned occupy different habitats, albeit in the same general region. The class of reproductive isolating mechanisms most relevant to this discussion is what has been called 'sexual or ethological' isolating mechanisms, in which the mutual attraction between the sexes of different species is weak or absent. As discussed above, sexual behaviour in the male and female involves highly complex synchronization, consisting of many components; the non-concordance of two species' mating patterns is a most efficient way of prohibiting the production of genetically less fit interspecific hybrids. It is more efficient than hybrid sterility, say, because, in preventing interspecific mating, sexual isolation eliminates the wasting of gametes and also eliminates the need for allocating resources to the developing (maladapted) hybrids (Ehrman and Parsons, 1976).

Returning to the courtship song of *Drosophila*, Ewing (1969) found that the calls of *D. pseudoobscura* and *D. persimilis* were quite distinct. The males of the former species produced two distinct songs (a low repetition rate song and a high repetition rate song) while males in the latter species produced almost exclusively only high repetition rate song.

In *D. pseudoobscura*, the sequence of courtship is almost always the following: low repetition rate song (LRR) followed by high repetition rate song (HRR), followed in turn by attempted copulation. If one interprets the unfolding of this sequence as reflecting a progressive increase in the male's readiness to copulate, then *D. persimilis* males (with only the HRR song) might differ from the *pseudoobscura* males in having a lower threshold for the production of this song. Following this reasoning (Ewing, 1969), it seems that the formation of a qualitative interspecific reproducing isolating mechanism was effected by a quantitative change in the threshold for song production in the males. The quantitative raising and lowering of thresholds for the elicitation of courtship behaviour in these insects is an example of a general mechanism by which behavioural adaptations develop in evolution (Manning, 1963).

As in any evolutionary adaptation, however, this change in the male's behaviour must be accompanied by a *correlated* adjustment in the mechanisms controlling the female's behaviour. While the behaviour patterns of males in any given species must be distinctly different from those of the males of other species, they must at the same time be acceptable and stimulating to the females of his own species.

One way in which the signalling characteristics of the male and the reception characteristics of the conspecific females could be correlated is by coupling the two processes to the same neural machinery (Ewing, 1969). The results of several behaviour-genetic studies now indicate that is the case in at least some organisms:

In studying the genetic mechanism controlling song production in *D. pseudoobscura* and *D. persimilis*, Ewing (1969) found that the genes which control overall song pattern are sex linked (contained on the X chromosome). He tentatively offered the interpretation that the same genes control the *production* of the song pattern in the male and the *reception* of the pattern in the female. In support of this view (Tan, 1946) is the fact that some of the genes controlling female responsiveness to species-specific stimuli in *pseudoobscura* and *persimilis* are also contained on the X chromosome. It may be that the genes on this chromosome control the neural circuitry that produces a biological clock or oscillator which males can use as a comparator for efferent signals and the females for afferent signals.

A similar linking of female and male acoustic processes was found in crickets (Hoy and Paul, 1973). These investigators studied the calls of *Teleogryllus oceanicus* and *Teleogryllus commodus* as well as their interspecific hybrids. The males of these two species produce species-specific calls, and while the females do not themselves call, they are attracted to the calling males. The males produced from the interspecific matings emitted songs that were quite distinct from the songs of either parent species. Significantly, hybrid female *Teleogryllus* found the song of their hybrid siblings more attractive than the songs of either parental species. The implication here, as for *Drosophila*, is that the production of the signal in the male, and its reception and translation by the female into behaviourally expressed preferences, are both coupled to the same genetic–physiological substrate.

The emphasis in this section has been on species-specific 'hard-wired' mechanisms for species recognition. There is also a set of *learned* mechanisms, sexual imprinting, that function to maintain species integrity by preventing interspecific mating. These processes are discussed by Bateson (this volume Chapter 2).

Male and Female Strategies in Mate Selection

Most of this discussion has concentrated on the mechanisms which enable the *males* of one species to *emit* signals different from the males of another species and on the mechanisms which permit the *female to respond* to conspecific male signals while rejecting, or at least ignoring, signals from other species. The biological reason for at least initially concentrating on the way in which females process male signals has to do with the differential reproductive strategies of males and females (Trivers, 1972).

Especially for species that do not have a monogamous mating system, the parental investment of a female is much greater than that of a male. In mammals, for example, once mating has been completed and pregnancy initiated, the female's reproductive physiology is drastically altered and becomes directed toward nurturing the developing young. The male mammal's investment can be as minimal as a brief copulatory encounter, although in some variations like the red fox *(Vulpes fulva)* the male may care for the young after birth (Brown, 1975). Even in monogamously mating species of birds, where the male cares for the developing young, the female must invest a great deal of energy in producing a gamete (ovum) that contains a large energy store for the embryo. In birds a single egg may weight up to 15–20% of the female's total body weight (Alcock, 1975), while males produce gametes (sperm) with virtually only genetic instructions and only enough metabolic stores to permit them the motility necessary to reach and fertilize the ovum (Trivers, 1972).

Because of this imbalance in the amount of reproductive energy spent by the two sexes, the cost of a reproductive error is often much more severe for the female than for the male (Williams, 1966). In the following discussion, I shall concentrate on those species of mammals in which one male mates with several females (the form of polygamy termed polygyny). If, for example, a *male* mammal inseminates an inappropriate female, he can recoup his loss within a short period (with the next ejaculation in a multiple ejaculating species like the rat). If, however, a *female* mates with an inappropriate (e.g., infertile male), she may be out of reproductive condition for the duration of the ovarian cycle, which can be many days (p. 680). Consequently, in a wide variety of species investigated (again, primarily those with a *polygamous* mating system), the female is more selective than the male while a male will generally mate with a wide variety of different females. This generalization holds true for taxa as diverse as guppies (Tinbergen, 1965), and mice (Doty, 1974).

Intraspecific Selection of Mates—Sexual Selection and Male Attractiveness

Because of the great reproductive expenditure of the female, she must not only select a conspecific mate, but she must also select the fittest mate *within* her own species (Williams, 1966). This selectivity of the female can lead to a competitive situation between the males of her species, and this competition among the males becomes especially intense in populations displaying polygamous mating systems and equal sex ratios (Brown, 1975). In such populations, for every male that mates, there is another male that must, for a time, go without a female. The individual selection of males that occurs by virtue of the competition for available females leads to the evolutionary process called 'sexual selection' (Campbell, 1972; Darwin, 1859, 1871; Fisher, 1958). This selective process leads to the evolution of behaviour in the male, the function of which is to attract females.

Morphological traits like the extravagant plumage of some birds and the 'ritualized' courtship displays of males in many species are thought to reflect the results of sexual selection. Although the male may win a female by virtue of his individual display *vis-à-vis* a single female, there are additional behavioural mechanisms that can improve his chances in obtaining a mate. These mechanisms are discussed in the succeeding sections.

Intraspecific Selection of Mates—Male Aggression

Since, in polygamously mating species, a female is obtained at the expense of another male, a prospective male could indirectly compete for female attention by attacking and driving away his competition. To the extent that females prefer males that occupy nutritionally rich and/or reproductively appropriate mating/nesting areas (cf. dickcissel, *Spiza americana* discussed by Zimmerman, 1966, 1971), aggression, the basis of the establishment of the territories, serves a useful reproductive function for the male.

In several species of birds, the males congregate within one area (a lek). Within the total area, however, there are subdivisions which are ecologically more advantageous than others. There is intense competition between males for preferred sites in the mating area, and highly elaborate competitive behaviour patterns emerge. Male grouse strut about and vocalize loudly at their opponents (Kruijt and Hogan, 1967; Lack, 1968). A male that ultimately comes to occupy the preferred site may perform up to 70% of the matings. (Robel, 1966 on *Tympanuchus cupido*).

As the breeding season approaches, male red deer *(Cervas elephas)* round up harems of females. Males compete intensely among themselves, on the basis of their large body size and their head displays which involve huge antlers. Males, from which the antlers were removed experimentally, dropped in their position in the dominance hierarchy (Lincoln, 1972), thus decreasing their chances of obtaining females.

Part of the theory of sexual selection involves the premise that inter-male competition for females is most intense in polygamous species. In these cases, some males mate with many females while other males consequently receive less reproductive attention. Where stable monogamous pair bonds are set up (and assuming an equal sex ratio), there are enough females to go around; consequently, inter-male competition, with its attendant behavioural and morphological ornamentation, is reduced (Selander, 1965). A comparison of the behaviour of roe deer and red deer illustrates the behavioural consequences of polygamous mating systems (Darling, 1964). Unlike the red deer which possess large antlers, and are aggressive only during rut, the roe deer *(Capreolus capreolus)* is mainly monogamous and does not form harems. In this species, both the male's gross body size and his antlers are much smaller than in the red deer.

A conclusion from these selected examples is that the development of mechanisms for male aggressive behaviour (especially in polygamously mating species) can be an important means for obtaining female sexual companions.

Intraspecific Selection of Mates—Male Cooperation

There is a more cooperative element in the mechanisms by which males can obtain females. To the extent that a male's ability to attract a female is proportional to the quantity of stimulation he provides, there are likely to be cases in which groups of males *combine* their individual signals (Wilson, 1975). This device of combined signalling sometimes occurs in communal mating grounds (leks) in which males congregate into one general area during mating season. Hjorth (1970) showed that for grouse, the combined displaying and calling can be perceived from a much greater distance than would be the case for a single individual. There are even cases of active synchronization in the behaviour of two males as in the joint jumping displays of pairs of blue-backed manakins *Chiroxiphia pareola* (Snow, 1963). Even when there are individual mating courts that are aggressively defended within the overall display ground, as in the black-and-white manakin, the resulting noise of simultaneously displaying males carries more than a hundred yards (Snow, 1956).

There are several mechanisms by which male-male behaviour can be synchronized, but one of the most effective is through *social facilitation*. Male bullfrogs *(Rana catesbeiana)* aggregate in ponds during the mating season (Capranica, 1965) where they emit a distinctive mating vocalization. One male will call. A second male responds to the call of the first male by calling back. The calling by the second in turn stimulates a third, and so on. This kind of social facilitation (or positive feedback) can generate a loud and frequent auditory signal which attracts females to the pond.

The advantage of male–male affiliative mechanisms balancing aggressive ones is that males can reside sufficiently closely to one another to cooperate in attracting females. Collias and Collias (1969) have shown that more females *per male* nest in large colonies of the village weaver *(Ploceus cucullatus)* than in small ones. Just as the winning and defence of individual territories requires an aggressive behavioural substrate, the combined displays require an affiliative system to operate. The integrated social structure of a particular species then reflects the balance of opposing agonistic and affiliative tendencies.

The conclusion from these studies of male courtship is that there are several kinds of behavioural mechanisms that promote the male's chances of obtaining a female: (1) the production of often exaggerated (ritualized) displays which directly attract the females; (2) development of aggressive mechanisms which serve to exlude competing males from the aggressor's area of reproductive activity; and (3) a balancing of the aggressive tendencies by affiliative patterns which allow males to combine their displays or signalling capabilities, the cumulative effect of which is to attract more females to the area. Although these three mechanisms are used to different degrees and in different combinations in different groups, the net effect of all three of these is to increase the probability of the male finding a willing mate. The first mechanism has to do with the male's relationship only with the female while the second and third deal with male-male interactions.

Intraspecific Selection of Mates—Male Rareness

There is a fourth mechanism by which males come to possess varying degress of attractiveness; this mechanism simultaneously combines both direct stimulating effects on the female with male–male interactions. This phenomenon, 'frequency-dependent' mating (Petit, 1951, and Ehrman, 1966), occurs when the number of successful matings of a particular genotype is inversely proportional to the frequency of the genotype in the potential mating pool. Also called, 'rare male advantage', the genotype that is rare in a population tends to be favoured at the expense of the common type. (Orange-eyed *Drosophila pseudoobscura* are preferred to purple—eyed males when the former are less frequent than the latter. When the orange-eyed males are more frequent, they are less preferred by the females, Ehrman, 1970.) One result of this kind of selection is to retain a balanced polymorphism in the population. Since the selective advantage of a gene increases as its frequency decreases, at low frequencies it will be highly favoured, and the gene will be maintained in the population even if it is selected against at intermediate frequencies. This process provides a reservoir of genetic variation in the gene pool.

Intraspecific Selection of Mates—Properties of the Female

The emphasis in this discussion so far has been on the characteristics of the male that make him more attractive to the female. For sexual selection to operate, there are also important properties of the female's behaviour that are necessary for her to obtain an optimal mate: she must be sensitive to the differences between conspecific males, she must consistently exert a preference, and her sensitivity-preference must have an heritable component. In a study by Ewing (1961) on artificial genetic selection for changes in body length, female *Drosophila's* consistent preferences functioned as pressure for sexual selection.

Recall that in *Drosophila* the male courtship consists of four components: (1) orientation, (2) wing vibration, (3) licking the female's genitals, and (4) attempts at copulation. In Ewing's study, the males selected for small size increased the proportion of their courtship time devoted to wing vibration. Why should the smaller males vibrate their wings more than larger males? Since the smaller flies had smaller wings, the stimulation from their vibrations was less intense than the vibratory stimulation of the larger flies. The selection experiment had been performed by placing ten pairs of flies in a vial. Since there were presumably genetic differences which produced differences in the vibration rates of the flies in any given bottle, there was an opportunity for the males to compete for the females on the basis of this display. When the experiment of selecting for small body size was repeated, with the variation of placing only a *single* pair of flies in each mating vial, there were flies of decreasing body lengths over successive generations; but there was *no concurrent increase* in vibration rates. After eight generations of selection with only a single pair of flies per vial, Ewing returned to the procedure of placing ten pairs per vial. The reintroduction of the opportunity for competition promptly resulted in an increase in wing vibration rate over succeeding generations. This experiment indicated that: (1) females are sensitive to wing vibration as a courtship display, and (2) given a competitive situation with the female acting as the agent of natural selection, males with higher vibration rates are selected, resulting in an increased mean vibration rate within the population.

In addition to possessing the ability to differentiate between the males' signals related to their presumed sexual prowess, the female organism often possesses auxiliary behavioural mechanisms for selecting her potential mate. She must often be able to 'remember' stimulation no longer present and be able to compare displays from several males. This ability is especially important in the cases where males are spread apart in separate territories and the female must pass through several males' mating stations before choosing her partner. By attaching a telemetering device to female ruffled grouse *(Bonasa umbellus)*, Brander (1967) was able to show that females visit most of the local males at their spatially separated display grounds. By successively sampling the various males' displays, the female might be able to store some representation of them and then could subsequently compare and choose among the males.

Another aspect of the female that may enhance her ability in obtaining males is her 'novelty' as a sexual partner. In polygamously mating species, (e.g., many mammals), a given male stands a better chance of being represented in the gene pool of the next generation by successively inseminating several different females than by repeatedly copulating with the same female. In the rat *(R. norvegicus)*, for example, a female will normally be impregnated by one ejaculatory series from a male (p. 681). In fact, further copulatory activities with that female can, under certain circumstances, disrupt the transport of his own sperm from the previous ejaculation (p. 685). Since a rested domestic rat can achieve up to seven ejaculations in one session (Larsson, 1956) he would be better off inseminating seven different females than concentrating on just one.

To support this notion that novel females are more stimulating than familiar females to the males of a polygamously mating species, there is a fair amount of evidence that male rats perform better, sexually, when they are offered a succession of different females than when they are repeatedly presented with the same female (Bermant *et al.*, 1968; Fisher, 1962; Fowler and Whalen, 1961; Wilson *et al.*, 1963). The increase in sexual performance with changing mates, termed the 'Coolidge effect', has also been demonstrated in male guinea pigs (Grunt and Young, 1952), rams (Beamer *et al.*, 1969), and bulls (Schein and Hale, 1965). These data imply that the period of sexual refractoriness that develops in a male following copulation with one female (Diakow, 1974) can be overcome by the introduction of a novel female, even one that had been previously mated to a second male (in rats, Hsiao, 1965). The strength of the effect varies across species (*cf.* Bermant and Davidson, 1974 for a review); and there are some contradictory comparative data (Dewsbury, 1975); however, for a normally polygamous or promiscuous male, the attractiveness of a new female would facilitate the spread of his genes among several different females.

Research on olfactory preferences in rodents provides several other examples of ways in which a novel female is more likely to attract a male. There are basic preferences in both male and female rats for olfactory cues from reproductively adequate mates. Sexually experienced male rats, for example, prefer the odour of an oestrous female to that of an anoestrous female (Carr *et al.*, 1966); similarly, female rats prefer the odour of normal males to that of castrates. Within the class of stimuli elicited by reproductively adequate animals, however, there are additional constraints that would support polygamous matings by males (but not polygamous mating by females). If an intact male rat has a history of mating with several different females, the odour of *novel females* is preferred (Carr *et al.*, 1970). (The preference for novel odours does not appear in inexperienced males.) His preference would lead a male to investigate, and consequently probably copulate with, different females. Conversely, the female rat, which becomes pregnant after one ejaculatory series, does not show a preference for new males. In fact, polygamously mated females preferred to approach the odour of a previous mating partner rather than that of a new one (Carr *et al.*, 1970).

In these studies of intraspecific mate choice, the behaviour of species with polygamous mating systems (e.g., many mammals) was emphasized. By definition no prolonged pair-bonds were involved. In the case where a single male and female remain bonded for a period of time, other behavioural criteria are employed so that an individual selects an adequate partner with which to mate and to share parental responsibilities. These mechanisms are discussed by Erickson, this volume Chapter 21.

PROPER TIME AND PLACE

Locations for Breeding

As has been discussed above, for biologically viable offspring to be produced, suitable (reproductively mature, heterosexual conspecific) mates are needed. Even perfect synchronization of two mates, however, will produce no offspring unless there is an appropriate physical environment. The earth is not uniform. There are geographical variations in light, temperature, and food. Over large ranges in the physical environment (i.e., between latitudes), species may adapt with altered patterns of reproduction. Concerning species that can extend over a range of latitudes, for example, Sadlier (1969) makes the following tentative generalization:

> The breeding season at high latitudes is shorter than at low, so that the possible number of parturitions is reduced. In many field studies, it has been noted that samples taken from higher latitudes inside a species' range had larger litter sizes. It has been assumed that this phenomenon is present to counteract the otherwise reduced productivity.

With the variations inherent in smaller geographical ranges, i.e. the area occupied by a single populations, a male can actively select the ecological context of breeding (p. 663) by virtue of his territorial behaviour. The combination of male territorial aggression and female selectivity results in two adapted organisms residing in a niche which is nutritionally viable for the production of offspring.

Temporal Factors—General

Even at a given location within the physical environment, conditions vary systematically as a function of time. (In Philadelphia, for example, there are approximately 9 h 22 min of sunlight per day at the end of December while, towards the end of June, there are 15 h of light per day.) Such seasonal variations in geophysical factors are critical for life processes. The annual changes in photoperiod produce fluctuations in mean monthly temperature (as much as 30 °C in some boreal regions) and in rainfall—thereby influencing the ecosystems (Ricklefs, 1973 for review). In this section of the chapter behavioural mechanisms will be related to the synchronization of the organism with respect to temporal variations in the physical environment.

Temporal Factors—Daily Rhythms

For many species, the primary environmental cycle is diurnal. Sexual behaviour for some rodents follows a daily temporal pattern similar to that for eating, drinking, and general activity (Richter, 1965). Feral and domestic rats, for example, are sexually most active around dusk (Calhoun, 1962a; Kuehn and Beach, 1963). This species is nocturnal, and its optic apparatus is specialized for activity at night.

The restriction of sexual activity in rats to a limited time of day is controlled by a circadian biological clock (or clocks). Since much of the work concerning the timing of reproductive events has focused on female rats, the discussion that follows below will be devoted to these rodents.

The female rat comes into behavioural oestrus once every four or five days (Long and Evans, 1922). Within this oestrous cycle, active heat lasts only for about fifteen hours, corresponding to part of the evening on the day of vaginal prooestrus.

By what mechanism is the female rat's mating behaviour programmed to coincide with a particular time of day? At least part of the answer is that the occurrence of sexual behaviour is tied to the female rat's ovarian cycle. (Lisk, Komisaruk, and Kelley and Pfaff, this volume Chapters 13, 11, and 7 respectively, detail the endocrine mediation of mammalian ovarian cycle.) From the classic work of Young and co-workers (Young, 1961), it is known that the ovarian hormones, oestrogen and progesterone, lead to the occurrence of mating behaviour. Oestrogen, secreted over the four-day cycle of the female rat, reaches a peak on the day of prooestrus (Smith, Freeman, and Neill, 1975). This background of oestrogenic stimulation seems to be necessary for the subsequent appearance of sexual behaviour on the evening of vaginal pro-oestrus. Progesterone is secreted at low levels during most of the oestrous (ovarian) cycle but begins to 'surge' shortly before the onset of darkness on the evening of prooestrus (Feder et al., 1968). This surge of progesterone is followed quickly by an intensive interest in mating by the female rat.

If sexual behaviour is facilitated by the progesterone surge during late prooestrus, what controls the timing of this hormones? The answer seems to be a surge of pituitary luteinizing hormone (LH) (Hoffman, 1973, review), which was in turn stimulated by a 'neural clock' (Everett and Sawyer, 1950). The basic temporal organization of this clock is endogenous. Like other circadian rhythms, it is a self-sustaining oscillation. Placing the female rat in constant darkness often does not disrupt the continuation of oestrous cycles at about four-day intervals (Hoffmann, 1967, 1969, 1970). However, like most circadian clocks, environmental light cycles can entrain (synchronize) the endogenous periodicity: a phase shift in the day–night cycle of twelve hours is followed, after several cycles, by the oestrous cycle becoming synchronized with the new day–night rhythm (Hemmingsen and Krarup, 1937).

It seems, therefore, that the restriction of the female rat's mating activity to a particular time of day is due, in part, to the timing of pituitary–gonadal secretions. These secretions (e.g., the LH surge) in turn are tied to a biological oscillator the period of which is approximately 24 h and which is entrained by the environmental lighting cycle.

The result of these neuroendocrine events is that mating behaviour, in the nocturnal rat, occurs around dusk (its behaviourally most active time) on the day of vaginal prooestrus. Later that night, ovulation occurs. This physiological event tends to occur towards the *end* of the night of prooestrus (Young *et al.*, 1941); and, like the surge of progesterone, ovulation is also triggered by the surge of LH. By the time ovulation has occurred, female receptivity has reached its peak (Young *et al.*, 1941; Kuehn and Beach, 1963) and mating will have occurred.

To summarize briefly: the temporal coordination of all of these biological events is tied to the operation of an endogenously organized biological clock (or clocks) the operation of which is translated into overt biological rhythms by hormonal mediators.

There are several adaptive features in the linking of several reproductive activities within an organism (e.g., receptivity and ovulation) to a circadian oscillation. The coupling of the several physiological and behavioural reproductive events to a common clock (or set of clocks) within the individual ensures that the neuroendocrine events required for reproduction will proceed in an orderly and integrated fashion. There is a second adaptive feature to the control of reproduction by biological clocks. Since reproductive behaviour must, by definition, be social, (at least two separate organisms must be coordinated), biological clocks can facilitate the necessary interorganismic integration. Because each animal's circadian rhythm can be entrained to a potent, stable geophysical variable like the light cycle, the biological periodicities of two organisms living in the same physical environment will come to have a common phase relationship to each other.

The importance of this rhythmic integration was highlighted by an experiment (Richter, 1970). A male and female rat were allowed to 'free-run', i.e., their biological rhythms were not anchored to an environmental light cycle. Under their free-running conditions, their circadian (about 24 h) rhythms began to diverge from the precise 24 h period that exists under entrainment by light and the rats mated only when their activity rhythms overlapped.

Temporal Factors—Seasonal Rhythms

Many species show not only *circadian* variations in sex but also annual variations. Since one of the geophysical causes for variations in temperature, rainfall, and thus the availability of food and other biological resources, is the relation of the earth to the sun, daylength is a stable cue which is highly correlated with seasonal, biological rhythms. In temperate regions especially where seasonal variations in the environment are great, reproduction is not constant throughout the year but fluctuates seasonally (Sadlier, 1969).

As was the case for the circadian cycles of sexual behaviour in female rats, annual cycles of reproductive behaviour in some organisms are tied to hormonal cycles. The relation of circadian cycles to seasonal cycles is even more intimate than the analogy suggests; the mechanism controlling both may be a circadian clock (Elliott et al., 1972).

According to the theory of *photoperiodism* (Bunning, 1973), the circadian clock can be used to measure daylength. In Bunning's theory, there are two distinct effects of the external light cycle. The first is the process of 'entrainment' by which the approximately 24 h (circadian) rhythm inherent in the endogenous clockwork mechanism *is tuned to a precise 24 h rhythm* (by the phase-shifting process underlying entrainment to the 24 h solar light cycle). Once this endogenous rhythm is entrained to precisely 24 h, it can itself act as a *measuring device to determine daylength*. As a hypothetical case, assume that the 24 h clock sequentially goes through two phases, of 12 h each. (Phase I is called a photically non-inducible phase; phase II is a photically inducible phase.) In winter (or early spring), the daylength is short; light stimulates the clock only during the first (non-inducible) phase. As the duration of light per day increases during the approach of spring, light into phase II impinges upon the hypothetical organism during the second (photoinducible) phase of the clock's operation as well as the first. This increasing imposition of light informs the organism that daylength is increasing and activates the neuroendocrine system to resume reproductive activity.

The photoperiodic hypothesis may explain maintenance of the reproductive state in male hamsters. Gaston and Menaker (1967) found that testis growth was sensitive to environmental light cycles. Approximately 12.5 h of light per day were required to maintain testis size; with less light, the testes regressed. To determine whether the photoperiodic hypothesis could account for these results, Elliot et al. (1972) performed the following experiment. After maintaining the subjects for 17 weeks in a control condition with 14 h of light a day (LD 14:10), the animals were divided into several groups, each placed under a different lighting schedule. In each group, light was delivered in blocks of six hours each; however, there were different amounts of darkness between the six hour light periods. One group received a photoperiod of 6 h of light followed by 18 h of darkness (LD 6:18). The total photic day was therefore 24 h. Another group received 6 h of light followed by 30 h of darkness (LD 6:30). This corresponded to a photic cycle length of 36 h.

The testes of the animals regressed under LD 6:18. These results support Gaston and Menaker's original finding that at least 12.5 h of light per day are required for testicular maintenance, since the organisms in this group received only 6 h of light per day. However, testis weight was *maintained* in the LD 6:30 condition. The results for this group support the photoperiodic hypothesis. Assume that at the start of the experimental light treatments there is a circadian clock that is entrained so that phase I (non-inducible) coincides with the onset of light (phase 2 begins 12 h later). The circadian clock then makes one cycle, and phase 1 starts again, this time 24 h after the light came on. The second 6 h block of light, however, came 36 h after the first one started; by this time, the clock has reached the start of phase 2 (of its second circadian day). Since phase 2 is the photoinducible phase, the clock interprets the two short 6 h blocks of light as being long (= able to stimulate both phase 1 and phase 2). Consequently, the testes remain patent, a condition appropriate to long daylengths. The biological clock has been 'tricked' because phase 1 was stimulated only in the first circadian day while phase 2 was stimulated only in the second circadian day.

Although the experimental procedure presented here is not to be found in nature, the results of these manipulations indicate that, normally (i.e. in nature), a circadian clock can be used to indicate that daylength is increasing.

To the extent that the appearance of sexual behaviour is controlled by endocrine events, the control of these humoral events by a biological oscillator is an efficient way for sexuality to be tied to season of the year. There may be, in addition, other mechanisms that would account for seasonality in some species (Rusak and Zucker, 1975). One highly adaptive feature of the control of tuning reproductive clocks to light is that relevant physiological states can begin to develop before the onset of the ecologically critical event (e.g., abundant food in late spring) and thus be ready for full operation by the time that the correct time for breeding approaches. Hamsters normally display testicular regression during the winter months. The gonads begin to grow considerably before the time when mating actually occurs (reviewed in Rusak and Zucker, 1975).

Temporal Factors—Effects of Behaviour on Breeding Cycles

The experiments presented in the previous section have shown how seasonal fluctuations in breeding and sexual behaviour are controlled by a biological clock which modulates endocrine secretions. Frequently, however, the relations between physiology and behaviour are reciprocal: just as neuroendocrine cycles can influence behaviour, behavioural stimuli also control physiological variables. Sexual behaviour follows the alteration of hormone levels in the breeding season; however, the effects of behavioural stimuli may in turn advance the time of breeding.

The advancement of breeding by social stimulation (or, in one sense of the term, 'synchronization' of breeding activities) is known to occur in a variety of species. Male rhesus monkeys show some degree of testicular regression during the non-breeding season (Sade, 1964); however, both behavioural and testicular gonadal function increased following exposure to an endocrinologically patent female (Vandenbergh, 1969). Breeding synchrony may have occurred in *Lemur catta* (Jolly, 1967) in that all nine females in the breeding group came into oestrus within 10 days of each other. If a ram is introduced to a group of ewes early in the breeding season, the females tend to come into oestrus together (Schinkel, 1954; Sinclair, 1950; Thibault et al., 1966). In birds, the observation that reproductive success is higher in large colonies than in small ones might be the result of the greater 'social stimulation' augmenting and synchronizing breeding in the large colonies. This theory proposed by Darling in 1938 may not be applicable to all the observed cases in birds (Brown, 1975); however, there seem to be some species in which this theory does hold (reviewed by McClintock, 1974).

If the breeding season is fairly accurately tied to the annual geophysical cycle, then what function would there be in causing (even slight) alterations of precise breeding times by social stimulation? In her review of the literature, McClintock (1974) derived several possible functions for breeding synchrony.

(1) As the breeding season approaches and food becomes increasingly available, the improved nutrition may bring more females into reproductive readiness. When a critical number of females reach this state, they would mutually support each other's reproductive state and help induce it in those members just about to enter breeding condition. The animals' reproduction would thus be tied to an optimal food supply.

(2) Even without being tied to variations in the microhabitat, there might be local synchronization in the timing of breeding. Peaks in local birth rate might function to saturate the predator population with young (Patterson, 1965).

(3) The synchronization that occurs from coordination of breeding might lower the amount of intragroup aggression (Nelson, 1970).

In a biological phenomenon as taxonomically widespread as breeding synchrony, there are probably several different physiological mechanisms operating. A common feature to all of these mechanisms is that one organism must be able to 'broadcast' its reproductive condition and this 'signal' must induce the same reproductive state in a recipient organism. A recently completed series of studies on female rats may prove to be a useful analogue for studying reproductive synchronization (McClintock, 1974).

In this study, groups of 6–8 female rats were placed in one of three compartments. Tubing was placed between the three boxes so that the rats could communicate via olfactory cues at least. An exhaust fan system was set up so that air was drawn from the first box *(upwind)*, through the second *(middle)* box, into the third box *(downwind)*, and then exhausted out of the room. Normal, cycling female rats were placed in the upwind and downwind boxes. In these groups, the animals received 14 h of light per day (14L : 10D).

In part I of the experiment, females that had been brought into constant oestrus by exposure to constant light were placed in the middle box. During the 20 days there, these animals were exposed to constant light (LL). In part II of the experiment, the light-induced constant oestrous females in the middle box were replaced by normal cycling females which were exposed to normal

LD cycles. Through both phases of the experiment, the oestrous cycles of all subjects were monitored. The results of this study are presented in Fig. 1.

Of the animals living under constant light in the middle box in part I, 80% were in oestrus (i.e. exhibited both cornified vaginal smears and a lordosis reflex to manual stimulation). Over the 20 days in this part of the study, the percentage of animals in the downwind box grew steadily to a maximum, in the last few days, of 83% in oestrus (over the last 9 days, the average was 56%). The percentage of females in the downwind box displaying oestrus was significantly higher than the percentage of oestrous females living in the upwind box, where the average during the last 9 days was only 25% (p < 0.02; chi square test).

In part II of the study, when the constant oestrous animals were replaced with animals displaying normal cycles (16% in heat on the average), the number of downstream animals in oestrus dropped to approximately 24%, which was not significantly different from the percentage of upwind animals in heat. These data support the notion that olfactory cues from animals in constant oestrus are sufficient to induce this state in other female rats, although other sensory modalities—like sound emitted by the oestrous females—might have played a role.

GETTING THE ORGANISMS TOGETHER: FINE-GRAINED SYNCHRONIZATION

Once an appropriate sexual partner has been selected (*cf.* p. 659) and the organism situated in a reproductively supportive physical and temporal environment (*cf.* p. 668), actual copulation can proceed. Research into the functions of, and mechanisms controlling, copulation generally falls into two classes:
1. Studies on the way in which copulatory stimulation facilitates the reproductive motivation of the male and female.
2. Studies on the mechanical reflex coordination of the genital apparatus.

Augmentation of Sexual Motivation

As was discussed in the previous sections, sexual motivation (i.e., the readiness to mate) in females and males is not always at maximal levels. There are temporal fluctuations (seasonal cycles superimposed upon the gonadal cycle), and full readiness for mating is sometimes realized only after initial sexual contact with the sexual partner. As female *Drosophila* mature, their receptivity increases rapidly between 24–48 h after eclosion (Manning, 1967), probably as a function of endogenous changes in the secretory activity of the corpus allatum. Although their subsequent receptivity remains fairly constant thereafter, the females require some copulatory stimulation from males before they will accept the male. Analogously, the female rat comes into heat

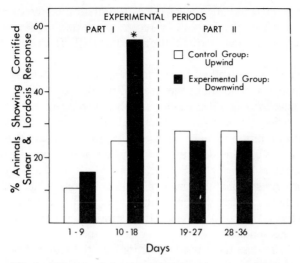

Fig. 1. Olfactory induction of oestrus in rats. In Part I of the study, the 'stimulus' animals in the *middle box* were in photically induced constant oestrus. In Part II of the study, new animals were placed in the *middle box*. They were exposed to a 14:10 LD cycle and displayed normal vaginal oestrus cycles

as a function of her ovarian cycle; however, there is often an enhancement of her mating behaviour following initial copulatory stimulation from the male (Beach, 1948).

Applying the 'ecological method' (i.e. comparing the responses of phylogenetically distant species to common environmental pressures, Lockard, 1971), the copulation-induced augmentation of mating in both *Drosophila* and rats has been found to have some common features. First, the increase in receptivity is a function of the kind of stimulation that a male of the species gives during copulation. Bennett-Clark *et al.* (1973) found that female *Drosophila melanogaster* were more receptive to male courtship if, immediately prior to the introduction of the males, the females were presented with an electronically simulated analogue of the courting song. Similarly, female rats show an increased probability of presenting the receptive posture (lordosis) to male rats if they were first primed with two seconds of experimenter-delivered cervical stimulation. Cervical stimulation of this kind is the type that a male delivers during his copulatory intromissions (Rodriguez-Sierra *et al.*, 1975).

These experiments demonstrate that female rats and fruit flies possess a kind of 'reproductive memory' for stimulation; the effects of stimulation persist even after the stimulation itself has terminated. In the experiment on *Drosophila*, for example, the effects of five minutes of simulated courtship song exerted a facilitating effect on mating for five minutes after the priming stopped. Thereafter, there was no effect of the premating stimulation.

In the experiment in which mechanical stimulation of the cervix facilitated mating in female rats, the increase in receptivity lasted for several hours after the two seconds of vaginal stimulation had ceased (Rodrigoez-Sierra *et al.*, 1975).

The mechanisms controlling the various classes of sexual responses, as well as the mechanisms controlling the more general sexual drive, are complex. Female rodents, for example, are not simply receptive or unreceptive (Adler, 1974). In a variety of mammals, the female is currently thought to display several different kinds of sexual responses, relevant to her sexuality. The following terms and definitions describing a female's sexual behaviour have been offered by Beach (1976).

(1) *Receptivity* is defined in terms of female responses 'necessary and sufficient for the male's success in achieving intravaginal ejaculations'.

(2) *Attractivity* refers to the female's 'stimulus value in evoking sexual responses by the male'.

(3) *Proceptivity* denotes 'various reactions by the female towards the male which constitute her assumption of initiative in establishing or maintaining sexual interaction'.

The separability of these behavioural components can be demonstrated in several contexts:

A female displaying spontaneously occurring constant vaginal cornification will often display lordosis 100% of the time to the experimenter's manual stimulation. However, the probability of a *male rat* eliciting lordosis can vary considerably; and even when a male can occasionally 'force' a lordosis from one of these female rats, she will often emit rejecting behaviour towards the copulating male (Adler and Bell, 1969). In the experiments of Rodriguez-Sierra *et al.*, (1975) described above, when the experimenter-delivered cervical stimulation increased the probability of a male rat subsequently eliciting lordosis from the female, the latter sometimes went through several minutes, immediately after the stimulation, during which she fought off the male and rolled over on her back.

The sexual drive is not only complex, it is probably not a unitary construct (Hinde, 1959). It is known that a variety of exteroceptive stimuli (like mildly painful shock) can potentiate and/or accelerate a male rat's sexual behaviour (Barfield and Sachs, 1968; Caggiula and Vlahoulis, 1974; Sachs and Barfield, 1974). This kind of stimulation does seem to motivate behaviour and not merely evoke reflex-like components of the male's sexual response. In one study, the female was removed from the test cage after each series of mounts and the male required to press a bar to regain access to the female. Just as shock induces copulation in the presence of the female, in this study the shocks elicited the operant's bar-pressing response, the reinforcement for which was the addition of the female into the cage (Sachs *et al.*, 1974). Peripheral shock therefore seems to genuinely 'arouse' the animal and not simply produce shortened reflex latencies. Despite the evidence for a general motivational effect, however, such exteroceptive stimulation does not simply activate a *specifically sexual* drive state (*cf*. Meyerson and Malmnas, this volume Chapter 16). When a female rat was not present, shocks increased general exploration and investigation of objects like food, pieces of wood, and water bottles in the test cage (Caggiula and Eibergen, 1969).

General arousal is an important factor in sexual activity. Lethargic male rats can be induced to mate by peripherally administered electric shock (Crowley *et al.*, 1973). There is, however, a fine balance between general and specifically sexual elements of behavioural activation. Too much general activity would decrease the male's tendencies to attend to the female and would thus diminish his sexual capacity. Such a maladaptive increase in general activity seems to have occurred in selection studies with *Drosophila melanogaster* (Manning, 1961). In this experiment, Manning placed 50 pairs of flies in a vial and selected the 10 fastest mating pairs and the 10 slowest. Continuing selection for 25 generations, Manning developed a line of fast-mating flies, a line of slow-mating flies, and an unselected control line which was intermediate in mating speed.

After developing the two selected lines, he tested the activity of the flies by admitting them to an arena where the number of squares entered by a fly in a given time was scored. The flies from the slow lines had much higher scores on this measure of general activity than did the fast-mating lines. There were also differences between fast and slow males in more specifically *sexual* measures like frequency of copulatory licking and latency for initiating courtship. The fast flies licked more and initiated courtship faster than the slow males. The fast-mating males thus had a *higher level of sexual activity* and a *lower level of general activity* than the slow-mating males. Under normal conditions, these two activities would presumably be coordinated at an optimum level. Unbalancing the coordination, as in artificial selection for the 'slow' lines, disrupts overall sexual performance.

Integration of Copulatory Reflexes

Even when the male and female are at their respective peaks of sexual readiness, there are purely mechanical problems that must be overcome. Consider the mating sequence in rats. The female will approach the male from a distance and then quickly dart away (McClintock and Adler, in prep.). The female's darting possibly represents a soliciting pattern (Beach, 1976); and if the cage is sufficiently large, the darting away is almost followed by a male pursuit and mount. Some of the mounts of the male rat are accompanied by a penile insertion (intromission), and the final insertion of a series is accompanied by the ejaculation of sperm and the seminal material that will form a vaginal plug in the female. The mount (with or without intromission) lasts for only a fraction of a second (Bermant, 1965); the period between successive copulatory contacts lasts a minute or more (Diakow, 1974).

Each of these phases of the complex coordinating of the genital apparatus of male and female rats has a function. The male rat's pattern of multiple intromissions preceding ejaculation is necessary for the induction of pregnancy (p. 681). For the male to be able to insert his penis into the vaginal orifice, however, the female must raise her rump and deflect her tail laterally (Diakow, 1975; Pfaff and Lewis, 1974). Moreover, the male must develop an erection and contract his somatic musculature so that the penis enters the vaginal orifice.

The elevation of the female's rump and the deflection of her tail occur when she assumes the lordosis posture (the concave curvature of her back) diagnostic of receptivity. Lordosis itself is a hormone-sensitive spinal reflex (Pfaff and Lewis, 1974; see also Hart, Komisaruk, and Kelley and Pfaff, this volume Chapter 10, 11, and 7 respectively). As is the case with other sexual reflexes, there are supraspinal inhibitory influences on the spinal elements controlling lordosis. These inhibitory mechanisms are in turn disinhibited by endogenous hormonal and exteroceptive behavioural stimuli associated with mating.

The behaviour that supports the male's intromission also has a spinal reflexological component (Hart, 1968 and Hart this volume Chapter 10 for description and methodology consisting of clusters of genital responses. Although the specific responses that appeared in each cluster varied, there were only a few basic patterns. A typical response cluster included three or four erections, one to three quick flips of the penis, and one to four long flips of the penis. After the response cluster was completed, the animal remained completely quiet for at least two or three minutes even though constant pressure on the penile area was still being exerted. Despite the constant stimulus to the penis, and the presumably constant level of hormone circulating in the blood, the genital reflexes occurred periodically; the two or three minutes between clusters seemed programmed by the spinal cord itself.

The spinally programmed pacing mechanism for sexual reflexes is, however, modified by other neural control systems. (It is noteworthy that no one studying the spinal flips in transected male rats has ever observed ejaculation or even seminal emission.) Experiments which demonstrate the existence of 'mount bouts' (Sachs and Barfield, 1970) support the view that there are higher order timing elements in the male rat's nervous system which affect copulatory pacing. The mount bout is a sequence of one or more mounts, with or without penile insertion, that is not interrupted by any non-copulatory behaviour (except genital grooming or orientation of the male towards the female). If the pacing of the male's copulation were totally determined by spinal reflexes and the elicitation of these reflexes by tactile stimulation, then males that did not receive penile stimulation should show grossly distorted pacing of the mount bouts. When Sachs and Barfield (1970), however, prevented males from gaining intromission by anaesthetizing the penis or by occluding the vagina of the female, the male nonetheless displayed a normal patterning of its mount bouts.

The model of copulatory behaviour presented thus far is that there are spinal and supraspinal elements controlling the topography and timing of copulatory responses. These copulatory automatisms in male and female are only effective if they occur in a synchronized manner, with the male and female's genital apparatus positioned correctly with respect to each other. Painstaking analysis of high-speed film of rat copulation (Diakow, 1975; Pfaff and Lewis, 1974) have begun to unravel the complexity of the relation between mount, lordosis, and penile insertion.

In order to investigate the neurophysiological basis for copulatory reflexes, we have shown that there are at least three main sensory nerves in the genital region of female rats that may be involved in its mating sequence: the pelvic, pudendal, and genito-femoral nerves. (Komisaruk et al., 1972). One of these nerves, the pudendal, receives afferent input ipsilaterally from the perineal region surrounding the vagina. The sensory field of this nerve extends from the base of the clitoral sheath to the base of the tail in the midline, and laterally along the inner surface of the thigh. There were two characteristics of this nerve's sensory field that are relevant for the occurrence of intromission. First, the total size of the sensory field was significantly greater (approximately 30%) in castrated females given exogenous oestrogen injections than in uninjected castrate controls (Komisaruk et al., 1972). A similar increase in field size was found by Kow and Pfaff (1973/74). Second, the most sensitive portion within the sensory field was not invariably the peri-vaginal area but a spot approximately 1 cm caudal to the tip of the clitoral sheath (Adler et al., in press). These two features of the pudendal nerve's sensory field may represent adaptive modifications of the female rat's sensory processing to facilitate the occurrence of penile intromission.

The enlarged oestrous sensory field may facilitate a slightly misplaced penile thrust to activate the pudendal nerve, which is involved in orienting the female to the male. The 'off centre' organization of the sensory field may also play a role in facilitating intromission: the most sensitive area of this field corresponds to a point on the female's perineum that the penis contacts during a mount with intromission. This perineal contact possibly facilitates the penis to locate the vaginal orifice. (Adler et al., in press).

SETTING THE STAGE FOR PREGNANCY

In this analysis of the functions and mechanisms of sexual behaviour we have followed the steps by which appropriate mates are selected from those available in the general environment (p.659), how the sexual activities of these organisms are synchronized with the physical and temporal aspects of that environment (p. 668), and how the organisms coordinate their genital apparatus (p. 674). The final set of behavioural adaptations (which involves the more reflexive movement of copulation) sets up the conditions necessary for the union of sperm and egg and triggers the conditions for the next stages of reproduction, pregnancy, and parenthood. Behaviourally-derived stimulation is especially important in this regard because the physiological processes of ovulation, fertilization, and pregnancy do not proceed automatically in all species. Behaviour, and the stimulation derived from behaviour, often play critical roles in their induction.

Consider the progression of events in the ovarian cycle of mammals (*cf.* Lisk, this volume Chapter 13). On p. 669 data were presented demonstrating an endogenous biological clock which controlled the timing of spontaneous ovulation in the rat.

The event of ovulation is embedded in an ovarian cycle consisting of three main stages:

(1) an initial *follicular phase*, during which the ovarian follicles grow;

(2) *ovulation*, when the mature follicle releases the egg;

(3) the *luteal phase*, when the ruptured follicle is transformed into the corpus luteum, which in turn secretes progesterone. In different species, stimulation derived from behaviour plays an important role in many, if not all, of these stages.

Behavioural Induction of Ovulation

One of the most striking examples of behavioural control in the oestrous cycle is seen in some species (e.g., cat, rabbit, ferret, mink, some species of mice, and perhaps tree shrews) in which ovulation is not spontaneous but depends upon stimuli delivered by the male during courtship and copulation (Rowlands, 1966).

In a broad and careful phylogenetic survey of Muroid and Cricetine rodents, Dewsbury and co-workers have related the patterns of copulatory behaviour of male rodents to the induction of ovulation and pregnancy in the female (Dewsbury, 1975).

Behaviourally-derived stimuli can even influence ovulation in species which normally ovulate spontaneously (Aron *et al.*, 1966). For example, in female rats displaying normal oestrous cycles, copulatory stimulation can advance the time when ovulation will occur and can sometimes increase the number of eggs released (Rodgers, 1971; Rodgers and Schwartz, 1972, 1973). Behavioural stimuli exert an even stronger effect under some experimental conditions. In female rats, for example, ovulation can be experimentally inhibited by placing these animals under conditions of constant light (Brown-Grant *et al.*, 1973; Hoffman, 1973) or by injecting a number of pharmacological agents during a critical period of prooestrus (Everett and Sawyer, 1950). Female rats thus treated become induced ovulators': they do not ovulate spontaneously but will do so if they receive enough copulatory stimulation (Adler, 1974). Although the female rat is normally a 'spontaneous ovulator', she nonetheless possesses the neuroanatomical and neuroendocrinal machinery for induced ovulation.

These data imply that the differences between various categories of reproductive function in related species (e.g. the difference between female rodents that are induced ovulators *versus* those that are spontaneous ovulators) can be attributed to slight quantitative differences in the neuroendocrine thresholds for triggering pituitary–ovarian events (Everett, 1964). The sufficiency of a female's endogenous endocrine cycles for inducing ovulation, independent of copulatory stimulation, will determine the categorization of a species as spontaneous or induced ovulator.

Behavioural Induction of Progestational Hormone Secretion

In the mammalian ovarian cycle, once successful ovulation has occurred, either of two sequences can follow. A female can go through the luteal phase of the cycle and return to the start of another oestrous cycle, or she can become fertilized and enter the prolonged luteal phase characteristic of pregnancy. In the females of some species (e.g., in some primates), the spontaneous luteal phase of each ovarian cycle is long; and there is enough progesterone to permit uterine implantation of a fertilized egg. If no egg implants, the uterus, which has been developing under the influence of progesterone, sheds its inner lining, the endometrium, and another cycle begins. (An apocryphal story attributes to William Osler the statement that menstruation is the weeping and wailing of a disappointed endometrium.) In the rat, the hamster, and several species of mice, however, there is no spontaneous luteal phase of any functional consequence; in these organisms, some aspect of the male's copulation triggers the progestational state underlying pregnancy (Adler, 1974; Dewsbury, 1975; Diamond, 1970; Diamond and Yanagimachi, 1968; McGill and Coughlin, 1970).

In the remainder of this section, I will present data, primarily from our laboratory, on how the male rat's behaviour facilitates the induction of pregnancy in the female and will describe some of the mechanisms that produce these adaptive behavioural patterns. By concentrating on one species, an attempt will be made to integrate behavioural and physiological aspects of reproduction into one coherent picture.

Recall that the copulatory behaviour of the male rat consists of a series of mounts and dismounts from the female. On some of these mounts, penile intromission occurs; and on the final intromission, the male ejaculates sperm and a vaginal plug. Following a period of behavioural inactivity (the postejaculatory interval), the male resumes copulating. The pattern of mount, intromission, ejaculation, and refractory period can be repeated several times in one session (*cf.* p. 677).

Since one of the most consistent features of the copulatory pattern of this species is the series of multiple intromissions preceding each ejaculation (Dewsbury, 1975), the question arises: what function do these multiple intromissions possess for successful reproduction?

In several experiments, the probability of pregnancy was determined for females that received a *normal complement of intromissions* preceding the male's ejaculation (high intromission group); these data were compared to the probability of inducing pregnancy in an experimental group of females that were permitted only *a reduced number of preejaculatory intromissions* (low intro-

mission group), Adler, 1969; Wilson et al., 1965). About 20 days after copulation, females in both groups were sacrificed and their uteri examined for the
presence of viable foetuses. In one study (Wilson et al., 1965), approximately
90% of the females in the high intromission group were pregnant while only
20% of the females in the low intromission group were pregnant. Thus, multiple
intromissions appear to be necessary for the induction of pregnancy.

How do multiple copulatory intromissions stimulate pregnancy? Part of
the answer is to be found in the organization of the female rat's four- to five-
day oestrous cycle. Unlike most primates, the ovarian cycle of the female
rat does not automatically go through a functional luteal phase; that is, the
mature follicle ovulates but does not secrete enough progesterone to permit
uterine implantation of a fertilized egg. If the female is to become pregnant,
some event must trigger the progestational state. Initially we hypothesized
that the stimulation derived from multiple intromissions triggers a neuroendocrine reflex which results in the secretion of progesterone. To test this
hypothesis, we compared the number of females in both groups which failed to
show regular four-day oestrous cycles (Adler, 1969; Wilson et al., 1965).
Almost 100% of the females in the *high intromission group* (n = 9) failed to show
four-day oestrous cycles following stimulation; whereas only 22% of the
females in the *low intromission group* failed to show cycles (n = 9). Since
cessation of behavioural cyclicity is one of the signs of progestational hormone
secretion, we concluded that multiple intromissions stimulate the release of
progesterone. Because the proportion of females in each group that stopped
showing behavioural oestrous cycles was approximately the same as the proportion that had developing pups in the previous experiment, multiple intromissions appeared to stimulate the induction of pregnancy by stimulating the
secretion of gestational hormones. This interpretation was supported by
progesterone assays (Adler et al., 1970). Within 24 h after mating, females in
the high intromission group had significantly more progesterone in their
peripheral blood than did females in the low intromission group. It is now
known that cervical stimulation induces twice-daily surges of pituitary prolactin
release and that this daily prolactin is necessary for secretion of the ovarian
progesterone necessary for pregnancy (Smith et al., 1976).

We also wanted to study the dynamics of this behaviourally initiated neuroendocrine reflex. The first step was to determine what aspects of male intromissions are responsible for initiating pregnancy. Since females in both groups
received ejaculations with sperm and vaginal plugs, ejaculation could not
account for the induction of the progestational state; on the other hand,
ejaculation may be a necessary part of the stimulus. The results of several experiments, however, suggest otherwise. In one study, males were treated with
guanethidine sulphate before being placed with females. These males could
copulate but could not deposit any semen (sperm or plug material) during the
ejaculatory response. Nonetheless, females mated to these males became progestational (Adler, 1969).

Moreover, with increasing numbers of intromissions (even without ejaculation), the proportion of females becoming progestational increased (Adler, 1969). With four or fewer intromissions, fewer than 10% of the females were progestational; with 13–16 intromissions, approximately 85% of the females became progestational. These data indicate that the occurrence of multiple copulatory intromissions is necessary and sufficient to trigger the hormonal state of pregnancy.

We are now attempting to follow the behavioural stimulus through successive levels of the female's neuroendocrine system to determine the mechanism by which copulatory intromissions trigger the secretion of the gestational hormones.

From the electrophysiological study of genital sensory processes, we determined that it was the pelvic nerve that innervated the vagino-cervical area, (Komisaruk et al., 1972). These data support the hypothesis that the pelvic nerve is the afferent channel for the induction of progesterone secretion. Further evidence for this conclusion comes from experiments in which the pelvic nerves were cut. In these studies, the female rats did not become progestational after mechanical stimulation of the cervix (Kollar, 1953; Carlsson and De Feo, 1965; Spies and Niswender, 1971).

We are now attempting to trace the copulatory stimulus into the central nervous system components of the neuroendocrine reflex. Since a *number* of intromissions are required to trigger the progestational state (Adler, 1969), there must be some sort of storage mechanism by which the stimulation from each brief (250 ms) penile insertion is retained and combined with stimulation from succeeding intromissions.

To determine the limits of the storage capacity of this system, an experiment was performed in which the rate of stimulation was varied (Edmonds et al., 1972). For a given group of females, both the number of intromissions permitted (two, five, or ten) and the interval between intromissions varied: the inter-intromission-interval values ranged from the control rate of *ad libitum* copulation (approximately 40s) up to one hour. The results are summarized in Fig. 2.

With ten intromissions, 100% of the females became progestational. This result is especially striking because the intromissions could be spaced one every half hour without a diminution in their effectiveness. The results for females receiving five intromissions also indicate that spaced intromissions are as effective as intromissions delivered at the control rate and, in addition, that intromissions at the rate of one every four or five minutes may be *more* effective in stimulating the progestational response than the control rate. One intromission delivered every half hour provided a density of stimulation of only one part per 7,200 (one intromission—250ms—per half hour). This potency points to an exquisitely adapted form of neuroendocrine integration by which species-specific stimuli (the multiple intromissions) are stored by an adaptively specialized neural mechanism.

The operation of this entire pregnancy system can be conceptualized as a

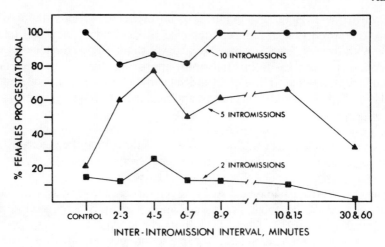

Fig. 2. Effects of different inter-intromission intervals on the induction
of progestational hormone secretion in female rats ($N = 213$)

biological amplifier in which each stage lengthens the temporal characteristics
of the previous one. Stimulation from the brief penile intromissions is stored
and accumulated. The stimulation leads to a central nervous system (CNS)
event, the duration of which is undetermined but which may run for several
hours (Barraclough and Sawyer, 1959). Pituitary involvement may last 12 days
(Pencharz and Long, 1933); the ovary secretes large amounts of progesterone
for 19 days (Morishige *et al.*, 1973). The final stage, uterine pregnancy, continues
for more than 20 days. In this sequence, the intromissions trigger the tonic
secretion of progesterone.

The storage of the initial copulatory stimulation in the female rat resembles
the other examples of reproductive mnemonic devices which were discussed
earlier in the chapter. Adaptively specialized storage systems are, in fact,
frequently occurring phenomena in reproductive physiology. The phenomenon
of delayed pseudopregnancy represents a classic example (Everett, 1968); if
proper parameters are used, electrical stimulation of the brain results in the
induction of a progestational state in female rats, but only after a delay of hours
or days. Another example of reproductive storage occurs in the hamster, in
which copulatory stimulation facilitates the subsequent parturation, more
than 20 days after the stimulus (Diamond, 1972). Although exogenous progesterone injections can trigger the progestational response and permit a pregnancy to follow artificial insemination, parturition is not normal unless
copulatory stimulation from a male hamster is provided at the time of insemination. The mechanism by which the stimulus is stored in the female's neuroendocrine system is not yet known precisely in any of these examples, but
phenomenologically they all represent the storage and amplification of a
triggering stimulus.

Behavioural Induction of Sperm Transport in Females

When first studying the copulatory influences on pregnancy in rats, we concentrated on the function of multiple intromissions in stimulating the neuroendocrine reflex that resulted in progesterone secretion and subsequent gestation. Since all of the female rats in our experiment, in both the high and low intromission groups, had sperm and plug deposited in their vaginas, it was an easy assumption that sperm transport and fertilization were normal (Adler, 1969). In one experiment, however, we checked the condition of ova in the fallopian tubes of the female rats three days after copulation.

Females which had received many preejaculatory intromissions all had developing ova in the blastocyst stage, whereas females which had received an ejaculation preceded by only one intromission had unfertilized and degenerating ova (Adler, 1968; 1969).

From subsequent studies (Adler, 1969; Adler and Zoloth, 1970), we discovered (1) that a number of preejaculatory intromissions were necessary to induce the normal transport of sperm from the vagina into the uterus of female rats that had just received an ejaculation. Besides requiring the preejaculatory intromissions, the postejcaulatory transport of sperm in female rats has two other behavioural prerequisites. (2) A prolonged ejaculatory response is required. (In one experiment, males that dismounted in less than 2 s following ejaculation produced uterine sperm counts that were significantly lower than those produced by males that stayed on the female for 2 or more s, Matthews and Adler, in press.) We hypothesized that prolonged ejaculatory responses ensure that the vaginal plug will be tightly placed against the cervix (Blandau, 1945; Matthews and Adler, in press. (3) It was also discovered that a period of behavioural quiescence by the male following ejaculation is necessary for the process of sperm transport in the female to be completed. Maximal numbers of sperm do not reach the uterus until 6–8 min following ejaculation (Adler and Zoloth, 1970; Matthews and Adler, in press). If, during this time, a female rat receives copulatory intromissions, the numbers of sperm in the uterus are reduced, and the size of her litter diminished (Adler, 1974). These behavioural influences on sperm transport in female rats are schematically summarized in Fig. 3.

The potential disruption of sperm transport by postejaculatory copulatory stimulation may have functional significance for the organization of reproduction in this species. Theoretically, one male could 'cancel' the effects of another male's copulation. If the second male begins copulating too soon after the previous male has completed an ejaculatory series, his multiple intromissions may prevent the first male's sperm from reaching the uterus, presumably by dislodging the plug. The second male's sperm would then be deposited upon *his* ejaculation and could fertilize the ova. To test this possibility, we arranged a series of mating tests involving albino female rats (Adler and Zoloth, 1970). An albino female was allowed to mate first with an albino male and was then

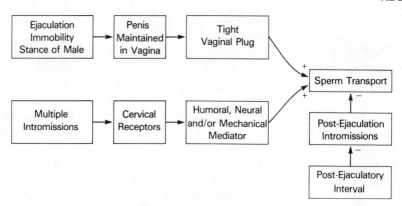

Fig. 3. Factors involved in sperm transport through the reproductive tract of female rats. The figure schematizes the effects of three components of the male rat's copulatory behaviour: the pre-ejaculatory multiple intromissions, the duration of the ejaculatory response, and the post-ejaculatory refractory period. The ' + ' signs represent facilitative effects while the ' − ' signs represent inhibitory effects. In this schema, the multiple intromissions and prolonged ejaculatory response both facilitate sperm transport. The physiological mechanism responsible for producing the post-ejaculatory refractory period, on the other hand, inhibits (or prevents) the male from delivering post-ejaculatory intromissions. If these post-ejaculatory intromissions *did* occur, they would inhibit sperm transport. The post-ejaculatory interval therefore disinhibits sperm transport

mated with a pigmented male for a second ejaculatory series. Paternity could be established soon after the pups are born since pups sired by albino fathers are light coloured and have clear eyes, whereas pups of pigmented fathers have dark skins and pigmented eyes. If a pigmented male is substituted for an albino male within the first few minutes after the albino's initial ejaculation, approximately 60% of the offspring are pigmented. If, however, 45 to 60 min elapse between copulations, only 23% of the offspring are pigmented. Therefore, a male rat can, if he begins copulating soon enough, prevent the insemination of a given female by another male that had copulated previously (Adler and Zoloth, 1970).

Thus, for effective sperm transport, the female rat must have no cervical stimulation for several minutes after receiving an ejaculation. What then prevents a male which has just ejaculated from resuming his intromission during this critical time? We suggest that it is the male's postejaculatory refractory period that prevents him from resuming copulation too soon (Adler and Zoloth, 1970). The male rats in our laboratory require an average of 4.5 min after ejaculating before they deliver the first intromission of their next ejaculatory series. Since three intromissions on the average are required to dislodge the vaginal plug totally (Lisk, 1969), and since sperm transport is relatively complete within six to eight minutes, the postejaculatory refractory period is of the correct magnitude to permit effective sperm transport into the uterine lumen.

The hypothesized function of the postejaculatory refractory period may have ecological significance for rodent population dynamics. Under conditions of crowding, laboratory rats show persistent social pathology (Calhoun, 1962a). One type of behavioural abnormality is a kind of pansexual behaviour in which males mount at a much higher rate than usual. In these crowded colonies, reproduction decreases, partly because of the pathological increase in mounting. Even where crowding is not a problem, colonies of rats with a higher percentage of males produce fewer pups than colonies with fewer males (Calhoun, 1962b). One of the reasons for reduced reproductive performance in such colonies may be copulatory interference with sperm transport.

Reproductive processes are also blocked in other species; the odour of strange males inhibits implantation in female mice (Parkes and Bruce, 1961). Sperm are rejected by the bursa copulatrix of *Drosophila* females during inter-specific mating (Dobzhansky *et al.*, 1968); and prolonged auditory stimulation can reduce fertility in rats (Zondek and Tamari, 1967). All of these examples of disruptions in reproductive processing may be 'pharmacological' in the sense that normally behavioural processes—like the postejaculatory interval in male rats—protect the organism from reproductive dysfunction.

Mechanisms Responsible for Adaptive Copulatory Patterns in Rats

If the postejaculatory refractory period of the male rat is an integral part of the copulatory process leading to sperm transport and successful pregnancy, its occurrence may be the result of an active physiological process of a type that normally ensures an adaptive behavioural inhibition. Several experiments now point to the operation of just such an active inhibitory process during the postejaculatory interval, when the male rat displays a pattern of 'tonic immobility' (Dewsbury, 1967). Along with this behaviour pattern, the hippo-campal and cortical EEG display the kind of spindling and slow wave electrical activity (Kurtz and Adler, 1973) that often signals physiological inhibition (Gellhorn, 1967). Another feature of the postejaculatory interval which indicates its active nature is the 22 kHz vocalization emitted by the male during his 'absolute refractory period' (Barfield and Geyer, 1975). When the EEG and vocalizations were recorded simultaneously, a correlation of approximately 0.95 was found between the 'inhibitory EEG spindling' and the emission of the of the 22 KHz vocalizations.

On the basis of behavioural and physiological indices like those presented in the preceding paragraph, Kurtz was able to develop an opponent-process model to describe the male rat's copulatory pattern (Kurtz and Adler, 1973). The performance of the successive intromissions culminating in ejaculation is induced by a positive appetitive system. The function of this system is to produce the series of copulatory events necessary for ejaculation in the male and the induction of pregnancy in the female. The behavioural refractoriness of the male during his postejaculatory interval (necessary to permit sperm trans-port in the female) is under an inhibitory system, reflected by the EEG spindling.

A pattern of multiple control is also found in the sexual behaviour of the female rat. There is an active (proceptive) phase in which she solicits and elicits male mounts (McClintock and Adler, in prep.). During the male's mount with intromission, the penile contact with the cervix induces a momentary behavioural inhibition of the female (*cf.* Komisaruk, this volume Chapter 11; also Diakow, 1974). Since cervical stimulation from intromission is necessary to induce pregnancy, it seems adaptive that the female rat should be inhibited from moving and should be less responsive to certain classes of stimuli while receiving an intromission. In Chapter 11 of this volume, Komisaruk suggests that lordosis is an extensor reflex which would stabilize the female in her position on the substrate (Komisaruk, 1974).

Finally, there is evidence that prolonged copulatory stimulation can, over the long run, inhibit or reduce female receptivity. The kind of cortical spindling that was described in male rats has also been found in female rats, as they approach sexual satiety (Kurtz, 1975). Furthermore, the diminution of receptivity following copulation is a phenomenon not restricted to rats but has been found in females of a wide variety of species including hamsters guinea pigs, turkeys, lizards, fruit flies, and some cockroaches (Barth, 1968; Carter and Schein, 1971; Crews, 1973; Goldfoot and Goy, 1970; Hardy and DeBold, 1972; Manning, 1967; Schein and Hale, 1965). Sexual behaviour in the female is thus a product of opposing systems. It is by the precise integration of positive and inhibitory behavioural mechanisms that behaviour is adaptively organized in sexually reproducing organisms.

SUMMARY AND CONCLUSION

Although there are many variations in the specific form of sexual behaviour, and the physiological mechanisms controlling it, every sexually reproducing species must solve these basic problems of sexual synchronization: (1) the promotion of intraspecific mating, (2) the selection by an organism of a reproductively appropriate mate within the species, (3) the tying of reproductive activities to a spatially and temporally adequate set of environmental conditions, (4) the coordination of the reproductive moods and copulatory movements of the mating pair, and (5) the setting up of conditions compatible with the next stages of reproduction, pregnancy, and parenthood. The purpose of of this chapter has been to outline some of the ways that the mechanisms controlling sexual behaviour contribute to this synchronization. Reproductive behaviour represents a mechanism for 'moving' an organism through its reproductive life cycle in an orderly and adaptive manner.

ACKNOWLEDGEMENTS

Preparation of this manuscript was supported by NIH Grant HD-04522 and NSF Grant BNS76-10198.

The author wishes to acknowledge the valuable criticisms and comments on the manuscript from Shelley Adler and from Drs. J. Anisko, B. Bertram, C. R. Gallistel, J. B. Hutchison, M. McClintock, and P. Rozin.

Invaluable technical assistance was provided by Elizabeth Spitzer, Richard Eisenberg, and David Hunter.

REFERENCES

Adler, N. T. (1968) Effects of the male's copulatory behavior in the initiation of pregnancy in the female rat, *Anat. Rec.*, **160**, 305.

Adler, N. T. (1969) The effect of male's copulatory behavior on successful pregnancy of the female rat. *J. Comp. Physiol. Psychol.*, **69**, 613.

Adler, N. T. (1974) The behavioral control of reproductive physiology. In: *Reproductive Behavior*, W. Montagna and W. A. Sadler (eds.), Plenum, New York.

Adler, N. T. and Bell, D. (1969) Constant estrus in rats: vaginal, reflexive, and behavioral changes, *Physiol. Behav.*, **4**, 151–3.

Adler, N. T., Komisaruk, B., and Davis, P. (in press). Sensory field of the pudendal nerve as a function of the estrous cycle in female rats, *Horm. Behav.*

Adler, N. T., Resko, J. A., and Goy, R. W. (1970) The effect of copulatory behavior on hormonal change in the female rat prior to implantation, *Physiol. Behav.*, **5**, 1003–7.

Adler, N. T. and Zoloth, S. R. (1970) Copulatory behavior can inhibit pregnancy in female rats, *Science*, **168**, 1480–2.

Alcock, J. (1975) *Animal Behavior. An Evolutionary Approach*, Sinauer, Sunderland, Mass.

Alexander, R. D. (1968) Arthropods. In: *Animal Communication*, T. Seboek (ed.), Indiana University Press, Bloomington.

Alleva, J. J., Waleski, M. V., and Alleva, F. R. (1971) A biological clock controlling the estrous cycle of the hamster, *Endocrinology*, **88**, 1368–79.

Aron, C., Asch, G., and Roos, J. (1966) Triggering of ovulation by coitus in the rat, *Int. Rev. Cytol.*, **20**, 139–72.

Barfield, R. J. and Geyer, L. A. (1975) The ultrasonic postejaculatory vocalization and the postejaculatory refractory period of the male rat, *J. Comp. Physiol. Psychol.*, **88**, 723–34.

Barfield, R. J., and Sachs, B. D. (1968) Sexual behavior: stimulation by painful electrical shock to skin in male rats. *Science*, **161**, 392–6.

Barraclough, C. A. and Sawyer, C. H. (1959) Induction of pseudopregnancy in the rat by reserpine and chlorpromazine, *Endocrinology*, **65**, 563–71.

Barth, R. H., Jr. (1968) The comparative physiology of reproductive processes in cockroaches. Part I. Mating behaviour and its endocrine control, *Adv. Reprod. Physiol.*, 167–207.

Beach, F. A. (1948) *Hormones and Behavior*, Paul B. Hoeber, Inc., New York.

Beach, F. A. (1976) Sexual attractivity, proceptivity, and receptivity in female mammals, *Horm. Behav.*, **7**, 105–38.

Beamer, W., Bermant, G., and Clegg, M. (1969) Copulatory behavior of the ram, *Ovis aries* II: Factors affecting copulatory satiation, *Anim. Behav.*, **17**, 706–11.

Bennet-Clark, H. C. and Ewing, A. W. (1968) The wing mechanism involved in the courtship of *Drosophila*, *J. Exp. Biol.*, **49**, 117–28.

Bennet-Clark, H. C., Ewing, A. W., and Manning, Aubrey (1973) The persistence of courtship stimulation in *Drosophila melanogaster*, *Behav. Biol.*, **8**, 763–9.

Bermant, G. (1965) Sexual behavior of male rats: Photographic analysis of the intromission response, *Psychon. Sci.*, **2**, 65–6.

Bermant, G., and Davidson, J. M., eds. (1974) *Biological Basis of Sexual Behaviour*, Harper and Row, New York.

Bermant, G., Lott, D., and Anderson, L. (1968) Temporal characteristics of the Coolidge Effect in male rat copulatory behavior, *J. Comp. Physiol. Psychol.*, **65**, 447–52.

Blandau, R. J. (1945) On the factors involved in sperm transport through the cervix uteri of the albino rat. *American Journal of Anatomy*, **77**, 253–72.

Brander, R. B. (1967) Movements of female ruffed grouse during the mating season, *Wilson Bull.*, **79**, 28–36.

Brown, J. L. (1975) *The Evolution of Behaviour*, Norton, New York.

Brown-Grant, K., Davidson, J. M., and Grieg, F. (1973) Induced ovulation in albino rats exposed to constant light, *J. Endocrinol.*, **57**, 7–22.

Bunning, E. (1973) *The Physiological Clock: Circadium Rhythms and Biological Chronometry* (3rd edn. revised), Springer-Verlag, New York.

Caggiula, A. R. and Eibergen, R. (1969) Copulation of virgin male rats evoked by painful peripheral stimulation, *J. Comp. Physiol. Psychol.*, **69**, 414–9.

Caggiula, A. R., Vlahoulis, M. (1974) Modifications in the copulatory performance of male rats produced by repeated peripheral shock, *Behav. Biol.*, **11**, 269–74.

Calhoun, J. (1962a) *The Ecology and Sociology of the Norway Rat*, Public Health Service Publication No. 1008, Public Health Service, Bethesda, Md.

Calhoun, John B. (1962b) Population density and social pathology, *Sci. Am.*, **206**, 139–48.

Campbell, B. (1972) *Sexual Selection and the Descent of Man*, Aldine Publishing Co., Chicago.

Capranica, R. R. (1965) *The Evoked Vocal Response of the Bullfrog*, MIT Press, Cambridge, Mass.

Carlsson, R. R. and DeFeo, V. J. (1965) Role of the pelvic nerve *vs.* the abdominal sympathetic nerves in the reproductive function of the female rat, *Endocrinology*, **77**, 1014–22.

Carr, W. J., Krames, L., and Costanzo, D. J. (1970) Previous sexual experience and olfactory preference for novel *versus* original sex partners in rats, *J. Comp. Physiol. Psychol.*, **71**, 216–22.

Carr, W. J., Loeb, L. S., and Wylie, N. R. (1966) Responses to feminine odors in normal and castrated male rats, *J. Comp. Physiol. Psychol.*, **62**, 336–8.

Carter, C. S. and Schein, M. W. (1971) Sexual receptivity and exhaustion in the female golden hamster. *Horm. Behav.*, **2**, 191–200.

Collias, N. E. and Collias, E. C. (1969) Size of breeding colony related to attraction of mates in a tropical passerine bird, *Ecology*, **50**, 481–8.

Crews, David (1973) Coition-induced inhibition of sexual receptivity in female lizards *(Anolis carolinensis)*, *Physiol. Behav.*, **11**, 463–8.

Crow, J. F. and Kimura, M. (1970) *An Introduction to Population Genetics Theory*, Harper and Row, New York.

Crowley, W. R., Popolow, H. B., and Ward, B. O., Jr. (1973) From dud to stud: Copulatory behavior elicited through conditioned arousal in sexually inactive male rats, *Physiol. Behav.*, **10**, 391–4.

Darling, F. F. (1938) *Bird Flocks and the Breeding Cycle*, University Press, Cambridge.

Darling, F. F. (1964) *A Herd of Red Deer*, Anchor Books, Doubleday, Garden City, N. Y.

Darwin, C. (1859) *On the Origin of Species*, Murray, London.

Darwin, C. (1871) *The Descent of Man and Selection in Relation to Sex*, Modern Library, Random House, New York.

Dewsbury, D. A. (1967) A quantitative description of the behavior of rats during copulation, *Behavior*, **29**, 154–78.

Dewsbury, D. A. (1975) Diversity and adaptation in rodent copulatory behavior, *Science*, **190**, 947–55.

Diakow, C. (1974) Male–female interactions and the organization of mammalian mating patterns. In: *Advances in the Study of Behavior*, 4, D. S. Lehrman, J. S. Rosenblatt, R. A. Hinde, and E. Shaw (eds.), Academic Press, New York.

Diakow, C. (1975) Motion picture analysis of rat mating behavior, *J. Comp. Physiol. Psychol.*, **88**, 704–12.

Diamond, M. (1970) Intromission pattern and species vaginal code in relation to induction of pseudopregnancy, *Science*, **169**, 995–7.

Diamond, M. (1972) Vaginal stimulation and progesterone in relation to pregnancy and parturition, *Biol. Reprod.*, **6**, 281–7.

Diamond, M. and Yanagimachi, R. (1968) Induction of pseudopregnancy in the golden hamster, *J. Reprod. Fert.*, **17**, 165–8.

Dobzhansky, T. (1955) *Evolution, Genetics, and Man*, Wiley, New York.

Dobzhansky, T. (1970) *Genetics of the Evolutionary Process*, Columbia Univ. Press, New York and London.

Dobzhansky, T., Ehrman, L., and Kastritsis, P. A. (1968) Ethological isolation between sympatric and allopatric species of the *Obscura* group of *Drosophila*. *Anim. Behav.*, **16**, 79–87.

Doty, R. L. (1974) A cry for the liberation of the female rodent: courtship and copulation in *Rodentia*, *Psychol. Bull.*, **81**, 159–72.

Edmonds, S., Zoloth, S. R., and Adler, N. T. (1972) Storage of copulatory stimulation in the female rat, *Physiol. Behav.*, **8**, 161–4.

Ehrman, L. (1960) A genetic constitution frustrating the sexual drive in *Drosophila paulistorum*, *Science*, **131**, 1381–2.

Ehrman, L. (1966) Mating success and genotype frequency in *Drosophila*, *Anim. Behav.*, **14**, 332–9.

Ehrman, L. (1970) The mating advantage of rare males in *Drosophila*, *Proc. Nat. Acad. Sci.*, **65**, 345–8.

Ehrman, L. and Parsons, P. A. (1976) *The Genetics of Behavior*, Sinauer, Sunderland, Mass.

Elliott, J. A., Stetson, M. H., and Menaker, M. (1972) Regulation of testis function in golden hamsters: a circadian clock measures photoperiodic time, *Science*, **178**, 771–3.

Everett, J. W. (1964) Central neural control of reproductive functions of the adenohypophysis, *Physiol. Rev.*, **44**, 373–431.

Everett, J. W. (1968) Delayed pseudopregnancy in the rat, a tool for the study of central neural mechanisms in reproduction. In *Perspectives in Reproduction and Sexual behaviour*, M. Diamond (ed.), Indiana University Press, Bloomington and London.

Everett, J. W. and Sawyer, C. H. (1950) A 24-hour periodicity in the LH-release apparatus of female rats, disclosed by barbiturate sedation, *Endocrinology*, **47**, 198–218.

Ewing, A. W. (1961) Body size and courtship behavior in *Drosophila melanogaster*, *Anim. Behav.*, **11**, 93–9.

Ewing, A. W. (1969) The genetic basis of sound production in *Drosophila Pseudoobscura* and *D. Persimilis*, *Anim. Behav.*, **17**, 555–60.

Ewing, A. W. (1970) The evolution of courtship songs in *Drosophila*, *Rev. Comp. Anim.*, **4**, 3–8.

Feder, H. H., Resko, J. A., and Goy, R. W. (1968) Progesterone levels in the arterial plasma of pre-ovulatory and ovariectomized rats, *J. Endocrinol.*, **41**, 563–9.

Fisher, A. (1962) Effects of stimulus variation on sexual satiation in the male rat, *J. Comp. Physiol. Psychol.*, **55**, 614–20.

Fisher, R. A. (1958) *The Genetical Theory of Natural Selection*, ed. (2nd revised) Dover, New York.

Fowler, H. and Whalen, R. (1961) Variation in incentive stimulus and sexual behavior in the male rat, *J. Comp. Physiol. Psychol.*, **54**, 68–71.

Gaston, S. and Menaker, M. (1967) Photoperiodic control of hamster testis, *Science*, **158**, 925–8.

Gellhorn, E. (1967) *Principles of Autonomic-Somatic Integration: Physiological Basis and Psychological and Clinical Implications*, Univ. of Minnesota Press, Minneapolis.

Goldfoot, D. A. and Goy, R. W. (1970) Abbreviation of behavioral estrus in guinea pigs by coital and vagino-cervical stimulation, *J. Comp. Physiol. Psychol.*, **72**, 426–34.

Grunt, J. and Young, W. C. (1952) Psychological modification of fatigue following orgasm (ejaculation) in the male guinea pig, *J. Comp. Physiol Psychol.*, **45**, 508–10.

Hardy, D. F. and DeBold, J. F. (1972) Effects of coital stimulation upon behavior of the female rat, *J. Comp. Physiol. Psychol.*, **78**, 400–8.

Hart, B. L. (1968) Sexual responses and mating behavior in the male rat. *J. Comp. Physiol. Psychol.*, **65**, 453–60.

Hemmingsen, A. M. and Krarup, N. B. (1937) Rhythmic diurnal variations in the oestrous phenomena of the rat and their susceptibility to light and dark, *Kongelige Danske Videnskabernes Selskab Biologiske Meddleelson*, **13**, 1–61.

Hinde, R. A. (1959) Unitary drives, *Anim. Behav.*, **7**, 130–41.

Hjorth, I. (1970) Reproductive behavior in Tetraonidae, with special reference to males, *Viltrevy*, **7**, 271–328.

Hoffman, J. C. (1967) Effects of light deprivation on the rat estrous cycle, *Neuroendocrinology*, **2**, 1–10.

Hoffman, J. C. (1969) An effect of early lighting history on later response to light deprivation in the rat, *Federation Proc.*, **28**, 382.

Hoffman, J. C. (1970) Light and reproduction in the rat: effects of photoperiod length on albino rats from two different breeders, *Biol. Reprod.*, **2**, 255–61.

Hoffman, J. C. (1973) The influence of photoperiods on reproductive functions in female mammals, *Handbook of Physiology—Endocrinology II*, part 1, 57–77.

Hoy, R. R. and Paul, R. L. (1973) Genetic control of song specificity in crickets, *Science*, **180**, 82–3.

Hsiao, S. (1965) The effect of female variation on sexual satiation in the male rat, *J. Comp. Physiol. Psychol.*, **60**, 467–9.

Jolly, A. (1967) Breeding synchrony in wild *Lemur catta*. In: *Social Communication among Primates*, S. Altman (ed.), University of Chicago Press, Chicago.

Kollar, E. J. (1953) Reproduction in the female rat after pelvic nerve neurectomy, *Anat. Rec.*, **115**, 641–58.

Komisaruk, B. R. (1974) Neural and hormonal interactions in the reproductive behavior of female rats. In: *Reproductive Behavior*, W. Montagna and W. Sadler (eds.), Plenum Press, New York.

Komisaruk, B. R., Adler, N. T., and Hutchison, J. B. (1972) Genital sensory field: enlargement by estrogen treatment in female rats, *Science*, **178**, 1295–8.

Kow, L. M. and Pfaff, D. W. (1973/74) Effects of estrogen treatment on the size of receptive field and response threshold of pudendal nerve in the female rat, *Neuroendocrinology*, **13**, 299–313.

Kruijt, J. P. and Hogan, J. A. (1967) Social behavior on the lek in black grouse, *Lyrurus tetrix tetrix* (L.), *Ardea*, **55**, 203–40.

Kuehn, R. E. and Beach, F. A. (1963) Quantitative measurement of sexual receptivity in female rats, *Behaviour*, **21**, 282.

Kurtz, R. G. (1975) Hippocampal and cortical activity during sexual behavior in the female rat, *J. of Comp. Physiol. Psychol.*, **89**, 158–69.

Kurtz, R. G. and Adler, N. T. (1973) Electrophysiological correlates of copulatory behavior in the male rat: evidence for a sexual inhibitory process, *J. Comp. Physiol Psychol.*, **84**, 225–39.

Lack, D. (1968) *Ecological Adaptations for Breeding in Birds*, Methuen, London.

Larsson, K. (1956) *Conditioning and Sexual Behavior*, Almquist and Wiksell, Stockholm.

Larsson, L. and Sodersten, P. (1973) Mating in male rats after section of th dorsal penile nerve, *Physiol. Behav.*, **10**, 567–71.

Lincoln, G. A. (1972) The role of antlers in the behaviour of red deer, *J. Exp. Zool.*, **182**, 233–50.

Lisk, R. D. (1969) Cyclic fluctuations in sexual responsiveness in the male rat, *J. Exp. Zool.*, **171**, 313–9.

Lockard, R. B. (1971) Reflections on the fall of comparative psychology: is there a message for us all? *Am. Psychol.*, **26**, 168–79.

Long., J. A. and Evans, H. M. (1922) The estrous cycle in the rat and its associated phenomena, *Mem. Univ. Calif.*, **6**, 1–128.

McClintock, M. (1974) Sociobiology of reproduction in the Norway rat *(Rattus norvegicus)*. Estrous synchrony and the role of the female rat in copulatory behavior, Unpublished doctoral dissertation, University of Pennsylvania.

McClintock, M. K., and Adler, N. T. The sexual behavior of the wild and domestic Norway rat: I. The role of the female and the effect of domestication. (Submitted for publication.)

McGill, T. E. and Coughlin, R. C. (1970) Ejaculatory reflex and luteal activity induction in *Mus musculus*, *J. Reprod. Fert.*, **21**, 215–20.

Manning, A. (1961) The effects of artificial selection for mating speed in *Drosophila melanogaster*, *Anim. Behav.*, **9**, 82–92.

Manning, A. (1963) Evolutionary changes in behaviour genetics, *Genetics Today*. Proceedings of the XI International Congress of Genetic, Pergamon Press, The Hague, Netherlands.

Manning, A. (1965) Drosophila and the evolution of behavior. *Viewpoints in Biology*, **4**, 125–69, Butterworths, London.

Manning, A. (1967) The control of sexual receptivity in female *Drosophilia*, *Anim. Behav.*, **15**, 239–50.

Matthews, M., and Adler, N. T. (in press). Facilitative and inhibitory effects of copulatory behavior on sperm transport in female rats.

Mayr, E. (1963) *Animal Species and Evolution*, Belknap, Cambridge, Mass.

Mayr, E. (1969) *Principles of Systematic Zoology*, McGraw-Hill, New York.

Morishige, W. K., Pepe, G., and Rothchild, I. (1973) Serum luteinizing hormone, prolactin, and progesterone levels during pregnancy in the rat, *Endocrinology*, **92**, 1527–30.

Muller, H. J. (1942) Isolating mechanisms, evolution, and temperature, *Biol. Symposia*, **6**, 71–125.

Nelson, J. B. (1970) The relationship between behavior and ecology in the sulidae with reference to other sea birds, *Oceanogr. Mar. Biol. Ann. Rev.*, **8**, 501.

Parkes, A. S. and Bruce, H. M. (1961) Olfactory stimuli in mammalian reproduction, *Science*, **134**, 1049–54.

Patterson, I. J. (1965) Timing and spacing of broods in the black headed gull *Larus ridibundus*, *Ibis*, **107**, 433.

Pencharz, R. I. and Long, J. A. (1933) Hypophysectomy in the pregnant rat, *Am. J. Anat.*, **53**, 117–35.

Petit, C. (1951) Le role de l'isolement sexuel dans l'evolution des populations de *Drosophila melanogaster*, *Bulletin Biologique de la France et de la Belgique*, **85**, 392–418.

Pfaff, D. W. and Lewis, C. (1974) Film analyses of lordosis in female rats, *Horm. Behav.*, **5**, 317–35.

Richter, C. P. (1965) *Biological Clocks in Medicine and Psychiatry*, Charles C. Thomas, Illinois.

Richter, C. P. (1970) Dependence of successful mating in rats on functioning of the 24-hour clocks of the male and female, *Comm. Behav. Biol.*, A, **5**, 1–5.

Ricklefs, R. E. (1973) *Ecology*, Chrion Press, Newton, Mass.

Robel, R. J. (1966) Booming territory size and mating success of the greater prairie chicken, *Anim. Behav.*, **14**, 328–31.

Rodgers, C. H. (1971) Influence of copulation on ovulation in the cycling rat, *Endocrinology*, **88**, 433–6.

Rodgers, C. H. and Schwartz, N. B. (1972) Diencephalic regulation of plasma LH, ovulation, and sexual behavior in the rat. *Endocrinology*, **90**, 461–5.

Rodgers, Charles H. and Schwartz, N. B. (1973) Serum LH and FSH levels in mated and unmated proestrous female rats, *Endocrinology*, **92**, 1475.

Rodriguez-Sierra, J. F., Crowley, W. R., and Komisaruc, B. R. (1975) Vaginal stimulation in rats induces prolonged lordosis responsiveness and sexual receptivity. *J. Comp. Physiol. Psychol.*, **89**, 79–85.

Rowlands, I. W., ed. (1966) *Comparative Biology of Reproduction in Mammals*, Zoological Society of London Symposia, Number 15.

Rusak, B. and Zucker, I. (1975) Biological rhythms and animal behavior, *Ann. Rev. Psychol.*, **26**, 137–71.

Sachs, B. D. and Barfield, R. J. (1970) Temporal patterning of sexual behavior in the male rat, *J. Comp. Physiol. Psychol.*, **73**, 359–64.

Sachs, B. D. and Barfield, R. J. (1974) Copulatory behavior of male rats given intermittent electric shocks: theoretical implications, *J. Comp. Physiol. Psychol.*, **86**, 607–15.

Sachs, B. D., Macaione, R., and Fegy, L. (1974) Pacing of copulatory behavior in the male rat: effects of receptive females and intermittent shocks, *J. Comp. Physiol. Psychol.*, **87**, 326–31.

Sade, D. S. (1964) Seasonal cycle in size of testes of freeranging *Macaca mulatta*, *Folia Primatol.*, **2**, 171–80.

Sadler, R.M.F.S. (1969) *The Ecology of Reproduction in Wild and Domestic Mammals*, Methuen, London.

Schein, M. W. and Hale, E. B. (1965) Stimuli eliciting sexual behavior. In: *Sex and Behavior*, F. A. Beach (ed.), J. Wiley and Sons, New York.

Schinkel, P. G. (1954) The effect of the ram on the incidence and occurrence of oestrus in ewes, *Aust. Vet. J.*, **30**, 189–95.

Selander, R. K. (1965) On mating systems and sexual selection, *Am. Natur.*, **99**, 129–40.

Sinclair, A. N. (1950) A note on the effect of the presence of rams on the incidence of oestrus in maiden Merino ewes during spring mating, *Aust. Vet. J.*, **26**, 37–9.

Smith, M. S., Freeman, M. E., and Neill, J. D. (1975) The control of progesterone secretion during the estrous cycle and early pseudopregnancy in the rat: Prolactin gonadotropin and steroid levels associated with rescue of the corpus luteum of pseudopregnancy, *Endocrinology*, **96**, 219–27.

Smith, M. S., McLean, B. K., and Neill, J. D. (1976) Prolactin: The initial luteotropic stimulus of pseudopregnancy in the rat, *Endocrinology*, **98**, 1370–8.

Snow, D. W. (1956) Courtship ritual: the dance of the manakins, *Anim. King.*, **59**, 86–91.

Snow, D. W. (1963) The display of the blue-backed manakin, *Chiroxiphia pareola*, in Tobago, W. I., *Zoologica*, **48**, 167–76.

Spies, H. G. and Niswender, G. D. (1971) Levels of prolactin, LH, and FSH in the serum of intact and pelvic-neurectomized rats, *Endocrinology*, **88**, 937–43.

Tan, C. C. (1946) Genetics of sexual isolation between *Drosophila pseudoobscura* and *Drosophila persimilis*, *Genetics*, **31**, 558–63.

Thibault, C., Courit, M., Martinet, L., Mauleon, P., DuMesnil Du Buisson, F., Ortavant, P., Pelletier, J., and Signoret, J. P. (1966) Regulation of breeding season and oestrous cycles by light and external stimuli in some mammals, *J. Anim. Sci.*, **25**, Suppl., 119–42.

Tinbergen, N. (1965) Some recent studies of the evolution of sexual behavior. In: *Sex and Behavior*, F. A. Beach (ed.), J. Wiley and Sons, New York.

Trivers, R. L. (1972) Parental investment and sexual selection. In: *Sexual Selection and the Descent of Man*, B. Campbell (ed.), Aldine, Chicago.

Vandenbergh, J. G. (1969) Endocrine coordination in monkeys: male sexual responses to females, *Physiol. Behav.*, **4**, 261–4.

Williams, G. C. (1966) *Adaptation and Natural Selection*, Princeton University Press, Princeton, N. J.

Wilson, E. O. (1975) *Sociobiology: The Synthesis*, Belknap, Cambridge, Mass.

Wilson, J. R., Adler, N. T., and LeBoeuf, B. (1965) The effects of intromission frequency on successful pregnancy in the female rat, *Proc. Nat. Acad. Sci.*, **53**, 1392–5.

Wilson, J., Kuehn, R., and Beach, F. A. (1963) Modification in the sexual behavior of male rats produced by changing the stimulus female, *J. Comp. Physiol. Psychol.*, **56**, 636–44.

Young, W. C. (1961) The hormones and mating behavior. In *Sex and Internal Secretions* Vol. 1, Williams and Wilkins Co., Baltimore.

Young, W. C., Boling, J. L., and Blandau, R. J. (1941) The vaginal smear picture, sexual receptivity, and time of ovulation in the albino rat, *Anat. Rec.*, **80**, 37–45.

Zimmerman, J. L. (1966) Polygyny in the dickcissel, *Auk*, **83**, 534–46.

Zimmerman, J. L. (1971) The territory and its density-dependent effect in *Spiza americana*, *Auk*, **88**, 591–612.

Zondek, B. and Tamari, I. (1967) *The Effects of External Stimuli on Reproduction*, G. E. W. Wolstenholme (ed.), Little, Brown, Boston.

CHAPTER 21

Sexual Affiliation in Animals: Pair Bonds and Reproductive Strategies

CARL J. ERICKSON

INTRODUCTION

In many animal species the male and female associate with one another well beyond the relatively brief period required for successful formation of a zygote. In some instances the relationship is established long before sexual maturity and is continued for many years until a partner dies or becomes lost. The nature of extended affiliation varies with the species and with the period of the life cycle. Morever, the interactions characterizing these relationships may range from an apparently casual maintenance of social proximity to more intricate patterns of cooperative defence, food seeking, and reproductive activity. The present chapter will examine the processes through which relationships between the sexes are established and maintained. Most attention will be given to those animal species in which parental care is shared by both sexes. Although shared parental care is found most commonly in monogamous relationships, no effort will be made to confine discussion to those species in which monogamous breeding is the typical mode of reproduction; the behavioural interactions of the sexes will be of primary concern. Avian studies provide a rich source of material and will be the centre of much discussion, but the issues to be considered are of general relevance to many animal social systems characterized by complex long-term affiliation between the sexes.

LONG-TERM SEXUAL RELATIONSHIPS AND THEIR FUNCTIONS

Among some animal species affiliative relationships between the sexes may persist for many years. In his *Historia Animalium* Aristotle observed that unless widowed, the female dove remains faithful to her mate throughout her lifetime. And in the medieval bestiaries the constancy of doves was frequently cited as a moral example for wayward parishioners. Recent observations underscore the durability of avian relationships. In 1971 Richdale and Warham (1973) found a pair of Buller's mollymawks, *Diomedia bulleri*, breeding together as they had in 1948 and in 1961. It is possible, of course, that they had taken other mates in the intervening years, but studies of several other species also reveal a remarkable constancy among some birds. John Coulson (pers. commun.) has observed a pair of kittiwakes, *Rissa tridactyla*, breeding together for fourteen consecutive seasons. Swans, too, are particularly well known for their fidelity to a single mate. Of the hundreds of Bewicks swans, *Cygnus bewickii*, wintering at the Slimbridge Wildfowl Trust during the past ten years, there has been no recorded instance of divorce among breeding pairs (Mary Evans, pers. commun.). Although new mates sometimes are selected if one member of a pair is lost, in no case have both individuals returned to the colony with new partners.

Extended sexual affiliations are most common when both parents are required to care for the young (Crook, 1965; Lack, 1968; Orians, 1969). Shared parental care is likely when offspring are altricial, when resources such as food are scarce or remote, or when the breeding season is short and the climate is harsh. A survey of animal groups indicates that shared parental activity is very characteristic of birds (Lack, 1968), some fishes such as the cichlids (Baerends and Baerends-van Roon, 1950; Lamprecht, 1972, 1973), and a few mammals (Eisenberg, 1966). Among the latter, relationships in which both parents care for the young are typical of most canids (Kleiman and Eisenberg, 1973) and of a few primates such as the marmosets (Kleiman, 1975) and gibbons (Carpenter, 1940).

Under some circumstances an extended monogamous relationship may be advantageous even if parental care is provided by one sex alone. In the higher latitudes or elevations the breeding season is often very brief, and in arid regions optimal conditions for producing young may be unpredictable in their time of appearance and duration. By selecting and retaining a mate prior to the breeding season, animals avoid delay when favourable breeding conditions do appear. For example, some species of ducks pair in the fall or winter before migrating to the far north in the spring to produce their offspring (Lack, 1968). A similar tactic may be found among some Australian grassfinches *(Estrildidae)*. Many of these species breed immediately after a rainfall when the conditions for reproductive success appear to be greatest. But rainfall is unpredictable; therefore, the birds must be prepared to breed when favourable circumstances suddenly appear (Butterfield, 1970). Unlike most other avian species, these finches have gonads that are active throughout the year. Hence, the birds are always physiologically ready to engage in reproductive activity, even during the period of moult (Immelmann, 1963). Moreover, they often pair at an unusually early age. It is very likely that this early pairing allows the animals to take full advantage of irregular and rapidly appearing breeding conditions. The brown booby, *Sula leucogaster*, is another species confronted with irregular breeding conditions. On Ascension Island food resources for this inshore feeder may be only marginal for months at a time before an abundance suddenly appears close by. Simmons (1970) has suggested that this accounts in large part for the long-term pair relationships of the species.

A mate may be retained, not only throughout a single breeding season, but from season to season as well; and, again, this mate retention can provide an advantage in terms of reproductive efficiency. For instance, if partners are familiar with one another as individuals, the rituals of species and sexual identification become superfluous and can be discarded. Unfortunately, few investigators have compared the courtship performances of familiar and unfamiliar pairs. In a laboratory study Erickson and Morris (1972) found that male ring doves perform significantly less of the bow-cooing display to former mates than to unfamiliar females. This display is thought to contribute to reproductive isolation. Moynihan (1955, p. 15) noted that when the nests of black-headed gulls, *Larus ridibundus*, were destroyed by high spring tides the majority of pairs seemed to revert to 'behaviour typical of early, but not the earliest, stages in the pairing process'. Interestingly, Aristotle noted that among pigeons, young couples are more likely to 'kiss' before copulation than are older couples. I know of no evidence confirming this observation; but if valid, the difference in behaviour could reflect the fact that older partners are also likely to be more familiar with one another as individuals. Thus, they would not require the information identifying species and sex which is ordinarily communicated through some forms of precopulatory interaction.

In some instances extended relationships are not associated with the breeding season and appear to have no direct bearing on the reproductive efficiency and success of a pair. For example, female white wagtails, *Motacilla alba alba*, join males on their winter territories and appear paired with them (Zahavi, 1971). Snow (1958) has described similar winter pairing in the blackbird, *Turdus merula*. But there is no evidence that the male and female remain together as a pair during the breeding season, and Snow's observations suggest that they do not. Winter pairing seems to benefit the female by providing her with a food supply within the territory of the male; the male, in turn, gains the aid of the female in defending the territory. In the shrimp, *Hymenocera picta*, the male and female spend much time in close proximity to one another. Individual recognition and social preference are maintained through pheromones detected by sensillae on the antennules (Seibt and Wickler, 1972; Wickler and Seibt, 1972; Seibt, 1973; Wickler, 1973; Seibt, 1974). But these investigators have found no indication that these relationships have any direct bearing upon the reproductive activities of the individuals involved.

Even when a male and female breed with one another, their relationship may provide advantages not directly related to reproduction. Mutual grooming may relieve them of ectoparasites and detritus; and, as a pair, they can more successfully defend themselves from predators. In several insular species of birds the sexes differ markedly in the size and shape of their beaks. These differences can reduce the competition between male and female in the food resources they exploit (Selander, 1966), and in some instances this variation could also allow the male and female to acquire food more efficiently by foraging together than by each foraging alone. The extinct huia, *Neomorpha acutirostris*, of North Island in New Zealand exhibited a striking sexual dimorphism in beak structure. The female bore a long, slender, decurved beak that was more than twice the length of the heavy, blunt beak of the male. Males could chisel through the tough bark of dead trees while females could probe the softer, rotten wood beneath, thus mutually aiding one another (Buller, 1872, cited by Darwin, 1874). The pack hunting of various canid species provides further evidence of cooperation between the sexes in obtaining food.

These examples underscore the need for caution in making any *a priori* suppositions regarding the functions of sexual affiliation, but in most of the species that have been carefully investigated pair affiliation does have a direct impact upon the efficiency of reproductive processes. Complex, cooperative relationships are found most often among monogamous animals in which the behavioural coordination of male and female spans the sexual and parental phases of the reproductive cycle. When the two sexes cooperate in multiple phases of the reproductive cycle, the following difficulties of social adjustment must be resolved if young are to be efficiently produced and successfully reared:

1. *The problem of synchrony.* The male and female must pass together through the successive stages of breeding. For instance, among those bird species in which both sexes cooperate in all phases of reproduction, the male and female must be prepared to court, copulate, build a nest, incubate eggs, and care for young in the same sequence, and they must simultaneously make the transitions from one reproductive phase to the next.

2. *The problem of complementarity.* The contributions of the two sexes to the reproductive effort are seldom simply additive; males and females usually differ qualitatively and quantitatively in the character of their participation and their roles are complementary. Thus any thorough examination of the cooperative relationship must account for these role differences and determine their source.

3. *The problem of compatibility.* Individual members of each sex differ markedly from one another in their reproductive behaviour. Consequently, the individuals comprising some pairs may be more compatible than others. An individual may be forced to accommodate to the particular style of the partner, and he (she) may 'persuade' the partner to adjust to his (her) own idiosyncracies. These mechanisms may involve simple adjustments to social cues, or they may require learning processes which allow an individual to anticipate the peculiarities of a partner's behaviour. Conceivably, fundamental physiological changes, such as those involving hormone secretion, occur in response to experience with a particular individual mate and contribute to the social adjustment of the pair. Finally, there is the interesting possibility that individuals detect and select compatible mates on the basis of courtship patterns

or other features.

In short, when both sexes cooperate in many aspects of reproductive behaviour, the outcome of their efforts depends upon the blend of their contributions into an effective social unit. The quality and ultimate success of such a parental unit may be either more or less than that predicted from the performances of each of the partners when previously mated with other animals. In the remainder of this chapter I shall discuss some of the processes which promote effective cooperation between the sexes.

INTERSEXUAL SYNCHRONY

More than forty years have passed since Allen (1934) first recognized the importance of synchrony for reproductive success and discussed the problem at length. It is now clear that the processes through which synchrony is achieved can vary markedly with the species and with the demands of particular breeding circumstances. An instructive example has been provided in a series of studies that examined the transition from courtship to nest construction in the ring dove.

During nest construction it is the male ring dove that selects the nesting material and carries it to the nest site. The female remains at the nest site and forms this material into the characteristic structure. On occasion, females gather nesting material and sometimes males weave the nest, but such reversals are very infrequent. Ring dove pairs do not build a nest immediately upon being placed together; this is the case even if a nest site and nesting material are readily available. Instead, they spend several days in active courtship. Some pairs will begin nest construction as early as the third or fourth day; others delay nest building for a week or more. Yet we seldom see one member of the pair engaged in nest building much in advance of the other. How is this synchrony achieved?

Careful examination of the interactions of males and females during their first few days together provided the first clue (Martinez-Vargas and Erickson, 1973). During this initial period the male spends much time engaged in a 'nest soliciting' display. This behaviour is usually performed at the site where the nest will be built. Typically, on the first day the female shows little response to the display, but by the second or third day she joins the displaying male at the nest site, and she may engage in nest solicting beside him. If the male leaves the nest site, however, it is likely that the female will leave as well. This sequence is repeated for several days until a significant change takes place toward the end of the first week. Again, the male goes to the nest site and nest-solicits as on previous days; and, as before, the female joins him there. But in contrast to her behaviour during the first few days, the female remains behind when the male leaves the nest. The female's attachment to the nest site represents a noteworthy transition because it is about this time that the male begins to collect nesting material and to deliver it to her for nest construction.

These observations indicated that the synchronized commencement of nest building depends upon the social interplay of the animals. But we suspected that major changes in hormone secretion were also involved in the emergence of the behaviour. For example, Lehrman (1958) had found preliminary evidence that ovarian hormones stimulate nest building by the female. If such physiological determinants influence the behaviour, how do they affect the synchrony of the partners? A series of experiments has clarified this issue considerably.

It is now apparent that the female's attachment to the nest site is directly linked to a change in ovarian activity. Korenbrot *et al.*, (1974), using a radioimmunoassay, have found a marked elevation in plasma oestradiol at about the time that the female becomes established at the nest site; and Silver *et al.*, (1974) have traced a concomitant rise in progesterone as well. The effects of these hormones on the behaviour of females were studied by Martinez-Vargas and Erickson (1973). While females remained in visual isolation from males, they were given daily injections of oestradiol benzoate (OB) and progesterone. Then after five days of treatment they were introduced to males in test cages. In contrast to untreated females, those that received oestrogen and progesterone became firmly established at the nest site on the first day with the males. Most interesting was the fact that the untreated male partners paired with these hormone-primed females gathered nesting material and carried it to the females at the nest site. Thus it appears that the transition of the female from courtship to nest building reflects the increased secretion of oestrogen and progesterone. On the other hand, the initiation of male participation seems to reflect more directly the changes in behaviour of the female; and the synchrony of the male and female in changing from courtship to nest building appears to be due to the male following the lead of the female.

This does not mean that the behaviour of the male is independent of his own gonadal hormones. Martinez-Vargas (1974) found that castrated male ring doves would not gather nesting material even when their female mates had been injected with OB and progesterone. If castrated males were given either testosterone proprionate (TP) or OB however, they readily collected nesting material and delivered it to the female at the nest site. More recently, Erickson and Hutchison (1977) have found that intrahypothalamic implants of TP are also effective for inducing nest-material collection in castrated male ring doves. Thus male courtship (Erickson *et al.*, 1967) and male nesting behaviour (Martinez-Vargas, 1974; Erickson and Martinez-Vargas, 1975) both appear to be dependent upon gonadal hormone, but the transition from one breeding phase to the other appears to be largely attributable to the behaviour of the female.

During the course of normal breeding the secretion of oestrogen and progesterone in the female ring dove does not occur autonomously. It is highly dependent upon the male, and more particularly, upon the behaviour of the male. If females are exposed to actively courting male ring doves for seven days, they exhibit a marked increase in follicular size, oviduct weight, and frequency of ovulation. Presumably the ovarian changes are also associated with the increased secretion of oestrogen and progesterone mentioned above. If females are exposed to castrated, non-courting males for a similar period, the physiological changes in the females are markedly less (Erickson and Lehrman, 1964; Erickson, 1970).

In summary, nest building is initiated when male-stimulated ovarian hormones establish the female at the nest site. Although the aid of the male in nest construction is dependent upon his own gonadal hormones, the emergence of his participation with that of his mate seems more directly tied to the behaviour changes of the female; and any internal changes in the male at this time are probably of secondary importance.

Many questions concerning the breeding synchrony of ring doves remain. For example, during the several days in which active nest construction occurs, the nest-building behaviour does not occur as a continuous activity. In our laboratory where cages are illuminated from 8.00 a.m. to 10.00 p.m. nest construction typically occurs between 10.30 a.m. and 1.30 p.m.; but pairs vary somewhat in the time at which they initiate and terminate nest building on each day. We do not yet know whether the times of initiation and termination are determined principally by the social stimulus of thë male or of the female, or whether both partners have internal circadian processes which synchronize through a mutual influence of one upon the other.

THE PROBLEM OF COMPLEMENTARITY
AND COMPATIBILITY

Although both male and female may contribute substantially to many phases of the reproductive process, including parental care, the participation of the two sexes usually differs systematically. In ring doves, as we have seen, the male selects nesting material and transports it to the nest site while the female is more directly involved in the construction of the nest. During incubation division of labour continues. The male sits on the eggs during the afternoon hours, and the female is on the nest throughout the remainder of the day. Hence, during nest construction the sexes perform qualitatively different patterns of behaviour at the same time of day while during egg incubation they perform qualitatively similar behaviour patterns at different times of the day. It seems clear, therefore, that the complementarity of effort is due, at least in part, to systematic differences in the behaviour of the two sexes; but the extent to which these differences are attributable to various physiological and experiential determinants is unknown.

The fine tuning of the ring dove's division of labour cannot, however, be attributed to general sexual differences alone. In every species females differ from one another in the quantity and quality of sexual and parental behaviour that they provide, and males exhibit similar variations. Yet the success of any reproductive effort may depend upon how effectively two individuals can mesh their contributions into a sensitively blended partnership. An individual may have to accommodate the particular style of a partner or induce cooperation in that partner. (The problem of social 'meshing' with regard to mother–infant relationships has been discussed by Hinde and Simpson, 1975.)

Individual adjustments such as these are apparent in the incubation behaviour of ring doves. Fig. 1 depicts the incubation patterns of a representative pair that was followed closely throughout two breeding cycles. Fig. 2 provides similar data for a comparable set of partners. Both pairs exhibited the characteristic incubation pattern of the Columbidae in which the male sits on the eggs during the later daytime hours. Also both pairs incubated effectively, at least to the extent that the eggs were always covered and the two birds seldom were on the nest simultaneously during incubation. Moreover, young were produced successfully in both instances. Nevertheless, there were some marked differences between the pairs. In pair A the male was on the nest during a much smaller portion of the day than was the male of pair B. Moreover, the male of pair B was on the nest for brief periods during the morning hours while the male of pair A seldom exhibited such behaviour. Many other differences could be indicated. It should be noted that the two pairs were relatively consistent from one breeding cycle to the next, suggesting that these patterns are rather stable features of the pairs displaying them.

In most pairs, such as those exemplified in Figs. 1 and 2, nest relief is performed smoothly, its timing apparently determined by the arrival of the relieving bird. When the sexes exchange watches at the nest, the bird to be relieved departs from the nest as the arriving bird comes into view, or it remains on the nest until the partner begins to settle on the eggs. Hence, nest relief usually involves little or no exposure of the eggs and no apparent conflict between the parents. Occasionally, however, one of the parents will leave the nest before its mate appears, or it will resist the attempts of its partner to take the nest. The frequency of such incidents may be indicative of the compatibility of the partners.

It will be interesting to know what the effects of exchanging mates among pairs (such as those of pairs A and B) will be. If interindividual adjustments are truly important for reproductive success, one would predict that exchanges between pairs of disparate styles would result in lower breeding success than exchanges between pairs exhibiting more similar incubation patterns. Such exchanges would provide some insight into the source of adjustment itself. For instance, it is unknown whether males conform to the incubation patterns of females, whether females conform to males, or whether adjustments are mutual. In preliminary studies Silver and Grabon (pers. commun.) have found some indication that males tend more often to conform to the incubation patterns of their mates. More research on this interesting problem should be pursued.

Female doves clearly have the capacity to make substantial behavioural adjustments to the incubation patterns of their partners. This can be seen

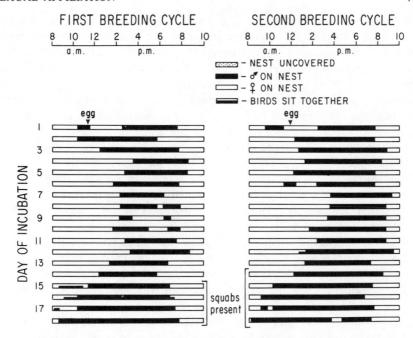

Fig. 1. Incubation of eggs by pair A

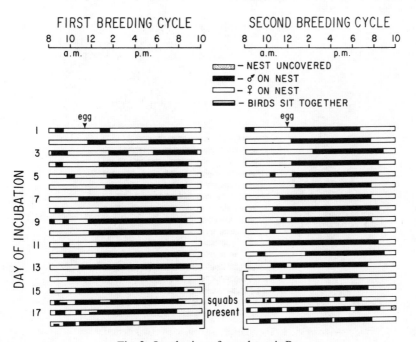

Fig. 2. Incubation of eggs by pair B

when one confines two females to the same cage. Under such circumstances both will lay eggs in the same nest and incubate them. Theresa Allen and I established a number of female/female pairs in order to examine the adjustment process. In all cases the eggs were covered continuously, even during the afternoon hours when males would normally be on the nest (Fig. 3). But incubation patterns were less consistent from day to day than those of male/female pairs, and they were less efficient to the extent that the two females of the monosexual pair were on the nest together much more often.

The process of adjusting to the peculiarities of a partner can be costly both in terms of efficiency and reproductive success. Therefore it may be advantageous to retain an individual as a mate in successive reproductive episodes once his idiosyncracies are familiar. Significantly, other conditions being equal, ring doves (Erickson and Morris, 1972), kittiwakes (Coulson, 1966), and red-billed gulls, *Larus novaehollandiae scopulinus*, (Mills, 1973) breed more successfully with a former mate than when paired with a stranger. If this difference in success reflects the compatibility of the parents, as Coulson has suggested, it indicates that the health and vigour of the young may be highly dependent upon the effectiveness with which their parents create an integrated social unit.

Successful adjustment is not an inevitable consequence of pair formation, and reproductive failure may be a direct reflection of social incompatibility. In some species, including those in which the majority of individuals return to

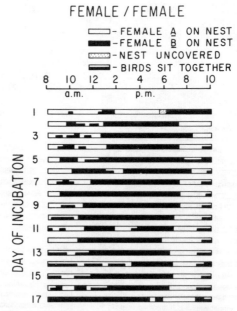

Fig. 3. Incubation of eggs by two females paired together

their previous mates year after year, 'divorce' is common. For example, Coulson (1966) found that approximately 25% of the kittiwakes in a Northumberland colony mated with new individuals when their former partners were present in the colony. Mills (1973) estimated the divorce rate at 27% in his study of red-billed gulls. Both investigators noted that the individuals selecting new mates had had a disproportionate number of breeding failures in the previous year. In the kittiwake colony 52% of the unsuccessful breeders selected new mates whereas only 17% of the successful birds took new partners. Delius (1965) found a similar relationship in skylarks, *Alauda arvensis*, between mate reten-tion and prior breeding success. Such correlations suggest an obvious adaptive strategy: if the relationship is successful, stay with it; if it is not, then opt for another. Coulson (1966) proposes, '... that there may be a degree of incom-patibility between individuals which results in unsuccessful breeding, and it is clearly an advantage for such pairs to split up in the hope that they will find a new partner who is more suitable.'

In the discussion above I have covered processes that foster adjustment between the sexes once a relationship has been established, but these processes may not exhaust the resources available to the animals for ensuring compatibility. Quite possibly, compatibility can be achieved in large part through the astute selection of a mate. In order to discuss this possibility it is appropriate to begin with a more general treatment of mate selection as it pertains to durable sexual relationships.

COMPATIBILITY THROUGH MATE SELECTION

When compared to other research areas involving reproductive behaviour, mate selection—and the more general problem of sexual selection—has been relatively neglected. Although Darwin (1874) drew attention to its significance as a source of morphological and behavioural characteristics, and although ethologists have long concerned themselves with the ritualization of various behaviour patterns through sexual selection (e.g., Huxley, 1923; Tinbergen, 1952), the ramifications of this process are only beginning to be realized (see, for example, Campbell, 1972).

In an important essay Trivers (1972) has provided a framework for evaluating mate selection in animals. Following Bateman (1948) and Williams (1966), Trivers developed the view that the reproductive cycle can be perceived as an investment—a parental investment of a male and female in their offspring. Specifically, Trivers defines parental investment as 'any investment by the parent in an individual offspring that increases the offspring's chance of surviving (and hence reproductive success) at the cost of the parent's ability to invest in other offspring' (p. 139). As the reproductive cycle proceeds, time and energy will be invested in the young; but the total amount of investment usually differs between the sexes, and the rate of investment can vary according to the demands of each phase of reproductive activity. In most polygynous species the parental investment of the male will be much smaller than that of the female; and if parental care is restricted to the female, the male's investment will be confined to the initial period of territory defence and copulation. In species such as the ring dove in which the male makes an important contribution to parental care, the total parental investments of the two sexes may be more similar. It is difficult to measure parental investment directly in the ring dove, but a familiarity with the breeding cycle provides an intuitive approximation that allows some predictions of their behaviour. Fig. 4 presents an estimate of the course of parental investment in this species. (The figure is a modification of a similar one presented by Trivers to portray the parental investment of an hypothetical monogamous species.) The precise form of the investments is not important for the present discussion. Two general features are significant,

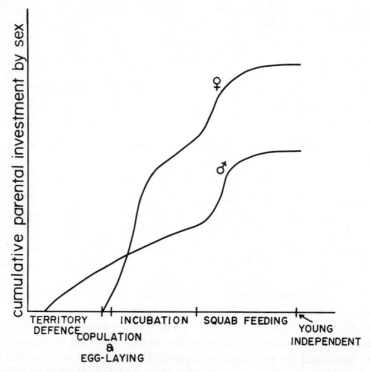

Fig. 4. Hypothetical cumulative parental investment of a male and female ring dove in their offspring as a function of time. Male's investment increases first in association with territory defence. Female's investment then rises steeply in association with ovulation and egglaying. Female's investment continues to rise more steeply than that of the male during incubation due to her greater time on the nest. Acceleration and then deceleration of the curves of both animals during squab care reflect the intuitive estimation that the contributions of both parents in this stage are approximately equal. (Fig. modified from Trivers, 1972, p. 147.)

however: (1) The total investment of the female is assumed to be greater than that of the male. (2) A relatively large proportion of the female's investment is expended early in the cycle; this is because the female bird must provide the embryo with all of its nutrients at the time of ovulation. These two features have several implications for the relationship between the animals. First, the cost of abandoning the mate and the reproductive cycle increases as the cycle progresses. Second, insofar as the female's investment is greater and rises more steeply during the early stages of breeding, the more important it becomes that she avoid or abandon, at an early stage, any mate incapable of parental care. The costs of abandoning a mate during courtship (prior to a heavy commitment of resources) are much less than those that would be incurred in abandoning the partner later in the cycle. Thus individuals that can, in some way, detect the parental capacities of a potential mate through observation of his courtship should have an advantage over those that cannot. Furthermore, if an individual has abundant parental capabilities, it should be to his advantage to communicate this fact to potential mates at an early stage.

In a study of common terns, *Sterna hirundo*, on the Massachusetts coast, Nisbet (1973) provided circumstantial evidence for the notion that courtship is predictive of performance in later stages of the reproductive cycle. In this species the male provides most of the food for the young during the period shortly after hatching. Since males may vary markedly in their ability to locate and capture food, it is of considerable importance to the breeding success of the female that she select a male mate who is capable of performing this task.

According to Nisbet the courtship of the common tern passes through three phases. In the first phase, males carry fish throughout the colony while displaying to females; the females are sometimes fed the fish but only irregularly. In the second phase the males and females may be seen paired on the feeding grounds, and the male often feeds the female. During the third phase the female remains in the male's territory, and she is fed there by the male until the clutch of eggs is complete. Nisbet found an appreciable variation among the pairs in the total weight of the clutch, in the amount of food fed to the chicks by the male, in the weight of the brood, and in the number of chicks fledged. There was also considerable variation among the pairs in the weight of the third egg and weight of the third chick. (Common terns lay but three eggs, and it is this final egg that seems most to reflect the nutritive investment of the parents.) Nisbet found that all of these variables were positively correlated with the amount of food fed to the female by the male during courtship, and in some instances the correlations were highly significant statistically. Thus, the male's courtship reliably predicted his later parental effectiveness. It should be noted, however, that Nisbet provided no clear evidence that females systematically preferred the more promising males.

Trivers (1972) suggested that through courtship an individual might communicate his parental willingness and ability as well as his potential compatability to a prospective partner. At present there is virtually no published evidence to support such a view, yet the suggestion is sufficiently interesting to warrant further discussion here.

Selection for Parental Willingness or Readiness

Some of our physiological studies of the male ring dove suggest an organization of behavioural systems that could permit females to select males on the basis of their preparedness for parental behaviour. It should be noted that throughout the following discussion I shall use the term parental behaviour broadly to denote nest building, incubation of the eggs, and care of the squabs.

Once a female ring dove has ovulated and is, in a sense, committed to pursuing the breeding cycle, it is essential to the reproductive success of the female for the male to join her in nest building, incubation, and squab care. Yet for reasons of age, health, or seasonal responsiveness, males may differ widely in their readiness to engage in these activities. Consequently, it is important that the female identify prior to ovulation those males that are adequately prepared.

Much of the variability in the reproductive activity of male birds appears to be linked to gonadal activity, and it now seems to be clear that the courtship, twig gathering, and incubation behaviour of the male ring dove are dependent, at least in part, upon secretions from the testes (Stern and Lehrman, 1969; Erickson, 1970; Martinez-Vargas, 1974). There is also some evidence that the gonads are important in squab care (Patel, 1936), and most probably it is the androgens that are the effective testicular hormones influencing these behaviour patterns. It is essential to note, however, that although courtship declines rather rapidly after castration, these other behaviour patterns may continue to be performed for some time after removal of the gonads. Because the behaviour can occur long after the gonadal secretions have cleared the circulation, we can assume that these gonadal hormones sensitize the neural systems associated with the various reproductive activities. Once they are sensitized, these systems and their related behaviour patterns have some momentum and can be activated for an extended period by appropriate stimuli (and, in some reproductive phases, in association with other hormones) in the absence of the gonadal hormones. Thus it is not necessary to assume that the gonads are actively secreting hormone when the male engages in the collection of nesting material, incubation of the eggs, and squab care; it is sufficient that the neural systems for these behaviour patterns have been exposed to the relevant hormone within a rather recent period.

Martinez-Vargas (1974) and Erickson and Hutchison (1977) found that when male ring doves were castrated, collection of nesting material declined, but in most cases six to eight weeks were required for this behaviour to reach a low level. In some males the behaviour continued declining very slowly for a period of months. Similarly, Stern and Lehrman (1969) showed that while fewer progesterone-treated male ring doves incubated eggs when castrated than when intact, fully one-third of the castrated males did incubate eggs one month after castration. Silver *et al.*, (1973) also found that untreated castrated males incubated less than intact males when tested one month following gonadectomy. In summary, the parental activities of the male ring dove appear to be dependent upon the gonads, but the behaviour patterns can persist at high levels following hormone withdrawal. This organization ensures that all androgen-dependent systems will remain functional throughout the six-week breeding period even if androgen secretion should fail at any time during the interval following insemination of the female.

Courtship will be indicative of the male's parental sensitization to the hormone only if there are certain relationships among the androgen-dependent systems. For example, if the courtship system were more sensitive to androgen than other systems, a low level of secretion could activate full-blown courtship but be inadequate to sensitize the systems for twig gathering and other later breeding behaviour. On the other hand, if the courtship system requires the highest level of androgen in order to become activated, then the appearance of courtship behaviour would be a guarantee that the systems governing subsequent breeding behaviour had also been properly sensitized. Courtship, then, could provide a gauge of the male's general preparation for full reproductive behaviour.

Erickson (1965) and Hutchison (1970) have shown that courtship does, in fact, seem relatively insensitive to androgen therapy, for it declines very rapidly following castration. Within a week or ten days the bow-cooing and nest-soliciting displays are severally reduced or eliminated. Moreover, several weeks of replacement therapy with rather large doses of TP are required to restore the behaviour to precastration levels (Erickson, 1965; Hutchison, 1970); and as the interval between castration and replacement therapy increases, the effectiveness of TP decreases (Hutchison, 1969, 1974). In contrast, the collection of nesting material by castrated males can be restored with relative ease, by either systemic treatment or intrahypothalamic application of TP (Martinez-Vargas, 1974; Erickson and Hutchison, 1977). Furthermore, this behaviour can be fully restored several months after castration at a time when the restoration of courtship would be quite difficult.

Thus the data currently available support the notion that courtship is indicative of the male's physiological preparation for the performance of subsequent reproductive behaviour.

Although courtship and parental behaviour patterns may share a common physiological substrate permitting courtship performance to be predictive of later parental participation, it should also be noted that courtship and parental behaviour are independently influenced by a variety of other factors, both internal and external to the animal, which can diminish the relationship between the two phases of reproductive activity. Hence the predictive value of courtship is likely to be less than perfect, and some males will probably fail to fulfil their 'promises'. Nevertheless, those courting males that indicate some paternal inclination should be preferred to those that offer no promise at all.

Selection for Parental Proficiency or Ability

Earlier it was suggested that individuals may reselect as mates those former partners that had proven their capacity to produce and raise young successfully. Conversely, they may reject those mates with whom they have been unsuccessful. In instances where an unfamiliar mate must be chosen, the courtship of the potential partner may reveal his or her special proclivities or prior experience regarding parental care. For example, the male common tern must select very small food types when the chicks are newly hatched; but as the chicks grow in size, larger morsels must be delivered. It would be particularly interesting to know whether males exhibit the full array of their food-capturing capabilities during the period of courtship. A male that does so should more fully demonstrate his parental proficiency to the female.

In many species the efficiency and success of breeding are increased through reproductive experience. Therefore, it should be advantageous for animals to select mates that have acquired such experience, especially if those individuals have previously bred successfully. Lehrman and Wortis (1960, 1967) demonstrated in the ring dove that prior reproductive experience greatly enhances behavioural responsiveness to hormones and promotes higher levels of breeding success. They showed that the experience of both male and female contribute to this success. It is not yet known, however, if birds will detect and prefer unfamiliar reproductively experienced individuals as partners. If experienced unfamiliar animals are, in fact, preferred to inexperienced unfamiliar individuals, it would imply that modifications in courtship become the basis upon which the selection of a mate is made.

It is generally thought that courtship is relatively fixed, stereotyped, and not open to much modification. Yet there is some evidence that this is not the case. As mentioned earlier, Aristotle noted that young pigeons are more inclined to 'kiss' prior to copulation than are older (and perhaps more familiar) couples, and in our laboratory we found (Erickson and Morris, 1972; Erickson, 1973) that the courtship of male ring doves when courting familiar females is quite different from that exhibited when courting unfamiliar females. Moreover, inasmuch as courtship and the various aspects of parental care may have physiological determinants in common, breeding experience, which affects these determinants, may influence several phases of reproductive activity.

Selection for Compatibility

Earlier it was suggested that the compatibility of partners might be established, in part, through mate selection. If courtship is indeed indicative of parental idiosyncrasies, then the behavioural displays could become the basis upon which compatible mates are chosen. Initially, such a notion might seem to assume considerable intelligence on the part of the selecting animal since it suggests that he can perceive his own style and select a mate to complement it. But such assumptions are unnecessary. For example, if could be the case that a particular female ring dove is motivated, for whatever reason, to engage in nest building especially early in the day. If the mechanism controlling this behavioural rhythm also influences the daily rhythm of her responsiveness to male courtship, she may be especially responsive to those few males that court especially early in the day. If males that court early also gather twigs early, then the female will have selected a compatible nest builder simply by responding to his unusually early courtship.

As of this writing, I know of no field or laboratory studies indicating that parental proficiency and style are reflected in courtship or form the basis of mate selection. The question deserves investigation. It would be particularly interesting to know, for instance, whether such contingencies have any bearing upon the highly individualized mate preferences shown by beagles, as studied by Beach and Le Boeuf (1967). Hopefully, studies now underway in our laboratory will provide some insight into these general issues.

ANIMAL PAIR BONDS

Many kinds of social behaviour may be largely or entirely reserved for exchanges between one or a few individuals. Indeed, intersexual relationships are defined by such restricted social interactions. These social exchanges are not necessarily limited to reproductive activity, for in many instances the behavioural interactions have no obvious bearing upon reproductive performance. For example, partners commonly remain in close proximity to one another while maintaining some distance from other individuals (e.g., zebra finches—Caryl, 1975). Also, they often become less aggressive towards one another while increasing their attacks upon others of their species. This aggression may be limited to members of the same sex (as in the snow bunting, *Plectrophenax nivalis subnivalis*, studied by Tinbergen, 1939) or it may be directed towards individuals of both sexes (Stettner *et al.*, 1966; Stettner *et al.*, 1971; Erickson, 1973). Allogrooming or allopreening as well as greeting ceremonies are often confined to the partner Fischer, 1965; Sparks, 1967). In some species idiosyncratic social exchanges develop. In American goldfinches, *Carduelis tristis*, for example, the flight calls of paired males and females become similar to one another (Mundinger, 1970). (But see Hailman's comments in Farner, 1973, p. 361.) Particularly interesting are those species in which male and female develop complex antiphonal duets. Although vocal duetting has been attributed to a few mammals such as the tree shrew, *Tupaia palawanensis* (Williams *et al.*, 1969), and siamang, *Symphalangus syndactylus* (Lamprecht, 1970), it is most widespread and reaches its greatest complexity among the birds (Hooker and Hooker, 1969; Thorpe, 1972).

While the indices of intersexual relationships described above are derived from the social behaviour patterns of interacting animals, these relationships are also often reflected in the behaviour of animals when partners are absent. For instance, searching behaviour and vocalization may appear (Lorenz, 1966a; 1970b). Thorpe and North (1965) cite the case of a pair of antiphonally singing bou-bou shrikes who had established a large repertoire of duets. When one of the partners disappeared, the remaining individual sang not only his own portion of the duet but that of his mate as well. Butterfield (1970) noted that the songs and calls of male zebra finches were more frequent when the birds were separated from their mates. Moreover, an absence of the mate seemed to produce emotional disturbances; although food intake increased slightly, there was a reduction in body weight after four weeks of separation and a significant increase in defecation.

Increasingly, ethologists, psychologists, and ecologists are using the term 'pair bond' to describe the extended intersexual relationships characterized by the social interactions discussed above. Because of the diversity of their principal interests representatives of the three disciplines tend to concentrate their attention upon different aspects of these relationships and, as a result, have generated some confusion through their varied use of the term. As I have suggested elsewhere (Erickson, 1974), it is my opinion that ecologists have focused upon the 'pair' while the behavioural scientists have attended to the 'bond'. Ecologists usually apply the term whenever a male and female remain together beyond some minimum period, their principal concerns being the duration of affiliation and the number of individuals engaged in the relationship. On the other hand, behavioural scientists are generally less interested in these temporal and numerical aspects than in the processes through which individuals create and maintain their relationships. Typically, the latter use the term 'bond' more conservatively, reserving it for instances in which there is clear evidence that the animals recognize one another as individuals and establish a preference for one another when involved in specific types of activity (cf., Lorenz, 1966a; 1970b). Hence, the ecologist often applies the label 'pair bond' when the ethologist or psychologist would not. Clearly, investigators should be aware of the potential ambiguity in their use of the term, and they should specify their meaning when applying it to descriptions of animal behaviour. Too often the application has been misleading or confusing. To give one example, in a study of pigeon breeding behaviour, Castoro and Guhl (1958) state, without further clarifying comment, 'After billing ensued, copulation was successful and the pair bond established.' It is unclear from this statement whether the authors are attributing pair-bond establishment to billing or copulation as causal agents (thereby leaving the defining dependent variables unspecified) or whether they equate pair-bond establishment with billing or copulation (thereby making the term redundant). Moreover, they provide no indication as to whether individual recognition is a feature of the pair-bond formation to which they refer.

Some authors have clearly expressed the wish to define the pair bond operationally in terms of the social interactions of the sexes. For example, Lorenz (1966b) states, 'It is quite erroneous to say that such [greeting] ceremonies are "the expression of" a bond; indeed they themselves constitute it.' More commonly, however, the pair bond is identified as a state within the animals which influences, and is influenced by, the social interactions of the pair. In the remainder of this chapter I should like to discuss some of the problems commonly associated with pair-bond formation and maintenance.

Copulation, allogrooming, courtship feeding, courtship displays, greeting ceremonies, and a variety of other types of interaction have been identified, on the one hand, as dependent variables affected by the pair bond and, on the other hand, as independent variables which strengthen or weaken it. Huxley (1914) was among the first to suggest the dependency of intersexual relationships upon specific kinds of social interaction. In his classic study of the great crested grebe, *Podiceps cristatus*, he states:

> What is the good of all these divings and posturings, these actions of courtship, the expressions of emotion? To what end are colours and structures developed solely to be used in them, and what return is got for the time and energy spent in carrying them out? They are common to both sexes, and so have nothing to do with any form of true sexual selection; they are self-exhausting processes, not leading up to or connected with coition, and so cannot be sexual excitants in the ordinary sense of the term.
>
> It must be, however, that they fulfil some function; and I believe I know what this function is. I believe that the courtship ceremonies serve to keep the two birds together, and to keep them constant to each other. (p. 516)

I have quoted this passage at length, not only because of its importance as a seminal observation, but because it clearly demonstrates a persisting inference about intersexual affiliation and its causes. It should be apparent that Huxley's deduction is not based upon any directly observed correspondence of events suggesting such a causal link. It is at best a speculative inference derived from an observed *absence* of correspondence between the displays and clearly discerned functional consequences regarding reproduction. Nonetheless, similar inferences have become a frequent exercise in many contemporary papers, and it is commonplace for investigators to assume that the pair bond is affected by various social interactions for which no other functional outcome is clearly apparent. In fact, it has become common to propose an influence on the pair bond when the behaviour under consideration does have obvious functions, as in the case of copulation or cooperative nest-building activity. Generally, the 'strength' of the bond is thought to be affected. Thus, in his study of gannets Nelson (1965) suggested that '... mutual fencing is a "friendly" meeting or pair-bond strengthening ceremony ...' (p. 274). Holmes (1973) discusses '... nest scraping, neck preening, and other behaviour

patterns that serve to strengthen pair bonds in western sandpipers *C. mauri* ...'
(p. 121), while Parmelee and Payne (1973) mention a '... weakening of the
pair bond associated with the male taking over the role of incubation ...'
(p. 224).

The issue of pair-bond strength and the factors controlling it has recently
become an issue of more than casual interest. In reply to the papal encyclical
Humanae Vitae, Wickler (1972) has drawn on studies of animal behaviour to
argue that human sexual intercourse may serve important functions beyond
procreation, one of which is to strengthen the pair bond between a man and
woman. He states, '... it is very likely that man is the only one to use this
[ventro-ventral] mating position—which was no doubt made possible to
him for other biological reasons—in order to strengthen the profound personal
relationship between the sexes.' (p. 45).

Statements regarding pair-bond strength are common in contemporary
discussions of intersexual affiliation; unfortunately, few investigators have
provided a clear definition of 'strength'. Wickler (1973), one of these few
exceptions, has suggested the following indices as measurable aspects of a
bond:

(1) The intensity of attraction (unilateral or mutual) between the partners,
measured by their persistency in gradually overcoming different obstacles
in order to come (or stay) close to the partner. (This seeking and maintaining of proximity to an individual is called attachment by Bowlby.)
(2) The degree of exclusiveness with which a given behaviour is directed
toward the partner. This relative exclusiveness will be different with respect
to different behavior patterns.
(3) The degree of synchronization between the partners, which again will
be different with respect to different kinds of behavior. (p. 66)

Investigators can profitably follow Wickler's lead in attempting to measure
intersexual affiliation through precise objective analysis. Moreover, attempts
to link the measured behaviour patterns to antecedent social interactions such as courtship or allogrooming will be particularly welcome. I
feel, however, that to describe the changing patterns of intersexual interaction
in terms of 'strength', 'force', or 'intensity' presupposes, at our current level of
understanding, an organization of behavioural processes which can distract
us from a more fruitful analysis of these relationships. For example, such
quantitative terminology suggests that social bonds gather a kind of momentum
derived from the social reinforcement inherent in some types of social interaction. Viewed in this way the pair bond seems to represent an internal motivated state which transcends the social transactions of the moment; it becomes, in
a sense, a kind of motivational flywheel accelerated and decelerated by multiple
inputs summed and stored over time. There is, however, no evidence at the
present time to support the notion that intersexual relationships are, in fact,
sustained by such monolithic forces. Furthermore, quantitative terminology

too often suggests the view that 'strong' bonds are more valuable to animals than those that are weak or absent. But one must be on guard against the assumption that 'strong' pair bonds are intrinsically beneficial. Social relationships can only be evaluated in context. Many species exhibit no extended sexual affiliation nor do they show any of the characteristics associated with intersexual attachment, and for them to do so would probably seriously limit their capacity for producing young. Even among those species that typically maintain extended relationships, it may be advantageous to terminate a relationship and select a new mate if the partner is infertile, a poor parent, or otherwise incapable of providing offspring. In these latter instances a 'strong' pair bond would be disadvantageous to the reproductive success of the individuals involved.

Perhaps we can view intersexual relationships more usefully and more simply as constellations of social exchanges that vary mainly in their patterning. Once the patterns are thoroughly described we can move on to consideration of their functions and causes. Until then it might be prudent to avoid the use of terms like 'strength'.

THE PROBLEM OF INDIVIDUAL RECOGNITION AND PREFERENCE

When prepared to breed, the male and female of some decapod crustaceans seclude themselves in a cavity of a sponge or coral and subsequently remain there together as a pair throughout their lifetimes. It is not necessary to assume the operation of complex behavioural processes to explain their fidelity to one another; it is more than likely that the relationship is sustained simply because the partners grow too large to escape from their nuptial chamber. Among four families of the deep-sea angler (Suborder Ceratioidea) males and females maintain a lifelong monogamous affiliation, but in this instance the pair is maintained because the head parts of the male fuse with the female's body, and he becomes an obligatory parasite upon her. These examples represent unusual circumstances, and apart from relatively transient circumstances (e.g., copulatory locks) no physical constraints of this kind influence the intersexual affiliation of birds and mammals. Yet they underscore the great variety of processes that can contribute to long-term relationships.

The processes through which the intersexual relationships of most animals are established and maintained remain largely unknown. Undoubtedly many durable relationships involve individual recognition and an acquired preference for the partner, but it is virtually impossible on the basis of reproductive behaviour alone to distinguish the attachment of individuals to one another from the attachment to the territory, nest, and young. Even in those cases in which the male and female birds complement one another with elegant precision in courtship, copulation, nest building, nest relief, and care of the young, it is entirely conceivable that the interactions could be accomplished without the slightest appreciation of the identity of the partner. For instance, if a male and female return to the same nest site for successive breeding cycles and breeding seasons, it is often difficult to discriminate the attachment to the nest site from the bond that may exist between the individuals themselves. The confusion of these variables is a difficulty that has been recognized by ornithologists for many years. For example, Schüz (1934, cited by Lack, 1940) concluded that the tendency of the white stork, *Ciconia ciconia*, to return to its mate of the previous season was due largely, if not entirely, to the common attachment to the nest site. (Tinbergen, 1953; Nelson, 1965; and Delius, 1965 have also discussed this problem.)

In the field, the observer most easily discerns the capacity for individual recognition when the animals are not directly involved in reproductive activity. Individuals may enage in obvious searching upon the absence of the partner and may exhibit characteristic exchanges of behaviour such as allogrooming or greeting ceremonies when contact is re-established. These activities are indicative of recognition if they are restricted to a single individual or to a limited group of individuals (such as a harem) and if they occur regardless of whether the partners are near or away from the territory, nest site, or young (Lorenz, 1966a). Tinbergen (1953) cites instances in which herring gulls, *Larus argentatus*, alight beside their mates upon returning from the sea, even if the mates had moved some distance during their absence.

In some species experimental techniques can be used to evaluate geographical influences upon the relationship. Morris and Erickson (1971) performed a simple experiment on ring doves to examine the extent to which the association of partners could be attributed to a common attachment to a geographical area. Pairs were placed in separate laboratory cages and allowed to mate and raise young twice in succession. At the completion of the second breeding cycle all birds were individually isolated for periods ranging up to eight months. At the end of this isolation period the birds were tested for mate recognition and mate preference. Three males and three females were taken from isolation and placed in a large outdoor aviary in a nearby forest. All birds had previously mated with one of the animals of opposite sex in the group. The birds were then observed to determine which of the previously mated doves located themselves in close proximity to one another and which of these doves copulated, built nests together, and incubated the same eggs. This procedure continued until fifteen pairs (five groups) had been examined. Without exception all birds paired with the same individuals with which they had mated in the laboratory. It should be noted that these mates were not selected originally by the birds themselves but were assigned to them by the investigators. Nonetheless, it was these assigned mates that were chosen as partners in the outdoor tests. This indicates that as a consequence of exposure to one another in the laboratory, the doves had acquired a preference for particular individuals as mates. Moreover, the possible influence of a common attachment to a nest site or territory was eliminated by testing the animals in an unfamiliar environment very unlike that in which they had originally paired, thereby demonstrating that ring doves learn to recognize their own mates as individuals and that they acquire a preference for them as partners.

Although in some species the common attachment to a nest site may be necessary for maintenance of a relationship, in other instances the converse may be the case, tenacity to the nest site being dependent upon the relationship of the partners. Delius (1965) found that skylarks were more likely to change their nest sites within the breeding area when former partners failed to return after the winter months.

In spite of the observation that some species such as the ring dove are capable of recognizing one another as individuals and of developing preferences for particular partners as mates, it does not necessarily follow that these processes sustain the relationship in the early stages of pair formation. It is quite possible that individual recognition and attachment emerge only gradually and that the cooperative relationship of the pair during the initial stages is determined to a large extent by the exigencies of building the nest and caring for the young. Carpenter (1929) alluded to this possibility in a brief study of intersexual affiliation in pigeons. He proposed that initially the fidelity of the pair is determined by the necessities of parental care and the lack of opportunity for pairing with other individuals. He suggested that after a period of time, however, a 'sentiment' develops between the individuals. In some cichlids the initial stages of pair formation can be terminated by transferring the partners to another aquarium or by changing the lighting. Only as their association continues does the relationship persist in spite of changes in the external milieu (Lorenz, 1966a). In short, environmental constraints or rudimentary processes could provide a provisional basis for maintaining the relationship in its early phases. This system could be gradually supplemented or supplanted through a relatively slow process of familiarization. The observations of Goforth and Basket (1965) on mourning doves, *Zenaidura macroura*, support this hypothesis. They found that a piece of yellow tape placed on the head of a female early in the incubation phase of the first reproductive cycle of the season caused the male to abandon both female and nest. But when this was done during a comparable phase of a subsequent breeding cycle, the association of the pair was not disrupted. Similarly, a brief separation of the individuals during the first cycle was more likely to disrupt the relationship than separation in later cycles.

The processes that sustain a relationship may differ between the sexes. There is little evidence bearing upon this issue, but Carpenter (1929) concluded that in pigeons fidelity is more characteristic of the female than of the male. Males, he suggested, maintain a monogamous relationship only because they are occupied with the nest and young. Recently Erickson (1973), demonstrated, however, that as male ring doves spent more and more time with their female partner, they showed an increasing tendency to attack females that were not their mates. The aggression continued to increase throughout two breeding cycles, and it occurred even when the males were tested in a neutral area away from their mates. The study also revealed that at an early stage males begin to be less aggressive to their mates than to other females, but the males continued to court both the eventual mate and another available female until well into the first reproductive cycle. Only in the second cycle with the same mate was courtship entirely reserved for the mate. The results suggested that in some instances considerable exposure was required before males learned to distinguish their own mates in areas away from the home aviary, for a few errors in identification occurred even after completion of two reproductive cycles with a female.

It is clear, then, that at least in some species members of a pair do come to recognize one another. In recent years there has been an increasing interest in the means by which this is accomplished. In the shrimp, *Hymenocera picta*, chemical cues are important in individual indentification (Seibt, 1974). Among birds, vocalization seems to be important. Tinbergen (1953) noted that herring gulls sitting with their eyes closed would become alert upon hearing the cry of their approaching mate, but they would remain unaffected by the cries of other approaching gulls. Similarly, incubating laughing gulls, *Larus atricilla*, exhibit a clear response to either the 'long-call' or the 'ke-hah' call of returning mates while the calls of neighbours and strangers are ignored (Beer, 1970). And White (1971) found that gannets, *Sula bassana*, respond selectively to the landing calls of their mates.

Morphological diversity provides an obvious basis for visual recognition, and the head and facial features may be of particular importance in identification. Heinroth (1911, cited by Tinbergen, 1953) reports an incident in which a male swan attacked his mate when she was feeding with her head under water. When the female raised her head, he broke off the attack. The pattern of bill markings on some species, such as Bewick's swan, provides reliable identification of individuals for human observers (Mary Evans, pers. commun.) but whether it does so for the swans themselves seems to be unknown.

Clearly, stable intersexual relationships may be promoted and maintained by a wide variety of processes. In many species the partners are obviously capable of identifying one another as individuals and of developing preferences for one another as breeding partners. Such capacities are most readily demonstrated through experimental procedures or through observation of behaviour not directly involving reproduction. Maintenance of proximity and participation in reproductive activity are not, in themselves, sufficient evidence for these capacities, although many investigators seem to assume otherwise. Where the term 'pair bond' implies the involvement of these capacities for identification, the criteria by which they have been established should be clearly specified.

SUMMARY AND CONCLUSION

Intersexual affiliation takes many forms. In some species several mates are taken simultaneously or successively; in others, a single partner may be retained throughout—and even beyond—an individual's reproductive lifetime. Within each species there are additional variations in reproductive strategy. Typically, the two sexes differ with respect to the time and energy they invest in their offspring. Moreover, individual members of each sex differ from one another in morphology and behaviour. When the reproductive success of a species depends upon extensive intersexual cooperation and when individuals comprising the two sexes of that species exhibit substantial behavioural variation, then processes of social adaptation must be brought into play to achieve an efficient, productive blend of effort. In this chapter I have discussed some of the means through which interindividual compatibility can be achieved. Processes of social adjustment have been classified into two groups: (1) processes that aid partners in adjusting to one another once a relationship has been established, and (2) processes of mate selection that contribute to compatibility.

Although complementary differences in physiology and experience promote the effective blending of behaviour by the two sexes, the fine tuning of social integration may depend upon the capacity to recognize the mate as an individual and upon the ability to anticipate his or her characteristic behaviour. Partners may be retained from one breeding episode to another because their individual behaviour patterns are known and have been found acceptable. In some instances, however, individuals that have proved inadequate as partners may be rejected in favour of unfamiliar but more promising mates. Quite possibly, animals communicate to potential mates their enthusiasm, proficiency, and style *vis à vis* future parental performance; but at the present time there is little evidence to indicate whether these qualities are, in fact, transmitted or detected during mate selection.

The problem of long-term sexual affiliation is complex and deserves more attention than it has received. Hopefully, with increasing communication among ecologists, ethologists, psychologists, and reproductive physiologists a deeper understanding of these relationships can be achieved.

ACKNOWLEDGEMENTS

This chapter is dedicated to the memory of my teacher and friend, Daniel S. Lehrman.

Preparation of this manuscript was aided by a grant from the National Institute of Child Health and Human Development, Research Grant HD-04482.

I am indebted to P. P. G. Bateson, J. Hanby, R. A. Hinde, J. B. Hutchison, M. J. A. Simpson, J. E. R. Staddon, and E. A. Steel for stimulating discussion during preparation of this paper. I am especially grateful to Bonnie E. Erickson for her thoughts, criticisms, and suggestions.

REFERENCES

Allen, A. A. (1934) Sex rhythm in the ruffed grouse (*Bonasa umbellus* Linn.) and other birds, *Auk*, **51**, 180–91.
Baerends, G. P. and Baerends-van Roon, J. M. (1950) An introduction to the study of the ethology of child fishes, *Behaviour*, Suppl., 1.

Bateman, J. J. (1948) Intrasexual selection in *Drosophila, Heredity*, **2**, 349–68.

Beach, F. A. and Le Boeuf, B. J. (1967) Coital behaviour in dogs. 1. Preferential mating in the bitch, *Anim. Behav.*, **15**, 546–58.

Beer, C. G. (1970) Individual recognition of voice in the social behavior of birds. In: *Advances in the Study of Behavior* Vol. 3, D. S. Lehrman, R. A. Hinde, and E. Shaw (eds.), Academic Press, New York, pp. 27–74.

Butterfield, P. A. (1970) The pair bond in the zebra finch. In: *Social Behaviour in Birds and Mammals*, J. Crook (ed.), Academic Press, New York, pp. 249–78.

Campbell, B., (1972) *Sexual Selection and the Descent of Man 1871–1971*, Aldine, Chicago.

Carpenter, C. R. (1929) Mating and brooding behavior of pigeons, Unpubl. *M. A. Thesis*, Duke University.

Carpenter, C. R. (1940) A field study in Siam of the behavior and social relations of the gibbon, *Hylobates lar*, *Comp. Psychol. Monogr.*, **16**, 212.

Caryl, P. G. (1975) Aggressive behaviour in the zebra finch *Taeniopygia guttata*. I. Fighting provoked by male and female social partners, *Behaviour*, **52**, 226–52.

Castoro, P. L. and Guhl, A. M. (1958) Pairing behavior of pigeons related to aggressiveness and territory, *Wilson Bull.*, **70**, 57–69.

Coulson, J. C. (1966) The influence of the pair-bond and age on the breeding biology of the kittiwake gull *(Rissa tridactyla)*, *J. Anim. Ecol.*, **35**, 269–79.

Crook, J. H. (1965) The adaptive significance of avian social organizations, *Symp. Zool. Soc. London*, **14**, 181–218.

Darwin, C. (1874) *The Descent of Man and Selection in Relation to Sex* (revised edn.), D. Appleton, New York.

Delius, J. D. (1965) A population study of skylarks *Alauda arvensis*. *Ibis*, **107**, 466–92.

Eisenberg, J. F. (1966) The social organization of mammals, *Handb. Zool.*, VIII, (10/7), Lieferung 39, 92 pp.

Erickson, C. J. (1965) A study of the courtship behavior of male ring doves and its relationship to ovarian activity of females, Unpubl. *Ph.D. Dissertation*, Rutgers University.

Erickson, C. J. (1970) Induction of ovarian activity in female ring doves by androgen treatment of castrated males, *J. Comp. Physiol. Psychol.*, **71**, 210–5.

Erickson, C. J. (1973) Mate familiarity and the reproductive behavior of ringed turtle doves, *Auk*, **90**, 780–95.

Erickson, C. J. (1974) Natur und Function der Paarbindung. In: *Grzimeks Tierleben*, Kindler Verlag, Munich, pp. 438–48.

Erickson, C. J., Bruder, R. H., Komisaruk, B. R., and Lehrman, D. S. (1967) Selective inhibition by progesterone of androgen-induced behavior in male ring doves *(Streptopelia risoria)*, *Endocrinology*, **81**, 39–44.

Erickson, C. J., and Hutchison, J. B. (1977) Induction of nest-material collecting in male Barbary doves by intracerebral androgen, *J. Reprod. Fertil*, **50**, 9–16.

Erickson, C. J. and Lehrman, D. S. (1964) Effect of castration of male ring doves upon ovarian activity of females, *J. Comp. Physiol. Psychol.*, **58**, 164–6.

Erickson, C. J. and Martinez-Vargas, M. C. (1975) The hormonal basis of co-operative nest building. In: *Neural and Endocrine Aspects of Behaviour in Birds*. P. Caryl, P. Wright, and D. W. Vowles (eds.), Elsevier, Amsterdam, in press.

Erickson, C. J. and Morris, R. L. (1972) Effects of mate familiarity on the courtship and reproductive success of the ring dove *(Streptopelia risoria)*, *Anim. Behav.*, **20**, 341–4.

Farner, D. S., ed. (1973) *Breeding Biology of Birds*, National Academy of Sciences, Washington, D. C.

Fischer, H. (1965) Das Triumphgeschrei der Graugans *(Anser anser)*, *Z. Tierpsychol.*, **22**, 247–304.

Goforth, W. R. and Baskett, T. S. (1965) Effects of experimental color marking on pairing of captive mourning doves, *J. Wildl. Mgmt.*, **29**, 543–53.

Hinde, R. A. and Simpson, M. J. A. (1975) Qualities of mother–infant relationships in monkeys. In: *Parent–Infant Interaction, Ciba Foundation Symposium 33 (new series)*, Elsevier, Amsterdam, pp. 39–67.

Holmes, R. T. (1973) Social behaviour of breeding western sand pipers *Calidris mauri*, *Ibis*, **115**, 107–23.

Hooker, T. and Hooker, B. I. (1969) Duetting. In: *Bird Vocalizations*, R. A. Hinde (ed.), Cambridge University Press, London, pp. 185–205.

Hutchison, J. B. (1969) Changes in hypothalamic responsiveness to testosterone in male barbary doves *(Streptopelia risoria)*, *Nature, London*, **222**, 176–7.

Hutchison, J. B. (1970) Differential effects of testosterone and oestradiol on male courtship in barbary doves *(Streptopelia risoria)*, *Anim. Behav.*, **18**, 41–51.

Hutchison, J. B. (1974) Post-castration decline in behavioural responsiveness to intra-hypothalamic androgen in doves, *Brain Res.*, **81**, 169–81.

Huxley, J. (1914) The courtship habits of the great crested grebe *Podiceps cristatus*; with an addition to the theory of sexual selection, *Proc. Zool. Soc. London*, 492–562.

Huxley, J. S. (1923) Courtship activities in the red-throated diver *(Colymbus stellatus Pontopp.)*; together with a discussion of the evolution of courtship in birds. *J. Linn. Soc.*, **35**, 253–92.

Immelmann, K. (1963) Drought adaptations in Australian desert birds, *Proc. XIII Int. Ornith. Cong. Ithaca*, 649–57.

Kleiman, D. G. (1975) The reproductive cycle and sociosexual interactions in pairs of golden lion marmosets (Primates, Callitrichidae). Paper presented at the Eastern Conference on Reproductive Behavior, Nags Head, North Carolina, May 1975.

Kleiman, G. and Eisenberg, J. F. (1973) Comparisons of canid and felid social systems from an evolutionary perspective, *Anim. Behav.*, **21**, 637–59.

Korenbrot, C. C., Schomberg, D. W., and Erickson, C. J. (1974) Radioimmunoassay of plasma estradiol during the breeding cycle of ring doves *(Streptopelia risoria)*, *Endocrinology*, **94**, 1126–32.

Lack, D. (1940) Pair-formation in birds, *Condor*, **42**, 269–86.

Lack, D. (1968) *Ecological Adaptations for Breeding in Birds*, Methuen, London.

Lamprecht, J. (1970) Duettgesang beim Siamang, *Symphalangus syndactylus* (Hominoidea, Hylobatinae), *Z. Tierpsychol.*, **27**, 186–204.

Lamprecht, J. (1972) Paarbruch bei Cichliden. Zur Spontaneität der Aggression, *Naturwiss.*, **59**, 275–6.

Lamprecht, J. (1973) Mechanismen des Paarzusammenhaltes beim Cichliden *Tilapia mariae* Boulenger 1899 (Cichlidae, Teleostei), *Z. Tierpsychol.*, **32**, 10–61.

Lehrman, D. S. (1958) Effect of female sex hormones on incubation behavior in the ring dove *(Streptopelia risoria)*, *J. Comp. Physiol. Psychol.*, **51**, 142–5.

Lehrman, D. S. and Wortis, R. P. (1960) Previous breeding experience and hormone-induced incubation behavior in the ring dove, *Science*, **132**, 1667–8.

Lehrman, D. S. and Wortis, R. P. (1967) Breeding experience and breeding efficiency in the ring dove, *Anim. Behav.*, **15**, 223–8.

Lorenz, K. Z. (1966a) *On Aggression*, Translated by M. K. Wilson, Grosset and Dunlap, New York.

Lorenz, K. Z. (1966b) Evolution of ritualization in the biological and cultural phase, *Phil. Trans. Roy. Soc. London*, Ser. B., **251**, 273–84.

Lorenz, K. Z. (1970a) Contributions to the study of the ethology of social Corvidae (1931), In: *Studies in Animal and Human Behaviour Vol. I*, Translated by R. Martin, Methuen, London, pp. 1–56.

Lorenz, K. Z. (1970b) Companions as factors in the bird's environment, pp. 101–258. In: *Studies in Animal and Human Behaviour Vol. I*, Translated by R. Martin, Methuen, London, pp. 101–258.

Martinez-Vargas, M. C. (1974) Nest building in the ring dove *(Streptopelia risoria)*: hormonal and social factors, *Behaviour*, **50**, 123–51.

Martinez-Vargas, M. C. and Erickson, C. J. (1973) Some social and hormonal determinants of nest-building behaviour in the ring dove *(Streptopelia risoria)*, *Behaviour*, **45**, 12–37.

Mills, J. A. (1973) The influence of age and pair-bond on the breeding biology of the red-billed gull *Larus novachollandiae scopulinus*, *J. Anim. Ecol.*, **42**, 147–69.

Morris, R. L. and Erickson, C. J. (1971) Pair bond maintenance in the ring dove *(Streptopelia risoria)*, *Anim. Behav.*, **19**, 398–406.

Moynihan, M. (1955) Some aspects of reproductive behaviour in the black-headed gull *(Larus ridibundus)* and related species, *Behaviour*, Suppl., 4.

Mundinger, P. C. (1970) Vocal imitation and individual recognition of finch calls, *Science*, **168**, 480–2.

Nelson, J. B. (1965) The behaviour of the gannet, *Brit. Birds.*, **58**, 233–88, 313–36.

Nisbet, I. C. T. (1973) Courtship-feeding, egg-size, and breeding success in common terns, *Nature*, **241**, 141–2.

Orians, G. H. (1969) On the evolution of mating systems in birds and mammals, *Am. Natur.*, **103**, 589–603.

Parmelee, D. F. and Payne, R. B. (1973) On multiple broods and the breeding strategy of arctic sanderlings, *Ibis*, **115**, 218–26.

Patel, M. D. (1936) The physiology of the formation of the pigeon's milk, *Physiol. Zool.*, **9**, 129–52.

Richdale, L. E. and Warham, J. (1973) Survival, pair bond retention, and nest-site tenacity in buller's mollymawk, *Ibis*, **115**, 257–63.

Seibt, U. (1973) Die beruhigende Wirkung der Partner-Nähe bei der monogamen Garnele *Hymenocera picta*, *Z. Tierpsychol.*, **33**, 424–7.

Seibt, U. (1974) Mechanismen und Sinnesleistungen für der Paarzusammenhalt bei der Garnele *Hymenocera picta* Dana, *Z. Tierpsychol.*, **35**, 337–51.

Seibt, U. and Wickler, W. (1972) Individuen-Erkennen und Partnerbevorzugung bei der Garnele *Hymenocera picta* Dana, *Naturwiss.*, **59**, 40–1.

Selander, R. K. (1966) Sexual dimorphism and differential niche utilization in birds, *Condor*, **68**, 113–51.

Silver, R., Feder, H. H., Lehrman, D. S. (1973) Situational and hormonal determinants of courtship, aggression, and incubation behavior in male ring doves *(Streptopelia risoria)*, *Horm. Behav.*, **4**, 163–72.

Silver, R., Reboulleau, C., Lehrman, D. S., and Feder, H. H. (1974) Radioimmunoassay of plasma progesterone during the reproductive cycle of male and female ring doves *(Streptopelia risoria)*, *Endocrinology*, **94**, 1547–54.

Simmons, K. E. L. (1970) Ecological determinants of breeding adaptations and social behaviour in two fish-eating birds, In: *Social Behaviour in Birds and Mammals*, Academic Press, London, pp. 37–77.

Snow, D. W. (1958) *A Study of Blackbirds*, Allen and Unwin, London.

Sparks, J. (1967) Allogrooming in primates: a review. In: *Primate Ethology*, D. Morris (ed.), Doubleday, Garden City.

Stern, J. M. and Lehrman, D. S. (1969) Role of testosterone in progesterone-induced incubation behaviour in male ring doves *(Streptopelia risoria)*, *J. Endocrinol.*, **44**, 13–22.

Stettner, L. J., Garreffa, L. F., and Missakian, E. (1971) Factors effecting monogamous behavior in the Bobwhite Quail *(Colinus virginianus)*, *Comm. Behav. Biol.*, **6**, 137–162.

Stettner, L. J., Missakian, E., and Loren, M. (1966) Monogamous reactions in laboratory-mated bob-white quail *(Colinus virginianus)*, *J. Comp. Physiol. Psychol.*, **62**, 160–2.

Thorpe, W. H. (1972) Duetting and antiphonal song in birds, *Behaviour*, Suppl., 18.

Thorpe, W. H. and North, M. E. W. (1965) Origin and significance of the power of vocal imitation: with special reference to the antiphonal singing of birds, *Nature*, **208**, 219–22.

Tinbergen, N. (1939) The behavior of the snow bunting in spring, *Trans. Linn. Soc. New York*, **5**, 1–94.

Tinbergen, N. (1952) Derived activities: their causation, biological significance, origin, and emancipation during evolution, *Quart. Rev. Biol.*, **27**, 1–32.

Tinbergen, N. (1953) *The Herring Gull's World*, Collins, London.

Trivers, R. L. (1972) Parental investment and sexual selection. In: *Sexual Selection and the Descent of Man 1871–1971*, B. Campbell (ed.), Aldine, Chicago, pp. 136–230.

White, S. (1971) Selective responsiveness by the gannet *(Sula bassana)* to played-back cells, *Anim. Behav.*, **19**, 125–31.

Wickler, W. (1972) *The Sexual Code*, Doubleday, New York.

Wickler, W. (1973) Ethological analysis of convergent adaptation, *Ann. N. Y. Acad. Sci.*, **223**, 65–9.

Wickler, W. and Seibt, U. (1972) Über den Zusammenhang des Paarsitzens mit anderen Verhaltensweisen bei *Hymenocera picta* Dana, *Z. Tierpsychol.*, **31**, 163–70.

Williams, G. C. (1966) *Adaptation and Natural Selection*, Princeton, Princeton University Press.

Williams, H. W., Sorenson, M. W., and Thompson, P. (1969) Antiphonal calling of the tree shrew *Tupaia palawanensis*, *Folia. primat.*, **11**, 200–5.

Zahavi, A. (1971) The social behaviour of the white wagtail *Motacilla alba alba* wintering in Israel, *Ibis*, **113**, 203–11.

CHAPTER 22

Olfactory Cues in Mammalian Sexual Behaviour

ERIC B. KEVERNE

INTRODUCTION

Communication in relationship to all behaviour, be it sexual, aggressive or territorial, depends upon multiple sensory cues, the functions of each overlapping extensively. Clearly, it is extremely unlikely that sexual interactions among mammals will depend exclusively on one sense, although effects can be shown experimentally when only specific sensory information is available. In this context, olfactory cues have been shown to play an important part in mammalian sexual behaviour, and have led to the use of the term 'pheromone' and 'pheromonal response' in defining such behaviour. Pheromones are substances secreted by an animal externally with specific effects on the behaviour or physiology of another individual of the same species. Although originally introduced by Karlson and Butenant (1959) in the context of insect communication, the meaning of the word pheromone has since been extended to include chemical communication in a broader sense and also in relation to mammalian behaviour. The use of this same terminology has led to certain misunderstandings, since laymen and scientists alike tend to associate sexual pheromones with the silkworm moth, *Bombyx mori*. The female of this species attracts her males from miles around, and in mammals nothing quite so spectacular or stereotyped has so far been described, nor is ever likely to be.

Yet another complication of using the term pheromone in the repertoire of mammalian behaviour stems from the two types of response it encompasses, and which are not necessarily mutually exclusive. If the pheromone produces a more or less immediate change in the behaviour of the recipient, it is said to have a releaser effect (Wilson, 1963) and sex attractants constitute a large and important category of the releaser pheromones. Primer pheromones, on the other hand, alter the physiology and consequent behavioural repertoire of the animal. This type of response is slow to develop and demands a prolonged stimulation which is mediated through the nervous and endocrine systems involving the anterior pituitary. Thus olfactory cues can influence sexual behaviour in at least two ways, one involving neocortical neural circuitry and requiring a .degree of computing and processing in mammals, and the other probably acting directly on subcortical limbic structures bringing about certain measurable physiological changes. Removal of the mammalian olfactory bulb may, therefore, decrease the likelihood of finding an attractive mate, but can also result in underdeveloped gonads, influence ovulation, the oestrous cycle, and implantation, and also impair sexual performance. Thus, when we consider olfactory cues and mammalian sexual behaviour it is important to know which response we are describing, and while this is fairly evident when the animal is presented with specific odour cues, it is not so clear when the process involves olfactory deprivation, especially by bulbectomy. A comprehension of this problem requires at least an elementary knowledge of neuroanatomy, and since this will be referred to throughout the chapter, the projections and connections of the olfactory system will be briefly outlined.

THE CENTRAL OLFACTORY CONNECTIONS

Most mammals, the exceptions being higher primates and man, possess a dual olfactory system. Sensory receptors in the olfactory epithelium in the nasal cavity give rise to axons, the fila olfactoria, which ascend into the cranium through the cribriform plate to synapse on mitral cells in the main olfactory bulbs. A second set of receptors, located in the epithelial lining of the vomeronasal organ, also send axons, the vomeronasal nerve, through the cribriform plate. The vomeronasal nerves run medially between the main olfactory bulbs, and synapse in the accessory olfactory bulb. The accessory olfactory bulb is itself spatially and histologically distinct from the main olfactory bulb and usually lies on the dorsal surface of the main bulbs.

The central projections of the main and accessory olfactory bulbs also remain distinct, and this has been shown using both histological (autoradiography and degeneration studies) and electrophysiological studies. The primary projections of the main olfactory bulb pass ipsilaterally in the lateral olfactory tract to the piriform cortex. A substantial number of axons also pass to the contralateral olfactory bulb via the anterior limb of the anterior commissure. Piriform cortex projections have been described to the entorhinal cortex, basolateral amygdala, lateral preoptic area, the medial forebrain bundle, habenula and medialis dorsalis nucleus (MD) of the thalamus (Cragg, 1961; Powell et al., 1965). However, using both light and electron-microscopic techniques, Heimer (1972) observed almost complete absence of terminal degeneration in the lateral hypothalamus, with the exception of the nuclei gemini of the mamillary bodies, following lesions to the pyriform cortex. This contrasted with an abundance of terminal degeneration in the MD of the thalamus, its projection from the piriform cortex leaving the stria medullaris

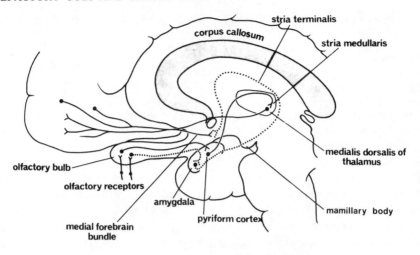

Olfactory connections of the brain

Fig. 1. The dual olfactory projections as they might occur in the primate brain. Dotted line represents a fairly direct olfacto-hypothalamic projection while the continuous line permits olfactory information access to the frontal neocortex via the thalamus

at the level of the habenula nucleus (Fig. 1—continuous line). These recent results suggest that the major projections from the piriform cortex are, if not entirely, at least primarily extrahypothalamic, the primary projection being to the MD of the thalamus which in turn projects to the orbito-frontal cortex (Pribram *et al.*, 1953). Thus a rather precise and well-differentiated relationship seems to emerge from more recent experimental studies by the electronmicroscope and reduced silver methods, whereas classical histological studies indicated diffuse olfactodiencephalic projections.

The central projections of the accessory olfactory bulb have only recently received careful investigation. In contrast to the main bulb, accessory bulb projections are directly into the limbic system and terminate in the ipsilateral cortico-medial nuclei of the amygdala (Fig. 1—dotted line) in the hamster (Scalia and Winans, 1975), rabbit (Broadwell, 1975), and rat (Allen and Keverne, unpubl. results). From the amygdaloid complex, fibres run in the stria terminalis to the anterior hypothalamus, preoptic area, and septal nuclei. De Olmos (1972) divided the stria terminalis into three components and mapped the projections of specific lesions after degeneration had occurred. His results indicated that projections from the cortico-medial nuclei of the amygdala travel in the stria to the medial hypothalamus (VMH) and the medial preoptic area. Thus the accessory olfactory pathway has a direct projection to limbic structures but unlike the main bulb, appears not to have access to the thalamus and in turn neocortical regions.

SIGNALLING PHEROMONES AND SEXUAL INTERACTION

Rodents

Rat

A great deal of work has been conducted on the sexual behaviour of rodents, and from this it is clear that olfactory cues from the female could be serving to attract the male. In the wild rat under semi-natural conditions, the female when in oestrus has been observed to extend her territorial range, leaving her scent on the ground and rocks (Calhoun, 1962). These scent markings were examined by males and could have provided the necessary cues for tracking the female to her burrow. In the laboratory, the involvement of olfactory cues in such sexual rapprochements has been examined, and LeMagnen (1952) showed that the adult male rat had a preference for the odour from a receptive female over the odour of a non-receptive, dioestrous female. Moreover, castrated or prepubertal male rats did not display this preference (Stern, 1970), but were capable of discriminating between the odours when given a non-sexual reinforcement (Carr and Caul, 1962). In other words, it would appear that the sexual attractant, although perceived at all times, is only attractive and responded to when the animal's hormonal status is appropriate, which is not surprising when we consider the marked dependence of sexual behaviour on gonadal hormones in the rat.

A question of some importance is whether the response to attractive female odours is genetically determined, and to what extent this has been influenced as a result of reinforcing sexual interactions which the male rat has learned to associate with a receptive female's odour. If the time males spend investigating female urine is anything to go by, then oestrous female urine is the source of the attractant and in this context sexual experience is most important. Thus sexually naive rats have been observed to spend just as much time investigating urine from oestrous females as dioestrous controls (Carr et al., 1965), while sexually experienced males spent twice as much time investigating the oestrous urine. Following sexual experience, the former naive males also showed increased investigation times of oestrous urine (Lydell and Doty, 1972). Similar procedures provide some similarities in the female rat, namely sexual experience and/or receptivity were necessary for females to prefer intact male urine over castrate male urine, while the naive non-receptive females showed no such preference. Learning, therefore, clearly plays an important part in the rat's response to sexual odours, and can be shown in the female as well as in the male. Since there is no behavioural evidence for the female rat actively seeking out the male, then the significance of male urine as a releaser pheromone is perhaps questionable. On the other hand, the finding that fresh but not ageing oestrous urine is more attractive than dioestrous urine indicates a potential temporarily discrete odour cue for the sexually experienced male rat, which may accurately indicate a given female's state of sexual receptivity (Lydel and Doty, 1972). Nevertheless, this fails to account for how the sexually inexperienced male finds his first female mate by the use of odour cues alone, unless olfactory imprinting has in some way determined this (Marr and Gardner, 1965; Marr and Lilliston, 1970).

Reconsidering the ability of male rats to selectively respond to odour cues from oestrous *versus* non-oestrous females, it will be remembered that actual discrimination was independent of the male's hormonal status (Carr and Caul, 1962). These behavioural results are parallelled by the electrophysiological findings that responses to female urine odours by unit recordings in the olfactory bulb and hypothalamic preoptic area are also independent of androgen in sexually inexperienced male rats (Pfaff and Gregory, 1971). Nevertheless, more units in the preoptic area than in the olfactory bulb responded differentially to oestrous compared to ovariectomized female urine odours in sexually experienced rats, while the reverse was the case for non-urine odours (Pfaff and Pfaffman, 1969). Thus, it is possible that the differential responses by single units in the hypothalamus are related to behavioural functions such as determine sexual performance. While neither the differential unit responses nor sex odour discrimination depend on androgen levels, androgens are essential for the male rat's mating behaviour. The olfactory sense may, therefore, only serve to make finer adjustments in the regulation of the mating pattern in the intact male rat.

Certainly, interruption of the afferent olfactory connections of male rats by olfactory bulb lesions has been shown to produce some changes in the male's mating pattern (Heimer and Larsson, 1967; Bermant and Taylor, 1969; Hitt *et al.*, 1973). The animals showed a prolonged latency in their responses to oestrous females, and a reduction in the number of ejaculations. Although olfactory stimuli were not, therefore, essential for the male rat's mating behaviour, olfactory impulses were nevertheless shown to exert influences upon this behaviour. These influences could be due to the olfactory bulbs themselves exerting some tonic neural effect on the hypothalamus, which is known to be involved in mating behaviour. Such behavioural influences might also be due to the loss of specific olfactory cues, since peripheral anosmia at the level of the olfactory mucosa produces similar mating pattern impairments (Larsson, 1971).

In the female rat, there is also evidence for olfactory influences on mating behaviour. Some 40% of female Wistar rats will show precocious mating on day three of their five-day cycle, while olfactory bulb removal prevents this early mating behaviour. This impairment of precocious mating does not occur in those females pretreated with oestradiol (Aron, Roos and Asch, 1970). Perhaps this is evidence that olfactory stimuli in some way modulates the threshold of reactivity to oestrogen of those neural structures mediating sexual behaviour, but it should be remembered that there are marked strain differences. Thus in Long–Evans (Moss, 1971) and Sprague–Dawley strains

(Edwards and Warner, 1972) bilateral removal of the olfactory bulbs enhances the expression of lordosis behaviour, with increases in the lordosis to mount ratio, while bulbectomy in Charles River COBS strain stops mating in about half the females (Curry, 1974). What, then, are the olfactory cues which are producing such divergent effects by their absence? In all probability, the answer cannot be attributed to an abolished or attenuated perception of pheromonal factors, since peripherally induced anosmia does not affect the expression of lordotic behaviour in female rats (Edwards and Warner, 1972). More likely, it seems possible that bulbectomy influences sexual behaviour by eliminating the olfactory neural input to the limbic areas involved in sexual behaviour in the female rat.

Mice

In mice, the social environment has been shown to influence urination in that males produce more urine than females in male–female encounters, while females produce scant amounts of urine in female–female encounters (Reynolds, 1971). Assuming the presence of attractant pheromones in the urine, urination could play an adaptive part in social encounters, being plentiful in the presence of a partner of the opposite sex where proximity and attraction are of biological advantage. Although no pheromones have been identified in male mouse urine, it seems clear that it does possess attractive properties which are dependent on the endocrine status of the male. Thus, in preference experiments more females spent more time sniffing the urine from intact adult males than that from castrates (Scott and Pfaff, 1970). The attractant components of male urine appear to have their origin in the preputial gland, since fewer female mice were shown to spend time sniffing the urine from preputialecto-mized males, or other females, while the homogenized preputial gland itself attracted a significantly large number of females (Bronson and Caroum, 1971). The male preputial gland appeared therefore to secrete an attractant pheromone into the urine, and lipid extracts of male preputial gland were even more effec-tive in attracting females. The sniffing response to this attractant pheromone in preputial homogenates depended upon the female's hormonal status and upon prior sexual experience (Caroum and Bronson, 1971). Sexually naive female mice, not under the influence of oestrogen, showed no preference for either preputial or muscle fat (control) homogenates. Sexual experience resulted in a strong and consistent preference for the preputial odour, regardless of the oestrous status of the female. Oestrogenized, sexually naive females showed a significant attraction to preputial homogenantes, but this was less consistent than the response resulting after sexual experience. Of particular interest was the finding that the strong effect of sexual experience on female attraction to preputial homogenates could be blocked by progesterone. The dose of progesterone administered was similar to that required to maintain pregnancy in the mouse, so it was not surprising to find that pregnant females were not attracted by the odour of male preputial glands. This may be of selective value, since male urine is also known to contain a pregnancy blocking primer pheromone (Bruce, 1960), and thus attracting pregnant females would result in biological wastage.

Perhaps of selective value is the finding that dominant male urine is more attractive to oestrous females than the urine from subordinate male mice (Jones and Nowell, 1974), while the same urine is aversive to both subordinate and dominant male mice, particularly the former. This would presumably serve the dual purpose of attracting females to the more biologically fit males, yet deterring other males which might offer a potential block to the pregnancy.

The attractant properties of male urine for female mice is parallelled by female urine serving to influence male mice, especially the urine from oestrous females (Davies and Bellamy, 1974). The attractiveness of female urine to male mice, as measured by duration of investigatory visit, was increased after storage at minus 10 °C, and, after prepubertal castration, males showed no preference for oestrous over dioestrous urine. Thus in the mouse, as in the rat, there appears to be mutual attraction of the sexes by substances present in the urine of both males and females. This attraction is dependent upon the endocrine status of both partners; namely the urine has to be from an oestrous female, while the male requires high androgen levels in order to display a response; and male urine is more potent to oestrous then anoestrous females especially that taken from a dominant male.

Clearly, olfactory cues appear to be important in mutual attraction in mice, but is there also a role for olfaction in mediating sexual performance? Bilateral removal of olfactory bulbs has resulted in a severe attenuation of hormonally induced sexual receptivity in the female (Thompson and Edwards, 1972), and completely abolished the display of masculine sexual behaviour in male mice (Rowe and Edwards, 1972). Although it is tempting to argue that olfaction is specifically involved in the mediation of mouse copulatory behaviour, caution should be exercised. In mice, bulbectomy modified most forms of social interaction, including aggression and maternal behaviour, and unilateral bulbectomy in the female also caused impairment of mating behaviour, so it seems unlikely that these effects were due to the loss of olfactory cues *per se*. Nevertheless, this does not exclude a possible contributory influence of olfactory cues on mating performance, especially in the male where unilateral bulbectomy failed to affect the normal display of male mating behaviour.

Hamster

When the female golden hamster is sexually receptive, an abundant, highly odorous substance, which has a releasing effect on the sexual behaviour of the male hamster, exudes from her genitalia. The male hamster sniffs and licks this secretion before and intermittently throughout mating (Dieterlen, 1959). If the vaginal secretion from the oestrous female is applied to the fur of a male, other males respond to him as to a female and attempt to mate with him (Lisk *et al.*, 1972), while even an anaesthetized male hamster can be transformed into a subject of sexual appeal by this procedure (Murphy, 1973). It would seem, therefore, that substances in the vaginal mucous of the female act to elicit a number of behaviour patterns associated with mating in the male. Even sexually naive males increased their mounting of other males when female vaginal secretions were applied, but these naive males failed to distinguish between oestrous and dioestrous smears. Thus the ability of the sexually experienced male hamster to distinguish the female in oestrus may be learned, which is of some adaptive significance for the male because the non-oestrous female is dominant if a fight ensues. Attempts at mating when the female is not in oestrus can result in vigorous fights, in which the male may be maimed or killed if no escape is available (Darby *et al.*, 1975).

The vaginal discharge itself seems not to be critical for the ongoing mating sequence, but rather for its initiation (Devor and Murphy, 1973). An anosmic male when placed with a receptive female does not commence mating. If copulation has already begun, however, then anosmia, induced by rapid occlusion of the nostril, does not interrupt the mating sequence. Such sexually experienced anosmic males can therefore mate, but this depends on the interval before reintroduction to the female. In about half the cases where this interval between nostril occlusion and returning the male to the female was less than 123 s, the now anosmic male resumed mating, indicating that olfactory stimuli are not necessary to maintain mating behaviour. Since mount frequencies, intromissions, and ejaculation latency were not compared for the anosmic and normal males, it is not clear whether olfactory input in the hamster might also influence sexual performance.

Procedures involving peripheral anosmia by zinc sulphate in the hamster seem to vary in their effects on male sexual behaviour. Powers and Winans (1973) reported normal patterns of mating behaviour in hamsters rendered anosmic in this way. Nevertheless, other workers have failed to observe any mating in the male hamster following peripheral anosmia with zinc sulphate (Lisk *et al.*, 1972; Devor and Murphy, 1973). With contradictions of this nature it is difficult to establish the role of the olfactory input in hamster sexual behaviour. Perhaps some of the differences stem from the recovery period allowed following zinc sulphate administration in behavioural testing. Within 24 h of treatment, there is general agreement that anosmia occurs and mating is abolished (Lisk *et al.*, 1972; Devor and Murphy, 1973), while recovery of mating is seen in 48–96 h, during which time hamsters are still anosmic to food retrieval (Powers and Winans, 1973). It is possible that the animals treated with zinc sulphate are debilitated for a number of hours following application (Sieck and Baumbach, 1974) and the initial loss of mating is not due to the peripheral anosmia. It is also possible that these experimental procedures, although intended to cause olfactory deafferentation alone, actually cause deafferentation or blockage of both olfactory and vomeronasal systems.

The idea that the vomeronasal organ and its projections to the accessory olfactory nucleus are of importance in mammalian sexual behaviour (excluding primates) has recently gained support (Estes, 1972). Experimental studies (Powers and Winans, 1975) have shown that mating behaviour of the male hamster can be seriously impaired following destruction of the vomeronasal nerve, but is unaffected by olfactory deafferentation alone. Bilateral surgical section of the vomeronasal nerves alone, abolished mating behaviour in some 40% of the subjects, but subsequent olfactory deafferentation with zinc sulphate was necessary to abolish mating in all hamsters. When we consider the differential neural projections of the olfactory bulb and vomeronasal organ (see p. 729), they seem to give rise to separate, although parallel, afferent pathways connected with the periform lobe and amygdala (Scalia and Winans, 1975).

Guinea Pig

In the domestic guinea pig behavioural observations provide suggestive evidence for a communicatory function of urine. Both males and females engaged in a behaviour termed 'perineal drag' in which the anogenital region is drawn across the ground. This behaviour occurs frequently in sexual and aggressive encounters. Both males and females urinate during these bouts of marking and at the same time the male deposits material from his scrotal glands, while the female may deposit vaginal secretions. Urination also occurs when a non-receptive female is pursued by a male, at which time she often raises her perineal region and sprays urine, which sometimes strikes the male in the face. The male reacts by vigorous head shaking and then by sniffing and licking the female's urine (pers. observ.). This frequently stops the male pursuing the unreceptive female further.

Although it has been suggested that olfactory cues are not of significance in distinguishing the sexes (Ibsen, 1965), certain marking behaviour by both male and female guinea pigs is probably of some communicative significance. In a choice situation, sexually experienced male guinea pigs preferred conspecific urine to that of other species, and female urine was investigated for longer than male urine (Beauchamp, 1973). As the female urine aged, it lost its attractiveness and after 48 h was no more attractive than water (Beauchamp and Berüter, 1973). It is possible that male attraction to female urine, which in this case was from non-receptive females, could serve to maintain social group structure. Under natural circumstances, females are probably only receptive for a few hours every 66–70 days. Urine could, therefore, maintain social cohesion during long periods when stimuli from sexually receptive females are absent. However, it is difficult to comprehend how odour cues from unreceptive females serve both to attract the male and maintain group cohesion, yet halt his sexual pursuits when sprayed at the male during mounting attempts. Moreover, it would be of some interest to determine if receptive female urine was more attractive than that from unreceptive female guinea pigs.

There is some evidence that olfactory imprinting might influence adult sexual behaviour in the guinea pig. It has been shown that there are periods during ontogeny when animals are particularly sensitive to learning certain stimulus characteristics of the species, and in this context olfactory preference can be modified by early exposure of the species to an experimental odour. In experiments where male guinea pigs were reared in the presence of artificial odours (acetophenone or ethyl benzoate), the response of the males to oestrous females was affected by such odours (Carter, 1972). Such responses as the latency to approach or mount the female, and number of mounts, were not clearly influenced by the odour rearing conditions, but frequencies of contact and sexual behaviour did show significant differences related to the odour conditions. The odour under which male guinea pigs were reared influenced their performance with oestrous females when adult, the highest scores being obtained in the presence of the familiar artificial odour.

Lesioning of the olfactory bulb in the female guinea pig results in their mating less readily than controls (Donovan and Kopriva, 1965). Some of the bulbectomized females showed several periods of oestrus without copulating, although they were continuously housed with proven stud males. Peripheral anosmia induced by zinc sulphate in the male guinea pig does not abolish mating, although it reduces the likelihood of the males responding to the onset of oestrus in the female (pers. unpubl. observ.). Moreover, male guinea pigs rendered anosmic in this way also showed reduced nuzzling and following of the female, less urine marking of the female or territory, and fewer markings with the perineal scrotal gland. In fact, most motor behaviours were depressed, especially within the first 24 h following intranasal zinc sulphate flushing. Unfortunately there is no adequate control for zinc sulphate flushing of the olfactory mucosa, which appears to be very stressful in the guinea pig. It is therefore uncertain whether failure to detect the onset of female oestrus was due to the absence of a specific olfactory cue, or as seems more likely, to the depressed behaviour of the males as a result of the operative procedure.

Canidae

Scent marking in the Canidae probably serves a number of functions including demarcation of territory, the marking of social contacts, the formation of consort pairs and the legitimization of the leader (Schenkel, 1947). So far as sexual attraction is concerned, there is evidence for olfactory influences of the female on the male, and a number of sources for attractants have been suggested.

Elimination of urine in members of the family Canidae differs between the sexes and females generally squat deeply, sometimes touching the surface with their ano-genital region. The raccoon dog, domestic dog, coyote, and bat-eared fox females only mark during the period preceding oestrus, and during oestrus itself (Kleiman, 1966). Males have been attracted over long distances to oestrous bitches (Fuller and Dubois, 1962), and female urine, used as a lure, attracted a high percentage of male foxes and coyotes (Gier, 1960). Sexually active males have been shown to discriminate between urine from a bitch in heat and that from a non-oestrous female, but one male which failed to mate also failed to respond differentially to the two types of urine (Beach and Gilmour, 1949). The bitch urinates more frequently when in heat and only part of the bladder contents are expelled at each micturition, hence making a series of odour trails which lead to her home. By following any one of these trails, the male could eventually come into the female's presence, and would be less likely to join an unreceptive female which marks less frequently, and produces urine which is less attractive.

In an attempt to trace the source of this attractant, Gier (1960) conducted a series of experiments involving surgical removal of the reproductive tract. Removal of the uterus, ovaries, and anal glands was without effect on the attractiveness of the oestrogenized female, but removal of the entire reproductive tract including the vulva resulted in a loss of attractiveness. Doses of oestradiol that were adequate to bring a normal bitch into heat induced courtship behaviour in females with their reproductive tract removed without influencing male interest. The male would smell and turn away, and if the female became too insistent, would react aggressively. The results indicated that the attractant odour was produced in the vulva of the female. Beach and Merari (1968) found males would investigate cotton balls impregnated with vaginal discharge from oestrogen treated females for longer periods than those from anoestrous females. However, when oestrogen-primed bitches were injected with progesterone, the stimulus value of their vaginal secretions was greatly enhanced. It was suggested (Beach and Merari, 1970) that progesterone altered the chemical composition of the vaginal secretions which in turn brought about the changes in the male's behaviour. These behavioural changes included an increase in sniffing and licking of the vulva when females received oestrogen and progesterone, and male arousal hence involved the gustatory as well as the olfactory sense.

Yet another source of sexual attractants is found in the anal gland secretions of the oestrous bitch (Donovan, 1967, 1969). Anal gland secretions were collected from males, oestrous, and anoestrous females, and presented to male dogs. The dogs sniffed, but quickly lost interest in all of the secretions, except those from a female in oestrous, to which it was reported they responded excitedly. Anal gland secretions from females in oestrous were wiped over the rump of an anoestrous female and when she was penned with a male, he exhibited great sexual excitement, licking the female's vulva and attempting to mount and copulate. When the same procedure was performed with secretions from anoestrous females, the male evidenced little interest. The anal gland secretions of one canine, the red fox, have undergone chemical scrutiny and Albone and Fox (1971) identified a series of saturated carboxylic acids (C_2 to C_6) and trimethylamine, but no concurrent behavioural studies were conducted with authentic acids to confirm that these were involved in sexual attraction.

From examination of published data, it would appear that three possible sources of sexual attractants have been located in the female carnivore and they include urine, vaginal secretions, and anal gland secretions. However, since the three sources are in close proximity it has to be ascertained that no cross-contamination occurred. Moreover, since both anal gland and vaginal secretions contain some similar components (short chain aliphatic acids), this might explain the attractant properties of both. While urine is the more appropriate vehicle for depositing attractants around the female's home range, oestrous vaginal secretions could still serve to trigger the male's sexual arousal and confirm the presence of the oestrous bitch. However, in experienced male dogs, mating behaviour does not seem to depend exclusively on olfactory cues, since peripherally anosmic dogs can readily copulate (Hart and Haugen, 1971). This does not necessarily imply that odour cues serve no function in attracting males to oestrous bitches, but, unlike the hamster, sexual performance is not dependent on an olfactory input.

Ungulates

There is an increasing amount of evidence to suggest that olfaction is of fundamental importance for the stimulation of sexual behaviour in many ungulate species, and a variety of similar responses are observed following genital inspection. This olfactory response, originally termed Flehmen by Schneider (1930) is almost invariably in response to close genital olfaction. Hart et al., (1946) demonstrated that olfactory cues were of importance in eliciting the sexual behaviour of bulls. With the non-oestrous cow, the bull showed no interest, but smearing the cows' genital area with a mixture of vaginal mucous and urine from an oestrous 'donor' cow resulted in the full mounting and servicing of an artificial vagina twice in five minutes. Similarly, when plastic gloves, used to rectally palpate a cow in oestrus and containing faecal matter and anal gland secretions, were rubbed around the tail of an anoestrous cow, the bull selected this cow from a row of animals and sniffed and stopped behind the experimental cow (Donovan, 1967).

Olfactory stimulation of the stallion is derived from different parts of the mare's body, including the external genitalia, the muzzle, and particularly the groin and neighbouring parts (Berliner, 1959). Unlike the adult, young stallions show a poor sexual response to a dummy, but sexual behaviour can be elicited when the dummy is sprinkled with urine from an oestrous mare. Some 37% of the young stallions were stimulated to mount the dummy when it was sprinkled with oestrous mare urine (Wierzbowski and Hafez, 1961).

The method by which rams detect ewes in oestrus has long been considered to involve olfactory cues. Kelley (1937) concluded that rams were able to detect oestrous ewes by a characteristic odour of vaginal secretions, and claims to have confused rams by wiping the swabs from the perineal region of oestrous ewes onto the vulva of non-oestrous ewes. Lindsay (1965), using rams with olfactory lobes ablated, found anosmic rams to approach both oestrous and non-oestrous ewes at random. Normal rams were able to select among the two categories, and preferentially approached oestrous ewes. However, the ability of anosmic rams to mate successfully was not impaired, but their precopulatory behaviour was modified, with practically no foreplay preceding the actual mating attempt.

Signoret and Mesnil de Buisson (1961) have experimentally partitioned the stimuli which elicit the mating stance in the sow. The mating sow shows an immobilizing reflex in the presence of the boar and in 50% of cases the same reflex can be triggered by exerting pressure on the back of the female in the male's absence. Acoustic signals produced by the boar were of some importance in promoting the mating stance, but olfactory signals were of primary importance. Sows in pens impregnated by the odour of the boar were readily induced to give a mating stance in 81% of cases, but the pheromones responsible were not identified.

Chemical analysis of compounds isolated from the fat of mature pigs showed the presence in the boar of an odoriferous 5α-androst-16-en-3-one, (androstenone) which was absent from the fat of the castrate boar and the female (Patterson, 1968a). The corresponding steroid alcohol, 3α-hydroxy-5α-androst-16-ene (androstenol), occurs in considerable concentration in the submaxillary salivary gland of the boar (Patterson, 1968a), and both steroids are present in the saliva, imparting a musky odour to the breath of the animal. During the mating behaviour of the boar, the male approaches the sow giving a series of grunts, noses the vulva and champs his jaws, producing copious saliva production at the mouth. This led to the suggestion that olfactory cues might have originated from male salivary gland secretion (Hafez et al., 1962). Trials using aerosol sprays containing the two delta-16-androgen steroids have shown that in the absence of the boar, the characteristic response of the oestrous female to the 'back pressure' test can be elicited in some 50% of cases which were previously negative in the absence of a boar (Melrose et al., 1971).

Other workers (Eibl and Wettke, 1964) have shown that a few millilitres of seminal fluid from a boar, deposited on the snout of a sow showing incomplete signs of heat, will make the animal responsive to 'back pressure' in the majority of cases. It has also been suggested that the preputial gland is the site of sex-odour production, which is dependent on the presence of male sex-hormones (Dutt et al., 1959). Melrose et al. (1971) found that a mixture of preputial fluid and urine was effective in promoting a response to 'back pressure' in up to 62% of oestrous sows that had not previously responded in the absence of the boar. It is therefore most interesting to find marked differences between the biochemical composition of the salivary gland and the boar preputial fluid, where under conditions of acid pH, low molecular weight fatty acids predominate, whilst under conditions of alkaline pH, the principal odoriferous components are phenols, ammonia, and amines (Patterson, 1968b). The proportions of the various components also varies depending on the degree of bacterial activity in the mixture (Melrose *et al.*, 1971).

In the red deer, *Cervus elaphus*, the vaginal mucous at oestrus has a strong, penetrating smell, and throughout the mating season there was a second odour which was sweet and musky, which may have been the stag's rutting odour following mounting. In the early stages of oestrus, fluid mucous dripped from the vagina and from the end of the deer's tail (Guinness *et al.*, 1971). Stags were observed to sniff areas where oestrous females had been lying, and following urination of the oestrous hind, the stag would rush up, sniff out the exact spot, and then show Flehman. As oestrus progressed the hind gradually became more reluctant to run away, and would allow the stag to place his chin on her rump during the chase, or lick her vulva. In the pronghorn deer, *Antilocapra americana*, males mark with their subauricular organ which is also presented to females in courtship and is licked by females (Muller-Schwarze and Silverstein, 1974). A number of components have been identified in the subauricular secretion but in tests of mixtures, isovaleric acid was the dominant compound and in tests of the individual compounds, isovaleric acid was the most active constituent (Muller-Schwarze *et al.*, 1974).

In the Asiatic elephant, *Elephas maximus maximus*, secretions from the clitoris, vagina, or urine may be involved in chemical communication (Jainudeen *et al.*, 1971). After touching a female in the vicinity of the urogenital sinus, the male frequently places his trunk into his mouth, a chain of events comparable to the Flehman reaction shown in ungulates and termed urine testing (Eisenberg *et al.*, 1971). Observations of sexual behaviour during male–female encounters indicates that the male played an active role in detecting oestrus, and the frequency of urine testing altered significantly during various phases of the cycle. During dioestrus, after the initial urine test, the male paid no further attention to his partner for the rest of the observation period. In prooestrus, frequency of olfactory testing increased, and in oestrus the testing decreased considerably, followed by a dramatic increase in frequency as the females passed out of oestrus. The female, on the other hand, touches and sniffs the male most frequently in the area of his temporal gland, at the mouth mucosa, and in the vicinity of the penis sheath. Secretions from the preputial glands of the male may also have an influence on the behaviour of the female. Females seen standing downwind of the male, but not in visual contact, would turn and approach the male following the unsheathing of his penis. It was considered that odours born downwind from the male were active in inducing the approach of the female (Eisenberg *et al.*, 1971).

SIGNALLING PHEROMONES INVOLVED IN PRIMATE BEHAVIOUR

From the available evidence it appears that olfactory signals play an important part in communication between the sexes amongst the Prosimian primates. In tree shrews *Tupaia longipes*, males have been observed to nuzzle the ano-genital region of females daily (Conaway and Sorenson, 1966). As females neared oestrus, following and nuzzling, and attempted mounts increased. During oestrus, following of the females was intense and sometimes lasted for an hour or longer, during which time the male kept his nose closely in line with the vulva of the female and, whenever she stopped, attempted to mount. Similar behaviour has been described for *T. montana* (Sorenson and Conaway, 1968). Olfactory marking is particularly well developed in the Lemuridae and many possess specialized apocrine scent glands (Montagna, 1962). Petter (1965) observed marking of branches with combined brachial and axillary gland secretions in *Lemur catta* and *Hapalemur griseus*. Male ring-tailed lemurs have also been observed to rub their tails in the forearm gland and shake this in the face of another animal (Jolly, 1966; Evans and Goy, 1968). *Lemur catta* females have been observed to perform genital marking with the vaginal labia widely reflected, and the inner surface pressed firmly against the marked surface. The possible function of these olfactory signals in the synchronization of oestrus and activation of ovulation has been suggested (Evans and Goy, 1968). Other species of Lemuroidea, *Lemur macaco*, *Propithecus verreauxi*, have also been observed to perform olfactory marking, particularly with urine, a feature in common with the male loris, *Loris tardigradus lydekkerianus*, (Ilse, 1955) and the lesser bush-baby, *Galago senegalensis moholi* (Doyle *et al.*, 1967).

Urine marking in the bush-baby occurred particularly in relationship to examination of the female genitalia, and increased at the beginning of oestrus. Courtship, which was probably released by olfactory cues, was initiated by the male and during oestrus the female had a white vaginal discharge which perceptibly excited the male (Doyle *et al.*, 1967). It has also been suggested that urine marking in the male serves a sexual function (Sauer and Sauer, 1963).

Among the Anthropoidea, urine marking has been described in the squirrel monkey, *Saimiri sciureus* (Castell and Maurus, 1967). According to Latta *et al.* (1967) there was no evidence to suggest that urine marking served a territorial function, but urine marking was elicited by sexual excitement. Genital inspection of females by males, and areas occupied by females during urine washing, was more frequent on their receptive days. The authors believed that olfactory cues served to indicate the presence of a receptive female in the group. Baldwin (1968) suggested that the smell of female odours excited male sexual activity, and that olfactory cues may be important in coordinating the seasonal reproductive cycle in squirrel monkeys.

Scent marking seems to play an important role in the sexual communication of marmosets (Epple, 1970) and olfactory signals are of importance in most species (Epple, 1967; Hampton *et al.*, 1966). Scent marking regularly precedes and follows copulation, and scent marking as well as intensive sniffing and licking of the partner's marks and genitals is a regular component of courtship behaviour in males and females (Epple, 1967). It was suggested that changes in the level of circulating hormones may stimulate production of scent and/or change its chemical constituents, which in turn would provide information on the sexual and social status of the individual (Epple, 1970). It was the view of Marler (1965) that olfactory communication played little part in the distance communication of monkeys and apes, although he pointed out that urine of oestrous females seemed to convey information about their condition to males in the group. Certainly, field studies of several anthropoid species have revealed that scenting of the female's ano-genital region by males was a common, almost routine occurrence in: *Cercopithecus aethiops* (Booth, 1962); the howler monkey, *Alouatta palliata* (Altmann, 1959); the dusky titi, *Callicebus molock* (Moynihan, 1966); the night monkey, *Aotus trivirigatus* (Moynihan, 1967); and the patas monkey, *Erythrocebus patas* (Hall *et al.*, 1965). In the talapoin monkey, *Miopithecus talapoin*, males were observed to look at or smell the female's sexual skin area more frequently and for longer periods around midcycle than during the early follicular or late luteal phase of the menstrual cycle (Scruton and Herbert, 1970). The authors suggested that this greater attention paid by the males to the female's external genitalia could be related to coincident changes in the female's vaginal odour. Carpenter (1942) first observed that the vaginal overflow of the rhesus monkey, *Macaca mulatta*, possesses a characteristic odour which he thought might provide additional stimuli attracting males to females. This may be related to the persistent close following of females by males as observed in field studies (Lindburg, 1967) from which it has been suggested males receive some sort of cue as to the state of female receptivity. Jay (1965) perceived a strong smelling vaginal discharge in toque macaques, *Macaca sinica*, and observed males to examine the genitalia of most females in the group each day. Bonnet macaques, *Macaca radiata*, have rarely been seen to present for copulation unless solicited by the male (Simonds, 1965). This involved flipping the tail aside, olfactory examination of the genitalia, and, on occasions, insertion of a finger into the vagina followed by smelling and tasting of the secretions (Rahaman and Parthasarathy, 1969). In the pigtail macaque, *Macaca nemestrina*, the male displayed the Flehmen posture following olfactory inspection of the female's genitalia (van Hooff, 1962). In the stump-tailed macaque, *Macaca arctoides*, sniffing, fingering, and licking of the perineal region occurs prior to copulation (Blurton-Jones and Trollope, 1968). This sniffing of the genital region by the male appears to be readily performed, since the male sniffs the female each time she presents, even if copulation has just occurred (Bertrand, 1969). The male may also insert a finger into the female's vagina, sometimes pulling out a whitish mucoid discharge which he throws away after olfactory inspection. This olfactory inspection is not necessarily followed by mounting. Although olfactory cues from the urine of receptive females are not ruled out, it would appear from these studies that in the macaques, communication of sexual status is by way of vaginal secretions.

Among other species of higher primates, notably the chimpanzees, *(Pan troglodytes)* van Lawick-Goodall (1968) drew attention to the increased frequency of male olfactory inspection of the female's vagina at the approach of her oestrous condition. Sometimes this simply involved sniffing the vaginal opening, but males have also been observed to insert a finger into the vagina and then to sniff the finger. Occasionally males used their hands to part the lips of the vulva before they looked and sniffed. That this behaviour was related to the oestrous cycle of the female was suggested by the increased genital inspections at the first signs of sexual swelling. Similar genital inspection involving sniffing and insertion of the index finger has also been described for the chimpanzees of the Mahali Mountains (Nishida, 1970). Captive lowland gorillas, *Gorilla gorilla gorilla*, in the Basel zoo have been reproted to have a distinctive odour during their periods of oestrus (Hess, 1973). Males have been observed to touch the female's genitalia and then sniff their hand or finger particularly during the preoestrous period, while oro-genital contact is common during oestrus as a prelude to copulation.

To test the proposition that olfactory cues can be employed to determine the female primate's sexual status, use has been made of operant conditioning techniques. Male rhesus monkeys were required to press a lever in order to raise a partition which physically separated them from a female partner, but through which they could both see and smell the partner. Males had to work with some dedication, pressing the lever 250 times to gain access to the female. Most males regularly responded for ovariectomized partners treated with oestrogen, but rarely responded when faced with untreated ovariectomized females (Michael and Keverne, 1968).

Those males which showed little interest in ovariectomized partners were made temporarily anosmic. This was brought about by insertion of nasal plugs impregnated with bisthmus iodoform paraffin paste, which induces a local anaesthetic effect on the olfactory mucosa and additionally blocks odour eddies reaching the mucosal receptors. Temporarily depriving these males of their sense of smell did not markedly affect either their pressing for, or behaviour with, the oestrogen-treated females. Clearly, other sensory information was sufficient to maintain interest with these sexually familiar partners. Anosmia did however, result in these males failing to recognize any change in attractiveness of their ovariectomized partners after these females were administered oestrogen. Such females were, nevertheless, sexually stimulating to normal males.

When the olfactorily deprived males had their sense of smell restored they readily began pressing for access to these females. That is to say, anosmia did not impair males' sexual arousal and sexual activity with familiar oestrogenized females, but anosmic males were not able to detect the onset of attractiveness which oestrogen promoted in their unfamiliar partners. These results were consistent with the hypothesis that oestrogenized female rhesus monkeys produced substances which stimulated the sexual interest of their partners via the olfactory sense.

The preoccupation of males with the female's genital region suggested this might be an obvious place at which to start looking for male sex attractants. We therefore studied the effects on male behaviour of transferring vaginal secretions from oestrogenized 'donor' monkeys to ovariectomized, unattractive 'recipient' partners. Application of vaginal secretions to the sexual skin area of receptors, which were themselves quite unattractive to males, nevertheless resulted in a marked stimulation of the male partner's sexual activity (Michael and Keverne, 1970). Oestrogen-primed vaginal secretions have now been applied to the sexual skin area of ovariectomized recipient rhesus monkeys on 249 separate occasions, and a one hour behaviour test observed on each occassion in an acoustically isolated testing booth housed behind a one-way screen. These tests involved 11 pairs of animals and the secretions significantly increased the male partner's sexual behaviour above pretreatment periods when only distilled water was applied (Fig. 2). In the pre-treatment period 8 ejaculations were recorded in 200 tests and these increased to 139 during 249 tests when vaginal secretions were smeared on the sexual skin of unreceptive recipients. Of even greater significance was the increase in male mounting attempts from 174 during the pretreatment period to 2, 292 during applications to the same female partners. This high number of mounting attempts with few ejaculations was an indication of the unreceptive condition of the ovariecto-

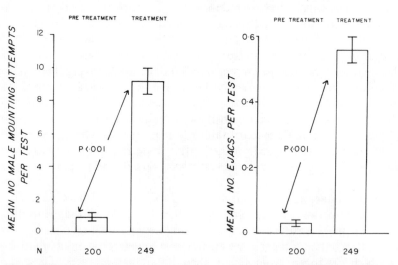

THE ENHANCEMENT OF SEXUAL ACTIVITY OF MALE RHESUS MONKEYS BY THE APPLICATION OF OESTROGEN STIMULATED VAGINAL SECRETIONS TO THE SEXUAL SKIN OF THEIR PARTNERS. (II pairs)

Fig. 2. Effects of applying vaginal secretions from oestrogenized 'donor' females to the sexual skin area of ovariectomized 'recipient' females on the sexual stimulation of male rhesus monkeys. Data for 11 pairs involving 5 males, 5 females and 5 donors. Fig. reproduced by permission of Blackwell Scientific Publications

mized recipients, and clearly demonstrates the male's increased sexual interest in these 'pheromone'-treated females.

To determine the chemical nature of the substances in vaginal secretions responsible for these powerful behavioural effects, extraction and fractionation procedures were used in conjunction with behavioural assay methods. The early stages of this procedure involved the use of ether extracts of secretions, collected by lavage with water from oestrogen-treated donor females (Keverne and Michael, 1971). Ovariectomized rhesus monkeys were again the recipients for these extracts and the very low levels of sexual activity during the pre-treatment period were in marked contrast to the high levels seen during the application of ether extracts. A gas chromatographic comparison of ether extracts of the vaginal secretion from ovariectomized untreated females indicated that the amounts of volatile components were absent or low, while oestrogen treatment stimulated production of volatile components (Fig. 3) and improved the sex attractant properties of vaginal secretions (Michael

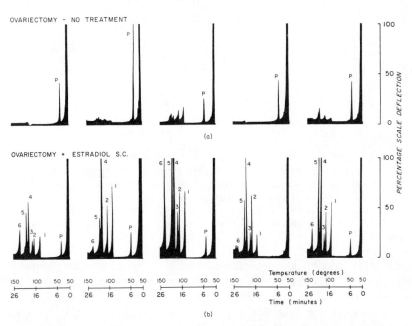

Fig. 3. Gas chromatograms of extracts of rhesus monkeys vaginal secretions: (a) represents chromatograms from five ovariectomized, untreated females with low volatile acid contents and without behavioural activity; (b) chromatograms of secretions collected from ovariectomized females during treatment with oes-tradiol. Volatile acids in the secretions markedly increased and these secretions possessed behavioural activity. Peak P is *n*-pentanol marker. (Michael, Keverne, and Bonsall, *Science*, **172**, 964–6, Fig. 1, 1971. Copyright 1971 by the American Association for the Advancement of Science.)

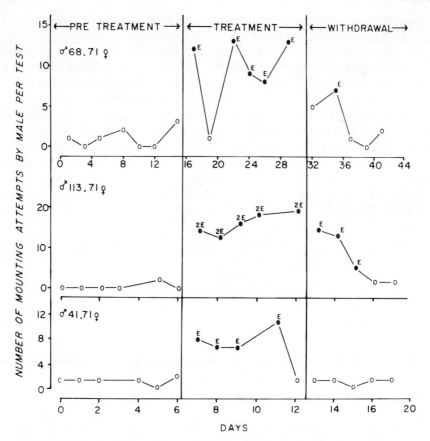

Fig. 4. Sexual stimulation of three male rhesus monkeys during treatment of their female partners with a synthetic mixture of aliphatic acids applied to their sexual skin area. o = test without ejaculation; ●E = one ejaculation in the test. ●2E = two ejaculations in the test. (Michael, Zumpe, Keverne and Bonsall (1972) *Rec. Prog. Horm. Res.*, **28**. Fig. reproduced with permission of Academic Press.)

et al., 1971). Identification of these volatile components was obtained by preparative gas chromatography and mass spectrometry (Curtis, *et al.*, 1971). The resultant mass spectra were compared with authentic samples, and the identification of the first five peaks was established as acetic, propionic, isobutyric, butyric, and isovaleric acids. A mixture of authentic acids was made up to match their concentration in a pool of vaginal washings, and a small sample of this mixture when tested for behavioural activity was demonstrated to possess sex attractant properties (Fig. 4).

The effectiveness of these pheromones in stimulating sexual behaviour in the rhesus monkey does, however, vary according to social conditions: with some partners and in certain tests no sexual stimulation occurs. As more males

RELATIVE EFFECTIVENESS OF VAGINAL AND SYNTHETIC PHEROMONES ON
THE SEXUAL BEHAVIOUR OF MALE RHESUS MONKEYS (9 pairs)

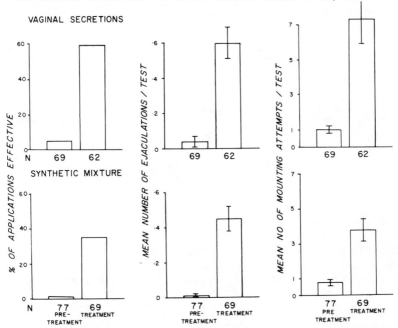

Fig. 5. Comparison of the effectiveness of vaginal secretions and synthetic pheromones on the sexual behaviour of male rhesus monkeys (9 pairs). Treatment using both methods produced a significant response, but vaginal secretions were more effective than synthetic pheromone. (Keverne (1976) *J. Soc. Cos. Chem.*, **27**, 11–23. Fig. reproduced with permission of Blackwell Scientific Publications.)

are tested it is becoming evident that the response to pheromones varies between individuals and is also dependent in part upon the female partner with which they are paired. When the behavioural effects of fresh vaginal secretions and a synthetic mixture of their acid content were compared in the same nine pairs of animals, vaginal secretions appeared to be more effective in stimulating the male's sexual behaviour (Fig. 5). Although both vaginal secretions and the synthetic pheromone complex stimulated male sexual activity at significantly higher levels than in the pretreatment tests, vaginal secretions were effective in 59% of applications compared with only 35% during application of synthetic pheromone to the same female partners.

The variation in effectiveness of these olfactory cues for stimulating sexual behaviour is best considered by an examination of the individuals involved. In doing this, it can be seen that the lower proportion of effective tests during applications of the synthetic pheromone was due to its failure to stimulate mounting behaviour in certain pairs (Fig. 6).

The relative effectiveness of fresh vaginal secretions and the synthetic

RELATIVE EFFECTIVENESS OF VAGINAL AND SYNTHETIC PHEROMONES ON THE
STIMULATION OF MALE SEXUAL ACTIVITY (male and female variables)

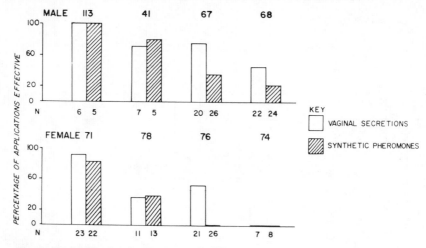

Fig. 6. Variability in the response of different males to vaginal and synthetic
pheromones and their relative effectiveness when applied to different female
partners. (Keverne (1976) *J. Soc. Cos. Chem.*, **27**, 11–23. Fig. reproduced by
permission of Blackwell Scientific Publications.)

acid mixture varied with the male partners from 100% in the case of male 113,
to 45% success with male 68. With males 113 and 41, acids and vaginal secretions
were equally effective. Similarly, if we compare the female partners, then application of olfactory pheromones to female 71, stimulated most male sexual
behaviour (Fig. 6). With female 76 only vaginal secretions stimulated male
behaviour, while neither synthetic acid mixture nor vaginal secretions stimulated any male's sexual behaviour with female 74. With male 67 and 68, the
synthetic acid mixture was approximately half as effective as the fresh secretion.
This was due to these males being paired for some of their tests with female
76 where, although secretions have stimulated sexual activity in 52% of tests,
the acid mixture has always been ineffective.

Thus it can be seen that the male's response to applied olfactory attractants
varies between individuals and is also, in part, dependent on the female partner
with whom they are paired. Whereas some females readily evoke a sexual
response from the male, others when treated in the same manner fail to do so
(see also Goldfoot *et al.*, 1976). Hence, the response to pheromones in these
highly evolved social primates is not stereotyped. Furthermore, it can be seen
that for certain pairs (Fig. 6), the synthetic acid mixture is not as effective in
stimulating the male's sexual activity as the original vaginal secretions. This
could mean there are components in untreated fresh vaginal secretions that
are lacking in the synthetic mixture.

In considering this proposition, phenylpropanoic (PPA) and *para*hydroxy-

IMPROVED EFFECTIVENESS OF SYNTHETIC PHEROMONES BY THE ADDITION
OF PHENYLPROPANOIC AND PARAHYDROXYPHENYLPROPANOIC ACIDS

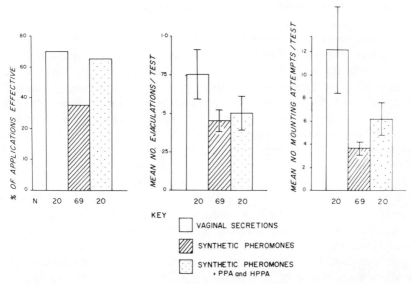

KEY

☐ VAGINAL SECRETIONS

▨ SYNTHETIC PHEROMONES

▨ SYNTHETIC PHEROMONES
  + PPA and HPPA

Fig. 7. Improvement in the effectiveness of synthetic pheromones when phenylpropanoic and *para*hydroxyphenylpropanoic acids are added. (Keverne (1976) *J. Soc. Cos. Chem.*, **27**, 11–23. Fig. reproduced by permission of Blackwell Scientific Publications.)

phenylpropanoic acids (HPPA) are both odorous compounds identified in the rhesus monkey's vaginal secretion. However, neither is effective in stimulating male sexual activity when applied alone to the sexual skin area of an ovariectomized female partner. Nevertheless, by addition of PPA and HPPA to the synthetic acid mixture an enhancement of the effectiveness of synthetic pheromone has been obtained (Fig. 7). Sexual interactions were shown by the female in more tests (65%) than when just synthetic mixtures of acids alone were applied (37% of tests). The mixture containing enhancers was almost as effective as the untreated vaginal secretions (70% of tests), although the amount of sexual behaviour stimulated was not so high. Untreated vaginal secretions when applied to the sexual skin of ovariectomized females in this test series stimulated 252 male mounting attempts and 15 ejaculations compared with 123 mounting attempts and 9 ejaculations during 20 tests when the synthetic mixture plus enhancers was applied.

From these results there is an indication that these phenolic components (PPA and HPPA) have an enhancing effect on the sexual stimulating properties of the synthetic pheromones. Nevertheless, it remains true that in some pairs the simple acid mixture appears to be completely effective. It is my opinion that the odour of the oestrous vaginal secretion is the true attractant and the synthetic acid mixture, mimicking the most odorous of the components, can in certain cases act as sufficient stimulus for some males. Others require additional volatile components such as PPA and HPPA, while still others require the whole untreated oestrous vaginal secretion. Hence, the odour cue is in itself complex (Keverne, 1974).

Moreover, the source of the odour cue does not appear to be either glandular or an exudate through the vaginal wall, but microbial action plays an important part in producing the odours in the vaginal secretions, since aliphatic acid concentrations increases during incubation of the vaginal lavage, while autoclaving or the addition of penicillin prevents production of these fatty acids (Michael *et al.*, 1972). It seems probable, therefore, that the production of these pheromones depends upon the bacteria of the vagina, and that the ovarian hormones exert their influence on acid production in the intact animal by determining the availability of nutrients in the form of cornified cells and mucous.The ovarian hormones may also affect the availability of the pheromone by changes in the tonus of the muscle folds in the vaginal wall, influencing flow rates to the exterior, where oestrogen-dependent changes in the colouration of the sexual skin facilitate dissemination. Reddening of the sexual skin is caused by increased vascularity and is associated with a localized increase in skin temperature. Hence, at times of intense reddening, under the influence of oestrogen, there would be an improved surface for the volatilization of sex-attractant pheromones.

An additional complication is to be found in the plasticity in the behavioural response of the male to the odour cue. It has already been shown that this can be modified by a partner preference, but perhaps of even more interest is the different behaviours which these odour cues can stimulate. The variability of the male's behavioural response to the same odour cue with different female partners is shown in Fig. 8. With the pairs 67, 76; 41, 71; and 68; 71 oestrogen-primed vaginal secretions markedly stimulated male sexual activity. With the pairs 67, 78; 41, 79; 68, 78 an increase was produced in the social responsiveness of the male and he was prepared to groom his female partner no longer, although no stimulation of sexual activity occurred. With the pairs 67, 74; 41, 79; 68, 78 no stimulation of sexual activity occurred during the treatment with pheromone, but a marked reduction was observed in each male's aggressive behaviour towards his partner. It could be argued that we are dealing with more than one odour cue, and the vaginal secretion contains a grooming stimulant, and an aggression-reducing pheromone, in addition to the sex attractant. My own feeling is that the coding for the behavioural response is not restricted to the olfactory cue, but is integrated in higher areas of the neocortex. This opinion is reinforced by the variability in the male's response both to ether extracts of secretions (Fig. 8, those pairs marked with an asterisk), and in some cases to the synthetic acid mixture itself, which clearly rules out different odour cues.

It is most important that this lack of a sterotyped response to olfactory

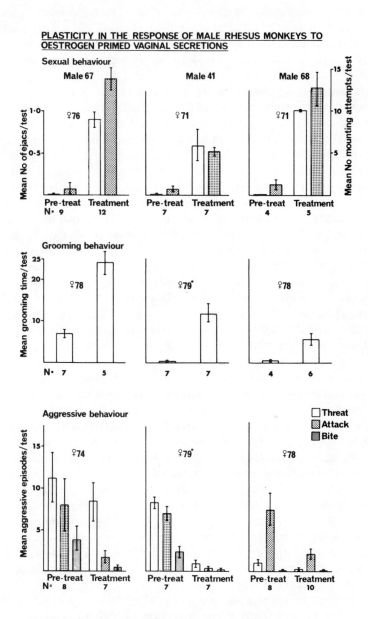

Fig. 8. Increases in sexual behaviour, grooming behaviour, or the reduction of aggression by applications of pheromone to the male rhesus monkey, but depending on the female partner. Those pairs marked with an asterisk had ether extracts of vaginal secretions applied. (Keverne (1976) *J. Soc. Cos. Chem.*, **27**, 11–23. Fig. reproduced by permission of Blackwell Scientific Publications.)

attractants is emphasized in this highly evolved social primate, particularly if consideration is to be given to the human situation and a search for human pheromones is started (Michael *et al.*, 1975). These aliphatic acids are present in human vaginal secretions albeit in differing proportions to the rhesus monkey (Michael *et al.*, 1972), and the human male can distinguish variance in these odours between the phases of the menstrual cycle of the rhesus monkey. Moreover, there is some evidence of cyclical production of these aliphatic acids in the human female (Michael *et al.*, 1975). This does not, however, imply any causal relationship between these odour cues and the sexual behaviour of the human male. If we are to consider the complexity and plasticity in the response of the male rhesus monkey, then the further social and cultural evolution of man may make the search for an olfactory aphrodisiac with sexual-releasing properties a fruitless task. Indeed, it may be argued that stimulation or provocation by female odours could be disruptive to our social order, and perhaps this is why we take such pains to disguise our body odours. This is not to say that these odours play no part in human sexual behaviour, but to give them significance at the level of sex attractants underestimates the complexity of human behaviour. What then might be the effect of these odour cues in human behaviour? Fig. 9 shows data which have been extracted from a number of experiments on rhesus monkeys which I feel have some bearing on the kind of level these odour cues might be seen to act on the human. Following withdrawal of the sex attractant from the female partner, males usually lose sexual interest in the female and make no further mounts, but occasionally (a and b, Fig. 9) males maintain their sexual arousal and, paradoxically, show increased mounting and thrusting prior to a loss of sexual interest. Similarly, if the oestrogenized female donor is given progesterone, her vaginal secretions lose their sexual stimulating properties when applied to the recipient, but prior to the male's loss of sexual interest there is a marked increase in the male's mounting and thrusting (Fig. 9c). Since the only change in all these experiments is the odour of the female partner, I interpret this increased mounting behaviour as an increase in male sexual performance to compensate for the odour deficit of the female partner; that is an increase in tactile input compensating for decreases in another sensory cue, namely olfactory. Following reversal of anosmia there may be an increase in male ejaculations with no marked increase in mounting (Fig. 9d). Here the restoration of the olfactory sense with an attractive female initially improves the sexual performance of the male, and briefly increases his ejaculatory score.

These results are appropriate to Raisman's (1972) concept of a dual olfactory system. It is possible that sexual attraction involving releaser pheromones is brought about by olfactory connections to the pyriform cortex and other cortical regions, via the medialis dorsalis of the thalamus, before a neural connection is obtained with the limbic system and finally the hypothalamus (Fig. 1). This neural circuitry I envisage as serving a filtering function with the cortex analogous to a computer incorporating certain 'go' and 'no go' pro-

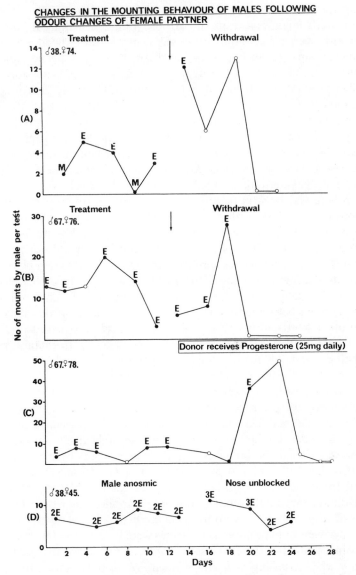

Fig. 9. Changes in the sexual performance (mounting patterns) of male rhesus monkeys following odour changes of their female partner. (Keverne (1976) *J. Soc. Cos. Chem.*, **27**, 11–23. Fig. reproduced by permission of Blackwell Scientific Publications.)

grammes. As we have already seen, the rhesus monkey's behaviour incorporates a number of 'no go' programmes, as for example the modifying effects of partner preferences, past experiences with certain females, and the presence of other males, etc. If we consider the human with infinitely complex behaviour patterns involving traditions, rituals, religions, and past experiences, there are many variables which might constitute 'no go' programmes, making it pointless to look for any overt behavioural response. If, on the other hand, we consider sexual performance (as in Fig. 8 for the rhesus monkeys) it is possible that a more direct neural input to the hypothalamus is involved, possibly mono-synaptic or probably involving only a few synapses. Certainly there is convincing anatomical evidence that even in primates the bed nucleus of the stria terminalis, particularly that part which lies in the medial region, forms a definite part of the olfactory system (Fig. 1); the projection originally being thought to be via the anterior limb of the anterior commissure (Meyer and Allison, 1949). More evidence is now in favour of the connection from the olfactory bulb passing directly to the cortico-medial nuclei of the amygdala and from here via the stria terminalis to the preoptic-anterior hypothalamic area (Cowan *et al.*, 1965). Either way, that area of the hypothalamus known to mediate hormonal-induced sexual behaviour in primates (Everitt and Herbert, 1975), receives a fairly direct olfactory input, and since this is not passing via the cortex, it seems unlikely that any complex processing is taking place. Could such a neural pathway, forming a direct link-up with the hypothalamus, serve as a means whereby olfactory information might modify both non-human primates' and our behaviour at a level below the threshold of conscious awareness? In other words, although we might not consciously perceive odours as overtly attractive, they could be influencing our sexual performance, perhaps by adjusting thresholds for hypothalamic activity.

While it seems likely that odour cues can influence our sexual behaviour, there is also the possibility that sexual odours might influence other behaviours. As I mentioned for the rhesus monkey, other behaviour patterns including aggression can be modified when the sex attractant is applied. In the human, too, there is evidence that subjects when making judgements on the basis of interview reports can be influenced in their assessment by exposure to sex odours (Cowley *et al.*, 1975). A psychological test was designed which required the participants in the experiment to express favourable or unfavourable opinions about the suitability of a number of applicants of both sexes for a position of responsibility. Exposure to male or female sex-odours influenced female judgement of male applicants. Males were little affected by the presence of the compounds, but there was some evidence to suggest that they reacted differently when assessing men and women. While not wanting to end on a note of sensational speculation, it is worth considering that if the olfactory system has direct access to our 'emotional brain' at a level below conscious awareness, a number of science fiction writers (Comfort, 1961) and psychiatrists (Wiener, 1966) might turn out to be prophets of the future.

SUMMARY AND CONCLUSIONS

The importance of olfactory cues in the sexual behaviour of a number of mammalian species has been reviewed and certain generalizations may be made.

The first concerns odour cues themselves. In the context of male sexual behaviour, it is hardly surprising that oestrous female urine and vaginal secretions are an important source of olfactory information. Urine odours may serve to attract males from a distance, as for example in the dog, while vaginal secretions provide specific information as to the endocrine status of the located female. This may be especially important in group-living species such as ungulates and primates. Of course, odour cues are but one of many sensory components which aid the male in determining the female's sexual status, and in no sense may be considered to serve as automatic releasers of sexual behaviour. This is an important distinction which should be emphasized between the pheromonal response of mammals and that of insects. Although the behavioural response of mammals to olfactory cues conveniently falls under the rubric of pheromone, as originally defined by Karlson and Butenandt, by usage the term has become associated with the innate stereotyped response observed in many insect species. The type of response olfactory cues produce in mammals can vary according to the social context in which perceived, and this clearly illustrates the problem in defining the complex pheromonal response of many mammalian species—a complexity which is to be anticipated with the greater development of the neocortex. It is this development of neocortex and its possible involvement in the decoding of olfactory information which leads to the second area of general comment; namely, the neuroanatomical basis of responses to odour cues.

Considering the dual neuroanatomical pathways of the olfactory system, a number of possible mechanisms are available for olfaction to influence male sexual behaviour. It is possible that only one of the olfactory pathways is involved in transmitting sexually meaningful stimuli, and in this context the vomeronasal accessory system is the most likely candidate because of its close anatomical relationships with the anterior hypothalamus. Nevertheless, the main olfactory bulb projects indirectly to the limbic system and it is difficult to believe it has no role to play in sexual behaviour. Indeed, a consideration of behavioural studies in hamsters suggests an important role, since only when the main olfactory, in addition to the vomeronasal systems are impaired does complete absence of mating behaviour occur in 100% of animals (Powers and Winans, 1975). A more likely possibility is, therefore, that impulses carried by both systems in some way summate to reach thresholds for the activation of sexual behaviour. The hamster appears, however, to be an exception among mammals in its dependence on the olfactory systems for initiation of sexual behaviour and this may be related to the male's subordination and susceptibility to attack from unreceptive females.

Olfactory cues are not, however, serving as stimuli for the release of fixed-action patterns of behaviour. More likely, the perception of odour cues appears to bias the animal in such a way that sexual, as opposed to any other behavioural responses, are made to certain complex environmental stimuli. Even in the hamster, therefore, mating behaviour is not under the exclusive control of olfactory stimuli. Rather, certain naturally occurring odours powerfully influence the particular response a male will make to the panoply of sensory cues associated with the female (Darby et al., 1975).

An alternative proposal to explain the dual olfactory projections is that each pathway mediates different aspects of male sexual behaviour. Thus, the main olfactory pathway could be involved in what broadly may be termed 'the onset of sexual arousal', and since this olfactory system has access via the thalamus to neocortical systems, neural circuitry is available for integration with experiential and other sensory information. Thus olfactory cues would only lead to the onset of sexual arousal at times appropriate to the survival of the species. This allows for a degree of plasticity in the behavioural response to odour cues, and equally accounts for the variability in responsiveness to sexual attractants observed amongst mammals. If odour cues were to release a stereotyped fixed-action pattern, as is invariably the case amongst insects, then the possible hazards this might entail could endanger the species.

On the other hand, once sexual attraction has been accomplished, and clearly this involves a great deal of overlap of multiple sensory and experiential factors, then odour cues may influence sexual performance via the accessory olfactory pathway. Such odour cues require little neural processing, and a direct input to the limbic system could modulate thresholds for hormonal activation. Although hormonal regulation of sexual behaviour in the rat has been localized in the preoptic-anterior hypothalamus, the accessory bulb projection terminating in the cortico-medial amygdala is but one synapse away from this area of the hypothalamus. Moreover, electrical stimulation of the cortico-medial amygdala itself has been shown to produce penile erection in the monkey (Robinson and Mishkin, 1968), while lesions in this region impair mating in male rats (Kaada, 1972). With the increased dependence in mammals on visual cues, such a direct olfactory projection to the limbic system subserving sexual performance would maximize the likelihood of fertile matings at the time of oestrus. This does not mean to say that the two olfactory systems as described are functionally independent, and the proposal outlined above does not exclude summatory or inhibitory interactions at the hypothalamic level.

Since most lesion studies involve both systems, an examination of the experimental data reveals very little, but where were care has been taken to distinguish between the vomeronasal-accessory and main bulb olfactory systems, there is support for this proposal. Hamsters with vomeronasal lesions show mainly changes in sexual performance (only 4 out of 26 showed no sexual behaviour in the 10 min provided) while main bulb deafferentation in addition to such lesions, eliminated mounts, intromission, and ejaculations in all males (Powers and Winans, 1975). It can thus be argued that if males are displaying any sexual interest in females, they are attracted and aroused, and hence the deficits in behaviour are essentially in terms of performance.

This chapter has been concerned with the ways in which olfactory cues influence sexual behaviour, and, in the main, most of these effects have been demonstrated in the male. However, olfaction is important in the female too, though perhaps not in the same way. Attraction to the male, as indicated by odour preference experiments where oestrous females preferred normal male urine to that from castrates, may be mediated by the main olfactory bulb projections. However, since pursuit of the sexual object is primarily the active role of the male in most mammalian species, while attractivity is vested mainly in the female, then olfactory cues may not be as important in female sexual behaviour. Primer pheromones, on the other hand, seem in most instances to act only on the female (e.g. Bruce effect, Whitten effect, Lee Boot effect), but the precise neural pathways involved are not yet established. It is interesting to speculate that such effects may be subserved by the accessory olfactory system. An extraordinary close relationship seems to exist between the accessory olfactory bulb and the medial hypothalamus by way of the stria terminalis projection from the cortical amygdaloid nucleus. Within the limits of present knowledge this appears to be the most likely pathway via which the olfactory system could have a direct influence on the hypothalamus and pituitary axis.

Man and the higher primates present something of a problem in our understanding of the ways in which olfactory cues influence behaviour. The absence of a vomeronasal-accessory bulb system in the adult might lead one to believe that olfactory information has no direct access to the limbic brain and therefore such olfactory cues might only influence behaviour after filtering through neocortical pathways. Behaviourally this would explain why olfactory cues appear to be of little importance in determining human interactions. On the other hand, from the data presented in this chapter it would appear that olfactory information can also influence primate sexual performance. This being so, there is reason to suppose such information is acting below the threshold of conscious processing. Perhaps, therefore, in man and higher primates, olfactory information also has direct access to the limbic brain and thereby has exceptional privilege over other sensory systems as a modulator of behaviour.

ACKNOWLEDGEMENTS

The original work reported here was conducted at the Institute of Psychiatry, University of London in the Primate Research Laboratories (Director R. P. Michael). I would like to thank Debby Hickman for typing the manuscript and Raith Overhill for the drawing of the figures.

REFERENCES

Albone, E. S. and Fox, M. W. (1971) Anal gland secretion of the red fox, *Nature*, **233**, 569–70.

Altmann, S. A. (1959) Field observations on a howling monkey society, *J. Mammal*, **40**, 317–30.

Aron, C., Roos, J., and Asch, G. (1970) Effect of removal of the olfactory bulbs on mating behaviour and ovulation in the rat, *Neuroendocrinology*, **6**, 109–17.

Baldwin, J. D. (1968) The social behaviour of squirrel monkeys *(Saimiri sciureus)* in a semi-natural environment, *Folia Primat.*, **11**, 35–79.

Beach, F. A. and Gilmore, R. (1949) Responses of male dogs to urine from females in heat, *J. Mammal*, **30**, 391–2.

Beach, F. A. and Merari, A. (1968) Coital behaviour in dogs. IV. Effects of progesterone in the bitch, *Proc. Nat. Acad. Sci.*, **61**, 442–6.

Beach, F. A. and Merari, A. (1970) Coital behaviour in dog. V. Effects of oestrogen and progesterone on mating and other forms of social behaviour in the bitch, *J. Comp. Physiol. Psychol.*, Suppl., I, 1–22.

Beauchamp, G. (1973) Attraction of male guinea pigs to conspecific urine, *Physiol. Behav.*, **10**, 589–94.

Beauchamp, G. and Berüter, J. (1973) Source and stability of attractive components in guinea pig *(Cavia porcellus)* urine, *Behav. Biol.*, **9**, 43–7.

Berliner, V. R. (1959) The oestrous cycle of the mare. In: *Reproduction in Domestic Animals*, H. H. Cole and P. T. Cupps (eds.), Academic Press, New York. pp. 267–89.

Bermant, G. and Taylor, L. (1969) Interactive effects of experience and olfactory bulb lesions in male rat copulation, *Physiol. Behav.*, **4**, 13–7.

Bertrand, M. (1969) The behavioural repertoire of the stump-tailed macaque, *Bibliotheca Primatologica*, II, 265.

Blurton-Jones, N. G. and Trollope, J. (1968) Social behaviour of stump-tailed macaques in captivity, *Primates*, **9**, 365–94.

Booth, C. (1962) Some observations on behaviour of *Cercopithecus* monkeys, *Ann. N. Y. Acad. Sci.*, **103**, 477–87.

Broadwell, R. D. (1975) Olfactory relationships of the telencephalon and diencephalon in the rabbit, *J. Comp. Neurol.*, **163**, 329–46.

Bronson, F. J. and Caroum, D. (1971) Preputial gland of the male mouse: attractant function, *J. Reprod. Fert.*, **25**, 279–82.

Bruce, H. M. (1960) A block to pregnancy in the mouse caused by the proximity of strange males, *J. Reprod. Fert.*, **1**, 96–103.

Calhoun, J. B. (1962) The ecology and sociology of the Norway rat, *U.S.P.H.S. Publ. no. 1008*, Washington D. C.

Caroum, D and Bronson, F. H. (1971) Responsiveness of female mice to preputial attractant: effects of sexual experience and ovarian hormones, *Physiol. Behav.*, **7**, 659–62.

Carpenter, C. R. (1942) Sexual behaviour of free ranging rhesus monkeys *(Macaca mulatta)*. II. Periodicity of oestrous, homosexual antoerotic and non-conformist behaviour. *J. Comp. Psychol.* **33**, 143–62.

Carr, W. J. and Caul, W. F. (1962) The effect of castration in the rat upon the discrimination of sex odours, *Anim. Behav.*, **10**, 20–7.

Carr, W. J., Loeb, L. S., and Dissinger, M. L. (1965) Response of rats to sex odours, *J. Comp. Physiol. Psychol.*, **59**, 370–7.

Carr, W. J., Loeb, L. S., and Wylie, N. R. (1966) Responses to feminine odours in normal and castrated male rats. *J. Comp. Physiol. Psychol.*, **62**, 336–8.

Carter, C. S. (1972) Effects of olfactory experience on the behaviour of the guinea pig *(Cavia poroellus)*, *Anim. Behav.*, **20**, 54–60.

Castell, R. and Maurus, M. (1967) Das Sogenannte Urinmarkieren von Totenkopfaffen *(Saimiri sciureus)* in Abhangigkeit von umwetbedingten und Emotionalen factoren, *Folia Primat.*, **6**, 170–6.

Comfort, A. (1961) *Come Out to Play*, Egre & Spottiswood.

Conaway, C. H. and Sorenson, N. W. (1966) Reproduction in tree shrews, *Symp. Zool. Soc. Lond.*, **15**, 471–92.

Cowan, W. M., Raisman, G., and Powell, T. P. S. (1965) The connections of the amygdala, *J. Neurol. Neurosurg. Psychiat.*, **28**, 137–51.

Cowley, J. J., Johnson, A. L., and Brooksbank, B. W. L. (1975) The effect of two odorous compounds on performance in an assessment of people test, *Proc. Cong. E. C. R. O.* Paris, 1974.

Cragg, B. G. (1961) Olfactory and other afferent connections of the hippocampus in the rabbit, rat, and cat, *Exp. Neurol.*, **3**, 588–600.

Curry, J. J. (1974) Alterations in incidence of mating and copulation-induced ovulation after olfactory bulb ablation in female rats, *J. Endocrinol.* **64**, 245–50.

Curtis, R. F., Ballantine, J. A., Keverne, E. B., Bonsall, R. W., and Michael, R. P. (1971) Identification of primate sexual pheromones and the properties of synthetic attractants, *Nature*, **232**, 396–8.

Darby, E. M., Devor, M., and Chorover, S. L. (1975) A presumptive sex pheromone in the hamster: some behavioural effects, *J. Comp. Physiol. Psychol.*, **88**, 496–502.

Davies, V. J. and Bellamy, D. (1974) Effects of female urine on social investigation in male mice, *Anim. Behav.*, **22**, 239–41.

De Olmos, J. (1972) The amygdaloid projection field in the rat. In: *Neurobiology of the Amygdala*, B. Eleftheriou (ed.), Plenum Press, N. Y. pp. 145–204.

Devor, M. and Murphy, M. R. (1973) The effect of peripheral olfactory blockade on the social behaviour of the male golden hamster, *Behav. Biol.*, **9**, 31–42.

Dieterlen, F. (1959) Das verhalten der Syrischen Goldhamsters *(Mesocricetus auratus)*, *Z. für Tierpsychol.*, **16**, 47–103.

Donovan, B. T. and Kopriva, P. C. (1965) Effect of removal or stimulation of the olfactory bulbs on the estrous cycle of the guinea pig, *Endocrinology*, **77**, 213–7.

Donovan, C. A. (1967) Some clinical observations on sexual attraction and deterrence in dogs and cattle, *Vet. Med. Anim. Clin.*, **62**, 1047–51.

Donovan, C. A. (1969) Canine anal glands and chemical signals (Pheromones), *J.A.U.M.A.*, **155**, 1995–6.

Doyle, G. A., Pelletier, A., and Bekker, T. (1967) Courtship, mating, and parturition in the lesser bush baby *(Galago senegalensis moholi)* under semi-natural conditions, *Folia Primat.*, **7**, 169–97.

Dutt, R. H., Simpson, E. C., Christian, J. C., and Barnhart, C. E. (1959) Identification of preputial glands as the site of reproduction of sexual odours in the boar., *Anim. Sci.*, **18**, 1557.

Edwards, D. A. and Warner, P. (1972) Olfactory bulb removal facilitates the hormonal induction of sexual receptivity in the female rat, *Horm. Behav.*, **3**, 321–32.

Eibl, K. and Wettke, K. (1964) Artificial insemination of pigs using CO_2-inactivated boar semen, *Vet. Rec.*, **76**, 856–8.

Eisenberg, J. F., McKay, G. M., and Jainudeen, M. R. (1971) Reproductive behaviour of the Asiatic elephant *(Elphas maximus maximus L)*, *Behaviour*, **38**, 193–225.

Epple, G. (1967) Vergleichende untersuchugen uber sexual und sozialverhalten der krallenaffen (Hapaliadae). *Folia Primat.*, **7**, 37–65.

Epple, G. (1970) Quantitative studies on scent marking in the marmoset *(Callithrix jacchus)*, *Folia primat.*, **13**, 48–62.

Estes, R. D. (1972) The role of the vomeronasal organ in mammalian reproduction, *Extrait de Mammalia*, **36**, 315–41.

Evans, C. S. and Goy, R. W. (1968) Social behaviour and reproductive cycles in captive ring-tailed lemurs *(Lemur catta)*, *J. Zool. Lond.*, **156**, 181–97.

Everitt, B. J. and Herbert, J. (1975) The effects of implanting testosterone propionate into the central nervous system on the sexual behaviour of adrenalectomised female rhesus monkeys, *Brain Res.*, **86**, 109–20.

Fuller, J. L. and Dubois, E. M. (1962) The behaviour of dogs. In: *The Behaviour of Domestic Animals* E. S. E. Hafez (ed.), Bailliere, Tindall and Cox, London, pp. 247–86.

Gier, H. T. (1960) Estrous cycle in the bitch; vaginal fluids, *Vet. Scope*, **5**, 2–9.

Goldfoot, D. A., Kravetz, M. A., Goy, R. W., and Freeman, S. K. (1976) Lack of effect of vaginal lavages and aliphatic acids on ejaculatory responses in rhesus monkeys. Behavioural and chemical analysis. *Horm. Behav.*, 7, 1–28.

Guinness, F., Lincoln, G. A., and Short, R. V. (1971) The reproductive cycle of the female red deer *(Cervus elaphus)*, *J. Reprod. Fert.* 27, 427–38.

Hafez, E. S. E., Samption, L. J., and Jakway, J. S. (1962) The behaviour of swine. In: *The Behaviour of Domestic Animals*, E. S. E. Hafez (ed.), Bailliere, Tindall and Cox, London, pp. 334–69.

Hall, K. R. L., Boelkins, R. C., and Goswell, M. J. (1965) Behaviour of patas, *Erythrocebus patas*, in captivity with notes on the natural habitat, *Folia primat.*, 3, 22–49.

Hampton, J. K., Hampton, S. H., and Landwehr, B. I. (1966) Observations on a successful breeding colony of the marmoset *(Oedipomidas oedipus)*, *Folia primat.*, 4, 265–87.

Hart, B. L. and Haugen, C. (1971) Scent marking and sexual behaviour maintained in anosmic male dogs, *Behav. Biol.*, 6, 131–5.

Hart, G. H., Mead, S. W., and Regan, W. M. (1946) Stimulating the sex drive of bovine males in artificial insemination, *Endocrinology*, 39, 221–3.

Heimer, L. (1972) The olfactory connections of the diencephalon in the rat, *Brain Behav. Evol.*, 6, 484–523.

Heimer, L. and Larsson, K. (1967) Mating behaviour of male rats after olfactory bulb lesions, *Physiol. Behav.*, 2, 207–9.

Hess, J. P. (1971) Observations on the sexual behaviour of captive lowland gorillas, *Symp. on Primate Behaviour*, Michael and Crook (eds.), A.S.A.B. Meeting, Academic Press.

Hitt, J. C., Bryon, D. M., and Modianos, D. T. (1973) Effects of rostral medial forebrain bundle and olfactory tubercle lesions upon sexual behaviour of male rats, *J. Comp. Physiol. Psychol.*, 82, 30–6.

Hooff, J. A. R. Van (1962) Facial expressions in higher primates, *Symp. Zool. Soc. London*, 8, 97–125.

Isben, H. L. (1956) The guinea-pig. In: *The Care & Breeding of Laboratory Animals*, E. J. Farris (ed.), Wiley and Sons.

Ilse, R. (1955) Olfactory marking of territory in two young female loris *(Loris tardigradus lydekkerianus)* kept in captivity in Poona, *Br. J. Anim. Behav.*, 3, 118–20.

Jainudeen, M. R., Eisenberg, J. F., and Tilakeratne, N. (1971) Oestrous cycle of the Asiatic elephant, *(Elephas maximus)* in captivity, *J. Reprod. Fert.*, 27, 321–8.

Jay, P. (1965) Field studies. In: *Behaviour of Non-Human Primates* A. M. Schrier, H. F. Harlow, and F. Stollnitz (eds.), pp. 525–92. Academic Press, New York, pp. 525–92.

Jolly, A. (1966) *Lemur Behaviour, A Madagascar Field Study*, Univ. of Chicago Press, Chicago.

Jolly A. (1967) Breeding synchrony in the wild *Lemur catta*. In: *Social Communication Among Primates*, S. Altmann (ed.), pp. 2–15. Univ. Chicago Press, Chicago, pp. 2–15.

Jones, R. B. and Nowell, N. W. (1974) A comparison of the aversive female attractant properties of urine from dominant and subordinate male mice, *Anim. Learn. Behav.*, 2, 141–4.

Kaada, B. R. (1972) Stimulation and regional ablation of the amygdaloid complex with reference to functional representations. *In: The neurobiology of the amygdala*, B. E. Elefthariou (ed.), Plenum Press, New York, pp. 205–281.

Kaada, B. R., Rasmussen, E. W., and Bruland, H. (1968) Approach behaviour towards a sex-incentive following fore-brain lesions in the rat, *Int. J. Neurol.*, 6, 203–323.

Karlson, P. and Butenandt, A. (1959) Pheromones (ectohormones) in insects, *Ann. Rev. Entomol.*, 4, 39–58.

Kelley, R. B. (1937) Studies in fertility of sheep, *Bull. Counc. Industr. Res. Aust.*, no. 112.

Keverne, E. B. (1974) Sex-attractants in primates, *New Scientist*, 63, 22–4.

Keverne, E. B. and Michael, R. P. (1971) Sex attractant properties of ether extracts of vaginal secretions from rhesus monkeys, *J. Endocrinol.*, 51, 313–22.

Kleiman, D. (1966) Scent marking in the Canidae, *Symp. Zool. Soc. London*, **18**, 167–77.

Larsson, K. (1969) Failure of gonadal and gonadotrophic hormones to compensate for an impaired sexual function in anosmic male rats, *Physiol. Behav.*, **4**, 733–7.

Larsson, K. (1971) Impaired mating performances in male rats after anosmia induced peripherally or centrally. *Brain Behav. Evol.* **4**, 463–471.

Latta, J., Hopf, S., and Ploog, D. (1967) Observations on mating behaviour and sexual play in the squirrel monkey *(Saimiri sciureus)*. *Primates*, **8**, 229–46.

Lawick-Goddall, J. van. (1968) The behaviour of free living chimpanzees in the Gombe Stream Reserve, *Anim. Behav. Monogr.*, **1**, Part 3, pp. 165–311.

Le Magnen, J. (1952) Les phenomens olfacto-sexuals chez le rat blanc, *Arch. Sci. Physiol.*, **6**, 295–332.

Leonard, J. W. and Scott, C. M. (1971) Origin and distribution of amygdalofugal pathways in the rat: An experimental neuroanatomical study, *J. Comp. Neurol.*, **141**, 313–330.

Lindburg, D. G. (1967) A field study of the reproductive behaviour of the rhesus monkey *Macaca mulatta)*, *Ph.D. Thesis*, Univ. of California, Berkley.

Lindsay, D. R. (1965) The importance of olfactory stimuli in the mating behaviour of the ram, *Anim. Behav.*, **13**, 75–8.

Lisk, R. D., Ziess, J., and Ciacco, L. A. (1972) The influence of olfaction on sexual behaviour in the male golden hamster *(Mesocricetus auratus)*, *J. Exp. Zool.*, **181**, 69–78.

Lydell, K. and Doty, R. L. (1972) Male rat odour preferences for female urine as a function of sexual experience, urine age, and urine source, *Horm. Behav.*, **3**, 205–12.

Marler, P. (1965) Communication in monkeys and apes. In: *Primate Behaviour*, I. de Vore (ed.), Holt, Reinehart and Winston, New York, pp. 544–84.

Marr, J. N. and Gardner, L. E. (1965) Early olfactory experience and later social behaviour in the rat: preference, sexual responsiveness and care of the young. *J. genet. Psychol.*, **107**, 167–174.

Marr, J. N. and Lilliston, L. (1970) Social attachment in rats by odour and age, *Behaviour*, **33**, 277–82.

Melrose, D. R., Reed, H. C. B., and Patterson, R. L. S. (1971) Androgen steroids associated with boar odour as an aid to the detection of oestrus in pig A. I, *Br. Vet. J.*, **127**, 495–502.

Meyer, M. and Allison, A. C. (1949) An experimental investigation of the connections of the olfactory tracts in the monkey, *J. Neurol. Neurosurg. Psychiat.*, **12**, 274–87.

Michael, R. P., Bonsall, R. W., and Warner, P. (1975) Human vaginal secretions: volatile fatty acid content, *Science*, **186**, 1217–9.

Michael, R. P. and Keverne, E. B. (1968) Pheromones in the communication of sexual status in primates, *Nature*, **218**, 746–9.

Michael, R. P. and Keverne, E. B. (1970) Primate sex pheromones of vaginal origin, *Nature*, **225**, 84–5.

Michael, R. P. and Keverne, E. B. (1971) An annual rhythm in the sexual activity of the male rhesus monkey *(Macaca mulatta)* in the laboratory, *J. Reprod. Fert.*, **25**, 95–8.

Michael, R. P., Keverne, E. B., and Bonsall, R. W. (1971) Pheromones: Isolation of male sex attractants from a female primate. *Science*, **172**, 964–6.

Michael, R. P., Keverne, E. B., Zumpe, D., and Bonsall, R. W. (1972) Neuroendocrine factors in the control of primate behaviour, *Rec. Prog. Horm. Res.*, **28**, 665–707.

Montagna, W. (1962) The skin of lemurs, *Ann. N. Y. Acad. Sci.*, **102**, 190–209.

Morris, N. M. and Udry, J. R. (1975) An experimental search for pheromonal influences on human sexual behaviour, *Proc. Eastern Conference on Reproductive Behaviour*.

Moss, R. L. (1971) Modification of copulatory behaviour in the female rat following olfactory bulb removal, *J. Comp. Physiol. Psychol.*, **74**, 374–82.

Moynihan, M. (1966) Communication in the titi monkey *(Callicebus)*. *J. Zool. London*, **150**, 77–127.

Moynihan, M. (1967) Comparative aspects of communication in New World primates.

In: *Primate Ethology*, D. Morris (ed.), Weidenfeld and Nicolson, London, pp. 236–66.

Muller-Schwartz,D., Muller-Schwartz, C., Singer, A. G., and Silverstein, R. M. (1974) Mammalian pheromone: Identification of active component in the subauricular scent of the male pronghorn, *Science*, **183**, 860–2.

Muller-Schwartze, D. and Silverstein, R. M. (1974) Duftsignale bei Huftieren, *Umschau* 74, 3, 88–9.

Murphy, M. R. (1973) Effects of female hamster vaginal discharge on the behaviour of male hamsters, *Behav. Biol.*, **9**, 367–75.

Nishida, T. (1970) Social behaviour and relationships among wild chimpanzees of the Mahali Mountains, *Primates*, **11**, 47–87.

Patterson, R. L. S. (1968a) Identification of 3 hydroxy-5-androst-16-ene as the musk odour component of boar sub-maxillary salivary gland and its relationship to the sex odour taint in pork meat, *J. Sci. Fd. Agric.*, **19**, 434–8.

Patterson, R. L. S. (1968b) Acidic components of boar preputial fluid, *J. Sci. Fd. Agric.*, **19**, 38.

Petter, J. J. (1965) The lemurs of Madagascar. In: *Primate Behaviour*, I. de Vore (ed.), Holt, Rinehart and Winston, New York, pp. 292–319.

Pfaff, D. and Gregory, E. (1971) Olfactory coding in olfactory bulb and medial forebrain bundle of normal and castrated male rats, *J. Neurophysiol.*, **34**, 208–16.

Pfaff, D. and Pfaffman, C. (1969) Behavioural and electrophysiological responses of male rats to female rat urine odours. In *Olfaction and Taste*, C. Pfaffman (ed.), pp. 258–67.

Powell, T. P. S., Cowan, W. M. and Raisman, G. (1965) The central olfactory connections. *J. Anat.* **99**, 791–813.

Powers, J. B. and Winans, S. S. (1973) Sexual behaviour in peripherally anosmic male hamsters, *Physiol. and Behav.*, **10**, 361–8.

Powers, J. B. and Winans, S. S. (1975) Vomeronasal organ: critical role in mediating sexual behaviour in male hamsters, *Science*, in press.

Pribram, K. H., Chow, K. L., and Semmes, J. (1953) Limit and organisation of the cortical projection from the medial thalamic nucleus in the monkey, *J. Comp. Neurol.*, **98**, 433–48.

Rahaman, H. and Partharsarathy, M. D. (1969) Studies on the sexual behaviour of bonnet monkeys, *Primates*, **10**, 149–62.

Raisman, G. (1972) An experimental study of the projection of the amygdala to the main olfactory bulb and its relationship to the concept of a dual olfactory system, *Exp. Brain Res.*, **14**, 395–408.

Reynolds, E. (1971) Urination as a social response in mice, *Nature*, **234**, 481–3.

Robinson, B. W. and Mishkin, M. (1968) Penile erection evoked from stimulation of fore-brain structures in *Macaca mulatta*, *Neurology*, **19**, 184–98.

Rowe, F. A. and Edwards, D. A. (1972) Olfactory bulb removal: Influences on the mating behaviour of male mice, *Physiol. and Behav.*, **8**, 37–41.

Sauer, E. G. F. and Sauer, E. M. (1963) The South West African bush baby of the *Galago senegalensis* group. *So. W. Afr. J. Sci.*, **12**, 5–35.

Scalia, F. and Winans, S. S. (1975) The differential projections of the olfactory bulb and accessory olfactory bulb in mammals, *J. Comp. Neurol.*, **161**, 31–56.

Schenkel, R. (1947) Ausdruck-studien an wölfen, *Behaviour*, **1**, 81–129.

Schneider, K. M. (1930) Das Flehmen, *Zool. Gart.* 43, 4, 183–98.

Scott, J. W. and Pfaff, D. W. (1970) Behavioural and electrophysiological responses of female mice to male urine odours, *Physiol. Behav.*, **5**, 407–11.

Scruton, D. H. and Herbert, J. (1970) The menstrual cycle and its effect on behaviour in the talapoin monkey *(Miopithecus talapoin)*, *J. Zool. Lond.*, **162**, 419–36.

Sieck, M. H. and Baumbach, H. D. (1974) Differential effects of peripheral and central anosmia producing techniques on spontaneous behaviour patterns, *Physiol. Behav.*, **13**, 407–25.

Signoret, J. P. and Mesnil de Buisson, F. (1961) Etude du comportement de la truie en oestrous, *IV Int. Cong. Adnim. Reprod. Artif. Insem.* The Hague, pp. 171–5.

Simonds, P. E. (1965) The bonnet macaque in South India. In: *Primate Behaviour*, I. de Vore (ed.), Holt, Rinehart and Winston, New York, pp. 175–96.

Sorenson, M. W. and Conaway, H. (1968) The social and reproductive behaviour of *Tupaia montana* in captivity. *J. Mammal.*, **49**, 502–12.

Stern, J. J. (1970) Responses of male rats to sex odours, *Physiol. Behav.*, **5**, 510–24.

Thompson, M. L. and Edwards, D. A. (1972) Olfactory bulb ablation and hormonally-induced mating in spayed female mice, *Physiol. Behav.*, **8**, 1141–6.

Thorpe, P. A. (1975) The presence of retinohypothalamic projection in the ferret, *Brain Res.*, **85**, 343–6.

Wiener, H. (1966) External chemical messengers. 1. Emission and reception in man, *N. Y. J. Med.*, **66**, 3153–70.

Wierzbowski, S. and Hafez, E. S. (1961) Analysis of copulatory reflexes in the stallion. *Pr. IV Intern. Congr. Anim. Reprod.* The Hague, pp. 176–9.

Wilson, E. O. (1963) Pheromones, *Sci. Am.*, **208**, 100–14.

CHAPTER 23

Biosocial Determinants of Gender Identity Differentiation and Development

JOHN MONEY AND MARK SCHWARTZ

INTRODUCTION

The study of the determinants of gender identity cannot genuinely be dichotomized into the biological and the social. All determinants of human behaviour are biological. Thus postnatal influences on the central nervous system (CNS) which are a product of social environment can be considered just as much a biological determinant as can genetic, hormonal, and other prenatal factors. Therefore, the accurate term for social determinants is 'biosocial determinants'. The concept of biosocial determinants is basic to the study of the development of human behaviour. Indeed, there is no human behaviour that is the exclusive product of nonsocial determinants. No matter what the determinant of human behaviour, it always must manifest itself in interaction with a social environment.

The basic theoretical point at issue in this chapter is not whether some determinants are social and some are not, but whether, and to what degree, social stimuli that have permanent and ineradicable effects differ from those that have transient effects on the CNS that might be replaced or eradicated later in life.

This chapter reviews research findings with respect to the way in which biosocial determinants conjoin with genetic and hormonal determinants in the developmental differentiation of adult gender identity and role. The term biosocial is used in this chapter to denote modification of cells and tissue in structure and function during the course of development. Prenatal differentiation of the reproductive system has been well documented. Postnatal cellular differentiation of the nervous system, resulting from biosocial input, has been less well documented. The term *gender role* was first used by Money *et al.* (1955) where it was defined as follows: 'All those things a person says or does to disclose himself or herself as having the status of boy or man, girl or woman, respectively. It includes, but is not restricted to sexuality, in the sense

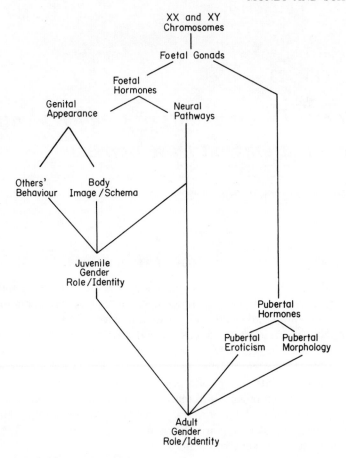

Fig. 1. Sequential and cumulative components of gender-
role/identity differentiation

of eroticism.' The ideal definition of role would be one that comprises both the
subjective (self-experiences) and the objective part which other people listen
to or observe. Unfortunately, in both popular and scientific usage, the unity
of the subjective and objective as two sides of the same coin was not accepted.
Today, most people dichotomoze identity and role, so as to parallel their
dichotomization of mind and body.

SEQUENTIAL PRENATAL COMPONENTS OF
GENDER/IDENTITY DIFFERENTIATION

Fig. 1 shows the sequential and cumulative determinants that lead to the
differentiation of adult gender identity. The prenatal determinants are the
focus of this section. Fig. 1 can be interpreted metaphorically as a relay race,
each entry being the equivalent of a runner who carries the programme for

gender-identity differentiation and passes it on to a successor. There is a certain amount of crossover, rather than simple running in parallel streams. With each change in the transmission of the programme of gender-identity differentiation, there exists the possibility that an error may be introduced and subsequently transmitted. By cataloguing potential errors and their consequences, one may begin to identify the relative contribution of each factor to gender identity and gender identity transpositions and anomalies.

It is a general rule that if there is a Y chromosome in the fertilizing sperm, the baby will be anatomically male. If the Y chromosome is absent and there are instead two X chromosomes, the baby will be female. If the Y chromosome is absent, and there is not a second X, the baby will be female without ovaries. The mechanism by which the message of the chromosomes is transduced into the internal and external reproductive system is not known in all its details. However, it is known that the Y chromosome programmes the differentiation of the bipotential cells of the primitive gonad into testes, beginning at around the sixth week of gestation. Differentiation of the primitive gonad into an ovary does not begin until the twelfth week, and apparently requires the presence of both X chromosomes, and no Y. The internal reproductive analagen are at the outset dually represented (Fig. 2) in all mammalian embryos (Jost, 1971, 1972), whereas the external organs are homologously derived from the same bipotential anlagen. In other words, all mammals are hermaphroditic in the early weeks of gestation. The masculine or Wolffian ducts differentiate into the vas deferens, epididymis, and ejaculatory ducts. The female or Müllerian ducts differentiate into the uterus, Fallopian tubes, and upper vagina. Whether the Wolffian or Müllerian system will differentiate is programmed by the presence or absence of hormones from the foetal testes. These hormones are, to continue the analogy of the relay race, the next runners.

The foetal testes secrete two hormones, androgen and Müllerian-inhibiting substance. The latter ensures that the Müllerian ducts will regress instead of proliferating into a uterus and Fallopian tubes. Androgen ensures that the Wolffian ducts will proliferate into the internal male organs, and that the undifferentiated anlagen of the external genitalia will differentiate as male. It is also probable, though not completely proved, that foetal androgen may programme pathways in the CNS which subsequently regulate the threshold for the emergence of various sexually dimorphic activities.

Fig. 3 illustrates that until the eighth week of foetal life, the external genitalia of the human foetus are developmentally bipotential. Androgen secretion from the foetal testes induces the bipotential genital tubercle to differentiate into the penis instead of the clitoris. Walsh et al. (1974) reported some evidence which suggests that the circulating androgen, testosterone, is converted to 5α-dihydrotestosterone (DHT) for differentiation of the external genitalia. The shaft behind the tubercle elongates and becomes the spongy tissue of the corpora cavernosa. In the absence of androgen, the shaft remains small as the main body of the clitoris. The skin that becomes the hood of the clitoris

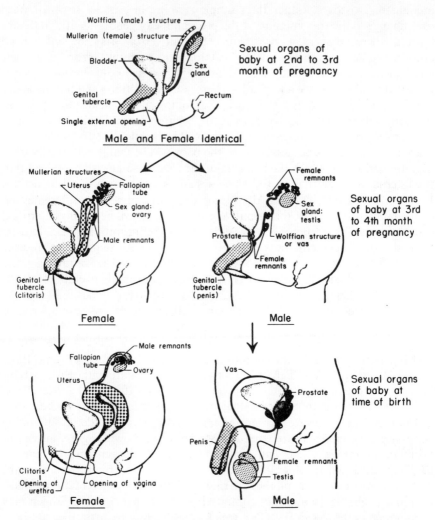

SEXUAL DIFFERENTIATION IN THE HUMAN FOETUS

Fig. 2. The internal reproductive anlagen are at the outset dually represented. The male and female organs have the same beginnings and are homologous with one another

and labia minora in the female, in the male wraps around the penis to cover it and to form the foreskin. In the female, the labioscrotal swellings remain separate and form the labia majora; in the male, they fuse in the midline and form the scrotum.

One might expect female differentiation to be programmed by the hormones of the foetal ovaries. So far as is known, however, the foetal ovaries do not secrete hormones prenatally. Proliferation of the Müllerian structures as well

EXTERNAL GENITAL DIFFERENTIATION IN THE HUMAN FOETUS

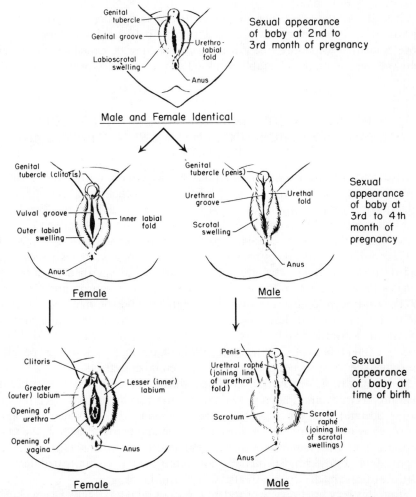

Fig. 3. The external sex organs of male and female differentiate from the same anlagen and cannot be distinguished if a baby is born with differentiation unfinished

as differentiation of the genital tubercle into the clitoris is, according to present evidence, independent of foetal ovarian hormones. If maternal hormones play a role, then that role has not yet been demonstrated. What counts in prenatal sexual differentiation, is the absence of androgens. Thus it appears that the initial bipotentiality of the internal and external reproductive systems is resolved according to the 'Adam principle'—adding something to make a male. The term, Adam principle, is used heuristically to denote the fact that developmentally something extra must be added to make a male. Initially the something extra is a Y chromosome as exemplified by the fact that even if there are two X chromosomes, the addition of a Y produces a morphological phenotype that is male.

Since something extra must be added to make a male, there is a greater chance of error, impairment, or insufficiency, both prenatally and later in development. Postnatally, the Adam principle may be called on to explain why the male is more vulnerable to psychosexual non-conformity than is the female.

DIFFERENTIATION OF THE BIPOTENTIAL NERVOUS SYSTEM AND DIMORPHIC BEHAVIOUR IN RODENTS AND PRIMATES

Divergent evidence from various animal studies has established that prenatal androgen may have a direct neural effect by influencing the threshold for subsequent elicitation of various sexually dimorphic behaviours (see Goldman, and Plapinger and McEwen, this volume Chapter 5 and 6 respectively).

In rodents, this effect can be achieved not only by prenatal androgen injection but, according to species, by neonatal injections also. Mating tests show that androgen treated females behave in a more masculine way than do untreated females (Young, 1962; Whalen and Edwards, 1967; Swanson and Crossley, 1971). Androgen-treated females also resemble control males on various dimorphic non-mating tests, including tests for some forms of aggressive behaviour (Edwards, 1969, 1970), wheel running (see review by Gorski, 1971), and open-field behaviour (Swanson, 1967). Exposure to testosterone after the critical period does not produce these masculinizing effects.

Male rats can be deprived of androgen during the critical period either by castration (Grady and Phoenix, 1963) or by injecting an antiandrogen (cyproterone acetate) into the neonatal pups (Neumann, 1970). When this antiandrogen is injected into the mother rat in the late prenatal period, the male pups are born with feminized external genitalia. In their behaviour, male rats deprived of testosterone neonatally are more similar to untreated females than are males which were not treated with the antiandrogen.

From this very brief review of rodent behavioural data, it may be concluded that sexually dimoprhic forms of behaviour, and presumably the neural substrates that mediate them, are bipotential in the foetus, and that differentiation is determined by the presence or absence of androgen.

The neural regulation of hypophyseal gonadotropin secretions in males and females differs markedly (see Boldman, this volume Chapter 5); the cyclic gonadotropin secretion of the female being regulated by the ventromedial and preoptic areas of the hypothalamus (Gorski, 1971). Female rats exposed to neonatal testosterone are permanently acyclic, and males castrated immediately after birth are cyclic in their gonadotrophin release (for a review of experiments on the role of prenatal androgen on CNS differentiation see Harris, 1964,

1970; Whalen, 1966; Gorski, 1968, 1971; Money and Ehrhardt, 1972 and Plapinger and McEwen, this volume Chapter 6). Neonatal testosterone can apparently directly alter neurons in the hypothalamus that mediate cyclicity Dörner and Staudt, 1968;). There is some evidence (Pfaff, 1966) of dimorphism in the structure of the brainstem, neocortex, hippocampus, and amygdala, which is also differentiated by the presence or absence of androgen.

In brief, the neural regulation of the hypophyseal gonadotropin secretion and of sexual behaviour is bipotential in the rodent during the foetal period. Differentiation is established by a process analogous to the sexual differentiation of the mammalian reproductive tract.

Since Harlow (1965) documented several instances of dimorphic behaviour in the rhesus monkey, this species has proved particularly useful for foetal androgenization studies (Phoenix et al., 1967). Infant male monkeys, for example, display more rough and tumble play and threat postures different from those of the female. Such differences are not entirely sex exclusive. Both male and female monkeys will at times show identical behaviour. Sex differences are a matter of threshold and frequency of display.

Rhesus monkeys injected with testosterone during the critical period of pregnancy give birth to hermaphroditic daughters with a clitorine penis (Fig. 4). The mounting, play, and threat behaviour of the androgenized females during infancy resemble those of control males. The only androgenized females that develop and retain the display of mature mounting in adolescence are those whose mothers have been injected with testosterone for long periods (Goy and Phoenix, 1972). When adult hermaphroditic females are ovariectomized and injected with testosterone (Eaton et al., 1973), they mount stimulus females and can occasionally achieve intromission and ejaculation with emission. Thus the degree of behavioural masculinization depends on the total duration and amount of foetal exposure to androgen.

Prenatal androgen does not render rhesus monkeys acyclic, though the onset of menstruation is retarded. Whether the incongruency between rodents and primates on this variable is due to timing, dosage, or species differences is not known.

It appears, therefore, that in primates as well as rodents, the reproductive system, the nervous system, and behaviour are all initially bipotential. The differentiating agent is androgen, and the critical period is in early foetal life. It is likely that this phenomenon is phyletic, occuring in all mammals, including humans.

PRENATAL HORMONES IN HUMAN CLINICAL STUDIES

Tomboyism and the Adrenogenital Syndrome

One cannot experimentally manipulate the prenatal environment in human beings. Therefore, the researcher relies on the study of individuals with defects

Fig. 4. Musculinized external sexual organs of a genetic female rhesus monkey with two ovaries, uterus, and Fallopian tubes. Masculinization was induced by injection of the pregnant mother with the androgen, testosterone propionate. (Photo courtesy of Robert Goy and Charles Phoenix.)

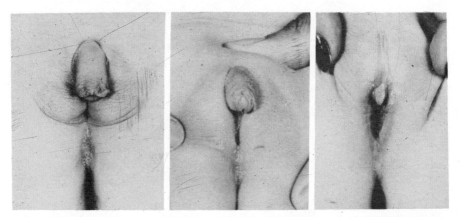

Fig. 5. Left, and centre, are two degrees of urogenital fusion and clitoral enlargement in the adrenogenital syndrome; right, genital appearance following clitoridectomy and exteriorization of the vagina

in sexual differentiation—nature's own experiments in intersexuality. One form of intersexuality is the andrenogenital syndrome in genetic females. This is a genetic recessive condition in which the adrenal cortex of the foetus fails to synthesize its proper hormone, cortisol. (The most common site for the enzyme defects is the 21-hydroxylating system which results in the salt-losing and regular form of the disease. An 11-hydroxylating defect occurs in some patients who are also hypertensive.) Instead, it secretes an excess of androgen. Affected females are born with an enlarged clitoris, variable in size. In some cases masculinization is complete, so that the genotypic female has a penis and empty scrotum. The internal reproductive system is female. In some cases, there is an associated deficit in salt retention. Fig. 5 shows the enlarged clitoris before and after the surgical correction performed soon after birth.

If cortisone therapy is begun neonatally and maintained continuously, excess postnatal androgen production ceases, and female puberty, secondary sex characteristics, and reproductive function are normal, although menses may have a late onset (Jones and Verkauf, 1971). Because of their history of foetal masculinization, the behavioural and psychosexual development of treated adrenogenital girls is of special interest. Fig. 6 shows an adolescent girl longitudinally treated for adrenogenital syndrome. More than 50 such girls have been followed longitudinally at The Johns Hopkins Hospital and another 20 at Children's Hospital in Buffalo (Ehrhardt and Baker, 1974). The tomboyish behaviour of an unbiased sample of these girls throughout childhood is listed in Table 1. In general, their kinetic energy expenditure is characterized as the equivalent of rough and tumble play observed in androgenized female monkeys. In comparison with matched controls (Ehrhardt et al., 1968) and female siblings (Ehrhardt and Baker, 1974) the girls report high energy expenditure which includes getting into organized group competitive sports, usually with boys. They become involved in boys' neighbourhood football,

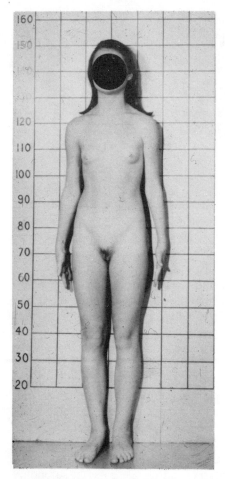
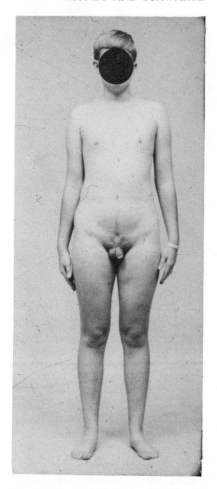

Fig. 6. Adolescent girl cortisol-treated since birth for the adrenogenital syndrome and surgically feminized in infancy. At birth the genital defect and that of the patient in Fig. 7 were identical

Fig. 7. This boy and the girl (Fig. 6) are a matched pair of genetic and gonadal females, born hermaphroditic with the adrenogenital syndrome. They are concordant for diagnosis, but discordant for gender identity and role

baseball, and/or basketball, either as the only girl, or with no more than two other girls. They are accepted by the boys because of their superior athletic skills. The girls do not assert themselves to obtain a high rank in the dominance hierarchy of boys, possibly because of a realistic recognition that they would not be tolerated if they did.

Adrenogenital girls do not find much in common with ordinary girls who live according to traditional sex stereotypes. In particular, they do not share the interest of these girls in releasing parentalism in dollplay and they have little

Table 1. Variables of tomboyism

1. Kinetic energy expenditure
2. Dominance assertion
3. Toy and sports preferences
4. Preferred styles in clothes, cosmetics, and grooming
5. Parentalism in play
6. Career ambition
7. Body image
8. Arousal by visual and narrative erotic imagery

enthusiasm for other stereotypic girls' games. In addition, the adrenogenital girls during childhood have a lower interest in babies (Ehrhardt and Baker, 1974), and fewer fantasies concerning romance and marriage, when compared to their female siblings.

Tomboyism does not necessarily mean that the girls have conflict with respect to their basic gender identity, although 35% of the Ehrhardt and Baker group thought that it might have been easier to be a boy.

Despite their tomboyism, adrenogenital girls do not manifest a lowered threshold for aggressive types of behaviour such as fighting, dominance assertion, or delinquency (Money and Schwartz, 1976). (The concept of threshold—for the release or inhibition of behaviour—is used throughout this chapter. It is the only adequate concept with which to provide an alternative to the concept of internal motivational state, which we eschew. A release threshold may be attributable to genetic programming, prenatal hormonal programming, toxic programming, or programming by any other determinants. It allows one also to formulate a developmental or longitudinal theory in terms of stages or experiences that are programmed serially, hierarchically or cybernetically.)

Adrenogenital girls gravitate away from their agemates who are not tomboyish, and towards those who are more tomboyish like themselves. The tomboyism of the girls who do not have the adrenogenital syndrome is less intense; in addition, it is less persistent and fades with the advent of adolescence as romantic interest in boys develops. The adrenogenital girls do not undergo the same transition toward lessening of tomboyism with an interest in boys, so they often become relatively isolated from their agemates.

Erotic preference of adrenogenital girls and women treated since childhood with cortisone is presently being investigated; the preliminary evidence (Money and Schwartz, 1977) indicates the possibility that there is a greater incidence of bisexuality and homosexuality than would be expected by chance. If this finding should be upheld, it will augment the finding of earlier research (Ehrhardt et al., 1968), which found a higher incidence of bisexuality and homosexuality in a group of adrenogenital girls and women who did not receive the benefit of cortisone therapy for postnatal control of their disease until late in childhood.

The actual mechanisms that mediate tomboyish behaviour have not been established, but it is very likely that they relate to threshold changes in the acquisition and expression of gender-specific behaviour, induced by prenatal androgenization, presumably in hypothalamic and limbic system pathways.

Normal males have been found to have larger hearts and lungs (Tanner, 1970) and a higher oxygen consumption per kilogram of body weight than girls of the same muscular mass (Garn and Clark, 1953). It is possible that alteration of these organs could also contribute to the increased energy expenditure of adrenogenital girls.

The Adrenogenital Syndrome in Genotypic Males

Excess prenatal androgen does not alter the external genitalia of the male. Therefore, some adrenogenital boys are not diagnosed until the excessive adrenal androgen induces early pubertal virilization. When the syndrome is diagnosed in early childhood, and cortisone treatment is begun, the boys will not look noticeably different from their peers. A group of 25 males with the adrenogenital syndrome has been followed at The Johns Hopkins Hospital (Money and Alexander, 1967), and 10 more at Buffalo (Ehrhardt and Baker, 1974).

Adrenogenital males have a higher energy expenditure level in sports and rough outdoor activities on a long-term basis as compared to unaffected boys. They are usually involved in more athletic activities and they rate themselves athletically superior to siblings and peers. This superiority is verified by their family members as is also their leader or captain status.

MATCHED PAIRS OF HERMAPHRODITES

Matched Pairs with the Adrenogenital Syndrome

A matched pair of hermaphrodites is one in which both individuals are concordant for genotypic sex, prenatal history, and diagnosis, but discordant for sex of rearing and postnatal history. Fig. 7 shows a genotypic female with the adrenogenital syndrome who is the counterpart of the girl in Fig. 6. Because of the enlarged phallus at birth, both babies were thought to be boys with undescended testes. In one case, the correct diagnosis was established at the age of eight weeks, and the child was surgically corrected and reannounced as a girl. In the second case, the correct diagnosis was missed until $3\frac{1}{2}$ years of age. It was then decided that the child had already differentiated a masculine gender identity. The sex of rearing was retained, and surgical masculinization, already begun elsewhere, was continued.

Both children were maintained on cortisone therapy. At the time of puberty, the girl feminized under the influence of her own ovarian hormones. The boy masculinized under the influence of exogenous androgen, though he would have done so spontaneously, under the influence of adrenocortical androgen, had cortisone therapy been withdrawn.

The gender identity and gender role of each of these individuals was feminine and masculine respectively. Each showed that prenatally determined tomboyish traits can be postnatally incorporated into either a feminine or a masculine gender identitiy and role. As a matched pair, they, and other matched pairs like them, show how great is the postnatal, social contribution to gender identity differentiation, sexual eroticism included.

Matched Pairs with the Androgen Insensitivity Syndrome

A second matched pair of hermaphrodites is shown in Fig. 8, again concordant for genotypic sex, prenatal history, and diagnosis, but discon-cordant for sex of rearing and postnatal history. In this example both individuals are karyotypically 46 XY, with the androgen-insensitivity syndrome.

In this syndrome, the body's cells lack in their nuclei a protein to which androgen is bound. Unable to use androgen, the foetus differentiates mor-phologically as a female. One exception is that the Müllerian ducts vestigiate because the testes are present, and they do not fail to secrete their Müllerian-inhibiting substance. The uterus, Fallopian tubes, and innermost part of the vagina are therefore not differentiated. At puberty there is no menstruation, but the breasts develop in normal female fashion under the influence of testi-cular oestrogen. The secondary sexual characteristics are female.

In the complete form of the androgen-insensitivity syndrome, the vulva looks normally female at birth. The child is reared as a girl and differentiates a feminine gender identity. There is also an incomplete form of the syndrome in which the external genitalia look ambiguous at birth, with a phallus that may be either an enlarged clitoris or a tiny, hypospadiac penis. It is from among cases such as these that the matched pair of Fig. 8 is drawn, one reared as a boy, the other as a girl. At puberty both the girl and the boy began spontaneously to feminize. For the girl, surgical feminization was an uncomplicated procedure, and she continued to live as a woman without interruption of her feminine gender identity. For the boy, surgical masculinization was, as always in the case of a small hypospadiac phallus, less than satisfactory. Even more distressing was the fact that his body could not be properly masculinized with injections of testosterone for its cells were as insensitive to injected androgen as to that secreted by his own testes. The boy was condemned by nature to live out his life looking juvenile, beardless, and more feminine than masculine in other secondary sexual appearance, even after surgical breast removal. Nevertheless, this boy's masculine gender identity held so tenaciously that it was impossible to consider sex-reassignment as a way of resolving his dilemma.

His case, along with that of his matched partner, demonstrates that in the presence of the 46, XY karyotype, the events of prenatal life do not preordain postnatal differentiation of gender identity and role, which is heavily dependent on postnatal social input. The same principle applies in matched pairs of 46, XY karyotype in which spontaneous pubertal development is masculinizing.

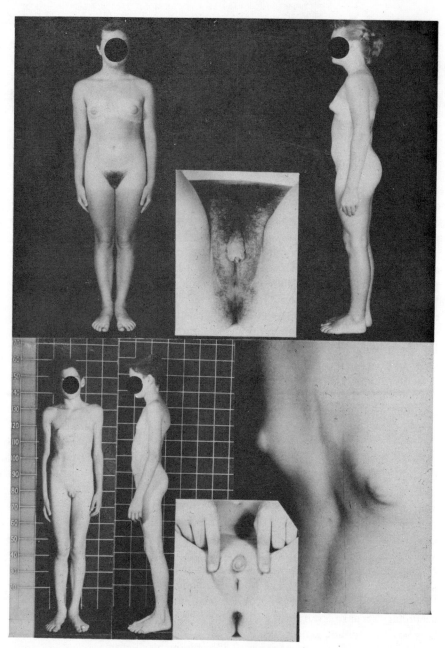

Fig. 8. A second matched pair of genetic and gonadal male hermaphrodites, concordant for diagnosis, but discordant for assigned sex, rearing, and gender identity. Both have the partial androgen-insensitivity syndrome, which accounts for adolescent breast development. The chromosomal male in the upper part was reared female since birth and developed a female gender identity. The chromosomal male in the lower part was reared male and developed a male gender identity. This boy underwent surgery to flatten his chest. The girl had a clitoridectomy and vaginoplasty

It applies also in the case of non-hermaphroditic individuals, as is evidenced in the case of the twins which follows.

Ablatio Penis

Fig. 9 shows identical twins (Money and Ehrhardt, 1972; Money, 1975) whose embryogenesis and foetal development was normal 46, XY. The one who is now the girl had the penis accidently ablated during attempted circumcision by cautery at the age of seven months. The child was formally sex-reassigned at 17 months, and soon thereafter the first stage of surgical feminization of the genitalia was undertaken. The final stage of vaginoplasty will be done when the body is fully grown. At the regular age of puberty, body feminization will be complete as a sequel to hormonal replacement therapy with oestrogen.

Now prepuberal in age, the girl has a tomboyish gender identity and role, as expected in view of her prenatal exposure to endrogen. Nonetheless, she has a feminine gender identity and role, distinctly different from that of her brother. The final and conclusive evidence awaits the appearance of romantic interest and erotic imagery.

GENDER-IDENTITY DIFFERENTIATION

Implications from Hermaphroditic Postnatal Biographies

The study of hermaphroditic biographies, and the biographies of cases of ablatio penis, points to the early postnatal years as constituting a very important developmental epoch in gender-identity differentiation. There is a parallel here with native language. According to the criterion of his ability to use language, a child by the age of five, at the latest, has an effective grasp of the principles of linguistics embedded in his native tongue. From that age onwards, however, there is still enough flexibility for a second language to be acquired. The earlier the second language is acquired, the closer it resembles a native language, spoken idiomatically and without an accent. Nonetheless, the second language will not eradicate the first which will always remain subject to rapid reacquisition, even years later, should it have fallen into disuse.

By the age of five, a child's gender identity is embedded firmly, like the native language. As a schema in the brain, gender identity programmes a developing boy's own masculinely appropriate behaviour and imagery. Simultaneously, it programmes the feminine counterpart as the complement of the boy's own reactions in relationships with the other sex. The reverse applies to the developing girl.

Sequential Postnatal Components of Gender-identity Differentiation

A second look at Fig. 1 shows how the prenatal and the postnatal components of gender-identity differentiation fit together sequentially. The appearance

Fig. 9. Identical twins whose embryogenesis and foetal development was normal 46, XY. The one who is now a girl had the penis accidently ablated during attempted circumcision by cautery at the age of seven months

of the genital anatomy bifurcates in its influence as it carries the gender-identity programme forward. It does so by influencing the behaviour of others, first of all with the headline announcement, 'It's a boy', or 'It's a girl'. Eventually the genital anatomy also influences the child directly, by way of tactile and visual aspects of the body image.

From 18 months until four years of age a child is especially responsive to enviromental determinants of gender identity and gender-role difierentiation. During this period, a child becomes aware of his or her anatomy and begins to make comparisons with other people who use the same gender-differentiating nouns and pronouns. The appearance and feel of the sex organs has a self-influence by way of influencing one's body image. It is especially important that gender-identifying cues are not contradictory or confused during this period. Although the data are still inconclusive, evidence points to this period as critical for the development of gender identity transpositions, as in transexualism, transvestism, and homosexuality. A predisposition of prenatal hormone origin may conceivably be a prerequisite.

The juvenile gender identity finally develops into the adult gender role identity. At puberty, the new tide of sex hormones does not determine anything at all about gender identity as masculine or feminine. Hormones simply activate what is already there by changing the threshold for sexual behaviour, erotic imagery, and the subjective feeling of eroticism.

Regarding the etiology of deviant gender identity and sexual behaviour, it is conventional to ask dichotomous questions as for example, 'Is homosexuality due to hormonal error, or to a distant father and overprotective mother?' The proper approach would be to question the proportional contribution of each of the multideterminants shown in Fig. 1.

SUMMARY AND CONCLUSIONS

Gender identity is not immanent in the genes nor in prenatal hormones. It is neither biologically determined, nor environmentally determined, but the product of both. Yet it is not sufficient to explain the development of gender identity, or any other behaviour, simply as a complex interaction of environment and biology, for there is an environmental biology and a biological environment. The scientific way is to identify some of the contributing variables, and the relative importance of each.

The research reviewed in this chapter has been focused on identifying several of the components from genetics to social stimuli, contributing to the interaction of nature and nurture, and has attempted to identify the relative importance of each to the establishment of gender identity. Eventually, one hopes to specify how the biochemical and genetic influences organize structural and anatomical characteristics which then developmentally interact with environmental variables.

With respect to the development of gender identity, the evidence reviewed in this chapter indicates that genetic and prenatal hormonal determinants do not, in general, override postnatal determinants. However, in any particular individual case that comes to professional attention, the technical limitations in medicine and science limit the chance of establishing an etiological diagnosis. Thus, there are still very few individual cases in which a diagnosis can be established such that genetic or hormonal determinants can be specified as having overriden postnatal social determinants (or *vice versa*), in the differentiation of gender identity. The task for further research is to identify more and more syndromes of gender identity disorder and impairment. Until this is done, there will continue to be an unspecified multitude of people with problems of gender identity for whom nothing more can be said than that they are idiosyncratically different or deviant—etiology unknown.

The major theoretical point in this chapter is that it is necessary for investigators of human behaviour to abandon the unicausational models of physics and chemistry, and rid themselves of the conceptual pitfalls of instincts, drives, and motivation (which have the same conceptual status as phlogiston) and to get down to identifying the actual mechanisms of behaviour.

ACKNOWLEDGEMENTS

This work was supported by USPHS grant number HD-00325 and by funds from the Grant Foundation, New York.

REFERENCES

Baker, S. W. and Ehrhardt, A. A. (1974) Prenatal androgen, intelligence, and cognitive sex. In: *Sex Differences in Behavior*, R. C. Friedman, R. M. Richart, R. Vande Wiele (eds.), John Wiley and Sons, New York.

Dalton, K. (1968) Antenatal progesterone and intelligence, *Br. J. Psychiat.*, 114, 1377–82.

Diamond, M. and Dale, E. (1967) Distribution of radiolabeled steroid after administration to the neonatal rat, *Anat. Rec.*, 157, 234.

Dörner, G. and Staudt, J. (1968) Structural changes in preoptic anterior hypothalamic area of the male rat following neonatal castration and androgen substitution, *Neuroendocrinology*, 3, 136–40.

Eaton, G. G., Goy, R. W., and Phoenix, C. H. (1973) Effects of testosterone treatment in adulthood on sexual behavior of female pseudohermaphrodite rhesus monkeys, *Nature New Biol.*, 242, 119–20.

Edwards, D. A. (1969) Early androgen stimulation and aggressive behavior in male and female mice, *Physiol. Behav.*, 4, 333–8.

Edwards, D. A. (1970) Post-neonatal androgenization and adult aggressive behavior in female mice, *Physiol. Behav.*, 5, 465–7

Ehrhardt, A. A., and Baker, S. W. (1974) Fetal androgens, human central nervous system differentiation, and behavior sex differences. In: *Sex Differences in Behavior*, R. C. Friedman, R. M. Richart, R. L. Vande Wiele (eds.), John Wiley and Sons, New York.

Ehrhardt, A. A., Epstein, K., and Money, J. (1968) Fetal androgens and female gender identity in the early treated adrenogenital syndrome, *Johns Hopkins Med. J.*, 122, 160–7.

Ehrhardt, A. A. and Money, J. (1967) Progestin-induced hermaphroditism: IQ and psychosexual identity in a study of ten girls, *J. Sex Res.*, 3, 83–100.

Garn, S. M. and Clark, L. L. (1953) The sex differences in the basic metabolic rate, *Child Devel.*, 24, 215–24.

Gorski, R. A. (1968) Influence of age on the response to paranatal administration of a low dose of androgen, *Endocrinology*, 82, 1001–4.

Gorski, R. A. (1971) Gonadal hormones and the perinatal development of neuroendocrine function. In: *Frontiers in Neuroendocrinology*, L. Martini and W. F. Ganong (eds.), Oxford University Press, New York.

Goy, R. W. (1968) Organising effects of androgen on the behaviour of rhesus monkeys. In: *Endocrinology and Human Behavior*, R. P. Michael (ed.), Oxford University Press, New York.

Goy, R. W. and Phoenix, C. H. (1972) The effects of testosterone propionate administered before birth on the development of behavior in genetic female rhesus monkeys. In: *Steroid Hormones and Brain Function*, C. Sawyer and R. Gorski (eds.), University of California Press, Berkeley.

Goy, R. W., Phoenix, C. H., and Young, W. C. (1962) A critical period for the suppression behavioral receptivity in adult female rats by early treatment with androgen, *Anat. Rec.*, 142, 307.

Grady, K. L. and Phoenix, C. H. (1963) Hormonal determinants of mating behavior; the display of feminine behavior by adult male rats castrated neonatally, *Am. Zool.*, 3, 482–3.

Grady, K. L., Phoenix, C. H., and Young, W. L. (1965) Role of the developing rat testis in differentiation of the neural tissues mediating mating behavior, *J. Comp. Physiol. Psychol.*, 59, 176–82.

Harlow, H. F. (1965) Sexual behavior in the rhesus monkey. In: *Sex and Behavior*, F. A. Beach (ed.), John Wiley and Sons, New York.

Harris, G. W. (1964) Sex hormones, brain development, and brain function, *Endocrinology*, 75, 627–48.

Harris G. W. (1970) Hormonal differentiation of the developing central nervous system with respect to patterns of endocrine function, *Phil. Trans. Roy. Soc. London*, 13, 259, 165–77.

Jones, H. W. Jr. and Verkauf, B. S. (1971) Congenital adrenal hyperplasia: age at menarche and related events at puberty, *Am. J. Obstet. Gynec.*, 109, 292–8.

Jost, A. (1971) Embryonic sexual differentiation. In: *Hermaphroditism, Genital Anomalies, and Related Endocrine Disorders* (3rd edn.), H. W. Jones Jr. and W. W. Scott, Williams and Wilkins, Baltimore.

Jost, A. (1972) A new look at the mechanisms controlling sex differentiation in mammals, *Johns Hopkins Med. J.*, 130, 38–53.

Money, J. (1975) Ablatio penis: normal male infant sex-reassigned as a girl, *Arch. Sex. Behav.*, 4, 65–72.

Money, J. and Alexander, D. (1967) Eroticism and sexual function in developmental anorchia and hyporchia with pubertal failure, *J. Sex Res.*, 3, 31–47.

Money, J. and Ehrhardt, A. A. (1972) *Man and Woman, Boy and Girl: The Differentiation and Dimorphism of Gender Identity from Conception to Maturity*. The Johns Hopkins University Press, Baltimore.

Money, J., Hampson, J. G., and Hampson, J. L. (1955) An examination of some basic sexual concepts: the evidence of human hermaphroditism. *Bull. Johns Hopkins Hosp.*, 97, 301–319.

Money, J. and Lewis, V. (1966) IQ, genetics and accelerated growth: adrenogenital syndrome, *Bull. Johns Hopkins Hosp.*, 118, 365–73.

Money, J. and Schwartz, M. F. (1976) Fetal androgens in the early treated adrenogenital syndrome of 46 XX hermaphroditism: Influence on assertive and aggressive types of behavior, *Aggressive Behavior*, 2, 19–30.

Money, J. and Schwartz, M. F. (1977) Dating, romantic and nonromantic friendships and sexuality in 17 early-treated adrenogenital females, ages 16 to 25. In: *Congenital Adrenal Hyperplasia*, P. A. Lee, L. P. Plotnick, A. A. Kowarski, and C. J. Midgeon (eds.), University Park Press, Baltimore.

Neumann, F. (1970) Antiandrogens, *Res. Reprod.*, **2**, (# 3), 3–4.

Pfaff, D. W. (1966) Morphological changes in the brains of adult male rats after neonatal castration. *J. Endocrinol.*, **36**, 415–6.

Phoenix, C. H., Goy, R. W., and Young, W. C. (1967) Sexual behavior: general aspects. In: *Neuroendocrinology*, Vol. II, L. Martini and W. F. Ganong (eds.), Academic Press, New York.

Swanson, H. H. (1967) Alteration of sex-typical behavior in hamsters in open field and emergence tests by neonatal administration of androgen or oestrogen, *Anim. Behav.*, **15**, 209–16.

Swanson, H. H. and Crossley, D. A. (1971) Sexual behaviour in the golden hamster and its modification by neonatal administration of testosterone propionate. In: *Hormones in Development*, M. Hamburg and E. J. W. Barrington (eds.), Appelton-Century-Crofts, New York.

Swanson, H. E. and van der Werff ten Bosch, J. J. (1964) The 'early-androgen' syndrome: Differences in response to prenatal and postnatal administration of various doses of testosterone propionate in female and male rats, *Acta Endocrinol.*, **47**, 37–50.

Tanner, J. M. (1970) Physical growth. In: *Carmichael's Manual of Child Psychology*, (3rd edn.), P. H. Musser (ed.), John Wiley and Sons, New York.

Walsh, P. C., Madden, J. D., Harrod, M. J., Goldstein, J. L., Macdonald, P. C., and Wilson, J. D. (1974) Familial incomplete male pseudohermaphroditism, Type 2: Decreased dihydrotestosterone formation in pseudovaginal perineoscrotal hypospadias, *New Eng. J. Med.*, **291**, 944–9.

Whalen, R. E. (1966) Differentiation of the neural mechanisms which control gonadotropin secretion and sexual behavior. In: *Perspectives in Reproduction and Sexual Behavior*, M. Diamond (ed.), Indiana University Press, Bloomington.

Whalen, R. E. and Edwards, D. A. (1967) Hormonal determinants of the development of masculine and feminine behavior in male and female rats. *Anat. Rec.*, **157**, 173–80.

Young, W. C. (1961) The hormones and mating behavior. In: *Sex and Internal Secretions* (3rd edn.), W. C. Young (ed.), Williams and Wilkins, Baltimore.

CHAPTER 24

Tactile Experience and Sexual Behaviour: Aspects of Development with Special Reference to Primates

M. J. A. Simpson

INTRODUCTION

In 1965, Mason wrote 'The evidence is conclusive that normal development of primate social behaviour is dependent on experience (Harlow, 1962; Nissen, 1953; Yerkes and Elder, 1936), but the specific factors involved have yet to be determined.' (Mason, 1965a). A comprehensive review about abnormal behaviour in primates (Mitchell, 1970) cited more than sixty studies where various kinds of rearing conditions produced abnormalities in the subsequent social behaviour of non-human primates, mostly rhesus monkeys. In his summary, Mitchell (1970) includes the following sentences:

Rearing in social isolation produces severe behavioural pathology in all primates. The most important source of stimulation that is absent in such a rearing condition is physical contact with another animal involving a complex combination of skin or fur contact, clinging, movement, oral contact, and warmth. Isolation-reared primates change as they mature from rocking digit-sucking, grimacing, self-clutching recluses to pacing, socially aggressive, self-threatening, masturbating, self-mutilating menaces who often make bizarre movements. When the isolate animal reaches sexual maturity, its sexual behaviour is often abnormal.

Any treatment, like rearing in social isolation, can work in several ways to 'produce' 'behavioural pathology', which may manifest itself in sexual and other situations. But can we isolate the 'specific factors involved'? To label and list sources of stimulation that are lacking, or altered by particular treatments is to make a start. But animals, including infants (see reviews in Lewis and Rosenblum 1974) are not passive receptacles which somehow produce results, pathological or otherwise, as a result of stimulation poured into them. They interact with their surroundings, and thereby modify the stimulation they receive (Held and Hein, 1963) moment by moment (examples in Hinde, 1970; Simpson, 1968; and Lewis' introduction to Lewis and Rosenblum, 1974). This chapter takes the view that an understanding of an individual's social skills can illuminate his behaviour in specifically sexual situations. Thus many studies concerned with the effects of social experience on social behaviour become potentially relevant.

In 1974, in a concise review about the relationship between early social experience and subsequent social development, Suomi wrote: 'It has consistently been demonstrated that the more socially complex an infant monkey's rearing environment, the more socially competent and sophisticated behaviours the monkey will develop'. This point was illustrated as follows: A monkey reared with only its mother is likely to develop species-appropriate sexual and (for females) maternal behaviour but not aggressive behaviour (Alexander, 1966; Suomi and Harlow, 1971). Mother-peer-raised monkeys are likely to develop most species-appropriate social behaviours (Harlow and Harlow, 1969). The differences in social capabilities are most evident when equal-aged monkeys reared in different environments are permitted to interact with each other. In such situations, partial isolates are usually dominant over total isolates (Rowland, 1964), peer-reared subjects are usually dominant over partial isolates (Pratt, 1969), and mother-peer-reared subjects are usually dominant over peer-reared subjects (Suomi *et al.* in prep.). Dominance is assumed to reflect the monkey's social competence, in this argument.

In his discussion about how his results confirmed the relationship between social complexity in an infant's rearing environment and the subsequent sophistication of its social behaviour, Suomi (1974) made the reservation that the complexity could hardly be considered as a one-dimensional variable. He also wrote that one-dimensional test situations are not likely to detect fully social capabilities which are obviously mediated by numerous variables, and suggested that our tests of capabilities should be both intensive and extensive: that is, each test should include detailed behavioural records, and there should be several tests.

The problem about such general and quantitative-seeming terms as 'partial isolation for the first year of life', or 'social complexity', or 'sophistication of its subsequent social behaviour' is that they seem to take us away from the processes involved, for it is difficult to apply the concepts implied to concrete instances of behaviour. When an infant rhesus monkey is isolated, what does he actually do with his body and with the fixtures in his cage? In order to show sophistication in his social behaviour, must a monkey be able to attend to two companions at once (e.g. Anderson and Mason, 1974), or connect two social events separated by time and by other events (e.g. discussion in Simpson, 1973), or be able to approach a female in a tactful manner and avoid precipitating an aggressive outburst in his group?

In his sentence: 'Male mounting behaviour probably does not develop as a unitary pattern; rather the various constituents seem to appear at different stages in ontogeny, and are differently related to experience and to eliciting conditions', Mason (1965a) suggests a multiprocess, multistrand model of behavioural development. A pessimist could object that with such a model we risk abandoning our clear-cut operational procedures, like total social isolation, and our bold concepts, like social sophistication, for a morass of behavioural detail.

This chapter takes the optimistic view we can master the detailed behavioural data generated by developmental studies by organizing our data around concepts of ability and skill. Those abilities and skills which persist through different developmental stages, and appear in different behavioural contexts at any one stage, would constitute the strands of Mason's (1965a) sentence above. For example, it may prove possible to study an individual's attention span at all ages, and in all situations where he acts on his surroundings. Then his performance in various playful, aggressive, sexual, and other situations in which he finds himself can be understood in terms of how well he manages the attentional and other skills involved.

The remainder of this chapter is organized as follows. First I will attempt to make provisional definitions of ability and skill. They are provisional in the sense that they are set up as guidelines for animal studies that, when they are actually made, may make it possible to improve the definitions. Then I will show how existing methods of studying the social behaviour of adult animals can be used to reveal the operation of social skills. The process of attending to the consequences of one's actions is then considered as an ability and as a skill. I will then consider briefly the tactile skills involved in infrahuman primate social behaviour, and I conclude with observations from Plooij's pers. comm. study of 'games' between chimpanzee mothers and their infants. Finally I will reconsider my stratagem of not making a precise and explicit definition of the word 'sexual' by discussing what may be special about human sexual experience.

ABILITIES AND SKILLS

It is difficult to define ability or skill in a rigorously operational way, and at the same time preserve the essence of what we feel is meant by the terms. Bruner's (1971) study of the development of hand use in human children was my inspiration for this section, and he approaches a definition with his sentence (p. 65): 'Skilled activity is a programme specifying an objective or terminal state to be achieved, and requiring the serial ordering of a set of constituent, modular sub-routines.' What is implied in the requirement that the constituent subroutines are serially ordered is that there are several orders and combinations in which they *could* be produced, and that some of those orders will fail, and some succeed, and that some of the successful ones will be more efficient than others. The Oxford English Dictionary's phrase 'practised ability' for skill reminds us that experience can improve skills, and suggests a distinction between skills and abilities: that the latter are not necessarily improved by practice. For the purpose of this chapter, a skill is an ability that can be improved by experience.

For example, a human infant's initial ability to fix its gaze on the corner of a triangle (e.g. Kessen, 1967), may initially be independent of practice at looking, though of course it may depend on many other factors, even perhaps including systemic androgens (e.g. Andrew, 1972a, and this volume Chapter 8). It seems obvious that fixing one's gaze on a stationary object is an ability, and that catching a ball is a skill, at least for primates and dogs, if not for praying mantises (see Mittelstaedt, 1962). It also seems superficially easy to break the skill of catching a ball into a number of constituent subroutines, including the ability to fix the gaze on a point, to follow the moving ball with head and eyes, to place the hands (or mouth) appropriately, and so on. Some of these component subroutines may themselves prove to be skills.

One hypothesis in this chapter is that attending to something for a finite period of time (e.g. following the ball) is an ability common to many skills, including ball-catching and social behaviour. Moreover, such an ability, in its unpractised, and later in its skilled forms, may be recognizable through several stages of development, and in several behavioural contexts.

Such a study seems promising, because the success or failure of many complex and elaborate *adult* activities may be explained in terms of the development of comparatively few component abilities, and because we are encouraged to look for abilities that can be followed through development, rather than to apply vague and complex categories (including sexual) which may appear in their complete (and thus convincingly recognizable) form in adult animals only, and in some adult individuals only occasionally, and in some in a peculiar and idiosyncratic form.

But how are we to achieve a description of, for example, attention span, which enables us to recognize and assess and compare its functioning in different behavioural contexts?

At present, the fact that this seems almost impossibly difficult must be faced. The best I can do is examine the difficulties. At least the recognition of this personal failure reminds us that, in practice, it is often when our skills fail us that we become most aware of them. The failure of a particular male monkey's sexual approach could be referred to a failure in social skill: he may have precipitated an outbreak of aggression in his group by failing to present to a nearby male as he made the approach. The failure of a mount by the male could be referred to the fact that he used his hind feet to grasp the 'wrong' pair of his partner's four ankles, or to his grasping the hind pair (correct) at the 'wrong' level (see Mason, 1965a; Harlow, 1969, 1974). Such failures would be valuable starting points for a developmental study if they directed our attention to comparable failures in other spheres of activity. For example, the above-mentioned male may have provoked comparable outbursts of aggression in feeding as in sexual situations; and his coordination may have been inept when climbing in the terminal branches of flexible trees as well as when climbing onto female partners.

This consideration of failures suggests a general strategy, where we look for common aspects of failures in different spheres of activity. This of course is something we do everyday as we try to understand our own difficulties, and the art of explaining and correcting social failures by breaking social behaviour into its component skills is practised by psychotherapists, and has been articulated in scientific form by Argyle and his co-workers (see, for example, Argyle, 1975).

There is a paradoxical sense in which developing mammals are often operating in situations where their current levels of ability and skill are just failing them for much of the time. For example, one four-week-old rhesus monkey infant seemed able to follow his mother with his eyes so long as both were on the ground and moving only in the horizontal plane, but he seemed to lose his mother when she climbed up a sloping pole. (Piaget's concepts of accomodation and assimilation as discussed by Piaget, 1952, and expounded by Flavell, 1963, can be seen as one way of theorizing about a situation where the developing individual is repeatedly pushing itself to the limits of its abilities.)

It is possible (see Simpson, 1976) that when play involves repetition and practice, the practice may be organized in such a way that those abilities and skills that are currently unreliable are being exercised. Thus what appears at first to be mere repetition may be the individual's attempt to provide the control that allows him to focus his attention onto that aspect of his ability that is at present unreliable.

Experimental studies of developing skills and abilities could profit by arranging problems so that many subjects of one age would fail where all older ones would succeed (e.g. Bruner, 1971). If we can be sure that a subject who is failing is nevertheless well motivated to work at the problem, we can work by 'titrating' the difficulty of the task against the individual's particular level of skill.

Skills in Adult Social Behaviour

We often find that a socially experienced animal behaves not only according to its own physiological state and the states of its companions (e.g. Herbert, 1968; Everitt and Herbert, 1969), but it also seems to take into account many other aspects of the situation, such as social relations with the other animals in the group (e.g. Anderson and Mason, 1974). Akers *et al.* (in prep.) describe special strategies used by oestrous female rhesus monkeys to attract the male's attention. A female may try being busy with pebbles near the male, or pretend to threaten something in a direction that will lead the male to look at her.

At a banal level, while the female may be driven by her oestrous state to initiate encounters with the male, she also acts with circumspect persistence in attempting to attract, and perhaps also to assess, his interest (see also Simpson, 1973; and MacKay's 1972 discussion). This observation becomes interesting if we can devise methods which show when an animal is acting persistently towards some goal, even when she does not achieve it, and if we can describe her circumspect behaviour in terms of those aspects of the situation that she takes into account.

Behaviour directed towards a goal varies in some way which can be correlated with the animal's position relative to that goal. If a male chimpanzee courtship gesture, such as reaching up to, grasping, shaking and twitching a branch (see McGinnis 1973 and Fig. 1 in this chapter), has the aim of getting a particular female to approach, then male branching will stop when the female approaches. However, the converse statement, that all behaviour which is ended by a particular event has that event as its goal, need not always be true (see Hinde and Stevenson-Hinde, 1969). Female approach may end male branching not because her approach is his goal, but because her approach elicits behaviour in the male, such as mounting, which makes it difficult for him to branch.

Thus sequences of goal-directed behaviour are special kinds of sequences of behaviour, and studies of goal-directed behaviour need as their basis information about how events usually follow each other in the behaviour sequences. I shall use male chimpanzee courtship to show the kinds of basic information that analyses of behaviour sequences can provide.

While the oestrous female is still two or three metres from the male (Fig. 1), there are several courtship gestures that the male may give, including *gazing* at her, reaching up to a branch and shaking it *(branch)*, hunching his shoulders *(hunch)*, standing bipedally *(bipedal stance)*, and rocking from side to side *(rock)*. The male's penis and hair will be erect (the hair starts up from arms and shoulders like bristles on a bottle-brush).

One sequence might be described as: gaze, branch, branch, branch, gaze, branch, branch, branch, female approaches and crouch presents, and then the male mounts. A second sequence, involving the same couple on the next day, could go as follows: branch, branch, gaze, gaze, branch, branch, branch, branch, gaze, branch, branch, rock, branch, branch, gaze, bipedal stance, then the male attacks female by chasing her and stamping on her back, and the female flees screaming.

Analysis of the two particular episodes just described would have been preceded by broader analyses that would have established the degree to which certain gestures, perhaps called courtship gestures, occur around mating times, and not around feeding or grooming times, and thus whether or not they could be placed in a separate group (van Hooff, 1971, provides one example; Morgan *et al.*, 1976 discuss techniques for discovering the degree to which elements in sequences form 'clusters').

A next step might be to combine data from separate courtship episodes. Table 1 combines the data from the two episodes in this account. (See Slater, 1973, for a general discussion of such analyses.) The table suggests certain generalizations, some of which could be tested statistically, given adequate

Fig. 1. Adult male chimpanzee Humphrey gazes and branches at oestrous female Winkle, who is four metres from Humphrey and licking concrete. Humphrey's pale pink erection is accentuated by a white stripe which extends the line of his penis down across his black scrotum. (From a photograph by the author.)

numbers in the cells (see Slater, 1973). Branching tends to be repeated, perhaps because it is a frequent event, and perhaps it is repeated more often than would be expected by chance. Gazing tends not to repeat itself, perhaps because, unlike branching, it is continuous throughout the episode. The one occasion when the female approached was preceded by branching. The occasion when the female was attacked was preceded by the male's bipedal stance.

For present purposes, let us ignore three methodological issues (dealt with by Slater, 1973): (1) the difficulties of discovering, by statistical techniques, how much of the apparent sequential organization (e.g. attack after bipedal

Table 1. Results from two hypothetical chimpanzee courtship episodes combined to show how often column events follow row events. (Thus one female approach was preceded by a branch, and eight of the fourteen branches led to further branches.)

Preceding event	Following event					
	Gaze	Branch	Rock	Biped. st.	Male attack	Female appr.
Gaze	1	5	0	1	0	0
Branch	4	8	1	0	0	1
Rock	0	1	0	0	0	0
Bipedal stance	0	0	0	0	1	0
Male attack	0	0	0	0	0	0
Female approach	0	0	0	0	0	0

stance, not after branching) could have arisen merely by chance; (2) the difficulties of describing sequences which include states, like gazing, having duration; and events, like branching, which can be regarded as instantaneous; and (3) the possibility that the partner is doing other things *during* each stage of the encounters that may affect the sequence (see also Simpson, 1968).

For my argument, there are two points of interest. First, I have 'lumped' the events from two episodes, in an attempt to fill the cells of Table 1 with sufficiently large numbers. Implicitly, differences in the contexts of the two episodes are now swamped out of the analysis, in the attempt to arrive at the kind of 'what-usually-follows-what' generalizations made by Table 1. Second, the table leaves open the question whether the data are adequately described as 'male branching elicits female approach, and female approach elicits male mounting', or whether we should add 'the male *tries* a variety of courtship gestures, including branching, *until* the female approaches'.

The first point, the effects of particular contexts, will not be answered by acts of 'lumping' which combine possibly different contexts. In analysing behaviour in context, we should always be ready to search for rules that enable us to predict the outcomes of particular occasions as accurately as possible. For example, the second courtship episode may have ended in attack because the female was slower to respond, and this outcome might have been predicted from our knowledge of the rules governing the patience of adult male chimpanzees. Here the necessary contextual information is about the timing of events, and it is information about the pair only. There could also be relevant aspects of the situation external to the pair: on the first occasion there may have been no attack because the male was being inhibited by the presence of another dominant male nearby.

When we ask about the degree to which the male's courtship behaviour is goal-directed, we are asking whether the male is persistently branching with so little apparent immediate effect simply because a certain amount of stimulation must be piled onto the female before she will approach, or because the female happens not to be looking at the male, and the branching is part of a strategy, whose goal is to attract the female's attention. (Of course, the answer to both questions could be positive.)

How do we recognize goal-directed behaviour? MacKay (1972) has distinguished between 'acting in such a way that' and 'acting in order to'. By accidentally tripping over a footstool, I act in such a way that I startle my dog. But I clap my hands, and then dash the footstool to the ground, in order to discover what stimulus will startle my deaf dog. What MacKay calls 'variational criteria' are needed to demonstrate goal-directed behaviour (see also Thorpe, 1963, and Hinde and Stevenson-Hinde, 1969). With reference to the male chimpanzee's courtship: we might discover that it is the female's approach that stops the male's branching behaviour, for he stops as soon as she approaches, and he stops several seconds before he begins to do anything else that might interfere with his branching. We might also find that he stopped branching if the female looked at him, and that he branched more vigorously than before when she looked away again, and that the violence of his branching was further increased if she walked away from him. (For an analogous argument about the use of tail-beats by one Siamese fighting fish to make its rival turn away, see Simpson, 1968).

Our original sequential study has helped us to focus on the finer details of the interaction: we move from the generalization 'male branching eventually elicits female approach' to add details which lead us to interpret the branching as goal-directed.

Note that, in this case, a single 'what-follows-what' study has become the basis for regarding chimpanzee courtship as a skill. In addition to saying that male branching often leads to female approach, we may become able to appreciate differences in branching skill, where some males, for example, are more effective than others in using branching to attract and hold the female's attention. Note also that sequential studies provide an initial foothold for studies of goal-directed behaviour only if there is some uniformity in the behaviour we are studying (Thorpe, 1963). For goal-directed behaviour to be recognizable by us, there must be some limit to the variation in the behaviour involved. In the male chimpanzee courtship case, many males branch. In human wooing, males may use singing, trips to the fair, rides in sports cars, chasing and rough and tumble play, tickling, etc., etc., and a sequential study using such categories might fail, until it exploited the fact that all the above activities moved and excited the diaphragm and underlying viscera, and that such excitement was also emotionally exciting (see Reich, 1942), and that excited people are more likely to comply in sexual adventures.

Finally, it is always worth remembering the distinction between courtship as a skill, and courtship as a sequence comprising a number of skills and abilities. For example, in order to be able to carry out effective sequences of courtship, a male chimpanzee must be able to sit, stand, climb, interact smoothly with other chimpanzees, etc. To consider courtship as a skill in itself, rather than as a sequence of behaviour in which other physical and social skills are expressed, is to presume that some males can combine the component actions in more effective sequences than other males can, and that practice can improve the effectiveness of male courtship sequences.

Attending to Consequences

I have suggested that adult social interactions may involve several skills and abilities, including the ability to control and sustain attention, and the ability to manage interactions that involve close contact between the participants. I now consider the ability to attend to one thing at a time, and I suggest how this could be affected by experience during an individual's development.

I propose that the development of the ability to manage attention depends partly on an experience of feedback from the environment, and from parts of the individual's own body, consequent upon things done by that individual to his surroundings and his body. This idea arises out of the work on the effects of movement-induced feedback on the development of perceptuomotor skills. Held and Hein's (1963) study provides one example of such work. They showed that active kittens who moved themselves through a patterned environment became able to avoid visual cliffs sooner than passive kittens, yoked to the active ones, who were thereby moved through the same surroundings. From such experiments (see also Hinde, 1970) it was argued that, for adequate perceptuomotor development, more was needed than the mere flow of stimulation over the kitten's receptors: there should in addition be some linkage between that flow of stimulation and the pattern of movements that contributed to such stimulation.

Many kinds of linkage can be subsumed by the term movement-induced. The linkage can be described by some function connecting the individual's movements with the environment's response: extension of my arm when I hold a ball in my hand produces a corresponding decrease in the size of my retinal image of that ball. For a real-life description of such a linkage between act and consequence, we should add some description of the reliability or variability of the linkage. If I push the same ball with the tip of a finger when I am swimming in turbulent surf, there may quite often be a decrease in the size of my retinal image of the ball as I extend my arm (55 out of 100 occasions, perhaps). But there will also be several occasions when the ball disappears altogether, and others when the surf throws the ball at my head. For an immature individual or one learning a new skill (McFarland's 1973) discussion of a paper by Connolly), such environmental turbulence can be compounded by the turbulence arising out of the difficulties the individual has in controlling his own limbs, eye muscles, etc.

I would add that there should be some optimum degree of uncertainty in the linkage, for the maintenance of the developing individual's interest in his surroundings. Complete predictability and rigidity could lead rapidly to loss of interest, and so could complete uncertainty arising out of surroundings that were too random in their responses.

In attempting to build up some picture of the general features of consequences that hold the attention of the developing individual I would also add the point that real-life consequences often take appreciable amounts of time to unfold. Moving my hand away from my head may reduce the apparent size of the ball in my hand as I do so, but throwing the ball at someone else can lead to consequences taking several seconds to unfold.

I suggest that surroundings that respond to the infant's actions with 'stories' (trains of events with a temporal pattern only appreciated by attention over some time-span) make it worthwhile for the infant to maintain and perhaps develop the ability to hold attention for appreciable spans of time.

As soon as one proposes that individuals attend to their surroundings for finite periods of time, one needs also to propose some means whereby they start and end each bout of attention. An individual interested in stories needs to know where to find the beginnings and how to recognize the ends. One simple hypothesis is that developing individuals are interested only in the stories they themselves elicit. An infant rhesus monkey, for example, might follow such rules as 'attend to your playmate for the next five seconds after hitting him, and if he does nothing, hit him again'. Here I am raising problems of the segmentation or framing (see also Simpson, 1976) of experience which are beyond the scope of this chapter, but which may become central in developmental studies.

The results of isolation experiments on primates can be interpreted in the light of this discussion. Chimpanzees reared in total social isolation for their first two years, and then confronted, at about seven years, with problem-solving tasks failed both because their attention spans seemed to be short, and because they spent much of the time performing interfering stereotyped movements (Menzel, *et al.*, 1970, see also below). Perhaps the events in those first two years never rewarded sustained attention: nothing that the infant chimpanzee did to his surroundings made any difference to them, and thus his surroundings were not worth attending to. The chimpanzees' stereotypes, and also those of isolation-reared rhesus monkeys (Mitchell, 1970, p. 228; Mitchell *et al.*, 1966 for examples), can be seen as attempts by the animals to provide themselves with events interesting enough to attend to. In rhesus monkeys, eyeball pushing could lead to some quick distortion of the visual field, followed by a slower recovery process, and these changes could be sufficiently variable from occasion to occasion (e.g. depending on the physiological state of the animal), and sufficiently prolonged, to reward sustained attention. In explaining floating limb, where a foot, for example, seems to gently float upwards as if of its own accord, we could speculate that the monkey has indeed succeeded in dissociating its attention from the motor activity of its leg so as to enjoy watching its foot as something interesting.

To conclude this section: descriptions of experiences relevant to the development of an infant's abilities to attend may need to include more than a catalogue of things done by and to the infant. Also relevant may be the reliability with which consequences, in whatever field of activity, are linked to actions; the limits within which those consequences vary; and the extent to which consequences appear as stories unfolding in time.

The Effects of Tactile Experience

In addition to providing direct experience of genital sensations, experiences of physical contact with others could work in two less direct ways. First, such experiences could *prevent* the development of inappropriate and incompatible behaviour patterns that interfered with effective adult social behaviour (e.g. being suicidally aggressive, or curling up into a ball: cf. Mitchell's 1970 review). Contact with mother and/or peers could prevent the development of some of the self-clasping and self-sucking habits seen in isolated rhesus monkeys and chimpanzees (see Harlow, 1969; Riesen, 1971). Second, contact, and the ready availability of mother and/or peers for contact, by having a calming effect on an infant, may *permit* him to initiate various kinds of interaction with his peers, and to appreciate the consequences of those interactions without being so frightened that he learns nothing from the experiences (see especially Mason, 1965b).

In human life, the combination of direct genital experience, and the other kinds of contact experienced in various social contexts, could interact in quite complex ways. This can be illustrated by considering Bakwin's (1952, 1973) observations that male and female human infants (including some between 5 and 12 months old) sometimes masturbate until they attain what their mothers clearly recognize as a climax or orgasm (see also Kinsey *et al.*, 1948). Why do not all infants thus focus on their genitals as a source of pleasure? That an infant's genitals are potentially a source of comfort to it has long been known by the unscrupulous nursemaids mentioned by Freud (1905), and is apparent when a chimpanzee mother succeeds in calming her screaming male infant's tantrum by rubbing its scrotum (pers. observ.). We can speculate that genital pleasure for primate infants remains a diffuse and undifferentiated aspect of pleasurable social experience while the infant is relatively uncoordinated, while being picked up and cuddled is a readily available source of comfort, and while the infant's parents accept any genital reactions as a matter of course. If, however, parental reactions suggest to the infant that public genital contact with others and himself are somehow wrong, then it might attempt to ignore genital sensations arising in a social context, and he could also become a specialist in private self-stimulation. In the latter situation, an infant might early develop a sharply focused genital sexuality, and later have some difficulty integrating this into its social life. In short, the ontogeny of its sexuality might parallel that described for his culture by Freud (1905).

To return to the simpler case of the developing male rhesus monkey infant, and to restrict discussion to the development of his ability to coordinate mounts successfully, we can suggest the following developmental process. This discussion assumes that the infant's hormonal state, tactile sensitivity, and anatomy are normal. His mother's body would provide a freely available, large, and relatively uniform surface, especially when she was stretched out on a warm day. In such situations an eight-week male rhesus monkey often crawls and slides all over his mother's body, dragging his belly and rather large scrotum over her as he does so. The different sensations coming from different parts of the infant's body will be consequences of differences in his own body, in so far as he restricts his movements to the relatively uniform parts of his mother's surface. As the infant becomes able to refer special sensations to his genital area, he may also discover how sliding movements enhance the sensations, which end abruptly when he falls off the edge of his mother, but may be maintained and enhanced further by to and fro thrusting movements on one part of her.

By about eight weeks, male infants begin to play actively with their peers (Harlow, 1969, 1974), which, unlike mothers, are small and present very discontinuous surfaces. While moving his genital 3 cm over mother made little difference, the same distance on a like-sized female peer may separate a soft warm perineal area from a hard cold bony hip. If, through experience with the relatively uniform surface provided by mother, the male has learned how different parts of himself feel, he will be able to interpret the more complex tactile feedback from different parts of his peer's body. It is possible that an infant unable to locate sensations in particular parts of his *own* body could be confused by the sensations coming from a peer, especially if his first experience of that peer was after he was a year old. The difficulties of surrogate-reared male rhesus monkeys in orienting their mounts (Mason, 1965a; Harlow, 1974) could be explained in terms lack of opportunity to discover how different parts of themselves and their partners felt.

The sexual difficulties experienced by chimpanzees reared alone from 12 h to 3 years are comparable to those of isolation-reared rhesus monkeys, though chimpanzees may recover and become able to copulate. Rogers and Davenport (1969) suggest that sexual behaviour in the chimpanzee is less rigid and stereotyped than in the rhesus monkey, and more amenable to modification. Some detailed observations by Nissen (see Riesen, 1971) on captive born, nursery-reared chimapnzees show the difficulties chimpanzees have in orienting components of sexual behaviour. Thus, one three-year-old inexperienced male was able to half-mount, and place his erect penis over his partner's sex skin, but then he would raise one foot and use his toe to stroke his penis. Another male showed all the components of chimpanzee male copulatory behaviour, but persistently missed penetration by a few degrees in angle, and a few centimetres in distance. The problems involved a mixture of inappropriate orientation, and lack of flexibility in the behaviour.

In a natural situation, male chimpanzee infants as young as one-year-old mount and penetrate adolescent females (van Lawick-Goodall, 1968; and pers. observ.). There are thus many opportunities to learn to adjust their mounts to a variety of situations, and a one-year-old can hardly miss the relatively large sexual swelling and its vaginal opening of an adolescent, and she may also cooperate in positioning herself.

Isolation-reared rhesus females often collapse when mounted, although female infants of about 10 weeks stand rigid when mounted by their peers (details in Harlow, 1974). Experience of having male peers mount correctly and rewardingly at a fairly early age may be necessary to prevent this rigid stance from disappearing from the female monkey's repertoire.

It is interesting, in terms of the foregoing discussion, that when infants reared in social isolation for up to 10 of their first 10 months are given bitches as surrogate mothers, some males (5 out of 6 studied so far) become able to perform adequate, though not perfectly normal mounts (Mason, pers. commun.; and see also Mason and Kenney, 1974). Such infants will not have had the opportunity to practise mounting with peers, but their experience with the tolerant bitches may have made possible the self-differentiation hypothesised above.

The following studies of chimpanzees allow us to extend the discussion about the extent to which observational studies of tactile experience might be possible. Davenport (in press) found that so long as chimpanzees were reared with their mothers in the first year, even under very restricted environmental conditions, the development of sterotyped self-stimulatory patterns was prevented. Such patterns occurred in infants separated very early and reared in peer groups, or reared by humans. Thus it seems that there is something special about the responses of the chimpanzee mothers to their infants.

The following observations by Plooij (pers. commun.) suggest what is special. In studying free-ranging chimpanzees at the Gombe Stream, he found that three infants, at about six weeks, started to bite anything appearing in front of their faces: their own hands or feet; and parts of their mothers' bodies, especially the hair on her arms, knees, and thighs. An effective elicitor of the biting behaviour, which may have been reflexive at this stage, was tactile stimulation of the face, and especially the perioral region (Fig. 2a and b). At first, such elicited bites were not necessarily directed at the eliciting stimulus: the infant might bite his own limbs when something touched his face.

One-third of the early bites were accompanied by playfaces in the infant, and mothers elicited the bites and playfaces by stroking the infant's face, or placing her index finger against or on his mouth. If the mother stopped stroking or took her finger away, the infant would increasingly often reach for her finger or hand, and bite it, and then the mother might again stroke his face (see also Fig. 2).

By twelve weeks, the playface and biting were no longer reflex-like. The infant would initiate interaction by directing his bites especially towards the mother's hands, as if he had learned that hands were specially likely to do

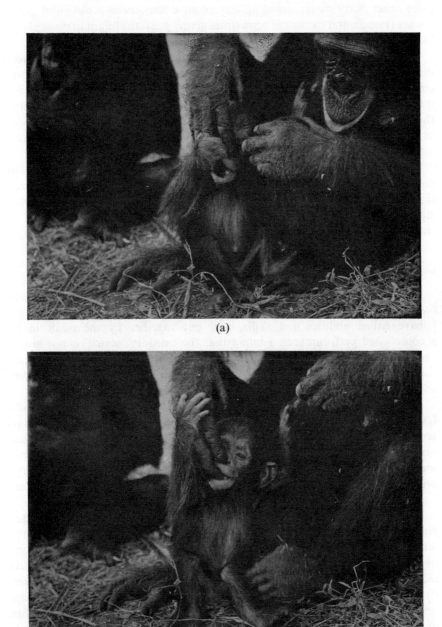

(a)

(b)

Fig. 2. 2½-month-old infant chimpanzee Sasha with her mother Nova: (b) was taken shortly after (a). One of Nova's fingers is between Sasha's lips. (Photographs by Anne Simpson.)

something back. Through the fourth month, the mother began to touch and poke other body parts, including the infant's belly, neck-pocket and groin-pocket (Fig. 3), and she would sometimes gently gnaw the infant in these places. She also started repeated games of gnawing and retreating with her mouth.

Plooij calls the special kinds of stimulation provided by a chimpanzee mother, and not by peers or by the humans who looked after Davenport's chimpanzee infants, the mother's 'availability to the infant'. This phrase is intended to emphasize that the mother's reactions to the infant's bites direct the behaviour of the infant once and for all onto her, and not onto his own body or onto objects. In terms of the discussion of feedback linked to the infant's actions, it is she who provides the most interesting consequences.

One may speculate that once a chimpanzee infant finds interactions with mother to be rewarding, it will soon begin to interact with other chimpanzees (Fig. 4). Plooij's study is an encouraging one, for it shows us how to carry out a study of the development of an individual's tactile interactions with its surroundings.

Sexual Experience

In suggesting that sequences of adult behaviour, including those that we so readily recognize as sexual, are built up out of the component strands which I have called abilities and skills, and put together by the adult in his accomplished performances, I imply that the category 'sexual' is not always very useful in developmental studies. I intend that implication, and I expect that it may prove mistaken to attempt to classify all experiences that influence adult sexual behaviour in a category called sexual experience.

If I could argue with Freud (1905) about his theory of infantile sexuality, I would suggest that it would be better considered as a theory of infant sensuality, oral, anal, and genital. I would also suggest that oral, anal, and genital experiences could have oral, anal, and genital sequelae, not just sexual sequelae, and that those who take Freud's sexual focus too seriously risk bringing up children who fit Freud's theories too well (see also Berger and Luckombe, 1967; and p. 796 above).

But Freud would know the work of Kinsey et al. (1948), and of Masters and Johnson (1966), and he could rightly object that, for adults at least, there does seem to be something special about sexual experience. In the sixties, some of us in the West felt that the orgasm was something of a touchstone of satisfactory sexual experience. To quote Kinsey et al. (1948) 'orgasm is distinct from any other phenomenon that occurs in the life of the animal, and its occurrence can ordinarily, if not invariably be taken as evidence of the sexual nature of the individual's response.' And Freud might add that infants have been observed to have orgasms (e.g. p. 796 above; Bakwin, 1952 and 1973), and that, in an admittedly arduous and prolonged session of effective stimulation with an artificial penis, an adult female rhesus monkey showed many of the physio-

Fig. 3. 18-month-old female infant Moeza being tickled by her mother Miff. (Photograph by Anne Simpson.)

Fig. 4. Sasha reaching and looking out towards Moeza. Nova turned to groom Miff shortly after the pictures in Fig. 2 were taken. (Photograph by Anne Simpson.)

logical signs of the orgasm described by Masters and Johnson (1966) for the human female. (Burton, 1971 carried out the experiment, but note that Herbert, 1970 describes a mating session where the male gives a total of approximately 30 thrusts, in approximately 6 separate mountings before he ejaculates; not the 1,000 thrusts given by Bruton's artificial penis. See also Zumpe and Michael, 1968; Michael, 1971).

The idea that, at least in human males, the development of their sexual behaviour is powerfully influenced by their experiences of their orgasms remains possibly true, and it is compatible with the skills and abilities hypothesis of this chapter. But any treatment of sexual experience should ask whether the mere occurrence of orgasms guarantees the value of the experience (see also Brecher and Brecher, 1967). Singer and Singer (1972), and Singer (1973) have shown that, for many, the reliable achievement of orgasms is only one of the goals of human sexual activity. Reich (1942) reminded us men that having orgasms (being 'erectively potent' in his terms) was not the same as letting go in sexual activity (being 'orgastically potent').

An enquiry into the nature of human sexual experience is beyond the scope of this chapter. Such an enquiry should recognize that there is more to be discovered about the experience than can be observed in what people do, and what happens to them (e.g. Singer, 1973). Such a study should also consider what sexual experience has in common with other experiences that human beings value, and how far it is special. I would begin by classifying sexual encounters as opportunities for discovery and rediscovery in self-committed activity. It has often been suggested that people and animals value and enjoy opportunities for gaining information from their surroundings and companions in exploration and play (Berlyne, 1960) and from academic and aesthetic pursuits (Humphrey, 1973, 1974). Getting information sometimes implies asking questions (Humphrey and Keeble, 1976) and the act of asking a question implies ignorance or uncertainty. (Of course we can be *given* information *gratis*, but it is still arguable that the information will not be assimilated unless we have some kind of question, however vague, in mind.)

In asking a question one is admitting ignorance in so far as one does not knew the answer, and one may indeed be unable to formulate the question in detail. One's best formulation of the question: 'What will make this television receiver work again?', may be the act of giving it a good thump on the side. And in playful, courtship, sexual and aggressive situations, to ask a question is often to commit, rather than admit, ignorance. The word 'commit' is intended to emphasize that much may be at stake: by exploring, an animal may discover where his predators live, if he is not eaten in the process; in his courtship he runs the risk of rejection; in fighting, the risk of losing or being killed. Some of the negative outcomes of such encounters also provide information worth having, and I expect that being able to enjoy such risky ventures has considerable survival value.

Finally, I can return to what may be special about human sexual behaviour by suggesting that the experience of orgasm can add to sexual experiences in rather a special way. The transiently changed state of consciousness involved in orgasm has often been noted (Kinsey *et al.*, 1948). On returning to an everyday state of consciousness one is not always able to remember exactly what the experience was like: in that sense it is to some degree a self-erasing experience. From that it follows that each new sexual encounter always seems to offer opportunities for discovery and rediscovery.

CONCLUSION

When I began this chapter, it seemed obvious to me that tactile experience was relevant to the development of sexual behaviour, perhaps because mammalian sexual behaviour would be incomplete without contact between the participants. It is also obvious that behaviour patterns producing tactile experience in infants have been little described. It seemed less obvious that the concept 'sexual' was a confusing one for a biologist, and that the term 'experience' has several meanings, all of which a biologist should recognize, in order to give a perspective to his work. For only with experience, understood as events that affect and control, can he work easily, and such are the events that have dominated developmental studies of experience. But the term experience can also refer to our thoughts and feelings about the events in which we become involved, and such thoughts and feelings may be more important to us, as individuals, than our own behaviour. Moreover, these thoughts and feelings may powerfully influence what we regard as sexual as we rear our children and carry out our observations and experiments, and thus influence our behaviour towards our children and experimental subjects.

It is easy to think of experience actively in terms of our control of a situation, or passively, in terms of the situation's control of us. But to the dimension of control we should add that of predictability. Human ventures whose outcomes are not wholly predictable in advance are often the most exciting and pleasurable, whether they be sexual or not. Moreover, experiences from which developing individuals learn must, by definition of learning, be those whose outcomes were not wholly predictable in advance. Such experiences are under the individual's control in so far as he launches himself into them, but thereafter he can learn from the ensuing consequences only by allowing them to influence him. Many important developmental processes may work to organize the individual's experience so that he has sufficient attentional control of what happens to him that he can learn with profit from the events he sets in train.

As one way of studying experience by observational methods, a skills approach was suggested. Because there are skills which can be recognized at different ages and in different behavioural contexts, such an approach seems a promising one for a developmental study. For example, it may prove possible to study an individual's attention span at all ages, and in all situations, whenever that individual acts on his surroundings. In contrast, a complex behaviour pattern, like a consummated sexual encounter, may occur only when the individual is adult, may depend upon and be influenced by the partner's reactions, and may occur only a few times in that individual's life. His performance in each encounter may nevertheless be understood in terms of the operation of a number of component skills, including attentional, tactile, and social ones, the development of each of which could have been followed through his whole life, in many situations.

ACKNOWLEDGEMENTS

I thank John and Rose Hutchison and Anne Simpson for their criticism, help, and encouragement given at all stages as I wrote this paper.

REFERENCES

Akers, J., Conaway, C., and Kling, A. (in preparation) The role of the female *(M. mulatta)* in sexual behaviour.

Alexander, B. K. (1966) The effects of early peer-deprivation on juvenile behavior of rhesus monkeys. *Unpubl. Doctoral Dissertation*, University of Wisconsin.

Anderson, C. O. and Mason, W. A. (1974) Early experience and complexity of social organization in groups of young rhesus monkeys *(Macaca mulatta)*, *J. Comp. Physiol. Psychol.*, **87**, 681–90.

Andrew, R. J. (1972a) Recognition processes and behavior, with special reference to the effects of testosterone on persistence. In: *Advances in the Study of Behavior*. Vol. 4, D. S. Lehrman, R. A. Hinde, and E. Shaw (eds.), Academic Press, New York and London, pp. 175–208.

Andrew, R. J. (1972b) The information potentially available in mammalian displays. In: *Non-verbal Communication*, R. A. Hinde (ed.), Cambridge University Press, Cambridge England.

Argyle, M. (1975) *Bodily Communication*, Methuen, London.

Bakwin, H. (1952) Masturbation in infants, *J. Pediatr.*, **40**, 675–8.

Bakwin, H. (1973) Erotic feelings in infants and young children, *Am. J. Dis. Child.*, **126**, 52–4.

Berger, P. L. and Luckman, T. (1967) *The Social Construction of Reality. A Treatise in the Sociology of Knowledge*, Penguin Books Inc., Harmondsworth, England, Baltimore, and Victoria.

Berlyne, D. A. (1960) *Conflict, Arousal,* and *Curiosity*, McGraw-Hill, New York.

Brecher, R. and Brecher, E. (1967) *An Analysis of Human Sexual Response*, Deutsch, London.

Bruner, J. S. (1971) The growth and structure of skill. In: *Motor Skills in Infancy*, K. J. Connolly (ed.), Academic Press, London and New York. and (1974) In: *Beyond the Information Given: Studies in the Psychology of Knowing*, J. M. Anglin (ed.), Allen and Unwin, London.

Burton, F. D. (1971) Sexual climax in female *Macaca mulatta*, *Proc. 3rd int. Congr. Primat.*, **3**, 180–91.

Crook, J. H. (1970) Social organisation and the environment: aspects of contemporary social ethology, *Anim. Behav.*, **18**, 197–209.

Davenport, R. K. (in press) Some behavioral disturbances of great apes in captivity. In: *Perspectives on Human Evolution*, J. Goodall and D. Hamburg (eds).

Everitt, B. J. and Herbert, J. (1969) The role of ovarian hormones in the sexual preference of rhesus monkeys, *Anim. Behav.*, **17**, 738–46.

Flavell, J. H. (1963) *The Development Psychology of Jean Piaget*, van Nostrand, London, Toronto, and New York.

Freud, S. (1905) *Three Essays on the Theory of Sexuality. The Complete Psychological Works of Sigmund Freud* Vol. 7, Hogarth, London.

Harlow, H. F. (1962) The heterosexual affectional system in monkeys, *Am. Psychol.*, **17**, 1–9.

Harlow, H. F. (1969) Age-mate or peer affectional system. In: *Advances in the Study of Behaviour*, Vol. 2, D. S. Lehrman, R. A. Hinde, and E. Shaw (eds.), Academic Press, N. Y. and London, pp. 333–83.

Harlow, H. F. (1974) Sexual behavior in the rhesus monkey. In: *Sex and Behavior*, F. A. Beach (ed.), R. E. Frieger Publishing Co., N. Y., pp. 234–65.

Harlow, H. F. and Harlow, M. K. (1969) Effects of various mother–infant relationships on rhesus monkey behaviours. In: *Determinants of Infant Behaviour* Vol. 4, B. M. Foss (ed.), Methuen, London, pp. 15–36.

Hebb, D. O. (1958) *A Textbook of Psychology*, Saunders, London.

Held, R. and Hein, A. V. (1963) Movement-produced stimulation in the development of visually guided behavior, *J. Comp. Physiol. Psychol.*, **56**, 872–6.

Herbert, J. (1968) Sexual preference in the rhesus monkey. *Anim. Behav.*, **16**, 120–8.

Herbert, J. (1970) Hormones and reproductive behaviour in rhesus and talapoin monkeys, *J. Reprod. Fert.*, Suppl., 11, 119–40.

Hinde, R. A. (1970) *Animal Behaviour: A Synthesis of Ethology and Comparative Psychology*, McGraw-Hill, N. Y.

Hinde, R. A. (1970) *Biological Bases of Human Social Behaviour*, McGraw-Hill, N. Y.

Hinde, R. A. and Simpson, M. J. A. (1975) Qualities of mother–infant relationships in monkeys. *Ciba Foundation Symposium 1974*, Associated Scientific Publishers, Amsterdam.

Hinde, R. A. and Stevenson-Hinde, J. G. (1969) Integration of response sequences. In: *Advances in the Study of Behavior*, D. S., Lehrman, R. A. Hinde, and E. Shaw, Academic Press, New York and London.

Hooff, J.A.R.A.M. van (1971) *Aspecten van het sociale Degrag ende Communicatie bij humane en hogere niet-humane Primaten: A Structural Analysis of the Social Behavior of a Semi-captive Group of Chimpanzees*, Bronder-Offset, Rotterdam.

Humphrey, N. K. (1973a) The illusion of beauty, *Perception*, **2**, 429–39.

Humphrey, N. K. (1974) Species and individuals in the perceptual world of monkeys, *Perception*, **3**, 105–14.

Humphrey, N. K. and Keeble, G. R. (1976) How monkeys acquire a new way of seeing, *Perception*, **5**, 51–6.

Kessen, W. (1967) Sucking and looking: two organized congenital patterns of behavior in the human newborn. In: *Early Behavior: Comparative and Developmental Approaches*, H. W. Stevenson, E. H. Hess, and H. L. Rheingold (eds.), John Wiley and Sons, New York, London, and Sydney.

Kinsey, A. C., Pomeroy, W. B., and Martin, C. E. (1948) *Sexual behavior in the human male*. Saunders, Philadelphia and London.

Lawick-Goodall, J. van (1968) The behaviour of free-living chimpanzees in the Gombe Stream Reserve, *Anim. Behav. Monogr.*, **1**, 161–301.

Lewis, M. and Rosenblum, L. A., eds. (1974) *The Effect of the Infant on its Caregiver*, Wiley, N. Y.

Mackay, D. M. (1972) Formal analysis of communicative processes. In: *Non-verbal Communication*, R. A. Hinde (ed.), Cambridge University Press, Cambridge, England.

Mason, W. A. (1965a) The social development of monkeys and apes. In: *Primate Behavior:*

Field Studies of Monkeys and Apes, I. DeVore (ed.), Holt, Rinehart and Winston, N. Y. pp. 514–43.

Mason, W. A. (1965b) Determinants of social behavior in young chimpanzees. In: *Behavior of Nonhuman Primates: Modern Research Trends*, A. M. Schrier, H. F. Harlow, and F. Stolnitz (eds.), Academic Press, N. Y. and London, pp. 335–64.

Mason W. A. and Kenney, M. D. (1974) Redirection of filial attachments in rhesus monkeys: dogs as mother surrogates, *Science*, **183**, 1209–11.

Masters, W. H. and Johnson, V. E. (1966) *Human Sexual Response*, Churchill, London.

McFarland, D. J. (1973) Discussion of Connolly's contribution in *Constraints on Learning: Limitations and Predispositions*, R. A. Hinde and J. G. Stevenson-Hinde (eds.), Academic Press, London and New York.

McGinnis, P. (1973) *Patterns of sexual behavior in a community of free-living chimpanzees*, *Ph.D. Thesis*, Cambridge.

Menzel, E. W. (1971) Communication about the environment in a group of young chimpanzees, *Folia Primat.*, **15**, 220–32.

Menzel, E. W. (1973) Leadership and communication in young chimpanzees, *Symp. IVth Int. Congr. Primat.*, **1**, 192–225.

Menzel, E. A., Devenport, R. K., and Rogers, C. M. (1970) The development of tool using in wild-born and restriction-reared chimpanzees, *Folia Primat.*, **12**, 273–83.

Michael, R. P. (1971) Neuroendocrine factors regulating primate behavior. In: *Frontiers in Neuroendocrinology*, L. Martini and W. F. Ganong (eds.), Oxford Univ. Press, Oxford, N. Y. London, Toronto, pp. 359–98.

Mitchell, G. (1970) Abnormal behavior in primates. In: *Primate Behavior: Developments in Field and Laboratory Research* Vol 1, L. A. Rosenblum (ed.), 195–249.

Mitchell, G., Raymond, E. J., Rupenthal, G. C., and Harlow, H. F. (1966) Long term effects of total social isolation upon behavior of rhesus monkeys, *Psychol. Rep.*, **18**, 567–80.

Mittelstaedt, H. (1962) Control systems of orientation in insects, *Ann. Rev. Entomol.*, **7**, 177–98.

Morgan, B. J. T., Simpson, M. J. A., Hanby, J. P., and Hall-Craggs, J. (1976) Visualising interaction and sequential data in animal behaviour: theory and application of cluster analysis, *Behaviour*, **56**, 1–43.

Nissen, H. W. (1953) 'Instinct as seen by a psychologist.' 'A re-examination of the concept of instinct.' With W. C. Allee, and M. F. Nimkoff, *Psychol. Rev.*, **60**, 287–97.

Nissen, H. W., Chow, K. L., and Semmes, J. (1951) Effects of restricted opportunity for tactile, kinesthetic, and manipulative experience on the behaviour of chimpanzees. *Am. J. Psychol.*, **64**, 485–507.

Piaget, J. (1952) *The Origins of Intelligence in Children*, International University Press, New York.

Pratt, C. L. (1969) The developmental consequences of variations in early social stimulation, *Ph.D.* University of Wisconsin.

Reich, W. (1942) *The Function of the Orgasm*, (trans. T. P. Wolfe), Panther, London.

Riesen, A. H. (1971) Nissen's observations on the development of sexual behavior in captive-born, nursery-reared, chimpanzees, In: *The Chimpanzee* Vol. 4, G. H. Bourne (ed.), Karger, Basel, pp. 1–18.

Rogers, C. M. and Davenport, R. K. (1969) Effects of restricted rearing on sexual behavior in chimpanzees, *Develop. Psychol.*, **1**, 200–4.

Rowell, T. E. (1972a) *Social Behaviour of Monkeys*, Penguin, London.

Rowell, T. E. (1972b) Female reproduction cycles and social behavior in primates. In: *Advances in the Study of Behavior* Vol. 4, D. S. Lehrman, R. A. Hinde, and E. Shaw (eds.), Academic Press, N. Y. and London, pp. 69–105.

Rowland, G. L. (1964) The effects of total social isolation upon learning and social behavior in rhesus monkeys, *Ph.D. Thesis*, University of Wisconsin.

Sackett, G. P. (1970) Unlearned responses, differential rearing conditions, and the development of social attachments by rhesus monkeys. In: *Primate Behavior: Developments in Field and Laboratory Research* Vol. 1, L. A. Rosenblum (ed.), Academic Press, N. Y. and London, pp. 111–40.

Simpson, M. J. A. (1968) The display of the Siamese fighting fish, *Betta Splendens, Anim. Behav. Monogr.*, **1**, 1–73.

Simpson, M. J. A. (1973) Social displays and the recognition of individuals. In: *Perspectives in Ethology* Vol. 1, P. P. G. Bateson and P. H. Klopfer (eds.), Plenum, pp. 225–79.

Simpson, M. J. A. (1976) The Study of Animal Play. In: *Growing Points in Ethology*, R. A. Hinde and P. P. G. Bateson (eds.), Cambridge University Press, Cambridge, England.

Singer, I. (1973) *The Goals of Human Sexuality*, Norton, N. Y.

Singer, J. and Singer, I. (1972) Types of female orgasm, *J. Sex. Res.*, **8**, 255–67.

Slater, P. J. B. (1973) Describing sequences of behavior. In: *Perspectives in Ethology* Vol. 1, P. P. G. Bateson and P. H. Klopfer (eds.), 131–53.

Suomi, S. J. (1974) Social interactions of monkeys reared in a nuclear family environment *versus* monkeys reared with mothers and peers, *Primates*, **15**, 311–20.

Suomi, S. J. and Harlow, H. F. (1971) Abnormal behavior in young monkeys. In: *The Exceptional Infant* Vol. 2, J. Hellmuth (ed.), Brunner, Mazel, N. Y., pp. 483–529.

Thorpe, W. H. (1963) *Learning and Instinct in Animals*, Methuen, London.

Yerkes, R. M. and Elder, J. H. (1936) Oestrus, receptivity, and mating in the chimpanzee, *Comp. Psychol. Monog.*, **13**, 1–39.

Zumpe, D. and Michael, R. P. (1968) The clutching reaction and orgasm in the female rhesus monkey *(Macaca mulatta)*, *J. Endocrinol.*, **40**, 117–23.

Index

Note: Where possible animal species are indexed under their common names.